FIRST-YEAR COURSE
THIRD EDITION

Glencoe
Accounting

CONCEPTS/PROCEDURES/APPLICATIONS

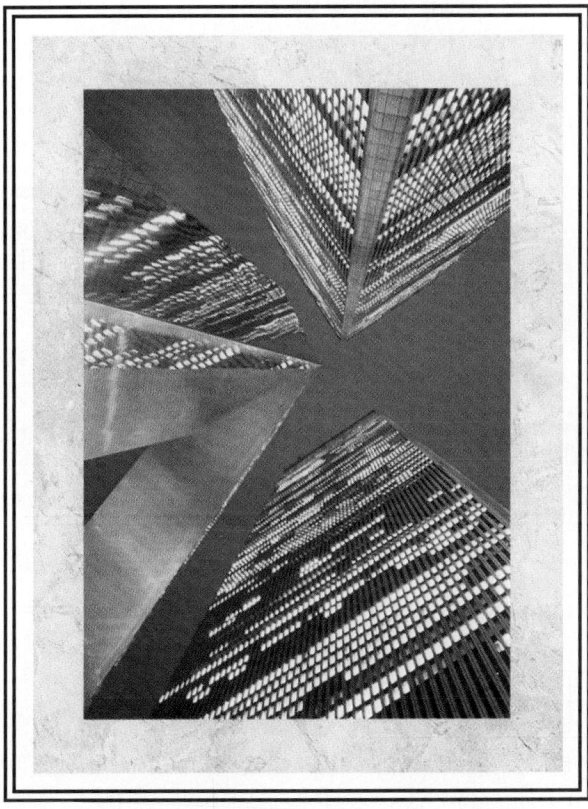

Donald J. Guerrieri
Norwin Senior High School
North Huntingdon, Pennsylvania

F. Barry Haber
Fayetteville State University
Fayetteville, North Carolina

William B. Hoyt
Wilton High School
Wilton, Connecticut

Robert E. Turner
McNeese State University
Lake Charles, Louisiana

GLENCOE
Macmillan/McGraw-Hill

New York, New York   Columbus, Ohio   Mission Hills, California   Peoria, Illinois

Contents

Photo Credits

T3, T12-T13, T20(b), T21(t), T23, T24(b),T34, T37(b), T39, T40-41, T44, 1A-1D,
38A-38D, 210A-210D, 414A-414D, 462A-462D, 568A-568D, KS Studios; T31(L),
David R. Frazier Photography; T31(r), Peter Miller/The Image Bank; T35, Henley
& Savage/The Stock Market; T42, Blair Seitz/Photo Researchers; T45,Courtesy
of Southwest Airlines

Glencoe Accounting
Teacher's Wraparound Edition

Imprint 1996

Send all inquiries to:
Glencoe/McGraw-Hill, 936 Eastwind Drive, Westerville, OH 43081

ISBN 0-02-800490-6

Printed in the United States of America.

4 5 6 7 8 9 10 11 12 13 14 15   RRW/MC   04 03 02 01 00 99 98 97 96

Dear Accounting Teachers:

Welcome to the exciting world of *Glencoe Accounting*, a comprehensive instructional program designed to meet the needs of today's teachers and students. Each member of this authorship team is an accounting teacher and, as such, knows your curriculum needs in the teaching/learning process. Our experience also provides us with insight into the methods and techniques that work best in the accounting classroom. The goal of our program can be summed up in one word: SUCCESS. We want you to be successful in your teaching and all your students to be successful in their learning.

Accounting is still the language of business, and *Glencoe Accounting* stresses the fundamental principles and procedures needed to build a solid foundation for understanding. We have taken a leadership role in addressing recent innovative approaches to education, such as Tech Prep and the issues raised by the Accounting Change Commission. Our textbook and supplementary materials have been developed to maximize teaching and learning to help you and your students be successful.

We believe that students learn best when they are actively involved in the learning process. Integrating learning techniques such as cooperative learning, case-study approaches to problem solving, and alternative assessment methods into daily classroom activities will provide creative and challenging learning experiences for all students.

The *Glencoe Accounting* program provides you with proven classroom materials that assist students in mastering accounting principles and procedures while also motivating and challenging them to learn. Our program builds a solid foundation in accounting fundamentals so students become thinkers, decision makers, and problem solvers, not merely recorders of financial information. We want you and your students to end each year feeling good about your accomplishments.

Preparing students to become productive members of a technological work force is truly a challenge. We address the impact of technology on accounting and other aspects of our society throughout the textbook with computer experiences and illustrations. Our accounting software is state-of-the art, and our software options and multimedia offer an innovative approach to accounting education.

Let's enjoy sharing what we know with our students. When you have a good time teaching, your students will have a good time learning. Have a successful year!

The Authors

Donald J. Guerrieri

William B. Hoyt

F. Barry Haber

Robert E. Turner

Student Components

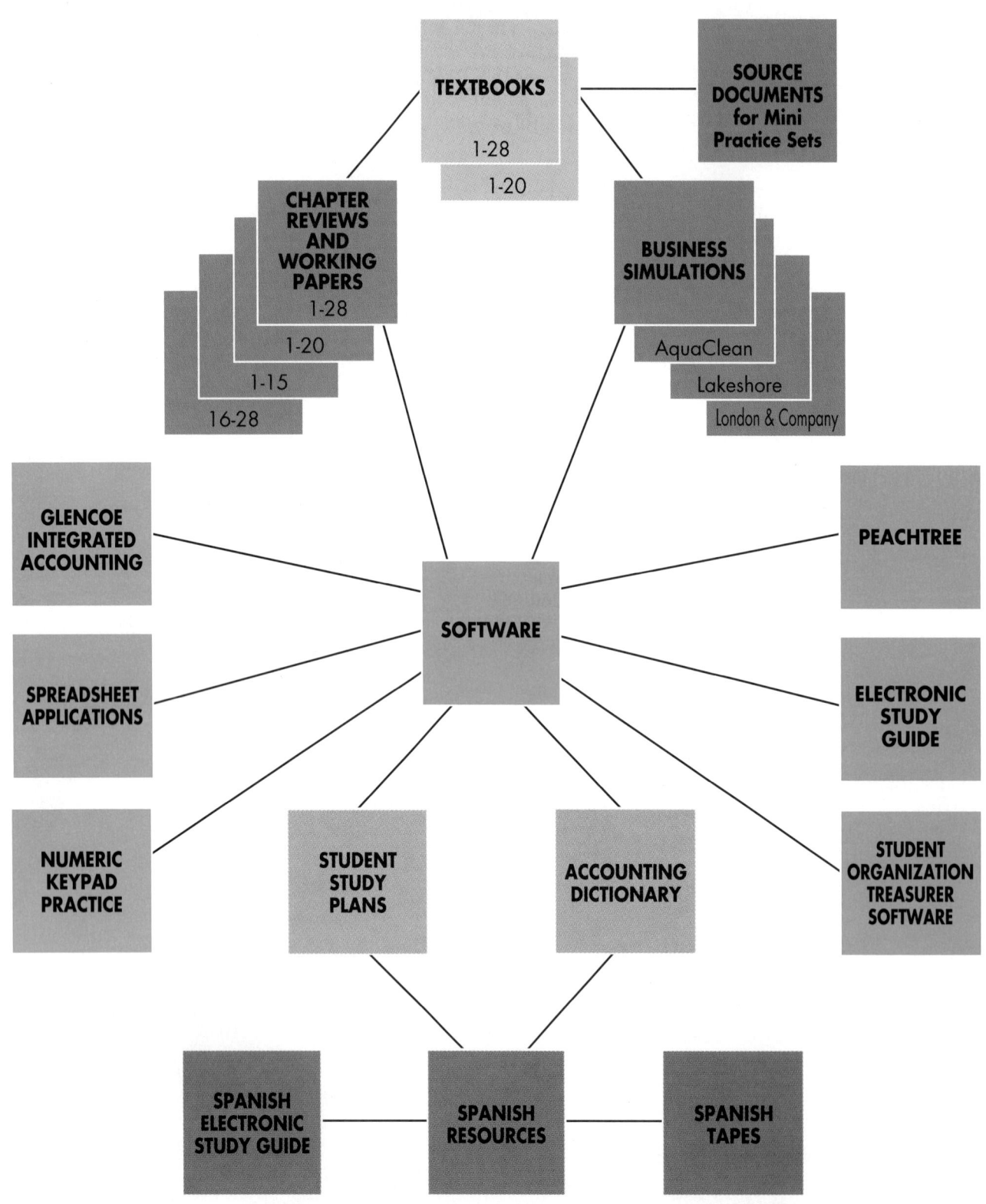

TEXTBOOKS

1-28

1-20

SOURCE DOCUMENTS for Mini Practice Sets

CHAPTER REVIEWS AND WORKING PAPERS

1-28

1-20

1-15

16-28

BUSINESS SIMULATIONS

AquaClean

Lakeshore

London & Company

GLENCOE INTEGRATED ACCOUNTING

SPREADSHEET APPLICATIONS

NUMERIC KEYPAD PRACTICE

SOFTWARE

STUDENT STUDY PLANS

ACCOUNTING DICTIONARY

PEACHTREE

ELECTRONIC STUDY GUIDE

STUDENT ORGANIZATION TREASURER SOFTWARE

SPANISH ELECTRONIC STUDY GUIDE

SPANISH RESOURCES

SPANISH TAPES

Teacher Components

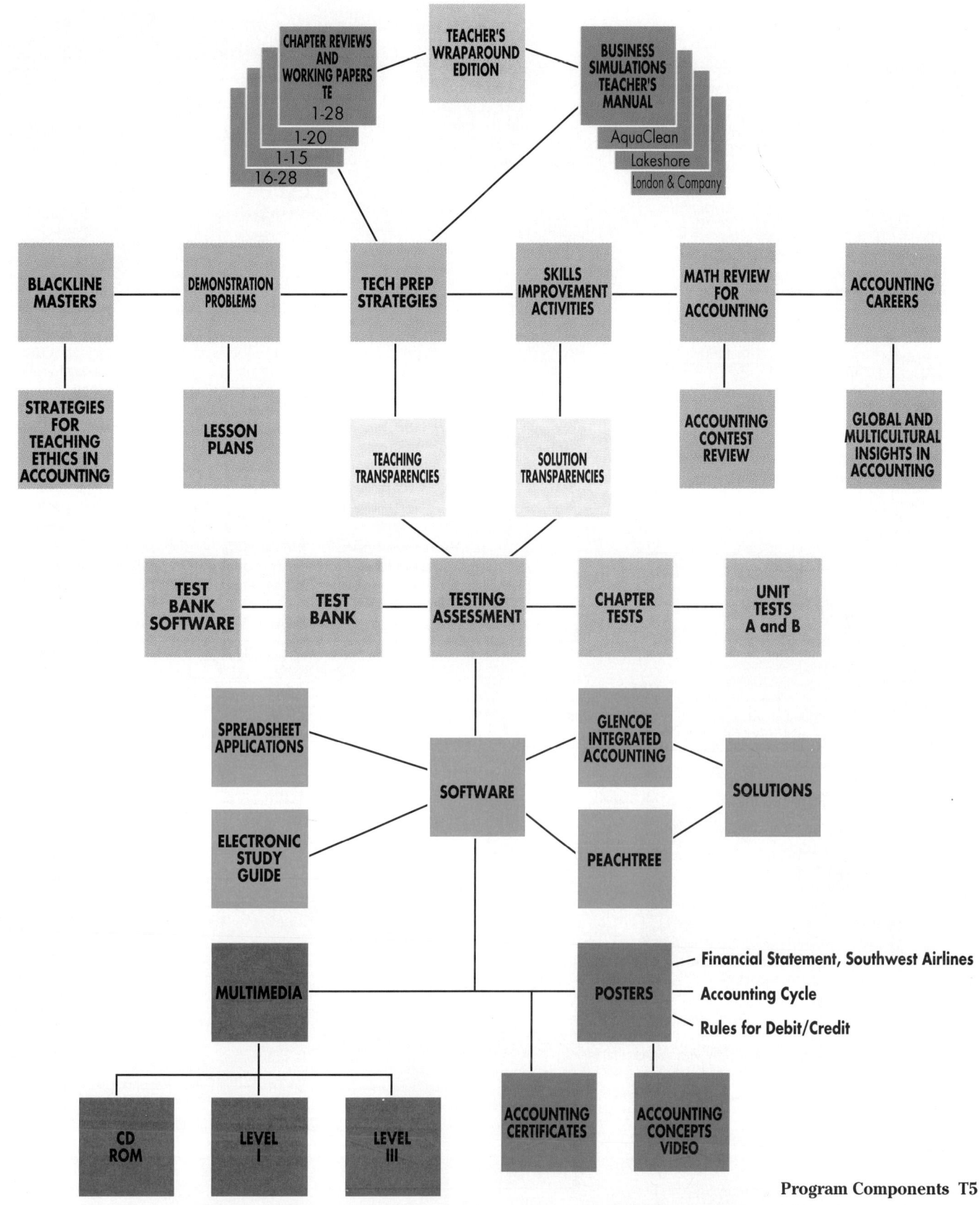

CHAPTER REVIEWS AND WORKING PAPERS TE
1-28
1-20
1-15
16-28

TEACHER'S WRAPAROUND EDITION

BUSINESS SIMULATIONS TEACHER'S MANUAL
AquaClean
Lakeshore
London & Company

BLACKLINE MASTERS

DEMONSTRATION PROBLEMS

TECH PREP STRATEGIES

SKILLS IMPROVEMENT ACTIVITIES

MATH REVIEW FOR ACCOUNTING

ACCOUNTING CAREERS

STRATEGIES FOR TEACHING ETHICS IN ACCOUNTING

LESSON PLANS

TEACHING TRANSPARENCIES

SOLUTION TRANSPARENCIES

ACCOUNTING CONTEST REVIEW

GLOBAL AND MULTICULTURAL INSIGHTS IN ACCOUNTING

TEST BANK SOFTWARE

TEST BANK

TESTING ASSESSMENT

CHAPTER TESTS

UNIT TESTS A and B

SPREADSHEET APPLICATIONS

GLENCOE INTEGRATED ACCOUNTING

SOFTWARE

SOLUTIONS

ELECTRONIC STUDY GUIDE

PEACHTREE

MULTIMEDIA

POSTERS
— Financial Statement, Southwest Airlines
— Accounting Cycle
— Rules for Debit/Credit

CD ROM

LEVEL I

LEVEL III

ACCOUNTING CERTIFICATES

ACCOUNTING CONCEPTS VIDEO

INSIDE THE STUDENT EDITION

Understanding the Lesson

The textbook organization provides a structure that is easy for students to follow and to understand. New learning is based on previous knowledge, with each new concept building on a prior concept and thus reinforcing material learned in earlier chapters. Much like an accounting cycle where records are maintained through a sequence of procedures and activities, the text instruction follows an organized flow of concept development, as shown in Figure 1.

```
Unit Opener
Assessment          Chapter Opener
Practice            Chapter Objectives
Summary             Vocabulary Development
Self-Checks  Concept Development
```

Figure 1

```
Introduction of Concept
Self-Check          Explanation of Concept
Illustration of Concept
```

Figure 2

Each chapter in the student textbook lends itself to comprehension and independent learning. Looking through the textbook, you will notice that major concepts are called out with topical headings and information is presented in an easy-to-follow, well-organized manner. Explanations in simple language guide students through concepts and procedures that are accompanied by illustrations showing step-by-step accounting procedures. Each concept is developed using a sequence of instruction that fully explains and illustrates each major concept (see Figure 2). The readable type size and the variety of illustrations and examples, as well as the effective use of full-color printing, invite student reading.

Chapter learning objectives are measurable and outcome based. Objectives help students read with a goal in mind.

The textbook organization parallels the steps in the accounting cycle, leading students through accounting records in a sequential, logical manner. This sequence is the same that would be followed in keeping records for a real business. The illustration of the cycle is repeated in each chapter to reinforce the order of steps and to help students integrate new learning into prior knowledge.

Chapter openers link the material in the current chapter to information the student has already learned.

New terms are defined when they are first used and within the context of a key concept.

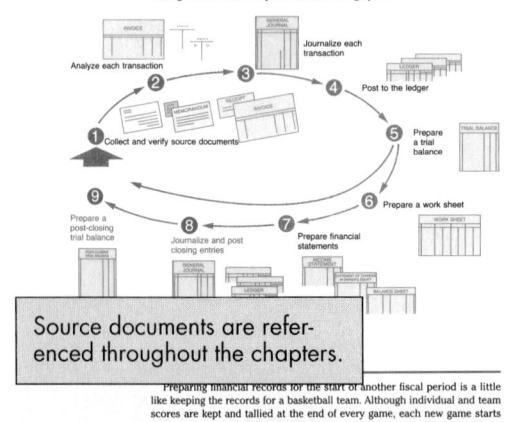

Source documents are referenced throughout the chapters.

The new vocabulary terms to be presented in the chapter are identified.

Chapter

COMPLETING THE ACCOUNTING CYCLE FOR A SOLE PROPRIETORSHIP

In Chapter 8, you learned how to prepare the end-of-period financial statements for a sole proprietorship service business. The income statement reports the business's revenue, expenses, and net income or net loss for a fiscal period. The statement of changes in owner's equity summarizes the effects of the business transactions for the period on the owner's capital account. The balance sheet reports the financial position of the business as of the end of the fiscal period.

In this chapter, you will complete the accounting cycle for Global Travel Agency. The accounting cycle is completed by journalizing the closing entries and preparing a post-closing trial balance.

Learning Objectives

When you have completed Chapter 9, you should be able to do the following:
1. Explain why the temporary capital accounts are closed at the end of the fiscal period.
2. Explain the purpose of
3. Explain the relationship count and the capital a
4. Analyze and journalize
5. Post closing entries to
6. Prepare a post-closing
7. Define the accounting t

New Terms

closing entries
post-closing trial balance
Income Summary account
compound entry

The Eighth and Ninth Steps in the Accounting Cycle

During a fiscal period, the temporary capital accounts are used to record transactions involving revenue, expenses, and withdrawals. At the end of the period, the balances in these accounts are transferred to the capital account to summarize the changes in owner's equity and to bring that account up to date.

The balances in the temporary capital accounts are transferred by recording a series of closing entries. **Closing entries** are journal entries made to close out, or reduce to zero, the balances in the temporary capital accounts and to transfer the net income or net loss for the period to the capital account.

After the closing entries have been journalized and posted, a trial balance is prepared to prove the equality of the general ledger after the closing process. The trial balance prepared after closing is called a **post-closing trial balance.** As you can see in Figure 9-1, the closing process and the post-closing trial balance complete the accounting cycle.

Preparing financial records for the start of another fiscal period is a little like keeping the records for a basketball team. Although individual and team scores are kept and tallied at the end of every game, each new game starts with a score of zero. Similarly, although entries are recorded in the accounts

168

CHAPTER 9 Completing the Accounting Cycle for a Sole Proprietorship   169

Abundant illustrations and examples visually reinforce understanding and comprehension of new accounting concepts and procedures.

REMEMBER notes summarize important concepts or procedures to help students identify material that is especially important for them to know.

Accounting concepts are developed in simple language and in a direct style to facilitate student understanding.

ACCOUNTING Tips

Revenue represents the *right* side of the capital account.

ACCOUNTING Notes

Closing entries are sometimes called clearing entries because one of their functions is to *clear* the revenue and expense accounts and leave them with zero balances.

ACCOUNTING TIPS and ACCOUNTING NOTES appear throughout the textbook and provide students with practical advice or interesting facts about business or the practice of accounting.

Students are given self-check opportunities to apply what they have just learned and to receive immediate feedback. Answers to the Check Your Learning activities are provided at the end of the student textbook.

An enumerated summary provides a quick review of the major concepts presented in the chapter.

A variety of chapter activities help students integrate knowledge and apply what they have learned. Chapter review activities begin with a vocabulary review that requires students to write sentences using the new terms in the chapter.

Review questions require students to focus on the key accounting concepts of the chapter.

Short activities develop students' decision-making, communications, human relations, math, and analysis skills.

Practice and Apply

Students need a variety of practice materials to help them transfer textbook learning to practical applications. The *Glencoe Accounting* program provides plentiful practice activities ranging from short exercises to mini-practice sets covering an accounting cycle.

In appropriate chapters, computer application problems are identified by a microcomputer icon or a spreadsheet icon to indicate that students may also complete these problems with either the general ledger integrated software or the spreadsheet software packages accompanying the *Glencoe Accounting* program. In addition, the five mini-practice sets can be completed on the computer.

Each chapter contains single-focus exercises that give students practice in applying key accounting concepts and procedures before they move on to full-scale problems. These exercises generally follow the same order as chapter content and can be completed either after the related concepts have been taught or as a group when the whole chapter has been completed. The *Teacher's Wraparound Edition* contains margin notes informing you when each exercise may be completed.

The last problem in each chapter is a "challenge" problem that can be used as a class assignment or as an independent project. The challenge problem is identified with a maze symbol in the student textbook.

Five or more chapter problems are arranged in ascending order of difficulty. With few exceptions, the problems do not "piggyback" on each other, so you can assign problems as needed without worrying that a preceding problem has not been completed. The problems have been written to help students develop critical thinking skills as they apply the chapter concepts and procedures. Additional problems for each chapter are provided at the end of the textbook.

Today's accounting courses include much more than just instruction in accounting theory and procedures. Also included are computer instruction and a variety of activities geared toward helping students develop and enhance such skills as communications, decision making, and critical thinking. Five in-book mini-practice sets (called Application Activities) give students the opportunity to integrate their knowledge of accounting concepts and procedures presented in two or more chapters. Accounting stationery is provided in the student workbook for each mini-practice set. Source documents for each mini-practice set are also available to add realism to these culminating activities.

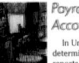

FOCUS ON Features

Each chapter ends with a special feature designed to help students relate the study of accounting to certain aspects of the world around them. These special features fall into three categories: Focus on Computers, Focus on Careers, and Focus on Ethics.

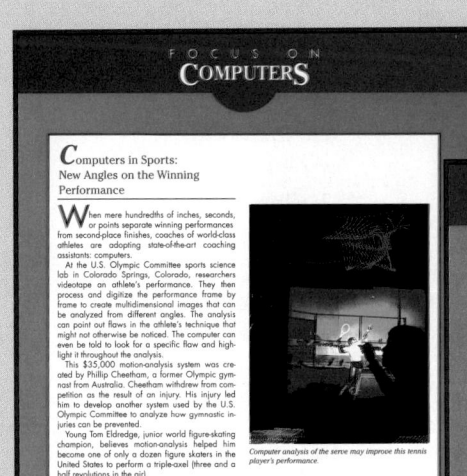

FOCUS ON ETHICS features describe common ethical issues in business and accounting and provide students an opportunity to identify the ethical dilemmas involved. Students are encouraged to develop a decision model to help them evaluate alternative actions to reach an ethical decision.

Software Piracy: A Matter of Ethics

Financial Report or Financial Repair

Pocketing Differences

Is the Boss Always Right?

Money Shuffling

Computer Viruses: The Enemy Within

Does Friendship Always Come First?

FOCUS ON COMPUTERS features integrate computer awareness into accounting instruction and introduce various aspects of current computer technology.

Automation: A Business's Life Support System

U.S. Forestry Service Fights Fires with *Computers?*

Passwords to Computer Security

Planning for Disasters

Computers in Sports: New Angles on the Winning Performance

Bar Codes: An Idea on the Fast Track

Hardware and Software: Buying Smart

Arresting Facts about Computer Fraud

Data Access vs. Privacy: A Delicate Balance

Computers in Government

Code Words for a Cashless Society

Home Is Where the Office Is

Computer Graphics

Telecommunications

FOCUS ON CAREERS features introduce students to a wide range of interesting, attainable career choices in the field of accounting.

Accounting: A Mobile Career

Accounting Clerks: Patient, Persistent, Good with Figures

Today's CPA

Credit Managers Take Risks in Stride

IRS: A Fertile Field of Career Opportunities

Playing a Supporting Role: The Theatrical Accountant

Forensic Accountants: Fraud Sleuths

Introduction

Today's students have many different learning styles and needs. As a result, instructional programs need a variety of ways to stimulate students' interest, facilitate their understanding, and motivate their learning. This *Teacher's Wraparound Edition* is a completely new teaching tool for accounting. It is designed to assist both new and experienced teachers and provides a wealth of teaching suggestions and resources to help you provide the best possible accounting instruction for all your students.

The *Teacher's Wraparound Edition* highlights several contemporary issues facing accounting educators in the 1990s, such as the use of technology, global awareness, cooperative learning, alternative assessment, and basic skills improvement. It also shows how Glencoe's comprehensive accounting program addresses these issues. The *Teacher's Wraparound Edition* provides a description of the content and use of the numerous teacher and student components comprising the *Glencoe Accounting* program. Suggested time schedules for six-week and nine-week grading periods are included.

The Four-Step Teaching Plan

Each chapter in the *Teacher's Wraparound Edition* is divided into instructional sections according to a four-step teaching plan designed to help you develop the chapter concepts and procedures in an organized manner. This widely accepted instructional method follows a mastery approach to developing student understanding of concepts and procedures. When utilized consistently, this four-step plan provides an instructional framework that makes it easy for you to teach and easy for your students to learn. The four steps in the instructional plan are Focus, Teach, Close, and Assess.

1 FOCUS

Gaining students' attention and interest is an important element in helping them to learn new ideas. The first step in the teaching plan is to focus students' attention by piquing their interest through a beginning activity. The FOCUS activity usually can be completed within the first several minutes of class and provides a motivational lead-in to the concepts that will be presented in the chapter.

2 TEACH

The second step in the teaching plan is TEACH. This section is the central part of the teaching plan. Teaching suggestions employing a variety of approaches, strategies, and activities appear in the side margins of the *Teacher's Wraparound Edition*. These suggestions are provided to support your classroom instruction through supplementary accounting information, suggestions for the use of visuals, comments on the use of technology, and interesting facts that may be used to hold students' interest.

For students who may need extra help learning a concept or procedure, Reteaching Strategies are provided at points throughout the chapter. Reteaching provides a means of presenting the same concept or procedure differently to accommodate students' different learning styles. Cooperative learning and critical thinking activities also provide opportunities for different instructional methods.

3 CLOSE

CLOSE is the third step in the teaching plan and is used to determine whether students have mastered the objectives of the chapter. Students have the opportunity to practice and apply what they have learned through a variety of activities. These activities include a vocabulary review, review questions, short cases developing basic skills, exercises, and problems. Providing students with a variety of ways to demonstrate what they have learned also gives you several opportunities to evaluate their learning and to identify students who need additional reinforcement through reteaching and practice activities.

4 ASSESS

The final step in the teaching plan is to evaluate student understanding of the concepts and procedures presented. Several evaluation techniques are available. Individual tests are available for each chapter. Unit tests are available in both objective and problem versions. Test Bank software allows you to generate your own test and to customize it as needed.

Because students have different learning styles, different means are sometimes needed for assessing their knowledge. The *Tech Prep Strategies in Accounting* booklet provides alternative assessment strategies.

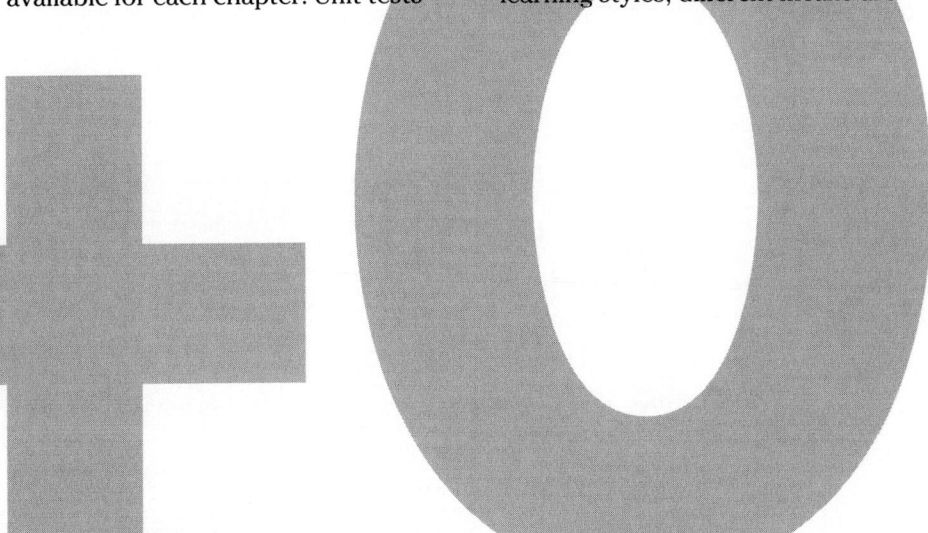

Unit Planning Guide

To provide the best possible learning experience for students, you need to know the variety of materials that are available to supplement your teaching. You cannot plan your lessons effectively unless you know what materials are available and the appropriate time to utilize each. This information is provided in the unit planning guides, which give you a comprehensive reference to unit and chapter teaching resources. Using these guides, you can easily identify unit objectives, chapter learning objectives, and the resources available to you for each chapter or unit. Refer to this guide as you plan each lesson so that you can make the best use of the numerous instructional materials that are included in the *Glencoe Accounting* program.

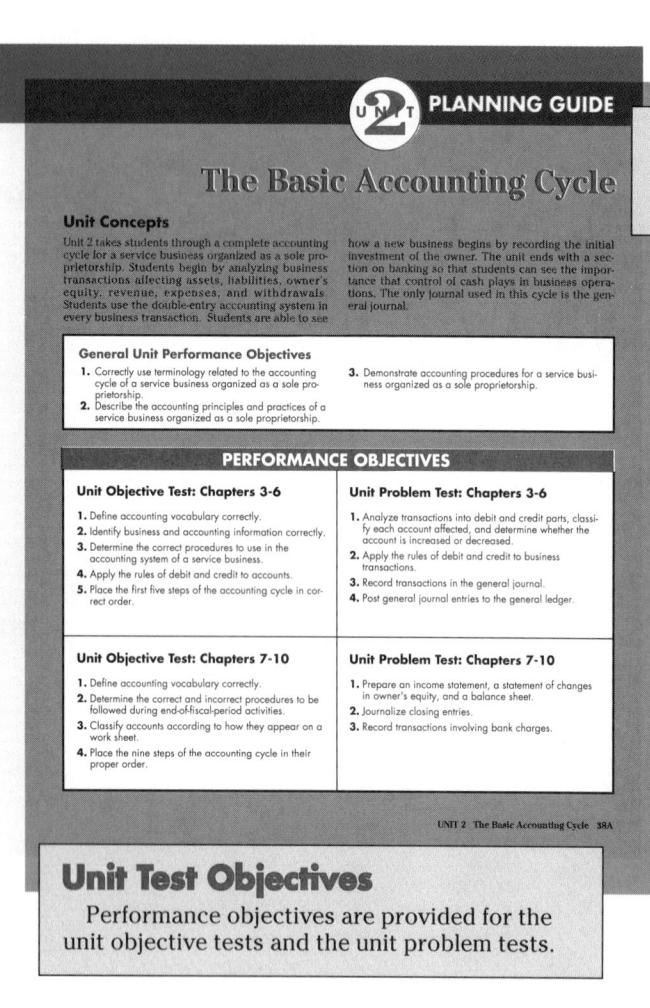

Unit Overview
Each unit planning guide begins with an overview of the unit content.

Chapter Objectives
Learning objectives are listed for each chapter in the student textbook.

Unit Test Objectives
Performance objectives are provided for the unit objective tests and the unit problem tests.

Computer Activities

A separate listing of computerized activities helps you identify opportunities to enhance student learning and comprehension through the use of optional computer software that includes general ledger and spreadsheet applications, an electronic study guide, and chapter content presented in CD ROM lessons.

Individual Course Objectives

Local or state course objectives can be referenced for planning your instruction.

UNIT 2 COMPUTERIZED ACCOUNTING ACTIVITIES

Chapter	Glencoe Integrated Accounting	Spreadsheet Applications	Electronic Study Guide Model Exercises/Problems	CD Rom
3			Exercise 3-1 3-2 Problem 3-1	Menu Selection 3
4			Exercise 4-1 4-2 Problem 4-1	Menu Selection 4
5	Problem 5-1 5-4	Problem 5-3 (General Journal)	Exercise 5-1 Problem 5-2	Menu Selection 5
6	Problem 6-4		Exercise 6-1 6-2 6-3	Menu Selection 6
Mini Practice Set	Application Activity 1			
7		Problem 7-3 (Six-Column Work Sheet)	Exercise 7-1 7-2 Problem 7-1	Menu Selection 7
8	Problem 8-5		Exercise 8-1 8-2	Menu Selection 8
9	Problem 9-5		Exercise 9-2 Problem 9-1	Menu Selection 9
10	Problem 10-4	Problem 10-4 (Bank Statement)	Problem 10-3	Menu Selection 10
Mini Practice Set	Application Activity 2			
Basic Math Review			Menu Option 29	

38D UNIT 2 The Basic Accounting Cycle

CHAPTER REINFORCEMENT

State/Local Objectives	Demonstration Problems	Check Your Learning	Basic Skills	Exercises	Problems	Challenge Problem	Additional Problems
	3-1 3-2	p.44 p.46	Math p.54	3-1 3-2 3-3	3-1 3-2 3-3 3-4	3-5	3A p.631
	4-1 4-2 4-3	p.66 p.75	Analysis p.77	4-1 4-2 4-3	4-1 4-2 4-3 4-4	4-5	4A p.632
	5-1 5-2 5-3 5-4 5-5 5-6	p.88 p.91 p.97 p.100	Decision Making p.101	5-1 5-2 5-3	5-1 5-2 5-3 5-4	5-5	5A p.633
	6-1 6-2 6-3 6-4 6-5 6-6	p.112 p.117	Communi-cation p.122	6-1 6-2 6-3	6-1 6-2 6-3 6-4	6-5	6A p.633
	7-1 7-2 7-3 7-4 7-5 7-6	p.135 p.140	Math p.142	7-1 7-2 7-3	7-1 7-2 7-3	7-4 7-5	7A p.634
	8-1 8-2 8-3 8-4 8-5	p.154 p.157 p.160	Decision Making p.162	8-1 8-2	8-1 8-2 8-3 8-4 8-5	8-6 8-7	8A p.634
	9-1 9-2 9-3 9-4 9-5	p.173 p.176	Human Relations p.181	9-1 9-2	9-1 9-2 9-3 9-4 9-5	9-6	9A p.635
	10-1 10-2 10-3 10-4 10-5	p.194 p.199	Analysis p.202	10-1 10-2 10-3 10-4	10-1 10-2 10-3 10-4	10-5	10A p.635

UNIT 2 The Basic Accounting Cycle 38C

Reinforcement Materials

A comprehensive list of chapter reinforcement materials provides a quick reference for planning your instruction and for individualizing learning experiences to meet students' different learning needs.

Using the TWE as a Resource

The *Teacher's Wraparound Edition* of *Glencoe Accounting* provides you and your students with the best possible learning opportunities and experiences. One of the goals of this resource is to help you communicate to students that accounting is a part of every business and that an understanding of accounting will benefit them in their personal and business lives, regardless of whether they choose to pursue accounting as a career. Another goal of this resource is to coordinate for you the numerous teacher and student components that comprise the *Glencoe Accounting* program.

Margin Features

Conveniently located teaching resources "wrapped around" the actual student pages include a variety of materials to support your classroom instruction.

INTRODUCING THE UNIT previews unit content and suggests resource materials that may be used to individualize instruction.

INTRODUCING THE CHAPTER links previous learning to the new chapter and previews chapter content. **VOCABULARY DEVELOPMENT** offers suggestions for helping students learn the new terms in each chapter.

TEACHING RESOURCES and **OTHER RESOURCES** list major components of the accounting program.

Features of the Four-Step Teaching Plan

The steps in this teaching plan offer a means of organizing your instruction and helping students to learn more efficiently.

1 FOCUS

The **FOCUS** activity provides a means of gaining students' attention and getting them ready to learn. This activity consists of two parts.

MAJOR CONCEPTS lists the key chapter concepts and can be used to preview your class presentation.

BUSINESS CONNECTION provides a short anecdote relating some part of the chapter content to a real business situation with actual companies. Use this anecdote to begin class discussion of the chapter or to relate the concepts presented in the chapter to the business world.

2 TEACH

The **TEACH** section of each chapter includes several instructional elements.

CONCEPT DEVELOPMENT provides strategies for teaching the accounting concepts presented in the chapter. Follow these suggestions for introducing, developing, or expanding a key concept.

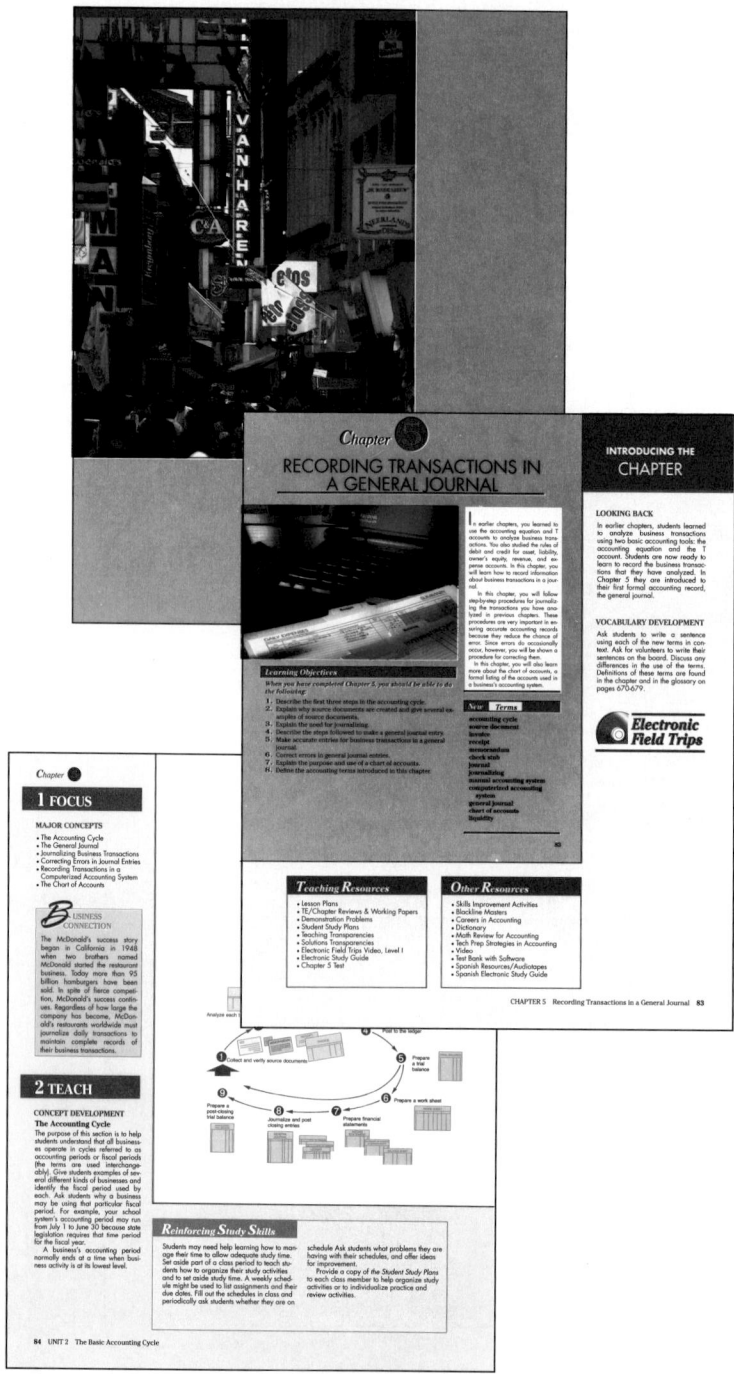

TEACHING TIPS provide information to supplement your classroom instruction.

USING VISUALS offers suggestions for explaining, applying, or analyzing chapter concepts through chapter figures and tables, demonstration problems, teaching transparencies, and blackline masters.

DID YOU KNOW? features provide interesting accounting or business information that may be used as the basis for a class discussion.

ACCOUNTING PRACTICE identifies the point in the chapter when students may complete an end-of-chapter exercise.

ACCOUNTING ISSUES/BUSINESS ISSUES present topics relating to contemporary concerns within the accounting profession or affecting business in general.

MAKING CONNECTIONS uses examples and activities to link accounting to a variety of experiences, both personal and business.

In addition to the preceding features that provide instructional support for chapter content, additional special features include alternative strategies for helping students to learn.

REINFORCING STUDY SKILLS suggests activities for helping students to improve their study habits.

MEETING SPECIAL NEEDS offers suggestions for assisting students with learning/physical disabilities and other special needs.

COOPERATIVE LEARNING suggests tasks to be completed in a group environment.

CRITICAL THINKING activities encourage students to apply what they have learned to solve basic accounting problems or to make decisions.

RETEACHING STRATEGIES suggest alternative methods of presenting concepts or procedures.

A **POP QUIZ** is included near the end of each chapter and provides a short test of the major points presented in the chapter.

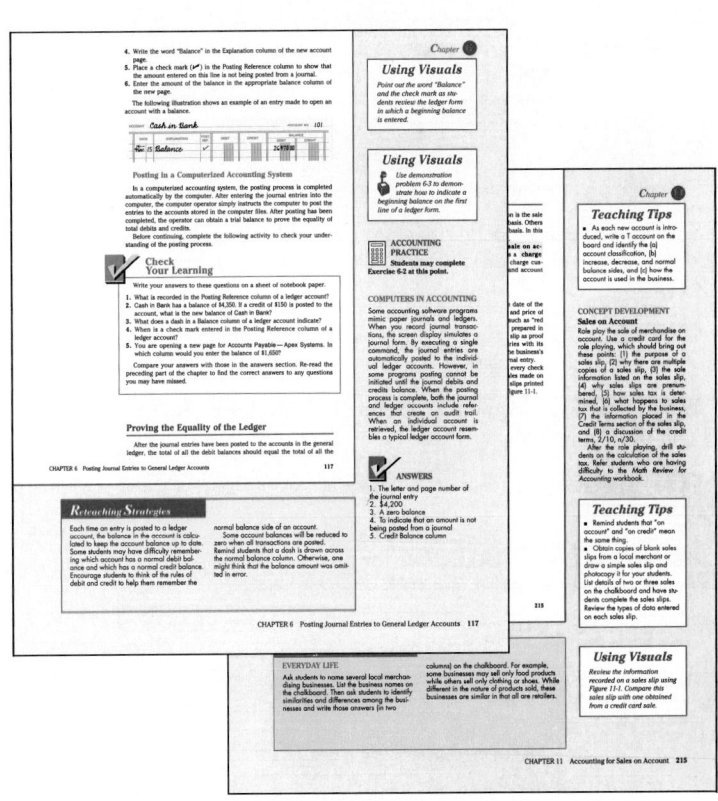

3 CLOSE

The **CLOSE** section provides a variety of opportunities for students to demonstrate new learning.

PRACTICE AND APPLY encompasses all end-of-chapter activities. Answers to these activities are provided in the margin of the *Teacher's Wraparound Edition.*

Each activity has a purpose, such as language development for the vocabulary review, evaluation of comprehension and retention through review questions, and development of basic skills through short cases.

EXERCISES are keyed to chapter objectives and may be completed after students have learned all chapter content or at appropriate points within the chapter (see Accounting Practice). Review activities are also provided in the student workbook, *Chapter Reviews and Working Papers.*

ADDITIONAL REINFORCEMENT reminds you that an *Electronic Study Guide* is available for review and that the on-line multimedia program will benefit students through its review of chapter concepts, vocabulary reinforcement, and exercises.

PROBLEMS are keyed to chapter objectives and provide an opportunity for students to apply their knowledge to preparing accounting records.

4 ASSESS

Several evaluation techniques are available to assess students' comprehension of and ability to apply chapter concepts.

CHAPTER TESTS provide objective questions and problems for each chapter.

UNIT TESTS are available as unit objective tests and as unit problem tests.

TEST BANK software may be used to customize chapter tests.

ALTERNATIVE STRATEGIES for evaluating students' progress are suggested in the tech prep booklet.

Making Connections

These suggestions and activities enable you to bring the outside world into your accounting classroom.

EVERYDAY LIFE relates information that students may already know to some aspect of accounting, thus providing a link from their personal knowledge to new learning. Use this activity to help students connect their own experiences to accounting information.

INTERDISCIPLINARY subjects, such as history, social studies, science, and mathematics are related to accounting in this series of informational vignettes that will help students see how various subjects are interconnected.

COMMUNICATIONS focuses on the needs of accounting workers to communicate with other people. These activities provide suggestions for helping students develop both written and oral communication skills.

AROUND THE WORLD offers insights into the global marketplace and how accounting plays a key role in global business. These activities provide an opportunity to discuss how accounting is affected by foreign business operations.

BUSINESS ETHICS provides examples of common situations that call for employees to make a decision about a potentially unethical action. These activities can be used to promote lively class discussions about actions that constitute ethical behavior.

Making Connections

EVERYDAY LIFE

Many students are responsible for purchasing their own car insurance. Ask students whether they must pay the premium for the insurance at the beginning or at the end of the insurance period. The response will be that they prepay. Ask students if they consider the cost of the premium to be an asset or an *expense*. Most students will consider it an expense. To illustrate how prepaid insurance is an asset, ask students to describe the benefit of purchasing insurance. The major benefit is *protection*, which is an asset until the insurance coverage expires.

Interdisciplinary Connections

SCIENCE

Keeping accounting records means collecting a lot of data in the form of numbers. Most businesses use computers to collect and record their accounting data. Data is also collected and recorded in other fields that also use computers for record keeping. One of the many ways that scientists use computers' ability to handle huge quantities of data is to record scientific observations, such as those made for weather forecasting, spacecraft guidance systems, earthquake predictions, and medical technology. Have students think of other ways computers could be used in science.

Making Connections

COMMUNICATIONS

Once the accountant has prepared a financial statement, he or she must present it to the client and explain it in terms that the officers, stockholders, and investors of the corporation will understand. Have students practice writing several paragraphs in which they explain the different sections of a financial statement and what that statement says about the company.

Making Connections

AROUND THE WORLD

How do people in other countries prepare to be accountants? In well-developed countries, they go to business school and then pass certification exams before they are allowed to practice. Many developing countries, however, have no formal certification process, little higher education for accounting study, and no published accounting textbooks. Lack of an accounting profession prevents businesses from joining the global economy and thus contributes to poor economic conditions in the developing nation. The United Nations is one group that is working toward improving accounting education throughout the world.

Making Connections

BUSINESS ETHICS

You work at an accounting firm that provides accounting services to a number of small businesses. A friend, Jason Marks, has recently started his own business selling office supplies and equipment. One of Jason's competitors is a client of your accounting firm. Jason asks you to give him a printout of this competitor's customer list. What should you do?

(Answer: Accounting information is privileged and confidential. You would betray your client's trust were you to share this information with outsiders. Jason is wrong to ask for the information, and you would be wrong to give it to him.)

Teaching Resources

The *Glencoe Accounting* program offers a variety of teacher support materials for use in tailoring your course to best meet your course objectives and to maximize student learning.

Teacher's Wraparound Edition

The *Teacher's Wraparound Edition* provides an organized teaching plan as well as numerous teaching/learning suggestions printed in the margin beside and below actual student pages.

Teacher's Edition of Chapter Reviews and Working Papers

Solutions to all chapter review pages, chapter exercises, chapter problems, mini-practice sets, and additional chapter problems are contained in the Teacher's Edition of the student workbook, *Chapter Reviews and Working Papers*.

Teacher's Manuals for Business Simulations

Separate teacher's manuals are available for the three business simulations accompanying *Glencoe Accounting*. Each manual provides teaching suggestions for both manual and microcomputer completion, as well as solutions to the simulation.

Teaching Transparencies

Visual learners are more responsive to graphics and illustrations than to the printed word. Fifty full-color instructional transparencies will not only enhance your class presentations of key accounting concepts and procedures but also will help your students to better comprehend your lessons.

Solutions Transparencies

Checking students' accounting papers can be a time-consuming task. To make that task easier, solutions transparencies are available for all exercises, problems, mini-practice sets, and additional reinforcement problems.

Accounting Contest Review

The *Accounting Contest Review* booklet helps you prepare your students to take local, regional, state, and national accounting tests. The booklet reviews accounting concepts and provides practice questions to help students prepare to compete in the accounting examinaton.

Strategies for Teaching Ethics in Accounting

This booklet introduces a Decision Model as well as strategies for teaching and integrating ethics into accounting. Student worksheets are provided for the case studies as well as a simulation for teacher implementation.

Lesson Plans

The *Lesson Plans* booklet provides a lesson plan for each chapter in the student textbook, including chapter learning objectives, the four-step teaching plan, and the major features of each lesson.

Demonstration Problems

The demonstration problems can be used in a variety of ways. Four to five demonstration problems are available for each chapter. They can be used to make transparencies for introducing new concepts or procedures, for make-up work, as short quizzes, or as extra practice.

Source Document Booklet

Business forms provide the financial information used in the accounting system of any business. Source Documents are available for the Mini Practice Sets in both the first year text and the advanced text for use in analyzing the entries to be made in the corresponding journals.

Rules for the Withdrawals Account

A withdrawal is an amount of money or an asset taken out of the business by the owner. Since withdrawals do not occur as frequently as expenses, no separate classification is used for the withdrawals account. Rather, it is classified as a temporary owner's equity account. Withdrawals decrease capital, so the rules of debit and credit are the same as for expense accounts.

Withdrawals Account	
Debit	Credit
+	−
1 Increase Side	2 Decrease Side
3 Balance Side	

Rule 1: The withdrawals account is increased by debits.
Rule 2: The withdrawals account is decreased by credits.
Rule 3: The normal balance for the withdrawals account is a debit balance.

Before you go any further, do the activity that follows to see if you understand the rules of debit and credit for revenue, expense, and withdrawals accounts.

Check Your Learning

Answer these questions about revenue, expense, and withdrawals accounts.

1. What is the normal balance side of any account?
2. What effect does a debit have on an expense account?
3. What is the normal balance for a revenue account?
4. What effect does a credit have on a revenue account?
5. What is the normal balance for an expense account?
6. What effect does a credit have on a withdrawals account?
7. What is the normal balance for a withdrawals account?

Compare your answers to those in the answers section. Re-read the preceding part of the chapter to find the correct answers to any questions you may have missed.

Summarizing the Rules of Debit and Credit

Revenue represents the increase side of the capital account. As a result, revenue accounts are increased on the credit side and decreased on the debit side. The normal balance for revenue accounts is a credit balance. The rules of debit and credit for expense and withdrawals accounts are opposite the rules for revenue accounts. Expenses and withdrawals represent the decrease side of the capital account. Expense and withdrawals accounts then are increased on the debit side and decreased on the credit side. The normal balance for expense and withdrawals accounts is a debit balance. These basic accounting relationships are shown in the T accounts in Figure 4-3.

Skills Improvement Activities

The *Skills Improvement Activities* booklet provides a handy resource for extra activities designed to improve students' analysis, communications, decision-making, human relations, listening, math, problem-solving, and proofreading skills. Answers are provided for all activities.

Tech Prep Strategies

The *Tech Prep Strategies in Accounting* booklet describes the goals of a tech prep program in accounting and offers suggestions for creating a tech prep program for your accounting course. This booklet includes a description of an actual tech prep program that could serve as a model program, suggestions for integrating applied academic skills into the accounting course, background information on providing cooperative learning activities in your classroom, accounting cases that can be used to enrich student learning, and alternative methods of assessing student achievement.

Student Study Plans

Students often need direction in learning how to study most efficiently. Study plans are available to help guide their efforts. Provide a copy of each chapter's study plan to each member of the class.

Math Review for Accounting

The *Math Review for Accounting* is an excellent resource for use with students who may need to review basic math skills at various times during their study of accounting. Math drills will help students who are weak in the math skills needed to complete basic accounting problems.

Accounting Careers

Students who enroll in accounting are often exploring the idea of a career in the field. The *Accounting Careers* booklet provides an overview of accounting occupations and contains guidelines for education and experience required for various occupations. Sources of additional information can be shared with students who are interested in pursuing accounting as a career.

Southwest Airlines: Business Case Studies

A booklet of real-life cases based on business activities at Southwest Airlines gives students a unique glimpse into real-world business and accounting concerns. A Southwest Airlines financial statement poster accompanies the case studies.

Blackline Masters

A package of blackline masters is available for use in duplicating additional accounting forms, making transparencies for instructional purposes, or providing handouts.

Posters

Posters that are suitable for use on classroom bulletin boards or for recruiting displays show the accounting cycle, the rules of debit and credit, and financial statement analysis.

Spanish Supplements

A major segment of our population speaks Spanish as their first language. Certain supplements in this program have been translated into Spanish to help you meet the needs of your Spanish-speaking students. These supplements include *Spanish Resources*, which includes for each chapter an overview, objectives, vocabulary, summary, and review questions. The *Spanish Audiotapes* correspond to the resources booklet. The *Spanish Electronic Study Guide* provides chapter reviews from the student workbook.

Global and Multicultural Insights in Accounting

This booklet provides strategies on integrating global and multicultural issues into the accounting classroom. Individual worksheets are provided on such areas as business close-ups, doing business and financial reporting in other cultures, and developing global understandings.

Accounting Awards

Certificates are available to award your students for their accomplishments using the *Glencoe Accounting* program.

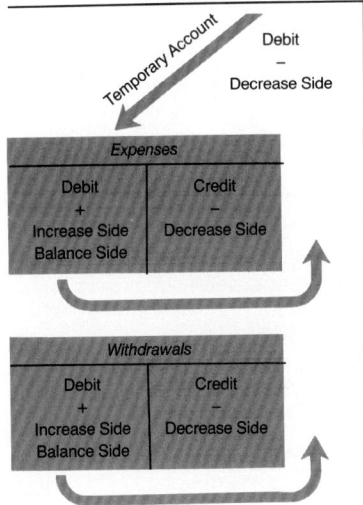

Permanent Account
Capital

Temporary Account

Debit	Credit
−	+
Decrease Side	Increase Side
	Balance Side

Expenses

Debit	Credit
+	−
Increase Side	Decrease Side
Balance Side	

Withdrawals

Debit	Credit
+	−
Increase Side	Decrease Side
Balance Side	

A debit balance is recorded on the debit side. | A credit balance is recorded o

Figure 4-3 Rules of Debit and Credit for Temporary Capital Accounts

R E M E M B E

Debits are used to:	Credits are use
1. Decrease (−) revenues.	1. Increase (+) revenues.
2. Increase (+) expenses.	2. Decrease (−) expenses
3. Increase (+) withdrawals.	3. Decrease (−) withdr

Analyzing Transactions Involving Revenue, Expenses, and Withdrawals

The Global Travel Agency transactions in Chapter 3 dealt with ass liability accounts and with the owner's equity account Jan Harter, Cap keep track of revenue, expenses, and withdrawals, Jan Harter has ex the number of accounts used by the business. The following list shows all the account titles used by Global T been classified as assets, liabilities The accounts have also been nu quickly located.

Business Simulations

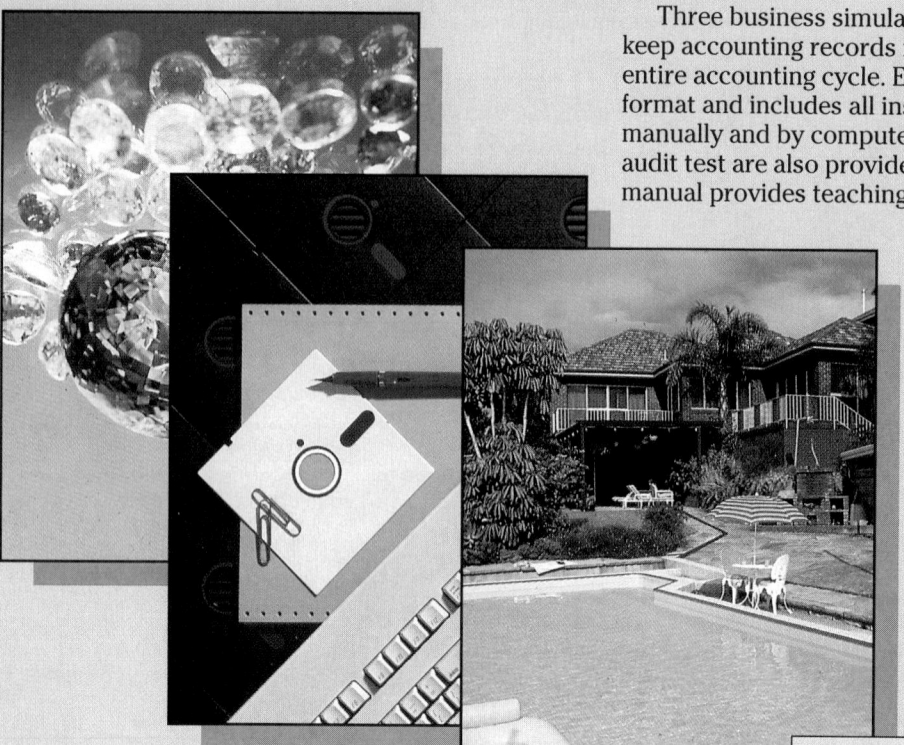

Three business simulations provide opportunities for students to keep accounting records for different types of businesses through an entire accounting cycle. Each simulation comes in a text-workbook format and includes all instructions for completing the simulation both manually and by computer. Source documents, all stationery, and an audit test are also provided in the text-workbook. A separate teacher's manual provides teaching suggestions and complete solutions.

London & Company

London & Company is a closely held, merchandising corporation that sells jewelry and fine gifts at the retail level. In this simulation, students analyze source documents, record transactions in special journals, and complete all work for a full accounting cycle. The simulation requires students to journalize entries for special procedures such as payroll, cash funds, depreciation, uncollectible accounts, inventories, and notes.

Estimated completion time is 15 to 17 hours manually and 5 to 7 hours using the optional microcomputer software.

Lakeshore Computer Center

In this simulation, students complete an accounting cycle for a merchandising business organized as a closely held corporation. This retail business sells computer hardware and software. Students analyze source documents, record transactions in special journals, post to general and subsidiary ledgers, and complete the end-of-period work for the business.

The estimated completion time is 16 to 20 hours manually and 5 to 7 hours using the optional microcomputer software.

AquaClean Pool Service

In this simulation, students complete an accounting cycle for a sole proprietorship, service business that provides pool cleaning services. Students analyze source documents, record transactions in the general journal, post to the general ledger, prepare a work sheet and financial statements, and complete the entries for end-of-cycle activities.

Estimated completion time is 5 to 7 hours manually and 2 to 3 hours using the optional microcomputer software.

Assessment/Testing

Just as students have differing learning styles, so too do they respond differently to testing situations. The *Glencoe Accounting* program provides a variety of materials that can be used to evaluate students' progress throughout the course.

Chapter Tests

Chapter tests combine objective questions and problems that require students to apply the accounting procedures they have learned in the chapter. Chapter tests are available in printed booklets that are sold separately. Order one booklet per student.

Unit Tests

Unit tests are useful for evaluating students' understanding of accounting concepts and procedures over the study of several chapters. Two types of unit tests are available: unit objective tests and unit problem tests. All unit tests are available in two versions: A and B. Both versions cover the same material, and you can alternate the versions from one year to the next or from one class to the next.

Unit objective tests provide matching, multiple choice, and true-false questions covering concepts and procedures. Unit problem tests focus on the accounting procedures taught in the chapters covered.

Alternative Assessment

The *Tech Prep Strategies in Accounting* booklet provides suggestions for devising alternative methods of evaluating student progress, such as team testing, group problem solving, and role playing.

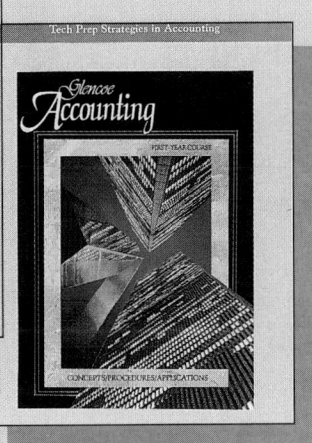

Test Bank

Test-preparation software enables you to develop tailor-made chapter, unit, semester, or final tests. You can customize your tests as desired, choosing from the bank of questions already provided on the software and/or adding your own questions to a test.

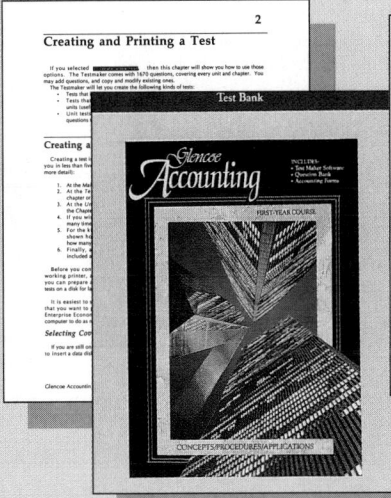

Software

An up-to-date integrated accounting program is at the heart of the *Glencoe Integrated Accounting Software*. This software provides fully integrated general ledger, accounts receivable, accounts payable, and payroll applications.

Glencoe Integrated Accounting Software

The *Glencoe Integrated Accounting Software* program disk, combined with template disks, allows students to complete these activities:

- End-of-chapter problems
- In-book mini-practice sets
- Standalone business simulations

Glencoe Integrated Accounting Software introduces students to the real world of accounting in today's business environment. With this integrated software package, students have access to the following accounting features:

- general ledger
- accounts receivable
- accounts payable
- payroll
- bank reconciliation
- depreciation
- cost of inventory
- financial statement analysis

Glencoe Integrated Accounting Software contains a variety of user features that make it easy to learn and easy to teach. These features make it easy for you to plan lessons that introduce your students to the basic elements of accounting.

- User friendly—Pull-down menus, context-sensitive help windows, a pop-up calculator, and visually appealing data entry screens help your students master computerized accounting.

- Pre-entered data—Problem set disks include all accounts and opening balances for selected text problems, mini-practice sets, and standalone business simulations. Students spend their time practicing accounting procedures, not keying data.

- Automated problem checking—A solutions disk allows you to automate the task of checking your students' work. This disk identifies and reports errors for easy analysis. Installed on a network, inspecting the work of an entire class requires only a few minutes.

- Three versions are available: DOS, Windows, and Macintosh.

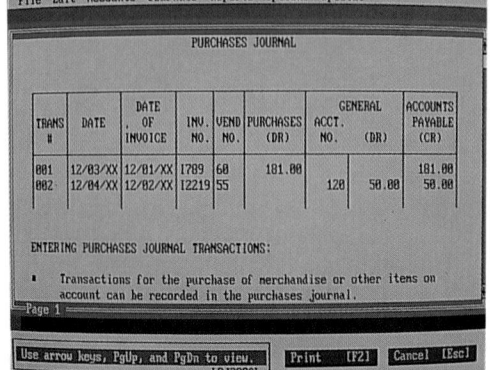

Computerized Accounting Texts

Glencoe offers you a variety of options for teaching computerized accounting procedures, ranging from hardcover textbooks to softcover text-workbooks. Our software texts have been developed to enhance computerized accounting concepts and will complement any curriculum.

Computerized Accounting

Glencoe's *Computerized Accounting* provides students with a smooth transition from manual accounting procedures to the computerized accounting process in the context of real-world business procedures. Three hardcover versions are available for DOS, Macintosh, and Windows. *Computerized Accounting* teaches general ledger accounting concepts and applications using *Glencoe Integrated Accounting*, version 2.0. The spreadsheet chapters are taught using Microsoft Works and Claris Works for Macintosh; and Microsoft Works and Lotus 1-2-3 for DOS and Windows. TurboTax is the commercial software used to teach the income tax chapter. The topics covered in *Computerized Accounting* are listed below.

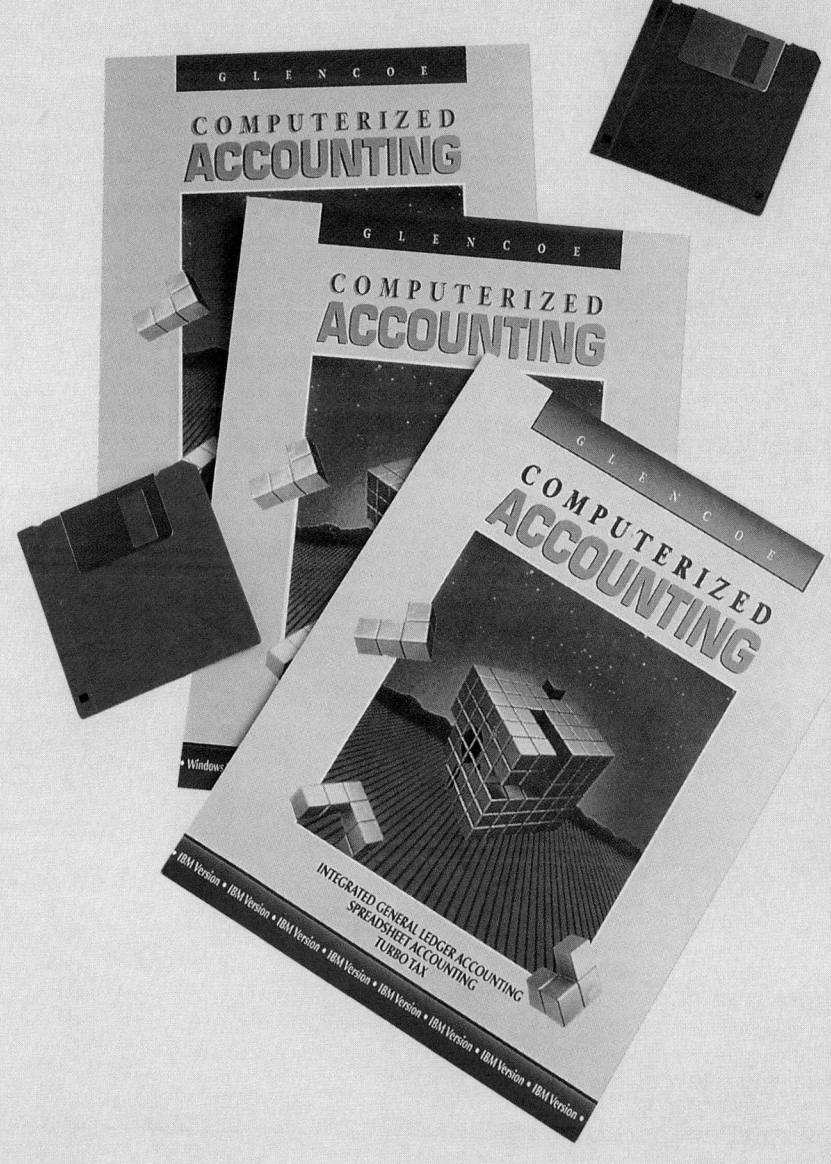

Chapter 1	Introduction to Computerized Accounting
Chapter 2	Exploring the Accounting System
Chapter 3	Recording Transactions in the General Journal
Chapter 4	Recording Transactions in the Sales and Cash Receipts Journals
Chapter 5	Recording Transactions in the Purchases and Cash Payments Journals
Chapter 6	Completing the Accounting Cycle
Chapter 7	Using Special Accounting Tools
Chapter 8	Advanced Accounts Payable Transactions
Chapter 9	Advanced Accounts Receivable Transactions and Partnerships
Chapter 10	Transactions and Financial Statements for Corporations
Chapter 11	Recording the Payroll
Chapter 12	Advanced Financial Statement Analysis
Chapter 13	Using the Inventory System
Chapter 14	Using the Inventory System
Chapter 15	Introduction to Spreadsheet
Chapter 16	Working with and Building Spreadsheets
Chapter 17	Income Tax: Personal and Business

Complementing the hardcover edition of *Computerized Accounting* is the student *Study Guides and Working Papers*. This workbook contains a study guide section for each chapter and the necessary working papers to compete end-of-chapter problems and application activities. Also available is a Teacher's Resource Portfolio containing supplementary teaching materials designed to help you reinforce the accounting concepts presented. Among the materials contained in the portfolio are teaching suggestions, teaching transparencies, supplemental problems, blackline teaching masters, lesson plans, and input forms.

Rounding out the *Computerized Accounting* program are a variety of software offerings. Problem set disks with beginning data for problems in the first fourteen chapters are available for use with *Glencoe Integrated Accounting*.

Also available is solution software to let you quickly and easily check students' work at the computer. For the remaining chapters of Computerized Accounting, spreadsheet and tax template disks are available to help students learn how to work with various types of spreadsheet and tax software they will encounter in the business world.

If your course requires a softcover text, Glencoe offers softcover DOS, Macintosh, and Windows versions of the hardcover text. *Computerized Accounting—DOS with Study Guides and Working Papers, Computerized Accounting—Macintosh with Study Guides and Working Papers,* and *Computerized Accounting —Windows with Study Guides and Working Papers* contain all the featured content of the hardcover texts. These text-workbooks are consumable, with the study guide pages and working papers bound with the text chapters.

Peachtree Accounting

This standalone text-workbook consists of tutorial and application problems specifically designed for use with your Peachtree software. Contents include an introduction to Peachtree software, general ledger, invoicing, purchase orders, accounts receivable, accounts payable, and inventory. Problem set disks containing beginning data for the text-workbook problems are available. Peachtree solution software is available to allow you to automate the process of checking student's work. A teacher's manual and key completes the Peachtree Accounting text-workbook option.

Software

Spreadsheet Applications

Spreadsheet software is available with *Glencoe Accounting, First-Year Course,* enabling students to gain realistic experience in using spreadsheets for a variety of accounting tasks. Students have the option of completing these tasks using either commercial software or simulated software. No additional print materials are required.

Problem templates are provided for DOS, Windows, and Macintosh platforms. Students working in a DOS or Windows environment may use either Lotus 1-2-3 or Microsoft Works spreadsheet and students working in a Macintosh environment may use either Microsoft Works or Claris Works spreadsheet.

The simulated software, which contains the major features of popular commercial spreadsheets, is easy to use and requires no previous knowledge of spreadsheets. Both the spreadsheet program and template data for designated problems in the student textbook are contained on one disk. No separate spreadsheet software is necessary.

The designated spreadsheet exercises and problems are identified in the student textbook with a spreadsheet icon. The spreadsheet activities range from working with the basic accounting equation to completing a 10-column work sheet to analyzing financial statements.

Electronic Study Guide

The *Electronic Study Guide* software is a self-paced computerized review and reinforcement program that helps students assess their own learning as they review textbook concepts, vocabulary, and procedures. No additional print materials are required. For each chapter of the textbook, students reinforce their knowledge of the material just studied using these study aids:

- Objective questions
- Exercises
- Problems
- Chapter summary

With the *Electronic Study Guide,* students can do the following:

- Practice answering different types of questions
- Determine immediately if their answers are correct
- Display feedback—an explanation of the answers
- Display a page number to read more about the topic
- Print the results of their work
- Practice doing exercises and problems
- Work at their own pace

Teaching Accounting with Multimedia Programs

The *Glencoe Accounting* program is an exciting, comprehensive package of learning and teaching materials. One of the newest, most exciting parts of this package is the multimedia component. Multimedia programs are offered for three levels of equipment: Level I videodisc players, computers equipped with CD ROM drives, and Level III interactive multimedia equipment.

Level I Video

Level I is the most basic type of system and may consist only of a videodisc player, a bar code scanner, and a television receiver. Live video and simple interactive applications are possible at this level. Level I of the multimedia program is called *Electronic Field Trips*.

Electronic Field Trips

This videodisc program contains 18 video segments relating to major accounting concepts. Each segment opens with live video that shows students the relationship between an accounting concept and the real world of business. Graphics are used to teach and exemplify a concept, and interactive questions focus students' attention on the topic of the segment and require them to apply their learning from the video. The accounting concepts included in the *Electronic Field Trips* program are listed below.

Segment 1 Accounting All Around You
Segment 2 Career Opportunities in Accounting
Segment 3 Business Ethics
Segment 4 Global Perspectives
Segment 5 Entrepreneurship
Segment 6 Computerized Accounting
Segment 7 Business Transactions
Segment 8 The Accounting Cycle
Segment 9 Banking and Internal Control
Segment 10 Sales and Cash Receipts
Segment 11 Purchases and Cash Payments
Segment 12 Adjusting Entries
Segment 13 Closing Entries
Segment 14 Payroll Accounting
Segment 15 Partnerships and Corporations
Segment 16 Depreciation
Segment 17 Inventory
Segment 18 Financial Statements and Analysis

How to Use the Program

A separate booklet of bar codes provides access to each video segment. Each segment is planned for approximately four minutes of running time. Additional time will be required for class discussion and for responses to and discussion of the interactive questions at the end of the segment.

The *Electronic Field Trips* segments provide an excellent introduction to key accounting concepts taught in the textbook. You may use these videos in several ways.

- Use the video as a novel introduction to pique students' interest.
- Integrate all or part of the segment into your chapter lecture, accessing each section of the video as needed to emphasize a concept.
- Assign a video segment as an independent study project in a lab setting.
- Use the videos as reviews of key concepts.

CD ROM

Many students today are visual learners who rely less on reading a textbook to gain knowledge and more on illustrations and other visual images to acquire understanding of a subject. The CD ROM program is ideal for visual learners, although all students will benefit from its use.

The CD ROM program can be used on a DOS or Macintosh standalone computer with a CD ROM drive. The program contains lessons for each chapter in the textbook and incorporates video images, animation, and graphics to enliven the content of each lesson.

The CD ROM software allows you to manage the entire line of multimedia lessons plus the accounting software for completing chapter problems and simulations.

Textbook Support

The CD ROM disk contains a lesson for each chapter in the textbook. The activities in each lesson can be used either for instruction, for review, or both. Each lesson provides a chapter preview, vocabulary review, presentation of lesson concepts, a review of key points, and interactive chapter exercises with built-in reinforcement.

Chapter Overview and Preview of Chapter Objectives

Each lesson begins with an overview of the chapter and a preview of the chapter objectives. These objectives are also listed in the student textbook.

Vocabulary Review

Understanding the language of accounting is key to mastering accounting concepts and procedures. Vocabulary study is enhanced and reinforced through activities that help students learn new terms, including vocabulary reviews and computer games that focus on chapter terms.

Chapter Lesson

The chapter content is separated into three primary concepts. Graphics and animation are used to convey new concepts to students. Static textbook illustrations come to life in computer animations showing how accounting records are kept.

Chapter Review

The points enumerated in the chapter summary are included as a review activity in the CD ROM lesson.

Interactive Chapter Exercises and Reteaching

The exercises that appear at the end of each chapter in the student textbook can be completed on the computer using the CD ROM program. Each exercise has a reteaching element that functions much as a "Help" screen does in many software programs. If students are unable to complete an exercise or want additional information about concepts or procedures related to the exercise, they may access a reteaching segment that provides support for the content of the exercise and references to the textbook in case students need to consult it for additional information.

Glencoe Accounting Software

In addition to content lessons for each of the textbook chapters, the CD ROM disk also contains all other *Glencoe Accounting* software, including the *Electronic Study Guide*, *Glencoe Accounting Integrated Software, commercial templates*, and the *Spreadsheet Applications Software*.

Spanish Language Resources

The CD ROM program has built-in features designed to assist Spanish-speaking students for whom English is a second language. Students using the program may choose to hear the audio portion of certain sections in either Spanish or English. This option is available for the chapter learning objectives, explanations of the lesson concepts, and the reteaching sections that accompany the end-of-chapter, interactive exercises. See page T4 for a chart listing the Spanish resources available with *Glencoe Accounting*.

Level III Interactive Multimedia

A Level III program is the most versatile multimedia project through its use of live video, graphics, and interactive lesson activities. The Glencoe Level III program requires a videodisc player, a computer equipped with multimedia components, a keyboard, and a mouse. See the manual accompanying the multimedia program for a complete description of hardware requirements.

The Level III program gives you access to the CD ROM lessons and to the Level I video, *Electronic Field Trips*. These videos can be used to introduce a chapter in the textbook, to bring realism to the CD ROM lessons, and to stimulate student interest in a new topic of accounting.

PROGRAM RESOURCES

Advanced Accounting

To be successful in the competitive business environment, today's students need not only to gain accounting knowledge but also to develop an understanding of the use of the computer in applying that knowledge. The *Glencoe Accounting Advanced Course* provides a strong foundation in basic accounting theory and procedures and includes instruction on computerized accounting systems. Traditional methods for teaching accounting are combined with current applications of technology to ensure that students achieve mastery of basic accounting concepts and procedures while they gain computer literacy and a general understanding of how to use the computer to perform various accounting activities.

The *Glencoe Accounting Advanced Course* is designed for both college-bound and vocational students. Much of the same material that students will study in a beginning college accounting course is included in the advanced text, but the material is written at a level suitable for high school students. Further, the coverage of practical accounting procedures helps prepare students for entry-level employment. Finally, the integration of computer applications throughout the text demonstrates the computer's use as a tool in accounting.

Table of Contents

Student Components

Teacher Components

STUDENT TEXT

SOURCE DOCUMENTS FOR MINI PRACTICE SETS

TEACHER'S ANNOTATED EDITION

CHAPTER REVIEWS AND WORKING PAPERS

HERITAGE HOME CENTER BUSINESS SIMULATION

TEACHER'S RESOURCE MANUAL

TEACHING TRANSPARENCIES

CHAPTER REVIEWS AND WORKING PAPERS TEACHER'S EDITION

HERITAGE HOME CENTER BUSINESS SIMULATION TE

PEACHTREE

GLENCOE INTEGRATED ACCOUNTING

SOFTWARE

SPREADSHEET APPLICATIONS

CHAPTER TESTS

TEST BANK

ELECTRONIC STUDY GUIDE

STUDENT ORGANIZATION TREASURER SOFTWARE

NUMERIC KEYPAD PRACTICE

SOLUTIONS

SOFTWARE

TEST BANK SOFTWARE

Marketing Your Accounting Program

Accounting: A Diamond in the Secondary Curriculum

Diamonds are seldom valued until the "prospector" uncovers the treasure, chips away the unwanted debris, and polishes the gem to highlight its brilliance. Only when the gem is highly polished and properly displayed is it truly valued.

The secondary accounting course is such a gem. Its value could have significant influence on most students; yet it is often buried in the overly congested road to education called the high school "Program of Studies." If not properly presented, accounting could become an obscure course offering, seldom valued or understood as a worthy course offering.

Sometimes accounting is viewed as a boring, number crunching, pencil pushing experience that does not challenge students. Nothing could be farther from the truth! Accounting should be an interesting, challenging, enjoyable, and rewarding experience for all students.

When the learning outcomes that all students should master throughout their entire education are identified, it becomes obvious that most of these competencies and skills are addressed within secondary accounting courses. These competencies and skills are not presented as separate units, chapters, or even topics, but rather, they are integrated within the accounting course as relevant, ongoing learning experiences.

Some of the basic education skills that are incorporated and reinforced in secondary accounting include reading, mathematics, economics, and communications. The accounting program also emphasizes the development of personal attributes such as motivation, ethics, values, and responsibility. Higher level skills such as analytical reasoning, problem solving, critical thinking, interpersonal relationships, and creativity can be integrated into various activities and projects.

Computer applications are an integral part of the accounting program to prepare students with the skills and knowledge needed for a technology-oriented market. Through the use of spreadsheets and similar software programs, accounting students can use technology for analysis, problem solving, and "what if" kinds of business situations.

The accounting curriculum provides students with the foundation skills necessary for entry-level employment in the business world.

> *Accounting should be an interesting, challenging, enjoyable, and rewarding experience for all students.*

At the same time, cooperative skills, attitudes, and business applications are being developed that enable students to become productive citizens in a global society. When presented properly, secondary accounting can provide the kinds of job-related experiences that all students need.

Often, however, accounting courses do not receive proper recognition for their practical contribution to secondary education. This is often due to two factors. Initially, guidance counselors and administrators are not adequately informed of the curriculum content, or the value for students in taking an accounting course. They are not aware that accounting develops and reinforces attitudes, skills, and competencies required for all students. Secondly, since graduation requirements have increased, students have less time in their schedule for elective course offerings such as accounting.

It is imperative that accounting teachers make known the course content (both obvious and hidden) and the value in taking an accounting course for educational and employment pursuits. This message should be communicated to the entire education community, which includes the board of education, building administrators, guidance counselors, teaching colleagues, parents, and most importantly, students.

To achieve support from all aspects of the education community, three essential stages of development are required. First, there must be COMMUNICATION. Without information and understanding, nothing will be accomplished. Second, there must be SUPPORT and MOTIVATION. Individuals or groups must be excited about the information presented. If there is not motivation to react, then there will be no reaction. Third, there must be ACTION. If action or reaction does not take place, communication is of little value.

Communication with Students and Colleagues

Secondary teachers realize that the best spokespersons for the accounting course are accounting students. Their enthusiasm for the course will be communicated to fellow students through daily conversations and discussions. Unfortunately, all students will not have contact with present or former accounting students; therefore, accounting teachers must make additional efforts to convey the message and to develop creative approaches in finding opportunities to reach all secondary students.

Promotional ideas such as recruitment posters, flyers, guest speakers, and preregistration "sales pitches" on course selections have proved to be somewhat successful. But the time has now come for accounting teachers to be innovative and creative. In a more competitive educational environment, effective PR is now a unique challenge.

An example of one effective approach to help students become aware of accounting is to develop a brief presentation (10 to 15 minutes) on the history of accounting and how a variety of accounting procedures were used during various periods of world history. You may wish to approach the social studies/history teachers and ask for permission to make a presentation to their classes. At the conclusion of the presentation, a modern view of accounting along with a profile of the secondary accounting course may be included.

Another approach is to meet with students in computer applications and programming classes within the school. Begin by asking the students to describe computer business applications with which they are familiar. Then discuss the many uses of computers in business and explain that accounting is at the heart of many of those applications. Be prepared to show examples of computerized applications such as a cash register receipt or a credit card sales receipt. Students who enjoy working with computers are likely to be interested in learning about accounting when they see the role of computers in accounting.

Communication with Administrators and Guidance Counselors

Another area of communication that has often been a concern for accounting teachers is with administrators and guidance counselors. The best way to get these individuals informed and involved is to have them attend a class. Have students offer the invitation. Counselors and administrators are more apt to accept invitations from students; and as a result, they may perceive classroom activities with a different perspective. At the conclusion of the class they will leave more informed and more supportive of the accounting program.

Communication with Parents and Students

An excellent way to communicate with both parents and students is to use a recruitment letter explaining what accounting is and why it is a worthwhile course. The names of

potential accounting students may be obtained from either the administration or guidance department's listing of students. The recruitment letter should be addressed to the individual student and placed in his/her homeroom teacher's mailbox for distribution to that student. Write a similar letter to the students' parents or guardians.

The recruitment letter will enable both students and parents to become informed about the benefits

> *Often . . . accounting courses do not receive proper recognition for their practical contribution to secondary education.*

in taking an accounting course. An added benefit is that parents usually appreciate the personal correspondence. Timing is of the utmost importance! Send out the recruitment letter prior to the scheduling for next year's courses.

Conclusion

Accounting teachers must continue the effort to present the accounting course much like the prospector does in displaying the gem. Only with a creative marketing plan will the entire education community become informed about accounting and grow to appreciate the fact that it is truly a "gem," a valuable course for all students.

Reprinted with permission and adapted from an article written by William B. Hoyt and published in *Business Education Forum* (February 1993).

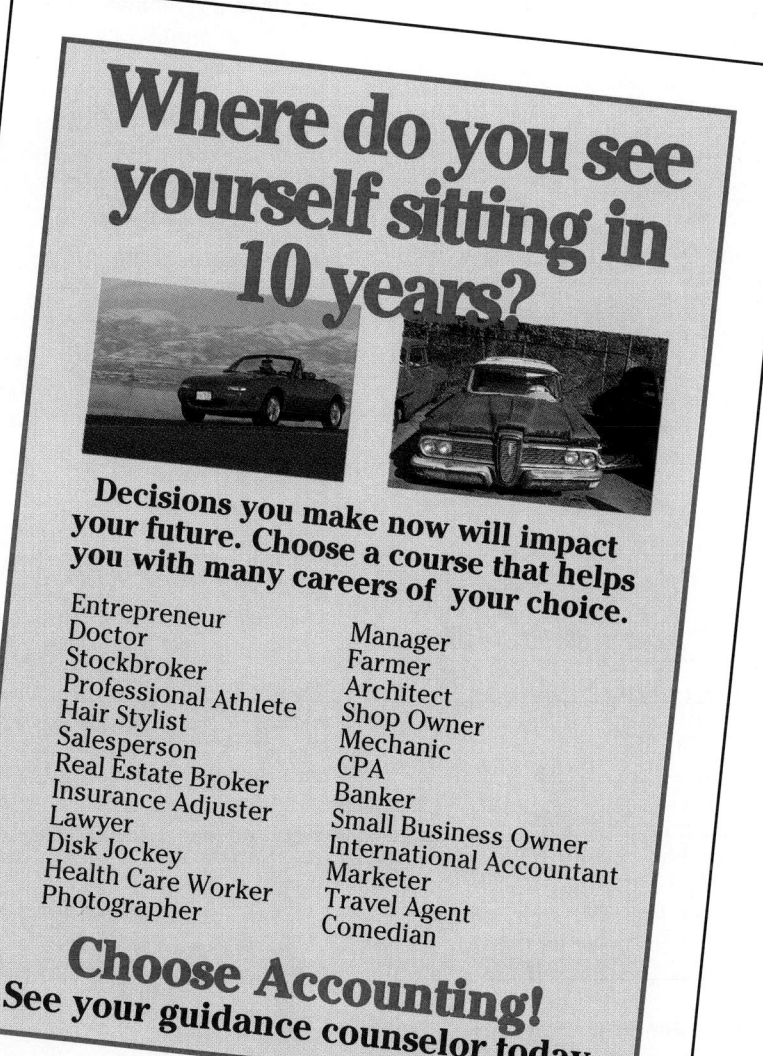

Integrating Computer Technology Into the Accounting Curriculum

Advances in computer technology are continually being made, and these advances dramatically affect all aspects of accounting. Accounting instruction should include an awareness of advances in computer technology and how these advances affect the processing of accounting data. Wherever possible, discuss computer technology with your students as an ongoing part of the accounting course. Advise students to be on the lookout for articles and advertisements in newspapers and magazines that focus on new developments in computer technology. *Glencoe Accounting* also includes several features to help you integrate computer technology into your accounting classroom.

- Focus on Computers vignettes appear throughout the student text. These vignettes demonstrate the role that technology plays in modern accounting, and they foster computer awareness. You can discuss the vignettes in class or use them as a springboard for further study.
- Computers in Accounting features in the Teacher's Wraparound Edition provide a real-world focus on how computers are used to process accounting information. You can also discuss with your students how the procedures they are learning to do manually are processed by computers.

Students also will benefit from using a computer to complete their accounting problems. They learn the role computers play in business and how computers are used to perform various accounting procedures. Generally students will learn best by first applying accounting procedures and preparing various accounting documents manually. Manual preparation helps them learn the *why* as well as the *how* of accounting. Transferring the manual procedure to the computer helps students see how computer technology augments accounting functions. The computer then becomes an instructional tool to enhance accounting instruction.

Accounting Software for the Classroom

A variety of educational and commercial software is available for use in the accounting classroom.

Review and Reinforcement Software

Tutorial programs help students review accounting terms, concepts, and procedures learned in a chapter. These computerized exercises can be used as review by students who need additional help with the chapter content, by students who have been absent from class discussion, or by students who want reinforcement of their mastery of the chapter content. When using electronic review and reinforcement, students can work independently to control the pace of their learning or in pairs to cooperatively increase their expertise.

Glencoe Accounting's Electronic Study Guide is a computerized system that will help your students study accounting basics on a chapter-by-chapter basis. Students get immediate feedback, learn where to find out more about a topic, and can print the results of their work.

Integrated Accounting Software

Students can use integrated accounting software to work end-of-chapter problems and mini-practice sets in the textbook and to complete separate business simulations. If you want your students to spend additional class periods on the computer, you should use a separate computerized accounting textbook in addition to your main text. With integrated accounting software, students can complete the accounting applications on the computer and learn the differences between manual and computerized accounting procedures.

Glencoe's *Integrated Accounting Software* is a complete, self-contained educational software program with disks containing beginning data for selected end-of-chapter problems, mini practice sets, simulations and computerized accounting texts. Separate solutions-checking disks enable you to use the computer to check students' work. A recent trend in the accounting classroom is to introduce students to a commercial integrated accounting package. A commercial package will give your students experience in using software found in business. A suggestion is to have your students use an educational package during Year l and a commercial package during Advanced Accounting. Glencoe has developed a *Peachtree Accounting* text with templates to give your students commercial software experience in either Year l or Advanced Accounting.

Spreadsheet Applications

Widely used in business today, the electronic spreadsheet is especially important in accounting. Spreadsheet applications software turns the computer into a tool that can perform calculations and analyze relationships among numbers. Spreadsheets can be used to calculate a variety of financial reports such as budget summaries, salary reports, income statements, balance sheets, and so on. They can be most helpful in situations in which the user wants to test a number of different financial variables.

Spreadsheet applications software is available with *Glencoe Accounting* for the first year course. This program enables students to gain realistic experience in using spreadsheets for a variety of accounting tasks. Students do not need any previous knowledge of spreadsheets. The activities are coordinated with selected end-of-chapter problems and range from working with the basic accounting equation to completing a 10-column worksheet to analyzing financial statements. Templates for DOS–Lotus 1-2-3 and Microsoft Works–and for Macintosh–Microsoft Works and Claris Works are available for the advanced course, and the activities also are coordinated with selected end-of-chapter problems.

Using Accounting Software with Limited Hardware

As with many other types of instructional tools, the more equipment available, the more flexibility your program can have. The ideal situation is to have one computer for each member of the accounting class. You also might have access several times a week to a school computer lab. If either of these situations exist, you have unlimited opportunities for providing a wide range of computer activities. It is possible, however, to provide some computer activities with limited computer hardware. Let's look at three different levels of computer inventory and how you can implement computer activities in the accounting course.

- One Computer for Twenty-five Students. Review and reinforcement programs usually contain short segments. With one computer, three to five students can be accommodated in an average class period by rotating students at the computer. Students also can use business accounting software to complete textbook problems and mini-practice sets. Rather than having each student complete each problem, form teams of two or possibly three students and assign a problem to each team. All students can then gain some computer experience without taking an excessive amount of classroom time.

The one-computer classroom is also ideal for demonstration using an electronic display device hooked up to a computer and an overhead projector. Remember that computerized student demonstrations of accounting principles are excellent learning situations that develop not only accounting content

knowledge but also software and communication skills as well.

- Three to Five Microcomputers for Twenty-five Students. Three to five students can be accommodated at each computer in an average class period. All students should be able to complete review and reinforcement activities as well as work through some textbook problems and mini-practice set activities. However, it is unlikely that students can complete business simulations during a single class period. It is possible, though, to have students work in teams of two or three persons to complete the simulations.
- Seven to Ten Microcomputers for Twenty-five Students. Review and reinforcement programs, textbook problems and mini-practice sets, and business simulations can all be completed on an individual basis. With proper scheduling, students should have sufficient time to complete several computer activities without intruding on instructional time.

Multimedia

As an accounting teacher, you know that your students have varying learning styles. Some students are print-dominant learners; others are non-print-dominant learners. To help you accommodate these varying learning styles and to integrate listening, hands-on application, and more frequent stimulation and interactivity into the accounting environment, *Glencoe Accounting* includes three multimedia components. These components are designed for use on a wide variety of available hardware configurations.

Level I Video

If your school has a basic system consisting of a videodisc player, a bar code scanner, and a television receiver, Level I of the *Glencoe Accounting* multimedia program can be an effective tool for classroom presentations.

This videodisc program, called *Electronic Field Trips*, contains 18 video segments relating to major accounting concepts. Students see the connection between accounting concepts and the real world of business.

Interactive questions focus students' attention and require them to apply what they have learned.

CD ROM

The Glencoe CD ROM program can be used on your DOS or Macintosh standalone computer with a CD ROM drive. The CD ROM program contains lessons for each chapter in the textbook and incorporates video images, animation, and graphics to make accounting come alive for your students. With the CD ROM software, you can manage the entire line of multi-media lessons plus the accounting software for completing chapter problems, mini-practice sets, and simulations.

Level III Interactive Multimedia

The Glencoe Level III program requires a videodisc player, a computer equipped with multimedia components, a keyboard, and a mouse. Live video, graphics, and interactive lesson activities make this program the most versatile of the three multimedia components. The Level III program gives you access to the CD ROM lessons and to the Level I video, *Electronic Field Trips*.

Computer Training for Accounting Teachers

You must have a general knowledge of computer operation, but you do not have to have a knowledge of internal hardware elements or programming languages. Resources exist in every school or district for help in using and troubleshooting equipment. These resources include other computer teachers, lab assistants and technology supervisors. Concentrate on becoming familiar with the operation of your software programs. Remember that software hotlines are one of your best resources when using any type of software. Glencoe's software HOTLINE is 1-800-437-3715.

Using Calculators

The calculator is a valuable tool in keeping accurate accounting records. When used properly, it can save time in performing computations and can help ensure accuracy. Your students may have access to electronic calculators, pocket or hand-held calculators, and pop-up calculators within computer software programs.

The ability to key numbers by touch is a skill that is valuable to accounting workers. You can help your students become proficient in using the calculator by giving them instruction and practice for one or two class periods.

Calculator Operations

To complete their accounting work quickly and accurately, students need to know how to perform the following operations on their calculators:

- Enter and clear a number.
- Clear an entire computation.
- Add and subtract whole numbers.
- Multiply and divide whole numbers.
- Add and subtract numbers with decimals.
- Use the percent key to find the percentage of a number.
- Use the memory keys.

Proficiency Using a Keypad

The numbers in a keypad are usually located in the same position on most electronic calculators and computer keyboards. The locations of return/enter keys and special function keys vary from one model to another.

On the ten-key numeric keypad, the home keys are the *4, 5,* and *6* keys. Have students place their three middle fingers on these keys. Show students how to position their fingers correctly. Give students a

> *The ability to key numbers by touch is a skill that is valuable to accounting workers.*

few drills using these keys by writing a series of numbers on the chalkboard. Have students key columns of numbers using just these keys and the enter key. Appendix A of the student workbook *Chapter Reviews and Working Papers* contains instructions and several exercises designed to help students develop proficiency in keying numbers by touch.

When students are comfortable with the home keys, add drills for the keys above and below each home key. Drill students on one set of keys at a time, for example, the *4, 7,* and *1* keys. Finally, drill students on all numbers. Begin the number drills with simple columns, then have students add, subtract, multiply, and divide numbers. Use numbers with decimals in some drills to give students practice on that key. Numeric Keypad software is included in the *Glencoe Accounting* program to provide students with instruction and practice in developing accuracy and speed using a computer numeric keypad.

Pocket Calculators

Many different kinds of pocket calculators exist, and they may work differently from larger calculators and pop-up computer calculators. Help students who are using pocket calculators by discussing the differences in their calculators. Students who have very small calculators may not be able to develop as much proficiency in keying numbers by touch because of the limitations of the keypad.

Estimation Skills

Remind students that errors may occur if numbers are keyed incorrectly. Discuss estimation as a technique for judging the appropriateness of an answer. Encourage students to estimate an answer before computing it on the calculator to make sure the answer is reasonable.

Tech Prep Strategies

A successful tech prep program addresses the needs of a diverse group of students so that they can acquire the skills and knowledge necessary to become productive members of a highly skilled and competitive work force.

To achieve effective learning, there must be an articulation for a sequence of study that provides for a smooth transition from secondary to post-secondary education. In addition, the tech prep program must offer some flexibility so that students are able to make choices throughout the program regarding formal education pursuits and appropriate work experiences.

Like business education, a tech prep program must have its roots in academic principles and procedures, and the program must address realistic work environments. A collaboration between education and business and industry is needed to define vocational and academic competencies and to determine proper course content and sequence.

Suggestions for implementing a tech prep program for accounting are contained in the *Tech Prep Strategies in Accounting* booklet, which includes a description of a model program, applied academic strategies, cooperative learning strategies, the case-study approach, and alternative assessment suggestions.

The "4 + 2" Model

Tech prep programs are intended to offer students flexibility in preparing either for college or for a vocational-technical career. This section describes a model program emphasizing vocational study and incorporating academic studies to prepare students for postsecondary education. An articulation agreement for dual enrollment is presented as an example of how you can implement secondary and postsecondary curriculums in accounting.

Applied Academic Strategies

Part 2 of the *Tech Prep Strategies* booklet addresses three types of interdisciplinary teaching strategies: computer applications, communications, and mathematics. In addition, the *Teacher's Wraparound Edition* includes short features, called "Interdisciplinary Connections," that you can use to integrate academic applications into your accounting instruction.

Cooperative Learning Strategies

Interaction facilitates learning. All students gain from small group learning activities in which everyone participates. Cooperative learning experiences contribute to academic achievement while also helping students develop essential social skills for working cooperatively in a group.

Part 3 of the *Tech Prep Strategies* booklet describes a variety of cooperative learning methods and provides several activities for your use in the accounting class. In addition, the *Teacher's Wraparound Edition* includes a cooperative learning activity in each text chapter.

Case-Study Approach

Management cases challenge students to hone their analysis skills and to address decision-making situations that go beyond chapter exercises, problems, and activities. Cases help students apply their accounting knowledge to real-world business activities. They also provide opportunities for cooperative learning experiences and small-group activities. Ten cases and solutions are given in the *Tech Prep Strategies* book. These cases are designed to help your students develop skills such as analysis, decision making, problem solving, and communications.

Alternative Assessment

You need ways to evaluate your accounting students on knowledge and skills that go beyond accounting concepts and procedures. Part 5 of the *Tech Prep Strategies* book suggests other skills—such as working in teams, thinking critically, making

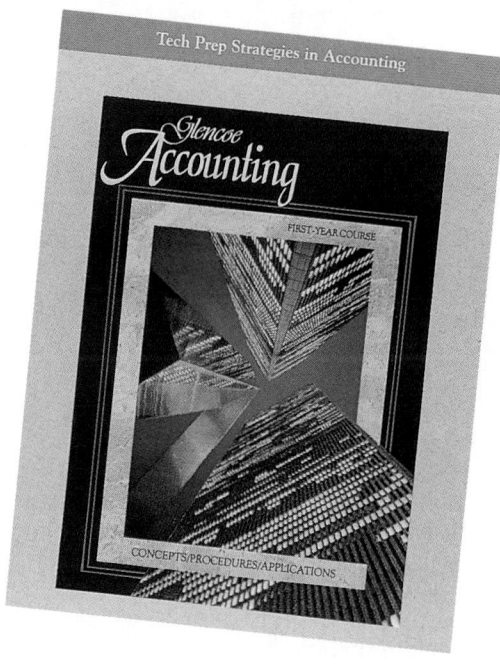

decisions—that should be evaluated and several assessments alternatives.

Improvement of Basic Skills

A separate booklet, *Skills Improvement Activities*, gives you a resource for practice activities to encourage students to improve their skills in such critical areas as problem solving and decision making, communications, human relations, and analysis.

The Future of Tech Prep

The jobs of the future will require more and more technical knowledge. Workers will need frequent retraining to keep up with technical changes, and education will also need to update its curriculum to accommodate new technology. The tech prep movement has been strongly supported by the National Business Education Association, whose organizational creed calls for the development of a world-class workforce. The *Glencoe Accounting* program complies with the concerns addressed by the NBEA.

Reinforcing Study Skills

Many students today have poor study skills, and, as a result, they need help in learning how to learn. In addition, poor reading, writing, and math skills contribute to both frustration and difficulty in learning.

Helping students develop the skill of learning will benefit them throughout their lives. In our rapidly changing, high technology world, future workers will be required to learn new technologies frequently. Having good learning skills will mean the difference between a productive worker who is able to change as the job changes and one who is forced into less skilled work because of a lack of technical skills.

The SQ3R Study Method

Students can use the SQ3R study method to increase their reading comprehension of any textbook because it gives them an organized approach to gaining information from printed material. It is especially helpful for a textbook presenting technical information and can help students improve their learning efficiency.

The letters SQRRR have the following meanings: Survey, Question, Read, Recite, and Review. Let's look now at each of these five steps in detail.

Step 1: Survey

As students begin each new chapter, have them *survey* it by first reading the chapter title and the chapter introduction. Second, they should review the learning objectives and the new terms. Third, they should read the chapter headings and think about how they relate to the learning objectives. As they look over the chapter, they should also look at all the figures and pictures and read the caption for each. Finally, they should look over the pages at the end of each chapter, noting in particular the Summary of Key Points. This procedure will give them a general idea of what the

chapter is about. Since each chapter is organized in a consistent format, students can follow this survey procedure throughout the course.

Step 2: Question

The essence of this step is to turn each heading into a question. For

> *Having good learning skills will mean the difference between a productive worker who is able to change and one who is forced into less skilled work because of a lack of technical skills.*

example, in Chapter 1 the first heading reads, "The United States Private Enterprise Economy." By turning this heading into a question, students ask themselves: "What is a private enterprise economy?" By beginning their study of each topic with a question, students are setting a purpose for studying the topic. They are now active participants in the search for answers rather than passive observers being given information. Using the question method helps students focus on the goal of their study.

Step 3: Read

Students read the topic at this step. As students read, they should keep their questions in mind and pay particular attention to the definitions of the highlighted terms. These definitions of new terms should be read slowly and more than once. Understanding the meanings of the terms is key to understanding the

---

Reinforcing Study Skills

Step Two of the SQ3R method is *Question*. To familiarize students with this approach, have them read each section or subsection head and turn it into a question that will focus their reading; for example, "What are the rules of debit and credit?" After reading the section, students should be able to answer the question they have generated.

Provide a copy of the *Student Study Plans* to each class member to help organize study activities or to individualize practice and review activities.

Reinforcing Study Skills

Setting purposes for reading often helps students focus on the main points. Have students read the chapter introduction and then, in their own words, explain what they think this chapter will be about. As students read, have them refer back to the Learning Objectives and try to meet each one as they go along.

Provide a copy of the *Student Study Plans* to each class member to help organize study activities or to individualize practice and review activities.

lesson. If basic language is not understood, students will have difficulty comprehending the accounting concepts throughout the course.

This method of reading will give more meaning to each topic, and students should be able to answer their questions; for example, "A private enterprise system is an economy in which people are free to produce the goods and services they choose and to use their money as they wish."

Step 4: Recite

In this step students do a *self-check* of what they have learned. They go back and restate the heading of the topic as a question and ask themselves if they can answer it. They should recite the answer to the question in their own words. This procedure helps students remember what information was important. Students should then complete the Check Your Learning activities following the topic. Self-check problems are a key part of the recite step, and students are able to verify their knowledge by checking the answers in the back of their textbook.

Step 5: Review

After students have read all the topics and have completed all the Check Your Learning activities, they then go back and review the entire chapter. You can help students review in class by discussing the material covered in the chapter, completing the vocabulary and review sections at the end of every chapter, completing the study guide pages in the working papers, or integrating the *Electronic Study Guide* into class activities.

As students move ahead in the lesson and work on the problems, they have many opportunities for review. An inability to solve the problems is a sure indicator that something is wrong. If this is the case with some students, they may need to go back to Step 1.

Summary

The SQ3R method will work if students use it. Discuss the method with students and illustrate its use each time you begin the first several chapters of the text. Give students a list of the steps and describe how the steps apply to studying a chapter. Also, continually remind students of SQ3R as you progress through the course and check to see if they are using it. Reviewing the SQ3R method and reinforcing its use are essential in helping your students develop good study skills.

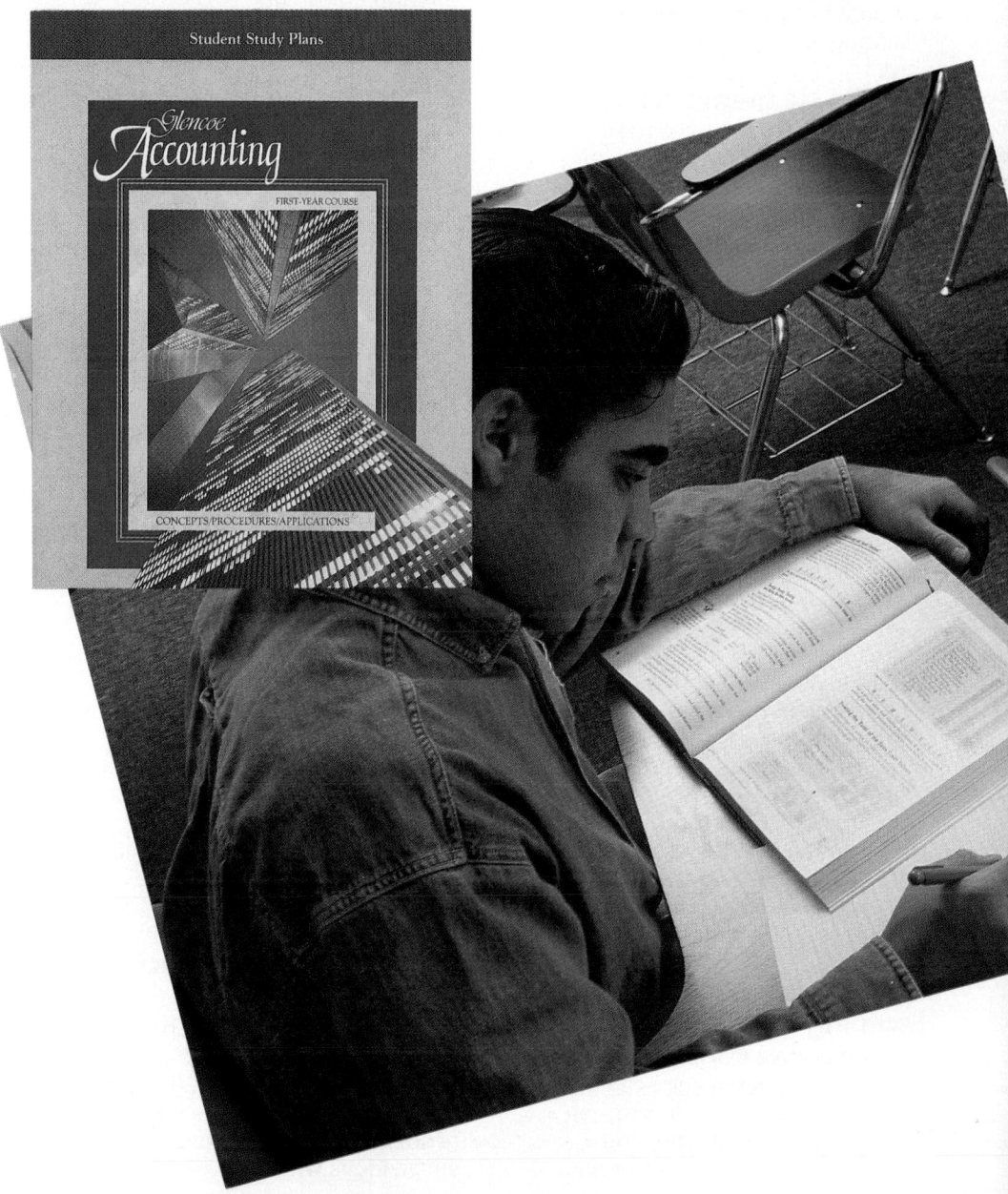

You can also use the method as a technique for instruction. In other words, you can follow each step when presenting a lesson, which reinforces the process of the study method for students and provides a means for improving study habits and increasing learning efficiency.

A sample study plan that you can use to teach your students SQ3R is provided in the *Student Study Plans* booklet. A blackline master outlining the steps of the plan is also available. The study plan provides step-by-step instructions on how to use the SQ3R study method for each chapter.

Using Cooperative Learning

Studies show that students learn faster and retain more information when they are actively involved in the learning process. Studies also show that in a classroom setting, adolescents often learn more from each other about subject matter than from a traditional teacher-led lecture and discussion. Cooperative learning is one method that gets students actively involved in learning and at the same time allows for peer teaching.

The Basic Elements of Cooperative Learning

Cooperative learning involves assigning students to small groups to work together within a traditional classroom setting. This learning structure is especially effective for more difficult learning tasks such as problem solving, critical thinking, and conceptual learning. The basic elements of a cooperative learning group are as follows:

- Cooperative learning emphasizes working toward group goals as opposed to the traditional emphasis on individual competition and achievement.
- Students discover that not only must they learn the material themselves, but also they are responsible for helping everyone in the group learn the material.
- The successes or failures of the group are shared by all members of the group.
- All members of the group have the same goal, and they must share equally the responsibilities for accomplishing that goal.

The Purposes of Cooperative Learning Groups

Cooperative learning contributes positively to increasing academic achievement; and while learning academics, students develop essential social skills so they can work together cooperatively. The use of cooperative learning groups accomplishes the following several purposes.

- Students achieve by helping each other, and they become actively involved in the learning process.
- Students take a more active role. Many students who are reluctant to participate in a large class discussion may take part in a small group interaction.
- Students' attitudes and motivation toward learning the subject matter of the course improve.
- Students with differing abilities can be assigned to each group. Capable students can share their ideas with less capable students, with the result being an improvement in the overall competency level of the class.

> *Cooperative learning . . . gets students actively involved in learning and at the same time allows for peer teaching.*

- Students learn valuable social and problem-solving skills that transfer to real-world occupations and work environments.
- Students improve their communication skills.
- Students are involved in the solution of problems they might not have been able to solve on their own.

Preparation and Social Skills

Before assigning a cooperative learning activity, prepare your students for the cooperative learning process and discuss the importance of social skills. The following suggestions will help you set the stage for effective cooperative learning.

Classroom Arrangement

Arrange the furniture in the room so that students can face each other as they work together.

Group Size

Decide on the size of the group. Groups work best when they are composed of two to five students.

Group Assignments

Assign students to groups. Each group should be mixed racially, socially, ethnically, and by gender and range of ability.

Rotation of Group Members

Change groups periodically. For example, you can change the groups every four to six weeks, every quarter, every semester, or for every new teaching unit.

Student Preparation

Prepare students for cooperation. Students need to understand that they are part of a group. The students work with each other to accomplish the same goal, but each student is individually accountable for learning.

Initial Activities

Start small. It is not necessary to incorporate all the characteristics of cooperative learning into the first activity. Some ideas will be easy to adapt while others may be more difficult. The first few days may seem disorganized, with some students upset, others mistrustful, and others off task. Be patient and keep at it.

Group Roles

Explain group roles. Students need to learn the cooperative skills that are fundamental to each role before they begin interacting in cooperative activities. The roles should be introduced to students one at a time so the students can learn the differences between them. Once all the roles have been learned, they should be rotated among the group members daily or weekly. Following are suggested tasks for each member of the group.

- **Recorder or Secretary**— Records group answers and serves as spokesperson for the group when appropriate.
- **Gatekeeper**—Ensures that all members participate and that no one individual dominates.
- **Praiser or Cheerleader**—Makes sure each group member's contribution is appreciated.
- **Taskmaster**—Guides the discussion or work to keep the group on target and encourages everyone to participate.

Responsibilities of the Teacher

The success of the cooperative learning groups depends on the teacher's ability to coach each of the groups. The teacher creates the environment and structures the process of learning, then guides the students' learning. Specifically, the teacher:

- Motivates the students to learn.
- States the goals of the instruction.
- Teaches the fundamental concepts.
- Interacts with and guides the work of many groups.
- Acts as a resource to the groups as needed.
- Monitors student behavior.
- Evaluates the group process.

> *The teacher creates the environment and structures the process of learning, then guides the students' learning.*

Evaluation of Group Activities

After group assignments are completed, students can be evaluated on individual performance through testing and applications and scored individually or as a group. Evaluation tools may include traditional tests and quizzes, group quizzes, and extra points for groups achieving overall high marks.

The accounting course provides many opportunities for cooperative learning. The "Cooperative Learning" section of the *Tech Prep Strategies in Accounting* booklet defines a list of 13 cooperative learning structures including co-op/co-op, jigsaw, brainstorming, and pairs check. For each of the 13 structures, two suggested activities and a description of the sequence of steps for implementing each activity illustrate how the structures can be adapted to the accounting curriculum.

Using Alternative Assessment

Evaluation of students' performance is fundamental to the teaching and learning process. In an accounting course, students' accounting skills typically are evaluated by using applications and written tests. These applications and tests are directed at individual students, and they provide a formal assessment of student performance. Such tests, however, do not evaluate students' communication and critical-thinking skills or problem-solving abilities. If classroom instruction is to parallel real-world applications, the evaluation of student performance should also relate to the personal skills that students will apply in the real world. Some of the alternatives to formal assessments include observation, questioning, presentations and discussion, projects, and portfolios and journals. These assessments are generally directed to the class as a whole and provide an informal evaluation of students' performance. These informal assessments are briefly described below along with a discussion of how the *Glencoe Accounting* program addresses each.

Observation

Observation of students at work is a natural part of the instructional process. You can observe each student's ability to work independently. You can also observe students' communication, human relations, and teamwork skills as they interact in cooperative learning groups or within a whole class setting.

Specific suggestions for group activities are included in this *Teacher's Wraparound Edition*.

Oral presentations and class discussions are especially effective for assessing students' knowledge, communication skills, and critical thinking abilities.

Questioning

Questioning, or the inquiry approach, is an excellent tool for assessing the competence of students and monitoring the development of meaningful understanding of concepts. Dialogue between the teacher and student is beneficial in identifying problems students are having in comprehending what is being taught.

You can evaluate analysis and problem-solving skills by having students explain how they solved a problem. Or, you can ask students to show their work at the chalkboard and evaluate their math skills. In either case, if a student does not give

ANALYSIS

WilsonJones

INDEX COMMUNICATIONS

the correct answer, you can identify why the answer is wrong and provide corrective guidance.

You can also analyze the questions that students ask during class and group work to assess their misunderstandings. In addition to the Check Your Learning questions and Reviewing Your Accounting Knowledge questions for every chapter, specific suggestions for questioning strategies are included in the side columns of this *Teacher's Wraparound Edition* and in the Making Connections activities, Critical Thinking activities, and Pop Quizzes.

Presentations and Discussions

Oral presentations and class discussions are especially effective for assessing students' knowledge, communication skills, and critical thinking abilities. Oral presentations give students the opportunity to present their own ideas to classmates, and you can then evaluate not only their communication skills but also their thought processes.

You can also evaluate students' verbal skills and listening skills through class discussions. The "Improving Your Skills" sections at the end of each chapter are excellent topics for class discussions. Specific suggestions for presentations and discussions are also included in the side columns of this *Teacher's Wraparound Edition* in the Cooperative Learning activities and Critical Thinking topics.

Projects

Projects allow you to assess multidimensional skills such as organizing, problem solving, and analysis. Projects involve students in real-world situations, and you can evaluate how well students manage a project from start to finish over several days of work.

In addition to evaluating the accuracy of the completed materials, you can evaluate a variety of factors such as the student's ability to find the data, compile it, and interpret it. The *Glencoe Accounting, First-Year Course*, offers five in-book mini-practice sets that give students the opportunity to integrate their knowledge of accounting concepts and procedures studied in two or more chapters. Further, three business simulations accompany the *Glencoe Accounting, First-Year Course* and give you an opportunity to evaluate students' skills in organizing their work, finding answers to questions, and completing the project on time. Descriptions of these simulations are included in this *Teacher's Wraparound Edition*.

Projects allow you to assess multidimensional skills such as organizing, problem solving, and analysis.

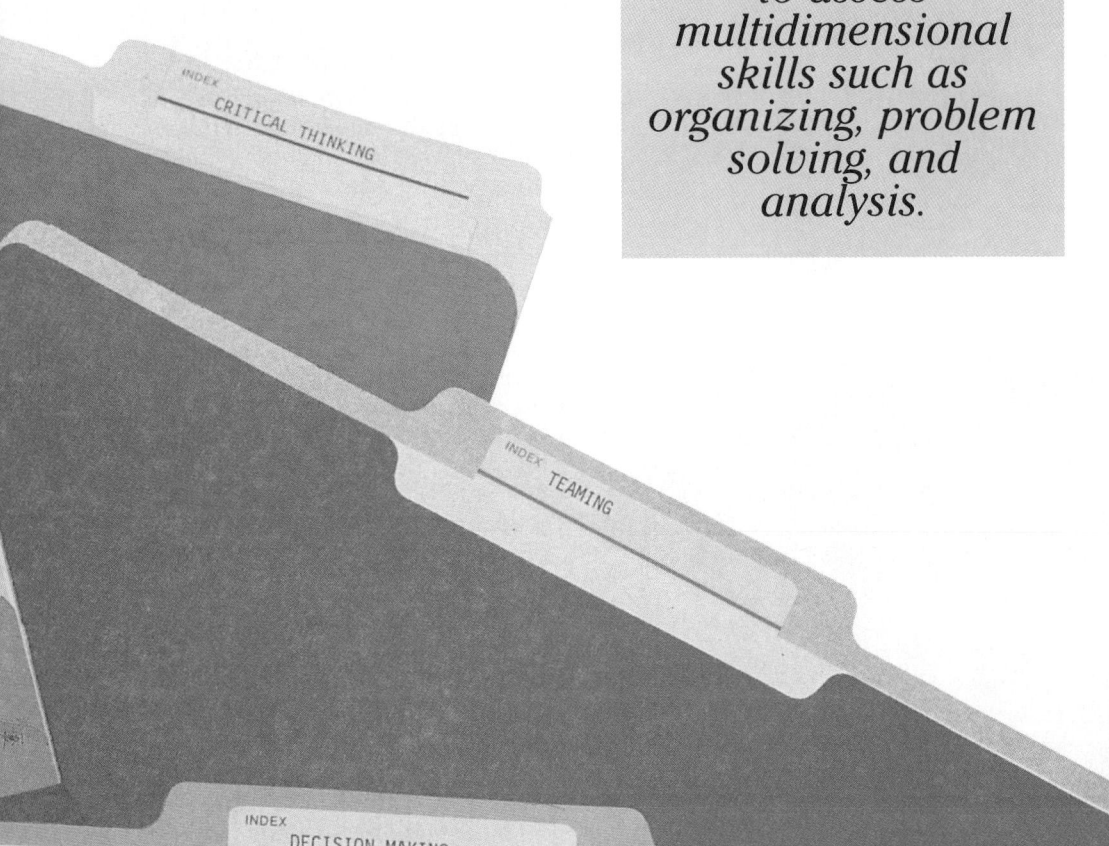

Portfolios and Journals

A portfolio and a journal are self-evaluations by the student who creates them. Ask students to collect samples of their work, then choose their best work and place it in an assessment portfolio to submit for evaluation.

A portfolio can include examples of basic skills activities; responses to the Focus on Computers, Careers, or Ethics features; memos or other documents for communications activities; and cooperative learning projects.

You can regularly read students' daily journals in which they record and reflect upon what they have learned.

Summary

The preceding suggestions are discussed in more detail in the *Tech Prep Strategies in Accounting* book. This book can be used as a reference for generating your own ideas and activities regarding assessment of student learning.

Meeting Special Needs

A typical class contains students whose learning and physical abilities vary widely. Students in your classroom may have auditory, visual, or physical difficulties, or they may have underdeveloped academic skills—all of which may interfere with their ability to learn in the same way or with the same efficiency as other students.

To ensure that each student is challenged and motivated, you must

Computer software can be especially effective for individual projects because it provides practice in applications and helps reinforce problem-solving skills

find more than one approach to teach accounting. Providing a positive learning environment for *all* your students may require you to modify your teaching methods when working with special needs students. Once you determine the special needs of your students, you can identify areas in the curriculum that may present barriers to some students. Although the quality or quantity of the material presented may not change, you may need to structure ways to remove those impediments to learning.

Physical Requirements

When an activity requires students to write on the chalkboard, students in wheelchairs may require a lowered chalkboard or a conveniently located overhead projector. For the visually impaired, an oral response is appropriate.

Teaching Style

Consider your teaching style. A lecture-question format may need to incorporate more visual clues such as transparencies, handouts, and so forth. The *Glencoe Accounting, First-Year Course*, offers a selection of visual learning aids including full-color transparencies, solution transparencies, demonstration problems, and blackline masters. The *Teacher's Wraparound Edition* offers suggestions for using these visuals.

Individualized Projects

Assigning students individual projects allows them to progress at their own pace. Computer software can be especially effective for individual projects because it provides practice in applications and helps reinforce problem-solving skills. The tutorial software allows learners to progress at their own pace.

Special Needs Strategies

The *Glencoe Accounting* program was designed to meet the needs of a variety of learners, including those with special needs.

- Students who speak English as a second language (ESL)
- Students with limited English proficiency
- Visual learners and visually handicapped students
- Hearing impaired students
- Students with learning disabilities
- Physically handicapped students
- Students with attention difficulties
- Students with oral expression disability
- Gifted students

The *Teacher's Wraparound Edition* provides a variety of teaching strategies to support the concepts presented in the chapter. You can select those activities and teaching strategies that are appropriate for the needs and abilities of your students and your teaching methods.

Improving Basic Skills

Accounting professionals function in a multidimensional business world that calls for them to use many different skills in addition to their accounting knowledge. To prepare students to function effectively in the business world, accounting education must also develop and improve basic skills that encompass the ability to speak, read, and write critically in a problem-solving atmosphere.

Among the skills presented in the *Glencoe Accounting* program are those in the following list.

- math
- analysis
- decision making
- problem solving
- communications
- listening
- human relations
- teamwork
- critical thinking

To prepare students to function effectively in the business world, accounting education must also develop and improve basic skills that encompass the ability to speak, read, and write critically in a problem-solving atmosphere.

Following the review section at the end of every chapter in both the first-year and advanced textbooks are short activities that encourage students to improve personal skills that will be key to their success on the job. These activities are entitled "Improving Your Human Relations Skills," "Improving Your Decision-Making Skills," and so on. The chart below references all of these personal skills activities and provides a page number for each.

In addition, the bottom margins of the *Teacher's Wraparound Edition* include a variety of activities on critical thinking, cooperative learning, and communications that give students additional opportunities to strengthen their basic skills. A separate booklet, *Skills Improvement Activities*, contains skill-building activities to promote more effective personal and business skills.

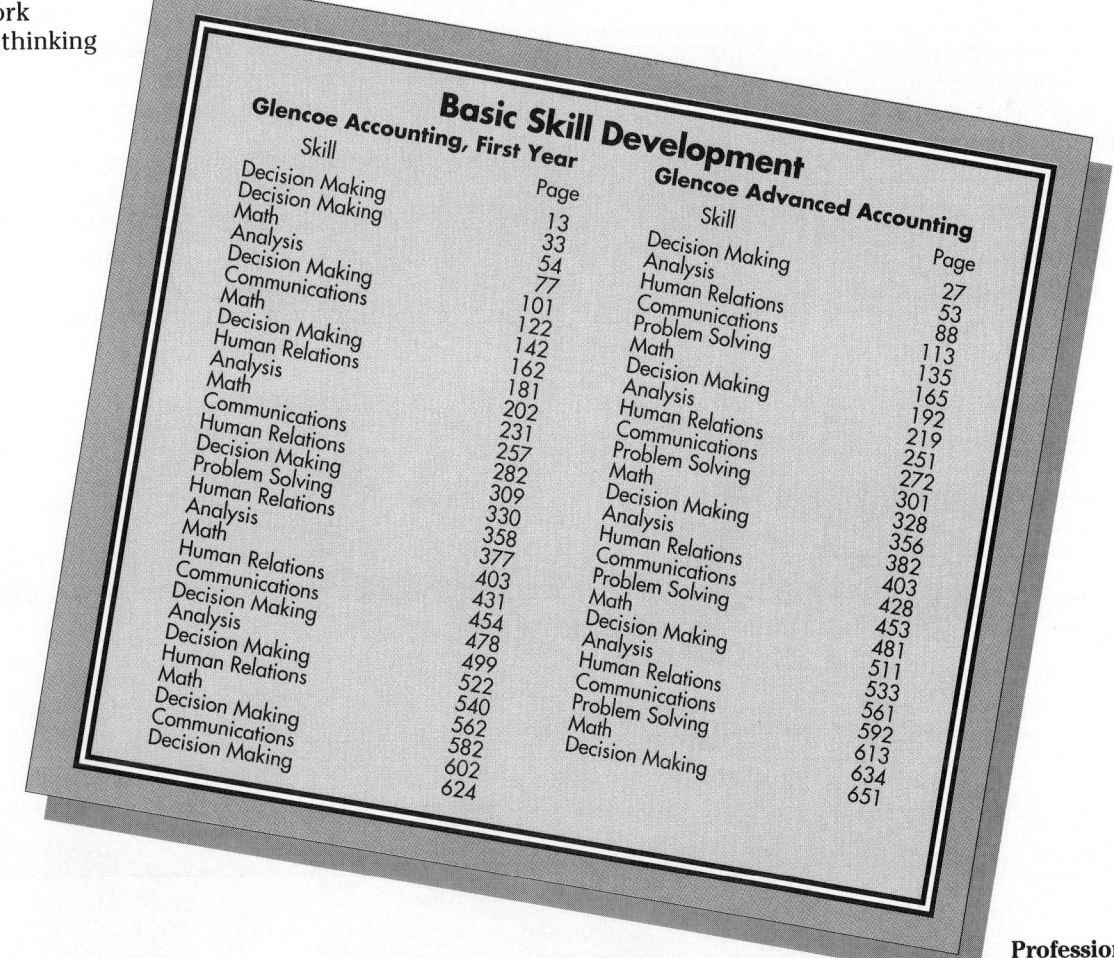

Basic Skill Development

Glencoe Accounting, First Year		Glencoe Advanced Accounting	
Skill	Page	Skill	Page
Decision Making			
Decision Making	13		
Math	33	Decision Making	27
Analysis	54	Analysis	53
Decision Making	77	Human Relations	88
Communications	101	Communications	113
Math	122	Problem Solving	135
Decision Making	142	Math	165
Human Relations	162	Decision Making	192
Analysis	181	Analysis	219
Math	202	Human Relations	251
Communications	231	Communications	272
Human Relations	257	Problem Solving	301
Decision Making	282	Math	328
Problem Solving	309	Decision Making	356
Human Relations	330	Analysis	382
Analysis	358	Human Relations	403
Math	377	Communications	428
Human Relations	403	Problem Solving	453
Communications	431	Math	481
Decision Making	454	Decision Making	511
Analysis	478	Analysis	533
Decision Making	499	Human Relations	561
Human Relations	522	Communications	592
Math	540	Problem Solving	613
Decision Making	562	Math	634
Communications	582	Decision Making	651
Decision Making	602		
	624		

Teaching Ethics in Accounting

Why do you need to teach your students about ethics in accounting when so much of your time must be spent on teaching basic accounting concepts and procedures? Students need to know that in their careers they will encounter ethical dilemmas requiring them to make decisions about an action. Students need to understand that unethical behavior is often perceived as unethical only *after* the action has been taken. The decision maker often has not considered the ramifications of the decision and how it will affect the people involved.

Can Ethics Be Taught?

Many teachers believe that ethics cannot be taught because students' ethical standards are set long before they reach the high school classroom. This idea is a misconception for two reasons. First, you are not teaching students to "be ethical." The purpose of introducing ethics into your accounting instruction is to help your students integrate ethical considerations into their decision-making framework. Students are helped to develop a process within which to consider both the business and the ethical ramifications of a decision *before* that decision is made.

A second misconception about teaching ethics to young adults relates to basic values. It is true that basic values are set in childhood, but people do make different decisions as they gain knowledge and insight into how their decisions reflect their basic values.

How Do You Teach Ethics in Accounting?

Most accounting teachers have little or no education in ethics as a discipline. Yet, you do know how to make decisions and most likely have personal experiences with decisions involving ethical ramifications. You need not be an ethics theorist to incorporate discussions of ethical actions into your accounting instruction.

Ethics Cases

To help you integrate ethics into your accounting instruction, the *Glencoe Accounting* program includes special features called "Focus on Ethics" in the student textbook. These features present typical situations that people encounter on the job. Their purpose is to give students an opportunity to put themselves in the situation and to make a decision about the most ethical course of action. In addition to the "Focus on Ethics" features, the *Teacher's Wraparound Edition* includes a short feature called "Business Ethics" in each chapter. These features may also be used for class discussion and decision making.

The Ethical Decision Model

Encourage students to use a structured decision model to help them analyze a situation, evaluate alternatives, consider ramifications of each decision, and choose among the alternatives. The five-step model described here offers one possibility.

The steps in the decision model are:

1. What are the ethical issues?
2. What are the alternatives?
3. Who are the affected parties?
4. How do the alternatives affect the parties?
5. What is your decision?

Use the first ethics feature in the student textbook (Chapter 4, page 82) as a sample and help students build the decision model. See page T82 for suggested answers to the decision model questions for this ethics feature. Students will also benefit from viewing the ethics segment on the *Electronic Field Trips* video that is part of the *Glencoe Accounting* multimedia program.

Class Participation and Discussion

Students need to understand that there is no right or wrong answer to the ethics cases. As they discuss each case, they are discussing possibilities. Students should feel that the class-room is a relatively "risk-free" environment in which to make ethical decisions because no employees will be harmed and no business or stockholders will lose money as a result of students' decisions.

You can also use these ethics cases to integrate writing activities into your accounting curriculum. Have students write their answers to the questions in the decision model. You might also have them write descriptions of situations in which they have been required to make an ethical choice. Be aware that students may write on many sensitive issues and help them choose more business-related topics if you prefer those topics for class discussion.

Using the Case-Study Approach

Case studies provide an opportunity for students to step into the shoes of business people who must make decisions about day-to-day business operations. Cases allow students to express independent answers or to work in cooperative learning groups that mimic real-world work groups. Using case studies can help you provide a superior learning experience for your students. Cases require students not only to draw on textbook learning but also to apply higher-level thinking skills to analyze a business situation and to determine a reasonable conclusion. As a result, they exercise a wide range of thinking skills and further develop their problem-solving skills.

Case studies can help students improve their skills in several areas.

■ *Analysis skills:* Students improve their ability to identify relevant information and to determine how it affects potential decisions.

■ *Cooperative learning:* Assigning cases to groups gives students practice in functioning within a work group and helps students learn to integrate others' opinions into their own ideas.

■ *Critical thinking:* Determining what information is pertinent and what is not helps students sharpen their skills in evaluating possible case solutions and in discriminating between alternative courses of action.

■ *Problem solving:* Cases set up real-life business problems for students to solve. The use of cases as a learning tool can help students integrate a model for solving problems into their own decision-making processes.

■ *Communication skills:* Whether working on cases independently or in a group, students can improve their communication skills through written analyses and/or oral presentations of findings and recommendations.

Part 4 of *Tech Prep Strategies in Accounting* discusses the use of case studies in accounting and also includes ten case studies for use in your classes. Teaching suggestions and answers to the cases are also given.

In addition, a case study booklet is also available using **Southwest Airlines** as the setting for business decision making.

The following chart summarizes the skills and attitudes addressed in each of the ten case studies in *Tech Prep Strategies in Accounting*.

Cases	Skills and Attitudes									
	Concepts	Technologies	Cooperative Learning	Analysis & Evaluation	Critical/Creative Thinking	Mathematical	Communication	Reporting	Interpersonal/Employability	Ethics
Case 1	•		•	•	•	•	•	•		
Case 2	•		•	•			•		•	•
Case 3			•		•		•		•	•
Case 4			•	•			•	•		
Case 5	•		•	•			•			
Case 6	•	•	•				•		•	•
Case 7						•			•	•
Case 8	•		•		•	•	•			
Case 9	•		•	•			•		•	•
Case 10	•		•	•			•	•		

> *Students exercise a wide range of thinking skills and further develop their problem-solving skills.*

Course Planning Guide

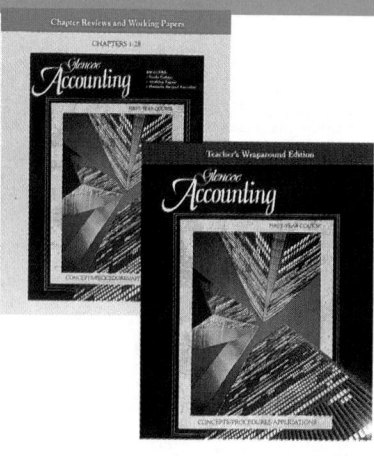

The "typical" accounting course is a one-year, two-semester course. Your school may also offer a second-year, advanced course. You may also teach in other configurations ranging from one quarter to one semester. The materials in the *Glencoe Accounting* program were developed to give you flexibility and a variety of options to meet the needs of your students and the length and goals of your accounting course.

One-Year Course of Study

Glencoe Accounting is a two-year program that includes student textbooks, workbooks, and extensive supplemental materials for both manual and integrated microcomputer applications. If your school does not offer a second-year course, you can be confident that your students will receive a strong foundation from the *First-Year Course*. The *First-Year Course* includes a comprehensive study of accounting including chapters on accounting for depreciation of plant and equipment, uncollectible accounts receivable, inventories, notes payable and receivable, partnerships, and corporations.

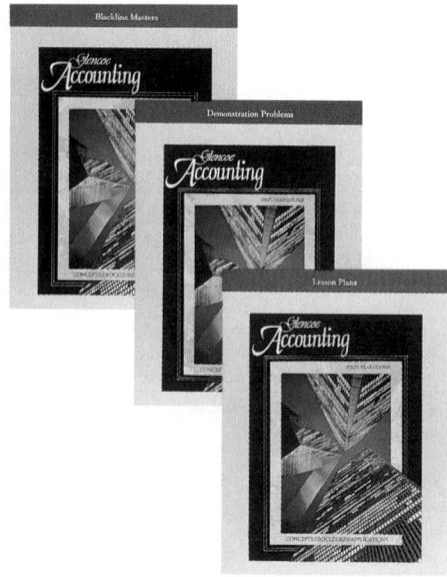

Computer Integration

The *First-Year Course* has 28 chapters and offers a variety of integrated computerized review, exercise, and problem activities. If you choose to spend more time on computer integration, the abridged edition, containing Chapters 1 through 20, might better suit your needs. The abridged edition covers accounting cycles for both service and merchandising businesses and includes payroll activities. This shorter book offers great flexibility while allowing you to schedule more time for computer activities in your course outline.

The use of the computer is fully integrated into accounting instruction through in-book problems and activities. You need purchase only the textbook and software to get your students started using the computer. See pages T22-T25 and pages T32-T33 for additional suggestions on integrating computer activities into your accounting course.

Individualized Instruction

If you wish to individualize accounting instruction, the organization of the text provides clearly written steps that are easy for students to follow on their own. Review activities are available in the *Chapter Reviews and Working Papers*. In addition, a booklet of student study plans is available. These study plans can be customized for your course so that you can individualize the instruction to meet the needs of each of your students.

Course Outlines

The two charts on the following pages are provided to help you develop a course outline and lesson plans for the entire first-year course. The first chart outlines a course of study for six-week grading periods; the second chart outlines a course of study for nine-week grading periods. Each chart identifies the estimated number of class periods required to complete each chapter and the mini-practice sets. The suggested number of classes includes the approximate time required for students to complete end-of-chapter activities, microcomputer activities, and chapter tests. Class periods are estimated at 50 minutes.

Simulations

Although three different business simulations are available for the first-year program, most teachers find that they do not have time to complete all three in a one-year course. If you choose to have students complete one or more business simulations, you will need to adjust the proposed outlines if you also wish to complete all the chapters in the textbook. Approximate completion times for each simulation are as follows:

AquaClean Pool Service—7 to 8 class periods manually, 4 to 5 by computer

Lakeshore Computer Center—16 to 18 class periods manually, 5 to 7 by computer

London & Company —18 to 20 class periods manually, 7 to 8 by computer

Many teachers choose to integrate at least one simulation into the regular class activities. The five mini–practice sets within the text provide an alternative to using all three simulations and at the same time give students additional real-life applications. These mini-practice sets may be completed manually or on the computer; source documents are available for these mini-practice sets.

Six-Week Grading Periods

GRADING PERIOD	CHAPTER AND APPLICATION ACTIVITY	NUMBER OF CLASSES
1	**Unit 1 - Introduction to Accounting**	
	Chapter 1 - Accounting in a Private Enterprise Economy	4
	Chapter 2 - Business Transactions and the Basic Accounting Equation	6
	Unit 2 - The Basic Accounting Cycle	
	Chapter 3 - Analyzing Transactions Affecting Assets, Liabilities, and Owner's Equity	5
	Chapter 4 - Analyzing Transactions Affecting Revenue, Expenses, and Withdrawals	5
	Chapter 5 - Recording Transactions in a General Journal	5
	Chapter 6 - Posting Journal Entries to General Ledger Accounts	5
2	Mini-Practice Set: App. Act. 1 - Setting up Accounting Records for a Sole Proprietorship	3
	Chapter 7 - Preparing a Six-Column Work Sheet	6
	Chapter 8 - Preparing Financial Statements for a Sole Proprietorship	6
	Chapter 9 - Completing the Accounting Cycle for a Sole Proprietorship	6
	Chapter 10 - Cash Control and Banking Activities	6
	Mini-Practice Set: App. Act. 2 - Completing the Accounting Cycle for a Sole Proprietorship	3
	AquaClean Pool Service (Optional)	
3	**Unit 3 - The Accounting Cycle for a Merchandising Business**	
	Chapter 11 - Accounting for Sales on Account	7
	Chapter 12 - Accounting for Cash Receipts	6
	Chapter 13 - Accounting for Purchases on Account	6
	Chapter 14 - Accounting for Cash Payments	6
	Chapter 15 - Recording General Journal Transactions	5
4	Mini-Practice Set: App. Act. 3 - Recording Business Transactions in Special Journals	3
	Chapter 16 - Preparing a Ten-Column Work Sheet	6
	Chapter 17 - Preparing Financial Statements for a Corporation	6
	Chapter 18 - Recording Adjusting and Closing Entries	5
	Mini-Practice Set: App. Act. 4 - Complete Accounting Cycle for a Merchandising Corporation	4
	Lakeshore Computer Center (Optional)	
	Unit 4 - Accounting for a Payroll System	
	Chapter 19 - Payroll Accounting	6
5	Chapter 20 - Payroll and Tax Records	6
	Mini-Practice Set: App. Act. 5 - Payroll Accounting	4
	Unit 5 - Accounting for Special Procedures	
	Chapter 21 - Accounting for Cash Funds	6
	Chapter 22 - Accounting for the Depreciation of Property and Equipment	7
	Chapter 23 - Accounting for Uncollectible Accounts Receivable	7
6	Chapter 24 - Accounting for Inventories	6
	Chapter 25 - Accounting for Notes Payable and Receivable	6
	London & Company (Optional)	
	Unit 6 - Accounting for Other Forms of Business Organization	
	Chapter 26 - Accounting for Partnerships	5
	Chapter 27 - Accounting for Corporations	6
	Chapter 28 - Analyzing and Interpreting Financial Statements	7
Total Class Sessions		180

PROFESSIONAL STRATEGIES

Nine-Week Grading Periods

GRADING PERIOD	CHAPTER AND APPLICATION ACTIVITY	NUMBER OF CLASSES
1	**Unit 1 - Introduction to Accounting**	
	Chapter 1 - Accounting in a Private Enterprise Economy	4
	Chapter 2 - Business Transactions and the Basic Accounting Equation	6
	Unit 2 - The Basic Accounting Cycle	
	Chapter 3 - Analyzing Transactions Affecting Assets, Liabilities, and Owner's Equity	6
	Chapter 4 - Analyzing Transactions Affecting Revenue, Expenses, and Withdrawals	6
	Chapter 5 - Recording Transactions in a General Journal	5
	Chapter 6 - Posting Journal Entries to General Ledger Accounts	6
	Mini-Practice Set: App. Act. 1 - Setting up Accounting Records for a Sole Proprietorship	2
	Chapter 7 - Preparing a Six-Column Work Sheet	5
	Chapter 8 - Preparing Financial Statements for a Sole Proprietorship	
2	Chapter 9 - Completing the Accounting Cycle for a Sole Proprietorship	5
	Chapter 10 - Cash Control and Banking Activities	5
	Mini-Practice Set: App. Act. 2 - Completing the Accounting Cycle for a Sole Proprietorship	3
	AquaClean Pool Service (Optional)	
	Unit 3 - The Accounting Cycle for a Merchandising Business	
	Chapter 11 - Accounting for Sales on Account	6
	Chapter 12 - Accounting for Cash Receipts	6
	Chapter 13 - Accounting for Purchases on Account	6
	Chapter 14 - Accounting for Cash Payments	6
	Chapter 15 - Recording General Journal Transactions	5
	Mini-Practice Set: App. Act. 3 - Recording Business Transactions in Special Journals	3
3	Chapter 16 - Preparing a Ten-Column Work Sheet	6
	Chapter 17 - Preparing Financial Statements for a Corporation	7
	Chapter 18 - Recording Adjusting and Closing Entries	5
	Mini-Practice Set: App. Act. 4 - A Complete Accounting Cycle for a Merchandising Corporation	
	Lakeshore Computer Center (Optional)	4
	Unit 4 - Accounting for a Payroll System	
	Chapter 19 - Payroll Accounting	7
	Chapter 20 - Payroll and Tax Records	6
	Mini-Practice Set: App. Act. 5 - Payroll Accounting	4
	Unit 5 - Accounting for Special Procedures	
	Chapter 21 - Accounting for Cash Funds	6
4	Chapter 22 - Accounting for the Depreciation of Property and Equipment	8
	Chapter 23 - Accounting for Uncollectible Accounts Receivable	7
	Chapter 24 - Accounting for Inventories	6
	Chapter 25 - Accounting for Notes Payable and Receivable	6
	London & Company (Optional)	
	Unit 6 - Accounting for Other Forms of Business Organization	
	Chapter 26 - Accounting for Partnerships	5
	Chapter 27 - Accounting for Corporations	6
	Chapter 28 - Analyzing and Interpreting Financial Statements	7
Total Class Sessions		180

FIRST-YEAR COURSE
THIRD EDITION

Glencoe Accounting

CONCEPTS/PROCEDURES/APPLICATIONS

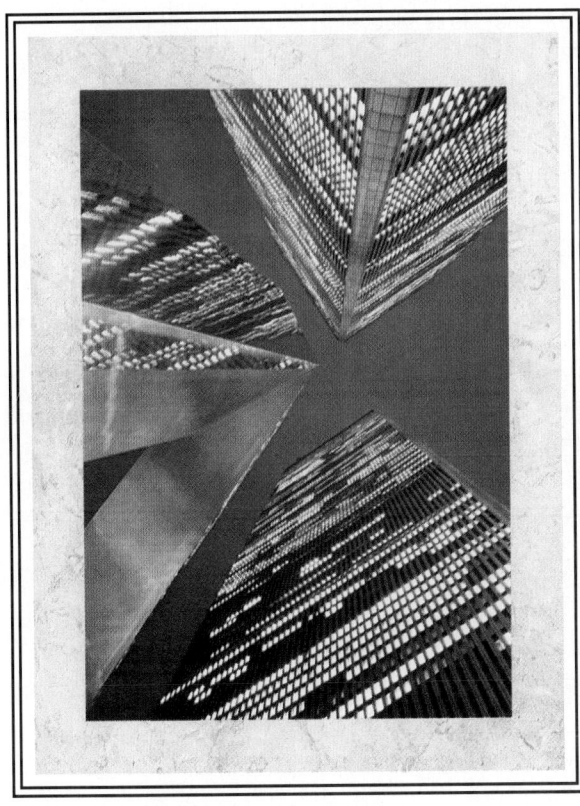

Donald J. Guerrieri
**Norwin Senior High School
North Huntingdon, Pennsylvania**

F. Barry Haber
**Fayetteville State University
Fayetteville, North Carolina**

William B. Hoyt
**Wilton High School
Wilton, Connecticut**

Robert E. Turner
**McNeese State University
Lake Charles, Louisiana**

GLENCOE
McGraw-Hill

New York, New York   Columbus, Ohio   Mission Hills, California   Peoria, Illinois

Donald J. Guerrieri is an accounting instructor at Norwin Senior High School, North Huntingdon, Pennsylvania. He has taught accounting at both the secondary and college levels. He also has experience working for a firm of certified public accountants Dr. Guerrieri has written numerous articles on the teaching of accounting for a variety of educational journals. He is also a program speaker at business education seminars and conferences.

F. Barry Haber is Professor of Accounting at Fayetteville State University, Fayetteville, North Carolina. Dr. Haber is a certified public accountant and is active in the American Institute of Certified Public Accountants, where he has served on the AICPA Minority Doctoral Fellows Committee. In addition to teaching accounting principles, Dr. Haber has authored three other textbooks, as well as various articles and cases in accounting.

William B. Hoyt is head of the Business Education Department at Wilton High School, Wilton, Connecticut. In addition to teaching accounting, he has been active in the development of microcomputer usage in business education courses. In this endeavor, he has taken part in panel discussions, given workshops, and written on the use of microcomputers in accounting instruction.

Robert E. Turner is the Vice President for Business Affairs at McNeese State University, Lake Charles, Louisiana. Mr. Turner has taught accounting and other business subjects at the high school and college levels. Mr. Turner has appeared on the programs of a number of business education conferences. He is also a frequent speaker at educational seminars around the country.

Library of Congress Cataloging-in-Publication Data

Glencoe accounting: concepts, procedures, applications: first-year
   course/   Donald J. Guerrieri . . . [et al.]. --3rd ed.
         p.   cm.
   Includes index
   ISBN 0-02-803617-4
   1. Accounting   I. Guerrieri, Donald J.
HF5635.G54   1995
657--dc20   93-44530
                                                                       CIP

Send all inquiries to:
Glencoe/McGraw-Hill
936 Eastwind Drive
Westerville, OH 43081

ISBN 0-02-803617-4

Printed in the United States of America.

4 5 6 7 8 9   RRW/MC   01 00 99 98 97 96 95

Contents

ACCOUNTING FOR A PAYROLL SYSTEM   **414**

ACCOUNTING FOR SPECIAL PROCEDURES   **462**

ACCOUNTING FOR OTHER FORMS OF BUSINESS ORGANIZATION

Preface

"The more things change, the more they stay the same." The world of accounting is a good application of this maxim. The computer has revolutionized the generation and processing of financial records. Transactions that were formerly recorded, posted, compiled, sorted, and summarized laboriously by hand are now processed by the computer in the twinkling of an eye. Earlier critical procedures such as balancing and ruling of accounts and time-worn books of original entry such as the combination journal have been discarded or relegated to less important positions by automation. Even the language of accounting has been enlarged to include such terms as *batching, spreadsheets,* and *integrated accounting systems.*

Yet, in spite of all the changes wrought by the computer, one thing remains the same—the traditional insistence on learning the "why" as well as the "how" of accounting. To gain career success in accounting today without a sound knowledge of computer technology and familiarization with basic computerized accounting procedures would be difficult. But to gain success without a clear, conceptual knowledge of accounting—the "why" and the "how"—would be impossible.

Glencoe Accounting: Concepts/Procedures/Applications, Third Edition continues to emphasize the proven method of learning essential concepts and procedures through manual accounting, reinforced liberally with realistic applications. The sound methodology, proven practices, and solid applications of yesterday have been combined with the new approaches, contemporary procedures, and forward-looking computer technology of today to truly prepare students for tomorrow. *Glencoe Accounting* is a comprehensive instructional program thoughtfully designed to help students succeed by meeting and even anticipating the demands of the modern world of accounting.

Course Objectives

Glencoe Accounting: Concepts/Procedures/Applications, Third Edition is intended for use in a one-year introductory financial accounting course. The primary thrust of the textbook is on learning the rules and procedures of accounting for profit-motivated businesses. Learning the "how" and "why" of accounting will not only enable one to keep the accurate financial records required to produce useful business information, but will give one the capacity to *use* that financial information to make wise business decisions.

After studying this textbook and successfully completing activities in the textbook and the related working papers, students will be able to:

1. Use the basic accounting principles and procedures that are applied to accounting records kept for businesses that operate in the private enterprise economy of the United States.
2. Explain and appreciate the importance of profit in helping to ensure continued business operations.
3. Describe the three major types of business organizations in a private enterprise economy and explain how accounting procedures differ for the three.
4. Develop proficiency in the use of the computer to maintain accounting records.
5. Describe the types of on-the-job activities that are required of entry-level accounting workers.

Organization of the Textbook

Glencoe Accounting: Concepts/Procedures/Applications, Third Edition is organized in 6 units of 28 chapters. The first unit of the textbook begins with a presentation in Chapter 1 of the role of accounting in our private enterprise economy and an explanation of several important accounting assumptions. Chapter 2 introduces students to the basic accounting equation. This introduction provides students with a solid foundation on which to build their understanding of accounting theory and procedures.

The second unit of the textbook, "The Basic Accounting Cycle," takes students through a complete accounting cycle for a service business organized as a sole proprietorship. In this unit, students first learn the rules of debit and credit using T accounts and the basic accounting equation. Chapters 3 and 4 present the rules of debit and credit for the permanent accounts and for the temporary capital accounts. In Chapter 5, students learn to use a general journal to record business transactions. The general journal is preferred to other types of journals as a first learning experience because it requires students to think through the effects of transactions rather than memorizing how types of transactions are recorded. The remaining chapters in the unit complete the accounting cycle: posting to the general ledger, preparing a six-column work sheet, generating financial statements, journalizing and posting closing entries, and developing a post-closing trial balance.

Unit 3 introduces students to a merchandising business that is organized as a small, privately held corporation. Since corporations provide more than half the jobs in this country, it is important for students to be aware of the differences between accounting for a sole proprietorship and accounting for a corporation. In this unit, students will learn how to use special journals to record transactions for a merchandising business. They will complete the accounting cycle for a merchandising business by preparing a ten-column work sheet, financial statements, adjusting and closing entries, and a post-closing trial balance.

In Unit 4, students will learn how to keep payroll records, including those maintained for employees and for the employer's payroll liabilities. Students will be introduced to the changes in the social security taxes that were enacted in 1991. They will learn to apply the FICA tax deduction in two parts: (1) social security tax and (2) medicare tax.

The fifth unit comprises five chapters covering various accounting procedures that occur infrequently in many businesses. These procedures include accounting for cash funds, depreciation of plant and equipment, uncollectible accounts receivable, inventories, and notes.

Unit 6 introduces students to other forms of business organizations. In Chapter 26, students will learn about accounting for a partnership. Chapter 27 covers basic accounting procedures for publicly held corporations. In the last chapter, students are introduced to the uses of financial information for decision making. This chapter presents a few simple analyses that can be completed using the financial information reported by publicly held corporations.

Additional problems that can be used for extra and remedial practice are found in the back of the text. Enrichment chapters provide information and basic practice on the use of the combination journal and specific information and applications on accruals and deferrals.

Special Features

Glencoe Accounting is designed to promote student interest, involvement, and success through a variety of learning features.

Accounting cycle approach. The textbook utilizes a traditional accounting cycle approach to introduce students to new concepts and procedures. This step-by-step development gives students the guidance they look for and clearly demonstrates the continuity and interrelationships of the accounting process.

Chapter objectives. Clearly defined and stated objectives are provided at the beginning of each chapter to help students know exactly what they are expected to learn. The mastery of these objectives is evaluated through end-of-chapter activities, applications, and examinations.

Vocabulary emphasis. The new accounting terms defined in each chapter are listed on the first page of the chapter. This list should be used to "preview" the meaning of each term for students. Research has shown that such vocabulary "previews" help students achieve greater understanding and retention of the material in the chapter. End-of-chapter vocabulary reviews reinforce understanding of key terms. A complete glossary of accounting terms serves as a useful reference tool for students.

Clear, conversational narrative. The textbook is written in a style that is appropriate for high school students. Simple analogies make concepts meaningful for students. Abundant illustrations and numerous examples guide students through the preparation of accounting records.

Early emphasis on transaction analysis. A solid foundation in the rules of debit and credit is provided early in the textbook. Understanding the "why" of transaction analysis ensures that the "how" comes naturally.

Guided examples. These frequently used learning aids walk students through sample transactions, step by numbered step, making the "why" behind each procedure very clear.

Frequent learning reinforcement. "Check Your Learning" reinforcement activities follow major sections in every chapter to help students assume the responsibility for their own learning. "Remember" notes summarize key points and help cement important facts in students' minds. "Accounting Tips" at appropriate intervals remind students of essential practices and procedures. "Accounting Notes" inform students of interesting facts about business and the practice of accounting.

Solid end-of-chapter activities. Vocabulary reviews reinforce key accounting terms. Review questions help students expand their understanding of accounting concepts. Short activities encourage students to improve their skills in such important areas as decision making, communications, analysis, math, and human relations. A variety of exercises and problems, ranging from easy to challenging, gives students of all abilities the chance to gain practical accounting experience and to enjoy success.

Five comprehensive application activities. These "mini practice sets," at appropriate points in the textbook, require students to integrate new knowledge with learned procedures and to apply their cumulative skills. The applications may be completed manually, with the computer, or both manually and with the computer.

Computer integration. Information about computerized accounting systems is integrated into the chapter narrative, providing computer awareness and system comparisons for all students. Short vignettes, called "Focus on Computers," introduce specific aspects of computer technology. A broad range of computer activities is available on optional software: end-of-chapter problems and application activities; simulations; spreadsheets; and a microcomputer program for review, remediation, and reinforcement of key accounting principles. All such activities are completely optional. While the computer integration is provided, the use of a computer is not required for successful completion of the course.

Career orientation. Seven "Focus on Accounting Careers" vignettes provide students with a look at interesting jobs in the accounting world.

Ethics in business and accounting. Vignettes on ethical business and accounting situations, called "Focus on Ethics," are provided throughout the text. These ethical dilemmas illustrate the kinds of problems working professionals often encounter.

Acknowledgments

We wish to thank those individuals and companies that provided advice and assistance in the development of this program. We owe a debt of gratitude to thousands of teachers and students who used the previous editions of this textbook and who offered encouragement, suggestions, and advice in making a good accounting program even better.

We especially thank the Accounting Advisory Committee, composed of ten master accounting teachers from across the country, who provided excellent guidance and advice in the development and review of this program.

Finally, we wish to thank our families, colleagues, and friends who offered constant encouragement and support as we worked on the third edition.

Donald J. Guerrieri
F. Barry Haber
William B. Hoyt
Robert E. Turner

Educational Consultants and Reviewers

We wish to acknowledge the contributions of the following:

DeVon Allmaras
Longmont High School
Longmont, Colorado

Gail Blair
William Floyd High School
Mastic Beach, New York

Thelma H. Brooks
Southeast Career Center
Columbus, Ohio

Johnsie Crawford
Brandon Senior High School
Brandon, Florida

Jackie Dean
Washington High School
Washington, North Carolina

Gloria Farris
Seneca High School
Louisville, Kentucky

Trudy Formanek
Colstrip High School
Colstrip, Montana

Shirley A. Helmick
Western Hills High School
Fort Worth, Texas

Ruth Hennessy
Comeaux High School
Lafayette, Louisiana

Norma Hernandez
Galena Park I.S.D.
Galena Park, Texas

Mitch Hummel
Cocalico High School
Denver, Pennsylvania

Jerry Livingston
A.C. Jones High School
Beeville, Texas

Nancy Lord
Southeast Career Center
Columbus, Ohio

Ellen Lunden
Grand Ledge High School
Grand Ledge, Michigan

Carolyn McGraw
Lakeland High School
Lakeland, Florida

David McDonald
Rincon High School
Tucson, Arizona

John Nigro
North Haven High School
North Haven, Connecticut

JoAnne Pamer
Burbank High School
Burbank, California

Nate Rosenberg
Palo Alto High School
Palo Alto, California

Debra Saffo
Southeast Career Center
Columbus, Ohio

Michael Sailes
Carver Area High School
Chicago, Illinois

Emma Jo Spiegelberg
Laramie High School
Laramie, Wyoming

Claudia Stuvland
Rogers High School
Puyallup, Washington

Sue Thomas
Norwood High School
Norwood, Massachusetts

Carl Wenzel
Geneva High School
Geneva, New York

Frank Wood
Arrowhead High School
Hartland, Wisconsin

Eleanor A. Young
Southeast Career Center
Columbus, Ohio

The first chapter in Unit 1 introduces students to the concept of financial record keeping and to the basic types of business organization. The second chapter presents the basic accounting equation and develops students' transaction analysis skills using the equation.

Chapter 1
Accounting in a Private Enterprise Economy
Focus on Computers

Chapter 2
Business Transactions and the Basic Accounting Equation
Focus on Careers

U N I T

INTRODUCTION TO ACCOUNTING

In this first unit on accounting, you will study the role that accounting plays in the private enterprise economy of the United States. In our private enterprise economy, businesses must earn a profit if they are to continue to operate. Keeping accounting records is an important part of operating a business. Accounting records help businesses operate efficiently—and profitably—by keeping track of how much is earned and how much is spent.

Accounting is so much a part of our business lives that much of its terminology has become a part of our everyday language. Throughout this textbook, you will learn why accounting has been called the "language of business."

Individualizing Instruction

To provide individualized activities within the unit, you may use any of the following:

- problems in *Math Review for Accounting*
- chapter study plans
- study guides in the student workbook
- end-of-chapter challenge problems (identified by a maze symbol)

- optional problems in the Additional Problems section at the back of the student textbook
- cases from *Tech Prep Strategies in Accounting*
- *Electronic Study Guide*

Introduction to Accounting

Unit Concepts

Unit 1 provides students with a general introduction to the private enterprise system, the business organizations comprising this system, and the role that accounting plays within the system. Four basic accounting assumptions are discussed, as are accounting careers, thus providing job information for students who may wish to enter the field of accounting.

The unit proceeds from the foundations of accounting into a discussion of property and property rights. Students then learn the basic accounting equation and how that equation is affected by various business transactions. Study of the basic accounting equation provides the foundation for learning the double-entry system of accounting.

General Unit Performance Objectives

1. Correctly use terminology related to accounting careers and to accounting principles and concepts.
2. Describe the educational requirements and general responsibilities of various accounting careers.
3. Use the basic accounting equation.
4. Determine the effects of business transactions on the basic accounting equation.

PERFORMANCE OBJECTIVES

Unit Objective Test: Chapters 1-2

1. Define accounting vocabulary correctly.
2. Identify business and accounting information correctly.
3. Apply accounting principles correctly.
4. Classify accounts.

Unit Problem Test: Chapters 1-2

1. Determine the increases and decreases in transactions affecting the basic accounting equation.
2. Calculate the missing amounts to complete the basic accounting equation.
3. Analyze the effects of business transactions on the basic accounting equation.

Chapter	Learning Objectives
1	1. Describe the three types of businesses operated to earn a profit in our private enterprise economy. 2. Discuss the three major forms of business organizations in our private enterprise economy. 3. Describe the role of accounting in our private enterprise economy. 4. Describe the variety of jobs available in accounting. 5. Recognize the major organizations that influence accounting practices. 6. Define the accounting terms introduced in this chapter.
2	1. Describe the relationship between property and property rights. 2. Explain the meaning of "equity" as it is used in accounting. 3. List the parts of the basic accounting equation and define each part. 4. Show how various business transactions affect the basic accounting equation. 5. Check the balance of the basic accounting equation after a business transaction has been analyzed and recorded. 6. Define the accounting terms introduced in this chapter.

CHAPTER REINFORCEMENT

State/Local Objectives		Demonstration Problems	Check Your Learning	Basic Skills	Exercises	Problems	Challenge Problem	Additional Problems
				Decision Making p.13	1-1 1-2 1-3 1-4			
		2-1 2-2 2-3 2-4 2-5	p. 19 p. 21 p. 27 p. 30	Decision Making p. 33	2-1 2-2 2-3	2-1 2-2 2-3 2-4 2-5	2-6	2A p.631

COMPUTERIZED ACCOUNTING ACTIVITIES

Chapter	Glencoe Integrated Accounting	Spreadsheet Applications	Electronic Study Guide Model Exercises/Problems	CD Rom
1			Exercise 1-4	Menu Selection 1
2		Problem 2-4 (The Accounting Equation)	Exercise 2-1 Problem 2-1 2-2	Menu Selection 2
Basic Math Review			Menu Option 29	

Chapter 1 introduces students to the need for financial record keeping and to the organization of business in our private enterprise economy. The concept of profit and loss, as well as the assumptions underlying financial accounting, provide the foundation for students to use the basic accounting equation in later chapters to analyze the effects of business transactions on business operations.

VOCABULARY DEVELOPMENT

Ask students to write a sentence using each of the new terms in context. Ask for volunteers to write their sentences on the board. Discuss any differences in the use of the terms. Definitions of these terms are found in the chapter and in the glossary on pages 670-679.

Electronic Field Trips

Chapter 1
ACCOUNTING IN A PRIVATE ENTERPRISE ECONOMY

Every business is somewhat like a stage production. For a play to be a success, everyone from the star to the electrician is held responsible for a task that must be performed a certain way. A stage production must run repeatedly for a certain length of time in order to make a profit. In our private enterprise economy, businesses are no different. Each business has many players, many tasks, and the need to perform successfully within certain time periods.

This textbook will describe how businesses operate in our private enterprise economy and the role accounting plays in business operations. Chapter 1 sets the stage for you to see the role accounting plays in our private enterprise economy.

Learning Objectives

When you have completed Chapter 1, you should be able to do the following:

1. Describe the three types of businesses operated to earn a profit in our private enterprise economy.
2. Discuss the three major forms of business organizations in our private enterprise economy.
3. Describe the role of accounting in our private enterprise economy.
4. Describe the variety of jobs available in accounting.
5. Recognize the major organizations that influence accounting practices.
6. Define the accounting terms introduced in this chapter.

New Terms

profit
loss
capital
service business
merchandising business
manufacturing business
sole proprietorship
partnership
corporation
charter
accounting system
business entity
going concern
fiscal period
accounting clerk
general bookkeeper
accountant
certified public accountant

2

Teaching Resources

- Lesson Plans
- TE/Chapter Reviews & Working Papers
- Student Study Plans
- Teaching Transparencies
- Solutions Transparencies
- Electronic Field Trips Video, Level I
- Electronic Study Guide
- Chapter 1 Test

Other Resources

- Skills Improvement Activities
- Blackline Masters
- Careers in Accounting
- Dictionary
- Math Review for Accounting
- Tech Prep Strategies in Accounting
- Video
- Test Bank with Software
- Spanish Resources/Audiotapes
- Spanish Electronic Study Guide

The United States Private Enterprise Economy

All societies have ways of providing their members with goods and services. These ways range from very simple to very complex. The simple end of the scale is a pure barter economy: "I'll give you two bushels of corn if you give me ten chickens." In a slightly more advanced economy, the corn might be exchanged for money. The amount of money exchanged for the corn would depend on the value the owner placed on the corn and on whether the buyer could buy corn from someone else for less.

The most complex type of economy is represented by the electronic exchange of money through an electronic funds transfer system, or EFTS. With EFTS, money can be speedily transferred from one account to another, from bank account to account holder, or from one country to another. A sophisticated, computerized banking system keeps records of the amount of money transferred and to whom.

The economy of the United States is an example of a highly developed, complex economy. The United States economy is referred to as a *private enterprise economy.* In such an economy, people are free to produce the goods and services they choose. Individual buyers are free to use their money as they wish. They may choose to spend it, save it, or invest it. Since the amount of money available is limited, however, businesses must compete to attract the dollars of buyers. One measure of success in attracting dollars is the amount of profit a business earns. The amount of money earned over and above the amount spent to keep the business operating is called **profit.** Businesses that have more operating costs than earnings operate at a **loss.** In a private enterprise economy, only the businesses that consistently earn a profit will have the economic resources to continue to operate.

Businesses Operated for Profit

Groups of people get together in our economy for many different reasons, but each group is organized for some common purpose and with some common goal in mind. Some organizations are service-oriented and do not operate to earn a profit. Examples of such *not-for-profit organizations* include churches, private colleges, professional or social clubs, charitable organizations such as the United Way, and federal, state, and local governments. Other groups are business-oriented and operate to earn a profit. Both types of groups need financial information if they are to operate efficiently. In this textbook, however, you will learn about business organizations operated to earn a profit.

There are three types of businesses in our private enterprise economy that operate for profit: service businesses, merchandising businesses, and manufacturing businesses. Each type of business needs money to get started and to maintain its operations. Money is needed to buy or to make products. Money is also needed for such operating costs as rent, telephone service, and employee wages. Some of this money can be borrowed, but most of it is supplied by one or more owners of the business. The money so invested in a business by an owner is called **capital.**

Service, merchandising, and manufacturing businesses are alike in many ways, as shown in Figure 1-1 on page 4. Each business combines capital with

---

1 FOCUS

MAJOR CONCEPTS
- The U.S. Private Enterprise Economy
- The Role of Accounting
- Career Opportunities in Accounting
- Organizations that Influence Accounting Practice

BUSINESS CONNECTION

Corporations often start out as sole proprietorships or partnerships. The Coca-Cola company was started as a sole proprietorship with an initial investment of $2,300. In the late 1880s, Asa Candler took the medicinal formula invented by another Atlanta pharmacist and marketed it as a soda fountain drink. Today Coke is sold all over the world.

2 TEACH

CONCEPT DEVELOPMENT
The U.S. Private Enterprise Economy
The purpose of this first chapter is to describe the economic system on which U.S. financial accounting and reporting standards are based. Knowledge of both economic and accounting concepts should enable the student to better understand the limitations of information provided by financial accounting. Students need to know that the practice of accounting requires judgment, is not an exact science, involves much estimation, and has different ways to achieve the same results.

Reinforcing Study Skills

Point out to students that reading factual or technical material requires different skills from those they use in recreational reading. Introduce students to the reading technique known as SQ3R: *Survey, Question, Read, Recite, Review.* A detailed explanation of this technique can be found in the Student Study Plans booklet. Have students apply the first step in SQ3R by *surveying* the section and subsection heads in Chapter 1. See the *Blackline Masters* booklet for a transparency master listing the characteristics of the SQ3R study method.

Provide a copy of the *Student Study Plans* to each class member to help organize study activities or to individualize practice and review activities.

Teaching Tips
■ Remind students that money is not always profit. Money could also be provided by additional investment or by borrowing.
■ Discuss profit as an important motivator in our private enterprise economy.

CONCEPT DEVELOPMENT
Background Brief

This chapter presents a general framework and overview of financial accounting as it is currently practiced. *Financial accounting* as studied in this text is unique to the U.S. private enterprise system and represents the branch of accounting that provides financial information primarily for decision makers outside a business.

Financial accounting is an information-processing system designed to collect, measure, and report financial effects on a business entity to decision makers outside (external to) the firm. These outsiders consist of owners, lenders, suppliers, potential investors, creditors, employees, customers, financial analysts, brokers, lawyers, economists, taxing authorities, labor unions, press, researchers, teachers, students, and the public.

Using Visuals

Direct students to study Figure 1-1. Then ask them to write a sentence summarizing the differences between the types of businesses. For example, "The two areas in which businesses differ are in their use of capital, labor, and materials, and whether they sell services, buy and sell products, or make and sell products."

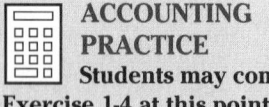

**ACCOUNTING
PRACTICE**
Students may complete Exercise 1-4 at this point.

	Service Business	Merchandising Business	Manufacturing Business
USES:	Capital and labor	Capital and labor	Capital, labor, and materials
HAS:	Operating costs	Operating costs	Operating costs
TO:	Provide services at a fee	Buy and sell finished products	Make and sell finished products
FOR:	Profit	Profit	Profit

Figure 1-1 Types of Businesses Operated for Profit

labor, has operating costs, and hopes to make a profit. They differ from one another, however, in some basic ways. A **service business** operates to provide a needed service for a fee. Service businesses include travel agencies, beauty salons, movers, repair shops, real estate offices, and medical centers. A **merchandising business** buys finished products and resells them to individuals or other businesses. Clothing stores, new and used car dealers, supermarkets, florists, and hobby shops are all examples of merchandising businesses. A **manufacturing business,** on the other hand, buys raw materials, such as wood or iron ore, and transforms them into finished products through the use of labor and machinery. It then sells the finished products to individuals or other businesses. Manufacturing businesses range from steel makers to the corner bakery.

In the United States, businesses come in many varieties and sizes. All of these businesses need to keep accounting records to help them operate both efficiently and profitably.

Making Connections

EVERYDAY LIFE

Ask students to name several local businesses that are profit-making organizations. Then ask them to name some local, nonprofit-making organizations. Ask students to cite similarities and differences between the two types of organizations. (For example, a similarity is that a nonprofit art museum sells products in its gift shop. Businesses also sell products or services. A major difference is in the purpose of each type of organization. The for-profit organization is operated to earn revenue and to return a profit to its owners. The nonprofit organization is operated to provide a service to the community and may be supported by taxes, donations, and revenue earned from selling products.)

Each type of business uses an accounting system to help guide the business's operations. In this accounting course, you will learn about the accounting systems used by service businesses.

Forms of Business Organization

To start a business, an owner must have a sufficient amount of money (capital) and must choose an appropriate form of business organization. With few exceptions, businesses in the United States are organized in one of three ways: as a sole proprietorship, a partnership, or a corporation.

▲ **The Sole Proprietorship** "Sole" means "single" or "one." "Proprietor" means "owner." A **sole proprietorship,** then, is a business owned by one person. It is the oldest and most common form of business organization. It is also the simplest and easiest form of business to start. Usually, only one person invests capital in a sole proprietorship. The business may be started with little or no legal paperwork (forms and documents required by law). The success or failure of the business depends heavily on the efforts and talent of its owner. Some examples of common sole proprietorships are small neighborhood grocery stores, gift shops, and repair shops.

▲ **The Partnership** A **partnership** is a business owned by two or more persons (called "partners") who agree to operate the business as co-owners. Business partners usually enter into a written, legal agreement. This agreement specifies the amount of money to be invested by each partner, the responsibilities of each partner, and how profits and losses are to be divided. Partnerships are often formed when the need for capital is greater than the amount of money one person can invest. Law firms, real estate offices, and "Mom and Pop" stores are frequently organized as partnerships.

▲ **The Corporation** A **corporation** is a business organization that is recognized by law to have a life of its own. In contrast to a sole proprietorship and a partnership, a corporation must get permission to operate from the state. This legal permission is called a **charter** and gives a corporation certain rights and privileges. The charter spells out the rules under which the corporation is to operate.

Many people think that only large businesses like IBM or McDonald's are corporations. This is not always the case. Some corporations are owned and operated by a few people or by one family. Corporations often start out as sole proprietorships or partnerships. The owner(s) of a business may choose to "incorporate" to acquire the money needed to expand the business's operations. To raise this money, shares of stock are sold to hundreds or even thousands of people. These shares represent investments in the corporation. Shareholders, who are also called stockholders, are, therefore, the legal owners of a corporation.

Whatever their form of organization, all businesses share common financial characteristics and methods of recording and reporting the transactions that occur during the operation of the business.

CHAPTER 1   Accounting in a Private Enterprise Economy   5

CONCEPT DEVELOPMENT
Forms of Business Organization
Discuss the types of business organizations and why they operate. A solid foundation about how and why businesses operate will make it easier for students to grasp the importance of a good, sound financial accounting system.

BUSINESS ISSUES
Small businesses sometimes have difficulty obtaining funding to operate their businesses successfully. One source of such funding is the Small Business Administration, a government agency that offers loans at attractive interest rates. An interesting statistic provided by the Small Business Administration is the number of businesses now owned by women. In the 1980s, the SBA confirmed that the average annual growth rate for small proprietorships owned by women was almost double the rate of those owned by men.

Teaching Tips
■ Point out to students that the official name of a corporation ends in Inc., Corp., or Ltd.

Using Visuals

A transparency listing the major characteristics of business organizations is available in the Glencoe Accounting *transparency packet. Also see the* Blackline Masters *booklet for a transparency master on the forms of business organization.*

Cooperative Learning

PAIRS CHECK

Create a list of the names of local businesses formatted in two columns. Divide students into pairs and ask each pair to categorize each business as a service, merchandising, or manufacturing business. You may want to supple-

ment your list with the names of well-known national businesses.

Refer to the "Cooperative Learning" section in the *Tech Prep* booklet for additional cooperative learning strategies.

Chapter 1

CONCEPT DEVELOPMENT

The Role of Accounting

Businesses in a private enterprise economy have making a profit as their major business goal. Accounting records provide information about profits, and losses, by tracking both the costs of operating a business and the income produced by the business. Accounting records allow business managers to analyze what is profitable and what is not. Because of its role in quantifying the results of business operations, an accounting system provides a common means of communicating financial information about the business.

Using Visuals

Ask students to state the ideas in Figure 1-2 in their own words. The diagram is drawn to look like steps, giving a visual clue that each activity named is a step in the accounting process.

Teaching Tips

■ Point out that accounting is an information system.

■ Ask students to discuss how financial condition might vary from one company to another.

■ The parties interested in accounting are owners, creditors, government units, employees, unions, and customers.

■ Accounting rule makers are the AICPA, FASB, SEC, and IRS.

Using Visuals

 A transparency providing a graphic depiction of the users of business financial information is located in the Glencoe Accounting transparency packet.

ACCOUNTING PRACTICE
Students may complete Exercise 1-2 at this point.

The Role of Accounting

Accounting plays a very important role in our private enterprise system because its function is to process financial information and to report on profits and losses. An **accounting system** is the process of recording and reporting financial events, or transactions. The steps involved in an accounting system are illustrated in Figure 1-2.

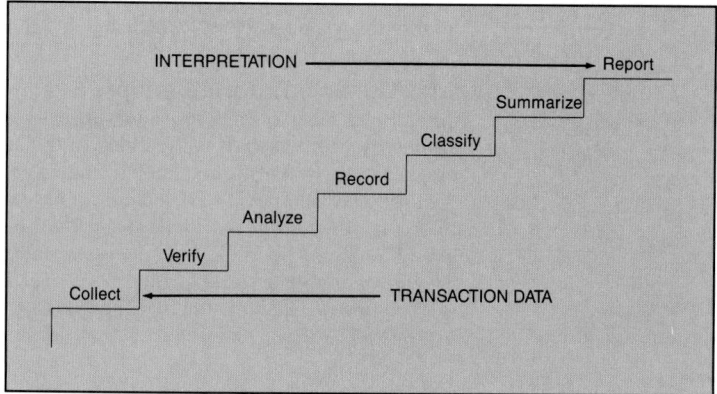

Figure 1-2 Steps in an Accounting System

As you can see, the first step in the process is to collect and verify the financial information for transactions. Each event or transaction having a financial impact on the business must be analyzed and recorded. The recorded information is then classified to make it more useful. After the information has been recorded and classified, it is summarized and presented in the form of accounting reports or statements. Examples of financial reports commonly prepared by accountants are presented in Figure 1-3. Accountants interpret the reports by looking for relationships and trends to help make the information more meaningful to the reader. Accounting is often called the "language of business" because it is a standard means of communicating financial information in a form that is clearly understood by all those interested in the operations and financial condition of a business.

The information in accounting reports has a wide audience. The owner of a business uses financial information to make decisions that affect day-to-day operations. People or institutions who loan money to a business use financial information to determine whether the business will be able to repay loans. Local, state, and federal governments may want to see financial records to determine whether a business is paying the proper amount of taxes. Finally, people who are thinking of investing money in a business want to know whether they can expect a return on their investments.

The Basis of an Accounting System

Accounting consists of many rules and procedures. These rules (or principles) and procedures guide the setting up and maintaining of financial records. Each business sets up its accounting system according to its specific needs, but all businesses follow the same basic rules and procedures.

6

Interdisciplinary Connections

SOCIAL STUDIES

Explain to students that business organization in a private enterprise economy is very different from that in a communist or state-run economy. The lack of people with business skills such as accounting is one difficulty that the former Soviet republics have had to solve as they try to shift to a market economy.

Eastgate Furniture Corporation
Income Statement for Year Ended December 31, 19 --

Revenue from sales:		
Gross sales		$650,000
Less: Sales returns and allowances	$ 1,500	
Sales discounts	4,500	6,000
Net sales		$644,000
Cost of goods sold:		
Merchandise inventory, Jan. 1, 19--		
Purchases		
Less: Purchases returns and allowances .		
Purchases discounts		
Net purchases		
Add freight in		
Cost of goods purchased		
Goods available for sale		
Merchandise inventory, Dec. 31, 19 --		
Cost of goods sold		
Gross profit from sales		
Operating expenses:		
Selling expenses:		
Sales salaries expense		
Rent expense, selling space		
Advertising expense		
Store supplies expense		
Depreciation expense, store equipment .		
Total selling expenses		
General and administrative expenses:		
Office salaries expense		
Rent expense, office space		
Insurance expense		
Office supplies expense		
Depreciation expense, office equipment .		
Total general and admin. expenses ..		
Total operating expenses		
Income from operations		
Less income taxes expense		
Net income		

Eastgate Furniture Corporation
Balance Sheet, December 31, 19 --

Assets

Current assets:			
Cash		$38,900	
Accounts receivable		9,900	
Merchandise inventory		23,000	
Prepaid expenses		4,400	
Total current assets			$ 76,200
Plant and equipment:			
Office equipment	$14,000		
Less accumulated depreciation	1,050	$12,950	
Store equipment	$27,550		
Less accumulated depreciation	4,600	22,950	
Total plant and equipment			35,900
Total assets			$112,100

Liabilities

Current liabilities:		
Accounts payable	$ 4,000	
Income taxes payable	2,100	
Total current liabilities		$ 6,100

Stockholders' Equity

Common stock, $5 par value, 4,000 shares		
authorized and outstanding	$20,000	
Retained earnings	86,000	
Total stockholders' equity		106,000
Total liab. and stockholders' equity		$112,100

Figure 1-3 Accounting Reports

An assumption is something taken for granted as true. When we go to a play, we assume that the show will be as advertised, that the actors can be heard by the audience, and that they are all speaking a language we understand. If our assumptions are wrong, the play will be disappointing or make no sense. Business "audiences" also must be able to make assumptions.

Accounting is based on four assumptions about business operations. These assumptions underlie all reports and are summarized by the terms "business entity," "going concern," "unit of measure," and "time period."

▲ **Business Entity** A **business entity** is an organization that exists independently of its owner's personal holdings. This means that accounting records contain only the financial information related to the business. The business owner's personal financial activities or other investments are not included in the reports of the business. For example, the personal residence of a business owner, valued at $75,000, is not reported in the accounting records of the business. Buildings owned by the business, however, are included in its financial records and reports.

▲ **Going Concern** In accounting, it is assumed that a business will continue to operate in the future. In other words, a business is said to be a **going concern.** Financial reports are prepared on the assumption that

COMPUTERS IN ACCOUNTING

Microcomputer usage in accounting firms has increased significantly because lower computer costs have made it possible for even small accounting firms to computerize their systems. Many CPAs use laptop computers, which they can connect to networks to link them to on-line databases that provide quick and comprehensive financial information.

Did you know?

Although corporations have more employees than smaller businesses, more people are employed by small- to medium-sized businesses. In the last several years, more new jobs have been created by small businesses than by corporations. How might students use this knowledge to help them make decisions about preparing for a career in accounting or business?

---

the business will operate long enough to carry out its operations and meet future obligations. That assumption is why a business might report that its long-term debts of $100,000 must be paid in the year 2010.

▲ **Unit of Measure**   The effects of business transactions are measured in money amounts. In the United States, the monetary unit of measure is the dollar. For accounting records, the dollar is assumed to have a fixed buying power. In other words, the effects of inflation or deflation are not reflected in the financial records of a business. Everything is recorded at cost. For example, a business purchased an office building for $150,000. The office building might now cost $180,000 to replace due to inflation. In the accounting records, however, the building would be listed at its original cost of $150,000.

▲ **Time Period**   Accounting reports are prepared for a specific period of time. A period of time covered by an accounting report is referred to as a **fiscal period.**   The fiscal period can cover any period of time—such as one month or three months—but the most common period is one year.

Accounting and the Computer

Before the invention of calculators and computers, all business transactions were recorded by hand. Now the computer performs routine record-keeping tasks and prepares reports that sometimes took accounting workers months to summarize manually. The computer is ideally suited to accounting work, and accountants were among the earliest users to recognize its practical applications. Found only in large businesses at first, computers are now commonplace. Microcomputers give even one-person businesses the option of using a computerized accounting system.

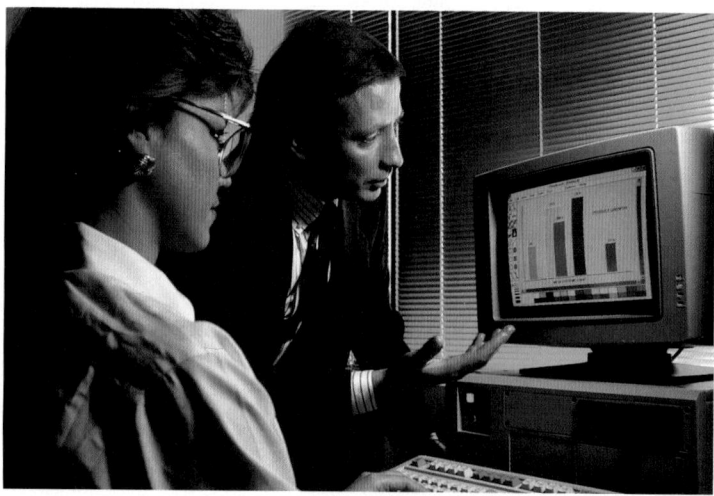

In today's business world, it is becoming increasingly important for accounting workers to be familiar with computerized accounting.

Critical Thinking

Not all fiscal periods begin and end with a calendar year. Consider a water park in the midwest offering water slides, a wave pool, and swimming pools. Ask students why a fiscal period from January through December might not be appropriate for this business. Then ask what period of time the fiscal period might cover. Would a similar business in southern Florida operate with the same fiscal period?

(Answer: A calendar year would not be appropriate because the water park is likely to operate only from May through September. A fiscal period of April through October would allow for both preopening and post-closing activities. A similar business in southern Florida might have a fiscal period of January through December, or even June through May, because the business would be open year round.)

Regardless of how or whether a business uses computers, the nature of accounting remains the same. Information may be recorded in a manual accounting system and a computerized accounting system in different ways, but the same financial reports will result. The rules and principles that you learn from this textbook will apply to both manual and computerized accounting systems.

Career Opportunities in Accounting

According to the *Occupational Outlook Handbook,* the number of jobs for bookkeeping and accounting workers is expected to increase substantially during the 1990s. Although the jobs will require varying amounts of education and experience, most of the jobs will fall into the categories of accounting clerk, general bookkeeper, or accountant. Let's take a look at the requirements of these jobs and their roles in business.

Accounting Clerk

Most entry-level jobs in accounting are clerical. The people who hold these jobs are generally called **accounting clerks.** According to the *Dictionary of Occupational Titles,* an accounting clerk does "routine computing, calculating, and posting of financial, statistical, and other numerical data, manually or by machine, to maintain accounting records and to record details of business transactions."

The job of an accounting clerk varies with the size of the company. In a small business, the clerk might handle most of the business's recordkeeping tasks. In a large company, clerks might specialize in one part of the accounting system. Minimum requirements for most accounting clerk positions are graduation from high school and one or two years of accounting courses. More and more employers want workers who can handle computerized accounting tasks. Some of the entry-level clerical jobs that you see in want ads call for accounting clerks in these categories: payroll, accounts receivable, accounts payable, general ledger, cash, inventory, and purchasing.

General Bookkeeper

Many small- or medium-sized businesses employ only one person to keep their accounting records. This person is usually called a **general bookkeeper.** In addition to processing and recording all the information from a company's transactions, a general bookkeeper often calculates wages and prepares checks for the payment of those wages. In companies with several accounting clerks, a general bookkeeper will often also be a supervisor.

Education requirements vary with the size of the company and the complexity of its accounting system. A general bookkeeper may or may not be required to have a four-year college degree in accounting. Experience or an associate's degree in accounting is sometimes enough to fulfill the job's requirements.

Accountant

The term **accountant** describes a fairly broad range of jobs. In general, an accountant is expected to make choices and decisions about the design

CONCEPT DEVELOPMENT
Career Opportunities in Accounting
The field of accounting provides many opportunities for future workers. The majority of new accounting jobs throughout the 1990s will require knowledge of both accounting and computer applications. Encourage students who are interested in accounting careers to speak with people who are currently employed in the field to find out about their education and training experiences. To help students pursue this information, contact local companies and ask for names of accounting employees who would be willing to talk to students about their careers.

Teaching Tips

■ Additional career information is provided in the special feature "Focus on Accounting Careers" and in the *Accounting Careers* booklet.

Making Connections

COMMUNICATIONS
Ask students to discuss some of the ways they would present themselves in a job interview for one of the positions discussed in this section. From student suggestions, make a list on the chalkboard of "Do's" and "Don'ts" for the job interview, including such nonverbal "messages" as dress, posture, and speaking style. A list of interview questions and techniques can be found in the *Blackline Masters* booklet.

Chapter 1

CONCEPT DEVELOPMENT
Organizations that Influence Accounting Practice

For financial information to have common meaning from one company to another, accounting rules must be standardized and followed by all companies. The accounting organizations listed here all contribute to the development of financial accounting standards. Your state society of certified public accountants will be willing to provide someone to discuss the major accounting organizations, such as the AICPA, FASB, SEC, and the IRS. Ask a local CPA for the society's address or for help in obtaining a speaker.

 ACCOUNTING PRACTICE
Students may complete Exercises 1-1 and 1-3 at this point.

---

of accounting systems and to prepare and explain financial reports. An accountant may also supervise the work of accounting clerks who perform routine recordkeeping functions.

Many accountants enter the field with either a bachelor's or a master's degree in accounting. It is not unusual, however, for accountants to have started at entry-level positions and studied for their degrees while on the job. Although accountants work in every kind of business, their work can be divided into four major categories: public accounting, managerial accounting, not-for-profit accounting, and teaching.

> **ACCOUNTING** *Notes*
> Accounting's "Big Six" certified public accounting firms are: Arthur Andersen & Co.; Coopers & Lybrand; Deloitte & Touche; Ernst & Young; Peat, Marwick, Main & Co.; and Price Waterhouse & Co.

▲ **Public Accounting**   Public accountants provide services to clients on a fee basis. Like medicine and law, public accounting requires a license, or certification by the state. To become a **certified public accountant,** or CPA, an accountant must pass a rigorous examination on accounting theory, accounting practices, auditing, and business law. CPAs provide a variety of services to their clients. They often prepare income tax returns and give financial advice about the operation of a business.

▲ **Managerial Accounting**   Unlike public accounting, *managerial accounting* takes place only inside a business firm. A managerial accountant may determine the cost of products, prepare budgets and tax returns, and provide financial information to the business's managers. By passing an examination similar to the CPA's, a managerial accountant may receive a Certificate in Management Accounting (CMA). A CMA, however, is not a license to practice and does not allow the accountant to perform services for the general public.

▲ **Not-for-Profit Accounting**   Groups that provide services to the general public and do not operate to make money are called not-for-profit organizations. Not-for-profit organizations include universities, churches, government agencies, and most hospitals. Although these organizations do not have profit as their main goal, they still require accounting services. They are concerned with the efficient use of the resources available to them. Not-for-profit accountants specialize in accounting for these organizations.

▲ **Teaching Accounting**   The field of education offers many opportunities for people with degrees and experience in accounting. High schools, colleges, and universities offer a wide variety of accounting courses that require qualified instructors.

Organizations that Influence Accounting Practice

In the United States, four groups have had a major impact on accounting practice. The four groups are the American Institute of Certified Public Accountants, the Financial Accounting Standards Board, the Securities and Exchange Commission, and the Internal Revenue Service.

10   UNIT 1   Introduction to Accounting

Making Connections

AROUND THE WORLD

In today's business environment, even small and medium-sized companies are expanding their markets to include foreign sales. Such businesses expect their accounting staffs or outside CPA firms to help them with international accounting rules. In a turnabout, CPA firms that have expertise in international accounting can sell their services to foreign companies wishing to do business here.

10   UNIT 1   Introduction to Accounting

The American Institute of Certified Public Accountants

The American Institute of Certified Public Accountants (AICPA) is a professional association. Its members are certified public accountants in public practice, business and industry, education, and government. The Institute's main concern has been the development of standards of professional practice for its members. Although the AICPA no longer issues official statements on accounting standards, it still has a strong influence.

Financial Accounting Standards Board

The Financial Accounting Standards Board (FASB) was established in 1973 to develop financial accounting standards for businesses and not-for-profit organizations. The FASB is authorized to issue two publications: *Statements of Financial Accounting Standards* and *Interpretations.* The *Statements* and *Interpretations* help in preparing and auditing financial reports.

Securities and Exchange Commission

The Securities and Exchange Commission (SEC) was established by Congress in 1934 to regulate the sale of stock certificates to the general public. The SEC was also given broad authority to regulate and control accounting and other information distributed by corporations. The SEC, however, has generally relied on the accounting profession to perform these functions. In only a few cases has the SEC exerted its legal power by disagreeing with a position taken by the AICPA or the FASB.

Internal Revenue Service

The Internal Revenue Service (IRS) has a widespread impact on many aspects of our economy. The IRS is charged with the collection of federal taxes, the enforcement of tax regulations, and the interpretation of tax laws relating to particular businesses or situations. Through these functions, the IRS has a direct effect on tax-related aspects of accounting.

Other Influences

Several other organizations continue to influence accounting practices and standards. The National Council on Governmental Accounting (NCGA) develops and interprets principles of accounting and financial reporting for state and local governments. The American Accounting Association (AAA), an organization of accounting professors and certified public accountants, is concerned with developing accounting standards. The Institute of Management Accountants is concerned with accounting for management purposes.

Summary of Key Points

1. In the United States private enterprise economy, businesses are concerned with earning a profit. Businesses that do not earn a profit over a period of time will not be able to continue operating.

Chapter 1

Teaching Tips
- The AICPA issues research studies and auditing standards and prepares the national CPA exam.
- The SEC issues Accounting Series Releases (ASRs).

ACCOUNTING ISSUES

Accounting practices are changed to keep business records up to date with current rules and regulations. One major source of change in accounting practices is tax law. When the U.S. Congress passes new tax legislation, the IRS will make changes in the rules affecting accounting practices to ensure adherence to the new tax code.

3 CLOSE

CHAPTER SUMMARY

This summary enumerates the key information in the chapter. It is a useful tool for reinforcement and review.

Pop Quiz

1. Money that an owner invests in a business is called _____.
2. What type of business is a supermarket?
3. What legal document gives a corporation permission to operate?
4. A business co-owned by two or more persons is called a _____.
5. What is a fiscal period?

ANSWERS

1. capital
2. merchandising
3. charter
4. partnership
5. the time period covered by an accounting report

2. The three types of businesses organized to earn a profit are service businesses, merchandising businesses, and manufacturing businesses.
3. The three major forms of business organization found in the United States are the sole proprietorship, the partnership, and the corporation.
4. Accounting is a systematic process of recording and reporting the financial information resulting from business transactions.
5. Accounting information is used by a wide variety of people to make decisions about how well or how poorly a business is operating.
6. Computers have affected the speed with which accounting is performed, but their use has not altered the basic accounting system.
7. There is a wide variety of jobs available in bookkeeping and accounting. The number of job openings in this area is expected to increase in the next decade.
8. Accounting practices are influenced and regulated by such groups as the AICPA, FASB, SEC, and IRS.

*R*eteaching *S*trategies

Students may have difficulty understanding just what an accounting "system" is. At this point in their study of accounting, the important concept to communicate is that accounting information is recorded and reports are prepared to summarize information *following a specific set of steps*. The "system" consists of both the steps, as outlined in Figure 1-2, and the tools (types of accounting forms and/or software programs) used to prepare the records.

Understanding accounting terminology is key to understanding an accounting system. Conduct an in-class exercise by giving a term and then calling on students to use that term in a sentence.

Review and Applications

Building Your Accounting Vocabulary

In your own words, write the definitions of each of the following accounting terms. Use complete sentences for your definitions.

accountant
accounting clerk
accounting system
business entity
capital
certified public
  accountant
charter

corporation
fiscal period
general bookkeeper
going concern
loss
manufacturing
  business

merchandising
  business
partnership
profit
service business
sole proprietorship

Reviewing Your Accounting Knowledge

1. The United States economy is referred to as a private enterprise economy. What is the major characteristic of our private enterprise economy?
2. What is one measure of business success?
3. What is the major difference between a merchandising business and a manufacturing business?
4. List the main difference between a partnership and a corporation.
5. What is the basic function of an accounting system?
6. Who are the users of accounting information?
7. List and briefly explain the four assumptions about business operations on which accounting is based.
8. What are some of the duties of an accounting clerk?
9. What are the four possible career areas in the field of accounting?
10. What organizations influence accounting as it is practiced in the United States?

Improving Your Decision-Making Skills

One way to make a decision is to follow a step-by-step pattern that is called the decision-making process. The steps in this process are

1. Face the problem (recognize the need for a decision).
2. Get information about the problem.
3. List alternative ways of dealing with the problem.
4. Evaluate the alternatives.
5. Reach a decision.
6. Act on the decision.

Suppose you are trying to decide whether a career in accounting is right for you. Using the steps in the decision-making process, describe the actions you would take at each step. Be specific about information you would need and where you would get it.

13

Improving Your Decision-Making Skills
Students' responses could include these options. *Step 1:* Decide whether to major in accounting in college or, for the non-college bound, whether to seek an accounting job after high school.
Step 2: Get information from guidance counselors (if college bound) or visit local businesses and talk to others in an accounting occupation (non-college bound).
Step 3: Alternatives: take a part-time job and attend school or take additional accounting courses and then decide.

Step 4: A part-time job may be out of the question for some students while others may need to work at something else before they can afford to take accounting courses.
Step 5: Students' decisions could be to go to college and decide later, find an entry-level accounting job or other work, or do nothing at all.
Step 6: Follow up on decisions by setting up interviews with guidance counselors or potential employers.

PRACTICE AND APPLY

• Concepts and Procedures

Exercise 1-1: Ch. Obj. 6

1. private enterprise economy
2. not-for-profit organization
3. shareholders
4. accounting reports
5. dollar
6. partners
7. stock
8. managerial accounting
9. electronic funds transfer system
10. organization

Exercise 1-2: Ch. Obj. 3

1. James Taylor would need to know the tradeoff between high profits and risk. He would be interested in the stability of earnings reported by Pacific Company over a period of years.
2. Rita Hays wants to be able to see if labor is getting its fair share of the firm's profits resulting from its employees' contributions.
3. Diane Hauser wants to know if the company will be a stable, long-term, dependable supplier.
4. Mark Siebert wants to be sure the company has the assets and profits or earning power to be able to repay the loan.
5. Jill Mercer wants to know if an investment in Pacific stock will provide a dependable source of retirement income.

Exercise 1-3: Ch. Obj. 3, 4

You may work as a bookkeeper in a small or medium-sized business. An associate's degree in accounting may be enough to become a bookkeeper. A position as an accountant will likely require a bachelor's or master's degree.

Applying Accounting Procedures

Exercise 1-1   Understanding Business and Accounting Terms

Instructions: Number a sheet of paper from 1 to 10. Write the word or words from the list below that best matches each numbered statement.

accounting reports	organization
dollar	partners
electronic funds transfer system	private enterprise economy
managerial accounting	shareholders
not-for-profit organization	stock

1. An economy in which people are free to produce the goods or services they choose
2. An organization that is service-oriented and that does not operate to earn a profit
3. The legal owners of a corporation
4. The end results of an accounting system
5. The unit of measure for financial information in the United States
6. Co-owners of a business
7. Shares of ownership in a corporation
8. A system that provides financial information to interested persons within an organization
9. A computerized system for transferring funds
10. A group of people who come together with a common goal in mind

Exercise 1-2   Using Financial Information

Instructions: Give one or more reasons why each of the following would be interested in the financial reports of the Pacific Company, a fishing fleet.

1. James Taylor is looking for an investment in which he can make a profit, even if a little risk is involved.
2. Rita Hays, the local union agent, is preparing the bargaining position for employee wage increases.
3. Diane Hauser, a buyer for a fish market, is seeking a new supplier from which to buy fresh fish.
4. Mark Siebert, a credit manager, has been asked to approve a loan for the Pacific Company.
5. Jill Mercer, a retired widow, is looking for an investment that will provide a steady income for her retirement years.

Exercise 1-3   Exploring Accounting Careers

Instructions: Read the following paragraph and assume that you are Lee Harms. On a sheet of paper, write what you think Lee's response would be.

A CAREER DAY MEETING

Two accounting students, Richard Cummings and Nancy Purcell, were discussing whether they should become accountants. They met Lee Harms, a CPA, at a career day meeting and asked her what types of employment opportunities they might find in accounting.

14

> Refer students to the Chapter 1 review pages in the workbook, *Chapter Reviews and Working Papers.*

Additional Reinforcement

Students who need additional practice or individualized help will benefit from the *Glencoe Accounting Electronic Study Guide* or the *Glencoe Accounting* on-line multimedia program, which provide reinforcement and reteaching for vocabulary, concepts, and procedures.

Exercise 1-4 Describing Types of Businesses

Instructions: On a sheet of paper, indicate whether each of the following businesses is a service business, a merchandising business, or a manufacturing business.

1. International Business Machines (IBM)
2. J. C. Penney Co., Inc.
3. Glendale Medical Center
4. Avis Rent-a-Car
5. Ford Motor Company
6. The Chase Manhattan Bank
7. Ace Hardware Stores
8. Michigan City Animal Hospital
9. Apple Computer, Inc.
10. K Mart Discount Department Store
11. Prudential Insurance Company of America
12. Bethlehem Steel Corporation

You may wish to provide services to the public for a fee by becoming a CPA. To work for a single business, you might need a Certificate in Management Accounting (CMA). Other opportunities exist in teaching and in government, universities, hospitals, and not-for-profit organizations.

Exercise 1-4: Ch. Obj. 1, 2

1. manufacturing
2. merchandising
3. service
4. service
5. manufacturing
6. service
7. merchandising
8. service
9. manufacturing
10. merchandising
11. service
12. manufacturing

4 ASSESS

A chapter test is available for use in assessing students' understanding of concepts in this chapter.

The testmaker software will enable you to develop tailor-made chapter, unit, semester, and final tests.

Alternative Assessment

For alternative assessment strategies, refer to *Tech Prep Strategies in Accounting.*

15

Teacher Notes

Use Chapter Test 1 here to assess students' understanding and retention of the concepts and procedures presented in the chapter.

Computer technology has radically changed accounting practices as decreasing prices and improving technology have placed computing power within reach of even the smallest business. Have students visit a local computer software store to scan the types of software packages available for maintaining accounting records. Ask students to share their observations in class.

QUESTIONS

1. What are some other uses for computers in business in addition to maintaining accounting records?
2. How might the owner of a small business decide which software is best for keeping the business's records?

ANSWERS

1. Among the many uses of computers are the scanning of prices at checkout counters, maintaining inventory records, tracking shipping (as in overnight mail and package delivery), and automating correspondence both within and outside a business.
2. The owner might read software evaluations in current computer magazines, ask other owners of small businesses for recommendations, call the software developer and ask questions about the software, or simply buy the software and try it.

*A*utomation:
A Business's Life Support System

In today's business world, time and money are precious resources. Wise decision making can help control spending and productivity. To this end, one of the wisest decisions management can make is to automate.

Small businesses have discovered that computers can help them in a big way. Consider these cases.

The estimator in a family-owned metal fabricating shop in the Midwest wrote his own computer program to help him prepare price estimates. He keys in the quantity and size of material, and the program prepares the estimate. By hand, estimates take 15 to 20 *minutes*; the electronic estimates take 15 to 20 *seconds*. Not only are the computer estimates faster—they're also more accurate.

A property management company oversees 65 properties, some of which are shopping centers. The work is done with just 4 bookkeepers, 8 property managers, and a network of computers. Without automation, the company president estimates they'd need 20 bookkeepers instead of 4 and 24 property managers instead of 8. The company saves over $400,000 a year in payroll costs alone. The company president says that savings is the difference between profit and bankruptcy.

Big businesses can save even more. Commercial banks move about $300 billion every day in international electronic funds transfers. The cost of a single international transfer is $10 to $12 if done on paper. Done electronically, the cost drops to about $2 per transfer.

Government agencies save time and money through automation, too. The U.S. Forest Service says that, since it automated, its environmental impact statements take 39% less time to prepare.

Buying or sending gifts over long distances is easy today with the help of computers.

Timber sales contracts take 27% less time. A study revealed that automation saved the Forestry Service $125 million in 1985.

To business owners, the question is not, "*Should I automate?*" Rather the question is, "How long will I survive without it?"

16

Chapter 2

BUSINESS TRANSACTIONS AND THE BASIC ACCOUNTING EQUATION

In Chapter 1 you learned that accounting has been called the "language of business." Accounting provides financial information that is essential for the success of any business. Accounting provides that financial information to a wide variety of users: owners, managers, employees, investors, and so on.

In this chapter, you will begin to learn some of the language of accounting. You'll learn about the basic accounting equation—the foundation of accounting. This equation expresses the relationship between property and the rights or claims to that property.

LOOKING BACK

Chapter 1 introduced students to the need for financial record keeping and to the forms of business organization—sole proprietorships, partnerships, and corporations—in our private enterprise economy. The chapter also introduced the concept of profit and loss, as well as some basic assumptions underlying financial accounting. In this chapter, students will build upon this foundation by learning to analyze typical business transactions using the basic accounting equation.

VOCABULARY DEVELOPMENT

Reinforce vocabulary through a team competition to define new terms. Appoint teams to participate in a "Vocabulary Bee." Teams take turns defining terms, with team members consulting with each other before giving a definition. If a team gives an incorrect definition, the team is eliminated. Definitions of these terms are found in the chapter and in the glossary on pages 670-679.

Electronic Field Trips

Learning Objectives

When you have completed Chapter 2, you should be able to do the following:

1. Describe the relationship between property and property rights.
2. Explain the meaning of "equity" as it is used in accounting.
3. List the parts of the basic accounting equation and define each part.
4. Show how various business transactions affect the basic accounting equation.
5. Check the balance of the basic accounting equation after a business transaction has been analyzed and recorded.
6. Define the accounting terms introduced in this chapter.

New Terms

property
property rights
credit
creditor
assets
equity
owner's equity
liabilities
basic accounting equation
business transaction
account
accounts receivable
accounts payable
capital
on account
revenue
expense
withdrawal

17

Teaching Resources

- Lesson Plans
- TE/Chapter Reviews & Working Papers
- Demonstration Problems
- Student Study Plans
- Teaching Transparencies
- Solutions Transparencies
- Electronic Field Trips Video, Level I
- Electronic Study Guide
- Chapter 2 Test
- Unit Objective Test for Chapters 1-2
- Unit Problem Test for Chapters 1-2

Other Resources

- Skills Improvement Activities
- Blackline Masters
- Careers in Accounting
- Dictionary
- Math Review for Accounting
- Tech Prep Strategies in Accounting
- Video
- Test Bank with Software
- Spanish Resources/Audiotapes
- Spanish Electronic Study Guide

Chapter 2

1 FOCUS

MAJOR CONCEPTS

- Property and Property Rights
- Financial Claims in Accounting
- Business Transactions
- Effects of Business Transactions on the Basic Accounting Equation
- Using a Computer in Accounting

BUSINESS CONNECTION

Fred DeLuca opened the first Subway Sandwiches & Salads shop in Bridgeport, Connecticut, in 1965, with one primary goal to stay in business. Two years later he adopted a growth-oriented philosophy and his franchise grew steadily. Today there are more than 8,000 Subway stores located throughout the U.S., Canada, Australia, Japan, Israel, Ireland, Mexico, Portugal, and South Korea. The Subway franchise could not have realized such substantial growth without earning revenue.

2 TEACH

CONCEPT DEVELOPMENT
Property and Property Rights

Emphasize these points: (1) the right to own property is fundamental to our private enterprise system, (2) the value of property is measured in dollars, and (3) accounting provides financial information about property and property rights.

To illustrate the relationship between property and property rights, use examples familiar to students—rollerblades, sports equipment, cars, clothing, sound systems, etc. Choose an example in which the owner has total financial control.

Using Visuals

 Use demonstration problem 2-1 to show the relationship between property and property rights.

18   UNIT 1   Introduction to Accounting

Property and Property Rights

The right to own property is basic to our private enterprise system. **Property** is anything of value that is owned or controlled. When you own an item of property, you have a legal right to that item. When you have control over an item, you have the right only to the use of the item. For example, you own a pair of skis you have bought. If you had rented the skis for a weekend instead of buying them, you would have control of the skis. You would have the right to use the skis for the weekend, but you would not own them. As you can see from this example, you can have certain rights, or claims, to the items that you either own or control.

When you purchase property, you acquire certain rights, or financial claims to that property.

Businesses also own and control property. One of the purposes of accounting is to provide financial information about property and a business's rights to that property. In accounting, property and property rights are measured in dollar amounts. Dollar amounts measure both the cost of the property and the **property rights,** or financial claims, to the property. For example, if you had paid $100 cash to buy the skis mentioned above, you would have a property right or financial claim of $100 to those skis. This relationship between property and property rights is shown in the equation that follows:

PROPERTY (COST)	=	PROPERTY RIGHTS (FINANCIAL CLAIMS)
Skis	=	Your Claim to Skis
$100	=	$100

When you buy property with cash, you acquire all of the property rights (financial claims) to that property at the time of purchase. What happens,

18

UNIT 1   Introduction to Accounting

Reinforcing Study Skills

Setting purposes for reading often helps students focus on the main points. Have students read the chapter introduction and then, in their own words, explain what they think this chapter will be about. As students read, have them refer back to the Learning Objectives and try to meet each one as they go along.

Provide a copy of the *Student Study Plans* to each class member to help organize study activities or to individualize practice and review activities.

however, when you buy property on credit? What happens to the financial claim when you don't pay for the property right away?

When you buy property and agree to pay for it later, you are buying on **credit.** The business or person selling you the property on credit is called a **creditor.** A creditor can be any person or business to which you owe money. When you buy property on credit, you do not have the only financial claim to the property. You share the financial claim to that property with your creditor. For example, suppose you want to buy a pair of ski boots that costs $150, but you have only $75. A store agrees to sell you the boots on credit. You pay the store $75 and sign an agreement to pay the remaining $75 over the next three months. Since you owe the store (the creditor) $75, you share the financial claim to the boots with the creditor. The creditor's financial claim to the ski boots is $75 and your claim is $75. The combined claims equal the cost of the property (the boots). Your purchase of the ski boots can be expressed in terms of the equation PROPERTY = PROPERTY RIGHTS.

PROPERTY	=	PROPERTY RIGHTS		
Ski Boots	=	Creditor's Financial Claim	+	Owner's Financial Claim
$150	=	$75	+	$75

As you can see, two (or more) people can have financial claims to the same property. The total financial claims always equal the total cost of the property. Before you read any further, answer the following questions to check your understanding of the relationship between property and property rights.

Check Your Learning

The equation below shows the relationship between property and its corresponding financial claims. Use the equation to answer the questions that follow. (Use notebook paper if you want to write your answer.)

Property = Creditor's Financial Claim + Owner's Financial Claim

1. What are the missing dollar amounts in each equation?
   a. Property (?) = Creditor's Claim ($1,000) + Owner's Claim ($6,000)
   b. Property ($2,000) = Creditor's Claim ($500) + Owner's Claim (?)
   c. Property ($30,000) = Creditor's Claim (?) + Owner's Claim ($22,000)
2. What is the amount of a creditor's claim to a radio if the radio cost $75 and the owner has paid $35 on it?
3. What is the amount of the owner's claim to a baseball glove if the glove cost $32 and the amount still owed is $12?
4. What was the cost of an automobile if the owner has a $3,000 claim and a creditor has an $11,000 claim?

The answers to these questions can be found in the answers section at the back of this book. Compare your answers to the answers for this activity. If you missed the answer to a question, find out why. Go back to the appropriate section of the chapter and study the material related to the answer you may have missed.

CONCEPT DEVELOPMENT
Financial Claims in Accounting

In accounting terms property equals assets, and claims to those assets equal equity, or property rights. Equity includes the claims of creditors (liabilities) and the owner (owner's equity).

Introduce the basic accounting equation and relate property to assets and property rights to equity. Creditors have first claim to assets, thus their claims are listed first on the equity side of the equation.

Teaching Tips

■ Check students' understanding of "entity" and review the definition if necessary.
■ Business entities refer to property as "assets."
■ An example of equity that may be familiar to students is the equity their parents have in their homes.
■ Equity includes (1) the creditor's claim to an asset and (2) the owner's claim to the same asset.

Using Visuals

Use demonstration problem 2-3 to reinforce the concept of the basic accounting equation.

Financial Claims in Accounting

As you learned in Chapter 1, every business is considered a separate entity. In other words, the property of a business is separate from the personal property of its owner(s). The accounting records of a business are kept only for transactions affecting the business itself. The owner's personal financial transactions are not a part of the business's records. For example, if the owner buys a car for her or his personal use, that car would not be recorded as property of the business.

In accounting, the property or items of value owned by a business are referred to as **assets.** Some examples of assets are cash, office equipment, manufacturing equipment, buildings, and land. There is also an accounting term for the financial claims to these assets. The total financial claims to the assets, or property, of a business are referred to as **equity.** If you have a financial claim to property, you are said to have equity in that property. Let's explore the meaning of this term.

Suppose Book Ends, a small bookstore, has just bought a new building for its operations. The building cost $45,000 and Book Ends made a cash down payment of $15,000 to the seller of the building. A local bank loaned the store the remaining $30,000. Both the book store and the bank now have financial claims to the building. As creditor, the bank has equity in the building equal to its investment of $30,000. Book Ends has equity equal to its down payment of $15,000. Over the years, as Book Ends repays the loan, its equity will increase. As less money is owed, the equity of the creditor (the bank) will decrease. When the loan is completely repaid, the creditor's financial claim will be canceled. In other words, the owner's equity will then equal the cost of the building. Book Ends will both own and control the property and will, therefore, have full property rights to it.

As you can see from this example, equity is simply the claims—of both creditor(s) and owner(s)—to the assets of a business. In accounting, there are separate terms for owner's claims and creditor's claims. The owner's claims to the assets of the business are called **owner's equity.** Owner's equity is measured by the dollar amount of the owner's claims to the total assets of the business.

The creditor's claims to the assets of the business are called **liabilities.** Liabilities are the debts of a business. They are measured by the amount of money owed by a business to its creditors. The relationship between assets and total equities—liabilities plus owner's equity—can be shown in the **basic accounting equation,** which is

$$\text{ASSETS} = \text{LIABILITIES} + \text{OWNER'S EQUITY}$$

Figure 2-1 shows the basic accounting equation applied to the example of Book Ends and the bank that gave it a loan. Notice that assets equal the combined claims to those assets.

R E M E M B E R

Total equities includes both the creditor's claims and the owner's claims.

Making Connections

EVERYDAY LIFE

Ask students to list their personal assets on a sheet of paper, then ask them to consider how they acquired those assets. Did they purchase them? Were they gifts? Then ask students to list any liabilities that they have and determine their equity.

Student responses regarding assets might include clothing, jewelry, cash in savings or checking accounts, bicycle, car, sports equipment, and stereo. Responses regarding liabilities might include money owed to parents or a friend, a layaway or charge account, and money due for car insurance.

ASSETS   =   EQUITIES

$45,000 Building $30,000 Loan $15,000 Investment

Property	=	Creditor's Claim	+	Owner's Claim
$45,000		$30,000		$15,000
ASSETS	=	LIABILITIES	+	OWNER'S EQUITY

Figure 2-1   The Basic Accounting Equation

Before you go on to learn about business transactions, do the Check Your Learning activity that follows to check your understanding of the basic accounting equation.

Check Your Learning

Use the basic accounting equation to answer these questions. (If you want to write your answers, use notebook paper.)

1. If a business has invested $50,000 in an asset that cost $75,000, what is the amount of its liability?
2. In accounting, there are two kinds of equity: ___?___ and owner's equity.
3. If a business has liabilities of $60,000 and assets of $218,000, what is the amount of owner's equity?

Compare your answers to those in the answers section. Re-read the preceding part of the chapter to find the correct answers to any questions that you may have missed.

Business Transactions

A **business transaction** is an economic event that causes a change in assets, liabilities, or owner's equity. Business transactions involve the buying, selling, or exchange of goods and services. Some businesses have hundreds, or even thousands, of business transactions every day. When a business transaction occurs, the financial position of the business changes. The change is reflected in the accounting system of the business as an increase or decrease in assets, liabilities, or owner's equity. Let's look at an example.

If a business buys a typewriter and pays cash for it, the amount of cash the business has is decreased. At the same time, the business has increased its equipment. In an accounting system, the increases and decreases caused by business transactions are recorded in specific accounts. An **account,** then, is a record of the increases or decreases in and the balance for a specific item such as cash or equipment.

CHAPTER 2   Business Transactions and the Basic Accounting Equation   **21**

**Effects of Business
Transactions on the Basic
Accounting Equation**

Five types of business transactions are used here to summarize the types of changes in assets, liabilities, or owner's equity resulting from business operations. Accounts are introduced as the means of analyzing the effects of business transactions.

Teaching Tips

■ As new types of business transactions are introduced throughout the textbook, follow these steps to promote student understanding:

1. Analyze the effects of each transaction.
2. Show the effects on the accounting equation.
3. Use a demonstration problem to show new concepts or procedures.
4. Have students work a similar problem.
5. Assign "Check Your Learning" activities. Have students re-read material they did not understand.

Using Visuals

Use demonstration problem 2-4 here to give students practice in classifying accounts.

Accounts represent things in the real world, such as money invested in a business, office furniture, or money owed to a creditor. For example, an account for office furniture represents the dollar cost of all the office furniture bought by the business.

Each business sets up its accounts and its accounting system according to its needs. There is no standard number of accounts a business should use. Some businesses have only a few accounts, while others have hundreds. Regardless of the number of accounts a business has, all its accounts may be classified as either assets, liabilities, or owner's equity. The following account titles are but a few examples of the types of accounts a business can have:

ASSETS	=	LIABILITIES	+	OWNER'S EQUITY
Cash in Bank		Accounts Payable		Paul Howard, Capital
Accounts Receivable				
Office Furniture				
Equipment				

Some of these account titles need more explanation. The second asset account listed is Accounts Receivable. **Accounts receivable** is the total amount of money to be received in the future for goods or services sold on credit. Accounts receivable is an asset because it represents something owned: a business's claim to the assets of another person or another business. It represents a future value that eventually will bring cash into the business. When the business eventually receives payment in cash, the claim will be canceled.

The liability account listed is Accounts Payable. **Accounts payable** is the amount of money owed, or payable, to a business's creditors. It is a future obligation requiring the payment of cash or services to another person or business. Finally, note that the owner's equity account in a business is identified by the owner's name followed by a comma and the word "Capital." **Capital** refers to the dollar amount of the owner's investment in the business.

ACCOUNTING *Notes*
The word *capital* has its roots in the Latin word *capitalis*, meaning "property." *Capital* first meant "main." Later the term came to stand for a person's wealth, which was the main source of a person's importance.

Effects of Business Transactions on the Basic Accounting Equation

When a business transaction occurs, an accounting clerk analyzes the transaction to see how it affects each part of the basic accounting equation. As an accounting clerk, you must select the information in a transaction that indicates any change in assets, liabilities, or owner's equity. You will find it easy to analyze the effects of a transaction if you follow the steps that are listed:

1. Identify the accounts affected.
2. Classify the accounts affected (asset, liability, or owner's equity).
3. Determine the amount of increase or decrease for each account affected.
4. Make sure the basic accounting equation remains in balance.

The business transactions that follow are examples of transactions that occur often in most businesses. To help you learn about various kinds of

---

Interdisciplinary Connections

MATHEMATICS

Although computers now handle many computations, accounting is still based in mathematics. Help students relate the basic accounting equation, *Assets = Liabilities + Owner's Equity*, to other equations they have worked with in algebra or other math classes. Note that any equation shows a balanced relationship.

Refer students to *Math Review for Accounting* for extra practice in basic math skills.

transactions, these examples are categorized as follows: (1) investments by the owner, (2) cash transactions, (3) credit transactions, (4) revenue and expense transactions, and (5) withdrawals by the owner.

Investments by the Owner

Paul Howard has decided to start a word processing service business. He plans to call the business WordService.

Business Transactions 1 and 2 concern investments made in the business by the owner. Transaction 1 is a cash investment; Transaction 2 is an investment of equipment.

Business Transaction 1: *The owner of WordService, Paul Howard, deposited $20,000 in a bank checking account under the name of WordService.*

Analysis:
1. Identify the accounts affected.

    Every transaction will affect at least two accounts. You can determine the accounts affected by analyzing the transaction to see which accounts are being changed. Here are the accounts used by WordService.

ASSETS	=	LIABILITIES	+	OWNER'S EQUITY
Cash in Bank		Accounts Payable		Paul Howard, Capital
Accounts Receivable				
Office Furniture				
Equipment				

Now look at Transaction 1 again. The business has received cash. Cash transactions are summarized in the account entitled Cash in Bank. Paul Howard is investing his personal funds in the business. An owner's investments in the business are summarized in the account called Paul Howard, Capital.

2. Classify the accounts affected.

    Cash in Bank is an asset account. Paul Howard, Capital is an owner's equity account.

3. Determine the amount of increase or decrease for each account affected.

    Cash in Bank is increased by $20,000. Paul Howard, Capital is increased by $20,000.

4. Make sure the basic accounting equation remains in balance.

	ASSETS	=	LIABILITIES	+	OWNER'S EQUITY
	Cash in Bank				Paul Howard, Capital
Trans. 1	+$20,000				+$20,000
Balance	$20,000	=	0	+	$20,000

The asset account Cash in Bank totals $20,000. Liabilities plus owner's equity also total $20,000. The basic accounting equation remains in balance.

R E M E M B E R

Each transaction affects at least two accounts.

Chapter 2

Business Transaction 2: *The owner, Paul Howard, invested an electric typewriter worth $300 in the business.*

Analysis:
1. Identify the accounts affected.
   The business has received an electric typewriter. Since a typewriter is equipment, the account Equipment is affected. Paul Howard has invested a personal asset in the business, so the account Paul Howard, Capital is also affected.
2. Classify the accounts affected.
   Equipment is an asset account and Paul Howard, Capital is an owner's equity account.
3. Determine the amount of increase or decrease for each account affected.
   Equipment is increased by $300. Paul Howard, Capital is increased by $300.
4. Make sure the basic accounting equation remains in balance.

	ASSETS		= LIABILITIES +	OWNER'S EQUITY
	Cash in Bank	Equipment		Paul Howard, Capital
Prev. Bal.	$20,000	0	0	$20,000
Trans. 2		+$300		+ 300
Balance	$20,000 +	$300	= 0 +	$20,300

The asset accounts Cash in Bank and Equipment total $20,300. Liabilities and owner's equity total $20,300, so the basic accounting equation is in balance.

Cash Payment Transactions

Transaction 3 is an example of a transaction in which an asset is purchased for cash. Any asset that is purchased for cash will be recorded as in this transaction. In similar transactions, the account title will change, depending upon the asset bought.

Business Transaction 3: *WordService issued a $4,000 check for the purchase of a microcomputer.*

Analysis:
1. Identify the accounts affected.
   The business has purchased a microcomputer. The Equipment account is used to summarize transactions involving any type of equipment. Since the business has paid out cash for the microcomputer, the account Cash in Bank is affected. (Payments made by check are always treated as cash payments and are summarized in the Cash in Bank account.)
2. Classify the accounts affected.
   Equipment and Cash in Bank are both asset accounts.
3. Determine the amount of increase or decrease for each account affected.
   Equipment is increased by $4,000. The account Cash in Bank is decreased by $4,000.
4. Make sure the basic accounting equation remains in balance.

24

UNIT 1   Introduction to Accounting

	ASSETS		= LIABILITIES +	OWNER'S EQUITY
	Cash in Bank	Equipment		Paul Howard, Capital
Prev. Bal.	$20,000	$ 300	0	$20,300
Trans. 3	– 4,000	+ 4,000		
Balance	$16,000 +	$4,300 =	0	+ $20,300

Transaction 3 affected only the assets side of the equation. WordService exchanged one asset (cash) for another asset (equipment). The total assets remain at $20,300. Liabilities plus owner's equity total $20,300, so the equation remains in balance.

Credit Transactions

Now that you have learned about cash transactions, let's look at how the use of credit affects the basic accounting equation. When a business buys on credit, it is often said to be buying **on account.** In the next three transactions, you will learn about a purchase on account, a payment on account, and a sale on account.

Business Transaction 4: *WordService bought office furniture on account from Office Interiors for $3,000.*

Analysis:
1. Identify the accounts affected.
   WordService has received additional property (office furniture), so the account Office Furniture is affected. The business has promised to pay for the office furniture at a later time. This promise to pay is a liability of WordService, therefore, the Accounts Payable account is affected.
2. Classify the accounts affected.
   Office Furniture is an asset account and Accounts Payable is a liability account.
3. Determine the amount of increase or decrease for each account affected.
   Office Furniture is increased by $3,000. Accounts Payable is also increased by $3,000.
4. Make sure the basic accounting equation remains in balance.

	ASSETS			= LIABILITIES +	OWNER'S EQUITY
	Cash in Bank	Office Furniture	Equipment	Accounts Payable	Paul Howard, Capital
Prev. Bal.	$16,000	0	$4,300	0	$20,300
Trans. 4		+$3,000		+$3,000	
Balance	$16,000 +	$3,000 +	$4,300 =	$3,000	+ $20,300

Assets now total $23,300. Liabilities plus owner's equity also total $23,300, so the equation remains in balance.

Business Transaction 5: *WordService issued a check for $1,000 in partial payment of the amount owed to its creditor, Office Interiors.*

Teaching Tips

■ Business Transaction 5:
Payment to creditor
(−) Liability
(−) Asset
■ For this "payment on account," the key words for students to look for are *issued a check, partial payment of amount owed,* and *creditor.*
■ Business Transaction 6:
Asset sold on account
(+) Asset
(−) Asset
■ For an item "sold on account," the key words are *sold* and *on account.*

**ACCOUNTING
PRACTICE**
**Students may complete
Exercises 2-2 and 2-3 at this point.**

Analysis:

1. Identify the accounts affected.
   The payment decreased the total amount owed to the creditor, so Accounts Payable is affected. A check was given in payment, so the account Cash in Bank is affected.
2. Classify the accounts affected.
   Accounts Payable is a liability account, while Cash in Bank is an asset account.
3. Determine the amount of increase or decrease for each account affected.
   Accounts Payable is decreased by $1,000. Cash in Bank is also decreased by $1,000.
4. Make sure the basic accounting equation remains in balance.

	ASSETS			= LIABILITIES	+ OWNER'S EQUITY
	Cash in Bank	Office Furniture	Equipment	Accounts Payable	Paul Howard, Capital
Prev. Bal.	$16,000	$3,000	$4,300	$3,000	$20,300
Trans. 5	− 1,000			− 1,000	
Balance	$15,000 +	$3,000 +	$4,300	= $2,000	+ $20,300

The asset accounts total $22,300, and liabilities plus owner's equity total $22,300, so the equation is in balance.

Business Transaction 6: *WordService sold the electric typewriter for $300 on account.*

Analysis:

1. Identify the accounts affected.
   Since WordService has agreed to receive payment for the typewriter at a later time, the Accounts Receivable account is affected. The business sold equipment, so the account Equipment is also affected.
2. Classify the accounts affected.
   Accounts Receivable is an asset account, as is Equipment.
3. Determine the amount of increase or decrease for each account affected.
   Accounts Receivable is increased by $300. Equipment is decreased by $300.
4. Make sure the basic accounting equation remains in balance.

	ASSETS				= LIABILITIES	+ OWNER'S EQUITY
	Cash in Bank	Accounts Receivable	Office Furniture	Equipment	Accounts Payable	Paul Howard, Capital
Prev. Bal.	$15,000	0	$3,000	$4,300	$2,000	$20,300
Trans. 6		+$300		− 300		
Balance	$15,000 +	$300 +	$3,000 +	$4,000	= $2,000	+ $20,300

The four asset accounts total $22,300. Liabilities plus owner's equity total $22,300, so the equation is in balance.

Before you go on to the next transaction, do the following activity to check your understanding of the transactions you have studied so far.

Making *Connections*

BUSINESS ETHICS

You work at Finkbine's, a small department store. Several of your co-workers take supplies such as pens, bags, boxes, hangers, etc., home from work for their personal use. How should you respond when these co-workers urge you to do the same?

(Answer: What your co-workers are doing is stealing. A few supplies may not seem like much, but the cost of those "lost" supplies will add up over time. Employee theft is one of the biggest problems faced by businesses today. Regardless of how small the items taken, the practice is still theft.)

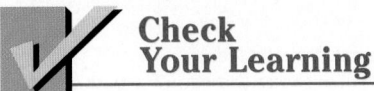

Check Your Learning

Use these accounts to analyze the business transactions of Swift Delivery Service.

ASSETS	=	LIABILITIES	+	OWNER'S EQUITY
Cash in Bank		Accounts Payable		Jan Swift, Capital
Accounts Receivable				
Office Furniture				
Delivery Equipment				

Identify the accounts affected by each transaction and the amount of increase or decrease for each account. Make sure the basic accounting equation is in balance after each transaction. Set up your transactions as shown for Transaction 6.

1. To get the business started, the owner, Jan Swift, deposited $30,000 in a checking account under the name of Swift Delivery Service.
2. The owner also invested a desk and chair valued at $700.
3. Swift Delivery Service issued a check for $10,000 for the purchase of delivery equipment.
4. The business bought office furniture on account for $5,000 from Eastern Furniture Company.
5. The old desk and chair invested by the owner were sold on account for $700.
6. Swift Delivery Service wrote a check for $2,000 in partial payment of the amount owed to a creditor.

Compare your answers to those in the answers section. Re-read the preceding part of the chapter to find the correct answers to any questions you may have missed.

Revenue and Expense Transactions

Most businesses have to earn profits to survive. In addition, business owners expect a return on their investment in a business. The most common way for a business to provide a return for its owner(s) is by selling goods and services. Income earned from the sale of goods and services is called **revenue.** Examples of revenue are fees earned for services performed and income earned from the sale of merchandise. Revenue increases owner's equity because it increases the business's assets.

In order to operate, most businesses must also buy goods and services. These goods and services are routine needs of the business (much as we need food, clothing, and shelter to keep ourselves operating). An **expense** is any price paid for goods and services used to operate a business. Examples of business expenses are rent, utility bills, and newspaper advertising. Expenses decrease owner's equity because they decrease the business's assets or increase liabilities.

Business Transaction 7: *WordService wrote a check for $500 to pay the rent for the month.*

CHAPTER 2   Business Transactions and the Basic Accounting Equation   27

Analysis:
1. Identify the accounts affected.
   WordService is receiving the use of a building it rents. Since rent is an expense, and expenses decrease owner's equity, the account Paul Howard, Capital is affected. The business is paying out cash for the use of the building, so Cash in Bank is affected.
2. Classify the accounts affected.
   Paul Howard, Capital is an owner's equity account. Cash in Bank is an asset account.
3. Determine the amount of increase or decrease for each account affected.
   Paul Howard, Capital is decreased by $500. Cash in Bank is decreased by $500.
4. Make sure the basic accounting equation remains in balance.

	ASSETS				= LIABILITIES +	OWNER'S EQUITY
	Cash in Bank	Accounts Receivable	Office Furniture	Equipment	Accounts Payable	Paul Howard, Capital
Prev. Bal.	$15,000	$300	$3,000	$4,000	$2,000	$20,300
Trans. 7	− 500					− 500
Balance	$14,500 +	$300	+ $3,000	+ $4,000	= $2,000	+ $19,800

The assets total $21,800. Liabilities and owner's equity total $21,800, so the equation remains in balance.

Business Transaction 8: *WordService received a check for $1,200 from a customer for preparing a report.*

Analysis:
1. Identify the accounts affected.
   WordService has received cash, so Cash in Bank is affected. The payment is revenue to WordService. Revenue increases owner's equity, so Paul Howard, Capital is also affected.
2. Classify the accounts affected.
   Cash in Bank is an asset account; Paul Howard, Capital is an owner's equity account.
3. Determine the amount of increase or decrease for each account affected.
   Cash in Bank is increased by $1,200. Paul Howard, Capital is also increased by $1,200.
4. Make sure the basic accounting equation remains in balance.

	ASSETS				= LIABILITIES +	OWNER'S EQUITY
	Cash in Bank	Accounts Receivable	Office Furniture	Equipment	Accounts Payable	Paul Howard, Capital
Prev. Bal.	$14,500	$300	$3,000	$4,000	$2,000	$19,800
Trans. 8	+ 1,200					+ 1,200
Balance	$15,700 +	$300	+ $3,000	+ $4,000	= $2,000	+ $21,000

The total assets equal the total of liabilities plus owner's equity: $23,000. The equation remains in balance.

Business owners and accounting workers today can quickly and easily determine account balances when business transaction data are stored in computer memory.

Using Visuals

Ask students to think of job activities that might be performed by an accounting worker who responds to customer calls. (Possible answers include providing account balances, taking information on late or lost payments, answering questions about payment due dates or interest costs.)

Withdrawals by the Owner

Generally, if a business earns revenue, the owner will take cash or other assets from the business for personal use. This transaction is called a **withdrawal.** Withdrawals are often made in anticipation of future profits. Many new small-business owners get into financial trouble because they "withdraw" without realizing that they must have more profits than withdrawals if they are to keep their businesses operating.

When business assets are decreased because of a withdrawal by the owner, the owner's financial claim to the business's assets is also decreased. A withdrawal decreases both assets and owner's equity. Look at Transaction 9 to see how a withdrawal affects the basic accounting equation.

Business Transaction 9: *Paul Howard withdrew $400 from the business for his personal use.*

Analysis:
1. Identify the accounts affected.
   A withdrawal decreases the owner's claim to the business's assets, so Paul Howard, Capital is affected. Cash has been paid out, so the Cash in Bank account is affected.
2. Classify the accounts affected.
   Paul Howard, Capital is an owner's equity account. Cash in Bank is an asset account.
3. Determine the amount of increase or decrease for each account affected.
   Paul Howard, Capital is decreased by $400. Cash in Bank is decreased by $400.

Teaching Tips

■ Discuss the major difference between a business expense and an owner's withdrawal of cash for personal use.
■ Business Transaction 9: Owner's withdrawal of cash
(−) Asset
(−) Equity
■ The withdrawal of cash from the business for personal use *reduces owner's equity.*

Making Connections

AROUND THE WORLD

As the global market has emerged, the need for international accounting standards has become apparent. The International Accounting Standards Committee has been charged with the task of developing accounting standards that can be used by businesses operating in many countries and in diverse economies. The emerging standards will be a blending of existing accounting practices as well as new ideas to accommodate global business activities.

Using Visuals

 Use demonstration problem 2-5 here to review or reinforce the analysis of various types of transactions.

ANSWERS

1. Jan Swift, Capital, − $50; Cash in Bank, − $50
2. Cash in Bank, + $1,000; Jan Swift, Capital, + $1,000
3. Jan Swift, Capital, − $600; Cash in Bank, − $600
4. Jan Swift, Capital, − $800; Cash in Bank, −$800
5. Cash in Bank, + $200; Accounts Receivable, − $200
Ending balances: Assets, $33,250 = Liabilities, $3,000 + Owner's Equity, $30,250

CONCEPT DEVELOPMENT

Using a Computer in Accounting

The computer is an indispensable tool for accounting firms and corporate accounting departments. The use of computer technology in accounting includes auditing, tax return preparation, electronic database management, image processing, word processing, electronic and voice mail, desktop publishing, spreadsheet analysis, networking, and portable computing. Time involved in computer training is beneficial for all accountants.

Teaching Tips

■ Contrast a manual accounting system with an electronic one. Remind students that regardless of the system used, the analysis of business transactions to determine the accounts affected remains a human activity.

---

4. Make sure the basic accounting equation remains in balance.

	ASSETS				= LIABILITIES +	OWNER'S EQUITY
	Cash in Bank	Accounts Receivable	Office Furniture	Equipment	Accounts Payable	Paul Howard, Capital
Prev. Bal.	$15,700	$300	$3,000	$4,000	$2,000	$21,000
Trans. 9	− 400					− 400
Balance	$15,300 +	$300 +	$3,000 +	$4,000 =	$2,000 +	$20,600

The total assets equal $22,600. Liabilities plus owner's equity are $22,600, so the equation remains in balance.

Before you go on to the end-of-chapter activities, do the following activity to check your understanding of the analysis of business transactions.

Check Your Learning

Use the accounts of Swift Delivery Service to analyze these business transactions. The previous balance for each is shown following the account title.

ASSETS	= LIABILITIES	+ OWNER'S EQUITY
Cash in Bank, $18,000	Accounts Payable	Jan Swift, Capital
Accounts Receivable, $700	$3,000	$30,700
Office Furniture, $5,000		
Delivery Equipment, $10,000		

Identify the accounts affected by each transaction and the amount of the increase or decrease for each acccount. Make sure the basic accounting equation is in balance after each transaction.

1. Paid $50 for advertising in the local newspaper.
2. Received $1,000 as payment for delivery services.
3. Wrote a $600 check for the month's rent.
4. Jan Swift withdrew $800 for her personal use.
5. Received $200 on account from the person who had purchased the old office furniture.

Compare your answers to those in the answers section. Re-read the preceding part of the chapter to find the correct answers to any questions you may have missed.

Using a Computer in Accounting

As you have just learned, each business transaction changes one or more parts of the basic accounting equation. The changes in the equation were summarized as increases or decreases in accounts. A simple worksheet was used to illustrate the various changes in the accounts. This worksheet,

---

Reteaching Strategies

Write the expanded accounting equation on the chalkboard: *Assets = Liabilities + Owner's Equity + Revenue − Expenses.* Point out that each part of the equation is a classification of the accounts used in recording business transactions. Conduct a drill where you call out an account name and ask students to tell you its classification. If students have difficulty with any one type of account, discuss how that account is used by the business and why it fits its classification.

called a *spreadsheet,* is used in accounting to perform financial calculations and to record transactions.

An electronic spreadsheet can be used by an accounting clerk to record the same changes. The accounting clerk can use a computer to show the effects of business transactions on the basic accounting equation quickly and accurately. If the computer is programmed properly, all the accounting clerk must do is determine (1) the accounts affected, (2) the amounts involved, and (3) whether the accounts are being increased or decreased. Once that data are entered, the computer will automatically calculate the new account balances and determine whether the equation is in balance. Figure 2-2 illustrates how the transactions you just studied would be prepared on a computer spreadsheet.

Figure 2-2 A Computerized Spreadsheet

Summary of Key Points

1. For all property that is owned or controlled, there are corresponding financial claims equal to the cost of the property.
2. The accounting term for a financial claim to a business's assets is *equity*.
3. The relationship between total assets and total equities is shown in the basic accounting equation: Assets = Liabilities + Owner's Equity.
4. Each business transaction changes one or more parts of the basic accounting equation.
5. When a business buys on account, the amounts owed are called accounts payable. When a business sells on account, the total amounts owed to the business are called accounts receivable.
6. Businesses must earn revenue to provide a return on the owner's investment and to allow the business to continue its operations. Revenue increases the owner's equity in the business.
7. The costs of items used in the operation of a business are called expenses. Expenses decrease the owner's equity in the business.
8. Withdrawals decrease the owner's financial claim.

Using Visuals

Ask students to look at the printout in Figure 2-2. Spreadsheet software is used by many businesses to track both financial and other quantifiable business data. Such software is especially useful in applications requiring re-calculation of amounts when one or more variables change.

3 CLOSE

CHAPTER SUMMARY

This summary enumerates the key information in the chapter. It is a useful tool for reinforcement and review.

Pop Quiz

1. The business or person selling property on credit is called a ____.
2. Creditors' claims to the assets of the business are called ____.
3. Define equity.
4. What is the amount of the owner's claim to an office computer that cost $3,000 and for which $1,000 is owed?
5. Investments by the owner are called ____.

ANSWERS

1. creditor
2. liabilities
3. The total financial claims to the assets or property of a business.
4. $2,000
5. capital

PRACTICE AND APPLY
- Language Development
- Comprehension and Retention
- Basic Skills

Building Your Accounting Vocabulary
See the Glossary on pages 670-679 for definitions of these terms.

Reviewing Your Accounting Knowledge
1. Property is anything of value that is owned or controlled. Property rights are financial claims to property and may be held by creditors and owners.
2. A business is a separate entity that can own and use property (assets). Business transactions are more easily identified when business and personal assets are separated.
3. Examples are cash, office furniture, office equipment, manufacturing equipment, buildings, and land—all of which are business assets because they are used in business operations.
4. Liabilities are creditors' claims for amounts owed, and owner's equity represents the owner's claim to assets. Examples are Accounts Payable (liability) and Paul Howard, Capital (owner's equity).
5. Accounts are used to show increases and decreases in balances for specific items such as cash, accounts receivable or payable, and owner's capital.
6. Accounts receivable shows cash to be received for goods or services sold on credit. Accounts payable shows debts to creditors for goods or services bought on credit.
7. At least two accounts must change for the equation to balance after a transaction is recorded.
8. (a) Identify the accounts affected, (b) classify the accounts affected, (c) determine the increase or decrease for each account, and (d) check that the equation remains in balance.
9. (a) Add all asset account balances, (b) add liability and owner's equity account balances, (c) compare totals. Total assets = total equities.

10. Businesses cannot continue to operate without revenue, which also provides a return on the owner's investment.
11. Revenue is earned from the sale of goods or services and represents money coming into the business. Expenses represent money paid out for goods or services used by the business. Revenue increases owner's equity; expenses decrease it.
12. Cash withdrawals decrease owner's equity because they decrease the assets owned by the business, which decreases the owner's financial claim.

Improving Your Decision-Making Skills
Liberty might raise capital to expand by forming a partnership with two or more co-owners who would invest in the business. Another option is to form a corporation and sell shares of stock to the public. A third option is to borrow money, creating a liability for the business.

 # Review and Applications

Building Your Accounting Vocabulary
In your own words, write a definition for each of the following accounting terms. Use complete sentences.

account	capital	owner's equity
accounts payable	credit	property
accounts receivable	creditor	property rights
assets	equity	revenue
basic accounting equation	expense	withdrawal
	liabilities	
business transaction	on account	

Reviewing Your Accounting Knowledge
1. What is the relationship between property and property rights?
2. Why are a business's assets separate from the owner's personal assets?
3. List five examples of business assets. Explain why they are business assets rather than personal assets.
4. Name two types of equity in a business, and explain what each type represents. Give an example of each.
5. Why are accounts used in an accounting system?
6. Explain the difference between accounts receivable and accounts payable.
7. Why are at least two accounts affected by each business transaction?
8. What steps should you follow in analyzing a business transaction?
9. How can you determine if the basic accounting equation is in balance?
10. Why is it important for a business to earn revenue?
11. Explain the difference between revenue and expenses.
12. Why does the withdrawal of cash by the owner for personal use decrease owner's equity?

Improving Your Decision-Making Skills
Liberty Fashions, a manufacturing company, was started by Helen Baker as a sole proprietorship. The company needs to expand its plant facilities at an estimated cost of $125,000. Helen does not have the money needed herself. What should she do now? Remember to follow the decision-making process you used in Chapter 1.

Applying Accounting Procedures
Exercise 2-1 Balancing the Accounting Equation
Determine the missing dollar amounts in each equation at the top of the next page. Use either the form in your workbook or plain paper and write in the missing amounts for each question mark.

ASSETS = LIABILITIES + OWNER'S EQUITY

1.	$17,000	=	$7,000	+	?
2.	$10,000	=	?	+	$ 7,000
3.	?	=	$9,000	+	$17,000
4.	$ 8,000	=	$2,000	+	?
5.	?	=	$6,000	+	$20,000

Exercise 2-2   Classifying Accounts

All accounts belong in one of the following classifications: Asset, Liability, Owner's Equity.

Instructions: For each of the following accounts, indicate the classification in which it belongs.

1. John Jones, Capital
2. Cash in Bank
3. Accounts Receivable
4. Accounts Payable
5. Computer Equipment

6. Calculator
7. Delivery Trucks
8. Building
9. Land
10. Typewriter

Exercise 2-3   Completing the Accounting Equation

The following accounts are used in a business owned and operated by Mike Murray.

Instructions: Look at the following list of accounts and determine the missing amount for each of the question marks.

ASSETS		=	LIABILITIES	+	OWNER'S EQUITY
Cash in Bank	$4,500		Accounts Payable ?		Mike Murray, Capital $9,250
Accounts Receivable	1,350				
Office Equipment	5,000				
	?				

Problem 2-1   Classifying Accounts within the Accounting Equation

Listed below, in alphabetical order, are the account titles and account balances for a business owned by Larry Hicks.

Accounts Payable	$7,000	Equipment	$12,000
Accounts Receivable	$2,000	Larry Hicks, Capital	$15,000
Cash in Bank	$5,000	Office Equipment	$ 3,000

Instructions: Using these account titles and balances,
(1) List and total the assets of the business.
(2) Determine the amount owed by the business.
(3) Give the amount of the owner's equity in the business.
(4) Determine whether the basic accounting equation is in balance for this business.

Problem 2-2   Determining Increases and Decreases in Accounts

Listed at the top of the next page are the account titles used by A-1 Carpet Cleaners.

33

Chapter 2

PRACTICE AND APPLY
• Concepts and Procedures

Exercise 2-1: Ch. Obj. 4
1. $10,000
2. $3,000
3. $26,000
4. $6,000
5. $26,000

Exercise 2-2: Ch. Obj. 3
1. owner's equity
2. asset
3. asset
4. liability
5. asset
6. asset
7. asset
8. asset
9. asset
10. asset

Exercise 2-3: Ch. Obj. 4, 5
Total assets, $10, 850
Accounts Payable, $1,600

Problem 2-1: Ch. Obj. 3, 4, 5
Assets, $22,000
Liabilities, $7,000
Owner's equity, $15,000

Additional Reinforcement

Students who need additional practice or individualized help will benefit from the *Glencoe Accounting Electronic Study Guide* or the *Glencoe Accounting* on-line multimedia program, which provide reinforcement and reteaching for vocabulary, concepts, and procedures.

Refer students to the Chapter 2 review pages in the workbook, *Chapter Reviews and Working Papers.*

Problem 2-2: Ch. Obj. 4

1. Cash in Bank, + $25,000; Kay Gentry, Capital, + $25,000
2. Cleaning Equipment, + $12,000; Cash in Bank, − $12,000
3. Office Equipment, + $2,500; Accounts Payable, + $2,500
4. Cash in Bank, − $800; Kay Gentry, Capital, − $800
5. Cash in Bank, + $1,000; Kay Gentry, Capital, + $1,000
6. Cash in Bank, − $600; Kay Gentry, Capital, − $600

Problem 2-3: Ch. Obj. 4, 5

Refer students to p. 31 as a reminder of how to record transactions in this form.

1. Cash in Bank, + $10,000; Tony LaBato, Capital, + $10,000
2. Cash in Bank, − $250; Supplies, + $250
3. Cash in Bank, − $900; Tony LaBato, Capital, − $900
4. Office Equipment, + $6,000; Accounts Payable, + $6,000
5. Cash in Bank, + $700; Tony LaBato, Capital, + $700
6. Cash in Bank, − $2,000; Accounts Payable, −$2,000
7. Accounts Receivable, + $500; Tony LaBato, Capital, + $500

Problem 2-4: Ch. Obj. 4, 5

SPREADSHEET PROBLEM **Students may complete Problem 2-4 using *Spreadsheet Applications,* the spreadsheet software that accompanies *Glencoe Accounting*.**

ASSETS	=	LIABILITIES	+ OWNER'S EQUITY
Cash in Bank		Accounts Payable	Kay Gentry, Capital
Accounts Receivable			
Cleaning Equipment			
Office Equipment			

Instructions: Use a form similar to the one that follows. For each transaction that follows:

(1) Identify the accounts affected.
(2) Classify the accounts.
(3) Determine the amount of the increase (+) or decrease (−) for each account affected.

The first transaction is completed as an example.

Trans.	Accounts Affected	Classification	Amount of Increase (+) or Decrease (−)
1	Cash in Bank Kay Gentry, Capital	Asset Owner's Equity	+$25,000 +$25,000

Transactions:

1. Kay Gentry, the owner, invested $25,000 cash in the business.
2. Bought cleaning equipment with cash, $12,000.
3. Purchased $2,500 worth of office equipment on account.
4. Wrote a check for the monthly rent, $800.
5. Received cash for services performed, $1,000.
6. The owner withdrew $600 cash from the business for personal use.

Problem 2-3 Determining the Effects of Transactions on the Accounting Equation

After becoming a CPA, Tony LaBato decided to start an accounting business.

Instructions: Use a form similar to the one that follows. For each of the following transactions:

(1) Identify the accounts affected, using the account titles on the form.
(2) Determine the amount of the increase or decrease for each account.
(3) Write the amount of the increase (+) or decrease (−) in the space under each account affected.
(4) On the following line, write the new balance for each account.

	ASSETS				=	LIABILITIES	+	OWNER'S EQUITY
Trans.	Cash in Bank	Accts. Rec.	Office Equip.	Acctg. Supplies	=	Accounts Payable	+	Tony LaBato, Capital
1	+$10,000							+$10,000

Transactions:

1. Tony LaBato began the business by depositing $10,000 in a checking account at the Lakeside National Bank in the name of the business, Tony LaBato, CPA.

34

Teacher Notes

_____
_____
_____
_____
_____

Transactions:

2. Bought accounting supplies for cash, $250.
3. Issued a check for $900 for the monthly rent on the office.
4. Bought $6,000 worth of new office equipment on account for use in the business.
5. Received $700 cash for accounting services performed for a customer.
6. Issued a $2,000 check to the creditor as partial payment for the office equipment purchased on account.
7. Performed accounting services and agreed to be paid for them later, $500.

SPREADSHEET   **Problem 2-4   Determining the Effects of Business Transactions on the Accounting Equation**

Andrea Hunt has decided to go into business for herself as a professional photographer.

PROBLEM   **Instructions:**   Use a form similar to the one below. For each of the following transactions:

(1) Identify the accounts affected.
(2) Write the amount of the increase (+) or decrease (−) in the space provided on the form.
(3) Determine the new balance for each account.

	ASSETS					=	LIABILITIES	+	OWNER'S EQUITY
Trans.	Cash in Bank	Accts. Rec.	Camera Equip.	Photo Supplies	Office Equip.	=	Accounts Payable	+	Andrea Hunt, Capital

Transactions:

1. Ms. Hunt, the owner, opened a checking account for the business by depositing $60,000 of her personal funds.
2. Paid the monthly rent of $3,000.
3. Bought supplies for developing photographs by writing a check for $300.
4. Bought $24,000 worth of camera equipment for cash.
5. Purchased office equipment on account for $4,000.
6. Received payment for photography services, $2,500.
7. Andrea Hunt invested an electric typewriter, which was valued at $450, in the business.
8. Withdrew $3,000 cash from the business for personal use.
9. Wrote a check to a creditor as partial payment on account, $2,000.
10. Took wedding photographs and agreed to accept payment later, $1,200.

Problem 2-5   Describing Business Transactions

The transactions for Oglesby Electrical Repair Service that follow are shown as they would appear in the basic accounting equation. In your own words, describe what has happened in each transaction. Transaction 1 is completed as an example.

Example:
1. The owner invested $30,000 in the business.

35

1. Cash in Bank +$60,000
Andrea Hunt, Capital +$60,000
Balances: $60,000 = $60,000
2. Cash in Bank −$3,000
Andrea Hunt, Capital −$3,000
Balances: $57,000 = $57,000
3. Cash in Bank −$300
Photo. Supplies +$300
Balances: $56,700 + $300 = $57,000
4. Cash in Bank −$24,000
Camera Equip. +$24,000
Balances: $32,700 + $24,000 + $300 = $57,000
5. Office Equip. +$4,000
Accounts Payable +$4,000
Balances: $32,700 + $24,000 + $300 + $4,000 = $4,000 + $57,000
6. Cash in Bank +$2,500
Andrea Hunt, Capital +$2,500
Balances: $35,200 + $24,000 + $300 + $4,000 = $4,000 + $59,500
7. Office Equip. +$450
Andrea Hunt, Capital +$450
Balances: $35,200 + $24,000 + $300 + $4,450 = $4,000 + $59,950
8. Cash in Bank −$3,000
Andrea Hunt, Capital −$3,000
Balances: $32,200 + $24,000 + $300 + $4,450 = $4,000 + $56,950
9. Cash in Bank −$2,000
Accounts Payable −$2,000
Balances: $30,200 + $24,000 + $300 + $4,450 = $2,000 + $56,950
10. Accounts Receivable +$1,200
Andrea Hunt, Capital +$1,200
Balances: $30,200 + $1,200 + $24,000 + $300 + $4,450 = $2,000 + $58,150

Problem 2-5: Ch. Obj. 4

2. Purchased office equipment with cash, $2,000
3. Bought repair tools on account for $8,000
4. Received payment for repair services, $700
5. Performed repair services and agreed to be paid later, $500
6. Owner invested an electric typewriter, valued at $200, in the business
7. Issued a $3,000 check to creditor as partial payment for repair tools bought on account
8. Oglesby Electrical Repair Service sold electric typewriter for $200 on account
9. Received payment on account for services previously performed, $500
10. Owner withdrew $1,000 cash from the business for personal use

Teacher Notes

Chapter 2

Problem 2-6: Ch. Obj. 5

CHALLENGE PROBLEM The last problem in each chapter is a challenge problem and is identified by this "maze" symbol.

1. Cash in Bank, $5,000
2. Business Equipment, $6,000
3. Accounts Payable, $4,000
4. Accounts Receivable, $10,000
5. Fran Henry, Capital, $17,000
6. Business Equipment, $14,000
7. Accounts Payable, $5,000
8. Cash in Bank, $4,000
Fran Henry, Capital, $17,000

4 ASSESS

A chapter test is available for use in assessing students' understanding of concepts in this chapter.

Unit objective and problem tests are available to assess students' knowledge of concepts in Chapters 1-2.

The testmaker software will enable you to develop tailor-made chapter, unit, semester, and final tests.

Alternative Assessment

For alternative assessment strategies, refer to *Tech Prep Strategies in Accounting*.

Trans.	ASSETS				=	LIABILITIES	+	OWNER'S EQUITY
	Cash in Bank	Accts. Rec.	Office Equip.	Repair Tools	=	Accounts Payable	+	Jane Oglesby, Capital
1	+$30,000							+$30,000
2	−$ 2,000		+$2,000					
3				+$8,000		+$8,000		
4	+$ 700							+$ 700
5		+$500						+$ 500
6				+$ 200				+$ 200
7	−$ 3,000					−$3,000		
8		+$200	−$ 200					
9	+$ 500	−$500						
10	−$ 1,000							−$ 1,000

CHALLENGE PROBLEM

Problem 2-6 Completing the Accounting Equation

Look at the following account titles and balances for a business owned by Fran Henry. Determine the missing amount for each of the question marks. Use the form in your workbook or plain paper and write in the missing amounts.

	ASSETS			=	LIABILITIES	+	OWNER'S EQUITY
	Cash in Bank	Accounts Receivable	Business Equipment	=	Accounts Payable	+	Fran Henry, Capital
1.	?	$ 2,000	$ 1,000		$ 500		$ 7,500
2.	$ 3,000	$ 9,000	?		$2,000		$16,000
3.	$ 8,000	$ 1,000	$10,000		?		$15,000
4.	$ 4,000	?	$ 4,000		$1,000		$17,000
5.	$ 9,000	$ 7,000	$ 6,000		$5,000		?
6.	$10,000	$14,000	?		$6,000		$32,000
7.	$ 6,000	$ 4,000	$10,000		?		$15,000
8.	?	$ 5,000	$ 9,000		$1,000		?

In #8, total assets are $18,000.

36

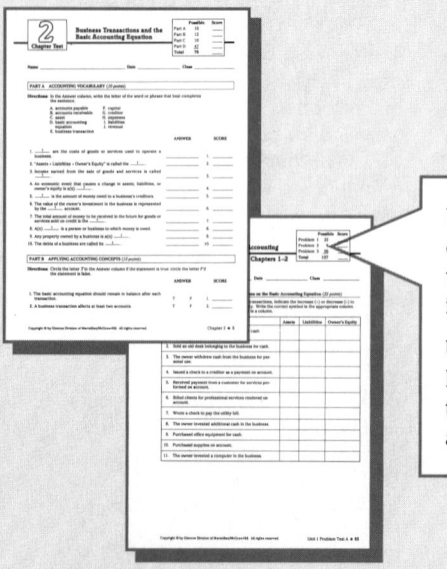

Use Chapter Test 2 here to assess students' understanding and retention of the concepts and procedures presented in the chapter.

Use Unit 1 Objective Test and/or Unit 1 Problem Test to assess students' retention of concepts presented in Chapters 1 and 2.

Accounting: A Mobile Profession

Accountants have been around for a long time. As early as 3600 B.C., priests in Babylonia kept accounts on clay tablets. In today's economic era, there are well over a million accountants in the United States. In spite of this, there simply are not enough accountants and accounting workers to go around.

A bachelor's degree with a major in accounting can lead to a variety of career choices. Today's accounting positions offer attractive salaries and are more challenging than ever before.

Public accountants offer professional services to the public for a fee. These services include tax preparation, auditing, management, consulting, and general accounting. To become a certified public accountant (CPA), you must pass a rigorous, state-administered examination in accounting theory and practice, auditing, and business law. Many public accountants leave the field to take high-level positions with clients.

Managerial accountants perform accounting functions for businesses. They might specialize in corporate taxes, operations, budgeting, investing, or internal auditing. Managerial accountants provide critical information for corporate executives and take active roles in long-range planning. Like the CPA, the managerial accountant can take an examination to become a certified management accountant (CMA). Managerial accountants are in a good position to learn about all aspects of a business's operations. As a result, many work their way into top management positions.

Not-for-profit accountants work for hospitals, school districts, colleges, or government agencies. They can be general accountants, auditors, controllers, bank examiners, or even IRS or FBI agents. Like accountants who work for profit-mak-

Positions in accounting are expected to increase faster than average through the 1990s.

ing businesses, these accountants offer consulting and other services to ensure the successful financial operation of the organization. Not-for-profit accounting, particularly in government, offers high job security, an important consideration for many people.

Today, accounting is more than simply balancing debits and credits. It may even be a stepping-stone to that corner office.

FOCUS ON
CAREERS

International accounting provides many new opportunities for accountants to become mobile. Many of these opportunities involve living and working in another country, as well as learning new skills not needed before—such as learning a new language, processing international payroll data, and preparing foreign country tax returns.

QUESTIONS

1. What are some personal traits that might be useful to a person who wants a career in accounting?
2. Why do accountants need to know both accounting theory and how to use computers?

ANSWERS

1. Accountants need to be careful and accurate, patient at completing detail work, and willing to work long hours during tax times.
2. Most businesses today use some type of computerized system for keeping accounting records. Students who wish to pursue a career in accounting need to feel comfortable with computers and to know how to use a variety of accounting software.

37

The chapters in Unit 2 cover the procedures for completing a basic accounting cycle, beginning with transaction analysis and ending with closing activities. The financial transactions and records introduced in this unit are for a sole proprietorship, service business.

UNIT 2

THE BASIC ACCOUNTING CYCLE

All businesses keep financial records. In Unit 2 you will learn how business transactions affect the financial records of a business. Learning to analyze business transactions correctly is the first step toward learning accounting. You will then learn how to record those transactions in the business's accounting records. The business used in the examples in this unit is a sole proprietorship. The business, called Global Travel Agency, provides travel services to its customers. After studying the chapters in this unit, you will have learned how to keep accounting records through a complete accounting cycle.

Individualizing Instruction

To provide individualized activities within the unit, you may use any of the following:

- problems in *Math Review for Accounting*
- chapter study plans
- study guides in the student workbook
- end-of-chapter challenge problems (identified by a maze symbol)

- optional problems in the Additional Problems section at the back of the student textbook
- cases from *Tech Prep Strategies in Accounting* book
- *Electronic Study Guide*

The Basic Accounting Cycle

Unit Concepts

Unit 2 takes students through a complete accounting cycle for a service business organized as a sole proprietorship. Students begin by analyzing business transactions affecting assets, liabilities, owner's equity, revenue, expenses, and withdrawals. Students use the double-entry accounting system in every business transaction. Students are able to see how a new business begins by recording the initial investment of the owner. The unit ends with a section on banking so that students can see the importance that control of cash plays in business operations. The only journal used in this cycle is the general journal.

General Unit Performance Objectives

1. Correctly use terminology related to the accounting cycle of a service business organized as a sole proprietorship.

2. Describe the accounting principles and practices of a service business organized as a sole proprietorship.

3. Demonstrate accounting procedures for a service business organized as a sole proprietorship.

PERFORMANCE OBJECTIVES

Unit Objective Test: Chapters 3-6

1. Define accounting vocabulary correctly.

2. Identify business and accounting information correctly.

3. Determine the correct procedures to use in the accounting system of a service business.

4. Apply the rules of debit and credit to accounts.

5. Place the first five steps of the accounting cycle in correct order.

Unit Problem Test: Chapters 3-6

1. Analyze transactions into debit and credit parts, classify each account affected, and determine whether the account is increased or decreased.

2. Apply the rules of debit and credit to business transactions.

3. Record transactions in the general journal.

4. Post general journal entries to the general ledger.

Unit Objective Test: Chapters 7-10

1. Define accounting vocabulary correctly.

2. Determine the correct and incorrect procedures to be followed during end-of-fiscal-period activities.

3. Classify accounts according to how they appear on a work sheet.

4. Place the nine steps of the accounting cycle in their proper order.

Unit Problem Test: Chapters 7-10

1. Prepare an income statement, a statement of changes in owner's equity, and a balance sheet.

2. Journalize closing entries.

3. Record transactions involving bank charges.

Chapter	Learning Objectives
3	1. List and apply the rules of debit and credit for asset, liability, and owner's equity accounts. 2. Use T accounts to analyze a business transaction into its debit and credit parts. 3. Determine the balances of the accounts affected by a business transaction. 4. Define the accounting terms new to this chapter.
4	1. Explain the difference between permanent accounts and temporary capital accounts. 2. List and apply the rules of debit and credit for revenue, expense, and withdrawals accounts. 3. Use the six-step method to analyze business transactions affecting revenue, expense, and withdrawals accounts. 4. Test a series of transactions for equality of debits and credits. 5. Define the accounting terms new to this chapter.
5	1. Describe the first three steps in the accounting cycle. 2. Explain why source documents are created and give several examples of source documents. 3. Explain the need for journalizing. 4. Describe the steps followed to make a general journal entry. 5. Make accurate entries for business transactions in a general journal. 6. Correct errors in general journal entries. 7. Explain the purpose and use of a chart of accounts. 8. Define the accounting terms introduced in this chapter.
6	1. Describe the steps followed in the posting process. 2. Accurately post business transactions from a general journal to the accounts in the ledger. 3. Prepare a trial balance. 4. Record correcting entries in the general journal. 5. Define the accounting terms new to this chapter.
Mini Practice Set 1	Analyze and record transactions covering a sole proprietorship service business.
7	1. Explain the purpose of the work sheet. 2. Describe the parts of a six-column work sheet. 3. Prepare a six-column work sheet. 4. Calculate net income and net loss amounts. 5. Define the accounting terms new to this chapter.
8	1. Explain the purpose of the income statement. 2. Prepare an income statement. 3. Explain the purpose of the statement of changes in owner's equity. 4. Prepare a statement of changes in owner's equity. 5. Explain the purpose of a balance sheet. 6. Prepare a balance sheet in report form. 7. Define the accounting terms new to this chapter.
9	1. Explain why the temporary capital accounts are closed at the end of the fiscal period. 2. Explain the purpose of the Income Summary account. 3. Explain the relationship between the Income Summary account and the capital account. 4. Analyze and journalize closing entries. 5. Post closing entries to accounts in the general ledger. 6. Prepare a post-closing trial balance. 7. Define the accounting terms new to this chapter.
10	1. Describe the internal controls used to protect cash. 2. Describe the forms used to open and use a checking account. 3. Accurately record information on check stubs. 4. Prepare a check correctly. 5. Reconcile a bank statement. 6. Journalize and post entries relating to bank service charges. 7. Define the terms new to this chapter.
Mini Practice Set 2	Analyze transactions and complete an accounting cycle for a sole proprietorship service business.

State/Local Objectives			Demonstration Problems	Check Your Learning	Basic Skills	Exercises	Problems	Challenge Problem	Additional Problems
			3-1 3-2	p.44 p.46	Math p.54	3-1 3-2 3-3	3-1 3-2 3-3 3-4	3-5	3A p.631
			4-1 4-2 4-3	p.66 p.75	Analysis p.77	4-1 4-2 4-3	4-1 4-2 4-3 4-4	4-5	4A p.632
			5-1 5-2 5-3 5-4 5-5 5-6	p.88 p.91 p.97 p.100	Decision Making p.101	5-1 5-2 5-3	5-1 5-2 5-3 5-4	5-5	5A p.633
			6-1 6-2 6-3 6-4 6-5 6-6	p.112 p.117	Communi- cation p.122	6-1 6-2 6-3	6-1 6-2 6-3 6-4	6-5	6A p.633
			7-1 7-2 7-3 7-4 7-5 7-6	p.135 p.140	Math p.142	7-1 7-2 7-3	7-1 7-2 7-3	7-4 7-5	7A p.634
			8-1 8-2 8-3 8-4 8-5	p.154 p.157 p.160	Decision Making p. 162	8-1 8-2	8-1 8-2 8-3 8-4 8-5	8-6 8-7	8A p.634
			9-1 9-2 9-3 9-4 9-5	p.173 p.176	Human Relations p.181	9-1 9-2	9-1 9-2 9-3 9-4 9-5	9-6	9A p.635
			10-1 10-2 10-3 10-4 10-5	p.194 p.199	Analysis p.202	10-1 10-2 10-3 10-4	10-1 10-2 10-3 10-4	10-5	10A p.635

UNIT 2 COMPUTERIZED ACCOUNTING ACTIVITIES

Chapter	Glencoe Integrated Accounting	Spreadsheet Applications	Electronic Study Guide Model Exercises/Problems	CD Rom
3			Exercise 3-1 3-2 Problem 3-1	Menu Selection 3
4			Exercise 4-1 4-2 Problem 4-1	Menu Selection 4
5	Problem 5-1 5-4	Problem 5-3 (General Journal)	Exercise 5-1 Problem 5-2	Menu Selection 5
6	Problem 6-4		Exercise 6-1 6-2 6-3	Menu Selection 6
Mini Practice Set	Application Activity 1			
7		Problem 7-3 (Six-Column Work Sheet)	Exercise 7-1 7-2 Problem 7-1	Menu Selection 7
8	Problem 8-5		Exercise 8-1 8-2	Menu Selection 8
9	Problem 9-5		Exercise 9-2 Problem 9-1	Menu Selection 9
10	Problem 10-4	Problem 10-4 (Bank Statement)	Problem 10-3	Menu Selection 10
Mini Practice Set	Application Activity 2			
Basic Math Review			Menu Option 29	

Teaching Tips

■ In Chapters 3-9, students will study the accounting cycle for a business organized as a sole proprietorship. The business earns revenue by providing travel arrangements for its clients. This chart of accounts shows the accounts used by the business, Global Travel Agency. Review the account titles with students and remind them that every business uses accounts to record its business transactions.

GLOBAL TRAVEL AGENCY
Chart of Accounts

ASSETS	101	Cash in Bank
	105	Accounts Receivable—Burton Co.
	110	Accounts Receivable—Greer's Market
	120	Computer Equipment
	130	Office Equipment
LIABILITIES	201	Accounts Payable—City News
	205	Accounts Payable—Modern Office Suppliers
OWNER'S EQUITY	301	Jan Harter, Capital
	305	Jan Harter, Withdrawals
	310	Income Summary
REVENUE	401	Fees
EXPENSES	501	Advertising Expense
	510	Maintenance Expense
	520	Rent Expense
	530	Utilities Expense

40

Chapter

ANALYZING TRANSACTIONS AFFECTING ASSETS, LIABILITIES, AND OWNER'S EQUITY

Learning Objectives

When you have completed Chapter 3, you should be able to do the following:

1. List and apply the rules of debit and credit for asset, liability, and owner's equity accounts.
2. Use T accounts to analyze a business transaction into its debit and credit parts.
3. Determine the balances of the accounts affected by a business transaction.
4. Define the accounting terms introduced in this chapter.

In Chapter 2, you learned that there is a relationship between property and the financial claims to that property. In accounting, this relationship is expressed by the basic accounting equation. You also learned that each business transaction causes a change in the basic accounting equation. This change is reflected as an increase or a decrease in assets, liabilities, or owner's equity. Even though a change does occur, the basic accounting equation remains in balance.

In this chapter, you will learn the rules of debit and credit for asset, liability, and owner's equity accounts. These rules state how increases and decreases are to be recorded. You will then learn to apply these rules as you analyze typical business transactions.

As you study Chapter 3, always keep in mind the basic accounting equation that follows:
ASSETS = LIABILITIES + OWNER'S EQUITY.

New Terms

double-entry accounting
T account
debit
credit
balance side

INTRODUCING THE
CHAPTER

LOOKING BACK

Unit 1 introduced students to the forms of business organization, types of businesses, and the basic building block in accounting theory, the accounting equation. An understanding of the relationship between the parts of the accounting equation—and how various business transactions affect the equation—is key to progressing to more complex aspects of accounting theory, which are introduced in Unit 2.

Chapter 3 establishes an important foundation for the study of accounting: *the analysis of business transactions.*

VOCABULARY DEVELOPMENT

Ask students to write a sentence using each of the new terms in context. Ask for volunteers to write their sentences on the chalkboard. Discuss any differences in the use of the terms. Definitions of these terms are found in the chapter and in the glossary on pages 670-679.

Electronic Field Trips

41

Teaching Resources

- Lesson Plans
- TE/Chapter Reviews & Working Papers
- Demonstration Problems
- Student Study Plans
- Teaching Transparencies
- Solutions Transparencies
- Electronic Field Trips Video, Level I
- Electronic Study Guide
- Chapter 3 Test

Other Resources

- Skills Improvement Activities
- Blackline Masters
- Careers in Accounting
- Dictionary
- Math Review for Accounting
- Tech Prep Strategies in Accounting
- Video
- Test Bank with Software
- Spanish Resources/Audiotapes
- Spanish Electronic Study Guide

Chapter 3

1 FOCUS

MAJOR CONCEPTS

- The Basis of an Accounting System
- The T Account
- The Rules of Debit and Credit
- Applying the Rules of Debit and Credit

BUSINESS CONNECTION

Dell Computer Corporation's rapid climb to success began in 1984 as PCs Limited when founder Michael Dell invested his savings of $1,000. This initial investment of capital (or owner's equity) grew into a corporation with 1993 sales of $2 billion. Today Dell employs over 4,000 people, markets more than 40 different PC designs, and distributes a full line of software and accessories in this country as well as in several foreign countries.

2 TEACH

CONCEPT DEVELOPMENT
The Basis of an Accounting System

Accounting records begin with the entry of a transaction into the records of the business. The double-entry system requires that the amount of each transaction be entered into at least two accounts. This double entry of amounts forms the basis for the "balance" that is maintained within the accounting equation.

CONCEPT DEVELOPMENT
The T Account

Emphasize that the T account is not a part of formal accounting records. Rather, it is a helpful tool for use in analyzing how a transaction affects specific accounts of the business. The T account can be likened to research notes that are made to assist one in writing a formal report.

The Basis of an Accounting System

You learned in Chapter 2 that every business transaction affects at least two accounts. When you recorded the dollar amount of a transaction in one account, you recorded that same amount in another account. You did this to keep the sides of the basic accounting equation equal, or in balance. In entering the transaction amount twice, you were using a "double-entry" system of recordkeeping.

In accounting, the financial recordkeeping system in which each business transaction affects at least two accounts is called **double-entry accounting.** Double-entry accounting forms the basis for the accounting concepts and procedures that you will study in this textbook. Although you will mainly study manual accounting systems, the rules of double-entry accounting apply as well to computerized accounting systems. In other words, whether you are keeping accounting records by writing information on accounting stationery or by entering information into a computer, the resulting reports are the same.

The T Account

In Chapter 2, you used the basic accounting equation to analyze business transactions. This method works well when a business has only a few accounts. It becomes awkward, however, when a business has several accounts and many transactions to analyze. A more efficient and convenient tool is the T account. The **T account,** so called because of its T shape, is used to show the increase or decrease in an account caused by a transaction. Accountants use T accounts to analyze the parts of a transaction.

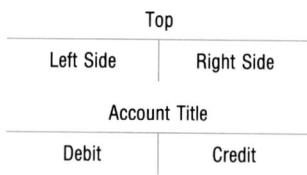

As you can see from the illustration, a T account has a top, a left side, and a right side. On the top of the T is the title of an account. The left side of the T is always used for debit amounts. A **debit** then is an amount entered on the *left* side of the T account. The right side of the T account is always used for credit amounts. A **credit** is an amount entered on the *right* side of the T account. The words "debit" and "credit" are simply the accountant's terms for "left" and "right." Remember, *debit = left side* and *credit = right side.*

The Rules of Debit and Credit

Debits and credits are used to record the increases and decreases in each account affected by a business transaction. Under the double-entry system, for each debit entry made in one account, a credit of an equal amount must be made in another account. The rules of debit and credit vary according to whether an account is classified as an asset, a liability, or an owner's equity account. Let's look first at the rules of debit and credit for accounts classified as assets.

42

UNIT 2   The Basic Accounting Cycle

Reinforcing Study Skills

Step Two of the SQ3R method is *Question.* To familiarize students with this approach, have them read each section or subsection head and turn it into a question that will focus their reading; for example, "What are the rules of debit and credit?" After reading the section, students should be able to answer the question they have generated.

Provide a copy of the *Student Study Plans* to each class member to help organize study activities or to individualize practice and review activities.

42   UNIT 2   The Basic Accounting Cycle

Rules for Asset Accounts

There are three rules of debit and credit for asset accounts:

1. An asset account is increased (+) on the debit side.
2. An asset account is decreased (−) on the credit side.
3. The normal balance for an asset account is a debit balance.

We can illustrate these rules using T accounts and the basic accounting equation. Look at the left-hand side of the equation below.

ASSETS = LIABILITIES + OWNER'S EQUITY

Asset Accounts

Debit	Credit
+	−
Increase Side	Decrease Side
Balance Side	

For asset accounts, the *increase* side is the debit (left) side of the T account. The *decrease* side is the credit (right) side of the T account. Notice the + and − signs. These signs are used to indicate the increase and decrease sides of the account. They do not mean the same thing as "debit" and "credit."

Each classification of account also has a specific side that is its normal balance side. This **balance side** is always the same as the side used to record increases to the account. Since the increase side of an asset account is always the debit side, asset accounts have a normal debit balance. The word "normal" used here means "usual." For example, in the normal course of business, total increases to assets are larger than total decreases. You would expect an asset account, then, to have a normal debit balance.

We can summarize the rules of debit and credit for asset accounts by using a T account.

Asset Accounts

Debit	Credit
+	−
1 Increase Side	2 Decrease Side
3 Balance Side	

Rule 1: Asset accounts are increased by debits.
Rule 2: Asset accounts are decreased by credits.
Rule 3: The normal balance for asset accounts is a debit balance.

Let's apply these rules now to an actual asset account. Look at the entries in the T account below for Cash in Bank.

Cash in Bank

Debit	Credit
+	−
$200	$ 70
150	40
$350	$110
Balance, $240	

The increases in the account are recorded on the left, or debit, side. The decreases in the account are recorded on the right, or credit, side. Total debits equal $350 ($200 + $150). Total credits equal $110 ($70 + $40). To find the balance, subtract total credits from total debits ($350 − $110). The debit balance is $240.

ANSWERS

1. Debit
2. Credit
3. Debit
4.   Office Equipment

Debit	Credit
+	−
$2,000	$500
1,500	
Bal. $3,000	

The balance is recorded on the debit side.

Teaching Tips

■ When introducing the rules of debit and credit for liability and the owner's capital accounts, write the accounting equation on the chalkboard. Draw T accounts for liabilities and capital to emphasize that these accounts are on the right side of the equation. The right sides of the T accounts for liabilities and capital are the increase sides, and the right sides are the normal balance sides.

Before you go any further, do the activity below to see if you understand the rules of debit and credit for asset accounts.

Check Your Learning

Answer these questions using the rules of debit and credit for asset accounts.

1. Asset accounts are increased on the left, or ___?___ , side.
2. Asset accounts are decreased on the right, or ___?___ , side.
3. The normal balance for asset accounts is a ___?___ balance.
4. On notebook paper, draw a T account for the asset account Office Equipment. Enter debits of $2,000 and $1,500. Enter a credit of $500. What is the balance, and on what side of the T account is it shown?

Compare your answers to those in the answers section. Re-read the preceding part of the chapter to find the correct answers to any questions you may have missed.

Rules for Liability and Owner's Equity Accounts

The rules for liability accounts and owner's equity accounts—specifically, the owner's capital account—are listed below:

1. The liability and capital accounts are increased (+) on the credit side.
2. The liability and capital accounts are decreased (−) on the debit side.
3. The normal balance for the liability and capital accounts is a credit balance.

Let's look again at the T accounts within the basic accounting equation, particularly those on the right-hand side. How do the T accounts for the liability and capital accounts differ from the T account for assets?

ASSETS		=	LIABILITIES		+	OWNER'S EQUITY	
Asset Accounts		=	Liability Accounts		+	Capital Account	
Debit	Credit		Debit	Credit		Debit	Credit
+	−		−	+		−	+
Increase Side	Decrease Side		Decrease Side	Increase Side		Decrease Side	Increase Side
Balance Side				Balance Side			Balance Side

The debit side of all three accounts is still on the left side of the T account, and the credit side of all three types of accounts remains on the right. Notice, however, that the increase (+) and decrease (−) sides of the liability and capital accounts are the opposite of those for assets. This is because accounts classified as liabilities and owner's equity are on the opposite side

44

Reteaching Strategies

If some students have difficulty remembering that debit is the left side of a T account and credit the right, help them develop a mnemonic device to aid their memory. For example, the word "credit" has an "r" and so does "right." Debit and left do not have an "r."

of the equation from accounts classified as assets. As a result, debit and credit rules on one side of the equation—and the T accounts within it—are mirror images of those on the other side.

We can summarize the rules of debit and credit for liability accounts and the owner's capital account by using a T account.

Liabilities and Capital

Debit	Credit
−	+
2 Decrease Side	1 Increase Side
	3 Balance Side

Rule 1: Liability and capital accounts are increased by credits.

Rule 2: Liability and capital accounts are decreased by debits.

Rule 3: The normal balance for liability and capital accounts is a credit balance.

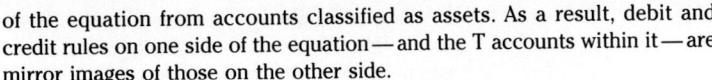

ACCOUNTING Notes

Assets appear on the *left* side of the basic accounting equation. The *left* (debit) side of an asset account is the side used to increase that account and its normal balance side.

Liabilities and the owner's capital account appear on the *right* side of the basic accounting equation. The *right* (credit) side of liability and capital accounts is the side used to increase those accounts. It is also the balance side.

Let's apply these rules now to actual accounts. First, look at the entries in the T account below for the liability account Accounts Payable.

Accounts Payable

Debit	Credit
−	+
$100	$200
75	175
$175	$375
	Balance, $200

The increases in the account are recorded on the right, or credit, side. The decreases in the account are recorded on the left, or debit, side. Total credits equal $375 ($200 + $175); total debits equal $175 ($100 + $75). To find the balance, subtract the total debits from the total credits ($375 − $175). The credit balance is $200.

Now look at the entries in the T account below for the owner's equity account Jan Harter, Capital. Remember, the rules of debit and credit for the capital account are the same as for a liability account.

Jan Harter, Capital

Debit	Credit
−	+
$350	$1,500
200	2,500
$550	$4,000
	Balance, $3,450

Increases to capital are recorded on the right, or credit, side of the account. Decreases are recorded on the left, or debit, side. The capital account has a normal credit balance. If you subtract the total debits from the total credits ($4,000 − $550), you have a credit balance of $3,450.

Summary of the Rules of Debit and Credit

Let's summarize the rules of debit and credit in terms of the basic accounting equation and T accounts.

ASSETS	=	LIABILITIES	+	OWNER'S EQUITY
Asset Accounts	=	Liability Accounts	+	Capital Account

Debit	Credit	Debit	Credit	Debit	Credit
+	−	−	+	−	+
Increase Side	Decrease Side	Decrease Side	Increase Side	Decrease Side	Increase Side
Balance Side			Balance Side		Balance Side

Chapter 3

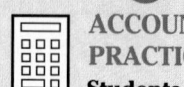

ACCOUNTING
PRACTICE
**Students may complete
Exercise 3-2 at this point.**

ANSWERS

1. Right
2. Left
3. Credit
4.   Accounts Payable

Debit	Credit
−	+
$600	$700
200	500
400	300
	Bal. $300

The balance is recorded on the credit side.

5.   Patrick Vance, Captial

Debit	Credit
−	+
$1,500	$9,000
700	3,000
	1,500
	Bal. $11,300

The balance is recorded on the credit side.

CONCEPT DEVELOPMENT

Applying the Rules of Debit and Credit

Encourage students to follow the six-step approach for analyzing transactions. These six steps take students through the cognitive process needed to analyze typical business transactions. Students should use the steps to evaluate the effects of a business transaction on the accounts of a business rather than trying to memorize each type of transaction.

Asset accounts are increased on the debit side and decreased on the credit side. The normal balance for an asset account is a debit. Liability and capital accounts are increased on the credit side and decreased on the debit side. The normal balance for liability and capital accounts is a credit.

Before you read any further, complete the following activity to see if you understand the rules of debit and credit for liability and capital accounts.

Check Your Learning

Answer these questions using the rules of debit and credit for liabilities and capital.

1. Liability and capital accounts are increased on the ___?___ side.
2. Liability and capital accounts are decreased on the ___?___ side.
3. The normal balance side for liability and capital accounts is the ___?___ .
4. On notebook paper, draw a T account for the liability account Accounts Payable. Enter debits of $600, $200, and $400. Enter credits of $700, $500, and $300. What is the amount of the balance, and on what side of the T account is it shown?
5. Draw a T account for the account Patrick Vance, Capital. Enter debits of $1,500 and $700. Enter credits of $9,000, $3,000, and $1,500. What is the amount of the balance, and on what side of the T account is it shown?

Compare your answers to those in the answers section. Re-read the preceding part of the chapter to find the correct answers to any questions you may have missed.

Applying the Rules of Debit and Credit

Now that you are familiar with the rules of debit and credit for asset, liability, and capital accounts, the next step is to apply those rules to the analysis of business transactions. When analyzing business transactions, you should ask yourself these six questions:

1. Which accounts are affected?
2. What is the classification of each account?
3. Is each account increased or decreased?
4. Which account is debited, and for what amount?
5. Which account is credited, and for what amount?
6. What is the complete entry?

R E M E M B E R

Debits are used to	Credits are used to
1. Increase (+) assets.	1. Decrease (−) assets.
2. Decrease (−) liabilities.	2. Increase (+) liabilities.
3. Decrease (−) owner's capital.	3. Increase (+) owner's capital.

Using Visuals

Use Demonstration Problems 3-1 and 3-2 to introduce students to the six-step approach to analyzing transactions presented in this chapter. Photocopy each problem for students so they may follow along as you analyze the transactions.

Reteaching Strategies

At this early stage in the accounting process, it is important for students to gain a clear understanding of how account balances are increased and decreased and how the normal balance side of an account is determined. Use hands to visually demonstrate that left is *opposite* right. Relating this idea to the accounting equation and the rules of debit and credit, left (the rules for assets) is opposite right (the rules for liabilities and owner's equity).

The business transactions that follow are for Global Travel Agency. Global Travel Agency is a small business that provides travel services to individuals and businesses. Global Travel is owned and operated as a sole proprietorship by Jan Harter. Jan has set up her accounting system to include the following asset, liability, and owner's equity accounts.

ASSETS	LIABILITIES	OWNER'S EQUITY
Cash in Bank	Accounts Payable	Jan Harter, Capital
Accounts Receivable		
Computer Equipment		
Office Equipment		

These accounts will be used to analyze several business transactions.

Business Transaction 1: *On October 1, Jan Harter took $25,000 from personal savings and deposited that amount to open a business checking account in the name of Global Travel Agency.*

1. Which accounts are affected?
The accounts affected are Cash in Bank and Jan Harter, Capital.
2. What is the classification of each account?
Cash in Bank is an asset account, and Jan Harter, Capital is an owner's equity account.
3. Is each account increased or decreased?
Cash in Bank is increased because the owner, Jan Harter, has deposited cash in the business checking account. Jan Harter, Capital is also increased because the owner's financial claim to the assets of the business has increased.
4. Which account is debited, and for what amount?

Cash in Bank	
Debit	Credit
+	−
$25,000	
Balance, $25,000	

Cash in Bank is an asset account. Increases in assets are recorded as debits. Cash in Bank is, therefore, debited for $25,000. Since this is an asset account, the normal balance is a debit balance.

5. Which account is credited, and for what amount?

Jan Harter, Capital	
Debit	Credit
−	+
	$25,000
	Balance, $25,000

Jan Harter, Capital is an owner's equity account. Increases in the owner's capital account are recorded as credits. Jan Harter, Capital is, therefore, credited for $25,000. The normal balance for the owner's capital account is a credit balance.

6. What is the complete entry?
Remember that in the double-entry system, each transaction affects at least two accounts. Cash in Bank is debited for $25,000 and Jan Harter, Capital is credited for $25,000. You can see from the T accounts on page 48 that the amount of the debit equals the amount of the credit.

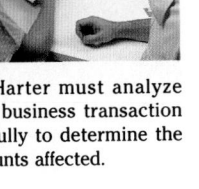
Jan Harter must analyze each business transaction carefully to determine the accounts affected.

CHAPTER 3   Analyzing Transactions Affecting Assets, Liabilities, and Owner's Equity   47

ACCOUNTING PRACTICE
Students may complete Exercise 3-3 at this point.

Teaching Tips
■ Keep the accounting equation on the chalkboard as you analyze transactions.
■ Business Transaction 1:
(+) Asset
(+) Capital

Did you know?
Why does the abbreviation for "debit" have an "r" in it when the word does not? The words "debit" and "credit" have their roots in Latin. Dr. is the abbreviation for the Latin *debere,* while Cr. is the abbreviation for the Latin *credere.*

Cooperative Learning

SEND-A-QUESTION
Ask each member of a team to write two typical business transactions for a video rental business on 3 x 5 cards. Have the members of the team analyze each transaction and on the back of the card write the accounts affected and whether they increase or decrease.

Then ask each team to pass its cards on to another team. The second team answers the questions and then compares their answers with those written on the backs of the cards.
Refer to the "Cooperative Learning" section of the *Tech Prep Strategies* booklet for additional cooperative learning strategies.

Teaching Tips

- Business Transaction 2:
(+) Asset
(−) Asset
- Point out to students that balances from previous transactions appear in a lighter typeface in the T accounts.
- Emphasize that the investment of cash or any other asset by the owner *always* increases owner's equity in the business.

Using Visuals

 If you have not already used demonstration problems 3-1 and 3-2, use them here to give students practice in analyzing transactions.

Cash in Bank			Jan Harter, Capital	
Debit	Credit		Debit	Credit
+	−		−	+
$25,000				$25,000

R E M E M B E R

In the double-entry accounting system, total debits must equal total credits in each business transaction.

Business Transaction 2: On October 2, Global Travel Agency issued Check 101 for $8,000 to buy a microcomputer system from Info-Systems, Inc.

1. Which accounts are affected?
Computer Equipment and Cash in Bank are affected.
2. What is the classification of each account?
Computer Equipment and Cash in Bank are both asset accounts.
3. Is each account increased or decreased?
Computer Equipment is increased because the purchase of the microcomputer increased the assets of the business. Cash in Bank is decreased because the business paid out cash.
4. Which account is debited and for what amount?

Computer Equipment	
Debit	Credit
+	−
$8,000	
Balance, $8,000	

Computer Equipment is an asset account. Increases in assets are recorded as debits. Computer Equipment is, therefore, debited for $8,000.

5. Which account is credited, and for what amount?

	Cash in Bank	
	Debit	Credit
	+	−
$25,000	$25,000	$8,000
− 8,000	Balance, $17,000	
$17,000		

Cash in Bank is also an asset account. Since decreases in asset accounts are recorded as credits, Cash in Bank is credited for $8,000.

6. What is the complete entry?
Computer Equipment is debited for $8,000 and Cash in Bank is credited for $8,000. The debit entry is equal to the credit entry.

Computer Equipment			Cash in Bank	
Debit	Credit		Debit	Credit
+	−		+	−
$8,000				$8,000

48

UNIT 2   The Basic Accounting Cycle

Critical Thinking

Ask students to list the assets and liabilities for their school's athletic department. Then ask each student to describe a transaction related to those assets or liabilities and to indicate which account is debited and which account is credited.
(Answers: Examples of assets are uniforms, shoes, playing equipment, permanent fixtures such as basketball hoops and boards, football field goals, soccer nets, lights, machines used to polish basketball floors or to maintain playing fields, etc. Possible transactions include the purchase of uniforms and equipment; season ticket sales; concession sales; referee, first aid, or security fees; etc.)

Business Transaction 3: *On October 4, Jan Harter took a $200 electric typewriter from home and invested it in the business as office equipment.*

1. Which accounts are affected?
   Office Equipment and Jan Harter, Capital are affected.
2. What is the classification of each account?
   Office Equipment is an asset account. Jan Harter, Capital is an owner's equity account.
3. Is each account increased or decreased?
   The investment of the typewriter increased the assets owned by the business. Office Equipment is thus increased. Since the typewriter is an investment by the owner of personal property, Jan Harter, Capital is also increased.
4. Which account is debited, and for what amount?

Office Equipment	
Debit	Credit
+	–
$200	
Balance, $200	

Office Equipment is an asset account. Since increases in assets are recorded as debits, Office Equipment is debited for $200.

5. Which account is credited and for what amount?

Jan Harter, Capital	
Debit	Credit
–	+
	$25,000
	200
	Balance, $25,200

$25,000
+   200
$25,200

Jan Harter, Capital is an owner's equity account. Increases in owner's equity are recorded as credits. Jan Harter, Capital is credited for $200.

6. What is the complete entry?
   Office Equipment is debited for $200 and Jan Harter, Capital is credited for the same amount. These amounts are shown in the T accounts below. The amount of the debit equals the amount of the credit.

Office Equipment			Jan Harter, Capital	
Debit	Credit		Debit	Credit
+	–		–	+
$200				$200

Business Transaction 4: *On October 9, Global Travel bought a new electronic typewriter on account for $1,500 from Modern Office Suppliers.*

1. Which accounts are affected?
   Office Equipment and Accounts Payable are affected. Remember, an item bought on account (on credit) is to be paid for in the future. The amount owed for the purchase is recorded in Accounts Payable until actual payment is made.

CHAPTER 3   Analyzing Transactions Affecting Assets, Liabilities, and Owner's Equity   **49**

Making Connections

COMMUNICATIONS

When setting up a record-keeping system for a client who has several business accounts, it is important for both the client and the accountant to be clear and specific about what each account includes. Have groups of two students role-play a conversation in which they set up and define the accounts needed by a small business that sells a service—such as mail boxes rented by the month—to the general public.

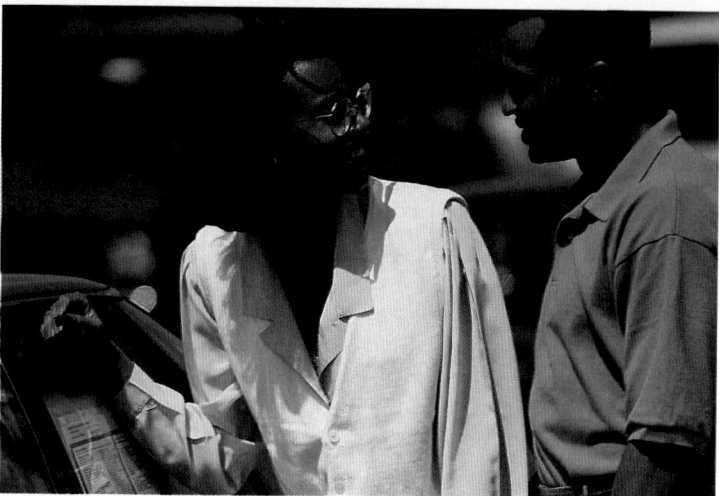

Many different types of items are purchased for use in a business's operations, such as a microcomputer or even a car.

2. What is the classification of each account?
Office Equipment is an asset account and Accounts Payable is a liability account.

3. Is each account increased or decreased?
Each account is increased. Office Equipment is increased because property is being acquired. Accounts Payable is increased because the business owes money on account.

4. Which account is debited, and for what amount?

Office Equipment	
Debit	Credit
+	−

$ 200	$ 200
+1,500	1,500
$1,700	Balance, $1,700

Office Equipment is debited for $1,500. Office Equipment is an asset account, and increases in assets are recorded as debits.

5. Which account is credited, and for what amount?

Accounts Payable	
Debit	Credit
−	+
	$1,500
	Balance, $1,500

Accounts Payable is a liability account. Increases in liability accounts are recorded as credits. The amount of the credit is $1,500.

6. What is the complete entry?
Office Equipment is debited for $1,500 and Accounts Payable is credited for $1,500. The changes caused by this transaction are summarized in the T accounts on the next page.

Making Connections

AROUND THE WORLD

Many U.S. businesses sell products developed for the domestic market in other countries. Few develop products especially for a foreign market. PepsiCo is an exception. The company has developed a new sugar-free drink called Pepsi Max for sale exclusively in international markets. Consumers in other countries dislike the taste of current diet soft drinks. PepsiCo spent two years developing its new formula for Pepsi Max, which has only one calorie.

Teaching Tips
■ Business Transaction 5:
(+) Asset
(−) Asset

Office Equipment		Accounts Payable	
Debit	Credit	Debit	Credit
+	−	−	+
$1,500			$1,500

Business Transaction 5: *On October 11, Global Travel sold the electric typewriter on account to Greer's Market for $200.*

1. Which accounts are affected?
   Accounts Receivable and Office Equipment are affected.
2. What is the classification of each account?
   Both Accounts Receivable and Office Equipment are asset accounts.
3. Is each account increased or decreased?
   Money that is to be received in the future increases Accounts Receivable. The sale of the typewriter decreases Office Equipment.
4. Which account is debited, and for what amount?

Asset

Accounts Receivable	
Debit	Credit
+	−
$200	
Balance, $200	

Increases in assets are recorded as debits. Accounts Receivable is an asset account, so it is debited for $200.

5. Which account is credited, and for what amount?

Asset

$ 200
+1,500
− 200
$1,500

Office Equipment	
Debit	Credit
+	−
$ 200	$200
1,500	
Balance, $1,500	

Decreases in assets are recorded as credits. Office Equipment is an asset account, so it is credited for $200.

6. What is the complete entry?
   Accounts Receivable is debited for $200 and Office Equipment is credited for the same amount. The debit amount equals the credit amount.

Accounts Receivable		Office Equipment	
Debit	Credit	Debit	Credit
+	−	+	−
$200			$200

Business Transaction 6: *On October 14, Global Travel mailed Check 102 for $750 as a partial payment to Modern Office Suppliers (for the $1,500 electronic typewriter bought in Transaction 4).*

1. Which accounts are affected?
   The accounts affected are Accounts Payable and Cash in Bank.

CHAPTER 3   Analyzing Transactions Affecting Assets, Liabilities, and Owner's Equity   **51**

Meeting Special Needs

ESL STUDENTS

Provide ESL students with a course outline that indicates when chapters are likely to be covered. Students may read slowly in their second language (English) and have to look up words in the dictionary. Giving ESL students a chance to preview the chapter—and in particular the new vocabulary—before you discuss it in class will get them tuned in to the topic and ready to absorb information from class discussions.

2. What is the classification of each account?
Accounts Payable is a liability account and Cash in Bank is an asset account.

3. Is each account increased or decreased?
The partial payment of a debt reduces the business's liability. There is a decrease, therefore, in Accounts Payable. Making a payment by check decreases the balance in Cash in Bank.

4. Which account is debited, and for what amount?

	Accounts Payable	
	Debit	Credit
$1,500	−	+
− 750	$750	$1 500
$ 750		Balance, $750

Decreases in liabilities are recorded as debits. Since Accounts Payable is a liability account, it is decreased. The amount of the decrease is the amount of the partial payment, $750.

5. Which account is credited, and for what amount?

	Cash in Bank	
	Debit	Credit
$25,000	+	−
− 8,000	$25,000	$8,000
− 750		750
$16,250	Balance, $16,250	

Decreases in assets are recorded as credits. Since Cash in Bank is an asset account, it is credited for $750, the amount of the check.

6. What is the complete entry?
Accounts Payable is debited for $750 and Cash in Bank is credited for the same amount. As you can see, the amount of the debit equals the amount of the credit.

Accounts Payable			Cash in Bank	
Debit	Credit		Debit	Credit
−	+		+	−
$750				$750

Business Transaction 7: On October 26, Global Travel received and deposited a check for $200 from Greer's Market. This is full payment for the electric typewriter that was sold on account on October 9.

1. Which accounts are affected?
Cash in Bank and Accounts Receivable are affected.

2. What is the classification of each account?
Cash in Bank and Accounts Receivable are both asset accounts.

3. Is each account increased or decreased?
Cash in Bank is increased by the receipt and deposit of the check. Accounts Receivable is decreased because the money Global Travel was to receive is now being paid.

4. Which account is debited, and for what amount?

52

Pop Quiz

1. What is the normal balance side of an asset account?
2. If office equipment is bought on account, which account is credited?
3. Does a credit to capital increase or decrease that account?
4. If an amount is paid on account, which account is debited?
5. If an asset is purchased for cash, which account is credited?

ANSWERS
1. debit or left
2. Accounts Payable
3. increase
4. Accounts Payable
5. Cash in Bank

Cash in Bank is debited for $200.

Cash in Bank		
$25,000	Debit	Credit
− 8,000	+	−
− 750	$25,000	$8,000
+ 200	200	750
$16,450	Balance, $16,450	

5. Which account is credited, and for what amount?

Accounts Receivable is decreased, so it is credited for $200.

Accounts Receivable		
$200	Debit	Credit
−200	+	−
$ 0	$200	$200
	Balance, $0	

6. What is the complete entry?
Cash in Bank is debited for $200 and Accounts Receivable is credited for $200. The amount of the debit equals the amount of the credit.

Cash in Bank		Accounts Receivable	
Debit	Credit	Debit	Credit
+	−	+	−
$200			$200

Summary of Key Points

1. Double-entry accounting is a system of recordkeeping in which each business transaction affects at least two accounts.
2. The T account is a tool for analyzing the debit and credit parts of a business transaction.
3. The top of the T is used for the account title; debits are entered on the left side of the T; credits, on the right.
4. Every account has an increase side and a decrease side.
5. For asset accounts, the increase side is the debit side and the decrease side is the credit side.
6. The normal balance for an asset account is a debit balance.
7. For liability accounts and the owner's capital account, the increase side is the credit side and the decrease side is the debit side.
8. The normal balance for both liability and capital accounts is a credit balance.
9. In double-entry accounting, the amount of the debit must equal the amount of the credit.

COMPUTERS IN ACCOUNTING

Computers now process the bulk of accounting transactions. When accounting information is computerized, the classification of accounts is still an important step in processing the accounting data. A system of double-entry accounting with checks and balances is still maintained. The data for each transaction is classified just as it would be in a manual accounting system. Then, codes are assigned to translate the classes of information into files that the computer can routinely access.

3 CLOSE

CHAPTER SUMMARY

This summary enumerates the key information in the chapter. It is a useful tool for reinforcement and review.

Reteaching Strategies

Provide students with a handout of the rules of debit and credit for use as a quick reference as they analyze transactions. Use Problem 3A in the Additional Problems section of the textbook (p. 631) for students who need extra practice analyzing transactions into their debit and credit parts.

Review and Applications

Building Your Accounting Vocabulary

Using your own words, write a definition of each of the following accounting terms. Use complete sentences for your definitions.

balance side   double-entry
credit   accounting
debit   T account

Reviewing Your Accounting Knowledge

1. Why is a transaction amount entered in at least two accounts?
2. Would double-entry accounting be used in a computerized accounting system? Why or why not?
3. Why do accountants use T accounts?
4. Name the three basic parts of a T account.
5. What is the left side of a T account called? the right side?
6. State briefly the rules of debit and credit for increasing and decreasing: (a) asset accounts, (b) liability accounts, (c) owner's capital account.
7. What is the normal balance side of asset accounts? liability accounts? the owner's capital account?
8. Classify the following accounts.
   a. Office Equipment   e. Cash in Bank
   b. Delivery Truck   f. Lee Jones, Capital
   c. Accounts Receivable   g. Office Supplies
   d. Store Supplies   h. Accounts Payable
9. Explain briefly what is meant by each of the following phrases.
   a. A debit of $100 to Cash in Bank.
   b. A credit balance.
   c. A credit of $500 to Accounts Payable.
   d. A debit balance.
10. What are the six questions that should be answered whenever a business transaction is analyzed?

Improving Your Math Skills

Calculators and computers do a lot of number crunching for us today, but it is still important to know your numbers if you plan to work in accounting. Complete the exercises that follow to check your skills.

1. Identify each place value in this number: 1,495.885.
2. Round the following numbers to the nearest hundredth.
   (a) 0.578   (c) 1.9001   (e) 10.38601
   (b) 4.89182   (d) 70.475   (f) 583.70121
3. Write the following amounts in words.
   (a) $2.00   (c) $31.56   (e) $1,492.61
   (b) $0.50   (d) $387.81   (f) $21.65

54

PRACTICE AND APPLY

- Language Development
- Comprehension and Retention
- Basic Skills

Building Your Accounting Vocabulary
See the Glossary on pages 670-679 for definitions of these terms.

Reviewing Your Accounting Knowledge
1. The amount is entered in at least two accounts to keep the equation in balance.
2. The double-entry system is used regardless of the method or technology used to record transactions because it allows for increases, decreases, and account balances.
3. T accounts are used to analyze effects of transactions before they are entered in the permanent records.
4. T accounts have a top (title), left side (debit), and right side (credit).
5. The left side of a T account is the debit side; the right side is the credit side.
6. (a) Assets are increased by debits and decreased by credits. (b) Liabilities are increased by credits and decreased by debits. (c) Capital is increased by credits and decreased by debits.
7. The normal balance side for assets is the debit side; for liabilities, the credit side; for capital, the credit side.
8. (a) Asset, (b) Asset, (c) Asset, (d) Asset, (e) Asset, (f) Owner's equity, (g) Asset, (h) Liability
9. (a) Cash in Bank was increased by $100. (b) The balance on the right side of a T account. (c) Accounts Payable was increased by $500. (d) The balance on the left side of a T account.
10. The six questions are: Which accounts are affected? What is the classification of each account? Is each account increased or decreased? Which account is debited, and for what amount? Which account is credited, and for what amount? What is the complete entry?

Improving Your Math Skills
1. Thousands / hundreds / tens / units / tenths / hundredths / thousandths
2. (a) 0.58 (b) 4.89 (c) 1.90 (d) 70.48 (e) 10.39 (f) 583.70
3. (a) two dollars, (b) fifty cents, (c) thirty-one dollars and fifty-six cents, (d) three hundred eighty-seven dollars and eighty-one cents, (e) one thousand four hundred ninety-two dollars and sixty-one cents, (f) twenty-one dollars and sixty-five cents

Applying Accounting Procedures

Exercise 3-1   Applying the Rules of Debit and Credit

Shultz's Speedy Delivery uses the following accounts.

Cash in Bank   Office Equipment   Accounts Payable
Accounts Receivable   Delivery Van   A. Schultz, Capital

Instructions: Use a form similar to the one below. For each account,
(1) Classify the account as an asset, liability, or owner's equity account.
(2) Indicate whether the increase side is a debit or a credit.
(3) Indicate whether the decrease side is a debit or a credit.
(4) Indicate whether the account has a normal debit or credit balance.

Account Title	Account Classification	Increase Side	Decrease Side	Normal Balance
Cash in Bank	Asset	Debit	Credit	Debit

Exercise 3-2   Identifying Accounts Affected by Transactions

Shirley Adams uses the following accounts in her business.

Cash in Bank   Office Furniture   Accounts Payable
Accounts Receivable   Office Supplies   Shirley Adams, Capital
Office Equipment

Instructions: For each of the following transactions,
(1) Indicate the two accounts affected.
(2) Indicate whether each account is debited or credited.

Transactions:
1. Sold an unneeded office typewriter to Jay's Department Store on account.
2. Purchased a computer on credit, promising to pay for it within 60 days.
3. Shirley Adams brought a filing cabinet from home and invested it in the business (office furniture).
4. Bought office supplies for cash.

Exercise 3-3   Identifying Increases and Decreases in Accounts

Alice Roberts uses the following accounts in her business.

Cash in Bank   Office Equipment   Accounts Payable
Accounts Receivable   Office Furniture   Alice Roberts, Capital

Instructions: Analyze each of the following transactions using the format shown below. Explain the debit, then the credit.

Example:
On June 2, Alice Roberts invested $5,000 of her own money into a business called Roberts Employment Agency.

a. The asset Cash in Bank is increased. Increases in assets are recorded as debits.
b. The owner's equity account Alice Roberts, Capital is increased. Increases in the capital account are recorded as credits.

55

Exercise 3-1: Ch. Obj. 1
Accts. Rec., Asset, Debit, Credit, Debit
Off. Equip., Asset, Debit, Credit, Debit
Delivery Van, Asset, Debit, Credit, Debit
Accts. Pay., Liability, Credit, Debit, Credit
A. Schultz, Cap., Owner's Equity, Credit, Debit, Credit

Exercise 3-2: Ch. Obj. 1
1. Accts. Rec. (Dr.), Off. Equip. (Cr.)
2. Off. Equip. (Dr.), Accts. Pay. (Cr.)
3. Off. Furn. (Dr.), S. Adams, Cap. (Cr.)
4. Off. Sup. (Dr.), Cash in Bank (Cr.)

Exercise 3-3: Ch. Obj. 2, 3

Additional **R***einforcement*

Students who need additional practice or individualized help will benefit from the *Glencoe Accounting Electronic Study Guide* or the *Glencoe Accounting* on-line multimedia program, which provide reinforcement and reteaching for vocabulary, concepts, and procedures.

Refer students to the Chapter 3 review pages in the workbook, *Chapter Reviews and Working Papers.*

Chapter 3

1. + Cash in Bank, Debit
   − Office Furniture, Credit
2. + Office Equipment, Debit
   + Accounts Payable, Credit
3. − Accounts Payable, Debit
   − Cash in Bank, Credit

Problem 3-1: Ch. Obj. 1, 2

1. Cash in Bank, +$40,000 Dr.;Norman Rocky, Cap., +$40,000 Cr.
2. Boat, +$27,000 Dr.; Accounts Payable, +$27,000 Cr.
3. Fishing Equip., +$3,750 Dr.; Norman Rocky, Cap., +$3,750 Cr.
4. Fishing Equip., +$7,500 Dr.; Cash in Bank, −$7,500 Cr.
5. Accts. Rec., +$1,200 Dr.; Fishing Equip., −$1,200 Cr.

Teaching Tips

- Remind students to read transactions carefully and to analyze the effect on the accounts of the business.

Problem 3-2: Ch. Obj. 1, 2, 3

Account balances
Cash in Bank	$40,515
Accounts Receivable	100
Office Equipment	1,585
Delivery Van	8,500
Accounts Payable	5,500
A. Schultz, Capital	45,200

Transactions:
1. Sold an unneeded office desk (office furniture) for $750 cash.
2. Bought a used computer from Computer, Inc., on account for $2,500.
3. Paid $750 on account to Computer, Inc.

Problem 3-1   Using T Accounts to Analyze Transactions

Norman Rocky decided to start his own business. He plans to use the following accounts.

Cash in Bank	Fishing Equipment	Accounts Payable
Accounts Receivable	Boat	Norman Rocky, Capital

Instructions: For each transaction,
(1) Determine which two accounts are affected.
(2) Prepare two T accounts for the accounts identified in Instruction #1.
(3) Enter the debit and credit amounts in the T accounts.

Transactions:
1. Norman Rocky invested $40,000 cash in a business called Rocky's Charter Service.
2. Bought a fishing boat on account for $27,000 from Charter Boats, Inc.
3. Norman Rocky invested his personal fishing equipment, valued at $3,750.
4. Rocky's purchased new fishing equipment for $7,500 cash.
5. Rocky's Charter Service sold some of the old fishing equipment on account to Fish & Bait Charters for $1,200.

Problem 3-2   Analyzing Transactions into Debit and Credit Parts

Abraham Schultz completed the following transactions soon after opening Schultz's Speedy Delivery.

Instructions:
(1) Prepare a T account for each account listed in Exercise 3-1.
(2) Analyze and record each of the business transactions using the appropriate T accounts. Identify each transaction by number.
(3) After recording all transactions, write the word "Balance" on the normal balance side of each T account. Then compute and record the balance for each account.

Transactions:
1. Mr. Schultz invested $45,000 cash in his business.
2. Bought a van on account for $8,500 to use for deliveries.
3. Purchased an office lamp for $85, Check 100.
4. Mr. Schultz invested a typewriter worth $200 in the business.
5. Made a $3,000 payment on the van bought on account, Check 101.
6. Sold the old typewriter on account for $200.
7. Bought a new typewriter for $1,500, Check 102.
8. Received a $100 payment for the typewriter sold on account.

Problem 3-3   Analyzing Transactions into Debit and Credit Parts

Helen Marquez owns a dog grooming business. The accounts she uses to record and report business transactions are listed on page 57.

Cash in Bank	Grooming Equipment	Accounts Payable
Accounts Receivable	Store Equipment	Helen Marquez, Capital
Grooming Supplies		

Instructions:

(1) Prepare a T account for each account listed above.

(2) Analyze and record each business transaction in the appropriate T accounts. Identify each transaction by number.

(3) After recording all transactions, compute and record the account balance on the normal balance side of each T account.

(4) Add the balances of those accounts with normal debit balances.

(5) Add the balances of those accounts with normal credit balances.

(6) Compare the two totals. Are they the same?

Transactions:

1. Helen Marquez invested $53,250 from savings into the business.
2. Bought grooming supplies for $550, Check 1000.
3. Bought grooming equipment on account from Dogs & Cats, Inc., for $2,675.
4. Ms. Marquez invested a dog drying lamp, value $150, in the business.
5. Bought a cash register for the store on account from Able Store Equipment for $1,250.
6. Sold the drying lamp on credit for $150.
7. Paid $500 on account to Able Store Equipment, Check 1001.
8. Purchased display shelves for the store for $650, Check 1002.
9. Paid $1,250 on account to Dogs & Cats, Inc., Check 1003.
10. Bought grooming supplies for $175, Check 1004.

Problem 3-4   Analyzing Transactions

Bob Hamilton completed the following transactions soon after opening his business, Your Cleaning Shop.

Cash in Bank	Office Equipment	Accounts Payable
Accounts Receivable	Cleaning Equipment	Bob Hamilton, Capital
Cleaning Supplies		

Instructions:

(1) Prepare a T account for each account used by Your Cleaning Shop.

(2) Analyze and enter each transaction in the appropriate T accounts.

(3) After recording all transactions, compute and record each balance.

(4) Make a list of the asset accounts and their balances.

(5) Add the asset account balances.

(6) Make a list of the liability and owner's equity accounts and balances.

(7) Add the liability and owner's equity account balances.

(8) Compare the totals. Are the totals the same?

Transactions:

1. Mr. Hamilton invested $10,000 of his personal savings in the business.
2. Bought cleaning supplies on account for $750 from Jack's Cleaning.
3. Bought an office desk for $175, Check 1001.
4. Mr. Hamilton invested his $100 calculator in the business.
5. Purchased a new carpet cleaning machine on account for $1,000 from Acme Industrial Equipment.

57

Problem 3-3: Ch. Obj. 1, 2, 3

Debit balances

Cash in Bank	$50,125
Accounts Receivable	150
Grooming Supplies	725
Grooming Equipment	2,675
Store Equipment	1,900
	$55,575

Credit balances

Accounts Payable	$ 2,175
H. Marquez, Capital	53,400
	$55,575

Problem 3-4: Ch. Obj. 1, 2, 3

Assets

Cash in Bank	$ 8,745
Accounts Receivable	100
Cleaning Supplies	785
Office Equipment	370
Cleaning Equipment	1,000
	$11,000

Liab. + Owners's Equity

Accounts Payable	$ 900
B. Hamilton, Capital	10,100
	$11,000

Problem 3-5: Ch. Obj. 1, 2, 3

CHALLENGE PROBLEM — The last problem in each chapter is a challenge problem and is identified by this "maze" symbol.

2. Off. Equip. Dr. (I)
Mary McColly, Cap. Cr. (I)
Invested off. equip. ($225) in bus.

3. Off. Equip. Dr. (I)
Accts. Pay. Cr. (I)
Bought equip. on account
($8,000)
4. Off. Equip. Dr. (I)
Cash in Bank Cr. (D)
Paid cash for equip. ($1,225)
5. Accts. Rec. Dr. (I)
Off. Equip. Cr (D)
Sold equip. on account ($225)
6. Off. Furn. Dr. (I)
Cash in Bank Cr. (D)
Paid cash for equip. ($900)
7. Off. Supp. Dr. (I)
Cash in Bank Cr. (D)
Paid cash for supplies ($95)
8. Accts. Pay. Dr. (D)
Cash in Bank Cr. (D)
Paid on account ($2,000)
9. Cash in Bank Dr. (I)
Accts. Rec. Cr. (D)
Rec. cash on account ($225)
10. Off. Furn. Dr. (I)
Accts. Pay. Cr. (I)
Bought furn. on account ($145)

4 ASSESS

A chapter test is available for use in assessing students' understanding of concepts in this chapter.

The testmaker software will enable you to develop tailor-made chapter, unit, semester, and final tests.

Alternative Assessment

For alternative assessment strategies, refer to *Tech Prep Strategies in Accounting.*

6. Bought a used typewriter for $195, Check 1002.
7. Made a $350 payment to Jack's Cleaning for the supplies purchased earlier, Check 1003.
8. Sold the old calculator on account for $100.
9. Paid Acme Industrial Equipment $500 on account, Check 1004.
10. Bought carpet spray for $35, Check 1005.

CHALLENGE
PROBLEM

Problem 3-5   Analyzing Transactions Recorded in T Accounts

Mary McColly owns and operates a word processing service. The T accounts that follow summarize several business transactions that occurred during May.

Instructions: Use a form similar to the one below. For each transaction,
(1) Identify the account debited and record the account title in the appropriate column.
(2) Indicate whether the account debited is being increased or decreased.
(3) Identify the account credited and write the account title in the appropriate column.
(4) Indicate whether the account credited is being increased or decreased.
(5) Write a short description of the transaction.

Trans. No.	Account Debited	Increase (I) or Decrease (D)	Account Credited	Increase (I) or Decrease (D)	Description
1	Cash in Bank	I	Mary McColly, Capital	I	Mary McColly invested $15,000 in the business

Cash in Bank

Debit +	Credit −
(1) $15,000	(4) $1,225
(9) 225	(6) 900
	(7) 95
	(8) 2,000

Accounts Receivable

Debit +	Credit −
(5) $225	(9) $225

Office Equipment

Debit +	Credit −
(2) $ 225	(5) $225
(3) 8,000	
(4) 1,225	

Office Furniture

Debit +	Credit −
(6) $900	
(10) 145	

Office Supplies

Debit +	Credit −
(7) $95	

Accounts Payable

Debit −	Credit +
(8) $2,000	(3) $8,000
	(10) 145

Mary McColly, Capital

Debit −	Credit +
	(1) $15,000
	(2) 225

58

Use Chapter Test 3 here to assess students' understanding and retention of the concepts and procedures presented in the chapter.

U.S. Forestry Service
Fights Fires with *Computers?*

We've all heard that "only you can prevent a forest fire." When a fire does start, however, it takes the U.S. Forestry Service to put it out. Around 1980, fire management specialists in the Forestry Service were determined to roll back soaring fire-fighting costs. To help them, they enlisted a brigade of computers. "Models" were developed to predict how fires spread and how different fire-fighting methods worked. These models were then entered into hand-held computers that fire fighters could carry with them.

By entering information about weather, wind speed, and terrain, fire fighters can determine how a particular fire will spread. The presence of a river or of strong winds makes a big difference in how fast a fire spreads. When fire fighters know how a fire will spread, they can then use computers to select the best tactics to control it. They'll also have a good idea of how many fire fighters and how much equipment will be needed to get the job done. Getting the jump on a fire means controlling it faster, and controlling the costs of fire management.

How well do the computers perform? Experts predict that, in one year alone, the new technology saved the Forestry Service $10 million. In that year, one major fire in Idaho cost less than $400,000 to put out. Without the aid of computers, experts say, the cost could have exceeded $3 million. One technology consultant estimates that the Forestry Service will see a 4900% return on its investment in computer technology over a five-year period.

Computers aren't as cuddly as Smokey the Bear. If they can help save our tax dollars and preserve our forests, however, Smokey may have to share the limelight.

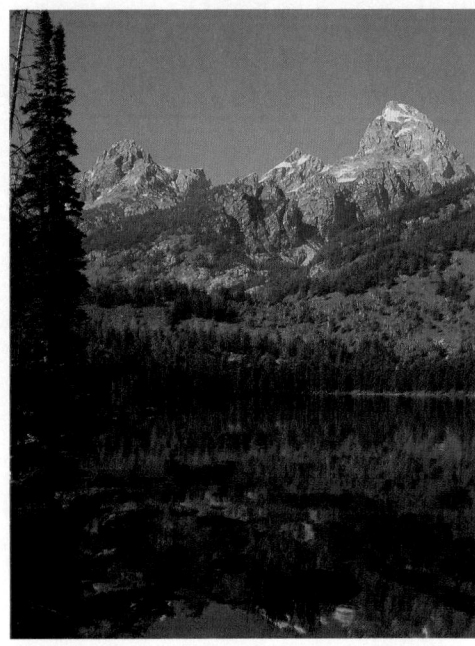

Computers help the U.S. Forestry Service manage the nation's forests.

Fighting forest fires is just one way in which computers help save money and improve performance. Computers are used today in almost every type of business, large or small, and by most government and nonprofit organizations as well.

Ask students to think of local businesses or government offices and identify those that use computers in their operations.

QUESTIONS

1. How might a retailer such as K-Mart use computer models to improve its performance?
2. How might one of the automakers use computer models in the production of a new car?

ANSWERS

1. The most common uses of models by retailers include the ordering of merchandise (using models to predict buying patterns and inventory needs) and decisions on where to locate (using models of the characteristics of locations of profitable stores).
2. Automakers use computer models to design their cars and to simulate testing conditions. These models allow them to refine the final image before the car goes into production.

59

ANALYZING TRANSACTIONS AFFECTING REVENUE, EXPENSES, AND WITHDRAWALS

LOOKING BACK

In Chapter 3 students learned the rules of debit and credit for asset, liability, and owner's equity accounts. T accounts were presented as a tool for analyzing the effects of business transactions on the basic accounting equation. In this chapter, students extend the rules of debit and credit to the revenue, expense, and withdrawals accounts.

VOCABULARY DEVELOPMENT

Have students read the list of new terms. Ask for ideas for each term's meaning. Write correct responses on the board. Review the meanings of terms that are not familiar to students. Definitions of these terms are found in the chapter and in the glossary on pages 670-679.

In Chapter 3, you learned the rules of debit and credit for accounts classified as assets, liabilities, and owner's equity. As you applied these rules of debit and credit, you saw that accounting is based upon a double-entry system: For every debit, there is an equal credit. You also learned that the T account is a tool used by accountants to analyze the effects of each business transaction on specific accounts. In other words, you saw how a debit in one account was always offset by an equal credit in another account.

In Chapter 4, you will learn about the temporary capital accounts for revenue, expenses, and withdrawals. You will then learn about the rules of debit and credit for revenue, expense, and withdrawals accounts. You will also learn how to apply these rules to analyze the effects of business transactions involving these accounts.

Learning Objectives

When you have completed Chapter 4, you should be able to do the following:

1. Explain the difference between permanent accounts and temporary capital accounts.
2. List and apply the rules of debit and credit for revenue, expense, and withdrawals accounts.
3. Use the six-step method to analyze business transactions affecting revenue, expense, and withdrawals accounts.
4. Test a series of transactions for equality of debits and credits.
5. Define the accounting terms introduced in this chapter.

New Terms

temporary capital accounts
permanent accounts
revenue principle

60

The Need for Specific Accounting Information

No pilot would take off in a plane equipped with only a speedometer and a gas gauge. These two instruments, although necessary, do not give all the kinds of information needed to keep such a complex machine on course and operating smoothly. Operating a business is a bit like operating a plane. Certain information is needed to keep the business on course. In this chapter, we will take a close look at three types of accounts that provide information about how well the business is doing. These accounts are the revenue, expense, and withdrawals accounts.

The Relationship of Revenue, Expenses, and Withdrawals to Owner's Capital

You learned earlier that the owner's capital account shows the amount of the owner's investment, or equity, in a business. Owner's capital can be increased or decreased, however, by transactions other than owner's investments. For example, the revenue, or income, earned by the business increases owner's capital. Expenses and withdrawals decrease owner's capital.

Revenue, expenses, and withdrawals could be recorded as increases or decreases in the capital account. This method, however, makes finding specific information about these items difficult. A more efficient way to record information about revenue, expenses, and withdrawals is to set up separate accounts for each of these items. By looking at the amounts recorded in the revenue and expense accounts, the owner can tell at a glance whether revenue and expenses are increasing or decreasing. Such information helps the business owner decide, for example, whether some expenses need to be cut to save money.

Temporary Capital Accounts

The revenue, expense, and withdrawals accounts are called **temporary capital accounts.** Temporary capital accounts start each new accounting period with zero balances. That is, the amounts in these accounts are not carried forward from one accounting period to another. Temporary accounts are not temporary in the sense that they are used for a short time and then discarded. They continue to be used in the accounting system, but the amounts recorded in them accumulate for only *one* accounting period. At the end of that period, the balances in the temporary accounts are transferred to the owner's capital account. (The procedure for moving these amounts to the capital account is discussed in Chapter 9.)

Let's use the temporary account Utilities Expense as an example. During an accounting period, utility costs for such items as electricity and telephones are recorded in Utilities Expense. By using this separate account, the owner can see at a glance how much money is being spent on this type of expense. The amounts accumulate in the account during the accounting period. At the end of the period, the total is transferred to the owner's capital account and subtracted from the balance of that account. (As you recall, expenses decrease owner's capital.) Utilities Expense, then, starts the next accounting period with a zero balance—ready to accumulate that period's costs.

1 FOCUS

MAJOR CONCEPTS

- The Need for Specific Accounting Information
- The Relationship of Revenue, Expenses, and Withdrawals to Owner's Capital
- The Rules of Debit and Credit for Temporary Capital Accounts
- Analyzing Transactions Involving Revenue, Expenses, and Withdrawals
- Summary of the Rules of Debit and Credit
- Testing for the Equality of Debits and Credits

BUSINESS CONNECTION

Keeping track of the sources of revenue is an important part of the accounting process and is a key element to business success. In the 1980s, a number of firms including Sears, ITT, XEROX, Westinghouse, and General Electric tried to increase their revenues by offering financial services such as real estate mortgages and consumer finance loans. Several of the companies have now sold off their financial services businesses because expected revenue did not materialize. Have students speculate on the reasons for revenue shortfalls.

2 TEACH

CONCEPT DEVELOPMENT

The Need for Specific Accounting Information

In a private enterprise economy, most businesses operate to make a profit. To determine whether a profit is being made, specific information is needed on the cost of operating the business and the revenue that is earned from the sale of products or services. The difference between revenue and expenses is income, which tells how well a business is doing. The accounting system provides this information.

Chapter 4

CONCEPT DEVELOPMENT
The Relationship of Revenue, Expenses, and Withdrawals to Owner's Capital

This chapter develops the relationship between the permanent accounts and the temporary capital accounts. This early exposure helps students assimilate the relationship of revenue and expenses to owner's capital. In addition, it helps to prepare students for the closing process, which they will study in Chapter 9.

Emphasize to students that during an accounting period, the increases and decreases in owner's capital are recorded in temporary accounts to maintain a separate record of the specific increases/decreases affecting capital. Use the basic accounting equation and show the revenue and expense accounts within the capital account to demonstrate the relationship between permanent and temporary accounts.

CONCEPT DEVELOPMENT
The Rule of Debit and Credit for Temporary Capital Accounts

To introduce the rules of debit and credit for revenue, expenses, and withdrawals, draw a T account for each classification on the chalkboard. Write the rules for revenue in that account. Discuss the effect of revenue on capital.

Next, write the rules for expenses in that T account. Discuss the effect of expenses on capital. Continue with the rules for withdrawals and their effect on capital.

Maintenance expense might include the costs of repairing equipment, painting, or taking care of the grounds around the office.

Permanent Accounts

In contrast to the temporary accounts, the owner's capital account is a permanent account. Assets and liabilities are also permanent accounts. **Permanent accounts** are continuous from one accounting period to the next. That is, at the end of an accounting period, the balances in these accounts are carried forward to the next period.

The permanent accounts report balances on hand or amounts owed on a regular basis. They show the day-to-day changes in assets, liabilities, and owner's capital. For example, during an accounting period many increases and decreases are recorded in the Cash in Bank account. The balance in this account reports the amount of cash on hand (in the bank) at any given time. At the end of the accounting period, the ending balance in this account becomes the beginning balance for the next accounting period. In other words, this account—and all other permanent accounts—continues from one accounting period to the next.

The Rules of Debit and Credit for Temporary Capital Accounts

In Chapter 3, you learned the rules of debit and credit for the asset, liability, and owner's capital accounts. In this chapter, we will continue the rules of debit and credit, this time for revenue, expense, and withdrawals accounts. Before looking at these rules, let's review quickly the basic accounting equation with T accounts showing the rules of debit and credit for assets, liabilities, and owner's capital.

Making Connections

EVERYDAY LIFE

Last spring Jerry started mowing lawns for his neighbors. By midsummer, Jerry was mowing five different lawns a week. He calculated his income for the remainder of the summer, hoping to earn enough money to buy a new mountain bike before school started. Jerry easily calculated his earnings, but he failed to account for any expenses. What expenses would Jerry have? What other reasons might Jerry not earn the total amount that he has calculated?

(Answers: Jerry's expenses would include gasoline and oil and mower repairs. Jerry may earn less than he has anticipated if the weather is rainy and he cannot mow for several days or if the weather is dry and the grass needs mowing less frequently.)

ASSETS	=	LIABILITIES	+	OWNER'S EQUITY
Asset Accounts	=	Liability Accounts	+	Capital Account

Debit	Credit	Debit	Credit	Debit	Credit
+	−	−	+	−	+
Increase Side	Decrease Side	Decrease Side	Increase Side	Decrease Side	Increase Side
Balance Side			Balance Side		Balance Side

R E M E M B E R

The normal balance for assets is a debit balance. The normal balance for liabilities and owner's capital is a credit balance.

Now let's look at the rules of debit and credit for accounts classified as revenue.

Rules for Revenue Accounts

Accounts set up to record business income are classified as revenue accounts. The following rules of debit and credit apply to revenue accounts:

1. A revenue account is increased (+) on the credit side.
2. A revenue account is decreased (−) on the debit side.
3. The normal balance for a revenue account is a credit balance.

Revenue earned from selling goods or services increases owner's capital. The relationship of the revenue account to the owner's capital account is shown by the T accounts in Figure 4-1. Can you explain why the T account for revenue is used to represent the credit (right) side of the capital account?

Permanent Account
Capital

Debit	Credit
−	+
Decrease Side	Increase Side
	Balance Side

Temporary Account

Revenue	
Debit	Credit
−	+
Decrease Side	Increase Side
	Balance Side

A credit balance is recorded on the credit side.

Figure 4-1 Rules of Debit and Credit for Revenue Accounts

CHAPTER 4   Analyzing Transactions Affecting Revenue, Expenses, and Withdrawals   63

Teaching Tips

■ Review the rules for recording increases and decreases in the owner's capital account. Increases in capital are recorded as credits, decreases as debits. Revenue increases capital and is thus recorded as a credit. Expenses and withdrawals decrease capital and thus are recorded as debits.
■ Emphasize that revenue represents an inflow of assets and an increase in equity.
■ Note for students that revenue, expense, and withdrawals accounts are *classified* as temporary. They are not temporary in their use by the business.
■ Temporary accounts are used to report results for a "period of time" (the income statement), which is why their balances are "temporary."
■ Temporary accounts start each new accounting period with a zero balance.

Using Visuals

Have students study Figure 4-1. Emphasize the visual relationship between capital and revenue; i.e., revenue increases capital and is thus recorded as a credit. Likewise, the revenue account is increased by a credit.

Using Visuals

 A teaching transparency of Figure 4-1 is available in the transparency binder accompanying Glencoe Accounting.

Critical Thinking

Tom Dunn started an automotive parts business two years ago. Except for a monthly salary, Tom has never taken money out of the business. He is now considering withdrawing $5,000 to pay off the mortgage on his family home. What factors should Tom consider before he makes a decision to withdraw cash from the business?

(Answers: Among responses students should mention are: Is the cash currently available? Will the cash be needed to pay liabilities? Will there still be enough cash left over to pay monthly expenses? Is future income anticipated to offset the withdrawal? After the withdrawal, will the business still realize a profit?)

Teaching Tips

■ The $200 in the T account for *Fees* is for demonstration only. Normally a revenue account would not have a debit balance. This entry could be explained as a correcting entry.

■ Emphasize that expenses represent an outflow of assets and a decrease in equity.

ACCOUNTING ISSUES

In an accrual-based accounting system, revenue is recorded when it is earned, not when it is received. Sometimes collecting the revenue earned gets to be a problem. Getting debtors to pay their bills on time can make a big difference to the smooth flow of business operations, especially to small and medium-sized companies. Without a steady stream of revenue, businesses may have a hard time paying their own debts.

The credit side of the capital account is used to increase that account. Since revenue increases capital, the revenue account is used to represent the credit side of the capital account.

We can summarize the rules of debit and credit for revenue accounts with a T account.

Revenue Accounts	
Debit	Credit
–	+
2 Decrease Side	1 Increase Side
	3 Balance Side

Rule 1: Revenue accounts are increased by credits.
Rule 2: Revenue accounts are decreased by debits.
Rule 3: The normal balance for revenue accounts is a credit balance.

Let's apply these rules of debit and credit to an actual revenue account. Look at the entries in the following T account for the revenue account called Fees.

Fees	
Debit	Credit
–	+
$200	$ 500
	1,000
	2,000
	Balance, $3,300

for a revenue account.

The increases to revenue are recorded on the right, or credit, side of the T account. The decreases to revenue are recorded on the left, or debit, side. To find the balance, subtract total debits ($200) from total credits ($500 + $1,000 + $2,000 = $3,500). You get a balance of $3,300 on the credit side, the normal balance side

R E M E M B E R

The normal balance side of any account is the same as the side used to increase that account.

Rules for Expense Accounts

Accounts that are set up to record the costs of goods and services used by the business are classified as expense accounts. Within an expense account itself, the following rules of debit and credit apply:

1. An expense account is increased (+) on the debit side.
2. An expense account is decreased (−) on the credit side.
3. The normal balance for an expense account is a debit balance.

Expenses are the costs of doing business. Expenses decrease owner's capital. Expenses, therefore, have the opposite effect from that of revenue on the owner's capital account. Look at the T accounts in Figure 4-2. Can you explain why the T account for expenses is used to represent the debit (left) side of the capital account?

Decreases in capital are shown on the debit side of that account. Since expenses decrease capital, expense accounts are used to represent the debit side of the owner's capital account.

64   UNIT 2   The Basic Accounting Cycle

Cooperative Learning

GROUP DISCUSSION

Assign students to small groups of 4 or 5. Ask each group to develop an idea for a service business and to identify some of the business's assets. Then instruct students to describe ten typical transactions for their business. Have students write the transactions and analyze each transaction using T accounts. Each T account should show the account balance on its normal balance side after all transactions are analyzed. Have each team select a spokesperson to present their "business" to the rest of the class. You may want to give students markers and blank transparency sheets to use in preparing their presentations.

Refer to the "Cooperative Learning" section of *Tech Prep Strategies in Accounting* for additional cooperative learning strategies.

Permanent Account
Capital

Figure 4-2 Rules of Debit and Credit for Expense Accounts

A debit balance is recorded on the debit side. | A credit balance is recorded on the credit side.

Using Visuals

Refer students to Figure 4-2. Have students describe in their own words the relationship between capital and the temporary accounts for revenue and expenses.

Using Visuals

A teaching transparency of Figure 4-2 is available in the transparency binder accompanying Glencoe Accounting.

Let's use a T account to summarize the rules of debit and credit for expense accounts.

Expense Accounts	
Debit	Credit
+	−
1 Increase Side	2 Decrease Side
3 Balance Side	

Rule 1: Expense accounts are increased by debits.
Rule 2: Expense accounts are decreased by credits.
Rule 3: The normal balance for expense accounts is a debit balance.

Teaching Tips

■ The $125 in the T account for *Advertising Expense* is for demonstration only. Expense accounts normally do not have credit balances. This entry could be explained as a correcting entry.

Now look at the entries recorded in the following T account for the expense account entitled Advertising Expense.

Advertising Expense	
Debit	Credit
+	−
$400	$125
200	
Balance, $475	

The increases to the expense account are recorded on the left, or debit, side of the T account. The decreases to the account are recorded on the right, or credit, side of the T account. When total credits ($125) are subtracted from total debits ($600), there is a balance of $475 on the debit side, which is the normal balance side for expense accounts.

R E M E M B E R

The normal balance of a revenue account is a credit. The normal balance for an expense account is a debit.

Did you know?

Some businesses reward their student employees for good grades. The student employees receive bonuses based on their grade-point averages. For example, a student who maintains a 2.5 to 3.0 GPA for a semester might get a bonus of $0.15 per hour for each hour worked during that semester. Students getting a 3.0 GPA, or higher, might get an additional $0.25 per hour.

Interdisciplinary Connections

LANGUAGE ARTS

Many accounting terms have a long linguistic history. *Debit* and *credit,* for example, derive from Latin but have been in the English language since the 1400s and 1500s. *Debit* is related to the word *debt.* Credit comes from the Latin for "belief" or "trust" and is related to such words as *credible* and *credence.*

ANSWERS

1. The normal balance side of any account is the side on which increases are recorded in that account.
2. A debit increases an expense account.
3. The normal balance for a revenue account is a credit balance.
4. A credit increases a revenue account.
5. A debit balance is the normal balance for an expense account.
6. A credit decreases the withdrawals account.
7. A debit balance is the normal balance for a withdrawals account.

ACCOUNTING PRACTICE
Students may complete Exercise 4-1 at this point.

Rules for the Withdrawals Account

A withdrawal is an amount of money or an asset taken out of the business by the owner. Since withdrawals do not occur as frequently as expenses, no separate classification is used for the withdrawals account. Rather, it is classified as a temporary owner's equity account. Withdrawals decrease capital, so the rules of debit and credit are the same as for expense accounts.

Withdrawals Account	
Debit	Credit
+	−
1 Increase Side	2 Decrease Side
3 Balance Side	

Rule 1: The withdrawals account is increased by debits.
Rule 2: The withdrawals account is decreased by credits.
Rule 3: The normal balance for the withdrawals account is a debit balance.

Before you go any further, do the activity that follows to see if you understand the rules of debit and credit for revenue, expense, and withdrawals accounts.

Check Your Learning

Answer these questions about revenue, expense, and withdrawals accounts.

1. What is the normal balance side of any account?
2. What effect does a debit have on an expense account?
3. What is the normal balance for a revenue account?
4. What effect does a credit have on a revenue account?
5. What is the normal balance for an expense account?
6. What effect does a credit have on a withdrawals account?
7. What is the normal balance for a withdrawals account?

Compare your answers to those in the answers section. Re-read the preceding part of the chapter to find the correct answers to any questions you may have missed.

Summarizing the Rules of Debit and Credit

Revenue represents the increase side of the capital account. As a result, revenue accounts are increased on the credit side and decreased on the debit side. The normal balance for revenue accounts is a credit balance. The rules of debit and credit for expense and withdrawals accounts are opposite the rules for revenue accounts. Expenses and withdrawals represent the decrease side of the capital account. Expense and withdrawals accounts then are increased on the debit side and decreased on the credit side. The normal balance for expense and withdrawals accounts is a debit balance. These basic accounting relationships are shown in the T accounts in Figure 4-3.

66

UNIT 2   The Basic Accounting Cycle

Permanent Account
Capital

Temporary Account

Debit
−
Decrease Side

Credit
+
Increase Side
Balance Side

Temporary Account

Expenses	
Debit + Increase Side Balance Side	Credit − Decrease Side

Withdrawals	
Debit + Increase Side Balance Side	Credit − Decrease Side

Revenue	
Debit − Decrease Side	Credit + Increase Side Balance Side

A debit balance is recorded on the debit side. | A credit balance is recorded on the credit side.

Figure 4-3 Rules of Debit and Credit for Temporary Capital Accounts

R E M E M B E R

Debits are used to:
1. Decrease (−) revenues.
2. Increase (+) expenses.
3. Increase (+) withdrawals.

Credits are used to:
1. Increase (+) revenues.
2. Decrease (−) expenses.
3. Decrease (−) withdrawals.

Analyzing Transactions Involving Revenue, Expenses, and Withdrawals

The Global Travel Agency transactions in Chapter 3 dealt with asset and liability accounts and with the owner's equity account Jan Harter, Capital. To keep track of revenue, expenses, and withdrawals, Jan Harter has expanded the number of accounts used by the business. The following list shows all the account titles used by Global Travel. As you can see, the accounts have been classified as assets, liabilities, owner's equity, revenue, and expenses. The accounts have also been numbered so that they can be easily and quickly located.

CHAPTER 4 Analyzing Transactions Affecting Revenue, Expenses, and Withdrawals   67

ASSETS
101 Cash in Bank
105 Accounts Receivable
120 Computer Equipment
130 Office Equipment

LIABILITIES
201 Accounts Payable

OWNER'S EQUITY
301 Jan Harter, Capital
305 Jan Harter, Withdrawals

REVENUE
401 Fees

EXPENSES
501 Advertising Expense
505 Maintenance Expense
510 Rent Expense
515 Utilities Expense

Using the rules of debit and credit for these accounts, let's analyze several business transactions. When you analyzed business transactions in Chapter 3, you asked six questions about each transaction. These same questions also apply to each transaction affecting revenue, expenses, or withdrawals.

1. Which accounts are affected?
2. What is the classification of each account?
3. Is each account increased or decreased?
4. Which account is debited, and for what amount?
5. Which account is credited, and for what amount?
6. What is the complete entry?

Business Transaction 8: *On October 15, Global Travel Agency mailed Check 103 for $550 to pay the month's rent.*

1. Which accounts are affected?
   The accounts affected are Rent Expense and Cash in Bank.
2. What is the classification of each account?
   Rent Expense is an expense account. Cash in Bank is an asset account.
3. Is each account increased or decreased?
   The payment of rent increases the business's costs, so Rent Expense is increased. The writing of a check reduces cash, so Cash in Bank is decreased.
4. Which account is debited, and for what amount?

Rent Expense	
Debit	Credit
+	−
$550	
Balance, $550	

Increases in expense accounts are recorded as debits. Rent Expense, therefore, is debited for $550.

5. Which account is credited, and for what amount?

Cash in Bank	
Debit	Credit
+	−
$16,450	$550
Balance, $15,900	

Decreases in assets are recorded as credits. Cash in Bank is, therefore, credited for $550.

6. What is the complete entry?

Rent Expense is debited for $550 and Cash in Bank is credited for $550. Remember, in the double-entry system, the debit amount of a transaction must equal the credit amount.

Rent Expense		Cash in Bank	
Debit	Credit	Debit	Credit
+	−	+	−
$550			$550

Business Transaction 9: *On October 16, Jan Harter bought a $75 advertisement on account from City News.*

1. Which accounts are affected?

Advertising Expense and Accounts Payable are affected.

2. What is the classification of each account?

Advertising Expense is an expense account; Accounts Payable is a liability account.

3. Is each account increased or decreased?

Buying advertising adds to expenses, so Advertising Expense is increased. Accounts Payable is increased because the amount the business owes is increased.

4. Which account is debited, and for what amount?

Advertising Expense	
Debit	Credit
+	−
$75	
Balance, $75	

Increases in expenses are recorded as debits. Advertising Expense is being increased by $75 and is, therefore, debited for that amount.

5. Which account is credited, and for what amount?

Accounts Payable	
Debit	Credit
−	+
	$750
	75
	Balance, $825

Increases in liabilities are recorded as credits. Accounts Payable is a liability and is, therefore, credited for the amount of the increase, $75.

CHAPTER 4   Analyzing Transactions Affecting Revenue, Expenses, and Withdrawals   69

Making Connections

BUSINESS ETHICS

Your company has a WATS line and allows its employees to make personal calls on the line before 8:00 a.m. and after 5:00 p.m. One of your friends asks if she can come to your office after work to call her sister, who lives in the next state. What should you do?

(Answer: Calls made on the WATS line are still an expense to the company. By allowing its employees to make personal calls, the company is actually providing an employee benefit, which should not be shared with non-employees. Explain to your friend that the WATS line is to be used only by those who work for the company.)

6. What is the complete entry?
Advertising Expense is debited for $75 and Accounts Payable is credited for $75.

Advertising Expense		Accounts Payable	
Debit	Credit	Debit	Credit
+	−	−	+
$75			$75

Business Transaction 10: *On October 18, Jan Harter completed travel plans requested by the Sims Corporation. She received $1,200 as payment for her services.*

1. Which accounts are affected?
Cash in Bank and Fees are affected.
2. What is the classification of each account?
Cash in Bank is an asset account and Fees is a revenue account.
3. Is each account increased or decreased?
Money received increases Cash in Bank. Fees received for services completed add to revenue, so the revenue account Fees is increased.
4. Which account is debited and for what amount?

Cash in Bank	
Debit	Credit
+	−
$16,450	$550
1,200	
Balance, $17,100	

Increases in assets are recorded as debits. The asset account Cash in Bank is debited for $1,200.

5. Which account is credited, and for what amount?

Fees	
Debit	Credit
−	+
	$1,200
	Balance, $1,200

Increases in revenue are recorded as credits. The revenue account Fees is credited for $1,200.

6. What is the complete entry?
Cash in Bank is debited for $1,200 and Fees is credited for the same amount.

Cash in Bank		Fees	
Debit	Credit	Debit	Credit
+	−	−	+
$1,200			$1,200

Global Travel Agency earns revenue by providing travel services to various customers.

Using Visuals

Direct students' attention to the photograph and its caption. Travel agencies earn revenue by providing services for their clients. Ask students to name other types of service businesses.

Teaching Tips

- Transaction 11 results in an increase to an asset and an increase to revenue.
  (+) Asset
  (+) Revenue

Using Visuals

A teaching transparency for business transaction 11 is available in the transparency binder accompanying Glencoe Accounting.

Business Transaction 11: *On October 20, Jan Harter completed travel plans for a customer. She billed the customer $450 for the work.*

1. **Which accounts are affected?**
   The customer has not yet paid for the job, so Accounts Receivable is affected. Fees is also affected.
2. **What is the classification of each account?**
   Accounts Receivable is classified as an asset account. Fees is a revenue account.
3. **Is each account increased or decreased?**
   Money to be received in the future increases Accounts Receivable. Accounts Receivable is, therefore, increased. Money to be received for a job is revenue, so Fees is increased. For accounting purposes, revenue is recognized and recorded on the date it is earned even if cash has not been received on that date. This is known as the **revenue principle.**
4. **Which account is debited, and for what amount?**

Accounts Receivable	
Debit	Credit
+	–
$450	
Balance, $450	

Increases in assets are recorded as debits. The asset account Accounts Receivable is debited for $450.

5. **Which account is credited, and for what amount?**

Fees	
Debit	Credit
–	+
	$1,200
	450
	Balance, $1,650

Increases in revenue are recorded as credits. The revenue account Fees is credited for $450.

CHAPTER 4 Analyzing Transactions Affecting Revenue, Expenses, and Withdrawals   **71**

Making Connections

AROUND THE WORLD

The Financial Accounting Standards Board plays a major role in developing accounting standards for U.S. businesses. Other countries have similar professional groups that evaluate the accounting needs within their own economies and monitor business's financial reports. For example, in Great Britain the counterpart to the FASB is the Accounting Standards Board.

Teaching Tips

■ Transaction 12 results in an increase to an expense and a decrease in an asset.
(+) Expense
(−) Asset

Using Visuals

A teaching transparency for business transaction 12 is available in the transparency binder accompanying Glencoe Accounting.

---

6. What is the complete entry?
Accounts Receivable is debited for $450 and Fees is credited for $450.

Accounts Receivable			Fees	
Debit	Credit		Debit	Credit
+	−		−	+
$450				$450

Business Transaction 12: *On October 28, Global Travel Agency paid a $125 telephone bill with Check 104.*

1. Which accounts are affected?
The cost of telephone service used by the business is an expense. The account Utilities Expense is affected. ("Utilities" are electricity, gas, heat, telephone service, and water.) Cash in Bank is also affected.

2. What is the classification of each account?
Utilities Expense is an expense account. Cash in Bank is an asset account.

3. Is each account increased or decreased?
The payment of a telephone bill increases expenses, so Utilities Expense is increased. The writing of a check reduces the amount of cash in the bank, so Cash in Bank is decreased.

4. Which account is debited, and for what amount?

Utilities Expense	
Debit	Credit
+	−
$125	
Balance, $125	

Increases in expenses are recorded as debits. Utilities Expense is debited for $125.

5. Which account is credited, and for what amount?

Cash in Bank	
Debit	Credit
+	−
$16,450	$550
1,200	125
Balance, $16,975	

Decreases in assets are recorded as credits. Cash in Bank is credited for $125.

6. What is the complete entry?
Utilities Expense is debited for $125 and Cash in Bank is credited for the same amount.

Utilities Expense			Cash in Bank	
Debit	Credit		Debit	Credit
+	−		+	−
$125				$125

72

ACCOUNTING | **Tips**

Revenue represents the *right* side of the capital account. The *right* (credit) side of the revenue account is, therefore, the side used to increase that account. Expenses and withdrawals represent the *left* side of the capital account. The *left* (debit) side of these accounts is then the side used to increase the accounts.

Business Transaction 13: *On October 29, Jan Harter wrote Check 105 for $450 to have the office repainted.*

1. Which accounts are affected?
Repainting is a cost of maintaining the office, so the Maintenance Expense account is affected. Cash in Bank is also affected since cash is being paid out.

2. What is the classification of each account?
Maintenance Expense is an expense account. Cash in Bank is an asset account.

3. Is each account increased or decreased?
Maintenance Expense is increased and Cash in Bank is decreased.

4. Which account is debited, and for what amount?

Maintenance Expense	
Debit	Credit
+	−
$450	
Balance, $450	

Increases in expenses are recorded as debits. Maintenance Expense is, therefore, debited for $450.

5. Which account is credited, and for what amount?

Cash in Bank	
Debit	Credit
+	−
$16,450	$550
1,200	125
	450
Balance, $16,525	

Decreases in assets are recorded as credits. Cash in Bank is, therefore, credited for $450.

6. What is the complete entry?
Maintenance Expense is debited for $450 and Cash in Bank is credited for $450.

Maintenance Expense		Cash in Bank	
Debit	Credit	Debit	Credit
+	−	+	−
$450			$450

Business Transaction 14: *On October 31, Jan Harter withdrew $400 cash for personal use by writing Check 106.*

1. Which accounts are affected?
Money taken out of the business by the owner is recorded in the withdrawals account. The accounts affected, therefore, are Jan Harter, Withdrawals and Cash in Bank.

CHAPTER 4   Analyzing Transactions Affecting Revenue, Expenses, and Withdrawals   **73**

2. What is the classification of each account?
Jan Harter, Withdrawals is classified as a temporary owner's equity account. Cash in Bank is an asset account.

3. Is each account increased or decreased?
Jan Harter, Withdrawals is used to accumulate amounts taken out of the business by the owner. The amount of money withdrawn by the owner increases the account, so Jan Harter, Withdrawals is increased. The writing of a check decreases Cash in Bank.

4. Which account is debited, and for what amount?

Jan Harter, Withdrawals	
Debit	Credit
+	−
$400	
Balance, $400	

Increases in withdrawals are recorded as debits. Jan Harter, Withdrawals is, therefore, debited for $400.

5. Which account is credited, and for what amount?

Cash in Bank	
Debit	Credit
+	−
$16,450	$550
1,200	125
	450
	400
Balance, $16,125	

Decreases in assets are recorded as credits. Cash in Bank is, therefore, credited for $400.

6. What is the complete entry?
Jan Harter, Withdrawals is debited for $400 and Cash in Bank is credited for $400.

Jan Harter, Withdrawals			Cash in Bank	
Debit	Credit		Debit	Credit
+	−		+	−
$400				$400

R E M E M B E R

Amounts taken out of the business decrease owner's capital. Therefore, increases in the withdrawals account are recorded as debits.

Before continuing, complete the following activity to check your understanding of how to analyze transactions involving revenue, expenses, and withdrawals.

Check Your Learning

Analyze this transaction using the six-step method you used in this chapter.

On March 1, J & L Enterprises mailed Check 107 for $2,000 to pay the month's rent.

1. Which accounts are affected?
2. What is the classification of each account?
3. Is each account increased or decreased?
4. Which account is debited, and for what amount?
5. Which account is credited, and for what amount?
6. What is the complete entry? Show in T account form.

Compare your answers to those in the answers section. Re-read the preceding part of the chapter to find the correct answers to any questions that you may have missed.

Summary of the Rules of Debit and Credit

The rules of debit and credit for the permanent accounts—assets, liabilities, and the owner's capital account—are summarized below using T accounts and the basic accounting equation.

ASSETS	=	LIABILITIES	+	OWNER'S EQUITY

Asset Accounts = **Liability Accounts** + **Capital Account**

Debit + Increase Side Balance Side	Credit − Decrease Side	Debit − Decrease Side	Credit + Increase Side Balance Side	Debit − Decrease Side	Credit + Increase Side Balance Side

Assets have **DEBIT BALANCES.**

Equities (liabilities and capital) have **CREDIT BALANCES.**

The rules of debit and credit for the temporary capital accounts—expenses, revenue, and the owner's withdrawals account—can also be summarized using T accounts.

TEMPORARY CAPITAL ACCOUNTS

Withdrawals

Debit + Increase Side Balance Side	Credit − Decrease Side

Expenses

Debit + Increase Side Balance Side	Credit − Decrease Side

Revenue

Debit − Decrease Side	Credit + Increase Side Balance Side

CHAPTER 4   Analyzing Transactions Affecting Revenue, Expenses, and Withdrawals   75

ANSWERS

1. Cash in Bank; Rent Expense
2. Cash in Bank is an asset account; Rent Expense is an expense account.
3. Cash in Bank is decreased; Rent Expense is increased.
4. Rent Expense is debited for $2,000.
5. Cash in Bank is credited for $2,000.
6. Rent Expense is debited for $2,000 and Cash in Bank is credited for $2,000.

Rent Expense

Debit + $2,000	Credit −

Cash in Bank

Debit +	Credit − $2,000

ACCOUNTING PRACTICE

Students may complete Exercise 4-3 at this point.

COMPUTERS IN ACCOUNTING

One of the advantages of a computerized accounting system is that you can make backup copies of all the accounting records and even safeguard them by storing them in another location. In 1993 the World Trade Center in New York was bombed and many companies not only lost the use of their office space, but they also lost valuable accounting records. As a result, their day-to-day business came to a standstill. Fortunately for one company, they had maintained computerized accounting records in a second location for backup purposes. The company quickly moved its employees into a new temporary location, retrieved the backup files, rented computers, and continued to meet its clients' needs while experiencing minimal downtime for business transactions.

Reteaching Strategies

The concept of why expenses decrease the balance of the capital account can be confusing to students. Review the rules for debit and credit. The rules for accounts on one side of the accounting equation are opposite the rules for accounts on the other side of the equation. The vertical rule in the T account separates debits and credits. The *effect* of entries recorded on the different sides of the T account are opposite each other. Since revenue is recorded as a credit because it increases capital, the effect of expenses is just the opposite. They are recorded as debits and decrease capital.

Use Problem 4A in the Additional Problems section (p. 632) for students who need extra practice analyzing transactions.

CHAPTER 4   Analyzing Transactions Affecting Revenue, Expenses, and Withdrawals   **75**

Chapter 4

CONCEPT DEVELOPMENT

Testing for Equality of Debits and Credits

Emphasize that total credits must equal total debits after all transactions have been recorded. Testing for the equality of debits and credits is one way to find out whether errors were made in recording the transactions.

Teaching Tips

■ Testing for the equality of debits and credits sets the stage for introducing the trial balance (in Chapter 6). You may want to introduce the trial balance here.

■ Point out the advantages of the double-entry system of accounting as a check on accuracy.

3 CLOSE

CHAPTER SUMMARY

This summary enumerates the key information in the chapter. It is a useful tool for reinforcement and review.

Testing for the Equality of Debits and Credits

In a double-entry accounting system, correct analysis and recording of business transactions should result in total debits being equal to total credits. Testing for the equality of total debits and credits is one way of finding out whether you have made any errors in recording transaction amounts. To test for the equality of total debits and credits, follow these steps:

1. Make a list of the account titles used by the business.
2. Opposite each account title, list the final or current balance of the account. Use two columns, one for debit balances and one for credit.
3. Add each amount column.

If you have recorded all the amounts correctly, the total of the debit column will equal the total of the credit column. The test for equality of debits and credits for the transactions in Chapters 3 and 4 shows that total debits are equal to total credits, so the accounting system is in balance.

ACCOUNT TITLE	DEBIT BALANCES	CREDIT BALANCES
Cash in Bank	$16,125	
Accounts Receivable	450	
Computer Equipment	8,000	
Office Equipment	1,500	
Accounts Payable		$ 825
Jan Harter, Capital		25,200
Jan Harter, Withdrawals	400	
Fees		1,650
Advertising Expense	75	
Maintenance Expense	450	
Rent Expense	550	
Utilities Expense	125	
Totals	$27,675	$27,675

Summary of Key Points

1. The accounts used by a business can be separated into permanent accounts and temporary capital accounts. Permanent accounts have balances that carry over from one accounting period to the next. Temporary capital accounts start each new accounting period with a zero balance.
2. Revenue, expense, and withdrawals accounts are temporary capital accounts; they are extensions of the owner's capital account.
3. Revenue accounts temporarily substitute for the credit side of the owner's capital account.
4. For revenue accounts, the increase side is the credit side and the decrease side is the debit side. The normal balance is a credit balance.
5. Expense and withdrawals accounts temporarily substitute for the debit side of the owner's capital account.
6. For expense and withdrawals accounts, the increase side is the debit side and the decrease side is the credit side. The normal balance for expense and withdrawals accounts is a debit balance.

Review and Applications

Building Your Accounting Vocabulary

In your own words, write the definition of each of the following accounting terms. Use complete sentences for your definitions.

permanent accounts   temporary capital
revenue principle   accounts

Reviewing Your Accounting Knowledge

1. Why are temporary capital accounts used?
2. What is the difference between a temporary capital account and a permanent account? Give three examples of each type of account.
3. State briefly the rules of debit and credit for increasing and decreasing: (a) revenue accounts, (b) expense accounts, (c) withdrawals account.
4. List the normal balance side of: (a) revenue accounts, (b) expense accounts, (c) withdrawals account, (d) asset accounts, (e) liability accounts, (f) the owner's capital account.
5. Why does a revenue account serve as a temporary substitute for the credit side of the owner's capital account?
6. What effect does a revenue transaction have on owner's capital?
7. Explain why the expense accounts serve as a temporary substitute for the debit side of the owner's capital account.
8. What effect does an expense transaction have on owner's capital?
9. How is a withdrawal different from an expense? How are they the same?
10. How would you test for the equality of debits and credits?

Improving Your Analysis Skills

The basic accounting equation is a simple mathematical equation: A = L + OE. The equation can be expanded to include revenue and expenses: A = L + OE + R − E. As with any equation, the parts can be rearranged to solve for different amounts. For example, to determine the amount of liabilities when assets and owner's equity are known, the equation becomes L = A − OE. Use the basic or expanded equation to find the amounts below.

1. Assets = $22,420; liabilities = $6,408
2. Liabilities = $9,470; revenue = $14,100; expenses = $7,000; owner's equity = $15,000
3. Assets = $18,400; liabilities = $4,900; revenue = $8,500; expenses = $2,300
4. Assets = $19,840; owner's equity = $12,400
5. Revenue = $22,500; liabilities = $12,880; expenses = $8,750; owner's equity = $15,000

77

---

10. To test for the equality of debits and credits, list all accounts used by the business and their balances, using separate columns for the debit and credit balances. Add each column and compare the two totals. They should be equal.

Improving Your Analysis Skills
1. Owner's equity = $16,012
2. Assets = $31,570
3. Owner's equity = $7,300
4. Liabilities = $7,440
5. Assets = $41,630

Building Your Accounting Vocabulary

See the Glossary on pages 670-679 for definitions of these terms.

Reviewing Your Accounting Knowledge

1. Temporary capital accounts are used to record specific revenue and expense information that would not be available if all such amounts were recorded in capital.
2. A temporary capital account is an extension of owner's equity and begins each accounting period with a zero balance. Permanent accounts carry balances from one period to another. Examples of temporary accounts: Withdrawals, Fees, Advertising Expense. Examples of permanent accounts: Cash in Bank, Accounts Receivable, Accounts Payable, Capital.
3. Revenue accounts are increased by credits and decreased by debits. Expense accounts are increased by debits and decreased by credits. The withdrawals account is increased by debits and decreased by credits.
4. (a) credit, (b) debit, (c) debit, (d) debit, (e) credit, (f) credit
5. Revenue is income earned by a business. Revenue increases the owner's capital account. Recording revenue in a separate account makes these increases easier to identify and to analyze.
6. Revenues increase capital.
7. Expenses are costs of doing business. Expenses decrease owner's capital. Recording expenses in separate accounts makes these decreases easier to identify and to analyze.
8. Expenses decrease capital.
9. Expenses are costs of doing business and are used to determine net income. Withdrawals are reductions in cash or other assets by the owner for personal use. Both reduce owner's equity, are increased by debits, and have normal debit balances.

PRACTICE AND APPLY

• Concepts and Procedures

Exercise 4-1: Ch. Obj. 2

2. Accounts Receivable: Asset, debit to increase, credit to decrease, debit balance

3. Airplanes: Asset, debit to increase, credit to decrease, debit balance

4. Accounts Payable: Liability, credit to increase, debit to decrease, credit balance

5. Edward Palmer, Capital: Owner's equity, credit to increase, debit to decrease, credit balance

6. Edward Palmer, Withdrawals: Owner's equity, debit to increase, credit to decrease, debit balance

7. Flying Fees: Revenue, credit to increase, debit to decrease, credit balance

8. Advertising Expense: Expense, debit to increase, credit to decrease, debit balance

9. Food Expense: Expense, debit to increase, credit to decrease, debit balance

10. Fuel and Oil Expense: Expense, debit to increase, credit to decrease, debit balance

11. Repairs Expense: Expense, debit to increase, credit to decrease, debit balance

Exercise 4-2: Ch. Obj. 2, 3

1. Utilities Expense, Dr. / Cash in Bank, Cr.

2. Accounts Receivable, Dr. / Service Fees, Cr.

3. John Albers, Withdrawals, Dr. / Cash in Bank, Cr.

4. Advertising Expense, Dr. / Cash in Bank, Cr.

Applying Accounting Procedures

Exercise 4-1   Applying the Rules of Debit and Credit

Edward Palmer uses the following accounts in his flying service business.

Cash in Bank	Edward Palmer,	Advertising Expense
Accounts Receivable	Capital	Food Expense
Airplanes	Edward Palmer,	Fuel and Oil Expense
Accounts Payable	Withdrawals	Repairs Expense
	Flying Fees	

Instructions: Use a form similar to the one that follows. For each account,

(1) Classify the account as an asset, liability, owner's equity, revenue, or expense account.

(2) Indicate whether the increase side is a debit or a credit.

(3) Indicate whether the decrease side is a debit or a credit.

(4) Indicate whether the account has a normal debit balance or a normal credit balance.

The first account is completed as an example.

Account Title	Account Classification	Increase Side	Decrease Side	Normal Balance
Cash in Bank	Asset	Debit	Credit	Debit

Exercise 4-2   Identifying Accounts Affected by Transactions

John Albers uses the following accounts in his business.

Cash in Bank	John Albers, Capital	Advertising Expense
Accounts Receivable	John Albers,	Rent Expense
Office Equipment	Withdrawals	Utilities Expense
Accounts Payable	Service Fees	

Instructions: For each of the following transactions,

(1) Identify the two accounts affected.

(2) Indicate whether each account is debited or credited.

Transactions:

1. Paid the electric bill for the month of July.

2. Billed a customer for services provided on account.

3. John Albers took cash from the business for his personal use.

4. Issued Check 567 to pay for a recent advertisement.

Exercise 4-3   Identifying Increases and Decreases in Accounts

The following accounts are used by Roy Jenny in his business, the Easy Rider Driving School.

Cash in Bank	Accounts Payable	Advertising Expense
Accounts Receivable	Roy Jenny, Capital	Gas and Oil Expense
Office Equipment	Roy Jenny, Withdrawals	Maintenance Expense
Cars	Instruction Fees	Utilities Expense

78

Refer students to the Chapter 4 review pages in the workbook, *Chapter Reviews and Working Papers.*

Additional Reinforcement

Students who need additional practice or individualized help will benefit from the *Glencoe Accounting Electronic Study Guide* or the *Glencoe Accounting* on-line multimedia program, which provide reinforcement and reteaching for vocabulary, concepts, and procedures.

Instructions: Analyze each of the following transactions using the format shown below. Explain the debit, then the credit.

Example:
On June 11, Roy Jenny paid the office cleaning bill of $100.

a. The expense account Maintenance Expense is increased. Increases in expenses are recorded as debits.
b. The asset account Cash in Bank is decreased. Decreases in assets are recorded as credits.

Transactions:
1. On April 3, Roy Jenny withdrew $500 from his business for his own use, Check 768.
2. On April 8, the business received $1,200 cash in instruction fees from various customers.
3. On April 12, the telephone bill of $85 was paid by issuing Check 769.

Problem 4-1   Using T Accounts To Analyze Transactions

Esther Wills plans to open her own law office. She will use the following accounts.

Cash in Bank	Esther Wills, Capital	Rent Expense
Accounts Receivable	Esther Wills,	Repairs Expense
Office Equipment	Withdrawals	Utilities Expense
Accounts Payable	Legal Fees	

Instructions: For each transaction,
(1) Determine which two accounts are affected.
(2) Prepare two T accounts for the accounts identified in Instruction #1.
(3) Enter the amount of the debit and the amount of the credit in the T accounts.

Transactions:
1. On May 7, Esther Wills received a check for $1,675 for professional legal services.
2. On May 12, Esther Wills paid the monthly rent of $450 by writing Check 100.
3. On May 15, Esther Wills withdrew $250 for her personal use, Check 101.
4. On May 29, Esther Wills had the business's computer repaired at a cost of $245 and was given until next month to pay.

Problem 4-2   Analyzing Transactions into Debit and Credit Parts

Edward Palmer completed the transactions that follow soon after opening the Palmer Flying Service.

Instructions:
(1) Prepare a T account for each account listed in Exercise 4-1.
(2) Enter a balance of $15,000 in the Cash in Bank account; also enter a balance of $15,000 in the Edward Palmer, Capital account.
(3) Analyze and record each business transaction, using the appropriate T accounts. Identify each transaction by number.

79

Exercise 4-3: Ch. Obj. 2, 3
1. (a) The owner's equity account Roy Jenny, Withdrawals is increased. Increases in withdrawals are recorded as debits. (b) The asset account Cash in Bank is decreased. Decreases in assets are recorded as credits.
2. (a) The asset account Cash in Bank is increased. Increases in assets are recorded as debits. (b) The revenue account Instruction Fees is increased. Increases in revenue accounts are recorded as credits.
3. (a) The expense account Utilities Expense is increased. Increases in expenses are recorded as debits. (b) The asset account Cash in Bank is decreased. Decreases in assets are recorded as credits.

Problem 4-1: Ch. Obj. 2, 3
1. Cash in Bank, Dr. $1,675
Legal Fees, Cr. $1,675
2. Rent Expense, Dr. $450
Cash in Bank, Cr. $450
3. Esther Wills, Withdrawals, Dr. $250 / Cash in Bank, Cr. $250
4. Repairs Expense, Dr. $245
Accounts Payable, Cr. $245

Teacher Notes

_____
_____
_____
_____
_____

Problem 4-2: Ch. Obj. 2, 3

Ending balances:
Cash in Bank, $3,435
Accounts Receivable, $550
Airplanes, $12,700
Accounts Payable, $75
Edward Palmer, Capital, $15,000
Edward Palmer, Withdr., $150
Flying Fees, $2,625
Advertising Expense, $75
Food Expense, $225
Fuel and Oil Expense, $240
Repairs Expense, $325

Problem 4-3: Ch. Obj. 2, 3, 4

Ending debit balances:

Cash in Bank	$10,032
Accounts Receivable	750
Bike Equipment	3,750
M. Ritter, Withdrawals	250
Equipment Repairs Expense	123
Rent Expense	225
Utilities Expense	95
Total	$15,225

Ending credit balances:

Accounts Payable	$ 2,000
M. Ritter, Capital	12,000
Rental Fees	1,225
Total	$15,225

Problem 4-4: Ch. Obj. 2, 3, 4

Ending debit balances:

Cash in Bank	$17,387
Accounts Receivable	92
Salon Supplies	75
Equipment	2,400
J. Nash, Withdrawals	150
Rent Expense	150
Utilities Expense	125
Wages Expense	110
	$20,489

Ending credit balances:

Accounts Payable	$ 2,400
J. Nash, Capital	17,500
Styling Fees	589
	$20,489

(4) After all the transactions have been recorded, write the word "Balance" on the normal balance side of each account.

(5) Compute and record the balance for each account.

Transactions:

1. Purchased an airplane for $12,700, Check 1001.
2. Wrote Check 1002 for fuel for the airplane, $125.
3. Received $1,850 cash for charter flight services.
4. Paid $150 (Check 1003) for in-flight lunches.
5. Placed an ad in the newspaper for $75 and agreed to pay for it later.
6. Edward Palmer withdrew $150 for personal use, Check 1004.
7. Provided flight services on account, $775.
8. Paid for plane repairs by writing Check 1005 for $325.
9. Refueled the airplane at a cost of $115, Check 1006.
10. Purchased in-flight lunches for $75, Check 1007.
11. Received $225 on account from a charge customer.

Problem 4-3   Analyzing Transactions into Debit and Credit Parts

Marna Ritter operates Ritter's Cycle Rental Service. She uses the following accounts to record and summarize her business transactions.

Cash in Bank	M. Ritter, Capital	Equipment Repairs
Accounts Receivable	M. Ritter, Withdrawals	Expense
Bike Equipment	Rental Fees	Rent Expense
Accounts Payable		Utilities Expense

Instructions:

(1) Prepare a T account for each account used by the business.

(2) Analyze and record each of the following transactions using the appropriate T accounts. Identify each transaction by number.

(3) After recording all transactions, compute and record the account balance on the normal balance side of each T account.

(4) Test for the equality of debits and credits.

Transactions:

1. Marna Ritter invested $12,000 cash in her new business.
2. Bought five new touring bikes on account for $3,750.
3. Allowed a group to charge bike rental fees in the amount of $750.
4. Had three bikes repaired at a cost of $123, Check 1.
5. Wrote Check 2 to pay the electric bill of $95.
6. Received $225 for bike rental fees.
7. Paid the $225 rent for the month, Check 3.
8. Paid $1,750 toward the touring bikes bought on account, Check 4.
9. Marna Ritter withdrew $250 cash for personal use, Check 5.
10. Received bike rental fees of $250.

Problem 4-4   Analyzing Transactions

Juanita Nash owns the Hi-Style Images beauty salon. She plans to use the following accounts for recording and reporting business transactions.

80

Teacher Notes

_____

_____

_____

_____

_____

Cash in Bank
Accounts Receivable
Salon Supplies
Equipment

Accounts Payable
Juanita Nash, Capital
Juanita Nash,
Withdrawals

Styling Fees
Rent Expense
Utilities Expense
Wages Expense

Instructions:
(1) Prepare a T account for each account listed above.
(2) Analyze and record each transaction using the appropriate T accounts. Identify each transaction by number.
(3) After recording all transactions, compute a balance for each account.
(4) Test for the equality of debits and credits.

Transactions:
1. Juanita Nash invested $17,500 cash in Hi-Style Images.
2. Bought equipment on account from Salon Products, Inc., for $2,400.
3. Bought salon supplies from Beauty Aids on account for $75.
4. Paid the rent for the month of $150, Check 1.
5. Wrote Check 2 to pay a part-time hair stylist $65.
6. Sent a bill for $67 to Pines Nursing Home for hair cuts and shampoos completed for patients at the home.
7. Deposited the daily receipts from styling services, $233.
8. Paid the gas and electric bill of $125, Check 3.
9. Sent Check 4 for $75 to Beauty Aids as payment on account.
10. Ms. Nash withdrew $150 for her personal use, Check 5.
11. Paid the part-time hair stylist $45, Check 6.
12. Mary Jones, a customer, charged a $25 hair set to her account.
13. Deposited daily receipts of $264 in the bank.

CHALLENGE

PROBLEM

Problem 4-5 Completing the Accounting Equation

With the addition of temporary capital accounts, the basic accounting equation can be expanded as follows:

Assets = Liabilities + Owner's Equity − Withdrawals + Revenue − Expenses

Instructions: Using this formula, determine the missing amounts for each of the question marks below. Use the form in your workbook or plain paper. The first one is completed as an example.

	Assets	= Liabilities +	Owner's Equity	− Withdrawals +	Revenue −	Expenses
1.	$64,400	$8,200	$56,300	$ 500	$10,000	$ 9,600
2.	$22,150	525	18,800	1,200	12,100	?
3.	17,500	75	21,650	?	4,115	3,250
4.	49,450	?	47,840	1,500	20,300	17,610
5.	21,900	1,150	20,005	950	?	16,570
6.	72,640	2,790	?	10,750	67,908	39,749
7.	?	1,988	41,194	6,196	52,210	42,597
8.	50,780	1,493	64,110	6,112	?	29,986
9.	?	3,840	61,774	?	40,163	21,637

(Expenses plus withdrawals equal $27,749.)

10.	64,070	?	49,102	4,875	53,166	?

(Total owner's equity after adding revenue and subtracting expenses and withdrawals is $50,643.)

81

Problem 4-5: Ch. Obj. 2

CHALLENGE

PROBLEM

The last problem in each chapter is a challenge problem and is identified by the "maze" symbol.

1. Assets, $64,400
2. Expenses, $8,075
3. Withdrawals, $5,090
4. Liabilities, $420
5. Revenue, $18,265
6. Owner's Equity, $52,441
7. Assets, $46,599
8. Revenue, $31,213
9. Assets, $78,028; withdrawals, $6,112
10. Liabilities, $13,427; expenses, $46,750

4 ASSESS

A chapter test is available for use in assessing students' understanding of concepts in this chapter.

The testmaker software will enable you to develop tailor-made chapter, unit, semester, and final tests.

Alternative Assessment

For alternative assessment strategies, refer to *Tech Prep Strategies in Accounting.*

Use Chapter 4 test here to assess students' understanding and retention of the concepts and procedures presented in the chapter.

Have students read the ethics case given in the textbook and jot down ideas about what they would do in the situation described. Then review the five-step decision model (see page T44). Emphasize that there are no "right" or "wrong" answers to the questions in the decision model.

After students have discussed the first four steps, have them vote on which alternative they feel is best, or, if one alternative has clearly been chosen during the discussion, review students' reasoning for choosing that course of action.

You may want to have students compare their final decision with the one they wrote down after first reading the vignette. Did following the five-step model reinforce their "instinctual" decision or lead them to choose a different course of action? Help students realize that following a decision model when they confront an ethical dilemma can help them to organize their thinking and arrive at a satisfactory solution.

QUESTIONS

1. What are the ethical issues in this situation?
2. What are the alternatives?
3. Who are the affected parties?
4. How do the alternatives affect the parties?
5. What is the decision?

ANSWERS

1. Violating copyright laws and denying fair compensation to a business and to a writer of a software program.
2. To refuse to copy the software or to make the copy for the friend.
3. You, your friend, the seller of the software program, the writer—or writers—of the software program.
4. If you copy the software, you save money and your friend saves money because you each have the software without paying full price for it. This alternative costs the business selling the software, and it costs the writer of the program, who receives a share of the selling price of each software program sold. If you do not copy the software, you lose the money your friend is willing to pay you for copying the software. Your

*S*oftware Piracy: A Matter of Ethics?

Y‍ou've just bought a new integrated software program. On the disk package, a formidable license agreement in small type sets forth your rights and obligations as the licensee of this program. At the heart of the agreement is the copyright statement. Federal *copyright laws* protect literary and artistic works from unauthorized use. The Software Protection Act of 1980 allows the owner of software to make one backup copy of the original disk in case the original is damaged, lost, or doesn't work.

Your friend has a deal for you. If you let him copy your backup disks and manual, he'll pay you half of what the program originally cost you. What a break! It took you many hours at the department store to earn the money to buy it, and you certainly could use that extra money.

How much could that little transaction between friends hurt a multimillion dollar software company?

One survey estimates that for every disk that's sold, ten are stolen. The Software Publishers Association estimates that over $1 billion a year is lost to software pirates. Software development is costly. It requires talented people and expensive equipment. When consumers don't respect the company's copyright protection, the law-abiding buyer helps pay the price. To help offset the company's losses from piracy, you paid more for the program at the store. If there weren't software pirates, your software probably would have cost much less.

It's not very likely that the software company will discover this violation of trust. Software publishers haven't yet come up with a solution to stop software piracy, but consumers can. When we refuse to participate in these illegal acts and honor

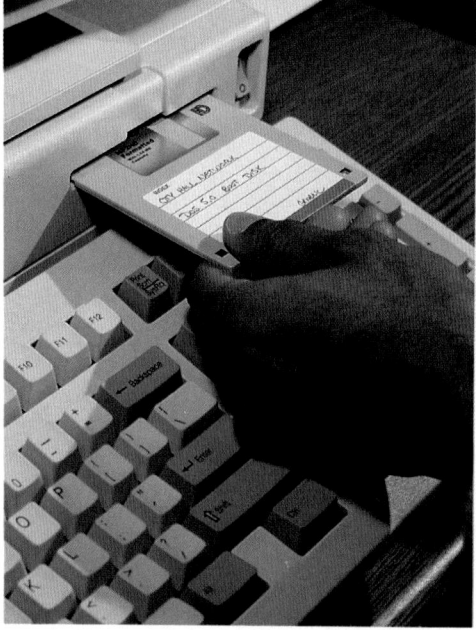

Piracy has become a serious problem for developers and sellers of software.

our purchase agreements, we demonstrate our respect for the creativity of the developers and acknowledge the investment that the company has made in bringing these innovative ideas to us.

In the end, isn't it really a question of ethics?

82

friend may also have to pay the full price of the software to obtain a copy.
5. Allow students to make their own decisions, but require them to defend the course of action they choose.

Chapter 5

RECORDING TRANSACTIONS IN A GENERAL JOURNAL

Learning Objectives

When you have completed Chapter 5, you should be able to do the following:

1. Describe the first three steps in the accounting cycle.
2. Explain why source documents are created and give several examples of source documents.
3. Explain the need for journalizing.
4. Describe the steps followed to make a general journal entry.
5. Make accurate entries for business transactions in a general journal.
6. Correct errors in general journal entries.
7. Explain the purpose and use of a chart of accounts.
8. Define the accounting terms introduced in this chapter.

In earlier chapters, you learned to use the accounting equation and T accounts to analyze business transactions. You also studied the rules of debit and credit for asset, liability, owner's equity, revenue, and expense accounts. In this chapter, you will learn how to record information about business transactions in a journal.

In this chapter, you will follow step-by-step procedures for journalizing the transactions you have analyzed in previous chapters. These procedures are very important in ensuring accurate accounting records because they reduce the chance of error. Since errors do occasionally occur, however, you will be shown a procedure for correcting them.

In this chapter, you will also learn more about the chart of accounts, a formal listing of the accounts used in a business's accounting system.

New Terms

accounting cycle
source document
invoice
receipt
memorandum
check stub
journal
journalizing
manual accounting system
computerized accounting
  system
general journal
chart of accounts
liquidity

83

INTRODUCING THE
CHAPTER

LOOKING BACK

In earlier chapters, students learned to analyze business transactions using two basic accounting tools: the accounting equation and the T account. Students are now ready to learn to record the business transactions that they have analyzed. In Chapter 5 they are introduced to their first formal accounting record, the general journal.

VOCABULARY DEVELOPMENT

Ask students to write a sentence using each of the new terms in context. Ask for volunteers to write their sentences on the board. Discuss any differences in the use of the terms. Definitions of these terms are found in the chapter and in the glossary on pages 670-679.

1 FOCUS

MAJOR CONCEPTS

- The Accounting Cycle
- The General Journal
- Journalizing Business Transactions
- Correcting Errors in Journal Entries
- Recording Transactions in a Computerized Accounting System
- The Chart of Accounts

BUSINESS CONNECTION

The McDonald's success story began in California in 1948 when two brothers named McDonald started the restaurant business. Today more than 95 billion hamburgers have been sold. In spite of fierce competition, McDonald's success continues. Regardless of how large the company has become, McDonald's restaurants worldwide must journalize daily transactions to maintain complete records of their business transactions.

2 TEACH

CONCEPT DEVELOPMENT
The Accounting Cycle

The purpose of this section is to help students understand that all businesses operate in cycles referred to as accounting periods or fiscal periods (the terms are used interchangeably). Give students examples of several different kinds of businesses and identify the fiscal period used by each. Ask students why a business may be using that particular fiscal period. For example, your school system's accounting period may run from July 1 to June 30 because state legislation requires that time period for the fiscal year.

A business's accounting period normally ends at a time when business activity is at its lowest level.

The Accounting Cycle

Accounting records are kept and then summarized for a certain period of time called a *fiscal period.* A fiscal period may be for any length of time, such as a month or even a quarter of a year. Most businesses, however, use a year as their fiscal period. The year does not have to be a calendar year; that is, from January 1 to December 31. Many businesses start their fiscal periods in months other than January. For example, many department stores have fiscal periods that begin February 1 and end January 31. Other businesses may have fiscal periods that begin July 1 and end June 30 of the following calendar year.

The fiscal period of a business is separated into activities that help the business keep its accounting records in an orderly fashion. These activities are called the **accounting cycle.** The steps in the accounting cycle are

1. Collect source documents and verify the financial information on them.
2. Analyze business transactions into their debit and credit parts.
3. Record the debit and credit parts of each business transaction in a journal.
4. Post each journal entry to the ledger accounts.
5. Prepare a trial balance.
6. Prepare a work sheet to summarize the financial information for the accounting period.
7. Prepare the financial statements.
8. Record and post the closing entries.
9. Prepare a post-closing trial balance.

Figure 5-1 Steps in the Accounting Cycle, with Steps 1, 2, and 3 Highlighted

84

UNIT 2   The Basic Accounting Cycle

The steps in the accounting cycle are shown in Figure 5-1. In this chapter, you will read about and use Steps 1, 2, and 3. Each of the remaining chapters in this unit will cover at least one more step in the accounting cycle. After studying Chapters 3 through 9, you will have completed the accounting cycle for a service business organized as a sole proprietorship. The business used in these chapters is Global Travel Agency, which you first read about in Chapter 3. Now let's look at the first step in the accounting cycle: collecting source documents and verifying the information on them.

Step 1: Collecting and Verifying Source Documents

Most business transactions take place during the daily operations of a business. When a business transaction occurs, a paper is prepared as evidence of that transaction. This paper is called a **source document.** The source documents for business transactions are sent regularly to the accounting clerk for use in keeping the business's accounting records. The accounting clerk begins the accounting cycle by collecting and verifying the source documents. The accounting clerk checks the accuracy of the documents first. One way is to verify the arithmetic on the source documents.

There are several types of source documents, which may be prepared in different ways. Some source documents are written by hand. Others may be prepared by machine or by computer. The type of source document prepared as a record of a transaction depends upon the nature of the transaction. Some commonly used source documents are (1) invoices, (2) receipts, (3) memorandums, and (4) check stubs.

An **invoice** is a form that lists specific information about a business transaction involving the buying or selling of an item. The invoice includes such information as the date of the transaction and the quantity, description, and cost of each item. For example, if Global Travel buys a new typewriter, the invoice prepared as a record of the transaction would include the information shown on the invoice in Figure 5-2 on page 86.

A **receipt** is a form prepared as a record of cash received by a business. For example, when Global Travel receives payment for a service completed for a client, a receipt is prepared to indicate the date the payment was received, the name of the person or business from whom the payment was received, and the amount of the payment. An example of a receipt is shown in Figure 5-2.

A **memorandum** is a brief message that is usually written to describe a transaction that takes place within a business. A memorandum like that shown in Figure 5-2 may also be prepared if no other source document exists for the business transaction.

A **check stub** is the part remaining in the business's checkbook after a check has been torn out. The check stub lists the same information that appears on a check: the date a check was written, the person or business to whom the check was written, and the amount of the check (see Figure 5-2). The check stub also shows the balance in the checking account before and after each check is written.

A business also receives bills for other items or services such as electricity, water, or telephones. One example is a utility bill, such as the one shown in Figure 5-2. This bill shows the charge for telephone service for the month of October.

CHAPTER 5   Recording Transactions in a General Journal   85

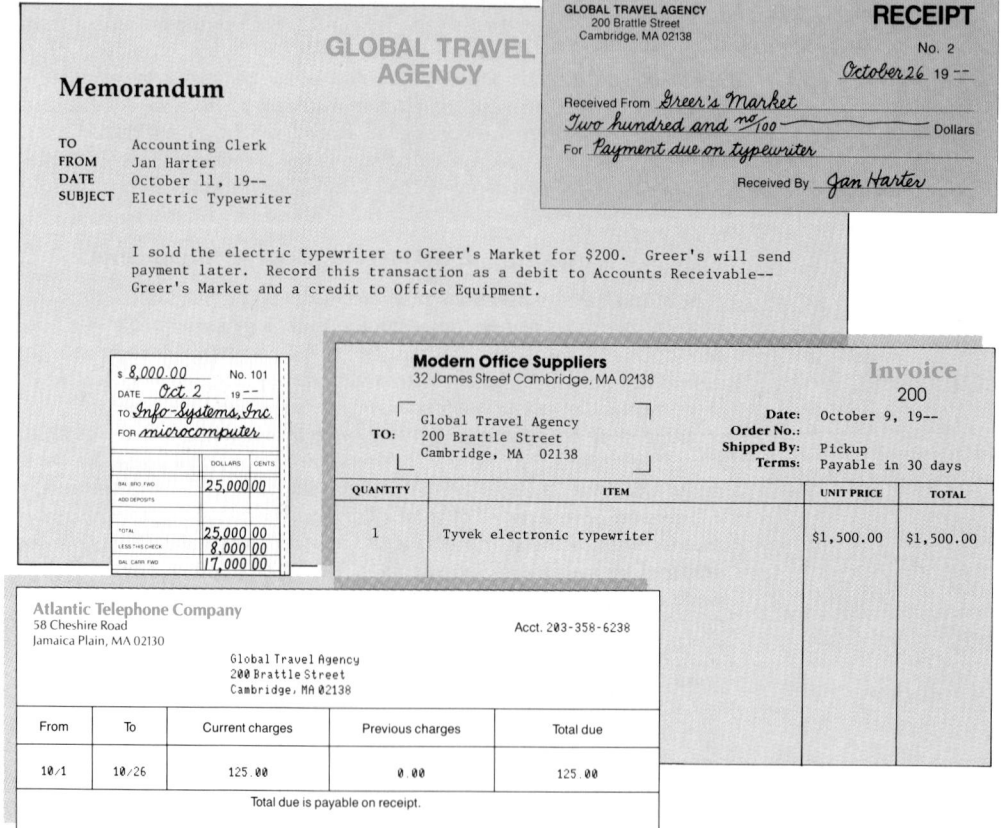

Figure 5-2   Examples of Source Documents

Step 2: Analyzing Business Transactions

After collecting and verifying source documents, the accounting clerk performs the second step in the accounting cycle. This is analyzing the information on the source documents to determine their debit and credit parts.

You have already learned how to analyze business transactions using the rules of debit and credit. When you first learned to analyze transactions, you were given a description of each transaction, such as the one that follows: Global Travel Agency bought a microcomputer for $8,000 and issued Check 101 in payment.

In real life, the accounting clerk must look at a source document to determine what has occurred during a business transaction. There is not enough space in this textbook to show you the source documents for all the transactions that you will study. As a result, you will continue to analyze descriptions of business transactions. You should remember, however, that source documents are evidence of business transactions, and they are the basis for the information recorded in the accounting system.

Step 3: Recording Business Transactions in a Journal

The third step in the accounting cycle is to record the debit and credit parts of each business transaction in a journal. A **journal** is a chronological record of a business's transactions. The process of recording these business transactions in a journal is called **journalizing.** Keeping a journal can be compared to keeping a diary in which all important events are written. The journal contains the most important information relating to a business transaction. It is the only place in which the complete details, including both the debit and credit parts of the transaction, are recorded. For this reason, the journal is often called a *record or "book" of original entry*.

Without accurate financial records, a business cannot keep track of either how well or how poorly it is doing. It cannot operate efficiently or, in the long run, profitably. A company without records, and a system for keeping them, is like a spaceship without an instrument panel and monitoring system. It cannot reach its destination if its operators receive no feedback.

Keeping accurate financial records begins with the recording of information from business transactions. The recording of such information is a part of each business's accounting system. Some businesses use a **manual accounting system** in which information is recorded by hand. Other businesses have a **computerized accounting system** in which information is recorded by entering it into a computer. Although some small businesses still use a manual accounting system, many use a computerized one. Large businesses rely almost entirely on computerized accounting systems because they must process vast amounts of financial information quickly.

Although computerized accounting systems are becoming more and more common for all businesses, understanding manual systems serves as background for understanding computerized systems. A basic procedure in a manual accounting system is the recording of daily business transactions in a journal.

The General Journal

Many kinds of journals are used in business. One of the most common is the general journal. As its name suggests, the **general journal** is an all-purpose journal in which all of a business's transactions may be recorded. The general journal you will be using throughout the accounting cycle for Global Travel, shown in Figure 5-3 on page 88, has two amount columns. The first amount column in the journal is used to record debit amounts. The second amount column is used to record credit amounts.

Each entry made in the general journal includes the following information, entered in this order:

1. The date of the transaction.
2. The title of the account debited.
3. The amount of the debit.
4. The title of the account credited.
5. The amount of the credit.
6. A brief reference to the source document for the transaction or an explanation of the entry.

Teaching Tips

■ Ask students to define "chronological."
■ In accounting, "financial or economic events" are business transactions.
■ Explain to students that "long run" refers to a time period of more than one year; "short run" refers to a time period of one year or less.

CONCEPT DEVELOPMENT
The General Journal
Recording transactions in a journal provides a chronological record of all transactions. This record begins the process of recording the financial information that is used to make management decisions and to determine whether the business is making a profit. Ask students to describe their ideas about why it is important for a business to keep accurate financial records.

Making Connections

LANGUAGE ARTS

A "journal" is sometimes called a "day-book," which is its literal meaning. The word came into Middle English from the French *journal*, meaning "daily," and was used to refer to any daily record. Ask students to think about how "journal" is related to such words as *journey* (a day's travel) and *journalism*.

Using Visuals

Refer students to Figure 5-3, which describes the information recorded in a general journal. Walk students through each part of a journal entry.

Using Visuals

 A teaching transparency illustrating the steps in recording a journal entry is available in the transparency binder accompanying Glencoe Accounting.

 ANSWERS

1. Fiscal period
2. Cycle; fiscal period
3. Source documents
4. General journal

CONCEPT DEVELOPMENT
Journalizing Business Transactions

Stress the six steps for analyzing business transactions in preparation for journalizing them. The key to understanding and learning about each type of transaction is for students to analyze financial effects using T accounts and the accounting equation. Once the effects of a transaction have been analyzed, the next step is to record those effects as a journal entry.

The preceding information must be entered for each transaction that you journalize. Look at the general journal shown in Figure 5-3 to find where each kind of information should be entered.

Figure 5-3 Two-Column General Journal

Before reading any further, complete the following activity to check your understanding of the material covering the first three steps of the accounting cycle.

Check Your Learning

Write your answers to the questions below on notebook paper.

1. A period of time into which a business separates its accounting records is called a(n) ___?___.
2. The accounting ___?___ includes all the activities that help a business keep its accounting records during its ___?___.
3. Papers prepared as records of business transactions are called ___?___.
4. An all-purpose journal in which all of a business's transactions can be recorded is the ___?___.

Compare your answers to those in the answers section. Re-read the preceding part of the chapter to find the correct answers to any questions you may have missed.

Journalizing Business Transactions

In Chapters 3 and 4, you learned a six-step method for analyzing business transactions. The steps are the answers to these questions:

1. Which accounts are affected?
2. What is the classification of each account?
3. Is each account increased or decreased?
4. Which account is debited, and for what amount?
5. Which account is credited, and for what amount?
6. What is the complete entry?

88   UNIT 2   The Basic Accounting Cycle

Continue to use these steps to determine the debit and credit parts of each journal entry. You may also want to use T accounts to help you analyze transactions. After analyzing many transactions, you will find that you need these tools less and less to determine the debit and credit parts of a journal entry.

Business Transaction 1: *On October 1, Jan Harter took $25,000 from personal savings and deposited that amount to open a business checking account in the name of Global Travel Agency, Memorandum 1.*

1. Which accounts are affected? The accounts affected are Cash in Bank and Jan Harter, Capital.
2. What is the classification of each account? Cash in Bank is an asset account, and Jan Harter, Capital is an owner's equity account.
3. Is each account increased or decreased? Both are increased.
4. Which account is debited, and for what amount?

Cash in Bank	
Dr.	Cr.
+	−
$25,000	

Using T accounts to show the effects of this transaction, we can see that Cash in Bank is debited for $25,000 since increases to asset accounts are recorded as debits.

5. Which account is credited, and for what amount?

Jan Harter, Capital	
Dr.	Cr.
−	+
	$25,000

Increases to the capital account are recorded as credits, so Jan Harter, Capital is credited for $25,000.

6. What is the complete entry? The complete entry for this transaction is shown in the general journal illustrated in Figure 5-4 on page 90. Be sure you understand how to journalize this transaction before you go on to Business Transaction 2.

Look again at the journal page shown in Figure 5-4. Notice that in the upper, right-hand corner there is a line for the page number. Journal pages are numbered in consecutive order; that is, 1, 2, 3, and so on. When you fill one page with journal entries, go on to the next page. Be sure to number each new page before you make any more journal entries.

R E M E M B E R

Six types of information must be entered in the general journal for each transaction: the date, the title of the account to be debited, the amount of the debit, the title of the account to be credited, the amount of the credit, and a reference to the source document or a brief explanation.

ACCOUNTING ISSUES

How much knowledge of financial matters should elected officials have? Colorado voters seem to think such knowledge is important. In November, 1990, after serving 10 years in the U.S. House of Representatives, Senator Hank Brown (R-Colorado) became the first accredited CPA elected to serve in the U.S. Senate. Like Brown, CPAs have much to offer in politics. Foremost, a basic understanding of accounting is valuable for managing the country's taxes and spending. Practical business experience is also valuable for balancing budgets and setting spending priorities. With accounting knowledge, you have much to offer whether you run as a candidate or work on a political campaign.

Cooperative Learning

BRAINSTORMING

Have students work in groups to list and describe the various source documents that a service business such as a hair salon would receive and generate for normal business activities (include source documents generated to order supplies). To help students gather ideas, have them ask questions at a local hair salon business.

Group responses should include the following: checks, cash receipts, credit card receipts, order forms, telephone messages, letters, shipping forms, packing slips, invoices.

Refer to the "Cooperative Learning" section of *Tech Prep Strategies in Accounting* for additional cooperative learning strategies.

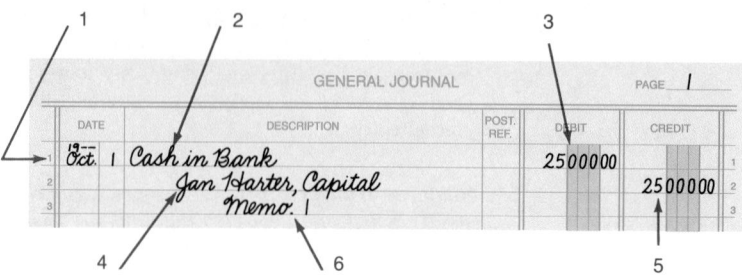

1. Enter the date of the transaction first. Note that the year and the month are written in the left side of the date section. The day is written in the right side. The year is written only once for all the journal entries on a page unless it changes. The day of each transaction is always entered, even when it is the same as the preceding transaction.

2. Write the title of the account to be debited at the extreme left of the Description column.

3. Write the amount of the debit in the Debit column. Do not use commas or decimals when entering amounts in a journal. If the amount is a whole number, enter zeroes in the cents part of the column.

4. Write the title of the account to be credited about 1/2 inch from the left edge of the Description column. Do not skip a line between the title of the account debited and the title of the account credited.

5. Write the amount of the credit in the Credit column.

6. Write the source document reference for the transaction on the line under the title of the account credited. Indent about 1 inch from the left edge of the Description column when writing the source document reference.

Figure 5-4 General Journal Entry for Business Transaction 1

Business Transaction 2: *On October 2, Global Travel Agency issued Check 101 for $8,000 to buy a microcomputer system from Info-Systems, Inc.*

1. Which accounts are affected? The accounts affected are Computer Equipment and Cash in Bank.
2. What is the classification of each account? Both are asset accounts.
3. Is each account increased or decreased? Computer Equipment is increased. Cash in Bank is decreased.
4. Which account is debited, and for what amount?

Computer Equipment	
Dr.	Cr.
+	−
$8,000	

Increases to asset accounts are recorded as debits, so Computer Equipment is debited for $8,000.

5. Which account is credited, and for what amount?

Cash in Bank	
Dr.	Cr.
+	−
	$8,000

Decreases to asset accounts are recorded as credits, so Cash in Bank is credited for $8,000.

6. What is the complete entry? The complete entry is shown in the general journal that follows. Note that there is no blank line between the journal entries.

	DATE	DESCRIPTION	POST. REF.	DEBIT	CREDIT	
1	19— Oct. 1	Cash in Bank		25 000 00		1
2		Jan Harter, Capital			25 000 00	2
3		Memo. 1				3
4	2	Computer Equipment		8 000 00		4
5		Cash in Bank			8 000 00	5
6		Check 101				6

GENERAL JOURNAL   PAGE 1

Before going on to the next transaction, complete the activity that follows to check your understanding of how to make an entry in the general journal.

Check Your Learning

Use a sheet of notebook paper to answer these questions about this transaction.

Today's date is September 14. The accounting clerk for Keeton Storage Co. is journalizing transactions. On September 12, Keeton issued Check 424 to Miami Office Supplies for the cash purchase of letterhead stationery. The amount of the check was $125.

1. Which date should be recorded in the journal entry for this transaction?
2. What is the title of the account to be debited and the amount of the debit?
3. What is the title of the account to be credited and the amount of the credit?
4. What is the source document reference or the explanation?

Compare your answers to those in the answers section. Re-read the preceding part of the chapter to find the correct answers to any questions you may have missed.

After analyzing a number of transactions, the rules of debit and credit will become second nature to you. Remember when you first learned to play a sport? You had to concentrate to remember how to do even simple actions. Learning to analyze business transactions is the same as learning anything else: the more you do it, the easier it gets.

Let's look now at the remaining transactions Global Travel completed during the month of October.

Business Transaction 3: *On October 4, Jan Harter took a $200 electric typewriter from home and invested it in the business as office equipment, Memorandum 2.*

Chapter 5

Using Visuals

Refer students to the journal entry for business transaction 2. Point out the source document references. Also, remind students not to leave a blank line between entries.

ANSWERS

1. September 12
2. Office Supplies, $125
3. Cash in Bank, $125
4. Check 424

Using Visuals

Use demonstration problem 5-1 to show students how to record an owner's additional investment in the business.

Reteaching Strategies

The debit part of a journal entry is always made first. Remind students that debit is left, and everything pertaining to the debit portion of the journal entry is recorded at the left. The name of the account to be debited is written at the left of the Description column, and the debit amount is written in the left, or Debit, amount column. Credit is right, and everything pertaining to the credit portion of the journal entry is recorded on the second line of the entry and to the right. The name of the account to be credited is indented about one-half inch to the right in the Description column, and the credit amount is written in the right, or Credit, column.

In this transaction, the owner is investing personal property in the business. The two accounts affected are Office Equipment and Jan Harter, Capital. Both accounts are increased by the transaction. The increase in office equipment is recorded as a debit to Office Equipment. The increase in owner's equity is recorded as a credit to Jan Harter, Capital. This transaction is shown in the following journal entry.

	GENERAL JOURNAL			PAGE 1
DATE	DESCRIPTION	POST. REF.	DEBIT	CREDIT
4	Office Equipment		20000	
	Jan Harter, Capital			20000
	Memo. 2			

Business Transaction 4: *On October 9, Global Travel bought a new electronic typewriter on account for $1,500 from Modern Office Suppliers, Invoice 200.*

With this transaction, Global Travel has increased its office equipment in return for money to be paid later to Modern Office Suppliers. Money owed to a creditor is recorded as an account payable. To keep the amounts owed to different creditors separate, Global Travel uses Accounts Payable followed by the creditor's name as the account title. The title of the account used to record this transaction then is Accounts Payable—Modern Office Suppliers. When making the journal entry, you may have to abbreviate the title to fit it all on one line. An acceptable abbreviation is Accts. Pay.—Modern Off. Supp. or AP—Modern Office Suppliers.

This transaction increases an asset and also increases a liability. As you recall, debits increase asset accounts and credits increase liability accounts. The journal entry for this transaction follows.

	GENERAL JOURNAL			PAGE 1
DATE	DESCRIPTION	POST. REF.	DEBIT	CREDIT
9	Office Equipment		150000	
	Accts Pay.—Modern Off. Supp.			150000
	Invoice 200			

Business Transaction 5: *On October 11, Global Travel sold the electric typewriter on account to Greer's Market for $200, Memorandum 3.*

With this transaction, Global Travel has increased one asset account and decreased another. Accounts Receivable is increased because Greer's Market now owes Global Travel $200. Increases to assets are recorded as debits, so Accounts Receivable is debited for $200. The title of the account used to record money owed by Greer's Market is Accounts Receivable—Greer's Market. This title may be abbreviated as Accts. Rec.—Greer's Market or as AR—Greer's Market to fit it on one line of the journal. The journal entry for this transaction follows.

Making Connections

AROUND THE WORLD

Twelve member nations of the European Community have joined to create a single European market called the European Economic Area. This combined market poses special difficulty for accountants, who must overcome the barriers caused by 12 separate sets of accounting rules. Accounting rules and financial statements prepared in one EEA country must be accepted in other EEA countries. U.S. companies that want to do business in this very large market must also understand the accounting rules in the EEA countries.

GENERAL JOURNAL		PAGE I	
DATE	DESCRIPTION	POST. REF.	DEBIT	CREDIT

			DEBIT	CREDIT	
13	11 Accts. Rec.–Greer's Market		2 0 0 00		13
14	Office Equipment			2 0 0 00	14
15	Memo. 3				15

Business Transaction 6: *On October 14, Global Travel mailed Check 102 for $750 as a partial payment to Modern Office Suppliers.*

This partial payment decreases the amount of money owed to Modern Office Suppliers, an account payable. Decreases to the liability account Accounts Payable are recorded as debits. Accounts Payable—Modern Office Suppliers is then debited for $750. The payment also decreases cash, so Cash in Bank is credited for $750. The complete journal entry follows.

GENERAL JOURNAL		PAGE I	
DATE	DESCRIPTION	POST. REF.	DEBIT	CREDIT

			DEBIT	CREDIT	
16	14 Accts. Pay.–Modern Off. Supp.		7 5 0 00		16
17	Cash in Bank			7 5 0 00	17
18	Check 102				18

Business Transaction 7: *On October 15, Global Travel mailed Check 103 for $550 to pay the month's rent.*

With this transaction, Global Travel increased its expenses. Increases to an expense account are recorded as debits. The account Rent Expense is debited for $550. The payment of the rent decreased the asset account Cash in Bank. Decreases to assets are recorded as credits. Cash in Bank is, therefore, credited for $550. The journal entry for this transaction follows.

GENERAL JOURNAL		PAGE I	
DATE	DESCRIPTION	POST. REF.	DEBIT	CREDIT

			DEBIT	CREDIT	
19	15 Rent Expense		5 5 0 00		19
20	Cash in Bank			5 5 0 00	20
21	Check 103				21

Business Transaction 8: *On October 16, Jan Harter bought an advertisement on account from City News for $75, Invoice 129.*

The purchase of the ad has increased the expense account Advertising Expense. An increase to an expense account is recorded as a debit. Advertising Expense is debited for $75. Buying the ad on account has also increased Global Travel's liabilities. An increase to a liability account is recorded as a credit. To keep this transaction separate from other accounts payable transactions, the account title Accounts Payable—City News is used. Accounts Payable—City News is, therefore, credited for $75. The journal entry for this transaction appears at the top of page 94.

CHAPTER 5 Recording Transactions in a General Journal **93**

GENERAL JOURNAL			PAGE		
DATE	DESCRIPTION	POST. REF.	DEBIT	CREDIT	
16	Advertising Expense		7500		22
	Accts Payable – City News			7500	23
	Invoice 129				24

Business Transaction 9: *On October 18, Global Travel completed travel plans for the Sims Corporation and received $1,200 as payment, Receipt 1.*

This transaction increases the asset account Cash in Bank. Increases to asset accounts are recorded as debits, so Cash in Bank is debited for $1,200. Fees earned for a service completed for a customer increase the revenue account Fees. Increases to a revenue account are recorded as credits, so Fees is credited for $1,200. The journal entry for this transaction follows.

GENERAL JOURNAL			PAGE		
DATE	DESCRIPTION	POST. REF.	DEBIT	CREDIT	
18	Cash in Bank		120000		25
	Fees			120000	26
	Receipt 1				27

Business Transaction 10: *On October 20, Jan Harter completed travel plans for Burton Co. She billed Burton $450 for the work, Invoice 1000.*

In this transaction, Global Travel has provided a service for money to be received in the future. The account Accounts Receivable is thus increased. The asset account Accounts Receivable—Burton Co. is debited for $450. Revenue for Global Travel has also increased, so the revenue account Fees is credited for $450. The journal entry for this transaction follows.

GENERAL JOURNAL			PAGE		
DATE	DESCRIPTION	POST. REF.	DEBIT	CREDIT	
20	Accts. Receivable–Burton Company		45000		28
	Fees			45000	29
	Invoice 1000				30

Business Transaction 11: *On October 26, Global Travel received and deposited a check for $200 from Greer's Market, Receipt 2.*

The deposit of the check in the business's checking account increases the asset account Cash in Bank. Asset accounts are increased by debits, so Cash in Bank is debited for $200. The receipt of money owed to Global Travel decreases the asset account Accounts Receivable. Accounts Receivable—Greer's Market is, therefore, credited for $200. The complete journal entry follows.

GENERAL JOURNAL			PAGE 1	
DATE	DESCRIPTION	POST. REF.	DEBIT	CREDIT
31 26	*Cash in Bank*		2 0 0 00	
32	*Accts. Rec. – Greer's Market*			2 0 0 00
33	*Receipt 2*			

Business Transaction 12: *On October 28, Global Travel paid a $125 telephone bill with Check 104.*

The payment of the telephone bill increases the expense account Utilities Expense. Expense accounts are increased by debits, so Utilities Expense is debited for $125. This payment decreases Global Travel's cash, so Cash in Bank is decreased by a credit of $125. The complete journal entry follows.

GENERAL JOURNAL			PAGE 1	
DATE	DESCRIPTION	POST. REF.	DEBIT	CREDIT
34 28	*Utilities Expense*		1 25 00	
35	*Cash in Bank*			1 25 00
36	*Check 104*			

R E M E M B E R

Every business transaction requires a debit and a credit entry. In a general journal, the debit part of the entry is made first. The credit part of the entry is entered next, and then the source document reference is written.

Business Transaction 13: *On October 29, Jan Harter wrote Check 105 for $450 to have the office repainted.*

The cost of having the office repainted is an expense to Global Travel. The expense account Maintenance Expense is thus increased with a debit of $450. The payment of the expense decreases the amount of cash, so Cash in Bank is credited for $450. The complete journal entry follows.

GENERAL JOURNAL			PAGE 2	
DATE	DESCRIPTION	POST. REF.	DEBIT	CREDIT
1 19-- Oct. 29	*Maintenance Expense*		4 50 00	
2	*Cash in Bank*			4 50 00
3	*Check 105*			

Business Transaction 14: *On October 31, Jan Harter withdrew $400 cash for her personal use by writing Check 106.*

In this transaction, the owner is taking an asset out of the business (cash) for personal use. The withdrawals account is used to record such amounts.

Critical Thinking

Mario Sanchez keeps the accounting records for his dry-cleaning business. He records all transactions in a general journal but often neglects to include a reference for each entry. He says it takes too long and that he cannot be bothered. Recently Mario received an invoice for a purchase made on September 14. Mario believes the invoice amount is incorrect. How would a journal entry reference help Mario verify the invoice amount quickly and easily?

(Answer: Mario could locate the transaction in the journal by its date, where he would find the purchase order number in the reference. Then he could quickly locate the purchase order and compare the items listed on the purchase order with those listed on the invoice.)

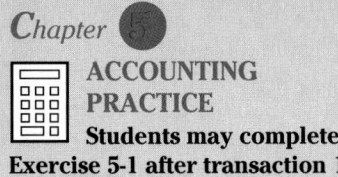
CONCEPT DEVELOPMENT

Correcting Errors in Journal Entries

Since errors are bound to happen, procedures have been developed for fixing them in the accounting records. These procedures maintain the audit trail that allows an outside reviewer of the accounting records to trace financial information from the source documents through the financial reports. Emphasize that errors should not be erased. Walk students through the two types of corrections shown in the journal entries.

CONCEPT DEVELOPMENT

Recording Transactions in a Computerized Accounting System

Computerized accounting systems vary according to the software used. Many software programs are available, but they all have in common a means of journalizing the financial information from business transactions. More sophisticated systems may be capable of entering some information directly from the point of sale, e.g., computerized cash registers that record sales directly into the accounting records.

The withdrawals account is increased by debits, so Jan Harter, Withdrawals is debited for $400. The business's cash is decreased by the withdrawal, so Cash in Bank is credited for $400. The complete journal entry follows.

	GENERAL JOURNAL			PAGE 2
DATE	DESCRIPTION	POST. REF.	DEBIT	CREDIT
31	Jan Harter, Withdrawals		400 00	
	Cash in Bank			400 00
	Check 106			

Correcting Errors in Journal Entries

Occasionally, errors in journalizing do occur. When an error is discovered, it must be corrected. Note, however, that *an error should never be erased.* An erasure looks suspicious. It might be seen as an attempt to cover up a mistake or, worse, to cheat or to change the accounting records.

If you find an error in a journal entry shortly after journalizing, the error is easy to correct. Use a ruler to draw a horizontal line through the entire incorrect item and write the correct information above the crossed-out error. A correction for an incorrect amount is shown in the journal below.

	GENERAL JOURNAL			PAGE 1
DATE	DESCRIPTION	POST. REF.	DEBIT	CREDIT
19-- Oct. 1	Cash in Bank		~~25 000 00~~ 52 000 00	
	Jan Harter, Capital			~~25 000 00~~ 52 000 00
	Memo. 1			

A correction for an incorrect account title is shown below.

	GENERAL JOURNAL			PAGE 1
DATE	DESCRIPTION	POST. REF.	DEBIT	CREDIT
19-- Oct. 1	Cash in Bank ~~Office Equipment~~		25 000 00	
	Jan Harter, Capital			25 000 00
	Memo. 1			

Recording Transactions in a Computerized Accounting System

Journalizing business transactions is basically the same whether a business uses a manual accounting system or a computerized accounting system. A journal entry recorded in a computer contains the same six types of information: the date, the title of the account debited, the debit amount, the title of the account credited, the credit amount, and the source document reference or explanation of the transaction. Figure 5-5 shows how Global Travel Agency's business transactions would appear in a computerized accounting system.

```
                    GENERAL JOURNAL                      Page   1

        DATE                  DESCRIPTION              DEBIT     CREDIT

        19XX
        Oct.  1  Cash in Bank                        25000.00
                    Jan Harter. Capital                         25000.00
                       Memo. 1
              2  Computer Equipment                   8000.00
                    Cash in Bank                                 8000.00
                       Check 101
              4  Office Equipment                      200.00
                    Jan Harter. Capital                           200.00
                       Memo. 2
              9  Office Equipment                     1500.00
                    Accts. Pay.--Modern Off. Supp.              1500.00
                       Invoice 200
             11  Accts. Rec.--Greer's Market           200.00
                    Office Equipment                             200.00
                       Memo. 3
             14  Accts. Pay.--Modern Off. Supp.        750.00
                    Cash in Bank                                  750.00
                       Check 102
             15  Rent Expense                          550.00
                    Cash in Bank                                  550.00
                       Check 103
             16  Advertising Expense                    75.00
                    Accts. Pay.--City News                         75.00
                       Invoice 129
             18  Cash in Bank                          1200.00
                    Fees                                          1200.00
                       Receipt 1
             20  Accts. Rec.--Burton Company           450.00
                    Fees                                           450.00
                       Invoice 1000
             26  Cash in Bank                           200.00
                    Accts. Rec.--Greer's Market                   200.00
                       Receipt 2
             28  Utilities Expense                      125.00
                    Cash in Bank                                   125.00
                       Check 104
             29  Maintenance Expense                    450.00
                    Cash in Bank                                   450.00
                       Check 105
             31  Jan Harter. Withdrawals                400.00
                    Cash in Bank                                   400.00
                       Check 106
```

Figure 5-5 General Journal Entries in a Computerized Accounting System

Check Your Learning

Use Figure 5-5 to answer the following questions. Write your answers on a sheet of notebook paper.

1. What account was debited in the October 16 transaction?
2. How many entries affected the Cash in Bank account during October?
3. What was the source document for the October 4 transaction?
4. On what date was a check written to pay the monthly rent?
5. How many entries affected the Fees account during October?
6. Describe the transaction recorded on October 20.

Compare your answers to those in the answers section.

COMPUTERS IN ACCOUNTING

A classic problem for traveling salespeople is sending in orders accurately and quickly for processing. Traditionally, the source documents for sales orders have been created with paper and pen or a typewriter, but today's salesperson may have the option of transferring the order with the use of a laptop computer. However, keyboarding errors can delay the processing of the order unnecessarily. Mary Kay Cosmetics, Inc., has found a solution to the problem. Sales representatives can now use a handheld computer that scans in bar codes from a preprinted sheet. Not only can the product number and price be scanned, but the customer name and address and simple commands can also be captured. Orders are processed quickly and accurately, eliminating unnecessary delays.

ANSWERS

1. Advertising Expense
2. 9
3. Memorandum 2
4. October 15
5. 2
6. Global Travel completed services for Burton Company and billed them $450, Invoice 1000.

Reteaching Strategies

Regardless of whether transactions are journalized manually or in a computerized system, the transactions are first recorded in a journal. The journal contains complete information about each of the daily transactions of the business in the order that they occur. If no journal was maintained and transactions were recorded directly in the ledger accounts, there would be no chronological listing of all transactions. It would also be difficult to locate complete information about a specific transaction. To do so, you would need to search through each ledger account to find the debit and credit entries related to that transaction.

CONCEPT DEVELOPMENT
The Chart of Accounts

Emphasize that the chart of accounts is simply a listing of all the accounts of a business. In a very small business having few accounts, the chart of accounts may be listed on one page and placed in the front of the ledger. In a large business having hundreds of accounts, the chart of accounts is usually maintained in its own folder (or file).

Remind students that accounts summarize actual transactions (business events). Asset accounts exist only as assets exist, liability accounts reflect debts, expense accounts reflect how assets were used, and so on.

You may want to tell students that the balance sheet accounts present a picture of what the business owns and owes and who has claims to the assets. The income statement accounts tell how the financial position of the business has changed because of operations.

Teaching Tips

■ Emphasize that the chart of accounts is listed two ways. First, accounts are listed by major classification: Assets, Liabilities, Owner's Equity, Revenue, and Expenses. This is the same order as accounts are located in the ledger. Second, accounts are listed by account number. Assets are listed according to their liquidity, or how easily they can be converted into cash. Other accounts are generally listed in alphabetical order.

At the touch of a button, an accounting worker can obtain printed copies of journal transactions.

The Chart of Accounts

In Chapter 3, you were shown a list of accounts used by Global Travel Agency. An "official" list of all the accounts used for journalizing a business's transactions is called a **chart of accounts.** Look at the chart of accounts in Figure 5-6. As you can see, each account is listed in the chart of accounts first by classification and then by account number.

You will also see in the chart of accounts an account you have not yet used, the Income Summary account. This account is used only at the end of the fiscal period when the balances in the temporary capital accounts are transferred to the owner's capital account. This process will be explained in detail in Chapter 9.

The Order of Accounts

In accounting, it is traditional to list accounts in the chart of accounts according to certain rules. Asset accounts are listed according to their liquidity. **Liquidity** refers to the ease with which an asset can be converted to cash. The accounts that can be most easily converted to cash are listed first. In the chart of accounts, Cash in Bank is the most "liquid" asset, so it is listed first. Since it is assumed that money owed to the business—accounts receivable—will soon be paid, Accounts Receivable accounts are listed next. The other asset accounts are then listed according to the next easiest to convert to cash, and so on. The accounts within each of the remaining classifications are listed in alphabetical order.

The Numbering of Accounts

An account number identifies an account much as a Dewey Decimal number identifies the location of a library book or a ZIP Code identifies the location of an address. Account numbers may have two, three, four, or more

Global Travel Agency
Chart of Accounts

ASSETS (100-199)
101   Cash in Bank
105   Accounts Receivable—Burton Co.
110   Accounts Receivable—Greer's Market
120   Computer Equipment
130   Office Equipment

LIABILITIES (200-299)
201   Accounts Payable—City News
205   Accounts Payable—Modern Office Suppliers

OWNER'S EQUITY (300-399)
301   Jan Harter, Capital
305   Jan Harter, Withdrawals
310   Income Summary

REVENUE (400-499)
401   Fees

EXPENSES (500-599)
501   Advertising Expense
510   Maintenance Expense
520   Rent Expense
530   Utilities Expense

Figure 5-6 Global Travel Agency's Chart of Accounts

digits. The number of digits used varies with the needs of the business. In this textbook, we will use three-digit numbers for accounts.

Think of each account number as a code. Each digit in the code has a special meaning. The first digit in an account number tells you the classification of an account. Asset accounts begin with the number 1; liability accounts, 2; owner's equity accounts, 3; revenue accounts, 4; and expense accounts, 5. The accounts are "filed" according to their classification. That is, the asset accounts appear first, the liability accounts appear second, and so on.

The second and third digits in the account number tell you the position of an account within its classification. For example, in Global Travel's chart of accounts, Cash in Bank has the number 101. The "01" tells you that the Cash in Bank account is the first asset account.

In an accounting system using three-digit account numbers, there can be up to ninety-nine accounts within each classification.

Assets	100-199
Liabilities	200-299
Owner's Equity	300-399
Revenue	400-499
Expenses	500-599

Look again at the account numbers in the chart of accounts for Global Travel (Figure 5-6). The account numbers are not consecutive. The "gap" between numbers allows a business to add other accounts as needed and still keep all the accounts properly ordered. Now that you know how accounts are numbered and organized, do the following activity.

ANSWERS

1. (a) assets; (b) assets; (c) owner's equity; (d) expenses; (e) revenue; (f) liabilities; (g) expenses
2. (a) Cash in Bank; (b) Accounts Receivable—Martinez Company; (c) Accounts Payable—Podaski Co.; (d) B. Watson, Capital; (e) Membership Fees; (f) Maintenance Expense; (g) Miscellaneous Expense
3. (a) 1; (b) 1; (c) 3; (d) 5; (e) 4; (f) 2; (g) 5

ACCOUNTING PRACTICE

Students may complete Exercise 5-3 at this point.

3 CLOSE

CHAPTER SUMMARY

This summary enumerates the key information in the chapter. It is a useful tool for reinforcement and review.

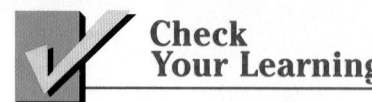

Check Your Learning

Write your answers to each of these questions on notebook paper.

1. What is the classification of each of the following accounts?
   a. Accounts Receivable—Martinez Company
   b. Cash in Bank
   c. B. Watson, Capital
   d. Miscellaneous Expense
   e. Membership Fees
   f. Accounts Payable—Podaski Co.
   g. Maintenance Expense
2. List the above accounts in the order in which they would be listed on a chart of accounts.
3. For each of the accounts in #1, list the first digit in the account number.

Compare your answers to those in the answers section. Re-read the preceding part of the chapter to find the correct answers to any questions you may have missed.

Summary of Key Points

1. Each business keeps its accounting records for a certain period of time called a fiscal period. A fiscal period can be any length of time, but most businesses use a year as their fiscal period.
2. The activities involved in keeping accounting records during a fiscal period make up the accounting cycle for a business.
3. The first step in the accounting cycle is to collect and verify source documents. Source documents are business papers prepared as evidence of business transactions.
4. The second step in the accounting cycle is to analyze the business transactions into their debit and credit parts.
5. Entering information from a business transaction in a journal is the third step in the accounting cycle. Each journal entry contains the date of the transaction, the title of the account debited, the amount of the debit, the title of the account credited, the amount of the credit, and a source document reference or brief explanation of the transaction.
6. If an error is made in a journal entry, a correction must be made. An account title or an amount is often the part of the journal entry that is incorrect. To correct either of these errors, use a ruler to draw a line through the incorrect part of the entry. Then write the correct information above the line.
7. Each business has a chart of accounts listing the accounts used in its accounting system by classification, account number, and account title.
8. Asset accounts are listed on the chart of accounts in the order of liquidity. Liquidity is the ease with which an asset can be converted to cash. The accounts in the other classifications are listed in alphabetical order.

Reteaching Strategies

To help students see the advantages of allowing gaps between account numbers, ask them to add the following accounts to the chart of accounts illustrated in Figure 5-6. Have students assign account numbers.

Mortgage Payable
Office Furniture
Postage Expense
Accounts Receivable—Sanders & Sons
Office Building

(Answers: Typical account numbers are: Mortgage Payable, 210; Office Furniture, 125; Postage Expense, 515; Accounts Receivable—Sanders & Sons, 115; Office Building, 140.)

Use Problem 5A in the Additional Problems section (p. 633) as an in-class exercise to review journalizing.

Review and Applications

Building Your Accounting Vocabulary

In your own words, write the definition of each of the following accounting terms. Use complete sentences for your definitions.

accounting cycle
chart of accounts
check stub
computerized
  accounting system

general journal
invoice
journal
journalizing
liquidity

manual accounting
  system
memorandum
receipt
source document

Reviewing Your Accounting Knowledge

1. What is meant by the term "fiscal period"?
2. List the nine steps of the accounting cycle.
3. What is the purpose of a source document?
4. List four source documents and explain when each is used.
5. Why is a journal often called a record or book of original entry?
6. Why is it important for businesses to keep accurate financial records?
7. How are the two amount columns of the general journal used to record dollar amounts?
8. What information is included in each general journal entry?
9. What procedure is used for correcting an error in a journal entry?
10. What two rules are followed in listing accounts in the chart of accounts?
11. What is the meaning of each digit in an account number?

Improving Your Decision-Making Skills

Miguel Ortega is planning to start his own bicycle repair shop, using the garage of his home as his place of business. Miguel has saved $7,000 to buy tools and equipment and get his business started. He also knows that he should have an accounting system for his new business. He has asked for your help in planning the accounting system. Can you suggest some titles for the accounts that Miguel will need in his accounting system?

Applying Accounting Procedures

Exercise 5-1 Analyzing Business Transactions

Patti Fair recently started a day care center. She uses the following accounts to record business transactions.

Cash in Bank
Accounts Receivable — Tiny Tots Nursery
Office Furniture
Delivery Van
Accounts Payable — Acme Truck Service
Patti Fair, Capital

Patti Fair, Withdrawals
Day Care Fees
Rent Expense
Utilities Expense
Van Expense

101

CHAPTER
REVIEW/ACTIVITIES

PRACTICE AND APPLY

- Language Development
- Comprehension and Retention
- Basic Skills

Building Your Accounting Vocabulary
See the Glossary on pages 670-679 for definitions.

Reviewing Your Accounting Knowledge

1. Time period covered by accounting records.
2. (a) Collect source documents and verify financial information. (b) Analyze business transactions. (c) Journalize transactions. (d) Post to ledger accounts. (e) Prepare a trial balance. (f) Prepare a work sheet. (g) Prepare financial statements. (h) Record closing entries. (i) Prepare a post-closing trial balance.
3. A source document is evidence that a business transaction occurred.
4. Four common source documents are invoices, receipts, memorandums, and check stubs. Invoices reflect the buying or selling of an item. Receipts record cash received by a business. Memorandums describe transactions that take place within a business. Check stubs record cash payments.
5. A journal is the only place in which complete details of a transaction are recorded.
6. Businesses need to keep accurate financial records so that they know how well they are doing.
7. The first amount column is used to record debit amounts; the second is used to record credit amounts.
8. The date of the transaction, the title of the account debited, the amount of the debit, the title of the account credited, the amount of the credit, and a reference to the source document or description of the entry.
9. Draw a horizontal line through the entire incorrect item and write the correct information above the crossed-out error.
10. Asset accounts are listed by liquidity; other accounts are generally listed alphabetically.
11. The first digit tells classification; the second and third digits tell position within the ledger.

Improving Your Decision-Making Skills
Miguel will need these accounts for his bicycle repair shop.

Assets	Liabilities	Owner's Equity	Revenue
Cash in Bank	Accounts Payable	Miguel Ortega, Capital	Repair Fees
Accounts Receivable		Miguel Ortega,	
Tools and Equipment		Withdrawals	
Bicycle Parts			

Chapter 5

PRACTICE AND APPLY

• Concepts and Procedures

Exercise 5-1: Ch. Obj. 1

2. Utilities Exp., Expense, Increase, Dr.; Cash in Bank, Asset, Decrease, Cr.
3. Cash in Bank, Asset, Increase, Dr.; Day Care Fees, Revenue, Increase, Cr.
4. Patti Fair, Withdr., Owner's Equity, Increase, Dr.; Cash in Bank, Asset, Decrease, Cr.
5. AR—Tiny Tots Nursery, Asset, Increase, Dr.; Day Care Fees, Revenue, Increase, Cr.
6. Office Furniture, Asset, Increase, Dr.; Patti Fair, Capital, Owner's Equity, Increase, Cr.

Exercise 5-2: Ch. Obj. 6

1. Cross out "Store" and write "Office" above it.
2. Cross out 3,000.00 and write 300.00 above it.

Exercise 5-3: Ch. Obj. 7

2. 201
3. 301
4. 401
5. 501
6. 305
7. 105
8. 510
9. 110
10. 205
11. 520
12. 120

Instructions: Use a form similar to the one that follows. For each transaction,

(1) Determine which accounts are affected.
(2) Classify each account.
(3) Determine whether the accounts are being increased or decreased.
(4) Indicate which account is debited and which account is credited in the general journal entry. The first transaction is completed as an example.

Trans.	Account Title	Account Classification	Account		General Journal	
			Increase	Decrease	Debit	Credit
1	Delivery Van	Asset	✔		✔	
	Cash in Bank	Asset		✔		✔

Transactions:

1. Bought a delivery van for cash.
2. Paid the telephone bill for the month.
3. Received cash from customers for day care services.
4. Patti Fair withdrew cash from the business for personal use.
5. Billed Tiny Tots Nursery for services provided.
6. Patti Fair invested a desk and chair in the business.

Exercise 5-2 Correcting Errors in Journal Entries

After journalizing several business transactions, the accounting clerk for Blake's discovered that errors had been made.

Instructions: Use the following information to correct the general journal transactions illustrated in the working papers accompanying this textbook.

1. On July 2, the debit should have been made to Office Supplies.
2. The amounts of the July 3 transaction should have been $300.

Exercise 5-3 Numbering Accounts

The list that follows describes the location of accounts used by Fit-Right Shoe Repairs.

Instructions: Use a form similar to the one that follows. For each account,
(1) Write the account description.
(2) Indicate an account number that would probably be assigned to the account. The first account is completed as an example.

Location of Account	Account Number
1. The first asset account	101

1. The first asset account
2. The first liability account
3. The owner's capital account
4. The first revenue account
5. The first expense account
6. The owner's withdrawals account

Refer students to the Chapter 5 review pages in the workbook, *Chapter Reviews and Working Papers.*

Additional Reinforcement

Students who need additional practice or individualized help will benefit from the *Glencoe Accounting Electronic Study Guide* or the *Glencoe Accounting* on-line multimedia program, which provide reinforcement and reteaching for vocabulary, concepts, and procedures.

7. The second asset account
8. The second expense account
9. The third asset account
10. The second liability account
11. The third expense account
12. The fourth asset account

COMPUTER **Problem 5-1   Preparing a Chart of Accounts**

PROBLEM

    The accountant for the Northwood Insurance Agency recommends the following accounts be used in recording transactions for the company.

210	Accounts Payable—BMI, Inc.	510	Rent Expense
105	Office Supplies	401	Commissions
501	Advertising Expense	110	Office Equipment
305	William Bair, Withdrawals	215	Accounts Payable—Fleming Co.
101	Cash in Bank	505	Office Expense
120	Office Furniture	301	William Bair, Capital
310	Income Summary		

Instructions: Prepare a chart of accounts for the Northwood Insurance Agency. Refer to Figure 5-6 on page 99 as an example.
(1) Write the heading, including the company name and the title "Chart of Accounts."
(2) List the assets including each account number and account title.
(3) List the liabilities including each account number and title.
(4) List the owner's equity accounts including the account number and title.
(5) List the revenue account by account number and title.
(6) List the expenses with each account number and title.

Problem 5-2   Recording General Journal Transactions

    Dan Decaro, an architect, owns and operates an architectural firm called Decaro and Co., Architects. The following accounts are needed to journalize the business's transactions.

Cash in Bank	Dan Decaro, Withdrawals
Accounts Receivable—Modern Builders	Professional Fees
Office Furniture	Equipment Rental Expense
Office Equipment	Salary Expense
Accounts Payable—Office Suppliers	Utilities Expense
Dan Decaro, Capital	

Instructions: Record the transactions that follow on page 1 of a general journal. For each transaction,
(1) Enter the date. Use the current year.
(2) Enter the title of the account debited.
(3) Enter the amount of the debit.
(4) Enter the title of the account credited.
(5) Enter the amount of the credit.
(6) Enter a source document reference.

Transactions:

Apr. 1 Wrote Check 410 for the secretary's salary, $270.
      3 Bought a $900 desk on account from Office Suppliers, Invoice 320.
      5 Received $500 for preparing house plans for a client, Receipt 10.

103

Problem 5-1: Ch. Obj. 7

COMPUTER **This computer image identifies a problem that students may com-**

PROBLEM **plete using the** *Glencoe Accounting, General Ledger* **software.**

Assets
101 Cash in Bank
105 Office Supplies
110 Office Equipment
120 Office Furniture

Liabilities
210 Accts. Pay.—BMI, Inc.
215 Accts. Pay.—Fleming Co.

Owner's Equity
301 William Blair, Capital
305 William Blair, Withdrawals
310 Income Summary

Revenue
401 Commissions

Expenses
501 Advertising Expense
505 Office Expense
510 Rent Expense

Problem 5-2: Ch. Obj. 4, 5

Apr.
1 Salary Exp. Dr., Cash in Bank Cr.
3 Off. Furn. Dr., AP—Office Suppliers Cr.
5 Cash in Bank Dr., Prof. Fees Cr.
7 Utilities Exp. Dr., Cash in Bank Cr.
11 AR—Modern Bldrs. Dr., Prof. Fees Cr.
12 Dan Decaro, Withdr. Dr., Cash in Bank Cr.
14 Off. Equip. Dr., Cash in Bank Cr.
16 AP—Office Suppliers Dr., Cash in Bank Cr.
25 Cash in Bank Dr., AR—Modern Bldrs. Cr.
30 Equip. Rental Exp. Dr., Cash in Bank Cr.

Teacher Notes

Problem 5-3: Ch. Obj. 4, 5

SPREADSHEET PROBLEM

Problem 5-3 can be completed using *Spreadsheet Applications*, the spreadsheet software that accompanies *Glencoe Accounting*.

June
1 Cash in Bank Dr., Ellen Day, Cap. Cr.
5 Computer Equip. Dr., AP—Star Systems Cr.
8 Cash in Bank Dr., Service Fees Cr.
10 Adv. Exp. Dr., Cash in Bank Cr.
13 Ellen Day, Withdr. Dr., Cash in Bank Cr.
17 AR—Connare Co. Dr., Service Fees Cr.
18 AP—Star Systems Dr., Cash in Bank Cr.
20 Off. Equip. Dr., Ellen Day, Cap. Cr.
22 Rent Exp. Dr., Cash in Bank Cr.
24 AP—Star Systems Dr., Cash in Bank Cr.
28 Cash in Bank Dr., AR—Connare Co. Cr.

Problem 5-4: Ch. Obj. 4, 5

COMPUTER PROBLEM

This computer image identifies a problem that students may complete using the *Glencoe Accounting, General Ledger* software.

Account numbers have been provided for Problem 5-4 so that it may be completed on the microcomputer.

Mar.
2 Cash in Bank Dr., Fees Cr.
3 Off. Furn. & Equip. Dr., Frank Palmer, Cap. Cr.
5 AR—Lisa Logan Dr., Fees Cr.
9 Salaries Exp. Dr., Cash in Bank Cr.
11 Frank Palmer, Withdr. Dr., Cash in Bank Cr.
14 Computer Equip. Dr., AP—Comp. Syst., Inc., Cr.
16 Rent Exp. Dr., Cash in Bank Cr.
18 Maint. Exp. Dr., Cash in Bank Cr.
21 Cash in Bank Dr., Fees Cr.
25 Util. Exp. Dr., Cash in Bank Cr.
28 Computer Equip. Dr., AP—Premier Proc. Cr.
31 Cash in Bank Dr., AR—Lisa Logan Cr.

Apr. 7 Wrote Check 411 to pay the electric bill of $110.
11 Billed a client, Modern Builders, $1,700 for drawing up office plans, Invoice 462.
12 Dan Decaro withdrew $325 for personal use, Check 412.
14 Bought a desk calculator from Dante Business Equipment Co. for $300, Check 413.
16 Wrote Check 414 for $450 to Office Suppliers in partial payment of the amount owed.
25 Received $850 from Modern Builders on account, Receipt 11.
30 Paid Office Equipment Leasing Co. $75 for the rental of an electronic typewriter, Check 415.

SPREADSHEET PROBLEM

Problem 5-3 Recording General Journal Transactions

Ellen Day operates Phoenix Computer Center, which provides computer services to small businesses. The following accounts are used to record Phoenix Computer Center's business transactions.

Cash in Bank	Ellen Day, Capital
Accounts Receivable—Connare Co.	Ellen Day, Withdrawals
Computer Equipment	Service Fees
Office Equipment	Advertising Expense
Accounts Payable—Star Systems	Rent Expense

Instructions: Record the transactions that follow on page 1 of a general journal.

June 1 Ellen Day invested $12,000 in the business, Memorandum 1.
5 Purchased $5,000 worth of computer equipment from Star Systems on account, Invoice 1632.
8 Received $1,600 for computer services completed for a customer, Receipt 101.
10 Paid the *Village Bulletin* $75 for running an ad, Check 101.
13 Ellen Day withdrew $300 for personal use, Check 102.
17 Billed the Connare Co. $700 for computer services, Invoice 102.
18 Paid Star Systems $2,500 as part payment on account, Check 103.
20 Ellen Day invested an electric typewriter valued at $350 in the business, Memorandum 2.
22 Wrote Check 104 for $600 to Shadyside Realty for the rent.
24 Paid Star Systems the remaining $2,500 owed, Check 105.
28 Received a $700 check from Connare Co. in full payment of its account, Receipt 102.

COMPUTER PROBLEM

Problem 5-4 Recording General Journal Transactions

Frank Palmer, a certified public accountant, owns and operates a public accounting office called Palmer Associates, CPAs. The following accounts are used to journalize the business's transactions.

101	Cash in Bank	301	Frank Palmer, Capital
110	Accounts Receivable—Lisa Logan	305	Frank Palmer, Withdrawals
120	Computer Equipment	401	Fees
130	Office Furniture & Equipment	505	Maintenance Expense
210	Accounts Payable—Comp Systems, Inc.	545	Rent Expense
220	Accounts Payable—Premier Processors	570	Salaries Expense
		580	Utilities Expense

104

Instructions: Record the following transactions on general journal page 7.

Mar. 2 Received $125 for preparing a client's tax return, Receipt 300.

3 Frank Palmer invested a desk, chair, and lamp, valued at $270, in the business, Memorandum 63.

5 Completed accounting work for Lisa Logan and billed her $1,600, Invoice A12.

9 Wrote Check 711 for $150 for the secretary's salary.

11 Frank Palmer withdrew $380 for personal use, Check 712.

14 Purchased a microcomputer, monitor, and printer for $2,600 from Comp Systems, Inc., on account, Invoice 911.

16 Paid the monthly rent of $400 by issuing Check 713.

18 Wrote Check 714 to Leone & Sons for painting the office, $290.

21 Received $3,600 for completing an audit for a client, Receipt 301.

25 Paid the $70 electric bill, Check 715.

28 Purchased on credit an additional disk drive for the computer from Premier Processors for $540, Invoice C457.

31 Received a check from Lisa Logan for $1,600 to apply on her account, Receipt 302.

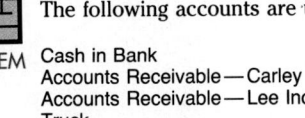

CHALLENGE

PROBLEM

Problem 5-5   Recording General Journal Transactions

Doug Hawk opened Hawk's Heating and Air Conditioning on November 1. The following accounts are used to record the business's transactions.

Cash in Bank	Accounts Payable—Lock-On Tool Co.
Accounts Receivable—Carley Cole	Doug Hawk, Capital
Accounts Receivable—Lee Industries	Doug Hawk, Withdrawals
Truck	Repair Revenue
Tools	Rent Expense
Office Equipment	Utilities Expense
Accounts Payable—First National Bank	

Instructions: Record the following transactions on page 1 of a general journal.

Nov. 1 Doug Hawk began business by investing the following assets in the business: Cash, $1,500; truck, $3,000; tools, $1,300; and office equipment, $200; Memorandum 101.

2 Paid the rent on the shop space, $400, Check 211.

4 Purchased a calculator from Marlo Equipment Co. for $150 by writing Check 212.

6 Completed repair work and received $600, Receipt 1001.

8 Bought $450 worth of tools on account from Lock-On Tool Co., Invoice 7872.

10 Doug Hawk withdrew $175 from the business for personal use, Check 213.

12 Completed $550 in repair work for Carley Cole on account, Invoice 10.

19 Received a check for $225 from Carley Cole to apply on account, Receipt 1002.

25 Wrote Check 214 to Lock-On Tool Co. for $450.

30 Completed repair work for $850 for Lee Industries. Accepted $425 cash (Receipt 1003) and a promise from Lee Industries to pay the balance in 30 days (Invoice 11).

105

Problem 5-5: Ch. Obj. 4, 5

CHALLENGE

PROBLEM

The last problem in each chapter is a challenge problem and is identified by this "maze" symbol.

Nov.

1 Cash in Bank, Truck, Tools, Off. Equip. Dr.; Doug Hawk, Cap. Cr.

2 Rent Exp. Dr., Cash in Bank Cr.

4 Off. Equip. Dr., Cash in Bank Cr.

6 Cash in Bank Dr., Repair Rev. Cr.

8 Tools Dr., AP—Lock-On Tool Co. Cr.

10 Doug Hawk, Withdr. Dr., Cash in Bank Cr.

12 AR—Carley Cole Dr., Repair Rev. Cr.

19 Cash in Bank Dr., AR—Carley Cole Cr.

25 AP—Lock-On Tool Co. Dr., Cash in Bank Cr.

30 Cash in Bank and AR—Lee Industries Dr., Repair Rev. Cr.

4 ASSESS

A chapter test is available for use in assessing students' understanding of concepts in this chapter.

The testmaker software will enable you to develop tailor-made chapter, unit, semester, and final tests.

Alternative Assessment

For alternative assessment strategies, refer to *Tech Prep Strategies in Accounting.*

Use Chapter Test 5 here to assess students' understanding and retention of the concepts and procedures presented in the chapter.

Computers not only keep confidential data protected but also play an important role in protecting other kinds of property from theft or misuse. Through security systems, computers monitor stores and other buildings. Computers can be used to verify authorized access to buildings as well as to computer files.

Why is such protection needed? Almost daily, stories about computer-related crimes appear in local newspapers. Ask students to be prepared to discuss the facts of such a story in class. Do students view such cases as crimes in the sense that theft is a crime?

QUESTIONS

1. What kinds of words make good passwords?
2. What other steps can companies take to minimize their security risks?

ANSWERS

1. "Nonsense" words make the best passwords. Nonsense words are combinations of letters that have no meaning. For example, glgj is a nonsense word. Perhaps the user could remember it as "general ledger general journal."
2. Perhaps the most effective step would be a very careful screening of potential employees who will have access to sensitive company information.

Passwords to Computer Security

Before the computer revolution, companies kept highly sensitive and confidential data under lock and key. In today's world of electronic data management, the computer's hard disk is the "file cabinet" and the "key" is a password.

Sometimes it is difficult to convince employees that a password is a security protection device. It's not uncommon to find a password taped to the computer. ("But I keep forgetting it!") Nor is it uncommon to hear a shared password shouted across a crowded office. ("Hey, Clare, run that password by me one more time.") Sometimes employees make a password so obvious that anyone would guess it. ("I know! I'll use my initials. No one knows my middle name." Oh, sure. Check the company phone directory!)

Passwords should be easy to remember, but hard to decode. They should be known to one person only. When several people share a computer, a company may want to add an extra protection product or method to the password system. Here are some devices companies can use.

- When the user logs on, *biometric devices* compare the user's fingerprints to those stored in its memory.
- *Key-reading devices* check a special identification card before allowing a user access to computer facilities.
- With *graphics passwords*, the computer screen might display, for example, a car. The user must then point to three parts in the correct sequence before gaining access to the system.
- A person calling in to a computer system may be connected to a *port protection device*, which requires the person to enter a password. If the password matches one in the device's memory, the caller is connected to the computer system. If it does not, the telephone call is terminated.

With the growing importance of computers, businesses are becoming more conscious of security.

- *Encryption* changes the text into an unrecognizable form through character substitution or transposition. For example, GEORGE would be HFPSHF by simply substituting for each letter the letter that follows it in the alphabet. A caller who doesn't know the encryption scheme can't read the data.

If confidentiality isn't respected or security is lax, the last word may be TOOLATE.

Chapter 6

POSTING JOURNAL ENTRIES TO GENERAL LEDGER ACCOUNTS

Learning Objectives

When you have completed Chapter 6, you should be able to do the following:

1. Describe the steps followed in the posting process.
2. Accurately post business transactions from a general journal to the accounts in the ledger.
3. Prepare a trial balance.
4. Record correcting entries in the general journal.
5. Define the accounting terms introduced in this chapter.

In Chapter 5, you learned how to analyze business transactions and enter those transactions in a general journal. The general journal is an all-purpose journal in which the details of a business's transactions are recorded. These details include the date, the accounts affected, the debit and credit amounts, and a source document reference.

After the information about a business's transactions has been journalized, that information is transferred to the specific accounts affected by each transaction. The process of transferring this information is called posting. Posting is the fourth step in the accounting cycle.

After posting has been completed, the balances of all the accounts must be proved to make sure the accounting system is still in balance. This is done by preparing a trial balance, the fifth step in the accounting cycle.

New Terms

posting
trial balance
ledger
ledger account form
proving the ledger
transposition error
slide
correcting entry

107

LOOKING BACK

In Chapter 5 students were introduced to the first formal record in the accounting system, the general journal. Students learned how to make journal entries to record information from business transactions. In this chapter students will proceed to the next step in the accounting cycle by learning to post journal entries to general ledger accounts.

VOCABULARY DEVELOPMENT

Discuss the definitions of the new terms in class. Ask students to give their definition of each term and to explain how each is used in accounting. Definitions of these terms are found in the chapter and in the glossary on pages 670-679.

Teaching Resources

- Lesson Plans
- TE/Chapter Reviews & Working Papers
- Demonstration Problems
- Student Study Plans
- Teaching Transparencies
- Solutions Transparencies
- Electronic Field Trips Video, Level I
- Electronic Study Guide
- Chapter 6 Test
- Unit Objective Test for Chapters 3-6
- Unit Problem Test for Chapters 3-6

Other Resources

- Skills Improvement Activities
- Blackline Masters
- Careers in Accounting
- Dictionary
- Math Review for Accounting
- Tech Prep Strategies in Accounting
- Video
- Test Bank with Software
- Spanish Resources/Audiotapes
- Spanish Electronic Study Guide

1 FOCUS

MAJOR CONCEPTS

- The Fourth and Fifth Steps in the Accounting Cycle
- The General Ledger
- The Posting Process
- Proving the Equality of the Ledger
- Finding Errors
- Correcting Entries

BUSINESS CONNECTION

The Limited, a clothing store targeting its sales to young women, has enjoyed enormous growth over the past decade. To stay on the cutting edge, businesses like The Limited must make the right merchandise decisions. Business owners and managers must continuously evaluate all aspects of the business, but they especially need to know what has sold well and what has not. Accounting records such as journals and ledgers provide the information needed for successful business decisions.

2 TEACH

CONCEPT DEVELOPMENT

The Fourth and Fifth Steps in the Accounting Cycle

Review the first three steps in the accounting cycle by drawing a circle on the chalkboard and labeling the three steps completed to this point (collecting and verifying financial information on source documents, analyzing transactions, and journalizing). Discuss steps 4 and 5 as you add them to the circle on the chalkboard.

Using Visuals

Draw students' attention to Figure 6-1. Reinforce the first three steps in the accounting cycle by asking class members to describe them. Point out steps 4 and 5.

The Fourth and Fifth Steps in the Accounting Cycle

Earlier, we referred to the general journal as a sort of business diary in which all of a business's transactions are recorded. You cannot, however, easily see the increases and decreases taking place in the business's accounts by looking at these journal entries. To provide a clear picture of how each account is affected by a business transaction, the information in a journal entry must be recorded in the accounts themselves. The process of transferring the information in a journal entry to an individual account is called **posting.** The purpose of posting is to show the effects of business transactions on the business's accounts.

After posting has been completed, a trial balance is prepared. A **trial balance** is a proof of the equality of total debits and total credits. As you can see in Figure 6-1, posting is the fourth step in the accounting cycle. Preparing a trial balance is the fifth step in the accounting cycle.

Figure 6-1   The Accounting Cycle, with Steps 4 and 5 Highlighted

The General Ledger

In a manual accounting system, the accounts used by a business are kept on separate pages or cards. These pages or cards are kept together in a book or file called a **ledger.** In a computerized accounting system, accounts are kept on magnetic tapes or disks, but the accounts as a group are

Reinforcing Study Skills

Some students find that an outline format is the best way to take notes, particularly notes from a textbook section or journal article. Making an outline for lecture motes may be more difficult, and students may have to use a combination of outline, narrative, and paragraph formats. Spend time with your students

helping them to develop an outline format that is useful for accounting notes.

Provide a copy of the *Student Study Plans* to each class member to help organize study activities or to individualize practice and review activities.

A company's general ledger accounts may be maintained on separate sheets in a ledger book.

still referred to as the ledger, or the ledger accounts. In either system, the ledger is often called a *general ledger.*

Posting to the ledger accounts creates a record of the effects of business transactions on each account used by a business. After journal entries have been posted, a business owner or manager can look at a specific account and easily find its current balance. If, for example, Jan Harter wants to know how much money Global Travel has in its bank account, she can simply look at the balance of the Cash in Bank account.

Before journal entries can be posted, however, all the accounts used in a business's accounting system must be opened in the ledger.

The Four-Column Ledger Account Form

In a manual accounting system, the accounting stationery used to record financial information about specific accounts is a **ledger account form.** There are several common ledger account forms. These forms—as well as other accounting stationery—are usually described by the number of amount columns they have. In other words, the number of columns refers only to those columns on the forms in which dollar amounts are recorded. For example, the ledger account form used for Global Travel's accounts is a four-column account form.

The four-column account form has spaces to enter certain information such as the account title, the account number, the date, an explanation of the entry, and the posting reference. It also has four columns in which to record dollar amounts. Look at the four-column account form shown in Figure 6-2 on page 110. Notice the four amount columns: the debit column, the credit column, the debit balance column, and the credit balance column. The first two amount columns are used to enter debit and credit amounts from journal entries. The last two amount columns are used to enter the new account balance after a journal entry has been posted. Which balance

CHAPTER 6   Posting Journal Entries to General Ledger Accounts

CONCEPT DEVELOPMENT
The General Ledger

Before learning how to post, students need to know what a ledger is. Emphasize that businesses have many accounts and that, collectively, these accounts are referred to as a ledger. Although a business may have more than one ledger, the main ledger is the general ledger.

A ledger may be likened to a card file, but one that is not arranged alphabetically. Rather, the accounts in the ledger are arranged by classification; in this section, Assets, Liabilities, Owner's Equity, Revenue, and Expenses. Show students examples of actual ledgers to help them form an image of the general ledger.

Using Visuals

Point out the ledger books in the photo. Although many businesses still use manual accounting systems, such ledger books are likely to be seen less frequently in the future as computerized accounting documents replace them.

Teaching Tips

■ A ledger is often called a book of "final" entry.
■ Two-column account forms are used infrequently today. With four-column forms, it is not necessary to balance and rule ledger accounts.

Making Connections

EVERYDAY LIFE

Ask students who have checking accounts to explain what happens to their account when they withdraw money or deposit a check. (The transaction is posted to the account and the balance either increases or decreases.) Ask students to explain why a bank must post transactions to checking and savings accounts daily.

(Answers: To keep customer bank account balances up to date. If a customer's checking or savings account balance is not up to date, an individual may be permitted to withdraw cash when the balance in the account is not sufficient to cover the withdrawal.)

Using Visuals

Review the general ledger form with students. Point out the column heads and the information that is recorded in each part of the form. Emphasize that the primary advantage of the four-column ledger account form is that the current balance of the account is always available.

Even the top managers of corporations are accountable to someone. Managers are responsible for presenting financial reports conforming to GAAP standards, safeguarding the assets of the company, ensuring compliance with laws, using company resources efficiently, meeting specified company goals, and maintaining controls to prevent fraud within the business. Who evaluates management performance? Audit committees, stockholders, creditors, potential investors, and government agencies all play a role in holding top managers accountable for their business decisions and activities.

column is used depends on the type of account. For example, the balance of an account having a normal debit balance—such as an asset or expense account—is entered in the debit balance column. The balance of an account having a normal credit balance—such as a liability or revenue account—is entered in the credit balance column. The balance column shows the current balance in the account. The ledger account balances, therefore, are kept up to date.

Figure 6-2   Four-Column Ledger Account Form

Opening Accounts in the Ledger

Before journal entries can be posted to the accounts in the ledger, an account must be opened for each account that appears on the chart of accounts. There are two steps to opening an account: (1) writing the account title on the account form and (2) writing the account number on the account form. Each account form will hold several entries, so it is not necessary to write the account title and number again until the first page is filled and a new page is needed. The accounts opened for Global Travel Agency's first three asset accounts are shown in Figure 6-3 as an example.

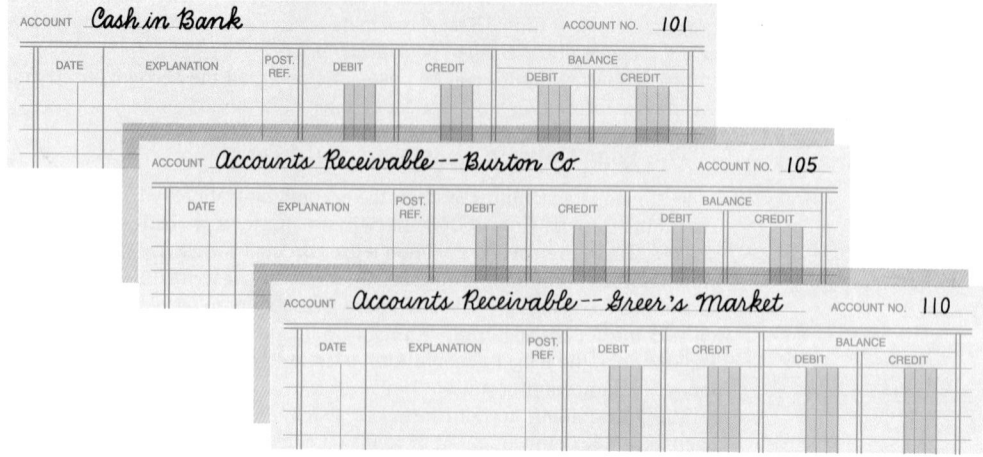

Figure 6-3   Opened General Ledger Accounts

In a computerized accounting system, the procedure is similar. An account is opened by entering the account title and number for each account on the chart of accounts. Computerized accounting systems vary, but all of them require that such information as the account numbers and titles be entered into the computer files.

Meeting Special Needs

HEARING IMPAIRMENTS

Students with a hearing disability need to have someone take notes for them so that they can concentrate on lip reading your presentation or following an interpreter. Try to identify a classmate who takes good notes and "contract" with that student to provide a duplicate set of notes for the hearing impaired student.

The Posting Process

How often posting occurs depends on the size of a business, the number of its transactions, and whether posting is done manually or by computer. Large businesses must post daily to keep their accounts up to date. Smaller businesses may be able to post weekly or even monthly. The posting process remains the same, though, regardless of how often it is done.

As in journalizing a transaction, posting to the accounts is completed from left to right. Let's look at the first journal entry for Global Travel to be posted to a ledger account.

Global Travel's first transaction affected two accounts: Cash in Bank and Jan Harter, Capital. The information in the journal entry for this transaction is transferred item by item from the journal to each of the accounts affected. As you read about each step in the posting process, refer to Figure 6-4.

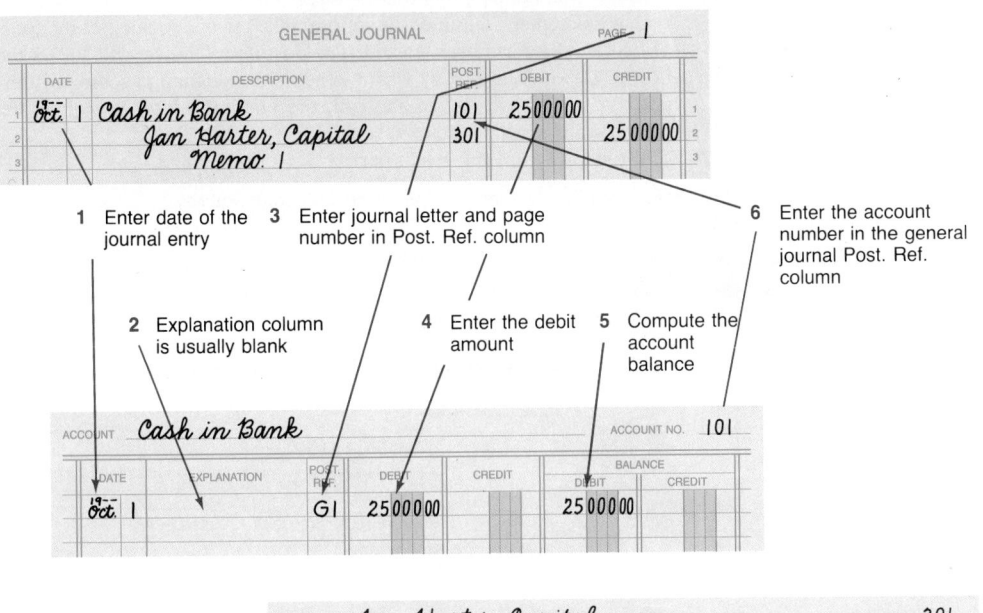

1 Enter date of the journal entry
2 Explanation column is usually blank
3 Enter journal letter and page number in Post. Ref. column
4 Enter the debit amount
5 Compute the account balance
6 Enter the account number in the general journal Post. Ref. column

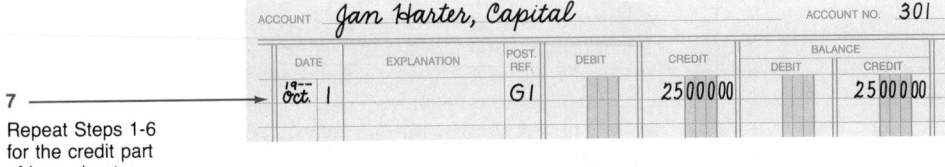

7 Repeat Steps 1-6 for the credit part of journal entry

Figure 6-4 Posting from the General Journal to Ledger Accounts

1. Write the date of the journal entry in the Date column of the account debited. Use the date of the journal entry, not the date on which the posting is done. Write the year and month in the left side of the Date column. It is not necessary to write the year and month for other postings to the same account unless one or both change. The day, however, is always entered.

CHAPTER 6 Posting Journal Entries to General Ledger Accounts   111

CONCEPT DEVELOPMENT
The Posting Process
Students need to understand why posting is necessary. The information in the journal is a chronological record of business transactions. Information is not organized in such a manner as to allow an owner or manager to quickly see how business transactions are affecting specific accounts. Ledger accounts are used for that purpose, and the information from the journal entries is transferred to the ledger accounts via the posting process.

Using Visuals
A teaching transparency showing the posting process is available in the transparency binder accompanying Glencoe Accounting.

Using Visuals
Refer students to Figure 6-4. Have them follow each arrow to determine how to transfer information from the journal to the ledger. Remind students that the date entered in the ledger form is always the date of the journal entry.

ACCOUNTING ISSUES
There are two schools of thought in presenting the order of posting. Some instructors believe that the amount should be entered first; others believe the data should be entered in the same order as the journal entry. Both are correct, but to ensure accuracy the method used should be easy for students to learn, minimize errors, and logical to follow. This textbook teaches students to enter the date first, moving from the left side of the ledger form to the right and entering all appropriate data. With this procedure, there is less chance that an item will be omitted.

Cooperative Learning

MAKE AND DEFEND
Divide students into groups and provide the following scenario. Ask each group to make a decision and to appoint a spokesperson to present and defend the decision to the class.

"Monica Nan recently started a small business selling handmade crafts. Initially she posted journal entries at the end of each month. Business has increased significantly, and Monica now wonders whether she should post more frequently, perhaps weekly or even daily? What recommendations would you make to Monica, and why?"

(Answers: All answers are correct if groups adequately defend their recommendations, which should refer to increased transactions and the need for timely information.)

Refer to the "Cooperative Learning" section of *Tech Prep Strategies in Accounting* for additional cooperative learning strategies.

Using Visuals

Use demonstration problem 6-1 here to demonstrate the posting process.

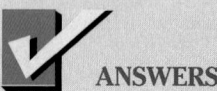

ANSWERS

1. The date; June 6, 19—
2. Accounts Payable—Monroe Products
3. $250; credit balance
4. 101

ACCOUNTING PRACTICE

Students may complete Exercise 6-1 at this point.

---

2. The Explanation column is usually left blank on the ledger account. Some businesses use this space to write in the source document number.
3. In the Posting Reference (Post. Ref.) column, write a letter for the journal from which the entry is being posted and the page number on which the journal entry is recorded. Use the letter "G" for the general journal.
4. Enter the debit amount in the Debit column of the ledger account.
5. Compute and record the new account balance in the appropriate balance column. Every amount posted will either increase or decrease the balance of that account. Remember that asset, withdrawals, and expense accounts have normal debit balances. Liability, owner's capital, and revenue accounts have normal credit balances.
6. Return to the journal and record the number of the account to which you just posted the debit part of the journal entry. Write the account number in the Posting Reference column on the same line as the debit entry.

    This step in the posting process is very important. The notation in the Posting Reference column of the journal tells anyone looking at the journal that an entry has been posted. The posting reference also shows the account to which the entry was posted. If the posting process is interrupted, perhaps by a telephone call, the posting reference signals the point at which posting stopped.
7. Repeat steps 1-6 for the credit part of the journal entry.

Before reading further, complete the following activity.

Check Your Learning

Use the following journal entry to answer these questions.

	DATE	DESCRIPTION	POST. REF.	DEBIT	CREDIT	
1	June 6	Accounts Payable—Monroe Products		1 000 00		1
2		Cash in Bank			1 000 00	2
3		Check 610				3

GENERAL JOURNAL PAGE 6

1. Assume that the ledger accounts have been opened. What is the first item of information that will be transferred to a ledger account?
2. What is the title of the first ledger account to which you will post?
3. If Accounts Payable—Monroe Products has a current balance (before posting) of $1,250, what will the balance be after this journal entry has been posted? Does this account have a debit balance or a credit balance?
4. If the accounts to which this entry will be posted are numbered 101 and 210, which number will be written in the Posting Reference column of the journal after the credit part of the entry has been posted?

Compare your answers to those in the answers section. Re-read the preceding part of the chapter to find answers to any questions you may have missed.

Reteaching Strategies

Students sometimes forget to complete the last step in the posting process—entering the ledger account number in the journal. Encourage students to think of the audit trail and the information the posting reference provides. When an account number is provided in the Posting Reference column of a journal, it shows that the entry has been posted to that account. When the journal and page number are provided in the Posting Reference column of a ledger account, it creates an audit trail that makes it easy to trace a transaction back to the journal entry and then ultimately back to its origination, the source document.

Use Problem 6A in the Additional Problems section of the textbook (p. 633) for students who need additional practice posting to the general ledger.

The journal entries made in Chapter 5 for Global Travel's business transactions are shown in Figure 6-5. The postings made to the general ledger accounts from these entries are shown in Figure 6-6 on pages 114-115. Study these illustrations to check your understanding of the posting process.

(accounts continue on pages 114-115)

Using Visuals

Figure 6-5 shows the general journal entries for transactions students have analyzed in earlier chapters. Walk students through the posting of several of these transactions (accounts continue on pages 114-115) to make sure they follow the posting process.

GENERAL JOURNAL			PAGE 1	
DATE	DESCRIPTION	POST. REF.	DEBIT	CREDIT
19-- Oct. 1	Cash in Bank	101	2500000	
	Jan Harter, Capital	301		2500000
	Memo. 1			
2	Computer Equipment	120	800000	
	Cash in Bank	101		800000
	Check 101			
4	Office Equipment	130	20000	
	Jan Harter, Capital	301		20000
	Memo. 2			
9	Office Equipment	130	150000	
	Accts. Pay.—Modern Off. Supp.	205		150000
	Invoice 200			
11	Accts. Rec.—Greer's Market	110	20000	
	Office Equipment	130		20000
	Memo. 3			
14	Accts. Pay.—Modern Off. Supp.	205	75000	
	Cash in Bank	101		75000
	Check 102			
15	Rent Expense	520	55000	
	Cash in Bank	101		55000
	Check 103			
16	Advertising Expense	501	7500	
	Accts. Payable—City News	201		7500
	Invoice 129			
18	Cash in Bank	101	120000	
	Fees	401		120000
	Receipt 1			
20	Accts. Rec.—Burton Company	105	45000	
	Fees	401		45000
	Invoice 1000			
26	Cash in Bank	101	20000	
	Accts. Rec.—Greer's Market	110		20000
	Receipt 2			
28	Utilities Expense	530	12500	
	Cash in Bank	101		12500
	Check 104			

GENERAL JOURNAL			PAGE 2	
DATE	DESCRIPTION	POST. REF.	DEBIT	CREDIT
19-- Oct. 29	Maintenance Expense	510	45000	
	Cash in Bank	101		45000
	Check 105			
31	Jan Harter, Withdrawals	305	40000	
	Cash in Bank	101		40000
	Check 106			

Figure 6-5 General Journal Entries for October Business Transactions

Interdisciplinary **Connections**

HISTORY

People have recorded business accounts in some way ever since they began to trade, thousands of years ago. Archaeologists found records of business contracts in the ruins of Babylon. In ancient Greece and Rome, people—probably well-educated slaves—kept records of the income and expenditures of wealthy families' farms and estates.

Chapter

Using Visuals

Reinforce the classifying of accounts by having students look at the account numbers and give each account's classification.

ACCOUNT Cash in Bank **ACCOUNT NO.** 101

DATE	EXPLANATION	POST. REF.	DEBIT	CREDIT	BALANCE DEBIT	BALANCE CREDIT
19-- Oct. 1		G1	25000 00		25000 00	
2		G1		8000 00	17000 00	
14		G1		750 00	16250 00	
15		G1		550 00	15700 00	
18		G1	1200 00		16900 00	
26		G1	200 00		17100 00	
28		G1		125 00	16975 00	
29		G2		450 00	16525 00	
31		G2		400 00	16125 00	

ACCOUNT Accounts Receivable -- Burton Co. **ACCOUNT NO.** 105

DATE	EXPLANATION	POST. REF.	DEBIT	CREDIT	BALANCE DEBIT	BALANCE CREDIT
19-- Oct. 20		G1	450 00		450 00	

ACCOUNT Accounts Receivable -- Greer's Market **ACCOUNT NO.** 110

DATE	EXPLANATION	POST. REF.	DEBIT	CREDIT	BALANCE DEBIT	BALANCE CREDIT
19-- Oct. 11		G1	200 00		200 00	
26		G1		200 00		

ACCOUNT Computer Equipment **ACCOUNT NO.** 120

DATE	EXPLANATION	POST. REF.	DEBIT	CREDIT	BALANCE DEBIT	BALANCE CREDIT
19-- Oct. 2		G1	8000 00		8000 00	

ACCOUNT Office Equipment **ACCOUNT NO.** 130

DATE	EXPLANATION	POST. REF.	DEBIT	CREDIT	BALANCE DEBIT	BALANCE CREDIT
19-- Oct. 4		G1	200 00		200 00	
9		G1	1500 00		1700 00	
11		G1		200 00	1500 00	

ACCOUNT Accounts Payable -- City News **ACCOUNT NO.** 201

DATE	EXPLANATION	POST. REF.	DEBIT	CREDIT	BALANCE DEBIT	BALANCE CREDIT
19-- Oct. 16		G1		75 00		75 00

ACCOUNT Accounts Payable -- Modern Office Suppliers **ACCOUNT NO.** 205

DATE	EXPLANATION	POST. REF.	DEBIT	CREDIT	BALANCE DEBIT	BALANCE CREDIT
19-- Oct. 9		G1		1500 00		1500 00
14		G1	750 00			750 00

Figure 6-6 Postings to General Ledger Accounts for the Month of October

Making Connections

BUSINESS ETHICS

You are an accounting clerk for Bryson Industries, a small manufacturer. The senior accounting clerk asked you to prepare the trial balance for the month. The totals on your trial balance are not equal and you cannot find the error that has been made. You are frustrated and consider changing one of the account balances in order to get the trial balance to balance.

(Answer: Changing the account balance would be dishonest. If you still cannot find the error after another try, ask the senior accounting clerk for assistance. Sometimes a fresh pair of eyes can more easily see what's wrong.)

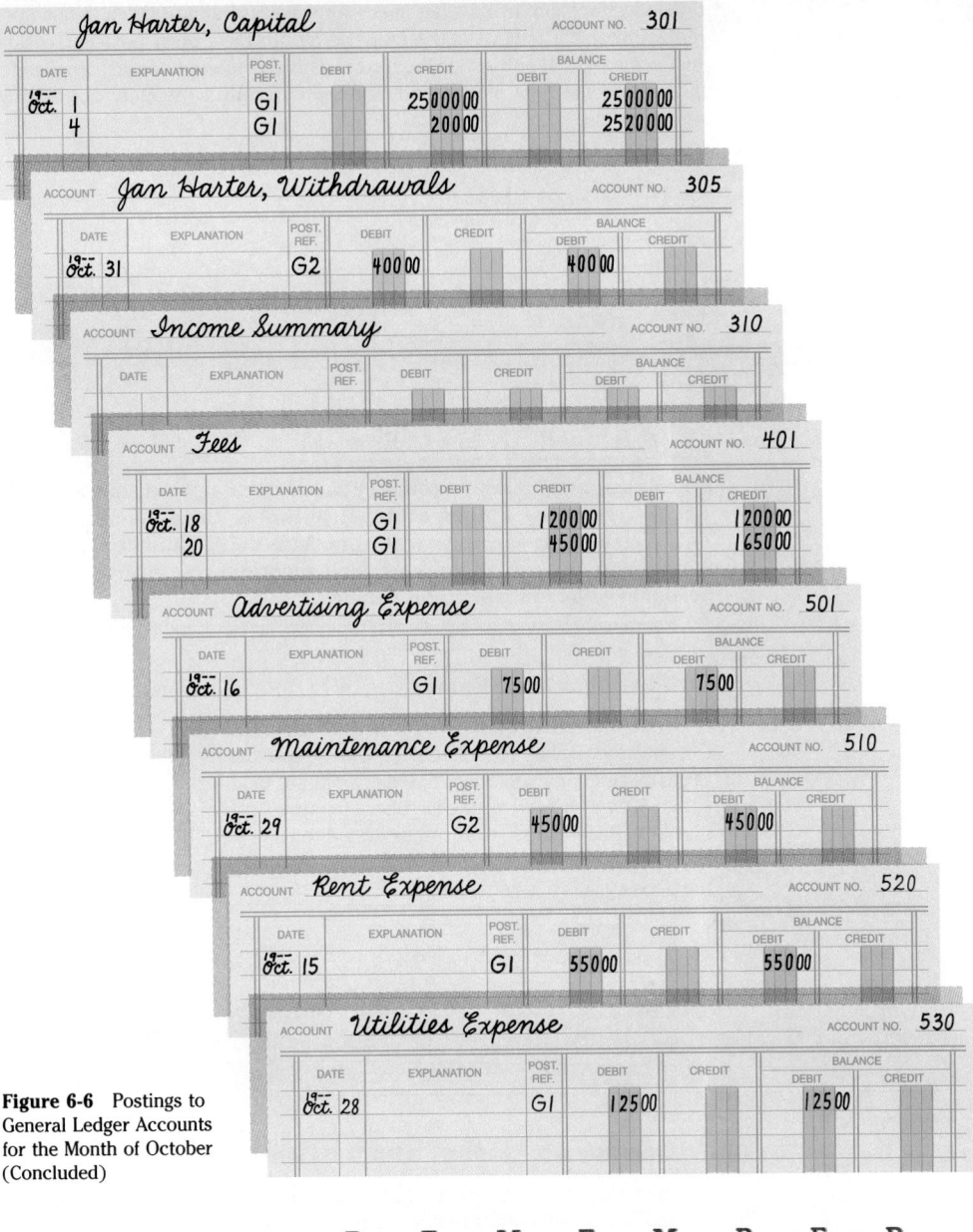

Figure 6-6 Postings to General Ledger Accounts for the Month of October (Concluded)

R E M E M B E R

For every journal entry, you will post to at least two ledger accounts. You will post to one account for the debit part of the entry and then to another account for the credit part.

CHAPTER 6 Posting Journal Entries to General Ledger Accounts 115

Chapter 6

Using Visuals

Review the rules of debit and credit by having students look at the accounts and give the increase/decrease and normal balance sides (debit or credit) of each account.

Critical Thinking

Last month Amelia mailed a check for $89.27 to pay the balance due for a doctor's bill. Today Amelia called to schedule an appointment, and she asked about her account balance. Amelia's account information did not show that the $89.27 had been received. However, Amelia has already received the canceled check from the bank. Give a reason(s) why Amelia's account still shows a balance due of $89.27.

(Answer: The check was received and the payment was processed, but (a) the transaction was not posted to Amelia's account, (b) the transaction may have been posted to the wrong account, (c) the transaction was never journalized, or (d) the transaction was analyzed incorrectly and recorded incorrectly in the journal.)

Using Visuals

Point out that the year is written at the top of the ledger form and is not repeated unless it changes. The month also is written once.

Using Visuals

Use demonstration problem 6-2 here to demonstrate how to indicate a zero balance in a ledger.

A ledger account usually has space for several postings. Often, blank lines remain after the journal entries for the month have been posted. To save space, the journal entries for the next month are entered on the same ledger page. Both the new month and day are entered in the Date column, as shown below.

ACCOUNT *Cash in Bank*   ACCOUNT NO. 101

DATE		EXPLANATION	POST. REF.	DEBIT	CREDIT	BALANCE DEBIT	BALANCE CREDIT
19-- Oct.	1		G1	25 000 00		25 000 00	
	31		G2		400 00	16 125 00	
Nov.	1		G2		50 00	16 075 00	

R E M E M B E R

When computing a new account balance, debit amounts are added to accounts having a normal debit balance. Credit amounts are subtracted from accounts with a normal debit balance. Likewise, credit amounts are added and debit amounts are subtracted from accounts with a normal credit balance.

Showing a Zero Balance in a Ledger Account

Sometimes a ledger account will have a zero balance. For example, on October 11, Global Travel sold an old typewriter for $200 on account to Greer's Market. On October 26, Greer's Market paid for the typewriter in full with a $200 check. When the October 26 journal entry is posted, the account Accounts Receivable—Greer's Market will have a zero balance. Look at the ledger account below. The dash across the debit balance column means that the account has a zero balance.

ACCOUNT *Accounts Receivable – Greer's Market*   ACCOUNT NO. 110

DATE		EXPLANATION	POST. REF.	DEBIT	CREDIT	BALANCE DEBIT	BALANCE CREDIT
19-- Oct.	11		G1	200 00		200 00	
	26		G1		200 00	—	

Opening an Account with a Balance

When the first page of an account is filled, a second page must be opened. To transfer information from one page of an account to the next, follow these steps:

1. Write the account title at the top of the new page.
2. Enter the account number.
3. Enter the complete date (year, month, and day) of the *last* entry on the previous account page.

Making Connections

AROUND THE WORLD

Business owners frequently look for ways to expand their markets. One means of expanding is by selling products or services in foreign markets. Business owners or managers who want to do business in another country will need to spend a lot of their time initially on the foreign operations. Aside from learning about governmental regulations (both U.S. and those of the foreign country), owners/managers will need to spend time finding office space, hiring staff, drafting business documents for use in foreign operations, setting up bank accounts, and adapting their accounting system for the foreign country.

4. Write the word "Balance" in the Explanation column of the new account page.
5. Place a check mark (✔) in the Posting Reference column to show that the amount entered on this line is not being posted from a journal.
6. Enter the amount of the balance in the appropriate balance column of the new page.

The following illustration shows an example of an entry made to open an account with a balance.

ACCOUNT	Cash in Bank				ACCOUNT NO.	101	
					BALANCE		
DATE	EXPLANATION	POST. REF.	DEBIT	CREDIT	DEBIT	CREDIT	
19-- nov. 15	Balance	✔			26 470 00		

Posting in a Computerized Accounting System

In a computerized accounting system, the posting process is completed automatically by the computer. After entering the journal entries into the computer, the computer operator simply instructs the computer to post the entries to the accounts stored in the computer files. After posting has been completed, the operator can obtain a trial balance to prove the equality of total debits and credits.

Before continuing, complete the following activity to check your understanding of the posting process.

Check Your Learning

Write your answers to these questions on a sheet of notebook paper.

1. What is recorded in the Posting Reference column of a ledger account?
2. Cash in Bank has a balance of $4,350. If a credit of $150 is posted to the account, what is the new balance of Cash in Bank?
3. What does a dash in a Balance column of a ledger account indicate?
4. When is a check mark entered in the Posting Reference column of a ledger account?
5. You are opening a new page for Accounts Payable—Apex Systems. In which column would you enter the balance of $1,650?

Compare your answers with those in the answers section. Re-read the preceding part of the chapter to find the correct answers to any questions you may have missed.

Proving the Equality of the Ledger

After the journal entries have been posted to the accounts in the general ledger, the total of all the debit balances should equal the total of all the

CONCEPT DEVELOPMENT
Proving the Equality of the Ledger

The ledger is "proved" after posting is completed by preparing a trial balance to show that total debits are equal to total credits. Emphasize to students that the trial balance is a part of the system of balances that are characteristic of a double-entry system of accounting. If errors appear at this stage, they must be found and corrected before other work may proceed.

Remind students that all accounts should be included in a trial balance, even those with zero balances. This practice follows computerized accounting systems, which print out all accounts.

Teaching Tips

■ The term "trial balance" was first defined on page 108. Review its meaning for students.

Using Visuals

Have students compare the ledger accounts on pages 113-115 with the trial balance shown in Figure 6-7. Note the use of a dash to show an account with a zero balance.

Using Visuals

Use demonstration problem 6-4 to show students how to prepare a trial balance.

CONCEPT DEVELOPMENT
Finding Errors

Students are usually frustrated when errors appear. Help them use the information in the text to approach finding errors in a logical manner. Most general ledger errors result from either computation errors or incorrect postings. Math errors can be found simply by re-adding or subtracting amounts. Errors in postings may take a bit more time to find. They are often caused by transpositions or slides, or occasionally by a debit amount being recorded as a credit or vice versa.

---

credit balances. Adding all the debit balances and all the credit balances and then comparing the two totals to see whether they are equal is called **proving the ledger.**

In earlier chapters, you proved the equality of total debits and credits simply by listing each account title and its balance and then adding all the debit balances and all the credit balances. This proof of the equality of total debits and credits is called a trial balance. As you recall, preparing a trial balance is the fifth step in the accounting cycle. The trial balance for Global Travel Agency for the month of October is shown in Figure 6-7.

Global Travel Agency Trial Balance October 31, 19--		
Cash in Bank	1612500	
Accts. Rec. – Burton Co.	45000	
Accts. Rec. – Greer's Market	—	
Computer Equipment	800000	
Office Equipment	150000	
Accts. Pay. – City News		7500
Accts. Pay. – Modern Office Suppliers		75000
Jan Harter, Capital		2520000
Jan Harter, Withdrawals	40000	
Income Summary		
Fees Income		165000
Advertising Expense	7500	
Maintenance Expense	45000	
Rent Expense	55000	
Utilities Expense	12500	
Totals	2767500	2767500

Figure 6-7   Trial Balance

Notice that this trial balance has been prepared on two-column accounting stationery. All of the debit balances are entered in the first amount column and all of the credit balances are entered in the second amount column. A trial balance may also be handwritten on plain paper, typed, or prepared on a computer.

If the total debits equal the total credits on the trial balance, the ledger has been proved. If the two amounts are not equal, an error has been made either in journalizing or posting. You must find the error and correct it before continuing with the next step in the accounting cycle.

Finding Errors

Most trial balance errors can be located easily and quickly by following these steps:

1. Re-add the trial balance columns. One or both of the columns may have been added incorrectly.
2. Determine the amount that you are out of balance by finding the difference between the trial balance debit and credit columns. If the difference

---

Making Connections

COMMUNICATIONS

Part of an accountant's work may be to present financial documents to business managers. Although it is embarrassing, mistakes do occur in recording transactions. Ask students to imagine they have found an error in a journal entry after it has been posted. How will they (a) correct the error and (b) explain the need for correction to the manager? Have students prepare and present the explanation they will give.

between the columns is 10, 100, 1,000, and so on, you have probably made an addition error. Suppose, for example, you have a debit column total of $35,245 and a credit column total of $35,345. The difference between the debit and credit columns is $100. Re-add the columns to find the error.

3. If the columns are added correctly, divide the column difference by 9. For example, suppose the difference between two totals is $27. That number is evenly divisible by 9 (27 ÷ 9 = 3). If the difference between the columns is evenly divisible by 9, you may have made a transposition error. A **transposition error** results when two numbers are accidentally reversed. If you have written the amount $325 as $352, for example, you have made a transposition error.

A difference divisible by 9 may also indicate a slide error. A **slide** occurs when a decimal point is moved by mistake. For example, if you write $1,800 as either $180 or $18,000, you have made a slide error.

To find the error, check the trial balance amounts against the balances in the general ledger accounts to make sure you have copied the balances correctly.

4. Check to make sure that you have not omitted one of the general ledger accounts. Look in the general ledger for an account balance equal to the amount of the column difference. For example, if the difference between the two columns is $725, look in the general ledger for an account having a balance of $725.

5. If all the general ledger accounts and their balances have been included in the trial balance, one of the account balances may be recorded in the wrong column. To find out if this is the case, divide the difference between the column totals by 2. For example, suppose that the difference between the two columns is $300; that amount divided by 2 is $150. Look in the debit and credit columns for an account balance matching this amount. Check to see whether a balance of $150 was entered in the wrong column.

6. If you still have not found the error, recompute the balance in each ledger account. You may have made an addition or subtraction error.

7. Finally, check the postings to verify that the correct amounts were posted from the journal entries. Check to make sure that the amounts were posted to the correct amount columns.

Correcting Entries

Accounting workers understand very well the truth in the saying, "To err is human. . . ." When mistakes are made in accounting, one rule applies: *Never erase an error.* Erasures look suspicious. Honest mistakes should be honestly corrected.

The method for correcting an error depends on when the error is found. You learned in Chapter 5 that when an error in a journal entry is discovered *before* posting, it may be corrected by drawing a single line through the incorrect item and writing the correction directly above. However, when an error in a journal entry is discovered *after* posting, the correction is made by a **correcting entry.**

CHAPTER 6   Posting Journal Entries to General Ledger Accounts   **119**

On November 15, Global Travel's accountant found an error in a journal entry made on November 2. A $100 check written to pay the electric bill had been journalized and posted to the Maintenance Expense account by mistake. The original journal entry is shown below in T-account form.

Maintenance Expense			Cash in Bank	
Dr.	Cr.		Dr.	Cr.
+	–		+	–
$100				$100

The T accounts below show how the transaction *should* have been recorded.

Utilities Expense			Cash in Bank	
Dr.	Cr.		Dr.	Cr.
+	–		+	–
$100				$100

As you can see, the $100 credit to Cash in Bank was correct. The error is in the debit part of the November 2 transaction. Maintenance Expense was incorrectly debited for $100. To correct the error, it must now be credited for that same amount. Utilities Expense should have been debited for $100. To correct the error, it is debited now.

The accountant wrote Memorandum 70 to notify the accounting clerk of the mistake. The correcting entry, recorded in the general journal, is shown below.

	GENERAL JOURNAL			PAGE 3	
DATE	DESCRIPTION	POST. REF.	DEBIT	CREDIT	
19-- Nov. 15	Utilities Expense		100 00		1
	Maintenance Expense			100 00	2
	Memo. 70				3

Posting a correcting entry is similar to any other posting. In the Explanation column of the ledger accounts, however, the words "Correcting Entry" are written. The illustration below and at the top of page 121 shows how the correcting entry was posted to the Maintenance Expense and Utilities Expense accounts.

ACCOUNT Maintenance Expense					ACCOUNT NO. 510	
DATE	EXPLANATION	POST. REF.	DEBIT	CREDIT	BALANCE DEBIT	CREDIT
19-- Oct. 29		G2			450 00	
Nov. 2		G2	100 00		550 00	
15	Correcting Entry	G3		100 00	450 00	

Pop Quiz

1. The process of transferring the information in the journal to specific accounts is called
____.
2. What does G1 in the Posting Reference column of a general ledger account indicate?
3. Should posting be done daily or weekly?
4. What purpose does a trial balance serve?
5. When is a correcting entry necessary?

ANSWERS

1. posting
2. general journal page 1
3. It depends upon the size of the business and the number of transactions; some businesses may only post monthly.
4. It proves the equality of total debits and credits.
5. When the journal entry is posted before the error is discovered.

ACCOUNT	*Utilities Expense*				ACCOUNT NO.	530	
DATE	EXPLANATION	POST. REF.	DEBIT	CREDIT	BALANCE		
					DEBIT	CREDIT	
19— Oct. 28		G1	125 00		125 00		
Nov. 15	*Correcting Entry*	G3	100 00		225 00		

Summary of Key Points

1. Posting is the fourth step in the accounting cycle. It is the process of transferring the information in a journal entry to the specific accounts in the ledger affected by that entry.
2. The accounts used by a business are kept in the ledger. In a manual accounting system, the ledger accounts are kept on pages or cards. In a computerized accounting system, the accounts are stored on magnetic tapes or disks.
3. The accounts in the ledger must be opened before posting can begin. An account is opened by writing the account title and its number at the top of the ledger account form.
4. A four-column ledger account form has four amount columns: one for a debit entry, one for a credit entry, one for a debit balance, and one for a credit balance.
5. After posting has been completed, the equality of the ledger must be proved. A proof of the equality of total debits and credits is called a trial balance. Preparing a trial balance is the fifth step in the accounting cycle.
6. The most common errors made in accounting records are addition or subtraction errors, transpositions, slides, omissions, and incorrect debiting or crediting.
7. Errors discovered after a transaction has been journalized and posted must be corrected by a correcting entry recorded in the general journal.

Using Visuals

Use demonstration problem 6-6 to give students practice in making correcting entries.

3 CLOSE

CHAPTER SUMMARY
This summary enumerates the key information in the chapter. It is a useful tool for reinforcement and review.

Reteaching Strategies

Correcting entries are necessary when an error is detected after a journal entry has been posted. The correcting entry must *undo* the error. Therefore, if an account was debited in error, it must be credited for the same amount to "cancel out" and, in effect, undo the error.

The second part of the correcting entry debits or credits the correct account. If the amount in the journal is incorrect, the correcting entry needs only to correct the amount. For example, if $100 was recorded instead of $1,000, the same accounts would be debited and credited for the difference—$900.

Review and Applications

Building Your Accounting Vocabulary

In your own words, write the definition of each of the following accounting terms. Use complete sentences for your definitions.

correcting entry	posting	transposition error
ledger	proving the ledger	trial balance
ledger account form	slide	

Reviewing Your Accounting Knowledge

1. What is the purpose of posting?
2. In what way can the information posted in the ledger accounts be helpful to the business owner?
3. What two steps are required to open a ledger account?
4. What determines the frequency of posting?
5. List the steps followed in posting.
6. What two things does the posting reference in a journal indicate?
7. How is a zero balance indicated in a ledger account?
8. List the steps you should follow to open the second page of a ledger account.
9. What steps would you follow to locate a trial balance error?
10. How should an accounting clerk correct an incorrect journal entry that has not yet been posted?
11. How should an accounting clerk correct a transaction that has been incorrectly journalized and posted?

Improving Your Communications Skills

Often the way we say things has a big impact on how our listeners respond to us. Angry words can bring an equally angry response, and no real communication will have taken place. Communication occurs when one person is able to express an idea in words and tone that are heard *and understood* in the way the speaker intended. See if you can identify why communication did not take place in the following examples. How would you have said things differently?

1. *Supervisor:* (Angrily) "You're late again, Wiley. If you're not here on time every day from now on, you're out of a job."
   Employee: "Aw, man. Get off my back. I'm tryin' as hard as I can."
2. *First Person:* "I'm tired of you always making the decisions on our projects. You never listen to what I want to do."
   Second Person: Well, you don't have to work with me anymore. I'll find someone else."

122

PRACTICE AND APPLY

- Language Development
- Comprehension and Retention
- Basic Skills

Building Your Accounting Vocabulary

See the Glossary on pages 670-679 for definitions of these terms.

Reviewing Your Accounting Knowledge

1. To show the effects of business transactions on a business's accounts.
2. Accounts give a clear picture of what is happening in the business, aiding in business decision making.
3. (a) Writing the account title and (b) writing the account number on the account form.
4. The size of a business, the number of its transactions, and whether posting is done manually or by computer.
5. (a) Enter the date of the journal entry. (b) Leave the Explanation column blank. (c) Enter the journal page reference. (d) Enter the debit amount. (e) Compute the account balance and record it in the appropriate balance column. (f) Write the debited account number in the journal Post. Ref. column. (g) Complete steps a-f for the credit part of the entry.
6. That an entry has been posted and the accounts to which it was posted.
7. By drawing a dash across the Debit or Credit Balance column.
8. (a) Write the account title at the top of the page. (b) Enter the account number. (c) Enter the complete date of the last entry on the filled account page. (d) Write "Balance" in the Explanation column of the new account page. (e) Place a check mark (√) in the Post. Ref. column to show that the amount entered is not a posting from a journal. (f) Enter the amount of the balance in the appropriate column.
9. (a) Re-add columns. (b) Check for transpositions, slides, or amounts entered in the wrong column. (c) Check ledger account balances for accuracy and omissions. (e) Recompute ledger account balances. (f) Verify journal postings.

10. By drawing a line through the incorrect information and writing the correction above.
11. With a correcting entry.

Improving Your Communication Skills

1. The supervisor should explain calmly how punctuality affects an employee's pay and job advancement. The supervisor should ask why the employee is late so often and whether a change in work hours would solve the problem. The employee's angry response prevented the situation from being discussed. A better approach would be, "I'm sorry I'm late again.

Would you have some time later today to talk with me about my work hours?"
2. The first person may feel that the second person controls the relationship and does not consider the first person's ideas. The second person responded negatively and reacted with a threat. People who are mature communicators are able to get past their immediate responses to anger or criticism and to try to find reasons for a problem. A good response would be, "I didn't realize that I always made the decisions. Let's talk about it."

Applying Accounting Procedures

Exercise 6-1   Posting to Ledger Accounts

Kati Karl operates an alterations business called Kati's Custom Alterations. Listed below are several transactions that took place during the fiscal period.

Instructions: Use a form similar to the one that follows. For each transaction below,

(1) Enter the title of the account affected (indicated in parentheses at the end of the transaction) on the form.

(2) Indicate whether the transaction amount would be posted to the debit column or the credit column of the ledger account.

(3) Indicate in which balance column (debit or credit) the new account balance would be recorded. The first transaction is given as an example.

Transactions:

1. Paid the telephone bill. (Utilities Expense)

2. Received cash for altering a coat for a customer. (Alterations Revenue)

3. Purchased thread, paying cash. (Supplies)

4. Ms. Karl withdrew cash from the business. (Kati Karl, Withdrawals)

5. Paid a creditor a portion of the amount owed. (Accounts Payable — ALCO, Inc.)

6. Received cash from Alvin Jones on account. (Accounts Receivable — A. Jones)

Trans.	Account Affected	Debit	Credit	Balance Debit	Balance Credit
1	Utilities Expense	✔		✔	

Exercise 6-2   Determining Account Balances

The transactions that follow affect the account Accounts Receivable — Pat Downey.

Instructions:

(1) Open the ledger account by writing in the account title and account number, 115.

(2) Record the account balance of $350 as of June 1 of the current year.

(3) Post the following transactions to the ledger account. All of the transactions were recorded on general journal page 1.

Transactions:

June 2   Received $200 from Pat Downey on account.

  5   Completed services for Pat Downey and billed her $70.

  21   Received a check for $220 from Pat Downey.

  29   Sent Invoice 417 to Pat Downey for services completed, $90.

Exercise 6-3   Correcting Errors

Several errors are described below. Use a form similar to the one that follows. For each error,

(1) Determine whether the error will affect the totals of the trial balance.

123

Additional Reinforcement

Refer students to the Chapter 6 review pages in the workbook, *Chapter Reviews and Working Papers.*

Exercise 6-3: Ch. Obj. 3, 4

2. No; Yes
3. No; Yes
4. No; Yes
5. Yes; No
6. Yes; No
7. Yes; No
8. Yes; No

Problem 6-1: Ch. Obj. 2

Account balances (Sept.):
Cash in Bank, $4,055.00
AR—Sarah Ashley, $375.00
AR—Rod McCune, $490.00
Dental Supplies, $330.00
Dental Equipment, $2,700.00
Furniture & Fixtures, $280.00
AP—Dental Distributors, $2,700.00
Giles Gilbert, Capital, $2,180.00
Giles Gilbert, Withdr., $600.00
Income Summary, 0
Professional Fees, $4,090.00
Utilities Expense, $140.00

Problem 6-2: Ch. Obj. 3

Trial balance totals: $8,970.00

Problem 6-3: Ch. Obj. 2, 3

Ending balances:
Cash in Bank, $5,080.00
AR—Sarah Ashley, 0
AR—Rod McCune, $300.00
Dental Supplies, $810.00
Dental Equipment, $4,000.00
Furniture & Fixtures, $915.00
AP—Dental Distributors, $2,650.00
Giles Gilbert, Capital, $2,255.00
Giles Gilbert, Withdr., $1,200.00
Income Summary, 0
Professional Fees, $7,720.00
Utilities Expense, $320.00
Trial balance totals: $12,625.00

---

(2) Indicate whether the error requires a correcting entry. The first one has been completed as an example.

Error	Does Error Affect Trial Balance Totals?	Correcting Entry Required?
1	Yes	No

Errors:

1. A $50 debit was not posted to the Office Supplies account.
2. A $200 purchase of store equipment was journalized and posted to Store Supplies.
3. A $30 job completed for Sarah James was recorded and posted to James Scott's account.
4. A $500 check received as payment for services was journalized and posted to the capital account.
5. A $69 debit to the withdrawals account was posted as $96.
6. A $100 debit to Cash in Bank was posted as $10.
7. After posting a $75 credit to a creditor's account, the account balance was incorrectly calculated.
8. A $25 debit to the Store Supplies account was posted as a credit.

Problem 6-1   Posting General Journal Transactions

Giles Gilbert, an orthodontist, operates Gilbert's Dental Services. The accounts used by the business have been opened and are included in the working papers accompanying this textbook. The general journal entries for the September business transactions are also included in the working papers.

Instructions: Post the transactions recorded in the general journal to the accounts in the general ledger.

Problem 6-2   Preparing a Trial Balance

Instructions: Use the general ledger accounts from Problem 6-1 to prepare a trial balance for the month ended September 30.

Problem 6-3   Journalizing and Posting
Business Transactions

You will need the general ledger from Problem 6-1 to complete this problem. During the month of October, Gilbert's Dental Services completed the transactions that follow.

Instructions:

(1) Journalize the transactions on page 2 of the general journal.
(2) Post the journal entries to the same general ledger accounts used in Problem 6-1.
(3) Prove the accuracy of the ledger by preparing a trial balance. Compare the totals to be certain they are in agreement.

Transactions:

Oct. 1 Bought several chairs and tables for the waiting room for $560, issuing Check 104.

124

Teacher Notes

_____

_____

_____

_____

_____

Oct. 3 Received a $490 check from Rod McCune on account, Receipt 103.
5 Issued Check 105 for $1,350 to Dental Distributors on account.
8 Sarah Ashley sent a check for $375 to apply on her account, Receipt 104.
10 Giles Gilbert withdrew $600 from the business, Check 106.
15 Purchased $480 worth of dental supplies for cash, Check 107.
17 Bought dental equipment costing $1,300 from Dental Distributors on account, Invoice AB629.
20 Paid the electric bill for the month of $180, Check 108.
22 Completed dental work for several patients receiving $3,330, Receipts 105-108.
25 Giles Gilbert invested an office desk, valued at $75, in the business, Memorandum 3.
31 Completed dental services for Rod McCune and billed him $300, Invoice 102.

Problem 6-4: Ch. Obj. 2, 3

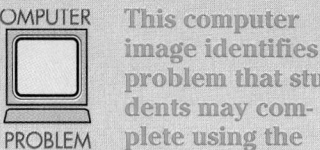

COMPUTER / PROBLEM This computer image identifies a problem that students may complete using the *Glencoe Accounting, General Ledger* software.

Ending balances:
Cash in Bank, $3,600.00
AR—Jenny Simms, $300.00
Legal Supplies, $285.00
Professional Library, $1,200.00
Office Furniture, $1,800.00
AP—Office Interiors, $500.00
Chris Courtney, Capital, $6,200.00
Chris Courtney, Withdr., $515.00
Income Summary, 0
Legal Fees, $1,200.00
Salaries Expense, $200.00
Trial balance totals: $7,900.00

Teaching Tips

■ When students are ready for Problem 6-4, remind them that invoices are numbered and that the creditor's invoice number is used as the source document for the journal entry.

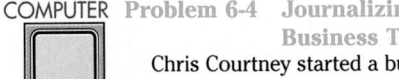

COMPUTER / PROBLEM **Problem 6-4   Journalizing and Posting Business Transactions**

Chris Courtney started a business to provide legal services to the community. The chart of accounts for Chris Courtney, Attorney at Law, is as follows.

ASSETS		OWNER'S EQUITY	
101	Cash in Bank	301	Chris Courtney, Capital
105	Accounts Receivable—Jenny Simms	305	Chris Courtney, Withdrawals
110	Legal Supplies	310	Income Summary
120	Professional Library		
125	Office Furniture	REVENUE	
		401	Legal Fees
LIABILITIES		EXPENSES	
201	Accounts Payable—Office Interiors	501	Salaries Expense

Instructions:
(1) Open an account in the general ledger for each account in the chart of accounts.
(2) Record the February transactions on page 1 of the general journal.
(3) Post each journal entry to the appropriate accounts in the ledger.
(4) Prove the ledger by preparing a trial balance.

Transactions:
Feb. 1 Chris Courtney invested $5,000 in the business, Memorandum 1.
3 Invested law books valued at $1,200 in the business, Memorandum 2.
5 Issued Check 101 for $300 for the purchase of legal supplies.
7 Bought a desk, chair, and table on account for $1,800 from Office Interiors, Invoice LX201.
9 Completed legal work for Jenny Simms on account, $400, Invoice 100.
12 Paid Office Interiors $900 on account, Check 102.
15 Issued Check 103 for $200 to pay the office secretary's salary.
18 Chris Courtney withdrew $500 cash from the business, Check 104.
20 Completed legal work for a client and received $800 cash, Receipt 100.

125

Teacher Notes

CHALLENGE

PROBLEM

The last problem in each chapter is a challenge problem and is identified by this "maze" symbol.

Store Supplies, Dr. $125
    Furniture & Fixtures, Cr. $125
Trina Lopez, Withdr., Dr. $1,200
    Trina Lopez, Capital, Cr. $1,200
Trina Lopez, Capital, Dr. $2,000
    Professional Fees, Cr. $2,000
Trina Lopez, Withdr., Dr. $3,000
    Trina Lopez, Capital, Cr. $3,000

Ending balances:
AR—Suzanne Sharpe, $225.00
Store Supplies, $245.00
Furniture & Fixtures, $2,000.00
AP—Vicki Dash, $2,000.00
Trina Lopez, Capital, $16,000.00
Trina Lopez, Withdr., $7,200.00
Professional Fees, $13,000.00

4 ASSESS

A chapter test is available for use in assessing students' understanding of concepts in this chapter.

Unit objective and problem tests are available to assess students' knowledge of concepts in Chapters 3-6.

The testmaker software will enable you to develop tailor-made chapter, unit, semester, and final tests.

Alternative Assessment

For alternative assessment strategies, refer to *Tech Prep Strategies in Accounting*.

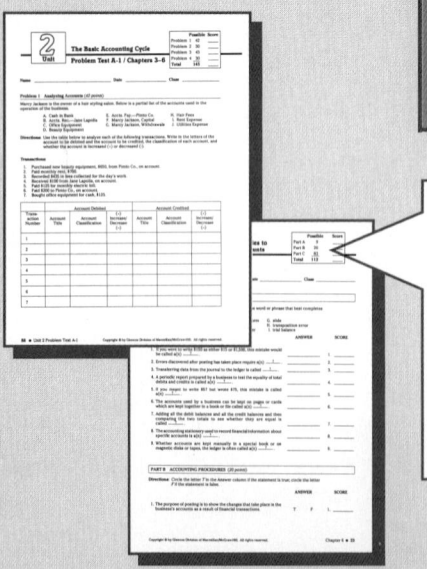

Use Chapter Test 6 here to assess students' understanding and retention of the concepts and procedures presented in the chapter.

Use Unit 2 Objective Test and/or Unit 2 Problem Test to assess students' retention of concepts presented in Chapters 3 through 6.

Feb. 24   Wrote Check 105 for $400 to Office Interiors on account.
    26   Received a check for $100 from Jenny Simms, Receipt 101.
    28   Chris Courtney took home $15 worth of supplies for personal use, Memorandum 3.

CHALLENGE

PROBLEM

Problem 6-5   Recording and Posting Correcting Entries

An auditor reviewed the accounting records of Lopez's Chiropractic Service. The auditor wrote a memo, outlined below, about a number of errors discovered in the June records. The general journal for June and a portion of the general ledger are included in the working papers.

Instructions:

(1) Record whatever correcting entries are required on general journal page 22. Some errors will not require correcting entries, but will require a general ledger correction. Use Memorandum 50 as the source document for all correcting entries and June 30 as the date.

(2) Post all correcting entries to the appropriate general ledger accounts.

Errors:

June   3   The purchase was for store supplies.
      7   A $200 payment to a creditor, Vicki Dash, was not posted to the account.
      9   The Furniture and Fixtures account should have been debited for $500.
    13   Trina Lopez withdrew $1,200 from the business for personal use.
    17   Cash totaling $2,000 was received for professional services completed for patients.
    19   A $75 receipt from Suzanne Sharpe was posted as $57.
    27   Trina Lopez invested an additional $3,000 in the business.

*A*ccounting Clerks: Patient, Persistent, Good with Figures

If you have these qualities—along with a high school diploma—clerical accounting could be in your future.

In today's work force, there are about two million clerical accounting workers—also known as accounting clerks or bookkeepers. Their tasks vary widely depending upon the size of the company that employs them. Generally speaking, accounting clerks are responsible for maintaining accurate records for all financial transactions (journalizing and posting) and preparing material for reports that measure the company's financial position or reports that facilitate corporate decision making.

In small companies, clerical accounting workers perform many of the steps in the accounting cycle: analyzing and recording business transactions, posting to ledgers, preparing a trial balance. They might also perform a wide variety of other accounting tasks: computing payrolls, writing checks to pay bills, making deposits to the business's checking account, reconciling bank statements, handling telephone inquiries about orders and bills, preparing statements for customers, placing orders for supplies or equipment, maintaining records of merchandise purchased and sold, and being responsible for change or petty cash funds.

In larger companies, there may be many accounting clerks. Since there are more people to perform basic accounting tasks, the accounting clerks tend to specialize. For example, an accounting clerk might only handle activities involving the purchase of items used or sold by the business. Other specialized clerical accounting positions include cash clerk, payroll clerk, accounts receivable or accounts payable clerk.

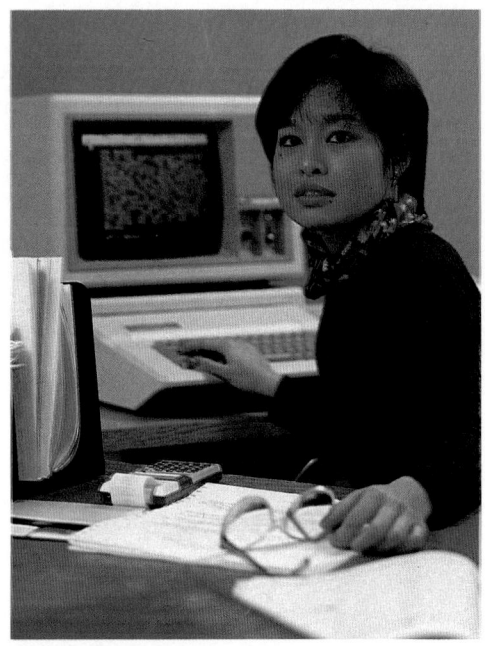

Clerical accounting workers perform a wide variety of tasks.

In today's business world, many companies use computers to process and maintain their accounting records. Even smaller businesses have access to microcomputers. Be sure, then, that you can add this line to your resume: Can perform accounting tasks on a computer.

Small neighborhood businesses such as pharmacies, dry cleaners, or hardware stores often employ students on a part-time basis to help with clerical accounting tasks. Ask if any students in your class are so employed. Have them share with the class the kinds of tasks they are asked to perform.

QUESTIONS

1. How does the work of an accounting clerk differ from that of a CPA?
2. Are there traits other than those mentioned in the text that would be desirable in an accounting clerk?

ANSWERS

1. An accounting clerk is involved primarily with recording the financial activity of a business on a day-to-day basis. The CPA interprets and evaluates this information with a view toward improving financial performance of the business.
2. In addition to being patient, persistent, and good with figures, accounting clerks should be logical, detail-oriented, and honest.
For additional information on accounting careers, refer to "Careers in Accounting" accompanying the *Glencoe Accounting* program.

127

APPLICATION ACTIVITY 1

This mini practice set covers the material that students have studied through Chapter 6. In this activity students will open general ledger accounts, analyze business transactions, journalize business transactions, post to ledger accounts, and prepare a trial balance.

Accounting stationery for completing this activity is included in the *Chapter Reviews and Working Papers.* Source documents are available to give realism to this activity.

COMPUTER

PROBLEM

Students may also complete this activity using *Glencoe Accounting, General Ledger Software.*

Teaching Tips

■ The Income Summary account has been omitted from this activity since students have not yet learned how it is used.

Mini Practice Set

APPLICATION ACTIVITY 1

Setting Up Accounting Records for a Sole Proprietorship

You have just completed your study of the first five steps in the accounting cycle. Now you will have the opportunity to apply what you have learned by setting up the accounting records for Jack Hires, Attorney at Law. The accounting stationery needed to complete this activity is included in the working papers accompanying this textbook.

When you have completed this activity, you will have done the following:

1. Analyzed business transactions.
2. Used the general journal to journalize business transactions.
3. Posted journal entries to the general ledger accounts.
4. Prepared a trial balance.

Jack Hires, Attorney at Law

Jack Hires, Attorney at Law, is organized as a sole proprietorship. The business is fully owned and operated by Jack Hires. The firm provides a wide range of legal services to local businesses and to individuals who live in the community. These services include criminal defense, personal injury, family law, bankruptcy, and general practice. Revenue earned by the firm is in the form of professional fees.

Chart of Accounts

The chart of accounts for Jack Hires, Attorney at Law, follows.

JACK HIRES, ATTORNEY AT LAW
Chart of Accounts

	101	Cash in Bank
	105	Accounts Receivable—Andrew Hospital
	110	Accounts Receivable—Indiana Trucking
ASSETS	115	Accounts Receivable—Sunshine Products
	130	Office Supplies
	135	Office Equipment
	140	Office Furniture
	145	Professional Library
LIABILITIES	205	Accounts Payable—Legal Services, Inc.
	210	Accounts Payable—Office Systems
OWNER'S EQUITY	301	Jack Hires, Capital
	305	Jack Hires, Withdrawals
REVENUE	401	Professional Fees
	505	Professional Expenses
EXPENSES	510	Rent Expense
	515	Utilities Expense

128

Jack Hires, Attorney at Law, began business operations on May 1 of this year. During the month of May, the business completed the transactions that follow.

Instructions: Use the accounting stationery in the working papers accompanying this textbook to complete this activity.

(1) Open a general ledger account for each account in the chart of accounts.
(2) Analyze each business transaction.
(3) Enter each business transaction in the general journal. Begin on journal page 1.
(4) Post each journal entry to the appropriate accounts in the general ledger.
(5) Prove the general ledger by preparing a trial balance.

Transactions:

May 1 Jack Hires invested $30,000 in the business by opening a checking account in the name of the business at City National Bank, Memorandum 1.
2 Bought a computer for the office for $3,500, Check 101.
2 Issued Check 102 for $125 for the purchase of office supplies.
3 Bought office furniture for $2,700 on account from Office Systems, Invoice 457.
7 Mr. Hires invested his personal law library worth $2,350 in the business, Memorandum 2.
9 Received $675 from Mr. and Mrs. James Market for representing them in court, Receipt 101.
11 Completed legal work for Andrew Hospital and agreed to be paid later, Invoice 101 for $750.
12 Bought additional law books on account from Legal Services, Inc., Invoice 876, $1,325.
14 Wrote Check 103 for $118 to pay the electric bill.
15 Jack Hires withdrew $500 for personal expenses, Check 104.
17 Completed legal services on account for Sunshine Products, Invoice 102, $1,250.
18 Bought a filing cabinet (office equipment) for $275, Check 105.
19 Received a check for $600 as payment legal services provided to a client, Receipt 102.
20 Provided legal services on account to Indiana Trucking, Invoice 103 for $600.
21 Prepared Receipt 103 for $625 received on account from Sunshine Products.
22 Paid the telephone bill of $145, Check 106.
25 Sent Check 107 for $1,350 to Office Systems as payment on account.
26 Received $245 for legal services, Receipt 104.
27 Paid the annual dues for membership in the American Bar Association, $350, Check 108.
30 Wrote Check 109 for the monthly rent, $750.
30 Withdrew $500 for personal expenses, Check 110.

129

Teacher Notes

LOOKING BACK

In the first half of this unit, students learned to analyze transactions, record journal entries, post to general ledger accounts, and prepare a trial balance. This chapter begins instruction on the end-of-period activities that complete the accounting cycle. Students will learn how to prepare a six-column work sheet for the sole proprietorship, service business introduced in earlier chapters.

VOCABULARY DEVELOPMENT

Ask students to write a sentence using each of the new terms in context. Ask for volunteers to write their sentences on the board. Discuss any differences in the use of the terms. Definitions of these terms are found in the chapter and in the glossary on pages 670-679.

Chapter

PREPARING A SIX-COLUMN WORK SHEET

In Chapter 6, you learned how to prepare a trial balance. At the end of a fiscal period, however, the owner of a business needs more information than a list of the account balances. The owner needs to know the business's financial position. In other words, has the business earned revenue greater than its expenses? Have expenses for the period increased or decreased? Has the business grown during the period?

The answers to such questions are found by preparing end-of-fiscal-period reports. Preparing a work sheet is the activity that begins the end-of-fiscal-period work. In this chapter, you will see how the work sheet is used to organize the information that has been recorded in the general ledger accounts during the fiscal period. You will also learn how to calculate the net income or the net loss for the fiscal period.

Learning Objectives

When you have completed Chapter 7, you should be able to do the following:

1. Explain the purpose of the work sheet.
2. Describe the parts of a six-column work sheet.
3. Prepare a six-column work sheet.
4. Calculate net income and net loss amounts.
5. Define the accounting terms introduced in this chapter.

New   Terms

work sheet
ruling
matching principle
net income
net loss

130

Teaching Resources

- Lesson Plans
- TE/Chapter Reviews & Working Papers
- Demonstration Problems
- Student Study Plans
- Teaching Transparencies
- Solutions Transparencies
- Electronic Field Trips Video, Level I
- Electronic Study Guide
- Chapter 7 Test

Other Resources

- Skills Improvement Activities
- Blackline Masters
- Careers in Accounting
- Dictionary
- Math Review for Accounting
- Tech Prep Strategies in Accounting
- Video
- Test Bank with Software
- Spanish Resources/Audiotapes
- Spanish Electronic Study Guide

The Sixth Step of the Accounting Cycle

The length of a fiscal period varies from one company to another. The maximum period covered by the accounting cycle, however, is one year. The first five steps of the accounting cycle are performed frequently during the cycle. The last four steps—preparing a work sheet, preparing financial statements, journalizing and posting closing entries, and preparing a post-closing trial balance—complete the accounting cycle. These steps begin the end-of-fiscal-period work. As you can see in Figure 7-1, this work begins with the sixth step of the accounting cycle: preparing a work sheet.

Figure 7-1 Steps in the Accounting Cycle, with Step 6 Highlighted

A **work sheet** is just what its name implies—a working paper used to collect information from the ledger accounts on one sheet of paper. Like the T account, the work sheet is a tool used by the accountant. The work sheet pulls together all the information needed to prepare the financial statements and complete the other end-of-fiscal-period activities.

Preparing a Work Sheet

A work sheet is prepared in pencil on standard multi-column accounting paper. The paper comes in several sizes and is usually printed without column headings. Blank spaces for column headings allow accounting clerks to write in headings needed by a particular business. The Global Travel Agency work sheet uses a six-column format with the column headings already filled in.

CHAPTER 7 Preparing a Six-Column Work Sheet   **131**

MAJOR CONCEPTS

- The Sixth Step of the Accounting Cycle
- Preparing a Work Sheet
- A Review of the Steps in Preparing a Six-Column Work Sheet

*B*USINESS CONNECTION

In 1969 Don Fisher opened a store to sell marked-down Levi's jeans and records. He called his new store The Gap. After a slow start, the company boomed in the early 1970s. Today The Gap continues to grow, and its trademark products are generic T-shirts and jeans. Like other businesses, The Gap must organize and summarize accounting information that is then analyzed for use in making business decisions that will help keep the business growing.

2 TEACH

CONCEPT DEVELOPMENT

The Sixth Step of the Accounting Cycle

This section gives students a brief review of the steps presented in earlier chapters and mentions the remaining four steps that will be covered in Chapters 7-9. Preparing the work sheet is the beginning of the end-of-period work. Review the meaning of "fiscal period" and stress the importance of consistency in time periods.

Point out that the work sheet is a "working paper" and thus is not part of the end-of-period financial

Continued

Using Visuals

Use Figure 7-1 to review the first five steps in the accounting cycle. Point out Step 6, highlighted in red, which is covered in this chapter.

The Sixth Step of the Accounting Cycle (Continued)

statements. Since it is a working document, the work sheet may be prepared in pencil. Emphasize that its purpose is to gather all necessary information on one piece of paper to assist in the preparation of the financial statements for the period.

CONCEPT DEVELOPMENT

Preparing a Work Sheet

A work sheet is prepared in sections. The first sections must balance before one can complete the remaining sections. The information that goes on the work sheet is obtained from the ledger accounts. Remind students that any errors in the journalizing and posting process should be corrected before the work sheet is prepared. Otherwise, those errors will be carried through the end-of-period documents.

The work sheet is an accounting tool. Accountants use it to gather, on one document, all of the information needed to prepare end-of-period reports.

The Global Travel work sheet has five sections: (1) the heading, (2) the Account Title section, (3) the Trial Balance section, (4) the Income Statement section, and (5) the Balance Sheet section. The Account Title section includes a column for the account number and a column for the account name. Find each of these parts on the work sheet shown in Figure 7-2.

The Trial Balance, Income Statement, and Balance Sheet sections each have debit and credit amount columns. The six amount columns give this work sheet its name: the six-column work sheet.

Global Travel Agency
Work Sheet
For the Month Ended October 31, 19--

ACCT. NO.	ACCOUNT NAME	TRIAL BALANCE		INCOME STATEMENT		BALANCE SHEET	
		DEBIT	CREDIT	DEBIT	CREDIT	DEBIT	CREDIT
1							
2							

Figure 7-2 Six-Column Work Sheet

The Heading

The heading of a work sheet is made up of three kinds of information, each centered on its own line. The heading includes

132

Making Connections

EVERYDAY LIFE

When completing class assignments, students often create a rough draft first. When writing reports, students first prepare an outline to organize the information to be contained in the report. They may choose to use a pencil rather than a pen so that they can erase mistakes and make revisions. The work sheet is a rough draft for the accountant. It is used to organize financial information prior to preparing the end-of-period financial statements. The columns of the work sheet help the accountant sort and classify information.

1. The name of the business.
2. The name of the accounting form.
3. The fiscal period covered by the work sheet.

It is easy to remember the function of the lines in the heading. Each line answers a "W" question: the name of the business (Who?), the name of the accounting form being prepared (What?), and the fiscal period covered (When?). Notice how these elements are positioned on the work sheet in Figure 7-2. Follow this format when preparing the heading of any work sheet.

The Account Title and Trial Balance Sections

Information for the Account Title and Trial Balance sections is taken from the general ledger accounts. In Chapter 6, as the fifth step of the accounting cycle, you prepared a trial balance by listing the account titles and their final balances. A trial balance can be prepared at any time during the fiscal period to prove the general ledger. When a trial balance is prepared at the end of a fiscal period, though, it is prepared as a part of the work sheet.

Look at the work sheet in Figure 7-3. The account numbers, titles, and balances were taken from Global Travel's general ledger. The account numbers and titles are listed on the work sheet in the same order as they appear in the general ledger. As you recall, asset accounts are placed first. After assets come the liability, owner's equity, revenue, and expense accounts. *All* the general ledger accounts are listed on the work sheet, even those having a zero balance. All the accounts are listed to avoid accidentally omitting an account and to ensure that the work sheet contains all the accounts needed to prepare the financial reports.

Global Travel Agency
Work Sheet
For the Month Ended October 31, 19--

ACCT. NO.	ACCOUNT NAME	TRIAL BALANCE DEBIT	TRIAL BALANCE CREDIT	INCOME STATEMENT DEBIT	INCOME STATEMENT CREDIT	BALANCE SHEET DEBIT	BALANCE SHEET CREDIT	
101	Cash in Bank	16 125 00						1
105	Accts. Rec. - Burton Co.	450 00						2
110	Accts. Rec. - Greer's Market							3
120	Computer Equipment	8 000 00						4
130	Office Equipment	1 500 00						5
201	Accts. Pay. - City News		75 00					6
205	Accts. Pay. - Mod. Off. Supp.		750 00					7
301	Jan Harter, Capital		25 200 00					8
305	Jan Harter, Withdrawals	400 00						9
310	Income Summary							10
401	Fees		1 650 00					11
501	Advertising Expense	75 00						12
510	Maintenance Expense	450 00						13
520	Rent Expense	550 00						14
530	Utilities Expense	1 25 00						15

Figure 7-3 Work Sheet with Account Titles and Trial Balance Amounts

R E M E M B E R

On the work sheet, be sure to enter the number, title, and final balance of every account that appears in the general ledger.

Using Visuals

Use demonstration problem 7-1 to show students how a heading is written on the work sheet.

Teaching Tips

■ Point out the importance of the three items of information in the heading. The "who," "what," and "when" will help students remember each line of the heading and the order of the lines.

■ Emphasize that a trial balance may be prepared at any time during the fiscal period but only after all posting has been completed.

■ Account numbers are listed on the work sheet to help in classifying accounts. Account numbers are also included so students can easily enter data from the work sheet directly into the computer, particularly for closing entries.

■ Remind students that erasing is permitted on a work sheet because it is a working document.

Using Visuals

Draw students' attention to Figure 7-3. Have them use the account numbers on the left of the form to tell you the classification of the accounts listed on the work sheet. Ask students what the dashes in the Trial Balance section mean.

Interdisciplinary Connections

MATHEMATICS

Remind students that many errors in work sheets and balance sheets are due to mistakes in adding, subtracting, and other computations. Point out that mathematical errors can occur even when using a calculator. Students need good math skills to check and double-check their work.

Refer students to *Math Review for Accounting* for review exercises to strengthen math skills.

The final balance for each account is entered in the Trial Balance section in the column that corresponds to its normal balance side. In other words, the final balances of accounts with normal debit balances are entered in the Trial Balance debit column. The final balances for accounts with normal credit balances are entered in the Trial Balance credit column. If an account has a zero balance at the end of the period, a dash is entered in the normal balance column. Notice in Figure 7-3 that a dash was entered in the Trial Balance debit column for Accounts Receivable—Greer's Market. Dashes were also recorded in the Trial Balance debit *and* credit columns for Income Summary. Income Summary does not have a normal balance side. You'll learn more about this account in Chapter 9.

Ruling and Totaling the Trial Balance Section

Ruling means "drawing a line." In accounting, a single rule drawn under a column of amounts means that the entries above the rule are to be added or subtracted. After all account titles and their balances have been entered on the work sheet, a single line is drawn under the last entry and across the entire Trial Balance section as shown in Figure 7-4. The debit and credit columns are now ready for totaling. If the ledger is in balance, the total debits will equal the total credits. Look again at Figure 7-4. The totals match, with each column totaling $27,675.00. Since total debits equal total credits, a double rule is drawn across both amount columns just beneath the totals, as shown in Figure 7-4. This double rule means that the amounts just above are totals and that no other entries will be made in the Trial Balance columns.

If the total debits do not equal the total credits, an error has been made. The error must be found and corrected before the work sheet can be completed. Procedures for locating errors were discussed in Chapter 6.

ACCT. NO.	ACCOUNT NAME	TRIAL BALANCE DEBIT	TRIAL BALANCE CREDIT	INCOME STATEMENT DEBIT	INCOME STATEMENT CREDIT	BALANCE SHEET DEBIT	BALANCE SHEET CREDIT
101	Cash in Bank	16 125 00					
105	Accts. Rec.—Burton Co.	450 00					
110	Accts. Rec.—Greer's Market	—					
120	Computer Equipment	8 000 00					
130	Office Equipment	1 500 00					
201	Accts. Pay.—City News		75 00				
205	Accts. Pay.—Mod. Off. Supp.		750 00				
301	Jan Harter, Capital		25 200 00				
305	Jan Harter, Withdrawals	400 00					
310	Income Summary	—	—				
401	Fees		1 650 00				
501	Advertising Expense	75 00					
510	Maintenance Expense	450 00					
520	Rent Expense	550 00					
530	Utilities Expense	125 00					
		27 675 00	27 675 00				

Global Travel Agency — Work Sheet — For the Month Ended October 31, 19--

Figure 7-4 Work Sheet with Trial Balance Section Completed

Before you read about the Income Statement and Balance Sheet sections of the work sheet, complete the following activity.

Meeting Special Needs

LEARNING DISABILITIES

Some students with learning disabilities have trouble with sequential tasks involving numbers and following step-by-step instructions. They may, for example, have trouble preparing a complete work sheet. For these students, it may be helpful to break up this task into smaller parts. Or, provide a "go-by" that lists the steps in completing the work sheet.

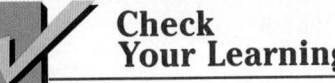

Check Your Learning

Answer the following questions about the work sheet on a sheet of notebook paper.

1. What part of the work sheet answers the questions who?, what?, when?
2. The account titles are listed on the work sheet in the same order as in the general ledger. What determines the order of the accounts in the general ledger?
3. How is a zero account balance indicated on the work sheet?

Compare your answers with those in the answers section. Re-read the preceding part of the chapter to find the correct answers to any questions you may have missed.

The Balance Sheet Section

The Balance Sheet section of the work sheet contains the balances of the asset, liability, and owner's equity accounts. As a result, these accounts are called the "balance sheet accounts." Once the Trial Balance section has been proved, the next step is to *extend,* or transfer, the amounts to the Balance Sheet section. In other words, the Trial Balance amounts for the asset, liability, and owner's equity accounts are simply copied to the appropriate Balance Sheet amount columns. Start on line 1 and extend each account balance in order. Debit amounts are extended to the Balance Sheet debit column, credit amounts to the Balance Sheet credit column. The work sheet in Figure 7-5 shows the balances extended to the Balance Sheet section.

Teaching Tips

■ Tell students to extend figures from the top of the work sheet down. They are less likely to miss an account balance.

■ Point out that permanent accounts are included in this section, and emphasize that each account balance remains in either the Debit or Credit column. If it is a debit in the Trial Balance section, it is a debit in the Balance Sheet section.

Global Travel Agency
Work Sheet
For the Month Ended October 31, 19--

ACCT. NO.	ACCOUNT NAME	TRIAL BALANCE		INCOME STATEMENT		BALANCE SHEET		
		DEBIT	CREDIT	DEBIT	CREDIT	DEBIT	CREDIT	
101	Cash in Bank	16 125 00				16 125 00		1
105	Accts. Rec.- Burton Co.	450 00				450 00		2
110	Accts. Rec.- Greer's Market							3
120	Computer Equipment	8 000 00				8 000 00		4
130	Office Equipment	1 500 00				1 500 00		5
201	Accts. Pay.- City News		75 00				75 00	6
205	Accts. Pay.- Mod. Off. Supp.		750 00				750 00	7
301	Jan Harter, Capital		25 200 00				25 200 00	8
305	Jan Harter, Withdrawals	400 00				400 00		9
310	Income Summary							10
401	Fees		1 650 00					11
501	Advertising Expense	75 00						12
510	Maintenance Expense	450 00						13
520	Rent Expense	550 00						14
530	Utilities Expense	125 00						15
		27 675 00	27 675 00					16

Figure 7-5 Work Sheet with Trial Balance Amounts Extended to Balance Sheet Section

Using Visuals

Use demonstration problem 7-4 to show students how to extend figures from one section of the work sheet to another.

The next step in completing the work sheet is to extend the account balances to the Income Statement section.

Using Visuals

With students looking at Figure 7-5, point out the account balances that have been extended from the Trial Balance section to the Balance Sheet section. Make sure students understand the term "extend."

Reteaching Strategies

Review the need for the Trial Balance section of the work sheet to be totaled, proved, and ruled before the account balances are extended to the other work sheet columns. The double rules at the bottom of the Trial Balance section indicate that the section is completed. The double rules are added only when the total debits equal the total credits.

To help students remember the source of information for preparing the work sheet, have them turn to pages 114-115 in Chapter 6 and compare the account balances there to the Trial Balance section of Figure 7-4.

Using Visuals

A teaching transparency showing the extension of amounts to the Balance Sheet section (Figure 7-5) is available for use here. See the transparency binder accompanying Glencoe Accounting.

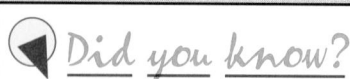
The Income Statement Section

The Income Statement section of the work sheet contains the balances of the revenue and expense accounts. These accounts are listed on the work sheet after the asset, liability, and owner's equity accounts. They are extended to the Income Statement section *after* the accounts are extended to the Balance Sheet section. Revenue accounts have a normal credit balance. The account balances for revenue accounts are, therefore, extended to the credit column of the Income Statement section. Since expense accounts have a normal debit balance, account balances for expenses are extended to the Income Statement debit column. Notice the amounts in the debit and credit columns of the Income Statement section in Figure 7-6.

Global Travel Agency
Work Sheet
For the Month Ended October 31, 19--

ACCT. NO.	ACCOUNT NAME	TRIAL BALANCE DEBIT	TRIAL BALANCE CREDIT	INCOME STATEMENT DEBIT	INCOME STATEMENT CREDIT	BALANCE SHEET DEBIT	BALANCE SHEET CREDIT	
101	Cash in Bank	1612500				1612500		1
105	Accts. Rec.—Burton Co.	45000				45000		2
110	Accts. Rec.—Greer's Market							3
120	Computer Equipment	800000				800000		4
130	Office Equipment	150000				150000		5
201	Accts. Pay—City News		7500				7500	6
205	Accts. Pay—Mod. Off. Supp.		75000				75000	7
301	Jan Harter, Capital		2520000				2520000	8
305	Jan Harter, Withdrawals	40000				40000		9
310	Income Summary							10
401	Fees		165000		165000			11
501	Advertising Expense	7500		7500				12
510	Maintenance Expense	45000		45000				13
520	Rent Expense	55000		55000				14
530	Utilities Expense	12500		12500				15
		2767500	2767500					16

Figure 7-6 Work Sheet with Trial Balance Amounts Extended to Income Statement Section

Totaling the Income Statement and Balance Sheet Sections

After all the amounts in the Trial Balance section have been extended to the Balance Sheet and Income Statement sections, those sections are totaled. As in the Trial Balance section, a single rule is drawn across the four debit and credit columns to indicate that the columns are ready to be added. Look now at Figure 7-7 on page 137. After the four columns are totaled, notice that the debit and credit columns in each section are *not* equal. Unlike the Trial Balance debit and credit totals, the column totals in these two sections will not be equal until the net income or net loss for the fiscal period is added.

Showing Net Income on the Work Sheet

Businesses must spend money to provide goods and services for customers and to pay the costs of operating the business. The costs of operating a business (such as telephone bills and rent) are expenses. In

Critical Thinking

Ask students whether or not the following errors would be revealed by a trial balance.

a. A credit entry was never posted.
b. An entire entry was never posted.
c. A transaction was not journalized.
d. A transaction was posted to the wrong account.
e. An amount was transposed during the posting process.
   (Answers: a. yes; b. no; c. no; d. no; e. yes)

Global Travel Agency
Work Sheet
For the Month Ended October 31, 19--

ACCT. NO.	ACCOUNT NAME	TRIAL BALANCE DEBIT	TRIAL BALANCE CREDIT	INCOME STATEMENT DEBIT	INCOME STATEMENT CREDIT	BALANCE SHEET DEBIT	BALANCE SHEET CREDIT
101	Cash in Bank	16 125 00				16 125 00	
105	Accts. Rec.- Burton Co.	450 00				450 00	
110	Accts. Rec.- Greer's Market	—					
120	Computer Equipment	8 000 00				8 000 00	
130	Office Equipment	1 500 00				1 500 00	
201	Accts. Pay.- City News		75 00				75 00
205	Accts. Pay.- Mod. Off. Supp.		750 00				750 00
301	Jan Harter, Capital		25 200 00				25 200 00
305	Jan Harter, Withdrawals	400 00				400 00	
310	Income Summary						
401	Fees		1 650 00		1 650 00		
501	Advertising Expense	75 00		75 00			
510	Maintenance Expense	450 00		450 00			
520	Rent Expense	550 00		550 00			
530	Utilities Expense	125 00		125 00			
		27 675 00	27 675 00	1 200 00	1 650 00	26 475 00	26 025 00

Figure 7-7 Work Sheet with Income Statement and Balance Sheet Sections Totaled

accounting, expenses are always matched against revenue for the same period. This is referred to as the **matching principle.** Matching the expenses of a period to the revenue earned during the same period provides a more reliable measure of profit. Matching expenses to revenue provides information on the cost (expense) of producing revenue for the period. This information helps the business owner or manager make decisions about such things as whether expenses are too high compared to the amount of revenue those expenses produced.

The Income Statement section of the work sheet includes both the revenue and the expenses for the fiscal period. After the columns have been totaled, total expenses (the debit column total) are subtracted from total revenue (the credit column total) to find the net income. **Net income** is the amount left after expenses for the period have been subtracted from revenue for the period. Global Travel Agency has a net income of $450.00 for the month of October.

$1,650.00
−1,200.00
$ 450.00

The amount of the net income must also be reflected in the Balance Sheet section of the work sheet. Remember, revenue and expense accounts are temporary capital accounts. Both revenue and expenses affect capital. Revenue increases capital, while expenses decrease capital. A net income, therefore, increases capital since total revenue is greater than total expenses. During the fiscal period, revenue and expense amounts are recorded in the temporary capital accounts set up for this purpose. At the end of the fiscal period, the net income—the difference between total revenue and total expenses—is transferred to the owner's capital account. Since the capital account is increased by credits, the amount of the net income is shown on the work sheet as an addition to the total of the Balance Sheet *credit* column.

$26,475.00
−26,025.00
$ 450.00

To check the accuracy of the net income amount, subtract the total of the Balance Sheet credit column from the total of the Balance Sheet debit column. Your answer should equal the amount of the net income. If the two

CHAPTER 7   Preparing a Six-Column Work Sheet   137

amounts match, enter the net income on the work sheet. If the amounts do not match, an error has been made. That error must be found and corrected. Check to be sure that all amounts have been extended correctly from the Trial Balance section and that the totals of all columns were added correctly.

To record the net income on the work sheet, follow these steps:

1. Skip a line after the last account title and then write the words "Net Income" in the Account Name column.   **A**
2. On the same line, enter the net income amount in the Income Statement debit column.   **B**
3. On the same line, enter the net income amount in the Balance Sheet credit column.   **C**

Look at the partial work sheet shown in Figure 7-8 to see how net income is recorded.

Global Travel Agency
Work Sheet
For the Month Ended October 31, 19--

ACCT. NO.	ACCOUNT NAME	TRIAL BALANCE		INCOME STATEMENT		BALANCE SHEET	
		DEBIT	CREDIT	DEBIT	CREDIT	DEBIT	CREDIT
401	*Fees*		1650 00		1650 00		
501	*Advertising Expense*	75 00		75 00			
510	*Maintenance Expense*	450 00		450 00			
520	*Rent Expense*	550 00		550 00			
530	*Utilities Expense*	125 00		125 00			
		2675 00	2675 00	1200 00	1650 00	2647500	2602500
A	*Net Income*			**B** 450 00			**C** 450 00

Figure 7-8   Partial Work Sheet Showing Net Income

Completing the Work Sheet

To complete the Income Statement and Balance Sheet sections, follow these steps. The completed work sheet for Global Travel is shown in Figure 7-9 on page 139.

1. Draw a single rule across all four columns on the line under the net income amount.   **D**
2. Add the net income amount to the previous total of the Income Statement debit column. Enter the new total and bring down the total of the Income Statement credit column to the same line. Total debits should equal total credits.   **E**
3. Repeat this process for the Balance Sheet section. Again, the total debit amount should equal the total credit amount.   **F**
4. Draw a double rule under the column totals and across all four columns. The double rule indicates that the debit and credit columns are equal and that no more amounts are to be entered in these columns.   **G**

Showing a Net Loss on the Work Sheet

When total expenses are greater than total revenue, a **net loss** occurs. A net loss decreases owner's equity. This decrease is shown as a debit to the capital account. When a net loss occurs, the Income Statement debit column

138

Making Connections

AROUND THE WORLD

Net income earned by a business is used in several ways. Some of it may be paid out to owners as a return on their investment. Much of it is used to finance business expansion wherever the opportunity arises, which for many companies is the international market.

For example, Pepsico recently announced plans to invest $500 million in Poland, $115 million in Hungary, and $750 million in Mexico. With these investments, Pepsico hopes to gain a large share of the market for soft-drink sales in these three countries.

Global Travel Agency
Work Sheet
For the Month Ended October 31, 19--

ACCT. NO.	ACCOUNT NAME	TRIAL BALANCE DEBIT	TRIAL BALANCE CREDIT	INCOME STATEMENT DEBIT	INCOME STATEMENT CREDIT	BALANCE SHEET DEBIT	BALANCE SHEET CREDIT	
101	Cash in Bank	16125 00				16125 00		1
105	Accts. Rec.-Burton Co.	450 00				450 00		2
110	Accts. Rec.-Greer's Market							3
120	Computer Equipment	8000 00				8000 00		4
130	Office Equipment	1500 00				1500 00		5
201	Accts. Pay.-City News		75 00				75 00	6
205	Accts. Pay.-Mod. Off. Supp.		750 00				750 00	7
301	Jan Harter, Capital		25200 00				25200 00	8
305	Jan Harter, Withdrawals	400 00				400 00		9
310	Income Summary							10
401	Fees		1650 00		1650 00			11
501	Advertising Expense	75 00		75 00				12
510	Maintenance Expense	450 00		450 00				13
520	Rent Expense	550 00		550 00				14
530	Utilities Expense	125 00		125 00				15
		27675 00	27675 00	1200 00	1650 00	26475 00	26025 00	16
A	Net Income			**B** 450 00			**C** 450 00	17
				1650 00	1650 00	26475 00	26475 00	18

D
G

E   F

Figure 7-9 Completed Work Sheet

$4,132.00
−3,904.00
$ 228.00

total (total expenses) is greater than the Income Statement credit column total (total revenue). The partial work sheet in Figure 7-10 shows a net loss. Expenses exceed revenue by $228.00.

To enter a net loss on the work sheet, follow the same general procedure as for entering net income:

1. Skip a line after the last account title and write the words "Net Loss" in the Account Name column.   **A**
2. On the same line, enter the net loss amount in the *credit* column of the Income Statement section.   **B** Enter this same amount in the *debit* column of the Balance Sheet section.   **C** (Remember to check the accuracy of the net loss amount by subtracting the Balance Sheet debit total from the Balance Sheet credit total. The difference should be the same as the amount of the net loss.)
3. Draw a single rule across all four columns.   **D**
4. Add the net loss amount to the previous totals and enter the new totals. Bring down the totals of the other two columns.   **E** Draw a double rule under the column totals across all four columns.   **F**

510	Maintenance Expense	1600 00		1600 00				13
520	Rent Expense	1400 00		1400 00				14
530	Utilities Expense	525 00		525 00				15
		5824 00	5824 00	4132 00	3904 00	31242 00	31470 00	16
A	Net Loss				**B** 228 00	**C** 228 00		17 D
				E 4132 00	4132 00	31470 00	31470 00	18 F

Figure 7-10 Partial Work Sheet Showing a Net Loss

Making Connections

COMMUNICATIONS

When showing a work sheet to a client, an accountant must be able to explain what exactly the figures mean. Have two students role-play a scene in which an accountant clearly explains to a client the concepts of *net income* and *net loss* and why they occur. The student taking the role of the accountant should evaluate expenses in relation to revenue. The student taking the role of the client should be prepared to ask questions about the work sheet and its use in preparing end-of-period statements.

Chapter 7

ACCOUNTING PRACTICE

Students may complete Exercise 7-3 at this point.

Teaching Tips

- Have students explain why a net income or net loss occurs to test whether they understand the concept or are just memorizing rules.

ANSWERS

1. Balance Sheet
2. net income or net loss
3. capital
4. Check to see that all debit and credit balances have been extended accurately. If all balances have been extended, check the addition of each column.

COMPUTERS IN ACCOUNTING

Computers make it possible to process accounting information in a fraction of the time it takes to process the same information manually. For example, Dr. Shaw sees as many as 50 patients a day. Her office personnel use a computer to record and post daily transactions. The posting process literally takes seconds, and then a trial balance is created to make sure the books balance. When it is time to prepare Dr. Shaw's financial statements, the computer can summarize the information collected from the daily transactions (the work sheet) and prepare the balance sheet and income statement.

CONCEPT DEVELOPMENT

A Review of the Steps in Preparing a Six-Column Work Sheet

Make a transparency of a blank work sheet and have students tell you where the information in Steps 1-8 should be placed on the work sheet.

R E M E M B E R

A *net income* amount is recorded in the debit column of the Income Statement section and in the credit column of the Balance Sheet section. A *net loss* amount is recorded in the credit column of the Income Statement section and in the debit column of the Balance Sheet section.

Check Your Learning

Answer these questions about the Income Statement and Balance Sheet sections of the work sheet.

1. Balances from the Trial Balance section of the work sheet are extended first to the ___?___ section.
2. The difference between total revenue and total expenses is ___?___ .
3. When the Balance Sheet debit and credit columns are first totaled, the totals are not equal. The totals are not equal because the amount of the net income or net loss for the period is not reflected in the ___?___ account.
4. If the difference between the Income Statement debit and credit totals does not match the difference between the Balance Sheet debit and credit totals, what should you do to find the error?

Compare your answers to those in the answers section. Re-read the preceding part of the chapter to find the correct answers to any questions you may have missed.

A Review of the Steps in Preparing a Six-Column Work Sheet

Follow these steps—in order—when preparing a six-column work sheet:

1. Write the heading on the work sheet.
2. In the Account Title and Trial Balance sections, list all account numbers and titles and each account balance from the general ledger.
3. Prove the equality of total debits and total credits in the Trial Balance section.
4. Extend the amounts of the Trial Balance section to the appropriate Balance Sheet and Income Statement columns.
5. Total the columns in the Income Statement and Balance Sheet sections.
6. Determine the amount of the net income or the net loss for the fiscal period.
7. Enter the amount of the net income or the net loss in the appropriate columns in the Income Statement and Balance Sheet sections.
8. Total and rule the Income Statement and Balance Sheet sections.

Reteaching Strategies

Net income occurs when you earn more (revenue) than you spend (expenses) during the accounting period. In other words, after all expenses are paid there is still some money left. Net income is also called a profit. Net loss is the result of spending more money (expenses) than the business earns (revenue) during an accounting period.

Assign two or three of your better students to help students who are having difficulties with the work sheet. Use Problem 7A in the Additional Problems section of the textbook (p. 634) for this extra practice.

Summary of Key Points

1. The preparation of a work sheet is the sixth step in the accounting cycle.
2. A work sheet is prepared to pull together all the information needed to complete the end-of-fiscal-period work.
3. The Trial Balance section of the work sheet is completed first. The Income Statement and Balance Sheet sections cannot be completed until the debit and credit totals in the Trial Balance section are equal.
4. Amounts are extended from the Trial Balance section to the Balance Sheet section and then to the Income Statement section.
5. The work sheet is used to calculate the net income or net loss for the fiscal period. Net income results when revenue is greater than the expenses. A net loss results when expenses are greater than revenue.

3 CLOSE

CHAPTER SUMMARY

This summary enumerates the key information in the chapter. It is a useful tool for reinforcement and review.

Pop Quiz

1. The Trial Balance section of the work sheet is prepared from the information in the ____.
2. True or False: Only the accounts showing a balance are recorded on the work sheet.
3. How can a business owner determine whether expenses are too high compared to the amount of revenue produced?
4. If total revenue is greater than total expenses, the result is ____.
5. When the Income Statement Debit column is greater than the Income Statement Credit column, a net ____ results.

ANSWERS

1. ledger
2. False
3. By matching the expenses of a period to the revenue earned during the same period
4. net income
5. loss

PRACTICE AND APPLY

- Language Development
- Comprehension and Retention
- Basic Skills

Building Your Accounting Vocabulary

See the Glossary on pages 670-679 for definitions of these terms.

Reviewing Your Accounting Knowledge

1. To pull together the information needed to complete end-of-fiscal-period work.
2. Heading (name of the business, title of the accounting form, date); Account Title section (list of account numbers and names in general ledger order); Trial Balance section (list of debit and credit account balances); Income Statement section (balances of revenue and expense accounts); Balance Sheet section (balances of asset, liability, and owner's equity accounts).
3. In the same order as in the general ledger.
4. To avoid accidentally omitting an account and to ensure that the work sheet contains all accounts needed to prepare financial reports.
5. That total debits are equal to total credits.
6. The asset, liability, and owner's equity accounts.
7. The revenue and expense accounts.
8. Matching expenses with revenue for a period provides data on the cost of producing revenue and provides valid data for making business decisions.
9. (a) Write "Net Income" or "Net Loss" on the second line after the last account title. (b) Enter the net income amount in the Debit column or the net loss amount in the Credit column of the Income Statement section. (c) On the same line, enter the net income amount in the Credit column or the net loss amount in the Debit column of the Balance Sheet section.
10. That the last figure is a total and that no other entries will be made in the columns.

Improving Your Math Skills

1. 0.5	7. 8/9
2. 0.2	8. 3/5
3. 0.33	9. 3/8
4. 0.8	10. 1/4
5. 0.875	11. 2/3
6. 0.3	12. 3/4

Review and Applications

Building Your Accounting Vocabulary

In your own words, write the definition of each of the following accounting terms. Use complete sentences for your definitions.

| matching principle | net loss | work sheet |
| net income | ruling | |

Reviewing Your Accounting Knowledge

1. Explain why a work sheet is prepared.
2. Name and briefly describe the five parts of a six-column work sheet.
3. In what order are the account titles listed on the work sheet?
4. Why are all accounts, including those with zero balances, listed on the work sheet?
5. What does the Trial Balance section of the work sheet prove when it has been totaled and ruled?
6. Which account balances are extended to the Balance Sheet section of the work sheet?
7. Which account balances are extended to the Income Statement section of the work sheet?
8. Why is the matching principle important?
9. Explain how net income and net loss are recorded on the work sheet.
10. What does a double rule on the work sheet indicate?

Improving Your Math Skills

Many types of work require you to convert fractions into decimals and vice versa. Practice your skills at converting decimals and fractions in the following problems.

Convert the following fractions into decimals.

1. $\frac{1}{2}$ 2. $\frac{1}{5}$ 3. $\frac{1}{3}$
4. $\frac{4}{5}$ 5. $\frac{7}{8}$ 6. $\frac{3}{10}$

Convert the following decimals into fractions.

7. 0.889   8. 0.60   9. 0.375
10. 0.25   11. 0.667   12. 0.75

Applying Accounting Procedures

Exercise 7-1   Entering Account Balances on the Work Sheet

The following accounts appear in the Account Title section of the work sheet.

142

Store Equipment
Rent Expense
Service Fees
Accounts Payable—Panters Supply
Vincent Lee, Capital

Advertising Expense
Accounts Receivable—John Long
Vincent Lee, Withdrawals
Maintenance Expense
Office Supplies

PRACTICE AND APPLY

• Concepts and Procedures

Instructions: Use a form similar to the one that follows. For each account,
(1) Classify the account.
(2) Use a check mark to indicate whether the account balance will be entered in the debit or the credit column of the Trial Balance section of the work sheet. The first account is shown as an example.

Account Title	Account Classification	Trial Balance	
		Debit	Credit
Store Equipment	Asset	✔	

Exercise 7-1: Ch. Obj. 1, 3

Rent Exp., Exp., TB Dr.
Service Fees, Rev., TB Cr.
AP—Painters Supply, Liab., TB Cr.
V. Lee, Cap., OE, TB Cr.
Adv. Exp., Exp., TB Dr.
AR—J. Long, Asset, TB Dr.
V. Lee, With., OE, TB Dr.
Main. Exp., Exp., TB Dr.
Off. Supplies, Asset, TB Dr.

Exercise 7-2 Extending Amounts

Instructions: Use the same account titles listed in Exercise 7-1. On a form similar to the one that follows, indicate to which column on the work sheet the account balance will be extended. The first account has been completed as an example.

Account Title	Income Statement		Balance Sheet	
	Debit	Credit	Debit	Credit
Store Equipment			✔	

Exercise 7-2: Ch. Obj. 3

Rent Exp., Inc. St., Dr.
Service Fees, Inc. St., Cr.
AP—Painters Supply, Bal. Sheet, Cr.
V. Lee, Cap., Bal. Sheet, Cr.
Adv. Exp., Inc. St., Dr.
AR—J. Long, Bal. Sheet, Dr.
V. Lee, With., Bal. Sheet, Dr.
Main. Exp., Inc. St., Dr.
Off. Supplies, Bal. Sheet, Dr.

Exercise 7-3 Calculating Net Income or Net Loss

The totals of the Income Statement debit and credit columns of several different work sheets are listed below. Calculate the amount of the net income or net loss for each set of work sheet amounts.

	Income Statement	
	Debit	Credit
1.	$2,342.00	$1,814.00
2.	914.00	1,173.00
3.	1,795.00	1,424.00
4.	6,933.00	8,256.00
5.	9,125.00	7,258.00
6.	1,182.00	2,089.00

Exercise 7-3: Ch. Obj. 4

1. $528 net loss
2. $259 net income
3. $371 net loss
4. $1,323 net income
5. $1,867 net loss
6. $907 net income

Problem 7-1 Preparing a Six-Column Work Sheet

The final balances in the ledger accounts of the Snowbird Playhouse for the fiscal period ended September 30 appear on page 144.

143

Additional Reinforcement

Students who need additional practice or individualized help will benefit from the *Glencoe Accounting Electronic Study Guide* or the *Glencoe Accounting* on-line multimedia program, which provide reinforcement and reteaching for vocabulary, concepts, and procedures.

Refer students to the Chapter 7 review pages in the workbook, *Chapter Reviews and Working Papers*.

Problem 7-1: Ch. Obj. 3
Trial Balance totals: $34,177.00
Income Statement subtotals:
   $11,772.00 Dr. / $17,663.00 Cr.
Balance Sheet subtotals:
   $22,405.00 Dr. / $16,514.00 Cr.
Net Income: $5,891.00

Problem 7-2: Ch. Obj. 3
Trial Balance totals: $50,729.00
Income Statement subtotals:
   $11,439.00 Dr. / $14,957.00 Cr.
Balance Sheet subtotals:
   $39,290.00 Dr. / $35,772.00 Cr.
Net Income: $3,518.00

		Debit Balances	Credit Balances
101	Cash in Bank	$7,469.00	
105	Stage Equipment	8,396.00	
110	Concession Equipment	5,340.00	
205	Accounts Payable—Atlas, Inc.		$ 1,920.00
210	Accounts Payable—King Co.		834.00
301	Sue Wellen, Capital		13,760.00
305	Sue Wellen, Withdrawals	1,200.00	
310	Income Summary		
401	Ticket Revenue		17,663.00
501	Advertising Expense	3,405.00	
505	Maintenance Expense	1,483.00	
510	Rent Expense	4,500.00	
515	Utilities Expense	2,384.00	

Instructions: Using the preceding account titles and balances, prepare a work sheet for the month ended September 30.
(1) Write the heading on the work sheet.
(2) List all of the account numbers, account titles, and each account balance in the Trial Balance section.
(3) Total and rule the Trial Balance section. (Remember, the two totals must equal before you can continue the work sheet.)
(4) Extend the amounts to the Balance Sheet section.
(5) Extend the amounts to the Income Statement section.
(6) Total the amount columns in the Income Statement and Balance Sheet sections.
(7) Enter the amount of net income or net loss in the appropriate columns in the Income Statement and Balance Sheet sections.
(8) Total and rule the Income Statement and Balance Sheet sections.

Problem 7-2   Preparing a Six-Column Work Sheet
   The ledger for the Four Star Travel Center shows the following account balances on June 30, the end of the fiscal period.

101	Cash in Bank	$10,589.00
105	Accounts Receivable—Frank Perkins	476.00
110	Accounts Receivable—Judy Mudre	385.00
115	Office Equipment	15,395.00
120	Computer Equipment	7,459.00
125	Office Furniture	2,486.00
201	Accounts Payable—Turner Co.	4,396.00
205	Accounts Payable—Spencer Corp.	2,840.00
210	Accounts Payable—LKH Co.	1,036.00
301	Karen Hart, Capital	27,500.00
305	Karen Hart, Withdrawals	2,500.00
310	Income Summary	
401	Commissions Revenue	14,957.00
501	Advertising Expense	3,940.00
505	Entertainment Expense	1,836.00
510	Miscellaneous Expense	924.00
515	Rent Expense	3,500.00
520	Utilities Expense	1,239.00

144

Teacher Notes

Instructions: Using the preceding account numbers, account titles, and balances, prepare a work sheet for the Four Star Travel Center. The Center operates on a three-month fiscal period.

SPREADSHEET

Problem 7-3   Preparing a Six-Column Work Sheet

The final balances in the ledger of the Tower Movie Theatre at the end of November are as follows.

PROBLEM

101	Cash in Bank	$13,394.50
105	Accounts Receivable — Kline, Inc.	357.00
110	Concession Equipment	9,305.75
115	Projection Equipment	4,395.00
120	Office Equipment	5,497.58
125	Office Furniture	1,385.70
205	Accounts Payable — K & D Supply	3,945.65
210	Accounts Payable — Janson Co.	2,846.90
215	Accounts Payable — Top Movie, Inc.	1,923.00
301	Pat Morganstern, Capital	30,426.48
305	Pat Morganstern, Withdrawals	2,500.00
310	Income Summary	
401	Admissions Revenue	11,596.00
405	Concession Revenue	4,496.00
501	Advertising Expense	3,675.00
505	Maintenance Expense	2,658.55
510	Miscellaneous Expense	864.59
515	Rent Expense	7,500.00
520	Telephone Expense	753.96
525	Utilities Expense	2,946.40

Instructions: Prepare a work sheet for the month ended November 30 for the Tower Movie Theatre.

CHALLENGE

Problem 7-4   Locating and Correcting Work Sheet Errors

A-1 Computer Repair Co.'s work sheet for the month ended September 30 appears in the working papers. The Trial Balance section of the work sheet has been completed, and the total debits and total credits are equal. The amounts have also been extended to the Balance Sheet and Income Statement sections. Unfortunately, as the amounts were extended, several errors were made.

PROBLEM

Instructions:

(1) Locate and correct all errors in the Income Statement and Balance Sheet sections. Cross out incorrect amounts and write the correct amount above the crossed-out amount or in the correct column.

(2) Complete the work sheet and determine the net income or net loss for the month.

CHALLENGE **Problem 7-5   Completing the Work Sheet**

The work sheet for Matt's Cleaning Service appears on page 146. Several amounts have been deleted from various columns.

Instructions: Calculate all missing amounts and complete the work sheet.

PROBLEM

145

SPREADSHEET

PROBLEM

Students may complete Problem 7-3 using *Spreadsheet Applications*, the spreadsheet software that accompanies *Glencoe Accounting.*

Trial Balance totals: $55,234.03
Income Statement subtotals:
  $18,398.50 Dr. / $16,092.00 Cr.
Balance Sheet subtotals:
  $36,835.53 Dr. / $39,142.03 Cr.
Net Loss: $2,306.50

Problem 7-4: Ch. Obj. 3, 4

CHALLENGE

PROBLEM

The last problem (or problems) in each chapter is a challenge problem and is identified by this "maze" symbol.

Income Statement subtotals:
  $6,737.00 Dr. / $13,742.00 Cr.
Balance Sheet subtotals:
  $27,779.00 Dr. / $20,774.00 Cr.
Net Income: $7,005.00

Teacher Notes

Problem 7-5: Ch. Obj. 3, 4

CHALLENGE PROBLEM

The last problem (or problems) in each chapter is a challenge problem and is identified by this "maze" symbol.

Income Statement subtotals:
$11,477.20 Dr. / $14,319.80 Cr.
Balance Sheet subtotals:
$51,081.45 Dr. / $48,238.85 Cr.

4 ASSESS

A chapter test is available for use in assessing students' understanding of concepts in this chapter.

The testmaker software will enable you to develop tailor-made chapter, unit, semester, and final tests.

Alternative Assessment

For alternative assessment strategies, refer to *Tech Prep Strategies in Accounting.*

Matt's Cleaning Service
Work Sheet
For the Month Ended March 31, 19--

ACCT. NO.	ACCOUNT NAME	TRIAL BALANCE DEBIT	TRIAL BALANCE CREDIT	INCOME STATEMENT DEBIT	INCOME STATEMENT CREDIT	BALANCE SHEET DEBIT	BALANCE SHEET CREDIT
101	Cash in Bank	1486240				1486240	
105	Accts. Rec.-Lynn Tarok	271491				271491	
110	Accts. Rec.-Jeffrey Holden					160400	
115	Office Furniture	988140					
120	Office Equipment					301745	
125	Computer Equipment						
130	Delivery Equipment					914650	
201	Accts. Pay.-Peterson Supply		601319				601319
205	Accts. Pay.-Atlas Co.						
210	Accts. Pay.-New Mark, Inc.		568309				568309
301	Jason Stone, Capital						3245000
305	Jason Stone, Withdrawals	200000					
310	Income Summary						
401	Commissions Revenue		1431980		1431980		
501	Advertising Expense	360500		360500			
505	Entertainment Expense			39491			
510	Maintenance Expense			183140			
515	Miscellaneous Expense	43265					
520	Rent Expense			500000			
525	Utilities Expense	21324		21324			
	Net Income			284260			
							5108145

Use Chapter Test 7 here to assess students' understanding and retention of the concepts and procedures presented in the chapter.

146

*P*lanning for Disasters

*S*arah was feeling proud of herself. After weeks of entering accounting data into her company's computer, she expected to reach the end of her project by the end of the day. As she was opening up the document for the final data entry, she accidentally wiped out everything. There were no backup disks. Disaster #1: Data Loss.

Greg, bookkeeper for *The Good Earth Gardeners*, got a promotion—to another company. No one else knew the system. Disaster #2: Personnel Loss.

Carlos's restaurant on the Florida Keys managed to bear the brunt of the hurricane. The building was still standing, but it was standing in several feet of water. The computer was inoperable and inaccessible. Disaster #3: Site Loss.

In the age of computer data management, companies need to ask themselves these questions: Have we assessed the short-term and long-term effects of data or computer loss? Do we have contingency plans? Is the plan in writing and has it been communicated to all who share the system?

For starters, here are some guidelines for disaster planning:
- Install computer locks and passwords.
- Always make backup disks of important data. How often data is saved should be measured by how much the company can afford to lose.
- Keep a fireproof safe on the premises or elsewhere for storing backup records.
- Appoint a security administrator who's responsible for communicating risks and alternative procedures, and reviewing them regularly with users.
- Keep an inventory of all hardware and software—and a list of suppliers that can supply and install compatible systems quickly. Establish alternative sites.
- Use surge protectors to safeguard against sudden electrical surges.

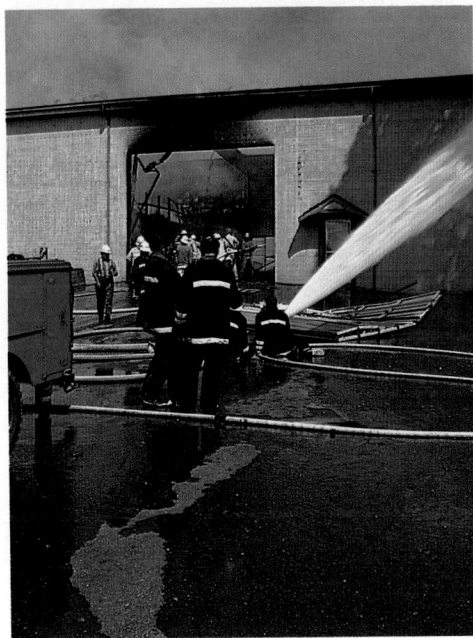

Proper planning may mean the difference between continuing operations or going out of business if a disaster strikes.

- Train personnel in order to minimize software errors.

Whether the computer disaster results from a fire or flood, theft, vandalism, power failure, or employee absenteeism, a company needs to plan for the worse case—because according to Murphy's Law, "If anything can go wrong, it will."

Disasters do happen. Even when planned for, fires, floods, or severe storms can disrupt business operations. Having backup files or documents in a safe place can make the difference between going out of business or being able to continue operating after a disaster.

QUESTIONS

1. Ask students to speculate on the problems a department store gutted by fire would face in restoring operations. How would these problems relate to the store's computer capabilities?
2. What are some possible off-site storage places to house key business documents?

ANSWERS

1. Rebuilding the store, replacing stock, hiring and training new employees since some would leave if the rebuilding process took months, documenting losses for filing insurance claims, documenting debts and paying bills, documenting amounts owed to the business and collecting those amounts. Computer records could provide enormous help in documenting purchases of merchandise and sales to customers, as well as providing vendor information, customer lists, and backup accounting information.
2. Bank vaults, companies providing storage facilities, fireproof safes in other buildings owned by the company.

147

Chapter **8**

PREPARING FINANCIAL STATEMENTS FOR A SOLE PROPRIETORSHIP

LOOKING BACK

Now that students have learned how to gather information and complete a work sheet, they are ready to prepare the end-of-period financial statements—the seventh step in the accounting cycle. Students will learn to prepare an income statement, a statement of changes in owner's equity, and a balance sheet in this chapter.

VOCABULARY DEVELOPMENT

Discuss the definitions of the new terms in class. Ask students to give their definition of each term and to explain how each is used in accounting. Definitions of these terms are found in the chapter and in the glossary on pages 670-679.

Electronic Field Trips

At the end of a fiscal period, financial reports are prepared to show the effects of business transactions for the period. In Chapter 7, you learned how to prepare a work sheet to summarize the financial information needed to prepare the financial reports. In this chapter, you will learn how to prepare those reports: namely, the income statement, the statement of changes in owner's equity, and the balance sheet.

Financial reports are prepared to give the business owner information on how successfully the business is operating. By comparing current financial reports with those from previous fiscal periods, the owner can make more informed decisions about how to run the business.

Learning Objectives

When you have completed Chapter 8, you should be able to do the following:

1. Explain the purpose of the income statement.
2. Prepare an income statement.
3. Explain the purpose of the statement of changes in owner's equity.
4. Prepare a statement of changes in owner's equity.
5. Explain the purpose of a balance sheet.
6. Prepare a balance sheet in report form.
7. Define the accounting terms introduced in this chapter.

New Terms

financial statements
income statement
statement of changes in owner's equity
balance sheet
report form

148

Teaching Resources

- Lesson Plans
- TE/Chapter Reviews & Working Papers
- Demonstration Problems
- Student Study Plans
- Teaching Transparencies
- Solutions Transparencies
- Electronic Field Trips Video, Level I
- Electronic Study Guide
- Chapter 8 Test

Other Resources

- Skills Improvement Activities
- Blackline Masters
- Careers in Accounting
- Dictionary
- Math Review for Accounting
- Tech Prep Strategies in Accounting
- Video
- Test Bank with Software
- Spanish Resources/Audiotapes
- Spanish Electronic Study Guide

The Seventh Step of the Accounting Cycle

To operate a business profitably, a business owner needs to have up-to-date financial information. Financial statements are prepared to provide such information. **Financial statements** are reports prepared to summarize the changes resulting from business transactions that have occurred during a fiscal period. As you can see from Figure 8-1, the preparation of financial statements is the seventh step in the accounting cycle. By analyzing these statements, a business owner can tell whether the business is on course, experiencing some difficulty, or headed for serious trouble.

Figure 8-1   The Accounting Cycle, with Step 7 Highlighted

Comparing information shown on the financial statements for different fiscal periods helps owners spot trends that indicate the "health" of a business. Are total assets or total liabilities increasing or decreasing? Is owner's equity increasing or decreasing? Is net income increasing or decreasing? If there is a net loss, is it a one-time occurrence or has it been going on for some time? If owner's equity and net income have decreased, or if the business has shown a net loss, an owner must find out the cause and try to correct the problem. Any business that shows losses over several reporting periods is in trouble, often severe trouble.

The primary financial statements prepared for a sole proprietorship are the income statement and the balance sheet. A third statement, the statement of changes in owner's equity, is also often prepared. Let's look now at how these reports are prepared and the information that is shown on each of them.

CHAPTER 8   Preparing Financial Statements for a Sole Proprietorship   149

---

1 FOCUS

MAJOR CONCEPTS

- The Seventh Step in the Accounting Cycle
- The Income Statement
- The Statement of Changes in Owner's Equity
- The Balance Sheet
- Preparing Financial Statements on the Computer

BUSINESS CONNECTION

Business owners use financial statements to evaluate how successfully the business is operating. In the 1980s, a number of firms such as Sears, ITT, Xerox, Westinghouse, and General Electric began offering financial services to try to increase revenues. Among the services offered were real estate lending and consumer finance. Some of the companies are now selling off their financial services groups because they were not as successful as anticipated. Financial statements help business managers make such decisions.

2 TEACH

CONCEPT DEVELOPMENT
The Seventh Step of the Accounting Cycle

Briefly review the first six steps in the accounting cycle. Step 6, preparing a work sheet, is the beginning of the end-of-period work. The work sheet is completed first so that information will be readily available for completing the financial statements.

Unlike the work sheet, which can be prepared in pencil, financial statements are formal documents that are prepared in ink, typewritten, or printed.

Teaching Tips
■ Remind students that the length of the fiscal period must remain constant for proper analysis of financial data.

Reinforcing Study Skills

The Learning Objectives at the beginning of the chapter set clear purposes for students' reading. Have students read the objectives. Then point out that the first six set out a two-step process for accomplishing specific tasks: first, to *explain* a report, and second, to *pre-* pare it. Students should keep this process in mind as they read the chapter.

Provide a copy of the *Student Study Plans* to each class member to help organize study activities or to individualize practice and review activities.

CONCEPT DEVELOPMENT
The Income Statement

Briefly review the "who," "what," and "when" of the income statement heading. Explain the use of a consistent time period for a fiscal period.

Remind students that the two amount columns on the income statement stationery do not represent debit and credit columns. Emphasize why expense account balances are entered in the first column and the total is entered in the second column. Make sure students know that these amounts are taken from the Income Statement section of the work sheet.

Point out that the net income (or net loss) was calculated on the work sheet.

Using Visuals

Refer to Figure 8-2. Stress the meaning of the date line, which reports information that covers a time period rather than a specific date.

Using Visuals

 Use demonstration problem 8-1 to show students how to complete the heading and the revenue section of the income statement.

Teaching Tips

■ Point out the accounting principle of matching the revenue earned to the expenses of earning that revenue.

■ The use of consistent fiscal periods allows for the accounting characteristic of comparability.

The Income Statement

The **income statement** reports the net income or net loss for the fiscal period it covers. As you recall from Chapter 7, net income or net loss is the difference between total revenue and total expenses. The main purpose of the income statement is to provide a report of the revenue earned and the expenses incurred over a specific period of time. For this reason, it is sometimes called a "profit-and-loss statement" or an "earnings statement."

The income statement may be handwritten, typed, or prepared on a computer. Since it is a formal report, the income statement is prepared in ink if it is done by hand. The income statement contains the following sections: (1) the heading, (2) the revenue for the period, (3) the expenses for the period, and (4) the net income or net loss for the period.

The Heading

Like the work sheet heading, the heading of an income statement has three parts, which answer the questions who? what? when? The parts of the heading are as follows:

1. The name of the business (who?).
2. The name of the report (what?).
3. The period covered (when?).

The heading for Global Travel Agency's income statement is shown in Figure 8-2. Notice that each line of the heading is centered on the stationery.

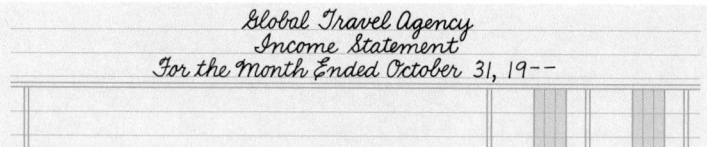

Figure 8-2 The Heading for an Income Statement

When preparing an income statement, be sure to follow the wording, capitalization, and punctuation shown in Figure 8-2. The wording of the date line is especially important. The reporting period on the income statement must be clearly identified. The reporting period covered by the income statement is the entire fiscal period. The net income (or loss) reported on the income statement is the profit (or loss) for the entire fiscal period.

The wording of the date line will vary from business to business. For Global Travel, the reporting period is one month. The heading, therefore, reads "For the Month Ended October 31, 19—." For a three-month period, the heading would read "For the Quarter Ended March 31, 19—." The date line for an income statement covering a full year would read "For the Year Ended June 30, 19—."

A business must be consistent in the fiscal period it uses as the basis for its financial reports. Owners want to be able to compare the data on financial statements from one fiscal period to the next. This is difficult to do if one statement covers a period of, say, one month while another covers a period of six months.

Making Connections

EVERYDAY LIFE

When an individual applies for a loan to purchase a car, the lending institution wants to know about the individual's financial position before it considers granting a loan. Ask students to list some questions the lending institution might ask about an individual's financial position and explain why.

(Answers: Typical responses might be: (1)

What is your weekly, monthly, or annual income? (2) Do you have any other current debts? (3) What assets do you own? The lending institution needs to know that the borrower can afford to make the payments on the loan. If the borrower's income is not sufficient to cover the loan plus regular living expenses, the lender can assume that the loan is a bad risk.)

Using Visuals

Have students read the caption under the photograph. Business owners and managers analyze financial reports frequently. If a business's income statement shows over several periods that the business is just breaking even, what decisions might the owner need to make? (Can expenses be cut to generate a net income? Can revenue be increased? Is there potential for growth in the future?)

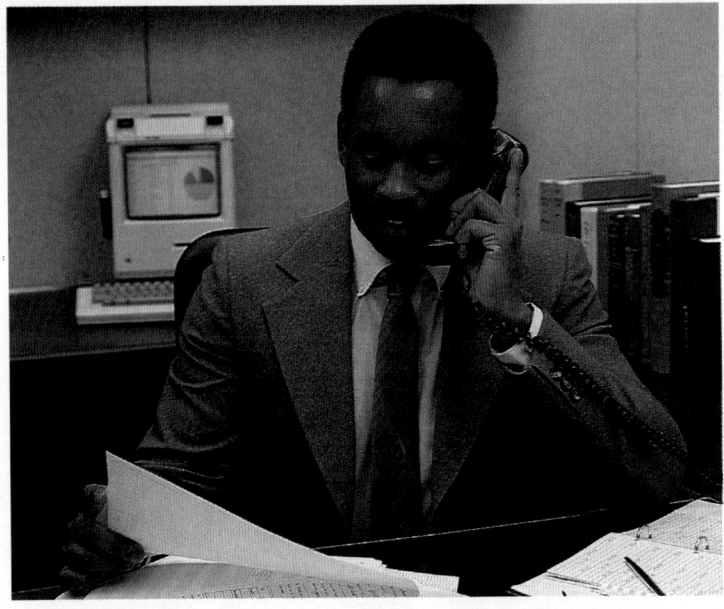

Owners use the information on financial statements to help them make more informed business decisions.

The Revenue Section

After the heading has been completed, the revenue earned for the period is entered on the income statement. This information is taken from the Income Statement section of the work sheet. Look at the income statement for Global Travel Agency shown in Figure 8-3 on page 152. The Income Statement section of the work sheet has been included to show you the source of the information used in preparing the income statement.

The income statement for Global Travel Agency is prepared on standard accounting stationery having a column for account titles and two amount columns. The two amount columns, however, are *not* used for debit and credit entries. Rather, they are used to separate individual account balances from totals. The first amount column is used to enter the balances of the individual revenue and expense accounts. The second amount column is used to enter totals: total revenue, total expenses, and net income (or net loss).

Refer to Figure 8-3 as you read the procedures for preparing an income statement:

1. Write the classification "Revenue:" on the first line at the left side of the form. **A**
2. Enter the titles of the accounts classified as revenue accounts. Enter the account titles beginning on the second line, indented about a half inch from the left edge of the column. **B**
3. Enter the balance of the revenue account(s)—in this case, the balance of the Fees account. Since Global Travel has only one revenue account, total revenue is the same as the balance of the one revenue account. The balance is thus written in the second, or totals, column. **C**

Teaching Tips

■ Totals are placed in the second amount column to make them stand out and be more easily read.
■ Remind students that the red letters correspond to parts of the illustration on page 152.

ACCOUNTING ISSUES

What do accountants need to know besides accounting? Today accountants must be knowledgeable about environmental laws and regulations. U.S. businesses have environmental obligations, and many now find themselves in a position to account for hazardous waste disposal and clean-up costs. CPAs need to advise clients on how to identify and report environmental costs such as these. Auditors are often responsible for detecting and reporting unrecorded liabilities for environmental obligations.

Interdisciplinary Connections

SCIENCE

While tiny "chips" can make today's computers almost invisible, early computers were huge and unwieldy, occupying entire rooms. The first all-electronic digital computer was ENIAC, completed in 1946 by Presper Eckert and John Mauchly of the University of Pennsylvania. It was estimated that in two hours, ENIAC could do physics calculations that would take 100 engineers a year. The same two scientists later designed UNIVAC I for the U.S. Census Bureau. It was the first computer that could handle both alphabetical and numerical data.

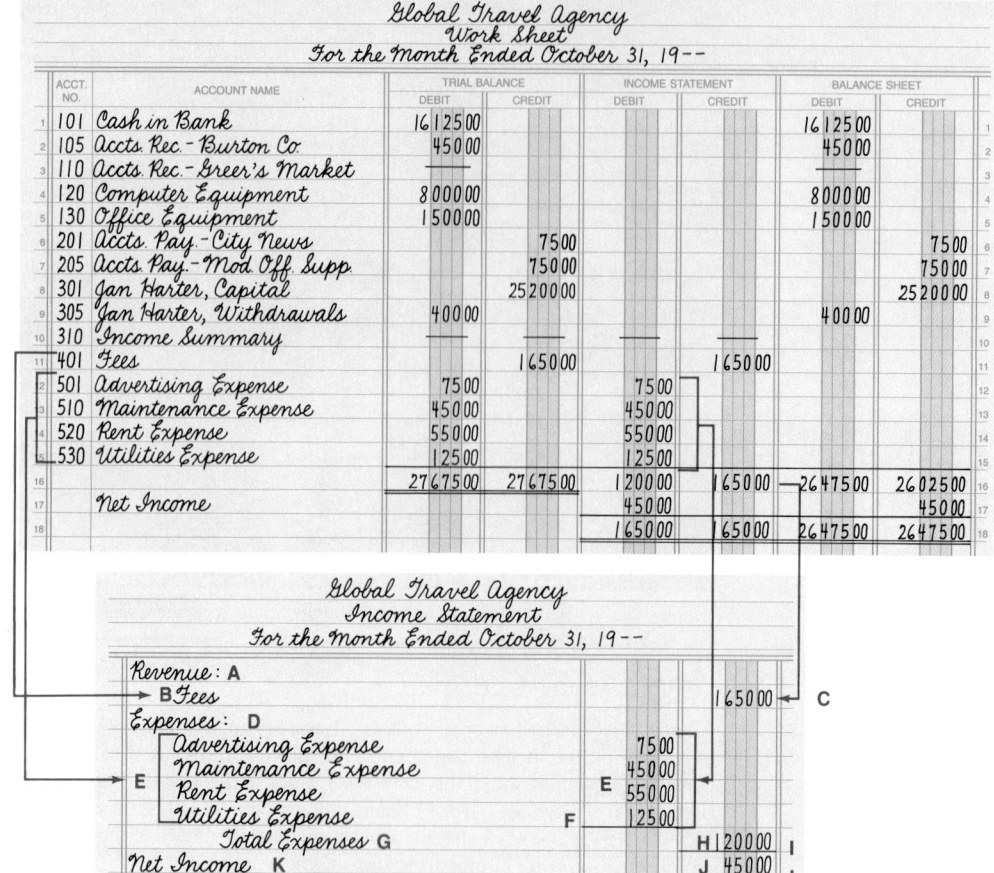

Figure 8-3 Preparing an Income Statement

Global Travel uses only one revenue account, Fees. Many businesses, however, have more than one revenue account, with a separate account for each different source of revenue. For example, a tennis club might have such revenue accounts as Membership Fees, Court Rental Fees, and Instruction Fees.

If a business has more than one revenue account, the individual account balances are entered in the first amount column. The total revenue is then written on a separate line in the second amount column. Figure 8-4 on page 153 illustrates the revenue section for a business that has more than one revenue account. Notice that the words "Total Revenue" are indented about one inch from the left edge of the form.

R E M E M B E R

The information needed to prepare the income statement is taken from the Income Statement section of the work sheet.

Revenue:		
Membership Fees	1000000	
Service Fees	350000	
Total Revenue		1350000

Figure 8-4 Income Statement with More Than One Revenue Account

The Expenses Section

After total revenue has been entered, the expenses incurred during the period must be reported. The expense account titles and the balances shown in the Income Statement section of the work sheet are used to prepare this section of the income statement. The listing of expenses on the income statement is shown in Figure 8-3 on page 152. Refer to this illustration as you read the instructions that follow:

<table><tr><td>

ACCOUNTING | *Tips*

To lessen the chance of error, write all numbers clearly. Be especially careful with numbers that look alike. For example, do not write 4's that look like 9's or 3's that look like 8's.

</td></tr></table>

1. On the line following the entry for total revenue, write the classification "Expenses:" at the left side of the form. **D**
2. Write the titles of the expense accounts, indented half an inch, in the order they appear on the work sheet. Since there are several expense accounts, enter the individual balances in the first amount column. **E**
3. Draw a single rule under the last expense account balance. **F**
4. Write the words "Total Expenses" on the line following the last expense account title, indented about one inch. **G**
5. Add the balances for all the expense accounts. Write the total expense amount in the second amount column, one line below the last expense account balance. **H**

The Net Income Section

After the amount of total expenses has been entered in the second amount column, the net income is entered. A net income, remember, occurs when total revenue is greater than total expenses.

1. Draw a single rule under the total expenses amount. **I**
2. Subtract the total expenses from the total revenue to find net income. Enter the amount of the net income in the second amount column under total expenses. **J**
3. On the same line in the wide column, write the words "Net Income" at the left edge of the form. **K**
4. If the amount of net income matches the amount shown on the work sheet, draw a double rule under the net income amount. **L** The income statement is now complete.

If the amount of net income shown on the work sheet and the amount shown on the income statement do not agree, an error has been made. Since the work sheet has been balanced and ruled, it is safe to assume that the error has occurred while preparing the income statement. An account balance may have been omitted or entered on the income statement incorrectly, or an error in addition or subtraction may have been made. The error must be found and corrected before the income statement can be completed (double ruled).

CHAPTER 8   Preparing Financial Statements for a Sole Proprietorship   **153**

Using Visuals

Using the example in Figure 8-4, point out that most businesses have more than one revenue account.

Teaching Tips

■ Call students' attention to the red letters that correspond with sections of the income statement in Figure 8-3.
■ Suggest that students use a calculator or adding machine with a tape as an aid to locating errors.
■ Ask students how they would go about locating an error on the income statement.

Using Visuals

Use demonstration problem 8-2 to give students practice in preparing an income statement.

Critical Thinking

Jane and Paul Schmidt own a pizza restaurant and all revenues are generated in the restaurant. They will begin offering carry-out service and free delivery next month. Explain why the Schmidts should maintain separate accounts for revenues generated from deliveries.

(Answer: By recording revenues in separate accounts, the Schmidts will be able to assess the income from each new service. For example, if the income for deliveries is substantial, the Schmidts might consider expanding the delivery area. If the free delivery does not generate sufficient revenue to justify the expense of the drivers, the Schmidts may want to discontinue the service.)

Chapter 8

Using Visuals

Using Figure 8-5, call students' attention to the treatment of a net loss.

Using Visuals

 Use demonstration problem 8-3 to show students how to record a net loss on the income statement.

 ANSWERS

1. Who? What? When?
2. For the Quarter Ended June 30, 19—
3. individual account balances; totals
4. net income; $236

Showing a Net Loss

If the total expenses are greater than the total revenue for the period, the result is a net loss. To determine the amount of net loss, subtract total revenue from total expenses. Enter the amount in the second amount column under total expenses. Write the words "Net Loss" on the same line at the left edge of the form. An illustration of how to report a net loss is shown in Figure 8-5.

Revenue:		
Fees		276500
Expenses:		
Advertising Expense	75000	
Maintenance Expense	29500	
Miscellaneous Expense	16400	
Rent Expense	140000	
Utilities Expense	39300	
Total Expenses		300200
Net Loss		23700

Figure 8-5   Income Statement Showing a Net Loss

R E M E M B E R

The net income or net loss amount reported on the income statement must match the amount calculated on the work sheet.

Before reading about the statement of changes in owner's equity, complete the following activity to check your understanding of the income statement.

 ### Check Your Learning

Answer these questions about the income statement. Write your answers on notebook paper.

1. What are the three "W" questions answered by the heading of the income statement?
2. What is the date line for an income statement prepared for the three months of April, May, and June?
3. The first amount column on the income statement is used to report ___?___ . The second amount column on the income statement is used to report ___?___ .
4. If expenses for a period are $19,351 and revenue is $19,587, does the business have a net income or a net loss? What is the amount of net income or net loss?

Compare your answers to those in the answers section. Re-read the preceding part of the chapter to find the correct answers to any questions you may have missed.

Reteaching Strategies

The date line in the heading of an income statement is critical because it identifies the fiscal period. Without the date line, you would not know whether the reported net income was earned in a month, a quarter, or a year.

Call a local stockbroker and ask for copies of quarterly and annual reports to share with your class. Have students look at the report dates and discuss the fiscal periods indicated by those dates.

The Statement of Changes in Owner's Equity

One of the most important things an owner wants to know is whether her or his equity in the business has increased or decreased during the fiscal period. Increases in owner's equity mean *increases* in assets, which in turn means the business has grown. Decreases in owner's equity mean *decreases* in assets and in turn a reduction in the size of the business.

During the period, transactions involving investments by the owner are recorded in the capital account. However, transactions affecting revenue, expenses, and withdrawals are recorded in separate accounts. At the end of the period, a financial statement is prepared to summarize the effects on the capital account of the various business transactions that occurred during the period. This statement is called the **statement of changes in owner's equity.**

The statement of changes in owner's equity is completed as a supporting document for the balance sheet. The information needed to prepare this statement is found in three places: the work sheet, the income statement, and the capital account in the general ledger. Look at Figure 8-6 below to see the statement of changes in owner's equity prepared by Global Travel Agency for the month ended October 31.

Global Travel Agency Statement of Changes in Owner's Equity For the Month Ended October 31, 19--				
Beginning Capital, October 1, 19--A			B ———	
C Add: Investment	D	2520000		
Net Income	E	45000		
Total Increase in Capital			F 2565000	
Subtotal			G 2565000	
Less: Withdrawals			H 40000	
Ending Capital, October 31, 19-- I			J 2525000	

Figure 8-6 Statement of Changes in Owner's Equity

The statement shows the changes in capital from the beginning of the fiscal period through the end of the period. As a result, the heading of the statement is similar to that for the income statement.

Follow these steps to complete the statement of changes in owner's equity:

1. On the first line, write the words "Beginning Capital," followed by the first day of the fiscal period. For Global Travel, that date is October 1, 19—. **A**
2. In the second amount column, enter the balance of the capital account at the beginning of the fiscal period. The source of this information is the capital account in the general ledger. Since Global Travel began operations during this fiscal period, there is no beginning capital balance. Enter a dash in the second amount column. **B**
3. Next, enter the *increases* to the capital account, namely, investments by the owner and net income. First, write the word "Add:" at the left side of the form. **C**

CHAPTER 8   Preparing Financial Statements for a Sole Proprietorship   **155**

CONCEPT DEVELOPMENT
The Statement of Changes in Owner's Equity

Emphasize that the purpose of this statement is to report all changes in owner's equity over an entire fiscal period. It is helpful to go through the statement and explain why each item is added or subtracted. Point out that information on this statement will be used to prepare a section of the balance sheet.

Teaching Tips

■ If needed, refer students to Chapter 4 for a review of the concepts relating to owner's equity. Remind students that total assets equal total equities.

Using Visuals

A teaching transparency showing the three financial statements is available for use in introducing the statement of changes in owner's equity. See the transparency binder accompanying Glencoe Accounting.

Using Visuals

Refer students to Figure 8-6. Explain that the capital account balance at the beginning of the fiscal period does not reflect the earnings (or loss) that occurred during the period. The beginning capital for this accounting period is the ending capital for the previous period. Since Global Travel did not exist before this fiscal period, the beginning capital amount is zero.

Using Visuals

Use demonstration problem 8-4 to give students practice in preparing a statement of changes in owner's equity.

Making Connections

COMMUNICATIONS

Have students imagine they are presenting a year-end financial statement to their client, a sole proprietor. In addition to the actual records, they must be ready to supply a written summary that can be readily understood by the business owner and gives a clear picture of where the business stands.

Using either the Global Travel Agency or Problem 8-5, have students write a memo to you summarizing the financial condition of either business.

The first addition would be any investments by the owner during the period. This information is found in the capital account in the general ledger. Jan Harter, the owner of Global Travel, invested a total of $25,200 in the business in the month of October. Write "Investment" following the word "Add." Enter the amount of the investment in the first amount column. **D**

On the next line, write the words "Net Income." Enter the amount of the net income—taken from the income statement—in the first amount column. Draw a single rule under the investment and net income amounts. **E**

4. Write the words "Total Increase in Capital" on the next line at the left edge of the form. Add the total investments and net income amounts and enter the total in the second amount column. Then draw a single rule under the amount. **F**

5. Write "Subtotal" on the next line, at the left edge of the form. Add the amounts for beginning capital and total increase in capital. Enter the total in the second amount column. **G** Since Global Travel did not have a beginning capital balance, this amount is the same as the total increase in capital amount.

6. The next section of the statement lists the *decreases* to the capital account: withdrawals and net loss. Since Global Travel did not have a net loss for the period, write the words "Less: Withdrawals" at the left edge of the account title column. Enter the amount of withdrawals for the period (taken from the work sheet) in the second amount column. Then draw a single rule under the amount. **H**

7. On the next line, write the words "Ending Capital," followed by the last day of the fiscal period. **I**

8. Subtract the withdrawals amount from the subtotal to determine the new, ending balance of the capital account. Finally, draw a double rule below the ending capital amount. **J**

The statement of changes in owner's equity is now complete. The ending capital balance determined on this statement will be used in preparing the balance sheet.

A statement of changes in owner's equity for an ongoing business that had a net loss for the period is shown in Figure 8-7. Notice that the investment by the owner increases the capital account, while the withdrawals and net loss decrease the capital account.

Beginning Capital, May 1, 19--		4630000
Add: Investment		100000
Subtotal		4730000
Less: Withdrawals	210000	
Net Loss	67500	
Total Decrease in Capital		277500
Ending Capital, May 31, 19--		4452500

Figure 8-7 Statement of Changes in Owner's Equity Showing a Net Loss

Before reading about the preparation of the balance sheet, complete the following activity to check your understanding of the statement of changes in owner's equity.

156

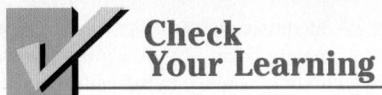

Check Your Learning

Answer the following questions about the statement of changes in owner's equity. Write your answers on notebook paper.

1. The statement of changes in owner's equity is prepared to reflect the changes in the ___?___ from the beginning of the period to the end.
2. The wording in the date line for the statement of changes in owner's equity is the same as that used for the ___?___ .
3. If the owner invested $20,000 during the period covered by this statement, and net income was $3,200, the ending balance in the capital account is ___?___ .
4. The information on the statement of changes in owner's equity is used in preparing the ___?___ .

Compare your answers to those in the answers section. Re-read the preceding part of the chapter to find the correct answers to any questions you may have missed.

The Balance Sheet

The **balance sheet** is a report of the final balances in all the asset, liability, and owner's equity accounts at the end of the fiscal period. These accounts, you'll remember, are the permanent accounts. The main purpose of the balance sheet is to provide a record of the business's assets and a summary of the claims (of both creditors and owners) against those assets *on a specific date.* In other words, the balance sheet states the financial position of a business at a specific point in time. It pinpoints what a business owns, owes, and is worth. For this reason, the balance sheet is sometimes called a "position statement."

Like the income statement and the statement of changes in owner's equity, the balance sheet may be handwritten, typed, or prepared by computer. A handwritten balance sheet is prepared in ink since it is a formal record.

The balance sheet prepared by Global Travel Agency is prepared in report form. In **report form,** the classifications of balance sheet accounts are shown one under the other.

The balance sheet is prepared from the information in the Balance Sheet section of the work sheet and from the statement of changes in owner's equity. Let's look now at the sections of the balance sheet: (1) the heading, (2) the assets section, and (3) the liabilities and owner's equity sections.

The Heading

Like the heading of the income statement, the heading of the balance sheet answers the questions who? what? when? The heading includes

1. The name of the business (who?).
2. The name of the financial statement (what?).
3. The date of the balance sheet (when?).

 ANSWERS

1. Capital account
2. Income statement
3. $23,200
4. Balance sheet

CONCEPT DEVELOPMENT
The Balance Sheet

This section explains the preparation of a balance sheet in report form. In the heading of the balance sheet, emphasize the date. Ask students why it is different from the dates on the previous two statements.

Point out the sources of information for preparing a balance sheet.

Assets	← Work Sheet
Liabilities	← Work Sheet
Owner's Equity	← Statement of Changes in OE

Use annual reports to show students examples of balance sheets from both large and small companies. Also show students statements in report form and account form. It is important for students to understand that the balance sheet is the same in principle no matter how large or small the company. When proving the equality of the balance sheet, refer back to the accounting equation presented in Chapter 2. The balance sheet proves the accuracy of the equation.

Teaching Tips

■ Compare the balance sheet to a photograph. The balance sheet shows a business's worth at a specific time.

Using Visuals

 A teaching transparency showing the three financial statements is available for use in introducing the balance sheet. See the transparency binder accompanying Glencoe Accounting.

Using Visuals

Call students' attention to the date lines on the forms in Figure 8-8. Have students explain why they are different.

Teaching Tips

■ Ask students to explain the accounting assumption relating to time periods and why this assumption is important.

As you recall, the income statement reports the amount of net income (or net loss) for the complete fiscal period. Unlike the income statement, the balance sheet refers to only one day in the fiscal period, usually the last day. The amounts shown on the balance sheet are the balances in the accounts as of that day. Look at the headings in Figure 8-8 to see the difference between the date lines on the income statement and on the balance sheet.

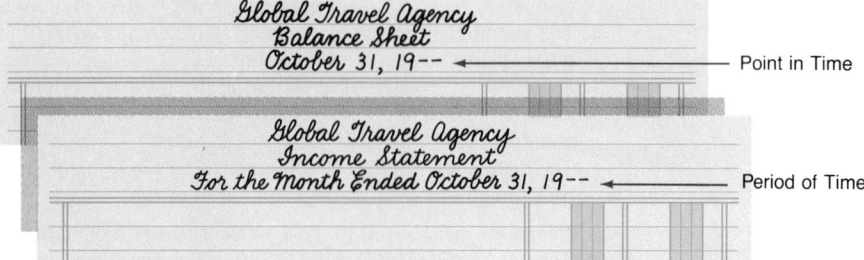

Figure 8-8 Headings of Financial Statements

The Assets Section

Refer to Figure 8-9 on page 159 as you read the procedures for preparing the balance sheet. The work sheet and statement of changes in owner's equity have been included in the illustration to show the sources of the information used to prepare the balance sheet.

1. Write the word "Assets" in the center of the first line.   **A**
2. Next, enter the asset account titles and their balances. The account titles and balances are listed on the balance sheet in the same order as they appear in the Balance Sheet section of the work sheet. Enter the individual account balances in the first amount column. Then draw a single rule under the last account balance.   **B**
3. On the next line, write the words "Total Assets," indented about half an inch. Add the individual balances and enter the total assets amount in the second amount column.   **C**

Do *not* draw a double rule under the total at this time. The double rule is not entered until the Liabilities and Owner's Equity sections have been completed and are shown to be equal to total assets.

The Liabilities and Owner's Equity Sections

The information for the Liabilities and Owner's Equity sections is taken from the work sheet *and* from the statement of changes in owner's equity. To complete these sections of the balance sheet, follow these steps:

1. Skip one line and then write the heading "Liabilities," centered.   **D**
2. List the liability account titles and their balances, using the same order as they appear in the Balance Sheet section of the work sheet. Enter the account balances in the first amount column. Draw a single rule under the last account balance.   **E**
3. On the next line, write the words "Total Liabilities," indented about half an inch. Total the individual balances and enter the total liabilities amount in the second amount column.   **F**

158

Making Connections

BUSINESS ETHICS

You applied for a loan to buy a new car. On the loan application, you overstated your salary and your length of employment. You then asked your employer to verify the application information should she be contacted about it. Were your actions proper?

(Answer: No, you should have been truthful on the application. Lenders use the information on loan applications to evaluate the person's creditworthiness. If you are not qualified, you should explore other avenues for acquiring the funds needed or revise your expectations about the type of car to buy.)

4. Skip a line and write the heading "Owner's Equity," centering it on the line. **G**

5. Write the title of the capital account and enter its balance in the second amount column. The balance is the amount of the ending balance shown on the statement of changes in owner's equity. **H**

Figure 8-9 Preparing a Balance Sheet

CHAPTER 8 Preparing Financial Statements for a Sole Proprietorship   159

Use the balance calculated on the statement of changes in owner's equity for the balance of the capital account on the balance sheet.

Proving the Equality of the Balance Sheet

You learned in earlier chapters that the basic accounting equation must always be in balance in a double-entry system of accounting. The balance sheet represents the basic accounting equation; thus, the Assets section must balance the Liabilities and Owner's Equity sections. To prove the equality of the balance sheet, follow these procedures:

1. Draw a single rule under the balance of the capital account. Write the words "Total Liabilities and Owner's Equity," indented about half an inch, on the next line. **I**
2. Add the total liabilities amount and the ending capital balance. Enter the total in the second amount column. **J** This total must agree with the total assets amount. If the totals are not equal, an error has been made—most likely in transferring amounts from the work sheet or from the statement of changes in owner's equity. Any errors must be found and corrected before the balance sheet can be completed.
3. If the totals are equal, draw a double rule under the total assets amount *and* under the total liabilities and owner's equity amount. **K** The balance sheet is now complete.

 ## Check Your Learning

Answer these questions about Figure 8-9, shown on page 159, using notebook paper.

1. What is the wording used in the date line of the balance sheet?
2. What are the three sections of the balance sheet?
3. How are the accounts listed on the balance sheet?
4. What is the source of the balance reported for Jan Harter, Capital?

Compare your answers to those in the answers section.

Preparing Financial Statements on the Computer

As we mentioned earlier, financial statements may be handwritten, typewritten, or prepared using a computer. Regardless of how they are prepared, the information shown on the statements remains the same.

The balance sheet shown in Figure 8-10 on page 161 is an example of a report prepared with a computer. In a computerized accounting system, the information for preparing financial statements is stored in the computer files. When financial reports are needed, it is not necessary to prepare a work sheet since all the information from business transactions is already

```
                    Global Travel Agency
                       Balance Sheet
                      October 31, 19--

                         Assets
Cash in Bank                              16125.00
Accts. Rec.--Burton Co.                     450.00
Accts. Rec.--Greer's Market                   0.00
Computer Equipment                         8000.00
Office Equipment                           1500.00
                                         ----------
        Total Assets                                  26075.00
                                                      =========


                        Liabilities
Accts. Pay.--City News                       75.00
Accts. Pay.--Modern Office Suppliers        750.00
                                         ----------
        Total Liabilities                               825.00

                       Owner's Equity
Jan Harter, Capital                                   25250.00
                                                      ----------
        Total Liabilities and Owner's Equity          26075.00
                                                      =========
```

Figure 8-10 Balance Sheet
Prepared by Computer

Point out the balance sheet in Figure 8-10.

stored in the computer. The computer operator simply gives a command indicating the reports needed. The computer calculates the net income or net loss and adjusts the capital account to correctly report any changes that have occurred during the period. Obviously, the information in the computer files must be kept up to date through regular journal entries or the reports generated from that information will not be accurate.

Summary of Key Points

1. The preparation of financial reports is the seventh step in the accounting cycle. The primary reports are the income statement and the balance sheet. The statement of changes in owner's equity is also often prepared.
2. The income statement reports the net income or net loss for the period. Net income or net loss is the difference between total revenue and total expenses over a specific period of time.
3. The statement of changes in owner's equity summarizes the effects of the period's business transactions on the capital account.
4. The balance sheet reports the final balances of asset, liability, and owner's equity accounts at the end of the fiscal period.
5. The work sheet is the source of information for preparing the income statement. The statement of changes in owner's equity is prepared from the work sheet, the income statement, and the capital account in the general ledger. The balance sheet is prepared from the work sheet and the statement of changes in owner's equity.
6. Financial reports may be handwritten on accounting stationery, typewritten, or prepared using a computer. If prepared by hand, the reports are written in ink.

COMPUTERS IN ACCOUNTING

CPAs are often away from their offices because they are working at home, traveling, or meeting with clients. To stay in touch with the people in their offices, many CPAs use a variety of equipment that takes advantage of the latest technology. Such equipment includes cellular mobile telephones, car phones, fax machines, pagers and beepers, voice mail, and laptop computers that can be linked to an office computer.

3 CLOSE

CHAPTER SUMMARY

This summary enumerates the key information in the chapter. It is a useful tool for reinforcement and review.

PRACTICE AND APPLY

- Language Development
- Comprehension and Retention
- Basic Skills

Building Your Accounting Vocabulary

See the Glossary on pages 670-679 for definitions of these terms.

Reviewing Your Accounting Knowledge

1. To show the effects of transactions for the period.
2. To report the revenue earned and the expenses incurred over a specific period of time.
3. Profit-and-loss statement or earnings statement.
4. So financial statements from one period can be compared with statements from other periods. Otherwise, comparisons would have little value.
5. The Income Statement section of the work sheet.
6. To show the changes that have occurred in the owner's capital account over a specific period of time.
7. The work sheet, the income statement, and the capital account in the general ledger.
8. To provide a record of the business's assets and a summary of the claims against those assets on a specific date.
9. The Balance Sheet section of the work sheet and the statement of changes in owner's equity.
10. The balance sheet date line refers to a specific date, usually the final day in the fiscal period. The date lines for the other two statements refer to the entire fiscal period.
11. The basic accounting equation.

---

8 Review and Applications

Building Your Accounting Vocabulary

In your own words, write the definition of each of the following accounting terms. Use complete sentences for your definitions.

balance sheet
financial statements
income statement
report form
statement of changes in owner's equity

Reviewing Your Accounting Knowledge

1. Why are financial statements prepared?
2. What is the purpose of the income statement?
3. What other names can be given to an income statement?
4. Why does a business need to be consistent in the fiscal period it uses as the basis for its financial reports?
5. What is the source of information used to prepare the income statement?
6. What is the purpose of the statement of changes in owner's equity?
7. What are the sources of information used to prepare the statement of changes in owner's equity?
8. What is the purpose of the balance sheet?
9. What are the sources of the information needed to prepare the balance sheet?
10. How does the date in the heading of a balance sheet differ from the date in the heading of an income statement and a statement of changes in owner's equity?
11. Which financial statement represents the basic accounting equation?

Improving Your Decision-Making Skills

Anna Choi is the accounting clerk for George Damaris, owner of Colonial Bakery. For several months, Anna has tried to convince George to install a computer. Anna believes that a computer would save time, especially when financial statements are being prepared. She has explained to George that all of the information for preparing financial statements can be stored in the computer files. Then, when the financial statements are needed, it is not necessary to prepare a work sheet. George believes that a computer will cost too much money. He also believes that if just one mistake is made in entering an amount, the financial statements will not provide a true picture of the business. What would you say to convince George that a computer should be installed for use in the business?

Applying Accounting Procedures

Exercise 8-1   Reporting Accounts on Financial Statements
The following list contains some of the account titles from the general ledger of the Winter Theater.

162

Improving Your Decision-Making Skills

Anna should explain that recording errors can also be made in manual accounting systems and will thus carry through to the financial statements. Anna should stress that a computerized accounting system actually reduces the chances of errors. Once amounts have been recorded *and* verified, they are stored in the computer's memory. Stored amounts are available for use at the push of a button and need not be re-entered when financial statements must be prepared. This decreases the chance of making keying errors.

Anna should also point out that preparing financial statements on the computer will be faster and any needed changes can be quickly made.

Accounts Payable—Boyden Company
Accounts Payable—Gail's Supplies
Accounts Receivable—Clinton Co.
Accounts Receivable—King Company
Admissions Revenue
Advertising Expense
Cash in Bank

Clem Winter, Capital
Clem Winter, Withdrawals
Concession Revenue
Miscellaneous Expense
Office Furniture
Projection Equipment
Rent Expense

Instructions: Use a form similar to the one that follows. For each account listed,

(1) Write the classification of the account.

(2) Use a check mark to indicate whether the account balance will be entered in the Trial Balance debit or credit column of the work sheet.

(3) Use a check mark to indicate on which financial statement (income statement or balance sheet) the account will appear. The first account is shown as an example.

Account Title	Account Classification	Trial Balance		Financial Statements	
		Debit	Credit	Income Statement	Balance Sheet
Accounts Payable—Boyden Co.	Liability		✔		✔

Exercise 8-1: Ch. Obj. 1, 5

Exercise 8-2: Ch. Obj. 3, 4
1. $42,300
2. $31,915
3. $20,270
4. $27,340
5. $6,060
6. $24,610

Problem 8-1: Ch. Obj. 1, 2
Net Income: $3,276.00

Problem 8-2: Ch. Obj. 3, 4
Ending Capital: $21,365.00

Exercise 8-2 Determining Ending Capital Amounts

The financial data affecting the capital accounts for several different businesses is summarized below.

Instructions: Use the form in your working papers or plain paper. Determine the ending capital balance for each business.

	Beginning Capital	Investments	Revenue	Expenses	Withdrawals
1.	$40,000	$ 500	$ 5,800	$3,400	$ 600
2.	24,075	0	14,980	6,240	900
3.	19,800	1,000	6,450	6,980	0
4.	0	26,410	5,920	4,790	200
5.	6,415	0	4,420	3,975	800
6.	20,870	1,200	12,980	9,240	1,200

Problem 8-1 Preparing an Income Statement

The work sheet for Matira's Delivery Service for the month ended April 30, 19—, appears on page 164.

Instructions: Using the work sheet, prepare an income statement for Matira's Delivery Service.

Problem 8-2 Preparing a Statement of Changes in Owner's Equity

Instructions: Using the work sheet for Matira's Delivery Service and the income statement prepared in Problem 8-1, prepare a statement of changes in owner's equity. Pat Matira made an additional investment in the business of $500 during the period.

163

Additional Reinforcement

Students who need additional practice or individualized help will benefit from the *Glencoe Accounting Electronic Study Guide* or the *Glencoe Accounting* on-line multimedia program, which provide reinforcement and reteaching for vocabulary, concepts, and procedures.

Refer students to the Chapter 8 review pages in the workbook, *Chapter Reviews and Working Papers.*

Chapter 8

Problem 8-3: Ch. Obj. 5, 6
Total Assets: $28,377.00

Problem 8-4: Ch. Obj. 2, 4, 6
Net Income: $1,940.00
Ending Capital: $19,819.00
Total Assets: $26,226.00

Problem 8-5: Ch. Obj. 2, 4, 6

COMPUTER

PROBLEM

This computer image identifies a problem that students may complete using the *Glencoe Accounting, General Ledger* software.

Matira's Delivery Service
Work Sheet
For the Month Ended April 30, 19--

ACCT. NO.	ACCOUNT NAME	TRIAL BALANCE DEBIT	TRIAL BALANCE CREDIT	INCOME STATEMENT DEBIT	INCOME STATEMENT CREDIT	BALANCE SHEET DEBIT	BALANCE SHEET CREDIT	
101	Cash in Bank	5391 00				5391 00		1
104	Accts. Rec.-J. Lincoln	423 00				423 00		2
106	Accts. Rec.-A. Jones	914 00				914 00		3
110	Office Equipment	2806 00				2806 00		4
115	Computer Equipment	6482 00				6482 00		5
120	Delivery Equipment	12361 00				12361 00		6
205	Accts. Pay.- Modern Supp.		4618 00				4618 00	7
210	Accts. Pay.-A&L Forms		2394 00				2394 00	8
301	Pat Matira, Capital		19589 00				19589 00	9
302	Pat Matira, Withdrawals	1500 00				1500 00		10
303	Income Summary							11
401	Delivery Fees		9309 00		9309 00			12
501	Advertising Expense	1852 00		1852 00				13
505	Delivery Expense	931 00		931 00				14
510	Miscellaneous Expense	246 00		246 00				15
515	Rent Expense	2400 00		2400 00				16
520	Utility Expense	604 00		604 00				17
		35910 00	35910 00	6033 00	9309 00	29877 00	26601 00	18
	Net Income			3276 00			3276 00	19
				9309 00	9309 00	29877 00	29877 00	20

Problem 8-3   Preparing a Balance Sheet

Instructions: Using the work sheet for Matira's Delivery Service and the statement of changes in owner's equity prepared in Problem 8-2, prepare a balance sheet in report form.

Problem 8-4   Preparing Financial Statements

The trial balance for the Joker Amusement Center has been prepared. It is included on the work sheet in the working papers accompanying this textbook.

Instructions:
(1) Complete the work sheet.
(2) Prepare an income statement for the quarter ended March 31.
(3) Prepare a statement of changes in owner's equity. Ken Graf made no additional investments during the period.
(4) Prepare a balance sheet in report form.

COMPUTER

PROBLEM

Problem 8-5   Preparing Financial Statements

The general ledger accounts for Jenkins Caterers follow. The balance in each account at the end of the fiscal period is also given.

101	Cash in Bank	$ 3,956
110	Accounts Receivable—Brian Doonan	1,328
114	Accounts Receivable—Fran Ullman	1,204
120	Catering Supplies	1,968
125	Office Equipment	10,957
130	Delivery Equipment	8,396

210	Accounts Payable—Adams Supply	3,976
215	Accounts Payable—Graham Co.	2,946
220	Accounts Payable—King Supply	1,285
301	Judy Jenkins, Capital	22,336
302	Judy Jenkins, Withdrawals	1,900
303	Income Summary	
401	Catering Revenue	4,989
403	Party Revenue	1,420
505	Advertising Expense	934
510	Delivery Expense	803
520	Maintenance Expense	1,483
525	Miscellaneous Expense	748
530	Rent Expense	1,850
535	Repair Expense	589
540	Utility Expense	836

Instructions:

(1) Prepare a work sheet for the month ended October 31.

(2) Prepare an income statement for the period.

(3) Prepare a statement of changes in owner's equity. Judy Jenkins made an additional investment of $1,000 during the period.

(4) Prepare a balance sheet.

CHALLENGE

PROBLEM

Problem 8-6   Preparing a Statement of Changes in Owner's Equity

You are the accounting clerk at the Raintree Company. The financial statements for the month of November have already been prepared. Unfortunately, the statement of changes in owner's equity was damaged when someone accidentally spilled a cup of coffee. Mary Fienwald, the accountant, has asked you to reconstruct that statement. Ms. Fienwald reminded you that the owner, Tyler Best, made an additional investment of $4,000 and withdrew $1,500 during the period.

Instructions: Use the balance sheet and income statement shown below and on page 166 to prepare a new statement of changes in owner's equity.

Raintree Company
Balance Sheet
November 30, 19--

Assets		
Cash in Bank	8297 00	
Accounts Receivable – Lester Maltese	693 00	
Accounts Receivable – Brian Cropp	478 00	
Store Equipment	16204 00	
Video Equipment	24869 00	
Total Assets		50541 00
Liabilities		
Accounts Payable – C & L Amusements	4013 00	
Accounts Payable – Gotham Company	3192 00	
Total Liabilities		7205 00
Owner's Equity		
Tyler Best, Capital		43336 00
Total Liabilities and Owner's Equity		50541 00

TB Totals: $36,952.00
Net Loss: $834.00
Ending Capital: $19,602.00
Total Assets: $27,809.00

Problem 8-6: Ch. Obj. 3, 4

CHALLENGE

PROBLEM

The last problem (or problems) in each chapter is a challenge problem and is identified by this "maze" symbol.

Ending Capital: $43,336.00

Teacher Notes

Chapter

Problem 8-7: Ch. Obj. 1, 2

CHALLENGE The last problem
(or problems) in
each chapter is a
challenge problem
PROBLEM and is identified
by this "maze"
symbol.

Total Expenses: $11,467.00

4 ASSESS

A chapter test is available for use in assessing students' understanding of concepts in this chapter.

The testmaker software will enable you to develop tailor-made chapter, unit, semester, and final tests.

Alternative Assessment

For alternative assessment strategies, refer to *Tech Prep Strategies in Accounting.*

Raintree Company Income Statement For the Month Ended November 30, 19--		
Revenue:		
Concession Revenue	1 930 00	
Game Revenue	8 295 00	
Total Revenue		10 225 00
Expenses:		
Advertising Expense	1 854 00	
Miscellaneous Expense	831 00	
Rent Expense	2 350 00	
Utility Expense	752 00	
Total Expenses		5 787 00
Net Income		4 438 00

CHALLENGE **Problem 8-7   Interpreting Financial Information**

PROBLEM
You are applying for a job with Foran Tree Service. The job includes preparing financial statements. In order to determine your ability to do the job, the owner, Carl Foran, has given you the following information.

At the beginning of the last fiscal period, the account Carl Foran, Capital had a balance of $46,105. At the end of the period, the account showed a balance of $49,386. During the period, Mr. Foran made an additional investment of $2,000 and had withdrawals of $500. The revenue for the period was $13,248.

Instructions: Use the stationery provided in the workbook or plain paper. Based on the information just given, determine the total expenses for the period.

166

Use Chapter Test 8 here to assess students' understanding and retention of the concepts and procedures presented in the chapter.

8 **Preparing Financial Statements for a Sole Proprietorship**

Chapter Test

	Possible	Score
Part A	10	
Part B	15	
Part C	3	
Part D	57	
Total	85	

Name _____ Date _____ Class _____

PART A   ACCOUNTING VOCABULARY *(10 points)*

Directions: In the Answer column, write the letter of the word or phrase that best completes the sentence.

A. balance sheet
B. Balance Sheet section of the work sheet
C. financial statements
D. income statement
E. Income Statement section of the work sheet
F. net income or net loss
G. on a specific date
H. report form
I. statement of changes in owner's equity
J. work sheet

	ANSWER	SCORE
1. The balance sheet reports financial information __?__.	___ 1 ___	
2. The information needed to prepare the income statement comes from the __?__.	___ 2 ___	
3. __?__ summarize the changes resulting from business transactions that have occurred during a fiscal period.	___ 3 ___	
4. The amount of the net income or net loss reported on the income statement must match the amount shown on the __?__.	___ 4 ___	
5. __?__ is reported on the income statement.	___ 5 ___	
6. A(n) __?__ is the financial statement that reports the final balances in all asset, liability, and owner's equity accounts at the end of the fiscal period.	___ 6 ___	
7. In the __?__, the classifications of balance sheet accounts are shown one under the other.	___ 7 ___	
8. The source of information for completing the balance sheet comes from the __?__.	___ 8 ___	
9. The __?__ is completed as a support document for the balance sheet.	___ 9 ___	
10. The __?__ reports a business's net income or net loss over an entire fiscal period.	___ 10 ___	

Copyright © by Glencoe Division of Macmillan/McGraw-Hill. All rights reserved.   Chapter 8 • 33

166   UNIT 2   The Basic Accounting Cycle

*F*inancial Report or Financial Repair?

Anyone who has ever applied for a bank loan has probably noticed as they prepare to sign the application, the formula line: "This is a true and accurate statement of financial dealings, and that knowingly making false statements on such a form is a crime." Following this warning is a description of the penalties which include fines or imprisonment or both. Perhaps some people might be anxious before they sign, hoping they have not left anything out of the application. Most people, however, would not *knowingly* misrepresent themselves, would they?

Imagine you find yourself in the following situation. Your Uncle Henry, whom you are very fond of, has been running a small restaurant for five years. Unfortunately, it has not been very profitable. Your uncle has been doing his own bookkeeping, but admits that he knows little about the formalities of it all. He decides that to move his restaurant "out of the red," he needs a loan so that he can expand and remodel his restaurant. Since Uncle Henry knows you are good with numbers and are taking some accounting classes, he asks you to look over the books and make an accounting report that he can present at the bank. Knowing how desperately your uncle wants and needs his business to succeed, you agree.

As you go over the books, however, you have a growing conviction that no bank will give your uncle the loan. As you stare at the numbers and agonize over telling your uncle, you notice that by rearranging the numbers just a little bit, your Uncle Henry's business could look a little more promising. After all, you rationalize, once the loan goes through and your uncle makes the planned improvements, business is bound to pick up. The bank does not need to know how things are now,

Most people at sometime in their life run into a situation in which it is difficult to decide between "right" and "wrong".

they just need to know that the loan will be repaid. After all, the amount of money your uncle needs is not really that much. . . .

What is the ethical dilemma in this case? What course of action would you choose? Perhaps for you the situation is a clear choice between right and wrong. Most people, however, run into situations in which it is difficult to decide what is "right" and what is "wrong." Commonly known as *situation ethics*, choosing what is right and wrong in a particular set of circumstances can lead to stress and anxiety, especially if something that you know is wrong under most circumstances suddenly seems okay. The best way to make an ethical decision, one that you can stand by and still live with yourself, is to outline all your options and choose one that does not compromise your beliefs.

In Uncle Henry's case, for example, you could more closely examine the possibility of his success by taking customer surveys, studying successful neighborhood restaurants, and then incorporating the findings into a business plan. This business plan could be submitted with an accurate financial report to help convince the bank to loan your uncle the money.

167

Have students read the ethics case given in the textbook and jot down ideas about what they would do in the situation described. Then review the five-step decision model (see page T44). Emphasize that there are no "right" or "wrong" answers to the questions in the decision model.

After students have discussed the first four steps, have them vote on which alternative they feel is best, or, if one alternative has clearly been chosen during the discussion, review student's reasoning for choosing that course of action.

You may want to have students compare their final decision with the one they wrote down after first reading the vignette. Did following the five-step model reinforce their "instinctual" decision or lead them to choose a different course of action? Help students realize that following a decision model when they confront an ethical dilemma can help them to organize their thinking and arrive at a satisfactory solution.

QUESTIONS
1. What are the ethical issues in this situation?
2. What are the alternatives?
3. Who are the affected parties?
4. How do the alternatives affect the parties?
5. What is your decision?

ANSWERS
1. Falsifying financial information submitted to a bank to qualify for a loan.
2. To submit a false report to the bank, develop a plan to recover business losses and submit this plan along with an accurate financial report to the bank.
3. You, Uncle Henry, the bank.
4. Answers will vary. For example, for the alternative of submitting a false report to the bank, you may be affected by feeling good if Uncle Henry obtained the money needed to make his restaurant successful. You would know, however, that the report was false, and you could be held liable should the bank discover the false information. You and Uncle Henry might also worry more about

the success of the restaurant. If the restaurant is not successful, the bank could lose money if Uncle Henry had too few assets to pay off the loan.
5. Accept any answer, but require students to defend the action they choose.

Chapter

COMPLETING THE ACCOUNTING CYCLE FOR A SOLE PROPRIETORSHIP

LOOKING BACK

In previous chapters students have learned the first seven steps in the accounting cycle—from analyzing and journalizing business transactions through preparing financial statements. In this chapter students will complete the accounting cycle for a sole proprietorship, service business by recording the closing entries and preparing a post-closing trial balance.

VOCABULARY DEVELOPMENT

Reinforce vocabulary through a team competition to define new terms. Include terms from earlier chapters as well. Appoint teams to participate in a "Vocabulary Bee." Teams take turns defining terms, with team members consulting with each other before giving a definition (use a time limit of a minute or so). If a team gives an incorrect definition, the team is eliminated. Definitions of these terms are found in the chapter and in the glossary on pages 670-679.

Electronic Field Trips

In Chapter 8, you learned how to prepare the end-of-period financial statements for a sole proprietorship service business. The income statement reports the business's revenue, expenses, and net income or net loss for a fiscal period. The statement of changes in owner's equity summarizes the effects of the business transactions for the period on the owner's capital account. The balance sheet reports the financial position of the business as of the end of the fiscal period.

In this chapter, you will complete the accounting cycle for Global Travel Agency. The accounting cycle is completed by journalizing the closing entries and preparing a post-closing trial balance.

Learning Objectives

When you have completed Chapter 9, you should be able to do the following:

1. Explain why the temporary capital accounts are closed at the end of the fiscal period.
2. Explain the purpose of the Income Summary account.
3. Explain the relationship between the Income Summary account and the capital account.
4. Analyze and journalize closing entries.
5. Post closing entries to accounts in the general ledger.
6. Prepare a post-closing trial balance.
7. Define the accounting terms introduced in this chapter.

New Terms

closing entries
post-closing trial balance
Income Summary account
compound entry

168

Teaching Resources

- Lesson Plans
- TE/Chapter Reviews & Working Papers
- Demonstration Problems
- Student Study Plans
- Teaching Transparencies
- Solutions Transparencies
- Electronic Field Trips Video, Level I
- Electronic Study Guide
- Chapter 9 Test

Other Resources

- Skills Improvement Activities
- Blackline Masters
- Careers in Accounting
- Dictionary
- Math Review for Accounting
- Tech Prep Strategies in Accounting
- Video
- Test Bank with Software
- Spanish Resources/Audiotapes
- Spanish Electronic Study Guide

The Eighth and Ninth Steps in the Accounting Cycle

During a fiscal period, the temporary capital accounts are used to record transactions involving revenue, expenses, and withdrawals. At the end of the period, the balances in these accounts are transferred to the capital account to summarize the changes in owner's equity and to bring that account up to date.

The balances in the temporary capital accounts are transferred by recording a series of closing entries. **Closing entries** are journal entries made to close out, or reduce to zero, the balances in the temporary capital accounts and to transfer the net income or net loss for the period to the capital account.

After the closing entries have been journalized and posted, a trial balance is prepared to prove the equality of the general ledger after the closing process. The trial balance prepared after closing is called a **post-closing trial balance.** As you can see in Figure 9-1, the closing process and the post-closing trial balance complete the accounting cycle.

Figure 9-1 The Accounting Cycle, with Steps 8 and 9 Highlighted

The Closing Process

Preparing financial records for the start of another fiscal period is a little like keeping the records for a basketball team. Although individual and team scores are kept and tallied at the end of every game, each new game starts with a score of zero. Similarly, although entries are recorded in the accounts

1 FOCUS

MAJOR CONCEPTS

- The Eighth and Ninth Steps in the Accounting Cycle
- The Closing Process
- The Income Summary Account
- Journalizing the Closing Entries
- Posting the Closing Entries to the General Ledger
- Preparing a Post-closing Trial Balance
- The Computer and Closing Entries

BUSINESS CONNECTION

In 1992 Nike's total sales rose to $3.4 billion, with earnings of $3.3 million. These earnings were reported after the company's accounting books were closed for the year. Comparing their operating results with earlier fiscal years, Nike reported that revenues and earnings had increased for the fifth consecutive year. Nike's success in 1992 was attributed to strong fourth-quarter sales in both its domestic and international markets.

2 TEACH

CONCEPT DEVELOPMENT
The Eighth and Ninth Steps in the Accounting Cycle
This section introduces the final steps in the accounting cycle. Review the first seven steps in the accounting cycle. Review the classification of accounts as permanent or temporary. *(Continued)*

Reinforcing Study Skills

Taking good notes is important in enabling students to recall and study what they have heard in lectures. Notes should be brief but complete enough to provide clear information when reading them hours or days after a lecture. Have pairs of students compare notes and their techniques for note-taking.

Provide a copy of the *Student Study Plans* to each class member to help organize study activities or to individualize practice and review activities.

Using Visuals

Use Figure 9-1 to review the steps in the accounting cycle.

ACCOUNTING PRACTICE
Students may complete Exercise 9-1 at this point.

Chapter 9

The Eighth and Ninth Steps in the Accounting Cycle (Continued)

Point out that temporary capital accounts are temporary only in that their balances are maintained for an accounting period and then the accounts are cleared to prepare them for the next cycle. Closing entries are made to clear the temporary capital accounts (reduce the balance to zero).

CONCEPT DEVELOPMENT
The Closing Process

Explain that temporary capital accounts start the fiscal period with zero balances. During the period, revenue, expenses, and withdrawals are recorded in the accounts, thus allowing these amounts to be compared with earlier periods.

Point out that the balance in the capital account at this point is not the same as the balance reported on the balance sheet. The only way to make a change in a ledger account is through a journal entry. Thus, journal entries must be made to reduce the temporary capital account balances to zero and to bring the capital account balance up to date.

Teaching Tips

- Closing entries are recorded and posted only at the end of the accounting period.
- Use a T account to demonstrate that the balance in capital does not match the balance shown on the balance sheet.

CONCEPT DEVELOPMENT
The Income Summary Account

There is no account in the general ledger entitled net income or net loss. Thus, an account is needed to serve as a temporary repository for the net income or loss before it is transferred to the capital account. The Income Summary account serves this purpose, which is (1) to summarize the net income or net loss for the accounting period in one account, and (2) to serve as a clearing account for the temporary revenue and expense accounts. The Income Summary account is, in effect, a simple income statement in the ledger.

---

during the fiscal period, the temporary capital accounts start each new fiscal period with zero balances.

In Chapter 8, you learned how to prepare an income statement. The income statement, you'll remember, reports the net income or net loss for *one accounting period.* The statement is prepared from information recorded and accumulated in the revenue and expense accounts. At the end of the period, then, the revenue and expense accounts must be closed or cleared because their balances apply to only one fiscal period. Closing entries are prepared to reduce the balances in the revenue and expense accounts to zero, thus preparing them for use during the next fiscal period.

Closing entries are also used to transfer the net income or net loss for the period to the capital account. Earlier you learned how to calculate the net income or loss on the work sheet. The net income or loss is then reported on the income statement and reflected in the ending balance of the capital account reported on the balance sheet. This ending capital balance is calculated on the statement of changes in owner's equity. No journal entries have yet been recorded to update the balance of the capital account in the general ledger. For example, the balance for Jan Harter, Capital shown on the work sheet is $25,200. The balance for Jan Harter, Capital reported on the balance sheet is $25,250. These two amounts are different because the withdrawals and the net income for the period have not yet been recorded in the capital account in the general ledger. This is done during the closing process.

The Income Summary Account

Before the closing entries are journalized and posted, there is no single account in the general ledger that shows the revenue and expenses for the fiscal period. This information appears in the balances of the individual revenue and expense accounts, but it is not shown in any one account in the general ledger.

There is, however, one general ledger account that, up to this point, has not been used. That is the Income Summary account. The **Income Summary account** is used to accumulate and summarize the revenue and expenses for the period. The account, then, serves as a simple income statement in the ledger. That is, the balance of the account equals the net income or net loss for the fiscal period.

Income Summary	
Dr.	Cr.
Expense Account Balances	Revenue Account Balances

Look at the T account for Income Summary. Expenses, which have debit balances, are transferred as debits to Income Summary. Revenues, which have credit balances, are transferred as credits to Income Summary.

Look back at the chart of accounts for Global Travel on page 40. You will notice that Income Summary is located in the owner's equity section of the general ledger. It is located there because of its relationship to the owner's capital account. Remember, revenue and expenses actually represent increases and decreases to owner's equity. The balance of Income Summary (the net income or net loss for the period) must be transferred to the capital account at the end of the closing process.

Making Connections

EVERYDAY LIFE

Personal budgets help you to plan how to spend your money. Assume you have set a budget for October and throughout the month you record all your expenditures. At the end of October, you compare the amount you actually spent with the amount you had budgeted to spend, and you find that your total expenditures exceeded the budgeted amount. Is this a net loss or a net income? Explain why

you would begin with zero balances when you record expenses for November.

(Answer: Net loss. By beginning with zero balances, you are recording only the expenses for November and not adding on to expenses for other months. Most people budget by the month so they can compare expenses from one month to another—just as businesses compare revenue and expenses from one month to another.)

Like the withdrawals account, Income Summary is a temporary capital account. Income Summary is quite different, however, from the other temporary capital accounts. First, Income Summary is used only at the end of the fiscal period. It is used only to summarize the balances from the revenue and expense accounts. Second, Income Summary does not have a normal balance, which means that it does not have an increase side or a decrease side. The debit and credit sides of the account are simply used to summarize the period's revenue and expenses. If the business has a net income, Income Summary will have a credit balance because the revenue recorded on the credit side will exceed the expenses recorded on the debit side. If the business has a net loss, the account will have a debit balance because the expenses recorded on the debit side will exceed the revenue recorded on the credit side.

Journalizing the Closing Entries

ACCOUNTING *Notes*
Closing entries are sometimes called clearing entries because one of their functions is to *clear* the revenue and expense accounts and leave them with zero balances.

Four separate journal entries are prepared to close the temporary capital accounts for Global Travel. They include

1. The balance of the revenue account is transferred to the credit side of the Income Summary account.
2. The expense account balances are transferred to the debit side of the Income Summary account.
3. The balance of the Income Summary account is transferred to the capital account (net income to the credit side; net loss to the debit side).
4. The balance of the withdrawals account is transferred to the debit side of the capital account.

The work sheet is the source of the information for the closing entries.

Closing the Balance of the Revenue Account into Income Summary

The first step in the closing procedure is to transfer the balance of the revenue account to Income Summary. The account balance for the revenue account is taken from the Income Statement section of the work sheet. Global Travel has only one revenue account, Fees, so the accounts affected by this first closing entry are Fees and Income Summary.

The balance for Fees shown on the work sheet is $1,650. To close Fees, the balance must be reduced to zero. Since Fees has a credit balance of $1,650, a debit of $1,650 to that account will result in a balance of zero. The closing entry for revenue is therefore a debit of $1,650 to Fees and a credit of $1,650 to Income Summary. This closing entry reduces the balance of the Fees account to zero and transfers the amount of total income to the Income Summary account.

Fees		Income Summary	
Dr.	Cr.	Dr.	Cr.
−	+		
Clo. $1,650	Bal. $1,650		Clo. $1,650

Interdisciplinary Connections

ECONOMICS

Each year, thousands of Americans open new businesses, many as sole proprietors. Up to 70 percent of new companies fail within two years, often because they lack a clear plan and good business advice. Many businesses fail because their owners have not evaluated their markets properly or they lack enough capital to carry them through the periods of peak demand.

Owners of small businesses can get economic and business advice from a variety of sources, including the federal government. The Small Business Administration, an agency of the federal government, provides information, advice, and practical help to small companies. Many states also offer business development advice.

Using Visuals

Call students' attention to the journal entry in Figure 9-2. Point out that the centered head "Closing Entries," describes the entries that follow and thus no description is needed for each of the closing entries.

Teaching Tips

■ Use T accounts to explain the closing of the expense accounts. Point out that one total is recorded in the Income Summary account because one total is recorded in the general journal entry that closes the expense accounts.

■ Show students how a compound entry saves space and posting time.

Using Visuals

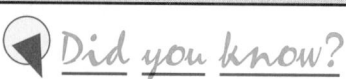

A teaching transparency is available to demonstrate a compound journal entry. See the transparency binder accompanying Glencoe Accounting.

Did you know?

Like individuals, businesses use budgets to plan their revenue and expenses. The word *budget* was used in England in the Middle Ages to mean "leather purse or wallet." In later times, the finance minister—called the chancellor of the exchequer—who presented an annual spending plan to the English Parliament was said to be "opening his budget."

The journal entry to close the revenue account into Income Summary is shown in Figure 9-2. To record the closing entry in the general journal:

	GENERAL JOURNAL			PAGE 3	
DATE	DESCRIPTION	POST. REF.	DEBIT	CREDIT	
	Closing Entries				1
19-- Oct. 31	*Fees*		165000		2
	Income Summary			165000	3

Figure 9-2 Closing the Revenue Account

1. Write the words "Closing Entries" in the center of the Description column. If you are recording the closing entries on a journal page that contains other entries, skip a line after the last entry. If you begin the closing entries on a new journal page, write the heading "Closing Entries" on the first line. This heading is the explanation for *all* the closing entries.
2. Enter the date (the last day of the fiscal period) in the Date column.
3. Enter the title of the account(s) debited and the amount of the debit.
4. Enter the title of the account credited and the amount of the credit.

Closing the Balances of the Expense Accounts into Income Summary

The second closing entry is made to transfer the balances of the expense accounts into Income Summary. The balances of the expense accounts are taken from the Income Statement section of the work sheet. The expense accounts used by Global Travel are Advertising Expense, Maintenance Expense, Rent Expense, and Utilities Expense.

Look at the T accounts that follow. Each expense account must be credited for the amount of its debit balance. (It is not necessary to use a separate closing entry for each expense account.) Income Summary then is debited for the total amount of expenses, $1,200.

Income Summary		Advertising Expense		Maintenance Expense	
Dr.	Cr.	Dr.	Cr.	Dr.	Cr.
		+	−	+	−
Clo. $1,200	Clo. $1,650	Bal. $75	Clo. $75	Bal. $450	Clo. $450

Rent Expense		Utilities Expense	
Dr.	Cr.	Dr.	Cr.
+	−	+	−
Bal. $550	Clo. $550	Bal. $125	Clo. $125

The journal entry to close the expense accounts appears in Figure 9-3.

Look again at the second closing entry. You will notice that it has one debit and four credits. A journal entry having two or more debits or two or more credits is called a **compound entry.** The compound entry saves both space and posting time. For example, each expense account could have been closed into Income Summary separately. That, however, would have required four entries, and postings, to Income Summary instead of one.

Making Connections

COMMUNICATIONS

Accountants need to be able to explain technical terms clearly to a lay person. Since this chapter deals with the final steps in the accounting cycle, have students prepare visual diagrams or other graphics that they would use to explain the whole cycle to a client. They should also prepare a short "caption" to accompany each diagram or graphic. These visuals could be made into transparencies for student presentations.

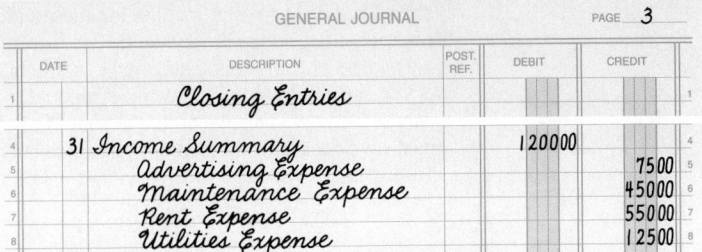

	GENERAL JOURNAL			PAGE 3	
DATE	DESCRIPTION	POST. REF.	DEBIT	CREDIT	
1	*Closing Entries*				1
4	31 Income Summary		1 2000 0		4
5	Advertising Expense			75 00	5
6	Maintenance Expense			4 50 00	6
7	Rent Expense			5 50 00	7
8	Utilities Expense			1 25 00	8

Figure 9-3 Closing the Expense Accounts

To close revenue accounts, debit each revenue account for the amount of its credit balance. Credit Income Summary for the amount of total revenue. To close expense accounts, debit Income Summary for the amount of total expenses. Credit each expense account for the amount of its debit balance.

Before going on, complete the following activity to make certain you understand how to close the revenue and expense accounts.

Check Your Learning

Write your answers to these questions on a sheet of paper.

1. A closing entry must be made for the account Ticket Revenue, which has a balance of $6,000.
   a. What is the title of the account debited?
   b. What is the title of the account credited?
   c. What is the amount of the debit? the credit?
2. A business has three expense accounts: Gas and Oil Expense (balance, $700), Miscellaneous Expense (balance, $600), and Utilities Expense (balance, $1,800). The end of the business's fiscal period is June 30.
   a. The date of the journal entry to close these accounts is ___?___.
   b. The account debited is ___?___.
   c. The amount of the debit is ___?___.
   d. The accounts credited are ___?___.
   e. The amounts of the credits are ___?___.

Compare your answers to those in the answers section. Re-read the preceding part of the chapter to find the answers to any questions you missed.

Closing the Balance of the Income Summary Account into Capital

The next journal entry is made to close the balance of the Income Summary account into the capital account. After closing the revenue and expense accounts, Income Summary has a credit balance of $450. This balance

---

---

is the amount of the net income for the period. It is the same amount that was calculated on the work sheet.

The first part of this closing entry is a debit of $450 to Income Summary. As you can see from the following T account, a debit of $450 to Income Summary reduces the balance of that account to zero. The amount of net income must be closed into the owner's capital account, so the second part of this closing entry is a credit of $450 to Jan Harter, Capital.

Income Summary		Jan Harter, Capital	
Dr.	Cr.	Dr.	Cr.
		−	+
Clo. $1,200	Clo. $1,650		Bal. $25,200
Clo. 450			Clo. 450

The journal entry to close the balance of Income Summary (the net income for the period) into the capital account is illustrated in Figure 9-4.

GENERAL JOURNAL PAGE 3

DATE	DESCRIPTION	POST. REF.	DEBIT	CREDIT
31	Income Summary		45000	
	Jan Harter, Capital			45000

Figure 9-4 Closing the Income Summary Account

If a business reports a net loss for the period, Income Summary would have a debit balance. The third closing entry, then, would be a debit to the capital account and a credit to Income Summary for the amount of the net loss. This situation is shown in Figure 9-5.

GENERAL JOURNAL PAGE 3

DATE	DESCRIPTION	POST. REF.	DEBIT	CREDIT
31	Jan Harter, Capital		25000	
	Income Summary			25000

Figure 9-5 Closing Income Summary for the Amount of Net Loss

Closing the Balance of the Withdrawals Account into Capital

The last closing entry made is to close the balance of the withdrawals account into capital. As you recall, withdrawals decrease owner's equity. The balance of the withdrawals account must be transferred to the capital account at the end of the period to show the decrease it causes in owner's equity. To close the withdrawals account, the amount of its balance—taken from the Balance Sheet section of the work sheet—is debited to capital. The withdrawals account is credited for the same amount to reduce its balance to zero. Jan Harter, Capital, therefore, is debited for $400, and Jan Harter, Withdrawals is credited for $400.

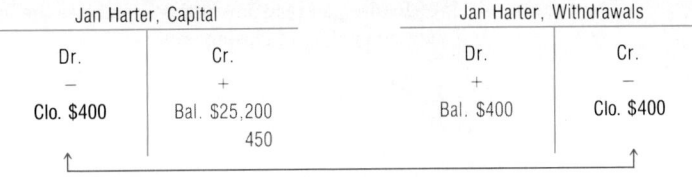

	Jan Harter, Capital			Jan Harter, Withdrawals	
	Dr.	Cr.		Dr.	Cr.
	–	+		+	–
	Clo. $400	Bal. $25,200		Bal. $400	Clo. $400
		450			

This journal entry is shown in Figure 9-6.

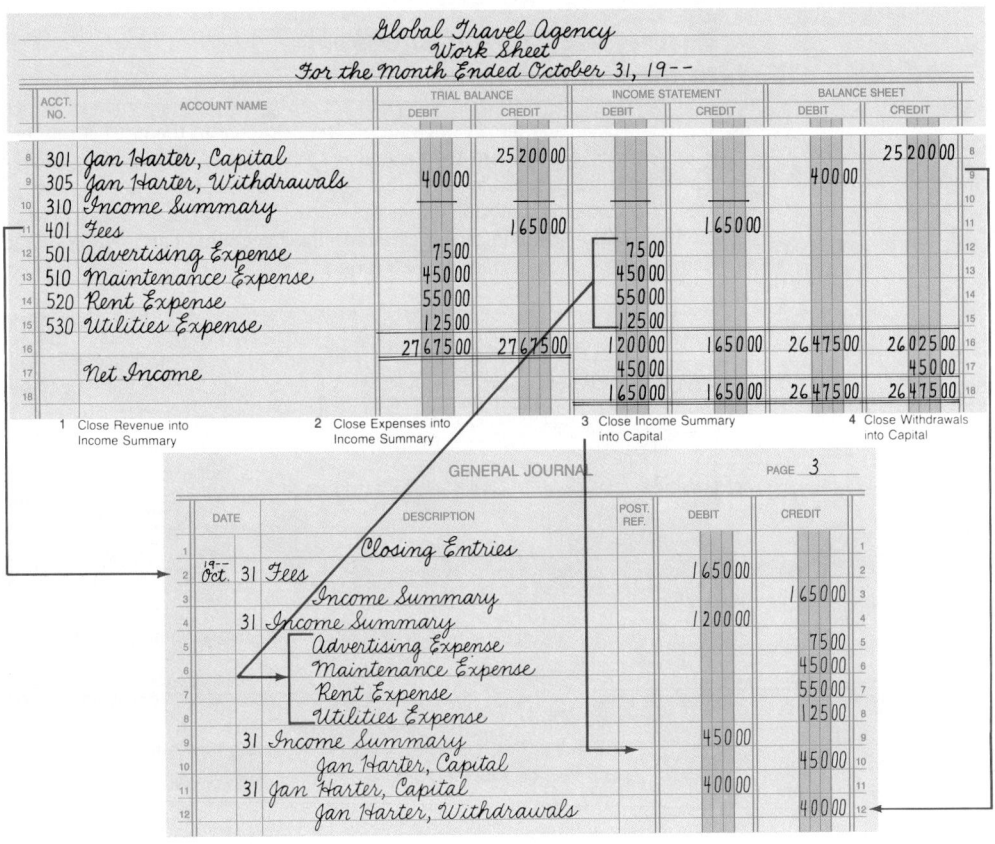

Figure 9-6 Closing the Withdrawals Account

The work sheet and the journal entries made to close the temporary capital accounts for Global Travel are shown in Figure 9-7.

Figure 9-7 Journalizing the Closing Entries

CHAPTER 9   Completing the Accounting Cycle for a Sole Proprietorship   175

Cooperative Learning

THINK-PAIR-SHARE

Permit students a specified amount of time to think about answers for the following questions and to discuss them with a partner. Ask students to share answers with the class.

1. What is the normal balance for the Income Summary account?
2. Which ledger accounts do not appear on the post-closing trial balance?

3. Is the post-closing trial balance dated for a point in time or for a period of time? Why?

(Answers: 1. Income Summary has no normal balance. 2. Temporary accounts. 3. A point in time because it represents ledger balances at a particular time.)

Refer to the "Cooperative Learning" section of *Tech Prep Strategies in Accounting* for additional cooperative learning strategies.

ANSWERS

1. Work sheet
2. Four
3. Income Summary
4. Increased
5. Three

CONCEPT DEVELOPMENT
Posting the Closing Entries to the General Ledger
Use T accounts to show students the effects of posting the closing entries shown in Figure 9-7. Remind students that the only way to bring ledger accounts up to date is to record and post journal entries.

Using Visuals

Have students read the photo caption and then respond to this question: Why might a business plan its closing process for a time of the year when business is slower than usual? (Answer: Closing takes time away from regular business activities, so it needs to be scheduled for a time when it will not interfere with regular activities if possible.)

Before you read any further, complete the following activity to check your understanding of closing entries.

Check Your Learning

Use notebook paper and answer these questions about Figure 9-7.

1. What is the source of information for the closing entries?
2. How many expense accounts are affected by the closing entries?
3. Which account serves as a "clearinghouse" during the closing process?
4. In the third closing entry, is the capital account being increased or decreased?
5. How many closing entries affect the Income Summary account?

Compare your answers to those in the answers section. Re-read the preceding part of the chapter to find the correct answers to any questions you may have missed.

Posting the Closing Entries to the General Ledger

After journalizing the closing entries, the next step in the closing process is to post those entries to the general ledger accounts. The posting procedure here is the same as for any other general journal entry, with one exception. When posting a closing entry, the words "Closing Entry" are written in the Explanation column of the general ledger account. The posting of the closing entries is shown in Figure 9-8 on pages 177-178.

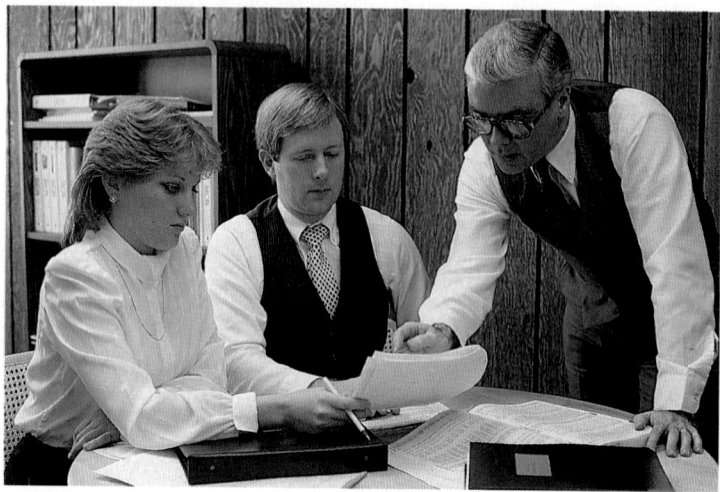

Closing entries divide the accounting activities of one fiscal period from those of another. This process provides financial data with which the owner or manager can evaluate the business's success.

Reteaching Strategies

When an owner takes cash or other assets from the business, it decreases owner's equity. The transaction is recorded in the withdrawals account rather than capital. At the end of the fiscal period, the balance in the withdrawals account needs to be transferred to the capital account to bring the capital balance up to date. After this final closing entry is made, the balance in the capital account matches the ending balance reported on the statement of changes in owner's equity and the balance sheet.

Assign Problem 9A in the Additional Problems section of the textbook (p. 635) to students who need extra practice recording closing entries.

Figure 9-8 Closing Entries Posted to the General Ledger

Using Visuals

Using Figure 9-8, trace the posting of each of the journal entries to the ledger accounts. Figure 9-8 continues on page 178.

ACCOUNTING ISSUES

In an effort to create an exam that tests broader types of knowledge in less time, the AICPA Board of Examiners recently changed the format of the CPA exam. Traditionally, the exam included only multiple choice questions. The new format includes questions that require yes or no answers (similar to true/false), matching questions, and questions requiring numerical responses. The new exam also tests the candidate's ability to write. Responses to essay questions are evaluated for both technical content and writing skills.

Making Connections

AROUND THE WORLD

Earning income is a major goal of successful business people, regardless of where they live in the world. One measure of success has long been the luxury automobile. Moscow, the center of a former state-controlled economy that determined who could do business and who could not, is now the home of the first Rolls-Royce dealership in Russia. The dealership was established by an American car dealer with two partners. Mercedes has been in Russia longer and now considers that country its fastest-growing market. Other companies represented in Russia are BMW, Ford, Jeep/Eagle, and Nissan, and others are on their way.

CONCEPT DEVELOPMENT
Preparing a Post-Closing Trial Balance

Emphasize that accounts listed on the post-closing trial balance should agree with the account balances found on the balance sheet. Note that temporary accounts are not listed on the post-closing trial balance.

Stress the purpose of the post-closing trial balance—to make sure the general ledger balances after closing entries have been posted.

Teaching Tips

- Remind students that "post" means "after."

Using Visuals

Compare the accounts in the post-closing trial balance shown in Figure 9-9 with the ledger accounts shown in Figure 9-8 (pages 177-178).

🖩 **ACCOUNTING PRACTICE**

Students may complete Exercise 9-2 at this point.

Figure 9-8 Closing Entries Posted to the General Ledger (Continued)

Preparing a Post-Closing Trial Balance

Preparing the post-closing trial balance is the last step in the accounting cycle. This trial balance is prepared to make sure the total debits in the ledger accounts are equal to total credits after the closing entries have been posted. The post-closing trial balance for Global Travel Agency is shown in Figure 9-9.

Notice that the only accounts and balances listed on the post-closing trial balance are the permanent accounts of the business. After the closing process, only permanent accounts have balances. Temporary capital accounts

Global Travel Agency
Post-Closing Trial Balance
October 31, 19--

Cash in Bank	16 125 00	
Accounts Receivable—Burton Co.	450 00	
Computer Equipment	8 000 00	
Office Equipment	1 500 00	
Accounts Payable—City News		75 00
Accounts Payable—Modern Office Suppliers		750 00
Jan Harter, Capital		25 250 00
Total	26 075 00	26 075 00

Figure 9-9 Post-Closing Trial Balance

Critical Thinking

Assume that you have been asked to review the financial statements and the post-closing trial balance for an accounting period. You notice that the Capital balance on the post-closing trial balance does not match the balance sheet amount. In checking the ledger account balances, you also notice that the revenue and expense accounts still have end-of-period balances. Is there a reason to explain this situation, or does this imply an error in the accounting records?

(Answer: The closing entries have not been posted to the ledger, which results in an incorrect Capital balance being reported on the post-closing trial balance. After posting, the Capital account balance should equal the amount shown on the balance sheet.)

have zero balances, so there is no need to list those accounts on the post-closing trial balance.

The Computer and Closing Entries

The closing entries we just discussed were prepared manually. In a computerized accounting system, closing entries may be completed entirely by the computer. A command from the computer operator instructs the computer to close the general ledger. The computer will close the temporary capital accounts, determine the amount of net income or net loss, and update the owner's capital account. After the closing is complete, the operator can instruct the computer to prepare a post-closing trial balance. The post-closing trial balance prepared by the computer lets the accounting clerk know that the temporary capital accounts have zero balances. A computer-prepared post-closing trial balance is illustrated in Figure 9-10.

```
                    Global Travel Agency
                  Post-Closing Trial Balance
                      October 31, 19--

Cash in Bank                        16125.00
Accts. Rec.--Burton Co.               450.00
Computer Equipment                   8000.00
Office Equipment                     1500.00
Accts. Pay.--City News                            75.00
Accts. Pay.--Mod. Off. Supp.                     750.00
Jan Harter, Capital                            25250.00

   Total                           26075.00  26075.00
                                   ========  ========
```

Figure 9-10   Post-Closing Trial Balance Prepared by Computer

You have now completed an accounting cycle for a service business organized as a sole proprietorship.

Summary of Key Points

1. The eighth and ninth steps in the accounting cycle are to record and post the closing entries and to prepare a post-closing trial balance. These steps complete the accounting cycle.
2. Closing is the process of transferring the balances in the temporary capital accounts to the capital account. The work sheet is the source of the balances of the temporary capital accounts.

CONCEPT DEVELOPMENT
The Computer and Closing Entries
Most accounting software programs do not require that journal entries be made as part of the closing process. The software program is set up to post automatically when that option is chosen. Such a process offers the advantage of fewer errors because no journal entries are necessary.

Using Visuals
Refer students to Figure 9-10, and have them compare the amounts with those in Figure 9-9. If possible, obtain a copy of a post-closing trial balance prepared on the computer from a local business and share it with the class.

COMPUTERS IN ACCOUNTING
Telecommunications enable CPAs to communicate faster and more efficiently. CPAs must often communicate from one computer to another and from one office to another. Electronic mail service (EMS) enables CPAs to send messages. Facsimile transmission (fax) is widely used to transfer data files with words, numbers, and graphics. One of the advantages of using EMS and fax is that the message or document can be sent even if the receiver is not present at the time of transmission.

3 CLOSE

CHAPTER SUMMARY
This summary enumerates the key information in the chapter. It is a useful tool for reinforcement and review.

Pop Quiz

1. What is the purpose of closing entries?
2. The ____ account serves as a simple income statement in the ledger.
3. Where do you find the information you need to record closing entries.
4. After closing entries are posted, all temporary accounts should have a ____ balance.
5. What is the purpose of the post-closing trial balance?

ANSWERS

1. To close out the balances in the temporary capital accounts and to transfer net income (or loss) to the capital account
2. Income Summary
3. the work sheet
4. zero
5. To make sure that total debit account balances and total credit account balances in the ledger accounts are still equal

3. Only temporary capital accounts are closed. The asset, liability, and owner's capital account are never closed.

4. The first closing entry transfers the balance of the revenue account(s) into Income Summary. The balances of the expense accounts are then closed into Income Summary. The balance of the Income Summary account (the net income or net loss for the period) is then closed into the capital account. The last closing entry transfers the balance of the withdrawals account into the capital account.

5. After the closing entries have been journalized, they are posted to the general ledger. A post-closing trial balance is then prepared to test the equality of total debits and credits in the ledger.

Teacher Notes

_____

_____

_____

_____

_____

Review and Applications

Building Your Accounting Vocabulary

In your own words, write the definition of each of the following accounting terms. Use complete sentences for your definitions.

closing entries   Income Summary   post-closing trial
compound entry   account   balance

Reviewing Your Accounting Knowledge

1. Why are the temporary capital accounts closed at the end of the fiscal period?
2. What is the purpose of the Income Summary account?
3. Explain the relationship between the Income Summary account and the capital account.
4. How is the Income Summary account different from the other temporary capital accounts?
5. List the steps involved in closing the temporary capital accounts.
6. What is the source of information for the closing entries?
7. How does the closing procedure for a net loss differ from the closing procedure for a net income?
8. In what way is the posting procedure for closing entries different from the posting procedure for other general journal entries?
9. What is the purpose of preparing a post-closing trial balance?
10. Why do only the balances of permanent accounts appear on the post-closing trial balance?

Improving Your Human Relations Skills

Recently Elena, a new employee, was assigned to work with you on several important projects in your office. You have found that Elena is not very well organized and often has to redo her part of an assignment. As a result of her poor work, you have already missed your first deadline.

1. What should you say to Elena?
2. How would you explain this problem to your supervisor?
3. What can be done to make sure you do not miss future deadlines?

Applying Accounting Procedures

Exercise 9-1   Understanding the Accounting Cycle

The nine steps in the accounting cycle are listed at the top of page 182, but not in the proper order.

Instructions: Rearrange these steps in the order in which they would be completed by a business during an accounting period. Use the form in the workbook or plain paper. Place a number (from 1 to 9) on the line preceding the step.

181

PRACTICE AND APPLY

- Language Development
- Comprehension and Retention
- Basic Skills

Building Your Accounting Vocabulary
See the Glossary on pages 670-679 for definitions of these terms.

Reviewing Your Accounting Knowledge
1. To reduce the account balances to zero for use in the new fiscal period.
2. To summarize the revenue and expenses for a fiscal period.
3. Income Summary is a temporary capital account used to record net income or net loss; its debit balance (loss) decreases capital while a credit balance increases capital (income).
4. It is used only at the end of the fiscal period to summarize the balances from the revenue and expense accounts and does not have a normal balance side.
5. (a) Transfer revenue to the credit side of Income Summary account. (b) Transfer the total of expenses to the debit side of Income Summary. (c) Transfer the Income Summary balance to Capital. (d) Transfer the balance of withdrawals to the debit side of Capital.
6. The work sheet.
7. A net loss results in a debit balance for Income Summary, which is transferred to the debit side of Capital.
8. The procedure is the same except for writing the words "Closing Entry" in the ledger accounts.
9. To test that total debits in the ledger are equal to total credits after closing entries are posted.
10. Only the permanent accounts have balances.

Improving Your Human Relations Skills
Students' answers will vary but may include the following.

1. Mention the importance of working together to complete projects successfully. Ask if you can help Elena by suggesting ways she can organize her portion of an assignment.
2. Explain that a portion of the project had to be redone. While it is not necessary to mention names or "fix blame," tell your supervisor you think you have the situation under control so that future deadlines can be met.
3. You should supervise Elena more closely and make sure that she understands what has to be done and by what date.

Chapter 9

PRACTICE AND APPLY

• Concepts and Procedures

Exercise 9-1: Ch. Obj. 1

a. 6
b. 2
c. 9
d. 8
e. 1
f. 5
g. 4
h. 3
i. 7

Exercise 9-2: Ch. Obj. 1, 2, 3

Problem 9-1: Ch. Obj. 4

Closing Entries:
Dr. Accounting Fees $15,865.00
Cr. Income Summary $15,865.00

Dr. Income Summary $6,190.00
Cr. Entertainment Exp. $3,400.00
Cr. Miscellaneous Exp. $560.00
Cr. Rent Expense $1,000.00
Cr. Utilities Exp. $1,230.00

Dr. Income Summary $9,675.00
Cr. Robert Holmes, Cap. $9,675.00

Dr. Robert Holmes, Cap. $2,350.00
Cr. Robert Holmes, Withdr.
$2,350.00

a. Complete the work sheet.
b. Analyze business transactions.
c. Prepare a post-closing trial balance.
d. Journalize and post the closing entries.
e. Collect and verify data on source documents.
f. Prepare a trial balance.
g. Post each entry to the general ledger.
h. Journalize business transactions.
i. Prepare the financial statements.

Exercise 9-2   Determining Accounts Affected by Closing Entries

The following list contains some of the accounts used by the Living Well Health Spa.

Accounts Payable—The Fitness Shop	Membership Fees
Accounts Receivable—Linda Brown	Miscellaneous Expense
Advertising Expense	Office Furniture
Cash in Bank	Rent Expense
Exercise Class Revenue	Repair Tools
Exercise Equipment	Ted Chapman, Capital
Income Summary	Ted Chapman, Withdrawals
Laundry Equipment	Utilities Expense
Maintenance Expense	

Instructions: Use a form similar to the one that follows. For each account,
(1) Indicate the statement on which each account is reported by writing "Balance Sheet" or "Income Statement" in the space provided.
(2) In the next column, use "Yes" or "No" to indicate whether the account is closed.
(3) In the last column, use "Yes" or "No" to indicate whether the account is included in the post-closing trial balance. The first account is shown as an example.

Account Title	Financial Statement	Is the account affected by a closing entry?	Does the account appear on the post-closing trial balance?
Accounts Payable—The Fitness Shop	Balance Sheet	No	Yes

Problem 9-1   Preparing Closing Entries

A portion of the work sheet for Holmes Accounting Service for the period ended September 30 appears on page 183.

Instructions: Using the information from the work sheet, prepare the journal entries to close the temporary capital accounts. Use journal page 7.
(1) Record the closing entry for the revenue account.
(2) Record the closing entry for the expense accounts.
(3) Record the closing entry for the Income Summary account.
(4) Record the closing entry for the withdrawals account.

182

Refer students to the Chapter 9 review pages in the workbook, *Chapter Reviews and Working Papers.*

Additional Reinforcement

Students who need additional practice or individualized help will benefit from the *Glencoe Accounting Electronic Study Guide* or the *Glencoe Accounting* on-line multimedia program, which provide reinforcement and reteaching for vocabulary, concepts, and procedures.

ACCT. NO.	ACCOUNT NAME	INCOME STATEMENT DEBIT	INCOME STATEMENT CREDIT	BALANCE SHEET DEBIT	BALANCE SHEET CREDIT	
101	Cash in Bank			7000 00		1
105	Accts. Rec. – Betty Foley			3000 00		2
115	Office Equipment			12000 00		3
120	Accounting Library			6000 00		4
201	Accts. Pay.–Ron Williams				900 00	5
301	Robert Holmes, Capital				19775 00	6
305	Robert Holmes, Withdrawals			2350 00		7
310	Income Summary					8
401	Accounting Fees		15865 00			9
501	Entertainment Expense	3400 00				10
510	Miscellaneous Expense	560 00				11
520	Rent Expense	1000 00				12
530	Utilities Expense	1230 00				13
		6190 00	15865 00	30350 00	20675 00	14
	Net Income	9675 00			9675 00	15
		15865 00	15865 00	30350 00	30350 00	16

Problem 9-2: Ch. Obj. 6
Post-Closing TB totals:
$30,200.00

Problem 9-2   Preparing a Post-Closing Trial Balance

Shown below are the accounts of Carrier's Repair Shop on June 30 after the closing entries have been journalized and posted.

Cash in Bank

Dr.	Cr.
+	−
$8,000	

Accounts Receivable— Kathy Clarke

Dr.	Cr.
+	−
$875	

Accounts Receivable— Malcolm, Inc.

Dr.	Cr.
+	−
$5,050	

Accounts Receivable— James Moreaux

Dr.	Cr.
+	−
$1,275	

Shop Equipment

Dr.	Cr.
+	−
$6,000	

Tools

Dr.	Cr.
+	−
$9,000	

Accounts Payable— Beste Tool & Die Co.

Dr.	Cr.
−	+
	$1,000

Accounts Payable— Oliver Equipment

Dr.	Cr.
−	+
	$2,500

J. C. Carrier, Capital

Dr.	Cr.
−	+
$1,500	$21,000
	7,200

J. C. Carrier, Withdrawals

Dr.	Cr.
+	−
$1,500	$1,500

Income Summary

Dr.	Cr.
$7,800	$15,000
7,200	

Repair Revenue

Dr.	Cr.
−	+
$15,000	$15,000

Rent Expense

Dr.	Cr.
+	−
$5,000	$5,000

Utilities Expense

Dr.	Cr.
+	−
$2,800	$2,800

183

Teacher Notes

Problem 9-3: Ch. Obj. 4
Net Income, $11,300.00

Problem 9-4: Ch. Obj. 5, 6
Ending Capital, $68,800.00

Problem 9-5: Ch. Obj. 4, 5, 6

COMPUTER

PROBLEM

This computer image identifies a problem that students may complete using the *Glencoe Accounting, General Ledger* software.

Instructions: Use the information in the T accounts to prepare the June 30 post-closing trial balance for Carrier's Repair Shop.

Problem 9-3   Journalizing Closing Entries

The following account titles and balances appeared on the work sheet for Whitman Contractors. The work sheet was for the month ended July 31.

	Income Statement		Balance Sheet	
	Debit	Credit	Debit	Credit
Cash in Bank			9,300	
Accounts Receivable—Projean Co.			3,000	
Accounts Receivable—Ford Bakery			10,000	
Office Equipment			8,000	
Construction Equipment			60,000	
Accounts Payable—Joseph's Elec.				5,000
Accounts Payable—Moran Cement Co.				1,500
Accounts Payable—Stoll Bldg. Supp.				15,000
C. Whitman, Capital				64,500
C. Whitman, Withdrawals			7,000	
Income Summary				
Construction Revenue		20,000		
Advertising Expense	1,700			
Gas and Oil Expense	4,300			
Miscellaneous Expense	700			
Repairs Expense	1,200			
Utilities Expense	800			

Instructions: Using the above information, record the closing entries for Whitman Contractors. Use general journal page 11.

Problem 9-4   Posting Closing Entries and Preparing a Post-Closing Trial Balance

Instructions: Use the closing entries prepared in Problem 9-3 to complete this problem.
(1) Post the closing entries recorded in Problem 9-3 to the appropriate general ledger accounts. The general ledger accounts for Whitman Contractors are included in the working papers accompanying this textbook.
(2) Prepare a post-closing trial balance.

COMPUTER

PROBLEM

Problem 9-5   Completing End-of-Period Activities

At the end of April, the general ledger for Tsung Management Company shows the following account balances.

110	Cash in Bank	$12,000	220	Accounts Payable—	
120	Accounts Receivable—			The Computer Shop	$15,500
	Hatter Company	3,000	301	Alan Tsung, Capital	54,675
130	Accounts Receivable—		302	Alan Tsung,	
	Jackson Co.	900		Withdrawals	4,000
140	Accounts Receivable—		303	Income Summary	
	Zest Realty Co.	1,800	401	Management Fees	9,600
150	Office Supplies	500	510	Advertising Expense	1,000
160	Office Equipment	13,000	520	Miscellaneous Expense	400
170	Computer Equipment	42,000	530	Rent Expense	1,200
210	Accounts Payable—		540	Utilities Expense	375
	Fox Office Supply	400			

184

Teacher Notes

Instructions: Using the preceding account titles and balances,

(1) Prepare the six-column work sheet. The period covered is one month.

(2) Prepare the financial statements. Alan Tsung made an investment of $10,000 during the month.

(3) Record the closing entries on page 12 of a general journal.

(4) Post the closing entries.

(5) Prepare a post-closing trial balance.

TB totals, $80,175.00
Net Income, $6,625.00
Ending capital, $57,300.00
P/C TB totals, $73,200.00

Problem 9-6: Ch. Obj. 4, 6

CHALLENGE PROBLEM

Problem 9-6 Correcting Errors in the Closing Entries

The work sheet and financial statements for Bennett Company for the month of November have been completed. They show that during this one-month period,

a. The net income for the period was $1,800.

b. The owner, Dale Bennett, made an additional investment of $5,000.

c. Dale Bennett withdrew $2,000.

d. The November 30 balance of Dale Bennett, Capital that appeared on the work sheet was $30,000.

e. Expenses for the month were as follows: Advertising Expense, $900; Miscellaneous Expense, $300; Rent Expense, $1,400; and Utilities Expense, $600.

The closing entries for the month were entered in the general journal as shown below.

The last problem in each chapter is a challenge problem and is identified by this "maze" symbol.

1. Third entry is incorrect; amount is $1,800, not $30,000
2. Debit balance, $28,200
3. Credit, $58,000
4. Credit, $29,800
5. Already included in the capital balance

GENERAL JOURNAL   PAGE 14

	DATE	DESCRIPTION	POST. REF.	DEBIT	CREDIT	
1		*Closing Entries*				1
2	19-- Nov. 30	*Fees*		5 000 00		2
3		*Income Summary*			5 000 00	3
4	30	*Income Summary*		3 200 00		4
5		*Advertising Expense*			900 00	5
6		*Miscellaneous Expense*			300 00	6
7		*Rent Expense*			1 400 00	7
8		*Utilities Expense*			600 00	8
9	30	*Income Summary*		30 000 00		9
10		*Dale Bennett, Capital*			30 000 00	10
11	30	*Dale Bennett, Capital*		2 000 00		11
12		*Dale Bennett, Withdrawals*			2 000 00	12

Instructions: Based on these closing entries, answer the following questions.

(1) What error has been made in recording the closing entries?

(2) After posting the entries shown, will Income Summary have a debit or a credit balance?

(3) After posting these entries, what will the balance of the capital account be?

(4) What *should* the balance of Dale Bennett, Capital be?

(5) Why does the additional investment of $5,000 *not* appear in the closing entries?

Make corrections in the journal entries in your working papers.

185

4 ASSESS

A chapter test is available for use in assessing students' understanding of concepts in this chapter.

The testmaker software will enable you to develop tailor-made chapter, unit, semester, and final tests.

Alternative Assessment

For alternative assessment strategies, refer to *Tech Prep Strategies in Accounting*.

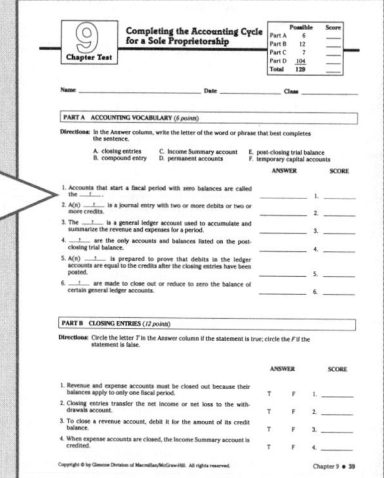

Use Chapter Test 9 here to assess students' understanding and retention of the concepts and procedures presented in the chapter.

F O C U S   O N
COMPUTERS

Computers play increasingly important roles in medicine today. One area that has been especially affected by computers is diagnosis of illness and injury. Many of the recent advances in medicine would not have been possible without computers. Ask students to think of ways in which computers are used to diagnose and treat patients. Ask students to share any recent experiences they may have had with computers in medicine, or have students read related articles.

QUESTIONS

1. What are computer networks and how can they help doctors and hospitals in the treatment of patients?
2. Identify several ways in which computers can be used in professional sports.

ANSWERS

1. Computer networks are systems of interconnected computers that can function individually or communicate with each other. Networks enable doctors and hospitals to share medical profiles, insurance information, and laboratory test results quickly.
2. Computers facilitate ticketing, assessing player performance, and developing game strategies.

*C*omputers in Sports: New Angles on the Winning Performance

When mere hundredths of inches, seconds, or points separate winning performances from second-place finishes, coaches of world-class athletes are adopting state-of-the-art coaching assistants: computers.

At the U.S. Olympic Committee sports science lab in Colorado Springs, Colorado, researchers videotape an athlete's performance. They then process and digitize the performance frame by frame to create multidimensional images that can be analyzed from different angles. The analysis can point out flaws in the athlete's technique that might not otherwise be noticed. The computer can even be told to look for a specific flaw and highlight it throughout the analysis.

This $35,000 motion-analysis system was created by Phillip Cheetham, a former Olympic gymnast from Australia. Cheetham withdrew from competition as the result of an injury. His injury led him to develop another system used by the U.S. Olympic Committee to analyze how gymnastic injuries can be prevented.

Young Tom Eldredge, junior world figure-skating champion, believes motion-analysis helped him become one of only a dozen figure skaters in the United States to perform a triple-axel (three and a half revolutions in the air).

As this technology becomes more widely used, will world records fall even faster? Will athletes be able to leap higher and longer, run faster, score more perfect 10s than ever before? How much does technique contribute to the winning performance? How much is the result of conditioning, training, body type, and the competitive spirit?

Computer analysis of the serve may improve this tennis player's performance.

186

Chapter 10

CASH CONTROL AND BANKING ACTIVITIES

Learning Objectives

When you have completed Chapter 10, you should be able to do the following:

1. Describe the internal controls used to protect cash.
2. Describe the forms used to open and use a checking account.
3. Accurately record information on check stubs.
4. Prepare a check correctly.
5. Reconcile a bank statement.
6. Journalize and post entries relating to bank service charges.
7. Define the terms introduced in this chapter.

An important part of the record-keeping for any business involves the records kept on the cash received and paid out. Cash is a business's most liquid asset. It is the asset needing the greatest protection, to prevent its loss or waste.

In this chapter, you will learn about the controls businesses use to protect their cash. One of the most commonly used controls is a checking account. The use of a checking account not only helps protect cash but also provides a separate record of cash transactions.

New Terms

internal controls
external controls
checking account
check
depositor
signature card
deposit slip
endorsement
restrictive endorsement
payee
drawer
drawee
voiding a check
bank statement
canceled checks
reconciling the bank statement
outstanding checks
outstanding deposits
bank service charge
stop payment order
NSF check
electronic funds transfer
    system (EFTS)

187

INTRODUCING THE
CHAPTER

LOOKING BACK

To this point, students have learned to keep the basic accounting records for a sole proprietorship, service business using a general journal. Another part of accounting relates to the handling of cash received and paid out by the business. In this chapter students will learn how to use a checking account and how to record banking charges in the accounting records for a business.

VOCABULARY DEVELOPMENT

Have students read the list of new terms. Ask for ideas for each term's meaning. Write correct responses on the board. Review the meanings of terms that are not familiar to students. Definitions of these terms are found in the chapter and in the glossary on pages 670-679.

Teaching Resources

- Lesson Plans
- TE/Chapter Reviews & Working Papers
- Demonstration Problems
- Student Study Plans
- Teaching Transparencies
- Solutions Transparencies
- Electronic Field Trips Video, Level I
- Electronic Study Guide
- Chapter 10 Test
- Unit Objective Test for Chapters 7-10
- Unit Problem Test for Chapters 7-10

Other Resources

- Skills Improvement Activities
- Blackline Masters
- Careers in Accounting
- Dictionary
- Math Review for Accounting
- Tech Prep Strategies in Accounting
- Video
- Test Bank with Software
- Spanish Resources/Audiotapes
- Spanish Electronic Study Guide

Chapter 10

1 FOCUS

MAJOR CONCEPTS

- Protecting Cash
- Opening a Checking Account
- Making Deposits to a Checking Account
- Writing Checks
- Proving Cash
- The Bank Statement
- Recording Bank Service Charges
- Special Banking Procedures
- Electronic Funds Transfer System

BUSINESS CONNECTION

Like other businesses, banks look for ways to gain customers and thus increase their business. One of the most popular bank services today is the ATM machine. Banks must join an ATM network to provide that service to their customers, who need an individual ID to access the ATM system. Two of the most extensive ATM networks are Cirrus and the Plus System, both of which offer quick and convenient banking. Ask students where the ATM machines are located in their community.

2 TEACH

CONCEPT DEVELOPMENT
Protecting Cash

When explaining the internal control of cash, refer to the list of examples given in items 1-6 and have students respond with how each example helps to protect cash. Mention that when the records of a business are being audited, internal controls of cash are reviewed in detail.

Using Visuals

Call students' attention to the photo caption, and ask students to think of several types of businesses that handle a large volume of cash each day and thus would make daily deposits to their checking accounts.

One way a business can control, or protect, its cash is by making all payments by check and depositing all cash received in a bank account.

Protecting Cash

In any business, ready cash (bills, coins, and checks) is used daily for a large number of transactions. A business receives cash in return for its goods or services. It pays out cash to purchase goods and services or to pay its expenses.

You learned in an earlier chapter that cash is a business's most liquid asset. It is important to protect that asset from loss, waste, theft, forgery, and embezzlement. Cash can be protected through internal controls and external controls. **Internal controls** refer to those steps the business takes to protect cash and other assets. For example, internal controls may include

1. Limiting the number of persons handling cash.
2. Separating accounting tasks involving cash (such as, not allowing the person who handles cash receipts and cash payments to also keep the accounting records showing the amounts received or paid out).
3. Bonding (insuring) employees who handle cash or cash records.
4. Using a safe or a cash register.
5. Depositing cash receipts in the bank daily.
6. Using checks to make all cash payments.

External controls are those controls provided outside the business. For example, banks maintain controls to protect the funds deposited by their customers. These controls include verifying the accuracy of signatures on checks and maintaining records of the transfer of money into and out of each customer's checking account.

188

UNIT 2   The Basic Accounting Cycle

Reinforcing Study Skills

Remind students that time management skills are important in helping them complete homework assignments and projects. One effective time management tool is a priorities chart. If prepared on a weekly basis, the chart will help students identify their most important tasks. Due dates for assignments and test dates would be priorities. Weeks in which short-term assignments are not due or in which major tests are not given are the best time to schedule work on a long-term assignment.

Provide a copy of the *Student Study Plans* to each class member to help organize study activities or to individualize practice and review activities.

Opening a Checking Account

A **checking account** is a bank account that allows a bank customer to deposit cash and to write checks against the account balance. A **check** is a written order from a depositor telling the bank to pay a stated amount of cash to the person or business named on the check. A **depositor** is a person or business that has cash on deposit in a bank. To open a checking account, a business owner must fill out a signature card and deposit cash in the bank.

A **signature card** contains the signature(s) of the person(s) authorized to write checks on the bank account. The signature card is kept on file by the bank so that it can be matched against signed checks presented for payment. The use of a signature card helps protect both the account holder and the bank against checks with forged signatures.

The signature card signed by Jan Harter to open the checking account for Global Travel Agency is shown in Figure 10-1.

ACCT. NO. **303443**
ACCOUNT NAME *Global Travel Agency*
ACCT. TYPE: ☑ CKG. ☐ SAV. ☐ C.R.
☐ OTHER _____
NO. SIGNATURES REQUIRED __1__
SOC. SEC. NO. OR TAXPAYER I.D. NO.
SIGNATURE *Jan Harter*

1 _____ SIGNATURE

2 _____ SIGNATURE

THE INDIVIDUALS WHO HAVE SIGNED ABOVE ARE AUTHORIZED TO USE THIS ACCOUNT ACCORDING TO THE RULES AND REGULATIONS THAT APPLY TO IT **AND** ANY SPECIAL INSTRUCTIONS ON FILE WITH THE BANK. EACH PERSON WHO SIGNS ACKNOWLEDGES THAT THESE RULES AND REGULATIONS HAVE BEEN RECEIVED AND AGREES TO THEIR TERMS. EACH PERSON ALSO AUTHORIZES THE BANK TO REQUEST A CONSUMER REPORT FROM ANY CONSUMER REPORTING AGENCY.

FOR BANK USE

IDENTIFICATION PRESENTED *Mass. State License*
COMMENTS *Sole Proprietorship – travel agency*
ACCOUNT ADDRESS *200 Brattle Street, Cambridge, MA 02138*
HOME PHONE *258-4512*   BUSINESS PHONE *258-2020*
☑ NEW ACCOUNT ☐ CAPTION CHANGE ☐ NEW SIGNATURE ☐ ADDITIONAL SIGNATURE
☐ INDIVIDUAL ☐ JOINT ☐ CORPORATE ☑ BUSINESS ☐ FIDUCIARY
☐ OTHER _____
NCPS _____   OPENED BY *GLC*   BRANCH _____
DATE OPENED OR CHANGED *10/1*   AMOUNT DEPOSITED $ *25,000.00*

Figure 10-1 Checking Account Signature Card

Making Connections

EVERYDAY LIFE

Assume you work for a sporting goods store that is open six days a week from 9 a.m. to 9 p.m. Due to a storewide sale, the store is making record daily sales and the manager has been too busy to make daily deposits at the bank. Have students explain why the manager should take the time each day to deposit the business's cash receipts.

Teaching Tips

■ There are 12 Federal Reserve districts in the United States. Ask students whether they know the district to which your area belongs. Discuss the Federal Reserve system in class or have students do brief research papers on the topic.

The American Express Company was formed in 1850 to transport goods and money quickly between the East Coast and the Midwest. The company issued its first travelers' checks in 1891. These checks replaced the traveler's letter of credit, which was a letter from one bank to another allowing the person named in the letter to withdraw money from the second bank.

When a depositor opens a checking account, checks are printed for the sole use of that depositor. Printed checks are packaged together in *checkbooks*. The checkbook chosen by Jan Harter is typical of those used by businesses. It looks like a spiral-bound notebook. Its pages are made up of detachable checks attached to check stubs. Each check — and its stub — is numbered in sequence. Prenumbered checks help a business keep track of every check that is written. Using checks with printed numbers is an important part of the internal control of cash.

In addition to the check number, each check is printed with the business's account number and an American Bankers Association (ABA) number. The ABA number is the fractional number printed in the upper right corner of a check, just below the check number. The ABA number is a code that identifies exactly where a check comes from. For example, look at the ABA number on the check in Figure 10-2.

Figure 10-2 Printed Check

The part of the number above the line and to the left of the hyphen stands for the city or state in which the bank is located. The number to the right of the hyphen indicates the specific bank on which the check is written. The number below the line is a code for the Federal Reserve district in which the bank is located.

The ABA number was developed to speed the sorting of checks by hand. An updated version of the ABA number is also printed on the bottom of each check for use in electronic sorting. The ABA number, the depositor's account number, and perhaps the check number are printed at the bottom of the check in a special ink and typeface. These specially printed numbers are referred to as MICR (*m*agnetic *i*nk *c*haracter *r*ecognition) numbers. Can you identify the MICR number on the check in Figure 10-2?

Cooperative Learning

CORNERS

Provide the following report topics and allow students to choose the topic they want to learn about. Group students based on the topic selected, and instruct each group to research the topic and prepare a report. Ask each group to present its report to the class.

• ATM Fraud
• Innovations in ATM Technology

• Mandatory Direct Payroll Deposit
• Automated Clearinghouse Security Risks and Fraud Prevention Systems
• Home Banking Services

Refer to the "Cooperative Learning" section of the *Tech Prep Strategies in Accounting* booklet for additional cooperative learning strategies.

Making Deposits to a Checking Account

A business should make regular deposits to protect the currency and checks it receives. Most businesses make daily deposits. A **deposit slip** is a bank form on which the currency (bills and coins) and checks to be deposited are listed. The deposit slip, also called a deposit ticket, gives both the depositor and the bank a detailed record of a deposit. Most banks provide their depositors with deposit slips on which the depositor's name, address, and account number are printed. A deposit slip for Global Travel Agency is shown in Figure 10-3. To complete a deposit slip, follow these steps:

1. Write the date on the Date line.
2. On the Cash line, list the total amount of bills and coins being deposited.
3. List checks separately by their ABA numbers. If many checks are being deposited, list the checks by amount on a calculator tape and attach the tape to the deposit slip. On the first Checks line, write "See tape listing," followed by the total amount of the checks.
4. Total the cash and checks, and write the total amount being deposited on the Total line.

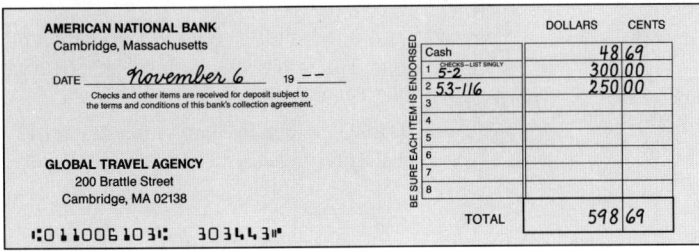

Figure 10-3 Deposit Slip

The deposit slip and the cash and checks being deposited are handed to a bank teller. Checks should be arranged in the order listed on the deposit slip. The teller verifies the deposit and gives the depositor a receipt. The deposit receipt may be a stamped and initialed (by the teller) copy of the deposit slip or a machine-printed form.

R E M E M B E R

On the deposit slip, list checks being deposited by their ABA numbers.

Endorsing Checks

When a business receives a check in payment for a product or service, it acquires the right to that check. The check is a form of property. To deposit the check in a checking account, the depositor endorses the check to transfer its ownership to the bank. An **endorsement** is an authorized signature that is written or stamped on the back of a check.

The endorsement on the check represents a promise to pay. For example, suppose the bank cannot collect the amount of the check from the account

CHAPTER 10   Cash Control and Banking Activities   **191**

CONCEPT DEVELOPMENT
Making Deposits to a Checking Account
The deposit slip is a summary of the cash receipts for a specific period of time, usually daily. The daily deposit should match the journal entries made for cash received. Emphasize the importance of using a restrictive endorsement. Call students' attention to the importance of controlling checks received from customers. Make sure students understand why businesses do not accept checks from every customer. (Some customers may have a history of writing checks without sufficient funds to cover them.)

Discuss the "why" behind recording each deposit in the checkbook (daily record of balance of Cash in Bank).

Teaching Tips

■ Obtain blank deposit slips from a local bank to give students experience in filling them out.

Using Visuals

Using Figure 10-3, point out the different amounts shown for cash and checks. Explain the meaning of the ABA numbers shown on the deposit slip.

Using Visuals

 Use demonstration problem 10-1 to show students how to fill out a deposit slip.

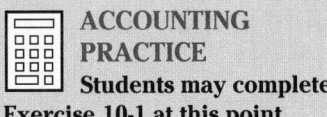 **ACCOUNTING PRACTICE**
Students may complete Exercise 10-1 at this point.

Interdisciplinary Connections

HISTORY

Modern banking developed from the moneychangers of the Middle Ages. Where traders from different countries met, the moneychangers made trading easier by exchanging their coins. Some people left money for safekeeping in the moneychangers' strongboxes, and soon the moneychangers began to lend their excess at interest.

ACCOUNTING PRACTICE

Students may complete Exercise 10-3 at this point.

CONCEPT DEVELOPMENT

Writing Checks

Emphasize the importance of completing the check stub before writing the check. Many people have shared the frustrating experience of having written a check without recording it and then being unable to determine their account balance. For businesses, the stub is even more important because it serves as a source document for journalizing entries involving cash payments.

Demonstrate filling out a check stub. Share several examples of original check stubs that have been filled out correctly. Show students the correct way to write a check.

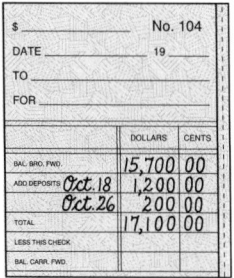

FOR DEPOSIT ONLY IN

Global Travel
Agency

Acct. 303443

Figure 10-4 Restrictive Endorsement

$		No. 104	
DATE		19	
TO			
FOR			
		DOLLARS	CENTS
BAL. BRO. FWD.		15,700	00
ADD DEPOSITS *Oct. 18*		1,200	00
Oct. 26		200	00
TOTAL		17,100	00
LESS THIS CHECK			
BAL. CARR. FWD.			

Figure 10-5 Recording a Deposit in the Checkbook

ACCOUNTING *Notes*
Checks dated on a Sunday or written for amounts less than $1 are as valid as checks dated on weekdays or written for larger amounts. A check doesn't have to be written on a bank form, either. Checks written on a blank sheet of paper or even a log are negotiable.

on which the check is written. The endorsement of the depositor authorizes the bank to deduct the amount of the check from the depositor's account. The depositor, of course, can go back to the person or business that wrote the check to collect payment on it.

Types of endorsements vary, but most businesses use restrictive endorsements. A **restrictive endorsement** restricts, or limits, how a check may be handled. To protect checks from being cashed by anyone else, Global Travel Agency stamps a restrictive endorsement on each check as soon as it is received. For example, by writing "For Deposit Only" as part of its endorsement, Global Travel limits any other use of the check. A typical restrictive endorsement is shown in Figure 10-4.

Recording Deposits in the Checkbook

The check stubs in the checkbook are a duplicate record of the Cash in Bank account. That is, the completed stubs contain the records of all checking account transactions: withdrawals, deposits, and bank service charges.

To record a deposit in the checkbook, follow these procedures:

1. Enter the date of the deposit on the Add Deposits line of the next unused check stub.
2. Enter the total amount of the deposit on the same line in the amount column.
3. Add the deposit amount to the amount on the Balance Brought Forward line. The result is the new checkbook balance. Enter the new balance on the Total line.

The check stub in Figure 10-5 illustrates how deposits are recorded in Global Travel Agency's checkbook.

Writing Checks

Writing checks is a simple procedure governed by a few important rules. These rules must be followed to ensure correct recordkeeping and proper handling of the money represented by the check.

First, *always write checks in ink.* Typewritten checks are also acceptable. Checks written in pencil are *not* acceptable. Checks typed or written in ink are difficult to change, while those written in pencil may be easily altered.

Next, always complete the check stub *before* writing the check. Following this procedure reduces the chance of forgetting to complete the stub. After the check is removed from the checkbook, the stub serves as a permanent record of the check.

Completing the Check Stub

Global Travel's check stub is divided into two parts. The upper half summarizes the details of the cash payment transaction. The lower half is a record of the effects of the transaction on the checking account. It contains the balance before the transaction, any current deposits, the transaction amount, and the balance after the transaction. To complete the check stub, follow these steps:

192

Critical Thinking

Carlos is the owner of a miniature golf business. When he needs to purchase supplies, he often takes money out of the cash register drawer to pay for the items. Also, Carlos occasionally takes $5 or $10 out to buy his lunch. Explain why these are poor business practices.

(Answer: Carlos should pay for all supplies by check so that he has a record of all pay-

ments made. He should also deposit all cash receipts in the bank to have a record of cash received. When Carlos takes money from the cash drawer for personal use, that amount will never be accounted for in the records of the business, thus presenting an inaccurate picture of the revenue and expenses of the business.)

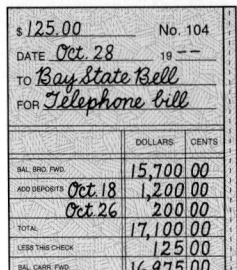

1. In the upper half of the stub, enter the amount of the check, the date, the name of the payee (on the To line), and the purpose of the check (on the For line). A **payee** is the person or business to whom a check is written.
2. If you have not already done so, enter the total balance on the Total line on the bottom half of the stub.
3. Enter the amount of the check on the line marked "Less This Check." This amount must be the same as the amount shown on the first line in the upper half of the stub.
4. Subtract the check amount from the total balance. Enter the new balance on the line marked "Balance Carried Forward."
5. Enter the new balance on the first line of the *next* check stub on the line labeled "Balance Brought Forward."

R E M E M B E R

Always complete the check stub *before* you write a check.

Filling Out the Check

After you have completed the check stub, write the check following the steps below. Remember to write the check in ink so that it cannot easily be changed.

1. Write the date on which the check is being issued.
2. Write the payee's name on the line marked "Pay To the Order Of." Start the payee's name as far left as possible.
3. Enter the amount of the check in numbers. Write clearly and begin the first number as close to the printed dollar sign as possible.
4. On the next line, write the dollar amount of the check *in words.* Start at the left edge of the line. Write any cents amount as a fraction. Draw a line from the cents fraction to the word "Dollars."
5. Sign the check. Only an authorized person—one who has signed the signature card for that account—may sign a check. The person who signs a check is the **drawer.** The bank on which the check is written is called the **drawee.**

The checkbook is now ready for the next transaction. A completed check and its stub are shown in Figure 10-6.

Figure 10-6 Completed Check and Stub

Some businesses use a check-writing machine when preparing a check. A check writer perforates the amount of the check in words on the Dollars line. These perforations protect a check from alteration, since the holes in the check are almost impossible to alter.

Voiding a Check

As a rule, if an error is made while writing a check, that check is not used. Corrected checks are not used because the corrections might look suspicious to banks. Instead, the incorrect check is marked "Void" and a new check is prepared. Writing the word "Void" in large letters across the front of a check (in ink) is known as **voiding a check.** When a check is voided, the stub is also voided.

The business needs to account for each check used, so a voided check is never destroyed. It is kept and filed in the business's records. One means of filing a voided check is to fold it and staple it to its check stub. A special file can also be set up for voided checks.

Before reading any further, complete the following activity to check your understanding of the information that appears on a check.

Check Your Learning

Study the check below and then answer the questions that follow. Write your answers on notebook paper.

Burton Company		No. 324
101 Tremont Street		5-3421
Boston, MA 02107	*November 12* 19 __	110
PAY TO THE ORDER OF *Global Travel Agency*		$ *450.00*
Four hundred fifty and no/100		DOLLARS
Patriot Bank		*Hilda G. Burton*
Boston, MA		

⑈011034213⑈ 293111⑈ 324

1. The payee of this check is ___?___ .
2. The drawer is ___?___ , and the drawee is ___?___ .
3. The number in the upper right corner, $\frac{5\text{-}3421}{110}$, is the ___?___ number.
4. The number 293111 at the bottom of the check is the ___?___ number.

Compare your answers to those in the answers section. Re-read the preceding part of the chapter to find the correct answers to any questions you may have missed.

Proving Cash

The balance in the Cash in Bank account in the general ledger is regularly compared with the balance in the checkbook. If all cash receipts have been deposited, all cash payments made by check, and all transactions journalized and posted, the Cash in Bank account balance should agree with the checkbook balance. Comparing these two cash balances regularly is part of the internal control of cash. Some businesses prove cash daily or weekly, while others prove cash on a monthly basis.

If the Cash in Bank balance does not agree with the checkbook balance, and the trial balance has been proved, the error is probably in the checkbook. A checkbook error is usually the result of: (1) faulty addition or subtraction, (2) failure to record a deposit or a check, or (3) a mistake in copying the balance brought forward amount.

If an error has been made in the checkbook, the proper place to enter the correction is on the next unused stub. For example, suppose Check 22 for $84.60 has been recorded on the check stub as $48.60. The error is found when cash is proved. By this time, several other checks have been written, so the next unused check stub is 31. In this case, the amount of the error ($84.60 − 48.60 = $36.00) should be subtracted from the balance brought forward amount on check stub 31. A note is written on check stub 22 to indicate that the error has been corrected on check stub 31.

$	No. 31
DATE	19
TO	
FOR	

	DOLLARS	CENTS
BAL. BRO. FWD.	4,750	00
ADD DEPOSITS		
Less Error corr	36	00
TOTAL *ck. 22*	4,714	00
LESS THIS CHECK		
BAL. CARR. FWD.		

The Bank Statement

A **bank statement** is an itemized record of all the transactions occurring in a depositor's account over a given period, usually a month. Typical bank statements include the following information: (1) the checking account

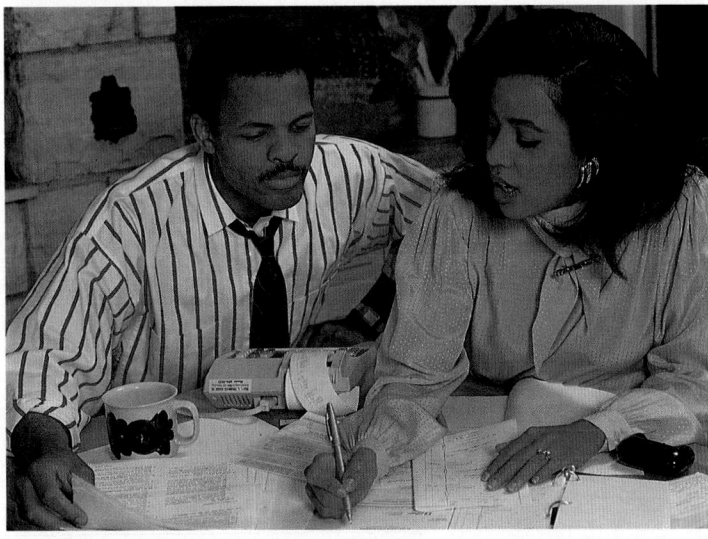

It is important to reconcile the bank statement to ensure that the business's cash records and the bank's records agree.

Chapter 10

CONCEPT DEVELOPMENT
Proving Cash
Discuss the reasons for comparing the checkbook balance with the Cash in Bank balance. Point out that cash should be proved before the Cash in Bank balance is compared with the bank statement balance.

CONCEPT DEVELOPMENT
The Bank Statement
Have students locate five items of information on the bank statement shown in Figure 10-7: the checking account balance, deposits made, checks paid, other deductions, and the account balance at the end of the period. Give a short explanation of each item. When you introduce the bank statement, you may want to bring an actual bank statement and canceled checks to class to show to students.

Remind students that bank service charges and NSF checks should be entered in the checkbook *before* reconciling the bank statement.

Point out that the bank statement reconciliation process updates both the checkbook balance and the bank statement balance. After both are updated, the balances should be the same.

Using Visuals

Refer students to the photograph and its caption. Ask students to explain how reconciling the bank statement is a part of internal control.

Making Connections

BUSINESS ETHICS

Martin wrote a check to pay for the repairs on his car even though he knew that he did not have enough money in his account to cover the amount of the check. However, in three days he would receive his pay check, which he planned to deposit in his account. Were Martin's actions justified?

(Answer: No. Knowingly writing an NSF is unethical and could prove to be costly to Martin. Today checks clear much more quickly than in the past. Martin's check may be presented for payment before Martin can deposit his pay check, which would result in a returned check, an NSF charge, and ill will on the part of the auto repair company.)

ACCOUNTING ISSUES

The continuously expanding and changing field of computers has had a dramatic effect on all aspects of auditing. Auditors must understand the accounting system and how the computer processes the transactions. Auditors must also be knowledgeable about the internal control procedures for computers. An auditor's training and education should include courses on the structure, design, and control of information systems.

balance at the beginning of the period, (2) a list of all deposits made by the business during the period, (3) a list of all checks paid by the bank, (4) a list of any other deductions from the depositor's account, and (5) the checking account balance at the end of the period. Find each of these items on Global Travel Agency's bank statement in Figure 10-7 below.

When a bank sends a statement to a depositor, it also returns the checks paid by the bank and deducted from the depositor's account. These returned checks are called **canceled checks.** Canceled checks are stamped or marked with the word "Paid" and the date of payment.

Upon receiving the bank statement, a business should promptly check the statement against its checkbook. The process of determining any differences between the balance shown on the bank statement and the checkbook balance is called **reconciling the bank statement.** The ending balance on the bank statement seldom agrees with the balance in the checkbook. There are several reasons for this.

There is frequently a two- or three-day delay between the preparation and delivery of a bank statement. During that delay, the business may have written additional checks. Often, checks written in one statement period do not reach the bank for payment until the next period. A deposit made when the statement is being prepared may not be listed on the statement. Finally, the depositor does not know about some bank transactions, such as service charges, until the statement is received.

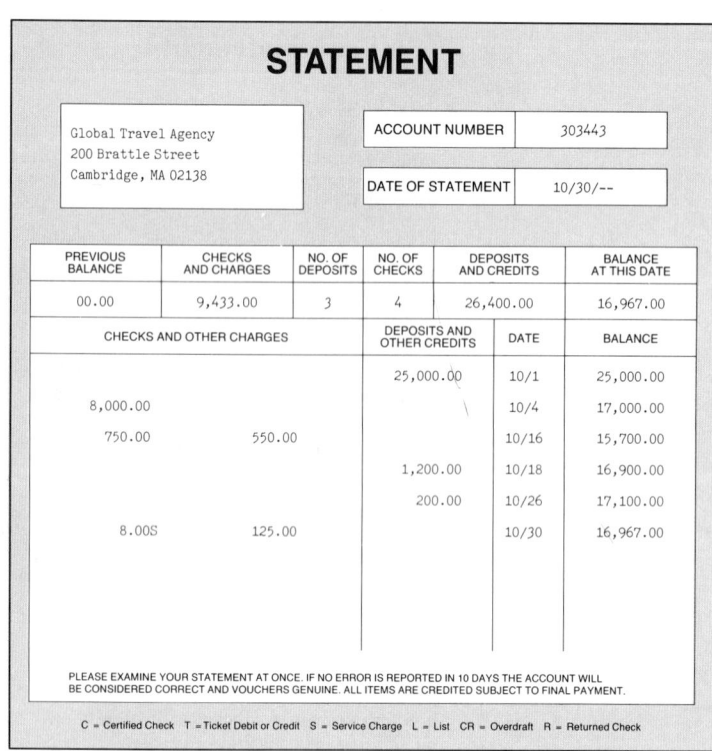

Figure 10-7 Bank Statement

UNIT 2   The Basic Accounting Cycle

The three situations most frequently causing differences between the bank statement balance and the checkbook balance involve outstanding checks, outstanding deposits, and bank service charges.

Outstanding Checks and Deposits

In banking terms, the word "outstanding" simply means "not yet received." **Outstanding checks,** therefore, are checks that have been written but not yet presented to the bank for payment. **Outstanding deposits** are deposits that have been made and recorded in the checkbook but that do not appear on the bank statement.

Bank Service Charges

The statement balance will also reflect any service charges made by the bank during the statement period. A **bank service charge** is a fee charged by the bank for maintaining bank records and for processing bank statement items for the depositor. This charge varies from bank to bank, but it is frequently based on the number of checks and deposits handled during the month or the balance kept in the depositor's account. The bank subtracts the service charge from the depositor's account and then notifies the depositor of the amount of the charge on the bank statement.

The checkbook balance must be adjusted to show the amount of the bank service charge. One way to adjust the balance in the checkbook is shown on the stub. The words "Less: Service Charge" are written on the line above the Total line. Next, the amount of the service charge is entered in the amount column — preceded by a minus sign. The balance is then recalculated and entered on the Total line.

	No. 107
$ _____	
DATE _____ 19 ___	
TO _____	
FOR _____	

	DOLLARS	CENTS
BAL. BRO. FWD.	16,125	00
ADD DEPOSITS		
Less: Serv. Chrg	– 8	00
TOTAL	16,117	00
LESS THIS CHECK		
BAL. CARR. FWD.		

R E M E M B E R

Before reconciling the bank statement, record in the checkbook any bank service charges or other deductions listed on the bank statement.

Reconciling a Bank Statement

Promptly reconciling the bank statement is a good way to guard against disorderly cash records or cash loss. Banks expect to be notified immediately of any error on the statement. Failure to do so within the time noted on the statement releases the bank from any responsibility for the error.

Most banks provide a form on the back of the bank statement for use in reconciling the bank statement. The reconciliation form for Global Travel's bank statement is shown in Figure 10-8 on page 198. This form documents the differences between the bank balance and the checkbook balance. Follow these steps when reconciling a bank statement:

1. Arrange the canceled checks in numerical order. Compare the canceled checks with those listed on the statement and with the stubs. As you find matching checks and stubs, place a check mark beside the check amount on the bank statement and on the check stub. Then list on the reconciliation form, by number and amount, all the stubs without check marks. These are the outstanding checks.

CHAPTER 10   Cash Control and Banking Activities   **197**

Making Connections

AROUND THE WORLD

School exists even for full-time business people. To help bankers from the former Soviet Union learn about banking practices in a private enterprise economy, the Russian-American Bankers Forum brought bankers from Russia, Kazakhstan, and Belarus to Fairfield University in Connecticut. The goal of the program was to help these banking "students" learn how to modernize their financial systems. The bankers learned about computerized banking operations and other modern banking practices. Computers are gaining in use in some of the former Soviet banks, but few banks have more than one branch and many computations are still made on an abacus.

Chapter 10

Using Visuals

Using Figure 10-8, walk students through the steps in reconciling the bank statement.

Using Visuals

A teaching transparency of a bank reconciliation statement is available in the transparency binder accompanying Glencoe Accounting.

Teaching Tips

- Most bank statements have reconciliation forms printed on their backs. Reconciliation forms vary from bank to bank. If possible, collect several samples to share with the class.

BANK RECONCILIATION FORM

PLEASE EXAMINE YOUR STATEMENT AT ONCE. ANY DISCREPANCY SHOULD BE REPORTED TO THE BANK IMMEDIATELY.

1. Record any transactions appearing on this statement but not listed in your checkbook.
2. List any checks still outstanding in the space provided to the right.
3. Enter the balance shown on this statement here. **16,967 00**
4. Enter deposits recorded in your checkbook but not shown on this statement. **—**
5. Total Lines 3 and 4 and enter here. **16,967 00**
6. Enter total checks outstanding here. **850 00**
7. Subtract Line 6 from Line 5. This adjusted bank balance should agree with your checkbook balance. **16,117 00**

CHECKS OUTSTANDING	
Number	Amount
105	450 00
106	400 00
TOTAL	850 00

Figure 10-8 Bank Reconciliation

2. Enter the ending balance shown on the bank statement.
3. Compare deposits listed on the bank statement to deposits listed in the checkbook. Enter the total of any outstanding deposits on the reconciliation form. Add this total to the bank statement balance and enter the amount on the form.
4. Subtract the total of the outstanding checks from the amount calculated in Step 3. The result is the adjusted bank balance.
5. Compare the adjusted bank balance to the adjusted checkbook balance. The two amounts should match.

If the adjusted bank balance does not match the adjusted checkbook balance, the error must be found and corrected. If the bank has made an error on the bank statement, notify the bank immediately. It is more likely, however, that the error is in the checkbook. Check the addition and subtraction on the check stubs to be sure they are correct.

When the adjusted balances match, the bank statement has been reconciled. The bank fees shown on the bank statement must then be recorded in the accounting records of the business. Before you read about the recording of bank service charges, complete the following Check Your Learning activity.

R E M E M B E R

If you are having problems reconciling a bank statement, double check for any outstanding checks or outstanding deposits that you may not have included in your calculations.

198

UNIT 2   The Basic Accounting Cycle

Check Your Learning

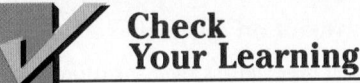

Valleyview Rental Center received its bank statement on April 27. The balance in the checkbook on April 27 is $2,944.20. The checking account balance shown on the statement is $3,085.95. A deposit of $345.00 was made on April 26, and on April 27 of $290.00. The service charge for the month was $5.25. Valleyview has these four outstanding checks:

Check 344	$202.00	Check 350	$ 25.00
Check 346	55.00	Check 351	500.00

1. What is the amount of the adjusted checkbook balance?
2. What is the amount of outstanding deposits?
3. What is the total amount of outstanding checks?
4. What is the amount of the adjusted bank balance?
5. Does the adjusted bank balance match the adjusted checkbook balance?

Compare your answers to those in the answers section. Re-read the preceding part of the chapter to find the answers to any questions you missed.

Recording Bank Service Charges

Like any other business, banks charge fees for their services. To the depositor, a service charge is an expense that must be recorded in the accounting records. Bank service charges are often recorded in the account Miscellaneous Expense. Since expenses decrease owner's equity, Miscellaneous Expense is debited for the amount of the service charge. Cash in Bank is also decreased by the amount of the service charge, so that account is credited. Remember, the amount of the service charge has already been deducted from the depositor's account, so it is not necessary to write a check for this expense. The journal entry for this transaction is shown in Figure 10-9. The bank statement is the source document for recording the bank service charge.

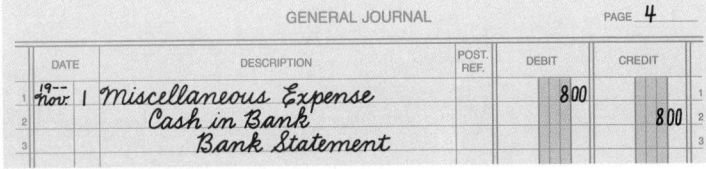

Figure 10-9 General Journal Entry for Bank Service Charge

Special Banking Procedures

Checks are usually written or received and deposited without any problems. A business, however, may not want its bank to pay a check that it has written and sent out. A business may also receive a check from a customer who does not have enough money to cover the amount of the check.

CHAPTER 10 Cash Control and Banking Activities   **199**

CONCEPT DEVELOPMENT
Special Banking Procedures
Have students suggest reasons for stopping payment on a check; for example, a check gets lost in the mail or a disagreement occurs on a transaction.

Explain the effect of an NSF check on the accounting records of the business. Analyze the transaction using T accounts. First, show how the receipt of the check was recorded. Next, establish the need to reverse the cash receipt entry. Finally, show the entry in T account form. Then illustrate the recording of an NSF check in the journal.

Point out that NSF check notices are received throughout the month, and a journal entry should be made each time a notice is received from the bank.

Teaching Tips

- Explain the effect of an NSF check on the accounting records of the business. Then demonstrate the recording of the NSF check in the journal.

Using Visuals

Use demonstration problem 10-5 to show students how to record an NSF check.

Using Visuals

Point out the account titles in Figure 10-10. Ask students to explain the effect of the NSF check on the business.

CONCEPT DEVELOPMENT
Electronic Funds Transfer System
Use a flow chart on the chalkboard to trace the route a check follows from the time it is written until it is returned with the bank statement. Make students aware of what takes place at each point in the flow. Emphasize that the ABA number on the bottom of each check is used in
(Continued)

Stopping Payment on a Check

Occasionally, a drawer will ask the bank (drawee) not to honor, or pay, a check. A **stop payment order** is a demand by the depositor that the bank not honor a certain check. The depositor must issue a stop payment order *before* the check has been presented to the bank for payment. Usually, the depositor must complete and sign a written stop payment order.

When payment is stopped on a check, the accounting clerk writes the words "Stopped Payment" on the appropriate check stub. The clerk must then *add* the amount of the stopped check to the current balance in the checkbook (on the next unused check stub). If appropriate, the accounting clerk then issues a new check.

Most banks charge a fee for stopping payment on a check. When this occurs, the amount of the fee must be subtracted from the checkbook balance and recorded in the business's accounting records. Most businesses record the amount of the fee as an expense in the Miscellaneous Expense account. The journal entry is similar to that made for the bank service charge.

Recording NSF Checks

An **NSF check** is one returned by the bank because there are *not* sufficient *f*unds in the drawer's checking account to cover the amount of the check. For example, suppose Global Travel received and deposited a check from a customer. If the customer does not have enough money in the bank to cover the check, the check will be returned to Global Travel. Global Travel will notify the customer that the check was returned by the bank. The customer must then deposit enough money in the bank to cover the check or find another means of paying its bill.

When the bank returns the NSF check to Global Travel, it deducts the amount of the check from Global Travel's checking account. Global Travel must then subtract the amount of the check from its checkbook balance.

A journal entry must also be made to record the return of the NSF check. Since the check represents payment for an amount owed to Global Travel, the amount of the check is recorded as an account receivable. Cash in Bank was originally debited for the amount of the check, so that account is now credited for the same amount. The journal entry is shown in Figure 10-10.

	GENERAL JOURNAL			PAGE___
DATE	DESCRIPTION	POST. REF.	DEBIT	CREDIT
18	Accts. Rec. — Burton Company		450 00	
	Cash in Bank			450 00
	NSF Check			

Figure 10-10 Recording the Return of an NSF Check

Electronic Funds Transfer System

As you learned earlier, when a bank sends a statement to a depositor, it also returns the checks paid by the bank. Let's look at the route a check follows from the time it is written until it is returned with the bank statement.

1. Global Travel Agency writes Check 103 to Abrams Real Estate for $550 for the month's rent.
2. Abrams Real Estate deposits the check in its acccount at the First National Bank.
3. First National Bank increases the balance in Abrams' checking account by $550.
4. First National Bank sends the $550 check to American National Bank, Global Travel Agency's bank, for collection.
5. American National Bank sends the First National Bank $550 and deducts this amount from Global Travel's account.
6. The paid check is returned to Global Travel Agency by American National Bank with the monthly bank statement.

As you can see, the exchange of checks and funds is a routine procedure. Since the number of checks written each day is in the millions, this transferring of funds from one bank to another is quite a job if handled manually. Today, banks use the electronic funds transfer system (EFTS) to handle the details of exchanging funds. The **electronic funds transfer system** enables banks to transfer funds from the account of one depositor to the account of another quickly and accurately without the immediate exchange of checks.

The full development of the electronic funds transfer system is not now being used because the general public does not wish to move to a system that is completely checkless.

Summary of Key Points

1. The use of a checking account is an important way for a business to protect cash. The checking account also serves as a duplicate record of all cash transactions.
2. Deposit slips are prepared when cash and checks are deposited in a bank account. Copies of deposit slips should be kept as proof of deposits.
3. Checks must be endorsed before they can be deposited. Most businesses stamp a restrictive endorsement on checks as soon as they are received. A restrictive endorsement limits how a check may be handled. The restrictive endorsement helps protect the checks received by a business from misuse.
4. Correctly written checks and accurate check stubs help prevent the loss of cash through carelessness or fraud.
5. As a part of its control of cash, a business regularly proves cash by comparing the Cash in Bank balance to the checkbook balance and finding the reason for any differences between the two amounts.
6. A bank statement is sent to each depositor, usually once a month. A bank statement should be reconciled promptly upon receipt. Any errors found on the bank statement must be reported to the bank immediately.
7. Bank service charges are recorded in the checkbook to keep the checkbook balance up to date.
8. After the bank statement has been reconciled, the service charges reported on the bank statement are journalized and then posted to the appropriate accounts.

Electronic Funds Transfer System (Continued)

an electronic system. Bring checks to class to show students this number. Also call students' attention to how the amount is entered at the bottom of the check for electronic sorting.

COMPUTERS IN ACCOUNTING

Telephone banking programs have been extremely popular, and, in an effort to improve customer service, many banks are now developing and testing systems for home banking services. Customers choose from a variety of electronic banking options such as paying bills and confirming account balances. In some systems, the customer communicates a transaction using a computer and modem. In other systems, the customer communicates the transaction via a touch-tone telephone. To make home banking convenient, accessible, and user friendly, some banks have collaborated with AT&T to develop a technology using the AT&T SmartPhone. With this telephone, users can choose options on a touch-sensitive LCD screen rather than entering commands through a keypad.

3 CLOSE

CHAPTER SUMMARY

This summary enumerates the key information in the chapter. It is a useful tool for reinforcement and review.

Pop Quiz

1. How can a business protect cash and other assets?
2. A fee that the bank charges for maintaining a checking account is a(n) ____.
3. How do you verify that the balance in your checking account agrees with the bank's records?
4. A check that is recorded in the checkbook but does not appear on the bank statement is a(n) ____.

5. How does a depositor notify the bank not to honor or pay a check?

ANSWERS

1. By establishing internal controls
2. Bank service charge
3. By completing a bank reconciliation statement
4. Outstanding check
5. By issuing a stop-payment order

PRACTICE AND APPLY

- Language Development
- Comprehension and Retention
- Basic Skills

Building Your Accounting Vocabulary

See the Glossary on pages 670-679 for definitions of these terms.

Reviewing Your Accounting Knowledge

1. Cash is the most liquid asset owned and is thus easily stolen.
2. Limit number of persons handling cash, separate accounting tasks involving cash, bond employees who handle cash or cash records, use a safe, deposit cash daily, use checks to make payments.
3. Verify signatures, keep checking account records.
4. (a) A signature card to match against signed checks; (b) a check to authorize payment of cash; (c) a deposit slip to record deposits; (d) a checkbook with prenumbered checks/stubs to record each payment.
5. To transfer ownership of the check to another person, business, or bank.
6. It serves as a permanent record of the check sent to the payee.
7. (a) Checking account balance at beginning of period; (b) deposits made during period; (c) checks paid by bank; (d) other deductions from depositor's account; (e) checking account balance at end of period.
8. (a) Subtract service charge from checkbook balance; (b) arrange canceled checks in numerical order; (c) compare canceled checks with statement and check stubs; (d) enter bank balance on reconciliation form; (e) compare deposits on bank statement with check stubs; (f) add outstanding deposits to bank balance; (g) subtract total outstanding checks from revised bank balance; (h) compare adjusted bank balance with adjusted checkbook balance.
9. Debit service charges to Miscellaneous Expense, credit Cash in Bank; debit NSF check to Accounts Receivable, credit Cash in Bank.
10. Write "Service Charge" and the amount on the line above the Total line; subtract from the balance.

10 Review and Applications

Building Your Accounting Vocabulary

In your own words, write the definition of each of the following accounting terms. Use complete sentences for your definitions.

bank service charge	electronic funds	reconciling the bank
bank statement	transfer system	statement
canceled checks	endorsement	restrictive
check	external controls	endorsement
checking account	internal controls	signature card
deposit slip	NSF check	stop payment order
depositor	outstanding check	voiding a check
drawee	outstanding deposit	
drawer	payee	

Reviewing Your Accounting Knowledge

1. Explain why it is important for businesses to protect their cash.
2. What internal controls can a business use to protect its cash?
3. What external controls can a business use to protect its cash?
4. Describe the types of forms that are needed to open and use a checking account.
5. What is the purpose of a check endorsement?
6. Why should you always complete the check stub *before* writing the check?
7. What information does a bank statement contain?
8. List the steps followed in reconciling a bank statement.
9. Explain how bank service charges and NSF checks are recorded in the accounting records of a business.
10. How is the bank service charge recorded in the checkbook?

Improving Your Analysis Skills

Maria Varga and John Wills are cashiers for Bacon Construction Co. Both Maria and John are responsible for receiving and paying out cash and are authorized to sign checks for the company. Maria is supposed to record all cash transactions in the company's accounting records, although John often helps. What is wrong with the cash control policies followed by Bacon Construction Co.? What suggestions can you make for improving these policies?

Applying Accounting Procedures

Exercise 10-1   Preparing a Deposit Slip

On August 14, Loretta Harper, owner of Harper Limousine Service, deposited the following items in the business's checking account.

202

Improving Your Analysis Skills

The internal cash controls for the Bacon Construction Company are weak. The major weakness is that there is no separation of the accounting tasks that involve cash. Both employees handle cash receipts and payments and record transactions. Here are a few suggestions to improve internal control of cash.

1. Only one person should be authorized to sign checks.

2. Only one person should be responsible for receiving cash.

3. Only one person should be responsible for recording cash transactions. This person should not be the same person responsible for receiving cash.

4. Employees handling cash and cash records should be bonded (insured).

5. Cash receipts should be deposited in the bank daily.

Cash: $784.29
Checks: Charles Ling, drawn on American Bank of Commerce, Dallas, ABA No. 32-7091; $39.44
Keith Lopez, drawn on People's Bank, Baton Rouge, ABA No. 84-268; $249.82
Marjorie Luke, drawn on Horizon Federal Savings and Loan, Shreveport, ABA No. 84-6249; $846.19

Instructions: Using this information, complete a deposit slip.

Exercise 10-2   Writing a Check

Carey Video Rentals received a bill from Northeast Telephone for $214.80 for September telephone services.

Instructions: Prepare Check 41 to pay the telephone bill. Use October 12 as the date and sign your name as drawer.

Exercise 10-3   Recording Deposits in the Checkbook

On January 20, Jon Preston, owner of Preston Fitness Center, deposited $1,434.86 in the business's checking account.

Instructions: Record this deposit on check stub 44 in Preston Fitness Center's checkbook.

Exercise 10-4   Recording Bank Service Charges in the Checkbook

The December bank statement for the Century Advertising Agency listed a bank service charge of $19.80.

Instructions: Record this service charge in the checkbook on check stub 24.

Problem 10-1   Handling Deposits

On February 4, Stanford Mott, owner of Mott Furniture Rental, deposited the following items in the company's checking account at the First National Bank in Ocala, Florida.

Cash: Currency, $374.00; Coins, $7.42
Checks: Bob Warner, drawn on Consumers Bank, Ocala, ABA No. 63-706; $64.98
Joan Walkman, drawn on Sun Bank, Gainesville, ABA No. 63-699; $349.81
Ernesto Garcia, drawn on Progressive Savings and Loan, Tampa, ABA No. 63-710; $29.44

Instructions:
(1) Endorse the checks with a restrictive endorsement. Use the name "Mott Furniture Rental."
(2) Fill out a deposit slip. Use the ABA number to identify each check.
(3) Record the deposit in the checkbook on check stub 651.

Problem 10-2   Maintaining the Checkbook

As the accounting clerk for Currie Construction, you write and sign checks and make deposits. The current checkbook balance, shown on check stub 104, is $3,486.29.

203

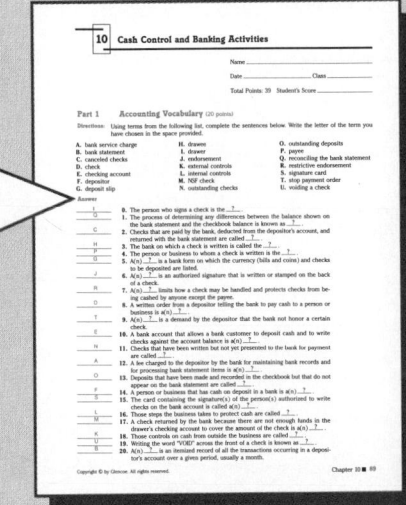

Exercise 10-1: Ch. Obj. 2
Total deposit, $1,919.74

Exercise 10-2: Ch. Obj. 2, 3
Balance, $1,427.16

Exercise 10-3: Ch. Obj. 2, 3
Balance, $5,538.13

Exercise 10-4: Ch. Obj. 3, 6
Balance, $10,090.18

Problem 10-1: Ch. Obj. 2, 3
Total deposit, $825.65
Balance, $4,132.19

Additional Reinforcement

Students who need additional practice or individualized help will benefit from the *Glencoe Accounting Electronic Study Guide* or the *Glencoe Accounting* on-line multimedia program, which provide reinforcement and reteaching for vocabulary, concepts, and procedures.

Refer students to the Chapter 10 review pages in the workbook, *Chapter Reviews and Working Papers.*

Problem 10-2: Ch. Obj. 3, 4
Ending balance, $2,086.89

Problem 10-3: Ch. Obj. 5, 6
Adjusted balances, $950.00

Problem 10-4: Ch. Obj. 5, 6

COMPUTER **This computer image identifies a problem that students may complete using the** *Glencoe Accounting, General Ledger* **software.**

PROBLEM

SPREADSHEET **Problem 10-4 can be completed using** *Spreadsheet Applications,* **the spreadsheet software that accompanies** *Glencoe Accounting.*

PROBLEM

Adjusted balances, $2,468.90

Instructions: For each transaction,
(1) Record the necessary information on the check stub. Determine the new balance and carry the balance forward.
(2) Write checks where requested. Sign your name as drawer.

Transactions:

Mar. 3 Issued Check 104 for $868.45 to Custom Construction for construction supplies.
3 Deposited $601.35 in the checking account.
6 Purchased building materials for cash by issuing Check 105 for $299.60 to Cunningham Lumber.
7 Paid Laverne Brothers $1,000.00 for completing a painting job, Check 106.
10 Made a deposit of $342.80 in the checking account.
10 Wrote Check 107 to Union Utilities for the February electric bill of $175.50.

Problem 10-3   Reconciling the Bank Statement

On May 31, George Fister, the accountant for Anco Financial Services, received the bank statement dated May 30. After comparing the company's checkbook with the bank statement, George found

1. The checkbook balance on May 31 was $960.
2. The ending bank statement balance was $1,380.
3. The bank statement showed a service charge of $10.
4. A deposit of $405 was made on May 30 but did not appear on the bank statement.
5. Check 468 for $529 and Check 472 for $306 were outstanding.

Instructions:
(1) Record the bank service charge in the checkbook.
(2) Reconcile the bank statement for Anco Financial Services.
(3) Journalize the entry for the bank service charge in the general journal.
(4) Post the bank service charge to the appropriate general ledger accounts.

SPREADSHEET **Problem 10-4   Reconciling the Bank Statement**

On July 31, June Hankins, owner of Hankins Photography Studio, received a bank statement dated July 30. After she compared the company's checkbook records with the bank statement, June found

PROBLEM

1. The checkbook had a balance of $2,551.34.
2. The bank statement showed a balance of $2,272.36.
3. The statement showed a bank service charge of $20.00.
4. A check from Ted Koonce for $62.44 that was deposited on July 18 was returned by the bank. There was no fee for handling the NSF check.
5. A deposit of $672.48 made on July 30 did not appear on the July bank statement.
6. These checks are outstanding:

Check 172 for $126.84   Check 183 for $192.80
Check 181 for $ 87.66   Check 187 for $ 68.64

204

Teacher Notes

Instructions: Using the preceding information,

(1) Record the service charge and the NSF check in the checkbook.
(2) Reconcile the bank statement for Hankins Photography Studio.
(3) Journalize the service charge and the NSF check on page 7 of a general journal.
(4) Post the journal entries to the appropriate general ledger accounts.

CHALLENGE   **Problem 10-5   Reconciling the Bank Statement**
                         Using the T Account Form

PROBLEM   On February 20, the Northam Computer Service Co. received its bank statement dated February 18. After examining it and the checkbook, these facts were determined.

1. The checkbook balance on February 20 was $880.84.
2. The ending bank balance was $344.58.
3. There was a service charge of $14.00 for the month.
4. The following checks were outstanding:

| Check 164 | $ 88.41 | Check 171 | $129.88 |
| Check 169 | 69.34 | Check 173 | 14.25 |

5. A $68.42 check from Tom McCrary that was deposited on February 13 was returned by the bank for insufficient funds. The bank charged Northam's account $7.00 for handling the NSF check. No journal entry has yet been made for the NSF check.
6. A deposit of $938.72 made on February 9 does not appear on the bank statement.
7. A check for $200.00 made out to Fontenot, Inc., was lost in the mail and has never been cashed. A stop payment order, which cost $10.00, was issued on February 15. No new check has yet been issued.

Instructions: Reconcile the bank statement. Using the T account form in the working papers, list changes to the bank statement balance on the left side and changes to the checkbook balance on the right side.

Problem 10-5: Ch. Obj. 5

CHALLENGE   The last problem in each chapter is a challenge problem and is identified by this "maze" symbol.

PROBLEM

Adjusted balances, $981.42

Teaching Tips

■ Do not hold students to a strict format for this bank reconciliation. Students should, however, know which items to add and which to deduct from each balance.

4 ASSESS

A chapter test is available for use in assessing students' understanding of concepts in this chapter.

Unit objective and problem tests are available to assess students' knowledge of concepts in Chapters 7-10.

The testmaker software will enable you to develop tailor-made chapter, unit, semester, and final tests.

Alternative Assessment

For alternative assessment strategies, refer to *Tech Prep Strategies in Accounting.*

Use Chapter Test 10 here to assess students' understanding and retention of the concepts and procedures presented in the chapter.

Use Unit 2 Objective Test, Chapters 7-10, and/or Unit 2 Problem Test, Chapters 7-10, to assess students' retention of concepts presented in these chapters.

Have students read the ethics case given in the textbook and jot down ideas about what they would do in the situation described. Then review the five-step decision model (see page T44). Emphasize that there are no "right" or "wrong" answers to the questions in the decision model.

After students have discussed the first four steps, have them vote on which alternative they feel is best, or, if one alternative has clearly been chosen during the discussion, review students' reasoning for choosing that course of action.

You may want to have students compare their final decision with the one they wrote down after first reading the vignette. Did following the five-step model reinforce their "instinctual" decision or lead them to choose a different course of action? Help students realize that following a decision model when they confront an ethical dilemma can help them to organize their thinking and arrive at a satisfactory solution.

QUESTIONS

1. What are the ethical issues in this situation?
2. What are the alternatives?
3. Who are the affected parties?
4. How do the alternatives affect the parties?
5. What is the decision?

ANSWERS

1. Taking money that does not belong to Christine, deciding what to tell the store manager about other discrepancies.
2. To take the money, to tell the store manager about the discrepancy.
3. Christine, the store manager, the customer who lost the money.
4. Answers will vary. For example, if Christine keeps the money, she will have an extra $34.50 to add to her college fund, but she may have to return it and face the consequences if the manager finds out or the customer returns for the money. The effect on the store manager may be a bad opinion of Christine if the customer returns for the money. If the customer returns for the correct change and is told that no mistake

*P*ocketing Differences

Christine recently got a job at the neighborhood grocery store as a cashier. She planned to use the money she earned to help pay for college. She enjoyed talking to people as she checked out their purchases, and she worked hard to become one of the fastest cashiers in the store.

Because she was quick, she had a large number of customers go through her aisle each day, and she took in a fair percentage of the day's earnings. Occasionally, when she totaled her receipts and cash at the end of her shift, she found herself either a little short or a little over. If she was a little short, of course, she reported the discrepancy to the manager according to the store's policy. Often if she was a little over, however, she kept the difference for her "college fund." She knew some of the other cashiers did the same thing. Since she had not heard of anyone getting into trouble over the matter, she assumed that management indulgently overlooked the practice.

One day as Christine was totaling up the day's transactions, she found she was over by $34.50. Whenever she had an excess in cash before, it had only been a few dollars. As she again counted the cash in her drawer, she noticed that she had a $50 bill mixed in with the $20 bills. Usually she placed the rare $50 or $100 bill under the checks. Christine wondered if she could have taken a $50 bill from a customer and, assuming it was a $20 bill, given incorrect change.

What is Christine's ethical dilemma? The $34.50 would be a nice bonus, but what if the customer realized his or her mistake and returned to the store? If she reports the difference to the manager, what if the manager asks about other discrepancies that Christine has had? What should Christine do?

Employees sometimes overlook the ethical implications of taking small items from their work place.

Often employees do not think of the ethical implications of taking small amounts of money or small items such as pens or note pads from the work place, but do realize the ethical aspects of taking home something more costly. Christine did not deliberate much over pocketing a dollar or two. A company pen costs about that much, and many employees take home pens without giving it a second thought. Christine's $34.50 difference, however, forced her to stop and think, and led her back to her earlier actions with smaller amounts of cash. Often, by deciding ahead of time what your own ethical stand on such issues will be, you can act consistently and ethically each time such a situation occurs.

206

has been made, the customer will likely have a poor opinion of the store and may not shop there anymore.
5. Accept any answer, but require students to defend the action they choose.

Mini Practice Set

APPLICATION ACTIVITY 2

Completing the Accounting Cycle for a Sole Proprietorship

You have just completed your study of the accounting cycle and the banking activities for a service business organized as a sole proprietorship. Now you will have the opportunity to apply what you have learned as you work through the accounting cycle for Jenny's Gymnastic Academy.

When you have completed this activity, you will have done the following:

1. Analyzed business transactions.
2. Journalized business transactions in the general journal.
3. Posted journal entries to the general ledger accoutns.
4. Prepared a trial balance and a work sheet.
5. Prepared financial statements.
6. Journalized and posted the closing entries.
7. Prepared a post-closing trial balance.
8. Prepared a reconciliation of the bank statement and recorded any bank service charges.

Jenny's Gymnastic Academy

Jenny's Gymnastic Academy is owned and managed by Jennifer Rachael. The business is organized as a sole proprietorship. The academy provides gymnastic programs for children ages 4-18. The business earns revenue from membership fees and fees charged for special classes.

Chart of Accounts

The chart of accounts for Jenny's Gymnastic Academy appears at the top of the next page.

Business Transactions

Jenny's Gymnastic Academy began business operations on March 1 of this year. During the month of March, the business completed the transactions that follow.

Instructions: Use the accounting stationery in the working papers accompanying this textbook to complete this activity.

(1) Open a general ledger account for each account in the chart of accounts.
(2) Analyze each business transaction.
(3) Enter each business transaction in the general journal. Begin on journal page 1.
(4) Post each journal entry to the appropriate accounts in the general ledger.

207

Trial balance, $41,553
Net income, $807
Ending Capital, $26,242
Balance sheet, $39,019
P/C TB, $39,019

JENNY'S GYMNASTIC ACADEMY
Chart of Accounts

ASSETS	101	Cash in Bank
	105	Accounts Receivable — Sally Chapin
	110	Accounts Receivable — Carla DiSario
	115	Accounts Receivable — George McGarty
	120	Accounts Receivable — Joyce Torres
	130	Office Supplies
	135	Office Furniture
	140	Office Equipment
	145	Gymnastic Equipment
LIABILITIES	205	Accounts Payable — Custom Designs
	210	Accounts Payable — The Gym House
	215	Accounts Payable — T & N Equipment
OWNER'S EQUITY	301	Jennifer Rachael, Capital
	305	Jennifer Rachael, Withdrawals
	310	Income Summary
REVENUE	401	Membership Fees
	405	Class Fees
EXPENSES	505	Maintenance Expense
	510	Miscellaneous Expense
	515	Rent Expense
	525	Utilities Expense

(5) Reconcile the bank statement that was received on March 31. The statement is dated March 30.
   a. The checkbook has a current balance of $19,580.00.
   b. The bank statement shows a balance of $19,831.00.
   c. The bank service charge is $15.00.
   d. A deposit of $140.00 made on March 30 does not appear on the bank statement.
   e. These checks are outstanding: Check 112 for $106.00 and Check 113 for $300.00.
(6) Make any necessary adjustments to the checkbook balance.
(7) Journalize and post the entry for the bank service charge.
(8) Prepare a trial balance and then complete the work sheet.
(9) Prepare an income statement.
(10) Prepare a statement of changes in owner's equity.
(11) Prepare a balance sheet.
(12) Journalize and post the closing entries.
(13) Prepare a post-closing trial balance.

Transactions:

Mar. 1 Jennifer Rachael invested $25,000 in Jenny's Gymnastic Academy, Memorandum 1, by opening a business checking account.
     2 Bought a cash register (office equipment) for $525, Check 101.
     2 Purchased $73 in office supplies and issued Check 102.

208

Teacher Notes

_____

_____

_____

_____

_____

Mar. 3 Received Invoice 2348 from Custom Designs for office furniture bought on account, $2,680.

4 Jennifer Rachael invested a used typewriter worth $135 in the business, Memorandum 2.

5 Purchased gymnastic equipment for $3,924, Check 103.

5 Received $950 for membership fees, Receipt 1.

6 Bought $8,495 of gymnastic equipment on account from The Gym House, Invoice 395.

8 Carla DiSario completed two classes, $36, Invoice 101, to be paid later.

9 Wrote Check 104 for $850 for the March rent.

10 Charged George McGarty $175 for special classes, on account, Invoice 102.

10 Received Invoice 5495 for a $2,375 microcomputer system bought on account from T & N Equipment.

11 Prepared Receipt 2 for $695 in membership fees received.

13 Received $36 from Carla DiSario on account, Receipt 3.

14 Sent Check 105 for $200 to The Gym House on account.

14 Jennifer Rachael invested $800 worth of gymnastic equipment in the business, Memorandum 3.

15 Wrote Check 106 for $750 to repaint a section of the gym.

16 Completed classes totaling $250 with Joyce Torres, Invoice 103, on account.

18 Jennifer Rachael withdrew $500 for personal use, Check 107.

19 Sent Check 108 for the electric bill of $183.

20 Received a check from George McGarty for $75 to apply on his account, Receipt 4.

21 Issued Check 109 for $45 for stamps (Miscellaneous Expense).

22 Received membership fees, Receipt 5 for $550.

24 Sent Check 110 for $500 to Custom Designs on account.

25 Paid $85 for the cleaning of the office, Check 111.

26 Completed classes with Sally Chapin, $185, to be paid later, Invoice 104.

27 Paid the $106 electric bill, Check 112.

28 Sold a piece of gymnastic equipment to another gym for $175 cash, Receipt 6.

30 Paid T & N Equipment $300 on account, Check 113.

30 Received $140 on account from Joyce Torres, Receipt 7.

31 Bought additional office supplies on account for $227 from T & N Equipment, Invoice 5643.

209

Teacher Notes

In Unit 3 students will study the accounting cycle for a merchandising business. The business used as an example throughout the chapters in this unit is organized as a privately held corporation.

Students will learn how to use special journals in this unit, beginning with the sales journal in Chapter 11. Students will also learn how to post from multicolumn special journals to the general ledger and to the subsidiary ledgers.

210

UNIT 3

THE ACCOUNTING CYCLE FOR A MERCHANDISING BUSINESS

In this unit, you will learn how to keep the accounting records for a business that sells merchandise to its customers. The business we will use in our examples in this unit is organized as a corporation. You will study the complete accounting cycle for a merchandising business called Champion Building Products, Inc. The accounting cycle for a merchandising business that is organized as a corporation is very much like that for the service business organized as a sole proprietorship that you studied in Unit 2.

Individualizing Instruction

To provide individualized activities within the unit, you may use any of the following:

- problems in *Math Review for Accounting*
- chapter study plans
- study guides in the student workbook
- end-of-chapter challenge problems (identified by a maze symbol)

- optional problems in the Additional Problems section at the back of the student textbook
- cases from *Tech Prep Strategies in Accounting*
- *Electronic Study Guide*

The Accounting Cycle for a Merchandising Business

Unit Concepts

In Unit 3, students go through a complete accounting cycle for a merchandising business organized as a corporation. Students learn about general purchasing procedures as well as accounting procedures. Since the business is a merchandising business with many business transactions, special journals are used. Students learn the types of transactions that are recorded in the special journals and the types of transactions that are recorded in the general journal. Adjusting entries are covered in this accounting cycle.

General Unit Performance Objectives

1. Correctly use terminology related to the accounting cycle of a merchandising business organized as a closely held corporation.
2. Describe the accounting procedures used in a merchandising business organized as a closely held corporation.
3. Demonstrate accounting procedures used for recording transactions in special journals and in general and subsidiary ledgers.

PERFORMANCE OBJECTIVES

Unit Objective Test: Chapters 11-15

1. Define the related accounting vocabulary correctly.
2. Determine correct and incorrect procedures for recording transactions in the special journals and in the general journal.
3. Classify the accounts of a merchandising corporation.
4. Analyze special journal entries.

Unit Problem Test: Chapters 11-15

1. Record the transactions in the special journals.
2. Foot, prove, total, and rule the special journals.
3. Post from the purchases and cash payments journals to the general ledger and the subsidiary ledger accounts.
4. Prepare a schedule of accounts payable.

Unit Objective Test: Chapters 16-18

1. Define the related accounting vocabulary correctly.
2. Determine correct and incorrect procedures for end-of-fiscal-period activities.
3. Determine the normal balances for accounts used by a merchandising corporation.
4. Analyze adjusting and closing entries.
5. Determine various financial statement amounts.
6. Select the correct financial statement for given accounts.

Unit Problem Test: Chapters 16-18

1. Record adjustments on a work sheet.
2. Prepare an income statement and a statement of retained earnings.
3. Record adjusting entries in the general journal.

ORGANIZER

Chapter	Learning Objectives
11	1. Explain the difference between a service business and a merchandising business. 2. Identify the special journals and explain how they are used in a merchandising business. 3. Record sales of merchandise on account in a multicolumn sales journal. 4. Post from the sales journal to customer accounts in the accounts receivable subsidiary ledger. 5. Foot, prove, and total the sales journal at the end of the month and post column totals to the general ledger. 6. Define the accounting terms new to this chapter.
12	1. Journalize cash received by a business in a cash receipts journal. 2. Post from the cash receipts journal to the accounts receivable subsidiary ledger and to the general ledger. 3. Foot, prove, total, and rule a cash receipts journal. 4. Post column totals from the cash receipts journal to the general ledger. 5. Prepare a schedule of accounts receivable. 6. Define the accounting terms new to this chapter.
13	1. Describe the procedures for processing a purchase on account. 2. Explain the use of the Purchases account. 3. Journalize a purchase on account in a purchases journal. 4. Post from the purchases journal to the accounts payable subsidiary ledger and to the general ledger. 5. Define the accounting terms new to this chapter.
14	1. Journalize various cash payments in a cash payments journal. 2. Post from the cash payments journal to the accounts payable subsidiary ledger and the general ledger. 3. Total, prove, and rule the cash payments journal. 4. Post special amount column totals to the general ledger. 5. Prepare a schedule of accounts payable. 6. Prove cash. 7. Define the accounting terms new to this chapter.
15	1. Explain the purpose of debit and credit memorandums. 2. Journalize transactions involving sales returns and allowances. 3. Journalize transactions involving purchases returns and allowances. 4. Journalize correcting entries. 5. Define the accounting terms new to this chapter.
Mini Practice Set 3	Analyze transactions and complete an accounting cycle for a merchandising business organized as a corporation.
16	1. Describe the parts of a ten-column work sheet. 2. Determine which general ledger accounts must be adjusted and calculate the amounts of the adjustments needed. 3. Prepare a ten-column work sheet. 4. Define the accounting terms new to this chapter.
17	1. Explain how the ownership for a corporation is recorded in comparison to that for a sole proprietorship. 2. Explain the relationship between the work sheet and the financial statements for a merchandising business organized as a corporation. 3. Explain how the financial statements for a corporation differ from those for a sole proprietorship. 4. Prepare an income statement for a merchandising corporation. 5. Prepare a statement of retained earnings for a merchandising corporation. 6. Prepare a balance sheet for a merchandising corporation. 7. Define the terms new to this chapter.
18	1. Record adjusting entries in the general journal. 2. Post adjusting entries to the general ledger. 3. Record closing entries for a merchandising corporation. 4. Post closing entries to the general ledger accounts. 5. Prepare a post-closing trial balance. 6. Describe the steps in the accounting cycle. 7. Define the accounting terms new to this chapter.
Mini Practice Set 4	Analyze transactions and complete an accounting cycle for a wholesale merchandising business organized as a corporation.

State/Local Objectives			Demonstration Problems	Check Your Learning	Basic Skills	Exercises	Problems	Challenge Problem	Additional Problems
			11-1 11-2 11-3 11-4 11-5 11-6	p. 217 p. 223 p. 228	Math p. 231	11-1 11-2 11-3 11-4	11-1 11-2 11-3 11-4 11-5	11-6	11A p. 635
			12-1 12-2 12-3	p. 242 p. 247	Communi- cations p.257	12-1 12-2 12-3	12-1 12-2 12-3 12-4	12-5	12A p. 636
			13-1 13-2 13-3 13-4	p. 270 p. 274 p. 280	Human Relations p.282	13-1 13-2 13-3	13-1 13-2 13-3 13-4	13-5	13A p. 637
			14-1 14-2 14-3	p. 293 p. 301 p. 307	Decision Making p. 309	14-1 14-2 14-3	14-1 14-2 14-3 14-4	14-5	14A p. 637
			15-1 15-2 15-3 15-4 15-5	p. 324 p. 327	Proof- reading p. 330	15-1 15-2 15-3 15-4	15-1 15-2 15-3	15-4 15-5	15A 15B p. 638
			16-1 16-2 16-3 16-4 16-5,16-6	p. 349 p. 354 p. 357	Human Relations p. 358	16-1 16-2	16-1 16-2 16-3 16-4	16-5	16A p. 639
			17-1 17-2 17-3 17-4 17-5 17-6	p. 366 p. 373	Analysis p. 377	17-1 17-2	17-1 17-2 17-3 17-4 17-5	17-6 17-7	17A p. 640
			18-1 18-2 18-3 18-4 18-5	p. 386 p. 394 p. 399	Math p. 403	18-1 18-2	18-1 18-2 18-3 18-4 18-5	18-6	18A 18B p. 640

COMPUTERIZED ACCOUNTING ACTIVITIES

Chapter	Glencoe Integrated Accounting	Spreadsheet Applications	Electronic Study Guide Model Exercises/Problems	CD Rom
11	Problem 11-5		Exercise 11-1 / 11-2 / Problem 11-1	Menu Selection 11
12	Problem 12-4	Problem 12-1 (Cash Receipts Journal)	Exercise 12-2 / 12-3 / Problem 12-1	Menu Selection 12
13	Problem 13-4		Exercise 13-1 / Problem 13-1	Menu Selection 13
14	Problem 14-4		Exercise 14-1 / 14-3 / Problem 14-1	Menu Selection 14
15	Problem 15-3	Problem 15-1 (General Journal)	Exercise 15-3 / 15-4 / Problem 15-1	Menu Selection 15
Mini Practice Set	Application Activity 3			
16		Problem 16-1 (Ten-Column Work Sheet)	Exercise 16-1 / 16-2	Menu Selection 16
17	Problem 17-5	Problem 17-1 (Income Statement)	Exercise 17-1 / 17-2 / Problem 17-1 / 17-2 / 17-3	Menu Selection 17
18	Problem 18-5	Problem 18-2	Problem 18-1 / 18-2	Menu Selection 18
Mini Practice Set	Application Activity 4			
Basic Math Review			Menu Option 29	

CHAMPION
BUILDING PRODUCTS, INC.

CHAMPION BUILDING PRODUCTS, INC.
Chart of Accounts

ASSETS	101	Cash in Bank
	105	Accounts Receivable
	110	Merchandise Inventory
	115	Supplies
	120	Prepaid Insurance
	150	Delivery Equipment
	155	Store Equipment
LIABILITIES	201	Accounts Payable
	205	Federal Income Tax Payable
	210	Sales Tax Payable
STOCKHOLDERS' EQUITY	301	Capital Stock
	305	Retained Earnings
	310	Income Summary
REVENUE	401	Sales
	405	Sales Discounts
	410	Sales Returns and Allowances
COST OF MERCHANDISE	501	Purchases
	505	Transportation In
	510	Purchases Discounts
	515	Purchases Returns and Allowances
EXPENSES	601	Advertising Expense
	605	Bank Card Fees Expense
	610	Delivery Expense
	615	Insurance Expense
	620	Maintenance Expense
	625	Miscellaneous Expense
	630	Rent Expense
	635	Salaries Expense
	640	Supplies Expense
	645	Utilities Expense
	650	Federal Income Tax Expense

Accounts Receivable Subsidiary Ledger	*Accounts Payable Subsidiary Ledger*
Amy Anderson	Aluminum Plus, Inc.
Shawn Flannery	Center City Supply
Gateway School District	Custom Doors, Inc.
Greensburg School District	Key Paint Company
Norwin School District	Starks Lumber Co.
Pelco Construction Co.	Viking Motors
St. Clair Roofing Co.	Wilson Electric, Inc.
Lisa Whitmore	

212

Chapter 11

ACCOUNTING FOR SALES ON ACCOUNT

In Unit 2, you learned to classify, record, and report accounting information for businesses that provided a service to their customers. In this unit, you will learn about a different type of business—one that sells merchandise to its customers.

As a business grows, the volume of its transactions increases and a more efficient system for recording transactions is needed. Special journals provide that more efficient system. Transactions that are similar are recorded in one journal.

In this chapter, you will study the sales journal and related records used to keep track of sales on account.

Learning Objectives

When you have completed Chapter 11, you should be able to do the following:

1. Explain the difference between a service business and a merchandising business.
2. Identify the special journals and explain how they are used in a merchandising business.
3. Record sales of merchandise on account in a multicolumn sales journal.
4. Post from the sales journal to customer accounts in the accounts receivable subsidiary ledger.
5. Foot, prove, and total the sales journal at the end of the month and post column totals to the general ledger.
6. Define the accounting terms introduced in this chapter.

New Terms

merchandising business
retailer
wholesaler
merchandise
inventory
sale on account
charge customer
credit card
sales slip
sales tax
credit terms
special journals
sales journal
accounts receivable subsidiary ledger
subsidiary ledger
controlling account
footing

213

INTRODUCING THE
CHAPTER

LOOKING BACK
In the first accounting cycle covered in this textbook (Chapters 3-9), students learned to keep the accounting records for a sole proprietorship business using a general journal and a general ledger. Building on that foundation, students are now ready to expand their knowledge to special journals and ledgers. In this second accounting cycle, students will analyze transactions and record them in four special journals and the general journal. They will post transactions to the general ledger and to the accounts receivable and accounts payable subsidiary ledgers.

VOCABULARY DEVELOPMENT
Ask students to write a sentence using each of the new terms in context. Ask for volunteers to write their sentences on the board. Discuss any differences in the use of the terms. Definitions of these terms are found in the chapter and in the glossary on pages 670-679.

Electronic Field Trips

Teaching Resources

- Lesson Plans
- TE/Chapter Reviews & Working Papers
- Demonstration Problems
- Student Study Plans
- Teaching Transparencies
- Solution Transparencies
- Electronic Field Trips Video, Level I
- Electronic Study Guide
- Chapter 11 Test

Other Resources

- Skills Improvement Activities
- Blackline Masters
- Careers in Accounting
- Dictionary
- Math Review for Accounting
- Tech Prep Strategies in Accounting
- Video
- Test Bank with Software
- Spanish Resources/Audiotapes
- Spanish Electronic Study Guide

1 FOCUS

MAJOR CONCEPTS

- Accounting for a Merchandising Business
- Sales on Account
- Using Special Journals in an Accounting System
- The Sales Journal
- Journalizing Sales on Account
- The Accounts Receivable Ledger
- Completing the Sales Journal
- Proving the Sales Journal at the End of a Page
- Using the Computer to Record and Post Sales on Account

BUSINESS CONNECTION

In today's fiercely competitive retailing environment, businesses must find fresh ways to woo customers. One way to attract customers is to offer a large inventory of products, which is what *megastores* do. Examples are Nike Town, Sony, and the Disney Stores. Although megastores have many more items to track through inventory, they record their sales transactions just as other merchandising businesses do, using a special journal devoted solely to sales of merchandise.

2 TEACH

CONCEPT DEVELOPMENT
Accounting for a Merchandising Business

Discuss the differences between a service business and a merchandising business. Have students give examples of merchandising businesses (such as those in the local mall or shopping area).

Discuss the differences between retailers and wholesalers. Introduce Champion Building Products, Inc., the business used throughout this unit. Ask students to name local businesses that are similar to Champion. Discuss the new accounts students will learn about in this chapter: Merchandise Inventory, Sales, and Sales Tax Payable.

Accounting for a Merchandising Business

A **merchandising business** buys goods—such as books, clothing, or furniture—and then sells those goods to customers for a profit. Most merchandising businesses operate either as retailers or as wholesalers, although there are many businesses that do both. A **retailer** is a business that sells to the final user; that is, to you as the consumer. Retailers include clothing stores, record shops, and automobile dealerships. A **wholesaler** is a business that sells to retailers. Electrical supply companies, automobile parts distributors, and food supply companies are all wholesalers.

In the chapters in Unit 3, you will study the accounting cycle for a merchandising business called Champion Building Products, Inc. Champion Building Products is a retail business that sells building materials and home improvement products. The chart of accounts for Champion Building Products is shown on page 212. Looking at this chart of accounts, you will notice several new accounts used by a merchandising business. As you study the accounting cycle for a merchandising business, you will learn how each of these accounts is used to record merchandising transactions. Some of the accounts in the chart of accounts are related to the fact that Champion Building Products is organized as a corporation. Let's introduce you now to the accounts Merchandise Inventory and Sales.

Merchandise Inventory

A merchandising business earns a profit by buying goods from a wholesaler or a manufacturing business and then selling these goods to its customers. The goods bought for resale to customers are called **merchandise.** The items of merchandise the business has in stock are referred to as **inventory.** At the beginning of each fiscal period, the amount of merchandise in stock is represented by the debit balance in the account Merchandise Inventory. Merchandise Inventory is an asset account.

Merchandise Inventory	
Dr.	Cr.
+	−
Increase Side	Decrease Side
Balance Side	

During business operations, the merchandise in stock will be sold and new items will be bought to replace the ones sold. Separate accounts, however, are used to record the sale of merchandise and the purchase of new merchandise.

Sales

Sales	
Dr.	Cr.
−	+
Decrease Side	Increase Side
	Balance Side

When a retail merchandising business sells goods to a customer, the amount of the merchandise sold is recorded in an account entitled Sales. Sales is the revenue account used by a merchandising business. As in other revenue accounts, increases to Sales are recorded as credits and decreases are recorded as debits. Sales may be either for cash or on account. Either type of transaction is recorded as a credit to Sales.

Understanding terminology is essential to retaining information gained from reading. To help students understand the new terms in this chapter related to sales transactions, use real-world examples of inventories, credit cards, sales slips, credit terms, and so on. Then ask students to give you other examples of these same terms.

Provide a copy of the *Student Study Plans* to each class member to help organize study activities or to individualize practice and review activities.

Sales on Account

In a merchandising firm, the most frequent type of transaction is the sale of merchandise. Some businesses sell only on a cash-and-carry basis. Others sell only on credit. Most sell on both a cash basis and a credit basis. In this chapter, you will learn about the sale of merchandise on credit.

The sale of goods that will be paid for later is called a **sale on account.** The customer to whom a sale on account is made is a **charge customer.** Some businesses issue **credit cards** to their charge customers. A credit card, imprinted with the customer's name and account number, entitles a charge customer to charge merchandise.

The Sales Slip

A **sales slip** is a form that lists the details of a sale: the date of the sale, the name of the customer, and the description, quantity, and price of the items sold. The description may be the physical details (such as "red wool socks"), a stock number, or both. A sales slip is usually prepared in multiple copies. The customer receives the original of the sales slip as proof of purchase. The number of copies kept by the business varies with its needs. A copy always goes to the accounting department. It is the business's record of the transaction and the source document for the journal entry.

Just as prenumbered checks help businesses keep track of every check written, prenumbered sales slips help them keep track of all sales made on account. Champion Building Products uses prenumbered sales slips printed with its name and address. Champion's sales slip is shown in Figure 11-1.

CHAMPION BUILDING PRODUCTS, INC.			
601 Mt. Lebanon Road			
Pittsburgh, PA 15230			

Date *December 1* 19— —   No. 80

SOLD TO	AMY ANDERSON 103 WOODSTONE DRIVE LAUGHLINTOWN, PA 15655		
Clerk FJK	Cash	Charge ✓	Terms *n/30*

Qty.	Description	Unit Price	Amount
1	Steel (white) door	350.00	350 00
2	Storm windows	70.00	140 00
1	Package insulation	10.00	10 00
		Sub Total	500 00
		Sales Tax	30 00
Thank You!		Total	530 00

Figure 11-1
Champion Building
Products' Sales Slip

Notice that the final amount on the sales slip is not simply the total cost of the items sold. A sales tax has been figured into the total.

The Sales Tax

Most states and some cities tax the retail sale of goods and services. This tax is called a **sales tax.** Taxable items vary from state to state, as do sales tax rates. The sales tax rate is usually stated as a percentage of the sale, such as 5%. Champion is located in a state with a 6% sales tax rate.

The sales tax is paid by the customer and collected by the business, which acts as the collection agent for the government. (Any governing body can levy taxes. Since, however, most sales taxes are levied by state governments, from now on we will refer to the taxing body as the state.) At the time of the sale, the business adds the amount of the tax to the selling price of the goods. Periodically, the business sends the collected sales taxes to the state. Until the state is paid, however, the sales taxes collected from customers represent a liability of the business. The business keeps a record of the sales tax owed to the state in the liability account Sales Tax Payable.

The amount of the sales tax is found by multiplying the total selling price of the merchandise by the sales tax rate. In the sales slip in Figure 11-1, for example, Amy Anderson bought $500 worth of merchandise. To find the sales tax, the sales clerk multiplied $500 by 6% (.06). The sales tax on the $500 sale was $30. The total transaction amount then was $530.

Not all sales of retail merchandise are taxed. In most states, sales made to government agencies, such as schools, are not taxed. For example, on December 5, Champion sold $1,240.50 worth of merchandise on account to the Norwin School District. Since schools are tax exempt, no sales tax was added to the amount of the sale.

Credit Terms

On the sales slip in Figure 11-1, there is a space to indicate the credit terms of the sale. **Credit terms** set out the time allowed for payment. The credit terms for the sale to Amy Anderson are *n/30*. The "n" stands for the *net*, or total, amount of the sale. The "30" stands for the number of days the customer has to pay for the merchandise. Amy Anderson must pay Champion the $530 within 30 days of December 1, or by December 31.

Analyzing Sales on Account

In the first part of this book, you recorded business transactions for Global Travel Agency, a service business organized as a sole proprietorship. When Global Travel completed travel arrangements and billed the customer, the accounts affected by the transaction were Accounts Receivable and Fees. Let's now look at how a revenue transaction involving a sale on account is recorded for a merchandising business.

December 1: *Sold merchandise on account to Amy Anderson for $500.00 plus sales tax of $30.00, Sales Slip 80.*

Three accounts are affected by this transaction: Sales, Sales Tax Payable, and Accounts Receivable. Sales is the revenue account used by a merchandising business. It is being increased, so it is credited. The amount of the credit is $500.00, the total amount of merchandise sold. The liability account Sales Tax Payable is being increased since Champion owes sales tax to the state. Sales Tax Payable is credited for $30.00. The asset account Accounts Receivable is being increased, so it is debited. The amount of the debit is $530.00, the total amount to be received from Amy Anderson.

This transaction is shown below in T-account form.

Accounts Receivable		Sales		Sales Tax Payable	
Dr.	Cr.	Dr.	Cr.	Dr.	Cr.
+	−	−	+	−	+
$530.00			$500.00		$30.00

When recording transactions involving sales on account, remember that the amount recorded as a debit to Accounts Receivable includes *both* the cost of the merchandise *and* the sales tax.

Before you learn how to record a sale on account, do the following activity.

Check Your Learning

Use notebook paper to write your answers to these questions.

1. The revenue account for a merchandising business is ___?___ .
2. A(n) ___?___ lists the details of a sale and is the source document for the journal entry.
3. Sales Tax Payable is classified as a(n) ___?___ account.
4. ___?___ list the amount of time a charge customer has to pay for a purchase.
5. Record the following transaction in T-account form: Sold merchandise on account to John Lowell for $50.00 plus $3.00 sales tax, Sales Slip 141.

Compare your answers to those in the answers section. Re-read the preceding part of the chapter to find the answers to any questions you may have missed.

Using Special Journals in an Accounting System

A merchandising business could choose to record all sales of merchandise on account in a general journal. As an example, let's look at three sales transactions for Champion Building Products.

December 1: Sold merchandise on account to Amy Anderson for $500.00, plus $30.00 sales tax, Sales Slip 80.

December 3: Sold merchandise on account to Pelco Construction Co. for $380.00, plus $22.80 sales tax, Sales Slip 81.

December 5: Sold merchandise on account to Norwin School District for $1,240.50, Sales Slip 82.

ACCOUNTING PRACTICE
Students may complete Exercise 11-1 at this point.

ANSWERS

1. Sales
2. Sales slip
3. Liability
4. Credit terms
5.   Accounts Receivable

Dr.	Cr.
+	−
$53.00	

Sales

Dr.	Cr.
−	+
	$50.00

Sales Tax Payable

Dr.	Cr.
−	+
	$3.00

CONCEPT DEVELOPMENT
Using Special Journals in an Accounting System

Explain why special journals are needed in businesses that have large numbers of repetitive transactions. List the four special journals that students will learn about in this unit. Emphasize that all special journals have three significant characteristics: (1) Each special journal is used to record a "special" type of business transaction. (2) Special journals simplify the journalizing process. (3) Special journals save time in posting.

Remind students that the general journal is still used by a business using special journals but only to record transactions that cannot be recorded in any of the special journals.

Reteaching Strategies

Reinforce the rules of debit and credit by introducing the new accounts in this chapter (e.g., Merchandise Inventory, Sales, and Sales Tax Payable) with T accounts. Draw T accounts on the chalkboard and label them with each new account title. Remind students of the information to be learned about each new account: (1) its classification; (2) its increase, decrease, and balance sides; and (3) how the account is used.

Teaching Tips
■ Demonstrate the debits and credits for these transactions on the chalkboard using general journal form.

Use Figure 11-2 to help stu-

Using Visuals

Use Figure 11-2 to help students make the transition between the general journal and the sales journal. This illustration shows how sales transactions would be recorded in a general journal and posted to the general ledger. Point out that each entry requires a credit to sales and that the account title must be written for each credit.

 Did you know?

You can now dial a telephone number using your computer keyboard. AT&T has a software program that allows business users to make telephone calls while working at their PCs. After entering the telephone number on the keyboard, the user picks up the telephone to talk. The advantage to businesses is that computer dialing is faster and makes it easier to respond to customer queries with information that is quickly accessible via the computer.

Look at Figure 11-2. You can see that there is a great deal of repetition in the journal entries and in the postings. These three sales on account required three journal entries (11 lines), three postings to Accounts Receivable accounts, two postings to Sales Tax Payable, and three postings to Sales. If

Figure 11-2   Sales Transactions Recorded in a General Journal

218   UNIT 3   The Accounting Cycle for a Merchandising Business

Critical Thinking

Which of the following errors would be detected when the balance in the Accounts Receivable account is compared with the total of the balances in the accounts receivable subsidiary ledger?

1. The transaction was never journalized.
2. The transaction was posted to the wrong account in the subsidiary ledger.

3. The amount was transposed when it was posted to the subsidiary ledger.
4. The transaction was journalized but was never posted to the subsidiary ledger.
5. The amount was recorded incorrectly in the journal.

(Answer: Answers 3 and 4 would be detected; 1, 2, and 5 would not.)

it took only three credit sales to generate all this, what would result from fifty credit sales? a hundred? several hundred? Obviously, a business having many sales on account needs a system for journalizing and posting that is less time consuming. For a merchandising business having a large number of transactions, a more efficient accounting system involves the use of special journals.

Special journals are multicolumn journals that have columns reserved for the recording of specific types of transactions. Special journals simplify the journalizing and posting process. In most cases, the details of a transaction can be recorded on one line rather than the three or four lines needed for a general journal entry. Each special journal has special amount columns reserved for recording debits and credits to the general ledger accounts named in the column headings.

Four common special journals are the sales journal, the cash receipts journal, the purchases journal, and the cash payments journal.

1. The sales journal is used to record sales of merchandise on account.
2. The cash receipts journal is used to record all cash received by the business.
3. The purchases journal is used to record the purchase on account of any item—whether merchandise or supplies and equipment used in operating the business.
4. The cash payments journal is used to record all payments of cash. Since most businesses pay by check, all checks written are recorded in the cash payments journal.

The general journal is also needed in an accounting system using special journals. The general journal is used to record any transactions that do not fit into the special journals. Now let's look at how to record sales on account in a sales journal.

The Sales Journal

A **sales journal** is a special journal used to record only the sale of merchandise on account. Cash sales of merchandise are recorded in a special journal called a cash receipts journal. You will learn about the cash receipts journal in Chapter 12.

The sales journal used by Champion Building Products is shown in Figure 11-3. Like the general journal, the sales journal has a space for the page number and columns for the date and the posting reference. There is a separate column in which to record the sales slip number and a column in which to record the name of the charge customer. There are also three special amount columns.

	SALES JOURNAL						PAGE____
DATE	SALES SLIP NO.	CUSTOMER'S ACCOUNT DEBITED	POST. REF.	SALES CREDIT	SALES TAX PAYABLE CREDIT	ACCOUNTS RECEIVABLE DEBIT	

Figure 11-3 Sales Journal

CONCEPT DEVELOPMENT

Journalizing Sales on Account
As each column of the sales journal is introduced, point out how the column is used. Illustrate the recording of the December 1, 3, and 5 transactions in the sales journal.

Using Visuals

A teaching transparency showing the sales journal in Figure 11-4 is available in the transparency binder accompanying Glencoe Accounting.

Using Visuals

Use Figure 11-4 to point out the special columns of the sales journal.

Using Visuals

Use demonstration problem 11-2 to show students how to record transactions in a sales journal or photocopy it to give students practice in recording such transactions.

The Sales Credit column is used to record the amount of the merchandise sold on account. The Sales Tax Payable Credit column is used to record the amount of the sales tax for a sale on account. The Accounts Receivable Debit column is used to record the total amount to be received from a customer for a sale on account. As you can see, the column headings indicate the general ledger accounts that are being debited and credited.

Journalizing Sales on Account

The information for Champion's first sale on account in December is as follows.

December 1: *Sold merchandise on account to Amy Anderson for $500.00 plus $30.00 sales tax, Sales Slip 80.*

The sales slip for this transaction appears in Figure 11-1 on page 215. To journalize the transaction in the sales journal, follow these steps. The sales journal entry for this transaction is shown in Figure 11-4.

1. Enter the sales slip date in the Date column.
2. Enter the sales slip number in the Sales Slip No. column.
3. Enter the name of the charge customer in the Customer's Account Debited column.
4. Enter the total selling price of the merchandise sold in the Sales Credit column. (This is the amount shown in the subtotal box of the sales slip.)
5. Enter the amount of the sales tax in the Sales Tax Payable Credit column.
6. Enter the total amount to be received from the charge customer in the Accounts Receivable Debit column. (This is the amount shown in the total box of the sales slip.)

		SALES JOURNAL					PAGE 12
DATE	SALES SLIP NO.	CUSTOMER'S ACCOUNT DEBITED	POST. REF.	SALES CREDIT	SALES TAX PAYABLE CREDIT	ACCOUNTS RECEIVABLE DEBIT	
Dec. 1	80	Amy Anderson		500 00	30 00	530 00	1
1	2	3		4	5	6	3

Figure 11-4 Recording a Sale on Account in the Sales Journal

You learned earlier that sales taxes are not imposed on sales of merchandise to government agencies. The next transaction involves such a sale.

December 5: *Sold merchandise on account to Norwin School District for $1,240.50, Sales Slip 82.*

There are only five steps involved in journalizing this transaction. The first four steps are the same as those for the sale on account to Amy Anderson. Step 5 is as follows:

5. Skip the Sales Tax Payable Credit column. Enter the total amount to be received from the customer in the Accounts Receivable Debit column.

For those sales that do not include a sales tax, the amounts entered in the Sales Credit column and in the Accounts Receivable Debit column are the same. This transaction is shown in Figure 11-5.

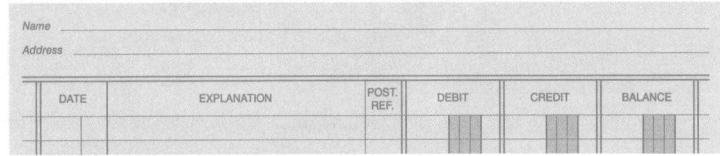

Figure 11-5 Recording a Sale Without Sales Tax in the Sales Journal

The Accounts Receivable Ledger

After a sale on account is journalized, it is posted to the customer's Accounts Receivable account. Businesses with only a few charge customers usually include an Accounts Receivable account for each customer in the general ledger. Large businesses, however, with many charge customers usually set up a separate ledger that contains accounts for all charge customers. This ledger is the **accounts receivable subsidiary ledger.** A **subsidiary ledger** is a ledger, or book, that is summarized in a controlling account in the general ledger. The accounts receivable subsidiary ledger is summarized in the Accounts Receivable account in the general ledger. Accounts Receivable is a **controlling account** because its balance must equal the total of all the account balances in the subsidiary ledger. The balance of Accounts Receivable thus serves as a control on the accuracy of the balances in the accounts receivable subsidiary ledger after posting.

The Accounts Receivable Subsidiary Ledger Form

The accounts receivable subsidiary ledger form used by Champion Building Products is shown in Figure 11-6.

| Name | | | | | |
| Address | | | | | |
DATE	EXPLANATION	POST. REF.	DEBIT	CREDIT	BALANCE

Figure 11-6 Subsidiary Ledger Account Form

Champion's subsidiary ledger account form has lines at the top for the name and address of the customer. In a manual accounting system, subsidiary ledger accounts are arranged in alphabetical order. They are not usually numbered. In a computerized system, however, each charge customer is assigned a specific account number.

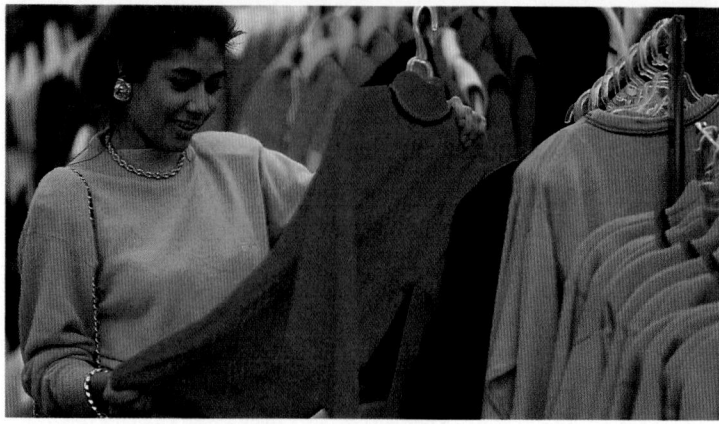

Almost all companies that sell on credit keep an individual accounts receivable record for each customer. Most companies place these customer accounts in a separate accounts receivable subsidiary ledger.

Notice that the subsidiary ledger form has only three amount columns. The Debit and Credit columns are used to record increases and decreases to the customer's account, as on a general ledger account form. The subsidiary ledger form, however, has only one Balance column. Since the Accounts Receivable controlling account is an asset, customer accounts in the accounts receivable subsidiary ledger will normally always have debit balances.

Posting to the
Accounts Receivable Subsidiary Ledger

To be certain that the balances in customers' accounts are always current, sales journal transactions are posted to the accou...s receivable subsidiary ledger daily. To post a transaction from the sales journal to the customer's subsidiary ledger account, follow the steps on page 223. Refer to Figure 11-7, which shows the posting to Amy Anderson's account, as you read these steps.

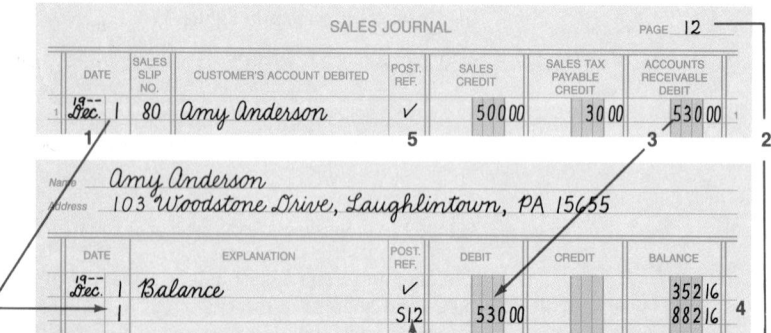

Figure 11-7 Posting a Sales Journal Entry to the Accounts Receivable Subsidiary Ledger

UNIT 3   The Accounting Cycle for a Merchandising Business

Making Connections

COMMUNICATIONS

Ask students to think of a small business that they would like to run, for example, a retail shop, an accounting firm, or a service business. Have students write a short, clear business plan explaining their product or service, describing their potential customers or clients, giving background information about their own experience, and explaining why they believe they can make their business a success.

1. Enter the date of the transaction in the Date column of the subsidiary ledger account. Be sure to use the same date as in the journal entry.
2. Enter the letter of the journal and the page number on which the transaction was recorded in the Posting Reference column of the subsidiary ledger account. "S" is the letter used for the sales journal.
3. In the Debit column of the subsidiary ledger form, enter the total amount to be received from the customer, as recorded in the Accounts Receivable Debit column.

Prev. Bal. $352.16
Debit   530.00
New Bal. $882.16

4. Compute the new balance and enter it in the Balance column. To find the new balance, add the amount in the Debit column to the previous balance amount.
5. Return to the sales journal and enter a check mark (✔)in the Posting Reference column. The check mark indicates that this transaction has been posted to the accounts receivable subsidiary ledger. Champion Building Products uses a manual accounting system, so its subsidiary ledger accounts are not numbered. In a computerized accounting system, the customer's account number, rather than a check mark, would be entered in the Posting Reference column.

R E M E M B E R

When posting from a special journal, post information moving from left to right across the ledger form. By following this procedure, you are less likely to forget to enter all the information from the journal entry.

Before you learn how to complete the sales journal, do the following activity to check your understanding of the sales journal and the accounts receivable subsidiary ledger.

Check Your Learning

Use notebook paper to write your answers to these questions.

1. What type of transaction is recorded in the sales journal?
2. What does a check mark in the Posting Reference column of the sales journal indicate?
3. How often are sales journal entries posted to the accounts receivable subsidiary ledger?
4. What is a controlling account?
5. How does an accounts receivable subsidiary ledger account form differ from a general ledger account form?

Compare your answers to those in the answers section. Re-read the preceding part of the chapter to find the answers to any questions you may have missed.

CONCEPT DEVELOPMENT
Completing the Sales Journal
Explain the need to total, prove, and rule the sales journal. Remind students that the use of special amount columns saves posting time since the column totals are posted, not the individual transactions.

Using Visuals

 Use demonstration problem 11-4 to show students how to total, prove, and rule a sales journal.

Completing the Sales Journal

All special journals have special amount columns in which debits and credits to frequently used accounts are recorded. The special amount columns in the sales journal are the Sales Credit, the Sales Tax Payable Credit, and the Accounts Receivable Debit columns. By recording transactions in these special columns, the accounting clerk can simply post the *column totals* to the general ledger accounts instead of posting each entry separately. Only three postings need to be made to the general ledger from the sales journal.

R E M E M B E R

The major characteristic of a special journal is that it saves time in posting.

Footing, Proving, Totaling, and Ruling the Sales Journal

Before amounts can be posted to the general ledger, the accounting clerk must calculate and verify the column totals. Here is the procedure for doing so. Use ink for all steps *except* Step 2.

1. Draw a single rule across the three amount columns, just below the last transaction.
2. Foot the amount columns. A **footing** is a column total written in small pencil figures. A footing must be verified. It is written in pencil so that it can be easily corrected if a mistake is discovered.
3. On a sheet of paper, test for the equality of debits and credits. The total of the debit column should equal the total of the two credit columns.

ACCOUNTING **Tips**
To lessen the risk of error, use a calculator, preferably one that prints out a tape to use in checking your work. Always clear the machine first.

Debit Column		Credit Columns	
Accounts Receivable	$13,328.45	Sales Tax Payable	$ 543.45
		Sales	12,785.00
Total	$13,328.45	Total	$13,328.45

4. In the Date column on the line below the single rule, enter the date on which the journal is being totaled.
5. On the same line in the Customer's Account Debited column, enter the word "Totals."
6. Enter the column totals — in ink — just below the footings.
7. Double-rule the three amount columns. A double rule, as you know, indicates that the totals have been verified.

The totaled and ruled sales journal for Champion Building Products is shown in Figure 11-8 on page 225.

After the sales journal has been footed, proved, totaled, and ruled, the column totals are posted to the general ledger.

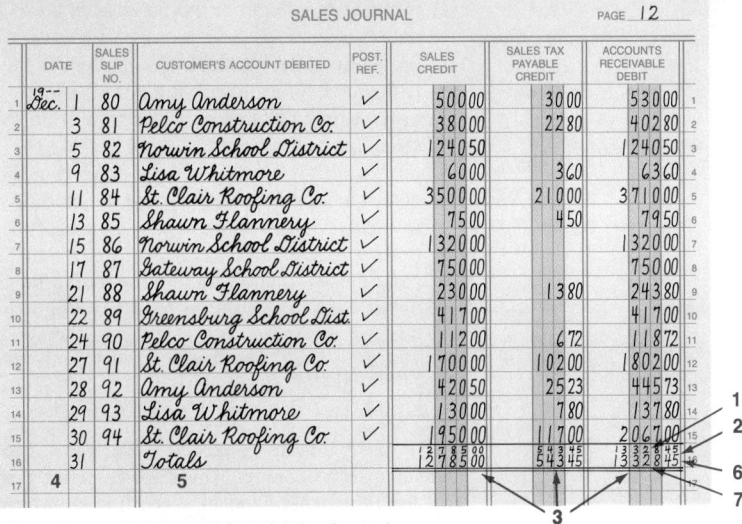

Figure 11-8   Totaled and Ruled Sales Journal

R E M E M B E R

Use a pencil when first totaling the columns. If an error is made in adding the columns, penciled numbers are much easier to correct.

Posting the Total of the Sales Credit Column

The procedure for posting the total of the Sales Credit column to the Sales account in the general ledger is as follows. Refer to Figure 11-9 as you read the steps on page 226.

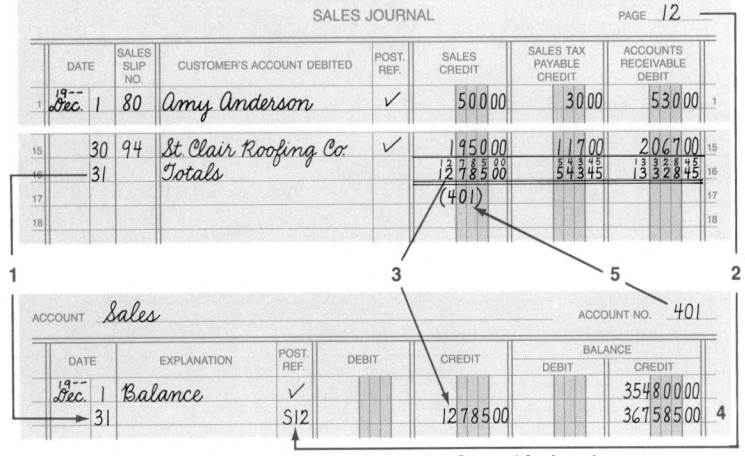

Figure 11-9   Posting the Sales Credit Total to the General Ledger Account

CHAPTER 11   Accounting for Sales on Account   **225**

Sidebar notes:

Chapter 11

Using Visuals

Point out the footings and the column totals in Figure 11-8. Reinforce the meanings of single and double rulings by asking students to explain what they mean in this illustration.

Teaching Tips

■ To emphasize the time saved in posting from a special journal, ask students to look at Figure 11-8 and count the number of postings saved by posting only the column totals.

Using Visuals

Use demonstration problem 11-5 to give students practice in posting from a special journal to accounts in the general ledger.

Using Visuals

Using Figure 11-9, walk students through the steps in posting the Sales Credit total to the general ledger account, Sales.

Making Connections

AROUND THE WORLD

Businesses do not have to be large to find foreign markets for their products. Many small and medium-sized businesses are looking to the global marketplace for new sales. For example, Golfworks—located in Newark, Ohio, and employing about 200 people—sells its golf clubs to retailers in several countries. Some of the most popular foreign markets are Canada, France, Japan, Great Britain, and Mexico.

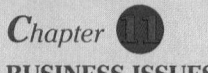

BUSINESS ISSUES

Education is only a part of the knowledge a CPA or other professional accountant must have to perform well in an accounting career. On-the-job experience also plays an important role in career success. Many businesses seek ways to retain their employees who have gained several years of accounting experience. Since approximately half of all graduating accounting students are female, one concern of many businesses is how to retain their female accountants, who often must choose between advancing in their careers and spending time caring for children. New programs that provide for flexible work schedules, child-care options, and alternative career paths can result in higher employee morale and lower turnover among both females and males, who also benefit from programs that provide greater work flexibility.

Using Visuals

Use Figure 11-10 to walk students through the posting of the Sales Tax Payable Credit total to the Sales Tax Payable account in the general ledger.

---

1. In the Date column of the Sales account in the general ledger, enter the date.
2. Enter the sales journal page number in the Posting Reference column. Remember to begin with the letter "S."
3. In the Credit column, enter the total from the Sales Credit column of the sales journal.
4. Compute the new balance and enter it in the Credit Balance column. To determine the new balance, add the amount entered in the Credit column to the previous balance.
5. Return to the sales journal and enter the Sales account number—in parentheses—below the double rule in the Sales Credit column. This indicates that the column total has been posted to the general ledger account.

$354,800.00
+ 12,785.00
$367,585.00

Posting the Total of the Sales Tax Payable Credit Column

The next total to be posted to the general ledger is that of the Sales Tax Payable Credit column. The steps in posting are listed below. The posting made to the general ledger account is shown in Figure 11-10.

1. In the Date column of the Sales Tax Payable account, enter the date.
2. Enter the sales journal page number in the Posting Reference column.
3. In the Credit column, enter the total from the Sales Tax Payable Credit column of the sales journal.
4. Compute the new balance and enter it in the Credit Balance column.
5. Return to the sales journal and enter the Sales Tax Payable account number—in parentheses—below the double rule in the Sales Tax Payable Credit column.

$ 852.15
+ 543.45
$1,395.60

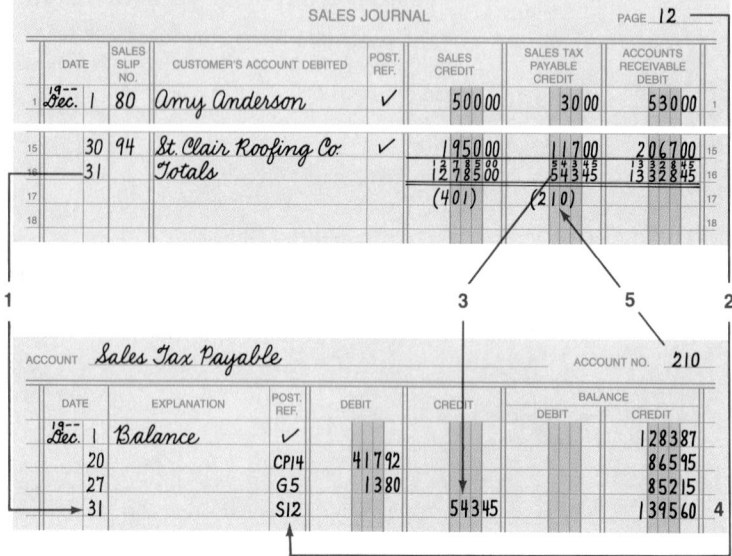

Figure 11-10   Posting the Sales Tax Payable Credit Total to the General Ledger Account

An account number in parentheses placed under a column total means that the column total has been posted to the general ledger account whose number is shown.

Posting the Total of the Accounts Receivable Debit Column

The last column of the sales journal to be posted to the general ledger is the Accounts Receivable Debit column. To complete the posting, follow the steps listed below. Refer to Figure 11-11 as you read these steps.

1. In the Date column of the Accounts Receivable account, enter the date.
2. Enter the sales journal page number in the Posting Reference column.
3. In the Debit column, enter the total from the Accounts Receivable Debit column of the sales journal.
4. Compute the new balance and enter it in the Debit Balance column.
5. Return to the sales journal and enter the account number of the Accounts Receivable account—in parentheses—below the double rule in the Accounts Receivable Debit column.

$ 9,380.36
+13,328.45
$22,708.81

Using Visuals

Use Figure 11-11 to walk students through the posting of the Accounts Receivable Debit column total to the Accounts Receivable account in the general ledger. Remind students that this account is a controlling account and that the details of the accounts receivable transactions are recorded in the accounts receivable subsidiary ledger through daily postings to those accounts.

Using Visuals

Use demonstration problem 11-5 to show posting from the sales journal to the Accounts Receivable account.

Figure 11-11 Posting the Accounts Receivable Debit Total to the General Ledger Account

Proving the Sales Journal at the End of a Page

The sales journal, like all special journals, is totaled and proved at the end of every month. Sometimes, however, a business has so many transactions in one month that it is impossible to fit them all on one journal page. When this occurs, the journal page is totaled and ruled before entries are recorded on the next page.

Follow the steps on page 228 to record the totals and carry them forward to the next page. These steps are illustrated in Figure 11-12 on page 228.

CONCEPT DEVELOPMENT
Proving the Sales Journal at the End of a Page
Explain that a special journal page may frequently become filled before the end of the month for businesses that have many sales transactions. Column totals at the end of page must be carried forward to the next journal page so that the total of the two (or three or more) pages can be posted as one amount to the general ledger accounts. The balances carried forward must be identified clearly on the new page so that an auditing trail can be maintained.

Meeting Special Needs

GIFTED STUDENTS

Have gifted students work in small groups to research the history, uses, and current practices of accounting. You might also have students interview local CPAs or accounting workers to determine how the proliferation of computers has affected the practice of accounting. Post their findings on a bulletin board.

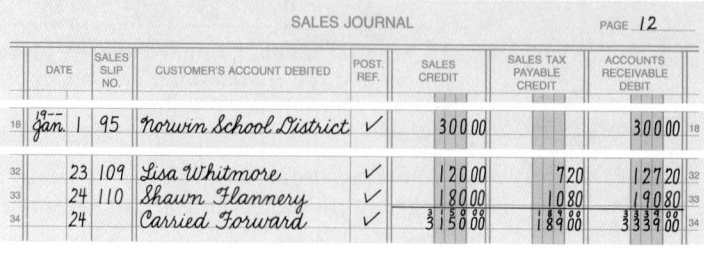

Figure 11-12   Proving the Sales Journal at the End of a Page

1. Foot the amount columns and prove the equality of debits and credits.
2. Enter the date of the *last* transaction in the Date column.
3. In the Customer's Account Debited column, write "Carried Forward."
4. Place a check mark (✔) in the Posting Reference column. This check mark indicates that these totals are not to be posted.
5. Enter the column totals in ink.
6. On the next journal page, enter the new page number.
7. On line 1, enter the complete date (year, month, and day) in the Date column. Use the same date as on the last line of the previous page.
8. Write "Brought Forward" in the Customer's Account Debited column.
9. Place a check mark (✔) in the Posting Reference column.
10. Enter the column totals from the previous page on line 1.

The journal page is now ready to record the next transaction. These same steps would be followed for any special journal.

Check Your Learning

Write your answers to these questions on a sheet of paper.

1. How many column totals in the sales journal are posted to general ledger accounts at the end of the month?
2. Why are the amount columns in the sales journal footed at the end of the month?
3. How would you indicate that the total of the Sales Credit column has been posted to the general ledger account?
4. Is the total posted to the Accounts Receivable account from the sales journal entered in the Debit or Credit column?
5. When the column totals in the sales journal are carried forward to a new page, what is entered in the Posting Reference column?

Compare your answers to those in the answers section. Re-read the preceding part of the chapter to find the answers to any questions you missed.

Using the Computer to Record and Post Sales on Account

Many businesses today use computerized accounting systems to keep their records of sales on account. In a computerized accounting system, each charge customer is assigned an account number. Every time a sale on account is made, the customer's account number is written or imprinted on the sales slip, which is the source document for entering sales information into the computer.

In a computerized system, the accounts receivable subsidiary ledger is stored in the computer's memory. Information about a particular account is called out of memory or is added to the account using the customer's account number. In most computerized accounting systems, entries made to a customer's account are automatically posted to the controlling account. The balance in Accounts Receivable is, therefore, always up to date. Examples of computer-generated general and subsidiary ledger accounts related to sales on account are shown in Figure 11-13.

```
                    Champion Building Products, Inc.
                          General Ledger

          Account 105 Accounts Receivable

                                      Post.
          Date                        Ref.    Debit      Credit

          12/01 Beginning Balance               9624.16
          12/27                        G5                   243.80
          12/31                        S12     13328.45
          12/31 Ending Balance                22708.81


                    Accounts Receivable Subsidiary Ledger

          Account 805 Amy Anderson

                                      Post.
          Date                        Ref.    Debit      Credit

          12/01 Beginning Balance                352.16
          12/01 Sales Slip 80          S12       530.00
          12/28 Sales Slip 92          S12       445.73
          12/31 Ending Balance                  1327.89


          Account 835 Pelco Construction Co.

                                      Post.
          Date                        Ref.    Debit      Credit

          12/01 Beginning Balance               3890.70
          12/03 Sales Slip 81          S12       402.80
          12/24 Sales Slip 90          S12       118.72
          12/31 Ending Balance                  4412.22
```

Figure 11-13   Computer-Generated General Ledger Accounts

Chapter 11

Chapter

3 CLOSE

CHAPTER SUMMARY

This summary enumerates the key information in the chapter. It is a useful tool for reinforcement and review.

Summary of Key Points

1. Retail firms buy merchandise to sell at a profit to consumers. Two of the accounts used by merchandising businesses are Merchandise Inventory and Sales.
2. A sales slip, prepared in multiple copies, lists the details of a sale on account. It is the source document for the journal entry.
3. Most states and some cities tax the retail sale of goods. Businesses collect these sales taxes and record them as a liability until they are paid to the state.
4. Special journals are used by businesses having a great many business transactions. The most common special journals are the sales journal, the cash receipts journal, the purchases journal, and the cash payments journal.
5. A sales journal is used to record all sales of merchandise on account.
6. The accounts receivable subsidiary ledger contains an account for each charge customer. The controlling account for this ledger is the Accounts Receivable account.
7. The individual amounts in the Accounts Receivable Debit column are posted daily to customer accounts in the accounts receivable subsidiary ledger.
8. At the end of the month, the totals of the special amount columns in the sales journal are posted to the accounts named in the column headings.
9. In a computerized accounting system, charge customers are assigned account numbers. The subsidiary ledger is stored in the computer's memory. All entries made to a customer's account are automatically posted to the controlling account in the general ledger.

230   UNIT 3   The Accounting Cycle for a Merchandising Business

Review and Applications

Building Your Accounting Vocabulary

In your own words, write the definition of each of the following accounting terms. Use complete sentences for your definitions.

accounts receivable
   subsidiary ledger
charge customer
controlling account
credit card
credit terms
footing

inventory
merchandise
merchandising
   business
retailer
sale on account

sales journal
sales slip
sales tax
special journal
subsidiary ledger
wholesaler

Reviewing Your Accounting Knowledge

1. How does a merchandising business differ from a service business?
2. What is the difference between a wholesaler and a retailer?
3. Classify the following accounts: Merchandise Inventory, Sales, and Sales Tax Payable.
4. What is the source document for recording sales on account in the sales journal?
5. What information is shown on a sales slip?
6. How does a merchandising business act as a collection agency for the state government?
7. What three accounts are affected by a sale on account?
8. When are special journals used in an accounting system?
9. Name and describe four commonly used special journals.
10. When are sales journal transactions posted to the accounts receivable subsidiary ledger?
11. Describe the procedure for totaling and proving the sales journal at the end of the month.
12. Describe the procedure for totaling and proving the sales journal at the end of a page.

Improving Your Math Skills

Percentages are used frequently in business. Sales taxes, discounts, interest rates, and income tax rates are just a few examples of the percentages used. Accountants especially must be able to calculate percentages with ease. Check your skill in using percentages by completing the following problems.

1. $6\frac{1}{2}$% of $1,185
2. 33% of $21,982
3. 12% of $2,400

4. $5\frac{1}{2}$% of $67.90
5. $7\frac{1}{4}$% of $2,000
6. $9\frac{3}{4}$% of $34,400

7. 122% of $8,920
8. $825 is ?% of $9,400
9. $441 is 6% of ?

231

CHAPTER
REVIEW/ACTIVITIES

PRACTICE AND APPLY

- Language Development
- Comprehension and Retention
- Basic Skills

Building Your Accounting Vocabulary
See the Glossary on pages 670-679 for definitions of these terms.

Reviewing Your Accounting Knowledge

1. A merchandising business buys items and resells them to customers for a profit. A service business provides a service to the general public for a fee.
2. A wholesaler sells to retailers; a retailer sells to the final user, the consumer.
3. Merchandise inventory, asset; Sales, revenue; Sales Tax Payable, liability.
4. The sales slip.
5. (a) Date of the sale; (b) customer's name; (c) description, quantity, and price of goods sold; (d) sales tax; (e) total sale price; and (f) credit terms.
6. The business adds the amount of the sales tax to the selling price of the goods and periodically sends the taxes collected to the government.
7. Sales, Sales Tax Payable, and Accounts Receivable.
8. When the volume of transactions requires a more efficient system for recording transactions that are similar in nature.
9. (a) Sales journal, used to record all sales of merchandise on account; (b) cash receipts journal, used to record all cash received; (c) purchases journal, used to record any purchase on account; and (d) cash payments journal, used to record all payments of and decreases to cash.
10. Daily.
11. (a) Draw a single rule across the amount columns below the last transaction; (b) foot the amount columns; (c) test equality of debits and credits; (d) enter the date; (e) on the same line in the Customer's Account Debited column, enter the word "Totals"; (f) enter the column totals in ink; (g) double-rule the three amount columns.

12. (a) Foot the amount columns and prove the equality of debits and credits; (b) enter the date of the last transaction in the Date column; (c) in the Customer's Account Debited column, write the words "Carried Forward"; (d) place a check mark in the Posting Reference column; (e) enter the column totals in ink; (f) on the next journal page, enter the new page number, (g) on line 1, enter the complete date (year, month, and day) in the Date column, using the same date as on the last line of the previous pages; (h) write the words "Brought Forward" in the Customer's Account Debited column; (i) place a check mark in the Posting Reference column; (j) enter the column totals from the previous page on line 1.

Improving Your Math Skills
1. $77.03
2. $7,254.06
3. $288.00
4. $3.73
5. $145.00
6. $3,354.00
7. $10,882.40
8. 8.78%
9. $7,350.00

CHAPTER 11   Accounting for Sales on Account   **231**

PRACTICE AND APPLY

• Concepts and Procedures

Exercise 11-1: Ch. Obj. 3

Sales slip:
202 $100.70
203 $159.00
204 $31.80
205 $530.00
206 $238.50
207 $84.80
208 $424.00
209 $42.40
210 $121.90
211 $328.60
212 $795.00

Exercise 11-2: Ch. Obj. 2

2. CRJ
3. SJ
4. CPJ
5. CRJ
6. CPJ
7. PJ
8. CPJ
9. PJ
10. GJ
11. GJ

Applying Accounting Procedures

Exercise 11-1   Computing Total Sales

Casey's Corner made the following sales on account during November. The state sales tax rate is 6%.

Sales Slip No.	Amount of Merchandise Sold	Sales Slip No.	Amount of Merchandise Sold
201	$300.00	207	80.00
202	95.00	208	400.00
203	150.00	209	40.00
204	30.00	210	115.00
205	500.00	211	310.00
206	225.00	212	750.00

Instructions: Use a form similar to the one that follows. For each transaction,

(1) Write the number of the sales slip in the first column.

(2) Write the total amount of merchandise sold in the Sales column.

(3) Compute the amount of the sales tax and enter it in the Sales Tax Payable column.

(4) Calculate the total amount of the sale and enter it in the Accounts Receivable column. The first transaction is completed as an example.

Sales Slip Number	Sales	Sales Tax Payable	Accounts Receivable
201	$300.00	$18.00	$318.00

Exercise 11-2   Identifying Special Journals

Instructions: Use a form similar to the one that follows. For each of the following transactions, identify the journal in which each transaction would be recorded by placing a check mark in the appropriate column. The first transaction is completed as an example.

Trans.	Sales Journal	Cash Receipts Journal	Purchases Journal	Cash Payments Journal	General Journal
1			✔		

Transactions:

1. Bought merchandise on account.
2. Received a payment from a charge customer.
3. Sold merchandise on credit.
4. Paid the utility bill for the month.
5. Received cash for merchandise sold.
6. Bought merchandise for cash.
7. Bought supplies on account.
8. Paid for merchandise purchased on account.
9. Bought store equipment and agreed to pay for it later.
10. Sold office equipment on account.
11. Recorded a correcting entry.

Refer students to the Chapter 11 review pages in the workbook, *Chapter Reviews and Working Papers.*

*A*dditional *R*einforcement

Students who need additional practice or individualized help will benefit from the *Glencoe Accounting Electronic Study Guide* or the *Glencoe Accounting* on-line multimedia program, which provide reinforcement and reteaching for vocabulary, concepts, and procedures.

Exercise 11-3 Labeling Column Headings for the Sales Journal

Instructions: In the sales journal given below, label all the column headings.

SALES JOURNAL   Page_____

Exercise 11-3: Ch. Obj. 2
Date
Sales Slip No.
Customer's Account Debited
Posting Reference
Sales Credit
Sales Tax Payable Credit
Accounts Receivable Debit

Exercise 11-4 Opening a Customer Account

On March 17, Jim Jackson, 160 Grove Street, Pittsburgh, PA 15230, opened a charge account at Avon Home Center. On the same day, he purchased on account an electric garage door opener for $110.00 plus sales tax of $6.60. Avon Home Center recorded the transaction on sales journal page 4.

Instructions: Open an account in the accounts receivable subsidiary ledger for Jim Jackson. Then record the amount of the sale in the account.

Exercise 11-4: Ch. Obj. 4
Account balance, $116.60

Problem 11-1: Ch. Obj. 3

Problem 11-2: Ch. Obj. 4

Problem 11-1 Recording Transactions in a Sales Journal

The 1776 Shop is a retail merchandising store specializing in eighteenth century furniture. During the month of October, it had the following charge sales.

Instructions: Record the charge sales for the month of October on sales journal page 10.

Transactions:

Oct. 1 Sold a curio cabinet to Laura Todd for $190.00 plus a sales tax of $6.65, Sales Slip 606.

5 Sold to Harry Long an early American rocker for $180.00 plus a sales tax of $6.30, Sales Slip 607.

7 Sold a country quilt rack to Martha Adams, $37.00 plus sales tax of $1.30, Sales Slip 608.

10 Sold Alex Hamilton a spindle magazine rack for $44.00 plus $1.54 sales tax, Sales Slip 609.

15 Sold a coat tree to Laura Todd, for $48.00, sales tax $1.68, Sales Slip 610.

18 Sold a butler's cart to Alex Hamilton for $107.00 plus $3.75 sales tax, Sales Slip 611.

23 Sold Martha Adams a colonial arm chair, $63.00 plus sales tax of $2.21, Sales Slip 612.

25 Sold a wall mirror to Harry Long for $82.00, plus $2.87 sales tax, Sales Slip 613.

30 Sold to Martha Adams for $27.00 plus a sales tax of $0.95 a log storage rack, Sales Slip 614.

31 Sold a $13.00 fireplace popcorn popper to Laura Todd, sales tax $0.46, Sales Slip 615.

Problem 11-2 Posting to the Accounts Receivable Subsidiary Ledger

You will need the sales journal completed in Problem 11-1 for this problem.

233

Teacher Notes

Problem 11-3: Ch. Obj. 5

Sales Cr. $2,450.00
Sales Tax Pay. Cr. $59.10
Accts. Rec. Dr. $2,509.10

Problem 11-4: Ch. Obj. 5

Page 20 totals:
Sales $698.00
Sales Tax Pay. $20.95
Accts. Rec. $718.95

Page 21 totals:
Sales $830.70
Sales Tax Pay. $24.93
Accts. Rec. $855.63

Instructions: Using three-column account forms, post each entry in the sales journal to the individual accounts in the accounts receivable ledger. The opened customer accounts are included in the working papers.

Problem 11-3   Posting Column Totals to the General Ledger

Towne Auto Parts had the following sales on account during September.

Instructions:

(1) Record each transaction on page 12 of the sales journal.

(2) Foot, prove, total, and rule the sales journal.

(3) Post the totals from the sales journal to the general ledger accounts.

Transactions:

Sept. 1   Sold a heavy-duty car battery to Roxanne Stein for $70.00, plus sales tax of $4.20, Sales Slip 425.

3   Sold David Fink a truck bumper, $205.00 plus $12.30 sales tax, Sales Slip 426.

5   Sold to Lakeside Township Municipality $480.00 in welding equipment, no sales tax, Sales Slip 427.

8   Sold to Oklahoma City School District $375.00 in van parts, no sales tax, Sales Slip 428.

10   Sold a case of automobile wax to the Auto Spa for $150.00 plus sales tax of $9.00, Sales Slip 429.

12   Sold $120.00 in auto parts, plus $7.20 sales tax, to Jax Auto Body Shop, Sales Slip 430.

15   Sold to David Fink $110.00 in auto parts, plus $6.60 sales tax, Sales Slip 431.

17   Sold $420.00 in bus parts to Oklahoma City School District, no sales tax, Sales Slip 432.

19   Sold to the Auto Spa $200.00 in waxes and cleaners, sales tax $12.00, Sales Slip 433.

21   Sold $45.00 in automobile accessories to Roxanne Stein, $2.70 sales tax, Sales Slip 434.

27   Sold to Jax Auto Body Shop $85.00 worth of paints and thinners, sales tax $5.10, Sales Slip 435.

30   Sold $190.00 in parts and equipment to Lakeside Township Municipality, no sales tax, Sales Slip 436.

**Problem 11-4   Proving the Sales Journal
at the End of a Page**

Johnson the Florist sells flowers on a retail basis. Although most of its sales are for cash, some charge sales are also made. The sales tax rate is 3%. The first eight transactions in February have already been recorded. The following transactions are the remaining charge sales for February.

Instructions:

(1) Record the first four transactions on page 20 of the sales journal.

(2) Foot, prove, and total the sales journal at the end of page 20.

(3) Carry forward the column totals to page 21.

(4) Record the remaining transactions in the sales journal.

(5) Foot, prove, and total the sales journal at the end of February.

234

Teacher Notes

Transactions:

Feb. 15 Sold "Bear Balloons" to Cindy Adams, $15.00 plus sales tax of $0.45, Sales Slip 119.

17 Sold wall wreaths to the First National Bank for $220.00, sales tax $6.60, Sales Slip 120.

18 Sold to Lynn Dunmire a bouquet of flowers for $32.00 plus $0.96 sales tax, Sales Slip 121.

20 Sold a "Pick-Me-Up" basket to Larry Farina for $26.50 plus sales tax of $0.80, Sales Slip 122.

22 Sold Marcia Macko a potted plant for $8.90 plus $0.27 sales tax, Sales Slip 123.

23 Sold a miniature rose bush to Wes Wertz, $7.80 plus sales tax of $0.23, Sales Slip 124.

24 Sold to Peggy Zelno a $28.00 floral wreath, sales tax $0.84, Sales Slip 125.

25 Sold Edward Bollinger one dozen long-stemmed roses, $18.00 plus $0.54 sales tax, Sales Slip 126.

26 Sold "Bear Balloons" to Holly Mills for $15.00, plus sales tax of $0.45, Sales Slip 127.

28 Sold a $55.00 door wreath to Betty Thomas, sales tax $1.65, Sales Slip 128.

Problem 11-5: Ch. Obj. 3, 4, 5

COMPUTER PROBLEM **This computer image identifies a problem that students may complete using the** *Glencoe Accounting, General Ledger* **software.**

SJ totals:
Sales $5,137.00
Sales Tax Pay. $64.96
Accts. Rec. $5,201.96

Acct. totals:
Accts. Rec. $7,445.56
Sales Tax Pay. $255.46
Sales $18,617.75

Problem 11-5   Recording and Posting Sales Transactions

The Pro Athlete, a retail sports supply store, has the following balances in the accounts receivable subsidiary ledger and the general ledger.

General Ledger (Partial)

Account Number		Account Balance
105	Accounts Receivable	$ 2,243.60
210	Sales Tax Payable	190.50
401	Sales	13,480.75

Accounts Receivable Subsidiary Ledger

Account Number		Account Balance
805	Arlington Heights High School, 3895 La Coste Boulevard, Arlington, TX 76107	$ 1,500.00
825	Bobbi Jo Gates, 350 Canyon Road, Houston, TX 77002	75.80
840	Jennifer Hope, 202 Casa View Drive, Abilene, TX 79604	110.50
860	Joseph Montoya, 1201 Blossom Lane, Dallas, TX 75221	248.90
870	Lou Ann Simmons, 1442 Cottonwood Road, Ft. Worth, TX 76101	308.40

Instructions:

(1) Open the three accounts in the general ledger and record the June 1 balances.

(2) Open the five accounts in the accounts receivable subsidiary ledger and record the June 1 balances.

(3) Record the following transactions on page 6 of the sales journal.

(4) Post each transaction to the accounts receivable subsidiary ledger.

(5) Foot, prove, total, and rule the sales journal.

(6) Post the column totals to the general ledger.

235

Problem 11-6: Ch. Obj. 3, 5

CHALLENGE   The last problem
in each chapter is
a challenge prob-
lem and is identi-
PROBLEM   fied by this
"maze" symbol.

SJ totals:
Sales $20,957.00
Sales Tax Pay. $1,257.42
Accts. Rec. $22,214.42

4 ASSESS

A chapter test is available for use in assessing students' understanding of concepts in this chapter.

The testmaker software will enable you to develop tailor-made chapter, unit, semester, and final tests.

Alternative Assessment

For alternative assessment strategies, refer to *Tech Prep Strategies in Accounting*.

Transactions:

June   1   Sold a tent to Jennifer Hope for $120.00 plus sales tax of $6.30, Sales Slip 555.

3   Sold Joseph Montoya a $350.00 set of golf clubs, sales tax $18.38, Sales Slip 556.

7   Sold to Bobbi Jo Gates jogging shoes and a warm-up suit, $105.00 plus $5.51 sales tax, Sales Slip 557.

9   Sold a graphite racquetball racquet for $90.00 plus sales tax of $4.73 to Lou Ann Simmons, Sales Slip 558.

11   Sold Jennifer Hope an aerobic suit, $52.00 plus $2.73 sales tax, Sales Slip 559.

13   Sold football helmets to Arlington Heights High School, total $3,200.00, Sales Slip 560.

15   Sold a backpack and hiking boots, totaling $115.00 plus $6.04 sales tax, to Bobbi Jo Gates, Sales Slip 561.

18   Sold to Joseph Montoya a $230.00 crossbow and arrows, sales tax $12.08, Sales Slip 562.

21   Sold a racquetball gear bag to Lou Ann Simmons for $24.00, sales tax $1.26, Sales Slip 563.

24   Sold a $130.00 pacer exercise bicycle to Jennifer Hope, plus $6.83 sales tax, Sales Slip 564.

27   Sold a Maxi Gympac to Arlington Heights High School for $700.00, Sales Slip 565.

30   Sold Joseph Montoya a fishing tackle box, $21.00 plus $1.10 sales tax, Sales Slip 566.

CHALLENGE   **Problem 11-6   Locating and Correcting Errors
in the Sales Journal**

PROBLEM   The Todaro Company posts transactions to the subsidiary ledger on a weekly basis. Before posting, however, the accounting supervisor checks all sales slips against the data entered in the sales journal. In April, a number of errors were discovered. You were asked to make the corrections.

Instructions:

(1) Compare each transaction described below with the sales journal entry. (The Todaro Company is located in a state with a 6% sales tax.)

(2) Correct any incorrect data.

(3) Foot, prove, total, and rule the sales journal.

Transactions:

Apr. 25   Suzette Simons purchased merchandise, $330.00, Sales Slip 3100.

25   On Sales Slip 3101, John Joyce bought $450.00 worth of merchandise.

26   Sold merchandise to Fred Woodburn on account, $170.00, Sales Slip 3102.

26   Sales Slip 3103, Carl Frost charged merchandise costing $200.00.

27   Bob Cummins purchased merchandise on account, $80.00, Sales Slip 3104.

28   Sold John Joyce merchandise on account, $30.00, Sales Slip 3105.

29   Sales Slip 3106, sold to Bob Cummins $425.00 of merchandise.

29   Carl Frost charged merchandise totaling $110.00, Sales Slip 3107.

30   Sold to Suzette Simons, Sales Slip 3108, merchandise, $90.00.

30   Sold merchandise to Fred Woodburn, $160.00, Sales Slip 3109.

236

Use Chapter Test 11 here to assess students' understanding and retention of the concepts and procedures presented in the chapter.

F O C U S   O N
CAREERS

*T*oday's CPA

Do you have a flair for working with numbers? Do you like interpreting facts and solving problems? If you do, you might want to consider a career as a certified public accountant. These professionals offer accounting advice and assistance to the public for a fee.

To become a certified public accountant (CPA), you'll need a bachelor's degree, a passing grade on a two-and-a-half day examination, plus a certificate from a state accountancy board. In 48 states, the board also requires an additional 40 hours of continuing education classwork a year. And, while not a written requirement, computer literacy is indispensable.

Over 300,000 CPAs practice in this country. Every year, about 10,000 new CPAs enter the field. Some are self-employed, but the majority work for accounting firms. Over half of the accountants entering the profession today are women.

CPAs have traditionally worked in the fields of taxation and auditing. Tax accountants prepare tax returns for their clients. Auditors verify the accuracy of financial statements prepared by business accountants.

Tax laws are becoming more demanding and small businesses are growing, and because of this, the demand for certified public accountants is increasing. This consumer demand is moving CPAs toward fields such as financial planning, computer auditing, tax law, or consulting services. In addition to being experts in accounting, CPAs may also need to be experts in a particular industry. CPAs who perform consulting services are increasingly being asked to participate in long-range planning, to give advice on marketing plans, to implement and evaluate computer systems, or to evaluate management personnel for promotion.

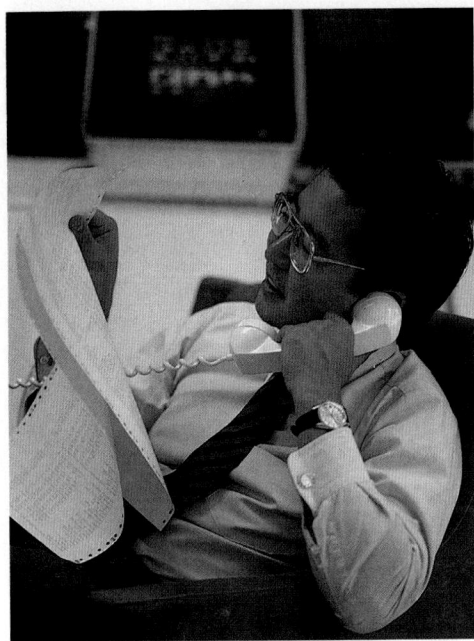

Today's CPAs play leading roles in a wide variety of industries.

Today's challenging business environment and computer technology are redefining the CPA profession. Public accounting firms that march to this different drummer are moving toward specialization. While this trend may require different employee qualifications, it can also present new opportunities to those of you who wish to enter the field in the coming years.

Accounting specialties such as taxation and auditing change frequently as new laws are passed or new accounting practices are required. Ask students to identify ways accountants can keep up to date with changes in their profession.

QUESTIONS

1. Can you name the "Big Six" accounting firms in the United States?
2. What are the specific requirements for certification as a CPA in your state?

ANSWERS

1. The "Big Six" include Arthur Andersen; Touche, DeLoitte, Haskins and Sells; Ernst and Young; Price Waterhouse; Coopers & Lybrand; and KPMG Peat Marwick.
2. Answers will vary according to state.

237

Chapter 12
ACCOUNTING FOR CASH RECEIPTS

LOOKING BACK

In Chapter 11 students learned that businesses having many transactions record them in special journals. Students learned that credit sales transactions are recorded in a special journal whose column totals are posted to the general ledger. Individual amounts are posted to customer accounts in the accounts receivable subsidiary ledger. In this chapter, students will continue their study of special journals by learning to use a cash receipts journal.

VOCABULARY DEVELOPMENT

Have students read the list of new terms. Ask for ideas for each term's meaning. Write correct responses on the chalkboard. Definitions for these terms are found in the chapter and in the glossary on pages 670-679.

Electronic Field Trips

In Chapter 11, you learned that many businesses record their business transactions in special journals. These journals streamline the journalizing and posting process through the use of special amount columns. The totals of the special amount columns are posted to the general ledger accounts at the end of the month.

In the last chapter, you were introduced to the first special journal, the sales journal. In this chapter, you will learn how to record various kinds of cash receipts in another special journal, a six-column cash receipts journal. You will also learn how to post from this journal to the general ledger and to the accounts receivable subsidiary ledger.

Learning Objectives

When you have completed Chapter 12, you should be able to do the following:

1. Journalize cash received by a business in a cash receipts journal.
2. Post from the cash receipts journal to the accounts receivable subsidiary ledger and to the general ledger.
3. Foot, prove, total, and rule a cash receipts journal.
4. Post column totals from the cash receipts journal to the general ledger.
5. Prepare a schedule of accounts receivable.
6. Define the accounting terms introduced in this chapter.

New Terms

- cash receipt
- receipt
- cash sale
- bank card
- cash discount
- contra account
- cash receipts journal
- schedule of accounts receivable

238

Teaching Resources

- Lesson Plans
- TE/Chapter Reviews & Working Papers
- Demonstration Problems
- Student Study Plans
- Teaching Transparencies
- Solutions Transparencies
- Electronic Field Trips Video, Level I
- Electronic Study Guide
- Chapter 12 Test

Other Resources

- Skills Improvement Activities
- Blackline Masters
- Careers in Accounting
- Dictionary
- Math Review for Accounting
- Tech Prep Strategies in Accounting
- Video
- Test Bank with Software
- Spanish Resources/Audiotapes
- Spanish Electronic Study Guide

Kinds of Cash Receipts

The cash received by a business is referred to as a **cash receipt.** The three most common sources of cash for a merchandising business are cash received from charge customers, cash sales, and bank card sales. Cash is also received, though much less frequently, from such transactions as the sale of an asset other than merchandise. Let's look at how these four kinds of cash receipts are handled.

Cash from Charge Customers

When a business receives a payment on account from a charge customer, that payment must be recorded. The business does so by first preparing a receipt. A **receipt,** shown in Figure 12-1, is a form that serves as a record of cash received.

Like sales slips, receipts are prenumbered and may be prepared in multiple copies. Champion Building Products prepares a receipt as the source document for the journal entry of the transaction.

Figure 12-1 Receipt for Cash Received from a Charge Customer

As you can see, the receipt lists the date the cash was received, the customer's name, the amount received, and an explanation of the transaction.

Cash Sales

A **cash sale** is a transaction in which a business receives full payment for the merchandise sold *at the time of the sale.* The proof of sale and the source document generated by this type of transaction differ from those for a sale on account.

Most retailers use a cash register to record (or "register") cash sales. Instead of using preprinted sales slips, records of cash sales are made on two rolls of tape inside the cash register. When a cash sale occurs, the details of the sale are printed on the two tapes at the same time. One tape is fed outside the machine, torn off, and handed to the customer as a receipt. The other tape remains in the register.

At the end of the day, the cash register is totaled and cleared. The total cash sales for the day and the total sales taxes collected on those sales are listed on the cash register tape. The tape also shows the total charge sales for the day. A proof is usually prepared to show that the amount of cash in the cash register equals the amount of cash sales recorded on the cash register tape. The proof and the tape are sent to the accounting clerk, who uses

Cash sales

Dec. 4
Tape 50

3,000.00 CA
180.00 ST

Sales tax

1 FOCUS

MAJOR CONCEPTS

- Kinds of Cash Receipts
- Cash Discounts
- The Cash Receipts Journal
- Journalizing Cash Receipts
- Posting from the Cash Receipts Journal
- Completing the Cash Receipts Journal
- Proving the Accounts Receivable Subsidiary Ledger
- Using the Computer with Accounts Receivable Transactions

BUSINESS CONNECTION

Many businesses sell merchandise to customers who pay for their purchases with bank credit cards. MasterCard, Inc., has issued 90 million credit cards in the United States and more than 163 million worldwide. Regardless of how a customer charges a credit sale, eventually that amount must be paid and the payment recorded in the accounting records as a cash receipt.

2 TEACH

CONCEPT DEVELOPMENT
Kinds of Cash Receipts
Bring actual charge-account receipts to class for students to analyze. Create a hypothetical situation in which cash is received from a charge customer and have students fill in the receipt. Remind students that the receipt is the source document for recording this type of transaction.
(Continued)

Reinforcing Study Skills

Review the SQ3R strategy with students: *Survey, Question, Read, Recite, Review.* Ask students to skim (survey) the main heads in the chapter and apply the second step by turning the heads into questions that students can answer in their reading. For example, "What are the different kinds of cash receipts?" "What are cash discounts?"

Provide a copy of the *Student Study Plans* to each class member to help organize study activities or to individualize practice and review activities.

Using Visuals

Using Figure 12-1, point out that cash receipt forms are numbered to help track all cash receipt transactions.

ACCOUNTING PRACTICE
Students may complete Exercise 12-1 at this point.

Kinds of Cash Receipts (Continued)

Try to borrow a used cash register from a local dealer. Have students create some cash sale transactions and enter them into the cash register. Remind students that the cash register has two rolls of tape, one for the customer and one for the business, and that every transaction is recorded on both tapes. After the cash register is totaled and cleared at the end of the day, the tape serves as the source document for recording total cash sales for the day.

Most retail merchandising stores today accept bank cards and, of course, cash in payment for merchandise sold.

the tape as the source document for the journal entry to record the day's cash sales.

Bank Card Sales

Many businesses today allow customers to use bank cards to buy merchandise. A **bank card** is a credit card issued by a bank and honored by many businesses. Bank cards are a sort of "super credit card" since they are accepted by many different businesses. The most widely used bank cards in North America are VISA® and MasterCard®.

Bank card sales are processed differently from a store's regular charge card sales. It is important to remember that a bank card holder has an account with the bank that issued the card, not with the business or businesses where the card is used. The bank pays the business and the bank card customer pays the bank. The business receives cash from the bank soon after it deposits its bank card sales slips. The business does not have to wait until the bank collects from the card holder. Bank card sales, therefore, are recorded as though they were cash sales.

When a bank card sale occurs, the sales clerk at Champion Building Products completes a multicopy bank card sales slip. The sales slip is inserted into the cash register, which records the details of the sale on both the sales slip and the cash register tape. When the cash register is totaled at the end of the day, the total bank card sales and the sales taxes for those sales are listed on the cash register tape. Since the cash register tape includes the bank card sales, those sales are included on the daily cash proof. Bank card sales are journalized from the same tape as the cash sales for the day.

Champion deposits all bank card sales slips in its checking account, using a special deposit slip. In its records, Champion treats deposits of bank card sales the same as cash deposits. There is, however, often a three- to four-day delay before the amount of the deposit is credited to Champion's checking

Bank card sales

Dec. 4
Tape 50

700.00 BCS
42.00 ST

Sales tax

240   UNIT 3   The Accounting Cycle for a Merchandising Business

account. This delay occurs because Champion's bank must collect from the other banks that issued the bank cards used by Champion's customers.

R E M E M B E R

The bank card holder has an account with the bank that issued the card, not with the business or businesses where the card is used.

Other Cash Receipts

Most of the cash receipts of a merchandising business result from the sale of merchandise. Cash may also be received from other transactions such as the sale of other assets or a loan from a bank. These types of cash transactions occur infrequently in most merchandising businesses.

When such transactions do occur, a receipt is prepared to indicate the source of the cash received. This receipt is similar to that prepared for cash received from a charge customer. All the information needed for the journal entry, however, is listed on the explanation line.

Cash Discounts

To encourage customers to pay promptly, some merchandising businesses offer a cash discount to their charge customers. A **cash discount** is the amount a customer can deduct if the merchandise is paid for within a certain time. A cash discount is an advantage to both buyer and seller. The buyer gets merchandise at a reduced cost; the seller receives cash quickly.

Businesses do not automatically offer cash discounts to all their customers. Some businesses may offer cash discounts only to their business customers. Champion offers a cash discount only to certain charge customers who buy merchandise in large quantities. Its credit terms for such customers are stated as *2/10, n/30.* This means that the customer can deduct 2% of the cost of the merchandise if it pays for the merchandise within 10 days of the sale date. Otherwise, the net (full) amount must be paid within 30 days. A cash discount, then, decreases the amount the business actually receives from the sale. Let's look at an example.

On December 5, Champion sold $1,240.50 worth of merchandise on account to the Norwin School District. In the sales journal, this transaction was recorded as a $1,240.50 credit to Sales and a $1,240.50 debit to Accounts Receivable. If Norwin pays within 10 days (by December 15), Champion will actually receive only $1,215.69, or the original price less the cash discount of $24.81 ($1,240.50 × 2%). Which accounts are involved in this cash receipt transaction?

Net amount	$1,240.50
Discount	− 24.81
Amount received	$1,215.69

Cash in Bank would be debited for $1,215.69, the amount of cash actually received. Accounts Receivable would be credited for the full $1,240.50 because the customer has paid for the merchandise that was sold. What happens to the discount amount?

CHAPTER 12 Accounting for Cash Receipts **241**

Teaching Tips

■ Emphasize these points about a contra account: (1) A contra account decreases the balance of the account it goes with. (2) The increase and balance side is always opposite the increase and balance side of the account it decreases.

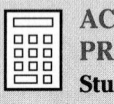

ACCOUNTING PRACTICE

Students may complete Exercise 12-2 at this point.

ANSWERS

1. Receipt; tape; tape
2. Debit side; it is a contra account to Sales, an account that has a normal credit balance.
3. $105; $3,395

The $24.81 discount could be debited to the Sales account since Champion will receive less revenue from this transaction than originally recorded. Instead, a separate account is used to have a complete record of all discounts taken by customers. The discount amount is entered in an account called Sales Discounts.

As you know, the normal balance side of the Sales account is the credit side. A cash discount, however, reduces the revenue earned from sales. The normal balance side of the Sales Discounts account, then, is the *debit* side.

Sales		Sales Discounts	
Dr.	Cr.	Dr.	Cr.
–	+	+	–
Decrease Side	Increase Side	Increase Side	Decrease Side
	Balance Side	Balance Side	

Accounts such as Sales Discounts are called contra accounts. A **contra account** is an account whose balance is a decrease in (is "*contra*ry to") another account's balance.

When the sale is made, a business does not know whether a charge customer will take advantage of the cash discount. A cash discount, therefore, can be recorded only when the customer actually pays for the merchandise within the time allowed. If sales taxes were paid, the discount is calculated on the amount of the merchandise sold, before taxes are added.

R E M E M B E R

Sales Discounts is a contra revenue account. Its normal balance is a debit balance.

Before going any further, do the following activity to check your understanding of the material you have just studied.

Check Your Learning

Write your answers to these questions on notebook paper.

1. What is the source document for the journal entry to record cash received from a charge customer? for a cash sale? for a bank card sale?
2. What is the normal balance side of the Sales Discounts account? Why?
3. The Phone Center's credit terms are 3/15, n/30. On April 2, it sold $3,500 worth of merchandise to a charge customer. The customer paid for the merchandise on April 8, taking advantage of the discount. What was the discount amount? How much cash was received?

Compare your answers to those in the answers section. Re-read the preceding part of the chapter to find the correct answers to any questions you may have missed.

Reteaching Strategies

When a customer uses a bank card to buy goods from a merchandising business, the customer is buying on credit. However, the business does not record the entry as an accounts receivable. The customer is receiving credit from the bank honoring the bank card and not from the merchandising business. The merchandising business will receive cash from the bank in a few days, so the transaction is recorded as a cash sale.

The Cash Receipts Journal

As you already know, when a business has a great many transactions, it can save time by using special journals. One special journal used is the sales journal; another is the cash receipts journal.

The **cash receipts journal** is a special journal used to record all transactions in which cash is received. The number of special amount columns varies, depending upon a business's needs. Every transaction recorded in the journal, however, requires a debit to the Cash in Bank account. The cash receipts journal, therefore, always includes a Cash in Bank Debit column.

The cash receipts journal used by Champion Building Products is shown in Figure 12-2. In addition to the date, source document, account title, and posting reference columns, it contains six amount columns. The General Credit column is used to record credits to accounts for which there is no special column. The amount of merchandise sold in cash and bank card sales is recorded in the Sales Credit column. The sales taxes collected for cash and bank card sales are entered in the Sales Tax Payable Credit column. The Accounts Receivable Credit column is used to record payments from charge customers. The Sales Discounts Debit column is used to record the amount of any cash discount taken by a charge customer. The Cash in Bank Debit column is used to record the amount of cash actually received.

DATE	DOC. NO.	ACCOUNT TITLE	POST. REF.	GENERAL CREDIT	SALES CREDIT	SALES TAX PAYABLE CREDIT	ACCOUNTS RECEIVABLE CREDIT	SALES DISCOUNTS DEBIT	CASH IN BANK DEBIT
1									
2									

Figure 12-2 Cash Receipts Journal

The entries in the Accounts Receivable Credit column are posted individually during the month to charge customers' accounts in the accounts receivable subsidiary ledger. The entries in the General Credit column are posted individually during the month to the general ledger accounts. At the end of the month, the totals of all the special amount columns are posted to the general ledger accounts named in the column headings.

Journalizing Cash Receipts

Now let's look at how various types of cash receipt transactions are recorded in the cash receipts journal.

Journalizing Cash from Charge Customers

Champion's first cash receipt transaction for December is cash received from a charge customer. The source document for this transaction is the receipt in Figure 12-1 on page 239.

CHAPTER 12   Accounting for Cash Receipts   **243**

CONCEPT DEVELOPMENT
The Cash Receipts Journal
Two major advantages of using the cash receipts journal are: (1) all of a business's cash receipts are recorded in one place—namely, the cash receipts journal; and (2) the cash receipts journal saves time in posting. Point out the six amount columns in the cash receipts journal and explain how each is used.

Using Visuals

Refer students to Figure 12-2 and discuss each of the column heads for the cash receipts journal.

Teaching Tips

■ Emphasize that the word "General" in the first amount column head in the cash receipts journal refers to the general ledger; thus, the amounts recorded as credits in this column are to accounts other than those listed in the remaining column heads of the journal.

CONCEPT DEVELOPMENT
Journalizing Cash Receipts
Remind students that business transactions must be analyzed before they are recorded in any journal. Use T accounts to help students analyze the December 1 business transaction (next page). Then have students look at Figure 12-2 and tell you which columns would be used to record this transaction.

Making Connections

COMMUNICATIONS

Many accounting workers are called upon to communicate with words as well as with numbers. Mastery of good writing skills is an important element of communicating successfully by memo, report, or letter. Capable writers use Standard English rather than informal or nonstandard English to communicate their messages. They also make sure that grammar, spelling, punctuation, vocabulary, and usage are all correct and appropriate for the audience and topic.

December 1: Received $79.30 from Lisa Whitmore on account, Receipt 301.

The accounts affected by this transaction are Cash in Bank and Accounts Receivable. Since Cash in Bank is being increased, it is debited for the amount of cash received, $79.30. Champion Building Products now expects to receive less money, so Accounts Receivable is being decreased. It is credited for $79.30.

The entry for this transaction is shown in Figure 12-3. Follow these steps when journalizing cash received from charge customers:

1. Enter the date of the receipt in the Date column.
2. Enter the receipt number in the Document Number column. Write the letter "R" (for receipt) in front of the receipt number.
3. Enter the name of the charge customer in the Account Title column.
4. Enter the amount received in the Accounts Receivable Credit column.
5. Enter the amount of cash received in the Cash in Bank Debit column.

The Posting Reference column will be completed when this entry is posted to the customer's account in the accounts receivable subsidiary ledger.

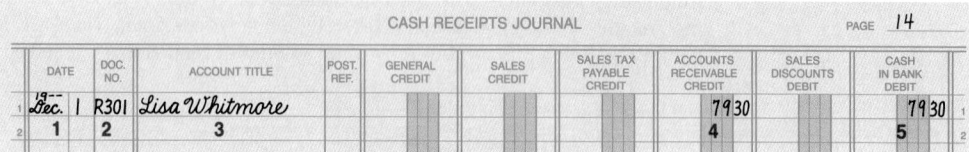

Figure 12-3 Recording Cash Received from a Charge Customer in the Cash Receipts Journal

Journalizing Cash Received on Account, Less a Cash Discount

The second cash receipt transaction involves a cash discount.

December 2: Received $1,166.20 from Greensburg School District in payment of Sales Slip 72 for $1,190.00, less the discount of $23.80, Receipt 302.

The accounts affected are Cash in Bank, Sales Discounts, and Accounts Receivable. Cash in Bank is being increased, so it is debited for $1,166.20, the amount of cash actually received. The Sales Discounts account is being increased. It is debited for $23.80, the amount of the cash discount. Payments on account from charge customers decrease Accounts Receivable. That account is credited for the *entire* amount of the original transaction, $1,190.00.

Follow these steps when journalizing cash receipts involving a cash discount. The journal entry for this transaction is shown on line 2 of Figure 12-4.

1. Enter the date of the receipt in the Date column.
2. Enter the receipt number in the Document Number column.
3. Enter the name of the charge customer in the Account Title column.

4. Enter the amount of the original transaction in the Accounts Receivable Credit column.

5. Enter the cash discount amount in the Sales Discounts Debit column.

6. Enter the actual amount of cash received in the Cash in Bank Debit column.

		CASH RECEIPTS JOURNAL							PAGE 14
DATE	DOC. NO.	ACCOUNT TITLE	POST. REF.	GENERAL CREDIT	SALES CREDIT	SALES TAX PAYABLE CREDIT	ACCOUNTS RECEIVABLE CREDIT	SALES DISCOUNTS DEBIT	CASH IN BANK DEBIT
19-- Dec. 1	R301	Lisa Whitmore					79 30		79 30
2	R302	Greensburg School Dist.					1 190 00	23 80	1 166 20
4	T50	Cash Sales	—		3 000 00	180 00			3 180 00
4	T50	Bank Card Sales	—		700 00	42 00			742 00
6	R303	Store Equipment		50 00					50 00

Figure 12-4 Recording Transactions in the Cash Receipts Journal

R E M E M B E R

When journalizing a cash receipt transaction with a sales discount, be sure to credit Accounts Receivable for the total amount of the original sales transaction.

Journalizing Cash Sales

As a rule, businesses journalize cash sales and make cash deposits daily. In this chapter, however, we will assume that Champion Building Products records its cash sales every two weeks.

December 4: Sold merchandise for $3,000.00 cash, plus $180.00 sales taxes, Tape 50.

The accounts affected by this transaction are Cash in Bank, Sales, and Sales Tax Payable. Cash in Bank is being increased. It is debited for $3,180.00, the cash received for the merchandise sold ($3,000.00) plus the sales taxes collected ($180.00). Sales is also being increased. It is credited for $3,000.00, the amount of merchandise sold. Sales Tax Payable is being increased since more money is now owed to the state. It is credited for $180.00.

The journal entry for this transaction is shown in Figure 12-4, line 3. The source document for the transaction is the cash register tape shown on page 239.

1. Enter the date written on the cash register tape in the Date column.

2. Enter the number of the tape in the Document Number column. Place a "T" (for tape) before the number.

3. Enter the words "Cash Sales" in the Account Title column.

4. Enter a dash in the Posting Reference column. The amounts recorded for cash sales are posted as part of the column totals at the end of the

Using Visuals

Refer to Figure 12-4. Ask students to explain why two entries have a dash in the Posting Reference column of the journal.

Using Visuals

 A teaching transparency showing the journal in Figure 12-4 is available in the transparency binder accompanying Glencoe Accounting.

 ACCOUNTING PRACTICE
Students may complete Exercise 12-3 at this point.

Teaching Tips

■ Explain that cash sales are recorded every two weeks in the examples used here merely to save space in journal illustrations.

Making Connections

BUSINESS ETHICS

You are an accountant at Bentley Products. One of your co-workers, Susan Cooper, a part-time accounting clerk, confides that she is also working part-time for Davis Toys, one of Bentley's competitors. Do you see any problem with Susan's working for two different companies that are in the same business?

(Answer: There may be a conflict of interest. Susan has access to financial information for both companies. It would be unethical for her to share one company's information with the other, even unwittingly.)

ACCOUNTING ISSUES

Are professional accountants different from other people? According to a survey of readers of the *Journal of Accountancy,* compared to the national average *Journal* readers are:

- five times more likely to have an undergraduate degree
- three times more likely to own two or more cars
- four times more likely to buy a new foreign car
- five times more likely to use a computer at work
- five times more likely to have a fax machine at home
- three times more likely to have taken a trip abroad

According to Bankcard Holders of America, there are more than 800 million charge cards and bank cards in use today.

month. The dash indicates that the entry is not posted individually to the general ledger accounts.

5. Enter the amount of merchandise sold in the Sales Credit column.
6. Enter the amount of sales taxes collected in the Sales Tax Payable Credit column.
7. Enter the total cash received in the Cash in Bank Debit column.

Journalizing Bank Card Sales

How often a business records bank card sales and deposits its bank card sales slips depends on the number of bank card sales it has. In this textbook, we will assume that Champion Building Products processes bank card sales every two weeks.

We mentioned earlier that a bank card sale is a form of cash sale. As you learn how to journalize bank card sales, notice the similarities between the two entries.

December 4: *Had bank card sales of $700.00, plus $42.00 sales taxes, Tape 50.*

The accounts affected are Cash in Bank, Sales, and Sales Tax Payable. Since the business receives cash when the bank card sales slips are deposited, Cash in Bank is being increased. It is debited for $742.00, the amount of merchandise sold ($700.00) plus the sales taxes on that merchandise ($42.00). Sales is also being increased. It is credited for $700.00, the total of the merchandise sold. Sales Tax Payable is being increased; it is credited for $42.00.

The journal entry for this transaction is shown in Figure 12-4, line 4. The source document for the entry is the cash register tape illustrated on page 240.

1. Enter the date of the cash register tape in the Date column.
2. Enter the number of the tape in the Document Number column. Remember to record a "T" before the number.
3. Enter the words "Bank Card Sales" in the Account Title column.
4. Enter a dash in the Posting Reference column. The bank card sales amounts are also posted to the general ledger as part of the column totals.
5. Enter the amount of merchandise sold in the Sales Credit column.
6. Enter the amount of sales taxes collected in the Sales Tax Payable Credit column.
7. Enter the total cash received in the Cash in Bank Debit column.

Journalizing Other Cash Receipts

Occasionally, a business will receive cash from a transaction that does not involve the sale of merchandise. However, since the business is receiving cash, the transaction is still entered in the cash receipts journal.

December 6: *Received $50.00 cash from Mandy Owens, an employee, for shelving no longer used by the business, Receipt 303.*

The accounts affected are Cash in Bank and Store Equipment. Cash in Bank is being increased by the amount received for the shelving, so it is debited for $50.00. Since Champion no longer owns the shelving, Store Equipment is being decreased and is credited for $50.00.

The journal entry for this transaction is shown on line 5 of Figure 12-4 on page 245.

1. Enter the date of the receipt in the Date column.
2. Enter the receipt number in the Document Number column.
3. Enter the title of the account credited in the Account Title column.
4. Enter the amount of the credit in the General Credit column. The General Credit column is used whenever the credit part of the entry cannot be entered in any other special amount column.
5. Enter the amount of cash received in the Cash in Bank Debit column.

Before you go any further, do the following activity to check your understanding of the material you have just studied.

Check Your Learning

Use notebook paper to write your answers to the questions about the following cash receipt transactions of Horizon Leather Goods.

1. On July 3, received $75.00 on account from Brooke Powell, Receipt 311. What should be entered in the Document Number column of the cash receipts journal?
2. On July 6, received $25.00 cash from Paul Robbins for a filing cabinet no longer used by the company, Receipt 312. In which column would the $25.00 credit be entered?
3. Cash sales for the week ended July 7 were $1,790.00, plus $89.50 in sales taxes, Tape 41. What amount should be recorded in the Sales Credit column?
4. Bank card sales for the week ended July 7 were $1,225.00, plus sales taxes of $61.25, Tape 41. How would you show that these amounts are not posted individually to the general ledger?
5. On July 10, received $923.44 on account from Stylecraft, Inc., in payment of Sales Slip 247 for $952.00, less a 3% cash discount of $28.56, Receipt 313. What amount should be recorded in the Cash in Bank Debit column?

Compare your answers to those in the answers section. Re-read the preceding part of the chapter to find the correct answers to any questions you may have missed.

Posting from the Cash Receipts Journal

During the month, two kinds of postings are made from the cash receipts journal. Cash receipts from charge customers are posted to the customer accounts in the accounts receivable subsidiary ledger. Entries in the General Credit column relating to cash receipts are posted to the appropriate general ledger accounts.

CHAPTER 12   Accounting for Cash Receipts **247**

Posting to the Accounts Receivable Subsidiary Ledger

The amounts entered in the Accounts Receivable Credit column are posted to the accounts receivable subsidiary ledger daily. This ensures that customer accounts are always up to date.

To post a cash receipt transaction to an account in the accounts receivable subsidiary ledger, follow these steps. Refer to Figure 12-5 as you read the steps.

1. Enter the date of the transaction in the Date column of the subsidiary ledger account.
2. Enter the letter of the journal and the page number on which the entry is recorded in the Posting Reference column. Use the letters "CR" for the cash receipts journal.
3. In the Credit column, enter the amount shown in the Accounts Receivable Credit column.
4. Compute the new balance and enter it in the Balance column. If the account has a zero balance, draw a line through the Balance column.
5. Return to the cash receipts journal and enter a check mark in the Posting Reference column.

Prev. Bal.	$79.30
Credit	−79.30
New Bal.	$ 0.00

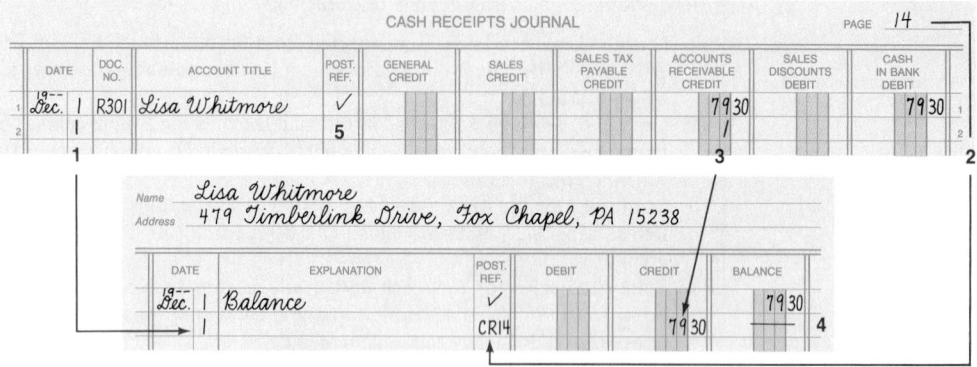

Figure 12-5 Posting from the Cash Receipts Journal to the Accounts Receivable Subsidiary Ledger

Follow these steps for all transactions that must be posted to the accounts receivable subsidiary ledger. Figure 12-6, on pages 249-250, shows the complete accounts receivable subsidiary ledger after all the entries in the cash receipts journal have been posted. Notice that the accounts include entries from both the sales journal and the cash receipts journal.

R E M E M B E R

When posting from the cash receipts journal to the accounts receivable subsidiary ledger, be sure to post the amount recorded in the Accounts Receivable Credit column.

Critical Thinking

When a business accepts a bank credit card for payment of a credit sale, the business usually pays between 2 and 6 percent of the sale amount to the bank that issued the credit card. What are the advantages to the business of allowing customers to use bank credit cards for their purchases? What are the disadvantages?

(Answers: When a business accepts a

bank credit card, the business can treat the sale as a cash sale since its money comes from the bank. The bank, rather than the business, has the responsibility of collecting the money from the customer. A disadvantage is that the business must pay a fee to the bank for taking on the responsibility of collecting from the customer.)

Using Visuals

Refer students to Figure 12-6, which continues onto the next page. Have students trace the amounts posted in the subsidiary ledger accounts from the completed journal on page 252.

Name: Amy Anderson
Address: 103 Woodstone Drive, Laughlintown, PA 15655

DATE	EXPLANATION	POST. REF.	DEBIT	CREDIT	BALANCE
19-- Dec. 1	Balance	✓			35216
1		S12	53000		88216
9		CR14		35216	53000
23		CR14		53000	—
28		S12	44573		44573

Name: Shawn Flannery
Address: 1350 Old Trail Road, Oakmont, PA 15139

DATE	EXPLANATION	POST. REF.	DEBIT	CREDIT	BALANCE
19-- Dec. 1	Balance	✓			21280
7		CR14		11280	10000
13		S12	7950		17950
21		S12	24380		42330
27		G5		24380	17950
29		CR14		10000	7950

Name: Gateway School District
Address: Mosside Boulevard, Monroeville, PA 15146

DATE	EXPLANATION	POST. REF.	DEBIT	CREDIT	BALANCE
19-- Dec. 1	Balance	✓			54000
10		CR14		46500	7500
15		G5		7500	—
17		S12	75000		75000

Name: Greensburg School District
Address: 301 Main Street, Greensburg, PA 15601

DATE	EXPLANATION	POST. REF.	DEBIT	CREDIT	BALANCE
19-- Dec. 1	Balance	✓			125880
2		CR14		119000	6880
15		G5	7500		14380
22		S12	41700		56080

Name: Norwin School District
Address: 251 McMahon Drive, North Huntingdon, PA 15642

DATE	EXPLANATION	POST. REF.	DEBIT	CREDIT	BALANCE
19-- Dec. 1	Balance	✓			76000
5		S12	124050		200050
12		CR14		200050	—
15		S12	132000		132000
26		CR14		132000	—

Figure 12-6 The Completed Accounts Receivable Subsidiary Ledger

CHAPTER 12   Accounting for Cash Receipts   249

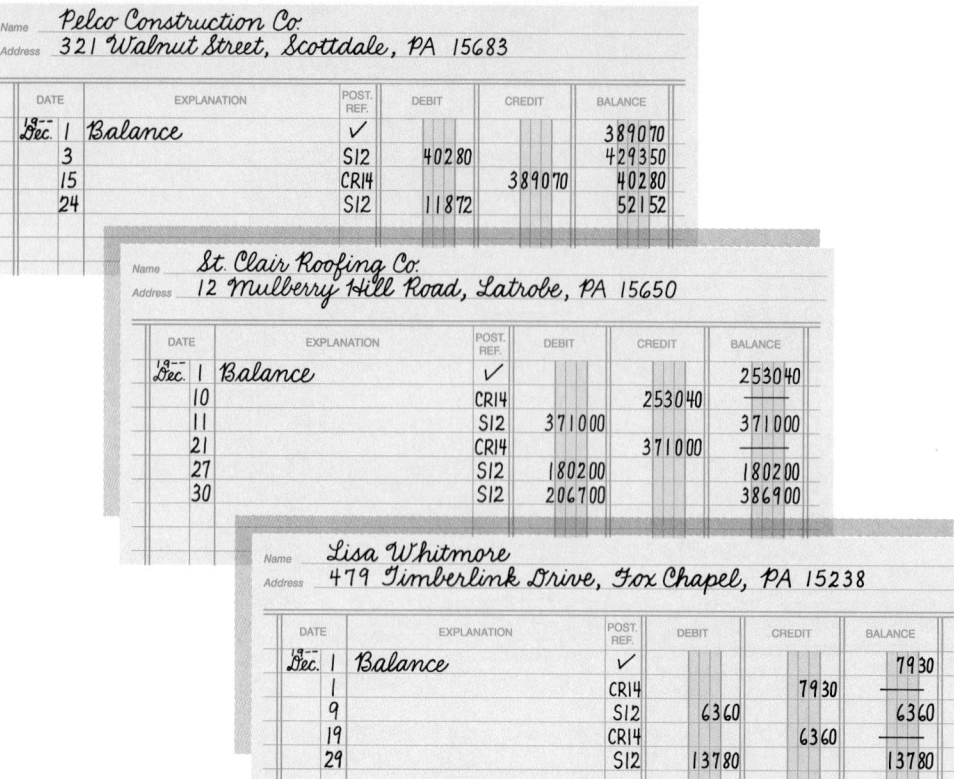

Figure 12-6   The Completed Accounts Receivable Subsidiary Ledger (Concluded)

Posting the General Credit Column

During the month, the transactions in the General Credit column of the cash receipts journal must be posted to the appropriate accounts in the general ledger. Refer to Figure 12-7 at the top of page 251 as you read these steps.

1. Enter the date of the transaction in the Date column of the general ledger account.
2. Enter the letter of the journal and the page number in the Posting Reference column. Be sure to use the letters "CR."
3. In the Credit column of the ledger account, enter the amount from the General Credit column of the journal.
4. Compute and enter the new account balance in the proper Balance column. If the account has a zero balance, draw a line through the appropriate Balance column.
5. Return to the cash receipts journal and enter the general ledger account number in the Posting Reference column.

Prev. Bal.	$26,277.45
Credit	− 50.00
New Bal.	$26,227.45

Making Connections

AROUND THE WORLD

How do people in other countries prepare to be accountants? In well-developed countries, they go to business school and then pass certification exams before they are allowed to practice. Many developing countries, however, have no formal certification process, little higher education for accounting study, and no published accounting textbooks. Lack of an accounting profession prevents businesses from joining the global economy and thus contributes to poor economic conditions in the developing nation. The United Nations is one group that is working toward improving accounting education throughout the world.

						SALES TAX	ACCOUNTS	SALES	CASH	
DATE	DOC. NO.	ACCOUNT TITLE	POST. REF.	GENERAL CREDIT	SALES CREDIT	PAYABLE CREDIT	RECEIVABLE CREDIT	DISCOUNTS DEBIT	IN BANK DEBIT	
Dec. 1	R301	Lisa Whitmore	✓				79 30		79 30	1
2	R302	Greensburg School Dist.	✓				1190 00	23 80	1166 20	2
4	T50	Cash Sales	—		3000 00	180 00			3180 00	3
4	T50	Bank Card Sales	—		700 00	42 00			742 00	4
6	R303	Store Equipment	155	50 00					50 00	5
			5							6

CASH RECEIPTS JOURNAL   PAGE 14

1   **3**   **2**

ACCOUNT	Store Equipment					ACCOUNT NO. 155		
DATE	EXPLANATION	POST. REF.	DEBIT	CREDIT	BALANCE			
					DEBIT	CREDIT		
Dec. 1	Balance	✓			2627 745			
6		CR14		50 00	2622 745		**4**	

Figure 12-7   Posting from the General Credit Column of the Cash Receipts Journal

The cash receipts journal entry for the December 6 transaction is now complete. All transactions recorded in the General Credit column are posted in the same manner.

Completing the Cash Receipts Journal

As with the sales journal, the cash receipts journal must be footed, proved, totaled, and ruled at the end of the month. The totals of the special amount columns are then posted to the general ledger.

In a manual accounting system, these end-of-the-month tasks are completed by accounting clerks. In a computerized system, the computer can simply be instructed to total the journal and post the data stored in the system.

Totaling, Proving, and Ruling the Cash Receipts Journal

To complete the cash receipts journal, follow the procedures on this page and on page 252:

1. Draw a single rule across the six amount columns, just below the last transaction.
2. Foot the columns.
3. Test for the equality of debits and credits.

Debit Columns		Credit Columns	
Sales Discounts	$ 180.11	General	$ 75.00
Cash in Bank	26,627.35	Sales	9,800.00
		Sales Tax Payable	588.00
		Accounts Receivable	16,344.46
	$26,807.46		$26,807.46

Using Visuals

Call students' attention to Figure 12-7 and to the steps for posting from the cash receipts journal to a general ledger account. Follow the red arrows and numbers.

CONCEPT DEVELOPMENT
Completing the Cash Receipts Journal
Remind students that totaling, proving, and ruling the cash receipts journal takes place *before* the column totals are posted. A total is posted to the account named in the column heading. After the amount has been posted, the general ledger account number is written in parentheses below the double rule in the appropriate column. Have students explain why a check mark rather than an account number is written below the double rule in the General Credit column.

Teaching Tips

■ Remind students that footings are completed in pencil because they are a test of total debits and credits.

4. In the Date column, just below the single rule, enter the last day of the month.
5. On the same line in the Account Title column, enter the word "Totals."
6. Enter the verified column totals — in ink — just below the footings.
7. Double-rule the amount columns.

The completed journal page is shown in Figure 12-8. The column totals can now be posted to the general ledger.

CASH RECEIPTS JOURNAL   PAGE

	DATE	DOC. NO.	ACCOUNT TITLE	POST. REF.	GENERAL CREDIT	SALES CREDIT	SALES TAX PAYABLE CREDIT	ACCOUNTS RECEIVABLE CREDIT	SALES DISCOUNTS DEBIT	CASH IN BANK DEBIT	
1	19-- Dec. 1	R301	Lisa Whitmore	✓				79.30		79.30	1
2	2	R302	Greensburg School Dist.	✓				1190.00	23.80	1166.20	2
3	4	T50	Cash Sales	—		3000.00	180.00			3180.00	3
4	4	T50	Bank Card Sales	—		700.00	42.00			742.00	4
5	6	R303	Store Equipment	155	50.00					50.00	5
6	7	R304	Shawn Flannery	✓				112.80		112.80	6
7	9	R305	Amy Anderson	✓				352.16		352.16	7
8	10	R306	Gateway School Dist.	✓				465.00	9.30	455.70	8
9	10	R307	St. Clair Roofing Co.	✓				2530.40	47.74	2482.66	9
10	12	R308	Norwin School District	✓				2000.50		2000.50	10
11	15	R309	Pelco Construction Co.	✓				3890.70		3890.70	11
12	16	R310	Supplies	115	25.00					25.00	12
13	18	T51	Cash Sales	—		2500.00	150.00			2650.00	13
14	18	T51	Bank Card Sales	—		400.00	24.00			424.00	14
15	19	R311	Lisa Whitmore	✓				63.60		63.60	15
16	21	R312	St. Clair Roofing Co.	✓				3710.00	70.00	3640.00	16
17	23	R313	Amy Anderson	✓				530.00		530.00	17
18	26	R314	Norwin School District	✓				1320.00	26.40	1293.60	18
19	29	R315	Shawn Flannery	✓				100.00		100.00	19
20	31	T52	Cash Sales	—		2700.00	162.00			2862.00	20
21	31	T52	Bank Card Sales	—		500.00	30.00			530.00	21
22	31		Totals		75.00	9800.00	588.00	16344.46	177.24	26630.22	22

Figure 12-8 Totaled Cash Receipts Journal

R E M E M B E R

Column totals are written in pencil first. Verified totals are written in ink.

Posting Column Totals to the General Ledger

There are six amount columns in the cash receipts journal used by Champion Building Products. Only five of the column totals, however, are posted to the general ledger. The total of the General Credit column is *not* posted. The entries in this column have already been posted to the general ledger accounts. To indicate that the total of this column is not posted, place a check mark in parentheses below the double rule in the General Credit column.

As shown in Figure 12-9, the totals of the other five amount columns are posted to the general ledger accounts named in the column headings. The column heading indicates whether the amount is to be posted to the Debit

CASH RECEIPTS JOURNAL   PAGE 14

	DATE	DOC. NO.	ACCOUNT TITLE	POST. REF.	GENERAL CREDIT	SALES CREDIT	SALES TAX PAYABLE CREDIT	ACCOUNTS RECEIVABLE CREDIT	SALES DISCOUNTS DEBIT	CASH IN BANK DEBIT	
1	Dec. 1	R301	Lisa Whitmore	✓				79 30		79 30	1
21	31	T52	Bank Card Sales	—		500 00	30 00			530 00	21
22	31		Totals		75 00	9800 00	588 00	1634446	177 24	2663022	22
23					(✓)	(401)	(210)	(105)	(405)	(101)	23

ACCOUNT **Cash in Bank**   ACCOUNT NO. 101

DATE	EXPLANATION	POST. REF.	DEBIT	CREDIT	BALANCE DEBIT	BALANCE CREDIT
Dec. 1	Balance	✓			2389927	
31		CR14	2663022		5052949	

ACCOUNT **Accounts Receivable**   ACCOUNT NO. 105

DATE	EXPLANATION	POST. REF.	DEBIT	CREDIT	BALANCE DEBIT	BALANCE CREDIT
Dec. 1	Balance	✓			962416	
27		G5		24380	938036	
31		S12	1332845		2270881	
31		CR14		1634446	636435	

ACCOUNT **Sales Tax Payable**   ACCOUNT NO. 210

DATE	EXPLANATION	POST. REF.	DEBIT	CREDIT	BALANCE DEBIT	BALANCE CREDIT
Dec. 1	Balance	✓				128387
20		CP14	41792			86595
27		G5	1380			85215
31		S12		54345		139560
31		CR14		588 00		198360

ACCOUNT **Sales**   ACCOUNT NO. 401

DATE	EXPLANATION	POST. REF.	DEBIT	CREDIT	BALANCE DEBIT	BALANCE CREDIT
Dec. 1	Balance	✓				35480000
31		S12		1278500		36758500
31		CR14		980000		37738500

ACCOUNT **Sales Discounts**   ACCOUNT NO. 405

DATE	EXPLANATION	POST. REF.	DEBIT	CREDIT	BALANCE DEBIT	BALANCE CREDIT
Dec. 1	Balance	✓			336611	
31		CR14	17724		354335	

Figure 12-9   Posting Column Totals from the Cash Receipts Journal

CONCEPT DEVELOPMENT
Proving the Accounts Receivable Subsidiary Ledger

Explain that a schedule of accounts receivable is simply a list of each charge customer, the balance in the customer's account, and the total amount due from all customers. All customers should be listed on the schedule, even if some of them have a zero account balance. Listing all customers makes it less likely that one will accidentally be omitted. This practice also corresponds to computerized accounting programs, which print out a list containing all customers and their balances.

A key point for students to remember is that the total of the schedule of accounts receivable must match the total of the Accounts Receivable controlling account in the general ledger.

Teaching Tips

■ A schedule of accounts receivable is reviewed carefully by managers to determine the customers who are not paying on time or who may have stopped buying from the business for some reason.

Using Visuals

Have students look at Figure 12-10 and then compare the account balances reported on the schedule to the account balances shown on pages 249-250 in the subsidiary ledger accounts.

ACCOUNTING **Tips**

When tracking an error, start at the end and work backward.

1. Re-add the balances in the schedule of accounts receivable.
2. Check the balances against the subsidiary ledger accounts.
3. Verify each customer's account balance.
4. Check the postings from the sales and cash receipts journals.
5. Verify the balance of the Accounts Receivable account.
6. Check the totals posted from the sales and cash receipts journals.

---

or Credit column of the account. After each total is posted, the new account balance is computed and entered in the correct Balance column. Finally, the numbers of the general ledger accounts are written in parentheses in the amount columns of the journal to indicate that the posting has been completed.

Proving the Accounts Receivable Subsidiary Ledger

The Accounts Receivable account is the controlling account for the accounts receivable subsidiary ledger. That is, it summarizes all the customer accounts in the subsidiary ledger. At the end of the month, after the posting has been completed, the balance of Accounts Receivable should equal the total of the balances of the individual subsidiary ledger accounts.

To prove the subsidiary ledger, the accounting clerk prepares a schedule of accounts receivable. A **schedule of accounts receivable** is a report listing each charge customer, the balance in the customer's account, and the total amount due from all customers.

In a manual accounting system, the schedule may be prepared on plain paper or accounting stationery. The schedule may also be prepared on a computer.

Figure 12-10 Schedule of Accounts Receivable

Champion's schedule of accounts receivable for December is shown in Figure 12-10. The heading identifies the statement and the date. Customer accounts are listed in alphabetical order, as they appear in the accounts receivable subsidiary ledger. All customers are listed, even those with zero balances, to ensure that no customer is omitted by mistake. According to the schedule, the total amount to be received from all customers is

$6,364.35. As you can see, this total matches the balance of the Accounts Receivable account in the general ledger. The accounts receivable subsidiary ledger has, therefore, been proved.

Using the Computer with Accounts Receivable Transactions

In a computerized accounting system, transactions affecting accounts receivable are handled much like other transactions. The information for each transaction is entered into the computer. When instructed to do so, the computer will post the transaction amounts to the general ledger controlling account and to the subsidiary ledger accounts. The subsidiary ledger accounts and the controlling account are then always up to date.

Many businesses then use the stored data to prepare and send statements of account to their charge customers. A *statement of account* summarizes the transactions affecting a charge customer's account over a period of time. The statement usually lists the customer's previous balance, all charge sales made, and any payments or other decreases to the account balance. A statement of account is usually prepared for a one-month period.

Many customers, particularly those who have not been offered cash discounts, wait to receive a statement of account before sending a payment check. Other customers only use the statement of account as a means of verifying their own records.

CHAMPION BUILDING PRODUCTS, INC.
601 Mt. Lebanon Road
Pittsburgh, PA 15230

STATEMENT OF ACCOUNT

TO: Amy Anderson
      103 Woodstone Drive
      Laughlintown, PA 15655

CLOSING DATE	PAYMENT DUE DATE	PREVIOUS BALANCE	NEW BALANCE
12/31/--	01/20/--	352.16	445.73

DATE	DESCRIPTION	AMOUNT
12/01	PURCHASE	530.00
12/09	PAYMENT -- THANK YOU	352.16-
12/23	PAYMENT -- THANK YOU	530.00-
12/28	PURCHASE	445.73

PREVIOUS BALANCE	NEW PURCHASES	PAYMENTS	NEW BALANCE
352.16	975.73	882.16	445.73

Figure 12-11   Computer-Generated Statement of Account

A statement of account that might be prepared by Champion Building Products, Inc., is illustrated in Figure 12-11. Compare this statement with the information listed in Amy Anderson's subsidiary ledger account in Figure 12-6.

CONCEPT DEVELOPMENT
Using the Computer with Accounts Receivable Transactions

Computerized accounting systems not only save time, especially in the posting process, but also are generally more accurate since information needs to be entered only once. The computer program takes the journal information and automatically posts it at the touch of a button to the subsidiary ledger and to the general ledger.

Computerized accounting programs also make it easier to create statements of amounts owed to send to customers since the statements can be generated directly from the information in the computerized customer accounts.

Using Visuals

Have students look at the various information contained in the statement of account. Bring samples of other similar statements to class and have students compare them to determine differences and similarities.

COMPUTERS IN ACCOUNTING

Computerized accounting systems pose numerous security risks. Internal computer controls are essential to guard against theft, unauthorized access to information, and threats to data integrity. Control procedures should include the following.

- Policy statements for computer security guidelines should be written and followed by all employees.
- Locking devices, password protection, and security software should be used to limit and control access to information.
- Data entered into the system should be validated.
- File storage and data backup procedures should be implemented so that data is not accidentally or intentionally destroyed.

Pop Quiz

1. What are the three most common sources of cash for a merchandising business?
2. What effect do cash discounts have on total sales?
3. A(n) ____ account decreases another account's balance.
4. If the cash receipts journal has no special column for the account to be credited, the amount is recorded in the ____ column.
5. What report is created to prove that the total of balances in the subsidiary ledger equals the Accounts Receivable balance?

ANSWERS

1. cash sales, bank card sales, and cash received from charge customers
2. cash discounts decrease total sales
3. contra
4. General Credit
5. schedule of accounts receivable

3 CLOSE

CHAPTER SUMMARY

This summary enumerates the key information in the chapter. It is a useful tool for reinforcement and review.

Summary of Key Points

1. The cash received by a business is first recorded on receipts and cash register tapes. These receipts and tapes are the source documents for the journal entries.
2. Bank card sales are recorded as though they were cash sales.
3. Some merchandising businesses give cash discounts to customers for paying their bills early. A customer who takes advantage of a cash discount may deduct a certain percentage of the cost of merchandise if it pays the bill within the discount period.
4. The Sales Discounts account is used to record the amount of any cash discounts taken by charge customers. It is referred to as a contra account because it reduces the balance of the Sales account.
5. The cash receipts journal is a special journal used to record all cash received by a business.
6. The cash receipts journal contains special amount columns for transactions that occur frequently. Credit amounts that cannot be entered in a special amount column are entered in the General Credit column.
7. Transactions are posted from the cash receipts journal to the accounts receivable subsidiary ledger daily. Transactions entered in the General Credit column are posted periodically during the month.
8. Column totals from the cash receipts journal are posted at the end of each month.
9. A schedule of accounts receivable lists all charge customers, their ending balances, and the total amount due from all customers. The total of the schedule of accounts receivable must match the balance of the Accounts Receivable account.

Review and Applications

Building Your Accounting Vocabulary

In your own words, write the definition of each of the following accounting terms. Use complete sentences for your definitions.

bank card	cash receipts journal	receipt
cash discount	cash sale	schedule of accounts
cash receipt	contra account	receivable

Reviewing Your Accounting Knowledge

1. What are the source documents for transactions recorded in the cash receipts journal?
2. Why are bank card sales considered to be a form of cash sale?
3. Give an example of a cash receipt that a merchandising business might have that did not result from the sale of merchandise.
4. Why would a business offer a cash discount to its customers?
5. What is the normal balance side of the Sales Discounts account?
6. Why does a cash receipts journal always have a Cash in Bank Debit column?
7. What accounts are affected when a business receives a payment from a charge customer who has taken advantage of a cash discount?
8. What are the two kinds of postings made from the cash receipts journal during the month?
9. When are amounts in the Accounts Receivable Credit column of the cash receipts journal posted to the accounts receivable subsidiary ledger?
10. Why is a check mark in parentheses placed below the double rule in the General Credit column of the cash receipts journal?
11. What is the purpose of preparing a schedule of accounts receivable?

Improving Your Communications Skills

Words that are similar in meaning are called *synonyms*. Using synonyms adds variety to communications. However, if your reader doesn't understand the word you use, you are not communicating. For this reason, it is usually a good idea to use familiar language in business writing. Rewrite each of the following sentences, supplying a synonym for the word in italics.

1. Some of the points that were raised during the meeting did not seem *germane*.
2. Please *expedite* the processing of these invoices.
3. To complete the report, it was necessary for Rosa to *procure* a copy of the monthly sales figures.
4. Andrew did a *prodigious* amount of work in a very short time.
5. The memo *aggrandized* the number of customer complaints.

257

Building Your Accounting Vocabulary
See the Glossary on pages 670-679 for definitions of these terms.

Reviewing Your Accounting Knowledge
1. Source documents for recording transactions in the cash receipts journal are receipts and cash register tapes.
2. Bank card sales are considered a form of cash sale because the business receives cash from the bank soon after it deposits its bank card sales slips. The bank collects from the card holder.
3. A merchandising business may also receive cash from the sale of other assets or a loan from a bank.
4. A business offers a cash discount to encourage prompt payment of sales slips or invoices.
5. The debit side is the normal balance side of the Sales Discounts account.
6. A cash receipts journal always has a Cash in Bank Debit column because every transaction recorded in the journal requires a debit to the Cash in Bank account.
7. The accounts affected when a business receives a payment from a charge customer who has taken advantage of a cash discount are: Cash in Bank, Sales Discounts, and Accounts Receivable.
8. During the month, cash receipts from charge customers are posted to the customer accounts in the accounts receivable subsidiary ledger. Cash receipts for the transactions entered in the General Credit column are posted to the appropriate general ledger accounts.
9. Amounts entered in the Accounts Receivable Credit column are posted to the accounts receivable ledger daily.

10. A check mark in parentheses is placed below the double rule in the General Credit column to indicate that the column total is not posted.
11. A schedule of accounts receivable is prepared to prove the subsidiary ledger.

Improving Your Communications Skills
Students' answers will vary, but may include the following synonyms.

1. relevant, suitable, pertinent, applicable, fitting
2. speed up, help along
3. get, obtain, acquire
4. enormous, extraordinary, huge, large
5. exaggerated, overstated

PRACTICE AND APPLY

• Concepts and Procedures

Exercise 12-1: Ch. Obj. 1

Exercise 12-2: Ch. Obj. 1
2. $0; $1,500.00
3. $27.60; $2,732.40
4. $114.00; $3,686.00
5. $0; $450.30
6. $15.55; $761.85
7. $27.26; $1,335.49

Exercise 12-3: Ch. Obj. 1
2. Sales Cr., Sales Tax Pay. Cr.,
Cash in Bank Dr.
3. Accts. Rec. Cr., Cash in Bank Dr.
4. Sales Cr., Sales Tax Pay. Cr.,
Cash in Bank Dr.
5. Accts. Rec. Cr., Sales Disc. Dr.,
Cash in Bank Dr.
6. General Cr., Cash in Bank Dr.

Applying Accounting Procedures

Exercise 12-1   Completing a Receipt Form
On December 15, The Rug Center received a check from the Barker Co. The $382.20 check was in payment of Sales Slip 493 for $390.00, less a 2% discount.

Instructions: Prepare a receipt for this cash receipt. The receipt is included in your working papers. Sign your name on the Received By line.

Exercise 12-2   Computing Cash Discounts
Expo Communications received the payments shown below for sales made on account. The companies that were offered cash discounts all paid within the discount period.

	Sale Amount	Credit Terms
1.	$4,600.00	2/10, n/30
2.	1,500.00	n/30
3.	2,760.00	1/10, n/30
4.	3,800.00	3/15, n/30
5.	450.30	n/30
6.	777.40	2/15, n/30
7.	1,362.75	2/10, n/30

Instructions: Use a form similar to the one that follows. For each sale amount,
(1) Indicate the credit terms for the sale in the second column.
(2) Compute the amount of the cash discount, if any.
(3) Determine the amount of cash actually received. The first payment has been completed as an example.

Sale Amount	Credit Terms	Cash Discount Amount	Amount of Cash Received
$4,600.00	2/10, n/30	$92.00	$4,508.00

Exercise 12-3   Analyzing Cash Receipt Transactions
Instructions: Listed below are several cash receipt transactions. Use a form similar to the one that follows. For each transaction, indicate in which columns of the cash receipts journal the transaction amounts should be recorded. The first transaction is given as an example.

Trans.	General Credit	Sales Credit	Sales Tax Payable Credit	Accounts Receivable Credit	Sales Discounts Debit	Cash in Bank Debit
1	✔					✔

Transactions:
1. Sold an old typewriter to an employee for $100.00 cash.
2. Recorded $2,500.00 in cash sales for the week plus $100.00 in sales taxes.
3. Received $50.00 on account from A. C. Reynolds.

258

Refer students to the Chapter 12 review pages in the workbook, *Chapter Reviews and Working Papers.*

Additional Reinforcement

Students who need additional practice or individualized help will benefit from the *Glencoe Accounting Electronic Study Guide* or the *Glencoe Accounting* on-line multimedia program, which provide reinforcement and reteaching for vocabulary, concepts, and procedures.

4. Recorded the week's bank card sales of $800.00 plus $32.00 sales tax.

5. Received $245.00 from the Porter Company in payment of merchandise purchased on account for $250.00, less a 2% cash discount.

6. As a favor to a neighboring business, sold office supplies for $25.00 cash.

SPREADSHEET

PROBLEM

Problem 12-1   Recording Transactions in the Cash Receipts Journal

ColorCraft Mart, a retail merchandising store, had the following transactions during the month of November.

Instructions: Record the cash receipts for November on page 11 of the cash receipts journal.

Transactions:

Nov. 1 Received a check for $100.00 from Johanna Ambrose on account, Receipt 300.

3 Richard Perry sent a $40.00 check to apply on his account, Receipt 301.

8 Received a check from Rachel Quinn for $269.50 as payment for a purchase of $275.00, less a 2% cash discount of $5.50, Receipt 302.

9 As a favor to Hoffman Realty, sold three reams of duplicating paper (office supplies) for $18.00, Receipt 303.

10 Prepared Receipt 304 for a $60.00 check from David Dinsmore on account.

12 Farrah Fletcher sent a check for $245.00 in payment of Sales Slip 1163 for $250.00 less a cash discount of $5.00, Receipt 305.

15 Cash sales for the first two weeks amounted to $1,150.00, plus sales taxes of $57.50, Tape 48.

15 Bank card sales for the period were $475.00, plus $23.75 in sales taxes, Tape 48.

15 Received a $125.00 check on account from Stephen Walsh, Receipt 306.

16 Richard Perry sent his check for $80.00 to apply on his account, Receipt 307.

18 A check for $70.00 was received from Johanna Ambrose on account, Receipt 308.

20 David Dinsmore sent a $110.00 check to apply to his account, Receipt 309.

22 Received a check for $30.00 from Stephen Walsh to apply on his account, Receipt 310.

24 Sold an old typewriter (office equipment) to an employee for $45.00, Receipt 311.

26 A check for $65.00 was received on account from David Dinsmore, Receipt 312.

30 Cash sales for the period totaled $1,400.00, plus $70.00 sales taxes, Tape 49.

30 Bank card sales were $500.00 plus sales taxes of $25.00, Tape 49.

Problem 12-2   Posting from the Cash Receipts Journal

You will need the cash receipts journal prepared in Problem 12-1 to complete this problem.

259

Problem 12-1: Ch. Obj. 1

SPREADSHEET

PROBLEM

Students may complete Problem 12-1 using *Spreadsheet Applications*, the spreadsheet software that accompanies *Glencoe Accounting*.

Column totals:
General $63.00
Sales $3,525.00
Sales Tax Pay. $176.25
Accts. Rec. $1,205.00
Sales Disc. $10.50
Cash in Bank $4,958.75

Teacher Notes

Problem 12-2: Ch. Obj. 2, 3, 4

Problem 12-3: Ch. Obj. 2, 3, 4, 5

Column totals:
General $152.00
Sales $3,450.00
Sales Tax Pay. $207.00
Accts. Rec. $1,280.00
Sales Disc. $16.20
Cash in Bank $5,072.80

Accts. Rec. bal. $855.00

Instructions:

(1) Post the individual amounts from the Accounts Receivable Credit column to the customers' accounts in the accounts receivable subsidiary ledger. The opened customer accounts are included in the working papers accompanying this textbook.

(2) Post the individual amounts from the General Credit column to the appropriate accounts in the general ledger.

(3) Foot, prove, total, and rule the cash receipts journal.

(4) Post the column totals to the general ledger accounts named in the column headings.

Problem 12-3   Journalizing and Posting
Cash Receipts Transactions

The Country Peddler, a retail merchandising store, uses special journals and an accounts receivable subsidiary ledger for recording business transactions. The accounts receivable subsidiary ledger and a portion of the general ledger are included in the working papers. The current account balances are recorded in the accounts. During the month of July, the Country Peddler had the cash receipts transactions that follow.

Instructions:

(1) Record the transactions in the cash receipts journal. Use page 7.

(2) Post the individual amounts from the Accounts Receivable Credit column to the customers' accounts in the accounts receivable subsidiary ledger.

(3) Post the individual amounts in the General Credit column to the general ledger accounts.

(4) Foot, prove, total, and rule the cash receipts journal.

(5) Post the column totals to the general ledger accounts named in the column headings.

(6) Prepare a schedule of accounts receivable.

Transactions:

July 1   Charlotte Cole sent a check for $50.00 to apply on her account, Receipt 401.

    3   Received cash on account from Kelly O'Brien, $75.00, Receipt 402.

    5   A $25.00 check was received from Jedd Girard to apply on his account, Receipt 403.

    6   Received a check for $291.00 from Joseph Zider in payment of a sales slip for $300.00, less a 3% cash discount, Receipt 404.

    7   Sold $15.00 worth of supplies, as a favor, to Lou's Pharmacy, Receipt 405.

    8   Charlotte Cole, a charge customer, sent a $20.00 check as payment on her account, Receipt 406.

    10   Received a check for $352.80 from Pat Eagleson in payment for merchandise totaling $360.00, less a 2% cash discount, Receipt 407.

    11   Jedd Girard sent a check for $80.00, on account, Receipt 408.

    13   A $60.00 check was received from Kelly O'Brien as a payment on account, Receipt 409.

    15   Dana Vella, a charge customer, sent a $75.00 check, Receipt 410.

    15   Recorded cash sales of $1,000.00, plus $60.00 in sales taxes, Tape 102.

Teacher Notes

15 Bank card sales totaled $350.00, plus $21.00 sales taxes, Tape 102.

20 Sold a duplicating machine (office equipment) for $125.00, Receipt 411.

23 A $70.00 check was received from Jedd Girard, Receipt 412.

24 Sold two reams of paper for $12.00, as a favor to Bill Davies, Receipt 413.

25 Kelly O'Brien sent a check for $45.00 as a payment on her account, Receipt 414.

26 A $35.00 check was received from Charlotte Cole, Receipt 415.

28 Dana Vella sent an $85.00 check, on account, Receipt 416.

31 Recorded cash sales of $1,500.00 plus $90.00 in sales taxes, Tape 103.

31 Bank card sales for the period were $600.00, plus $36.00 sales taxes, Tape 103.

Problem 12-4: Ch. Obj. 2, 3, 4, 5

COMPUTER PROBLEM This computer image identifies a problem that students may complete using the *Glencoe Accounting, General Ledger* software.

Problem 12-4 Recording and Posting Sales and Cash Receipt Transactions

On April 1, Pennwood Paints, a merchandising distributor of paints and paint products, has the following balances in its accounts receivable subsidiary ledger and general ledger.

General Ledger (Partial)

Account Number		Account Balance
101	Cash in Bank	$3,000.00
105	Accounts Receivable	5,826.33
110	Supplies	175.00
115	Office Equipment	1,200.00
210	Sales Tax Payable	326.50
401	Sales	9,984.45
405	Sales Discounts	47.52

Accounts Receivable Subsidiary Ledger

Account Number		Account Balance
820	James Coletti, 114 Putnam St., San Francisco, CA 94101	$ 479.56
832	Norma Fury, 5654 Beach St., San Francisco, CA 94101	350.60
840	Heritage Racquet Club, 890 Fremont Blvd., Monterey, CA 93940	2,684.16
846	Myra Kristan, 386 Bay St., Santa Cruz, CA 95060	150.75
860	O'Mara Enterprises, 547 University Ave., Berkeley, CA 94704	1,890.36
890	Nick Pomeroy, 103 Prospect Ave., Santa Clara, CA 95050	270.90

Instructions:

(1) Open the general ledger accounts and record the April 1 balances.

(2) Open the customer accounts in the accounts receivable subsidiary ledger and record the April 1 balances.

(3) Record the April transactions in the sales and cash receipts journals. Use page 4 for each journal.

(4) Post the individual amounts from the two journals to the accounts receivable subsidiary ledger on a daily basis. Post the amounts in the

261

Teacher Notes

SJ column totals:
Sales $5,905.00
Sales Tax Pay. $354.30
Accts. Rec. $6,259.30

CRJ column totals:
General $70.00
Sales $4,840.00
Sales Tax Pay. $290.40
Accts. Rec. $8,643.18
Sales Disc. $141.31
Cash in Bank $13,702.27

Accts. Rec. bal. $3,442.45

General Credit column of the cash receipts journal to the general ledger accounts daily.

(5) Foot, prove, total, and rule the journals.

(6) Post the column totals in the journals to the general ledger. Post the sales journal totals first.

(7) Prepare a schedule of accounts receivable.

Transactions:

Apr. 1 Received a check for $2,633.52 from Heritage Racquet Club in full payment of their account of $2,684.16, less a 2% cash discount of $50.64, Receipt 150.

2 Sold $200.00 worth of merchandise to Nick Pomeroy, plus sales taxes of $12.00, Sales Slip 401.

3 Norma Fury sent us a check for $350.60 in full payment of her account, Receipt 151.

5 Received a check for $75.00 from Myra Kristan to apply on account, Receipt 152.

6 O'Mara Enterprises sent a $1,854.69 check in full payment of Sales Slip 391 for $1,890.36, less a 2% discount of $35.67, Receipt 153.

7 Sold merchandise on account to Norma Fury for $415.00 plus $24.90 sales taxes, Sales Slip 402.

8 Sold to James Coletti on account, $310.00 in merchandise, sales taxes $18.60, Sales Slip 403.

9 Myra Kristan bought $175.00 worth of merchandise on account, sales tax $10.50, Sales Slip 404.

10 Cash sales for the first part of the month were $1,850.00 plus sales taxes of $111.00, Tape 20.

10 Bank card sales totaled $670.00 plus $40.20 sales taxes, Tape 20.

11 Sold $950.00 in merchandise on account to Heritage Racquet Club, $57.00 sales taxes, Sales Slip 405.

12 Sold $10.00 in memo pads (supplies), as a favor, for cash, Receipt 154.

13 James Coletti sent a check for $479.56 in payment of Sales Slip 397, Receipt 155.

14 Sold to O'Mara Enterprises on account $1,200.00 in merchandise, plus sales taxes of $72.00, Sales Slip 406.

15 Received a $270.90 check from Nick Pomeroy to apply on his account, Receipt 156.

16 Norma Fury sent a check to apply on her account, Receipt 157 for $125.00.

18 Sold an old typewriter to Doug Jones, an employee, for $60.00, Receipt 158.

19 Sold to James Coletti merchandise totaling $140.00, $8.40 sales taxes, on account, Sales Slip 407.

21 Received a check for $988.00 from Heritage Racquet Club in full payment of Sales Slip 405 for $1,007.00, less a 2% cash discount of $19.00, Receipt 159.

22 Recorded Receipt 160 for a check from James Coletti for $328.60, on account.

23 Received a check for $160.00 from Nick Pomeroy on account, Receipt 161.

262

25 Sold to Myra Kristan $215.00 worth of merchandise on account, sales taxes $12.90, Sales Slip 408.

26 Sold merchandise totaling $150.00 to Nick Pomeroy on account, sales tax $9.00, Sales Slip 409.

27 Received a check for $1,236.00 from O'Mara Enterprises in payment of Sales Slip 406 for $1,272.00 less a 3% cash discount of $36.00, Receipt 162.

28 Sold $770.00 in merchandise to Heritage Racquet Club on account, sales taxes of $46.20, Sales Slip 410.

29 Sold on account to O'Mara Enterprises $1,300.00 worth of merchandise, plus $78.00 sales taxes, Sales Slip 411.

29 Sold $80.00 in merchandise on account, plus $4.80 sales tax, to James Coletti, Sales Slip 412.

30 Cash sales for the period were $1,790.00, plus sales taxes of $107.40, Tape 21.

30 The amount of bank card sales was $530.00, plus $31.80 sales taxes, Tape 21.

CHALLENGE

PROBLEM

Problem 12-5 Analyzing Sales and Cash Receipt Errors

The Grenon Lumberyard uses special journals to record sales on account and cash receipts. During the past month, an accounting clerk made each of the errors described below. Explain how each error might be discovered.

1. A sale on account was journalized correctly but posted to the Credit column of the customer's account.

2. A sale of some office supplies for $36.00 cash was correctly recorded in the cash receipts journal but posted to the Office Supplies account as a debit of $36.00.

3. Made an addition error in totaling the Cash in Bank Debit column of the cash receipts journal.

4. A sale on account to Paul Forest was recorded correctly in the sales journal but posted to the account of Pauline Fredericks.

5. Made a subtraction error in determining the balance of a customer's account.

6. Recorded the sale of an old piece of office equipment in the Sales Credit column of the cash receipts journal.

7. A sale on account for $125.00 plus $6.25 sales tax was recorded in the sales journal as a debit of $125.00 to Accounts Receivable, a credit of $6.25 to Sales Tax Payable, and a credit of $131.25 to Sales.

8. The total of the Sales Tax Payable Credit column was posted to the Accounts Receivable account in the general ledger.

9. Recorded a cash receipt from a charge customer but forgot to post the amount to the customer's account.

10. Sold merchandise on account to a charge customer but forgot to include the amount of the sales tax in the sales journal entry.

263

Problem 12-5: Ch. Obj. 1, 2, 4

CHALLENGE

PROBLEM

The last problem in each chapter is a challenge problem and is identified by this "maze" symbol.

4 ASSESS

A chapter test is available for use in assessing students' understanding of concepts in this chapter.

The testmaker software will enable you to develop tailor-made chapter, unit, semester, and final tests.

Alternative Assessment

For alternative assessment strategies, refer to *Tech Prep Strategies in Accounting.*

Use Chapter Test 12 here to assess students' understanding and retention of the concepts and procedures presented in the chapter.

Bar coding is efficient, but it sometimes has drawbacks from the consumer's viewpoint. For example, one drawback is that sale items must be entered separately if the price has not been changed in the computer. Ask students to interview the owner or manager of a store using bar codes to determine some of the problems with this technology.

QUESTIONS

1. Why is bar code technology so attractive to grocery stores?
2. Name some local businesses other than grocery stores that use bar codes.

ANSWERS

1. The typical grocery store carries thousands of items, and any savings in tracking inventories are significant. Bar coding makes inventory maintenance easier, faster, and more cost efficient. In addition, bar coding means fewer mistakes in entering prices by the checkout person.
2. Students' answers will vary but should include clothing and shoe stores as well as drugstores, hardware stores, and general merchandise stores.

*B*ar Codes:
An Idea on the Fast Track

*A*t the grocery store checkout, the cashier whisks the label on a jar, box, or bag across a window. There's a flash and a beep, and a price appears on the cash register screen faster than human fingers could key in $2.43.

What you didn't see was the lightning-fast transfer of information between the cash register and the store's computer.

• A scanner uses a bright light to "read" the bar code, the striped symbols on the product label. The stripes represent the manufacturer and the product. (Numbers below the bars also represent the manufacturer and the product.)

• The pattern is decoded into data and sent to the computer.

• The computer "looks up" the price and sends it back to the cash register. The computer also updates the store's inventory for the product.

Supermarkets were the first to use bar code technology in the early 1970s, resulting in faster order processing, a detailed receipt of purchases, and far fewer errors. Now bar codes are turning up everywhere.

• The U.S. Postal Service uses bar codes to speed up mail sorting and routing.

• Hospitals match bar codes printed on patients' wristbands with codes on prescription drug labels to make sure the right medicine goes to the right patient.

• Airlines hope to cut down on lost luggage by using bar codes on claim checks and luggage tags and matching them to aircraft.

• Hand-held scanners attached to video cassette recorders allow users to program their VCRs by running the scanners over bar-coded listings printed in the TV schedule.

• State judicial systems use bar codes to monitor cases and work loads. Bar-coded files and docu-

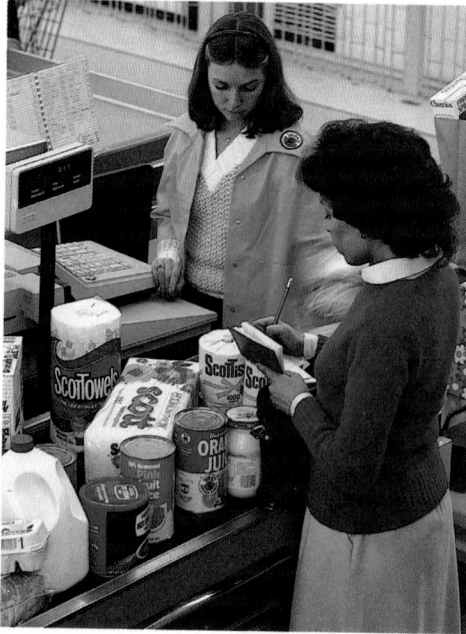

Scanning bar codes on merchandise speeds up the checkout process and helps the store keep an up-to-date inventory.

ments are scanned each time they're used. A central computer stores the information and prepares a weekly analysis of the entire judicial system.

• Courier and delivery companies use bar codes to track packages.

Yes, the beep goes on!

264

Chapter 13

ACCOUNTING FOR PURCHASES ON ACCOUNT

Learning Objectives

When you have completed Chapter 13, you should be able to do the following:

1. Describe the procedures for processing a purchase on account.
2. Explain the use of the Purchases account.
3. Journalize a purchase on account in a purchases journal.
4. Post from the purchases journal to the accounts payable subsidiary ledger and to the general ledger.
5. Define the accounting terms introduced in this chapter.

In the last two chapters, you have learned that businesses use special journals to record transactions that are alike and occur often. Special journals help accountants avoid accounting traffic jams. They channel incoming data into appropriate "lanes" and are a shortcut for much of the data headed for the general ledger.

The special journals you have studied so far cover only part of the daily flow of transactions. The sales and cash receipts journals are used for merchandise *leaving* the business. Merchandise and other items used to operate the business must also *enter* the business.

In this chapter, you'll learn about another special journal: the purchases journal. You will also learn about the subsidiary ledger used by businesses having large numbers of creditors.

New Terms

purchase requisition
purchase order
packing slip
invoice
processing stamp
purchase discount
discount period
Purchases account
cost of merchandise
purchases journal
tickler file
due date
accounts payable subsidiary
  ledger

265

LOOKING BACK

Students have now learned how to record sales and cash receipts transactions in special journals designed specifically for those transactions. They have also learned how to post to a subsidiary ledger account and to prepare a schedule of accounts receivable. In this chapter, students will continue their study of the special journals by learning to record purchases on account in a purchases journal.

VOCABULARY DEVELOPMENT

Discuss the definitions of the new terms in class. Ask students to give their definition of each term and to explain how each is used in accounting. Definitions of these terms are found in the chapter and in the glossary on pages 670-679.

Electronic Field Trips

Teaching Resources

- Lesson Plans
- TE/Chapter Reviews & Working Papers
- Demonstration Problems
- Student Study Plans
- Teaching Transparencies
- Solutions Transparencies
- Electronic Field Trips Video, Level I
- Electronic Study Guide
- Chapter 13 Test

Other Resources

- Skills Improvement Activities
- Blackline Masters
- Careers in Accounting
- Dictionary
- Math Review for Accounting
- Tech Prep Strategies in Accounting
- Video
- Test Bank with Software
- Spanish Resources/Audiotapes
- Spanish Electronic Study Guide

1 FOCUS

MAJOR CONCEPTS

- Purchasing Items Needed by a Business
- Purchases Discounts
- The Purchases Account
- The Purchases Journal
- Journalizing Purchases on Account
- The Accounts Payable Subsidiary Ledger
- Posting from the Purchases Journal
- Completing the Purchases Journal
- Handling Purchases on Account in a Computerized Accounting System

BUSINESS CONNECTION

Retailers such as JC Penney purchase merchandise from suppliers on account. In an effort to improve productivity, JC Penney made a strategic agreement with Haggar, one of its suppliers. Penney's provides constant communication about merchandise stocks to Haggar, which fills Penney's orders in nearly half the time. Haggar merchandise reaches JC Penney significantly faster, minimizing out-of-stock situations and potential lost sales. Both companies have benefited from the partnership efforts.

2 TEACH

CONCEPT DEVELOPMENT

Purchasing Items Needed by a Business

Remind students that the procedures for purchasing items on account vary from company to company. Use a general purchasing procedure flowchart to show the typical purchasing process. Discuss each step with students.

Invite a business person familiar with the purchasing procedures used by his or her business to speak to the class. Ask the speaker to bring samples of the purchasing forms used by the business.

Purchasing Items Needed by a Business

Businesses buy as well as sell. This is true at every level of business—from the corner grocery store to a giant international corporation. Regardless of its type, size, or purpose, a business needs supplies and equipment to operate. All businesses need such things as paper, pencils, pens, and other items for their employees' use. They also need various types of furniture and equipment—from desks, to typewriters, to cash registers, to delivery vans. Retail businesses need shopping bags for customers, sales slips, and cash register tapes. Retail businesses must also buy merchandise to resell to their customers. Although these items may be bought on a cash basis, they are usually bought on account.

The purchase of supplies, equipment, and merchandise can be divided into four stages: requesting the needed items, ordering from a supplier, verifying items received, and processing the supplier's bill. Let's take a look at each of these stages.

Requesting Needed Items

When equipment or supplies are needed or when the inventory of merchandise on hand becomes low, the person or department in charge of purchasing must be notified. In a small business, the owner does all the buying. In a large business, a separate purchasing department usually buys items for the entire company.

Most businesses require that a request for items to be purchased be in writing. A **purchase requisition** is a written request that a certain item or items be ordered. Like many business documents, a purchase requisition is usually a prenumbered, multicopy form.

A purchase requisition includes the quantity, description, and stock number of each item requested. A requisition may cover several different items. The form usually lists the date the requested items are needed and may have a space for the suggested supplier. The original of the completed form is sent to the purchasing department or the purchasing agent. One copy is kept by the person making the request. Figure 13-1 shows the purchase requisition form used by Champion Building Products.

PURCHASE REQUISITION		
FOR DEPARTMENT Home Improvements	NO. 9421	
NOTIFY Betty Connor ON DELIVERY	DATE Nov. 12, 19--	
	DATE WANTED Dec. 5, 19--	
QUANTITY	DESCRIPTION	STOCK NO.
4 gal.	Exterior paint, white	94682
4 gal.	Exterior paint, gray	94788
6 gal.	Exterior paint, brown	94281
6 gal.	Exterior paint, beige	94666
6 gal.	Exterior paint, peach	94711
ORDER FROM Key Paint Company	APPROVED BY Paul Andrews	
	PURCHASING AGENT	

Figure 13-1 A Typical Purchase Requisition

Reinforcing Study Skills

The reading strategy SQ3R can also be helpful when applied to smaller units of the text, such as paragraphs. As students read, they should ask themselves questions to guide their reading. For example, in the first section: (paragraph 1) "What items do businesses need to buy?" (paragraph 2) "What are the four stages of purchasing?"

Provide a copy of the *Student Study Plans* to each class member to help organize study activities or to individualize practice and review activities.

Placing an Order with a Supplier

After a purchase requisition is approved, a purchase order is prepared. A **purchase order** is a written offer to a supplier to buy certain items. Much of the information on the purchase order is taken directly from the purchase requisition. Other information may be obtained from the supplier's catalog. The purchase order contains the quantity, description, unit price, and total cost of each item being ordered. The *unit price* is the cost of a single item or of the smallest quantity—such as a dozen—in which an item can be bought. The purchase order also contains the supplier's name and address, the date the items are needed, and, perhaps, the method of shipping.

Look at the purchase order prepared by Champion Building Products in Figure 13-2. Like the purchase requisition, the purchase order is a prenumbered, multicopy form. The original of the purchase order is sent to the supplier from whom the items are being ordered. One copy of the purchase order may be sent to the department requesting the items. Another copy is kept by the purchasing department.

CHAMPION BUILDING PRODUCTS, INC.
601 Mt. Lebanon Road
Pittsburgh, PA 15230

Purchase Order

No.   9784

To Key Paint Company
1714 Peak Road
Cleveland, OH 44109

Date: November 15, 19--
Date Needed: December 5, 19--

Quantity	Item	Unit Price	Total
4 gal.	Exterior paint: white, # 94682	$6.98	$ 27.92
4 gal.	Exterior paint: gray, #94788	6.98	27.92
6 gal.	Exterior paint: brown, #94281	6.98	41.88
6 gal.	Exterior paint: beige, #94666	6.98	41.88
6 gal.	Exterior paint: peach, #94711	6.98	41.88
	TOTAL		$181.48

Figure 13-2   A Typical Purchase Order

Note that a purchase order is only an *offer* to buy items. Until the items ordered are actually received, the buyer does not know whether or not the supplier has accepted the offer and shipped the items. A supplier may not be able to fill the purchase order because an item is out of stock or has been discontinued. The mailing of a purchase order, therefore, does not require a journal entry.

CHAPTER 13   Accounting for Purchases on Account

267

Making Connections

EVERYDAY LIFE

Ask students if they have ever purchased anything on account. Some students (or their parents) may use credit cards. When buying on account, the customer receives a receipt for the items purchased. Then, when the invoice (or credit card statement) is received, the customer compares the amounts on receipts to the amounts shown on the invoice (or statement) to verify that the charges are accurate.

ACCOUNTING ISSUES

Students who are interested in pursuing an accounting degree would benefit from the 1992-93 *AICPA Directory of Accounting Education,* a directory containing up-to-date information about more than 700 undergraduate and graduate accounting programs in the United States. The directory lists the degrees offered; describes the programs for each degree; describes the characteristics of the school and student body; and provides names, addresses, and telephone numbers of administrators and faculty. To order the directory, call the American Institute of CPAs (AICPA) at 1-800-TO-AICPA and request product number 876795JA.

Using Visuals

Have students read the photo caption. Then ask them to suggest reasons why a packing slip might not agree with the list of items ordered.

Teaching Tips

- An invoice is prepared by the supplier's accounting department and mailed to the buyer's accounting department. To the seller, this document is a sales invoice; to the buyer, it is a purchase invoice.
- Explain why a business uses a date stamp.

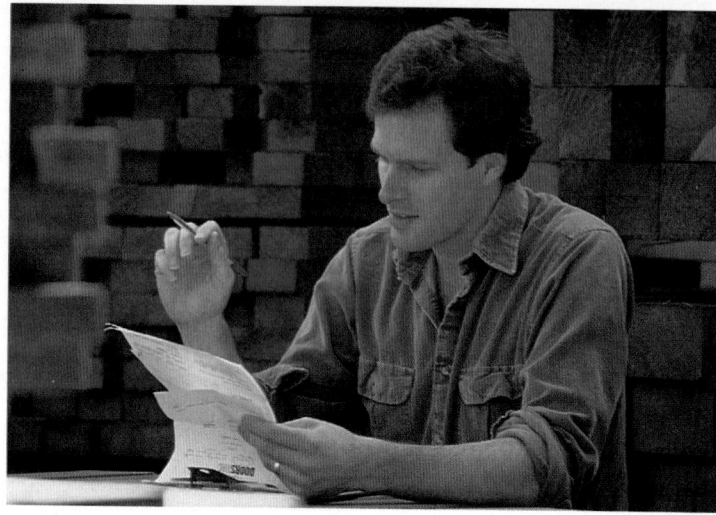

It is important to verify the packing slip to ensure that the business received the exact items and quantities ordered.

Verifying the Items Received

A supplier accepts a purchase order by shipping the items requested and billing the buyer for the items shipped. When an order is shipped to a buyer, a packing slip is included with the order. A **packing slip** is a form that lists the items included in the shipment.

When a shipment is received, it is immediately unpacked and checked against the quantities and items listed on the packing slip. If the contents of the shipment do not agree with those listed on the packing slip—in quantity or type of item—a notation about the mistake is made on the packing slip. The packing slip is then sent to the accounting department to be checked against both the purchase order and the supplier's bill. Checking a shipment of items against the packing slip and the purchase order is important to avoid costly mistakes. A buyer does not have to pay for items not ordered, not received, or received but damaged.

Processing the Supplier's Bill

When items are shipped to a buyer, the supplier prepares a bill called an invoice. An **invoice** lists the credit terms and the quantity, description, unit price, and total cost of the items shipped to the buyer. The invoice may also list the buyer's purchase order number and method of shipment.

Invoices are sent directly to the buyer's accounting department, where an accounting clerk uses a date stamp to indicate when the invoice was received. Next, the accounting clerk checks each detail on the invoice against the verified packing slip and the purchase order. This is done to make sure that Champion is billed for only the quantities and items actually ordered and received.

Once verified, the invoice becomes the source document for a journal entry. Before the invoice is recorded, however, the accounting clerk adds a

268

Making Connections

BUSINESS ETHICS

You work in the purchasing department of a large corporation and are responsible for placing orders for various items needed by the corporation. You contact one supplier and indicate that you will place most of your orders with that company if it gives you particular credit and discount terms. Is what you did ethical?

(Answers: Probably. Part of your job is to secure the items your company needs at the best possible price. The supplier is free to turn down your offer. If, however, the credit and discount terms are beyond those generally offered for large-volume discounts and if the supplier depends heavily upon your business, you may be guilty of coercion.)

processing stamp on the invoice. A **processing stamp** is just what the words indicate. It is a stamp placed on an invoice that outlines a set of steps to be followed in processing the invoice for payment. The information on the processing stamp includes: (1) the date the invoice is to be paid; (2) the discount amount, if any; (3) the amount to be paid (the net amount of the invoice less the discount); and (4) the check number. The accounting clerk completes the first three lines on the stamp at the time the invoice is received. The check number is entered later—when the check is issued.

Look at the invoice in Figure 13-3. Notice that a date has been stamped on the invoice to show when Champion received it. Notice, also, the processing stamp information.

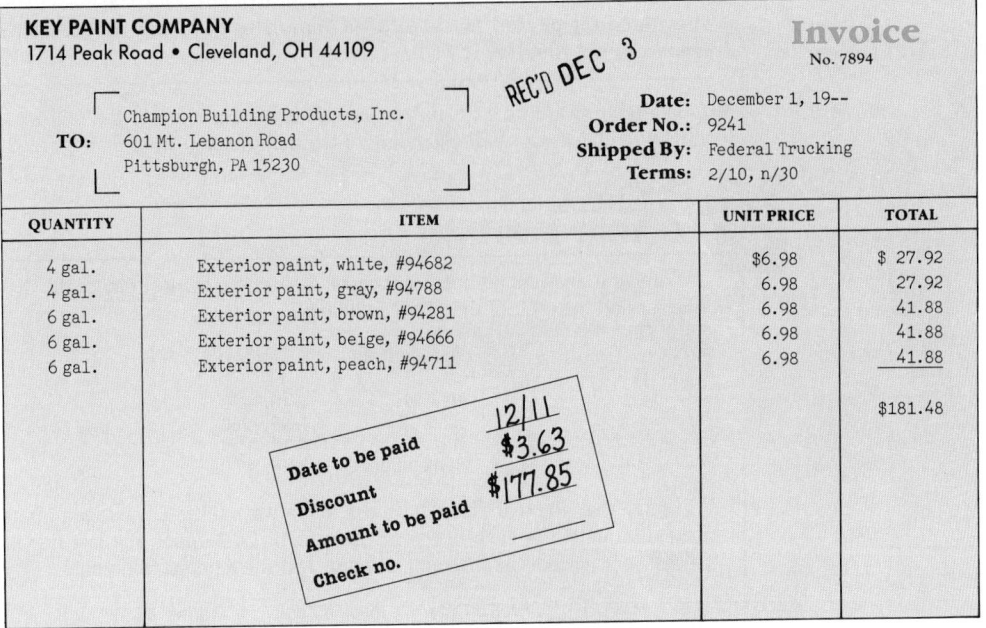

Figure 13-3 An Invoice

Purchase Discounts

Suppliers often offer credit customers a cash discount for early payment. From the buyer's point of view, this discount for early payment is a **purchase discount.** A purchase discount is calculated in the same way a sales discount was calculated in Chapter 12.

For example, Champion Building Products purchased $181.48 worth of merchandise on account from Key Paint Company. The invoice, dated December 1 and shown in Figure 13-3, lists credit terms of 2/10, n/30. If Champion pays for the merchandise within 10 days of the invoice date, it may deduct 2% from the total of the invoice. Those 10 days are referred to as the discount period. A **discount period** is the period of time within which an invoice must be paid if a discount is to be taken. If Champion does

Using Visuals
Call students' attention to the invoice in Figure 13-3. If students were keeping the accounting records for Champion Building Products, would this be a sales invoice or a purchase invoice? (Purchase invoice)

CONCEPT DEVELOPMENT
Purchases Discounts
Review the concept of buying and selling merchandise and the purpose of cash discounts. Discuss whether it is to the advantage of most businesses to take advantage of purchase discounts. For example, is it to the advantage of a business to pay a $1,000 invoice within a 10-day period and thereby save $20, or should the business conserve cash and postpone payment to the end of the 30-day period? Does $20 represent a reasonable charge for the use of $980 by the seller for a period of 20 days? For most businesses, the answer is no. The charge of $20 for 20 days is equal to a 37 percent annual interest charge. Place the following calculation on the chalkboard.

$$\$20 = \$980 \times ? \times 20/365$$

Use the formula $I = PRT$ and solve for the interest rate.

$$\frac{\$20}{\$980 \times 20/365} = .372 \text{ or } 37.2\%$$

Well-managed businesses usually pay within the discount period to avoid paying what are, in effect, very high interest charges.

Review credit terms, how discounts are calculated, how the amount to be paid is determined, and how to determine the last day in the discount period.

Critical Thinking

The accounting clerk for Richland Supplies, an auto supplies store, paid an invoice in March and then in April realized that some of the items listed on the invoice were back ordered and had never been received. Where would the accounting clerk find a record of the back-ordered items, and how could this error have been avoided?

(Answer: The back-ordered items would have been noted on the packing slip. The error could have been avoided if the accounting clerk had verified the invoice against the packing slip before approving payment of the invoice.)

ACCOUNTING PRACTICE

Students may complete Exercise 13-1 at this point.

ANSWERS

1. May 24
2. July 2
3. August 7
4. October 2
5. November 6; $70; $3,430
6. December 13; $18; $582
7. March 20; $19.04; $932.96
8. September 3; $145.10; $7,109.90

CONCEPT DEVELOPMENT

The Purchases Account

Use the problem-solving approach to establish the need for the Purchases account. The discussion should include these points: the need for a separate account, why the account decreases owner's equity, why the account is a temporary account, the normal balance side of the account, why the account is different from an expense account, and the classification of cost of merchandise.

Use a T account on the chalkboard to illustrate the rules of debit and credit for the Purchases account.

---

not pay for the merchandise within the discount period, it must pay the net, or total, amount within 30 days.

The discount amount is found by multiplying the invoice total by the discount percent. The discount amount is then subtracted from the invoice total to determine the actual amount to be paid. As you can see, by paying on or before December 11 (December 1 + 10 days), Champion can save $3.63.

Invoice Total	$181.48	Invoice Total	$181.48
Discount Percent	× .02	Discount Amount	− 3.63
Discount Amount	$ 3.63	Amount to be Paid	$177.85

R E M E M B E R

The discount period is calculated from the date the invoice was prepared, not the date it was received.

Before you learn how to analyze purchases on account, do the following activity to check your understanding of the material you have just covered.

Check Your Learning

Write your answers on notebook paper. Determine the last day of the discount period for each of the invoices below.

	Invoice Date	Terms
1.	May 14	2/10, n/30
2.	June 17	2/15, n/30
3.	July 28	1/10, n/30
4.	September 22	3/10, n/60

Assume that you work for a business that always takes advantage of purchase discounts. For each of the invoices below, determine the last day of the discount period, the discount amount, and the amount to be paid.

	Invoice Date	Invoice Total	Terms
5.	October 27	$3,500	2/10, n/30
6.	November 28	$ 600	3/15, n/30
7.	March 5	$ 952	2/15, n/30
8.	August 19	$7,255	2/15, n/30

Compare your answers to those in the answers section. Re-read the preceding part of the chapter to find the answers to any questions you missed.

The Purchases Account

Most of the purchases on account made by a merchandising business are for merchandise to be resold to customers. Since a merchandising business earns revenue by selling merchandise, it is important that the business keep a record of the cost of that merchandise. In Chapter 11, you learned that a

270

---

merchandising business uses a separate account to record the sale of merchandise. Likewise, when a merchandising business buys new goods to replace those sold to customers, it uses a separate account. The cost of new merchandise is recorded in the **Purchases account.** The balance in this account shows the cost of merchandise purchased during a fiscal period.

You learned in earlier chapters that revenue and expense accounts are temporary equity accounts. The Purchases account is also a temporary equity account. It is classified as a **cost of merchandise** account. The cost of merchandise is just what the words indicate. It is the actual cost to the business of the merchandise sold to customers.

Purchases	
Dr.	Cr.
+	–
Increase Side	Decrease Side
Balance Side	

Merchandise that is purchased for resale is a cost of doing business. Like expenses, the cost of purchases decreases owner's or stockholders' equity. The Purchases account, therefore, follows the same rules of debit and credit as expense accounts. That is, Purchases is increased by debits and decreased by credits. The normal balance of the Purchases account is a debit balance.

R E M E M B E R

The amount of merchandise bought during the period is recorded in the Purchases account. Purchases is classified as a cost of merchandise account.

The Purchases Journal

You learned earlier that when a business has similar transactions that occur often, it is easier to record those transactions in a special journal. The **purchases journal** is a special journal used to record all transactions in which items are bought on account. The purchases journal used by Champion Building Products appears in Figure 13-4. Like the sales and cash receipts journals, the purchases journal has special amount columns for recording purchases transactions that occur frequently.

Figure 13-4   The Purchases Journal

As you already know, a liability is created whenever a business purchases items on account. Regardless of what is bought, a purchase on account always requires a credit to the Accounts Payable account. The purchases journal, therefore, always includes an Accounts Payable Credit column.

The debit columns in the purchases journal are used to record two different types of purchases on account. We mentioned earlier that most of the

CHAPTER 13   Accounting for Purchases on Account   271

Chapter 13

CONCEPT DEVELOPMENT

Journalizing Purchases on Account

Review the design of the purchases journal. Remind students that the accounts listed in the Creditor's Account Credited column are accounts in the accounts payable subsidiary ledger. Point out that the column headings *Accounts Payable Credit* and *Purchases Debit* stand for those accounts in the general ledger. The account titles given in the General Account Debited column are also general ledger accounts.

Remind students that many of the journalizing concepts in this chapter are not new since they are similar to those for the sales journal and the cash receipts journal.

Teaching Tips

- Point out that the journal entry is made when the invoice (bill) is received, not when the purchase order is mailed. The invoice is the source document, not the purchase order.
- Remind students that every purchase of merchandise on account uses the same two columns: Purchases Debit and Accounts Payable Credit.

Using Visuals

 Use demonstration problem 13-1, Parts A and B, here to give students practice in analyzing purchases on account.

ACCOUNTING Notes

Each entry requires a credit to Accounts Payable; therefore, some accountants call the purchases journal the accounts payable journal.

---

purchases on account a business makes are for merchandise to be resold to customers. Since merchandise bought on account is recorded in the Purchases account, the purchases journal includes a Purchases Debit column. The total of this column is posted as a debit to the Purchases account in the general ledger at the end of each month.

The General Debit column is used to record purchases of all other items on account. Examples of items that would be recorded in the General Debit column are purchases of supplies or equipment on account. Each amount recorded in the General Debit column is posted directly to the general ledger account named in the General Account Debited column.

R E M E M B E R

Every purchase on account results in either a debit to the Purchases account (for merchandise bought on account) or a debit to a general ledger account (for all purchases other than merchandise). Accounts Payable is always credited for a purchase on account.

Journalizing Purchases on Account

After an invoice has been verified by the accounting clerk, the purchase is recorded in the purchases journal.

Recording the Purchase of Merchandise on Account

Champion's first purchase on account in December involves a purchase of merchandise on account. The source document for this transaction is the invoice in Figure 13-3 on page 269.

December 3: *Received Invoice 7894 from Key Paint Company for merchandise purchased on account, $181.48.*

Purchases	
Dr.	Cr.
+	–
$181.48	

Accounts Payable	
Dr.	Cr.
–	+
	$181.48

The accounts affected by this transaction are Purchases and Accounts Payable. The Purchases account is debited whenever any merchandise is bought for resale to customers. In this transaction, Purchases is debited for $181.48. Accounts Payable is increased since Champion now owes more money to its creditors. It is credited for $181.48.

The recording of this transaction in the purchases journal is shown in Figure 13-5. Refer to this illustration as you read these steps.

1. Enter the date in the Date column. Use the date Champion *received* the invoice, not the date the invoice was prepared.
2. Enter the number of the creditor's invoice in the Invoice No. column.
3. Enter the creditor's name in the Creditor's Account Credited column.
4. Enter the *total* of the invoice in the Accounts Payable Credit column.

Interdisciplinary Connections

FOREIGN LANGUAGE

The word *vendor*, which comes from the Latin *vendere*, "to sell," has relatives in several other languages. An Italian salesperson is a *venditore;* a Spanish one, a *vendedor.* An ele-gant saleswoman for a Paris fashion house is a *vendeuse.* Ask students what related English words they can think of (e.g., vending machine).

5. For a purchase of merchandise on account, enter the total amount of the invoice in the Purchases Debit column.

| | | | | | | | GENERAL | | |
DATE	INVOICE NO.	CREDITOR'S ACCOUNT CREDITED	POST. REF.	ACCOUNTS PAYABLE CREDIT	PURCHASES DEBIT	ACCOUNT DEBITED	POST. REF.	DEBIT	
Dec. 3	7894	Key Paint Company		1814 8	1814 8				1
1	2	3		4	5				2

PURCHASES JOURNAL — PAGE 12

Figure 13-5 Recording the Purchase of Merchandise on Account in the Purchases Journal

R E M E M B E R

The purchase of merchandise on account is recorded as a debit to Purchases and a credit to Accounts Payable.

After the invoice from Key Paint Company has been journalized, it is placed in a tickler file. A **tickler file** is a file that contains a folder for each day of the month. Invoices are placed in the folders according to their **due dates,** the dates that they must be paid. For example, an invoice due on December 11 would be placed in the folder marked "11."

R E M E M B E R

The due date is the date on which an invoice must be paid.

Journalizing Other Purchases on Account

Champion Building Products does not purchase supplies and other items on account often enough to set up special columns in the purchases journal. When such purchases do occur, they are recorded in the General Debit column of the purchases journal.

December 12: *Received Invoice 3417, dated December 10, from Center City Supply for supplies bought on account, $362.60, terms n/30.*

The accounts affected by this transaction are Supplies and Accounts Payable. The asset account Supplies is being increased, so it is debited for the amount of the purchase, $362.60. Champion now owes Center City Supply for the supplies purchased on account, so Accounts Payable is also being increased. Accounts Payable is credited for $362.60.

Supplies		Accounts Payable	
Dr.	Cr.	Dr.	Cr.
+	−	−	+
$362.60			$362.60

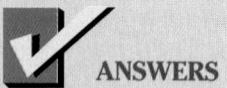
The journal entry for this transaction is shown in Figure 13-6, line 4. Refer to this illustration as you read the steps that follow:

1. Enter the date the invoice was received in the Date column.
2. Enter the invoice number in the Invoice No. column.
3. Enter the creditor's name in the Creditor's Account Credited column.
4. Enter the total of the invoice in the Accounts Payable Credit column.
5. Since there is no special amount column for supplies, write the title of the general ledger account being debited in the General Account Debited column.
6. Enter the total amount of the invoice in the General Debit column.

After journalizing the invoice, the accounting clerk places it in the tickler file. Center City Supply does not offer its credit customers a cash discount. "January 9" had, therefore, been recorded on the processing stamp on the invoice. The accounting clerk placed this invoice in the folder marked "9" to indicate the bill is to be paid on January 9.

			PURCHASES JOURNAL							PAGE 12	
	DATE	INVOICE NO.	CREDITOR'S ACCOUNT CREDITED	POST. REF.	ACCOUNTS PAYABLE CREDIT	PURCHASES DEBIT	GENERAL ACCOUNT DEBITED	POST. REF.	GENERAL DEBIT	
1	Dec. 3	7894	Key Paint Company		181 48	181 48				1
2	6	204C	Starks Lumber Co.		3495 66	3495 66				2
3	9	2419	Aluminum Plus, Inc.		7842 98	7842 98				3
4	12	3417	Center City Supply		362 60		Supplies		362 60	4
5	1	2	3		4		5		6	5

Figure 13-6 Recording the Purchase of Supplies on Account in the Purchases Journal

Before you learn how to post from the purchases journal, do the following activity to check your understanding of the material you have just studied.

Check Your Learning

Use notebook paper to write your answers to these questions.

1. In what account is the cost of merchandise purchased for resale to customers recorded?
2. Does the cost of merchandise increase or decrease owner's (stockholders') equity?
3. Increases to the Purchases account are recorded as ___?___ while decreases to the Purchases account are recorded as ___?___.
4. If merchandise is purchased on account, its cost is recorded as a debit to ___?___ and a credit to ___?___.
5. Store equipment bought on account is recorded as a debit to ___?___ and a credit to ___?___.
6. What types of purchases are recorded in the General Debit column of the purchases journal?

Compare your answers to those in the answers section. Re-read the preceding part of the chapter to find the answers to any questions you missed.

Businesses that make many purchases on account may prepare weekly, or even daily, printouts of the invoices that must be paid.

The Accounts Payable Subsidiary Ledger

In Chapters 11 and 12, you learned that when a business has many charge customers it is more efficient to set up a subsidiary ledger for those customers. Likewise, when a business has many creditors, it is more efficient to set up a subsidiary ledger for those creditors. The **accounts payable subsidiary ledger** is a ledger that contains accounts for all creditors and the amount that is owed to each. The individual creditors' accounts in the accounts payable subsidiary ledger are summarized in the general ledger controlling account Accounts Payable. The balance of the Accounts Payable controlling account and the total of all the account balances in the accounts payable subsidiary ledger must agree after all posting has been completed.

In a manual accounting system, creditors' accounts in the accounts payable subsidiary ledger do not have account numbers. Instead, the accounts are arranged in alphabetical order. In a computerized accounting system, each creditor is assigned an account number.

The ledger account form used for the accounts payable subsidiary ledger is the same form that is used for the accounts receivable subsidiary ledger. An accounts payable subsidiary ledger account is shown in Figure 13-7 on page 276. As you can see, the subsidiary ledger account form has lines at the top for the creditor's name and address.

In the accounts payable subsidiary ledger, the Debit column of the ledger account form is used to record decreases to the creditor's account. Any payments on account are recorded in the Debit column. The Credit column is used to record increases to the creditor's account. All purchases on account are recorded in the Credit column. The Balance column is used to record the total, up-to-date amount that is owed to the creditor. Since Accounts Payable is a liability account, suppliers' accounts in the accounts payable subsidiary ledger will normally have credit balances.

CHAPTER 13   Accounting for Purchases on Account   **275**

Making Connections

COMMUNICATIONS

Verbal as well as mathematical *accuracy* is essential in business. For example, in preparing purchase orders, packing slips, and invoices, it is important that descriptions of goods or services are stated clearly and that stock numbers and prices agree with the catalog or information sheet.

CONCEPT DEVELOPMENT

Posting from the Purchases Journal

Posting from the purchases journal is similar to posting from the other special journals. Remind students that they must post to two ledgers from the purchases journal: (1) to the accounts payable subsidiary ledger, and (2) to the general ledger.

Using Visuals

Use demonstration problem 13-3 here to give students practice in posting from the purchases journal to the accounts payable subsidiary ledger accounts.

Using Visuals

Walk students through each step of the posting procedure shown in Figure 13-7.

ACCOUNTING PRACTICE
Students may complete Exercise 13-3 at this point.

Posting from the Purchases Journal

After a transaction has been journalized, it must be posted. All the transactions in the purchases journal must be posted to the creditors' accounts in the accounts payable subsidiary ledger. In addition, the purchases of items other than merchandise must be posted to the appropriate general ledger accounts.

Posting to the Accounts Payable Subsidiary Ledger

Each transaction in the purchases journal is a purchase on account that must be posted to the accounts payable subsidiary ledger. The entry is posted as a credit to the account listed in the Creditor's Account Credited column. Transactions are posted daily to the accounts payable subsidiary ledger.

The first entry that must be posted involves the Key Paint Company account. Refer to Figure 13-7 as you read the steps that follow:

1. In the Date column of the subsidiary ledger account, enter the date of the transaction.
2. In the Posting Reference column, record the letter of the journal and the page number on which the transaction was recorded. "P" is the letter used for the purchases journal.
3. In the Credit column, enter the amount of the purchase as recorded in the Accounts Payable Credit column.
4. Compute the new balance. To do this, add the amount in the Credit column to the previous balance amount. Enter the new balance in the Balance column.
5. Return to the purchases journal and place a check mark (✔) in the *first* Posting Reference column (following the Creditor's Account Credited column).

Prev. Bal.	$1,835.12
Credit	+ 181.48
New Bal.	$2,016.60

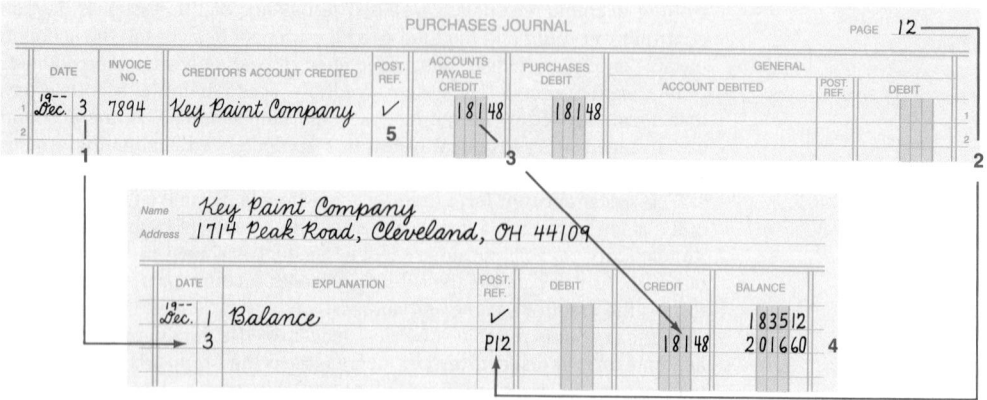

Figure 13-7 Posting from the Purchases Journal to the Accounts Payable Subsidiary Ledger

The first entry in the purchases journal has now been posted to the accounts payable subsidiary ledger. Follow the steps above whenever you post a purchase on account to the accounts payable subsidiary ledger.

Creditor accounts in the accounts payable subsidiary ledger normally have credit balances.

Posting from the General Debit Column

During the month, the accounting clerk also posts the transactions recorded in the General Debit column of the purchases journal. The transactions in this column are posted to the general ledger accounts named in the General Account Debited column. The first transaction to be posted involves the Supplies account.

The posting of this transaction is shown in Figure 13-8. Refer to Figure 13-8 as you read the steps that follow:

1. In the Date column of the general ledger account, enter the date of the transaction.
2. In the Posting Reference column, record the journal and page number of the transaction. Be sure to use the letter "P."

Prev. Bal.	$5,074.40
Debit	+ 362.60
New Bal.	$5,437.00

3. In the Debit column of the ledger account, enter the amount recorded in the General Debit column.
4. Compute and record the new balance in the Debit Balance column.
5. Return to the purchases journal and place the general ledger account number in the General Posting Reference column (following the General Account Debited column).

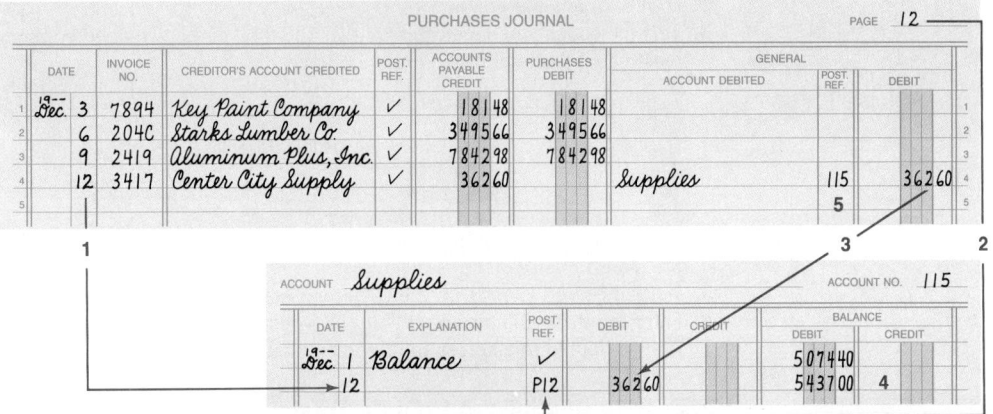

Figure 13-8 Posting from the Purchases Journal to the General Ledger

Completing the Purchases Journal

As you recall, a special journal eliminates the many postings to certain accounts by setting up special amount columns to represent those accounts. At the end of the month, the totals of these special columns are posted to the appropriate accounts in the general ledger. In the purchases journal, column totals are posted to the Accounts Payable and Purchases accounts.

CHAPTER 13   Accounting for Purchases on Account   277

Making Connections

AROUND THE WORLD

What happens to state-owned businesses when the government goes out of business? When the two Germanies were reunited and the state-controlled economy of the former East Germany ceased to exist, its businesses were auctioned to interested buyers from around the world. Buyers were required by the German government to guarantee jobs for current employees of the business. An estimated 13,000 businesses were sold.

Totaling, Proving, and Ruling the Purchases Journal

At the end of the month, the accounting clerk totals the purchases journal. The steps followed are the same as those for totaling the sales and the cash receipts journals. Refer to the purchases journal in Figure 13-9 as you read the steps that follow.

	DATE	INVOICE NO.	CREDITOR'S ACCOUNT CREDITED	POST. REF.	ACCOUNTS PAYABLE CREDIT	PURCHASES DEBIT	GENERAL — ACCOUNT DEBITED	POST. REF.	DEBIT	
1	Dec. 3	7894	Key Paint Company	✓	181 48	181 48				1
2	6	204C	Starks Lumber Co.	✓	3495 66	3495 66				2
3	9	2419	Aluminum Plus, Inc.	✓	7842 98	7842 98				3
4	12	3417	Center City Supply	✓	362 60		Supplies	115	362 60	4
5	15	11162	Viking Motors	✓	1200 00		Delivery Equipment	150	1200 00	5
6	22	295C	Starks Lumber Co.	✓	1008 36	1008 36				6
7	24	4681	Wilson Electric, Inc.	✓	5680 04	5680 04				7
8	28	11193	Viking Motors	✓	125 95		Store Equipment	155	125 95	8
9	29	2498	Aluminum Plus, Inc.	✓	3600 00	3600 00				9
10	31	349	Custom Doors, Inc.	✓	640 00	640 00	1 →			2
11	31		Totals		24 137 07	22 448 52			1 688 55	11
12	4		5				7 →		168855	6

PURCHASES JOURNAL   PAGE 12

Figure 13-9   The Completed Purchases Journal

1. Draw a single rule under the three amount columns: Accounts Payable Credit, Purchases Debit, and General Debit.
2. Foot each amount column.
3. Test the equality of debits and credits. The total of the two debit columns must equal the total of the credit column.

Debit Columns		Credit Column	
Purchases	$22,448.52	Accounts Payable	$24,137.07
General	1,688.55		
	$24,137.07		$24,137.07

4. In the Date column, on the line below the single rule, enter the last day of the month.
5. Write the word "Totals" in the Creditor's Account Credited column.
6. Enter the three column totals—in ink—just below the footings.
7. Draw a double rule across the three amount columns.

Posting the Special Column Totals of the Purchases Journal

After the purchases journal has been totaled and ruled, the accounting clerk posts the totals of the Accounts Payable Credit column and the Purchases Debit column to the general ledger accounts. The new account balances for each account are calculated an entered in the appropriate Balance column. The posting of these column totals is shown in Figure 13-10 on page 279.

After posting each column total, the accounting clerk places the account number to which the amount was posted, in parentheses, just below the double rule in the column. The total of the General Debit column is not posted because the individual amounts were posted during the month.

278

A check mark (✔), therefore, is placed in parentheses below the double rule in the General Debit column.

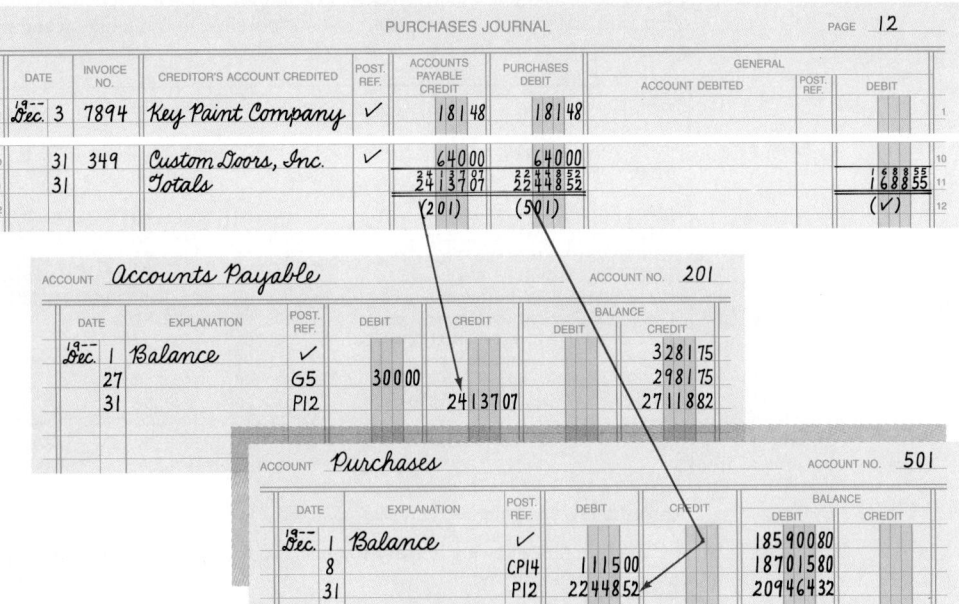

Figure 13-10   Posting Column Totals from the Purchases Journal to the General Ledger

Handling Purchases on Account in a Computerized Accounting System

You have just learned the manual method for recording entries for purchases on account, posting to subsidiary ledgers, and proving the totals of the purchases journal. A computerized system processes purchases on account in a manner similar to a manual system.

In a computerized accounting system, a number of purchase transactions are often grouped for processing. The transactions may be grouped daily, weekly, or biweekly. Each group of invoices is known as a *batch.* Each batch of transactions is assigned a *batch number.* Batch numbers are assigned in consecutive order. For example, Batch 121 might be assigned to the group of transactions for the first working week in December and Batch 122 for the second working week.

In a computerized system, each creditor has its own account number. The account number assigned to a business from which goods and services are bought on account is called a *vendor number.*

The batch number and the vendor number—as well as the account numbers for the accounts being debited and credited—are recorded on the processing stamp on each invoice. The information on the processing stamp is then entered into the computer through a keyboard terminal or perhaps an optical scanner. The computer prints a summary of the batched transactions. This summary, which looks much like the purchases journal, is shown

CHAPTER 13   Accounting for Purchases on Account   **279**

COMPUTERS IN ACCOUNTING

Electronic data interchange (EDI) systems provide a means for creating and transmitting purchase orders electronically. The orders are automatically logged in the records of both the buyer and the seller. Among the benefits are improved service and fast arrival of merchandise. With EDI, there is no question about when the purchase order was received and when the invoice was sent.

ANSWERS

1. December 15, 19—
2. Sung International Imports
3. Accounts Payable Credit; Purchases Debit
4. Accounts payable
5. Check mark
6. Accounts Payable Credit; Purchases Debit; general ledger accounts
7. Account number

in Figure 13-11. The summary is compared with batch proof information to determine if the accounting data was entered accurately. The computer calculates daily account balances and prints out any reports needed. All this is done with speed and accuracy that are not possible in a manual accounting system.

		PURCHASES	JOURNAL			PAGE	12
DATE	INV. NO.	CREDITOR'S ACCOUNT CREDITED	ACCTS. PAY. CREDIT	PURCHASES DEBIT	G.L. ACT#	G.L. DEBIT	
12/03	7894	Key Paint Co.	181.48	181.48			
12/06	204c	Starks Lumber Co.	3495.66	3495.66			
12/09	2419	Aluminum Plus, Inc.	7842.98	7842.98			
12/12	3417	Center City Supply	362.60		115	362.60	
12/15	11162	Viking Motors	1200.00		150	1200.00	
12/22	295c	Starks Lumber Co.	1008.36	1008.36			
12/24	4681	Wilson Electric, Inc.	5680.04	5680.04			
12/28	11193	Viking Motors	125.95		155	125.95	
12/29	2498	Aluminum Plus, Inc.	3600.00	3600.00			
12/31	349	Custom Doors, Inc.	640.00	640.00			
		TOTALS	24137.07	22448.52		1688.55	

Figure 13-11 Computerized Purchases Journal

Complete the following activity to check your understanding of the material you've just covered.

Check Your Learning

Use notebook paper to write your answers to these questions about this transaction.

On December 15, the Johnston Company received Invoice 29761, dated December 12, from Sung International Imports for merchandise bought on account for $600, terms 2/10, n/30.

1. The date of the entry in the purchases journal to record this transaction is ___?___ .
2. The creditor's account credited in the purchases journal is ___?___ .
3. The amount of this transaction, $600, is entered in the ___?___ column and the ___?___ column of the purchases journal.
4. This transaction is posted to the ___?___ subsidiary ledger.
5. After this transaction has been posted to the creditor's account, a ___?___ is placed in Post. Ref. column of the purchases journal.
6. At the end of the month, the totals of the ___?___ column and the ___?___ column are posted to the ___?___ .
7. To indicate that a special column total has been posted, the ___?___ is written in parentheses under each column total.

Compare your answers to those in the answers section. Re-read the preceding part of the chapter to find the correct answers to any questions you may have missed.

Reteaching Strategies

Remind students that they have already learned about subsidiary ledgers and controlling accounts. Ask them to compare the accounts payable subsidiary ledger to the accounts receivable subsidiary ledger. How are they similar? How are they different?

(Answers: The forms for the two ledgers are the same. The accounts payable sub-sidiary ledger is used to record amounts owed by the business, and the normal account balance is a credit. The accounts receivable subsidiary ledger is used to record amounts owed to the business by its customers, and the normal account balance is a debit.)

Summary of Key Points

1. Four documents involved in a purchase on account are: purchase requisition, purchase order, packing slip, and invoice. The purchase requisition is a request to order goods; the purchase order is an offer to buy goods; and the packing slip is a list of the goods shipped. An invoice lists the quantity, description, unit price, and total cost of the items shipped to the buyer. It must be checked against the purchase order and the packing slip before the purchase may be recorded.

2. When an invoice is received by the accounting department, a processing stamp is placed on the invoice. The information on the processing stamp includes: (a) the date the invoice is to be paid; (b) the discount amount, if any; (c) the amount to be paid (the total of the invoice less any discount); and (d) the check number.

3. Some suppliers offer a cash discount to their credit customers for early payment. Buyers refer to this discount as a purchase discount.

4. The Purchases account is used by merchandising businesses to record the cost of merchandise purchased during the fiscal period. Purchases is classified as a cost of merchandise account. The rules of debit and credit for Purchases are the same as those for expense accounts.

5. The purchases journal is a special journal used to record all purchases on account made by a merchandising business. The source document for a purchases journal entry is an invoice.

6. The purchases journal contains special amount columns for credits to Accounts Payable and debits to Purchases. Debit amounts that cannot be entered in a special column are entered in the General Debit column.

7. Journalized invoices are filed according to their due dates in a tickler file. A tickler file contains a folder for each day of the month.

8. The accounts payable subsidiary ledger contains an account for each creditor. The total of the account balances in the accounts payable subsidiary ledger must match the balance of the Accounts Payable controlling account in the general ledger.

9. Transactions are posted from the purchases journal to the accounts payable subsidiary ledger daily. Transactions entered in the General Debit column are posted periodically during the month.

10. The totals of the special amount columns in the purchases journal are posted to the general ledger at the end of each month.

CHAPTER SUMMARY

This summary enumerates the key information in the chapter. It is a useful tool for reinforcement and review.

Review and Applications

PRACTICE AND APPLY

- Language Development
- Comprehension and Retention
- Basic Skills

Building Your Accounting Vocabulary

See the Glossary on pages 670-679 for definitions of these terms.

Reviewing Your Accounting Knowledge

1. To verify that the company is being billed only for the quantities and items actually ordered and received.

2. (a) The date the invoice is to be paid; (b) the discount amount, if any; (c) the amount to be paid, or the net amount of the invoice less the discount; and (d) the check number.

3. To encourage them to pay early.

4. The Purchases account.

5. The Accounts Payable Credit column and the Purchases Debit column.

6. Accounts Payable is always credited when items are bought on account.

7. The debit amount is recorded in the General Debit column.

8. Invoices are filed in a tickler file according to their due dates.

9. Credit balances; accounts in a subsidiary ledger normally will have the same balance as the controlling account. Accounts Payable has a normal credit balance; thus accounts in the accounts payable subsidiary ledger also have credit balances.

10. Transactions involving customers' accounts and purchases of items other than merchandise.

11. The total of the General Debit column in the purchases journal is not posted because the transactions in the General Debit column are posted during the month.

Building Your Accounting Vocabulary

In your own words, write the definition of each of the following accounting terms. Use complete sentences for your definitions.

accounts payable	invoice	purchase requisition
subsidiary ledger	packing slip	Purchases account
cost of merchandise	processing stamp	purchases journal
discount period	purchase discount	tickler file
due date	purchase order	

Reviewing Your Accounting Knowledge

1. Why is an invoice checked against both the purchase order and the packing slip?
2. What information is included on a processing stamp?
3. Why would a supplier give a cash discount to its credit customers?
4. Which account is used only to record the cost of merchandise bought for resale?
5. What are the two special amount columns in a purchases journal?
6. Which account is always credited when items are bought on account?
7. When a store buys on account shelves for displaying merchandise, in which column of the purchases journal is the debit amount of the transaction recorded?
8. How are invoices filed in a tickler file?
9. Do accounts in the accounts payable subsidiary ledger have normal debit balances or credit balances? Why?
10. What two types of postings from the purchases journal are completed during the month?
11. Why is the total of the General Debit column in the purchases journal not posted?

Improving Your Human Relations Skills

Two weeks ago you took a part-time job as an accounting clerk at the Brandeis Company. Bryan Thomas is a co-worker who sits at the desk next to yours. One day at the afternoon break, Bryan told you that your co-workers were concerned with your work habits. He said that all the other employees took an extra five minutes at break time. And, no one in the office worries about completing work on time. If the work is not finished on time, it can be finished later and overtime will be paid. Bryan suggested that you conform to the work habits of your co-workers.

1. What do you think about Bryan's suggestion?
2. What would you say to Bryan about his suggestion?

282

Improving Your Human Relations Skills

Students' answers will vary but could include the following ideas.

1. This question deals with productivity and the work ethic. Bryan's suggestion indicates inappropriate office behavior. Discuss what employers expect from their employees ("a fair day's work for a fair day's pay"). Unproductive workers are a drain on the resources and profits of the company and are usually the first to lose their jobs. Productive workers are usually the first to be considered for promotion.

2. Bryan's comments are an example of negative peer pressure. Discuss ways of dealing with peer pressure. Ideally, students will learn, for their own well-being, to stand up for their beliefs. Students may suggest that nothing be said to Bryan, so as not to offend or "show up" their co-workers. Students may also suggest telling Bryan that they would not change their work habits.

Applying Accounting Procedures

Exercise 13-1 Determining Due Dates and Discount Amounts

Jason's Appliance Center frequently purchases merchandise on account. When invoices are received, a processing stamp is placed on the invoice indicating the due date, the amount of any discount, and the amount to be paid. The following invoices were received during August.

	Invoice Number	Invoice Date	Credit Terms	Amount of Invoice
1.	24574	August 5	2/10, n/30	$3,000.00
2.	530992	August 7	3/10, n/30	5,550.00
3.	211145	August 12	2/15, n/60	729.95
4.	45679	August 16	n/45	345.67
5.	34120	August 23	2/10, n/30	1,526.50
6.	00985	August 27	n/30	700.00

Instructions: Use a form similar to the one that follows. The first invoice has been completed as an example. For each invoice,
(1) Determine the due date. Assume that Jason's always pays invoices within the discount period.
(2) Compute the discount amount, if any.
(3) Compute the amount that is to be paid.

Invoice Number	Invoice Date	Credit Terms	Invoice Amount	Due Date	Discount Amount	Amount to be Paid
24574	Aug. 5	2/10, n/30	$3,000.00	Aug. 15	$60.00	$2,940.00

Exercise 13-2 Analyzing Purchases on Account

Listed below are several transactions of the South Shore Home Improvement Center.

Instructions:
(1) Open T accounts and record the April 1 balances for the following accounts: Office Supplies, $157.30; Store Equipment, $21,945.00; Accounts Payable, $1,354.50; and Purchases, $31,416.45.
(2) Record each of the following transactions in the T accounts.
(3) Determine the ending balance for each account.

Transactions:
Apr. 4 Purchased 13 boxes of wallpapering kits on account from the Enloe Corp., $700.00, Invoice 1248.
      7 Purchased a new cash register on account from Honeycutt Office Equipment, Invoice 384 for $1,200.00.
     12 Received Invoice 891 from Lopez Stationers for copy machine paper bought on account, $200.00.
     15 Bought 15 cartons of paint in assorted colors on account from Day Glow, Inc., for $3,400.00, Invoice 2847.
     30 Received a bill from W & R Company for typewriter ribbons and erasing tapes purchased on account for $250.00, Invoice 8469.

283

Chapter 13

PRACTICE AND APPLY
• Concepts and Procedures

Exercise 13-1: Ch. Obj. 1

Exercise 13-2: Ch. Obj. 1, 2
Balances:
Office Supplies, $607.30
Store Equip., $23,145.00
Accts. Pay., $7,104.50
Purchases, $35,516.45

Additional Reinforcement

Students who need additional practice or individualized help will benefit from the *Glencoe Accounting Electronic Study Guide* or the *Glencoe Accounting* on-line multimedia program, which provide reinforcement and reteaching for vocabulary, concepts, and procedures.

Refer students to the Chapter 13 review pages in the workbook, *Chapter Reviews and Working Papers.*

Exercise 13-3: Ch. Obj. 1

5
2
4
7
1
6
8
3

Problem 13-1: Ch. Obj. 3

Column totals:
Accounts Pay., $7,919.26
Purchases, $6,026.88
General, $1,892.38

Problem 13-2: Ch. Obj. 4

Accounts Payable total, $7,919.26

**Exercise 13-3   Understanding the Steps
in the Purchasing Process**

Listed below are the steps that Martinez Bicycles follows when it purchases items on account. The steps, however, are not listed in the order they occur.

Instructions: Use the form provided in the working papers. Place a number from 1 to 8 on the line to the left of each step to indicate when that step would be completed.

- Record information on processing stamp.
- Prepare purchase order.
- Receive and verify invoice.
- Place invoice in tickler file.
- Prepare purchase requisition.
- Record invoice in purchases journal.
- Post transaction to accounts payable subsidiary ledger.
- Receive order and verify packing slip.

Problem 13-1   Journalizing Purchases on Account

The Swan Music Center uses a purchases journal to record its purchases on account.

Instructions: Record the following transactions on page 4 of a purchases journal.

Transactions:

Jan. 3 Purchased merchandise on account from the Brass Corp. for $577.50, Invoice 2312.

5 Received Invoice 78934 from Hankins Sheet Music for merchandise bought on account, $478.98.

8 Bought $124.50 worth of supplies on account from Rosemont Office Supplies, Invoice 9876.

12 Purchased merchandise on account from Weber Drums, Invoice 777 for $390.65.

18 Anderson Equipment sent Invoice 44456 for $1,567.88 for office equipment purchased on account.

24 Bought on account from Parsons, Inc., merchandise costing $900.00, Invoice 6743.

26 Received an invoice for merchandise bought on account from Brass Corp., $789.25, Invoice 2468.

29 Received Invoice 9888 from Rosemont Office Supplies for supplies bought on account, $200.00.

31 Bought merchandise on account, $2,890.50, from Weber Drums, Invoice 804.

Problem 13-2   Posting from the Purchases Journal

Use the purchases journal prepared in Problem 13-1 to complete this problem. The opened general ledger accounts and the accounts payable subsidiary ledger appear in the working papers accompanying this textbook.

Instructions:

(1) Post amounts from the Accounts Payable Credit column to the creditors' accounts in the accounts payable subsidiary ledger.

284

Teacher Notes

---

(2) Post the transactions in the General Debit column to the general ledger accounts.

(3) Foot, prove, total, and rule the purchases journal.

(4) Post the totals of the special columns to the general ledger accounts.

Problem 13-3   Journalizing and Posting Purchases on Account

Frank's Book Nook uses a purchases journal to record its purchases on account. The opened accounts for the general ledger and the accounts payable subsidiary ledger appear in the working papers.

Instructions:

(1) Record the following transactions on page 8 of the purchases journal. The first few transactions in November were recorded on journal page 7.

(2) Post the transactions from the purchases journal to the accounts payable subsidiary ledger.

(3) Post the amounts in the General Debit column to the general ledger.

(4) Foot, prove, total, and rule the purchases journal.

(5) Post the totals of the special columns to the general ledger.

Transactions:

Nov. 6 Purchased merchandise on account from Redstone Publishers, $1,458.00, Invoice 2020.

8 Bought supplies on account from Central Supply for $420.24, Invoice 8091.

9 Received Invoice 3987 for merchandise purchased on account from All South Circulation Co., $240.80.

10 Bought $295.20 worth of merchandise on account from Redstone Publishers, Invoice 2093.

12 Wakefield, Inc., sent Invoice 7428 for merchandise purchased on account, $250.30.

19 Purchased on account from Lake Equipment display shelves for the store, $2,946.80, Invoice 6311.

24 Received an invoice for merchandise bought on account from Longview Publications, $1,700.00, Invoice 9009.

27 Purchased $2,900.50 worth of merchandise on account from Wakefield, Inc., Invoice 7583.

30 Received Invoice 8173 for $250.00 for supplies purchased on account from Central Supply.

COMPUTER

PROBLEM

Problem 13-4   Recording and Posting Purchases Transactions

On August 1, Modern Furniture, Inc., a retail merchandising business, had the following balances in the accounts payable subsidiary ledger and in the general ledger.

General Ledger (Partial)

Account Number		Account Balance
120	Office Supplies	$ 845.25
140	Office Furniture	2,013.95
145	Office Equipment	1,369.45
150	Store Equipment	3,496.00
155	Delivery Equipment	0.00
201	Accounts Payable	5,099.70
501	Purchases	146,592.75

285

Problem 13-3: Ch. Obj. 3, 4

Column totals:
Accounts Pay., $11,187.84
Purchases, $7,570.80
General, $3,617.04

Problem 13-4: Ch. Obj. 3, 4

COMPUTER

PROBLEM

This computer image identifies a problem that students may complete using the *Glencoe Accounting, General Ledger* **software.**

Accounts Payable Subsidiary Ledger

Account Number		Account Balance
910	Davis Business Center, 1066 Morris Blvd., St. Louis, MO 63104	$ 214.90
920	Eaves Office Products, 4277 Memorial Dr., Decatur, GA 30032	0.00
927	Forey, Inc., 90 South 9th St., Minneapolis, MN 55402	1,675.00
935	Hillman Brothers, Inc., 500 Texas Ave., Dallas, TX 75245	2,495.00
941	Jackson & Sons, Inc., 200 E. Broad St., Richmond, VA 23219	0.00
960	R & S Copiers, 700 Market St., St. Louis, MO 63101	714.80
980	Tom's Auto City, 5000 Delmar Blvd., St. Louis, MO 63112	0.00

Instructions:

(1) Open the general ledger accounts and record the August 1 balances.

(2) Open the accounts in the accounts payable subsidiary ledger and record the August 1 balances.

(3) Record the following transactions on purchases journal page 14.

(4) Post daily to the accounts payable subsidiary ledger and the general ledger.

(5) Total, prove, and rule the purchases journal.

(6) Post the totals of the special amount columns.

Transactions:

Aug. 1 Bought office equipment on account from Davis Business Center, $85.00, Invoice 804.

3 Jackson & Sons sent Invoice 2808 for $2,000.00 for merchandise purchased on account.

6 Received Invoice 1236 for office supplies purchased on account from Eaves Office Products, $600.00.

8 Bought on account from Hillman Brothers, Inc., merchandise costing $2,825.64, Invoice 3727.

10 Purchased a new delivery van on account from Tom's Auto City, Invoice 944 for $5,400.00.

16 Bought merchandise on account from Jackson & Sons, $540.00, Invoice 2847.

20 Received Invoice 1253 for $400.00 from Eaves Office Products for a new chair for the office.

25 Received from Jackson & Sons Invoice 2944 for $9,000.00 for merchandise purchased on account.

27 Purchased merchandise from Hillman Brothers, Inc., on account, $3,460.00, Invoice 3844.

29 Bought merchandise on account from Forey, Inc., Invoice 2074, $2,200.00.

30 Received Invoice 2999 from R & S Copiers for a copy machine bought on account for $780.00.

31 Purchased file folders on account for $84.00 from Eaves Office Products, Invoice 1301.

286

CHALLENGE

PROBLEM

Problem 13-5 Analyzing Errors in the Purchases Journal

The purchases journal for the month of May for Home Hardware Center appears in the working papers. After all amounts, including the column totals, had been posted, an error was discovered: On May 29, Home Hardware purchased a new keyboard for the office computer from the Arnold Company, Invoice 1468.

Instructions: Answer the following questions regarding this error.

(1) What is the error?
(2) Which account *should* have been debited?
(3) Why did the totals of the debit columns and the credit column still prove equal?
(4) Will the balance in the accounts payable subsidiary ledger agree with the balance in the controlling account in the general ledger? Why or why not?
(5) What would the column totals have been if the entry had been made correctly?
(6) How would you correct this error?

Chapter 13

Problem 13-5: Ch. Obj. 3, 4

CHALLENGE

PROBLEM

The last problem in each chapter is a challenge problem and is identified by this "maze" symbol.

4 ASSESS

A chapter test is available for use in assessing students' understanding of concepts in this chapter.

The testmaker software will enable you to develop tailor-made chapter, unit, semester, and final tests.

Alternative Assessment

For alternative assessment strategies, refer to *Tech Prep Strategies in Accounting*.

287

Use Chapter Test 13 here to assess students' understanding and retention of the concepts and procedures presented in the chapter.

FOCUS ON
COMPUTERS

Ask students to think of typical business activities that could be completed on a computer. Make a list on the chalkboard as they describe the activities. In addition to financial record keeping, examples might include correspondence, inventory, customer database, supplier database, product design, graphic presentations for financial reports, and so on.

QUESTIONS

1. What questions need to be answered before shopping for a computer?
2. Name several popular commercial accounting software programs.

ANSWERS

1. How will I use a computer? How much money am I willing to spend? How will I educate myself about what the computer can do? What software is available? Where should I shop for a computer? What options do I need? What kind of support will I get after I buy? What kind of warranty exists for the computer?
2. Several commercial accounting programs are available, including DacEasy, Peachtree Complete, ACCPAC Simply Accounting, and Quicken.

*H*ardware and Software: Buying Smart

Let's pretend. You own a small, home-based, start-up business in custom designing and silk-screening T-shirts. It's called "Ts for You." In the past six months, you've sold 2,000 shirts. All this just by running two ads in the local newspaper and by talking to friends.

A week ago, you decided to mail a letter to some local businesses. Since then the phone has been ringing off the hook. And there are labels to type, inventory to track, customer lists to develop, supplies to order.

Time to automate! How do you start?

The Computer and Accessories. Choosing and buying a computer is an important decision. You need to take time to do your homework and make intelligent choices.
• Go to the library and check the consumer reports.
• Seek out users who have needs similar to yours. Find out what equipment they have and how satisfied they are.
• Go to a reputable computer store. Ask a *lot* of questions. Try out the equipment. Find out about servicing.
• Shop for a good price.
• Don't be ambitious, but also don't underestimate your growing needs.
• If you decide to upgrade in the future, how easy will it be with the equipment you've chosen?

The Software. No matter what your needs are, there's probably a software package that will fit those needs.
• Make a list of the tasks you want to accomplish. Do you need a special-purpose program or an integrated one?
• Check software directories, magazines, and software databases at your library for reviews and information.
• Read the sales literature and ask your computer

Determine your computer needs first. Then consider such factors as memory, software, and price.

store or distributor for demonstrations. Is it easy to use?
• Check the age of the product. Has it been updated? How recently?
• Again, shop for a good price.

Not everyone needs a computer, just as not everyone needs a car. More and more, however, computers are becoming an essential part of business life. As with other products, it is important to buy the right product for the job.

288

Chapter

ACCOUNTING FOR CASH PAYMENTS

Y ou have now learned how to use the sales, cash receipts, and purchases journals to record business transactions. You have also learned how two subsidiary ledgers—the accounts receivable and accounts payable subsidiary ledgers—make an accounting system more efficient.

In this chapter, you will learn about a fourth special journal: the cash payments journal. Many business transactions involve the payment of cash. Creditors' invoices must be paid, expenses such as rent and utilities must be met, and various types of assets must be purchased. As a business's cash payments increase, a special journal for recording those payments becomes necessary.

You'll also learn how to determine whether the balance of the Cash in Bank account agrees with the business's checkbook records.

Learning Objectives

When you have completed Chapter 14, you should be able to do the following:

1. Journalize various cash payments in a cash payments journal.
2. Post from the cash payments journal to the accounts payable subsidiary ledger and the general ledger.
3. Total, prove, and rule the cash payments journal.
4. Post special amount column totals to the general ledger.
5. Prepare a schedule of accounts payable.
6. Prove cash.
7. Define the accounting terms introduced in this chapter.

New Terms

premium
FOB destination
FOB shipping point
bank card fee
cash payments journal
schedule of accounts payable
proving cash

289

1 FOCUS

MAJOR CONCEPTS

- The Management and Control of Cash
- Kinds of Cash Payments
- The Cash Payments Journal
- Journalizing Cash Payments
- Posting from the Cash Payments Journal
- Completing the Cash Payments Journal
- Proving the Accounts Payable Subsidiary Ledger
- Proving Cash

BUSINESS CONNECTION

It's back to the basics for the *Charlotte Observer*—basic accounting principles, that is. The North Carolina newspaper acknowledges that failure to observe basic accounting principles made an alleged embezzlement of $2 million possible. It is suspected that a veteran *Observer* employee conspired with two local businesses to generate false bills for supplies never received by the newspaper. Rolfe Neill, publisher of the *Observer*, acknowledges that valuable lessons were learned about basic accounting principles and inventory control.

2 TEACH

CONCEPT DEVELOPMENT
The Management and Control of Cash

Emphasize that (1) all cash payments must be authorized and supported by a source document, which also emphasizes the importance of source documents and systems for routing them; (2) all checks should be prenumbered and should be signed only after the amount and the payee have been entered on the check; and (3) all voided checks must be accounted for.

The Management and Control of Cash

If cash is the lifeblood of a business, the accounting department is its heart. All cash entering or leaving a business must at some time be pumped through the accounting department. If it is not, cash loss occurs. Earlier chapters have discussed various ways to guard against cash loss, particularly the use of a bank account in which to deposit all cash receipts.

Cash receipts, however, account for only half of the cash system. Procedures must also be set up and followed for managing cash payments. All cash payments should be authorized. Each authorization should be supported by an approved source document, such as an invoice. All payments should be made by prenumbered check. Checks should be signed only by an authorized person. Finally, every spoiled check should be accounted for, marked "Void," and filed in sequence.

Kinds of Cash Payments

A business makes many different cash payments every month. Merchandising businesses, for example, routinely pay out cash for the purchase of supplies, equipment, and merchandise. In addition, payments are made for expenses and to creditors.

At Champion Building Products, all cash payments are made by check. When a cash payment is to be made, the details are first recorded on the check stub. (The check stub becomes the source document for the journal entry to record the cash payment.) A check is then prepared and signed by an authorized person.

Cash Purchases

In Chapter 13, you learned that a business often buys merchandise, supplies, and equipment on account. Sometimes these items, particularly supplies, are bought with cash instead of on credit.

Insurance protection is also purchased for cash. Like families, businesses buy insurance to protect themselves against losses from theft, fire, or flood. Insurance policies can be bought for varying lengths of time, such as six months or one year. The amount paid for insurance is called the **premium.** A premium is paid in advance at the beginning of the insurance period. The asset account used to record the premium is called Prepaid Insurance. Prepaid Insurance is an asset account because insurance protection represents a benefit to a company if an insured loss occurs.

Cash Payments of Expenses

In accounting, expenses are the costs of goods or services used to operate a business. Rent, utilities, advertising, and salaries are examples of expenses. Most expenses are billed and paid monthly. Businesses routinely write checks to pay for these expenses when they are incurred.

290

UNIT 3   The Accounting Cycle for a Merchandising Business

Reinforcing Study Skills

Learning through active *listening* may be difficult for many students who are skillful readers. Encourage students to participate actively in listening to lectures or oral reports. As they listen, they should focus on both the information presented and the actual task of listening attentively. Active listeners do the following.

- Read assignments beforehand.
- Keep their minds on the presentation.

- Anticipate what the speaker will say next.
- Relate information to personal life experiences.
- Formulate questions.

Provide a copy of the *Student Study Plans* to each class member to help organize study activities or to individualize practice and review activities.

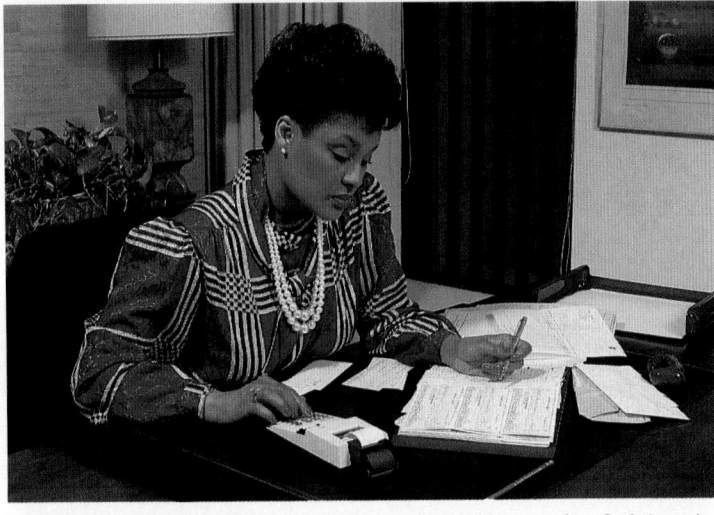

It is good cash management not to pay invoices before they are due. Cash is an important asset and should be held until the last moment.

CONCEPT DEVELOPMENT
Kinds of Cash Payments
Cash payments are made with checks, not with actual cash. The source document for most cash payment transactions is the check stub. Making payments by check is a good internal control practice.

Cash Payments for Items Bought on Account

When a business buys on account, it receives an invoice (bill) from the supplier. The credit terms on the invoice indicate when it is to be paid. After the invoice is journalized, the invoice is filed by its due date in a tickler file.

One of the daily tasks of an accounting clerk is to process invoices for payment. Each day, the clerk removes the invoices due for payment from the tickler file. Checks are then prepared, signed by an authorized person, and mailed to creditors.

The amount of the check written in payment of an invoice depends on the credit terms. In Chapter 13, you learned that businesses often take advantage of purchase discounts offered by suppliers.

For example, Champion Building Products purchased $181.48 worth of merchandise on account from Key Paint Company. When the invoice was received, it was recorded as a $181.48 debit to Purchases and a $181.48 credit to Accounts Payable. The invoice, dated December 1, listed credit terms of 2/10, n/30. If Champion pays for the merchandise on or before December 11, it may deduct 2% from the total of the invoice, or $3.63.

When the invoice is paid on December 11, Champion will debit Accounts Payable for the full $181.48 since it is paying for the merchandise purchased on account. Cash in Bank will be credited for $177.85, the actual amount of the check being written. Where should the amount of the purchase discount be recorded?

A purchase discount decreases the cost of merchandise bought on account. The discount, then, could be recorded as a credit to Purchases. Accountants prefer, however, to set up a separate account called Purchases Discounts. Purchases Discounts is classified as a cost of merchandise account. It is also a contra account; its normal balance is "contrary to" that of

ACCOUNTING **Notes**
Why do you have to write the amount of a check twice? It's easy to make a mistake when writing numbers, to write "$100" when you mean "$10," for example. It's much harder to make that kind of mistake in words. Few people would write "one hundred" when they mean "ten."

Making Connections

EVERYDAY LIFE

Many students are responsible for purchasing their own car insurance. Ask students whether they must pay the premium for the insurance at the beginning or at the end of the insurance period. The response will be that they *prepay.* Ask students if they consider the cost of the premium to be an asset or an *expense.* Most students will consider it an expense. To illustrate how prepaid insurance is an asset, ask students to describe the benefit of purchasing insurance. The major benefit is *protection,* which is an asset until the insurance coverage expires.

Teaching Tips

- FOB destination means that the seller pays. FOB shipping point means that the buyer pays.
- Another term for "transportation in" is "freight in."
- Transportation In is classified as a cost of merchandise account because it increases the cost of merchandise purchased for resale.

Purchases		Purchases Discounts	
Dr.	Cr.	Dr.	Cr.
+	–	–	+
Increase Side	Decrease Side	Decrease Side	Increase Side
Balance Side			Balance Side

the Purchases account. As you know, Purchases has a normal debit balance. The normal balance side of Purchases Discounts, therefore, is the credit side.

Taking advantage of all purchase discounts is good business practice. Over a period of time, such discounts can add up to a sizable reduction in costs.

R E M E M B E R

Purchases Discounts is a contra cost of merchandise account. It has a normal credit balance.

Other Cash Payments

When a company buys merchandise from a supplier, there is often a charge for shipping the goods. This shipping charge may be paid by either the buyer or the supplier. Who pays depends on the terms of the purchase.

Shipping terms are stated as either FOB destination or FOB shipping point. "FOB" stands for "free on board." **FOB destination** means that the supplier pays the shipping cost to the buyer's destination or location. **FOB shipping point** means that the buyer pays the shipping charge from the supplier's shipping point.

A shipping charge is considered an additional cost of the merchandise purchased for resale. As such, the shipping charge could be debited to the Purchases account. That account would then reflect two costs, the cost of the merchandise itself and the shipping costs paid by the buyer. However, most accountants prefer to have a separate record of shipping charges. The account set up to handle these charges is Transportation In. Transportation In is classified as a cost of merchandise account.

Transportation In	
Dr.	Cr.
+	–
Increase Side	Decrease Side
Balance Side	

Like purchases of merchandise, shipping charges are a cost of doing business. The Transportation In account thus follows the same rules of debit and credit as expense accounts. That is, Transportation In is increased by debits and decreased by credits. The account has a normal debit balance.

If the shipping terms are FOB shipping point, the transporting company gives the freight bill directly to the buyer at delivery. Usually, the buyer must pay the freight bill before it can take possession of the merchandise. In other words, although suppliers do not necessarily require on-the-spot payment, shippers do. The business writes a check for the amount of the shipping charges and records that amount as a debit to the Transportation In account.

Interdisciplinary Connections

HISTORY

Probably the world's most famous insurer is Lloyd's of London. Members of this international insurance group write insurance against loss or damage of anything from oil tankers to opera singers' voices. The company grew out of meetings in the early 1700s at Lloyd's Coffee House in London's financial district.

Cash Decreases for Bank Service Charges and Bank Card Fees

Most banks charge a monthly fee for servicing a business's checking account. Since checking account service charges occur only once a month and involve a small amount of money, they are usually debited to the Miscellaneous Expense account.

Champion's bank also charges a fee for handling bank card sales slips. This **bank card fee** is usually based on the total dollar volume of the bank card sales processed. The fee is stated as a percentage of the total bank card sales. The percentage rate varies from bank to bank. Accountants usually record the amount of the fee in an expense account entitled Bank Card Fees Expense.

Both amounts are automatically deducted from the business's checking account and appear on the monthly bank statement. No checks are involved, even though Cash in Bank is decreased. These two decreases are expenses and must be recorded as deductions to Cash in Bank. The bank statement is the source document for the journal entry.

Before you learn how to journalize cash payment transactions, do the following activity to check your understanding of the material you have just studied.

Check Your Learning

Write your answers to these questions on notebook paper.

1. What is the amount paid for insurance called?
2. What is the source document for most cash payments?
3. What is the normal balance of Purchases Discounts?
4. Why is it good business practice to take advantage of purchase discounts?
5. Does a purchase discount increase or decrease the cost of merchandise?

Compare your answers to those in the answers section. Re-read the preceding part of the chapter to find the correct answers to any questions you may have missed.

The Cash Payments Journal

So far, you have studied three special journals: the sales journal, the cash receipts journal, and the purchases journal. The cash payments journal is the fourth and last special journal.

The **cash payments journal** is a special journal used to record all transactions in which cash is paid out or decreased. These transactions include payments to creditors for items bought on account, cash purchases of merchandise and other assets, payments for various expenses, and cash decreases for bank service charges and bank card fees. The source documents for the journal entries are the check stubs and the bank statement.

Using Visuals

Use demonstration problem 14-1, Part A, here to give students practice analyzing cash payments transactions using T accounts.

ANSWERS

1. The premium
2. Check stub
3. Credit
4. Because over time such discounts can add up to a sizable reduction in costs
5. Decrease

CONCEPT DEVELOPMENT
The Cash Payments Journal

After studying three other types of special journals, students should be familiar with the use of a multicolumn journal. You may want to review the types of transactions recorded in each journal. Remind students that column headings relate to accounts in the general ledger.

Reteaching Strategies

Some students may need extra help with the calculation of purchases discounts. Write several examples on the chalkboard and have volunteers calculate the amount of the discount, the date payment is due, and the net payment. Have the students explain their calculations.

Refer students to *Math Review for Accounting* for extra practice in calculating percentages.

CONCEPT DEVELOPMENT

Journalizing Cash Payments

Without looking at the journal entry in Figure 14-2, have students analyze the December 1 transaction and determine which columns would be used to record the transaction. Point out that a cash payment will always result in a credit in the Cash in Bank Credit column.

The cash payments journal used by Champion Building Products is shown in Figure 14-1. The first four columns are for the date, the source document number, the title of the account, and the posting reference. The number of amount columns differs from business to business. Champion's journal has four amount columns.

The General Debit column is used for debits to all general ledger accounts for which there is no special column. The Accounts Payable Debit column is used to record all decreases to accounts in the accounts payable subsidiary ledger and to the Accounts Payable account. The Purchases Discounts Credit column is used to enter the amount of any purchase discount taken by Champion. Every transaction recorded in the cash payments journal involves a decrease to Cash in Bank. The cash payments journal, therefore, always has a Cash in Bank Credit column.

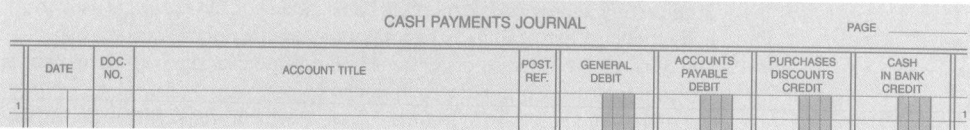

Figure 14-1   Cash Payments Journal

The entries in the General Debit column are posted individually to the general ledger during the month. At the end of the month, the totals of the three special amount columns are posted to the general ledger accounts named in the column headings.

R E M E M B E R

The cash payments journal is used to record all transactions that decrease Cash in Bank.

Journalizing Cash Payments

The six transactions that follow are typical of those recorded in the cash payments journal. Notice that each transaction results in a credit to Cash in Bank.

Journalizing Cash Purchases

A business may buy many things for cash. Here are two examples.

December 1: *Paid $1,500.00 to Keystone Insurance Co. for the premium on a six-month insurance policy, Check 1211.*

Two asset accounts are affected by this transaction: Prepaid Insurance and Cash in Bank. In this transaction, Prepaid Insurance is being increased. It is debited for $1,500.00, the amount of the premium. Cash in Bank is being decreased and is credited for $1,500.00.

	Prepaid Insurance			Cash in Bank	
	Dr.	Cr.		Dr.	Cr.
	+	–		+	–
	$1,500.00				$1,500.00

To journalize the cash payment for the purchase of an asset, follow these steps. This journal entry is shown in Figure 14-2.

CASH PAYMENTS JOURNAL PAGE 14

DATE	DOC. NO.	ACCOUNT TITLE	POST. REF.	GENERAL DEBIT	ACCOUNTS PAYABLE DEBIT	PURCHASES DISCOUNTS CREDIT	CASH IN BANK CREDIT	
19-- Dec. 1	1211	Prepaid Insurance		1500 00			1500 00	1
1	2	3		4			5	2

Figure 14-2 Recording a Cash Purchase in the Cash Payments Journal

1. Enter the date in the Date column of the cash payments journal.
2. Enter the number of the check in the Document Number column.
3. Enter the title of the account being debited in the Account Title column.
4. Enter the amount of the debit in the General Debit column.
5. Enter the amount of the credit in the Cash in Bank Credit column.

Merchandise for resale is usually purchased on account and, thus, recorded in the purchases journal. A business may, however, also buy merchandise for cash. In this case, the transaction is recorded in the cash payments journal.

December 2: *Purchased merchandise from Starks Lumber Co. for $1,115.00 cash, Check 1212.*

The accounts affected by this transaction are Purchases and Cash in Bank. Purchases is being increased because Champion has bought additional merchandise. It is debited for $1,115.00. The merchandise was purchased for cash, so Cash in Bank is being decreased. That account is credited for $1,115.00.

	Purchases			Cash in Bank	
	Dr.	Cr.		Dr.	Cr.
	+	–		+	–
	$1,115.00				$1,115.00

To record the purchase of merchandise for cash, follow the steps listed below. The journal entry is shown in Figure 14-3, line 2, on the next page.

1. Enter the date in the Date column.
2. Enter the number of the check issued for the payment in the Document Number column.
3. Enter the title of the account debited in the Account Title column.
4. Enter the amount of the purchase in the General Debit column.
5. Enter the amount of the check in the Cash in Bank Credit column.

Point out the journal entry in Figure 14-2, which is for the December 1 transaction.

Teaching Tips

■ Purchases of merchandise using cash rather than a check are infrequent and would be discouraged by an auditor for most businesses.

Cooperative Learning

CO-OP CO-OP

Divide students into groups of 2 or 3 persons. Ask each group to research and prepare a report about a real-life case where employees embezzled money or stole merchandise from their employer. The report should include a discussion of internal controls that could have been maintained to prevent the loss. Students must outline the necessary steps to complete the project and plan and negotiate their activities. When each group member has shared individual findings with other group members, the students combine the information, write a report, and choose a spokesperson to present their findings to the class.

Refer to the "Cooperative Learning" section of *Tech Prep Strategies in Accounting* for additional cooperative learning strategies.

			CASH PAYMENTS JOURNAL					PAGE 14	
	DATE	DOC. NO.	ACCOUNT TITLE	POST. REF.	GENERAL DEBIT	ACCOUNTS PAYABLE DEBIT	PURCHASES DISCOUNTS CREDIT	CASH IN BANK CREDIT	
1	19-- Dec. 1	1211	Prepaid Insurance		1500 00			1500 00	1
2	2	1212	Purchases		1115 00			1115 00	2
3	2	1213	Rent Expense		1250 00			1250 00	3
4	3	1214	Key Paint Company			1835 12	36 70	1798 42	4
14	25	1224	Center City Supply			85 91		85 91	14
15	26	1225	Transportation In		554 37			554 37	15
16	31	1226	Salaries Expense		7000 00			7000 00	16
17	31	—	Miscellaneous Expense		5 50			5 50	17
18	31	—	Bank Card Fees Expense		87 65			87 65	18

Figure 14-3 Journalizing Transactions in the Cash Payments Journal

R E M E M B E R

Purchases is debited whenever merchandise to be resold to customers is bought — whether the purchase is for cash or on account.

Journalizing Cash Payments of Expenses

Expenses are generally paid — by check — when they are incurred.

December 2: *Paid $1,250.00 to Berenson Realty for the December rent, Check 1213.*

Rent Expense and Cash in Bank are affected by this transaction. Rent Expense is being increased. It is, therefore, debited for $1,250.00. Cash in Bank is being decreased, so it is credited for $1,250.00.

Rent Expense			Cash in Bank	
Dr. +	Cr. −		Dr. +	Cr. −
$1,250.00				$1,250.00

The journal entry to record this transaction is shown in Figure 14-3, line 3. Refer to this illustration as you read these steps describing how to record the cash payment of an expense.

1. Enter the date in the Date column.
2. Enter the check number in the Document Number column.
3. Enter the name of the account being debited in Account Title column.
4. Enter the amount of the expense in the General Debit column.
5. Enter the amount of the check in the Cash in Bank Credit column.

Journalizing Payments on Account

On the due date of an invoice for merchandise or other items purchased on account, the accounting clerk prepares a check in payment. Frequently, the cash payment involves a purchase discount.

December 3: *Paid $1,798.42 to Key Paint Company for merchandise purchased on account, $1,835.12 less a discount of $36.70, Check 1214.*

The accounts affected by this transaction are Accounts Payable, Purchases Discounts, and Cash in Bank. Accounts Payable is being decreased by the payment to the creditor. It is debited for $1,835.12, the amount of the original purchase. Purchases Discounts is being increased because Champion is taking advantage of the discount offered by Key Paint. It is credited for $36.70. Cash in Bank is being decreased. It is credited for $1,798.42, the amount of cash actually paid out.

Accounts Payable		Purchases Discounts		Cash in Bank	
Dr.	Cr.	Dr.	Cr.	Dr.	Cr.
−	+	−	+	+	−
$1,835.12			$36.70		$1,798.42

This transaction is shown in the cash payments journal in Figure 14-3, line 4. Refer to this illustration as you read the following steps:

1. Enter the date in the Date column.
2. Enter the number of the check issued for the payment in the Document Number column.
3. Enter the creditor's name in the Account Title column.
4. Enter the amount of the debit in the Accounts Payable Debit column. (This is the same amount as the original purchase.)
5. Enter the amount of the purchase discount in the Purchases Discounts Credit column.
6. Enter the amount of the check in the Cash in Bank Credit column.

After the cash payment is journalized, the accounting clerk places the number of the check on the invoice's processing stamp, on the line marked "Check No." The paid invoice is then filed.

Businesses are not always able to take advantage of discounts offered by suppliers. In other instances, the supplier may not offer a discount at all. When this occurs, the check is written for the amount of the original purchase. Such a cash payment is illustrated in Figure 14-3, line 14.

Journalizing Other Cash Payments

Checks are also written to pay for shipping charges when merchandise is sent FOB shipping point.

December 26: *Issued Check 1225 for $554.37 to Fast Delivery Co. for shipping charges on merchandise bought from Aluminum Plus, Inc.*

The accounts affected by this transaction are Transportation In and Cash in Bank. The Transportation In account, remember, is used to record shipping charges on merchandise purchased from suppliers. Transportation In is being increased. It is, therefore, debited for $554.37. Cash in Bank is being decreased and is credited for $554.37.

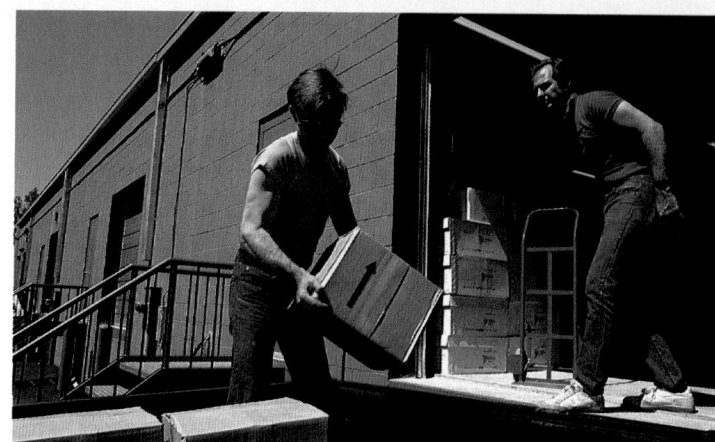

If shipping terms are FOB destination, the shipping charges are already built into the cost of the merchandise.

Transportation In		Cash in Bank	
Dr.	Cr.	Dr.	Cr.
+	–	+	–
$554.37			$554.37

To record a cash payment for shipping charges, follow the steps below. The journal entry is shown on line 15 of Figure 14-3 on page 296.

1. Enter the date in the Date column.
2. Enter the number of the check issued for the payment in the Document Number column.
3. Enter the title of the account being debited in the Account Title column.
4. Enter the amount of the shipping costs in the General Debit column.
5. Enter the amount of the check in the Cash in Bank Credit column.

R E M E M B E R

The word "General" in the column heading of a special journal refers to the general ledger. The account named in the Account Title column is the general ledger account affected by the transaction.

Journalizing Bank Charges

Bank service charges and bank card fees are automatically deducted from Champion's checking account. Champion does not write a check for these two expenses. Since they result in decreases to Cash in Bank, the transactions are recorded in Champion's cash payments journal.

▲ **Journalizing Checking Account Service Charges** On Champion's December bank statement, the bank included a $5.50 service

Making Connections

AROUND THE WORLD

Who are the world's largest industrial corporations? Number 1 in the world (in the early 1990s) is General Motors, followed by Exxon and Ford Motor Company. Number 4 is the Royal Dutch/Shell Group (Great Britain/The Netherlands). Other giant companies are Toyota Motor Corporation (Japan, Number 5), British Petroleum (Great Britain, Number 11), Daimler-Benz (Germany, Number 8), Elf-Aquitaine (France, Number 22), and Nestlé (Switzerland, Number 23).

charge. After the accounting clerk reconciled the bank statement, the service charge was recorded in the cash payments journal.

December 31: *Recorded the bank service charge of $5.50, December bank statement.*

The two accounts affected by this transaction are Miscellaneous Expense and Cash in Bank. Miscellaneous Expense is being increased because of the bank service charge. The account is debited for $5.50. The service charge reduces the checking account balance; therefore, Cash in Bank is being decreased. That account is credited for $5.50.

Miscellaneous Expense		Cash in Bank	
Dr.	Cr.	Dr.	Cr.
+	–	+	–
$5.50			$5.50

To record the bank service charge, follow these steps. The journal entry is shown on line 17 of Figure 14-3 on page 296.

1. Enter the date in the Date column.
2. Enter a dash in the Document Number column. This indicates that a check was not written for this transaction.
3. Enter the title of the account debited in the Account Title column.
4. Enter the amount of the service charge in the General Debit column.
5. Enter the amount of the cash decrease in the Cash in Bank Credit column.

▲ **Journalizing Bank Card Fees**   Most banks charge a fee for handling a business's bank card sales. Champion's bank charges a fee of 5% of the total bank card sales. During the time covered by the December bank statement, the bank processed $1,753.00 in bank card sales for Champion. The bank card fee was, therefore, $87.65 ($1,753.00 × .05). The fee was listed on the bank statement as a deduction from the checking account balance. This decrease in cash is recorded in the cash payments journal.

December 31: *Recorded the bank card fee of $87.65, December bank statement.*

The accounts affected by this transaction are Bank Card Fees Expense and Cash in Bank. Since Bank Card Fees Expense is being increased, it is debited for $87.65. Cash in Bank is credited for the same amount.

Bank Card Fees Expense		Cash in Bank	
Dr.	Cr.	Dr.	Cr.
+	–	+	–
$87.65			$87.65

To journalize the bank card fee, follow the same steps as in recording the bank service charge. Bank Card Fees Expense, however, is entered in the

---

Teaching Tips
- Some banks may send a separate memo notifying a business of the charge for processing bank card sales for the month.

Using Visuals
 Use demonstration problem 14-1, Part B, here to give students practice in recording transactions in a cash payments journal.

Teaching Tips

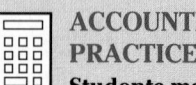

- Accountants often use parentheses around a number to be subtracted rather than a minus sign.

ACCOUNTING PRACTICE
Students may complete Exercise 14-1 after the section on journalizing bank card fees.

CONCEPT DEVELOPMENT
Posting from the Cash Payments Journal
As with posting from the other special journals, students will post from the cash payments journal to two ledgers: the accounts payable subsidiary ledger and the general ledger. Remind students to follow a logical sequence in posting to avoid omitting an item.

Account Title column of the cash payments journal. This journal entry is illustrated on line 18 of Figure 14-3 on page 296.

After the bank charges have been recorded, they must also be entered in the checkbook records. One way to adjust the balance on the check stub is shown on the stub. The deposit heading is crossed out, and the words "Bank Statement" written in its place. The accounting clerk adds the two bank charges and enters the total of $93.15 ($87.65 + $5.50) in the Amount column. A minus sign is also entered to show that the amount is to be subtracted from the balance brought forward.

$		No. 1227
DATE		19
TO		
FOR		

	DOLLARS	CENTS
BAL. BRO. FED. *Bk Stmt*	22,277	27
ADD DEPOSITS	− 93	15
TOTAL	22,184	12
LESS THIS CHECK		
BAL. CARR. FWD.		

Posting from the Cash Payments Journal

After cash payments have been journalized, they are posted. Payments on account are posted to the creditors' accounts in the accounts payable subsidiary ledger. Entries in the General Debit column are posted to the named accounts in the general ledger.

Posting to the Accounts Payable Subsidiary Ledger

To keep creditors' accounts current, amounts in the Accounts Payable Debit column are posted daily. The first Champion entry to be posted to the accounts payable subsidiary ledger is the December 3 payment to Key Paint Company.

To post an entry from the cash payments journal to the accounts payable subsidiary ledger, follow the steps below. Refer to Figure 14-4 as you read these steps.

1. Enter the date of the transaction in the Date column of the creditor's account.
2. In the ledger account's Posting Reference column, enter the letter of the journal and the page number on which the entry appears. "CP" are the letters for the cash payments journal.
3. In the Debit column, enter the amount recorded in the Accounts Payable Debit column of the journal.

Prev. Bal.	$2,016.60
Debit	−1,835.12
New Bal.	$ 181.48

4. Compute the new balance and enter it in the Balance column. If the account now has a zero balance, draw a line through the Balance column.
5. Return to the cash payments journal and enter a check mark (✔) in the Posting Reference column.

R E M E M B E R

The individual amounts in the Accounts Payable Debit column are posted daily to the creditors' accounts in the accounts payable subsidiary ledger.

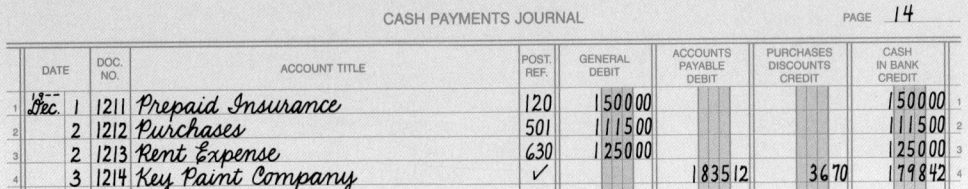

CASH PAYMENTS JOURNAL   PAGE 14

	DATE	DOC. NO.	ACCOUNT TITLE	POST. REF.	GENERAL DEBIT	ACCOUNTS PAYABLE DEBIT	PURCHASES DISCOUNTS CREDIT	CASH IN BANK CREDIT	
1	Dec. 1	1211	Prepaid Insurance	120	150000			150000	1
2	2	1212	Purchases	501	111500			111500	2
3	2	1213	Rent Expense	630	125000			125000	3
4	3	1214	Key Paint Company	✓		183512	3670	179842	4

Name   Key Paint Company
Address   1714 Peak Road, Cleveland, OH 44109

DATE	EXPLANATION	POST. REF.	DEBIT	CREDIT	BALANCE
Dec. 1	Balance	✓			183512
3		P12		18148	201660
3		CP14	183512		18148

Figure 14-4   Posting from the Cash Payments Journal to the Accounts Payable Subsidiary Ledger

All other payments on account are posted to creditors' accounts in the subsidiary ledger in the same manner. Figure 14-5 on pages 302-303 shows the complete accounts payable subsidiary ledger after all postings have been completed. Notice that the accounts contain entries from both the purchases journal and the cash payments journal.

Before continuing, do the following activity.

Check Your Learning

Use Figure 14-5 to answer these questions. Write your answers on a separate sheet of paper.

1. How many creditors does Champion Building Products have?
2. How much was owed to Aluminum Plus, Inc., on December 1?
3. How much was paid on account to Custom Doors, Inc., during December?
4. How many times during December did Champion purchase items on account from Key Paint Company?
5. How much was owed to Starks Lumber Co. on December 31?
6. Did Champion make a payment to Viking Motors during December?
7. In what journal was the December 28 transaction involving Wilson Electric, Inc., recorded?
8. How many postings were made to the accounts payable subsidiary ledger from the cash payments journal during December?

Compare your answers to those in the answers section. Re-read the preceding part of the chapter to find the correct answers to any questions you may have missed.

Using Visuals

Call students' attention to Figure 14-4. Ask students to describe the order of posting from this journal to the ledgers.

ANSWERS

1. 7
2. 0
3. $1,135.21
4. 1
5. $1,008.36
6. No
7. General journal
8. 7

Reteaching Strategies

Although no document number is given, the source document for the bank charges is the monthly bank statement. No checks are written to pay fees for services provided by the bank because the bank deducts the amount of its charges directly from the business's checking account. Some students may be familiar with the bank charge for printing personal-ized checks. Businesses also must pay such fees, which are journalized in the cash payments journal.

Use problem 14A, pages 637-638, for students who need additional practice journalizing cash payments transactions and posting from the cash payments journal.

Using Visuals

Have students look at the accounts shown in Figure 14-5. How do they know whether the amount shown in the Balance column is a debit balance or a credit balance?

Name Aluminum Plus, Inc.
Address 1550 Sixth Avenue, Pittsburgh, PA 15219

DATE	EXPLANATION	POST. REF.	DEBIT	CREDIT	BALANCE
19-- Dec. 9		P12		7842 98	7842 98
19		CP14	7842 98		—
29		P12		3600 00	3600 00

Name Center City Supply
Address 700 Penn Avenue, Pittsburgh, PA 15221

DATE	EXPLANATION	POST. REF.	DEBIT	CREDIT	BALANCE
19-- Dec. 1	Balance	✓			85 91
12		P12		362 60	448 51
24		CP14	85 91		362 60

Name Custom Doors, Inc.
Address 150 Forest Avenue, Columbus, GA 31907

DATE	EXPLANATION	POST. REF.	DEBIT	CREDIT	BALANCE
19-- Dec. 1	Balance	✓			1135 21
9		CP14	1135 21		—
31		P12		640 00	640 00

Name Key Paint Company
Address 1714 Peak Road, Cleveland, OH 44109

DATE	EXPLANATION	POST. REF.	DEBIT	CREDIT	BALANCE
19-- Dec. 1	Balance	✓			1835 12
3		P12		181 48	2016 60
3		CP14	1835 12		181 48
12		CP14	181 48		—

Name Starks Lumber Co.
Address 1900 Marietta Avenue, Lancaster, PA 17603

DATE	EXPLANATION	POST. REF.	DEBIT	CREDIT	BALANCE
19-- Dec. 1	Balance	✓			225 51
6		P12		3495 66	3721 17
7		CP14	225 51		3495 66
15		CP14	3495 66		—
22		P12		1008 36	1008 36

Figure 14-5 The Completed Accounts Payable Subsidiary Ledger

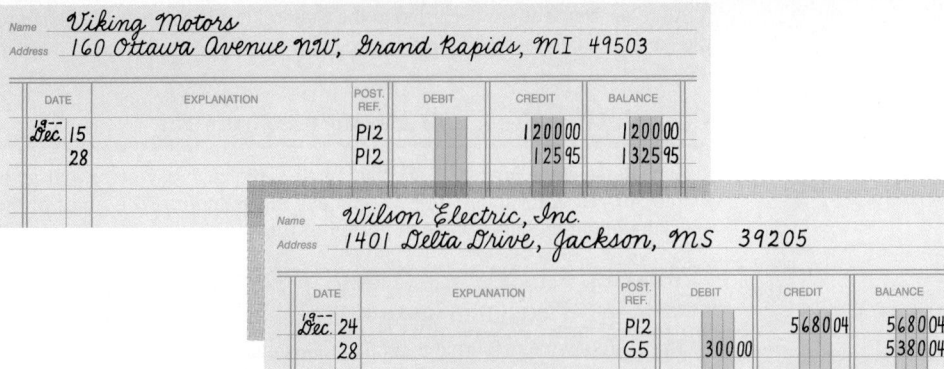

Figure 14-5 The Completed Accounts Payable Subsidiary Ledger (Concluded)

Using Visuals

Review the steps in posting in Figure 14-6. If posting took place on December 6, what date would be entered in the Date column of the general ledger form for this entry?

Using Visuals

Use demonstration problem 14-2 to give students practice in posting from the cash payments journal to general ledger and subsidiary ledger accounts.

Posting from the General Debit Column

Periodically during the month, the transactions in the General Debit column are posted to the appropriate general ledger accounts. The first December transaction in the General Debit column is the Prepaid Insurance transaction on December 1.

To post an entry from the cash payments journal to the general ledger, follow these steps. Refer to Figure 14-6 as you read the steps.

1. Enter the date of the transaction in the Date column of the general ledger account.
2. Enter the letter of the journal and the page number on which the transaction appears in the account's Posting Reference column. Be sure to use the letters "CP."
3. In the Debit column, enter the amount from the General Debit column of the journal.
4. Compute the new balance and enter it in the appropriate Balance column. (Since there is no previous balance, enter the amount recorded in the Debit column in the Debit Balance column.)
5. Return to the cash payments journal and enter the account number in the Posting Reference column.

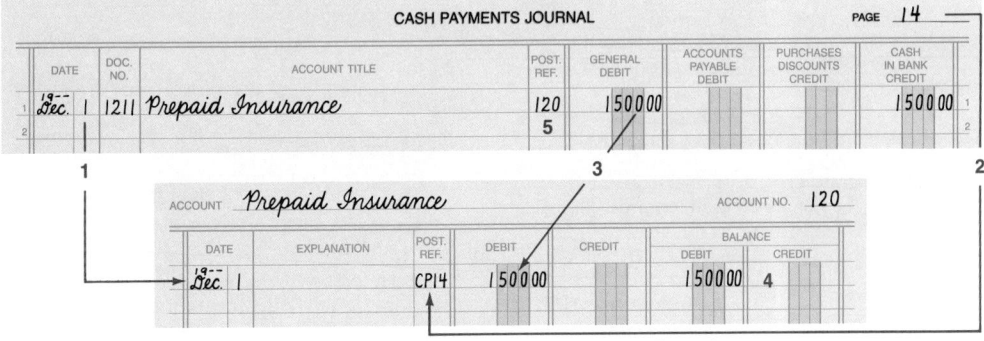

Figure 14-6 Posting from the General Debit Column of the Cash Payments Journal

---

Critical Thinking

Assume you are an accounting clerk for a local business and you misplace this month's invoice from a supplier. You telephone the supplier to get the current account balance. Why should you not write a check for payment without the invoice?

(Answers: Any payment must be supported by a source document for several reasons. (1) The items ordered and received need to be verified before payment is made. (2) The invoice may have included credit terms that would reduce the amount due. (3) The current account balance may include additional purchases that were not on the lost invoice. Those items will be listed on the next invoice and might be paid for twice. (4) The audit trail is incomplete without an invoice.)

CONCEPT DEVELOPMENT

Completing the Cash Payments Journal

As with other special journals, the cash payments journal must be totaled, proved, and ruled before the column totals can be posted to the general ledger. Remind students that rulings are made under amount columns only.

Using Visuals

Have students look at the completed cash payments journal in Figure 14-7. What do the numbers and check marks in the Posting Reference column signify?

Using Visuals

 A teaching transparency showing the journal in Figure 14-7 is available in the transparency binder accompanying Glencoe Accounting.

All other transactions recorded in the General Debit column are posted to the general ledger accounts in the same way.

Completing the Cash Payments Journal

As with the three preceding special journals, the cash payments journal is footed, proved, totaled, and ruled at the end of the month. The totals of the special amount columns are then posted to the general ledger accounts.

Totaling, Proving, and Ruling the Cash Payments Journal

The cash payments journal is totaled following the same procedures used for the other special journals. Before the journal can be ruled, the accounting clerk must prove the equality of debits and credits. The total of the debit columns must equal the total of the credit columns.

Debit Columns		Credit Columns	
General	$14,730.44	Purchases Discounts	$ 294.31
Accounts Payable	14,801.87	Cash in Bank	29,238.00
	$29,532.31		$29,532.31

The cash payments journal can now be double-ruled, as shown in Figure 14-7.

CASH PAYMENTS JOURNAL   PAGE 14

	DATE	DOC. NO.	ACCOUNT TITLE	POST. REF.	GENERAL DEBIT	ACCOUNTS PAYABLE DEBIT	PURCHASES DISCOUNTS CREDIT	CASH IN BANK CREDIT	
1	Dec. 1	1211	Prepaid Insurance	120	1500 00			1500 00	1
2	2	1212	Purchases	501	1115 00			1115 00	2
3	2	1213	Rent Expense	630	1250 00			1250 00	3
4	3	1214	Key Paint Company	✓		1835 12	36 70	1798 42	4
5	7	1215	Starks Lumber Co.	✓		225 51	4 51	221 00	5
6	9	1216	Custom Doors, Inc.	✓		1135 21	22 70	1112 51	6
7	12	1217	Key Paint Company	✓		181 48	3 63	177 85	7
8	15	1218	Utilities Expense	645	225 00			225 00	8
9	15	1219	Supplies	115	137 50			137 50	9
10	15	1220	Starks Lumber Co.	✓		3495 66	69 91	3425 75	10
11	15	1221	Federal Income Tax Expense	650	2437 50			2437 50	11
12	19	1222	Aluminum Plus, Inc.	✓		7842 98	156 86	7686 12	12
13	20	1223	Sales Tax Payable	210	417 92			417 92	13
14	24	1224	Center City Supply	✓		85 91		85 91	14
15	26	1225	Transportation In	505	554 37			554 37	15
16	31	1226	Salaries Expense	635	7000 00			7000 00	16
17	31	—	Miscellaneous Expense	625	5 50			5 50	17
18	31	—	Bank Card Fees Expense	605	87 65			87 65	18
19	31		Totals		14730 44	14801 87	294 31	29238 00	19

Figure 14-7 The Completed Cash Payments Journal

R E M E M B E R

Columns are first footed in pencil. Verified totals are then written in ink.

304   UNIT 3   The Accounting Cycle for a Merchandising Business

Posting Column Totals to the General Ledger

At the end of the month, the total of each special amount column is posted to the general ledger account named in the column heading. In the cash payments journal, column totals are posted to Accounts Payable, Purchases Discounts, and Cash in Bank. Figure 14-8 shows the posting of the three column totals to the general ledger accounts. Note that the account numbers for the three accounts are written in parentheses in the appropriate columns.

The total of the General Debit column is not posted. Each entry in that column has already been posted to a specific general ledger account. A check mark is, therefore, entered below the double rule in the General Debit column.

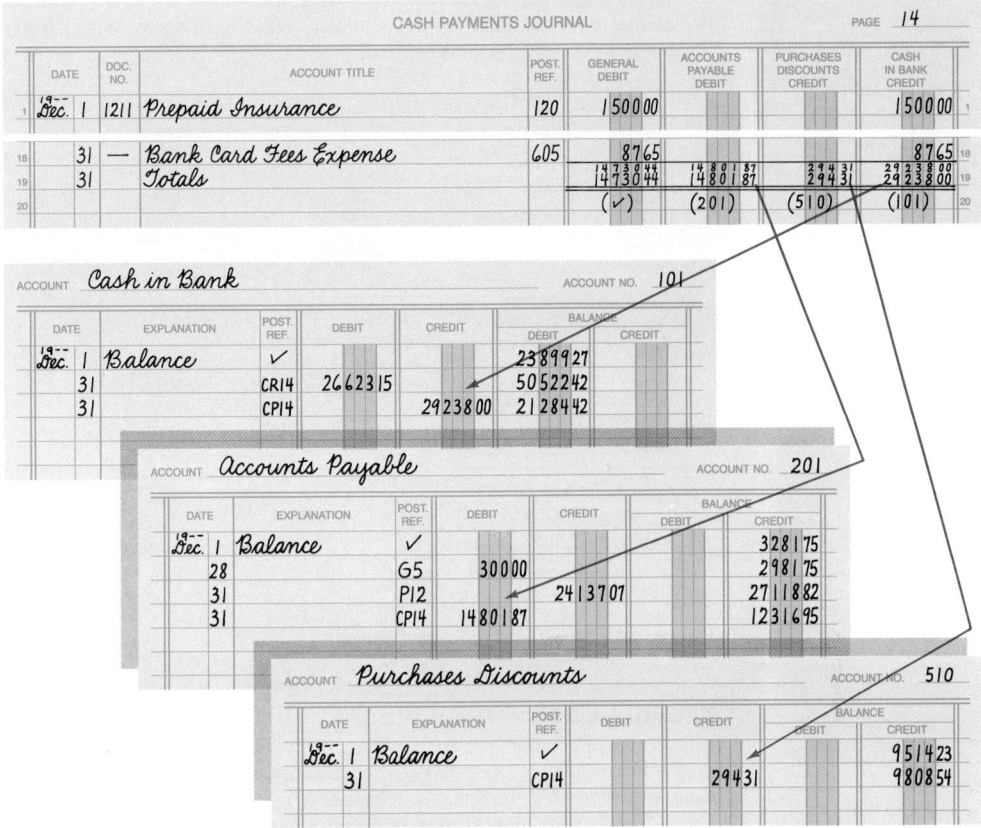

Figure 14-8 Posting Column Totals from the Cash Payments Journal

R E M E M B E R

To show that column totals are not posted, place a check mark in parentheses (✓) below the double rule.

CHAPTER 14 Accounting for Cash Payments

Chapter

Using Visuals

Have students look at Figure 14-8 and explain why a check mark appears under the total for the General Debit column.

Using Visuals

 Use demonstration problem 14-3 to show students how to post column totals from the cash payments journal to the general ledger accounts.

Making Connections

COMMUNICATIONS

When making written business presentations, students should allow the same kind of time for thorough proofreading and editing that they would give a formal essay or paper in another subject area. Errors in spelling or grammar—which careful proofreading can avoid—make a bad impression on the client/reader.

CHAPTER 14 Accounting for Cash Payments **305**

Proving the Accounts Payable Subsidiary Ledger

After the column totals have been posted, the accounting clerk prepares a **schedule of accounts payable.** This schedule lists all creditors in the accounts payable ledger, the balance in each account, and the total amount still owed to creditors. The accounts payable subsidiary ledger is proved when the total of the schedule of accounts payable agrees with the balance of the Accounts Payable account. Accounts Payable, you will remember, is the controlling account for the accounts payable subsidiary ledger.

Champion's schedule of accounts payable for December is shown in Figure 14-9. As in the schedule of accounts receivable, the accounts are listed in alphabetical order. All creditors are listed, even those with zero balances. Notice that the total listed on the schedule, $12,316.95, agrees with the balance of the Accounts Payable account.

ACCOUNT Accounts Payable					ACCOUNT NO. 201	
DATE	EXPLANATION	POST. REF.	DEBIT	CREDIT	BALANCE DEBIT	CREDIT
19-- Dec. 1	Balance	✓				3 281 75
28		G5	300 00			2 981 75
31		P12		24 137 07		27 118 82
31		CP14	14 801 87			12 316 95

Champion Building Products, Inc.
Schedule of Accounts Payable
December 31, 19--

Aluminum Plus, Inc.		3 600 00
Center City Supply		362 60
Custom Doors, Inc.		640 00
Key Paint Company		
Starks Lumber Co.	1 008 36	
Viking Motors	1 325 95	
Wilson Electric, Inc.	5 380 04	
Total Accounts Payable		12 316 95

Figure 14-9   Schedule of Accounts Payable

Proving Cash

Proving cash is the process of determining whether the amounts of cash recorded in a business's accounting records and in its checkbook agree. Ideally a business should prove cash each day. When a business uses special journals, however, the Cash in Bank account in the general ledger is not updated daily. Postings to the Cash in Bank account are not made until the end of the month. For many businesses, then, proving cash is done at the end of the month. The cash proof may be prepared on plain paper, on accounting stationery, or on a special cash proof form. The cash proof prepared by Champion's accounting clerk, shown in Figure 14-10, was prepared on two-column accounting stationery. To prove cash, follow the steps on page 307.

Champion Building Products, Inc.
Cash Proof
December 31, 19--

Beginning Cash in Bank balance		23899 27
Plus: Cash receipts for the month		26623 15
Subtotal		50522 42
Less: Cash payments for the month		29238 00
Ending Cash in Bank balance		21284 42
Check stub balance		21284 42

Figure 14-10 Cash Proof

1. On the first line, record the beginning balance of Cash in Bank according to the general ledger account.
2. Add the total cash received during the month. This is the total of the Cash in Bank Debit column of the cash receipts journal.
3. From the subtotal, subtract the cash payments for the month. This is the total of the Cash in Bank Credit column of the cash payments journal.
4. Compare this figure against the balance shown on the last check stub in the checkbook. If the ending balance of Cash in Bank and the balance on the check stub match, cash is proved.

The ending balance of Cash in Bank is $21,284.42. Since the balance shown on the last check stub is also $21,284.42, cash has been proved.
Now do the following activity.

Check Your Learning

Write your answers to these questions on notebook paper.

1. The total of the Purchases Discounts Credit column is posted to the ___?___ account in the general ledger.
2. Amounts in the General Debit column of the cash payments journal are posted to ___?___.
3. The Accounts Payable Debit column total is posted to the ___?___ account in the general ledger.
4. The Cash in Bank Credit column total is posted to the ___?___ account in the general ledger.
5. The accounts payable subsidiary ledger is proved when the total of the creditors' account balances agrees with the balance of the ___?___ account in the ___?___ ledger.
6. If the beginning Cash in Bank balance is $15,000, cash receipts for the month are $10,000, and cash payments for the month are $20,000, what is the ending Cash in Bank balance? If the checkbook balance is $5,000, has cash been proved?

Compare your answers to those in the answers section. Re-read the preceding part of the chapter to find the correct answers to any questions you may have missed.

CHAPTER 14 Accounting for Cash Payments **307**

Teaching Tips

■ Cash proofs are important for the control of cash. Cash proofs often point out errors in the accounting work.

Using Visuals

In Figure 14-10, point out that recording bank service charges in the cash payments journal means that they do not have to be subtracted on the cash proof. They do need to be recorded on a check stub to make sure that the checkbook balance is up to date.

COMPUTERS IN ACCOUNTING

CPAs often use flowcharts to describe complex business structures such as internal controls for cash payments or purchases. Preparing flowcharts by hand has always been slow and tedious. New easy-to-use computer programs now offer the capability of creating flowcharts quickly. Features of the software include a wide assortment of symbols to illustrate the business functions, the ability to print in both portrait and in landscape orientation, and the ability to view multiple flowcharts on the screen.

ANSWERS

1. Purchases Discounts
2. Individual accounts in the general ledger periodically
3. Accounts Payable
4. Cash in Bank
5. Accounts Payable; general
6. $5,000; yes

Reteaching Strategies

If any students are having difficulty with the posting process, ask for volunteers among students who have mastered posting to help those who are having difficulties. Give them several minutes of class time, while others are working on problems, to work together on posting.

The schedule of accounts payable is a check on the accuracy of the posting to the individual accounts in the accounts payable ledger. Review typical errors that may have occurred if the balance on the schedule of accounts payable does not match the balance of the Accounts Payable account.

3 CLOSE

CHAPTER SUMMARY

This summary enumerates the key information in the chapter. It is a useful tool for reinforcement and review.

Summary of Key Points

1. Good internal controls require that all cash payments be authorized, all payments be made by check, and all checks be signed by an authorized person.
2. The premium paid for insurance coverage is debited to the asset account Prepaid Insurance.
3. Suppliers may offer cash discounts to encourage their credit customers to pay promptly. The buyer calls this a purchase discount. It is a deduction from the cost of merchandise purchased and is recorded in the Purchases Discounts account. Purchases Discounts is a contra account that reduces the balance of the cost of merchandise account Purchases.
4. The cost of shipping charges for merchandise purchased from suppliers is considered an additional cost of merchandise. The cost of shipping charges is debited to the Transportation In account, which appears in the cost of merchandise section of the chart of accounts.
5. Banks charge fees for handling a business's checking account and for processing its bank card sales. These fees are automatically deducted from the business's checking account. Since the fees decrease Cash in Bank, they are recorded in the cash payments journal. The service charge and the bank card fee must also be deducted from the business's checkbook records.
6. The cash payments journal is a special journal used to record all transactions in which cash is paid out. The source documents for the journal entry are check stubs and the bank statement.
7. Transactions are posted from the cash payments journal to the accounts payable ledger daily. Transactions entered in the General Debit column are posted periodically during the month.
8. A schedule of accounts payable is a list of all creditors, the amount owed to each, and the total amount owed to all creditors. The total of the schedule of accounts payable must agree with the balance of the Accounts Payable controlling account.
9. At the end of the month, cash is proved by determining whether the balance of Cash in Bank according to the accounting records agrees with the balance shown in the checkbook.

Review and Applications

Building Your Accounting Vocabulary

In your own words, write the definition of each of the following accounting terms. Use complete sentences for your definitions.

bank card fee	FOB destination	proving cash
cash payments journal	FOB shipping point	schedule of accounts payable
	premium	

Reviewing Your Accounting Knowledge

1. List five procedures that a business should use to control its cash payments.
2. Why are shipping charges an additional cost of merchandise purchased for resale?
3. Classify the following accounts: Prepaid Insurance, Purchases Discounts, Transportation In.
4. On what amount is the bank card fee based?
5. To which accounts are bank service charges and bank card fees debited?
6. What kinds of transactions are recorded in the cash payments journal?
7. What information can you get from the accounts payable subsidiary ledger that cannot be found in the Accounts Payable controlling account?
8. When are transactions in the cash payments journal posted to the accounts payable subsidiary ledger? To the general ledger?
9. Is the balance of the Accounts Payable account in the general ledger always equal to the total of its subsidiary ledger? Explain.
10. Why is a schedule of accounts payable important?
11. List the steps followed to prove cash at the end of the month.

Improving Your Decision-Making Skills

Decision making is involved whenever you have to determine which of several tasks you should complete first. This process is known as *setting priorities.*

Paula Blake is an accounting clerk for the Hudson Company. When she arrived at work on Monday, September 14, she found the following tasks awaiting her. Read through the list and decide in which order *you* would complete the tasks.

1. File ten paid invoices in the creditors' files.
2. Prepare checks for three invoices with due dates of September 15.
3. Prepare a report for the supervisor listing the suppliers from whom the company purchases merchandise and the credit terms offered by each supplier. The report is needed for a meeting on Tuesday morning.
4. Open and sort the morning's mail.
5. Journalize and post the day's cash payments.
6. Reconcile the bank statement, which arrived this morning.

309

Building Your Accounting Vocabulary

See the Glossary on pages 670-679 for definitions of these terms.

Reviewing Your Accounting Knowledge

1. (a) All cash payments should be authorized. (b) Each authorization should be supported by an approved source document. (c) All payments should be made by prenumbered check. (d) All checks should be signed only by an authorized person or persons. (e) Every spoiled check should be accounted for, marked "void," and filed in sequence.

2. Shipping charges are a cost of doing business and add to the cost of the merchandise.

3. Prepaid Insurance, asset; Purchases Discounts, contra cost of merchandise; Transportation In, cost of merchandise.

4. On the total dollar volume of the bank card sales slips processed.

5. Miscellaneous Expense for service charges and Bank Card Fees Expense for bank card fees.

6. All transactions in which cash is paid out or decreased through automatic deductions.

7. Specific information for each creditor's account, such as the current balance.

8. Transactions are posted to the accounts payable ledger daily and to the general ledger periodically.

9. No. Transactions affecting creditors' accounts are posted daily while column totals are posted to the Accounts Payable account only at the end of the month.

10. It proves the accounts payable subsidiary ledger when the total of the schedule agrees with the balance of Accounts Payable.

11. (a) Determine the beginning balance of the Cash in Bank account. (b) Add the total cash received during the month. (c) From the subtotal, subtract the total cash payments for the month. (d) Compare this figure with the balance shown on the last stub in the checkbook. If the ending balance of Cash in Bank and the check stub match, cash is proved.

Improving Your Decision-Making Skills

The following is one possible priority list. Students may be able to justify other listings.

1. Open and sort the morning's mail (#4).
2. Prepare checks for three invoices with due dates of September 15 (#2).
3. Journalize and post the day's cash payments.
4. Prepare a report for the supervisor needed for a meeting on Tuesday morning.
5. Reconcile the bank statement, which arrived this morning.
6. File ten paid invoices in the creditors' files.

PRACTICE AND APPLY

• Concepts and Procedures

Exercise 14-1: Ch. Obj. 1

Exercise 14-2: Ch. Obj. 5
(1) Total AP, $13,873.08
(2) Yes.

Teaching Tips

■ Remind students to list creditors in alphabetical order.

Exercise 14-3: Ch. Obj. 6
Balance 11/30, $8,277.98
Check stub balance, $8,277.98

Applying Accounting Procedures

Exercise 14-1   Entering Amounts in the Cash Payments Journal

Listed below are several transactions of Modern Home Draperies that took place during the first week of July.

Instructions: Use a chart similar to the one that follows. For each transaction, indicate in which columns of the cash payments journal the transaction amounts would be recorded. The first transaction has been completed as an example.

Trans.	General Debit	Accounts Payable Debit	Purchases Discounts Credit	Cash in Bank Credit
1	✔			✔

Transactions:
1. Issued Check 342 to Reid Real Estate for the July rent.
2. Issued Check 343 to French Designs in payment of Invoice 20711 less a 2% discount.
3. Bought office supplies from Marks Corp., Check 344.
4. Wrote Check 345 for freight charges on merchandise bought from the Hayes Company.
5. Purchased merchandise for cash from the Wood Company, Check 346.
6. Recorded the bank service charge, June bank statement.
7. Recorded the bank card fee, June bank statement.

Exercise 14-2   Preparing a Schedule of Accounts Payable

The accounts payable ledger of The Corner Book Store included the accounts that follow.

Carswell Magazines	$1,157.20	Barker Publications	$ 186.35
Petrocelli Publishing	5,611.90	Ridgewood, Inc.	2,630.25
Beardsley Equipment	3,868.00	Jenkins Supplies	419.38

Instructions:
(1) Prepare a schedule of accounts payable for August.
(2) If the balance of the Accounts Payable account is $13,873.08, has the subsidiary ledger been proved?

Exercise 14-3   Proving Cash

On November 30, the total of the Cash in Bank Credit column of the cash payments journal is $19,975.12. The total of the Cash in Bank Debit column of the cash receipts journal is $20,956.47. The balance on check stub 1533 is $8,277.98.

Instructions: Use the space provided in the working papers. Prove cash for November. The balance of Cash in Bank on November 1 was $7,296.63.

Problem 14-1   Journalizing Cash Payments Transactions

Owens Office Supply Co., a retail merchandising business, makes all cash payments by check and uses a multicolumn cash payments journal.

310

Refer students to the Chapter 14 review pages in the workbook, *Chapter Reviews and Working Papers.*

---

*A*dditional *R*einforcement

Students who need additional practice or individualized help will benefit from the *Glencoe Accounting Electronic Study Guide* or the *Glencoe Accounting* on-line multimedia program, which provide reinforcement and reteaching for vocabulary, concepts, and procedures.

Instructions: Record the following transactions on page 8 of the cash payments journal.

Transactions:

July 1 Paid cash for a new $700.00 desk for the office, Check 497.
    2 Issued Check 498 to Able Realty to pay the July rent, $400.00.
    7 Bought $298.00 worth of office supplies for cash, Check 499.
  10 Issued Check 500 for $808.50 to Moore Paper Co. in payment of Invoice 798 for $825.00, less a 2% discount of $16.50.
  12 Prepared Check 501 for $921.50 in payment of AAA Envelope Co.'s Invoice 684 for $950.00, less a 3% discount of $28.50.
  14 Paid Sam's, Inc., $490.00 for Invoice 2478 for $500.00, less a $10.00 discount, Check 502.
  20 Paid the AAA Envelope Co. $600.00 on account, Check 503.
  22 Issued Check 504 for $8,820.00 to Crawford Paper Products in payment of Invoice 3-729 for $9,000.00, less a 2% discount of $180.00.
  26 Wrote Check 505 to Interstate Transit for shipping charges on merchandise purchased from Crawford Paper Products, $89.90.
  26 Purchased merchandise for cash, $629.00, Check 506.
  28 Paid Sam's, Inc., $254.80 for Invoice 2498 for $260.00, less a 2% discount of $5.20, Check 507.
  29 Sent Check 508 for $428.60 to Moore Paper Co. in payment of Invoice 868.
  30 Issued Check 509 in the amount of $372.40 to Crawford Paper Products for Invoice 3-800, $380.00 less $7.60 discount.
  31 Prepared Check 510 for $1,500.00 for salaries for the month.

Problem 14-2 Posting Transactions from the

You will need the cash payments journal from Problem 14-1 to complete this problem. The opened general ledger and accounts payable subsidiary ledger for Owens Office Supply Co. appear in the working papers accompanying this textbook.

Instructions:

(1) Post the amounts in the Accounts Payable Debit column to the creditors' accounts in the accounts payable subsidiary ledger.
(2) Post the amounts in the General Debit column to the accounts in the general ledger.
(3) Foot, prove, total, and rule the cash payments journal.
(4) Post the column totals to the general ledger.
(5) Prepare a schedule of accounts payable.

Problem 14-3 Recording Cash Payment Transactions

The Four Seasons Shop uses special journals and subsidiary ledgers to record its business transactions. The opened general ledger and accounts payable subsidiary ledger are included in the working papers.

Instructions:

(1) Record the following transactions in the cash payments journal, page 9.
(2) Post the transactions to the accounts payable subsidiary ledger and to the general ledger daily.

311

Problem 14-1: Ch. Obj. 1
Column totals:
General, $3,616.90
Accounts Pay., $12,943.60
Purchases Disc., $247.80
Cash in Bank, $16,312.70

Problem 14-2: Ch. Obj. 2, 3, 4, 5
AP balance, $583.67

Problem 14-3: Ch. Obj. 1, 2, 3, 4, 5, 6

Teacher Notes

Column totals:
General, $6,971.75
Accounts Pay., $12,948.35
Purchase Disc., $340.45
Cash in Bank, $19,579.65

AP balance, $4,453.45

Cash proof, $21,508.77

Problem 14-4: Ch. Obj. 1, 2, 3, 4, 5, 6

COMPUTER
PROBLEM
This computer image identifies a problem that students may complete using the *Glencoe Accounting, General Ledger* software.

(3) Total, prove, and rule the cash payments journal at the end of the month.
(4) Post the column totals to the general ledger.
(5) Prepare a schedule of accounts payable.
(6) Prove cash. The beginning Cash in Bank balance was $8,941.62. Total cash receipts for the month were $32,146.80. The balance shown on check stub 201 is $21,508.77.

Transactions:
May 2 Issued Check 185 to Lake Developers for the May rent of $800.00.
     3 Paid Brown Carpet Co. $4,753.00 for Invoice 2416 totaling $4,900.00, less the 3% discount of $147.00, Check 186.
     5 Purchased $900.00 worth of merchandise from Materials Unlimited for cash, Check 187.
     9 Paid the monthly telephone bill of $149.25, Check 188.
     9 Sent Check 189 to Jane Aday, Inc., $1,212.50, for Invoice 296-P for $1,250.00 less a 3% discount of $37.50.
    11 Issued Check 190 for office supplies costing $362.49.
    14 Paid the electric bill for the month, $128.47, Check 191.
    14 Sent Check 192 for $900.00 to Williams Company to apply on account.
    16 Issued Check 193 to Brigg's Brothers, Inc., for $3,492.00 in full payment of Invoice 3498 for $3,600.00 less a $108.00 discount.
    17 Paid Invoice 2741 from Central Manufacturing Corp., $1,200.00 less a discount of $24.00, Check 194 for $1,176.00.
    18 Purchased stamps (Miscellaneous Expense), $25.00, Check 195.
    22 Paid $1,800.00 for a one-year general liability insurance policy, Check 196.
    24 Purchased merchandise for $2,600.00 cash, Check 197.
    26 Sent Check 198 to Jane Aday, Inc., for $774.40. The check was in payment of Invoice 389-P for $798.35, less a 3% discount of $23.95.
    29 Purchased office supplies for cash, Check 199 for $128.40.
    30 Recorded the bank service charge of $15.00, May bank statement.
    30 The bank card fee for the month was $63.14, May bank statement.
    31 Sent Check 200 for $300.00 to Brown Carpet Co. to apply on account.

COMPUTER

PROBLEM

Problem 14-4 Processing Purchases and Cash Payments Transactions

The Concord Department Store uses special journals and subsidiary ledgers to record its business transactions. On October 1, the store had the following balances in its general ledger and accounts payable subsidiary ledger accounts.

General Ledger (Partial)

Account Number		Account Balance
101	Cash in Bank	$12,241.65
120	Prepaid Insurance	0.00
125	Supplies	1,400.00
140	Office Equipment	6,450.00
201	Accounts Payable	2,990.00
501	Purchases	60,198.00
505	Transportation In	1,577.00

312

Teacher Notes

_____

_____

_____

_____

_____

510	Purchases Discounts	1,200.00
605	Bank Card Fees Expense	684.19
620	Miscellaneous Expense	415.75
625	Rent Expense	10,800.00
635	Utilities Expense	1,959.25

Accounts Payable Subsidiary Ledger

Account Number		Account Balance
910	Belleview Company, 1145 Belvedere Avenue, Baltimore, MD 21239	$ 90.00
915	BKP Kitchen Products, 100 First Avenue, Kitty Hawk, NC 27949	1,400.00
935	Loup Corporation, 301 Joppa Road, Baltimore, MD 21204	0.00
937	Love's Women's Wear, 72 Rockaway Boulevard, Brooklyn, NY 11212	0.00
970	Randolph Linens, 601 Brattle Street, Randolph, MA 02368	0.00
978	Richmond Designs, 1722 Monument Avenue, Richmond, VA 23220	1,500.00

PJ totals:
Accounts Pay., $19,476.25
Purchases, $14,056.25
General, $5,420.00

CPJ totals:
General, $4,880.52
Accounts Pay., $11,670.00
Purchases Disc., $255.60
Cash in Bank, $16,294.92
AP balance, $10,796.25
Cash proof, $11,208.53

Instructions:
(1) Open the accounts and enter beginning balances in Concord Department Store's general ledger.
(2) Open the creditors' accounts in the accounts payable subsidiary ledger and record the beginning balances.
(3) Record the following transactions in the purchases journal (page 9) and the cash payments journal (page 10). For some transactions, you will have to determine the amount of the discount (if any) and the amount of the check written.
(4) Post to the accounts payable ledger daily from the purchases and cash payments journals.
(5) Post the entries in the General columns of the purchases and cash payments journals on a daily basis.
(6) At the end of October, the total of the Cash in Bank Debit column of the cash receipts journal, page 12, was $15,261.80. Post this total to the Cash in Bank account.
(7) Total the purchases journal and the cash payments journal.
(8) Post the column totals to the general ledger. Post the purchases journal totals first.
(9) Prepare a schedule of accounts payable.
(10) Prove cash. The balance shown on check stub 502 is $11,208.53.

Transactions:
Oct. 1 Purchased merchandise on account from BKP Kitchen Products, $2,000.00, Invoice K-691 dated Sept. 28, terms 3/15, n/30.
2 Issued Check 488 for $1,200.00 to Lyons Real Estate for the October rent.
4 Wrote Check 489 for $1,470.00 to Richmond Designs in payment of Invoice 78942 for $1,500.00, less a $30.00 discount.
7 Paid BKP Kitchen Products $1,400.00 on account, Check 490.
8 Sent Check 491 for $90.00 to the Belleview Company on account.
11 Issued Check 492 for $1,940.00 to BKP Kitchen Products in payment of Invoice K-691 for $2,000.00, less a discount of $60.00.
12 Paid the monthly telephone bill of $214.87, Check 493.

313

Teacher Notes

Problem 14-5: Ch. Obj. 1

CHALLENGE

PROBLEM

The last problem in each chapter is a challenge problem and is identified by this "maze" symbol.

Accounts Payable total, $9,119.95
Purchases Discounts total, $179.21

---

12 Purchased merchandise for cash from the Belleview Company, $1,945.60, Check 494.

13 Issued Check 495 to Tidewater Insurance Co. for a one-year fire insurance policy, $950.00.

14 Bought office equipment on account from Loup Corp., $5,300.00, Invoice K-4444 dated Oct. 10, terms n/30.

16 Issued Check 496 for $75.00 for carpet cleaning (Miscellaneous Expense).

18 Bought $120.00 worth of supplies from Loup Corp. on account, Invoice K-4462 dated Oct. 16, terms n/30.

20 Received Invoice 4215, dated Oct. 18 with terms of 2/20, n/60, from Love's Women's Wear for $945.20 worth of merchandise purchased on account.

20 Wrote Check 497 for $25.00 for freight charges on merchandise bought from Love's Women's Wear.

21 Purchased merchandise from Randolph Linens on account for $3,480.00, Invoice CP422 dated Oct. 18, terms 2/15, n/30.

21 Bought $3,200.00 worth of merchandise on account from Richmond Designs, Invoice 79211 dated Oct. 19, terms 3/10, n/30.

23 Paid the $321.00 electric bill, Check 498.

24 Received Invoice 2832 dated Oct. 22, terms 2/10, n/30, for merchandise purchased on account from Belleview Company, $800.00.

25 Bought merchandise on account from Randolph Linens for $1,684.25, Invoice CP478 dated Oct. 24, terms 2/15, n/30.

26 Paid cash for office supplies, $50.00, Check 499.

27 Sent Check 500 to Richmond Designs in full payment of Invoice 79211, less the discount.

28 Recorded the monthly bank service charge of $25.00, October bank statement.

28 Recorded the $74.05 bank card fee, October bank statement.

28 Bought merchandise totaling $600.00 from Randolph Linens on account, Invoice CP500 dated Oct. 27, terms 2/15, n/30.

30 Sent Check 501 to Randolph Linens in full payment of Invoice CP422, less the discount.

31 Purchased merchandise on account from BKP Kitchen Products for $1,346.80, Invoice K788 dated Oct. 29, terms 3/15, n/30.

CHALLENGE

PROBLEM

Problem 14-5   Examining the Cash Payments Journal

The completed cash payments journal of The Piece Goods Shop for the month of April appears on page 315. Some amounts and other information have been deleted from the journal.

Instructions: Fill in the missing information and complete the journal. The chart of accounts for The Piece Goods Shop includes the following accounts.

101	Cash in Bank		510	Purchases Discounts
115	Prepaid Insurance		605	Bank Card Fees Expense
120	Office Supplies		630	Miscellaneous Expense
201	Accounts Payable		650	Rent Expense
501	Purchases		660	Utilities Expense
505	Transportation In			

314

CASH PAYMENTS JOURNAL PAGE 7

	DATE	DOC. NO.	ACCOUNT TITLE	POST. REF.	GENERAL DEBIT	ACCOUNTS PAYABLE DEBIT	PURCHASES DISCOUNTS CREDIT	CASH IN BANK CREDIT	
1	Apr. 2	176	Rent Expense	650	750 00			750 00	1
2	3	177	Utilities Expense	660	167 50			167 50	2
3	5	178	Baker Curtains, Inc.	✓		250 00		250 00	3
4	9			501				788 50	4
5	9	180	Office Supplies		209 50				5
6	11	181	Andrews Fabrics	✓			22 50	727 50	6
7	13	182	Warneford, Inc.	✓		875 00		875 00	7
8	13	183	Buckeye Manufacturing	✓		1500 00	30 00	1470 00	8
9	16	184	Utilities Expense	660	87 50			87 50	9
10	17	185	First Avenue Fabrics			2430 00	48 60		10
11	18	186		630	23 00			23 00	11
12	19	187	Purchases		2133 20			2133 20	12
13	23	188	Prepaid Insurance	115					13
14	25	189	Andrews Fabrics	✓		1181 75		1146 30	14
15	27	190	Baker Curtains, Inc.	✓			42 66		15
16	30		Office Supplies	120	535 50			535 50	16
17	30	—	Miscellaneous Expense	630	10 00				17
18	30		Bank Card Fees Expense	605	59 00				18
19					6163 70			15104 44	19
					6163 70				20

---

4 ASSESS

A chapter test is available for use in assessing students' understanding of concepts in this chapter.

The testmaker software will enable you to develop tailor-made chapter, unit, semester, and final tests.

Alternative Assessment

For alternative assessment strategies, refer to *Tech Prep Strategies in Accounting.*

315

> Use Chapter Test 14 here to assess students' understanding and retention of the concepts and procedures presented in the chapter.

Have students talk with a credit manager of a retail outlet. What factors does the manager consider when deciding whether or not to extend credit to a customer?

QUESTIONS

1. Suggest the steps you would take to plan and negotiate a business loan to produce a new product.
2. How might the decision to extend credit to consumers be considered a marketing or selling decision rather than a financial decision?

ANSWERS

1. Among the steps you would take are to: define your product and its market, clearly identify production costs and the time required to get your product to market, target possible lenders, prepare a persuasive application, negotiate the best terms and conditions possible, learn from rejections, and maintain a positive relationship with your lender.
2. Since many consumers depend on credit, sales may be lost if credit is not available. The risk manager must weigh the cost of a lost sale against the chances of nonpayment of a loan.

Credit Managers Take Risks in Stride

If you're challenged by risk-taking and you feel you've got pretty good judgment, read on. This could be the career for you.

In today's economy, money is more than a measure of value for goods and services. It's also a tradeable commodity. From country to country, business to business, business to consumer, extending credit can make or break a business—and the credit manager's judgment and instincts can make the difference. No risk means no gain. The successful business makes credit available in order to expand its market share and increase its profits. Some bad debts (uncollectible accounts) are inevitable; keeping the bad debts to a minimum is the real challenge.

Any business that lends money or extends credit employs a credit manager: banks; credit bureaus; mortgage, finance, or investment companies; brokerages; department stores; businesses. The credit manager is the person who directs or coordinates activities of workers engaged in conducting credit investigations. He or she reviews and evaluates applications and data gathered by the staff, and rejects or approves the applications. Essentially, it's the credit manager's responsibility to determine whether a business or an individual is a good credit risk.

In businesses, credit managers are often accountants. Banks and other lending institutions hire college graduates with degrees in accounting and business. Once these employees complete a bank-officer trainee program and gain experience, their responsibilities grow.

In larger companies, credit management is subdivided into financial analysis and credit analysis. These positions require an advanced background in accounting and more experience. Few colleges offer training in credit management, so candidates

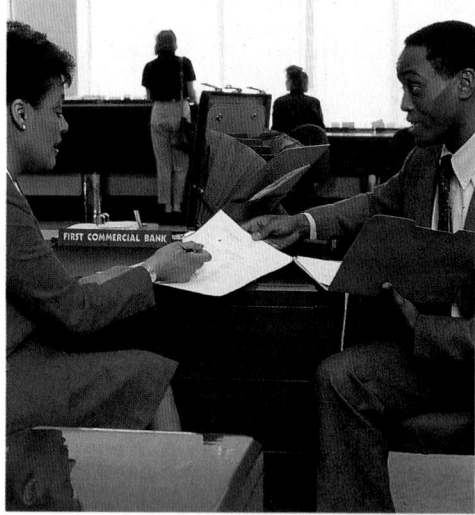

The ability to minimize risks is an essential skill for a credit manager.

often seek advanced training at the Credit Research Foundation or the National Association of Credit Management.

A day in the life of a credit manager presents opportunities to exercise critical assessments of a client's character and credibility, the economic climate, and the terms of repayment. The employer is banking on the fact that he or she won't make too many mistakes.

316

Chapter 15

RECORDING GENERAL JOURNAL TRANSACTIONS

In Chapters 11 through 14, you learned how to record business transactions in four special journals. Each special journal is designed to handle a specific kind of business transaction: sales of merchandise on account, the cash received by a business, the purchase of merchandise and other assets on account, and all cash payments or decreases to cash.

There are, however, some transactions that do not fit into one of these four categories. As a result, these transactions cannot be recorded in one of the special journals. They are instead recorded in the general journal, which you first learned about in Chapter 5.

In this chapter, you will learn how the general journal fits into an accounting system using special journals. You will also learn about the kinds of business transactions that are recorded in it.

Learning Objectives

When you have completed Chapter 15, you should be able to do the following:

1. Explain the purpose of debit and credit memorandums.
2. Journalize transactions involving sales returns and allowances.
3. Journalize transactions involving purchases returns and allowances.
4. Journalize correcting entries.
5. Define the accounting terms introduced in this chapter.

New Terms

sales return
sales allowance
credit memorandum
debit memorandum
purchases return
purchases allowance

INTRODUCING THE CHAPTER

LOOKING BACK

Special journals save time both in recording transactions and in posting to ledger accounts. Some transactions, however, do not fit in the special journals. Those transactions must be recorded in the general journal. Among the transactions students will learn to record in this chapter are those involving returns and allowances for both sales and purchases.

VOCABULARY DEVELOPMENT

Reinforce vocabulary through a team competition to define new terms. Appoint teams to participate in a "Vocabulary Bee." Use terms from earlier chapters to supplement the terms here. Teams take turns defining terms, with team members consulting with each other before giving a definition (use a time limit of a minute or so). If a team gives an incorrect definition, the team is eliminated. Definitions of these terms are found in the chapter and in the glossary on pages 670-679.

317

Teaching Resources

- Lesson Plans
- TE/Chapter Reviews & Working Papers
- Demonstration Problems
- Student Study Plans
- Teaching Transparencies
- Solutions Transparencies
- Electronic Field Trips Video, Level I
- Electronic Study Guide
- Chapter 15 Test
- Unit Objective Test for Chapters 11-15
- Unit Problem Test for Chapters 11-15

Other Resources

- Skills Improvement Activities
- Blackline Masters
- Careers in Accounting
- Dictionary
- Math Review for Accounting
- Tech Prep Strategies in Accounting
- Video
- Test Bank with Software
- Spanish Resources/Audiotapes
- Spanish Electronic Study Guide

1 FOCUS

MAJOR CONCEPTS

- Handling Business Transactions That Occur Infrequently
- Sales Returns and Allowances
- Purchases Returns and Allowances
- Correcting Entries

BUSINESS CONNECTION

Direct mail businesses like Lands' End process numerous transactions for sales returns. In fact, Lands' End guarantees customer satisfaction, and they accept returns for any reason, at any time. When a customer returns an item, Lands' End wants to know the reason, such as the item does not fit, the color or quality is not acceptable, the item is damaged, the incorrect item was shipped, etc. Information about sales returns helps Lands' End to analyze its operations so that it can better meet customers' needs.

2 TEACH

CONCEPT DEVELOPMENT
Handling Business Transactions That Occur Infrequently

Some business transactions do not fit one of the special journals. Those transactions must be recorded in the general journal. The name of the general journal means that it is an all-purpose journal that can be used to record any transaction.

CONCEPT DEVELOPMENT
Sales Returns and Allowances

Customers are not always satisfied with merchandise purchased. Merchandise may have been the wrong size or color or it may have been damaged. When customers return merchandise, the seller must issue a credit or return cash paid. A full return of the purchase price is a sales return. If the customer wants to keep the merchandise but receive a partial credit for some damage to the item, a sales allowance is granted.

(Continued)

Handling Business Transactions that Occur Infrequently

A business designs its special journals to handle particular kinds of transactions that occur frequently, usually daily. Any transaction that cannot be recorded in a special journal is recorded in the general journal. Examples of transactions that would be recorded in a general journal include sales returns and allowances, purchases returns and allowances, and correcting entries. These general journal entries will be explained in this chapter.

Sales Returns and Allowances

All merchandising businesses expect to have some customers who are not satisfied with their purchases. The reasons for dissatisfaction vary. An item may be damaged or defective. The color or size may be incorrect. Perhaps the customer made a mistake and bought the wrong item. Whatever the reason, merchants usually allow dissatisfied customers to return merchandise. Any merchandise returned for full credit or a cash refund is called a **sales return.**

Sometimes a customer discovers that merchandise is damaged or defective but still usable. When this happens, the merchant may reduce the sales price for the damaged merchandise. This price reduction granted by a business for damaged goods kept by the customer is called a **sales allowance.**

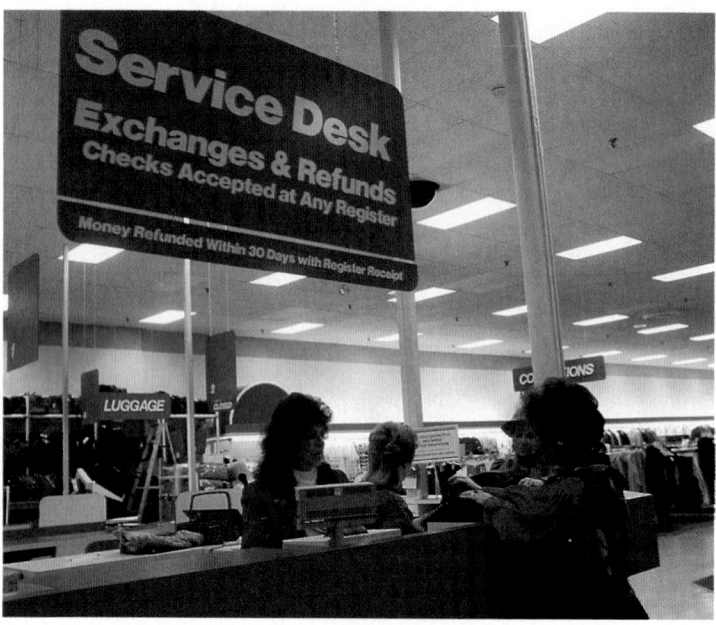

Many merchandising businesses have separate departments to handle customer returns of merchandise.

Reinforcing Study Skills

Remind students that the learning objectives listed at the beginning of each chapter provide a good "road map" for their approach to the chapter. As they read the chapter, students should try to reach each of the stated goals before going on to the next main objective. Reading for a specific objective should help students retain information more easily.

Provide a copy of the Student Study Plans to each class member to help organize study activities or to individualize practice and review activities.

If the sales return or sales allowance occurs on a charge sale, the business usually prepares a credit memorandum. A **credit memorandum** is a form that lists the details of a sales return or sales allowance. It is called a "credit" memorandum because the charge customer's account will be *credited* for (or decreased by) the amount of the return or allowance.

The credit memorandum, or credit memo, used by Champion Building Products is shown in Figure 15-1. This credit memo was prepared when Shawn Flannery returned merchandise he had bought on credit on December 21. Notice that the credit memo includes a description of the returned item, the reason for the return, and the amount to be credited to Shawn Flannery's account. Champion's credit memo also includes spaces for the date and sales slip number of the original sale. Notice too that the total on the credit memo includes the sales tax charged on the original sale.

ACCOUNTING Tips
Credit memos are prepared by the seller of the merchandise.

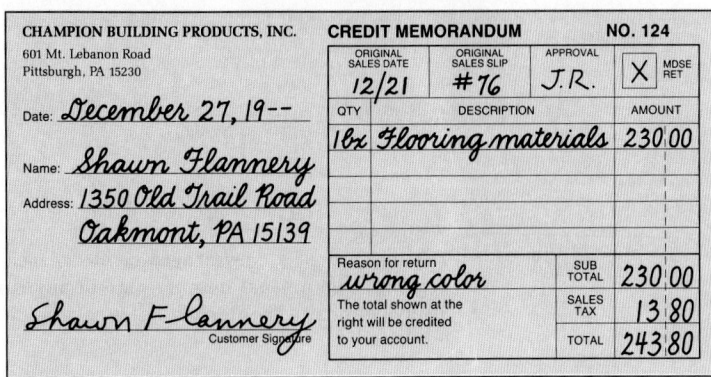

CHAMPION BUILDING PRODUCTS, INC.
601 Mt. Lebanon Road
Pittsburgh, PA 15230

CREDIT MEMORANDUM   NO. 124

ORIGINAL SALES DATE	ORIGINAL SALES SLIP	APPROVAL		
12/21	#76	J.R.	X	MDSE RET

Date: *December 27, 19--*

Name: *Shawn Flannery*

Address: *1350 Old Trail Road Oakmont, PA 15139*

QTY	DESCRIPTION	AMOUNT
1 bx	Flooring materials	230 00

Reason for return
wrong color

The total shown at the right will be credited to your account.

SUB TOTAL	230 00
SALES TAX	13 80
TOTAL	243 80

Shawn F. Lannery
Customer Signature

Figure 15-1   Credit Memorandum

The same form would have been used had Shawn Flannery been given a sales allowance. Of course, the amount credited to his account would have been less. Any credit granted for an allowance is the difference between the original sales price and the reduced price.

Champion's credit memos are prenumbered and prepared in duplicate. The original is given or sent to the customer. The copy kept by the business is the source document for the journal entry to record the transaction.

The Sales Returns and Allowances Account

Sales returns and sales allowances decrease the total revenue earned by a business. This decrease, however, is not recorded in the Sales account. Instead, a separate account called Sales Returns and Allowances is used. (Sales discounts, you'll remember, are also treated separately.) Sales Returns and Allowances summarizes the total amount of returns and allowances for damaged, defective, or otherwise unsatisfactory merchandise. Separating sales returns and allowances from Sales is efficient. There are, however, other reasons for having a separate account.

With a separate account for returns and allowances, Sales always represents the gross, or total, revenue for the period. Having a separate account

A sales return or allowance decreases the Sales account, but businesses record these amounts in a separate account to better track the amounts, which represent lost sales. The Sales account should always show the gross sales or revenue for the accounting period.

Using Visuals

Ask students to read the photo caption on page 318 and then to give examples of local businesses that have separate counters for returns and exchanges. Which local businesses do not use separate areas for returns? What are some possible reasons they may not use separate returns areas?

Teaching Tips

- Merchandise returned to a business must be in the same condition as when purchased or full credit may not be granted for a return.
- Ask students to think of specific items they have returned to a store for credit.
- Emphasize the association between "credit" memorandum and "credit" being granted to a customer by decreasing the customer's account balance with a "credit" entry.

Using Visuals

Call students' attention to the credit memo in Figure 15-1. Note the approval initials on the form. How does the requirement that returns be approved by an authorized person help to protect the business?

Making Connections

EVERYDAY LIFE

Most everyone has probably returned merchandise to a retailer. Perhaps they did not like the fit of clothing, or maybe their name was misspelled on the return address labels they ordered through a catalog. Ask students to describe occasions when they have returned merchandise.

Teaching Tips

■ Sales Returns and Allowances is a contra revenue account; therefore, its balance decreases the balance of the Sales account. Use T accounts to explain this relationship between the two accounts.

■ Emphasize that the Sales Returns and Allowances account is important to a seller because it shows total amounts granted for returns and allowances, which is an indicator of customer dissatisfaction with the seller's merchandise.

■ Remind students that they should learn three things about any new account: (1) its classification; (2) its increase, decrease, and normal balance sides; and (3) how the account is used in the business.

Using Visuals

 Use demonstration problem 15-1 to show students how to analyze sales returns and allowances transactions and record them in a general journal.

for sales returns and allowances allows management to better monitor customer dissatisfaction. The balance in the account may also signal merchandising problems. If the monthly balance of Sales Returns and Allowances is large in comparison to the balance of the Sales account, steps should be taken to discover why and to correct the cause. For example, management would want to know if any one supplier is responsible for a large number of returns, if returns and allowances are mainly from one department, or if merchandise is being mishandled inside the company.

Like Sales Discounts, Sales Returns and Allowances is classified as a contra revenue account. As a contra account, its balance decreases the balance of the revenue account Sales. Since the normal balance side of Sales is the credit side, the normal balance side of Sales Returns and Allowances is the debit side. This relationship is shown in the T accounts.

Sales		Sales Returns and Allowances	
Dr.	Cr.	Dr.	Cr.
–	+	+	–
Decrease Side	Increase Side	Increase Side	Decrease Side
	Balance Side	Balance Side	

R E M E M B E R

The balance of a contra account decreases the balance of its related account. The normal balance side of any contra account, therefore, is always opposite the normal balance side of the account it decreases.

Analyzing Sales Returns and Allowances Transactions

On December 21, Champion sold merchandise on account to Shawn Flannery for $230.00 plus sales tax of $13.80. The transaction was recorded in the sales journal and posted to the customer's account in the accounts receivable subsidiary ledger. The December 21 transaction is shown below in T-account form.

GENERAL LEDGER

Accounts Receivable		Sales Tax Payable	
Dr.	Cr.	Dr.	Cr.
+	–	–	+
$243.80			$13.80

SUBSIDIARY LEDGER

Sales		Shawn Flannery	
Dr.	Cr.	Dr.	Cr.
–	+	+	–
	$230.00	$243.80	

Cooperative Learning Strategies

MAKE AND DEFEND

Divide students into groups of 4 or 5 and provide the following scenario. Ask students to recommend changes to improve the retailer's return policy. Each group should list reasons to support its decisions. Have each group select a spokesperson to present and defend its recommendations to the class.

"The Music Emporium sells cassette tapes and compact disks. It accepts all returned merchandise with or without a receipt, and regardless of the date of purchase. It pays cash for all returns. The manager has noticed that returns over the last six months have been unusually high."

Refer to the "Cooperative Learning" section of *Tech Prep Strategies in Accounting* for additional cooperative learning strategies.

On December 27, Shawn Flannery returned the merchandise purchased on account for full credit. The credit memo shown in Figure 15-1 was prepared by Champion for this transaction.

December 27: *Issued Credit Memo 124 to Shawn Flannery for the return of merchandise purchased on account, $230.00 plus $13.80 sales tax.*

The accounts affected by this transaction are Sales Returns and Allowances, Sales Tax Payable, and Accounts Receivable in the general ledger and the accounts receivable subsidiary ledger account Shawn Flannery.

The Sales Returns and Allowances account is being increased since the amount of merchandise returned by customers has increased. It is, therefore, debited for $230.00, the original sales price of the merchandise. Since the merchandise sold and taxed earlier has been returned, Champion no longer owes the state the sales tax on the December 21 sale. Sales Tax Payable, then, is being decreased. It is debited for $13.80. Accounts Receivable is also being decreased because Champion no longer expects to receive cash from Shawn Flannery. It is credited for $243.80, the original sales price of the returned merchandise ($230.00) plus the sales tax ($13.80). Accounts Receivable is the controlling account for the accounts receivable subsidiary ledger. If the controlling account is being credited, one of the accounts in the subsidiary ledger must also be credited. That account is Shawn Flannery. Since Accounts Receivable was credited for $243.80, the Shawn Flannery account is also credited for $243.80.

GENERAL LEDGER

Accounts Receivable				Sales Tax Payable	
Dr.	Cr.			Dr.	Cr.
+	−			−	+
$243.80	$243.80			$13.80	$13.80

SUBSIDIARY LEDGER

Sales Returns and Allowances				Shawn Flannery	
Dr.	Cr.			Dr.	Cr.
+	−			+	−
$230.00				$243.80	$243.80

As you can see from the T accounts, the December 27 sales return transaction has, in effect, "wiped out" the earlier journal entry recording the sale to Shawn Flannery.

Journalizing Sales Returns and Allowances Transactions

Champion's special journals are not designed to handle returns of merchandise sold on account. The entry, therefore, is recorded in the general journal, as shown in Figure 15-2 on page 322.

> ## *Did you know?*
>
> At the age of 20, Luca Bartolomes Pacioli, a Franciscan monk, was tutoring two sons of a wealthy merchant. He prepared his own materials to tutor the brothers in both mathematics and bookkeeping applications, and he later began lecturing on his teachings. He developed an accounting system based on Arabic algebra using an equation that set the assets equal to the rights or claims of the individuals who provided financing for those assets. Now, more than 500 years later, we refer to this method of accounting as double-entry accounting, and Luca Pacioli is known as the Father of Accounting.

Critical Thinking

An electronic parts manufacturer offers a rebate on purchases to wholesalers if their returns are less than 20 percent. Why would a business offer this rebate?

(Answer: Returns are expensive for the business to process. When an order is initially received, the business incurs expenses in processing the order and shipping it to the customer. When the customer returns the merchandise, not only does the business lose the revenue, but it also incurs additional expenses for handling the return. By providing incentives to keep returns low, the business does not incur the expense of processing orders for unwanted merchandise and it avoids the expense of processing returns.)

Look at the third line of the journal entry. Since a general ledger controlling account and a subsidiary ledger account are affected by this transaction, both Accounts Receivable and Shawn Flannery are written on the same line in the Description column. The two account titles are separated by a diagonal line.

Notice also that a diagonal line was entered in the Posting Reference column. The diagonal line indicates that the amount (the $243.80 credit) is to be posted to *two* places. The amount will be posted *first* to the Accounts Receivable controlling account in the general ledger and *then* to the Shawn Flannery account in the accounts receivable subsidiary ledger. The diagonal line is entered in the Posting Reference column when the journal entry is made.

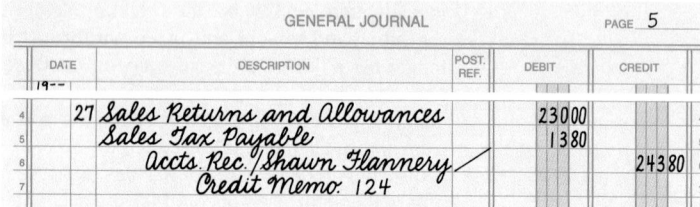

Figure 15-2 Recording a Sales Returns and Allowances Transaction in the General Journal

R E M E M B E R

Always record the title of the controlling account before you record the title of the subsidiary ledger account.

Sometimes a merchant will give a customer a cash refund instead of a credit for a sales return or allowance. Champion's policy is to give a cash refund only if the original sale was a cash sale. When a cash refund is given, the Cash in Bank account is affected instead of Accounts Receivable. The entry for a cash refund is recorded in the cash payments journal.

Posting Sales Returns and Allowances Transactions

After a sales returns and allowances transaction has been recorded in the general journal, it is posted to the appropriate accounts in the general ledger and the accounts receivable subsidiary ledger.

Figure 15-3 shows how the December 27 transaction is posted. Notice how the credit part of the transaction was posted. The $243.80 credit amount, remember, is posted to two accounts—the general ledger controlling account and a particular subsidiary ledger account. After the amount is posted to the general ledger account, the account number of Accounts Receivable is entered to the *left* of the diagonal in the Posting Reference column. After the amount is posted to the customer's account, a check mark (✔) is entered to the *right* of the diagonal line.

322

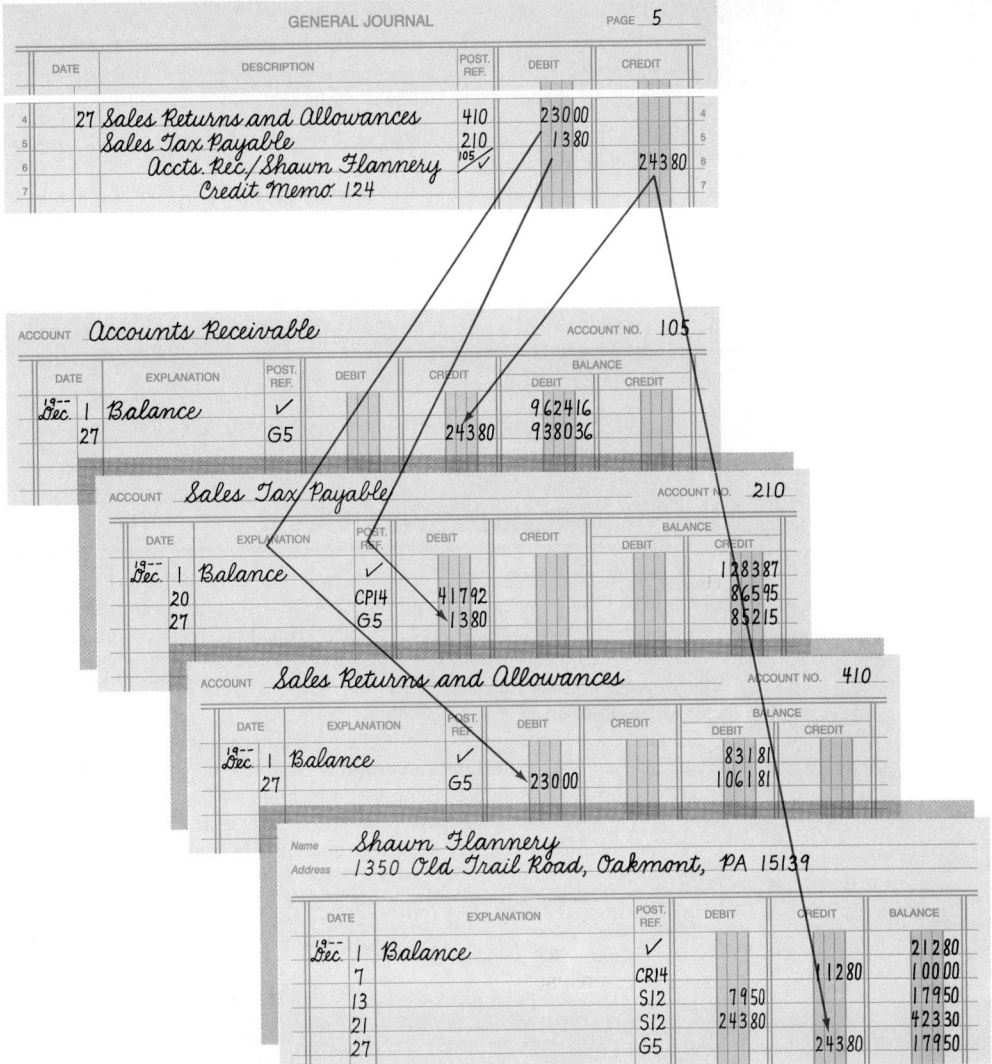

Figure 15-3 Posting a Sales Returns and Allowances Transaction

Before you go any further, complete the activity on page 324 to check your understanding of the material you have just read.

R E M E M B E R

Be sure to post the total amount of a sales return or allowance transaction to both Accounts Receivable and the customer's account in the subsidiary ledger.

CHAPTER 15   Recording General Journal Transactions **323**

ANSWERS

1. Sales return
2. Sales allowance
3. Credit memorandum
4. Sales
5. Debit

On notebook paper, complete each statement with the appropriate term.

1. When a business allows a charge customer to return merchandise for full credit, that transaction is called a(n) ___?___ .
2. A(n) ___?___ occurs when a business reduces the price for damaged merchandise that the charge customer chooses to keep.
3. The form that lists the details of a sales return or sales allowance transaction is called a(n) ___?___ .
4. Sales Returns and Allowances reduces the balance of ___?___ .
5. The normal balance side of the Sales Returns and Allowances account is the ___?___ side.

Compare your answers to those in the answers section. Re-read the preceding part of the chapter to find the answers to any questions you missed.

CONCEPT DEVELOPMENT
Purchases Returns and Allowances

Students have learned how the seller of merchandise grants credit to dissatisfied customers. Businesses are also customers and buy items such as merchandise, supplies, and equipment that may need to be returned to the supplier. Such returns for credit are purchases returns or allowances.

Emphasize the difference between a return and an allowance. Point out that the buyer prepares a debit memo to inform the seller that items purchased were unsatisfactory. Use a T account to emphasize the association between "debit" memorandum and a "debit" to the creditor's account.

A purchases return or allowance decreases Purchases, but a separate account is used to record such amounts so they can more easily be tracked in the accounting system. The Purchases account should always show the total amount of merchandise purchased for the accounting period and should not be "cluttered" with purchases returns and allowances.

Purchases Returns and Allowances

As you learned in Chapter 13, businesses buy many items for use in the operation of the business. In addition, merchandising businesses buy goods to resell to their customers. Occasionally, a business buys merchandise or other items on account that, upon inspection, turn out to be unacceptable. Like any other customer, a business may either return the items or take an allowance on them.

The form a business uses to notify its supplier (creditor) of a return or allowance is called a **debit memorandum,** or debit memo. A "debit" memo indicates the amount that the supplier's account in the accounts payable subsidiary ledger will be *debited,* or decreased. A debit memo prepared by Champion Building Products is shown in Figure 15-4. As you can see, the

DEBIT MEMORANDUM		No. 51
		Date: December 28, 19--
		Invoice No.: 4681

CHAMPION BUILDING PRODUCTS, INC.
601 Mt. Lebanon Road
Pittsburgh, PA 15230

To: Wilson Electric, Inc.
1401 Delta Drive
Jackson, MS 39205

This day we have debited your account as follows:

Quantity	Description	Unit Price	Total
3	Electric garage door openers, stock number EG 31	$100.00	$300.00

Figure 15-4 Debit Memorandum

Using Visuals

Point out the debit memorandum in Figure 15-4. Most debit memos are created between a retailer and a wholesaler, thus no sales tax is charged on those transactions.

Reteaching Strategies

Use the following scenario to help students understand returns and allowances. Ask students to name the accounts affected if Sachi decides to return the bike or if he decides to take the allowance of $10.

"Sachi's son had his heart set on a new bike. She purchased the bike, took it home, and checked the parts before assembling the bike. Sachi was disappointed when she noticed that the kick stand and the handle grips were both missing because she knew the retailer had no more of this particular model in stock. Sachi packed all the parts back into the box and took the bike back to the retailer. The retailer gave her two options: to get her money back or to keep the bike and receive a reduction of $10 because of the two missing items."

debit memo is prenumbered and has spaces to list the creditor's name, address, and invoice number. Champion prepares an original and one copy of each debit memo. The original is sent to the creditor. The copy becomes the source document for the journal entry.

A debit memo always results in a debit (decrease) to the Accounts Payable controlling account in the general ledger and to the creditor's account in the subsidiary ledger. The account credited depends on whether the debit memo is for merchandise or for some other asset bought on account.

Suppose that Champion prepared a debit memo for the return of a defective typewriter it had purchased on account. Since Champion no longer has the typewriter, the asset account Office Equipment is credited.

When Champion buys merchandise for resale to its customers, it debits the cost to the Purchases account. A return of that merchandise decreases the balance of Purchases. As for sales, however, a separate account is used to record the return of merchandise to a supplier: the Purchases Returns and Allowances account. A **purchases return,** then, occurs when a business returns merchandise bought on account to the supplier for full credit. A **purchases allowance** occurs when a business keeps unsatisfactory merchandise but pays less than its original purchase price.

Purchases Returns and Allowances appears in the cost of merchandise section of the chart of accounts. Like Purchases Discounts, it is a contra cost of merchandise account. Since the normal balance side of the Purchases account is the debit side, the normal balance side of Purchases Returns and Allowances is the credit side. This relationship is shown in the T accounts.

Purchases		Purchases Returns and Allowances	
Dr.	Cr.	Dr.	Cr.
+	–	–	+
Increase Side	Decrease Side	Decrease Side	Increase Side
Balance Side			Balance Side

Analyzing Purchases Returns and Allowances Transactions

On December 24, Champion Building Products purchased $5,680.04 in merchandise on account from Wilson Electric, Inc. On December 28, Champion returned some of that merchandise to Wilson Electric. Champion prepared and sent the debit memo shown in Figure 15-4.

December 28: Issued Debit Memo 51 for the return of merchandise purchased on account from Wilson Electric, Inc., $300.00.

Three accounts are affected by this transaction. The two general ledger accounts affected are Accounts Payable and Purchases Returns and Allowances. The accounts payable subsidiary ledger account affected is Wilson Electric, Inc.

Since Champion is returning merchandise purchased on account, it no longer owes money to the creditor for that merchandise. The liability account Accounts Payable, therefore, is debited for $300.00. Since the controlling account Accounts Payable is being debited, an account in the subsidiary ledger must also be debited. The Wilson Electric, Inc. account, therefore, is also debited for $300.00. Purchases Returns and Allowances is being increased since the amount of merchandise returned to suppliers has increased. It is credited for $300.00, the cost of the original merchandise purchased. This transaction is shown in T-account form.

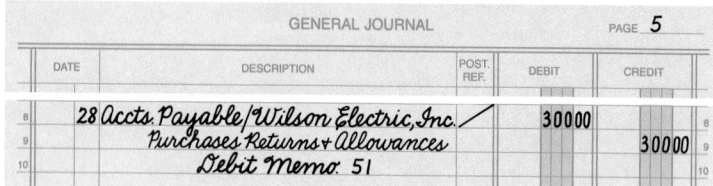

GENERAL LEDGER			Purchases Returns and Allowances		SUBSIDIARY LEDGER	
Accounts Payable					Wilson Electric, Inc.	
Dr.	Cr.		Dr.	Cr.	Dr.	Cr.
−	+		−	+	−	+
$300.00				$300.00	$300.00	

Journalizing Purchases Returns and Allowances Transactions

A return of merchandise, or any other item, bought on account is recorded in the general journal. The journal entry for this transaction is shown in Figure 15-5. Look at the debit part of the entry. The amount will be posted to both the general ledger controlling account and a subsidiary ledger account. Both account titles, then, are written on the same line in the Description column, separated by a diagonal. A diagonal line is also entered in the Posting Reference column to remind the accounting clerk to post the $300.00 debit to two accounts.

		GENERAL JOURNAL			PAGE 5	
	DATE	DESCRIPTION	POST. REF.	DEBIT	CREDIT	
8	28	Accts. Payable/Wilson Electric, Inc. /		300 00		8
9		Purchases Returns + Allowances			300 00	9
10		Debit Memo. 51				10

Figure 15-5 Recording a Purchases Returns and Allowances Transaction in the General Journal

R E M E M B E R

A diagonal line in the Posting Reference column indicates that an amount is to be posted to two accounts.

Posting Purchases Returns and Allowances Transactions

Figure 15-6 shows how a purchases returns and allowances transaction is posted to the general and subsidiary ledger accounts. Notice again that the $300.00 debit is posted to two accounts. After the posting, the account number for the controlling account is placed to the left of the diagonal in the Posting Reference column. The check mark to the right of the diagonal indicates that the amount has been posted to the appropriate account in the subsidiary ledger.

Making Connections

BUSINESS ETHICS

You are a sales clerk at Givens Department Store. A friend comes in to return an item she purchased recently. You know that your friend purchased the item on sale, but you nevertheless give her a full refund. Are your actions correct?

(Answer: No. Most companies have fairly liberal return policies, but returning more to a customer than that customer paid for the item is wrong. It will also have a detrimental effect on the company's income.)

GENERAL JOURNAL   PAGE 5

DATE	DESCRIPTION	POST. REF.	DEBIT	CREDIT
28	Accts. Payable/Wilson Electric, Inc.	201/✓	300 00	
	Purchases Returns + Allowances	515		300 00
	Debit Memo 51			

ACCOUNT Accounts Payable   **ACCOUNT NO.** 201

DATE	EXPLANATION	POST. REF.	DEBIT	CREDIT	BALANCE DEBIT	BALANCE CREDIT
Dec. 1	Balance	✓				3 281 75
28		G5	300 00			2 981 75

ACCOUNT Purchases Returns and Allowances   **ACCOUNT NO.** 515

DATE	EXPLANATION	POST. REF.	DEBIT	CREDIT	BALANCE DEBIT	BALANCE CREDIT
Dec. 1	Balance	✓				3 717 90
28		G5		300 00		4 017 90

Name Wilson Electric, Inc.
Address 1401 Delta Drive, Jackson, MS 39205

DATE	EXPLANATION	POST. REF.	DEBIT	CREDIT	BALANCE
Dec. 24		P12		5 680 04	5 680 04
28		G5	300 00		5 380 04

Figure 15-6 Posting a Purchases Returns and Allowances Transaction

Before reading further, complete the following activity to check your understanding of transactions involving purchases returns and allowances.

 ## Check Your Learning

Write your answers to these questions on notebook paper.

1. What form is used to notify a creditor about the return of items bought on account and the decrease in the creditor's account?
2. How does a purchases return differ from a purchases allowance?
3. What type of account is Purchases Returns and Allowances?
4. What does a diagonal line in the Posting Reference column of the general journal indicate?
5. In what section of the chart of accounts does Purchases Returns and Allowances appear?

Compare your answers to those in the answers section. Re-read the preceding part of the chapter to find the correct answers to any questions you may have missed.

Using Visuals

Call students' attention to the red arrows in Figure 15-6. Why is the debit amount in the general journal posted twice?

 ACCOUNTING PRACTICE
Students may complete Exercise 15-2 at this point.

 ANSWERS

1. Debit memorandum
2. A purchases return occurs when merchandise bought on account is returned to the supplier for full credit. A purchases allowance occurs when a business keeps unsatisfactory merchandise and pays less than its original cost.
3. Contra cost of merchandise account
4. The amount is to be posted to both the general ledger and the subsidiary ledger.
5. Cost of merchandise

Reteaching Strategies

Some students may confuse debit and credit memos since a debit memo results in a credit to Purchases Returns and Allowances while a credit memo results in a debit to Sales Returns and Allowances. A mnemonic device to help them remember which is which is to relate each to the Purchases and Sales accounts. Purchases has a normal debit balance and a debit memo is the source document for a purchases return or allowance. Sales has a normal credit balance and a credit memo documents a sales return or allowance.

CONCEPT DEVELOPMENT
Correcting Entries

Errors do occur in accounting records. Remind students that they should never erase an error unless it is on the work sheet. Errors must be corrected in a manner that allows an auditor to see the error and to see what was done to correct it.

Using Visuals

Use demonstration problem 15-5, Part A, to show students how to correct an error discovered before the journal entries were posted.

Correcting Entries

Unfortunately, errors are occasionally made when handling accounting records. Some ways to spot and correct errors were discussed in earlier chapters. One rule always applies to these and other corrections. *Never erase an error.*

Sometimes errors affect only subsidiary ledger accounts. For example, cash received on account from one customer may have been recorded in the cash receipts journal under another customer's name. The Accounts Receivable Credit column in the cash receipts journal is not affected by such an error. When the column total is posted, the balance of the Accounts Receivable account will match the total of the balances of all the customer accounts. The balances, however, in two customers' accounts in the accounts receivable subsidiary ledger will be incorrect.

This type of error is usually discovered in one of two ways. A customer often spots the error in a monthly statement. When auditing (examining) the business records, an accountant may also spot the error and inform the accounting clerk of it by memo. The accountant's memo becomes the source document for the correcting entry.

On December 15, Champion's accountant discovered an error affecting two customer accounts in the accounts receivable subsidiary ledger.

December 15: Discovered that $75.00 received from the Gateway School District, a charge customer, on November 30 had been incorrectly credited to the Greensburg School District account, Memorandum 68.

When the November 30 transaction was journalized and posted, Cash in Bank was debited for $75.00. Accounts Receivable and the Greensburg School District account were each credited for $75.00. The original journal entry is shown below in T-account form.

GENERAL LEDGER

Cash in Bank		Accounts Receivable	
Dr.	Cr.	Dr.	Cr.
+	−	+	−
$75.00			$75.00

SUBSIDIARY LEDGER

Greensburg School District	
Dr.	Cr.
+	−
	$75.00

The following T accounts show how the transaction *should* have been recorded:

GENERAL LEDGER

Cash in Bank		Accounts Receivable	
Dr.	Cr.	Dr.	Cr.
+	−	+	−
$75.00			$75.00

SUBSIDIARY LEDGER

Gateway School District	
Dr.	Cr.
+	−
	$75.00

As you can see, the only difference is the account that is credited in the accounts receivable subsidiary ledger. The Greensburg School District account was incorrectly credited. To correct the error, it must now be debited.

328   UNIT 3   The Accounting Cycle for a Merchandising Business

---

Meeting Special Needs

HEARING IMPAIRMENTS

When speaking with students who wear hearing aids, be sure to stand close to them. Hearing aids have a limited range. The hearing aids also amplify all sound, so try to restrict background noise as much as possible.

The Gateway School District account should have been credited. To correct the error, it must be credited now. The correcting entry, recorded in the general journal, is shown in Figure 15-7.

	DATE	DESCRIPTION	POST. REF.	DEBIT	CREDIT	
1	¹⁹— Dec. 15	Greensburg School District		75 00		1
2		Gateway School District			75 00	2
3		Memo. 68				3

GENERAL JOURNAL   PAGE 5

Figure 15-7 Journalizing a Correcting Entry to Subsidiary Ledger Accounts

Summary of Key Points

1. A general journal is also needed in an accounting system using special journals. All transactions that cannot be recorded in the special journals are entered in the general journal.
2. A business may allow its customers to return unsatisfactory merchandise for full credit (a sales return) or to keep the merchandise at a lesser price (a sales allowance).
3. Sales returns and allowances are debited to the Sales Returns and Allowances account. This account is a contra revenue account and has a normal debit balance.
4. A credit memo is prepared by the seller to list the details of a sales return or sales allowance. It is the source document for the general journal entry.
5. A debit memo is prepared by the buyer to notify a creditor of a return or allowance. It is the source document for the general journal entry.
6. A merchandising business may not be satisfied with merchandise purchased on account. It too may return the merchandise for full credit (a purchases return) or keep the merchandise at a reduced cost (a purchases allowance).
7. Purchases returns and allowances are credited to the Purchases Returns and Allowances account. This account is a contra cost of merchandise account and has a normal credit balance.
8. A diagonal line in the Posting Reference column of the general journal means that the debit or credit amount is to be posted to the two accounts named in the Description column. One account is a general ledger controlling account and the other is a subsidiary ledger account.
9. Errors in the accounting records that are discovered after posting require a correcting entry in the general journal.

Pop Quiz

1. Businesses use a separate account to record ____ and allowances.
2. What is the classification of the sales returns and allowances account?
3. What accounts are affected by a credit memo issued for a return of merchandise (including sales tax) sold on account?
4. If a business issues cash for a credit transaction, where is the transaction recorded?
5. What accounts are affected by a return of merchandise purchased on account?

ANSWERS
1. Returns
2. Contra revenue
3. Sales Returns and Allowances, Sales Tax Payable, Accounts Receivable, and the customer's account
4. Cash payments journal
5. Accounts Payable, Purchases Returns and Allowances, and the creditor's account

Review and Applications

Building Your Accounting Vocabulary

In your own words, write the definition of each of the following accounting terms. Use complete sentences for your definitions.

credit memorandum   purchases allowance   sales allowance
debit memorandum   purchases return   sales return

Reviewing Your Accounting Knowledge

1. Why is a general journal needed in an accounting system using special journals?
2. When special journals are used, what types of transactions are normally recorded in the general journal?
3. What is the difference between a sales return and a sales allowance?
4. What information is included on a credit memo?
5. Why is a separate general ledger account used to record sales returns and sales allowances?
6. To which subsidiary ledger is a sales return or allowance posted?
7. What form is prepared to notify a supplier that items purchased on account are being returned?
8. Which account is credited if a business returns an office calculator bought on account? Merchandise bought on account?
9. Classify these accounts: Sales Returns and Allowances and Purchases Returns and Allowances.
10. What does the Purchases Returns and Allowances account show?
11. How would you indicate that a purchases returns and allowances transaction has been posted to the subsidiary ledger account?

Improving Your Proofreading Skills

Reading carelessly when checking amounts of money and other figures often leads to problems. Compare each figure in Column A with the corresponding figure in Column B. On a separate sheet of paper, write the word "Different" if the two items *do not* agree. Write "Same" if the two items *do* agree.

	Column A	Column B
1.	$181,813	$181,831
2.	59874AX	58784AX
3.	10/11/51	10/11/52
4.	ECC-339	ECC-333
5.	306-54-6750	306-54-6750
6.	$160.36	$160.63
7.	998DIA	988DIA
8.	$5,622.40	$5,622.40

330

PRACTICE AND APPLY

- Language Development
- Comprehension and Retention
- Basic Skills

Building Your Accounting Vocabulary

See the Glossary on pages 670-679 for definitions of these terms.

Reviewing Your Accounting Knowledge

1. To record any transactions that cannot be recorded in a special journal.
2. Sales returns and allowances, purchases returns and allowances, and correcting entries.
3. A sales return occurs when merchandise is returned for credit or a cash refund. A sales allowance is a price reduction granted for damaged goods kept by the customer.
4. The date, the name of the customer, a description of the returned item, the reason for the return, and the amount to be credited to the customer's account.
5. So that the total amount of such transactions can be determined more easily.
6. To the accounts receivable ledger.
7. A debit memorandum.
8. Office Equipment is credited for the return of a calculator bought on account; Purchases Returns and Allowances is credited for a return of merchandise bought on account.
9. Sales Returns and Allowances, contra revenue account; Purchases Returns and Allowances, contra cost of merchandise account.
10. The total amount of credit granted by suppliers for unsatisfactory merchandise.
11. A check mark is entered in the general journal Posting Reference column to the right of the diagonal line.

Improving Your Proofreading Skills

1. different	5. same
2. different	6. different
3. different	7. different
4. different	8. same

Exercise 15-1 Analyzing a Credit Memo

Use the credit memo below to answer the following questions.

1. Who issued the credit memorandum?
2. Whose account is being credited?
3. On what date was the credit memorandum prepared?
4. What was the sales slip number and sales slip date of the original transaction?
5. What merchandise is being returned?
6. Why is the merchandise being returned?
7. What is the amount of the merchandise being returned?
8. Why is the sales tax included?
9. What is the total amount of credit being granted?
10. Assuming this merchandise was originally purchased on account, in which journal should the transaction be recorded?

PRACTICE AND APPLY

• Concepts and Procedures

Exercise 15-1: Ch. Obj. 1
Sports World Outlet
Deborah DeGregory
March 10
No. 4631; March 7
Sauna suit
Wrong size
$17.95
The customer no longer owes it.
$18.67
General Journal

Exercise 15-2: Ch. Obj. 3

Exercise 15-3: Ch. Obj. 2, 3, 4

Sports World Outlet
1990 California Avenue
Palo Alto, CA 94303

CREDIT MEMORANDUM   NO. 2270

ORIGINAL SALES DATE	ORIGINAL SALES SLIP	APPROVAL	X MDSE RET
3/7	4631	KKC	

Date: *March 10, 19--*

Name: *Deborah DeGregory*

Address: *1530 Beach Street*
Monterey, CA 93940

QTY	DESCRIPTION	AMOUNT
1	Sauna suit	17 95

Reason for return
wrong size

The total shown at the right will be credited to your account.

SUB TOTAL	17 95
SALES TAX	72
TOTAL	18 67

Deborah DeGregory
Customer Signature

Exercise 15-2 Analyzing a Purchases Returns and Allowances Transaction

Instructions: Enter the following transactions in T accounts.

Feb. 3 Purchased $400.00 in merchandise on account from FirmFlex, Inc.
     12 Discovered that the merchandise purchased on February 3 was defective. Issued Debit Memo 7 for the return of the defective merchandise.

Exercise 15-3 Identifying Special Journals for Selected Transactions

The Lighting Gallery, a lamp store, uses special journals and a general journal. The business had the following transactions during July.

Instructions: Use a form similar to the one at the top of the following page. Indicate in which journal each transaction would be recorded by placing a check mark in the correct column. The first transaction has been recorded as an example.

331

Refer students to the Chapter 15 review pages in the workbook, *Chapter Reviews and Working Papers.*

Exercise 15-4: Ch. Obj. 2, 3

Problem 15-1: Ch. Obj. 2, 3, 4

SPREADSHEET

PROBLEM

Students may complete Problem 15-1 using *Spreadsheet Applications*, the spreadsheet software that accompanies *Glencoe Accounting.*

Date of Transaction	Sales	Cash Receipts	Purchases	Cash Payments	General
July 1	✔				

Transactions:

July 1 Sold merchandise on account to Laurel County High School (no sales tax).

3 Purchased merchandise on account from Long Enterprises.

6 Paid the rent for the month.

8 A payment received from Jonathan Smith, Sr., was incorrectly journalized and posted to the account of Jonathan Smith, Jr.

10 Recorded the cash sales for the week, plus sales tax.

12 Purchased an electronic typewriter on account from Curry Office Equipment Company.

15 Returned part of the merchandise purchased on account from Long Enterprises.

18 Sold merchandise on account, plus sales tax, to Nancy Decker.

20 Received cash from Laurel County High School on account.

23 Nancy Decker returned for full credit the merchandise bought earlier on account, plus sales tax.

25 Paid cash to a creditor, Long Enterprises.

27 Recorded bank card sales for the week, plus sales taxes.

29 Paid shipping charges for merchandise purchased on account from Mason Electrical.

30 Returned the electronic typewriter, originally purchased on account, to Curry Office Equipment Company.

31 Recorded the bank service charge for the month.

Exercise 15-4   Analyzing Transactions

Instructions: Use a form similar to the one that follows. For each transaction in Exercise 15-3, indicate the account or accounts that will be debited and credited. The first transaction is given as an example.

Date of Transaction	Account(s) Debited	Account(s) Credited
July 1	Accounts Receivable/ Laurel County High School	Sales

Problem 15-1   Recording Transactions in the General Journal

The Rocking Horse, a retail merchandising store for children, uses a general journal in addition to special journals.

Instructions: Record the following transactions on page 7 of the general journal.

Transactions:

Nov. 1 Discovered that $35.00 of office supplies bought on account in October from The Office Mart was incorrectly journalized and posted to the Purchases account, Memorandum 7.

332

Teacher Notes

Nov. 6 Returned to the Kendra Corp. $75.00 in damaged merchandise purchased on account, Debit Memo 12.

9 Issued Credit Memo 16 for $150.00 to Seton Nursery School for merchandise returned by them (no sales tax was charged).

15 Discovered that a $200.00 receipt of cash from Helen Bush was incorrectly journalized and posted to the account of Harriet Bush, Memorandum 8.

20 Returned $370.00 in damaged merchandise to a creditor, the Berry Corp., Debit Memo 13.

25 Discovered that a typewriter purchased for $275.00 cash had been incorrectly journalized and posted to the Store Equipment account, Memorandum 9.

Problem 15-2 Recording and Posting General Journal Transactions

Brandi Specialty Products, Inc., had the following transactions during February.

Instructions:
(1) Record the transactions on page 2 of the general journal.
(2) Post the journal entries to the appropriate accounts in the general and subsidiary ledgers. The opened accounts needed to complete this problem are included in the working papers.

Transactions:
Feb. 2 Issued Credit Memo 102 to Wilton High School for $220.00 of merchandise returned by them (no sales tax was charged).

7 Discovered that a $90.00 payment on account from Jane Daerr had been incorrectly journalized and posted to the account of Jamie Darr, Memorandum 33.

12 Returned incorrect merchandise to the Noble Corp. for full credit, $275.00, Debit Memo 61.

18 Discovered that $100.00 in merchandise purchased on account from OS Systems, Inc., had been incorrectly journalized and posted to the Office Supplies account, Memorandum 34.

25 Gave credit to Paul Barron for the return of $56.00 of merchandise purchased on account, plus sales tax of $3.36, Credit Memo 103.

COMPUTER

PROBLEM

Problem 15-3 Recording and Posting Special Journal Entries

The Golf Doctor, a retail distributor of golf equipment and apparel, uses special journals and subsidiary ledgers to record its business transactions. The business's accounts receivable and accounts payable subsidiary ledgers and the general ledger are included in the accounting stationery accompanying this textbook. The current balances have been recorded in the accounts. A partial chart of accounts for The Golf Doctor follows.

101	Cash in Bank	405	Sales Discounts
105	Accounts Receivable	410	Sales Returns and Allowances
110	Supplies	501	Purchases
120	Computer Equipment	505	Purchases Discounts
130	Office Equipment	510	Purchases Returns and Allowances
205	Accounts Payable	605	Bank Card Fees Expense
210	Sales Tax Payable	620	Miscellaneous Expense
401	Sales	650	Rent Expense

333

Problem 15-2: Ch. Obj. 2, 3, 4
Accounts Receivable total, $2,590.64

Problem 15-3: Ch. Obj. 2, 3, 4

COMPUTER

PROBLEM

This computer image identifies a problem that students may complete using the *Glencoe Accounting, General Ledger* software.

Teaching Tips
■ Problem 15-3 is a comprehensive problem requiring students to use all five journals and the general and subsidiary ledgers.

Teacher Notes

SJ totals:
Sales, $2,300.00
Sales Tax Pay., $138.00
Accounts Rec., $2,438.00

CRJ totals:
General, $50.00
Sales, $6,320.00
Sales Tax Pay., $379.20
Accounts Rec., $2,260.00
Sales Disc., $30.00
Cash in Bank, $8,979.20

PJ totals:
Accounts Pay., $9,520.00
Purchases, $7,300.00
General, $2,220.00

CPJ totals:
General, $600.00
Accounts Pay., $3,917.00
Purchases Disc., $36.34
Cash in Bank, $4,480.66

Instructions:

(1) Record the May transactions in the sales journal (page 15), cash receipts journal (page 18), purchases journal (page 11), cash payments journal (page 19), and general journal (page 9).

(2) Post the individual amounts from the five journals to the accounts receivable and accounts payable subsidiary ledgers on a daily basis.

(3) Post the individual amounts from the General columns of the cash receipts, purchases, cash payments, and general journals on a daily basis.

(4) Foot, prove, total, and rule the special journals.

(5) Post the column totals of the special journals to the general ledger accounts. Use the following order for posting: sales, cash receipts, purchases, cash payments.

Transactions:

May 1 Issued Check 350 to Mega Byte Corp. for $1,400.00 in payment of Invoice MB131.

1 Received a check for $670.00 from Dora Dunn in payment of her account, Receipt 450.

2 Received a $312.00 check from Gayle Linwood in payment of her account of $318.00, less a discount of $6.00, Receipt 451.

3 Sent Check 351 for $212.66 to Pro Golf Apparel in payment of Invoice PGA05 for $217.00 less a 2% discount of $4.34.

4 Received a check from Dan Gable for $416.00 in payment of his account of $424.00 less an $8.00 discount, Receipt 452.

5 Issued Credit Memo 50 for $212.00 to Lance Muir for the return of $200.00 in merchandise purchased on account, plus $12.00 sales tax.

8 Purchased $1,600.00 in merchandise on account from Pro Golf Apparel, Invoice PGA15, dated May 7, terms 2/10, n/30.

9 Sold merchandise on account to Dora Dunn, $800.00 plus $48.00 sales tax, Sales Slip 330.

10 Sold $500.00 in merchandise on account to Lance Muir, sales tax $30.00, Sales Slip 331.

12 Received a check for $50.00 from the sale of an old calculator for cash, Receipt 453.

13 Purchased $2,500.00 in merchandise on account from Top-Flight Distributors, Invoice TF40, dated May 12, terms 3/10, n/30.

15 Sold merchandise on account to Gayle Linwood, $750.00 plus sales taxes of $45.00, Sales Slip 332.

17 Issued Debit Memo 38 to Top-Flight Distributors for the return of defective merchandise, $300.00.

17 Wrote Check 352 for $1,568.00 to Pro Golf Apparel in payment of Invoice PGA15 for $1,600.00 less a $32.00 discount.

18 Dora Dunn sent a check for $832.00 in payment of Sales Slip 330 for $848.00, less a discount of $16.00, Receipt 454.

21 Issued Check 353 to Branch Realty in payment of the monthly rent of $600.00.

22 Sold merchandise, $100.00 plus $6.00 sales tax, on account to Dan Gable, Sales Slip 333.

23 Purchased a $1,800.00 microcomputer from Mega Byte Corp., Invoice MB60, dated May 22, terms n/30.

24 Paid Top-Flight Distributors $700.00 on account, Check 354.

334

Teacher Notes

_____

_____

_____

_____

_____

May 27 Purchased merchandise on account from Pro Golf Apparel, $3,200.00, Invoice PGA47, dated May 24, terms 2/10, n/30.

29 Discovered that an April purchase of $400.00 in office equipment had been journalized and posted to the Computer Equipment account, Memorandum 25.

29 Sold $150.00 in merchandise to Gayle Linwood on account, $9.00 sales tax, Sales Slip 334.

30 Purchased $420.00 in computer supplies from Mega Byte Corp., Invoice MB72, dated May 29, terms n/30.

31 Recorded cash sales of $3,540.00, plus $212.40 in sales taxes, Tape 40.

31 Recorded bank card sales for the period, $2,780.00, plus $166.80 sales taxes, Tape 40.

Problem 15-4: Ch. Obj. 4

Problem 15-4 Examining Correcting Entries

The following correcting entries were recorded in the general journal of the Pilgrim Gift Shop during September. The shop makes no sales on account.

Instructions: Give a brief description of the error that was made when each transaction was *originally* recorded. In other words, why is the correcting entry being prepared?

CHALLENGE PROBLEM — *The last problem (or problems) in each chapter is a challenge problem and is identified by this "maze" symbol.*

Teaching Tips

■ The Sept. 12 transaction could be a correcting entry for either the accounts receivable or accounts payable subsidiary ledger.

		GENERAL JOURNAL		PAGE 14	
	DATE	DESCRIPTION	POST. REF.	DEBIT	CREDIT
1	19— Sept. 8	Purchases		114 00	
2		Transportation In			114 00
3		Memo. 209			
4	12	Jonas Conlan Co.		824 50	
5		Jonah Conway Corp.			824 50
6		Memo. 210			
7	14	Office Equipment		483 90	
8		Office Furniture			483 90
9		Memo. 211			
10	20	Federal Income Tax Payable		624 00	
11		Sales Tax Payable			624 00
12		Memo. 212			
13	26	Bank Card Fees Expense		127 90	
14		Miscellaneous Expense			127 90
15		Memo. 213			
16					

Problem 15-5: Ch. Obj. 2, 3, 4

CHALLENGE PROBLEM — *The last problem (or problems) in each chapter is a challenge problem and is identified by this "maze" symbol.*

Problem 15-5   Recording General Journal Transactions

You are an accounting clerk for Bayside Jewelers. The transactions that follow require journal entries. Record these entries on page 12 of the general journal.

Transactions:

Oct. 4 Received a letter from Imperial Gemstones stating that a 3% discount we took on its $4,200.00 invoice was disallowed because the payment was received after the end of the discount period, Memorandum 112.

335

4 ASSESS

A chapter test is available for use in assessing students' understanding of concepts in this chapter.

Unit objective and problem tests are available to assess students' knowledge of concepts in Chapters 11-15.

The testmaker software will enable you to develop tailor-made chapter, unit, semester, and final tests.

Alternative Assessment

For alternative assessment strategies, refer to *Tech Prep Strategies in Accounting.*

Oct. 8   A journal entry was recorded and posted for a payment of $1,176.00 made to the Berenson Corp. for its invoice of $1,200.00 dated September 26 with terms of 2/10, n/30. During a routine check, the accounting supervisor discovered an invoice from Berenson dated September 10 that has not yet been paid. Berenson will not allow discounts if there are earlier, unpaid invoices, Memorandum 113.

9   John Schmidt returned damaged merchandise purchased on account, $114.50, plus sales tax of 4%, Credit Memo 96.

10   Bayside returned a shipment of defective merchandise to Harkness Corporation. The invoice from Harkness for $998.40 has been recorded and posted, Debit Memo 94.

11   Received a notice from the Weber Co. stating that we had taken a discount of 3% on an invoice of $6,340.00 with terms of 2/10, n/30. The invoice was paid within the discount period, Memorandum 114.

336

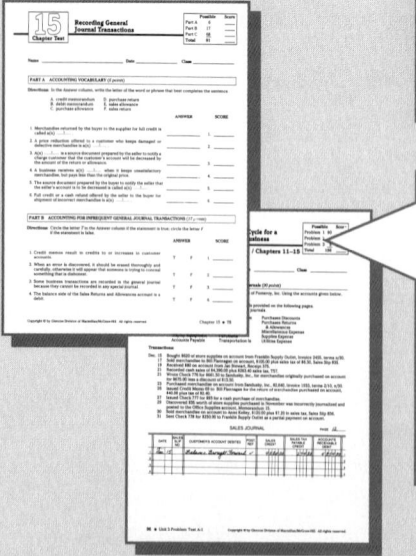

Use Chapter Test 15 here to assess students' understanding and retention of the concepts and procedures presented in the chapter.

Use Unit 3, Chapters 11-15, Objective Test and/or Unit 3, Chapters 11-15, Problem Test to assess students' retention of concepts presented in Chapters 11 and 15.

*A*rresting Facts
About Computer Crime

When the computer was first invented, *computer crime* referred to the theft or sabotage of computers. Today, the term means the unauthorized use of computer systems for unlawful purposes. The increasing use and importance of computers have given rise to a new breed of criminal.

Indeed, computer crime has become such a problem that laws in almost every state make it a risky business, resulting in convictions and serious sentences.

Computer-abetted crime is particularly troublesome because
• The crime is usually committed by someone who is authorized to use the system—a programmer, a clerk, or a bank teller, for example.
• It's difficult, though not impossible, to track down the culprit because, if the thief is clever enough, the records look tamper-free.
• Businesses don't like to reveal that they have been victims of computer crimes for fear of shaking the public's confidence in them.

Usually young, skilled, and male, computer criminals steal funds electronically. The electronic funds transfer system (EFTS) is particularly vulnerable. One embezzler who knew the bank's system transferred $10.8 million to a Swiss bank account before he was caught.

Some methods of computer crime are difficult to detect. Two unique methods are salami slicing and the Trojan horse.
• *Salami slicing*. An embezzler modifies a program to round down fractions of a penny in transactions such as salary calculations. These fractions are then added to the criminal's computer account. With several thousand employees, these fractions of a cent can add up.

No one knows for sure, but it is estimated that billions of dollars are lost to computer crime each year.

• *Trojan horse*. A hidden "criminal" program is used to scan data and steal passwords, which it then uses to enter and pillage accounts.

Computer crime can cost its victims millions of dollars. No matter how tempting it is for a computer thief to crack a system, however, there's always someone just as clever who can find the glitch and catch the thief.

Have students select a recent case of computer-abetted crime, as reported in the media. Have them prepare a summary of the case highlighting the nature of the crime, how it was carried out, the amount of money taken, and the penalty imposed (if the case has been litigated).

QUESTIONS

1. Categorize the types of computer crimes.
2. It is suspected that many companies fail to report computer-abetted crimes. Why would a firm not report such a crime when it would quickly report a break-in or theft?

ANSWERS

1. There are three categories: data can be changed or invented to produce inaccurate information; programs can be changed to create false information or illegal transactions; unauthorized persons can get access to a firm's computer and use it for personal benefit.
2. Companies are reluctant to admit computer crimes publicly, fearing the negative image this can create. Such an occurrence seems to suggest poor management.

337

APPLICATION ACTIVITY 3

Application Activity 3 is a reinforcement activity that helps students integrate their learning of how to use the special journals and the general journal to record business transactions for a merchandising business. In this activity, students are given business transactions to journalize and post. Students will use the four special journals, the general journal, the general ledger, and the accounts receivable and accounts payable subsidiary ledgers.

The accounting stationery for completing this activity is included in the student's *Chapter Reviews and Working Papers*. Most students will be able to complete this activity within two to three class periods.

Source documents are also available to add realism to this activity.

COMPUTER

PROBLEM

Students may also complete this activity on the microcomputer using the general ledger software accompanying *Glencoe Accounting*. Most students will be able to complete the activity on the microcomputer within one to two class periods.

Mini Practice Set

Recording Business Transactions in Special Journals

In Chapters 11 through 15, you have learned how to record the business transactions of a merchandising business in special journals. Now you will have the opportunity to review and apply what you have learned by working as an accounting clerk for The Apple Tree Boutique. The accounting stationery needed to complete this activity is included in the working papers accompanying this textbook.

When you have completed this activity, you will have done the following:

1. Analyzed business transactions.
2. Journalized business transactions in the four special journals and in the general journal.
3. Posted journal entries to the general ledger and to the accounts receivable and accounts payable subsidiary ledgers.
4. Posted the totals of the special journals to the general ledger.
5. Proved cash.
6. Prepared a schedule of accounts receivable and a schedule of accounts payable.

The Apple Tree Boutique

Todd and Toni Thomas own a merchandising business organized as a corporation called The Apple Tree Boutique. The retail store is a small, fashionable specialty shop for women's clothing. This husband-and-wife team has been operating successfully for five years.

Chart of Accounts

The chart of accounts for The Apple Tree Boutique appears on the next page. It includes the accounts receivable subsidiary ledger accounts and the accounts payable subsidiary ledger accounts.

Keeping the Accounting Records for

The Apple Tree Boutique

Since The Apple Tree Boutique has a large volume of business transactions, the business uses special journals and a general journal.

The previous accounting clerk, Dani Trio, has journalized and posted the business transactions for June 1 through June 15. Those transactions are included in the accounting stationery accompanying this textbook. The transactions that follow took place between June 16 and June 30.

Instructions: The forms for completing this activity are included in the working papers accompanying this textbook.

338

THE APPLE TREE BOUTIQUE
Chart of Accounts

	101	Cash in Bank
	105	Accounts Receivable
	110	Merchandise Inventory
ASSETS	115	Supplies
	120	Prepaid Insurance
	150	Store Equipment
	155	Office Equipment

LIABILITIES	201	Accounts Payable
	205	Sales Tax Payable

	301	Capital Stock
STOCKHOLDERS' EQUITY	305	Retained Earnings
	310	Income Summary

	401	Sales
REVENUE	405	Sales Discounts
	410	Sales Returns and Allowances

	501	Purchases
COST OF MERCHANDISE	505	Transportation In
	510	Purchases Discounts
	515	Purchases Returns and Allowances

	605	Advertising Expense
	610	Bank Card Fees Expense
	615	Miscellaneous Expense
EXPENSES	620	Rent Expense
	625	Salaries Expense
	630	Utilities Expense

ACCOUNTS RECEIVABLE SUBSIDIARY LEDGER		ACCOUNTS PAYABLE SUBSIDIARY LEDGER	
815	Sarah Locke	905	Ebony Creations
818	Allison McKensey	920	Jay-Jax Jeans
825	Marti Mitchell	930	Montini Fashions
870	Della Starr	960	Store & Office Suppliers
880	Elena Trevino	980	Vanity Designers

(1) Record the remaining June transactions in the sales journal (page 18), cash receipts journal (page 15), purchases journal (page 12), cash payments journal (page 21), and general journal (page 7).

(2) Post the individual amounts from the five journals to the accounts receivable and accounts payable subsidiary ledgers on a daily basis.

(3) Post the individual amounts from the General columns of the cash receipts, purchases, cash payments, and general journals on a daily basis.

(4) Foot, prove, total, and rule the special journals.

(5) Post the column totals of the special journals to the general ledger accounts. Use the following order for posting: sales journal, cash receipts journal, purchases journal, cash payments journal.

(6) Prove cash. The balance shown on check stub 216 is $11,269.34.

339

S. Journal totals:
Sales, $1,401.00
Sales Tax Pay., $84.06
Accts. Rec., $1,485.06

C. R. Journal totals:
General, $115.00
Sales, $9,364.39
Sales Tax Pay., $561.87
Accts. Rec., $2,300.55
Sales Disc., $0
Cash in Bank, $12,341.81

Teacher Notes

_____

_____

_____

_____

_____

Application Activity 3

P. Journal totals:
Accts. Pay., $6,626.30
Purchases, $4,861.00
General, $1,765.30

C.P. Journal totals:
General, $3,716.30
Accts. Pay., $7,821.04
Purch. Disc., $101.80
Cash in Bank, $11,435.54

Accounts Rec. balance, $791.20
Accounts Pay. balance, $3,527.26

(7) Prepare a schedule of accounts receivable and a schedule of accounts payable.

Transactions:

June 16 Sold $115.00 worth of merchandise on account to Marti Mitchell, plus $6.90 sales tax, Sales Slip 407.

17 Issued Check 210 for $1,315.27 to Montini Fashions in payment of Invoice M131.

18 Purchased $1,270.00 in merchandise on account from Jay-Jax Jeans, Invoice JJ215.

18 Sold merchandise on account to Sarah Locke, $80.00 plus $4.80 sales tax, Sales Slip 408.

18 Received a check for $95.40 from Della Starr to apply on account, Receipt 157.

19 Wrote Check 211 for $565.30 to Store & Office Suppliers in full payment of our account.

19 Paid Ebony Creations' Invoice EC462 for $425.73, less a 2% cash discount of $8.51, by issuing Check 212 for $417.22.

21 Discovered that a $680.00 cash purchase of merchandise in May had been journalized and posted incorrectly as a debit to Merchandise Inventory, Memorandum 21.

21 Sold on account to Elena Trevino $350.00 of merchandise plus sales tax of $21.00, Sales Slip 409.

22 Prepared Receipt 158 for a $79.50 check received on account from Allison McKensey.

23 Wrote Check 213 for $346.08 to Vanity Designers in payment of Invoice V340 for $353.14, less a $7.06 cash discount.

24 Issued Debit Memo 42 for $150.00 to Jay-Jax Jeans for damaged merchandise returned to them.

24 Received Invoice EC475 for $542.95 of merchandise purchased on account from Ebony Creations.

25 Recorded the $4.00 bank service charge from the June bank statement.

25 Recorded the bank card fee of $125.00 from the June bank statement.

25 Purchased $664.31 in merchandise from Vanity Designers on account, Invoice V372.

25 Bought a $1,200.00 cash register (store equipment) on account from Store & Office Suppliers, Invoice AB601.

26 Sold merchandise to Allison McKensey on account totaling $130.00, plus sales tax $7.80, Sales Slip 410.

26 Received $200.00 from Sarah Locke on account, Receipt 159.

27 Prepared Receipt 160 for a $150.00 check received from Elena Trevino on account.

28 Sold an old calculator (office equipment) for $40.00, Receipt 161.

30 Issued Check 214 for $2,412.00 for the salaries for the month.

30 Paid the annual insurance premium of $300.00 by issuing Check 215 to Reliable Insurance Agency.

30 Recorded cash sales of $1,700.00, $102.00 sales taxes, Tape 32.

30 Recorded bank card sales of $950.00, plus sales taxes of $57.00, Tape 32.

340

Teacher Notes

_____

_____

_____

_____

_____

Chapter 16

PREPARING A TEN-COLUMN WORK SHEET

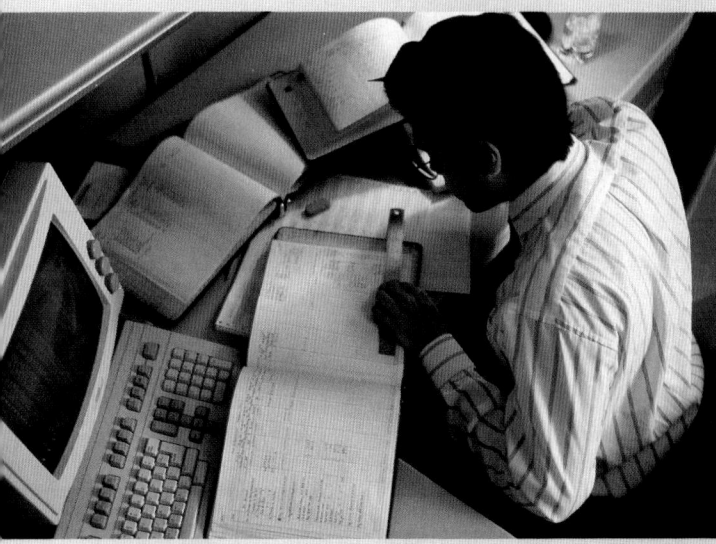

Learning Objectives

When you have completed Chapter 16, you should be able to do the following:

1. Describe the parts of a ten-column work sheet.
2. Determine which general ledger accounts must be adjusted and calculate the amounts of the adjustments needed.
3. Prepare a ten-column work sheet.
4. Define the accounting terms introduced in this chapter.

The work sheet you learned how to prepare in Chapter 7 had six amount columns. The work sheet you will learn to prepare in this chapter has *ten* amount columns. The four "new" columns are the debit and credit columns of the Adjustments and Adjusted Trial Balance sections.

These columns are used to calculate "adjustments" for account balances that are not up to date at the end of the fiscal period. For example, employees use supplies such as letterhead stationery and envelopes every day, but the Supplies account is not credited daily to record the cost of those supplies. Instead, at the end of the accounting period, the amount of supplies consumed is calculated and the Supplies account is "adjusted" by this amount.

In this chapter, you will learn which account balances must be adjusted at the end of the fiscal period. You will also learn how to calculate the needed adjustments and enter them on a ten-column work sheet.

New   Terms

adjustment
beginning inventory
ending inventory
physical inventory
cost of merchandise sold
gross profit

LOOKING BACK

Now that students have learned to analyze and record business transactions for a merchandising business using special journals, they are ready to learn about the end-of-period work for such a business. In this chapter students will learn to use a 10-column work sheet rather than the 6-column work sheet they learned about in Chapter 7.

VOCABULARY DEVELOPMENT

Have students read the list of new terms. Ask for ideas for each term's meaning. Write correct responses on the chalkboard. Review the meanings of terms that are not familiar to students. Definitions for these terms are found in the chapter and in the glossary on pages 670-679.

Electronic Field Trips

341

Teaching Resources

- Lesson Plans
- TE/Chapter Reviews & Working Papers
- Demonstration Problems
- Student Study Plans
- Teaching Transparencies
- Solutions Transparencies
- Electronic Field Trips Video, Level I
- Electronic Study Guide
- Chapter 16 Test

Other Resources

- Skills Improvement Activities
- Blackline Masters
- Careers in Accounting
- Dictionary
- Math Review for Accounting
- Tech Prep Strategies in Accounting
- Video
- Test Bank with Software
- Spanish Resources/Audiotapes
- Spanish Electronic Study Guide

1 FOCUS

MAJOR CONCEPTS

- Completing End-of-Fiscal-Period Work
- The Ten-Column Work Sheet
- Completing the Trial Balance Section
- Calculating Adjustments
- Completing the Adjusted Trial Balance Section
- Extending Amounts to the Balance Sheet and Income Statement Sections
- Completing the Work Sheet

BUSINESS CONNECTION

Inventory is the key to a successful holiday season at your local toy store. Buyers for Toys 'R Us, Kay Bee, Child World, and other toy merchants must determine which toys to stock months before the selling season begins. When the retailer buys the toys, they are recorded in the Purchases account. Much of the retailer's success depends on the buyer making the right inventory decisions. At the end of the fiscal period, the retailer calculates the cost of goods sold and the gross profit.

2 TEACH

CONCEPT DEVELOPMENT
Completing End-of-Fiscal-Period Work

When introducing this topic, it is helpful to review the steps in the accounting cycle. Point out that step 6, preparing a work sheet, is the beginning of the end-of-period work. Note that the accounting cycle presented in Chapters 2-9 included *nine* steps. The cycle presented in Chapters 11-18 includes *ten* steps. The step added is number 8, the journalizing and posting of adjusting entries.

Completing End-of-Fiscal-Period Work

The balances of the general ledger accounts summarize the effects of business transactions for an accounting period. They cannot, however, summarize the overall performance of a company. To evaluate performance, managers, stockholders, and creditors need more than a list of account totals. They need to know net income, the value of stockholders' (owners') equity, and the company's financial strength. Sound business decisions cannot be made without this vital information.

It is the purpose of all end-of-period reports to provide essential information that shows the financial position of a business organization. In Chapters 7 and 8, you learned about the steps taken at the end of every fiscal period to determine and report the financial condition of a sole proprietorship service business. The first step was to prepare a work sheet. In this chapter, you will prepare a work sheet typical of those used by merchandising businesses. This work sheet will be the basis for preparing end-of-period financial statements and journal entries.

The Ten-Column Work Sheet

The six-column work sheet in Chapter 7 had a heading and three amount sections: the Trial Balance section, the Income Statement section, and the Balance Sheet section. Each of these sections had a debit and a credit column. The Trial Balance section, remember, included all accounts listed in the chart of accounts, even those with zero balances. Each account was classified and its balance extended to the Balance Sheet or Income Statement section. Asset, liability, and owner's equity balances were extended to the Balance Sheet section. Revenue and expense balances were extended to the Income Statement section. The net income (or loss) was then determined.

The ten-column work sheet is prepared in much the same way. The ten-column work sheet, however, has five amount sections to complete instead of three. These five sections are (1) Trial Balance, (2) Adjustments, (3) Adjusted Trial Balance, (4) Income Statement, and (5) Balance Sheet.

Completing the Trial Balance Section

A trial balance is prepared to prove the equality of debits and credits in the general ledger. A trial balance may be prepared at any time during the fiscal period—provided that all amounts have been posted to the general ledger. Champion Building Products prepares its trial balance at the end of the fiscal period, using the first two columns of the work sheet.

To prepare the trial balance, the number and title of each account in the general ledger is entered on the work sheet in the Account Name section. The accounts are listed in the same order as they appear in the general ledger. The balance of each account is entered in either the Debit or the Credit column. After all balances have been entered, the Debit and Credit columns are ruled, totaled, and proved. A double rule is drawn across both columns once they are proved.

342

Reinforcing Study Skills

Skimming is a reading skill that helps in surveying or previewing new material, looking for specific information, and reviewing. In skimming a chapter, students should quickly read the title; skim the introduction, first and last paragraphs; find the relationships between section and subsection heads; and look for key terms.

Provide a copy of the *Student Study Plans* to each class member to help organize study activities or to individualize practice and review activities.

The Trial Balance section of Champion's work sheet is shown in Figure 16-1. Notice that every general ledger account is listed, even those with zero balances.

Today many businesses use computers to prepare their trial balances. Those trial balances are often printed out on extra-wide paper. The wide paper provides enough space so that the work sheet can be completed right on the printout. If the paper is not wide enough to complete the work sheet, the Trial Balance data must be copied onto multicolumn accounting paper before the work sheet can be completed.

ACCT. NO.	ACCOUNT NAME	TRIAL BALANCE DEBIT	TRIAL BALANCE CREDIT
101	Cash in Bank	21 284 42	
105	Accounts Receivable	6 364 35	
110	Merch. Inventory	84 921 10	
115	Supplies	5 549 50	
120	Prepaid Insurance	1 500 00	
150	Delivery Equipment	19 143 90	
155	Store Equipment	26 353 40	
201	Accounts Payable		12 316 95
205	Fed. Inc. Tax Payable		
210	Sales Tax Payable		1 983 60
301	Capital Stock		75 000 00
305	Retained Earnings		27 625 45
310	Income Summary		
401	Sales		377 385 00
405	Sales Discounts	3 550 42	
410	Sales Returns & Allow.	1 061 81	
501	Purchases	209 464 32	
505	Transportation In	4 215 80	
510	Purchases Discounts		9 808 54
515	Purchases Ret. & Allow.		4 017 90
601	Advertising Expense	2 864 50	
605	Bank Card Fees Expense	3 292 30	
610	Delivery Expense	2 693 96	
615	Insurance Expense		
620	Maintenance Expense	3 321 90	
625	Miscellaneous Expense	647 05	
630	Rent Expense	15 000 00	
635	Salaries Expense	84 000 00	
640	Supplies Expense		
645	Utilities Expense	3 158 71	
650	Fed. Inc. Tax Expense	9 750 00	
		508 137 44	508 137 44

Figure 16-1 The Trial Balance Section of the Work Sheet

R E M E M B E R

The debit and credit columns of the Trial Balance section must be equal. If they are not, you must find and correct any errors before continuing.

Making Connections

EVERYDAY LIFE

Ask students if they have ever seen a sign on a business saying "Closed for Inventory." Companies sometimes close for a day or two to complete a physical inventory of the merchandise on hand. Many times they hire temporary help to complete the task much faster. Ask students to describe occasions when a business in their community closed for taking inventory. Have any students participated in taking a physical inventory as part of their job responsibilities?

Chapter 16

CONCEPT DEVELOPMENT
Calculating Adjustments

This section explains the adjustments that must be made for a merchandising corporation. Emphasize *why* these adjustments must be made before the financial statements are prepared. Also stress that revenue and expenses must be matched in a fiscal period.

Briefly discuss the fact that consumed assets are an expense of doing business. Point out that items purchased are initially recorded as assets. As they are used (for example, office supplies), no amount is recorded and so an adjustment is needed at the end of the period to update the accounting records to reflect the supplies consumed.

Teaching Tips

■ Remind students of the principle of matching expenses to the revenue earned during an accounting period.

■ For each adjustment, have students identify which accounts are permanent and which are temporary.

■ Emphasize that all entries recorded in the Adjustments section of the work sheet must later be journalized and posted to the general ledger.

■ Adjustments are entered on the work sheet from the top down.

■ An important aspect of the accountant's job is to identify all accounts needing adjustment.

Calculating Adjustments

Not all changes in account balances are the result of daily business transactions. Some changes result from the passage of time or from the internal operations of the business. For example, insurance premiums are paid for a certain period of time and expire during that time period. Office supplies such as paper, pens, and pencils are bought for use by the business's employees. These supplies are used gradually during the accounting period. Supplies such as shopping bags and sales slips are also gradually used as sales are made. At the end of the period, the balances in accounts such as Prepaid Insurance and Supplies must be brought up to date.

Up to this point, the general ledger account balances have been changed through journal entries that are posted to the accounts. Those journal entries were made to record transactions that were supported by source documents. There are no source documents, however, for the changes in account balances caused by the passage of time or a business's internal operations. Such changes must be recorded through an adjustment to the account balance made at the end of the fiscal period. An **adjustment** is an amount that is added to or subtracted from an account balance to bring that balance up to date. For example, suppose that supplies costing $500 have been purchased during an accounting period. At the end of the period, $200 of these supplies are still on hand. The account balance for Supplies must be adjusted to show that the business has used $300 of supplies.

Every adjustment affects one permanent account and one temporary account. Items that are purchased for use in the operation of the business are recorded as assets (permanent accounts). As these assets are used up during business operations, they become expenses (temporary accounts) to the business. Accountants say that these assets are "expensed" because the costs of consumed assets are expenses of doing business. At the end of the fiscal period, therefore, an adjustment must be made to transfer the costs of the assets consumed to the appropriate expense accounts. As you recall, the expenses for a given fiscal period must be matched against the revenue for that period before net income (or net loss) can be determined.

The Adjustments section of the work sheet is used to calculate the amounts of the adjustments that must be made at the end of the fiscal period to bring various account balances up to date. After the work sheet has been completed and the financial reports prepared, the adjustments written on the work sheet will be recorded as journal entries. These journal entries will then be posted to the appropriate general ledger accounts. The balances in those accounts are thus brought up to date with the balances calculated on the work sheet. You will learn how to journalize adjustments in Chapter 18.

Determining the Adjustments Needed

How do you know which accounts must be adjusted at the end of the fiscal period? The account balances reported on the financial statements must reflect the actual balance for each account at the end of the fiscal period. If the balance shown for each account on the work sheet is not up to date *as of the last day of the fiscal period,* then that account balance must be adjusted.

Interdisciplinary Connections

ECONOMICS

The 1980s brought drastic changes to American businesses and the accountants who worked for them. Large accounting firms that were used to dealing with major manufacturing firms making cars, steel, and the like found their new customers to be service businesses or high-technology companies. CPAs also had to learn about international accounting rules as a result of increasing business interests of U.S. firms in other countries.

Look at the trial balance for Champion Building Products shown in Figure 16-1. The first account listed is Cash in Bank. Since all cash received or paid out during the period has been journalized and then posted to the Cash in Bank account, the balance in this account is up to date. The balance in the controlling account Accounts Receivable is also up to date since all amounts owed or paid by charge customers have been journalized and posted.

The next account on the trial balance is Merchandise Inventory. In Chapter 11, you learned that Merchandise Inventory is the account merchandising businesses use to report the cost of merchandise on hand to sell to customers. The balance reported in the Trial Balance section ($84,921.10) is the merchandise on hand at the *beginning* of the fiscal period.

The amount of merchandise on hand is constantly changing during the fiscal period. The changes are not recorded in the Merchandise Inventory account. During the period, Champion recorded the cost of additional merchandise purchased in the Purchases account. As inventory was reduced by the sale of merchandise, the amount of each sale was recorded in the Sales account. No entries were posted to Merchandise Inventory. At the end of the fiscal period, therefore, the balance in Merchandise Inventory does *not* reflect the amount of merchandise on hand as of the last day of the fiscal period. This account balance must be adjusted.

Adjusting the Merchandise Inventory Account

Merchandise Inventory is an asset account that is found only in a merchandising business. At the beginning of each fiscal period, the balance in Merchandise Inventory represents the amount of merchandise on hand and available for sale. This balance is the beginning inventory. **Beginning inventory** is the merchandise a business has on hand at the *beginning* of a fiscal period. The merchandise a business has on hand at the *end* of a fiscal period is its **ending inventory.** The ending inventory for one fiscal period is the beginning inventory for the next fiscal period.

During a fiscal period, the balance of Merchandise Inventory usually is not changed. The balance of Merchandise Inventory is changed only when a physical inventory is taken. A **physical inventory** is an actual count of all the merchandise on hand and available for sale. A physical inventory can be taken at any time. One is always taken, however, at the end of a fiscal period.

Once the actual number of items on hand is known, the cost of the ending inventory can be calculated. This is done by multiplying the quantity of each different item by its unit cost. The cost of the ending inventory is the total cost of all the items on hand. Knowing the ending inventory cost is very important. With it, the Merchandise Inventory account can be brought up to date, and the cost of merchandise sold can be determined. The **cost of merchandise sold** is just what the words indicate. It is the actual cost to the business of the merchandise sold to customers. The cost of merchandise sold is reported on the income statement. At the end of a fiscal period, the total cost of merchandise sold during the period is calculated and used to determine the gross profit. **Gross profit** is the difference between the revenue earned from sales and the total cost of the merchandise sold.

Let's use an example to show the importance of the beginning and ending inventory amounts. Suppose two students decide to sell school buttons at a

CHAPTER 16 Preparing a Ten-Column Work Sheet   **345**

Teaching Tips

■ Remind students that the Merchandise Inventory account is not used to record sales or purchases of merchandise during the period.

■ Briefly discuss taking an inventory. Have students relate job experiences or have students inventory the classroom.

■ Methods of determining the cost of an inventory are discussed in Chapter 24.

It is important for a business to take an actual count of the merchandise it has on hand at least once a year.

sports event. They have 14 buttons left from their last sale. These buttons cost them 45¢ each. The cost of their beginning inventory is thus $6.30 ($0.45 × 14). The students purchased 100 more buttons at 45¢ each, for a total cost of $45.00.

The two students sold their buttons at the sports event for 75¢ each. Since they were so busy, they did not keep track of each sale. After the sports event was over, the students totaled their money and found that they had sold $77.25 worth of buttons. But how much of that $77.25 was profit and how much was the cost of the buttons?

To find this out, the students first counted the remaining buttons. They had 11 left. These 11 buttons cost 45¢ each, so the cost of their ending inventory was $4.95 ($0.45 × 11).

Next, to determine their profit, the students needed to know the cost of the buttons they had sold. The students originally had 14 buttons costing $6.30. They had purchased 100 buttons costing $45.00. The total cost of all the buttons they had available for sale was $51.30 ($6.30 + $45.00). To find the cost of the buttons sold, the students subtracted the cost of the buttons they still had ($4.95) from the cost of all the buttons that they had available for sale ($51.30). The cost of the buttons they had sold was $46.35. Next, the students subtracted the cost of the buttons sold from their total sales amount ($77.25). The difference was their gross profit of $30.90 ($77.25 − $46.35). This calculation is shown below.

Sales		$77.25
Beginning Inventory (14 @ 45¢)	$ 6.30	
Plus Purchases (100 @ 45¢)	+45.00	
Cost of Merchandise Available for Sale	$51.30	
Less Ending Inventory (11 @ 45¢)	− 4.95	
Cost of Merchandise Sold		−46.35
Gross Profit		$30.90

At the end of a fiscal period, businesses calculate their gross profit the same way the two students did. As you can see from the calculations, both beginning and ending inventory amounts are needed to determine gross profit.

The purpose of the end-of-fiscal-period work is to report the results of the merchandising operation (the net income or net loss) for the period and to prepare the general ledger accounts for the next period. The ending inventory for one fiscal period, remember, becomes the beginning inventory for the next period. At the end of each period, therefore, the beginning inventory amount recorded in Merchandise Inventory must be replaced by the ending inventory amount. This is accomplished by an adjustment to Merchandise Inventory.

R E M E M B E R

Every adjustment affects one permanent account and one temporary account.

▲ Calculating the Adjustment for Merchandise Inventory

When the Trial Balance section of Champion's work sheet was prepared, the Merchandise Inventory account had a debit balance of $84,921.10. This was the amount of merchandise on hand at the beginning of the fiscal period. At the end of the period, a physical inventory (an actual count) was made of the merchandise still on hand. The cost of the ending inventory was calculated to be $81,385.70. This difference is the result of all the purchases and sales of merchandise during the period. The $81,385.70 amount must replace the beginning inventory amount to bring the Merchandise Inventory account up to date for the next fiscal period.

To bring the balance of Merchandise Inventory up to date, it must be decreased by $3,535.40 ($84,921.10 − $81,385.70). Merchandise Inventory has a normal debit balance. To decrease the balance, Merchandise Inventory is credited for $3,535.40.

In double-entry accounting, every credit must have an equal debit. Remember too that each adjustment affects one permanent account and one temporary account. If Merchandise Inventory (a permanent account) is being credited, a temporary account must be debited. In this adjustment, the Income Summary account is debited for $3,535.40. Why is Income Summary debited?

In Chapter 9, you learned that Income Summary is a temporary equity account used as a sort of clearinghouse. Income Summary does not have a normal balance since it is used only at the end of the fiscal period to summarize information from other accounts. In Chapter 9, you used Income Summary to summarize the total revenue and total expenses for the period. The difference between these two amounts (the net income or net loss) was then closed into the capital account.

Income Summary is also used to make the adjustment to the Merchandise Inventory account. The debit side of Income Summary is used to record total expenses for the period. The cost of merchandise sold is an expense for a merchandising business. Since the inventory has decreased, this means that

---

Did you know?

In the 1980s well-publicized cases involving unethical business practices by Wall Street investment bankers such as Michael Milken and Ivan Boesky caused several major business schools to begin offering courses on business ethics in their MBA programs. One alumnus of Harvard gave the school $30 million to be used for a business ethics curriculum. The alumnus was John Shad, head of Drexel Burnham Lambert, which went bankrupt as a result of several shady business deals.

Making Connections

AROUND THE WORLD

The computer is quickly connecting the world into one huge global marketplace. Ford Motor Company is taking advantage of computer connections to link its car designers from around the world. For example, a Ford engineer in England can send a part design to Michigan via computer file, where final revisions may be made. The final design can then be sent to a plant in Italy where a computerized milling machine can turn out the new part in hours. The computerized hookups allow Ford to use its resources efficiently, no matter where they are located.

Using Visuals

Use demonstration problem 16-1, Parts A and B, to show students how to analyze the adjustment for Merchandise Inventory.

Teaching Tips

■ Some accountants adjust the Merchandise Inventory account by closing out the beginning inventory balance and entering the new balance. See the *Blackline Masters* for supplementary material that can be used to teach other methods of adjusting Merchandise Inventory.

Using Visuals

Use demonstration problem 16-2 to show students how to enter the adjustment for Merchandise Inventory on the work sheet.

ACCOUNTING *Notes*

Letters are used to identify the adjustments to avoid confusing an adjustment number with an amount.

Champion sold $3,535.40 of merchandise in addition to the merchandise purchased during the period. The cost of merchandise sold is increased by this amount. A reduction in merchandise inventory is, therefore, debited to Income Summary and credited to Merchandise Inventory.

The adjustment for Champion's Merchandise Inventory account is illustrated in the T accounts.

Merchandise Inventory		Income Summary	
Dr.	Cr.	Dr.	Cr.
+	−		
Bal. $84,921.10	Adj. $3,535.40	Adj. $3,535.40	

If the cost of the ending inventory is greater than the cost of the beginning inventory, Merchandise Inventory would be debited and Income Summary would be credited. For example, suppose that the beginning inventory was $84,921.10 and the ending inventory was $87,371.50. Since the inventory has increased by $2,450.40 ($87,371.50 − $84,921.10), Merchandise Inventory must be debited for that amount. Income Summary, then, would be credited for $2,450.40. This adjustment is illustrated in the T accounts.

Merchandise Inventory		Income Summary	
Dr.	Cr.	Dr.	Cr.
+	−		
Bal. $84,921.10			
Adj. 2,450.40			Adj. $2,450.40

R E M E M B E R

If the ending inventory is less than the beginning inventory, Merchandise Inventory is credited for the amount of the difference. If the ending inventory is greater than the beginning inventory, Merchandise Inventory is debited for the amount of the difference.

▲ **Entering the Adjustment for Merchandise Inventory on the Work Sheet**   The T accounts used to analyze the adjustment to Merchandise Inventory will serve as a guide to entering the adjustment on the work sheet. Look at the partial work sheet in Figure 16-2. To record the adjustment for Merchandise Inventory

1. Enter the credit amount of the adjustment in the Adjustments Credit column on the Merchandise Inventory line. Label this amount (a).

   The work sheet adjustments are the source of the information for the journal entries that will be made later to record the amount of each adjustment. To help in locating amounts on the work sheet, the debit and credit parts of each adjustment are labeled. A small letter in parentheses is placed just above and to the left of the amounts. The first adjustment is labeled (a); the second, (b); the third, (c); and so on.
2. Enter the debit amount of the adjustment in the Adjustments Debit column on the Income Summary line. Label this amount (a) also.

Making Connections

COMMUNICATIONS

Accountants must not only communicate with their clients but must also deal with other people in their firm. Have students imagine one of these situations and then write an interoffice memo in which they (a) ask a colleague to complete a work sheet they have started, or (b) announce an upcoming meeting with a potential new client.

ACCT. NO.	ACCOUNT NAME	TRIAL BALANCE		ADJUSTMENTS	
		DEBIT	CREDIT	DEBIT	CREDIT
1 101	Cash in Bank	2128442			
2 105	Accounts Receivable	636435			
3 110	Merch. Inventory	8492110			(a) 353540
13 310	Income Summary			(a) 353540	

Figure 16-2 Recording the Adjustment for Merchandise Inventory on the Work Sheet

R E M E M B E R

The two parts of an adjustment are labeled with small letters in parentheses.

This adjustment, when journalized, will bring the balance in Merchandise Inventory up to date.

Before you go any further, do the following activity to see if you understand the adjustment for Merchandise Inventory.

Check Your Learning

Answer these questions on a sheet of notebook paper.

1. Why must the Merchandise Inventory account be adjusted at the end of a fiscal period?
2. When is a physical inventory taken?
3. If the ending inventory is greater than the beginning inventory, which account is debited in the adjustment? credited?
4. If the ending inventory is less than the beginning inventory, which account is debited in the adjustment? credited?

Compare your answers to those in the answers section. Re-read the preceding part of the chapter to find the correct answers to any questions you may have missed.

Adjusting the Supplies Account

A merchandising business buys various supplies to be used by employees in the everyday operations of the business. Among these supplies are pencils and pens, typing paper, shopping bags, sales slips, price tags, and cash register tapes. As these supplies are purchased, their cost is debited to Supplies.

Some supplies are used up every day. As they are consumed, they become expenses of the business. It's impossible to keep daily records of each item as it is used. The Supplies account, therefore, is not updated until the end of the fiscal period.

On the work sheet, the balance of the Supplies account is $5,549.50. This amount is the value of the supplies on hand on January 1 *plus* the additional supplies bought during the year.

CHAPTER 16   Preparing a Ten-Column Work Sheet   349

At the end of December, Champion Building Products took an inventory and found that there were actually $1,839.60 of supplies on hand. This means that $3,709.90 of supplies had been used during the year ($5,549.50 − $1,839.60 = $3,709.90).

The amount of supplies on hand has decreased by $3,709.90. Supplies (a permanent account) must be credited, therefore, for that amount. Supplies Expense (a temporary account) is used to record the cost of supplies used during the period. To update the account, Supplies Expense is debited for $3,709.90.

Supplies			Supplies Expense	
Dr.	Cr.		Dr.	Cr.
+	−		+	−
Bal. $5,549.50	Adj. $3,709.90		Adj. $3,709.90	

The adjustment to Supplies is shown in Figure 16-3, on lines 4 and 29. To enter the adjustment on the work sheet, follow the steps at the top of the next page.

ACCT. NO.	ACCOUNT NAME	TRIAL BALANCE DEBIT	TRIAL BALANCE CREDIT	ADJUSTMENTS DEBIT	ADJUSTMENTS CREDIT
101	Cash in Bank	21 284 42			
105	Accounts Receivable	6 364 35			
110	Merch. Inventory	84 921 10			(a) 3 535 40
115	Supplies	5 549 50			(b) 3 709 90
120	Prepaid Insurance	1 500 00			(c) 250 00
150	Delivery Equipment	19 143 90			
155	Store Equipment	26 353 40			
201	Accounts Payable		12 316 95		
205	Fed. Inc. Tax Payable	—			(d) 145 00
210	Sales Tax Payable		1 983 60		
301	Capital Stock		75 000 00		
305	Retained Earnings		27 625 45		
310	Income Summary	—		(a) 3 535 40	
401	Sales		377 385 00		
405	Sales Discounts	3 550 42			
410	Sales Returns & Allow.	1 061 81			
501	Purchases	209 464 32			
505	Transportation In	4 215 80			
510	Purchases Discounts		9 808 54		
515	Purchases Ret. & Allow.		4 017 90		
601	Advertising Expense	2 864 50			
605	Bank Card Fees Expense	3 292 30			
610	Delivery Expense	2 693 96			
615	Insurance Expense	—		(c) 250 00	
620	Maintenance Expense	3 321 90			
625	Miscellaneous Expense	647 05			
630	Rent Expense	15 000 00			
635	Salaries Expense	84 000 00			
640	Supplies Expense	—		(b) 3 709 90	
645	Utilities Expense	3 158 71			
650	Fed. Inc. Tax Expense	9 750 00		(d) 145 00	
		508 137 44	508 137 44	7 640 30	7 640 30

Figure 16-3 Recording Adjustments on the Work Sheet

Critical Thinking

When an inventory of supplies was completed at the end of the fiscal period, it was found that the amount of the supplies on hand was greater than the balance in the Supplies account. Explain how this could happen.

(Answer: When new supplies were purchased, the transaction was never journalized and posted to the Supplies account.)

1. Enter the credit amount of the adjustment (the supplies consumed) in the Adjustments Credit column on the Supplies line. Since this is the second adjustment, label it (b).
2. Enter the debit amount of the adjustment in the Adjustments Debit column on the Supplies Expense line. Label it (b).

Adjusting the Prepaid Insurance Account

On December 1, Champion purchased an insurance policy to protect the business from loss. The insurance coverage was for the six months December through May. The premium of $1,500.00 (or $250.00 per month) was debited to Prepaid Insurance.

The balance of the Prepaid Insurance account reported on Champion's work sheet is $1,500.00. This reflects the purchase of the insurance on December 1.

By the end of December, however, one month of the premium ($250.00) has expired. In other words, the amount of prepaid insurance has decreased by $250.00. Prepaid Insurance (a permanent account) must be credited for $250.00 to bring its balance up to date. That part of the premium that has expired is an expense of the business. The amount of the expired premium $250.00, therefore, is debited to Insurance Expense (a temporary account).

Prepaid Insurance			Insurance Expense	
Dr.	Cr.		Dr.	Cr.
+	–		+	–
Bal. $1,500.00	Adj. $250.00		Adj. $250.00	

The adjustment for Prepaid Insurance is shown on the partial work sheet in Figure 16-3, lines 5 and 24. To enter this adjustment on the work sheet, follow these steps:

1. Enter the credit amount of the adjustment in the Adjustments Credit column on the Prepaid Insurance line. Since this is the third adjustment, label it (c).
2. Enter the debit amount of the adjustment in the Adjustments Debit column on the Insurance Expense line. Label the amount (c).

Adjusting the Income Tax Expense Account

Champion Building Products is organized as a corporation. A corporation is considered to be a separate legal entity. Champion may own assets, must pay its own debts, and may enter into legal contracts. Under the law, a corporation is considered separate from its owners.

As a result, a corporation is required to pay federal income taxes on its net income. (Many states and cities also tax corporate income. For now, we will discuss only federal income taxes.) A corporation is put on a pay-as-you-go basis. That is, the corporation is required to estimate in advance its federal income taxes for the year. The corporation pays that estimated amount to the federal government in quarterly installments during the year. At the end of the fiscal year, the exact amount of net income and the tax on that income are determined. If the corporation owes additional taxes (as is usually the case), they are paid when the corporate income tax return is filed.

Teaching Tips

■ Businesses need insurance to protect their property from loss, just as individual property owners do. Ask students to suggest other types of insurance a business may have (for example, liability insurance or special insurance to cover computer equipment).

■ Discuss why Prepaid Insurance is an asset (because it provides a future benefit to the business).

Using Visuals

Use demonstration problem 16-4 to give students practice entering the adjustment for insurance expense on the work sheet.

Teaching Tips

■ Corporations estimate their net income tax for the year and make payments during that year. If the estimate is too high or too low, an adjustment is needed on the work sheet.

At the beginning of the fiscal period, Champion estimated that its income taxes would be $9,750.00. The business made quarterly payments of $2,437.50 in April, June, September, and December. These payments were recorded in the cash payments journal as debits to Federal Income Tax Expense and credits to Cash in Bank.

At the end of the fiscal period, Champion's accountant determined that Champion's federal income tax for the year was $9,895.00. Since Champion had already paid $9,750.00 in taxes, it only owes an additional $145.00.

The balance in the Federal Income Tax Expense account must be adjusted to show the additional tax expense for the period. To adjust Federal Income Tax Expense (a temporary account), that account is debited (increased) for $145.00. This amount is entered in the Adjustments Debit column on the Federal Income Tax Expense line. Since this is the fourth adjustment, the label (d) is used.

The $145.00 also represents an increase in Champion's liabilities. The additional tax will be paid in the future when the company files its income tax return. The balance in Federal Income Tax Payable (a permanent account) must, therefore, be adjusted. It is credited for $145.00. The $145.00 is entered in the adjustments Credit column on the Federal Income Tax Payable line. This entry is also labeled (d). This adjustment is shown on lines 9 and 31 on the work sheet in Figure 16-3 on page 350.

Federal Income Tax Expense			Federal Income Tax Payable	
Dr.	Cr.		Dr.	Cr.
+	−		−	+
Bal. $9,750.00				
Adj. 145.00				Adj. $145.00

Totaling and Ruling the Adjustments Section

After all adjustments have been entered, the Adjustments section of the work sheet is totaled and ruled. Each adjustment has an equal debit and credit, so the total of the Adjustments Debit and Credit columns must be the same. When the Adjustments section is proved, a double rule is drawn under the totals and across both columns, as shown in Figure 16-3 on page 350.

R   E   M   E   M   B   E   R

The Adjustments section of the work sheet, like the Trial Balance section, must be proved before the work sheet can be continued.

Completing the Adjusted Trial Balance Section

After all the adjustments are made, the Adjusted Trial Balance section is completed. This section shows the updated balances of all the general ledger accounts. To complete this section of the work sheet, the balance of each account in the Trial Balance section is combined with the adjustment, if any, in the Adjustments section. The new balance is then entered in the appropriate Adjusted Trial Balance column.

ACCT. NO.	ACCOUNT NAME	TRIAL BALANCE		ADJUSTMENTS		ADJUSTED TRIAL BALANCE	
		DEBIT	CREDIT	DEBIT	CREDIT	DEBIT	CREDIT
1	101 Cash in Bank	2128442				2128442	
2	105 Accounts Receivable	636435				636435	
3	110 Merch. Inventory	8492110			(a) 353540	8138570	
4	115 Supplies	554950			(b) 370990	183960	
5	120 Prepaid Insurance	150000			(c) 25000	125000	
6	150 Delivery Equipment	1914390				1914390	
7	155 Store Equipment	2635340				2635340	
8	201 Accounts Payable		1231695				1231695
9	205 Fed. Inc. Tax Payable				(d) 14500		14500
10	210 Sales Tax Payable		198360				198360
11	301 Capital Stock		7500000				7500000
12	305 Retained Earnings		2762545				2762545
13	310 Income Summary	—	—	(a) 353540		353540	
14	401 Sales		37738500				37738500
15	405 Sales Discounts	355042				355042	
16	410 Sales Returns & Allow.	106181				106181	
17	501 Purchases	20946432				20946432	
18	505 Transportation In	421580				421580	
19	510 Purchases Discounts		980854				980854
20	515 Purchases Ret. & Allow.		401790				401790
21	601 Advertising Expense	286450				286450	
22	605 Bank Card Fees Expense	329230				329230	
23	610 Delivery Expense	269396				269396	
24	615 Insurance Expense	—		(c) 25000		25000	
25	620 Maintenance Expense	332190				332190	
26	625 Miscellaneous Expense	64705				64705	
27	630 Rent Expense	1500000				1500000	
28	635 Salaries Expense	8400000				8400000	
29	640 Supplies Expense	—		(b) 370990		370990	
30	645 Utilities Expense	315871				315871	
31	650 Fed. Inc. Tax Expense	975000		(d) 14500		989500	
32		50813744	50813744	764030	764030	50828244	50828244

Figure 16-4 Extending Balances to the Adjusted Trial Balance Section of the Work Sheet

Let's take a look at how new balances are computed. If an account balance has *not* been adjusted, it is simply extended to the same column (Debit or Credit) in the Adjusted Trial Balance section. Look at Figure 16-4. The balances of the first two accounts—Cash in Bank and Accounts Receivable—were not adjusted. Since both accounts have debit balances, those balances are extended to the Adjusted Trial Balance Debit column.

If the account balance in the Trial Balance section has been adjusted, the new balance must be calculated. The amount of the adjustment (from the Adjustments section) must be added to or subtracted from the amount in the Trial Balance section. The first adjusted balance is that for Merchandise Inventory.

Before being adjusted, Merchandise Inventory had a debit balance of $84,921.10. Adjustment (a) is a credit of $3,535.40. To determine the updated balance, the credit adjustment is subtracted from the debit balance. The adjusted balance of $81,385.70 ($84,921.10 − $3,535.40) is extended to the Adjusted Trial Balance Debit column.

The adjusted balances for Supplies, Prepaid Insurance, and Federal Income Tax Expense are calculated in the same way.

Making Connections

BUSINESS ETHICS

Barry Thorn, a recent high school graduate, has just prepared his resume for an accounting position. Because his resume looked so short, he decided to "pad" it by adding false information. Barry has heard that prospective employers do not always check all resume information. Do you agree with Barry's approach? What problems may Barry encounter by giving false information?

(Answer: No, Barry should not have "padded" his resume. Potential employers often check the information on a resume, although that may happen after the person has been hired. Including false information on the resume is usually grounds for dismissal.)

If an account has a zero balance in the Trial Balance section, the amount listed in the Adjustments section is extended to the same column in the Adjusted Trial Balance section. Federal Income Tax Payable, for example, has a zero balance in the Trial Balance section. Adjustment (d) is a credit of $145.00. This amount is extended to the Adjusted Trial Balance Credit column.

After all account balances have been extended to the Adjusted Trial Balance section, both columns are totaled. If total debits equal total credits, this section has been proved. A double rule is drawn under the totals and across both columns. If total debits do not equal total credits, an error has been made. Re-add each column. If the error is not found, check the amounts extended from the Trial Balance and Adjustments sections. The error must be found and corrected before the work sheet can be completed.

Before you read any further, do the following activity.

Check Your Learning

Write your answers to these questions on notebook paper.

1. If the Trial Balance shows a balance of $3,357.45 for Supplies and the amount of supplies on hand is actually $853.75, what is the amount of the adjustment? What account is debited? What account is credited?
2. If a company paid an annual insurance premium on November 1 of $1,740.00 and the fiscal period ended on December 31, what is the amount of the adjustment? What account is debited? credited?
3. If the Income Summary account is credited in the Adjustments section of the work sheet, is the ending inventory greater or less than the beginning inventory?
4. If a business has made quarterly federal income tax payments of $945.00 and its tax has been calculated at the end of the year to be $3,895.00, what is the amount of the adjustment? This adjustment is entered as a debit to the ___?___ account and as a credit to the ___?___ account.

Compare your answers to those in the answers section. Re-read the preceding part of the chapter to find the answers to any questions you missed.

Extending Amounts to the Balance Sheet and Income Statement Sections

Beginning with line 1, each account balance in the Adjusted Trial Balance section is extended either to the Balance Sheet section or to the Income Statement section. These extensions are shown in Figure 16-5.

The Balance Sheet section contains the balances of all the permanent general ledger accounts. Here you will find all asset, liability, and stockholders' equity accounts (in this case, Capital Stock and Retained Earnings).

The Income Statement section contains the balances of all the temporary general ledger accounts. This section includes all revenue, cost of merchandise, and expense accounts as well as Income Summary.

ACCT. NO.	ACCOUNT NAME	ADJUSTED TRIAL BALANCE DEBIT	CREDIT	INCOME STATEMENT DEBIT	CREDIT	BALANCE SHEET DEBIT	CREDIT	
101	Cash in Bank	21284 42				21284 42		1
105	Accounts Receivable	6364 35				6364 35		2
110	Merch. Inventory	81385 70				81385 70		3
115	Supplies	1839 60				1839 60		4
120	Prepaid Insurance	1250 00				1250 00		5
150	Delivery Equipment	19143 90				19143 90		6
155	Store Equipment	26353 40				26353 40		7
201	Accounts Payable		12316 95				12316 95	8
205	Fed. Inc. Tax Payable		145 00				145 00	9
210	Sales Tax Payable		1983 60				1983 60	10
301	Capital Stock		75000 00				75000 00	11
305	Retained Earnings		27625 45				27625 45	12
310	Income Summary	3535 40		3535 40				13
401	Sales		377385 00		377385 00			14
405	Sales Discounts	3550 42		3550 42				15
410	Sales Returns & Allow.	1061 81		1061 81				16
501	Purchases	209464 32		209464 32				17
505	Transportation In	4215 80		4215 80				18
510	Purchases Discounts		9808 54		9808 54			19
515	Purchases Ret. & Allow.		4017 90		4017 90			20
601	Advertising Expense	2864 50		2864 50				21
605	Bank Card Fees Expense	3292 30		3292 30				22
610	Delivery Expense	2693 96		2693 96				23
615	Insurance Expense	250 00		250 00				24
620	Maintenance Expense	3321 90		3321 90				25
625	Miscellaneous Expense	647 05		647 05				26
630	Rent Expense	15000 00		15000 00				27
635	Salaries Expense	84000 00		84000 00				28
640	Supplies Expense	3709 90		3709 90				29
645	Utilities Expense	3158 71		3158 71				30
650	Fed. Inc. Tax Expense	9895 00		9895 00				31
		508282 44	508282 44	350661 07	391211 44	157621 37	117071 00	32

Figure 16-5 Extending Adjusted Trial Balance Amounts to the Balance Sheet and Income Statement Sections

Completing the Work Sheet

After all amounts have been extended to the Balance Sheet and Income Statement sections, a single rule is drawn across these last four columns. All four columns are then totaled. As you learned in Chapter 7, at this point the totals of the debit and credit columns in the Balance Sheet and Income Statement sections are not equal. The difference between the two column totals in each section is the amount of net income (or net loss) for the period.

After the net income (or net loss) is recorded, the last four columns are ruled and totaled as shown in Figure 16-6 on page 356. Notice that the words "Net Income" are written in the Account Name column on the same line as the net income amount.

If the totals of the two Income Statement columns are equal, and the totals of the two Balance Sheet columns are equal, a double rule is drawn across all four columns. The double rule indicates that these sections of the work sheet have been proved. The complete ten-column work sheet for Champion Building Products is shown in Figure 16-6.

CHAPTER 16 Preparing a Ten-Column Work Sheet — 355

Using Visuals

Point out the account numbers on the work sheet in Figure 16-5. Ask students how each account is classified and how the account number can help them decide whether the account balance is extended to the Balance Sheet or the Income Statement section.

CONCEPT DEVELOPMENT
Completing the Work Sheet

Review the steps in totaling and ruling an accounting form. Point out that the totals for the two financial statement sections do not match because the net income or net loss earned during the fiscal period covered by the work sheet has yet to be calculated.

Using Visuals

 A teaching transparency of Figure 16-5 is available in the transparency binder accompanying Glencoe Accounting.

Using Visuals

Direct students' attention to Figure 16-6, the completed work sheet. Walk students through the effect of a net income on the business; then ask them to analyze a net loss and to describe how it would be recorded on the work sheet.

COMPUTERS IN ACCOUNTING

The portable pen-based computer is designed to be addressed by writing rather than by typing on a keyboard. UPS (United Parcel Service) drivers use pen-based computers to record shipment data. Pen-based computers can also simplify an accountant's work. Accountants can use them to input data for a spreadsheet (work sheet) exercise. The computer reads the handwritten calculations and translates the data for processing, completing the calculations in a matter of seconds. Accountants also find the pen-based computer handy when they work with huge checklists while examining inventories in remote locations.

Using Visuals

A teaching transparency of Figure 16-6 is available in the transparency binder accompanying Glencoe Accounting.

Champion Building Products, Inc.
Work Sheet
For the Year Ended December 31, 19--

ACCT. NO.	ACCOUNT NAME	TRIAL BALANCE DEBIT	TRIAL BALANCE CREDIT	ADJUSTMENTS DEBIT	ADJUSTMENTS CREDIT	ADJUSTED TRIAL BALANCE DEBIT	ADJUSTED TRIAL BALANCE CREDIT	INCOME STATEMENT DEBIT	INCOME STATEMENT CREDIT	BALANCE SHEET DEBIT	BALANCE SHEET CREDIT
101	Cash in Bank	21 284 42				21 284 42				21 284 42	
105	Accounts Receivable	63 6435				63 6435				63 6435	
110	Merch. Inventory	84 921 10			(a) 3 535 40	81 385 70				81 385 70	
115	Supplies	5 549 50			(b) 3 709 90	1 839 60				1 839 60	
120	Prepaid Insurance	1 500 00			(c) 250 00	1 250 00				1 250 00	
150	Delivery Equipment	19 143 90				19 143 90				19 143 90	
155	Store Equipment	26 353 40				26 353 40				26 353 40	
201	Accounts Payable		12 316 95				12 316 95				12 316 95
205	Fed. Inc. Tax Payable				(d) 145 00		145 00				145 00
210	Sales Tax Payable		1 983 60				1 983 60				1 983 60
301	Capital Stock		75 000 00				75 000 00				75 000 00
305	Retained Earnings		27 625 45				27 625 45				27 625 45
310	Income Summary			(a) 3 535 40		3 535 40		3 535 40			
401	Sales		377 385 00				377 385 00		377 385 00		
405	Sales Discounts	3 550 42				3 550 42		3 550 42			
410	Sales Returns & Allow.	1 061 81				1 061 81		1 061 81			
501	Purchases	209 464 32				209 464 32		209 464 32			
505	Transportation In	4 215 80				4 215 80		4 215 80			
510	Purchases Discounts		9 808 54				9 808 54		9 808 54		
515	Purchases Ret. & Allow.		4 017 90				4 017 90		4 017 90		
601	Advertising Expense	2 864 50				2 864 50		2 864 50			
605	Bank Card Fees Expense	3 292 30				3 292 30		3 292 30			
610	Delivery Expense	2 693 96				2 693 96		2 693 96			
615	Insurance Expense			(c) 250 00		250 00		250 00			
620	Maintenance Expense	3 321 90				3 321 90		3 321 90			
625	Miscellaneous Expense	647 05				647 05		647 05			
630	Rent Expense	15 000 00				15 000 00		15 000 00			
635	Salaries Expense	84 000 00				84 000 00		84 000 00			
640	Supplies Expense			(b) 3 709 90		3 709 90		3 709 90			
645	Utilities Expense	3 158 71				3 158 71		3 158 71			
650	Fed. Inc. Tax Expense	9 750 00		(d) 145 00		9 895 00		9 895 00			
		508 137 44	508 137 44	7 640 30	7 640 30	508 282 44	508 282 44	350 661 07	391 211 44	157 621 37	117 071 00
	Net Income							40 550 37			40 550 37
								391 211 44	391 211 44	157 621 37	157 621 37

Figure 16-6 Champion Building Products' Completed Work Sheet

Pop Quiz

1. How do you determine which accounts need adjustment?
2. Is the cash account balance adjusted at the end of the fiscal period? Why or why not?
3. How does a business know how much the Merchandise Inventory balance has changed?
4. How does a business calculate gross profit?
5. What two accounts are affected when Merchandise Inventory is adjusted?

ANSWERS

1. If the balance on the work sheet is not up to date, the account must be adjusted.
2. No. Cash is continually updated through journal entries and posting.
3. By making a physical count of all merchandise on hand.
4. By subtracting the cost of merchandise sold from revenue.
5. Income Summary, Merchandise Inventory.

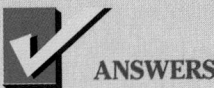

Complete the following activity to check your understanding of the ten-column work sheet.

Check Your Learning

Use Figure 16-6 on page 356 to answer these questions. Write your answers on a sheet of notebook paper.

1. How many adjustments did Champion Building Products make at the end of the fiscal period?
2. What is the adjusted balance of Merchandise Inventory? How was that balance calculated?
3. What amount was extended to the Income Statement section for Federal Income Tax Expense?
4. To what section of the work sheet was the balance of Prepaid Insurance extended? Why?
5. What was the balance of Federal Income Tax Payable reported on the Trial Balance section?
6. How was the net income for the period calculated?

Compare your answers to those in the answers section. Re-read the preceding parts of the chapter to determine the correct answers to any questions you may have missed.

Summary of Key Points

1. The work sheet is prepared to organize all the data needed to update the accounts and to prepare the financial statements and end-of-period journal entries. The work sheet lists all accounts and their updated balances and shows the net income (or net loss) for the period.
2. The Trial Balance section of the work sheet includes all accounts listed in the chart of accounts, even those with zero balances.
3. Changes in some accounts are not reflected by the recording of the daily business transactions. Some accounts, therefore, must be updated at the end of a fiscal period. The end-of-period changes to such accounts are called adjustments.
4. Every adjustment requires a debit and a credit of equal amount. Every adjustment will affect one permanent general ledger account and one temporary general ledger account.
5. The beginning inventory is the amount of merchandise a business has on hand at the beginning of a fiscal period. The ending inventory is the amount of merchandise on hand at the end of a fiscal period. The balance of Merchandise Inventory changes only when it is adjusted to reflect the actual amount of merchandise on hand.
6. A corporation must pay income taxes on its net income for the year.

ANSWERS
1. 4
2. $81,385.70; the credit adjustment of $3,535.40 was subtracted from the Trial Balance amount of $84,921.10
3. $9,895.00
4. Prepaid Insurance is an asset account; asset accounts are extended to the Balance Sheet section of the work sheet.
5. $0
6. The total of the Income Statement Debit column was subtracted from the total of the Income Statement Credit column.

3 CLOSE

CHAPTER SUMMARY

This summary enumerates the key information in the chapter. It is a useful tool for reinforcement and review.

Reteaching Strategies

To help students understand the adjustment for federal income taxes, obtain a copy of the tax tables and either photocopy or make a transparency of one table. Explain that corporations, like individuals, pay taxes throughout the year. At the end of the year, the corporation's total earnings and total deductions are calculated to determine the total tax owed. If the corporation has paid more tax than is owed, it will receive a refund. If the corporation has paid less tax than is owed, it will have to pay the additional amount. The Federal Income Tax Expense account is adjusted to reflect the actual amount of taxes paid to the federal government.

Review and Applications

Building Your Accounting Vocabulary

In your own words, write the definition of each of the following accounting terms. Use complete sentences for your definitions.

adjustment
beginning inventory

cost of merchandise
sold
ending inventory

gross profit
physical inventory

Reviewing Your Accounting Knowledge

1. Why is a work sheet prepared before the financial statements?
2. What are the titles of the five sections of the ten-column work sheet?
3. Why are general ledger accounts that have zero balances entered in the Trial Balance section of the work sheet?
4. Why are certain general ledger accounts updated at the end of the fiscal period?
5. Name four accounts of a merchandising corporation that are typically adjusted at the end of the fiscal period.
6. What is meant by "expensing" an asset?
7. Why does the balance of the Merchandise Inventory account not change during the fiscal period?
8. Why is a physical inventory always taken at the end of the fiscal period?
9. Why is the merchandise inventory adjustment recorded in the Income Summary account?
10. What does the Adjusted Trial Balance section of the work sheet contain?

Improving Your Human Relations Skills

Ray Boyd is an accounting clerk at Masterson's, a small variety store. Lisa Jung, the company accountant, orally gave Ray the data for the adjustments at the end of the fiscal period. Ray wrote the amounts down, but made a mistake in one of the figures. Ray recorded the adjustments on the work sheet, extended the amounts, and completed the work sheet. When Lisa received the work sheet, she immediately recognized that an error had been made. Lisa redid the work sheet, then reported Ray's sloppy work to his supervisor. Was this situation handled properly? Why or why not?

Applying Accounting Procedures

Exercise 16-1   Calculating Adjustments

Several accounts that must be adjusted at the end of the fiscal period are listed on the next page. The current account balance (before any adjustment) is given for each account. The ending inventories of merchandise and supplies are also given, along with the amount of insurance that has expired and the federal income tax expense for the period.

PRACTICE AND APPLY

• Language Development
• Comprehension and Retention
• Basic Skills

Building Your Accounting Vocabulary

See the Glossary on pages 670-679 for definitions of these terms.

Reviewing Your Accounting Knowledge

1. To enable the accountant to determine the net income (or net loss) for the fiscal period.
2. (a) Trial Balance, (b) Adjustments, (c) Adjusted Trial Balance, (d) Income Statement, and (e) Balance Sheet.
3. All accounts are listed in the Trial Balance section of the work sheet, even those with zero balances, to allow for their potential use for adjustments.
4. To show the changes caused by internal operations or the passage of time.
5. Merchandise Inventory, Supplies, Prepaid Insurance, and Federal Income Tax Expense.
6. At the end of the fiscal period, an adjustment is made to transfer the costs of the assets consumed to the appropriate expense accounts. This is called expensing an asset.
7. As merchandise is purchased, its cost is recorded in the Purchases account. As merchandise is sold, the entries are recorded in the Sales account.
8. To calculate the cost of the ending inventory and, therefore, the cost of merchandise sold.
9. Income Summary is a summary account used to record the total expenses and total revenue for the fiscal period. The cost of merchandise sold increases or decreases the expense for the period.
10. The updated balances of all the general ledger accounts.

Improving Your Human Relations Skills

This situation was not handled properly. First, Lisa could have verified that Ray had written down the correct amounts before asking him to complete the work sheet. She also could have given Ray a written list of the adjustment amounts. Either of these actions might have prevented the error in the first place.

When Lisa received the work sheet, she should have gone to Ray, pointed out the error, and allowed him to correct it. Both Lisa and Ray would have learned from this procedure. As it happened, Ray's performance was criticized, but he did not have the opportunity to correct his work and learn from the error.

Account Title	Current Balance	Adjustments Needed
Merchandise Inventory	$73,640	Ending inventory is $71,890.
Office Supplies	5,980	Office supplies on hand total $1,936.
Prepaid Insurance	1,980	Six months of premium ($165 per month) have expired.
Federal Income Tax Payable		
Income Summary		
Insurance Expense		
Office Supplies Expense		
Federal Income Tax Expense	5,800	Tax for the year is $5,994.

Instructions: Use a form similar to the one that follows.

(1) Determine the amount of the adjustment for each account.

(2) Enter the adjustment in the Adjustments Debit or Credit column. Label each adjustment (a), (b), (c), and so on.

(3) Calculate each new account balance and enter that amount in the Adjusted Trial Balance Debit or Credit column.

	Trial Balance		Adjustments		Adjusted Trial Balance	
Account Title	Dr.	Cr.	Dr.	Cr.	Dr.	Cr.
Merchandise Inventory	$73,640					

Exercise 16-2 Reporting Amounts on the Work Sheet

Instructions: Use a form similar to the one below. For each amount, place a check in each section of the work sheet in which it would appear.

1. Balance of Supplies on January 1 plus purchases during the period
2. Beginning merchandise inventory
3. Quarterly federal income tax installments paid
4. Expired portion of insurance premium
5. Supplies consumed during the period
6. Ending merchandise inventory
7. Value of Prepaid Insurance on January 1
8. Additional federal income taxes owed
9. Supplies inventory on December 31
10. Value of Prepaid Insurance on December 31
11. Total federal income tax expense for the period

Number of Item	Trial Balance	Adjustments	Adjusted Trial Balance	Income Statement	Balance Sheet
1	✔				

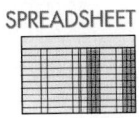
SPREADSHEET

PROBLEM

Problem 16-1 Completing a Ten-Column Work Sheet

The December 31 trial balance for the Hillard Supply Corporation is listed on page 360. Also listed is the data needed for the adjustments (ending merchandise inventory, supplies used during the period, expired insurance premium, and the additional federal income taxes owed).

359

PRACTICE AND APPLY

• Concepts and Procedures

Exercise 16-1: Ch. Obj. 2
Adjustments:
(a) $1,750
(b) $4,044
(c) $990
(d) $194

Exercise 16-2: Ch. Obj. 3
2. TB
3. TB
4. Adj.; ATB; IS
5. Adj.; ATB; IS
6. ATB; BS
7. TB
8. Adj.; ATB; BS
9. ATB; BS
10. ATB; BS
11. ATB; IS

Problem 16-1: Ch. Obj. 2, 3

Additional Reinforcement

Students who need additional practice or individualized help will benefit from the *Glencoe Accounting Electronic Study Guide* or the *Glencoe Accounting* on-line multimedia program, which provide reinforcement and reteaching for vocabulary, concepts, and procedures.

Refer students to the Chapter 16 review pages in the workbook, *Chapter Reviews and Working Papers.*

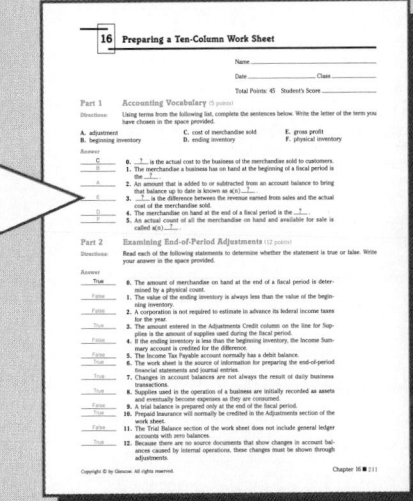

Column totals:
Adj., $11,971.12
ATB, $232,323.04
Net income, $23,283.74
IS, $145,967.20
BS, $109, 639.58

Problem 16-2: Ch. Obj. 2, 3

Column totals:
TB, $190,988.91
ADJ., $6,962.71
ATB, $191,198.91
Net income, $10,078.77
IS, $72,343.69
BS, $128,933.99

Instructions: Complete the ten-column work sheet for the Hillard Supply Corporation for the year ended December 31. The trial balance has already been entered on the work sheet.

	Trial Balance	
	Debit	Credit
Cash in Bank	$ 14,975.56	
Accounts Receivable	3,773.64	
Merchandise Inventory	86,865.10	
Supplies	2,940.60	
Prepaid Insurance	1,975.00	
Office Equipment	10,762.80	
Accounts Payable		$ 8,740.08
Federal Income Tax Payable		0.00
Sales Tax Payable		1,369.34
Capital Stock		45,000.00
Retained Earnings		30,928.42
Income Summary		
Sales		145,967.20
Purchases	93,874.75	
Insurance Expense	0.00	
Miscellaneous Expense	3,662.59	
Rent Expense	9,225.00	
Supplies Expense	0.00	
Federal Income Tax Expense	3,950.00	
	$232,005.04	$232,005.04

Data for Adjustments

Merchandise Inventory, December 31	$ 77,872.13
Supplies consumed during the period	2,171.15
Insurance premium expired during the period	489.00
Additional federal income taxes owed	318.00

Problem 16-2   Completing a Ten-Column Work Sheet

The December 31 trial balance for the J. J. Laine Corporation is listed below. Also listed is the data needed for the adjustments.

Instructions: Complete the ten-column work sheet for the J. J. Laine Corporation for the year ended December 31.

	Trial Balance	
	Debit	Credit
Cash in Bank	$13,865.69	
Accounts Receivable	4,385.03	
Merchandise Inventory	82,933.70	
Supplies	2,395.59	
Prepaid Insurance	1,350.00	
Store Equipment	30,756.69	
Accounts Payable		$ 8,489.48
Federal Income Tax Payable		0.00
Sales Tax Payable		1,590.58
Capital Stock		80,000.00
Retained Earnings		28,565.16
Income Summary		
Sales		71,487.20
Sales Returns and Allowances	945.59	
Purchases	39,495.69	
Transportation In	2,038.34	

Teacher Notes

Purchases Discounts		856.49
Insurance Expense	0.00	
Miscellaneous Expense	2,952.59	
Rent Expense	9,000.00	
Supplies Expense	0.00	
Federal Income Tax Expense	870.00	

Data for Adjustments

Merchandise Inventory, December 31	$78,672.13
Supplies on hand, December 31	394.45
Insurance premium expired during the period	490.00
Additional federal income taxes owed	210.00

Problem 16-3: Ch. Obj. 2, 3
Column totals:
TB, $186,836.19
ADJ., $4,416.90
ATB, $187,647.14
Net income, $23,057.84
IS, $140,665.40
BS, $70,039.58

Problem 16-4: Ch. Obj. 2, 3

Problem 16-3 Completing a Ten-Column Work Sheet

The balances of the general ledger accounts of Cropp Sound Shop, Inc., as of December 31 are listed below. Also listed are the adjustment data.

Instructions: Prepare a ten-column work sheet for the Cropp Sound Shop, Inc., for the year ended December 31.

Cash in Bank	$ 12,328.72
Accounts Receivable	1,734.84
Merchandise Inventory	23,648.50
Supplies	3,976.34
Prepaid Insurance	1,800.00
Store Equipment	14,395.38
Display Equipment	15,224.80
Accounts Payable	11,028.36
Federal Income Tax Payable	0.00
Sales Tax Payable	1,271.14
Capital Stock	25,000.00
Retained Earnings	9,408.24
Income Summary	
Sales	138,992.06
Sales Returns and Allowances	1,273.49
Purchases	87,118.33
Transportation In	1,174.30
Purchases Discounts	810.91
Purchases Returns and Allowances	325.48
Advertising Expense	2,438.56
Insurance Expense	0.00
Miscellaneous Expense	3,927.25
Rent Expense	9,750.00
Supplies Expense	0.00
Utilities Expense	4,395.68
Federal Income Tax Expense	3,650.00

Data for Adjustments

Ending merchandise inventory	$ 24,185.45
Ending supplies inventory	1,045.39
Insurance premium expired	675.00
Federal income tax expense for the year	3,924.00

Problem 16-4 Completing a Ten-Column Work Sheet

The balances of the general ledger accounts of the Springtime Floral Shop, Inc., as of December 31 are listed below.

Instructions: Prepare a ten-column work sheet for the Springtime Floral Shop, Inc., for the year ended December 31. The account titles have already been entered on the work sheet. The data for the adjustments is as follows.
(1) The cost of the ending merchandise inventory is $47,349.92.

361

Teacher Notes

_____

_____

_____

_____

_____

Adjustments:
(a) $1,858.58
(b) $2,406.99
(c) $1,242.00
(d) $435.00

Column totals:
TB, $233,573.81
ADJ., $5,942.57
ATB, $234,008.81
Net income, $28,744.95
IS, $145,726.95
BS, $117,026.81

Problem 16-5: Ch. Obj. 3

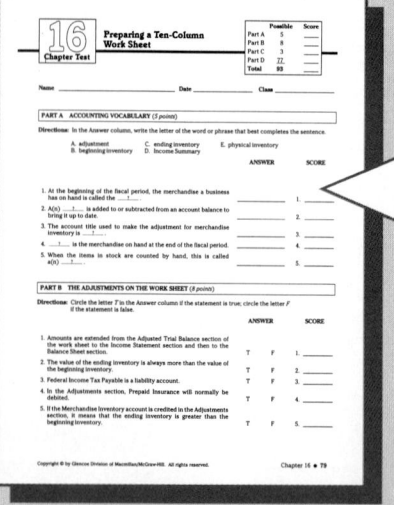

CHALLENGE

PROBLEM

The last problem in each chapter is a challenge problem and is identified by this "maze" symbol.

TB totals, $38,344.43
Adj. totals, $14,132.25

4 ASSESS

A chapter test is available for use in assessing students' understanding of concepts in this chapter.

The testmaker software will enable you to develop tailor-made chapter, unit, semester, and final tests.

Alternative Assessment

For alternative assessment strategies, refer to *Tech Prep Strategies in Accounting.*

Use Chapter Test 16 here to assess students' understanding and retention of the concepts and procedures presented in the chapter.

---

(2) The cost of the supplies on hand on December 31 is $619.35.
(3) The one-year insurance premium of $1,656.00 was paid on April 1.
(4) The total federal income taxes owed for the year are $7,835.00.

Cash in Bank	$ 15,382.72
Accounts Receivable	2,853.94
Merchandise Inventory	49,208.50
Supplies	3,026.34
Prepaid Insurance	1,656.00
Store Equipment	19,406.68
Display Equipment	25,504.20
Computer Equipment	5,496.00
Accounts Payable	13,378.36
Federal Income Tax Payable	0.00
Sales Tax Payable	2,043.14
Capital Stock	50,000.00
Retained Earnings	22,425.36
Income Summary	
Sales	144,939.66
Sales Discounts	203.85
Sales Returns and Allowances	1,385.49
Purchases	79,318.73
Transportation In	1,192.30
Purchases Discounts	295.81
Purchases Returns and Allowances	491.48
Advertising Expense	3,148.56
Bank Card Fees Expense	288.40
Insurance Expense	0.00
Maintenance Expense	1,381.03
Miscellaneous Expense	3,775.39
Rent Expense	10,350.00
Supplies Expense	0.00
Utilities Expense	2,595.68
Federal Income Tax Expense	7,400.00

CHALLENGE

PROBLEM

Problem 16-5   Locating Errors on the Work Sheet

The Hispino Card Shop began business as a corporation on December 1. It is now December 31, the end of the first fiscal period, and the work sheet for the corporation is being prepared.

Information for the Trial Balance and Adjustments sections has been recorded on the work sheet, which is included in the working papers. It is apparent from the totals on the work sheet that errors have been made in preparing these portions of the work sheet.

The accounting records show that

1. The merchandise on hand at the end of the month is valued at $13,350.00.
2. The supplies on hand on December 31 are valued at $419.75.
3. The insurance premium was paid on December 1. The premium was $980.00 and covers the period from December 1 to March 31.
4. The total federal income tax owed for the period is $243.00.

Instructions:

(1) Find and correct the error(s) in the Trial Balance section.
(2) On the line provided on the work sheet, write in the corrected totals for the Trial Balance section.
(3) Find and correct the error(s) in the Adjustments section.
(4) Write in the corrected totals for the Adjustments columns.

362

Data Access vs. Privacy:
A Delicate Balance

Scenario #1: It's 10:00 p.m. on a Friday evening. Early the next morning, Sandy is going camping with some friends. "Oh, no! I forgot to go to the bank."

No problem. The automatic teller machine (ATM) is always up and running. Sandy drives to the nearest bank, slips in her card, keys in her secret code number and the amount she wants, and—presto!—instant money. This machine knew who Sandy was, how much money she had in her account, and the new balance in her account after the transaction—in seconds.

Scenario #2: Company's coming for dinner in one hour. The carpet is covered with dog hairs. Your mother heads for the broom closet. "Oh, no! The vacuum cleaner isn't here. I forgot to pick it up at the repair shop."

No problem. You offer to go get it. Your mother gives you her credit card and you drive into town. The vacuum cleaner is ready. You hand your mother's credit card to the repair person, who validates it by sliding it through a little machine. The digital readout gives its approval in seconds. You get home just in time to race the cleaner across the rug.

In this fast-paced world, time is of the essence, and computers help us accomplish many time-consuming tasks efficiently. In order for organizations, businesses, and government agencies to accomplish their objectives, however, they must have access to a lot of personal data. To some, that is a threat to our right of privacy.

Information about our credit, health, and employment history could be embarrassing. It could even be harmful if confidentiality is not respected, if the information is incorrect, or if those who use it don't exercise good judgment and fairness.

Computers have dramatically increased the amount of data that can be collected, processed, and stored.

So while accessible databases save hours and dollars, they must be carefully guarded so they're used with our approval and with the right to review and to challenge incorrect facts.

There will probably be many debates on the issue of accessibility versus privacy. Can we have it both ways?

When making a purchase by telephone, you may be asked for a credit card account number so your account can be charged. Ask students about the advisability of giving such information over the telephone. What might the consequences be?

QUESTIONS

1. Name some sources from which a firm can gather names and addresses for its database of customers.
2. How has government reacted to the privacy issue relating to computer access?

ANSWERS

1. Since they are a matter of public record, such listings as the telephone book, vehicle registrations, and real estate transactions are excellent sources. Firms may also buy lists of individuals' names and addresses.
2. Several laws have been enacted to protect privacy. They include the Freedom of Information Act (1970), the Fair Credit Reporting Act (1970), The Electronic Communications Privacy Act (1986), and the Computer Matching and Privacy Act (1988).

363

Chapter

PREPARING FINANCIAL STATEMENTS FOR A CORPORATION

LOOKING BACK

In the previous chapter students learned to collect information on the work sheet in preparation for completing the end-of-period financial statements. In this chapter students will prepare three financial statements for a merchandising business organized as a privately held corporation: the income statement, the statement of retained earnings, and the balance sheet.

VOCABULARY DEVELOPMENT

Discuss the definitions of the new terms in class. Ask students to give their definition of each term and to explain how each is used in accounting. Definitions of these terms are found in the chapter and in the glossary on pages 670-679.

In Chapter 16, you learned that some accounts in the general ledger are not up to date at the end of the fiscal period. You learned how to determine which accounts had to be adjusted, how to calculate the amount of each adjustment, and how to enter adjustments on a ten-column work sheet.

The work sheet is a working paper. It organizes all the accounting data needed to prepare the financial statements and the end-of-period journal entries. In this chapter, you will use the information on the work sheet to prepare the financial statements for a merchandising corporation. You will learn what information is included on each statement and why the statements are important to stockholders, creditors, and managers. You'll also learn how the equity accounts of a corporation differ from those of a sole proprietorship.

Learning Objectives

When you have completed Chapter 17, you should be able to do the following:

1. Explain how the ownership for a corporation is recorded in comparison to that for a sole proprietorship.
2. Explain the relationship between the work sheet and the financial statements for a merchandising business organized as a corporation.
3. Explain how the financial statements for a corporation differ from those for a sole proprietorship.
4. Prepare an income statement for a merchandising corporation.
5. Prepare a statement of retained earnings for a merchandising corporation.
6. Prepare a balance sheet for a merchandising corporation.
7. Define the accounting terms introduced in this chapter.

New Terms

capital stock
stockholders' equity
retained earnings
net sales
net purchases
gross profit on sales
operating expenses
operating income
statement of retained earnings

364

Teaching Resources

- Lesson Plans
- TE/Chapter Reviews & Working Papers
- Demonstration Problems
- Student Study Plans
- Teaching Transparencies
- Solutions Transparencies
- Electronic Field Trips Video, Level I
- Electronic Study Guide
- Chapter 17 Test

Other Resources

- Skills Improvement Activities
- Blackline Masters
- Careers in Accounting
- Dictionary
- Math Review for Accounting
- Tech Prep Strategies in Accounting
- Video
- Test Bank with Software
- Spanish Resources/Audiotapes
- Spanish Electronic Study Guide

Accounting for a Corporation

A sole proprietorship is owned by one person. A corporation may be owned by one person or by hundreds of people. The ownership of a corporation is represented by shares of stock.

Recording the Ownership of a Corporation

As you recall, investments made by the owner of a sole proprietorship are recorded in the owner's capital account; for example, Jan Harter, Capital. An owner's investment of $25,000 in the sole proprietorship would be recorded as shown in the T accounts below. Cash in Bank is debited for $25,000 and Jan Harter, Capital is credited for the same amount.

Cash in Bank		Jan Harter, Capital	
Dr.	Cr.	Dr.	Cr.
+	−	−	+
$25,000			$25,000

An investment of this same amount in a corporation would be recorded by the corporation as shown in the following T accounts. Cash in Bank again is debited since the corporation is receiving cash. The account credited for the amount of the investment, however, is Capital Stock. **Capital stock** represents the total amount of investment in the corporation by its stockholders (owners).

Cash in Bank		Capital Stock	
Dr.	Cr.	Dr.	Cr.
+	−	−	+
$25,000			$25,000

Capital Stock is classified as a stockholders' equity account. **Stockholders' equity** is the value of the stockholders' claims to the assets of the corporation. The Capital Stock account is to a corporation what the owner's capital account is to a sole proprietorship. Capital Stock, then, has the same rules of debit and credit as an owner's capital account.

Capital Stock	
Dr.	Cr.
−	+
Decrease Side	Increase Side
	Balance Side

Reporting Stockholders' Equity in the Corporation

The form of business organization does not affect the amount of equity in the business. That is, one person may have an ownership interest in a sole proprietorship worth $20,000, or ten people may have shares of stock in a corporation worth $20,000. The difference between the two is in the way these two amounts are reported on the balance sheet.

The balance sheet of the sole proprietorship reports the balance of the owner's capital account. This amount is reported in the owner's equity section of the balance sheet. For a corporation, the owner's equity section of

CHAPTER 17 Preparing Financial Statements for a Corporation **365**

1 FOCUS

MAJOR CONCEPTS

- Accounting for a Corporation
- Preparing End-of-Period Financial Statements
- The Income Statement
- The Statement of Retained Earnings
- The Balance Sheet
- Financial Statements Prepared by Computer

BUSINESS CONNECTION

Closely held corporations generate billions of dollars of revenue each year. Among some of the largest privately held companies in the United States are the United Parcel Service, Meijer, Levi Strauss & Company, and S.C. Johnson Wax. These companies differ from publicly held corporations in that the stock representing their ownership is not traded on a public stock exchange.

2 TEACH

CONCEPT DEVELOPMENT
Accounting for a Corporation
Discuss the difference in equity accounts for the sole proprietorship versus the corporation. The corporation used as an example in this cycle is organized as a privately held corporation, so its capital stock is not traded on a public stock exchange. Publicly held corporations may issue several different kinds of stock, as well as declaring dividends and issuing bonds. Students will learn more about public corporations in Chapter 27.

Teaching Tips

■ Review the rules of debit and credit for the capital account and then relate them to the Capital Stock account.
■ Remind students that an ownership interest is the same as a financial claim to the assets of the business.

Reinforcing Study Skills

Taking notes while listening for information can be challenging, but shortcuts can make it easier. Some hints are: Have pen and paper ready to take notes at the beginning of every class. Make up your own "shorthand" using symbols and abbreviations. Write faster, but keep your writing legible. Use an outline format and use phrases, not complete sentences.

Provide a copy of the *Student Study Plans* to each class member to help organize study activities or to individualize practice and review activities.

the balance sheet is called stockholders' equity. The law requires that stockholders' equity be reported in two parts: (1) equity contributed by stockholders and (2) equity earned through business profits.

▲ Equity Contributed by Stockholders

The first part of stockholders' equity is the amount of money invested by the stockholders. Stockholders contribute to equity in the corporation by buying shares of stock issued by the corporation. As you just learned, stockholders' investments are recorded in the account Capital Stock.

▲ Equity Earned Through Business Profits

The second part of stockholders' equity is the amount of net income earned during the fiscal period and retained by the corporation. In a sole proprietorship, this is the amount of net income less any withdrawals by the owner. In a corporation, this amount represents the increase in stockholders' equity from net income held by the corporation and not distributed to the stockholders as a return on their investment. This amount is called **retained earnings.**

Retained Earnings	
Dr.	Cr.
−	+
Decrease Side	Increase Side
	Balance Side

Earnings retained by a corporation are recorded in the account Retained Earnings. Retained Earnings is classified as a stockholders' equity account. Like the Capital Stock account, it is increased by credits and decreased by debits. Retained Earnings has a normal credit balance.

In a sole proprietorship, net income is recorded as an increase in capital. This increase in capital represents an increase in the assets of the business. In a corporation, retained earnings represent the growth, or increase, in the assets of the corporation.

Before learning about the financial statements prepared by a merchandising corporation, complete the following activity to check your understanding of the material you have just studied.

Check Your Learning

Write your answers to these questions on a sheet of notebook paper.

1. An investment of $40,000 by Jane Settles in a sole proprietorship is recorded as a credit to the ___?___ account.
2. The sale of 50 shares of stock, for $2,500, by the Sims Corporation is recorded as a credit to the account ___?___ .
3. The value of stockholders' claims to the assets of the business is called ___?___ .
4. Stockholders' equity consists of two accounts: ___?___ and ___?___ .

Compare your answers to those in the answers section. Re-read the preceding part of the chapter to find the answers to any questions you may have missed.

The basic accounting equation applies to any business's accounting system: Assets = Liabilities + Stockholders' (Owner's) Equity. Increases in capital or in retained earnings also represent increases in assets, which keeps the basic accounting equation in balance.

Preparing End-of-Period Financial Statements

At the end of a fiscal period, a business prepares various financial statements. These statements summarize the changes that have taken place during the fiscal period and report the financial condition of the business at the end of the fiscal period. Managers use the information in these statements to evaluate past decisions and to help them make future decisions. Stockholders are interested in the business's performance and in its potential. Creditors want to know whether the business can pay its debts. Government agencies, employees, consumers, and the general public are also interested in the financial position of the business.

For these financial reports to be useful, the data must be presented in such a way that users can recognize similarities, differences, and trends from one period to another. The same types of statements, therefore, are prepared at the end of each fiscal period. The time period covered by the financial statements is the same from one period to another (for example, one month, one year, and so on).

Champion Building Products, a merchandising corporation, prepares three financial statements. These statements are the income statement, the statement of retained earnings, and the balance sheet. The first two statements report the changes that have taken place over the fiscal period. The balance sheet shows the financial position of the business on a specific date—the last day of the fiscal period. The data needed to complete all three statements are taken from the work sheet.

The Income Statement

As you know, the income statement reports the net income or net loss earned by a business in a fiscal period. In Chapter 8, you prepared an income statement for Global Travel Agency, a service business organized as a sole proprietorship. On that statement, Global Travel's total expenses were subtracted from its revenue to determine the net income or loss for the fiscal period.

A merchandising business, however, has an additional cost—the cost of the merchandise that was purchased and then resold to customers. That cost must be included when determining net income or loss. The income statement for a merchandising business, then, must be expanded. An income statement for a merchandising business has five sections: (1) Revenue, (2) Cost of Merchandise Sold, (3) Gross Profit on Sales, (4) Operating Expenses, and (5) Net Income (or Loss).

CHAPTER 17   Preparing Financial Statements for a Corporation   **367**

CONCEPT DEVELOPMENT
Preparing End-of-Period Financial Statements
The same financial statements are prepared at the end of each fiscal period. The same time period is used so that financial statements may be compared from one period to the next. For example, if the fiscal period is a calendar year, the financial statements would cover January through December each year, not January through December one year and April through March the next year.

Remind students that the work sheet is the source of information for preparing the financial statements, especially the Balance Sheet and Income Statement sections.

> ## *Teaching Tips*
> - The assumption of time period means that the same time span is used from one fiscal period to another.
> - The accounting characteristic of comparability allows data to be compared over a span of fiscal periods.

CONCEPT DEVELOPMENT
The Income Statement
Refer back to the income statement students learned in Chapter 8 (page 152), which had three parts: revenue, expenses, and net income (or loss). Two additional sections used by a merchandising business are added in this chapter: cost of merchandise sold and gross profit on sales.

When introducing the revenue section, discuss the difference between net sales and total revenue. Also discuss the function of a contra account.

When presenting the cost of merchandise sold section, refer back to the example of school buttons in Chapter 16 (page 346). Write each step on the chalkboard and have students explain each entry. Help students to think each step through logically rather than memorizing each label.

Making Connections

EVERYDAY LIFE

Avon Products, Inc., now accepts orders by mail, fax, or telephone. Their traditional direct sales approach, however, continues to generate much of the company's revenue. Many people, including teenagers, have become successful entrepreneurs selling Avon prod-ucts. To calculate their net income, Avon representatives must determine the cost of goods sold. The cost of goods sold includes the cost of purchasing Avon products from the Avon distribution centers and the shipping costs to have the products delivered to the sales representative's home.

Chapter 17

Using Visuals

Ask a student to read the photo caption to the class. Then ask students to name examples of people who might be interested in reviewing the financial reports of a specific corporation.

Teaching Tips

■ The income statement used for Champion Building Products has four amount columns. Photocopy a blank form and show students how to enter information in each column. Emphasize that calculations should move from left to right.

Using Visuals

Direct students' attention to Figure 17-1. Remind students that the heading of the income statement gives the fiscal period covered by that statement. How does this heading differ for a balance sheet?

Using Visuals

 Use demonstration problem 17-1 to show students how to complete the revenue section of the income statement. Remind students that the balance of a contra account reduces the balance of its related account (for example, sales returns and allowances reduces sales).

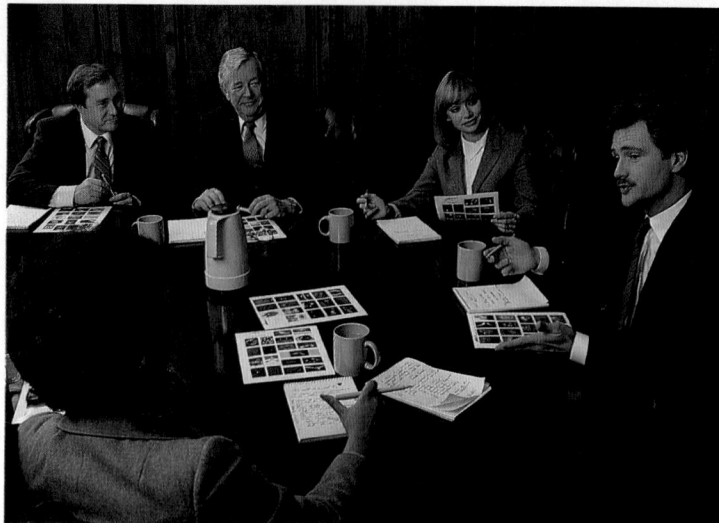

Financial statements are a central feature of accounting because they are the primary means of communicating important financial information to users.

The accounting stationery used for Champion's income statement has four amount columns. The far right column is used to enter totals. The other columns are used to enter balances that must be added or subtracted.

All of the information needed to prepare the income statement is taken from the work sheet, particularly the Income Statement section. As with all other financial statements, the income statement begins with a three-line heading. As you can see in Figure 17-1, the income statement for Champion Building Products has been prepared for the year ended December 31. After the heading has been written, the next information to be entered on the income statement is the revenue for the period.

Champion Building Products, Inc. Income Statement For the Year Ended December 31, 19--			
Revenue:			
Sales			377 385 00
Less: Sales Discounts	3 550 42		
Sales Ret. & Allow.	1 061 81	4 612 23	
Net Sales			372 772 77

Figure 17-1 The Heading and Revenue Section of the Income Statement

The Revenue Section

The first section on the income statement is the revenue section. This section reports the net sales for the period. Look at Figure 17-1 again. The balances of the revenue account Sales and the contra revenue accounts Sales Discounts and Sales Returns and Allowances are reported in this section. As

368 UNIT 3 The Accounting Cycle for a Merchandising Business

Cooperative Learning

NUMBERED HEADS TOGETHER

With the students numbered off in groups of 4 to 5 persons, ask each of the following questions. Allow a few minutes for discussion on each question, then choose a number and select a group to give an answer.

1. How does an income statement for a merchandising business differ from that for a service business?
2. How do you calculate net sales?

3. What is gross profit on sales?

(Answers: (1) The merchandising business reports cost of merchandise sold and gross profit on sales. (2) Subtract all sales discounts, returns, or allowances from total sales. (3) The amount of profit before expenses are deducted.)

Refer to the "Cooperative Learning" section of *Tech Prep Strategies in Accounting* for additional cooperative learning strategies.

368 UNIT 3 The Accounting Cycle for a Merchandising Business

you learned earlier, contra revenue accounts decrease the amount of revenue Champion receives from its sales transactions. **Net sales,** therefore, is the amount of sales for the period less any sales discounts, returns, or allowances. Refer to Figure 17-1 as you learn how to complete the revenue section.

1. On the first line, write the classification "Revenue:" at the left edge of the stationery.
2. On the second line, enter the title of the revenue account Sales, indented about one-half inch. Enter the balance of the account in the *third* amount column.
3. On the next lines, enter the deductions from Sales. Write the word "Less:" followed by the titles and balances of the two contra revenue accounts. (You may have to abbreviate the account titles.) Enter the balances of the accounts ($3,550.42 and $1,061.81) in the *second* amount column.
4. To find the total deduction from Sales, add the balances of the two contra revenue accounts. Write the total, on line 4, below the Sales balance in the *third* amount column.
5. On the next line, enter the words "Net Sales," indented about an inch. Subtract the total of the two contra accounts from the balance of the Sales account. Enter the amount in the *fourth* amount column. As you can see in Figure 17-1, Champion's net sales for the year are $372,772.77.

$3,550.42
+1,061.81
$4,612.23

$377,385.00
−   4,612.23
$372,772.77

The Cost of Merchandise Sold Section

Before a merchandising business can determine its net income or net loss, it must calculate the cost of the merchandise that was sold during the period. The cost of merchandise sold is calculated as follows:

```
  Beginning merchandise inventory
+ Net purchases during the period
= Cost of merchandise available for sale
− Ending merchandise inventory
= Cost of merchandise sold
```

As you can see from this equation, there are two steps involved in calculating the cost of merchandise sold. The first step is to determine the cost of all the merchandise that was available for sale. This is done by adding net purchases to the beginning inventory amount recorded in the Merchandise Inventory account. **Net purchases** is the amount of all costs related to merchandise purchased during the period. To calculate net purchases, the balance of Transportation In (the transportation charges for the period) is added to the balance of the Purchases account. The balances of Purchases Discounts and Purchases Returns and Allowances are then subtracted from that amount, leaving the net purchases.

```
  Purchases
+ Transportation In
= Cost of Delivered Merchandise
− Purchases Discounts
− Purchases Returns and Allowances
= Net Purchases
```

CHAPTER 17   Preparing Financial Statements for a Corporation   **369**

Using Visuals

Have students look at Figure 17-2 as you explain each of the account titles or descriptive phrases listed in the left column of the form.

Transportation charges increase the cost of merchandise. The contra cost of merchandise accounts—Purchases Discounts and Purchases Returns and Allowances—decrease the cost of the merchandise bought for resale.

The second step in calculating the cost of merchandise sold is to subtract the ending merchandise inventory amount from the cost of merchandise available for sale. The cost of merchandise sold section of the income statement is shown in Figure 17-2. Refer to this illustration as you read the following steps:

Teaching Tips

- Walk students through steps 1-11 and explain the purpose behind each step.

ACCOUNTING **Tips**

When adding a column of figures, start at the top of the column and add down. To verify that your total is correct, add the figures from the bottom up. When subtracting, first subtract in the normal manner. To verify your answer, add the answer to the number that was subtracted; the result should be the number that you subtracted from. This method of verifying works equally well manually or with a calculator.

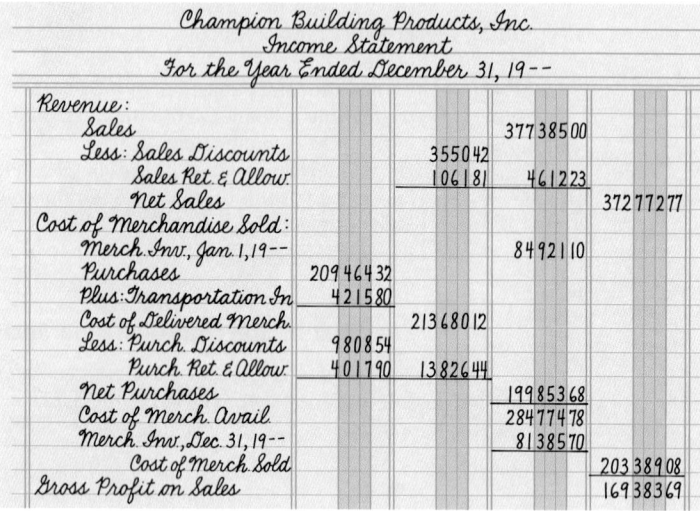

Figure 17-2 Income Statement Through Gross Profit on Sales

ACCOUNTING PRACTICE

Students may complete Exercise 17-1 after they have learned about the cost of merchandise sold section of the income statement.

1. On the line below net sales, write the words "Cost of Merchandise Sold:" at the left edge.
2. Next, write "Merchandise Inventory, January 1, 19—," indented about half an inch. Enter the amount of the beginning inventory in the *third* amount column. (The beginning inventory is found on the Merchandise Inventory line of the work sheet in the Trial Balance Debit column.)
3. Next, enter the title and balance of the Purchases account. Enter the balance amount in the *first* amount column.
4. On the next line, write the word "Plus:" followed by the title and balance of Transportation In. Enter the balance in the *first* amount column, below the Purchases amount.

$209,464.32
+   4,215.80
$213,680.12

5. Add the balances of the Purchases and Transportation In accounts. The result is the *Cost of Delivered Merchandise.* Enter the amount in the *second* amount column.
6. On the next line, enter the deductions from Purchases. Write the word "Less:" and the titles and balances of the two contra cost of merchandise accounts. Enter the balances in the *first* amount column.

370

UNIT 3   The Accounting Cycle for a Merchandising Business

Interdisciplinary Connections

HISTORY

During the "Commercial Revolution," between 1450 and 1700, money and goods, rather than land, became the measure of wealth. To finance trading voyages to Asia or the Americas, merchant-investors bought shares in a *joint-stock company.* As in modern corporations, shareholders shared both risks and profits from the voyage.

$ 9,808.54
+ 4,017.90
$13,826.44

7. To find the total deduction from Purchases, add the balances of the two contra cost accounts. Enter the total, on the same line, in the *second* amount column.

$213,680.12
− 13,826.44
$199,853.68

8. Subtract the total of the two contra cost accounts from the cost of delivered merchandise amount. The difference is the net purchases for the period. Enter the amount in the *third* amount column.

$ 84,921.10
+199,853.68
$284,774.78

9. Now, add the net purchases amount to the beginning inventory amount. The total is the *Cost of Merchandise Available for Sale.* Enter the total in the *third* amount column.

10. On the next line, write "Merchandise Inventory, December 31, 19—." Enter the amount of the ending inventory in the *third* amount column. (The ending inventory is found on the Merchandise Inventory line of the work sheet in the Balance Sheet Debit column.)

$284,774.78
− 81,385.70
$203,389.08

11. Subtract the ending inventory amount from the cost of merchandise available for sale. The difference is the *Cost of Merchandise Sold* during the period. Enter the amount in the *fourth* amount column.

As you can see in Figure 17-2, Champion sold merchandise costing $203,389.08 during the fiscal period.

The Gross Profit on Sales Section

In Chapter 16, you learned that the total amount received for all sales during the period actually represents two different amounts. The net, or total, sales amount includes the cost of the merchandise sold and the profit made from selling that merchandise. Once the cost of merchandise sold has been determined, the gross profit on sales can be calculated. The **gross profit on sales** is the amount of profit made during the period before expenses are deducted. Gross profit on sales is found by subtracting the cost of merchandise sold from net sales. In Figure 17-2, you can see that Champion had net sales of $372,772.77 and a cost of merchandise sold of $203,389.08. Champion's gross profit on sales is, therefore, $169,383.69.

$372,772.77
−203,389.08
$169,383.69

The Operating Expenses Section

The next section of the income statement shows the operating expenses for the period. **Operating expenses** are the cash spent or the assets consumed to earn revenue for the business. Look at Figure 17-3 on page 372. The titles and balances of all expense accounts *except* Federal Income Tax Expense are listed in the same order as on the work sheet. While it is a normal expense for a corporation, Federal Income Tax Expense is not considered to be an operating expense. Rather than cash spent to *earn* revenue, the account represents cash paid out as a *result* of the revenue earned.

Notice that the balances of the expense accounts are entered in the *third* amount column. The balances are then totaled. This total, $118,938.32, is entered in the *fourth* amount column.

The Net Income Section

The final section of the income statement reports the net income (or net loss) for the period, both before and after federal income taxes. It is customary to list the federal income tax amount separately on the income statement. This is done so that the amount of the operating income is more easily

CHAPTER 17   Preparing Financial Statements for a Corporation   **371**

Champion Building Products, Inc.
Income Statement
For the Year Ended December 31, 19--

Revenue	Revenue:				
	Sales				377 385 00
	Less: Sales Discounts		3 550 42		
	Sales Ret. & Allow.		1 061 81	4 612 23	
	Net Sales				372 772 77
Cost of Merchandise Sold	Cost of Merchandise Sold:				
	Merch. Inv., Jan. 1, 19--			84 921 10	
	Purchases	209 464 32			
	Plus: Transportation In	4 215 80			
	Cost of Delivered Merch.		213 680 12		
	Less: Purch. Discounts	9 808 54			
	Purch. Ret. & Allow.	4 017 90	13 826 44		
	Net Purchases			199 853 68	
	Cost of Merch. Avail.			284 774 78	
	Merch. Inv., Dec. 31, 19--			81 385 70	
	Cost of Merch. Sold				203 389 08
Gross Profit on Sales	Gross Profit on Sales				169 383 69
	Operating Expenses:				
	Advertising Expense		2 864 50		
	Bank Card Fees Expense		3 292 30		
	Delivery Expense		2 693 96		
	Insurance Expense		250 00		
Operating Expenses	Maintenance Expense		3 321 90		
	Miscellaneous Expense		647 05		
	Rent Expense		15 000 00		
	Salaries Expense		84 000 00		
	Supplies Expense		3 709 90		
	Utilities Expense		3 158 71		
	Total Oper. Expenses				118 938 32
	Operating Income				50 445 37
	Less: Fed. Income Taxes				9 895 00
Net Income	Net Income				40 550 37

Figure 17-3 Champion's Completed Income Statement

$169,383.69
−118,938.32
$ 50,445.37

$50,445.37
− 9,895.00
$40,550.37

seen on the business's income statement. **Operating income** is the taxable income of a corporation, or the amount of income earned before federal income taxes.

Look at Figure 17-3 again. To determine the operating income, the total operating expenses are subtracted from the gross profit on sales. As you can see, Champion's operating income for the period is $50,445.37. "Less: Federal Income Taxes" is written on the next line, indented one-half inch. The amount of income taxes, $9,895.00, is taken from the Income Statement Debit column of the work sheet. The amount of federal income taxes is subtracted from the operating income. The difference, $40,550.37, is the net income for the period. This amount must agree with the amount shown on the work sheet. If it does, a double rule is drawn under the amount to show that the income statement is proved and complete.

Before you go any further, do the following activity to see if you understand how the income statement is prepared.

Making Connections

COMMUNICATIONS

Once the accountant has prepared a financial statement, he or she must present it to the client and explain it in terms that the officers, stockholders, and investors of the corporation will understand. Have students practice writing several paragraphs in which they explain the different sections of a financial statement and what that statement says about the company.

Check Your Learning

Answer these questions on a sheet of notebook paper.

1. If the net purchases of a business are $17,347.90 and the beginning inventory is $61,350.50, what is the cost of merchandise available for sale?
2. If the gross profit on sales is $22,913.86 and total expenses are $15,164.19, what is the operating income?
3. What is the cost of merchandise sold if the beginning inventory is $14,947.00, net purchases are $83,611.50, and the ending inventory is $15,669.14?
4. If net sales are $137,412.00 and the cost of merchandise sold is $63,010.27, what is the gross profit on sales?
5. How is the net income calculated?

Compare your answers to those in the answers section. Re-read the preceding part of the chapter to find the correct answers to any questions you may have missed.

The Statement of Retained Earnings

In a corporation, there are two stockholders' equity accounts: Capital Stock and Retained Earnings. The Capital Stock account represents the stockholders' investment in the corporation. The balance of this account changes only when additional shares of stock are issued by the corporation. The Retained Earnings account summarizes the profits accumulated and kept by a corporation less any amounts paid to stockholders as a return on their investment.

In Chapter 8, you learned how to prepare a statement of changes in owner's equity. That statement showed the changes that had occurred in the owner's capital account during the fiscal period. A similar statement — the statement of retained earnings — is prepared for a corporation. A **statement of retained earnings** reports the changes that have taken place in the Retained Earnings account during the period. Changes result from business operations (net income or loss) and the distribution of earnings. A net income increases the balance of the Retained Earnings account. A net loss and any distribution of earnings decrease the balance of the account.

Like the statement of changes in owner's equity, the statement of retained earnings is prepared as a supporting document for the balance sheet. The balance of the Retained Earnings account calculated on this statement is used when preparing the balance sheet. The information needed to prepare this report is found on the work sheet.

The statement of retained earnings for Champion Building Products is shown in Figure 17-4 on page 374.

The first line of this statement shows the balance of the Retained Earnings account at the beginning of the fiscal period. This balance, $27,625.45, is taken from the Balance Sheet Credit column of the work sheet. Champion

ANSWERS

1. $78,698.40
2. $7,749.67
3. $82,889.36
4. $74,401.73
5. Net income is calculated by subtracting the federal income taxes from the operating income.

CONCEPT DEVELOPMENT

The Statement of Retained Earnings

When presenting this section, discuss the function of each of the two equity accounts: Capital Stock and Retained Earnings. The Capital Stock account represents the owners' interest in the business. Since the business example used in this accounting cycle is a closely held corporation, its stock normally is not bought or sold. The balance in the Capital Stock account will not change unless some of the stock is sold or additional money is invested in the stock.

The Retained Earnings account shows the profit earned by the business. In reality, some of the profit would most likely be returned to the stock owners as a return on their investment. Students will learn about distribution of earnings in Chapter 27.

Teaching Tips

■ Distribution of earnings is usually in the form of cash dividends. Students will learn more about dividends in Chapter 27.

Reteaching Strategies

Review the Cost of Goods Sold section of the income statement by writing the following account balances on the chalkboard. Ask students to make the calculations to determine Cost of Goods Sold.

Beginning Inventory, 1/1	$ 65,112
Purchases	114,549
Transportation In	2,546
Purchases Discounts	4,897
Purchases Ret. & Allow.	4,311
Ending Inventory, 12/31	68,335

(Answers: Cost of delivered merchandise, $117,095; net purchases, $107,887; cost of merchandise available for sale, $172,999; cost of merchandise sold, $104,664.)

CONCEPT DEVELOPMENT
The Balance Sheet
When introducing the balance sheet, remind students of the format they learned earlier, in Chapter 8 (page 159). The information for preparing the balance sheet is obtained from the Balance Sheet section of the work sheet *and* from the statement of retained earnings.

Reinforce the need for adjustments on the work sheet by pointing out how the account balances reported on the balance sheet differ from the beginning trial balance amounts. The account balances for Merchandise Inventory, Prepaid Insurance, Supplies, and Federal Income Tax Payable were all changed as a result of adjustments.

Champion Building Products, Inc.
Statement of Retained Earnings
For the Year Ended December 31, 19--

Retained Earnings, January 1, 19--		27 625 45
Net Income		40 550 37
Retained Earnings, December 31, 19--		68 175 82

Figure 17-4 Statement of Retained Earnings

earned a net income of $40,550.37 for the period. This amount is added to the balance of the Retained Earnings account. There are no deductions from Retained Earnings. The new balance of the Retained Earnings account, then, is $68,175.82.

The Balance Sheet

The balance sheet reports the final, updated balances of all asset, liability, and stockholders' equity accounts as of a specific date. It is prepared from the information in the Balance Sheet section of the work sheet and from the statement of retained earnings.

Champion's balance sheet is shown in Figure 17-5. This balance sheet has been prepared in report form. In the report form, as you will recall, the classifications are shown one under the other.

Champion Building Products, Inc.
Balance Sheet
December 31, 19--

Assets		
Cash in Bank	21 284 42	
Accounts Receivable	6 364 35	
Merchandise Inventory	81 385 70	
Supplies	1 839 60	
Prepaid Insurance	1 250 00	
Delivery Equipment	19 143 90	
Store Equipment	26 353 40	
Total Assets		157 621 37
Liabilities		
Accounts Payable	12 316 95	
Federal Income Tax Payable	145 00	
Sales Tax Payable	1 983 60	
Total Liabilities		14 445 55
Stockholders' Equity		
Capital Stock	75 000 00	
Retained Earnings	68 175 82	
Total Stockholders' Equity		143 175 82
Total Liabilities and Stockholders' Equity		157 621 37

Figure 17-5 Champion's Balance Sheet

The assets are listed first. The classification "Assets" is centered on the first line. The account titles and balances are then listed in the same order

---

Making Connections

AROUND THE WORLD

U.S. corporations that want to sell their stock to the public have long been required by the Securities and Exchange Commission to make their financial statements and other information public. Foreign companies wishing to sell stock here also must comply with U.S. accounting standards. Some foreign compa-

nies that have wanted to list their stock on a U.S. stock exchange have failed to do so because of the strict financial disclosure and accounting requirements in this country. Conformance to U.S. accounting standards is required for any corporation wishing to sell its stock on a U.S. stock exchange.

as they appear on the work sheet. The individual balances are entered in the first amount column. The total assets amount is entered in the second amount column. The double rule, however, is not entered until the Liabilities and Stockholders' Equity sections have been completed and are shown to be equal to total assets.

The Liabilities section is begun one blank line below the total assets amount. Again, the account titles and balances are listed as they appear on the work sheet. The individual balances are entered in the first amount column, and the total liabilities amount is entered in the second amount column.

$ 14,445.55
143,175.82
$157,621.37

Next, the Stockholders' Equity section is completed. Stockholders' equity consists of two accounts: Capital Stock and Retained Earnings. The balance of the Capital Stock account is taken from the Balance Sheet section of the work sheet. The balance of the Retained Earnings account is taken from the statement of retained earnings. Again, the individual balances are listed in the first amount column and the total in the second column.

Once these amounts have been entered, the total of the Liabilities section and the total of the Stockholders' Equity section are added. This total must agree with the total assets amount. If it does, the balance sheet is double ruled.

Financial Statements Prepared by Computer

Today most businesses rely on automated equipment or computers to maintain the general and subsidiary ledgers and to prepare the end-of-period financial statements. Computers offer businesses the advantages of speed and accuracy. Even small businesses can now afford the microcomputers specifically designed for the smaller business operation. There is a variety of accounting software available for microcomputers. Some businesses may prefer to have an outside computer company maintain their accounting records and prepare the statements.

If Champion's balance sheet had been prepared on a computer, the printout might look like that in Figure 17-6 on page 376. Other financial statements prepared by computer would look similar to this balance sheet.

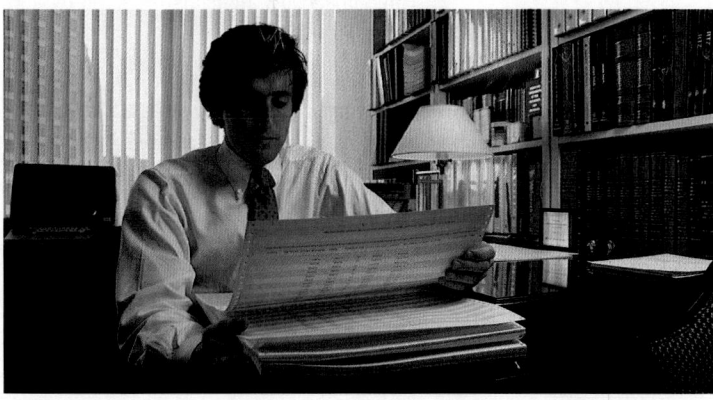

Computer know-how can increase an executive's access to information for decision making, as well as improve the speed with which decisions can be made.

Using Visuals

Figure 17-6 shows a computer-generated balance sheet. Try to collect samples of computer-generated financial statements from local businesses to share with your class.

COMPUTERS IN ACCOUNTING

After financial statements are prepared, owners and managers use the financial information to evaluate the operations of the business and to make decisions about the future of the business. Making decisions about the business usually involves several people throughout the company. Some of the individuals may be located in different cities or states, or even different countries. Instead of traveling to meetings, individuals can communicate with each other through teleconferencing. Teleconferencing enables several individuals in different locations to share written reports, video, audio, and drawings simultaneously.

3 CLOSE

CHAPTER SUMMARY

This summary enumerates the key information in the chapter. It is a useful tool for reinforcement and review.

```
                CHAMPION BUILDING PRODUCTS, INC.
                         BALANCE SHEET
                       DECEMBER 31, 19--
              ASSETS
Cash in Bank                            21284.42
Accounts Receivable                      6364.35
Merchandise Inventory                   81385.70
Supplies                                 1839.60
Prepaid Insurance                        1250.00
Delivery Equipment                      19143.90
Store Equipment                         26353.40
                                        --------
     Total Assets                                   157621.37
                                                    ========

              LIABILITIES
Accounts Payable                        12316.95
Federal Income Tax Payable                145.00
Sales Tax Payable                        1983.60
                                        --------
     Total Liabilities                               14445.55

          STOCKHOLDERS' EQUITY
Capital Stock                           75000.00
Retained Earnings                       68175.82
                                        --------
     Total Stockholders' Equity                     143175.82
                                                    ---------
     Total Liabilities and Stockholders' Equity     157621.37
                                                    ========
```

Figure 17-6 A Computer-Generated Balance Sheet

Summary of Key Points

1. Accounting for corporations differs from other forms of business only in reporting owner's equity on the balance sheet. Capital Stock replaces the individual owner's capital account. The Retained Earnings account is used to record the net income from business operations.
2. Three financial statements prepared by a merchandising corporation are the income statement, the statement of retained earnings, and the balance sheet.
3. The income statement for a merchandising business contains a section showing the cost of merchandise sold.
4. Net sales is the amount of total sales less deductions for sales discounts, returns, and allowances. Net purchases is the total cost of merchandise bought plus transportation charges less deductions for purchases discounts, returns, and allowances.
5. Gross profit on sales is the amount of net sales minus the cost of merchandise sold.
6. The federal income taxes paid by a corporation are listed separately on the income statement.
7. The statement of retained earnings reports the changes in the Retained Earnings account during the period.
8. The net income for the period is added to the balance of the Retained Earnings account.

Pop Quiz

1. The retained earnings account is classified as a(n) _____ account.
2. The net income held by a corporation is called _____.
3. An income statement for a service business reports revenue, expenses, and net income. What two additional types of information are reported for a merchandising business?
4. True or false: Federal income tax is considered an operating expense for a corporation.
5. The amount of income earned before federal taxes have been paid is called _____.

ANSWERS

1. stockholders' equity
2. retained earnings
3. cost of goods sold and gross profit on sales
4. false
5. operating income

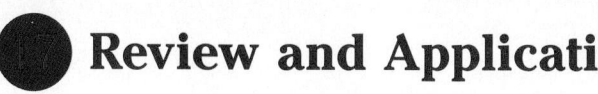

Review and Applications

Building Your Accounting Vocabulary

In your own words, write the definition of each of the following accounting terms. Use complete sentences for your definitions.

capital stock
gross profit on sales
net purchases
net sales

operating expenses
operating income
retained earnings

statement of retained
    earnings
stockholders' equity

Reviewing Your Accounting Knowledge

1. How does stockholders' equity differ from owner's equity?
2. What three financial statements are usually prepared by a merchandising corporation?
3. How does an income statement for a merchandising business differ from that for a service business?
4. How is net sales calculated? net purchases?
5. What is the difference between the cost of merchandise available for sale and the cost of merchandise sold?
6. How is the cost of merchandise sold calculated?
7. Why are the income taxes paid by a corporation listed separately on the income statement?
8. What is the difference between operating income and net income?
9. Why is the net income for the period added to Retained Earnings rather than to Capital Stock?
10. When does the balance of the Capital Stock account change?
11. Why is the income statement prepared before the statement of retained earnings and the statement of retained earnings prepared before the balance sheet?
12. What are the two stockholders' equity accounts included on the balance sheet?

Improving Your Analysis Skills

Joan Corrales is thinking of buying the Midtown Video Center. She has been given Midtown's financial statements for the past twelve months. What should Joan look for in these statements to help her make a decision about buying Midtown Video Center? Name as many items as you can.

Applying Accounting Procedures

Exercise 17-1   Determining the Cost of Merchandise Sold
The account balances at the top of page 378 were taken from the Income Statement section of the work sheet.

377

Building Your Accounting Vocabulary
See the Glossary on pages 670-679 for definitions of these terms.

Reviewing Your Accounting Knowledge

1. Owner's equity represents the owner of a sole proprietorship, as evidenced by the owner's Capital account; stockholder's equity represents the ownership of a corporation, as evidenced by the Capital Stock account (the stockholders' investments) and Retained Earnings (the income retained by the corporation).
2. Income statement, statement of retained earnings, balance sheet.
3. An income statement for a merchandising business includes the cost of the merchandise sold to customers. The income statement for a service business does not include cost of merchandise sold, nor does it calculate gross profit on sales.
4. Net sales is calculated by deducting sales returns, allowances, and discounts from total sales. Net purchases is calculated by adding transportation charges to the balance of Purchases and then subtracting purchases returns, allowances, and discounts.
5. The cost of merchandise available for sale is the amount of beginning merchandise inventory added to net purchases. When the ending merchandise inventory amount is deducted from this figure, the remainder is the cost of merchandise sold.
6. By subtracting the ending merchandise inventory from the cost of merchandise available for sale.
7. To more easily identify the amount of taxable income on the income statement.
8. Operating income is the amount left after expenses are deducted; net income is the amount left after both expenses and federal taxes are deducted.

9. Because the Retained Earnings account summarizes the profits accumulated and kept by a corporation, less any distributions made to stockholders.
10. Only when additional shares of stock are issued by the corporation.
11. The income statement is prepared first because net income is used to calculate the balance of Retained Earnings, which is reported on the statement of retained earnings. The balance of Retained Earnings calculated on the statement of retained earnings is then reported on the balance sheet.
12. Capital Stock and Retained Earnings.

Improving Your Analysis Skills
Income Statement
1. Have total sales increased, remained the same, or decreased?
2. Have sales returns and allowances increased (a signal of possible customer dissatisfaction)?
3. Has the merchandise inventory increased (a possible indication that certain products are not selling well or the inventory is too high)?
4. Have purchases returns and allowances increased (perhaps indicating unreliable suppliers)?

(Continued on next page)

5. Has gross profit on sales increased, remained the same, or decreased?
6. Have operating expenses increased (if expenses are going up faster than revenues, the company needs to know why)?
7. Has the company earned a net income?

Statement of Retained Earnings
Has the balance of Retained Earnings increased or decreased over the period?

Balance Sheet
1. Has the Cash in Bank balance changed?
2. Have accounts receivable increased (the company could be having trouble collecting its bills)?
3. Have liabilities increased (the more debt a company has, the less money and borrowing power it has for bad times)?

PRACTICE AND APPLY

• Concepts and Procedures

Exercise 17-1: Ch. Obj. 4
NP, $116,235.00
COMS, $111,413.40

Exercise 17-2: Ch. Obj. 4
1. $96,009.20
2. $15,615.69
3. $27,779.16
4. $17,132.25
5. $4,337.86
6. $17,653.39

Refer students to the Chapter 17 review pages in the workbook, *Chapter Reviews and Working Papers*.

| | Income Statement | |
	Debit	Credit
Purchases	$121,390.00	
Transportation In	1,406.00	
Purchases Discounts		$4,920.00
Purchases Returns and Allowances		1,641.00

The beginning merchandise inventory was $36,819.40 and the ending merchandise inventory was $41,641.00.

Instructions:
(1) Determine the amount of net purchases for the period.
(2) Determine the cost of merchandise sold.

Exercise 17-2 Calculating Amounts on the Income Statement

Instructions: For each group of figures that follows, determine the missing amount.

1. Beginning merchandise inventory — $81,269.40
   Net purchases — 14,739.80
   Cost of merchandise available for sale — ?

2. Net sales — $51,674.90
   Cost of merchandise sold — 36,059.21
   Gross profit on sales — ?

3. Purchases — $26,340.95
   Transportation In — 1,438.21
   Cost of delivered merchandise — ?

4. Cost of merchandise available for sale — $49,816.42
   Ending merchandise inventory — 32,684.17
   Cost of merchandise sold — ?

5. Gross profit on sales — $17,029.63
   Operating expenses — 12,691.77
   Operating income — ?

6. Operating income — $24,072.39
   Federal income taxes — 6,419.00
   Net income — ?

SPREADSHEET **Problem 17-1 Preparing an Income Statement**
The work sheet for the Kardos Corporation for the year ended December 31 is shown on the following page.

Instructions: Prepare an income statement. Refer to Figure 17-3 on PROBLEM page 372 if you need help in setting up the income statement.

Problem 17-2 Preparing a Statement of Retained Earnings

Instructions: Use the work sheet and the income statement from Problem 17-1 to prepare a statement of retained earnings for the Kardos Corporation.

378

Additional Reinforcement

Students who need additional practice or individualized help will benefit from the *Glencoe Accounting Electronic Study Guide* or the *Glencoe Accounting* on-line multimedia program, which provide reinforcement and reteaching for vocabulary, concepts, and procedures.

Hardos Corporation
Work Sheet
For the Year Ended December 31, 19--

ACCT. NO.	ACCOUNT NAME	TRIAL BALANCE DEBIT	TRIAL BALANCE CREDIT	ADJUSTMENTS DEBIT	ADJUSTMENTS CREDIT	ADJUSTED TRIAL BALANCE DEBIT	ADJUSTED TRIAL BALANCE CREDIT	INCOME STATEMENT DEBIT	INCOME STATEMENT CREDIT	BALANCE SHEET DEBIT	BALANCE SHEET CREDIT
101	Cash in Bank	1926184				1926184				1926184	
105	Accounts Receivable	780419				780419				780419	
110	Merchandise Inventory	8923624			(a) 510890	8412734				8412734	
115	Supplies	601990			(b) 491640	110350				110350	
120	Prepaid Insurance	235200			(c) 98000	137200				137200	
140	Store Equipment	1968725				1968725				1968725	
150	Computer Equipment	738940				738940				738940	
201	Accounts Payable		1463247				1463247				1463247
205	Fed. Inc. Tax Payable				(d) 62100		62100				62100
210	Sales Tax Payable		138006				138006				138006
301	Capital Stock		7000000				7000000				7000000
305	Retained Earnings		1631552				1631552				1631552
310	Income Summary			(a) 510890		510890		510890			
401	Sales		35487191				35487191		35487191		
405	Sales Discounts	410645				410645		410645			
410	Sales Returns & Allow.	141982				141982		141982			
501	Purchases	19384192				19384192		19384192			
505	Transportation In	479041				479041		479041			
510	Purchases Discounts		890947				890947		890947		
515	Purchases Ret. & Allow.		576291				576291		576291		
601	Advertising Expense	310640				310640		310640			
605	Bank Card Fees Expense	283109				283109		283109			
610	Insurance Expense			(c) 98000		98000		98000			
615	Maintenance Expense	340591				340591		340591			
620	Miscellaneous Expense	78362				78362		78362			
625	Rent Expense	1200000				1200000		1200000			
630	Salaries Expense	7956490				7956490		7956490			
635	Supplies Expense			(b) 491640		491640		491640			
640	Utilities Expense	398000				398000		398000			
645	Fed. Inc. Tax Expense	1029100		(d) 62100		1091200		1091200			
		47187234	47187234	1162630	1162630	47249334	47249334	33174782	36954429	14074552	10294905
	Net Income							3779647			3779647
								36954429	36954429	14074552	14074552

379

Problem 17-1: Ch. Obj. 4

SPREADSHEET PROBLEM — **Problem 17-1 can be completed using *Spreadsheet Applications*, the** spreadsheet software that accompanies *Glencoe Accounting*.

Net sales, $349,345.64
COMS, $189,068.85
Gross profit, $160,276.79
Operating exp., $111,568.32
Operating inc., $48,708.47
Net Income, $37,796.47

Problem 17-2: Ch. Obj. 5
Ending RE balance, $54,111.99

Teacher Notes

Problem 17-3   Preparing a Balance Sheet

Instructions: Use the work sheet from Problem 17-1 and the statement of retained earnings you prepared in Problem 17-2 to prepare a balance sheet for the Kardos Corporation.

Problem 17-4   Preparing Financial Statements

Instructions: The partially completed work sheet for Ocean Bluffs Marine, Inc., is included in the working papers.
(1) Complete the work sheet.
(2) Prepare an income statement.
(3) Prepare a statement of retained earnings.
(4) Prepare a balance sheet.

Problem 17-5   Completing a Work Sheet and Financial Statements

The trial balance for the R & L Corporation has been prepared on a ten-column work sheet that is included in the working papers accompanying this textbook.

Instructions:
(1) Complete the work sheet for the fiscal year ended March 31. Use the following information to make the adjustments.

Ending merchandise inventory	$46,821.00
Ending supplies inventory	1,084.00
Expired insurance	1,250.00
Total federal income taxes for the year	546.00

(2) Prepare an income statement.
(3) Prepare a statement of retained earnings.
(4) Prepare a balance sheet.

CHALLENGE PROBLEM   Problem 17-6   Evaluating the Effect of an Error on the Income Statement

The accounting clerk for Lakeside Camera Shop prepared the income statement that follows for the year ended December 31. The accounting supervisor at Lakeside noticed that the balance of the Transportation In account was omitted from this statement in error. That account has a balance of $519.40.

Instructions: Use the income statement shown on page 381 to answer these questions.
(1) In which section of the income statement should the account Transportation In have been shown?
(2) How is net purchases affected by this omission (understated or overstated)? By what amount?
(3) How does the omission of the Transportation In balance affect gross profit on sales? By what amount?
(4) What is the correct amount for the cost of merchandise sold for the period?
(5) What is the correct amount for net income?

380

Teacher Notes

_____

_____

_____

_____

_____

Lakeside Camera Shop
Income Statement
For the Year Ended December 31, 19--

Revenue:				
Sales			11577645	
Less: Sales Discounts		37461		
Sales Ret. & Allow.		108691	146152	
Net Sales				11431493
Cost of Merchandise Sold:				
Merch. Inv., Jan. 1, 19--			5122926	
Purchases		3362490		
Less: Purch. Discounts	41073			
Purch. Ret. & Allow.	120486	161559		
Net Purchases			3200931	
Cost of Merch. Avail.			8323857	
Merch. Inv., Dec. 31, 19--			4471470	
Cost of Merch. Sold				3852387
Gross Profit on Sales				7579106
Operating Expenses:				
Advertising Expense			92980	
Bank Card Fees Expense			132464	
Miscellaneous Expense			163921	
Rent Expense			620000	
Salaries Expense			2960929	
Supplies Expense			276418	
Total Oper. Expenses				4246712
Operating Income				3332394
Less: Fed. Income Taxes				279000
Net Income				3053394

CHALLENGE PROBLEM

Problem 17-7   Calculating Income Statement Amounts

Instructions: Look at the following balances. Determine the missing amount for each of the question marks. Use the form in your working papers or plain paper.

	Net Sales	Beginning Inventory	Net Purchases	Ending Inventory	Cost of Merchandise Sold	Gross Profit
1.	$246,000	?	$126,400	$ 48,300	$130,900	$115,100
2.	85,000	$20,000	?	10,000	45,000	40,000
3.	?	34,200	58,800	?	66,600	85,400
4.	26,295	36,887	12,199	39,895	?	?
5.	48,683	?	18,321	25,249	?	28,262
6.	?	29,246	?	35,896	58,055	74,907
7.	41,160	38,443	29,526	?	?	28,880
8.	?	40,976	607,379	38,503	?	269,644
9.	289,656	64,813	?	60,042	181,635	?
10.	519,078	?	214,122	156,753	229,872	?

Problem 17-7: Ch. Obj. 4

CHALLENGE PROBLEM   The last problem (or problems) in each chapter is a challenge problem and is identified by this "maze" symbol.

1. $52,800
2. $35,000
3. $152,000; $26,400
4. $9,191; $17,104
5. $27,349; $20,421
6. $132,962; $64,705
7. $55,689; $12,280
8. $879,496; $609,852
9. $176,864; $108,021
10. $172,503; $289,206

4 ASSESS

A chapter test is available for use in assessing students' understanding of concepts in this chapter.

The testmaker software will enable you to develop tailor-made chapter, unit, semester, and final tests.

Alternative Assessment

For alternative assessment strategies, refer to *Tech Prep Strategies in Accounting.*

Use Chapter Test 17 here to assess students' understanding and retention of the concepts and procedures presented in the chapter.

381

Have students read the ethics case given in the textbook and jot down ideas about what they would do in the situation described. Then review the five-step decision model (see page T44). Emphasize that there are no "right" or "wrong" answers to the questions in the decision model.

After students have discussed the first four steps, have them vote on which alternative they feel is best, or, if one alternative has clearly been chosen during the discussion, review students' reasoning for choosing that course of action.

You may want to have students compare their final decision with the one they wrote down after first reading the vignette. Did following the five-step model reinforce their "instinctual" decision or lead them to choose a different course of action? Help students realize that following a decision model when they confront an ethical dilemma can help them to organize their thinking and arrive at a satisfactory solution.

QUESTIONS

1. What are the ethical issues in this situation?
2. What are the alternatives?
3. Who are the affected parties?
4. How do the alternatives affect the parties?
5. What is the decision?

ANSWERS

1. Embezzling money at the request of a boss.
2. Continue to embezzle money to keep a well-paying job, report the boss to the hotel chain's management, report the situation to the police.
3. You, your boss, the hotel chain, the hotel's customers.
4. Answers will vary. For example, if you continue to embezzle money because your boss asks you to do so, you might have extra money and keep your job, but you would also be held liable for breaking the law. The hotel chain will continue to lose money if you do not report the situation. The hotel's customers are affected because they must pay higher costs to compensate for the hotel's higher operating costs.

*I*s the Boss Always Right?

Would you do exactly what your boss told you to do even if it went against your conscience? Many people who believe they would follow their own conscience above their bosses' find that if an actual questionable situation arises, their conscience often loses. Studies have shown that the power an employee attributes to his or her employer can lead an employee to act unethically if the boss requests it. Sometimes the thought of losing a job can cause people to act in ways that they normally would never think of acting.

For instance, suppose you found yourself in the following situation. While working on an accounting degree at your local community college, you found a position as a night auditor in a local hotel which is part of a national chain, but is owned and managed locally. After several months on the job, you have become very familiar with the system and the books. As you reviewed the previous year's books, you noticed discrepancies. Once you checked the books carefully, you realized that over time a large sum of money had been embezzled. Alarmed at what you had discovered, you took the books to the hotel manager. Much to your surprise, he only laughed and told you not to worry about it. He recommended that you continue auditing the books by following the pattern of the previous night auditor.

What is your ethical dilemma? Your boss has, in effect, asked you to continue embezzling money. If you refuse to comply, you will almost certainly lose your job, and it is a well-paying one. If you are fired or even if you quit, who would believe that it happened because you caught your boss embezzling? You could report your boss to the management of the national hotel chain, but would they believe you? Would they do anything about it?

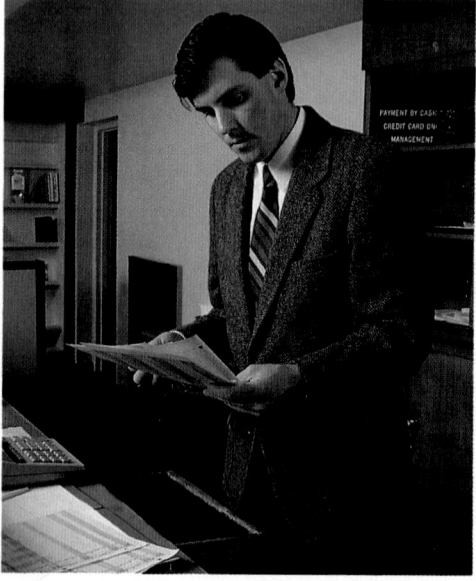

Discovering that someone you work with has done something unethical can place you in a difficult situation.

Could they even be in on the scheme?

Often an ethical situation can arise when you stumble upon the unethical actions of someone else. When this occurs, you have to be prepared to evaluate the situation, take a stand, and follow through. Such a situation can be even more difficult when the person you are up against is your boss. As in all ethical dilemmas, it is helpful to consider all your options before choosing what path you will take. Such a procedure ensures that you will have definite reasons for your actions that you can rely on should the going get tough.

5. Accept any answer, but require students to defend the course of action they choose.

Chapter

RECORDING ADJUSTING AND CLOSING ENTRIES

In Chapter 17, you learned how to prepare three financial statements for a merchandising business organized as a corporation. The income statement and the statement of retained earnings reported the changes that occurred as a result of business operations during the fiscal period. The balance sheet reported the financial position of the business as of the last day of the fiscal period.

In this chapter, you will complete the accounting cycle for a merchandising business. You will learn how to journalize and post the adjusting entries that were calculated on the work sheet in Chapter 16. You will also journalize and post the closing entries for Champion Building Products, Inc. After journalizing and posting the closing entries, you will prepare a post-closing trial balance.

INTRODUCING THE
CHAPTER

LOOKING BACK

In the past several chapters, students have learned how to record transactions for a merchandising business, prepare a work sheet, and prepare financial statements. In this chapter, students will complete the accounting cycle by recording adjusting and closing entries and preparing a post-closing trial balance.

VOCABULARY DEVELOPMENT

Have students read the list of new terms. Ask for ideas for each term's meaning. Write correct responses on the chalkboard. Review the meanings of terms that are not familiar to students. Definitions of these terms are found in the chapter and in the glossary on pages 670-679.

Electronic Field Trips

Learning Objectives

When you have completed Chapter 18, you should be able to do the following:

1. Record adjusting entries in the general journal.
2. Post adjusting entries to the general ledger.
3. Record closing entries for a merchandising corporation.
4. Post closing entries to the general ledger accounts.
5. Prepare a post-closing trial balance.
6. Describe the steps in the accounting cycle.
7. Define the accounting terms introduced in this chapter.

New Terms

adjusting entries
software
hardware

383

Teaching Resources

- Lesson Plans
- TE/Chapter Reviews & Working Papers
- Demonstration Problems
- Student Study Plans
- Teaching Transparencies
- Solutions Transparencies
- Electronic Field Trips Video, Level I
- Electronic Study Guide
- Chapter 18 Test
- Unit 3 Objective Test, Chapters 16-18
- Unit 3 Problem Test, Chapters 16-18

Other Resources

- Skills Improvement Activities
- Blackline Masters
- Careers in Accounting
- Dictionary
- Math Review for Accounting
- Tech Prep Strategies in Accounting
- Video
- Test Bank with Software
- Spanish Resources/Audiotapes
- Spanish Electronic Study Guide

1 FOCUS

MAJOR CONCEPTS

- Updating the General Ledger Accounts
- Journalizing Closing Entries
- Preparing a Post-Closing Trial Balance
- An Accounting Cycle for a Merchandising Business
- A Computerized Accounting System

BUSINESS CONNECTION

Wellfleet Communications is a highly successful business that has been named as the fastest-growing company in the United States. The company produces equipment to tie together local area networks (LANs). The company founder, Paul Severino, is credited with both market savvy and firm control of budgets and operations. Financial statements and other accounting information help provide the data Mr. Severino uses to help keep his company successful and growing.

2 TEACH

CONCEPT DEVELOPMENT
Updating the General Ledger Accounts

Review adjustments to Merchandise Inventory, Supplies, Prepaid Insurance, and Federal Income Tax Expense. Analyze each adjusting entry in T-account form. Review the placement of the adjustments on the work sheet. Remind students why the debit and credit parts are identified by a small letter in parentheses.

Point out that adjustments on the work sheet have not been recorded in any of the accounts affected by the adjustments. Journal entries must be made and then posted to bring the ledger accounts up to date.

Using Visuals

Using Figure 18-1, point out the accounts whose balances are adjusted.

Updating the General Ledger Accounts

In Chapter 16, you learned that some general ledger account balances are not completely up to date at the end of the fiscal period. For example, the balance of Merchandise Inventory reported in the Trial Balance section of the work sheet represents the beginning inventory rather than the ending inventory. The balance of the Supplies account does not reflect the supplies used up during the period. The Prepaid Insurance balance does not show that a part of the premium has expired. In addition, the amount recorded in Federal Income Tax Expense reflects the estimated taxes paid, not the actual amount that must be paid.

All of these accounts must be adjusted so that their balances are current as of the last day of the fiscal period. As you recall, the adjustments are made to bring account balances up to date and to expense the assets that have been consumed during business operations. These adjustments are planned, calculated, and recorded in the Adjustments section of the work sheet. The work sheet adjustments, however, do not update the general ledger accounts. Changes can be made to accounts only through journal entries.

Journalizing Adjustments

The journal entries that update the general ledger accounts at the end of a fiscal period are called **adjusting entries.** The source of the information for the adjusting entries is the Adjustments section of the work sheet. Figure 18-1 indicates that there are four adjustments entered in the Adjustments section of Champion Building Products' work sheet. Each of the adjustments shown on the work sheet affects two general ledger accounts: one

Champion Building Work For the Year Ended

ACCT. NO.	ACCOUNT NAME	TRIAL BALANCE DEBIT	TRIAL BALANCE CREDIT	ADJUSTMENTS DEBIT	ADJUSTMENTS CREDIT
110	Merch. Inventory	8 4 9 2 1 10			(a) 3 5 3 5 40
115	Supplies	5 5 4 9 50			(b) 3 7 0 9 90
120	Prepaid Insurance	1 5 0 0 00			(c) 2 5 0 00
205	Fed. Inc. Tax Payable		—		(d) 1 4 5 00
310	Income Summary		—	(a) 3 5 3 5 40	
615	Insurance Expense	—		(c) 2 5 0 00	
620	Maintenance Expense	3 3 2 1 90			
625	Miscellaneous Expense	6 4 7 05			
630	Rent Expense	1 5 0 0 0 00			
635	Salaries Expense	8 4 0 0 0 00			
640	Supplies Expense	—		(b) 3 7 0 9 90	
645	Utilities Expense	3 1 5 8 71			
650	Fed. Inc. Tax Expense	9 7 5 0 00		(d) 1 4 5 00	
		5 0 8 1 3 7 44	5 0 8 1 3 7 44	7 6 4 0 30	7 6 4 0 30

Figure 18-1 Partial Work Sheet with Adjustments for Champion Building Products

384   UNIT 3   The Accounting Cycle for a Merchandising Business

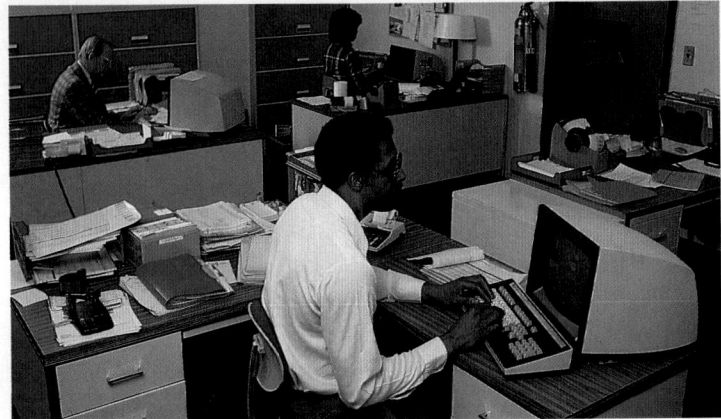

In many businesses, accounting workers are specialized. For example, an accounting clerk may process only accounts payable transactions or transactions affecting only general ledger accounts.

permanent account and one temporary account. Each adjustment also has a debit part and a credit part. The two parts of each adjustment are identified by a small letter in parentheses: (a), (b), (c), and (d). The debit and credit parts of each adjusting entry are found by matching the letters recorded on the work sheet. The accounts debited and credited in the Adjustments section of the work sheet will be recorded as debits and credits in the adjusting entries.

Adjusting entries are recorded in the general journal. Before recording the first adjusting entry, the words "Adjusting Entries" are written in the Description column of the journal. This heading, similar to the one for the closing entries, eliminates the need to write an explanation after each adjusting entry.

The first adjustment listed on the work sheet is labeled (a). In this adjustment, Income Summary is to be debited for $3,535.40 and Merchandise Inventory is to be credited for $3,535.40. The adjusting entry made to record this adjustment in the general journal is shown in Figure 18-2. Notice that the debit part of the entry is recorded first.

	DATE	DESCRIPTION	POST. REF.	DEBIT	CREDIT	
1		Adjusting Entries				1
2	19-- Dec. 31	Income Summary		3 535 40		2
3		Merchandise Inventory			3 535 40	3
4	31	Supplies Expense		3 709 90		4
5		Supplies			3 709 90	5
6	31	Insurance Expense		250 00		6
7		Prepaid Insurance			250 00	7
8	31	Federal Income Tax Expense		145 00		8
9		Federal Income Tax Payable			145 00	9

GENERAL JOURNAL   PAGE 6

Figure 18-2 Recording Adjusting Entries in the General Journal

Making Connections

EVERYDAY LIFE

When individuals prepare a 1040 or 1040A U.S. Individual Tax Form, in essence they are calculating an adjustment for their personal income tax expense. They are looking at the amount of income tax they have already paid to the government, analyzing how much their tax liability is, and determining if they must pay more money or if they are entitled to a refund.

ANSWERS

1. Income Summary; Merchandise Inventory; $2,000
2. Supplies Expense
3. Insurance Expense
4. Consumed
5. $720.00

Did you know?

The stock market goes up or down each day as measured by the Dow-Jones average. Charles Henry Dow and Edward D. Jones founded a company in New York that provided financial news services. Dow Jones & Company used messengers to deliver financial news to the Wall Street brokers. Their financial news sheet eventually became *The Wall Street Journal,* which continues to report financial information. Dow served as the newspaper's first editor, from 1885 to 1891.

The remaining adjustments are handled in the same way. First, the debit and credit parts of the adjustment on the work sheet are matched. Then the adjusting entry is recorded in the general journal. All the adjusting entries are recorded one after another in the journal with no explanations and no blank lines. The date for each adjusting entry is the last day of the fiscal period.

R E M E M B E R

In a general journal, the debit part of an entry is always recorded before the credit part. The credit part of the entry is indented about one-half inch from the left side of the Description column.

Before you read further, do the following activity to see if you understand how to journalize adjusting entries.

 ## Check Your Learning

The adjustments that follow are taken from the Adjustments section of a ten-column work sheet. Use these adjustments to answer the questions that follow.

	Adjustments	
	Debit	Credit
Merchandise Inventory		(a) 2,000.00
Supplies		(b) 400.00
Prepaid Insurance		(c) 300.00
Federal Income Tax Payable		(d) 720.00
Income Summary	(a) 2,000.00	
Insurance Expense	(c) 300.00	
Supplies Expense	(b) 400.00	
Federal Income Tax Expense	(d) 720.00	

1. The first adjusting entry is a debit to ___?___ and a credit to ___?___. The amount of the debit and the credit is ___?___.
2. When Supplies is credited for $400.00, which account is debited for the same amount?
3. The expense account used to record the adjustment for expired insurance premium is ___?___.
4. The $400.00 debit to Supplies Expense represents the supplies ___?___ during the accounting period.
5. How much additional federal income taxes are owed at the end of the accounting period?

Compare your answers to those in the answers section. Re-read the preceding part of the chapter to find the correct answers to any questions you may have missed.

Reteaching Strategies

The work sheet is a tool that helps you plan the necessary adjustments and prepare the financial statements at the end of the accounting period. Entering adjustments on the work sheet, however, does not change the balances of the accounts affected. Journal entries must be made and then posted to the ledger accounts. Adjusting entries are recorded in the general journal in the order that they appear on the work sheet.

Posting Adjusting Entries to the General Ledger

After the adjusting entries have been recorded in the general journal, they must be posted to the general ledger accounts. After the adjusting entries are posted, the balances of the general ledger accounts are the same as those reported on the financial statements—except for Retained Earnings. The balance of that account is not brought up to date until the closing entries are journalized and posted.

The first adjusting entry involves the Merchandise Inventory account and the Income Summary account. The posting of the first adjusting entry is shown in Figure 18-3. Notice that the words "Adjusting Entry" are written in the Explanation column of the two general ledger accounts.

After the first adjusting entry is posted, Merchandise Inventory has a balance of $81,385.70. The debit balance of $3,535.40 in the Income Summary account represents an increase to the cost of merchandise sold for the fiscal period.

Chapter

Using Visuals

Students are already familiar with the posting procedure, but you may want to review the steps with them in Figure 18-3. Point out the words "Adjusting Entry" written in the general ledger account to identify the entry.

Using Visuals

Use demonstration problem 18-2 to give students practice in posting adjusting entries to the general ledger.

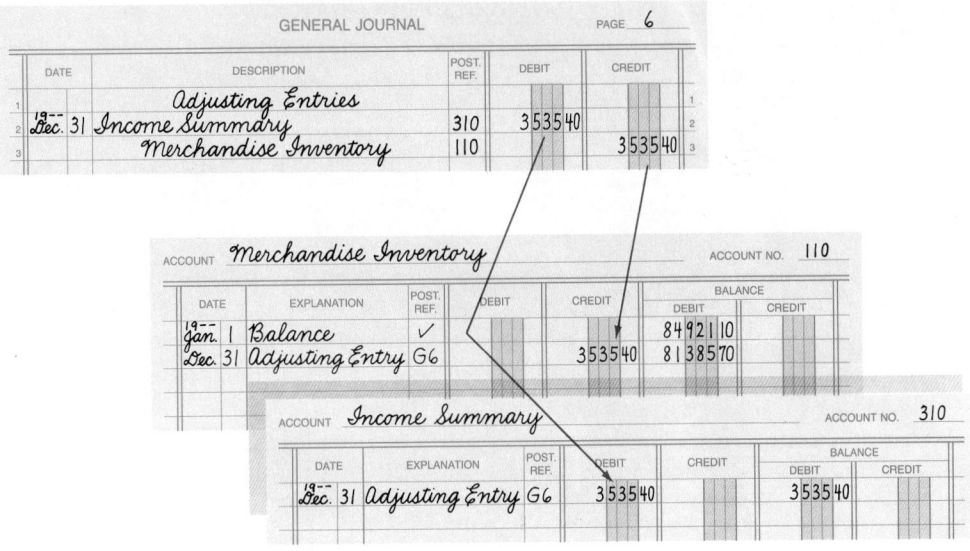

Figure 18-3 Posting the First Adjusting Entry to the General Ledger Accounts

The remaining adjusting entries are posted to the general ledger accounts in the same way. Figure 18-4, on pages 388-389, shows the general journal and the ledger accounts after the posting of the adjusting entries has been completed.

R E M E M B E R

After the adjusting entries in the general journal have been posted to the appropriate accounts in the general ledger, the balances in those accounts will be the same as the balances reported on the income statement and the balance sheet.

Interdisciplinary Connections

SOCIAL STUDIES/GOVERNMENT

Government must tax its citizens for its support. With passage of the 16th Amendment in 1913, the U.S. government imposed a permanent federal tax on income. The IRS, which collects income taxes, is part of the Treasury Department. Since World War II, individual income taxes have been the federal government's largest source of income: 45 percent in 1990. Corporate income taxes provided 11 percent of the federal government's income.

Using Visuals

Use Figure 18-4 to compare each general ledger account balance with the income statement and balance sheet prepared in Chapter 17 (pages 372 and 374). Note that the general ledger account balances agree with the financial statements after the adjusting entries have been posted.

BUSINESS ISSUES

In 1984, at the age of 20, Mike Olson began building snow boards in a one-horse barn in Seattle. Five years later he was $400,000 in debt. He abandoned his company, Gnu, to make a clean start under a new company name, Mervin Manufacturing. By 1993 his new company was producing a big chunk of the market share and was generating 3.5 million dollars a year. Bankruptcy laws help give people like Mike Olson a new start. Ask students to discuss whether they think such people who are later successful should pay back some of the debt they escaped under the bankruptcy laws.

GENERAL JOURNAL — PAGE 6

DATE	DESCRIPTION	POST. REF.	DEBIT	CREDIT
	Adjusting Entries			
Dec. 31	Income Summary	310	353540	
	Merchandise Inventory	110		353540
31	Supplies Expense	640	370990	
	Supplies	115		370990
31	Insurance Expense	615	25000	
	Prepaid Insurance	120		25000
31	Federal Income Tax Expense	650	14500	
	Federal Income Tax Payable	205		14500

ACCOUNT: Merchandise Inventory — ACCOUNT NO. 110

DATE	EXPLANATION	POST. REF.	DEBIT	CREDIT	BALANCE DEBIT	BALANCE CREDIT
Jan. 1	Balance	✓			8492110	
Dec. 31	Adjusting Entry	G6		353540	8138570	

ACCOUNT: Supplies — ACCOUNT NO. 115

DATE	EXPLANATION	POST. REF.	DEBIT	CREDIT	BALANCE DEBIT	BALANCE CREDIT
Dec. 1	Balance	✓			507440	
12		P12	36260		543700	
15		CP14	13750		557450	
16		CR14		2500	554950	
31	Adjusting Entry	G6		370990	183960	

ACCOUNT: Prepaid Insurance — ACCOUNT NO. 120

DATE	EXPLANATION	POST. REF.	DEBIT	CREDIT	BALANCE DEBIT	BALANCE CREDIT
Dec. 1		CP14	150000		150000	
31	Adjusting Entry	G6		25000	125000	

ACCOUNT: Federal Income Tax Payable — ACCOUNT NO. 205

DATE	EXPLANATION	POST. REF.	DEBIT	CREDIT	BALANCE DEBIT	BALANCE CREDIT
Dec. 31	Adjusting Entry	G6		14500		14500

ACCOUNT: Income Summary — ACCOUNT NO. 310

DATE	EXPLANATION	POST. REF.	DEBIT	CREDIT	BALANCE DEBIT	BALANCE CREDIT
Dec. 31	Adjusting Entry	G6	353540		353540	

ACCOUNT: Insurance Expense — ACCOUNT NO. 615

DATE	EXPLANATION	POST. REF.	DEBIT	CREDIT	BALANCE DEBIT	BALANCE CREDIT
Dec. 31	Adjusting Entry	G6	25000		25000	

Figure 18-4 Adjusting Entries Posted to the General Ledger

Making Connections

COMMUNICATIONS

Knowing about computers has become a necessary skill in most offices and businesses. Have students research and analyze some of the accounting software programs now available. They should look at these programs in terms of their being "user-friendly" and suitable for small businesses, large corporations, or individual users. Students should then prepare a business report summarizing their findings and listing their recommendations. This activity could also be used as a cooperative learning experience.

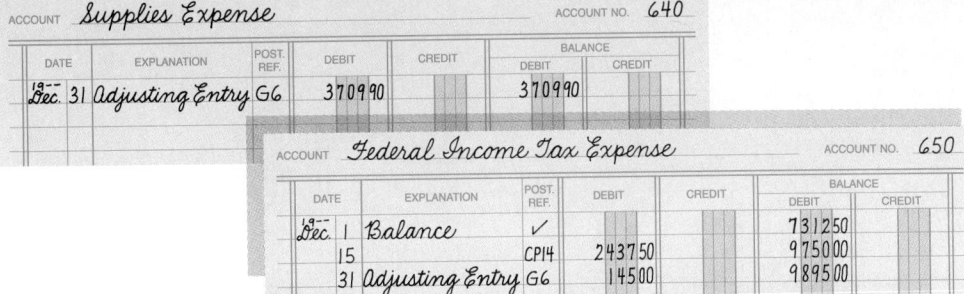

ACCOUNT	Supplies Expense						ACCOUNT NO.	640	
		POST.				BALANCE			
DATE	EXPLANATION	REF.	DEBIT	CREDIT	DEBIT		CREDIT		
Dec. 31	Adjusting Entry	G6	3709 90		3709 90				

ACCOUNT	Federal Income Tax Expense					ACCOUNT NO.	650	
		POST.			BALANCE			
DATE	EXPLANATION	REF.	DEBIT	CREDIT	DEBIT	CREDIT		
Dec. 1	Balance	✓			7312 50			
15		CP14	2437 50		9750 00			
31	Adjusting Entry	G6	145 00		9895 00			

Figure 18-4   Adjusting Entries Posted to the General Ledger (Concluded)

Journalizing Closing Entries

In Chapter 9, you learned how to journalize and post the closing entries for a service business operated as a sole proprietorship. In the chapters in this unit, you have been studying the accounting records for a merchandising business organized as a corporation. Regardless of how a business is organized or whether it sells goods or services, the procedures for journalizing closing entries are the same. In other words, all closing entries transfer the balances of the temporary accounts to a permanent account. After the closing entries have been posted, all of the temporary accounts will have zero balances. The general ledger will then be ready for use during the next accounting period.

All the information needed for the closing entries is found in the Income Statement section of the work sheet. As you recall, the Income Statement columns of the work sheet contain the balances of all the temporary accounts.

Steps for Closing the Ledger

In Chapter 9, you journalized four entries to close the temporary general ledger accounts of a sole proprietorship. Only three closing entries are required to close the temporary accounts for a merchandising business organized as a corporation. A business organized as a corporation does not have a withdrawals account. No closing entry, therefore, is needed for this account, reducing the number of closing entries to three.

The account balances that must be closed for Champion Building Products are shown in Figure 18-5 on page 390. The first closing entry is made to close the accounts that have balances in the Income Statement *Credit* column of the work sheet. These accounts are the revenue and contra cost of merchandise accounts. In this first closing entry, then, the revenue and contra cost of merchandise accounts are closed into Income Summary. The second closing entry is made to close into Income Summary the balances of the cost of merchandise, contra revenue, and expense accounts listed in the Income Statement *Debit* column. The third closing entry is made to close the balance of Income Summary into Retained Earnings. The amount of this third entry is the net income or net loss for the fiscal period.

CHAPTER 18   Recording Adjusting and Closing Entries

389

CONCEPT DEVELOPMENT
Journalizing Closing Entries
Ask students to explain the difference between permanent and temporary accounts. Then use the chalkboard or the overhead to show students the Income Statement section of a work sheet. Remind students that temporary accounts are reported on the income statement and that these accounts are closed at the end of the fiscal period.

Use T accounts to show the balances of all the accounts found in the Income Statement section of the work sheet. Include a T account for Retained Earnings since it is used in place of the capital account (as for a sole proprietorship) to receive the balance of Income Summary.

Teaching Tips

■ Remind students of the purpose of the Income Summary account: to serve as a mini income statement in the general ledger.
■ Point out that the Income Statement section of the work sheet is the source of information for the closing entries.

Using Visuals

A teaching transparency describing the permanent and temporary accounts for a merchandising business is available in the transparency binder accompanying Glencoe Accounting.

Making Connections

AROUND THE WORLD

One way for companies to do business in another country is through a joint venture. One example of a foreign joint venture is Airbus Industrie, a partnership of French, British, and German airplane manufacturing companies. Another ambitious joint venture has been the building of the "Chunnel," the undersea tunnel being built by Eurotunnel, a French-English company formed to build the connector between France and England.

Using Visuals

Have students look at Figure 18-5 and locate the accounts with credit balances in the Income Statement section of the work sheet. Then have them find the accounts with debit balances.

Follow these steps to analyze the closing entries.

1. Ask students to select each account affected by a closing entry.
2. Review how to close the account to bring its balance to zero.
3. Illustrate the closing of each temporary account using T accounts.
4. Discuss why the Income Summary account is used as a clearing account.
5. Use a general journal to show students how to record the closing entries. You may want to record each entry as it is analyzed.

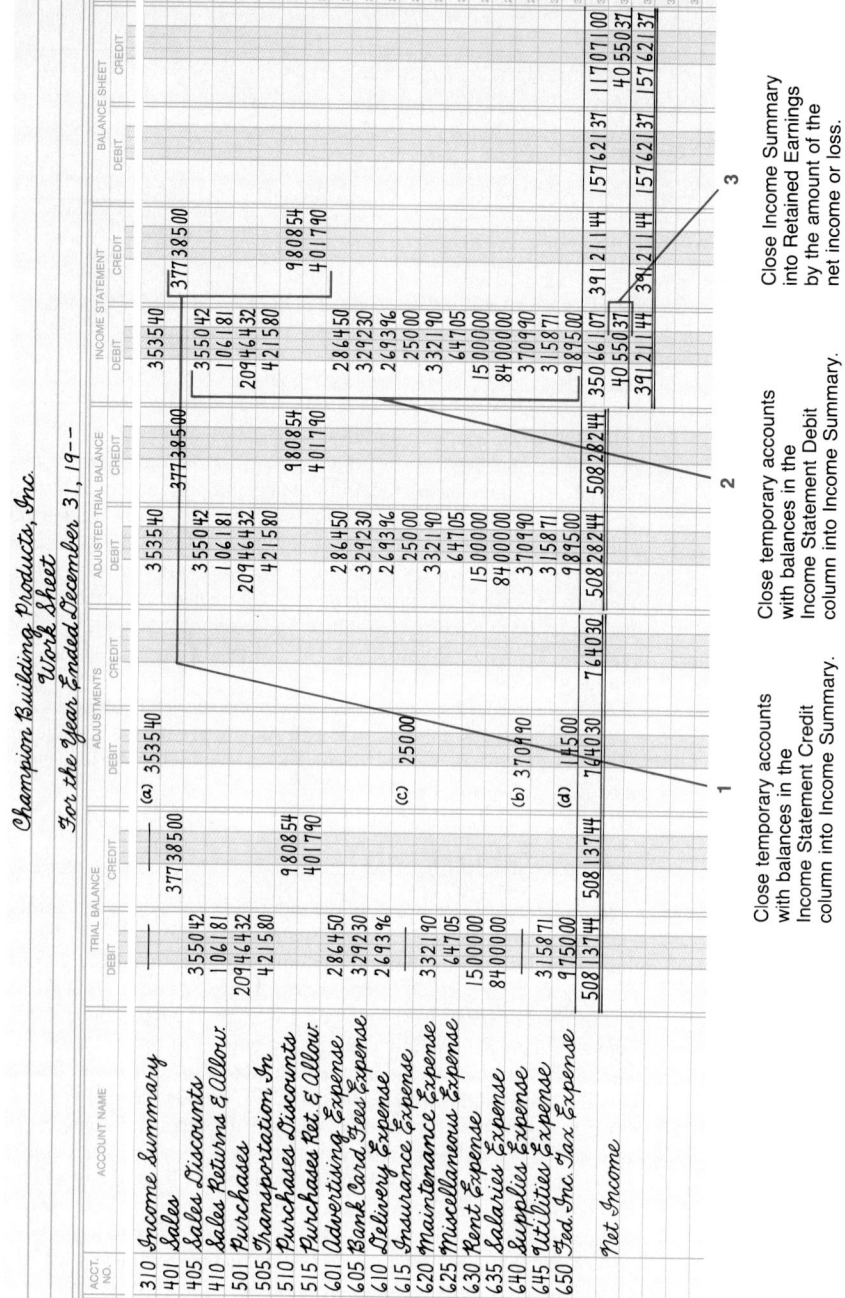

Figure 18-5 Closing Entries Needed for a Corporation

390   UNIT 3   The Accounting Cycle for a Merchandising Business

Let's now look more closely at each of these closing entries.

1. Close the temporary revenue and contra cost of merchandise accounts with credit balances into Income Summary. The first closing entry affects the following accounts: Sales, Purchases Discounts, Purchases Returns and Allowances, and Income Summary. When closing accounts with credit balances, each account is debited for the amount of its balance. Income Summary is credited for the total. To analyze this closing entry, look at the T accounts that follow.

Sales	
Dr.	Cr.
−	+
Clos. $377,385.00	Bal. $377,385.00

Income Summary	
Dr.	Cr.
Adj. $3,535.40	Clos. $391,211.44

Purchases Discounts	
Dr.	Cr.
−	+
Clos. $9,808.54	Bal. $9,808.54

Purchases Returns and Allowances	
Dr.	Cr.
−	+
Clos. $4,017.90	Bal. $4,017.90

After this closing entry is journalized and posted, the three temporary accounts — Sales, Purchases Discounts, and Purchases Returns and Allowances — will have zero balances. Income Summary will have a credit balance of $387,676.04.

R E M E M B E R

The sum of all the *credit* balances of the revenue and contra cost of merchandise accounts is the amount *credited* to **Income Summary**.

2. Close the contra revenue, cost of merchandise, and expense accounts with debit balances into Income Summary. When closing temporary accounts with debit balances, each account is credited for the amount of its balance. Crediting these accounts decreases each account balance to zero. The total of the balances is debited to Income Summary. To analyze this closing entry, look at the T accounts on page 392.

R E M E M B E R

The sum of all the *debit* balances of the contra revenue, cost of merchandise, and expense accounts is the amount *debited* to **Income Summary**.

Using Visuals

Have students look at the T accounts on this page and then offer reasons for why the accounts with debit balances are all added and the total closed to Income Summary rather than each account being closed individually. (To save space and time making separate journal entries)

ACCOUNTING Notes

Entrepreneurs must often try more than once to become successful. The owner of the Laugh-O-Gram Corporation in Kansas City did so poorly that he had to file for bankruptcy after two years. Not discouraged, that owner decided to try again. Walt Disney left Kansas City in 1923 for Hollywood with all his belongings—one set of clothes and some drawings.

Income Summary

Dr.	Cr.
Adj. $ 3,535.40	Clos. $391,211.44
Clos. 347,125.67	

Sales Discounts

Dr.	Cr.
+	−
Bal. $3,550.42	Clos. $3,550.42

Sales Returns and Allowances

Dr.	Cr.
+	−
Bal. $1,061.81	Clos. $1,061.81

Purchases

Dr.	Cr.
+	−
Bal. $209,464.32	Clos. $209,464.32

Transportation In

Dr.	Cr.
+	−
Bal. $4,215.80	Clos. $4,215.80

Advertising Expense

Dr.	Cr.
+	−
Bal. $2,864.50	Clos. $2,864.50

Bank Card Fees Expense

Dr.	Cr.
+	−
Bal. $3,292.30	Clos. $3,292.30

Delivery Expense

Dr.	Cr.
+	−
Bal. $2,693.96	Clos. $2,693.96

Insurance Expense

Dr.	Cr.
+	−
Adj. $250.00	Clos. $250.00

Maintenance Expense

Dr.	Cr.
+	−
Bal. $3,321.90	Clos. $3,321.90

Miscellaneous Expense

Dr.	Cr.
+	−
Bal. $647.05	Clos. $647.05

Rent Expense

Dr.	Cr.
+	−
Bal. $15,000.00	Clos. $15,000.00

Salaries Expense

Dr.	Cr.
+	−
Bal. $84,000.00	Clos. $84,000.00

Supplies Expense

Dr.	Cr.
+	−
Adj. $3,709.90	Clos. $3,709.90

Utilities Expense

Dr.	Cr.
+	−
Bal. $3,158.71	Clos. $3,158.71

Federal Income Tax Expense

Dr.	Cr.
+	−
Bal. $9,895.00	Clos. $9,895.00

After this closing entry has been journalized and posted, these temporary accounts will have zero balances. Income Summary will have a credit balance of $40,550.37.

Critical Thinking

Joan is always looking for shortcuts. She decided she would journalize adjusting and closing entries at the same time? Do you think Joan has a good idea? Explain.

(Answer: No, it is not a good idea. Every adjusting entry affects a temporary account. You do not want to journalize closing entries to close the temporary accounts until the ledger has been updated. Joan will need to journalize and post adjusting entries first. Only after all the necessary accounts—both permanent and temporary—have been updated can Joan journalize the entries to close the temporary accounts.)

3. Close Income Summary into Retained Earnings. After the second closing entry, Income Summary has a credit balance of $40,550.37. This balance represents the net income for the fiscal period. To close Income Summary, it must be debited for $40,550.37. Retained Earnings is credited for $40,550.37. This amount represents the increase in stockholders' equity from net income earned for the fiscal period.

Income Summary			Retained Earnings	
Dr.	Cr.		Dr.	Cr.
			−	+
				Bal. $27,625.45
Adj. $ 3,535.40	Clos. $391,211.44			Clos. 40,550.37
Clos. 347,125.67				
Clos. 40,550.37				

After the entry to close Income Summary into Retained Earnings has been posted, Income Summary will have a zero balance. The balance of Retained Earnings will be increased to $68,175.82.

The closing entries for Champion Building Products are shown in Figure 18-6. Notice that the words "Closing Entries" were written above the first entry to avoid having to write an explanation for each entry.

GENERAL JOURNAL   PAGE 6

	DATE	DESCRIPTION	POST. REF.	DEBIT	CREDIT	
11		Closing Entries				11
12	19-- Dec. 31	Sales		3773850 0		12
13		Purchases Discounts		980854		13
14		Purchases Returns and Allowances		401790		14
15		Income Summary			39121144	15
16	31	Income Summary		34712567		16
17		Sales Discounts			355042	17
18		Sales Returns and Allowances			106181	18
19		Purchases			20946432	19
20		Transportation In			421580	20
21		Advertising Expense			286450	21
22		Bank Card Fees Expense			329230	22
23		Delivery Expense			269396	23
24		Insurance Expense			25000	24
25		Maintenance Expense			332190	25
26		Miscellaneous Expense			64705	26
27		Rent Expense			1500000	27
28		Salaries Expense			8400000	28
29		Supplies Expense			370990	29
30		Utilities Expense			315871	30
31		Federal Income Tax Expense			989500	31
32	31	Income Summary		4055037		32
33		Retained Earnings			4055037	33

Figure 18-6
Closing Entries Recorded in the General Journal

Closing Entry to Transfer a Net Loss

At the end of an accounting period, it is possible for a business to have a net loss. The amount of the net loss would first be calculated on the work

CHAPTER 18   Recording Adjusting and Closing Entries   393 sheet. For example, suppose a business has a net loss of $5,000.00 for the period. To analyze the closing entry for this loss, look at the T accounts.

Income Summary				Retained Earnings	
Dr.	Cr.			Dr.	Cr.
				–	+
Adj. $ 3,612.00	Clos. $63,790.00			Clos. $5,000.00	Bal. $25,480.00
Clos. 65,178.00	Clos. 5,000.00				

To close Income Summary, it must be credited for $5,000.00. Retained Earnings is *debited* for $5,000.00 because the earnings retained by the business have *decreased* by the amount of the net loss. The closing entry made is a debit to Retained Earnings and a credit to Income Summary.

 ## Check Your Learning

Use notebook paper to write your answers to these questions.

1. The source of information for the closing entries is the ___?___ section of the work sheet.
2. To close temporary accounts having debit balances, ___?___ each account for the amount of its ___?___ .
3. The last closing entry is made to close the Income Summary account. For a corporation, the balance of Income Summary is closed into ___?___ .
4. If, before the last closing entry, Income Summary has a debit balance, that debit balance represents a ___?___ for the fiscal period.
5. If the balances of the revenue and contra cost of merchandise accounts in the Income Statement Credit column of the work sheet total $20,460.00, what closing entry is made to record this total?
6. If Income Summary has total debits of $145,700.00 and total credits of $160,200.00, what is its balance and what does it represent?

Compare your answers to those in the answers section. Re-read the preceding part of the chapter to find the answers to any questions you missed.

Posting Closing Entries

After closing entries are recorded in the general journal, they must be posted to the general ledger. For each entry posted, the words "Closing Entry" are written in the Explanation column of the general ledger account. A portion of Champion's general ledger showing the posted closing entries is shown in Figure 18-7 on pages 395-397.

R E M E M B E R

Use a systematic procedure when posting. **Begin with the date of the transaction. Continue posting by moving from the left of the account to the right. Remember to enter the account number in the Posting Reference column of the journal after you have posted a transaction.**

394

Figure 18-7 Partial General Ledger at the End of the Fiscal Period

The ledger accounts shown are:

ACCOUNT Retained Earnings — ACCOUNT NO. 305

DATE	EXPLANATION	POST. REF.	DEBIT	CREDIT	BALANCE DEBIT	BALANCE CREDIT
Dec. 1	Balance	✓				2762545
31	Closing Entry	G6		4055037		6817582

ACCOUNT Income Summary — ACCOUNT NO. 310

DATE	EXPLANATION	POST. REF.	DEBIT	CREDIT	BALANCE DEBIT	BALANCE CREDIT
Dec. 31	Adjusting Entry	G6	353540		353540	
31	Closing Entry	G6		3912144		38767604
31	Closing Entry	G6	34712567			4055037
31	Closing Entry	G6	4055037			

ACCOUNT Sales — ACCOUNT NO. 401

DATE	EXPLANATION	POST. REF.	DEBIT	CREDIT	BALANCE DEBIT	BALANCE CREDIT
Dec. 1	Balance	✓				35480000
31		S12		1278500		36758500
31		CR14		980000		37738500
31	Closing Entry	G6	37738500			—

ACCOUNT Sales Discounts — ACCOUNT NO. 405

DATE	EXPLANATION	POST. REF.	DEBIT	CREDIT	BALANCE DEBIT	BALANCE CREDIT
Dec. 1	Balance	✓			336611	
31		CR14	18431		355042	
31	Closing Entry	G6		355042		

ACCOUNT Sales Returns and Allowances — ACCOUNT NO. 410

DATE	EXPLANATION	POST. REF.	DEBIT	CREDIT	BALANCE DEBIT	BALANCE CREDIT
Dec. 1	Balance	✓			83181	
27		G5	23000		106181	
31	Closing Entry	G6		106181	—	

ACCOUNT Purchases — ACCOUNT NO. 501

DATE	EXPLANATION	POST. REF.	DEBIT	CREDIT	BALANCE DEBIT	BALANCE CREDIT
Dec. 1	Balance	✓			18590080	
8		CP14	111500		18701580	
31		P12	2244852		20946432	
31	Closing Entry	G6		20946432	—	

Using Visuals

Have students look at the ledger accounts in Figure 18-7 (pages 395, 396, 397). Why is it not necessary to write identifying remarks in the Explanation section of the accounts for entries other than adjusting or closing entries? (The posting reference column indicates the journal page on which the entry can be found and the source document will be identified in that entry. The terms "Adjusting Entry" and "Closing Entry" identify the work sheet as the source document for these entries.)

Transportation In — ACCOUNT NO. 505

DATE	EXPLANATION	POST. REF.	DEBIT	CREDIT	BALANCE DEBIT	BALANCE CREDIT
Dec. 1	Balance	✓			366143	
26		CP14	55437		421580	
31	Closing Entry	G6		421580	—	

Purchases Discounts — ACCOUNT NO. 510

DATE	EXPLANATION	POST. REF.	DEBIT	CREDIT	BALANCE DEBIT	BALANCE CREDIT
Dec. 1	Balance	✓				951423
31		CP14		29431		980854
31	Closing Entry	G6	980854			—

Purchases Returns and Allowances — ACCOUNT NO. 515

DATE	EXPLANATION	POST. REF.	DEBIT	CREDIT	BALANCE DEBIT	BALANCE CREDIT
Dec. 1	Balance	✓				371790
28		G5		30000		401790
31	Closing Entry	G6	401790			—

Advertising Expense — ACCOUNT NO. 601

DATE	EXPLANATION	POST. REF.	DEBIT	CREDIT	BALANCE DEBIT	BALANCE CREDIT
Dec. 1	Balance	✓			286450	
31	Closing Entry	G6		286450	—	

Bank Card Fees Expense — ACCOUNT NO. 605

DATE	EXPLANATION	POST. REF.	DEBIT	CREDIT	BALANCE DEBIT	BALANCE CREDIT
Dec. 1	Balance	✓			320465	
31		CP14	8765		329230	
31	Closing Entry	G6		329230	—	

Delivery Expense — ACCOUNT NO. 610

DATE	EXPLANATION	POST. REF.	DEBIT	CREDIT	BALANCE DEBIT	BALANCE CREDIT
Dec. 1	Balance	✓			269396	
31	Closing Entry	G6		269396		

Insurance Expense — ACCOUNT NO. 615

DATE	EXPLANATION	POST. REF.	DEBIT	CREDIT	BALANCE DEBIT	BALANCE CREDIT
Dec. 31	Adjusting Entry	G6	25000		25000	
31	Closing Entry	G6		25000	—	

Figure 18-7 Partial General Ledger at the End of the Fiscal Period (Continued)

Figure 18-7 Partial General Ledger at the End of the Fiscal Period (Concluded)

CHAPTER 18   Recording Adjusting and Closing Entries

397

Chapter 18

Using Visuals

As the photo caption indicates, many computerized accounting programs close the temporary account balances with no journal entries required. Ask students how such a feature would save time and prevent errors?

CONCEPT DEVELOPMENT
Preparing a Post-Closing Trial Balance

Students have already learned how to prepare a post-closing trial balance (in Chapter 9). Remind students that the post-closing trial balance is prepared as a check on the accuracy of the ledger account balances. If total debits do not equal total credits, the reason must be found and corrected before the accounting records are ready for use during the next fiscal period.

Teaching Tips

- The word "post" means after, and the post-closing trial balance is sometimes called the after-closing trial balance.

Using Visuals

Have students look at the accounts on the post-closing trial balance in Figure 18-8. Ask them to explain why no temporary accounts appear on this form.

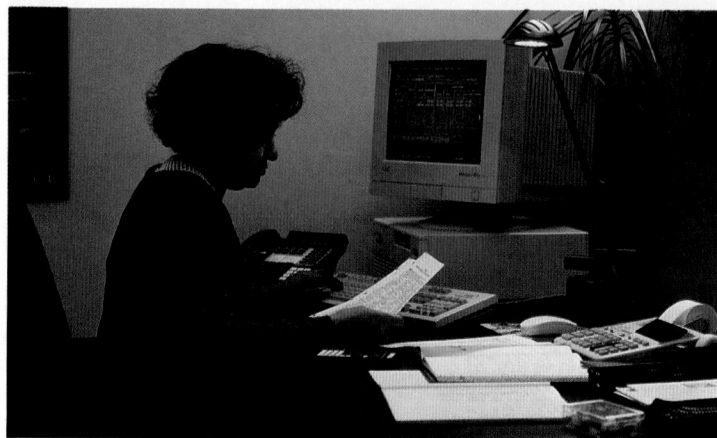

Some accounting software programs automatically calculate the closing entries and update the Retained Earnings account.

After all closing journal entries have been posted, all temporary accounts should have zero balances. As a check that the permanent general ledger accounts are in balance after posting, the final step in the closing process is to prepare a post-closing trial balance.

Preparing a Post-Closing Trial Balance

A post-closing trial balance is prepared at the end of the fiscal period to test the equality of the general ledger after all adjusting and closing entries have been posted. This trial balance proves that the permanent general ledger accounts are in balance at the close of the accounting period.

The post-closing trial balance for Champion Building Products is shown in Figure 18-8.

Champion Building Products, Inc. Post-Closing Trial Balance December 31, 19--		
Cash in Bank	2 128 42	
Accounts Receivable	6 364 35	
Merchandise Inventory	81 385 70	
Supplies	1 839 60	
Prepaid Insurance	1 250 00	
Delivery Equipment	19 143 90	
Store Equipment	26 353 40	
Accounts Payable		12 316 95
Federal Income Tax Payable		145 00
Sales Tax Payable		1 983 60
Capital Stock		75 000 00
Retained Earnings		68 175 82
Totals	157 621 37	157 621 37

Figure 18-8   Post-Closing Trial Balance

398   UNIT 3   The Accounting Cycle for a Merchandising Business

The account balances that appear on the post-closing trial balance are the same as those on the balance sheet.

Before continuing, complete the following activity to check your understanding of the material you have just studied.

Check Your Learning

Use Figures 18-7 and 18-8 to answer the following questions. Write your answers on a sheet of notebook paper.

1. What was the balance of the Retained Earnings account before closing?
2. What is the balance of the Retained Earnings account after closing?
3. Does the $40,550.37 credit to Retained Earnings represent a net income or a net loss?
4. How many transactions affected Income Summary on December 31?
5. Name three expense accounts affected by both an adjusting entry and a closing entry.
6. The accounts that appear on the post-closing trial balance are the same as those on what financial statement?

Compare your answers to those in the answers section. Re-read the preceding part of the chapter to find the answers to any questions you may have missed.

An Accounting Cycle for a Merchandising Business

You have just completed the study of an accounting cycle for a merchandising business organized as a corporation. The accounting cycle for a merchandising business follows the same steps as for a service business. Sole proprietorships, corporations, and partnerships will all have similar accounting cycles. The basic steps in the accounting cycle, listed below, are the same regardless of the type of ownership.

1. Collect and verify data from business transactions.
2. Analyze business transactions.
3. Journalize.
4. Post to the general ledger and to the accounts receivable and accounts payable subsidiary ledgers.
5. Prepare a trial balance.
6. Complete the work sheet.
7. Prepare the financial statements—income statement, statement of retained earnings, and balance sheet.
8. Journalize and post the adjusting entries.
9. Journalize and post the closing entries.
10. Prepare a post-closing trial balance.

CHAPTER 18   Recording Adjusting and Closing Entries   **399**

 ANSWERS
1. $27,625.45
2. $68,175.82
3. Net income
4. 4
5. Insurance Expense, Supplies Expense, and Federal Income Tax Expense
6. Balance sheet

CONCEPT DEVELOPMENT
An Accounting cycle for a Merchandising Business
As a review of the accounting cycle, trace one business transaction from the first step in the cycle to the last. For each step, ask students to name the types of accounting stationery used and what is recorded on it.

Teaching Tips
■ Explain that the accounting cycle for a merchandising business has 10 steps because adjustments have been added to the cycle that was first introduced in Chapter 5 (page 84).

ACCOUNTING PRACTICE
Students may complete Exercise 18-2 at this point.

Reteaching Strategies

After closing entries are posted for a corporation, the totals for the columns on the post-closing trial balance should equal the totals in the Balance Sheet section on the work sheet. Only the permanent accounts appear on the balance sheet and on the post-closing trial balance. Have students discuss in class the types of errors that may occur on a trial balance and what causes those errors.

CONCEPT DEVELOPMENT

A Computerized Accounting System

Computerized accounting systems vary from business to business. Large businesses usually have a system designed solely to fit their needs. Ask an accountant from a local business, or a local CPA, to speak to your class about how the computer is used in accounting in her or his company.

Teaching Tips

■ Errors occur in computerized accounting systems and must be corrected as they are found. Since computers copy original data files for posting and preparing financial statements, and thus would not make transposition or slide errors when copying, ask students to suggest the most likely errors that would occur in a computerized accounting system. (Input errors, either in amounts or in account numbers)

COMPUTERS IN ACCOUNTING

Electronic meeting rooms empower CPA firms and their clients to communicate more effectively and increase productivity. When complex projects require brainstorming, for example, several people can interact on a network of PCs in an open forum. Individuals submit ideas, pass them on through the system, receive ideas from others, add to those ideas, pass them on, and so forth. The ideas can be consolidated and ranked electronically, increasing the productivity level of the group tremendously. The group decision room technology is also valuable for strategic planning.

The steps in the accounting cycle are not affected by the type of accounting system used: manual or computerized. In a computerized accounting system, therefore, many of the routine procedures—such as posting—are performed by the computer. Let's look at the steps in the accounting cycle and see how those steps might be performed in a computerized accounting system.

A Computerized Accounting System

There are many different computerized accounting systems available to businesses today. Some businesses may need only a microcomputer, while others may need several large computers to store their accounting information. Whether large or small, all computers operate from computer programs that direct the operations of the computer. These computer programs are called **software.** The computers themselves and their related equipment, such as disk drives and printers, are called **hardware.**

A comparison of the steps in the accounting cycle for manual and computerized accounting systems appears in Figure 18-9.

Look again at the steps in the accounting cycle. The first two steps—collecting, verifying, and analyzing business transactions data—must be performed by an accounting clerk. Likewise, journal entries are made by an accounting clerk. In a computerized accounting system, the accounting clerk makes journal entries by inputting transaction data to the computer rather than writing it in a journal. Even in a computerized accounting system, the accounting clerk must still analyze transactions to determine the data to be entered into the computer.

The transaction data entered into the computer are maintained in a permanent file in the computer's memory. All the accounts used by a business are also stored in computer memory by account number. In a computerized accounting system, therefore, both the general ledger accounts and the subsidiary ledger accounts have account numbers.

When journal entries are made, the accounting clerk must identify for the computer the account numbers of the accounts involved. There is no need to enter account titles since that information is already stored in computer memory. After an account number is identified, the specific data for a transaction—the date, the amount debited or credited, and the source document reference—are entered into the computer.

When data for business transactions have been input, the accounting clerk instructs the computer to post those transactions to the ledger accounts stored in its memory. Computerized posting not only takes much less time than manual posting, but it also eliminates the errors that may be made in posting manually.

After the journal entries have been posted, the computer may be instructed to prepare a trial balance. The computer searches its ledger account files and prepares that trial balance using the current balance in each account. As in a manual accounting system, if transactions have not been posted or if errors have been made in entering information, the trial balance will not balance. Any errors must be found and corrected before continuing the work in the accounting cycle.

After the trial balance is proved, the information needed to prepare financial reports and to make adjusting and closing entries must be calculated. In some computerized systems, the trial balance is printed out on extra-wide paper and the work sheet is then completed manually on that paper. In other systems, adjustments are calculated manually and then entered into the computer. The computer calculates the new, end-of-period account balances and uses those account balances to prepare the financial statements. Notice that in a computerized accounting system, the adjusting entries are journalized and posted *before* the financial statements are prepared.

Steps	Manual	Computerized
1. Collect and verify data from business transactions	Same	Same
2. Analyze transactions	Same	Same
3. Journalize	Transaction data entered into journals	Transaction data input into computer
4. Post to general and subsidiary ledgers	Posted manually by accounting clerk	Posted by computer upon demand to ledger accounts stored in memory
5. Prepare trial balance	Account balances collected manually and trial balance prepared manually	Stored data used by computer to prepare trial balance upon demand
6. Complete the work sheet	Adjustments calculated manually; work sheet completed manually	Adjustments calculated manually, then entered into computer; work sheet not needed since computer stores data in its files for preparing financial statements
7. Prepare financial statements	Statements prepared manually in typed or handwritten form	Statements prepared by computer upon demand
8. Journalize and post adjusting entries	Entered into journal and posted after financial statements are prepared	Data entered and stored during adjustment of trial balance
9. Journalize and post closing entries	Entered into journal and posted to general ledger	Either entered into computer or program will close general ledger upon demand
10. Prepare post-closing trial balance	Prepared manually after general ledger is closed	Prepared by computer upon demand

Figure 18-9 Comparing Manual and Computerized Accounting Systems

CHAPTER 18 Recording Adjusting and Closing Entries   **401**

3 CLOSE

CHAPTER SUMMARY

This summary enumerates the key information in the chapter. It is a useful tool for reinforcement and review.

In some accounting systems, information for closing entries must be entered into the computer, which will then post the closing entries and prepare a post-closing trial balance. In other systems, the computer is programmed to calculate, at the operator's command, the closing entries needed and to close the temporary accounts automatically.

Summary of Key Points

1. Adjusting entries are prepared at the end of the accounting period to bring the general ledger accounts up to date.
2. The Adjustments section of the work sheet provides the information for journalizing adjusting entries.
3. After adjusting entries are recorded in the general journal, they are posted to the general ledger accounts.
4. Closing entries are made to transfer the balances of the temporary accounts into a permanent account. Three closing entries are required for a corporation.
5. The information for journalizing closing entries is taken from the Income Statement section of the work sheet.
6. After closing entries are posted, the general ledger accounts are then ready for use in the next accounting period.
7. After closing entries have been posted to the general ledger accounts, a post-closing trial balance is prepared. The account balances that appear on the post-closing trial balance are the same as those on the balance sheet.
8. The basic steps in the accounting cycle are the same for all businesses, regardless of how they are organized or whether they use a manual or a computerized accounting system.

Teacher Notes

_____

_____

_____

_____

_____

Review and Applications

Building Your Accounting Vocabulary

In your own words, write the definition of each of the following accounting terms. Use complete sentences for your definitions.

adjusting entries hardware software

Reviewing Your Accounting Knowledge

1. What is the purpose of adjusting entries?
2. Where would you find the information for journalizing the adjusting entries?
3. What is the purpose of closing entries?
4. Where can you find the information needed for journalizing the closing entries?
5. What are the three closing entries for a business organized as a corporation?
6. Why is Retained Earnings credited when the business earns a net income?
7. Why is Retained Earnings debited when the business has a net loss for an accounting period?
8. What type of general ledger accounts appear on the post-closing trial balance? On what financial statement will you find these same accounts?
9. Name the ten steps in the accounting cycle.
10. In what ways does a computerized accounting system differ from a manual accounting system?

Improving Your Math Skills

Accountants and other people who work with numbers often estimate answers before they find the actual answer. Grocery shoppers sometimes keep a running estimate in their heads of their purchases to avoid exceeding a pre-set dollar amount. Estimating an amount helps you know whether you've made a math error and need to double-check your answer. The easiest way to estimate is to round all numbers to whole numbers, either to the nearest ten or the nearest hundred. For example, to add 678, 792, 312, and 419 quickly, round to 700, 800, 300, and 400; then add to get 2,200. The actual answer is 2,201. Practice your estimating skills on the following problems. Then find the actual answers.

1. Add 315, 680, 234, 256, and 761.
2. Subtract 420, 336, and 790 from 2,140.
3. Divide 2,176 by 312.
4. Add 16, 78, 61, 92, 45, and 37.
5. Add 112, 90, 360, 47, and 163; then divide by 67.

403

Building Your Accounting Vocabulary
See the Glossary on pages 670-679 for definitions of these terms.

Reviewing Your Accounting Knowledge

1. To bring account balances in the general ledger up to date, ensuring that the expenses of the period are properly recorded.
2. The Adjustments section of the work sheet.
3. To transfer balances of temporary accounts to a permanent account.
4. The Income Statement section of the work sheet.
5. (a) Close the balances of the revenue and contra cost of merchandise accounts into Income Summary. (b) Close the balances of the contra revenue, cost of merchandise, and expense accounts into Income Summary. (c) Close the balance of Income Summary into Retained Earnings.
6. Because the net income amount represents an increase in stockholders' equity for the fiscal period.
7. Because the earnings retained by the business have decreased by the amount of the net loss.
8. Permanent general ledger accounts, which are reported on the balance sheet.
9. (a) Collect and verify data from business transactions. (b) Analyze business transactions. (c) Journalize business transactions. (d) Post journal entries to the general ledger and to the accounts receivable and accounts payable ledgers. (e) Prepare a trial balance. (f) Complete the work sheet. (g) Prepare financial statements. (h) Journalize and post the adjusting entries. (i) Journalize and post the closing entries. (j) Prepare a post-closing trial balance.

10. In a computerized accounting system, transaction data is input into a computer rather than written in a journal. This data is maintained in a permanent file in the computer's memory, along with all the accounts used by the business. Once the initial transaction data has been input, the computer performs all other steps in the accounting cycle upon instruction by the operator.

Improving Your Math Skills
1. Estimate, 2,250; actual, 2,246
2. Estimate, 600; actual, 594
3. Estimate, 7; actual, 7 (rounded to whole number)
4. Estimate, 330; actual, 329
5. Estimate, 12 (850 ÷ 70); actual, 12 (rounded to whole number)

PRACTICE AND APPLY

• Concepts and Procedures

Exercise 18-1: Ch. Obj. 1, 3

Exercise 18-2: Ch. Obj. 6

Problem 18-1: Ch. Obj. 1

Applying Accounting Procedures

Exercise 18-1 Identifying Accounts Affected by Adjusting and Closing Entries

The following account titles appear in the chart of accounts of Larkin's Department Store.

Accounts Payable	Prepaid Insurance
Accounts Receivable	Purchases
Bank Card Fees Expense	Purchases Discounts
Capital Stock	Purchases Returns & Allowances
Cash in Bank	Retained Earnings
Equipment	Sales
Federal Income Tax Expense	Sales Returns & Allowances
Federal Income Tax Payable	Sales Tax Payable
Income Summary	Supplies
Insurance Expense	Supplies Expense
Merchandise Inventory	Transportation In
Miscellaneous Expense	Utilities Expense

Instructions: Use a form similar to the one that follows to answer these questions about each account.

(1) Is the account affected by an adjusting entry?
(2) Is the account affected by a closing entry?
(3) Does the account appear on the post-closing trial balance?

Account Title	Is the account affected by an adjusting entry?	Is the account affected by a closing entry?	Does the account appear on the post-closing trial balance?
Accounts Payable	No	No	Yes

Exercise 18-2 Organizing the Steps in the Accounting Cycle

Instructions: Place the following steps of the accounting cycle in their proper order.

Analyzing transactions
Collecting/verifying transaction data
Completing the work sheet
Journalizing
Journalizing/posting adjusting entries
Journalizing/posting closing entries
Posting
Preparing financial statements
Preparing a post-closing trial balance
Preparing a trial balance

Problem 18-1 Journalizing Adjusting Entries

The following adjustments, shown at the top of page 405, appeared on the work sheet of Bayside Shoes.

Instructions: Record the adjusting entries for the year ended September 30. Use general journal page 4.

404

Refer students to the Chapter 18 review pages in the workbook, *Chapter Reviews and Working Papers.*

Additional Reinforcement

Students who need additional practice or individualized help will benefit from the *Glencoe Accounting Electronic Study Guide* or the *Glencoe Accounting* on-line multimedia program, which provide reinforcement and reteaching for vocabulary, concepts, and procedures.

ACCT. NO.	ACCOUNT NAME	TRIAL BALANCE DEBIT	TRIAL BALANCE CREDIT	ADJUSTMENTS DEBIT	ADJUSTMENTS CREDIT
3	110 Merchandise Inventory	14035 00		(a) 9000 00	
4	115 Supplies	607 50			(b) 300 00
5	120 Prepaid Insurance	3600 00			(c) 1200 00
8	205 Federal Income Tax Pay.		—		(d) 500 00
12	310 Income Summary				(a) 9000 00
22	615 Insurance Expense	—		(c) 1200 00	
27	640 Supplies Expense	—		(b) 300 00	
28	645 Utilities Expense	3160 00			
29	650 Federal Income Tax Exp.	2350 00		(d) 500 00	

SPREADSHEET PROBLEM — Problem 18-2 can be completed using *Spreadsheet Applications*, the spreadsheet software that accompanies *Glencoe Accounting*.

Problem 18-3: Ch. Obj. 1, 2

SPREADSHEET PROBLEM

Problem 18-2 Journalizing Closing Entries

The following amounts appeared in the Income Statement section of the work sheet of Broadway Rugs. Inc.

Instructions: Record the necessary closing entries for the year ended June 30. Use general journal page 13.

ACCT. NO.	ACCOUNT NAME	INCOME STATEMENT DEBIT	INCOME STATEMENT CREDIT
13	310 Income Summary		7000 00
14	401 Sales		90000 00
15	405 Sales Discounts	1000 00	
16	410 Sales Ret. & Allow.	2400 00	
17	501 Purchases	25000 00	
18	505 Transportation In	3000 00	
19	510 Purchases Discounts		500 00
20	515 Purchases Ret. & Allow.		1500 00
21	610 Insurance Expense	300 00	
22	620 Miscellaneous Expense	6000 00	
23	630 Rent Expense	12000 00	
24	640 Supplies Expense	450 00	
25	650 Utilities Expense	14000 00	
26	660 Federal Income Tax Exp.	5532 00	
27		69682 00	99000 00
28	Net Income	29318 00	
29		99000 00	99000 00

Problem 18-3 Journalizing and Posting Adjusting Entries

The following adjustments are from the Adjustments section of the work sheet of The Fabric Barn.

405

Problem 18-4: Ch. Obj. 3, 4
Retained Earnings, $53,280

Problem 18-5: Ch. Obj. 1, 2, 3, 4, 5

COMPUTER

PROBLEM

This computer image identifies a problem that students may complete using the *Glencoe Accounting, General Ledger* software.

TB totals, $261,826.57

Instructions:

(1) Using the adjustment information, journalize the adjusting entries on page 17 of a general journal. Use September 30 as the date for the adjusting entries.

(2) Post the adjusting entries to the general ledger accounts, which are included in the working papers accompanying this textbook.

	Adjustments		
	Debit	Credit	
Merchandise Inventory		(a)	9,000.00
Prepaid Insurance		(b)	120.00
Supplies		(c)	1,480.00
Federal Income Tax Payable		(d)	962.00
Income Summary	(a) 9,000.00		
Insurance Expense	(b) 120.00		
Supplies Expense	(c) 1,480.00		
Federal Income Tax Expense	(d) 962.00		
	11,562.00	11,562.00	

Problem 18-4   Journalizing and Posting Closing Entries

The following account balances appeared in the Income Statement section of the work sheet of the Sandwich Glass Shoppe.

Instructions:

(1) Journalize the closing entries for the year ended June 30. Use page 14 of a general journal.

(2) Post the closing entries to the general ledger accounts, which are included in your working papers.

	Income Statement	
	Debit	Credit
Income Summary	4,000.00	
Sales		150,000.00
Sales Returns and Allowances	5,000.00	
Purchases	90,000.00	
Transportation In	5,000.00	
Purchases Discounts		1,000.00
Purchases Returns and Allowances		1,500.00
Miscellaneous Expense	300.00	
Rent Expense	6,000.00	
Supplies Expense	1,630.00	
Utilities Expense	3,000.00	
Federal Income Tax Expense	4,700.00	
	119,630.00	152,500.00
Net Income	32,870.00	
	152,500.00	152,500.00

COMPUTER

PROBLEM

Problem 18-5   Completing End-of-Period Activities

The general ledger accounts for Better Entertainment, Inc., as of December 31, the end of the fiscal period, appear in the working papers.

Instructions:

(1) Prepare a trial balance on a ten-column work sheet.

(2) Complete the work sheet. Use the following adjustment information.

Teacher Notes

Merchandise inventory, December 31	$20,000.00
Supplies inventory, December 31	900.00
Unexpired insurance, December 31	1,800.00
Total federal income taxes for the year	2,965.00

(3) Prepare an income statement from the work sheet information.
(4) Prepare a statement of retained earnings.
(5) Prepare a balance sheet.
(6) Journalize and post the adjusting entries. Begin on general journal page 14.
(7) Journalize and post the closing entries.
(8) Prepare a post-closing trial balance.

CHALLENGE **Problem 18-6   Preparing Adjusting and Closing Entries**

PROBLEM
In the middle of the end-of-period activities, the accountant for the Leather Goods Shop was called away because of a death in the family. Before leaving, the accountant had prepared the work sheet and the financial statements. However, the business manager can only locate a trial balance and the income statement.

Instructions:
(1) Journalize the adjusting and closing entries on page 16 of a general journal.
(2) Using the information provided, prepare a post-closing trial balance.

Leather Goods Shop
Income Statement
For the Year Ended December 31, 19--

Revenue:			
Sales		$299,156	
Less: Sales Ret. & Allowances		9,500	
Net Sales			$289,656
Cost of Merchandise Sold:			
Merchandise Inventory, 1/1/--		$ 64,800	
Purchases	$168,624		
Plus: Transportation In	8,236		
Cost of Delivered Merchandise		$176,860	
Less: Purchases Discounts	$ 2,950		
Purchases Ret. & Allow.	2,108	5,058	
Net Purchases		171,802	
Cost of Merchandise Available		$236,602	
Merchandise Inventory, 12/31/--		60,400	
Cost of Merchandise Sold			176,202
Gross Profit on Sales			$113,454
Operating Expenses:			
Advertising Expense		$ 4,000	
Insurance Expense		1,800	
Miscellaneous Expense		1,600	
Salaries Expense		26,900	
Supplies Expense		2,744	
Utilities Expense		4,200	
Total Operating Expenses			41,244
Operating Income			$ 72,210
Less: Income Taxes			14,913
Net Income			$ 57,297

407

Adjustments:
(a) $5,000.00
(b) $3,200.00
(c) $1,200.00
(d) $25.00

Net income, $41,285.00

Retained Earnings, $66,685.00
Bal. Sheet totals, $120,236.57
P/C TB totals, $120,236.57

Problem 18-6: Ch. Obj. 1, 2, 3, 4, 5

CHALLENGE The last problem in each chapter is a challenge problem and is identified by this

PROBLEM "maze" symbol.

P/C TB totals, $129,419.00

---

4 ASSESS

A chapter test is available for use in assessing students' understanding of concepts in this chapter.

Unit objective and problem tests are available to assess students' knowledge of concepts in Chapters 16-18.

The testmaker software will enable you to develop tailor-made chapter, unit, semester, and final tests.

Alternative Assessment

For alternative assessment strategies, refer to *Tech Prep Strategies in Accounting*.

Leather Goods Shop
Trial Balance
December 31, 19--

Cash in Bank	$ 12,035	
Accounts Receivable	6,106	
Merchandise Inventory	64,800	
Supplies	3,916	
Prepaid Insurance	5,400	
Equipment	46,106	
Accounts Payable		$ 4,690
Federal Income Tax Payable		—
Sales Tax Payable		416
Capital Stock		40,000
Retained Earnings		24,603
Income Summary	—	—
Sales		299,156
Sales Returns and Allowances	9,500	
Purchases	168,624	
Transportation In	8,236	
Purchases Discounts		2,950
Purchases Returns and Allowances		2,108
Advertising Expense	4,000	
Insurance Expense	—	
Miscellaneous Expense	1,600	
Salaries Expense	26,900	
Supplies Expense	—	
Utilities Expense	4,200	
Federal Income Tax Expense	12,500	
	$373,923	$373,923

Use Chapter Test 18 here to assess students' understanding and retention of the concepts and procedures presented in the chapter.

Use Unit 3 Objective Test, Chapters 16-18, and/or Unit 3 Problem Test, Chapters 16-18, to assess students' retention of concepts presented in these chapters.

F O C U S   O N
CAREERS

IRS: A Fertile Field of Career Opportunities

When you think of accounting, it's hard not to think of taxes. When you think of taxes, it's hard not to think of the Internal Revenue Service (IRS). If you're considering a career in accounting, you might want to consider what the IRS has to offer.

A four-year degree with 15 credit hours of accounting and 9 credit hours of business-related subjects will qualify you for a position as a special agent. For those who wish to follow this career path, the IRS provides one year of paid, intensive training after college. After the training period, agents work alone and with other agencies, such as the FBI or drug enforcement agencies. This law enforcement position usually involves criminal investigations. Special agents investigate tax fraud and illegal gains made by mobsters, drug traffickers, and racketeers.

Accounting majors with 15 credit hours of accounting and 6 credit hours of business law could become revenue agents. Revenue agents go out in the field to businesses to ensure that their staff accountants are maintaining proper records. Experienced revenue agents who choose not to pursue management positions can become international corporate accountants or computer audit specialists.

If you wish to delay college, you could find a position as a clerk or typist. You can then work your way up, picking up college accounting credits at night. The IRS encourages continuing education and promotion from within.

If you're in college, apply for an internship, a summer job, or a cooperative position. Cooperative positions pay college students salaries and benefits, and when you graduate, there's a job waiting for you.

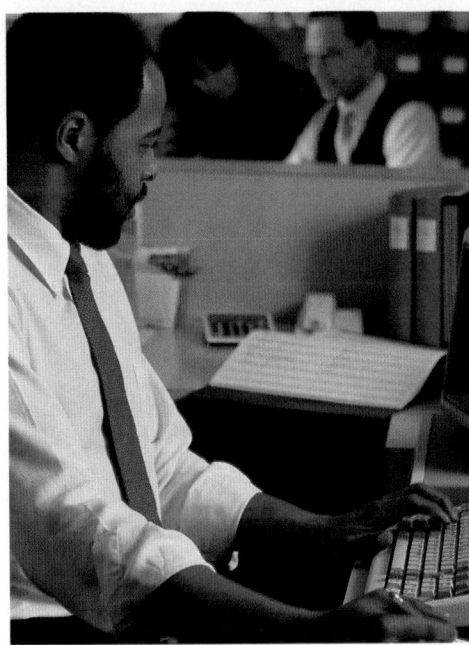

The Internal Revenue Service offers many opportunities for persons with a background in accounting.

The IRS employs more accountants than any corporation. Many accountants in the private sector who specialize in taxes or auditing began their careers by working for the IRS. It just may be the best training ground for your future in accounting. Why not investigate it!

Invite a representative of the local IRS office, or a local CPA, to speak to your class. To prepare for the visit, help students develop career-related questions to ask the speaker.

QUESTIONS

1. Each week *The Wall Street Journal* carries a column called "Tax Report." Ask students to summarize an article of interest and share it with the class.
2. The IRS employs several thousand people, many of whom must have accounting educations and practical experience. Have students research the requirements for an employee of the IRS.

ANSWERS

1. Answers will vary.
2. Answers will vary depending on the job researched by the student.

409

Mini Practice Set

APPLICATION ACTIVITY 4

A Complete Accounting Cycle for a Merchandising Corporation

In Unit 3, you studied the complete accounting cycle for a merchandising corporation that uses special journals. Now you will have the opportunity to review and apply what you have learned as you work through the accounting cycle for The Lighthouse Gallery, Inc.

When you have completed this activity, you will have done the following:

1. Analyzed business transactions.
2. Journalized business transactions in the four special journals and in the general journal.
3. Posted journal entries to the general ledger and to the accounts receivable and accounts payable subsidiary ledgers.
4. Posted the totals of the special journals to the general ledger.
5. Proved cash.
6. Prepared a schedule of accounts receivable and a schedule of accounts payable.
7. Prepared a trial balance and a work sheet.
8. Prepared financial statements.
9. Journalized and posted adjusting and closing entries.
10. Prepared a post-closing trial balance.

The Lighthouse Gallery, Inc.

The Dempsey family owns and operates a wholesale merchandising business organized as a corporation. The business, called The Lighthouse Gallery, Inc., sells a wide variety of lamps and lighting fixtures to service and retail businesses.

Chart of Accounts

The chart of accounts for The Lighthouse Gallery is shown on the following page. The accounts receivable subsidiary ledger accounts and the accounts payable subsidiary ledger accounts are also listed.

Keeping the Accounting Records
for The Lighthouse Gallery, Inc.

The Lighthouse Gallery, Inc., has a large volume of business transactions. The business, therefore, uses special journals and a general journal to record its business activity.

Susan Scott, The Lighthouse Gallery's previous accounting clerk, has already journalized and posted the business transactions for December 1 through December 15. The transactions recorded thus far are included in the accounting stationery accompanying this textbook. The transactions for December 16 through December 31 are shown on the following pages.

APPLICATION ACTIVITY 4

Application Activity 4 is a comprehensive activity that requires students to complete an accounting cycle for a merchandising business that is organized as a corporation. In this activity, students are required to analyze and record the business transactions for The Lighthouse Gallery, Inc., a store that sells lamps and lighting fixtures. Students must decide which journal to use to record each of the transactions. They must also post to the general ledger and the accounts receivable and accounts payable subsidiary ledgers.

The accounting stationery needed to complete this activity is included in the student's *Chapter Reviews and Working Papers*. Most students should be able to complete the activity manually within three to four class periods.

Source documents are also available to add realism to this activity.

COMPUTER

PROBLEM

As with other application activities, an optional microcomputer diskette is available for use in completing this activity. Most students will be able to complete this activity on the microcomputer within two class periods.

Teacher Notes

THE LIGHTHOUSE GALLERY, INC.
Chart of Accounts

S. Journal totals:
Sales, $13,424.00
Sales Tax Pay., $805.44
Accounts Rec., $14,229.44

ASSETS	101	Cash in Bank
	105	Accounts Receivable
	110	Merchandise Inventory
	115	Supplies
	120	Prepaid Insurance
	125	Office Equipment
	130	Store Equipment
LIABILITIES	201	Accounts Payable
	205	Federal Income Tax Payable
	210	Sales Tax Payable
STOCKHOLDERS' EQUITY	301	Capital Stock
	305	Retained Earnings
	310	Income Summary
REVENUE	401	Sales
	405	Sales Discounts
	410	Sales Returns and Allowances
COST OF MERCHANDISE	501	Purchases
	505	Transportation In
	510	Purchases Discounts
	515	Purchases Returns and Allowances
EXPENSES	605	Advertising Expense
	610	Bank Card Fees Expense
	615	Insurance Expense
	620	Miscellaneous Expense
	625	Rent Expense
	630	Salaries Expense
	635	Supplies Expense
	640	Utilities Expense
	650	Federal Income Tax Expense

ACCOUNTS RECEIVABLE SUBSIDIARY LEDGER

805	Bulb-Tronics Suppliers
830	Lumination Outlet
860	Serendipity Shop
865	Sparky Electrical Contractors
870	The Kilowatt House

ACCOUNTS PAYABLE SUBSIDIARY LEDGER

910	Brass Lamps, Ltd.
920	Creative Lamps, Inc.
930	Electrical Reflector Co.
940	Reddi-Bright Manufacturing
950	Stained Glass Outlet
960	Taylor Office Suppliers

Instructions: The forms for completing this activity are included in the working papers accompanying this textbook.
(1) Record the remaining December transactions in the sales, cash receipts, purchases, cash payments, and general journals.
(2) Post the individual amounts from the five journals to the accounts receivable and accounts payable subsidiary ledgers daily.

411

Teacher Notes

CR Journal totals:
General, $230.00
Sales, $11,194.47
Sales Tax Pay., $671.67
Accounts Rec., $14,007.90
Sales Disc., $225.90
Cash in Bank, $25,878.14

P Journal totals:
Accounts Pay., $14,110.00
Purchases, $13,905.00
General, $205.00

CP Journal totals:
General, $7,033.80
Accounts Pay., $14,765.00
Purch. Disc., $193.20
Cash in Bank, $21,605.60

AR balance, $8,497.44
AP balance, $6,645.00

TB totals, $181,004.37

Adjustments:
(a) $5,416.55
(b) $1,181.46
(c) $1,800.00
(d) $300.00

Net income, $26,900.99

Retained Earnings, $39,900.99

P/C TB totals, $74,205.70

---

(3) Post the individual amounts from the General columns of the cash receipts, purchases, cash payments, and general journals daily.

(4) Foot, prove, total, and rule the special journals at the end of the month.

(5) Post the column totals of the special journals to the general ledger. Use this order for posting: sales, cash receipts, purchases, and cash payments.

(6) Prove cash. The balance shown on check stub 619 is $22,752.83.

(7) Prepare a schedule of accounts receivable and a schedule of accounts payable.

(8) Prepare a trial balance on a ten-column work sheet for the year ended December 31.

(9) Complete the work sheet. Use the following adjustment information.

Merchandise inventory, December 31	$24,850.43
Supplies inventory, December 31	120.00
Unexpired insurance, December 31	660.00
Total federal income taxes	4,500.00

(10) Prepare an income statement from the work sheet information.

(11) Prepare a statement of retained earnings.

(12) Prepare a balance sheet.

(13) Journalize and post the adjusting entries.

(14) Journalize and post the closing entries.

(15) Prepare a post-closing trial balance.

Transactions:

Dec. 16 Received Invoice 410 from Reddi-Bright Manufacturing for merchandise purchased on account, $1,475.00.

16 Paid the quarterly federal income tax installment of $1,050.00, Check 610.

16 Issued Check 611 for $2,548.00 to Brass Lamps, Ltd., in payment of Invoice 112 for $2,600.00 less a discount of $52.00.

17 Paid the monthly salaries by issuing Check 612 for $4,750.00.

17 Purchased $80.00 of supplies from Taylor Office Suppliers on account, Invoice 830.

17 Received a check for $1,965.60 from Bulb-Tronics Suppliers in payment of Sales Slip 479 for $2,003.40 less a cash discount of $37.80, Receipt 358.

19 Sold merchandise on account to Bulb-Tronics Suppliers, $2,600.00 plus $156.00 sales tax, Sales Slip 484.

19 Prepared Receipt 359 for a $1,716.00 check received from Lumination Outlet in payment of Sales Slip 480 for $1,749.00 less a $33.00 cash discount.

20 Purchased merchandise on account from Brass Lamps, Ltd., Invoice 215, $1,560.00.

20 Wrote Check 613 to Creative Lamps, Inc., to apply on account, $375.00.

21 Prepared Credit Memo 44 for $106.00 for the return of $100.00 in merchandise by Bulb-Tronics Suppliers, plus sales tax of $6.00.

23 Sold merchandise to Lumination Outlet on account, $1,580.00 plus sales tax of $94.80, Sales Slip 485.

Teacher Notes

_____

_____

_____

_____

_____

Dec. 23 Received a check from Serendipity Shop to apply on account, Receipt 360 for $300.00.

23 Paid Electrical Reflector Co. for Invoice 326 for $1,890.00 less a $37.80 discount, Check 614 for $1,852.20.

25 Received from The Kilowatt House a check for $1,102.40 in payment of Sales Slip 483 for $1,123.60 less a cash discount of $21.20, Receipt 361.

26 Returned defective merchandise purchased on account from Brass Lamps, Ltd., $150.00, Debit Memo 28.

26 Received Invoice 335 from Electrical Reflector Co. for merchandise purchased on account totaling $1,630.00.

28 Wrote Check 615 for $120.00 to the *Daily Examiner* for a monthly advertisement.

28 Sparky Electrical Contractors sent a check for $450.00 to apply on account, Receipt 362.

29 Paid Stained Glass Outlet $1,625.00 on account, Check 616.

29 Sold to The Kilowatt House $1,990.00 of merchandise on account, plus $119.40 sales tax, Sales Slip 486.

30 Issued Check 617 to Reddi-Bright Manufacturing for $700.00 to apply on account.

30 Sold merchandise totaling $560.00 plus $33.60 sales tax to the Serendipity Shop on account, Sales Slip 487.

31 Recorded the bank service charge of $10.00 and the bank card fee of $150.00, December bank statement.

31 Paid transportation charges of $51.60 for merchandise shipped from Electrical Reflector Co., Check 618.

31 Recorded cash sales of $3,995.10 plus $239.71 in sales tax, Tape 41.

31 Recorded bank card sales of $1,736.27 plus sales tax of $104.18, Tape 41.

413

Teacher Notes

The payroll unit comprises two chapters that provide full and realistic coverage of general payroll records and related accounting procedures. While manual payroll and accounting procedures are emphasized, students also learn about computerized payroll systems.

U N I T 4

ACCOUNTING FOR A PAYROLL SYSTEM

You have now learned how to record business transactions for businesses that provide services and for those that sell merchandise. Regardless of the type of business, all businesses that employ people must also keep records on the money paid to their employees and on the taxes paid to local, state, and federal governments. In this unit, you will learn how to keep records on employee earnings and how to record the payment of wages in the accounting records of the business.

414

Individualizing Instruction

To provide individualized activities within the unit, you may use any of the following:

- problems in *Math Review for Accounting*
- chapter study plans
- study guides in the student workbook
- end-of-chapter challenge problems (identified by a maze symbol)

- optional problems in the Additional Problems section at the back of the student textbook
- cases from *Tech Prep Strategies in Accounting*
- *Electronic Study Guide*

Accounting for a Payroll System

Unit Concepts

Unit 4 covers the procedures used to maintain a payroll system. Students learn about the various methods for paying employees, the records prepared for the payroll, and the individual forms kept for each employee. The unit also covers procedures for recording the payroll and the payroll taxes required of employers and employees. Students become familiar with the government regulations—both federal and state—for withholding amounts, dates when payments must be made, and forms that must be submitted with payments.

General Unit Performance Objectives

1. Correctly use terminology related to accounting for a payroll system.
2. Describe the principles and practices of accounting for a payroll system.
3. Demonstrate the accounting procedures used in a payroll system.

PERFORMANCE OBJECTIVES

Unit Objective Test: Chapters 19-20

1. Define the related accounting vocabulary correctly.
2. Determine the correct and incorrect procedures for payroll activities.
3. Distinguish between a salary expense and a payroll tax expense.
4. Analyze payroll transactions.

Unit Problem Test: Chapters 19-20

1. Compute gross earnings for employees paid on a salary plus commission basis.
2. Compute gross earnings for employees paid on an hourly wage and piece work basis.
3. Complete a payroll register.
4. Record the payment of a payroll in the cash payments journal.
5. Calculate and record the employer's payroll tax liabilities.

ORGANIZER

Chapter	Learning Objectives
19	1. Explain the importance of accurate payroll records. 2. Calculate gross earnings and net pay. 3. Explain the types of deductions from employees' gross earnings. 4. Prepare a payroll register. 5. Prepare an employee's earnings record. 6. Define the accounting terms new to this chapter.
20	1. Record payroll information in the cash payments journal. 2. Describe and calculate the employer's payroll taxes. 3. Record the employer's payroll taxes in the general journal. 4. Identify tax reports that are prepared regularly by the employer. 5. Define the accounting terms new to this chapter.
Mini Practice Set 5	Prepare and maintain payroll records for a merchandising business organized as a corporation.

EXPANDED PAYROLL BOOK
FOR 1 TO 35 EMPLOYEES

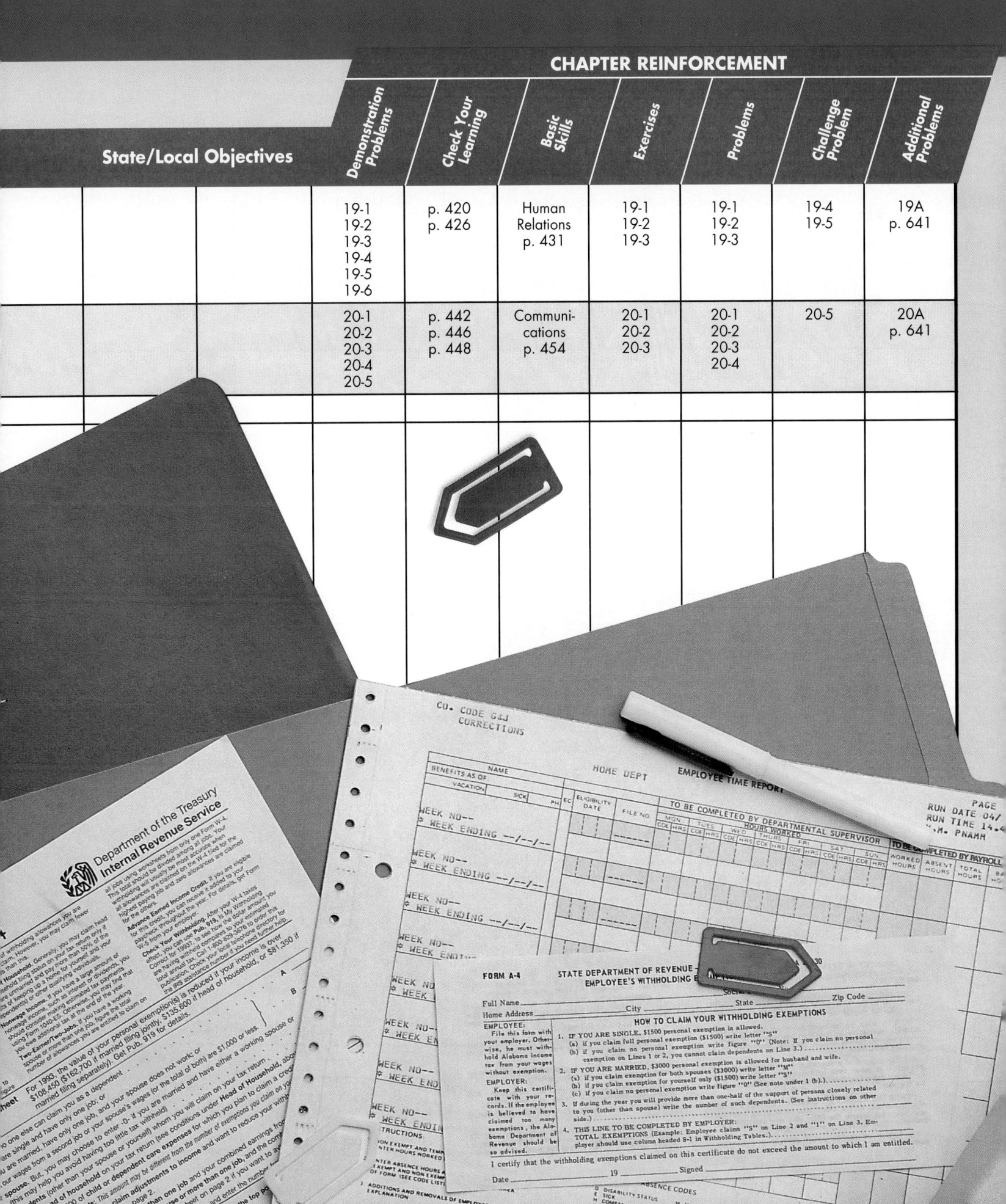

State/Local Objectives	Demonstration Problems	Check Your Learning	Basic Skills	Exercises	Problems	Challenge Problem	Additional Problems
	19-1 19-2 19-3 19-4 19-5 19-6	p. 420 p. 426	Human Relations p. 431	19-1 19-2 19-3	19-1 19-2 19-3	19-4 19-5	19A p. 641
	20-1 20-2 20-3 20-4 20-5	p. 442 p. 446 p. 448	Communications p. 454	20-1 20-2 20-3	20-1 20-2 20-3 20-4	20-5	20A p. 641

UNIT 4 COMPUTERIZED ACCOUNTING ACTIVITIES

Chapter	Glencoe Integrated Accounting	Spreadsheet Applications	Electronic Study Guide Model Exercises/Problems	CD Rom
19	Problem 19-3	Exercise 19-2 Problem 19-1 (Payroll Register)	Exercise 19-2 19-3	Menu Selection 19
20	Problem 20-4	Problem 20-2	Exercise 20-1 20-2	Menu Selection 20
Mini Practice Set	Application Activity 5			
Basic Math Review			Menu Option 29	

Chapter 19
PAYROLL ACCOUNTING

INTRODUCING THE
CHAPTER

LOOKING BACK

Students have now learned to analyze transactions and keep the accounting records for both service and merchandising businesses. In addition to the records that must be maintained for external business transactions, accounting records of internal activities such as payroll must also be kept. In this chapter students will learn about various methods of calculating gross earnings, deductions from gross earnings, and payroll records that are maintained for each employee.

VOCABULARY DEVELOPMENT

Reinforce vocabulary through a team competition to define new terms. Appoint teams to participate in a "Vocabulary Bee." Teams take turns defining terms, with team members consulting with each other before giving a definition (use a time limit of a minute or so). If a team gives an incorrect definition, the team is eliminated. Definitions of these terms are found in the chapter and in the glossary on pages 670-679.

Electronic Field Trips

Most businesses have employees who help keep the business operating. In a private enterprise economy, people are free to work for any business they choose so long as they meet the requirements for employment. Businesses in turn must follow certain guidelines in paying their employees for the services they perform. For example, both federal and state laws require businesses to keep accurate payroll records and to prepare various reports on those earnings.

Most companies set up a system to ensure that their employees are paid on time and that their employees' paychecks are accurate. In this chapter, you will learn about such a system. You will learn how employee earnings and deductions from those earnings are calculated, as well as how paychecks are prepared. You will also learn about the earnings records kept for each employee.

Learning Objectives

When you have completed Chapter 19, you should be able to do the following:

1. Explain the importance of accurate payroll records.
2. Calculate gross earnings and net pay.
3. Explain the types of deductions from employees' gross earnings.
4. Prepare a payroll register.
5. Prepare an employee's earnings record.
6. Define the accounting terms introduced in this chapter.

New Terms

payroll
pay period
payroll clerk
gross earnings
salary
wage
time card
electronic badge readers
piece rate
commission
overtime rate
deduction
exemption
payroll register
net pay
direct deposit
employee's earnings record
accumulated earnings

416

Teaching Resources

- Lesson Plans
- TE/Chapter Reviews & Working Papers
- Demonstration Problems
- Student Study Plans
- Teaching Transparencies
- Solutions Transparencies
- Electronic Field Trips Video, Level I
- Electronic Study Guide
- Chapter 19 Test

Other Resources

- Basic Skills Activities
- Blackline Masters
- Careers in Accounting
- Dictionary
- Math Review for Accounting
- Tech Prep Strategies in Accounting
- Video
- Testmaker Software
- Spanish Resources/Audiotapes
- Spanish Electronic Study Guide

The Importance of Payroll Records

A **payroll** is a list of a business's employees and the payments due to each employee for a specific pay period. A **pay period** is the amount of time for which an employee is paid. Most businesses use weekly, biweekly, semimonthly, or monthly pay periods.

The employee payroll is a major expense for most companies. To ensure that they have accurate records of their payroll costs, most businesses set up a payroll system for use in recording and reporting employee earnings information. A payroll system should accomplish two basic goals: (1) the collection and processing of all the information needed to prepare and issue payroll checks, and (2) the production of the necessary payroll records for accounting purposes and for reporting to government agencies, management, and others.

Businesses with many employees often hire a person who is responsible for preparing the payroll. This person is called a **payroll clerk.** The payroll clerk makes sure that employees are paid on time, employees are paid the correct amounts, payroll records are completed, payroll reports are filed, and payroll taxes are paid.

All payroll systems have certain tasks in common. Each payroll system includes (1) the calculation of earnings, (2) the calculation of deductions, (3) the recording of these amounts in the employer's payroll and accounting records, (4) the preparation of payroll checks, and (5) the reporting of employee earnings information to federal and state governments. In this and the next chapter, you will learn about these common payroll tasks.

Calculating Gross Earnings

Most employees are paid for the specific amount of time they have worked during a pay period. The total amount of money earned by an employee in a pay period is the employee's **gross earnings.** Gross earnings can be calculated in several ways. Some employees are paid on a salary basis; others are paid hourly wages, piece rates, or commissions. Employees may also be paid on a salary-plus-commission basis. In addition, if employees work extra hours during a pay period, the amount of overtime pay must be included in the calculation of gross earnings. Let's look at each of these ways of calculating gross earnings.

Salary

ACCOUNTING *Notes*
Salt was used as money in Roman times. Our word *salary* comes from the Latin word for "salt."

One common method of paying employees, especially those who are managers or supervisors, is by salary. A **salary** is a fixed amount of money paid to an employee for each pay period. In other words, an employee who is paid a salary is paid a fixed amount regardless of the number of hours worked during the pay period. The amount of the salary is the same as gross earnings, so no additional computations are needed. For example, Paula is paid a salary of $2,000 a month. Her gross earnings are thus $2,000 for each monthly pay period. Paula may work 160 hours one month and 180 hours the next, but her gross earnings will remain at $2,000 a month.

CHAPTER 19   Payroll Accounting   417

MAJOR CONCEPTS

- The Importance of Payroll Records
- Calculating Gross Earnings
- Determining Deductions from Gross Earnings
- Completing the Payroll Register
- Preparing Payroll Checks
- The Employee's Earnings Record
- A Computerized Payroll System

BUSINESS CONNECTION

Employee payroll is a major expense for a business. In order to cut expenses and improve the financial position of the company, General Motors announced in December of 1991 that over a four-year period it would close six of its 32 assembly plants and cut 79,500 employees from the payroll.

CONCEPT DEVELOPMENT

The Importance of Payroll Records

Payroll is often one of a business's largest expenses. Inaccuracies in payroll calculations could cost a business thousands of dollars both in payroll amounts and in taxes businesses pay on their payrolls. Discuss the importance of control of payroll expenses and the business cost of wasted employee time.

Teaching Tips

■ Biweekly = every two weeks; semimonthly = twice a month.

CONCEPT DEVELOPMENT

Calculating Gross Earnings

Six methods of determining gross earnings are presented in this section. These methods include salary, hourly wage, piece rate, commission, salary plus commission, and overtime. Emphasize why employers choose different ways of compensating employees.

Reinforcing Study Skills

Taking good notes does not stop with the end of a lecture. Suggest to students that their notes will be more helpful later on if they edit them carefully within a day of writing them. At that point they should still be able to clarify their notes and fill in the gaps from memory

or by asking a classmate or the instructor.

Provide a copy of the *Student Study Plans* to each class member to help organize study activities or to individualize practice and review activities.

The hourly wage paid to some employees may be governed by a contract between the employer and a union.

Hourly Wage

$$\begin{array}{r} \$\ 4.45 \\ \times\quad 36 \\ \hline 26.70 \\ 133.5\quad \\ \hline \$160.20 \end{array}$$

Another common way of determining gross earnings is the hourly wage. A **wage** is an amount of money paid to an employee at a specified rate per hour worked. The number of hours worked multiplied by the hourly wage equals the gross earnings for the pay period. For example, Karen Nielson is paid $4.45 per hour. Last week she worked 36 hours. Karen's gross earnings were thus $160.20 (see the calculations in the margin).

R E M E M B E R

Gross earnings are calculated by multiplying the hourly rate by the total hours worked.

No. *11*						
Name *Karen Nielson*						
Soc. Sec. No. *045-68-5733*						
Week Ending *6/30/--*						
DAY	IN	OUT	IN	OUT	IN	OUT	TOTAL
M	7:58	12:25	1:32	4:18			7¼
T	8:00	12:00	12:45	4:00			7¼
W	7:56	12:01	1:10	4:15			7
Th	8:01	11:55	1:02	4:16			7¼
F	7:45	12:02	1:05	3:58			7¼
S							
S							
				TOTAL HOURS		36

	Hours	Rate	Amount
REGULAR	36	$4.45	$160.20
OVERTIME	0		
		TOTAL EARNINGS	$160.20

Figure 19-1 A Time Card Completed by an Employee

To keep accurate records of the number of hours worked during each pay period, many businesses have their employees complete time cards. A **time card** is a record of the time an employee arrives at work each day, the time the employee leaves, and the total number of hours worked each day. The times may be recorded manually or by a time clock that registers each employee's arrival and departure times. For example, look at the time card Karen Nielson completed, shown in Figure 19-1.

Employee arrival and departure times are seldom exactly on the hour. As a result, most companies com-

418

Making Connections

EVERYDAY LIFE

Many different jobs exist in our economy. Many students will be familiar with jobs that pay an hourly rate. Pay for other jobs may be calculated in different ways. For example, sales is a type of job that usually pays a commission on total sales for the month. Ask students to describe jobs they are familiar with and to explain how employees are paid for doing those jobs.

pute arrival and departure times to the nearest quarter hour (15 minutes). A quarter hour begins or ends on the hour, 15 minutes after the hour, 30 minutes after the hour, and 45 minutes after the hour. With this system, employees are paid for working to the nearest quarter hour, regardless of the time they enter and leave work. For example, on Monday Karen arrived for work at 7:58, left for lunch at 12:25, returned from lunch at 1:32, and left work at 4:18. Karen will be paid for working from 8:00 to 12:30 and from 1:30 to 4:15.

R E M E M B E R

When determining the number of hours worked, round arrival and departure times to the nearest quarter hour.

Some businesses are using computer technology at the point where employees enter and leave. This is done by **electronic badge readers.** Each employee's time card or identification badge has a magnetic strip on which is encoded certain employee information. When the time card is entered, the badge reader scans the magnetic strip. The identity of the employee, the department or area in which the employee works, and the arrival or departure time are entered directly into the computer. This electronic equipment enables a business to prepare a daily printout on employee work hours.

Regardless of how records on employee work hours are prepared, most companies have supervisors check the accuracy of the labor costs.

Piece Rate

$ 4.60
× 40
$184.00

$ 535
× .12
$64.20

$184.00
+ 64.20
$248.20

In many factories and manufacturing plants, employees are paid a specific amount of money for each item, or piece, they produce during a pay period. The amount paid for each piece produced is called the **piece rate.** Most companies also pay an hourly wage in addition to the piece rate. For example, Leon is paid an hourly rate of $4.60 plus 12¢ for each piece he produces. Leon worked 40 hours last week and produced 535 items. His gross earnings for the week were $248.20 (see the calculations in the margin).

Commission

$ 7,184
× .05
$359.20

A **commission** is an amount paid to an employee based on a percentage of the employee's sales. Many companies pay their sales employees a commission to encourage them to increase their sales. For example, Kate is paid a 5% commission on all her sales. Last week Kate's total sales were $7,184.00. Kate's gross earnings for the week were $359.20.

Salary Plus Commission or Bonus

$ 4,640
× .03
$139.20
+200.00
$339.20

Some companies pay their salespeople a base salary plus a commission or a bonus on the amount of their sales. For example, Jerry is paid a salary of $200.00 per week plus a commission of 3% of his sales. Jerry's sales were $4,640.00 last week. His gross earnings were $339.20.

CHAPTER 19 Payroll Accounting   419

Using Visuals

Use demonstration
problem 19-4 to show
students how to calcu-
late overtime pay.

ACCOUNTING
PRACTICE
**Students may complete
Exercise 19-2 at this point.**

ANSWERS

1. (a) $173.16; (b) $201.24; (c)
$250.38
2. $441.50
3. $227.10

CONCEPT DEVELOPMENT
Determining Deductions from
Gross Earnings

Point out that some payroll deductions are required by law, while others are voluntary. Before explaining
each deduction, describe the employer's role as a "collection agent"
for federal, state, and local governments. Remind students that deductions are part of the total earnings of
the employees.

$ 4.60	
× 40	
$184.00	
$ 6.90	
× 3	
$ 20.70	
+184.00	
$204.70	

Overtime Pay

The number of hours an employee may work in a weekly pay period is
regulated by state and federal laws. Generally, these laws require employers
to pay overtime for all hours over 40 per work week. The **overtime
rate,** set by the Fair Labor Standards Act of 1938, is $1\frac{1}{2}$ times the employee's regular hourly rate of pay. For example, Ben worked 43 hours last
week; his hourly rate of pay is $4.60. Ben was paid for 40 hours at his regular
rate of $4.60. He was also paid for the additional 3 hours at a rate of $6.90
($4.60 × 1.5). Ben's gross earnings for the week were thus $204.70.

Employees who are paid a salary may also be entitled to overtime pay. If
a salaried employee is to be paid overtime, the employee's hourly rate of
pay must be determined. For example, Ellen's salary is $600.00 per week for
a 40-hour week. Her hourly rate is determined by dividing $600.00 by 40
($600.00 ÷ 40 = $15.00 per hour). Ellen's gross earnings for a 44-hour week
would be $600.00 plus $90.00 for the 4 overtime hours at $22.50 per hour
($15.00 × 1.5), for a total of $690.00.

R E M E M B E R

**Employees who work more than 40 hours per work week must be paid
overtime. The overtime rate is $1\frac{1}{2}$ times the employee's regular hourly
rate of pay.**

Before continuing, complete the following activity to check your understanding of the material you have just studied.

Check
Your Learning

Use notebook paper to calculate the answers to these questions.

1. If an employee is paid $4.68 per hour and is paid overtime for all hours
worked over 40, what is the gross pay for each of the following?
   a. 37 hours   **b.** 42 hours   **c.** 49 hours
2. Tom is paid a salary of $200.00 per week plus a commission of 7% on
sales. Tom's total sales last week were $3,450.00. What were his gross
earnings?
3. Clare earns $4.75 per hour plus 10¢ for each item she produces. If Clare
produced 371 items last week and worked 40 hours, what were her gross
earnings?

Compare your answers to those in the answers section. Re-read the preceding part of the chapter to find the correct answers to any questions you
may have missed.

Determining Deductions from Gross Earnings

The first time you received a paycheck, you may have been surprised to
see that the amount of the check was not the same as the amount of your

420

Reteaching Strategies

Accurate payroll records must be maintained
for several reasons.

- To ensure that the employee salaries and
wages are computed accurately.
- To ensure that the wages and salaries are
paid to employees promptly.
- Because the business must comply with tax
law provisions.

Refer students who are having difficulty with

the mathematical calculations to *Math Review
for Accounting.* Give students extra practice
in calculating gross earnings by making up
several problems and writing them on the
chalkboard. Ask students who have learned
the calculations to help those who have not
yet mastered the various means of calculating
gross earnings.

gross earnings. Various amounts are taken out of all employees' gross earnings. An amount that is subtracted from gross earnings is called a **deduction.** Deductions include those required by law and those an employee voluntarily wishes to have withheld from earnings.

Deductions Required by Law

An employer is required by law to withhold payroll taxes on its employees' gross earnings. These taxes include the federal income tax and the social security tax. In addition, many cities and states require employers to withhold city or state income taxes.

▲ Federal Income Tax

Most people who work must pay the federal government a tax based on their annual incomes. To ensure that taxpayers have the funds to pay their taxes, employers are required to withhold a certain amount of money from each employee's earnings. In other words, the employer acts as a collection agent for the federal government. The employer periodically sends the money that has been withheld from all employees' earnings to the Internal Revenue Service (IRS).

The amount of taxes withheld from each employee's paycheck is an estimate of the amount the employee will owe in taxes at the end of the tax year. The exact amount of taxes is determined when the employee prepares a tax return. If too much money has been withheld, the IRS will refund the amount of the overpayment. If too little money has been withheld, the employee is required to pay the additional amount when the income tax return is filed. Generally, to avoid penalties, an employee must pay in at least 90% of the actual taxes owed.

The amount withheld for federal income taxes each pay period depends on three things: (1) the employee's marital status, (2) the number of exemptions claimed by the employee, and (3) the employee's gross earnings. The first two items of information are found on each employee's Form W-4. This

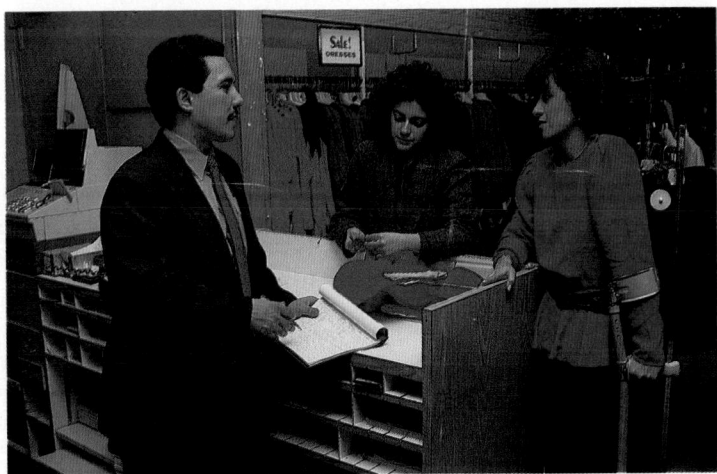

Employees who earn a stated amount of money for each item sold or a percent of the total value of their sales are paid a "straight" commission.

Using Visuals

A teaching transparency showing deductions from gross earnings is available in the transparency binder accompanying Glencoe Accounting.

Teaching Tips

■ Discuss procedures for paying personal income, social security, and medicare taxes and the concept of withholding. You may want to bring in outside materials such as *Understanding Taxes,* published by the IRS, to share with your students.

■ The payroll tax money withheld from employees' earnings is deposited either weekly or monthly depending on the amount of the payroll.

■ Discuss the 90 percent requirement and use examples on the chalkboard.

■ Give students examples of exemptions and discuss how the number of exemptions influences the amount of tax paid.

Using Visuals

Read the photo caption to the class. Ask students who work on commission to describe how their pay is calculated.

BUSINESS ISSUES

The concept of wages dates back to the time of the Greek philosopher Plato who believed that a man should earn enough so that he could live the same as his parents. Plato also believed that no one should be paid more than five times the lowest paid worker's earnings. Some CEOs make more than 200 times the salary of the lowest paid employee in their firm. A recent study indicates that companies are moving toward compensating top executives based on the performance of the company. One nonfinancial performance measure that is being considered is employee and customer satisfaction.

Making Connections

COMMUNICATIONS

Many accountants today offer a much broader range of services than accounting firms have traditionally provided. These services include researching and giving advice on where and how to find capital and developing written studies on the feasibility of proposed projects. Ask students to suggest other creative ways in which accountants can offer new services.

Teaching Tips

■ Discuss qualifications for dependents. Point out that each dependent claimed results in a specific decrease in taxable earnings.

Using Visuals

Walk students through the form in Figure 19-2. Try to obtain blank copies of this form and have students complete them in class.

Teaching Tips

■ Discuss why most students are not exempt from paying income taxes.
■ Write other examples of earnings and exemptions on the chalkboard and have students calculate the taxes owed.

---

form, called the Employee's Withholding Allowance Certificate, must be filled out by each employee upon starting a job. A new W-4 form should also be filed if the employee's marital status or exemptions change. Employers are required to keep a current Form W-4 on file for each employee.

Karen Nielson's completed Form W-4 is shown in Figure 19-2. As you can see, an employee must include her or his name, address, social security number, and marital status. In addition, the employee must list the number of exemptions claimed (see line 4 on the form). An **exemption** is an allowance claimed by a taxpayer that reduces the amount of taxes that must be paid. Usually, a taxpayer is allowed one personal exemption and one exemption for each person the taxpayer supports, such as a child or an elderly parent. The greater the number of exemptions claimed by a taxpayer, the lower the amount deducted from earnings for federal income taxes.

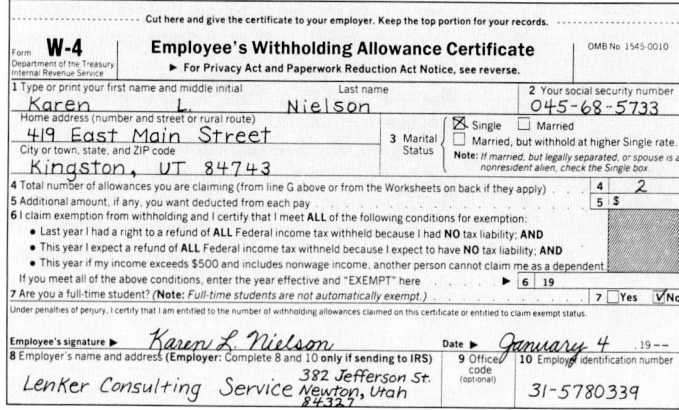

Figure 19-2 Employee's Withholding Allowance Certificate

A few employees may not be required to pay federal or state income taxes in a given year. To qualify as an "exempt" employee, a person must have paid no federal income tax the previous year and state that no tax is expected to be paid in the current year. A person cannot claim to be exempt if he or she is claimed as a dependent by another person, has any nonwage income, or expects to have more than $500 in income. If a person writes "Exempt" on Form W-4, the employer will not withhold amounts for federal or state income taxes.

An employee's gross earnings also affect the amount withheld for federal income taxes. Once gross earnings have been calculated, most employers use tax tables supplied by the IRS each year to calculate the amount of federal tax to withhold from each employee's earnings. The partial tax tables shown in Figure 19-3 (pages 424-425) are for use with single and married persons who are paid weekly. Other tax tables are also available.

Let's look at an example of how tax tables are used to calculate the amount of tax to be withheld. Karen Nielson is single and claims no exemptions. One week she earned $160.20. This amount falls between $160 and $165 on the tax table for single persons. Reading across this line to the column for zero withholding allowances, you find that $17.00 is to be withheld from Karen's gross earnings for the week for federal taxes.

Interdisciplinary Connections

ECONOMICS/SOCIAL STUDIES

Each year, the media announce "Tax Freedom Day," the day when an average worker will have earned enough to pay all his or her taxes for the year. The exact date varies with state and city income tax rates, but it usually falls between mid-April and early May. In 1990 the nationwide average was May 5.

▲ **Social Security Tax** In addition to withholding employees' federal income taxes, employers must also collect social security taxes for the federal government. The present social security system was established by the Federal Insurance Contributions Act (FICA) in 1935. This tax is often referred to as FICA tax.

The social security system finances programs that provide income to certain individuals:

1. The old-age and disability insurance programs provide income to retired and disabled persons and their dependent children.
2. The survivors benefits program provides income to the spouse and dependent children of a deceased worker.
3. The medicare program provides certain health insurance benefits for the elderly.

The social security tax is an exact tax, not an estimated tax. The FICA tax rate is a percentage of the gross earnings of the employee. The rate is set by Congress, which has the power to change the rate at any time. Most employees must pay social security taxes, even those who claim to be exempt from federal income taxes. The present rate is 7.65% and is expected to remain at this rate through 1999.

Beginning in 1991, the FICA tax is divided into two parts and each must be recorded on payroll documents. The total FICA tax rate is 7.65%. This must now be separated to include 6.2% for social security and 1.45% for medicare. The social security part covers old age, survivors, and disability insurance. The medicare part covers hospital and medical insurance.

6.2%	Social Security Tax
1.45%	Medicare Tax
7.65%	Total FICA Tax

The FICA tax is deducted from each employee's earnings each pay period until the maximum taxable amount for the year is reached. This maximum amount is changed each year based on the average level of the nation. For 1994 the maximum amount that may be taxed for the social security tax is $60,600. There is no maximum for the medicare tax. The maximum amount of social security tax that, therefore, may be withheld is $3,757.20.

$$\begin{array}{r} \$60,600.00 \\ \times \quad .062 \\ \hline \$3,757.20 \end{array}$$

▲ **State and Local Income Taxes** Most states also have an income tax on earnings to provide funds for the state. Many cities tax the incomes of the people who live or work in the city. In some areas, state and/or city tax rates are set as a percentage of gross earnings. In other areas, the tax amounts to be deducted are calculated using tax tables similar to the ones used by the federal government.

Voluntary Deductions

Most employers agree to deduct other amounts from their employees' paychecks. Once the employee asks that deductions be made, they are withheld from each paycheck until the employee notifies the employer to stop.

CHAPTER 19 Payroll Accounting   **423**

ACCOUNTING Notes
Under the Tax Reform Act of 1986, most individuals over the age of five should have a social security number. A person has the same social security number for life. This number is used when reporting an employee's earnings to state and federal governments. The employee's lifetime earnings—as well as all social security taxes paid—are also recorded by this number.

Chapter ⬤

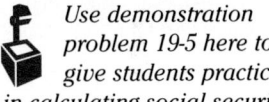

Teaching Tips

■ Mention the procedure for securing a social security number by filling out a Form SS-5.
■ When discussing social security and medicare taxes, emphasize that these taxes are not optional for either the employee or the employer. You may also want to discuss the role the U.S. Congress plays in setting social security and medicare tax rates and the maximum earnings on which taxes are to be withheld.
■ All employees begin paying social security and medicare taxes at the beginning of each tax year.

Using Visuals

Use demonstration problem 19-5 here to give students practice in calculating social security and medicare taxes.

Teaching Tips

■ Discuss any payroll taxes imposed by your local and state governments.

ACCOUNTING PRACTICE
Students may complete Exercise 19-3 at this point.

Teaching Tips

■ When introducing voluntary deductions, emphasize that the employer decides which deductions will be included in the payroll system. Common voluntary deductions are for credit union savings or payments, savings bonds, health or life insurance premiums, charitable contributions, union dues, and so on.

Making Connections

BUSINESS ETHICS

Ask your students to assume the role of payroll clerk for a small business. A friend and co-worker asks how much another employee is paid per hour. Ask students what to do?

(Answer: Payroll information is extremely confidential. Sharing payroll information with others is a violation of the trust of one's employer. The payroll clerk might ask *why* the information is wanted. If discrimination in pay scales is suspected, the issue should be discussed with the employee's supervisor.)

Using Visuals

To help students learn to use
the tax tables in Figure 19-3,
give them several examples
and have them find the
appropriate tax amounts.

SINGLE Persons - WEEKLY Payroll Period

If the wages are -		And the number of withholding allowances claimed is -										
At least	But less than	0	1	2	3	4	5	6	7	8	9	10
		The amount of income tax to be withheld is -										
145	150	15	8	1	0	0	0	0	0	0	0	0
150	155	16	9	2	0	0	0	0	0	0	0	0
155	160	16	10	3	0	0	0	0	0	0	0	0
160	165	17	10	4	0	0	0	0	0	0	0	0
165	170	18	11	4	0	0	0	0	0	0	0	0
170	175	19	12	5	0	0	0	0	0	0	0	0
175	180	19	13	6	0	0	0	0	0	0	0	0
180	185	20	13	7	0	0	0	0	0	0	0	0
185	190	21	14	7	1	0	0	0	0	0	0	0
190	195	22	15	8	1	0	0	0	0	0	0	0
195	200	22	16	9	2	0	0	0	0	0	0	0
200	210	23	17	10	3	0	0	0	0	0	0	0
210	220	25	18	11	5	0	0	0	0	0	0	0
220	230	26	20	13	6	0	0	0	0	0	0	0
230	240	28	21	14	8	1	0	0	0	0	0	0
240	250	29	23	16	9	2	0	0	0	0	0	0
250	260	31	24	17	11	4	0	0	0	0	0	0
260	270	32	26	19	12	5	0	0	0	0	0	0
270	280	34	27	20	14	7	0	0	0	0	0	0
280	290	35	29	22	15	8	2	0	0	0	0	0
290	300	37	30	23	17	10	3	0	0	0	0	0
300	310	38	32	25	18	11	5	0	0	0	0	0
310	320	40	33	26	20	13	6	0	0	0	0	0
320	330	41	35	28	21	14	8	1	0	0	0	0
330	340	43	36	29	23	16	9	2	0	0	0	0
340	350	44	38	31	24	17	11	4	0	0	0	0
350	360	46	39	32	26	19	12	5	0	0	0	0
360	370	47	41	34	27	20	14	7	0	0	0	0
370	380	49	42	35	29	22	15	8	2	0	0	0
380	390	50	44	37	30	23	17	10	3	0	0	0
390	400	52	45	38	32	25	18	11	5	0	0	0
400	410	53	47	40	33	26	20	13	6	0	0	0
410	420	55	48	41	35	28	21	14	8	1	0	0
420	430	56	50	43	36	29	23	16	9	2	0	0
430	440	58	51	44	38	31	24	17	11	4	0	0
440	450	59	53	46	39	32	26	19	12	5	0	0
450	460	61	54	47	41	34	27	20	14	7	0	0
460	470	64	56	49	42	35	29	22	15	8	1	0
470	480	67	57	50	44	37	30	23	17	10	3	0
480	490	70	59	52	45	38	32	25	18	11	4	0
490	500	73	60	53	47	40	33	26	20	13	6	0
500	510	75	63	55	48	41	35	28	21	14	7	1
510	520	78	66	56	50	43	36	29	23	16	9	2
520	530	81	68	58	51	44	38	31	24	17	10	4
530	540	84	71	59	53	46	39	32	26	19	12	5
540	550	87	74	61	54	47	41	34	27	20	13	7
550	560	89	77	64	56	49	42	35	29	22	15	8
560	570	92	80	67	57	50	44	37	30	23	16	10
570	580	95	82	70	59	52	45	38	32	25	18	11
580	590	98	85	73	60	53	47	40	33	26	19	13
590	600	101	88	75	63	55	48	41	35	28	21	14
600	610	103	91	78	66	56	50	43	36	29	22	16
610	620	106	94	81	68	58	51	44	38	31	24	17
620	630	109	96	84	71	59	53	46	39	32	25	19
630	640	112	99	87	74	61	54	47	41	34	27	20
640	650	115	102	89	77	64	56	49	42	35	28	22
650	660	117	105	92	80	67	57	50	44	37	30	23
660	670	120	108	95	82	70	59	52	45	38	31	25
670	680	123	110	98	85	72	60	53	47	40	33	26
680	690	126	113	101	88	75	63	55	48	41	34	28
690	700	129	116	103	91	78	65	56	50	43	36	29
700	710	131	119	106	94	81	68	58	51	44	37	31
710	720	134	122	109	96	84	71	59	53	46	39	32
720	730	137	124	112	99	86	74	61	54	47	40	34
730	740	140	127	115	102	89	77	64	56	49	42	35
740	750	143	130	117	105	92	79	67	57	50	43	37
750	760	145	133	120	108	95	82	70	59	52	45	38
760	770	148	136	123	110	98	85	72	60	53	46	40
770	780	151	138	126	113	100	88	75	63	55	48	41
780	790	154	141	129	116	103	91	78	65	56	49	43
790	800	157	144	131	119	106	93	81	68	58	51	44
800	810	159	147	134	122	109	96	84	71	59	52	46
810	820	162	150	137	124	112	99	86	74	61	54	47
820	830	165	152	140	127	114	102	89	77	64	55	49
830	840	168	155	143	130	117	105	92	79	67	57	50
840	850	171	158	145	133	120	107	95	82	69	58	52
850	860	173	161	148	136	123	110	98	85	72	60	53
860	870	176	164	151	138	126	113	100	88	75	62	55
870	880	179	166	154	141	128	116	103	91	78	65	56
880	890	182	169	157	144	131	119	106	93	81	68	58
890	900	185	172	159	147	134	121	109	96	83	71	59
900	910	187	175	162	150	137	124	112	99	86	74	61
910	920	190	178	165	152	140	127	114	102	89	76	64
920	930	193	180	168	155	142	130	117	105	92	79	67
930	940	196	183	171	158	145	133	120	107	95	82	69

Figure 19-3 IRS Tax Tables

Critical Thinking

The tax tables on pages 424 and 425 are for
a weekly payroll period. Why could you not
use these tables to calculate tax deductions
for an individual who is paid biweekly?
  (Answer: The deductions in the tables are
based on the estimated annual earnings. A
weekly table assumes that if you earn "x"
amount of dollars in one week, you will earn
52 times that amount in a year. If you used a
weekly table for biweekly wages, the annual
income would be overstated twofold.)

MARRIED Persons - **WEEKLY** Payroll Period

If the wages are -		And the number of withholding allowances claimed is -										
At least	But less than	0	1	2	3	4	5	6	7	8	9	10
		The amount of income tax to be withheld is -										
145	150	4	0	0	0	0	0	0	0	0	0	0
150	155	5	0	0	0	0	0	0	0	0	0	0
155	160	6	0	0	0	0	0	0	0	0	0	0
160	165	6	0	0	0	0	0	0	0	0	0	0
165	170	7	0	0	0	0	0	0	0	0	0	0
170	175	8	1	0	0	0	0	0	0	0	0	0
175	180	9	2	0	0	0	0	0	0	0	0	0
180	185	9	3	0	0	0	0	0	0	0	0	0
185	190	10	3	0	0	0	0	0	0	0	0	0
190	195	11	4	0	0	0	0	0	0	0	0	0
195	200	12	5	0	0	0	0	0	0	0	0	0
200	210	13	6	0	0	0	0	0	0	0	0	0
210	220	14	8	1	0	0	0	0	0	0	0	0
220	230	16	9	2	0	0	0	0	0	0	0	0
230	240	17	11	4	0	0	0	0	0	0	0	0
240	250	19	12	5	0	0	0	0	0	0	0	0
250	260	20	14	7	0	0	0	0	0	0	0	0
260	270	22	15	8	2	0	0	0	0	0	0	0
270	280	23	17	10	3	0	0	0	0	0	0	0
280	290	25	18	11	5	0	0	0	0	0	0	0
290	300	26	20	13	6	0	0	0	0	0	0	0
300	310	28	21	14	8	1	0	0	0	0	0	0
310	320	29	23	16	9	2	0	0	0	0	0	0
320	330	31	24	17	11	4	0	0	0	0	0	0
330	340	32	26	19	12	5	0	0	0	0	0	0
340	350	34	27	20	14	7	0	0	0	0	0	0
350	360	35	29	22	15	8	1	0	0	0	0	0
360	370	37	30	23	17	10	3	0	0	0	0	0
370	380	38	32	25	18	11	4	0	0	0	0	0
380	390	40	33	26	20	13	6	0	0	0	0	0
390	400	41	35	28	21	14	7	1	0	0	0	0
400	410	43	36	29	23	16	9	2	0	0	0	0
410	420	44	38	31	24	17	10	4	0	0	0	0
420	430	46	39	32	26	19	12	5	0	0	0	0
430	440	47	41	34	27	20	13	7	0	0	0	0
540	550	64	57	50	44	37	30	23	16	10	3	0
550	560	65	59	52	45	38	31	25	18	11	4	0
560	570	67	60	53	47	40	33	26	19	13	6	0
570	580	68	62	55	48	41	34	28	21	14	7	1
580	590	70	63	56	50	43	36	29	22	16	9	2
590	600	71	65	58	51	44	37	31	24	17	10	4
600	610	73	66	59	53	46	39	32	25	19	12	5
610	620	74	68	61	54	47	40	34	27	20	13	7
620	630	76	69	62	56	49	42	35	28	22	15	8
630	640	77	71	64	57	50	43	37	30	23	16	10
890	900	131	118	106	96	89	82	76	69	62	55	49
900	910	134	121	108	98	91	84	77	70	64	57	50
910	920	136	124	111	99	92	85	79	72	65	58	52
920	930	139	127	114	101	94	87	80	73	67	60	53
930	940	142	129	117	104	95	88	82	75	68	61	55
940	950	145	132	120	107	97	90	83	76	70	63	56
950	960	148	135	122	110	98	91	85	78	71	64	58
960	970	150	138	125	112	100	93	86	79	73	66	59
970	980	153	141	128	115	103	94	88	81	74	67	61
980	990	156	143	131	118	105	96	89	82	76	69	62
990	1,000	159	146	134	121	108	97	91	84	77	70	64
1,000	1,010	162	149	136	124	111	99	92	85	79	72	65
1,010	1,020	164	152	139	126	114	101	94	87	80	73	67
1,020	1,030	167	155	142	129	117	104	95	88	82	75	68
1,030	1,040	170	157	145	132	119	107	97	90	83	76	70
1,040	1,050	173	160	148	135	122	110	98	91	85	78	71
1,050	1,060	176	163	150	138	125	112	100	93	86	79	73
1,060	1,070	178	166	153	140	128	115	103	94	88	81	74
1,070	1,080	181	169	156	143	131	118	105	96	89	82	76
1,080	1,090	184	171	159	146	133	121	108	97	91	84	77
1,090	1,100	187	174	162	149	136	124	111	99	92	85	79
1,100	1,110	190	177	164	152	139	126	114	101	94	87	80
1,110	1,120	192	180	167	154	142	129	117	104	95	88	82
1,120	1,130	195	183	170	157	145	132	119	107	97	90	83
1,130	1,140	198	185	173	160	147	135	122	109	98	91	85
1,140	1,150	201	188	176	163	150	138	125	112	100	93	86
1,150	1,160	204	191	178	166	153	140	128	115	102	94	88
1,160	1,170	206	194	181	168	156	143	131	118	105	96	89
1,170	1,180	209	197	184	171	159	146	133	121	108	97	91
1,180	1,190	212	199	187	174	161	149	136	123	111	99	92

Figure 19-3 IRS Tax Tables (Concluded)

CHAPTER 19 Payroll Accounting

425

Chapter 19

✓ ANSWERS

1. federal income tax; social security and medicare tax; city or state income tax
2. marital status; number of exemptions
3. (a) $2.00; (b) $10.00
4. (a) Social sec., $13.89; (b) social sec., $10.04;

CONCEPT DEVELOPMENT
Completing the Payroll Register

Explain that a payroll register is completed for each pay period. All the payroll information for a pay period is included in the payroll register, which becomes the source document for journalizing payroll entries.

Teaching Tips

- Remind students that information recorded in a payroll register is not posted. Only journal entries are posted.
- Remind students that total earnings are the gross earnings for the pay period.

Some common voluntary deductions include those for union dues, health insurance payments, life insurance payments, pension fund contributions, credit union deposits and payments, and charitable contributions.

Before continuing, complete the following activity to check your understanding of deductions from gross earnings.

Check Your Learning

Use notebook paper to write the answers to these questions.

1. List three deductions from employee earnings that are required by law.
2. What two items of information for computing federal income taxes are recorded on an employee's Form W-4?
3. Using the tax tables on pages 424-425, find the amount of taxes for these employees.
   a. Employee 1: Married; claims 2 exemptions; gross weekly earnings, $224.
   b. Employee 2: Single; claims 1 exemption; gross weekly earnings, $162.
4. Calculate the amount of social security tax that each employee in Question 3 must pay.

Compare your answers to those in the answers section. Re-read the preceding part of the chapter to find the correct answers to any questions you may have missed.

Completing the Payroll Register

We mentioned earlier that federal and state laws require businesses to keep accurate records of the amounts paid to employees. A payroll register is one form that is used. The **payroll register** is a form that summarizes information about employees' earnings for each pay period. The payroll clerk is usually responsible for preparing the payroll register.

The payroll register shown in Figure 19-4 is used by Lenker Consulting Service. As you can see, each employee's I.D. number and name are listed along with her or his marital status and the number of exemptions claimed. Refer to this illustration as you read the following descriptions of the other columns in the payroll register:

1. Total Hours Column. The information in this column is taken from each employee's time card. Regular and overtime hours are added together and the total number of hours entered in this column.
2. Rate Column. The employee's current rate of pay is written in this column. The employee's earnings record is the source of information for each employee's rate of pay.
3. Earnings Columns. The earnings section of the payroll register is divided into three columns: regular earnings, overtime earnings, and total earnings. To complete these columns, the payroll clerk must multiply the employee's total hours worked by the employee's hourly rate.

426

UNIT 4   Accounting for a Payroll System

Reteaching Strategies

Students sometimes need reinforcement to understand the concept of exemptions. Explain that an exemption is an allowance that reduces your tax liability. In addition to having an allowance for yourself, you are entitled to additional allowances for each person to whom you provide more than one-half of their support during the year. For example, an individual may be able to claim an allowance for himself or herself, for a child, and for a parent who lives in the household.

EMP. NO.	NAME	MAR.	EXEMP	TOTAL HOURS	RATE	EARNINGS REGULAR	OVERTIME	TOTAL	SOC. SEC. TAX	MEDICARE TAX	FED. INC. TAX	STATE INC. TAX	HOSP. INS.	OTHER	TOTAL	NET PAY	CK. NO.
012	Cropp, B.	M	0	39	4.25	165 75		165 75	10 28	2 40	7 00	4 97	3 20	(B) 5 00	32 85	132 90	183
014	Lee, V.	S	0	43	4.10	164 00	18 45	182 45	11 31	2 65	20 00	6 57	—	—	40 53	141 92	184
017	Moore, L.	S	1	41	4.45	178 00	6 67	184 67	11 45	2 68	13 00	6 65	2 10	—	35 88	148 79	185
011	Nielson, K.	S	0	36	4.45	160 20		160 20	9 93	2 33	17 00	4 77	3 20		37 23	122 97	186
018	Thorton, S.	M	1	31	4.25	131 75		131 75	8 17	1 91	5 00	2 74	3 20	(B) 5 00	29 02	107 73	187
	TOTALS					799 70	25 12	824 82	51 14	11 97	60 00	25 70	11 70	(B) 10 00	170 51	654 31	

Other Deductions: Write the appropriate code letter to the left of the amount: B—U.S. Savings Bonds; C—Credit Union; UD—Union Dues; UW—United Way.

Figure 19-4 Payroll Register

For example, Employee 12 worked 39 hours during the week ended June 30. Employee 12, whose hourly rate is $4.25, earned $165.75 for the week. Since no overtime hours were worked, regular earnings and total earnings are the same.

$ 4.25
× 39
$165.75

If an employee works overtime, the overtime earnings are entered in the middle column. Employee 14, for example, worked 3 overtime hours, earning $18.45. That employee's regular and overtime earnings are added and entered in the total earnings column.

$164.00
+ 18.45
$182.45

4. Deductions Columns. On this payroll register, the deductions section is divided into seven columns. (The number of columns in this section varies from company to company.) Look at the deductions recorded for Employee 12. The deductions include those required by law—social security tax, medicare tax, federal income tax, and state income tax—and voluntary deductions for hospital insurance and U.S. savings bonds. After the amount of each deduction is calculated for an employee, the amounts are added and the total is entered in the total deductions column.

$10.28
2.40
9.00
4.97
3.20
+ 5.00
$34.85

5. Net Pay Column. **Net pay** is the amount of money left after all deductions are subtracted from gross earnings. For example, Employee 12's net pay is $130.90.

$165.75
− 34.85
$130.90

6. Check Number Column. Most employees are paid by check. After the payroll checks have been prepared, the check numbers are recorded in this column.

Notice also that each amount column is totaled and the totals entered on the last line of the payroll register. The totals recorded for earnings, deductions, and net pay should be cross-checked to verify the amounts.

R E M E M B E R

Gross (total) earnings minus deductions equals net pay.

Preparing Payroll Checks

Once the payroll register has been checked for accuracy, a paycheck is prepared for each employee. Most businesses prefer to pay their employees

CHAPTER 19   Payroll Accounting

427

Using Visuals

Have students look at the payroll register in Figure 19-4. Go through the information in each column and explain the source of the amounts written in the columns.

Using Visuals

 A teaching transparency showing the payroll register in Figure 19-4 is available in the transparency binder accompanying Glencoe Accounting.

Using Visuals

 Use demonstration problem 19-6 to give students practice in filling out a payroll register.

CONCEPT DEVELOPMENT
Preparing Payroll Checks

Explain why employers often use separate checking accounts for their payroll checks. Discuss the advantages of this procedure (include the control of cash).

Ask students who work whether they have the option of having their paychecks deposited directly to their checking accounts. Direct deposit is becoming more popular today. Ask students to think of advantages of this procedure for the employer, for the employee, and for the bank.

Teaching Tips

■ Assign Problem 19A, page 641, to students who need additional practice preparing a payroll register.

Making Connections

AROUND THE WORLD

U.S. businesses are not the only companies that invest in foreign countries. The German car maker Mercedes has announced that it will build a new plant in the United States near Tuscaloosa, Alabama. The new plant is planned to open in 1996 and will employ 1,500. Additional jobs will be created as other businesses locate nearby to provide parts and supplies to the Mercedes plant.

by check as a means of cash control. When a company has only a few employees, paychecks are often written on the company's regular checking account. Companies with several employees, however, generally have a separate checking account for payroll.

When a separate payroll account is used, funds must be put into this payroll account each pay period. This is usually done by writing a check on the company's regular checking account for the amount of the total net pay. This check is then deposited in the payroll checking account.

The payroll register is the source of information for preparing the paychecks. Along with the paycheck, each employee must be given a written explanation showing how the employee's net pay was calculated. A payroll check has an additional stub that is used for this purpose. A typical payroll check and stub are shown in Figure 19-5. Notice that the amounts recorded on the stub are the same as the amounts recorded in the payroll register for that employee. After each paycheck is written, its number is recorded in the payroll register.

Figure 19-5 Completed Payroll Check and Stub

Some companies offer their employees the option of direct deposit of their paychecks. With **direct deposit,** the employee's net pay is deposited in her or his personal bank account. No paycheck is prepared. The employee does receive a record of the amount of money deposited and the amounts withheld for taxes and other deductions. Direct deposits are usually made through electronic funds transfer. With this system, the employer provides the employee's bank with a computer tape or card showing the wages that should be added to the employee's account. When the tape or card is run through the bank's computer system, the balance in the employee's account is automatically increased.

The Employee's Earnings Record

In addition to the payroll register, the employer must keep an individual payroll record for each employee. This payroll record is kept on a form

UNIT 4   Accounting for a Payroll System

called an **employee's earnings record.** An example of an employee's earnings record appears in Figure 19-6. The same amount columns that appear on the payroll register appear on the earnings record. In addition, there is a column on the earnings record for the employee's accumulated earnings. **Accumulated earnings** are each employee's year-to-date gross earnings, the employee's gross earnings from the beginning of the year through each pay period. For example, Karen Nielson's accumulated earnings as of June 30 are determined by adding her gross earnings for this pay period ($160.20) to her accumulated earnings for the previous pay period ($4,423.41).

$4,423.41
+ 160.20
$4,583.61

The earnings records are kept on a quarterly basis. This makes it easier for a business to complete government reports that are often required each quarter. At the end of each quarter, the amount columns on the earnings record are totaled. The final amount in the accumulated earnings column is carried forward to the top of the employee's earnings record for the next quarter, as shown in Figure 19-6.

Call students' attention to the employee earnings record in Figure 19-6. Compare the amounts in this record with the payroll register and the payroll check and stub on pages 427-428.

Teaching Tips
- Emphasize the need for accurate, up-to-date payroll records.

Using Visuals
Call students' attention to the employee earnings record in Figure 19-6. Compare the amounts in this record with the payroll register and the payroll check and stub on pages 427-428.

EMPLOYEE'S EARNINGS RECORD FOR QUARTER ENDING __ June 30, 19--

Nielson, Karen L.
Last Name   First   Initial
Address 419 East Main Street
Kingston, UT 84743

EMPLOYEE NO. 11   MARITAL STATUS S   EXEMPTIONS Ø
POSITION Office Clerk
RATE OF PAY $4.45   SOC. SEC. NO. 045-68-5733

| PAY PERIOD | | EARNINGS | | | DEDUCTIONS | | | | | | | NET PAY | ACCUMULATED EARNINGS |
NO.	ENDED	REGULAR	OVERTIME	TOTAL	SOCIAL SECURITY	MEDICARE	FED. INC. TAX	STATE INC. TAX	HOSP. INS.	OTHER	TOTAL		
													2309 14
1	4/7/--	178 00		178 00	11 04	2 58	19 00	5 16	3 20		40 98	137 02	2487 14
2	4/14/--	175 77		175 77	10 90	2 55	19 00	5 10	3 20		40 75	135 02	2662 91
3	4/21/--	178 00		178 00	11 04	2 58	19 00	5 16	3 20	(B) 5 00	45 98	132 02	2840 91
4	4/28/--	178 00	13 34	191 34	11 86	2 78	22 00	5 55	3 20		45 39	145 95	3032 25
5	5/5/--	166 87		166 87	10 35	2 42	18 00	4 84	3 20		38 81	128 06	3199 12
6	5/12/--	178 00		178 00	11 04	2 58	19 00	5 16	3 20		40 98	137 02	3377 12
7	5/19/--	175 77		175 77	10 90	2 55	19 00	5 10	3 20	(B) 5 00	45 75	130 02	3552 89
8	5/26/--	178 00		178 00	11 04	2 58	19 00	5 16	3 20		40 98	137 02	3730 89
9	6/2/--	178 00	11 67	189 67	11 76	2 75	21 00	5 50	3 20		44 21	145 46	3920 56
10	6/9/--	151 30		151 30	9 38	2 19	16 00	4 39	3 20		35 16	116 14	4071 86
11	6/16/--	178 00		178 00	11 04	2 58	19 00	5 16	3 20	(B) 5 00	45 98	132 02	4249 86
12	6/23/--	173 55		173 55	10 76	2 52	19 00	5 03	3 20		40 51	133 04	4423 41
13	6/30/--	160 20		160 20	9 93	2 33	17 00	4 77	3 20		37 23	122 97	4583 61
QUARTERLY TOTALS		2249 46	25 01	2274 47	141 04	32 99	246 00	66 08	41 60	(B) 15 00	542 71	1731 76	

Other Deductions: B – U.S. Savings Bonds; C – Credit Union; UD – Union Dues; UW – United Way.

EMPLOYEE'S EARNINGS RECORD FOR QUARTER ENDING __ September 30, 19--

Nielson, Karen L.
Last Name   First   Initial
Address 419 East Main Street
Kingston, UT 84743

EMPLOYEE NO. 11   MARITAL STATUS S   EXEMPTIONS Ø
POSITION Office Clerk
RATE OF PAY $4.45   SOC. SEC. NO. 045-68-5733

| PAY PERIOD | | EARNINGS | | | DEDUCTIONS | | | | | | | NET PAY | ACCUMULATED EARNINGS |
NO.	ENDED	REGULAR	OVERTIME	TOTAL	SOCIAL SECURITY	MEDICARE	FED. INC. TAX	STATE INC. TAX	HOSP. INS.	OTHER	TOTAL		
1													4583 61

Figure 19-6 Employee's Earnings Record

CHAPTER 19 Payroll Accounting

429

CONCEPT DEVELOPMENT
A Computerized Payroll System

When discussing this section, try to set up a viewing of a payroll program being run on a computer. If you do not have access to a computer, try to arrange a visit to a local company that is willing to give a demonstration of its computerized payroll accounting system.

Point out that computer input is usually in numeric form, which is why information for each employee is identified by that employee's identification number rather than by name. Emphasize that the two main advantages of using a computer to record payroll information are (1) speed of operation and (2) reduced chance of error.

Teaching Tips

- Bring in payroll printouts for students to view.

COMPUTERS IN ACCOUNTING

Tax preparation software makes the filing of income tax returns easy, accurate, and complete. Several commercial software packages are available. Some software programs use IRS-approved, computerized forms and guide you through the return so that you do not overlook opportunities for deductions. The data is automatically transferred from federal tax forms to state tax forms. With compatible communications accessories such as a modem and communication software, the return can be filed electronically, enabling the taxpayer to receive a refund within an average of three weeks instead of the usual 12.

---

3 CLOSE

CHAPTER SUMMARY

This summary enumerates the key information in the chapter. It is a useful tool for reinforcement and review.

A Computerized Payroll System

In recent years, computers have become an important part of payroll preparation and reporting for many businesses. Computers can process large quantities of payroll information quickly and accurately, thus helping to ensure that employees are paid on time and that their paychecks are accurate. Many businesses purchase their own computers, while others hire outside firms to process their payrolls for them.

When a company uses a computerized payroll system, basic information about each employee is stored in the computer's files. This information includes the employee's identification number, name, social security number, and method of calculating gross earnings. A payroll clerk normally inputs each employee's I.D. number and the number of hours worked during the pay period. The computer uses this information, along with the stored data on each employee's deductions and exemptions, to compute gross earnings, deductions, and net pay. The computer then prepares the payroll register.

The computer will also print the paychecks and the earnings information on the check stubs. If the employee is paid by direct deposit, the computer prepares the tape listing the amount of each employee's wages. The computer also prints the written record of earnings that each employee receives. The computer then prepares the employee's earnings records.

Many companies have their payrolls prepared by banks that use computerized payroll systems. When the payroll is prepared by a bank, information about each employee is stored in the bank's computers. When it is time for the payroll to be prepared, the number of hours worked by each employee must be communicated to the bank. The bank prepares the paychecks and sends the company a record of its employees' earnings for use in recording payroll information in the accounting system.

Summary of Key Points

1. Most employers have a payroll system to ensure that employees are paid on time and that their paychecks and payroll records are accurate. Employers are required to keep accurate records of all payroll information.
2. Gross earnings may be calculated by various methods: salary, hourly wage, piece rate, commission, or a combination of these methods.
3. An employee who works more than 40 hours per work week must be paid overtime. The overtime rate is $1\frac{1}{2}$ times the regular rate of pay.
4. Deductions from gross earnings are those required by law—such as federal income taxes, social security tax, medicare tax, and city or state income taxes—and those requested by the employee—such as union dues, insurance payments, and charitable contributions.
5. A payroll register is prepared for each pay period to summarize the payroll information for all employees. In addition, an individual earnings record is kept for each employee and updated each pay period.
6. Computers are used in many businesses for payroll preparation. In a computerized payroll system, the computer does all the calculations and prints the payroll register, the employee paychecks and stubs, and the employee's earnings records.

Pop Quiz

1. An employee's taxes are based on ____.
2. If an employee earns $817 for a 40-hour week and also receives overtime pay, how much would the employee earn for an hour of overtime?
3. How can you inform an employer not to withhold federal or state taxes from your pay?
4. True or false: The employer is legally required to withhold mandatory and voluntary payroll deductions.
5. What two payroll records must the employer keep under federal and state laws?

ANSWERS

1. Gross earnings
2. $30.64
3. Write "Exempt" on Form W-4.
4. False. Employers are not required to withhold voluntary deductions.
5. A payroll register and an employee's earnings record for each employee

Review and Applications

Building Your Accounting Vocabulary

In your own words, write the definition of each of the following accounting terms. Use complete sentences for your definitions.

accumulated earnings
commission
deduction
direct deposit
electronic badge reader

employee's earnings record
exemption
gross earnings
net pay
overtime rate
pay period

payroll
payroll clerk
payroll register
piece rate
salary
time card
wage

Reviewing Your Accounting Knowledge

1. What are the two goals of a payroll system?
2. What five tasks are included in a payroll system?
3. What is the difference between a salary and a wage?
4. Why do some businesses pay their employees on a commission basis?
5. What three federal taxes are businesses required to withhold from employees' wages?
6. List three things that determine the amount withheld from employee earnings each pay period for federal income taxes.
7. What is a Form W-4?
8. Describe the programs that are financed by the social security syster
9. Explain the statement "the social security tax is an exact tax."
10. Name some common voluntary deductions that are withheld from employee paychecks.

Improving Your Human Relations Skills

Lenny Alvarez has a part-time job at a local department store. One of his classmates, Paul Tuan, also works at the same store after school and on weekends. One day Paul found Lenny between classes and told him that he would be half an hour late for work that evening. Paul asked Lenny to take his time card and punch in for him so that he would not lose pay for being late. Lenny believes that it is dishonest to punch in for Paul but he wants to remain friendly with him. What should Lenny say to Paul?

Applying Accounting Principles

Exercise 19-1   Calculating Total Hours Worked

Instructions: Part of a time card appears on page 432. Determine the total number of hours worked for the week. Use the form provided in the working papers.

431

PRACTICE AND APPLY

• Concepts and Procedures

Exercise 19-1: Ch. Obj. 2
Total hours, 41 1/4

Exercise 19-2: Ch. Obj. 2

SPREADSHEET

PROBLEM

Exercise 19-2 can be completed using *Spreadsheet Applications,* the spreadsheet software that accompanies *Glencoe Accounting.*

Regular earnings, $946.88
Overtime, $52.84
Gross earnings, $999.72

Exercise 19-3: Ch. Obj. 2, 3
Net pay:
Brown, $139.66
Lutz, $165.25
Lynch, $183.06
Quinn, $204.45
Sell, $175.84
Total pay, $868.26

DAY	IN	OUT	IN	OUT
M	8:03	12:30	1:30	5:10
T	7:49	12:07	12:59	5:05
W	7:58	12:15	12:45	4:30
TH	8:30	12:02	12:35	5:15
F	7:59	12:04	1:04	5:30

SPREADSHEET

PROBLEM

Exercise 19-2   Calculating Gross Earnings

Heywood Music Center has five employees. They are paid on a weekly basis with overtime for all hours worked over 40 per week. The overtime rate is $1\frac{1}{2}$ times the regular rate of pay. Employee names and other payroll information are given below.

David Brown: Single; 1 exemption; rate per hour, $4.95
Tonya Lutz: Single; 1 exemption; rate per hour, $5.25
Pat Lynch: Single; 2 exemptions; rate per hour, $4.80
Betty Quinn: Married; 2 exemptions; rate per hour, $4.90
Richard Sell: Married; 3 exemptions; rate per hour, $4.90

The time cards show that the total hours worked by each employee the week ending July 17 are listed here.

Brown: $33\frac{1}{2}$ hours   Quinn: $44\frac{1}{4}$ hours
Lutz: 38 hours   Sell: $39\frac{1}{2}$ hours
Lynch: 43 hours

Instructions: Use a form similar to the one that follows. Calculate the amount of regular earnings, overtime earnings, and gross earnings for each employee. The first employee's earnings have been completed as an example.

Employee	Total Hours	Pay Rate	Regular Earnings	Overtime Earnings	Gross Earnings
Brown, David	$33\frac{1}{2}$	$4.95	$165.83	—	$165.83

Exercise 19-3   Determining Taxes on Gross Earnings

Use the gross earnings computed in Exercise 19-2 to complete this exercise.

Instructions: Determine the amounts to be withheld from each employee's gross earnings for FICA and income taxes. Use the tax charts on pages 424-425 for the federal income tax. The state income tax is 1.5% of gross earnings. The rate for social security tax is 6.2%, and the medicare tax is 1.45%. Use the formula provided in the working papers.

SPREADSHEET

PROBLEM

Problem 19-1   Preparing a Payroll Register

Win's Sport Shop has four employees. They are paid on a weekly basis with overtime paid for all hours over 38. The overtime rate is $1\frac{1}{2}$ times the

Refer students to the Chapter 19 review pages in the workbook, *Chapter Reviews and Working Papers.*

Additional Reinforcement

Students who need additional practice or individualized help will benefit from the *Glencoe Accounting Electronic Study Guide* or the *Glencoe Accounting* on-line multimedia program, which provide reinforcement and reteaching for vocabulary, concepts, and procedures.

regular rate of pay. The employee names and other information needed to prepare the payroll are as follows.

Megan Berg: Single; 0 exemptions; rate per hour, $4.95; employee no. 108
Don Holt: Married; 1 exemption; rate per hour, $5.25; employee no. 112; union member
Lisa Roberts: Married; 2 exemptions; rate per hour, $5.70; employee no. 102; union member
Steven Varga: Single; 1 exemption; rate per hour, $4.80; employee no. 109; union member

During the week ended July 7, Berg worked 39 hours, Holt worked 41 hours, and Varga and Roberts each worked 35 hours.

Instructions:

(1) Prepare a payroll register. List employees in alphabetical order by *last* name. Use the tax charts on pages 424-425 to determine the federal income taxes. There is no state income tax. Compute FICA taxes at 6.2% for social security and 1.45% for medicare. Union members pay weekly dues of $3.80.

(2) After the payroll data is entered in the payroll register, total the columns and check the accuracy of the totals. Date of payment, July 7, 19--.

Problem 19-2   Preparing Payroll Checks and Employee's Earnings Records

Use the payroll register from Problem 19-1 to complete this problem.

Instructions:

(1) Prepare a paycheck and stub for each employee. Record the paycheck numbers in the payroll register.

(2) Record the payroll information in the employee's earnings records.

COMPUTER

PROBLEM

Problem 19-3   Preparing the Payroll

Dan's Audio Center has a total of six employees and pays its employees on a weekly basis. Hourly employees are paid overtime for all hours over 40. The overtime rate is $1\frac{1}{2}$ times the regular rate of pay.

Dan's Audio Center pays its employees by one of three methods: hourly rate, salary, or salary plus a 5% commission on total sales. The following table lists the employees and the method by which their wages are computed.

	Method of Computing Earnings		
Employee	Hourly	Salary	Salary Plus Commission
Chris Carroll		$270.00	
Pat Cashin	$4.95		
Tyler Davis			$160.00 plus 5%
Debbie Strong			$140.00 plus 5%
Jason Witty	$4.65		
Steven Wong			$140.00 plus 5%

Employee deductions include federal income taxes (use the charts on pages 424-425), FICA taxes at 6.2% for social security and 1.45% for medicare, state income taxes of 1.5% of earnings, and a hospital insurance premium of $2.43 for single employees and $4.37 for married employees. Also, Steven Wong and Tyler Davis have $6.00 withheld each week for the purchase of U.S. savings bonds.

433

Problem 19-1: Ch. Obj. 2, 3, 4

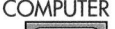
SPREADSHEET

PROBLEM

Problem 19-1 can be completed using Spreadsheet Applications, the spreadsheet software that accompanies *Glencoe Accounting.*

Teaching Tips

■ In this and all other problems in this chapter, remind students to round the overtime rate and tax amounts to the nearest cent.

Net pay:
Berg, $158.57
Holt, $193.27
Roberts, $180.44
Varga, $140.34

Payroll register totals:
Reg. Earnings, $755.10
Overtime, $31.07
Total Earnings, $786.17
Social Sec., $48.74
Medicare, $11.41
FIT, $42.00
Union Dues, $11.40
Total Deductions, $113.55
Net Pay, $672.62

Problem 19-2: Ch. Obj. 5

Problem 19-3: Ch. Obj. 2, 3, 4, 5

COMPUTER

PROBLEM

This computer image identifies a problem that students may complete using the Glencoe Accounting, General Ledger software.

Teacher Notes

Pat Cashin, 41 3/4 hours
Jason Witty, 37 1/2 hours
Pat Cashin's overtime rate: $7.43

Payroll register totals:
Reg. Earnings, $1,345.69
Overtime, $13.00
Total Earnings, $1,358.69
Social Sec., $84.23
Medicare, $19.71
FIT, $61.00
SIT, $20.38
Hospital Ins., $20.40
Savings Bonds, $12.00
Total Deductions, $217.72
Net Pay, $1,140.97

Problem 19-4: Ch. Obj. 2, 3, 4

CHALLENGE

PROBLEM

The last problem (or problems) in each chapter is a challenge problem and is identified by this "maze" symbol.

Totals:
Regular, $1,809.66
Overtime, $7.80
Total, $1,817.46
Social Sec., $112.69
Medicare, $26.36
FIT, $120.00
SIT, $32.70
Hospital Ins., $25.00
Total Deductions, $316.75
Net Pay, $1,500.71

During the pay period ended October 14, the salespeople at Dan's Audio Center sold the following amounts of merchandise: Debbie Strong, $1,925.80; Steven Wong, $2,135.65; and Tyler Davis, $1,204.76. The hourly employees completed the following time cards.

No. 73							
Name *Jason Witty*							
Soc. Sec. No. *093-48-7423*							
Week Ending *10/14/--*							
DAY	IN	OUT	IN	OUT	IN	OUT	TO
M	8:58	12:03	12:55	5:09			
T	8:55	11:55	1:00	4:00			
W	9:30	12:10	1:04	3:30			
Th	8:57	12:03	12:59	6:00			
F	8:58	12:00	1:00	6:05			
S	9:00	12:00					
S							

	TOTAL HOURS		
	Hours	Rate	Amo
REGULAR			
OVERTIME			
	TOTAL EARNINGS		

No. 92						
Name *Pat Cashin*						
Soc. Sec. No. *087-46-3875*						
Week Ending *10/14/--*						
DAY	IN	OUT	IN	OUT	IN	OUT	TOTAL
M	8:55	12:06	1:01	5:35			
T	7:58	11:01	12:03	6:38			
W	9:03	1:10	2:00	6:00			
Th	7:59	11:55	1:10	4:51			
F	9:01	12:06	1:05	3:47			
S	9:00	12:03					
S							

	TOTAL HOURS		
	Hours	Rate	Amount
REGULAR			
OVERTIME			
	TOTAL EARNINGS		

Instructions:
(1) Prepare a payroll register for the week ended October 14. The date of payment is also October 14. Each employee's I.D. number, marital status, and number of exemptions claimed is listed on her or his employee's earnings record.
(2) Prepare a payroll check and stub for each employee.
(3) Record the payroll information for each employee on her or his employee's earnings record.

CHALLENGE

PROBLEM

Problem 19-4   Preparing the Payroll Register

North Shore Office Products has seven employees who are paid weekly. The hourly employees are paid overtime for all hours worked over 40, at a rate $1\frac{1}{2}$ times their regular rate of pay. The payroll information for each employee is listed below.

Lynn Ferchi:	Married; 2 exemptions; employee no. 105
Judy Fox:	Married; 2 exemptions; employee no. 137
John French:	Single; 1 exemption; employee no. 135
Sonya Knox:	Married; 4 exemptions; employee no. 141
David Kovic:	Single; 0 exemptions; employee no. 139
Pat Printer:	Single; 1 exemption; employee no. 113
Guy Whitten:	Married; 3 exemptions; employee no. 129

Lynn Ferchi is the store manager and is paid a salary of $300.00 per week plus 1% of all sales made in the store. Judy Fox and John French are salespeople who are paid a salary of $200.00 per week plus a 6% commission on all sales over $500.00 per week. Sonya Knox and David Kovic are office

434

workers and are paid an hourly wage of $5.20. Pat Printer is the assistant manager of the store and is paid a weekly salary of $295.00. Guy Whitten is a stock person who is paid $4.40 per hour.

The payroll deductions include federal income tax, social security tax of 6.2%, medicare tax of 1.45%, and state income tax of 1.8%. Sonya Knox and Guy Whitten have $12.50 deducted each week for hospital insurance.

During the week ended March 24, Judy Fox had sales of $2,184.90 and John French had sales of $2,341.70. During the week, Sonya Knox worked 41 hours, David Kovic worked 38½ hours, and Guy Whitten worked 34 hours.

Instructions: Prepare a payroll register for the week ended March 24. Use the tax tables provided in the chapter.

CHALLENGE PROBLEM **Problem 19-5   Preparing the Payroll Register**

Belco Products, Inc., is a small manufacturer of plastic products. The company has 10 employees, all of whom are paid weekly. Overtime is paid at a rate of 1½ times the regular rate of pay for all hours worked over 40. Production employees are paid an hourly rate plus 20¢ for each piece over 300 produced per week. The payroll information for each employee appears below.

	Emp. No.	Marital Status	No. of Exemp.	Method of Payment
Lee Chan	108	M	1	Salary $52,520 a year
Rita Cortez	116	S	0	$5.75 per hour
Stanley Garfield	137	S	2	$6.00 per hour plus piece rate
Jan Hunt	144	M	3	$5.90 per hour plus piece rate
John McGarrell	156	S	1	$5.50 per hour
Pat Ritzmann	173	M	6	Salary $59,800 a year
Sarah Schoenle	178	M	1	$6.20 per hour plus piece rate
Peggy Sellers	186	M	4	$6.20 per hour plus piece rate
Carol Stack	189	S	2	Salary $500 a week
Gary Wright	192	M	3	Salary $275 a week plus 3% of sales

Additional information needed to complete the payroll for the week ended December 21 is shown here.

	Hours Worked	Pieces Produced	Sales	Accumulated Earnings
Lee Chan				$50,500.00
Rita Cortez	43			12,750.00
Stanley Garfield	40	356		13,016.75
Jan Hunt	35	269		8,610.90
John McGarrell	41			11,350.50
Pat Ritzmann				57,500.00
Sarah Schoenle	42	402		16,400.50
Peggy Sellers	40	325		14,982.19
Carol Stack				25,000.00
Gary Wright			$21,025.00	44,394.25

The payroll deductions include federal income tax, social security tax of 6.2%, medicare tax of 1.45%, and state income tax of 1.5%. The maximum taxable earnings for social security are $60,600. All employees have hospital insurance deductions of $5.25 for single employees and $7.50 for married employees.

Instructions: Prepare a payroll register for the week ended December 21.

435

CHALLENGE

PROBLEM

The last problem (or problems) in each chapter is a challenge problem and is identified by this "maze" symbol.

Totals:
Regular, $4,994.85
Overtime, $52.74
Total, $5,047.59
Social Sec., $312.95
Medicare, $73.19
FIT, $519.00
SIT, $75.73
Hospital Ins., $66.00
Total Deductions, $1,046.87
Net Pay, $4,000.72

4 ASSESS

A chapter test is available for use in assessing students' understanding of concepts in this chapter.

The testmaker software will enable you to develop tailor-made chapter, unit, semester, and final tests.

Alternative Assessment

For alternative assessment strategies, refer to *Tech Prep Strategies in Accounting.*

Use Chapter Test 19 here to assess students' understanding and retention of the concepts and procedures presented in the chapter.

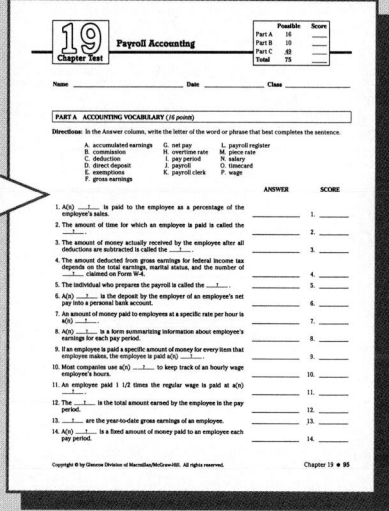

FOCUS ON
COMPUTERS

In his 1992 campaign, President Clinton promised to replace the out-of-date computer system then in the White House. Have students research the progress the President has made on buying new computers. Ask them to try to find the cost of improving the White House computer system.

QUESTIONS

1. If, as indicated in the text, 18 files are kept for every living citizen of the United States, how many files exist today given today's population total?
2. Give an example of how computers are used in your state or local government.

ANSWERS

1. Given a U.S. population of 253 million, 4,554,000,000 files exist.
2. Answers will vary but could involve population counts, voting records, vehicle registration, tax information, services billing, and the like.

*C*omputers in Government

Imagine what it's like for the federal government to keep track of all its citizens, property, services, and legislation; enforce its laws; monitor its businesses; and protect its borders.

While it's not known exactly how much information the federal government maintains, here's one statistic that will help to put things in perspective. The computer archives of government agencies keep an average of 18 files on every living citizen. Without the aid of computers, the paperwork and people needed to process it would be out of control.

The United States government is the biggest computer user in the world. Here are some examples of how computers help various agencies within our federal government function.

The *Internal Revenue Service* processes over 95 million tax returns a year. They're sorted at the rate of 30,000 an hour, thanks to high-speed bar code readers; checked by computers; and stored on magnetic tape.

In 1890 Herman Hollerith's tabulating machine helped the *U.S. Census Bureau* count the population. It took six weeks to tabulate a population of 62,622,250. Today, computers keep a running count of our population, deaths, and births.

The *Securities and Exchange Commission* processes 6 million pages of documents every year to regulate the transactions of public corporations. It can retrieve instantly any data filed by the 10,000 corporations it regulates.

The *Social Security Administration* keeps records on 100 million workers and issues monthly checks to 36 million people. Without the help of computers, these tasks would require the efforts of thousands of clerks.

The *Federal Bureau of Investigation (FBI)* stores a database of over 8 million records. These

Computers can perform calculations quickly and accurately. The Cray Supercomputer, shown here, can perform 600 million calculations per second.

records are accessed by local police at the rate of 540,000 calls every day.

The *U.S. Forestry Service* operates in a shared information environment. All full-time personnel are computer literate. They use electronic mail, manage fires and supplies, and prepare environmental impact statements on computers.

Computers help our government manage a mountain of data.

436

Chapter 20

PAYROLL AND TAX RECORDS

In Chapter 19, you learned that employers use a payroll system to ensure that their employees are paid on time and that the amounts they are paid are accurate. Many businesses hire a payroll clerk whose sole responsibility is to prepare the payroll.

You also learned in Chapter 19 that various amounts are withheld from employees' earnings for taxes and other voluntary deductions. Employers are also required to pay taxes on their employees' earnings. You will learn about those taxes in this chapter. You'll also learn how to record the various journal entries affecting payroll in the business's accounting records.

LOOKING BACK

In Chapter 19 students learned to calculate both earnings and deductions. In this chapter students will learn to journalize and post the salaries expense and the payroll tax expenses for a pay period. In addition, students will be introduced to some of the reports and forms that employers are required to file with the government.

VOCABULARY DEVELOPMENT

Discuss the definitions of the new terms in class. Ask students to give their definition of each term and to explain how each is used in accounting. Definitions of these terms are found in the chapter and in the glossary on pages 670-679.

Electronic Field Trips

Learning Objectives

When you have completed Chapter 20, you should be able to do the following:

1. Record payroll information in the cash payments journal.
2. Describe and calculate the employer's payroll taxes.
3. Record the employer's payroll taxes in the general journal.
4. Identify tax reports that are prepared regularly by the employer.
5. Define the accounting terms introduced in this chapter.

New Terms

unemployment taxes
federal tax deposit coupon
Form 941
Form W-2
Form W-3
Form 940

437

Teaching Resources

- Lesson Plans
- TE/Chapter Reviews & Working Papers
- Demonstration Problems
- Student Study Plans
- Teaching Transparencies
- Solutions Transparencies
- Electronic Field Trips Video, Level I
- Electronic Study Guide
- Chapter 3 Test
- Unit 4 Objective Test for Chapters 19-20
- Unit 4 Problem Test for Chapters 19-20

Other Resources

- Skills Improvement Activities
- Blackline Masters
- Careers in Accounting
- Dictionary
- Math Review for Accounting
- Tech Prep Strategies in Accounting
- Video
- Test Bank with Software
- Spanish Resources/Audiotapes
- Spanish Electronic Study Guide

MAJOR CONCEPTS

- Journalizing and Posting the Payroll
- Computing the Employer's Payroll Taxes
- Paying the Payroll Tax Liabilities
- Filing the Employer's Quarterly Federal Tax Return
- Filing the Employer's Annual Tax Reports

BUSINESS CONNECTION

On August 24, 1992, Hurricane Andrew left 250,000 people homeless and destroyed property estimated at over $20 billion in Florida and $1.5 billion in Louisiana. Some businesses were completely destroyed. Mike Kurtz Plumbing lost its entire office, including its computers. The IRS granted relief to taxpayers who were unable to meet their federal tax obligations by extending the deadline for submission of tax forms.

2 TEACH

CONCEPT DEVELOPMENT
Journalizing and Posting the Payroll

Put the entire entry on the chalkboard, using T accounts, and explain each part of the entry. Emphasize these points.

1. The amount of total gross earnings for the pay period is entered in the cash payments journal as a debit to Salaries Expense.
2. Deductions are liabilities of the employer because the employer has possession of the employees' money and owes it to various companies and government agencies.
3. The amount of money "taken home" by employees is called the net pay. The Cash in Bank account is credited for this amount.
4. The entry to record the payment of the payroll is a compound entry. Cash is decreased by the payment, so the entry is recorded in the cash payments journal.

Journalizing and Posting the Payroll

In Chapter 19, you learned that a check is written to transfer the total net pay amount from the business's regular checking account to the business's payroll checking account. For Lenker Consulting Service, the check written on June 30 was for $654.31. The check is deposited in the payroll account, and all paychecks for the period are drawn on this payroll account. When that check is recorded in the cash payments journal, the payroll transaction amounts are entered into the employer's accounting system. The payroll register contains all the information needed to make the journal entry to record the payroll.

Analyzing the Payroll Transaction

Let's analyze the effect of the payment of the payroll on the employer's accounting system. Each pay period, the business pays out a certain amount of money to its employees in the form of wages. Employee wages are a normal operating expense of a business. The expense account used to record employees' earnings is often called Salaries Expense.

Salaries Expense	
Dr.	Cr.
+	–
$824.82	

The payment of the payroll increases the expenses of the business. To increase the amount in Salaries Expense, the account is debited for the total gross earnings for the pay period. For example, the total amount of gross earnings shown on Lenker's payroll register for the week ended June 30 is $824.82 (see Figure 20-1 on page 440). This amount is recorded as a debit to Salaries Expense.

R E M E M B E R

The total gross earnings each pay period is debited to Salaries Expense.

Various deductions, such as those for income and FICA taxes, are withheld from employees' gross earnings each pay period. The employer holds the amounts deducted from gross earnings until the specified times for paying them to the appropriate government agencies and businesses. These amounts are, therefore, *liabilities* of the employer since they are to be paid some time in the future.

Each type of payroll liability is recorded in a separate account. For example, total employees' federal income taxes withheld are recorded in Employees' Federal Income Tax Payable, employees' FICA taxes are recorded in Social Security Tax Payable and Medicare Tax Payable, and so on. The liability accounts used by Lenker Consulting Service to record payroll deductions are

> Employees' Federal Income Tax Payable
> Employees' State Income Tax Payable
> Social Security Tax Payable
> Medicare Tax Payable
> Hospital Insurance Premiums Payable
> U.S. Savings Bonds Payable

Amounts deducted from employees' earnings and held for payment by the employer are recorded as liabilities in the accounting records.

Let's look now at the credit part of the journal entry needed to record the payment of the payroll. The credit part of the journal entry is made up of several items. The largest item is for the amount of net pay. This is the amount actually paid out in cash by the employer to the employees. Cash in Bank, therefore, is credited for the total amount of net pay.

The difference between gross earnings and net pay equals the employer's payroll liabilities. Each payroll liability account is credited for its total amount shown on the payroll register. The following T accounts illustrate the effect of the payroll transaction. You can see that the credit part of the entry for Lenker Consulting Service is made up of seven parts.

Cash in Bank		Employees' Federal Income Tax Payable		Employees' State Income Tax Payable	
Dr.	Cr.	Dr.	Cr.	Dr.	Cr.
+	–	–	+	–	+
	$654.31		$60.00		$25.70

Social Security Tax Payable		Medicare Tax Payable		Hospital Insurance Premiums Payable		U.S. Savings Bonds Payable	
Dr.	Cr.	Dr.	Cr.	Dr.	Cr.	Dr.	Cr.
–	+	–	+	–	+	–	+
	$51.14		$11.97		$11.70		$10.00

As you can see from these T accounts, the business has paid out $654.31 in cash (the total net pay). The business owes the federal government $60.00 for employees' federal income taxes, $51.14 for the employees' social security taxes, and $11.97 for the employees' medicare taxes. The business also owes employees' state income taxes of $25.70. The insurance company is owed $11.70. Finally, the federal government is owed $10.00 toward the purchase of U.S. savings bonds by the employees. The total of *all* these amounts is equal to the total gross earnings debited to Salaries Expense: $824.82.

$654.31
60.00
51.14
11.97
25.70
11.70
+ 10.00
$824.82

Recording the Payroll in the Cash Payments Journal

The totals line of the payroll register is the source of information for recording the payroll transaction in the cash payments journal. Figure 20-1 on page 440 illustrates this entry. The amount of total gross earnings is debited to Salaries Expense. Each of the payroll liability accounts is credited for its individual column total. (Several different types of deductions may be recorded in the Other Deductions column of the payroll register. If so, the total for each *type* of deduction is determined and credited to the liability account.) Cash in Bank is credited for the amount of net pay.

Figure 20-1   Recording the Entry for Payroll in the Cash Payments Journal

This entry could also be recorded in a general journal. As you can see in Figure 20-2, the journal entry is basically the same as the entry recorded in the cash payments journal. The only difference is that Cash in Bank is listed separately instead of being recorded in a special amount column.

Figure 20-2   Recording the Entry for Payroll in a General Journal

Posting the Payroll Entry to the General Ledger

As you remember, amounts entered in the General columns of the cash payments journal are posted to the general ledger accounts individually.

Amounts entered in the special amount columns of the cash payments journal are posted as totals at the end of the month. The credit to Cash in Bank on June 30 is included in the Cash in Bank Credit column total that is posted at the end of the month. The posting of the journal entry for the payroll is shown in Figure 20-3.

440   UNIT 4   Accounting for a Payroll System

CASH PAYMENTS JOURNAL   PAGE 12

DATE	DOC. NO.	ACCOUNT TITLE	POST. REF.	GENERAL DEBIT	GENERAL CREDIT	ACCOUNTS PAYABLE DEBIT	PURCHASES DISCOUNTS CREDIT	CASH IN BANK CREDIT
June 30	362	Salaries Expense	630	824 82				654 31
		Social Security Tax Payable	220		51 14			
		Medicare Tax Payable	225		11 97			
		Emp. Fed. Inc. Tax Payable	210		60 00			
		Emp. State Inc. Tax Payable	215		25 70			
		Hospital Ins. Prem. Pay.	230		11 70			
		U. S. Savings Bonds Payable	235		10 00			

ACCOUNT *Salaries Expense*   ACCOUNT NO. 630

DATE	EXPLANATION	POST. REF.	DEBIT	CREDIT	BALANCE DEBIT	BALANCE CREDIT
June 16		✓			16 990 30	
23		CP11	690 80		17 681 10	
30		CP12	824 82		18 505 92	

ACCOUNT *Employees' Federal Income Tax Payable*   ACCOUNT NO. 210

DATE	EXPLANATION	POST. REF.	DEBIT	CREDIT	BALANCE DEBIT	BALANCE CREDIT
June 23	Balance	✓				135 61
30		CP12		60 00		195 61

ACCOUNT *Employees' State Income Tax Payable*   ACCOUNT NO. 215

DATE	EXPLANATION	POST. REF.	DEBIT	CREDIT	BALANCE DEBIT	BALANCE CREDIT
June 23	Balance	✓				294 28
30		CP12		25 70		319 98

ACCOUNT *Social Security Tax Payable*   ACCOUNT NO. 220

DATE	EXPLANATION	POST. REF.	DEBIT	CREDIT	BALANCE DEBIT	BALANCE CREDIT
June 23	Balance					189 45
30		CP12		51 14		240 59

ACCOUNT *Medicare Tax Payable*   ACCOUNT NO. 225

DATE	EXPLANATION	POST. REF.	DEBIT	CREDIT	BALANCE DEBIT	BALANCE CREDIT
June 23	Balance					59 89
30		CP12		11 97		71 86

ACCOUNT *Hospital Insurance Tax Payable*   ACCOUNT NO. 230

DATE	EXPLANATION	POST. REF.	DEBIT	CREDIT	BALANCE DEBIT	BALANCE CREDIT
June 23	Balance	✓				35 10
30		CP12		11 70		46 80

ACCOUNT *U. S. Savings Bonds Payable*   ACCOUNT NO. 235

DATE	EXPLANATION	POST. REF.	DEBIT	CREDIT	BALANCE DEBIT	BALANCE CREDIT
June 23	Balance	✓				40 00
30		CP12		10 00		50 00

Figure 20-3   Posting the Payroll Entry to the General Ledger

CHAPTER 20   Payroll and Tax Records   441

Using Visuals

Have students trace the posting of the cash payments journal entries in Figure 20-3.

ACCOUNTING ISSUES

The federal income tax is a government tax based on annual incomes; and employers are required to withhold the tax from employees' wages. Each year, vast amounts of income are not reported to the Internal Revenue Service. An estimated $11 billion spent on child care alone goes unreported. Many Americans do not realize that when they hire individuals to perform domestic services such as house cleaning, gardening, or babysitting that an employer-employee relationship might exist and that they may be required to withhold federal income taxes and other appropriate payroll taxes.

ANSWERS

1. gross earnings
2. liabilities
3. net pay
4. cash payments

CONCEPT DEVELOPMENT
Computing the Employer's Payroll Taxes

Students often have difficulty identifying the difference between the Salaries Expense account and the Payroll Tax Expense account. Point out that these payroll taxes are paid entirely by the employer. They are based on the total gross earnings of all employees, but the money to pay these taxes is not subtracted from the employees' paychecks.

Using Visuals

Read the photo caption to students. Ask students to suggest reasons why payroll is the most likely business activity to be computerized.

Before reading any further, do the following activity to check your understanding of the journal entry made to record the payroll.

Check Your Learning

Write your answers to these questions on notebook paper.

1. The amount recorded and posted to the Salaries Expense account is the total ___?___ for the pay period.
2. The amounts deducted from the gross earnings of the employees are considered ___?___ of the business until they are paid.
3. Cash in Bank is credited for the total ___?___ for the period.
4. If a business uses special journals, the payment of wages is recorded in the ___?___ journal.

Compare your answers to those in the answers section. Re-read the preceding part of the chapter to find the correct answers to any questions you may have missed.

Computing the Employer's Payroll Taxes

In addition to withholding money for taxes from employees' wages, the employer must also *pay* taxes on its employees' wages. The employer's taxes are considered operating expenses of the business. They usually consist of the employer's FICA taxes, the federal unemployment tax, and the state unemployment tax.

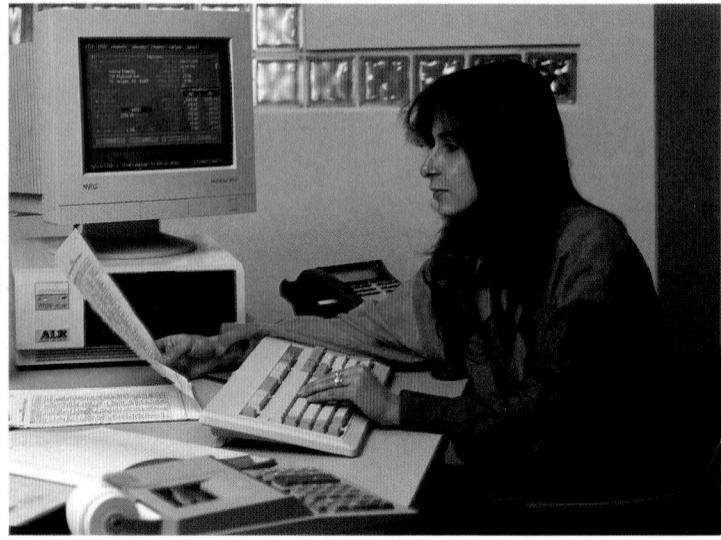

Payroll records are frequently the first of a business's accounting records to be computerized.

Reteaching Strategies

The journal entry to record the payment of payroll is easy when you get the information from the payroll register. Ask students to refer to the payroll register on page 427. The total earnings is the amount debited to salaries expense. Each of the liabilities that the employer owes because of the money withheld from employee earnings is found under Deductions in the payroll register. The Net Pay in the payroll register is the amount credited to the cash account.

The Employer's FICA Taxes

Under the Federal Insurance Contributions Act, the employee and the employer must both pay the FICA taxes on the employee's earnings. As you recall, an employee pays set percentages of her or his gross earnings for social security tax and medicare tax. The employer likewise pays the same set percentages on the employee's total gross earnings as taxes. The current rates are 6.2% for social security tax and 1.45% for medicare tax.

At Lenker Consulting Service for the week ended June 30, the employees' total social security taxes were $51.14 and the total medicare taxes were $11.97. The employer's taxes on the employees' earnings are $51.14 and $11.96 (6.2% of $824.82 and 1.45% of $824.82). Occasionally, a difference of a few cents results because the employer's taxes are calculated on the total gross earnings of all employees while employees' taxes are calculated individually. This is why the employees' contribution to the medicare tax is $11.97 and the employer's contribution is $11.96.

The social security taxes are paid on an employee's gross earnings up to $60,600. The medicare taxes are paid on all gross earnings. After an employee has earned $60,600, both the employee and the employer are exempt from paying social security taxes for the remainder of the year. The payroll clerk must check the accumulated earnings on each employee's earnings record to determine when that employee has reached one of these maximum taxable amounts. If the payroll is prepared by computer, the maximum taxable amount is entered into the computer memory at the beginning of the year. When an employee reaches the limit, the computer automatically drops that tax for the employee.

R E M E M B E R

Both employees and employers pay FICA taxes on employees' gross earnings. The same percentage rates are used for both calculations.

Federal and State Unemployment Taxes

The Federal Unemployment Tax Act (FUTA) requires employers to pay unemployment taxes, which are based on a percentage of their employees' gross earnings. **Unemployment taxes** are collected to provide funds for workers who are temporarily out of work. For example, workers who lose their jobs during an economic recession are paid unemployment compensation to help them live until they can find other jobs.

The employer must pay both a federal unemployment tax and a state unemployment tax. The maximum federal unemployment tax is 6.2% on the first $7,000 of an employee's annual wages. The percentage rates for state unemployment taxes vary among states, as do maximum taxable amounts. Employers are allowed to deduct up to 5.4% of their state unemployment taxes from federal unemployment taxes. Most employers then pay a federal tax of .8% (6.2% − 5.4%).

Teaching Tips

■ You may want to discuss the current tax rates and earnings maximums if they are different from the rates presented in the text.

■ Briefly discuss the need for unemployment taxes. A discussion of the unemployment compensation system in your state may be helpful to your students.

■ Remind students that the amount of unemployment taxes paid is based on gross earnings of the employees. Unemployment taxes are paid only by the employer, not the employee.

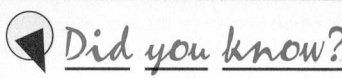 Did you know?

The United States is the fastest-growing industrialized nation in the world. Here is how the population changes each hour:

- 466 people are born
- 249 people die
- 101 people immigrate

The net population change is an increase of 318 people.

ACCOUNTING
PRACTICE
**Students may complete
Exercise 20-2 after the section on
unemployment taxes.**

Using Visuals

 *Use demonstration
problem 20-2 to show
students how to record
the journal entries for the
employer's payroll taxes.*

Teaching Tips

■ Explain that the entry to
record the employer's payroll
taxes is made in the general journal because these taxes have
been incurred but not paid.

Using Visuals

*Call on students to explain
the source of the information
in each line of the journal
entry in Figure 20-4.*

Using Visuals

*A teaching transparen-
cy showing the journal
entry to record the
employer's payroll tax liabilities is available in the transparency binder accompany-
ing Glencoe Accounting.*

$824.82
× .008
$ 6.60
$824.82
× .054
$ 44.54

For Lenker Consulting Service, the federal unemployment tax for the week ended June 30 is found by multiplying the total gross earnings of $824.82 by .8%. Lenker's federal unemployment taxes are $6.60.

The state unemployment tax for the week ended June 30 is determined by multiplying the total gross earnings by 5.4%. Lenker's state unemployment taxes are $44.54.

In a few states, employees are required to pay unemployment taxes. The percentage amounts vary from one state to another.

Journalizing the Employer's Payroll Taxes

The payroll taxes that are paid by the employer are considered to be expenses of doing business. The total payroll taxes are, therefore, recorded in the expense account Payroll Tax Expense. Like the taxes and other deductions withheld from employees' earnings, the employer's taxes are collected and held until they are required to be paid. The employer's payroll taxes thus represent *liabilities* of the business.

$ 51.14
11.96
6.60
+ 44.54
$114.24

The Social Security Tax Payable account and the Medicare Tax Payable account are used to record both the employees' FICA taxes and the employer's FICA taxes. The employer's unemployment taxes are recorded in the accounts Federal Unemployment Tax Payable and State Unemployment Tax Payable.

T accounts can be used to analyze the debit and credit parts of the entry for payroll taxes. The following T accounts illustrate the entry for Lenker Consulting Service's payroll taxes.

Payroll Tax Expense		Social Security Tax Pay		Medicare Tax Payable	
Dr.	Cr.	Dr.	Cr.	Dr.	Cr.
+	-	-	+	-	+
$114.24			$51.14		$11.96

Federal Unemployment Tax Payable		State Unemployment Tax Payable	
Dr.	Cr.	Dr.	Cr.
-	+	-	+
	$6.60		$44.54

Since no check is being written at this time, the employer's payroll tax liabilities are recorded in the general journal. The source document for the journal entry is the payroll register. This general journal entry is shown in Figure 20-4.

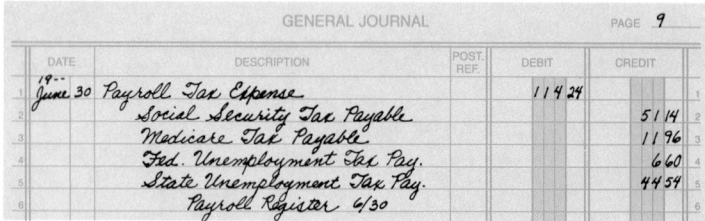

Figure 20-4 Recording the Entry for the Employer's Payroll Taxes

---

Critical Thinking

Paying employees to work overtime is often less expensive for employers than hiring additional personnel. In terms of payroll tax, why would it be cheaper to pay overtime wages than to hire new employees?

(Answers: The employer is liable for taxes up to a specified amount of the employee's annual earnings. For example, currently an employer is required to pay federal unem-

ployment taxes only on the first $7,000 of an employee's earnings during a calendar year. Tax rates for state unemployment tax and social security and medicare taxes are similar. An employer can avoid increased tax liabilities by hiring fewer employees and paying each of them more money in annual wages because of overtime.)

The date used for this journal entry is the same as the ending date of the pay period. The Payroll Tax Expense account is debited for the total amount of the employer's taxes. The individual payroll tax liability accounts are credited for the amount of each tax.

Posting Payroll Taxes to the General Ledger

After the journal entry has been made to record the payroll tax amounts, these amounts are posted to the appropriate general ledger accounts. The posting of the employer's payroll taxes is shown in Figure 20-5.

Figure 20-5 Posting Payroll Taxes to the General Ledger

Using Visuals

Use demonstration problem 20-3 to give students practice recording the entry for the employer's payroll tax liabilities.

Using Visuals

Have students look at the ledger accounts in Figure 20-5. Point out the two equal entries in the Social Security Tax Payable account.

Chapter 20

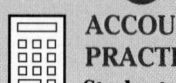

ACCOUNTING PRACTICE
Students may complete
Exercise 20-3 at this point.

ANSWERS

1. $56.00
2. Social Security Tax Payable, Medicare Tax Payable, Federal Unemployment Tax Payable, State Unemployment Tax Payable
3. employer
4. social security, $2,075.07

CONCEPT DEVELOPMENT
Paying the Payroll Tax Liabilities

Explain the procedures used and point out the obligation of the employer to pay the correct amount at the specified time. These taxes are paid weekly, monthly, or quarterly, depending on the amount and state requirements.

Also discuss with students any state or local taxes that must be withheld from gross earnings in your area.

Teaching Tips

■ Both the employer's and the employees' share of social security and medicare taxes are paid at the same time.

Notice that the Social Security Tax Payable and the Medicare Tax Payable accounts have two entries for the June 30 payroll. The first entry in each account was posted from the cash payments journal. It is the amount of taxes withheld from the *employees'* earnings. The second entry is the amount of taxes paid by the *employer* on the employees' total gross earnings for the pay period.

Check Your Learning

Use notebook paper to write your answers to the following questions.

1. If the federal unemployment tax rate is .8%, how much has the employer paid in federal unemployment taxes on one employee's accumulated earnings of $14,264.91?
2. What are the titles of the liability accounts used to record the employer's payroll taxes?
3. Payroll taxes are usually paid only by the ___?___.
4. What is the amount of the employer's social security taxes on employees' gross earnings of $33,468.92?

Compare your answers to those in the answers section. Re-read the preceding part of the chapter to find the answers to any questions you missed.

Paying the Payroll Tax Liabilities

At regular intervals, the payroll taxes and the amounts withheld from employees' earnings are paid by the employer. These amounts include (1) FICA and employees' federal income taxes, (2) employees' state income taxes, (3) federal and state unemployment taxes, and (4) amounts voluntarily withheld from employees' earnings.

FICA and Federal Income Taxes

The payment made for social security and medicare taxes includes both the employees' and the employer's tax amounts. The payment for employees' federal income taxes is the total amount of taxes withheld from employees' earnings for federal income tax. These two amounts are sent in one payment to the appropriate government agency or to a bank designated by the Internal Revenue Service to receive such payments. The payment must be made when the total of the two taxes owed is $500.00 or more. The business writes one check for the total amount owed. For Lenker Consulting Service, this is monthly. Larger businesses may pay these taxes weekly.

After recording the June 30 payroll and the employer's payroll taxes, Lenker Consulting Service found that its employees' federal income tax, social security tax, and medicare tax liabilities totaled $571.16. This amount included the employees' federal income taxes of $195.61, social security taxes of $291.73, and medicare taxes of $83.82.

A **federal tax deposit coupon** (Form 8109) is also prepared and sent with the check to show the amount of taxes being sent to the federal government. The Form 8109 prepared by Lenker Consulting Service is shown in Figure 20-6. Notice the ovals on the right side of the form. One oval is filled in

446

UNIT 4   Accounting for a Payroll System

Reteaching Strategies

The maximum wage for social security and medicare taxes can change each year based on inflation and the cost of living. The employer must contribute an amount equal to the amount that each employee pays.

Use Problem 20A, page 641, to give students extra practice in calculating payroll taxes.

446   UNIT 4   Accounting for a Payroll System

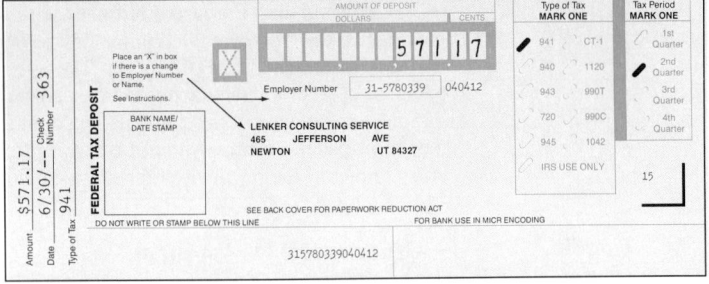

Figure 20-6 Federal Tax Deposit Coupon (Form 8109)

Using Visuals

Point out the federal tax deposit coupon in Figure 20-6. The check accompanying the deposit coupon is made out to a local bank that is a member of the Federal Reserve System. This bank then forwards the funds to the IRS.

to indicate which tax is being paid, and one oval is filled in to indicate the tax period covered. The oval for the FICA and federal income tax payment is the one labeled "941."

The check written to pay social security, medicare, and employees' federal income taxes is recorded in the cash payments journal. The entry is shown on lines 10, 11, and 12 in Figure 20-7. Since the liability accounts Employees' Federal Income Tax Payable, Social Security Tax Payable, and Medicare Tax Payable are being decreased by the payment, those accounts are debited. Employees' Federal Income Tax Payable is debited for $195.61, Social Security Tax Payable is debited for $291.73, and Medicare Tax Payable is debited for $83.82. Cash in Bank is also being decreased by the payment, so that account is credited for the total amount being paid out, $571.16.

Using Visuals

 Use demonstration problem 20-4 to give students practice in journalizing the entry to record the payment of the payroll tax liabilities.

			CASH PAYMENTS JOURNAL						PAGE 12	
DATE	DOC. NO.	ACCOUNT TITLE	POST. REF.	GENERAL DEBIT	GENERAL CREDIT	ACCOUNTS PAYABLE DEBIT	PURCHASES DISCOUNTS CREDIT	CASH IN BANK CREDIT	
June 30	363	Emp. Fed. Inc. Tax Payable		195 61				571 16	10
		Social Security Tax Payable		291 73					11
		Medicare Tax Payable		83 82					12
30	364	Emp. State Inc. Tax Pay.		319 98				319 98	13
30	365	Fed. Unemploy. Tax Pay.		63 41				63 41	14
30	366	State Unemploy. Tax Pay.		272 29				272 29	15
30	367	Hosp. Ins. Premiums Pay.		46 80				46 80	16
30	368	U.S. Savings Bonds Pay.		50 00				50 00	17

Figure 20-7 Recording the Journal Entries for the Payment of Payroll Liabilities

Using Visuals

Point out that checks are written to pay the payroll liabilities (recorded in Figure 20-7) and are then recorded in the cash payments journal.

State Income Taxes

The amounts withheld by the employer for employees' state income taxes are also paid regularly. The entry to record the payment of a state income tax liability is shown on line 12 in Figure 20-7.

Federal and State Unemployment Taxes

Most businesses pay the federal unemployment tax quarterly. If a business has accumulated federal unemployment taxes of less than $100 for the year, only one annual payment is necessary. A federal tax deposit coupon

---

Making Connections

AROUND THE WORLD

Trade sanctions kept many companies from investing in South Africa in recent years. With changes in the South African government, many companies are taking a new look at business opportunities in that country. One U.S. company that quickly jumped on the bandwagon is Pillsbury, which is forming a joint venture with Foodcorp, a South African company, to make and market Pillsbury products in South Africa.

Chapter 20

Using Visuals

 Use demonstration problem 20-5 to give students practice in recording the payment of payroll liabilities.

Teaching Tips

■ All payments for other deductions are to be made by the employer in a timely manner.

 ANSWERS

1. Six
2. The payments were made to different government agencies and businesses.
3. $571.16
4. $51.14
5. $1,323.64
6. $0

(Form 8109) is also prepared and sent with the check for federal unemployment taxes. The oval filled in for this payment is labeled "940," which is the number assigned to FUTA taxes. The journal entry made to record the payment of federal unemployment taxes is shown on line 13 in Figure 20-7.

State unemployment taxes are also paid on a quarterly basis. The requirements for paying unemployment taxes vary from state to state. The journal entry to record the payment of the state employment taxes is shown on line 14 in Figure 20-7.

Other Liability Amounts

In addition to the payments for taxes, an employer is also responsible for making payments to appropriate organizations for all voluntary deductions from employees' earnings. For Lenker Consulting Service, these deductions are for insurance premiums and U.S. savings bonds. Other companies may withhold amounts from employees' earnings for union dues, charitable contributions, and so on.

On June 30, Lenker Consulting Service prepared checks to pay the amounts withheld for employees' insurance premiums ($46.80) and the amounts withheld for the employees' purchase of U.S. savings bonds ($50.00). The journal entries for these two cash payments are shown on lines 15 and 16 in Figure 20-7.

Posting the Journal Entries for Payment of Payroll Liabilities

After all the payments for the employer's payroll liabilities have been recorded, the entries are posted to the appropriate general ledger accounts. The postings made to Lenker Consulting Service's general ledger accounts are shown in Figure 20-8 on pages 449-450.

 ### Check Your Learning

Use Figure 20-8 on page 449 to answer these questions.

1. How many different entries were made on June 30 to record the checks written by Lenker Consulting Service to pay its payroll liabilities?
2. Why wasn't just one check written to pay all the payroll liabilities?
3. What was the amount of the check written to pay the FICA and employees' federal income taxes?
4. What was the total liability for unemployment taxes for the June 30 payroll?
5. How much cash did Lenker Consulting Service pay out on June 30 for its payroll liabilities?
6. What is the balance of Hospital Insurance Premiums Payable after all entries have been posted for June 30?

Compare your answers with those in the answers section. Re-read the preceding part of the chapter to find the correct answers to any questions you may have missed.

Reteaching Strategies

Some students may have difficulty remembering the various taxes that businesses must pay on their payrolls. Having students categorize the taxes may help them remember. For example, in the illustration given in the textbook, four federal taxes are paid: employee federal income taxes, social security taxes, medicare taxes, and the federal unemployment tax. Two state taxes are paid: employee state income taxes and the state unemployment tax. The optional withholdings will vary by company.

Assign Problem 20A, page 641, to students who need extra practice calculating and recording the payroll taxes.

CASH PAYMENTS JOURNAL PAGE 12

DATE	DOC. NO.	ACCOUNT TITLE	POST. REF.	GENERAL DEBIT	GENERAL CREDIT	ACCOUNTS PAYABLE DEBIT	PURCHASES DISCOUNTS CREDIT	CASH IN BANK CREDIT
June 30	363	Emp. Fed. Inc. Tax Payable	210	195 61				571 16
		Social Security Tax Pay.	220	291 73				
		Medicare Tax Payable	225	83 82				
30	364	Emp. State Inc. Tax Pay.	215	319 98				319 98
30	365	Fed. Unemploy. Tax Pay.	235	63 41				63 41
30	366	State Unemploy. Tax Pay.	240	272 29				272 29
30	367	Hosp. Ins. Premiums Pay.	230	46 80				46 80
30	368	U.S. Savings Bonds Pay.	235	50 00				50 00

ACCOUNT Employees' Federal Income Tax Payable **ACCOUNT NO.** 210

DATE	EXPLANATION	POST. REF.	DEBIT	CREDIT	BALANCE DEBIT	BALANCE CREDIT
June 23	Balance	✓				135 61
30		CP12		60 00		195 61
30		CP12	195 61			

ACCOUNT Employees' State Income Tax Payable **ACCOUNT NO.** 215

DATE	EXPLANATION	POST. REF.	DEBIT	CREDIT	BALANCE DEBIT	BALANCE CREDIT
June 23	Balance	✓				294 28
30		CP12		25 70		319 98
30		CP12	319 98			

ACCOUNT Social Security Tax Payable **ACCOUNT NO.** 220

DATE	EXPLANATION	POST. REF.	DEBIT	CREDIT	BALANCE DEBIT	BALANCE CREDIT
June 23	Balance	✓				189 45
30		CP12		51 14		240 59
30		G9		51 14		291 73
30		CP12	291 73			

ACCOUNT Medicare Tax Payable **ACCOUNT NO.** 225

DATE	EXPLANATION	POST. REF.	DEBIT	CREDIT	BALANCE DEBIT	BALANCE CREDIT
June 23	Balance	✓				59 89
30		CP12		11 97		71 86
30		G9		11 96		83 82
30		CP12	83 82			

ACCOUNT Hospital Insurance Premiums Payable **ACCOUNT NO.** 225

DATE	EXPLANATION	POST. REF.	DEBIT	CREDIT	BALANCE DEBIT	BALANCE CREDIT
June 23	Balance	✓				35 10
30		CP12		11 70		46 80
30		CP12	46 80			

ACCOUNT U.S. Savings Bonds Payable **ACCOUNT NO.** 230

DATE	EXPLANATION	POST. REF.	DEBIT	CREDIT	BALANCE DEBIT	BALANCE CREDIT
June 23	Balance	✓				40 00
30		CP12		10 00		50 00
30		CP12	50 00			

Figure 20-8 Posting the Payments of Payroll Liabilities to the General Ledger

CHAPTER 20 Payroll and Tax Records

449

Using Visuals

Have students look at Figure 20-8 and trace the posting of the entries in the cash payments journal to the general ledger accounts. The figure continues onto page 450.

Cooperative Learning

CORNERS

Let students choose one of the following topics: Social Security and Medicare Taxes, Federal Unemployment Taxes, State Unemployment Tax, Federal Income Tax, or State Income Taxes. Students work in groups to learn as much as they can about the topic. For each topic students should learn about the following:

• Who pays the tax—employee or employer?
• The current tax rate.
• The forms the employer is required to submit.
• When the employer must pay the taxes.

Ask a spokesperson from each group to present the group findings to the class.

Refer to the "Cooperative Learning" section of Tech Prep Strategies in Accounting for additional cooperative learning strategies.

Figure 20-8   Posting the Payments of Payroll Liabilities to the General Ledger (Concluded)

Filing the Employer's Quarterly Federal Tax Return

Each employer must file a **Form 941,** the employer's quarterly federal tax return. This document reports the accumulated amounts of federal income taxes and FICA taxes withheld from employees' earnings for the quarter. The data for completing Form 941 is obtained from the employees' earnings records and from the tax payments made during the quarter. The employer's quarterly federal tax return prepared by Lenker Consulting Service for the quarter ended June 30 is shown in Figure 20-9 on page 451.

Filing the Employer's Annual Tax Reports

Each employer must complete certain other forms on an annual basis. These forms report payroll information to employees and to various government agencies. The most common forms prepared are the wage and tax statement, the transmittal of income and tax statements, and the employer's federal and state unemployment tax returns.

Wage and Tax Statement

The wage and tax statement is also called Form W-2. **Form W-2** summarizes an employee's earnings and tax deductions for the previous calendar year. This information includes: (1) gross earnings for the year, (2) federal income tax withheld, (3) FICA tax withheld, and (4) state and local income taxes withheld. The form must be prepared and given to each employee by January 31 of the following year. If an employee ends employment before December 31 and requests Form W-2, it must be furnished to the employee within 30 days. A copy of Karen Nielson's Form W-2 from Lenker Consulting Service is shown in Figure 20-10 on page 452.

The number of Form W-2 copies prepared depends on whether state and local income taxes are withheld from employees' earnings. When state and local income taxes are *not* withheld, four copies (A through D) are prepared. The employer sends Copy A to the Internal Revenue Service and gives

450

UNIT 4   Accounting for a Payroll System

Using Visuals

Point out the lines on the form in Figure 20-9 that correspond to various payroll amounts students have learned to calculate in this chapter (e.g., taxable social security wages).

Form **941** — **Employer's Quarterly Federal Tax Return**

Department of the Treasury Internal Revenue Service — 4141 — ▶ For Paperwork Reduction Act Notice, see page 2. — Please type or print.

Your name, address, employer identification number, and calendar quarter of return. (If not correct, please change.)

Name (as distinguished from trade name): **Lenker Consulting Service**
Trade name, if any:
Address and ZIP code: **465 Jefferson Avenue, Newton, UT 84327**

Date quarter ended: **June 30, 19--**
Employer identification number: **31-5780339**

OMB No. 1545-0029

T / FF / FD / FP / I / T

If address is different from prior return, check here ▶ ☐

IRS Use: 1 1 1 1 1 1 1 1 1 1 1 1 2 3 3 3 3 3 3 4 4 4
5 5 5 6 7 8 8 8 8 8 9 9 9 10 10 10 10 10 10 10 10 10

If you are not liable for returns in the future, check here . . . ▶ ☐ — Date final wages paid . . . . ▶

Complete for First Quarter Only		
1a Number of employees (except household) employed in the pay period that includes March 12th ▶	1a	
b If you are a subsidiary corporation AND your parent corporation files a consolidated Form 1120, enter parent corporation employer identification number (EIN) . . ▶ 1b –		
2 Total wages and tips subject to withholding, plus other compensation . . . . ▶	2	9,252 96
3 Total income tax withheld from wages, tips, pensions, annuities, sick pay, gambling, etc. . . ▶	3	773 55
4 Adjustment of withheld income tax for preceding quarters of calendar year (see instructions) . ▶	4	0 00
5 Adjusted total of income tax withheld	5	773 55
6 Taxable social security wages paid . . . . . $ 9,252 96 × 15.02% (.1502)	6	1,389 79
7a Taxable tips reported . . . . $ _____ × 15.02% (.1502)	7a	0 00
b Taxable hospital insurance wages paid . . $ _____ × 2.9% (.029). .	7b	0 00
8 Total social security taxes (add lines 6, 7a, and 7b)	8	1,389 79
9 Adjustment of social security taxes (see instructions for required explanation)	9	0 00
10 Adjusted total of social security taxes (see instructions) . . . . ▶	10	1,389 70
11 Backup withholding (see instructions)	11	0 00
12 Adjustment of backup withholding tax for preceding quarters of calendar year . . . . . ▶	12	0 00
13 Adjusted total of backup withholding	13	0 00
14 Total taxes (add lines 5, 10, and 13) . . . . ▶	14	2,163 34
15 Advance earned income credit (EIC) payments, if any	15	0 00
16 Net taxes (subtract line 15 from line 14). **This must equal line IV below** (plus line IV of Schedule A (Form 941) if you have treated backup withholding as a separate liability)	16	2,163 34
17 Total deposits for quarter, including overpayment applied from a prior quarter, from your records . ▶	17	2,163 34
18 Balance due (subtract line 17 from line 16). This should be less than $500. Pay to IRS . . . . ▶	18	0 00
19 If line 17 is more than line 16, enter overpayment here ▶ $ _____ and check if to be: ☐ Applied to next return **OR** ☐ Refunded.		

Record of Federal Tax Liability (Complete if line 16 is $500 or more.) See the instructions under rule 4 for details before checking these boxes.
Check only if you made eighth-monthly deposits using the 95% rule ▶ ☐   Check only if you are a first time 3-banking-day depositor ▶ ☐

Tax liability   ▼ Do NOT Show Federal Tax Deposits Below ▼

Date wages paid	First month of quarter		Second month of quarter		Third month of quarter	
1st through 3rd	A		I		Q	
4th through 7th	B		J		R	
8th through 11th	C		K		S	
12th through 15th	D					
16th through 19th	E					
20th through 22nd	F		N		V	
23rd through 25th	G		O		W	
26th through the last	H		P		X	
Total liability for month	I	720.08	II	726.44	III	716.82

(Do Not Show Tax Deposits Here)

IV Total for quarter (add lines *I*, *II*, and *III*). **This must equal line 16 above** . . . . ▶

Under penalties of perjury, I declare that I have examined this return, including accompanying schedules and statements, and to the best of my knowledge and belief, it is true, correct, and complete.

Signature ▶ *Ralph M. Lenker*   Title ▶ Owner   Date ▶ 6/30/--

Figure 20-9 Form 941, Employer's Quarterly Federal Tax Return

CHAPTER 20 Payroll and Tax Records — 451

Interdisciplinary Connections

HISTORY/SOCIAL STUDIES

Social Security was America's first social insurance program, part of President Franklin D. Roosevelt's New Deal. It was started in 1935 during the Great Depression as a way to give additional income to retired people. Today Social Security also pays benefits to the disabled and to survivors of workers who have died.

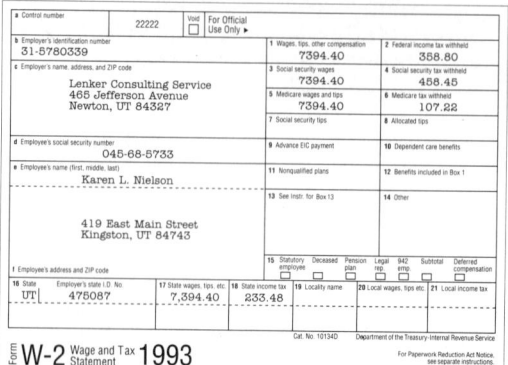

Figure 20-10 Form W-2, Wage and Tax Statement

Copies B and C to the employee. The employee must file Copy B with her or his federal income tax return; Copy C is for the employee's own files. The employer keeps Copy D.

When income taxes are withheld for either the state or local government, two more copies of Form W-2 are prepared. The employer sends one copy to the appropriate state or city agency. The other copy is given to the employee to be filed with state or city income tax returns.

Transmittal of Income and Tax Statements

Form W-3, the transmittal of income and tax statements, is filed by the employer with the Internal Revenue Service. **Form W-3** summarizes the information contained on the employees' Forms W-2. The employer must file Form W-3 by February 28 for the preceding year's taxes. Along with Form W-3, the employer must include Copy A of each employee's Form W-2. The federal government feeds information from the forms into computers for use in checking individual income tax returns. Lenker Consulting Service's Form W-3 is shown in Figure 20-11.

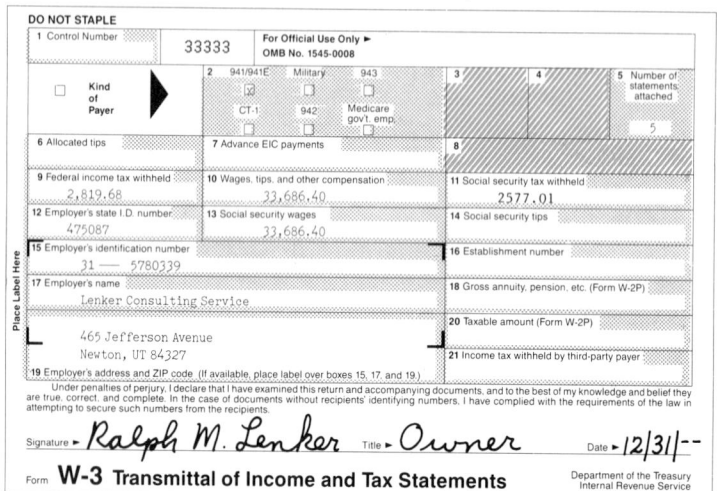

Figure 20-11 Form W-3, Transmittal of Income and Tax Statements

Employer's Federal and State Unemployment Tax Returns

Each employer is also responsible for filing **Form 940,** an employer's annual unemployment tax return. The information on this return includes both federal and state unemployment taxes paid during the year. This form must be filed by January 31 for the preceding calendar year. The requirements for filing state unemployment tax returns vary from state to state.

Summary of Key Points

1. The payroll register is the source of information for preparing the entry to record the payment of the payroll. This entry is recorded in the cash payments journal.
2. Employees' wages are considered to be a normal operating expense for the business. The amount of the total gross earnings is debited to the Salaries Expense account.
3. Amounts deducted from employees' earnings and held by the employer are liabilities of the business. The employer must make regular payments of the amounts withheld to the appropriate government agencies or to other businesses or organizations.
4. Employers are required to pay taxes on the total amount of their employees' gross earnings. These amounts are operating expenses of the business. Employer's payroll taxes include social security and medicare taxes, federal unemployment taxes, and state unemployment taxes.
5. FICA taxes are paid by both the employee and the employer. The same percentages used to calculate employees' deductions are used to determine the employer's FICA taxes. The employer's FICA taxes are calculated on the total gross earnings amount.
6. The entry to record the employer's payroll taxes is made in the general journal.
7. Employers must report earnings and tax information to employees once a year on Form W-2.
8. Each employer is required to file quarterly and annual tax reports on employee earnings and on taxes paid by the employee and the employer.

COMPUTERS IN ACCOUNTING

Processing a company's payroll is time consuming and expensive. As an alternative to processing payroll in house, companies can choose a computer service bureau to run the payroll system for them. Among the advantages of using a bureau are:

- The risk of costly error is eliminated.
- The salary data remains confidential.
- Company personnel are not burdened with the payroll procedures.

3 CLOSE

CHAPTER SUMMARY

This summary enumerates the key information in the chapter. It is a useful tool for reinforcement and review.

Pop Quiz

1. In which journal is the transaction for the payment of payroll recorded?
2. Who is responsible for paying social security and medicare taxes?
3. Who is responsible for paying federal and state unemployment taxes?
4. True or false: If an employer withholds voluntary deductions from an employee's earnings, the employer gives that money back to the employee at the end of the year.

5. How often does the employer file Form 941?

ANSWERS

1. cash payments journal
2. both employee and employer
3. the employer
4. False. The employer sends deductions to appropriate organizations.
5. quarterly (four times a year)

PRACTICE AND APPLY

- Language Development
- Comprehension and Retention
- Basic Skills

Building Your Accounting Vocabulary
See the Glossary on pages 670-679 for definitions of these terms.

Reviewing Your Accounting Knowledge

1. Total gross earnings is charged to Salaries Expense because employee wages (such as net pay, federal taxes, social security and medicare taxes, and insurance payments) are an operating expense of the business.
2. They are to be paid at a time in the future.
3. Cash in Bank.
4. The employer's portion of social security and medicare taxes is determined by multiplying total gross earnings by current tax rates (6.2% and 1.45% in this textbook).
5. The current maximum combined tax rate for federal and state unemployment taxes is 6.2%. Most states have a tax rate of 5.4%, leaving a federal tax rate of .8%.
6. Because the total amount of the tax is an operating expense to the business.
7. The general journal.
8. The employee's earnings records and the tax payments made during the quarter are the source of information for preparing Form 941.
9. Employees must receive W-2 forms by January 31 of the following year. If an employee ends employment before December 31 and requests a Form W-2, it must be furnished within 30 days.
10. Copies B and C of Form W-2 are given to the employee. The employee files Copy B with the federal income tax return. The employee keeps Copy C. If state or local taxes are withheld, two additional copies are provided for attachment to state or local tax returns.
11. Because the federal government feeds information from these forms into computers for use in checking individual tax returns.

Review and Applications

Building Your Accounting Vocabulary

In your own words, write the definition of each of the following accounting terms. Use complete sentences for your definitions.

federal tax deposit coupon	Form W-3	unemployment
Form W-2	Form 940	taxes
	Form 941	

Reviewing Your Accounting Knowledge

1. Why is the amount of the total gross earnings rather than total net pay charged to the Salaries Expense account?
2. Why are the amounts withheld from employees' paychecks liabilities of the employer?
3. What account is credited for the total amount of the employees' net pay?
4. How is the amount owed by the employer for FICA taxes determined?
5. Why do few employers pay the full 6.2% federal unemployment taxes?
6. Why is the employer's share of payroll taxes recorded in Payroll Tax Expense?
7. In what journal is the entry for the employer's payroll taxes recorded?
8. What is the source of information for preparing Form 941?
9. When do employees receive Form W-2 from their employers?
10. Explain how an employee uses the different copies of Form W-2.
11. Why does the federal government require the employer to submit copies of the employees' Forms W-2 with Form W-3?

Improving Your Communications Skills

In business communications, courtesy makes a good impression on people and encourages them to respond favorably. Courteous messages are stated in polite, positive words and use the "you" approach whenever possible. Rewrite the following sentences, changing them to courteous statements.

1. Give us more information if you want us to act on your complaint.
2. You will not get the discount unless you pay the bill in 10 days.
3. We cannot extend to you more than a $200 line of credit just now.
4. Send us your check or we can't ship your order.
5. We cannot deliver your order because our plant is closed until July 15.

Applying Accounting Procedures

Exercise 20-1 Calculating Employee Tax Deductions

Instructions: Use the form provided in the working papers. For each of the following gross earnings amounts, determine: (1) employees' federal income tax to be withheld (use the tax tables on pages 424-425 of the textbook); (2) FICA taxes to be withheld (the rate for social security tax is 6.2% and the rate for medicare tax is 1.45%); (3) state income tax to be withheld (the state tax rate is 1.5%).

454

Improving Your Communications Skills
Students' answers may vary. Possible solutions include the following.
1. Please provide us with the following information (list of specifics) so that we may process your complaint speedily and thoroughly.
2. If the bill is paid within 10 days, you may deduct the discount from the total amount.
3. At this time, we are pleased to extend to you a $200 line of credit.
4. We will ship your order as soon as we receive your check.
5. We will deliver your order when our plant reopens on July 15.

	Marital Status	Exemptions	Gross Earnings
1.	M	2	$183.74
2.	S	0	$216.48
3.	S	1	$243.84
4.	M	1	$162.80
5.	S	1	$149.99

Exercise 20-2 Calculating Employer's Payroll Taxes

Instructions: Use the form provided in the working papers. For each of the following total gross earnings amounts, determine the employer's FICA taxes (social security 6.2%, medicare 1.45%), the federal unemployment tax (.8%), and the state unemployment tax (5.4%).

1. $ 914.80
2. $1,113.73
3. $2,201.38
4. $ 791.02
5. $1,245.75

Exercise 20-3 Identifying Entries for Payroll Liabilities

The following list includes several common payroll-related items. These items are included either in the entry to record the payment of the payroll or the entry to record the employer's payroll taxes.

Employees' federal income taxes
State unemployment tax
U.S. savings bonds
Employer's FICA taxes
Federal unemployment tax

Employees' state income taxes
Union dues
Employees' FICA taxes
Life insurance premiums

Instructions: Use the form provided in the workbook. Place a check mark in the column that describes the entry in which the item is recorded.

Problem 20-1 Recording the Payment of the Payroll

The totals of the payroll register for Aurora Garden Shop are shown below. On November 30, the accountant wrote Check 731 to pay the payroll.

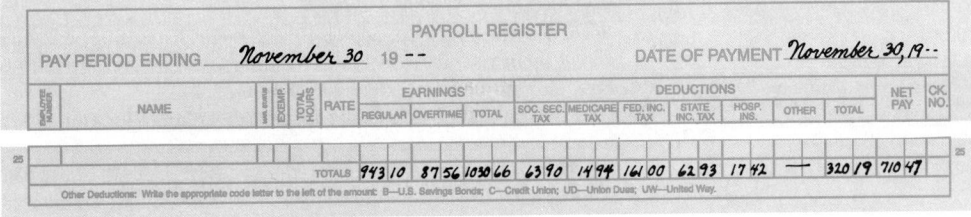

PAYROLL REGISTER

PAY PERIOD ENDING *November 30* 19 --   DATE OF PAYMENT *November 30, 19--*

	NAME			RATE	EARNINGS			DEDUCTIONS						NET PAY	CK. NO.
					REGULAR	OVERTIME	TOTAL	SOC. SEC. TAX	MEDICARE TAX	FED. INC. TAX	STATE INC. TAX	HOSP. INS.	OTHER	TOTAL	
25	TOTALS				943 10	87 56	1030 66	63 90	14 94	161 00	62 93	17 42	—	320 19	710 47	25

Other Deductions: Write the appropriate code letter to the left of the amount: B—U.S. Savings Bonds; C—Credit Union; UD—Union Dues; UW—United Way.

Instructions:

(1) Record the payroll entry in the cash payments journal.
(2) Post the entry to the general ledger accounts.

SPREADSHEET

PROBLEM

Problem 20-2 Journalizing Payroll Transactions

The Potter Company's payroll register for the week ended June 28 appears on the next page.

455

Exercise 20-1: Ch. Obj. 1

Exercise 20-2: Ch. Obj. 2

Exercise 20-3: Ch. Obj. 2, 3

Problem 20-1: Ch. Obj. 1
CPJ entry:
Salaries Exp., Dr. $1030.66
Social Sec. Tax Pay., Cr. $63.90
Medicare Tax Pay., Cr. $14.94
Empl. FIT Pay., Cr. $161.00
Empl. St. Inc. Tax Pay., Cr. $62.93
Hospital Ins. Pay., Cr. $17.42
Cash in Bank, Cr. $710.47

Problem 20-2: Ch. Obj. 1, 2, 3

SPREADSHEET

PROBLEM

Problem 20-2 can be completed using *Spreadsheet Applications*, the spreadsheet software that accompanies *Glencoe Accounting*.

CPJ entry:
Salaries Exp., Dr. $965.85
Social Sec. Tax Pay., Cr. $59.88
Medicare Tax Pay., Cr. $14.01
Empl. FIT Pay., Cr. $56.00
Empl. St. Inc. Tax Pay., Cr. $19.32
Union Dues Pay., Cr. $18.60
Cash in Bank, Cr. $798.04

GJ entry:
Payroll Tax Exp., Dr. $133.77
Social Sec. Tax Pay., Cr. $59.88
Medicare Tax Pay., Cr. $14.01
Fed. Unempl. Tax Pay., Cr. $7.73
State Unempl. Tax Pay., Cr. $52.16

Additional Reinforcement

Students who need additional practice or individualized help will benefit from the *Glencoe Accounting Electronic Study Guide* or the *Glencoe Accounting* on-line multimedia program, which provide reinforcement and reteaching for vocabulary, concepts, and procedures.

Refer students to the Chapter 20 review pages in the workbook, *Chapter Reviews and Working Papers*.

Problem 20-3: Ch. Obj. 1, 2, 3
Net pay, $2,770.75
Payroll Tax Exp., $531.92
Soc. Security Tax Pay., $238.12
Medicare Tax Pay., $55.69
FUTP, $30.72
SUTP, $207.39
May 16 check, $1,226.62

Problem 20-4: Ch. Obj. 1, 2, 3, 4

COMPUTER PROBLEM

This computer image identifies a problem that students may complete using the *Glencoe Accounting, General Ledger* software.

Net pay, $10,333.17
Payroll Tax Exp., $1,687.40
Social Sec. Tax Pay., $755.37
Medicare Tax Pay., $176.66
FUTP, $97.47
SUTP, $657.90
Total FUTP check, $561.58
Total SUTP check, $3,790.63
Total employees' FIT, social security and medicare taxes, $2,543.06

PAYROLL REGISTER

PAY PERIOD ENDING June 28 19--   DATE OF PAYMENT June 28, 19--

EMPLOYEE NUMBER	NAME	MAR. STATUS	EXEMP	TOTAL HOURS	RATE	EARNINGS REGULAR	OVERTIME	TOTAL	SOC. SEC. TAX	MED. TAX	FED. INC. TAX	STATE INC. TAX	HOSP. INS.	OTHER	TOTAL	NET PAY	CK. NO.
12	Blondi, M.	M	1	38	4.95	188 10		188 10	11 66	2 73	3 00	3 76		(uw) 4 65	25 80	162 30	1
14	Dilloway, S.	S	1	41	4.90	196 00	7 35	203 35	12 61	2 95	17 00	4 07			36 63	166 72	2
19	Lake, M.	S	0	42½	5.60	224 00	21 00	245 00	15 19	3 55	29 00	4 90		(uw) 4 65	57 29	187 71	3
13	Lapolla, J.	M	2	36	5.25	189 00		189 00	11 72	2 74	—	3 78		(uw) 4 65	22 89	166 11	4
18	Zeoli, N.	S	1	26	5.40	140 40		140 40	8 70	2 04	7 00	2 81		(uw) 4 65	25 20	115 20	5
25																	25
	TOTALS					937 50	28 35	965 85	59 88	14 01	56 00	19 32	—	18 60	167 81	798 04	

Other Deductions: Write the appropriate code letter to the left of the amount: B—U.S. Savings Bonds; C—Credit Union; UD—Union Dues; UW—United Way.

(1) Record the entry for the payment of the payroll on page 15 of the cash payments journal. Check 573 was written on June 28 to pay the payroll.

(2) Use the information in the payroll register to compute the employer's payroll taxes. These include FICA taxes (6.2% for social security, 1.45% for medicare) and federal (.8%) and state (5.4%) unemployment taxes.

(3) Record the entry for the employer's payroll taxes on page 7 of the general journal.

Problem 20-3 Recording and Posting Payroll Transactions

The Clune Marina completed the following payroll transactions during the first two weeks of May. Clune's pays its employees on a biweekly basis.

Instructions:

(1) Record the May 13 transactions in the cash payments journal (page 12) and in the general journal (page 14).

(2) Post both payroll entries to the appropriate general ledger accounts.

(3) Journalize and post the May 16 transactions.

Transactions:

May 13   Wrote Check 636 to pay the payroll of $3,840.58 (gross earnings) for the pay period ended May 13. The following amounts were withheld: FICA taxes, $238.12 for social security and $55.69 for medicare; employees' federal income taxes, $639.00; employees' state income taxes, $96.02; insurance premium, $21.00; U.S. savings bonds, $20.00.

     13   Recorded the employer's payroll taxes (FICA tax rate, 6.2% for social security and 1.45% for medicare; federal unemployment tax rate, 0.8%; state unemployment tax rate, 5.4%).

     16   Paid the amounts owed to the federal government for employees' federal income taxes and FICA taxes, Check 637.

     16   Purchased U.S. savings bonds for employees for $100.00, Check 638.

     16   Paid $148.00 to the American Insurance Company for employees' insurance, Check 639.

COMPUTER PROBLEM

Problem 20-4 Recording and Posting Payroll Transactions

The Book Worm pays its employees twice a month. Employee earnings and tax amounts for the pay period ended March 31 are listed below.

Gross Earnings	Soc. Sec. Tax	Medicare Tax	Emp. Fed. Inc. Tax	Emp. State Inc. Tax
$12,183.40	$755.37	$176.66	$679.00	$239.20

456

Teacher Notes

(1) Prepare Check 713 (payable to "Book Worm Payroll Account") to transfer the net pay amount to the payroll checking account.

(2) Journalize and post the payroll transaction.

(3) Journalize and post the entry to record the employer's payroll taxes. Use general journal page 19. The social security tax rate is 6.2%, and the medicare tax rate is 1.45%; the state unemployment tax rate is 5.4%; and the federal unemployment tax rate is .8%.

(4) Prepare checks dated March 31 to pay the following payroll liabilities:
- (a) Federal unemployment taxes, payable to First City Bank (Check 714).
- (b) State unemployment taxes, payable to the State of Missouri (Check 715).
- (c) Employee's federal income taxes and FICA taxes, payable to First City Bank (Check 716).

(5) Journalize and post the entries for the payment of the payroll liabilities.

(6) Prepare Forms 8109 for the two federal tax deposits made in #4.

Problem 20-5   Recording Payroll Transactions

The Wiesel Company pays its employees each week. The payroll register for the week ended September 16 is shown below.

PAYROLL REGISTER

PAY PERIOD ENDING September 16 19--   DATE OF PAYMENT September 16, 19--

EMPLOYEE NUMBER	NAME	MAR STATUS	EXEMP	TOTAL HOURS	RATE	EARNINGS REGULAR	EARNINGS OVERTIME	EARNINGS TOTAL	SOC. SEC. TAX	MED. TAX	FED. INC. TAX	STATE INC. TAX	HOSP. INS.	OTHER	TOTAL	NET PAY	CK. NO.
102	Abbott, D.	M	2	39	5.20	202 80		202 80	12 57	2 94	—	4 06	3 80	(c) 5 00	28 37	174 43	1
116	Concannon, A.	S	0	42	4.80	192 00	14 40	206 40	12 80	2 99	23 00	4 13	2 45	(B) 5 00	50 37	156 03	2
109	Flowers, D.	M	1	41	5.35	214 00	8 03	222 03	13 77	3 22	9 00	4 44	3 80		34 23	187 80	3
121	Jackson, P.	S	1	36	4.95	178 20		178 20	11 05	2 58	13 00	3 56	2 45	(c) 10 00	42 64	135 56	4
117	Oller, W.	S	0	31	5.10	158 10		158 10	9 80	2 29	16 00	3 16	2 45	(B) 5 00	38 70	119 40	5
123	Repicky, J.	S	1	40	5.10	204 00		204 00	12 65	2 96	17 00	4 08	2 45	(c) 15 00	54 14	149 86	6
141	Toomey, B.	M	2	33	5.35	176 55		176 55	10 95	2 56	—	3 53	3 80		20 84	155 71	7
139	Welsh, T.	S	0	41	5.10	204 00	7 65	211 65	13 12	3 07	18 00	4 23	2 45	(UW) 3 00	43 87	167 78	8
					TOTALS	1,529 65	30 08	1,559 73	96 71	22 61	96 00	31 19	23 65	B ─ ─ C 30 00 UW 3 00	313 16	1,246 57	

Other Deductions: Write the appropriate code letter to the left of the amount: B—U.S. Savings Bonds; C—Credit Union; UD—Union Dues; UW—United Way.

Instructions:

(1) Record the payment of the payroll on page 16 of the cash payments journal. Check 831 was written on September 16 to pay the payroll.

(2) Compute the employer's payroll taxes (FICA tax rates, 6.2% social security, 1.45% medicare; state unemployment tax rate, 5.4%; federal unemployment tax rate, 0.8%). The following employees have accumulated earnings of $7,000 or more: Abbott, Concannon, Flowers, Repicky, and Welsh. Record the entry for the employer's payroll taxes on page 8 of the general journal.

(3) Record the payment of all FICA and employees' federal income taxes, Check 832. The previous account balances were: Employees' Federal Income Tax Payable, $189.00, and Social Security Tax Payable, $191.48, and Medicare Tax Payable, $44.92.

(4) Record the income tax payment to the state, Check 833. The balance in the account Employees' State Income Tax Payable before the September 16 payroll was $178.40.

(5) Record the payments for amounts withheld from employees:
- (a) Check 834 to Tri-County Credit Union (previous balance, $270.00).
- (b) Check 835 for hospital insurance (previous balance, $260.15).

457

Chapter 20

Problem 20-5: Ch. Obj. 1, 2, 3

CHALLENGE PROBLEM The last problem in each chapter is a challenge problem and is identified by this "maze" symbol.

(2) Payroll Tax Exp., $151.11
Soc. Security Tax Pay., $96.71
Medicare Tax Pay., $22.61
FUTP, $4.10
SUTP, $27.69

(3) Social security, medicare, and employees' FIT, $760.04

(4) State income tax payment, $209.59

(5) Credit union, $300.00
Hospital ins., $283.80

4 ASSESS

A chapter test is available for use in assessing students' understanding of concepts in this chapter.

Unit objective and problem tests are available to assess students' knowledge of concepts in Chapters 19-20.

The testmaker software will enable you to develop tailor-made chapter, unit, semester, and final tests.

Alternative Assessment

For alternative assessment strategies, refer to *Tech Prep Strategies in Accounting.*

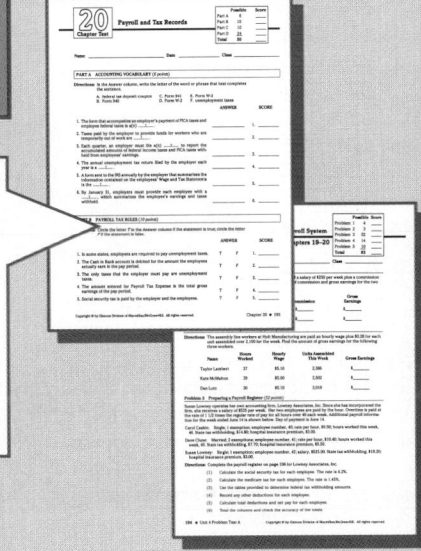

Use Chapter Test 20 here to assess students' understanding and retention of the concepts and procedures presented in the chapter.

Use Unit 4 Objective Test and/or Unit 4 Problem Test to assess students' retention of concepts presented in Chapters 19-20.

F O C U S   O N
ETHICS

Have students read the ethics case given in the textbook and jot down ideas about what they would do in the situation described. Then review the five-step decision model (see page T44). Emphasize that there are no "right" or "wrong" answers to the questions in the decision model.

After students have discussed the first four steps, have them vote on which alternative they feel is best, or, if one alternative has clearly been chosen during the discussion, review students' reasoning for choosing that course of action.

You may want to have students compare their final decision with the one they wrote down after first reading the vignette. Did following the five-step model reinforce their "instinctual" decision or lead them to choose a different course of action? Help students realize that following a decision model when they confront an ethical dilemma can help them to organize their thinking and arrive at a satisfactory solution.

QUESTIONS

1. What are the ethical issues in this situation?
2. What are the alternatives?
3. Who are the affected parties?
4. How do the alternatives affect the parties?
5. What is the decision?

ANSWERS

1. Deceiving employees, using money earmarked for one purpose to do something else, using illegal means to save a business.
2. The business owner can use the employees' money to pay off debts, seek financial counseling to set up a plan to get out of debt, apply for a loan, or contact creditors to negotiate a repayment schedule.
3. The business owner, employees, IRS, creditors, customers.
4. Answers will vary. For example, if the business owner uses the employees' withholding funds, she could pay off the debts immediately but might not have the money to pay the IRS when taxes are due. She would be running the risk of being prosecuted for breaking the law. If the business owner cannot obtain a

*M*oney Shuffling

Ask the average taxpayer how he or she feels about the IRS, and you will garner few positive responses. Paying taxes, however, is part of living in the United States. Most employees expect to see money withheld from their paychecks, assuming in good faith that the money will be passed along to the IRS. With some planning, perhaps some money will be refunded when the returns are filed.

What if, however, your money was not going to the government? What if, instead, the money withheld from your check was being used to pay off company debts, to pacify threatening creditors, or to buy into a high-risk investment? Such a situation might occur more often than you think. For example, a business owner who is losing money may feel that she could get her business under control by temporarily directing her employee's withholding funds into other channels, such as using the money to pay off some pressing debts. "After all," her rationalization might go, "the IRS does not need this money right now, but I do. Things will ease up soon, and by that time I will have the money to pay the taxes."

What is the ethical dilemma in this situation? If you were an accounting clerk managing payroll for this particular business, what course of action would you take? Would you go along with the owner's plan? One way to decide might be to ask yourself the question, to whom does the money belong? Legally, it belongs to the government; it is only being held by the employer. In essence, the employer transferred the money to the employee in the form of a salary; the employee transferred the money to the government by designating that a certain amount be withheld from his or her salary. If the employer "borrows" the money from

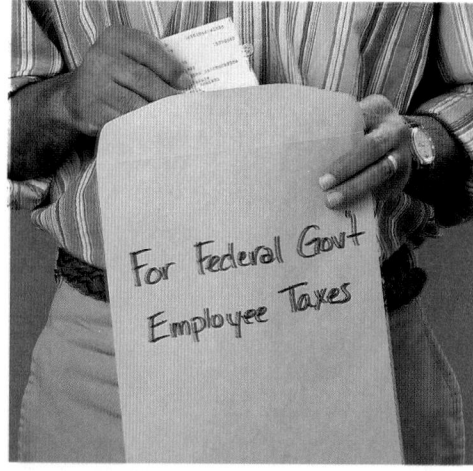

Looking at all the available options can help you resolve ethical questions.

the government, but returns it before the taxes are due, however, who is to know?

Before making a decision, it is wise to consider the other options. For example, if the unpaid debts are a result of bad business practices, the owner could seek financial counseling to determine the best solution to the problem. If the situation is really just a cash flow problem, and money is expected soon, a loan could be taken to pay off the most pressing debts, and then the loan could be repaid when the cash comes in. Perhaps the time span of repayment could be renegotiated with the creditors. Often, receiving a payment, even if it is less than the amount due, will assure a creditor that efforts are being made to repay, and the creditor may be willing to rework the terms.

458

loan, the creditors could suffer because they might not be repaid. The employees and customers would be affected if the business owner were unable to get out of debt and had to close the business.
5. Accept any answer, but require students to defend the course of action they choose.

Mini Practice Set

APPLICATION ACTIVITY 5

Payroll Accounting

In Unit 4, you studied the procedures involved in a payroll system—from determining and recording employees' earnings to preparing employers' tax reports. Now you will have the opportunity to review and apply what you have learned as you prepare the payroll and maintain payroll records for a business called The Greens.

When you have completed this activity, you will have done the following:

1. Calculated employees' gross earnings.
2. Determined deductions from employees' gross earnings.
3. Calculated employees' net pay.
4. Prepared a payroll register.
5. Written payroll checks and stubs for employees.
6. Recorded payroll information on employees' earnings records.
7. Journalized and posted the payroll transaction.
8. Calculated the employer's payroll taxes.
9. Journalized and posted the employer's payroll tax transaction.
10. Journalized and posted the payment of FICA taxes and federal income taxes.
11. Prepared Form 8109.
12. Journalized and posted the payment of a monthly insurance premium.

The Greens

The Greens is a golf shop located in Concord, Massachusetts. It is a merchandising business, organized as a corporation, owned and operated by the Jackson family. The store has been in operation for almost five years. During that time, its sales have increased each year, and the business is now showing a good profit.

Payroll Information

The store presently employs eight people. A Form W-4 is on file for each employee. The list that follows summarizes the data on those documents.

Chris Carroll:	Single; claims 1 exemption
Ralph DeLuca:	Single; claims 1 exemption
Christina Frei:	Single; claims 1 exemption
Gary Gula:	Single; claims 0 exemptions
Anne Holland:	Married; claims 2 exemptions
Marcy Jackson:	Married; claims 2 exemptions
Betty Quinn:	Married; claims 3 exemptions
Yourself:	Single; claims 1 exemption

The business pays its employees on a weekly basis. Overtime is paid at the rate of $1\frac{1}{2}$ times the regular rate of pay for all hours worked over 40. The weekly pay period runs from Monday through Saturday, with employees

459

MINI
PRACTICE SET

APPLICATION ACTIVITY 5

Application Activity 5 is a reinforcement activity that helps students integrate their learning of how to keep payroll records and how to record the cost of the payroll in the accounting records of a business. In this activity, students are required to calculate employee earnings and deductions, prepare a payroll register and employee's earnings records, write payroll checks, record the payment of the payroll, record the employer's payroll tax liabilities and the payment of those liabilities, and record the payment of a monthly insurance premium withheld from employees' pay.

The accounting stationery for completing this activity is included in the student's *Chapter Reviews and Working Papers*. Most students should be able to complete this activity manually within three class periods.

Source documents are available to add realism to this activity.

COMPUTER

PROBLEM

An optional microcomputer diskette is available for completing this activity on the microcomputer. Most students should be able to complete the microcomputer version within one or two class periods.

Teacher Notes

Application Activity 5

Hours worked:
Carroll, 22 hours
DeLuca, 36 hours
Gula, 34 1/2 hours
Quinn, 42 hours

being paid on Saturday for that week's work. The store is closed for business on Sunday.

The employees are paid by one of three methods: hourly rate, salary, or salary plus a 10% commission on the amount of merchandise sold. The following table lists the employees, the method by which their wages are computed, and other pertinent information.

Employee	Emp. No.	Position	Employee Status	Rate of Pay
Marcy Jackson	010	Manager	Full-time	$500.00/week
Anne Holland	011	Salesperson	Full-time	$175.00/week plus 10% commission
Christina Frei	012	Accounting clerk	Part-time	$200.00/week
Gary Gula	013	Stock clerk	Full-time	$4.95/hour
Betty Quinn	016	Salesclerk	Full-time	$5.15/hour
Ralph DeLuca	018	Salesclerk	Full-time	$5.15/hour
Chris Carroll	019	Stock clerk	Part-time	$4.90/hour
Yourself	022	Accounting clerk	Part-time	$200.00/week

Federal and state tax tables are used to determine income taxes to be withheld. These tables are included in the working papers that accompany this textbook. The current rates for other taxes are as follows.

FICA: Employee and employer contributions:
      Social Security: 6.2%
      Medicare: 1.45%
State unemployment tax: 5.4%
Federal unemployment tax: 0.8%

Preparing the Payroll for The Greens

The business entered the third quarter of its fiscal year at the beginning of July. It is presently the last week of July. Christina Frei, the accounting clerk, is on vacation. In her absence, you are to prepare this week's payroll.

Today is Saturday, July 29. The time cards for the employees who are paid on an hourly basis are included in the working papers accompanying this textbook. The hours worked by those employees are listed below and on the following page.

Chris Carroll

	IN	OUT	IN	OUT
M	2:00	5:00		
T	2:00	6:00		
W	3:00	5:00		
TH	2:00	6:00		
F	2:00	6:00		
S	9:00	2:00		

Ralph DeLuca

	IN	OUT	IN	OUT
M	9:00	12:00	12:30	5:00
T	9:00	11:30	12:00	5:00
W	9:00	1:00		
TH	9:00	12:00	12:30	4:00
F	8:30	1:00	1:30	3:00
S	9:00	1:30		

Gary Gula

	IN	OUT	IN	OUT
M	9:00	12:00	1:00	3:00
T	9:00	12:00	1:00	5:00
W	8:00	12:00	1:00	5:00
TH	9:00	12:00	1:00	3:30
F	9:00	12:00	1:00	4:00
S	9:00	12:00		

Betty Quinn

	IN	OUT	IN	OUT
M	9:00	12:00	12:30	5:00
T	9:00	12:30	1:00	6:00
W	9:00	12:00	1:00	4:30
TH	8:30	12:30	1:00	5:00
F	9:00	11:30	12:00	5:00
S	9:00	1:00		

460

Teacher Notes

_____

_____

_____

_____

_____

Instructions:

(1) Complete the timecards for the four hourly employees. Enter the total hours worked at the bottom of each card.

(2) Anne Holland recorded sales this week of $1,241.00. Calculate her commission and add it to her salary to determine her gross earnings.

(3) Enter the payroll information for all employees in the payroll register. Each employee was recently assigned an employee number because Marcy Jackson is planning to computerize the payroll system. Since this payroll is being prepared manually, list the employees in the payroll register in alphabetical order by *last name*.

(4) Use the following information to complete the payroll register:

(a) Use the federal and state tax charts to determine income tax amounts to be withheld.

(b) Chris Carroll, Ralph DeLuca, Gary Gula, and Anne Holland each have a $5.00 deduction for the purchase of U.S. savings bonds.

(c) Christina Frei, Marcy Jackson, and Betty Quinn each have $3.00 deducted for donations to the United Way.

(d) All employees pay an insurance premium each week. Married employees pay $4.55 and single employees pay $2.75.

(e) None of The Greens' employees has reached the maximum taxable amount for the FICA taxes.

(5) Calculate the net pay for each employee.

(6) Total all amount columns in the payroll register. Prove the accuracy of the totals.

(7) Write Check 972 on the business's regular checking account for the amount of the total net pay. Make the check payable to The Greens Payroll Account. In Christina's absence, Marcy Jackson will sign the check for you. Complete the deposit slip for the payroll account.

(8) Record the payroll transaction in the cash payments journal, page 19. Use information contained in the payroll register and Check 972 as the source documents. Post the transaction to the general ledger accounts.

(9) Write the paychecks for the employees. Use the information in the payroll register to complete the check stubs. After a check has been written for an employee, enter the check number in the payroll register.

(10) Enter this week's payroll information on the employee's earnings records for Chris Carroll and Anne Holland only. Be sure to add the current gross earnings amount to the accumulated total.

(11) Calculate and record the employer's taxes for this pay period in the general journal, page 15. The source of information is the payroll register.

(12) Make a deposit for the taxes owed to the federal government. The total includes the amounts withheld for employees' federal income tax, social security tax, and medicare tax. Complete Form 8109 by entering the amount owed. Write Check 973, payable to the First Federal Bank of Boston, for the taxes.

(13) Enter the transaction in the cash payments journal.

(14) Pay the monthly insurance premium by writing Check 974 to Yankee Insurance Company for $164.40. Record the payment in the cash payments journal.

(15) Complete the posting from the cash payments journal.

461

Holland's commission, $124.10

Payroll register column totals:
Regular, $1,869.08
Overtime, $15.46
Total, $1,884.54
Social Security, $116.83
Medicare, $27.33
FIT, $126.00
SIT, $66.79
Hospital Insurance, $27.40
Savings Bonds, $20.00
United Way, $9.00
Total Deductions, $393.35
Net Pay, $1,491.19

Employer's taxes:
Social Security, $116.84
Medicare, $27.33
FUTP, $15.08
SUTP, $101.77
Total deposit for taxes owed, $899.74

Teacher Notes

_____

_____

_____

_____

_____

The chapters in this unit cover the accounting procedures for cash, depreciation of plant assets, receivables, inventories, and notes. In Chapter 21 students learn how to establish, reconcile, and replenish change funds and petty cash funds. In Chapter 22 students learn accounting procedures for long-term assets. Chapter 23 presents methods of accounting for uncollectible accounts. Chapter 24 reviews the Merchandise Inventory account and presents systems for determining inventory cost. In the last chapter of the unit, Chapter 25, students learn about notes payable and notes receivable.

462

UNIT 5

ACCOUNTING FOR SPECIAL PROCEDURES

In addition to accounting for everyday business transactions, many businesses must also account for financial events that occur less frequently. Among these financial events are accounting for cash funds, accounting for the depreciation of certain assets, accounting for accounts receivable that cannot be collected, accounting for the cost of inventories, and accounting for money that is borrowed or loaned by the business.

Individualizing Instruction

To provide individualized activities within the unit, you may use any of the following:

- problems in *Math Review for Accounting*
- chapter study plans
- study guides in the student workbook
- end-of-chapter challenge problems (identified by a maze symbol)

- optional problems in the Additional Problems section at the back of the student textbook
- cases from *Tech Prep Strategies in Accounting*
- *Electronic Study Guide*

Accounting for Special Procedures

Unit Concepts

Unit 5 provides additional information on accounting procedures for cash funds, depreciation of plant assets, uncollectible accounts receivable, inventories, and notes payable and receivable. Students learn about the principles of accounting for each of these special procedures. They learn how to calculate amounts for depreciation, uncollectible accounts receivable, inventories, and notes. They learn about the accounts to be debited and credited and the corresponding entries. Students also become familiar with the financial statements needed for these procedures.

General Unit Performance Objectives

1. Correctly use terminology related to accounting for special procedures.
2. Describe the principles and practices of accounting for special procedures.
3. Demonstrate accounting applications for special procedures.

PERFORMANCE OBJECTIVES

Unit Objective Test: Chapters 21-25

1. Define accounting vocabulary correctly.

2. Determine the correct and incorrect accounting procedures for recording transactions involving cash funds, depreciation, inventory amounts, uncollectible amounts, and notes.

3. Select the correct accounting procedures for depreciation, uncollectible accounts, inventory amounts, cash funds, and notes.

4. Analyze transactions involving depreciation, uncollectible accounts, and notes receivable and payable.

Unit Problem Test: Chapters 21-25

1. Journalize the transactions to establish and replenish a petty cash fund.

2. Calculate estimated annual depreciation for plant assets.

3. Record transactions involving depreciation, uncollectible accounts, and notes in a general journal.

4. Calculate the cost of inventory on hand at the end of the fiscal period using four different costing methods.

ORGANIZER

Chapter	Learning Objectives
21	1. Record the entry to establish a change fund. 2. Prove the cash in the cash register drawer at the end of each business day. 3. Record the entry to establish a petty cash fund. 4. Prepare a petty cash requisition to replenish the petty cash fund. 5. Use a petty cash register to record petty cash disbursements. 6. Record the journal entry to replenish the petty cash fund. 7. Determine whether cash is short or over and record the amount of the shortage or overage. 8. Define the accounting terms new to this chapter.
22	1. Identify plant assets. 2. Explain the need to depreciate plant assets. 3. Calculate the annual estimated depreciation expense of a plant asset. 4. Calculate depreciation for a partial year. 5. Determine the book value of a plant asset. 6. Record adjusting entries in the general journal for depreciation. 7. Define the accounting terms new to this chapter.
23	1. Explain the difference between the direct write-off method and the allowance method of accounting for uncollectible accounts. 2. Journalize the entry to record the direct write-off of an uncollectible account receivable. 3. Explain how the adjustment for uncollectible accounts using the allowance method is recorded on the work sheet. 4. Journalize the adjusting entry for estimated uncollectible accounts. 5. Journalize the entry to write off an uncollectible account using the allowance method. 6. Journalize the entry to record the collection of a written-off account. 7. Describe two methods that can be used to estimate bad debts expense. 8. Define the accounting terms new to this chapter.
24	1. Explain the importance of maintaining consistent inventory records. 2. Explain the difference between a periodic and a perpetual inventory system. 3. Determine the cost of a merchandise inventory using the following methods: specific identification; first in, first out; last in, first out; and weighted average cost. 4. Assign a value to merchandise inventory using the lower-of-cost-or-market rule. 5. Define the accounting terms new to this chapter.
25	1. Explain how promissory notes are used by businesses. 2. Determine the due date, interest expense, and maturity value of a promissory note. 3. Explain the difference between interest-bearing and non-interest-bearing notes. 4. Record journal entries for notes payable and notes receivable. 5. Define the accounting terms new to this chapter.

State/Local Objectives			Demonstration Problems	Check Your Learning	Basic Skills	Exercises	Problems	Challenge Problem	Additional Problems
			21-1 21-2 21-3 21-4 21-5 21-6	p. 468 p. 475	Decision Making p. 478	21-1 21-2 21-3 21-4	21-1 21-2 21-3 21-4 21-5	21-6	21A p. 642
			22-1 22-2 22-3 22-4 22-5	p. 487 p. 489 p. 494	Analysis p. 499	22-1 22-2 22-3 22-4	22-1 22-2 22-3 22-4 22-5 22-6	22-7	22A p. 643
			23-1 23-2 23-3 23-4 23-5 23-6	p. 509 p. 513 p. 517	Decision Making p. 522	23-1 23-2 23-3	23-1 23-2 23-3 23-4 23-5	23-6	23A p. 643
			24-1 24-2 24-3 24-4	p. 532 p. 535	Human Relations p. 540	24-1 24-2 24-3 24-4	24-1 24-2 24-3 24-4 24-5	24-6 24-7	24A p. 643
			25-1 25-2 25-3 25-4 25-5 25-6 25-7 25-8 25-9	p. 550 p. 552 p. 554 p. 558 p. 561	Math p. 562	25-1 25-2 25-3 25-4	25-1 25-2 25-3 25-4 25-5	25-6 25-7	25A p. 644

UNIT 5 COMPUTERIZED ACCOUNTING ACTIVITIES

Chapter	Glencoe Integrated Accounting	Spreadsheet Applications	Electronic Study Guide Model Exercises/Problems	CD Rom
21		Exercise 21-2	Exercise 21-2 Problem 21-1 21-2	Menu Selection 21
22	Problem 22-6	Exercise 22-3	Exercise 22-2 22-4 Problem 22-2	Menu Selection 22
23	Problem 23-5	Exercise 23-2	Exercise 23-1 23-3 Problem 23-3	Menu Selection 23
24		Problem 24-4	Exercise 24-1 24-2 24-3 24-4	Menu Selection 24
25	Problem 25-5	Exercise 25-4	Exercise 25-5 Problem 25-4	Menu Selection 25
Basic Math Review			Menu Option 29	

LOOKING BACK

In prior chapters students have learned to maintain accounting records for the typical transactions that occur frequently in most businesses. These transactions have focused on daily revenue and expense transactions as well as payroll records. In this unit students will study accounting procedures that occur with less frequency. Students begin their study with cash funds and the controls that businesses maintain for those funds.

VOCABULARY DEVELOPMENT

Ask students to write a sentence using each of the new terms in context. Ask for volunteers to write their sentences on the board. Discuss any differences in the use of the terms. Definitions of these terms are found in the chapter and in the glossary on pages 670-679.

Chapter 21

ACCOUNTING FOR CASH FUNDS

In earlier chapters, you learned that businesses use a checking account for depositing cash receipts and making cash payments. The use of a checking account is an important internal control for any business. Merchandising businesses, however, need to have some cash on hand to make change for customers who pay cash for their purchases. In addition, most businesses find it easier to use cash for small, incidental cash payments rather than writing a large number of checks for very small amounts.

In this chapter, you will learn about two cash funds businesses use to handle these situations: a change fund and a petty cash fund. Since errors in making change do occur in merchandising businesses, you will also learn how to record the amounts of those errors in the accounting records for the business.

Learning Objectives

When you have completed Chapter 21, you should be able to do the following:

1. Record the entry to establish a change fund.
2. Prove the cash in the cash register drawer at the end of each business day.
3. Record the entry to establish a petty cash fund.
4. Prepare a petty cash requisition to replenish the petty cash fund.
5. Use a petty cash register to record petty cash disbursements.
6. Record the journal entry to replenish the petty cash fund.
7. Determine whether cash is short or over and record the amount of the shortage or overage.
8. Define the accounting terms introduced in this chapter.

New Terms

change fund
petty cash fund
petty cash disbursement
petty cashier
petty cash voucher
petty cash requisition
petty cash register

464

Teaching Resources

- Lesson Plans
- TE/Chapter Reviews & Working Papers
- Demonstration Problems
- Student Study Plans
- Teaching Transparencies
- Solutions Transparencies
- Electronic Field Trips Video, Level I
- Electronic Study Guide
- Chapter 21 Test

Other Resources

- Skills Improvement Activities
- Blackline Masters
- Careers in Accounting
- Dictionary
- Math Review for Accounting
- Tech Prep Strategies in Accounting
- Video
- Test Bank with Software
- Spanish Resources/Audiotapes
- Spanish Electronic Study Guide

The Change Fund

Many businesses, including such retail stores as drugstores and supermarkets, need change funds. A **change fund** is an amount of money, consisting of varying denominations of bills and coins, that is used to make change in cash transactions. For example, a customer who pays for a $13.80 purchase with a $20.00 bill must be given change of $6.20.

Establishing a Change Fund

When a business first establishes a change fund, the amount of change needed for the fund is estimated. The size of the fund does not change unless the business finds that it needs more or less change than its original estimate. The change fund is established by writing a check for the amount of the fund. The check is made payable to the person who will be in charge of the change fund. That person cashes the check and places the bills and coins in the cash register drawer. Let's look at an example.

December 1: The accountant for East Side Book Store wrote Check 150 for $100.00 to establish a change fund.

When a check is written to establish a change fund, a new asset account is needed to record the amount of the fund. This asset account is usually called Change Fund. The Change Fund account appears immediately after Cash in Bank in the chart of accounts.

Look at the T accounts that follow. The asset account Change Fund is debited for the amount of the check written to establish the fund ($100.00). As you already know, any check written by the business decreases Cash in Bank, so that account is credited for the amount of the check.

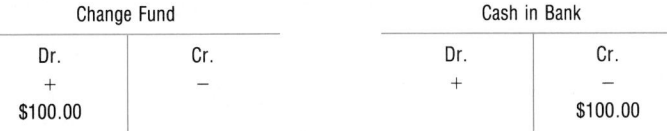

Change Fund		Cash in Bank	
Dr.	Cr.	Dr.	Cr.
+	−	+	−
$100.00			$100.00

East Side Book Store uses special journals to record its business transactions. All checks written by the business are recorded in its cash payments journal. The journal entry made to record the establishment of the change fund for East Side Book Store is shown in Figure 21-1.

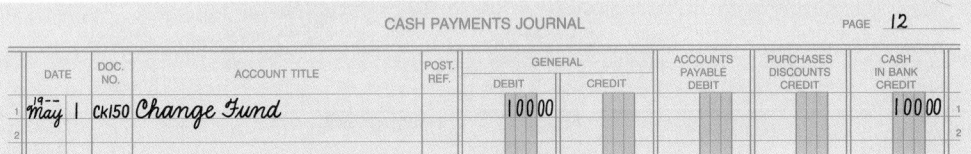

				GENERAL		ACCOUNTS PAYABLE DEBIT	PURCHASES DISCOUNTS CREDIT	CASH IN BANK CREDIT	
DATE	DOC. NO.	ACCOUNT TITLE	POST. REF.	DEBIT	CREDIT				
19-- May 1	Ck150	Change Fund		100 00				100 00	1
									2

Figure 21-1 Recording the Journal Entry To Establish a Change Fund

The Change Fund account is usually debited only once — when the business first establishes its change fund. If the business needs to increase the size of the change fund later, a check is written for the amount of the cash

1 FOCUS

MAJOR CONCEPTS
- The Change Fund
- The Petty Cash Fund

*B*USINESS CONNECTION

In the mid 1980s, Baskin Robbins tried an innovative approach to cash control. A cash register attached to a steel vault was installed in several California stores. When a customer's payment was inserted into a slot, the correct change and a receipt were automatically returned without the cash drawer ever opening! Though the system was highly successful in eliminating mistakes and deterring theft, Baskin Robbins could not justify the $16,000 cost of each terminal. Advances in technology may provide a more cost-effective cash register in the future.

2 TEACH

CONCEPT DEVELOPMENT
The Change Fund
When introducing the change fund, point out that any retail business using a cash register needs to keep a small amount of money in the cash register for making change. The change fund consists of varying denominations of bills and coins.

Using Visuals

Call students' attention to the photo. Ask students who work with change funds to describe how the fund is used.

Using Visuals

Point out the entry to record the change fund in Figure 21-1. Ask students why the cash payments journal is used.

All merchandising businesses need to have cash on hand in order to make change for customers.

*R*einforcing *S*tudy *S*kills

The techniques used for reading a textbook can also be applied to reading articles in professional journals and other periodicals. To preview an article, read the title and the notes about the author. Then apply the techniques of skimming the first and last paragraphs, noticing the points in heads and subheads, and looking at graphics.

Provide a copy of the *Student Study Plans* to each class member to help organize study activities or to individualize practice and review activities.

Using Visuals

Use demonstration problem 21-1 to show students how to record the establishment of a change fund.

CONCEPT DEVELOPMENT
Using the Change Fund
Students should have a basic understanding of the process of using the change fund and how the cash proof form is used to verify the accuracy of the fund.

Using Visuals

Review the cash proof shown in Figure 21-2. Point out that total cash sales and net cash received as recorded on the cash proof must agree.

Using Visuals

Use demonstration problem 21-2 to guide students through the completion of a cash proof form.

ACCOUNTING PRACTICE
Students may complete Exercise 21-1 at this point.

increase. For example, suppose that East Side Book Store finds that it needs a change fund of $125.00. A check would be written for $25.00. In the journal entry, Change Fund would be debited for $25.00, bringing the account balance to $125.00. Cash in Bank would be credited for $25.00.

Using the Change Fund

The amount of cash in the change fund is put in the cash register drawer at the beginning of the day. When a cash sale occurs, the salesclerk rings up the sale on the cash register, which automatically records the transaction on the cash register tape. At the end of the day, the cash in the cash register drawer is counted. The amount of cash in the change fund is set aside for use as change for the next day. The balance of the cash from the drawer is deposited in the business's checking account. Let's look at an example.

Suppose East Side Book Store has $470.00 in its cash register drawer at the end of the day on May 15. The cash sales, and the taxes on those sales, shown on the cash register tape total $370.00. A cash proof is prepared to verify that the amount of cash in the drawer is equal to the total cash sales for the day plus the change fund cash. Look at the cash proof shown in Figure 21-2. As you can see, the amount of cash in the drawer at the end of the day minus the amount of cash in the change fund equals the total sales shown on the cash register tape.

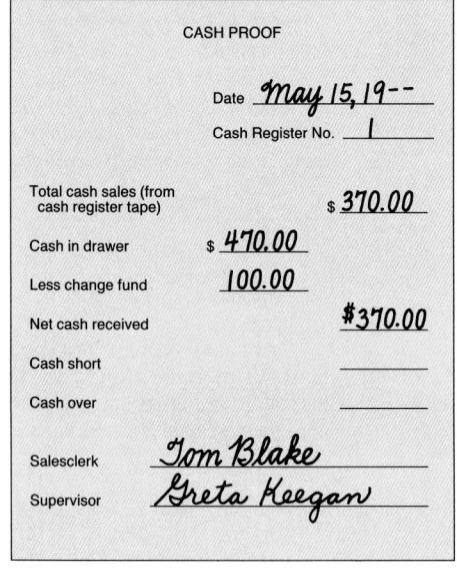

Figure 21-2 Cash Proof Form

Most businesses require that salesclerks sign the cash proof to indicate that they have counted the cash in the drawer and verified its accuracy. The supervisor also checks these amounts and signs the cash proof. The cash proof form is attached to the cash register tape, which is the source document for journalizing the cash sales for the day in the cash receipts journal.

Making Connections

EVERYDAY LIFE

Ask students to share their experiences of receiving incorrect change from a cashier. In each case, would the change fund have been short or over as a result of the error?

Recording Cash Short and Over

Many cash transactions occur during each business day. Occasionally, a salesclerk makes an error and gives the incorrect amount of change to a customer. When this happens, the amount of cash in the cash register drawer, less the beginning change fund, will not agree with the cash sales amount recorded on the cash register tape. If the salesclerk gives a customer too much change, the amount of cash in the drawer at the end of the day will be *short.* If the salesclerk gives a customer too little change, the cash amount will be *over.*

The amounts of cash either gained or lost through errors made in giving change to customers must be recorded in the business's accounting records. The account used to record these amounts is Cash Short and Over. Cash Short and Over is a temporary owner's equity account. Cash shortages result in losses or expenses to the business; they are recorded as debits to Cash Short and Over. Cash overages are gains or revenue for the business; they are recorded as credits to Cash Short and Over. Note that Cash Short and Over does not have a normal balance side. If cash overages occur more often than cash shortages, Cash Short and Over will have a credit balance. If there are more cash shortages (as usually happens), it will have a debit balance. At the end of the fiscal period, the balance of Cash Short and Over is closed into Income Summary.

Cash Short and Over	
Dr.	Cr.
Cash	Cash
Shortages	Overages

Cash shortages or overages are recorded in the cash receipts journal when the cash sales for the day are recorded. Look at the journal entry in Figure 21-3. In this transaction, the cash register tape showed that cash sales were $520.00 and the sales taxes were $26.00—for a total of $546.00. The actual cash in the cash register drawer, after the amount of the change fund was subtracted, was $545.00. In the journal entry, Sales is credited for $520.00, the total selling price of the merchandise sold. Sales Tax Payable is credited for $26.00. Cash in Bank is debited for $545.00. Since the amount of the debit must equal the amount of the credit, Cash Short and Over is debited for $1.00, the amount of the shortage.

$546.00 sales
−545.00 cash
$ 1.00 short

CASH RECEIPTS JOURNAL — PAGE 15

DATE	DOC. NO.	ACCOUNT TITLE	POST. REF.	GENERAL DEBIT	GENERAL CREDIT	SALES CREDIT	SALES TAX PAYABLE CREDIT	ACCOUNTS RECEIVABLE CREDIT	CASH IN BANK DEBIT	
22	31	T30	Cash Short and Over		1 00		520 00	26 00		545 00	22
23											23

Figure 21-3   Recording a Cash Shortage in the Cash Receipts Journal

The journal entry to record a cash overage is similar to that for a cash shortage, except that Cash Short and Over is *credited* for the amount of the overage. For example, suppose, in the previous example, that the amount of cash in the drawer had been $547.00 after the amount of the change fund had been subtracted. In the journal entry, Cash in Bank would be debited for $547.00 and Cash Short and Over would be credited for $1.00. The credits to Sales and Sales Tax Payable would be the same.

$547.00 cash
−546.00 sales
$ 1.00 over

✓ ANSWERS

1. Merchandising businesses, including such retail stores as supermarkets and drug stores
2. Change Fund is debited for $25.00; Cash in Bank is credited for $25.00.
3. Short; $5
4. Cash in Bank Debit, $390.75; Cash Short and Over Debit, $3.00; Sales Credit, $375.00; Sales Tax Payable Credit, $18.75
5. Cash in Bank Debit, $647.10; Sales Credit, $620.00; Sales Tax Payable Credit, $24.80; Cash Short and Over Credit, $2.30

CONCEPT DEVELOPMENT
The Petty Cash Fund

Students have learned that one way to protect cash is to deposit all cash receipts and to pay all bills by check. It is impractical, however, to write checks for small amounts, such as payment for newspaper delivery or for small purchases of supplies. Instead, businesses use a petty cash fund for making cash payments for small, incidental purchases. Some working students may have experience with a petty cash fund. If so, ask them what they can tell the class about it.

Teaching Tips

■ Petty cash funds are sometimes referred to as "imprest funds."

R E M E M B E R

When amounts are entered in the General columns of the cash receipts journal, the title of the account being debited or credited must be written in the Account Title column.

Before you read any further, do the following activity to check your understanding of accounting for change funds and cash shortages and overages.

Check Your Learning

Write your answers to these questions on notebook paper.

1. What kinds of businesses need change funds?
2. If a business has a change fund of $75 and wants to increase the amount of the fund to $100, which accounts are debited and credited in the cash payments journal? For what amounts?
3. Hingham Convenience Store has a change fund of $150.00. Cash sales and the sales taxes for one day totaled $982.00. At the end of the day, the cash in the cash register drawer totaled $1,127.00. Is cash short or over? By what amount?
4. Describe the debits and credits made to record the following transaction in the cash receipts journal: Sales, $375.00; sales taxes, $18.75; net cash, $390.75.
5. Describe the debits and credits made to record the following transaction in the cash receipts journal: Sales, $620.00; sales taxes, $24.80; net cash, $647.10.

Compare your answers to those in the answers section. Re-read the preceding part of the chapter to find the correct answers to any questions you may have missed.

The Petty Cash Fund

In earlier chapters, you learned that most businesses control cash by writing checks for all payments made. Writing checks for very small payments, however, is costly, time consuming, and impractical for many businesses. Many businesses keep some cash on hand for making small, incidental cash payments. This cash on hand is called a **petty cash fund.** Typical cash payments made from a petty cash fund are for purchases of postage stamps and small amounts of supplies and for such expenses as small delivery bills and taxi or bus fare for employees on business errands.

The word "petty" indicates that only small amounts of cash are paid out of this fund. When setting up a petty cash fund, each business determines the maximum amount that will be paid out by a petty cash disbursement. A **petty cash disbursement** is any payment made from the petty cash fund. All payments over the maximum amount are paid by check. The person responsible for maintaining the petty cash fund and for making cash disbursements is called the **petty cashier.**

Reteaching Strategies

Provide a cash drawer with play money, and explain that the money in the drawer is the change fund. Ask a volunteer to count the money, then have one student act as the cashier, making change for each sale, as students role play a few business transactions.

When the role playing is over, ask the volunteer to count the money again. Ask the students to complete a cash proof form, and, if necessary, indicate the amount of cash short or over.

Establishing the Petty Cash Fund

Before a petty cash fund is established, a business must determine the amount of cash needed in the fund. The business estimates the amount of cash that will be needed for a certain period of time, usually a month. This estimate is based on the company's past experiences in making cash payments of small amounts. Let's look at an example of how a petty cash fund is established.

On May 1, East Side Book Store decided to establish a petty cash fund. Crystal Casteel, an office clerk, was appointed petty cashier. The business decided that the petty cash fund would contain $100.00 and that any amounts over $10.00 would be paid by check. The company accountant, Greta Keegan, wrote Check 151 for $100.00, payable to "Petty Cashier—Crystal Casteel," to establish the fund. Crystal Casteel cashed the check and placed the money, consisting of small denominations of bills and coins, in a petty cash box. For better internal control over the fund, the petty cash box is kept in an office safe or a locked desk drawer. Crystal is now responsible for the $100.00 in the petty cash fund. She will make all petty cash disbursements.

When a petty cash fund is established, a new asset account—Petty Cash Fund—is created. Petty Cash Fund appears in the chart of accounts after the Cash in Bank and Change Fund accounts.

The establishment of East Side's petty cash fund is illustrated in the T accounts. Petty Cash Fund is debited for $100.00, the amount of the fund. Cash in Bank is credited for $100.00, the amount of the check. The Petty Cash Fund account usually is debited only once: when the petty cash fund is established.

Petty Cash Fund		Cash in Bank	
Dr.	Cr.	Dr.	Cr.
+	–	+	–
$100.00			$100.00

The cash payments journal entry to establish a petty cash fund is shown in Figure 21-4.

	DATE	DOC. NO.	ACCOUNT TITLE	POST. REF.	GENERAL DEBIT	GENERAL CREDIT	ACCOUNTS PAYABLE DEBIT	PURCHASES DISCOUNTS CREDIT	CASH IN BANK CREDIT	
1	19-- May 1	Ck150	Change Fund		100 00				100 00	1
2	1	Ck151	Petty Cash Fund		100 00				100 00	2

CASH PAYMENTS JOURNAL   PAGE 12

Figure 21-4   Recording the Journal Entry To Establish a Petty Cash Fund

When petty cash disbursements occur more often than expected and the petty cash fund is used up before the end of the specified time period, the company may decide to increase the dollar size of the petty cash fund. The journal entry to record the increase is similar to the entry to establish the petty cash fund shown in Figure 21-4. When the petty cash fund is increased, Petty Cash Fund is debited and Cash in Bank is credited for the amount of the increase.

CHAPTER 21   Accounting for Cash Funds   469

CONCEPT DEVELOPMENT
Making Petty Cash Payments

An important point for students to understand is that the petty cash fund operates on an imprest basis, which means the sum of all the paid vouchers, plus the amount of cash in the petty cash box, must be equal to the amount for which the fund was originally established. A petty cash voucher must be completed as a record of each cash disbursement.

Using Visuals

Call students' attention to Figure 21-5. Emphasize that the account to be debited for this petty cash disbursement is Supplies.

 ACCOUNTING PRACTICE
Students may complete Exercise 21-3 after the section on making petty cash payments.

CONCEPT DEVELOPMENT
Replenishing the Petty Cash Fund

Guide students through the reconciliation of the petty cash fund and the journal entry that is made to replenish the fund. Use demonstration problem 21-6 to give students practice in journalizing the entry to replenish the petty cash fund.

ACCOUNTING *Notes*
For internal control of petty cash, most businesses purchase prenumbered petty cash vouchers.

Making Petty Cash Payments

The petty cashier is responsible for making payments from the petty cash fund. Whenever a cash payment is made, a petty cash voucher is completed. A **petty cash voucher** is a proof of payment from the petty cash fund.

An example of a petty cash voucher is shown in Figure 21-5. Petty cash vouchers are usually prenumbered. If they are not, the petty cashier numbers them as they are issued. The petty cash voucher includes the following information: (1) the date of the payment, (2) the person or business to whom the payment is made, (3) the amount of the payment, (4) the reason for the payment, (5) the account to be debited, (6) the signature of the person approving the payment (usually the petty cashier), and (7) the signature of the person receiving the payment. After the petty cash disbursement is made, the paid voucher is usually filed in the petty cash box until the fund is reimbursed.

Figure 21-5 Petty Cash Voucher

Replenishing the Petty Cash Fund

As payments are made out of the petty cash fund, the amount of cash in the petty cash box decreases. Some businesses set a minimum amount that must be kept in the petty cash box. When the amount of cash in the fund reaches that minimum amount, petty cash is replenished. Replenishing the petty cash fund restores the fund to its original cash balance.

The petty cash fund is usually replenished once a month or when its balance reaches the minimum amount. The petty cash fund is also replenished at the end of the business's fiscal period, even if the minimum balance has not been reached. At the end of a fiscal period, the business's financial statements must report the financial condition of the business at that time. The petty cash fund, therefore, is replenished to update the balances of the accounts affected by petty cash payments. The petty cash fund is then at its original amount for the start of the next fiscal period.

The first step in replenishing the petty cash fund is to reconcile the cash balance in the fund.

▲ **Reconciling the Petty Cash Fund**   The petty cash fund is reconciled to determine whether the fund is in balance. To reconcile the fund, the petty cashier first adds all the paid petty cash vouchers. This total is then subtracted from the original cash balance of the fund. The difference

470

UNIT 5   Accounting for Special Procedures

Interdisciplinary Connections

LANGUAGE ARTS

The word *petty,* as in "petty cash," comes from the French *petit,* or small, and is used in several other terms. A trial jury, for example, is a petty (or petit) jury, in contrast to a grand jury. Petty larceny is less serious than grand larceny. Ask students to think of other related words (e.g., petite, petticoat).

is the *reconciled petty cash balance,* or the amount of money that *should be* in the petty cash box. If a count of the cash in the petty cash box agrees with the reconciled balance, the fund is in balance. If the two amounts do not agree, the petty cash fund is either short or over.

On May 1, Crystal Casteel, the petty cashier for East Side Book Store, totaled all the petty cash vouchers. The total petty cash disbursements for the month were $87.75. As you recall, the original amount of money established for East Side's petty cash fund was $100.00. The reconciled petty cash balance was then calculated as follows:

Original balance	$100.00
Total of paid petty cash vouchers	− 87.75
Reconciled petty cash balance	$ 12.25

When Crystal counted the actual amount of cash in the petty cash box, she found that there was $12.25. The petty cash fund, therefore, is in balance.

▲ Preparing a Petty Cash Requisition Form

When the petty cash fund is replenished, the amounts paid out of petty cash must be recorded in the appropriate general ledger accounts.

After the petty cash fund has been reconciled, the petty cashier prepares a petty cash requisition. A **petty cash requisition** is a form requesting money to replenish the petty cash fund. A typical petty cash requisition is illustrated in Figure 21-6 below. This form serves as the source of information for the check written to replenish the petty cash fund. The check stub then serves as the source document for the entry recorded in the cash payments journal.

```
                    PETTY CASH REQUISITION


        Accounts for which
        payments were made:                        Amount


            Supplies                               $24.45
            Advertising Expense                      14.80
            Delivery Expense                         19.00
            Miscellaneous Expense                    11.75
            Travel Expense                           17.75


        TOTAL CASH NEEDED TO
           REPLENISH FUND                          $87.75


        Requested by: Crystal Casteel      Date 5/31/--
                        Petty Cashier

        Approved by: Greta Keegan          Date 5/31/--
                        Accountant

                              Check No. 168
```

Figure 21-6 Petty Cash Requisition

Making Connections

AROUND THE WORLD

Suzuki Motor Corporation has a relatively small share of the automotive market in the United States. Its market share in other countries, though, is impressive. The company's market strategy is to sell cars in the areas of the world where cars are not yet used much. For example, Suzuki has a 76-percent market share in India and 66 percent in Pakistan. China is another large market for Suzuki, which sells more cars there than any other Japanese car manufacturer.

Chapter 21

CONCEPT DEVELOPMENT
Using a Petty Cash Register

Many businesses keep files of vouchers issued for petty cash disbursements and do not record them in a petty cash register. Businesses that have frequent petty cash disbursements may need to record them in a petty cash register. Remind students that this register is not a journal; it is not a record of original entry and no amounts are transferred (posted) from the register to any accounts.

To prepare the petty cash requisition, the petty cashier first sorts the paid petty cash vouchers according to the accounts to be debited. The vouchers for each account are totaled. The account title and the total amount to be debited to that account are then recorded on the petty cash requisition. Look at Figure 21-6 on page 271 again. During May, East Side Book Store made petty cash disbursements affecting the general ledger accounts Supplies, Advertising Expense, Delivery Expense, Miscellaneous Expense, and Travel Expense.

The total of all the paid petty cash vouchers is the amount of cash needed to replenish the petty cash fund. When the accountant receives the petty cash requisition from the petty cashier, a check is written for the total of the paid vouchers. The check is made payable to the petty cashier, who cashes the check and places the money in the petty cash box.

R E M E M B E R

The *only* time Petty Cash Fund is debited is when the fund is initially established or when the amount of money in the fund is increased.

Using a Petty Cash Register

Some businesses like to have a written record of all the paid petty cash vouchers. A **petty cash register** is a record of all disbursements made from the petty cash fund. The petty cash register is a supplemental record used to summarize the types of petty cash disbursements. It is not an accounting journal because no amounts are posted from this register to general ledger accounts.

▲ **Recording Petty Cash Vouchers in a Petty Cash Register** Not all businesses having a petty cash fund use a petty cash register. Those who do might use a form similar to that shown in Figure 21-7. This illustration shows how East Side Book Store's petty cash vouchers would be recorded.

Notice that the establishment of the petty cash fund on May 1 is noted on line 1 of the register. Each petty cash payment is identified by date, voucher number, and a brief explanation. The amount of each disbursement is entered in the Payments column *and* in the appropriate Distribution of Payments column. There are three special amount columns: Supplies, Delivery Expense, and Miscellaneous Expense. The General Amount column is used for petty cash payments that cannot be entered in one of the three special amount columns.

▲ **Totaling and Proving the Petty Cash Register** When the petty cash fund is replenished, the petty cash register is totaled and proved. Refer to Figure 21-7 as you read the following steps on totaling and proving a petty cash register:

1. Enter the date the fund is being replenished in the Date column. Also enter the word "Totals" in the Explanation column.
2. Single rule the amount columns.

Making Connections

BUSINESS ETHICS

Marcy is the petty cashier for the company where she works. Recently, she told you that she often borrows money from the petty cash fund. She always leaves an IOU and repays the fund within a few days. How would you respond to Marcy?

(Answer: Explain to Marcy that what she is doing is unethical. The petty cash fund was set up to pay for business expenses, not to serve as a convenient source of funds for employees. Marcy may need some advice on managing her money.)

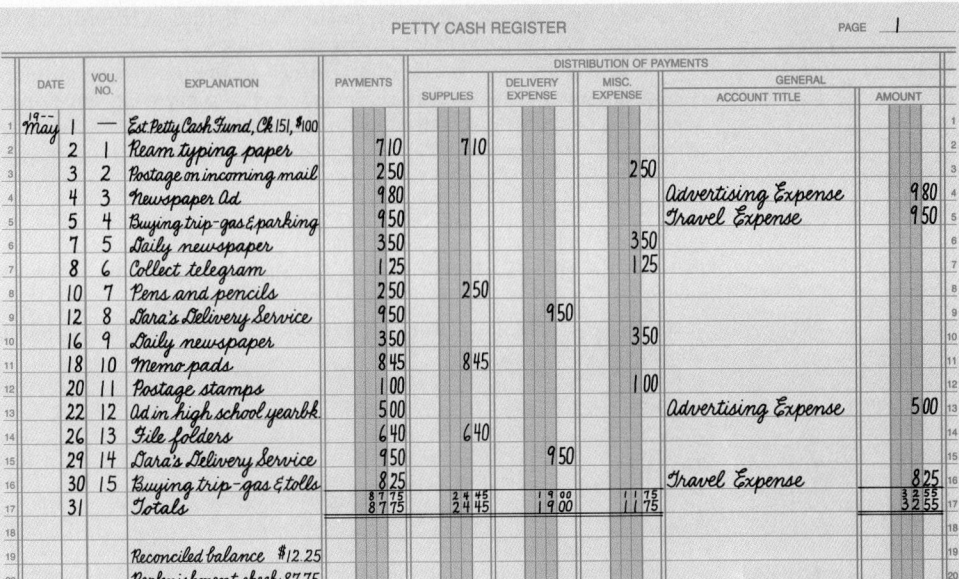

DATE	VOU. NO.	EXPLANATION	PAYMENTS	DISTRIBUTION OF PAYMENTS				
				SUPPLIES	DELIVERY EXPENSE	MISC. EXPENSE	GENERAL — ACCOUNT TITLE	AMOUNT
19-- May 1	—	Est Petty Cash Fund, Ck 151, $100						
2	1	Ream typing paper	7 10	7 10				
3	2	Postage on incoming mail	2 50			2 50		
4	3	Newspaper Ad	9 80				Advertising Expense	9 80
5	4	Buying trip-gas&parking	9 50				Travel Expense	9 50
7	5	Daily newspaper	3 50			3 50		
8	6	Collect telegram	1 25			1 25		
10	7	Pens and pencils	2 50	2 50				
12	8	Dara's Delivery Service	9 50		9 50			
16	9	Daily newspaper	3 50			3 50		
18	10	Memo pads	8 45	8 45				
20	11	Postage stamps	1 00			1 00		
22	12	Ad in high school yearbk	5 00				Advertising Expense	5 00
26	13	File folders	6 40	6 40				
29	14	Dara's Delivery Service	9 50		9 50			
30	15	Buying trip-gas&tolls	8 25				Travel Expense	8 25
31		Totals	87 75	24 45	19 00	11 75		32 55
			87 75	24 45	19 00	11 75		32 55
		Reconciled balance $12.25						
		Replenishment check 87.75						
		Total $100.00						

Figure 21-7   A Typical Petty Cash Register

3. Foot each amount column.
4. Verify that the total of the Payments column is equal to the total of the Distribution of Payments columns. In this example, total payments equal $87.75. The total of the Supplies, Delivery Expense, Miscellaneous Expense, and General columns also equals $87.75 ($24.45 + $19.00 + $11.75 + $32.55). Once verified, the totals are then recorded below the footings.
5. Draw a double rule under the amount columns to show that the totals have been proved.
6. Next, enter the petty cash fund replenishment information. Skip one line. Then write the reconciled petty cash balance (the amount of cash that should be in the petty cash box before it is replenished). For East Side Book Store, that amount is $12.25.
7. On the next line, write the amount of the check written to replenish the petty cash fund.
8. Add the balance in the petty cash fund and the amount of the check. The sum should equal the original amount of the petty cash fund.

As you can see, the petty cash register helps the petty cashier keep track of the petty cash disbursements by account. When the petty cash fund is replenished, the totals of the special columns and the amounts recorded in the General column would be listed on the petty cash requisition form.

Using a Petty Cash Envelope

Small businesses sometimes use a petty cash envelope for recording petty cash disbursements. A form very similar to the petty cash register is

CHAPTER 21   Accounting for Cash Funds   **473**

Cooperative Learning

GROUP DISCUSSION

Assign students to groups of four or five and ask them to recommend internal controls for the management of petty cash.

(Answer: Group suggestions will vary, but the following internal controls should be included: (a) Determine the maximum amount and/or types of expenses to be paid from the petty cash fund. (b) Keep the money in a safe or in a locked box. (c) Use prenumbered petty cash voucher forms. (d) Record all disbursements in a petty cash register or on a petty cash envelope. (e) Replenish the fund at the end of each accounting period.)

Refer to the "Cooperative Learning" section of *Tech Prep Strategies in Accounting* for additional cooperative learning strategies.

printed on the front of the petty cash envelope. Entries to record cash disbursements are the same as for a petty cash register.

The paid petty cash vouchers are placed in the petty cash envelope. When the petty cash fund is replenished, the petty cash envelope—containing all the paid vouchers for the period—is sealed and filed. A new envelope is used to record the next period's petty cash disbursements.

Journalizing the Check To Replenish the Petty Cash Fund

When the check is written to replenish the petty cash fund, it must be recorded in the cash payments journal. The check stub is the source document for recording the journal entry. Look at the cash payments journal shown in Figure 21-8.

	DATE	DOC. NO.	ACCOUNT TITLE	POST. REF.	GENERAL DEBIT	GENERAL CREDIT	ACCOUNTS PAYABLE DEBIT	PURCHASES DISCOUNTS CREDIT	CASH IN BANK CREDIT	
1	19-- May 1	Ck150	Change Fund		100 00				100 00	1
2	1	Ck151	Petty Cash Fund		100 00				100 00	2
19	31	Ck168	Supplies		24 45				87 75	19
20			Advertising Expense		14 80					20
21			Delivery Expense		19 00					21
22			Miscellaneous Expense		11 75					22
23			Travel Expense		17 75					23

Figure 21-8 Recording the Replenishment of the Petty Cash Fund in the Cash Payments Journal

The date of the transaction is the date of the check. As you can see, Cash in Bank is credited for $87.75, the amount of the check. The individual accounts are debited for the amount of the paid petty cash vouchers as listed on the petty cash requisition. For example, the Supplies account is debited for $24.45.

The petty cashier is the only person who has access to the petty cash fund and the only person authorized to disburse cash from the fund.

474

UNIT 5   Accounting for Special Procedures

Making Connections

COMMUNICATIONS

Most computer word-processing programs offer a "spell-check" and sometimes a "grammar-check" feature. Remind students that these features do not eliminate the need for them to do their own careful proofreading of written reports for grammar, spelling, and choice of the correct word. Spell-check programs accept any word that is spelled correctly!

When replenishing the petty cash fund, always credit **Cash in Bank** and debit the accounts for which petty cash payments have been made. The **Petty Cash Fund** account is not affected by this transaction.

Before you read any further, do the following activity to check your understanding of how to establish and replenish a petty cash fund.

Check Your Learning

Use notebook paper to write your answers to these questions.

1. The Shutter Bug, a retail camera shop, established a petty cash fund of $80.00. The petty cashier had paid vouchers totaling $73.00. What is the reconciled amount of the petty cash fund?
2. Lovell's Flower Shop wrote a check for $60.00 to establish a petty cash fund. Which account is debited and which account is credited in the journal entry to record this transaction?
3. During January, Lovell's paid the following petty cash vouchers: Supplies, $16.00; Advertising Expense, $9.00; Delivery Expense, $15.90; and Miscellaneous Expense, $8.75. When the petty cash fund is reconciled, how much money should be in the petty cash box?
4. Using the information given in Question 3, which accounts are debited and credited to record the replenishment of the petty cash fund? What are the amounts of each debit and credit?
5. What is the purpose of a petty cash requisition?

Compare your answers to those in the answers section. Re-read the preceding part of the chapter to find the answers to any questions you missed.

Handling Cash Short and Over in the Petty Cash Fund

The petty cashier may occasionally make an error when paying out cash from the petty cash fund. When this happens, the amount of cash in the petty cash box will not agree with the reconciled petty cash balance.

As with the change fund, any amounts of cash gained or lost through errors made by the petty cashier must be recorded in the business's accounting records. As you remember, cash shortages represent expenses for the business, while cash overages represent revenues. The Cash Short and Over account is used to record these cash shortages and overages.

Let's look at an example. At the end of June, Crystal Casteel, the petty cashier at East Side Book Store, classified and totaled the petty cash vouchers. The accounts affected by the petty cash disbursements were as follows:

Supplies	$15.75
Advertising Expense	25.00
Delivery Expense	20.45
Miscellaneous Expense	12.30
Travel Expense	9.50

The total petty cash disbursements for June were $83.00. Crystal then reconciled the petty cash fund.

Original balance	$100.00
Total of paid petty cash vouchers	− 83.00
Reconciled petty cash balance	$ 17.00

When Crystal counted the actual cash left in the petty cash box, however, she found that there was only $15.50. The petty cash fund was short $1.50. Instead of needing $83.00 to bring the petty cash fund up to the original $100.00, $84.50 is needed ($83.00 + $1.50). The $1.50 cash shortage is considered to be an expense and will be debited to Cash Short and Over.

When Crystal prepared the petty cash requisition form, she listed the accounts to be debited for the petty cash disbursements. She also indicated that the Cash Short and Over account was to be debited for $1.50. The cash payments journal entry to record the replenishment is shown in Figure 21-9.

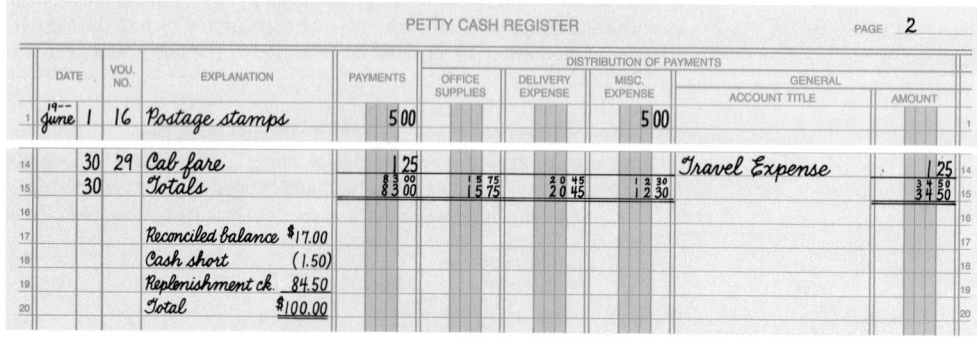

Figure 21-9 Recording a Petty Cash Fund Shortage in the Cash Payments Journal

A petty cash overage would be recorded in a similar manner. If, for example, the actual cash in the petty cash box had been $17.75, there would have been a cash overage of $0.75. Cash Short and Over would have been credited for that amount in the journal entry. Instead of needing $83.00 to replenish the fund, only $82.25 would have been requested.

If a business uses a petty cash register, the cash shortage or overage is also reported in that record. Look at Figure 21-10 to see how the June cash shortage of $1.50 was recorded on the petty cash register page.

Figure 21-10 Recording a Cash Shortage in the Petty Cash Register

476

Summary of Key Points

1. A change fund is an amount of money, consisting of various denominations of bills and coins, that is used to make change for cash transactions.
2. The asset account Change Fund is usually debited only once—when the change fund is established.
3. A cash proof is prepared at the end of each business day to determine whether the cash in the cash register drawer, less the amount of the change fund, is equal to the cash sales shown on the cash register tape.
4. A petty cash fund is the cash a business has on hand for making small, incidental cash payments.
5. The asset account Petty Cash Fund is usually debited only once—when the petty cash fund is established.
6. A petty cash voucher is prepared by the petty cashier when a disbursement is made from the petty cash fund.
7. The petty cashier prepares a petty cash requisition to request that the petty cash fund be replenished.
8. Some companies want a record of all petty cash disbursements on one form. Such companies may use a petty cash register or a petty cash envelope to record all petty cash disbursements.
9. When errors are made in making change for cash customers or paying out cash from the petty cash fund, cash is said to be short or over. Shortages and overages are recorded in the account Cash Short and Over.

3 CLOSE

CHAPTER SUMMARY
This summary enumerates the key information in the chapter. It is a useful tool for reinforcement and review.

Pop Quiz

1. The amount of money used to make change in cash transactions is called a(n) _____ account.
2. The Cash Short and Over account is classified as a(n) _____.
3. Cash shortages and overages are recorded in the _____ journal.
4. What is a petty cash voucher?
5. Where are disbursements made from the petty cash fund recorded?

ANSWERS
1. Change fund
2. Temporary owner's equity account
3. Cash receipts
4. Proof of payment from the petty cash fund
5. Petty cash register

21 Review and Applications

PRACTICE AND APPLY

- Language Development
- Comprehension and Retention
- Basic Skills

Building Your Accounting Vocabulary

See the Glossary on pages 670-679 for definitions of these terms.

Reviewing Your Accounting Knowledge

1. The Change Fund account is debited and the Cash in Bank account is credited.

2. When too much change is given to a customer or when theft or the wrongful or negligent entering of amounts on the register tape occur.

3. A cash shortage is treated like an expense because it is considered a cost of doing business.

4. A temporary owner's equity account. It does not have a normal balance side.

5. To make small, incidental payments using cash rather than having to write checks for the payments.

6. Postage stamps, small amounts of supplies, and newspaper delivery.

7. The Petty Cash Fund account is debited and the Cash in Bank account is credited.

8. The Petty Cash Fund account is usually debited only once—when the fund is established. It may also be debited if the business decides to increase the amount of the fund.

9. To update the balances of the accounts for which payments have been made.

10. The petty cash fund is reconciled to determine whether the fund is in balance. The total of the paid petty cash vouchers is subtracted from the original balance of the fund. The difference, or reconciled amount, should agree with the cash in the petty cash box.

11. (a) Reconcile the fund. (b) Prepare a petty cash requisition. (c) Have the accountant write a check for the total amount needed to replenish the fund. (d) Record the transaction in the cash payments journal.

12. Because no amounts are posted from this register to the ledger accounts.

Building Your Accounting Vocabulary

In your own words, write the definition of each of the following accounting terms. Use complete sentences for your definitions.

change fund   petty cash register   petty cash voucher
petty cash fund   petty cash requisition   petty cashier
petty cash
   disbursement

Reviewing Your Accounting Knowledge

1. Which accounts are debited and credited when a change fund is established?
2. When does a cash shortage occur?
3. Explain why a cash shortage is treated like an expense.
4. What type of account is Cash Short and Over?
5. Why would a business want to set up a petty cash fund?
6. List three payments that might be made from a petty cash fund.
7. Which accounts are debited and credited to establish a petty cash fund?
8. How often is the Petty Cash Fund account debited?
9. Why should the petty cash fund be replenished at the end of the fiscal period?
10. What is meant by reconciling the petty cash fund?
11. Explain the procedure for replenishing the petty cash fund.
12. Why is the petty cash register not considered a journal?

Improving Your Decision-Making Skills

Alec Grey was recently appointed petty cashier for the Jerez Company. Alec is concerned because some employees have asked him to cash small personal checks for them from the petty cash fund. Other employees have asked to borrow money from the fund until payday. Alec believes he would be wrong to cash personal checks or lend money from the petty cash fund. How can he handle this situation without creating hard feelings among the employees?

Applying Accounting Procedures

Exercise 21-1   Preparing a Cash Proof

The change fund for Messina's Grocery Store is $200.00. On March 31, total cash sales from cash register 6 are $964.00 and sales taxes are $57.84. A count of cash shows $1,216.84 in the cash register drawer.

Instructions: Use the form in your working papers to prepare a cash proof. Sign your name as salesclerk.

Improving Your Decision-Making Skills

Alec could handle this situation by creating guidelines that specifically state that disbursements will be made only for company-related payments. He should make sure that all employees receive a copy of the guidelines and that a copy is posted on the company bulletin board.

SPREADSHEET **Exercise 21-2 Calculating Cash Short and Over**

PROBLEM

Buddie's Gift Shop has a change fund of $125.00. The cash sales, sales tax, and amount of cash in the cash register drawer for the week of February 11-16 are shown below.

Instructions: Determine the total sales amount, net amount of cash received, and any cash shortage or overage. Use notebook paper or the form provided in your working papers.

Date	Cash Sales	Sales Tax	Cash in Drawer
Feb. 11	$183.50	$ 7.34	$315.84
12	199.75	7.99	332.49
13	206.10	8.24	338.34
14	223.15	8.93	358.18
15	234.30	9.37	366.62
16	288.90	11.56	435.46

Exercise 21-3 Preparing a Petty Cash Voucher

Riddle's Card Shop has a petty cash fund of $75.00. On October 3, the store ran out of tape for the cash register. Paul Howard, an employee, went to Adco Office Supplies to buy the cash register tape (office supplies). The total cost was $2.67.

Instructions: Reimburse Paul Howard by completing petty cash voucher 13 in your workbook. Sign your name as petty cashier.

Exercise 21-4 Replenishing a Petty Cash Fund

Arts and Crafts, Inc., has a petty cash fund of $80.00. During the first six months of the period, the business had the petty cash disbursements below.

Instructions: Use notebook paper or the form in your workbook.

(1) For each period, determine the total petty cash payments, the reconciled petty cash balance, the amount of cash short or over (if any), and the amount of the check needed to replenish the fund.

(2) Determine the balance of Cash Short and Over at the end of the six months. Is this balance revenue or an expense for Arts and Crafts?

Date	Supplies	Delivery Expense	Miscellaneous Expense	Advertising Expense	Actual Cash in Petty Cash Box
Jan. 31	$29.15	$ 9.42	$16.40	$10.00	$15.03
Feb. 28	14.62	11.09	19.63	13.95	20.70
Mar. 31	20.65	12.16	14.10	17.00	14.31
Apr. 30	15.63	8.73	12.98	19.67	24.89
May 31	9.95	4.05	26.07	23.95	14.48
June 30	19.46	13.60	18.42	17.41	10.11

Problem 21-1 Establishing a Change Fund

On April 1, Chang Nee opened Nee's Chinese Restaurant. He wrote Check 115 to establish a change fund of $150.00. At the end of the business day on April 1, the shop's cash register tape (T1) showed cash sales of $340.00, plus sales taxes of $17.00. An actual cash count of the money indicated that $505.00 was in the cash register drawer.

479

PRACTICE AND APPLY

• Concepts and Procedures

Exercise 21-1: Ch. Obj. 2
Net cash, $1,016.84
Cash short, $5.00

Exercise 21-2: Ch. Obj. 2, 7

SPREADSHEET **Problem 21-2 can be completed using *Spreadsheet Applications*, the spreadsheet software that accompanies *Glencoe Accounting.***

PROBLEM

Net cash:
Feb. 11, $190.84
Feb. 12, $207.49; $0.25 short
Feb. 13, $213.34; $1.00 short
Feb. 14, $233.18; $1.10 over
Feb. 15, $241.62; $2.05 short
Feb. 16, $310.46; $10.00 over

Exercise 21-3: Ch. Obj. 5

Exercise 21-4: Ch. Obj. 4, 7
Replenishment Checks:
Jan. 31, $64.97
Feb. 28, $59.30
Mar. 31, $65.69
April 30, $55.11
May 31, $65.52
June 30, $69.89

Balance of Cash Short and Over:
Debit balance, $2.39; expense

Refer students to the Chapter 21 review pages in the workbook, *Chapter Reviews and Working Papers.*

Problem 21-1: Ch. Obj. 1, 2
Cash short, $2.00

Problem 21-2: Ch. Obj. 3, 4, 6
Total petty cash vouchers, $95.00

Problem 21-3: Ch. Obj. 3, 4, 6
Petty cash requisition:

Office Supplies	$14.00
Adv. Expense	25.00
Del. Expense	16.90
Misc. Expense	12.60
Total	$68.50

Instructions:

(1) Record the entry to establish the change fund on page 1 of the cash payments journal.

(2) Prepare a cash proof for April 1. Sign your name on the Salesclerk line.

(3) Record the cash sales for April 1 in the cash receipts journal, page 1.

Problem 21-2 Establishing and Replenishing a Petty Cash Fund

Medical Health Services established a petty cash fund for payments of $10.00 or less. The following transactions involve the fund.

(1) Record the entry to establish the petty cash fund on page 6 of the cash payments journal.

(2) Record the entry for replenishing the petty cash fund in the cash payments journal.

Transactions:

June 1   Wrote Check 501 for $100.00 to establish a petty cash fund.

30   The accountant wrote Check 549 to replenish the petty cash fund. Paid petty cash vouchers included: Medical Supplies, $40.00; Delivery Expense, $27.00; Miscellaneous Expense, $12.00; and Office Expense, $16.00.

Problem 21-3 Establishing and Replenishing a Petty Cash Fund

Gateway Studios, a film producing company, decided to establish a petty cash fund. On September 1, the accountant, Al Rosen, wrote Check 418 for $70.00 to establish the fund. The following disbursements were made.

Instructions:

(1) Record the entry to establish the petty cash fund in the cash payments journal, page 9.

(2) Make a list of the paid petty cash vouchers.

(3) Classify the petty cash disbursements by account. Calculate the total amount paid out for each account.

(4) Prepare a petty cash requisition, signing your name on the Petty Cashier line. On September 30, an actual count of the cash in the petty cash box indicated a balance of $1.50.

(5) Record the entry in the cash payments journal to replenish the petty cash fund on September 30. Use Check 441.

Transactions:

Sept. 1   Purchased memo pads for the office, $2.75, Voucher 101 (Office Supplies).

3   Prepared Voucher 102 for a $7.50 newspaper ad (Advertising Expense).

5   Wrote Voucher 103 for the postage on an outgoing package, $1.75 (Miscellaneous Expense).

8   Paid Dandy Delivery Service $5.65, Voucher 104 (Delivery Expense).

10   Issued Voucher 105 for pens and pencils, $3.75 (Office Supplies).

12   Paid $2.20 for postage stamps, Voucher 106 (Miscellaneous Expense).

15   Wrote Voucher 107 to Dandy Delivery Service, $6.75 (Delivery Expense).

480

Teacher Notes

_____

_____

_____

_____

_____

Sept. 20 Paid the news carrier $4.25 for delivery of the daily newspaper, Voucher 108 (Miscellaneous Expense).

  22 Bought typing paper for $7.50, Voucher 109 (Office Supplies).

  25 Paid $4.50 to Dandy Delivery Service, Voucher 110 (Delivery Expense).

  27 Prepared Voucher 111 for a $10.00 ad (Advertising Expense).

  28 Bought $4.40 in postage stamps, Voucher 112 (Miscellaneous Expense).

  30 Prepared Voucher 113 for a $7.50 ad (Advertising Expense).

Problem 21-4   Using a Petty Cash Register

Use the information in Problem 21-3 to complete this problem.

Instructions:

(1) Enter the information about the establishment of the petty cash fund on line 1 of a petty cash register, page 1.

(2) Record the petty cash disbursements in the petty cash register.

(3) Total and prove the petty cash register on September 30.

(4) Check 441 was issued to replenish the petty cash fund. Record the replenishment information in the petty cash register.

Problem 21-5   Handling a Petty Cash Fund

Copy World, a duplicating service business, is owned and operated by Kathleen Houser. A petty cash fund was established on December 1 when the accountant wrote Check 563 for $100.00. The accounts for which petty cash disbursements are likely to be made include: Office Supplies, Photo Supplies, Advertising Expense, Delivery Expense, and Miscellaneous Expense.

Instructions:

(1) Record the entry to establish the petty cash fund on page 12 of a cash payments journal.

(2) Record the establishment of the fund on the first line of the petty cash register, page 1.

(3) Record each petty cash disbursement in the petty cash register.

(4) Foot, prove, total, and rule the petty cash register on December 31.

(5) Reconcile the petty cash fund. An actual cash count of the fund shows a balance of $1.50.

(6) Prepare a petty cash requisition. Sign your name as Petty Cashier.

(7) Record the cash payments journal entry to replenish the petty cash fund by issuing Check 580.

(8) Record the replenishment information in the petty cash register.

(9) The accountant believes the petty cash fund should be increased by $25.00. Record the issuance of Check 581 on December 31.

Transactions:

Dec. 1 Bought an $8.00 ad in the local newspaper, Voucher 101.

  2 Prepared Voucher 102 for $7.50 to pay Mercury Messenger for packages delivered.

  3 Bought adding machine tape for 75¢, Voucher 103.

  5 Paid $9.50 for flowers for an employee's birthday, Voucher 104.

  7 Prepared Voucher 105, $5.25, for a typewriter ribbon.

  9 Paid $4.40 for postage stamps, Voucher 106.

481

Problem 21-4: Ch. Obj. 5, 6

Replenishment of fund:

Fund	$70.00
Vouchers	68.50
Balance	$ 1.50

Problem 21-5: Ch. Obj. 3, 4, 5, 6, 7

Petty cash requisition:

Office Supplies	$20.30
Photo Supplies	14.80
Adv. Expense	13.00
Del. Expense	22.50
Misc. Expense	27.15
Cash short	0.75
Total	$98.50

Teacher Notes

Teaching Tips

■ Remind students that voided source documents are never destroyed. The word "void" is written across the document, which is then filed.

Problem 21-6: Ch. Obj. 5

CHALLENGE

PROBLEM

The last problem in each chapter is a challenge problem and is identified by this "maze" symbol.

Replenishment of fund:	
Office Supplies	$ 30.50
Del. Expense	20.20
Misc. Expense	15.65
General	40.70
	$107.05
Cash short	(2.20)

4 ASSESS

A chapter test is available for use in assessing students' understanding of concepts in this chapter.

The testmaker software will enable you to develop tailor-made chapter, unit, semester, and final tests.

Alternative Assessment

For alternative assessment strategies, refer to *Tech Prep Strategies in Accounting.*

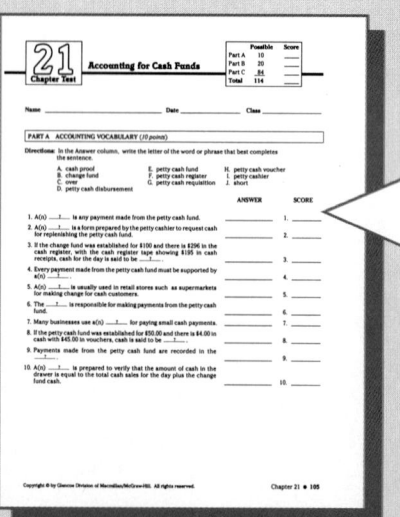

Use Chapter Test 21 here to assess students' understanding and retention of the concepts and procedures presented in the chapter.

Dec. 12 Bought photo supplies for $9.00, Voucher 107.
15 Paid $8.50 to have the shop's windows washed, Voucher 108.
18 Bought memo pads, pencils, and pens for office use, $6.30, issuing Voucher 109.
20 Prepared Voucher 110 for $7.50 to pay Mercury Messenger for packages delivered.
23 Prepared Voucher 111 incorrectly and voided it.
23 Bought stationery for $8.00, Voucher 112.
27 Paid the news carrier $4.75 for the daily newspaper, Voucher 113.
29 Issued Voucher 114 to Mercury Messenger for packages delivered, $7.50.
30 Bought photo supplies, $5.80, issuing Voucher 115.
31 Issued Voucher 116 for a newspaper ad, $5.00.

CHALLENGE

PROBLEM

Problem 21-6   Locating Errors in a Petty Cash Register

The Decorating Den is owned and operated by Lou Montgomery. On July 1, a petty cash fund of $125.00 was established with Check 411. The store prepares a petty cash voucher for each petty cash disbursement. The vouchers are then entered in a petty cash register, which is included in the working papers. When the petty cash register was totaled on July 31, the accounting clerk discovered that the footings of the distribution of payments columns did not equal total payments.

Instructions:

(1) Compare the following petty cash disbursement information with the entries in the petty cash register.

(2) Correct any errors you find in the petty cash register by drawing a line through the incorrect item and writing the correction above it.

(3) Total all columns after corrections have been made.

(4) Record the replenishment information on the register. The amount in the petty cash box on July 31 is $15.75.

Date	Vou. No.	Paid to	For	Account	Amount
July 2	1	Paperama	Shopping bags	Store Supplies	$9.45
3	2	Windsor's	ZIP Code book	Miscellaneous Expense	5.20
5	3	Post Office	Stamps	Miscellaneous Expense	6.25
6	4	Prater Delivery	Delivery charge	Delivery Expense	3.50
8	5	Howard Mfg.	Wallpaper book	Samples Expense	8.10
10	6	Windsor's	Typing paper	Office Supplies	6.30
10	7	Daily Examiner	Newspaper ad	Advertising Expense	7.50
11	8	Paperama	Coffee filters	Miscellaneous Expense	2.10
13	9	May Stationers	Writing tablets	Office Supplies	8.93
14	10	Swift Carriers	Delivery charge	Delivery Expense	5.85
19	11	Void			
19	12	Post Office	Postage due	Miscellaneous Expense	2.10
21	13	Prater Delivery	Delivery charge	Delivery Expense	3.50
24	14	Town Taxi	Delivery charge	Delivery Expense	7.35
26	15	Windsor's	Pens/pencils	Office Supplies	6.14
29	16	Daily Examiner	Newspaper ad	Advertising Expense	8.00
30	17	Windsor's	Typing ribbons	Office Supplies	9.13
31	18	M&M Supply	Order booklets	Store Supplies	7.65

482

Code Words for a Cashless Society

While a cashless society still seems straight out of science fiction, the symptoms have already invaded our way of life.

Electronic funds transfer systems (EFTS) use computers, telephone lines, and satellites to process financial transactions. Using an EFTS,

• Your employer can deposit your paychecks directly to your personal bank account.

• You can pay loans or make investments by transferring funds directly from your bank account to another bank or financial institution.

According to one survey, more funds are now transferred *every month* than all transactions done by traditional means before the EFTS was introduced.

Automated teller machines (ATMs) are interactive systems that let you access your bank account simply by entering a bank card, an identification number, and transaction codes. At an ATM, you can get account updates, withdraw or deposit funds, or transfer funds from one account to another.

In major cities across the country, networks, such as CIRRUS, link local banks to national computer systems. With a card and an identification code, you can withdraw cash instantly from your bank in Boston while you're vacationing in Los Angeles.

It's been estimated that in half of all United States households, at least one person uses an ATM.

Point-of-sale (POS) *systems* have not caught on quite so fast. Like ATMs, but located in retail stores, POS terminals connect your account with the store's account. You simply present your debit card to the clerk, who enters it into the terminal. The cost of your purchase is transferred from your account to the store's account.

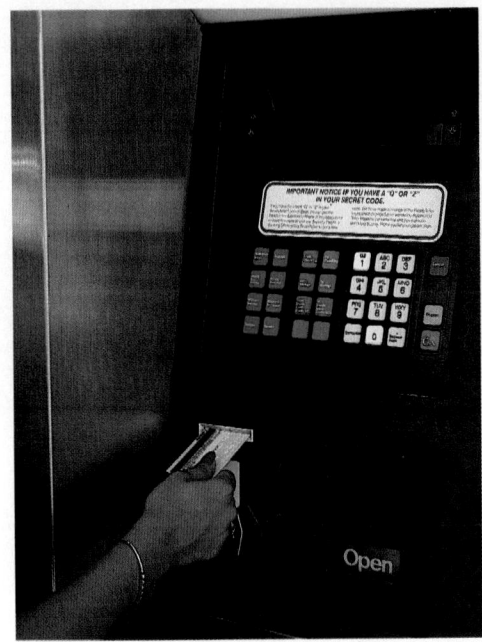

Whenever you use an automatic teller machine, you are using an input device connected to a mainframe computer.

Unlike with credit cards, there's no time lag between purchase and payment. You don't have to write a check (and half a dozen people won't need to process it). The store is paid instantly, with no exchange of cash. POS terminals are expensive, so retailers banking on a cashless operating system may have to wait a bit.

Living in a cashless society might be in your not-too-distant future.

One problem with ATMs has been security at machine locations. Ask students to determine whether there have been problems with theft at ATMs in their communities. If so, what have the authorities done to improve security?

QUESTIONS

1. How does a debit card differ from a bank credit card?
2. Why would an employer want to offer direct deposit to its employees?

ANSWERS

1. A debit card transfers money from the cardholder's account to the card issuer's account. A bank credit card charges the cardholder's account for purchases. The cardholder must then pay the bank.
2. Direct deposit is a convenience offered to many employees. It saves the employer and employee time and the need to handle large amounts of cash.

Chapter **22**

ACCOUNTING FOR THE DEPRECIATION OF PLANT AND EQUIPMENT

LOOKING BACK

In Chapter 21 students learned to account for two cash funds that are used by many businesses: the change fund and the petty cash fund. In this chapter students will learn that certain assets provide long-term economic benefits to a business. The cost of those assets is allocated over the life of each asset through depreciation. Students will learn to classify assets as current or long-term assets and to calculate depreciation using the straight-line method.

VOCABULARY DEVELOPMENT

Have students read the list of new terms. Ask for ideas for each term's meaning. Write correct responses on the board. Review the meanings of terms that are not familiar to students. Definitions of these terms are found in the chapter and in the glossary on pages 670-679.

Electronic Field Trips

Businesses own many different types of assets used to earn revenue for the business. Cash is one asset, as are office supplies, equipment, buildings, land, and merchandise. One type of asset requires special treatment in a business's accounting records. The assets in this group—such as office equipment, store equipment, delivery equipment, and buildings—all have two things in common. First, they are long-term assets that are expected to produce benefits for the business for more than one year. Second, they are purchased for use in operating the business rather than for resale.

When assets are used by a business for several years, the costs of those assets must be allocated, or spread, over the number of years of the assets' productive lives. In this chapter, you will learn how that is done.

Learning Objectives

When you have completed Chapter 22, you should be able to do the following:

1. Identify plant assets.
2. Explain the need to depreciate plant assets.
3. Calculate the annual estimated depreciation expense of a plant asset.
4. Calculate depreciation for a partial year.
5. Determine the book value of a plant asset.
6. Record adjusting entries in the general journal for depreciation.
7. Define the accounting terms introduced in this chapter.

New Terms

current assets
plant and equipment
depreciation
disposal value
straightline depreciation
accumulated depreciation
book value

484

Teaching Resources

- Lesson Plans
- TE/Chapter Reviews & Working Papers
- Demonstration Problems
- Student Study Plans
- Teaching Transparencies
- Solutions Transparencies
- Electronic Field Trips Video, Level I
- Electronic Study Guide
- Chapter 22 Test

Other Resources

- Skills Improvement Activities
- Blackline Masters
- Careers in Accounting
- Dictionary
- Math Review for Accounting
- Tech Prep Strategies in Accounting
- Video
- Test Bank with Software
- Spanish Resources/Audiotapes
- Spanish Electronic Study Guide

Plant and Equipment

Throughout this textbook, you have learned about various assets that are used in the operation of a business. These assets can be classified as either current assets or plant and equipment. **Current assets** are assets that are either used up or converted to cash during the normal operating cycle of the business, usually one year. Cash is a current asset. Accounts receivable is also a current asset because the business expects to collect cash from charge customers within a short period of time, usually 30-60 days. Merchandise is a current asset because it is sold within a short period of time, increasing cash or accounts receivable when sold.

Plant and equipment, or simply *plant assets,* are long-lived assets that are used in the production or sale of other assets or services over several accounting periods. Plant assets include land, buildings, delivery equipment, store equipment, and office equipment.

R E M E M B E R

Plant assets are used for more than one accounting period. Current assets are consumed or converted to cash in one accounting period.

You learned in Chapter 16 that assets such as supplies and prepaid insurance are consumed in the operation of a business. The costs of those assets are converted to expenses at the end of the period. Like other expenses, they must be matched with the revenue earned during the same period (the matching principle of accounting). Since current assets are used or consumed during one accounting period, the costs of those assets are easily matched to the revenue for the period. Plant assets, however, are used for a number of accounting periods. A business, then, must have a method of spreading, or allocating, the cost of a plant asset over the number of accounting periods during which the asset will be used to produce revenue. The method most businesses use is called depreciation.

Allocating the Cost of Plant Assets

The number of years a plant asset can be used—its useful life—varies from one asset to another. A delivery truck, for example, might have a useful life of six years. A microcomputer might have a useful life of only three years, since it might become obsolete within that period.

Allocating the cost of a plant asset over that asset's useful life is called **depreciation.** For accounting purposes, all plant assets except land depreciate, or decrease in value. The cost of land is not depreciated, since land is considered to have an unlimited useful life.

When a plant asset is depreciated, its cost is spread out over its useful life. For example, suppose that a plant asset costs $40,000 and has a useful life of ten years. The cost of the asset will be depreciated over those ten years. A portion of the $40,000 will be transferred to an expense account each year. At the end of ten years, most of the total cost of the plant asset will have been expensed.

CHAPTER 22   Accounting for the Depreciation of Plant and Equipment   **485**

Allocating the Cost of Plant Assets (Continued)

example of how the cost of a $300 calculator can be spread over a five-year period. You may want to let students suggest ways to determine the amount to allocate each year. Have them justify their reasoning.

ACCOUNTING PRACTICE
Students may complete Exercise 22-1 after the section "Plant and Equipment."

Using Visuals

Read the photo caption to students. Ask students to discuss the meaning of "tangible." Have students suggest examples of long-term, tangible assets.

Teaching Tips

■ Depreciation is an accounting term used to describe the allocation of cost. Depreciation does not change the actual market value of the asset. Some assets, especially buildings, appreciate in value as they are being depreciated.
■ Emphasize the phrase "allocating the cost."
■ Remind students that the term "expensed" means that the cost of an asset has been converted into an expense.

CONCEPT DEVELOPMENT
Estimating Depreciation of a Plant Asset

Stress that depreciation must be estimated because it is impossible to know at the time of purchase two major facts: (1) the useful life of an asset and (2) the disposal value, which is the value of an asset at replacement time.

Mention that certain guidelines are used to estimate depreciation: (1) past experience, (2) published information by the IRS, and (3) manufacturers' estimates.

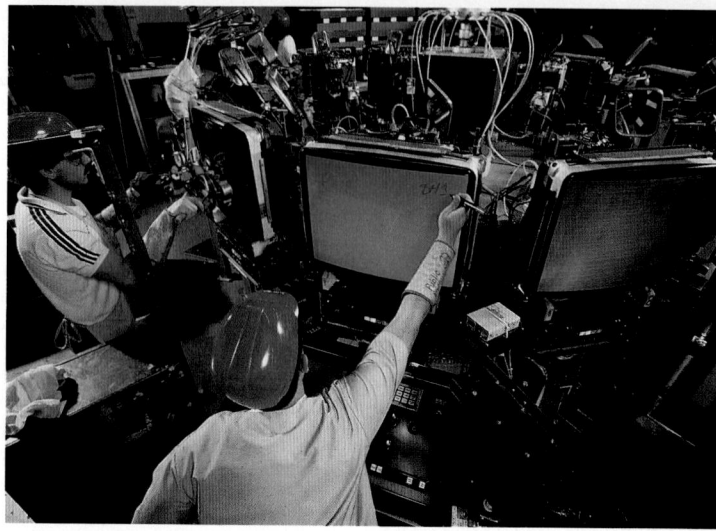

Plant assets are long-term tangible assets that are used for more than one accounting period. These assets are purchased for use in the business rather than for resale.

Estimating Depreciation of a Plant Asset

It is important to remember that depreciation is a way of *estimating* how fast an asset is used up or loses value. No one can predict such amounts with certainty. Depreciation amounts are estimates of the decrease in value or usefulness of a plant asset over a period of time. There are four factors that affect the estimate of depreciation. Two are based on certainty and two are estimates based on past experience. The four are (1) the cost of the plant asset, (2) the estimated useful life of the asset, (3) the estimated disposal value of the asset, and (4) the depreciation method used.

Plant Asset Cost

The cost of a plant asset is the price paid for the asset plus any sales taxes, delivery charges, and installation charges. The total cost is the amount debited to the plant asset account—for example, Delivery Equipment—at the time of purchase.

Estimated Useful Life of a Plant Asset

The *estimated useful life* of a plant asset is the number of years the asset is expected to be used before it wears out, becomes outdated, or is no longer needed by the business. In determining the estimated useful life of a plant asset, the accountant may consider past experiences with the same type of asset. The Internal Revenue Service (IRS) also publishes guidelines on the estimated useful service lives for many assets.

486

UNIT 5 Accounting for Special Procedures

Making Connections

EVERYDAY LIFE

Ask students who have a personal computer at home whether the value of their computer is the same today as when they purchased it. They probably already realized that the market value of their computer has depreciated because of the ongoing improvements in technology. Ask those students with home computers to contact a computer store to determine the approximate value of their computer.

Disposal Value of a Plant Asset

At some point, a plant asset will need to be replaced, sold, or discarded. Usually this occurs while the asset still has some monetary value. For example, if a business needs to buy a new delivery truck, the old delivery truck can often be traded in on the new truck. The estimated value of a plant asset at its replacement time is called **disposal value.** Disposal value is also called trade-in value or salvage value.

The disposal value assigned to a plant asset is an estimate that is based on previous, actual disposal values of similar assets. In addition, the IRS publishes guidelines on disposal values that many businesses use.

Depreciation Method

There are several methods that can be used in accounting for the depreciation of a plant asset. In this first-year accounting course, you will learn about a simple and widely used accounting method for estimating the amount of depreciation called the straight-line method. **Straight-line depreciation** is a method of equally distributing the depreciation expense on a plant asset over its estimated useful life.

Other methods of computing depreciation include units-of-production and accelerated methods. Units-of-production estimates useful life measured in units of use rather than units of time. Accelerated depreciation methods are based on the theory that an asset loses more value in the early years of its useful life than in the later years. Under the sum-of-the-years'-digits method, the depreciable cost of an asset is multiplied each year by a fraction to calculate the depreciation expense. The declining-balance method uses a depreciation rate that is usually either 1½ or 2 times the straight-line depreciation rate. If the rate used is twice the straight-line depreciation rate, the method is called "double-declining-balance."

Before going further, do the following activity to check your understanding of depreciation.

Check Your Learning

Use a sheet of notebook paper to answer these questions.

1. What is a current asset? Give two examples of current assets.
2. What is a plant asset? Give two examples of plant assets.
3. Explain what depreciation is.
4. Why do businesses use depreciation? What accounting principle is involved?
5. What are the four factors that affect the estimate of depreciation?
6. Which two factors in question 5 do you think are estimates? Which two are certain?

Compare your answers to those in the answers section. Re-read the preceding part of the chapter to find the correct answers to any questions you may have missed.

CHAPTER 22 Accounting for the Depreciation of Plant and Equipment   487

Reteaching Strategies

Students often confuse the depreciation of assets for income tax purposes with the actual depreciation in the market value of an item. Explain market value and book value, then give students several examples comparing the two. For example, suppose a business depreciates a building over a period of 19 years. Each year the book value of the building decreases. However, suppose real estate values in the area are increasing. The market value of the building would also increase.

CONCEPT DEVELOPMENT
Calculating Estimated Depreciation

Explain and illustrate how estimated annual depreciation is calculated using the example in the textbook. You may want to review the recording of a transaction that involves the purchase of delivery equipment.

Remind students that the depreciation amount is an estimate. An adjustment will be made when the asset is removed or replaced.

Using Visuals

Use demonstration problem 22-1 to give students practice in calculating depreciation.

Teaching Tips

■ Give students several examples of long-term assets and ask them to calculate the estimated amount to be depreciated and the estimated annual depreciation expense.

ACCOUNTING PRACTICE
Students may complete Exercise 22-2 at this point.

CONCEPT DEVELOPMENT
Calculating Depreciation Expense for Part of a Fiscal Year

Follow these steps when teaching depreciation for part of a fiscal year.

1. Review the calculations for a full year.
2. Develop a situation in which a plant asset may require a partial year's calculation (delivery truck purchased in April rather than January).
3. Stress that depreciation must be calculated for the number of months the plant asset is owned during the fiscal year.
4. Develop formula for partial year.
5. Illustrate formula.
6. Allow students to practice applying the formula for a full year and/or part of a fiscal year.
7. Permit students to refer to the formula while practicing.

Calculating Estimated Depreciation

Superior Appliance Center purchased a delivery truck on January 5 for $16,500.00 cash. The truck has an estimated disposal value of $1,500.00 and an estimated useful life of five years. The purchase of the truck is recorded in Superior's cash payments journal as a debit of $16,500.00 to Delivery Equipment and a credit for the same amount to Cash in Bank.

The cost of the truck will be depreciated over each year of the truck's useful life. To estimate the amount of depreciation for each year, the amount to be depreciated must first be determined. This amount is calculated by subtracting the estimated disposal value from the original cost of the asset. The estimated amount to be depreciated for Superior's new delivery truck is calculated as follows:

Original Cost	–	Estimated Disposal Value	=	Estimated Amount To Be Depreciated
$16,500.00	–	$1,500.00	=	$15,000.00

ACCOUNTING *Notes*
Some accountants refer to disposal value as salvage, scrap, or residual value.

Superior must subtract the estimated disposal value because that amount represents a part of the cost of the asset that the business expects to recover. That amount, therefore, cannot be treated as an expense.

The next step is to calculate the annual depreciation expense. Superior uses the straight-line method of calculating depreciation. In that method, remember, the depreciation expense is distributed equally over the asset's useful life. To determine the annual expense, the estimated amount to be depreciated is divided by the number of years of the asset's estimated useful life. As you recall, the delivery truck has an estimated useful life of five years.

Estimated Amount To Be Depreciated	÷	Estimated Useful Life	=	Estimated Annual Depreciation Expense
$15,000.00	÷	5	=	$3,000.00

As you can see from this calculation, the estimated annual depreciation expense for the delivery truck is $3,000.00.

Calculating Depreciation Expense for Part of a Fiscal Year

The $3,000.00 depreciation expense we just calculated was for a full year. Suppose that Superior had purchased the delivery truck in April instead of in January. In that case, Superior would have owned the delivery truck for only 9 months of the year. The amount of the depreciation expense for the first year, therefore, must be calculated for 9 months instead of 12 months. Depreciation expense for a partial year is calculated as follows:

Estimated Annual Depreciation Expense	×	Fraction of Year	=	Estimated Depreciation Expense for Partial Year
$3,000.00	×	$\frac{9}{12}$	=	$2,250.00

488

UNIT 5 Accounting for Special Procedures

Cooperative Learning

PAIRS CHECK

Ask students to use the straight-line method to calculate the annual depreciation on the following plant assets. When the students have completed the calculations, they should compare their answers with those of a partner. If any answers differ, the pairs should work together to find the correct answer.

a. Copy machine: original cost, $22,100; disposal value, $4,500; useful life, 4 years.

b. Delivery van: original cost, $18,500; disposal value, $7,000; useful life, 5 years.
c. Fork lift: original cost, $25,900; disposal value, $10,900; useful life, 8 years.

(Answers: (a) $4,400; (b) $2,300; (c) $1,875)

Refer to the "Cooperative Learning" section of *Tech Prep Strategies in Accounting* for additional cooperative learning strategies.

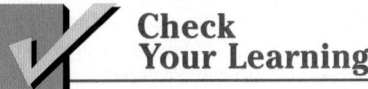

Check Your Learning

Handy Home Improvements bought a truck on January 4 at a cost of $23,000.00. The truck has an estimated disposal value of $5,000.00 and an estimated useful life of five years. Use a sheet of notebook paper to calculate the answers to the following questions.

1. What is the estimated amount to be depreciated on this truck?
2. What is the estimated annual depreciation expense?
3. What is the estimated monthly depreciation expense?
4. If the truck had been bought on May 3, instead of on January 4, what would the estimated depreciation expense be for the partial year?

Compare your answers to those in the answers section. Re-read the preceding part of the chapter to find the correct answers to any questions you may have missed.

Plant Asset Records

Most businesses maintain a record of each plant asset and the depreciation that has been recorded for that asset. Figure 22-1 shows the plant asset record for the delivery truck purchased by Superior Appliance Center. As you can see, this record provides detailed information about the delivery

PLANT ASSET RECORD

ITEM Delivery Truck   GENERAL LEDGER ACCOUNT Delivery Equipment

SERIAL NUMBER 2911-50041   MANUFACTURER VanPower

PURCHASED FROM Lake City Trucks   EST. DISPOSAL VALUE $1,500.00

ESTIMATED LIFE 5 years   LOCATION Company Garage

DEPRECIATION METHOD Straight-line   DEPRECIATION PER YEAR $3,000.00   RATE OF DEPRECIATION 20%

| DATE | EXPLANATION | ASSET | | | ACCUMULATED DEPRECIATION | | | BOOK VALUE |
		DEBIT	CREDIT	BALANCE	DEBIT	CREDIT	BALANCE	
1/5/93	Purchased	16,500		16,500				16,500
12/31/93						3,000	3,000	13,500
12/31/94						3,000	6,000	10,500
12/31/95						3,000	9,000	7,500
12/31/96						3,000	12,000	4,500
12/31/97						3,000	15,000	1,500

Figure 22-1 Plant Asset Record

CHAPTER 22   Accounting for the Depreciation of Plant and Equipment   489

ACCOUNTING PRACTICE

Students may complete Exercise 22-4 at this point.

CONCEPT DEVELOPMENT

Accounting for Depreciation Expense at the End of a Fiscal Year

Stress that plant asset records are used to determine depreciation for a fiscal year.

Note that the total cost of the plant assets, as recorded in the general ledger, must agree with the total value of plant assets on the depreciation summary form. This agreement is one proof that the accountant is recording all the depreciation for the fiscal year.

Mention that a credit to a plant asset account, such as Delivery Equipment, signals that the asset was sold, traded in, or discarded.

truck. The plant asset record also includes: (1) the date of purchase, (2) the original cost, (3) the estimated useful life, (4) annual depreciation, (5) accumulated depreciation, and (6) book value at the end of each year.

Each year a plant asset is used by a business, its value is decreased through the recording of depreciation expense. The amount of depreciation expense accumulates from one year to the next. **Accumulated depreciation** is the total amount of depreciation for a plant asset that has been recorded up to a specific point in time. The bottom of the plant asset record in Figure 22-1 on page 489 contains a depreciation schedule. At the end of the third year, for example, the accumulated depreciation that has been recorded for the delivery truck is $9,000.00.

The far right column of the depreciation schedule shows the book value of the plant asset. **Book value** is the original cost of a plant asset less its accumulated depreciation. For example, at the end of the third year, the book value of the delivery truck is $7,500.00 ($16,500.00 − $9,000.00). Notice too that the book value of the delivery truck at the end of five years is $1,500.00, which is the truck's estimated disposal value. With the straight-line method, the truck will not be depreciated beyond its estimated disposal value.

R E M E M B E R

After a plant asset is purchased, its cost is allocated over its estimated useful life.

Accounting for Depreciation Expense at the End of a Fiscal Year

During a fiscal period, a business may buy several plant assets. The costs of these assets are recorded as debits to the appropriate asset account. When a plant asset is purchased, the accountant sets up a depreciation schedule for the asset such as the one shown in Figure 22-1 on page 489. The amount of depreciation taken for the plant asset, however, is usually not recorded in the accounting records until the end of the fiscal period. At that time, an adjusting entry is made to record the depreciation expense for each plant asset.

The information for calculating the adjustments for depreciation is taken from the plant asset records. Many businesses prepare a summary of total depreciation expense for each type of plant asset. For example, a business may have ten delivery trucks, with each truck having its own plant asset record. At the end of the fiscal period, the depreciation expense for all the trucks will be totaled. The total will then be entered on a summary form under the title of the asset account, in this case, Delivery Equipment. Superior Appliance Center's depreciation summary form is shown in Figure 22-2.

Businesses that use computerized accounting systems store plant asset information in the computer. When a summary of total depreciation is

---

```
            1993 SUMMARY OF ESTIMATED DEPRECIATION EXPENSE
                        December 31, 1993

                                      Estimated
                                    Depreciation     Depreciation
            Asset          Cost        Expense          To Date

Building                50000.00       2500.00         8125.00
Delivery Equipment      16500.00       3000.00         9000.00
Office Equipment        10000.00       1000.00         3000.00
Store Equipment        250000.00      25000.00        75000.00

Totals                 326500.00      31500.00        95125.00
```

Figure 22-2 Depreciation Summary Form

needed, the computer calculates the totals and prints them out for use in making adjustments for depreciation expense.

Look again at the summary in Figure 22-2. As you can see, Superior's total depreciation expense for the year is $31,500.00. This amount is the total of all depreciation expense for all plant assets. The total accumulated depreciation for all of Superior's plant assets is $95,125.00.

Adjusting for Depreciation Expense

At the end of a fiscal period, adjusting entries are recorded to show the amount of depreciation expense for each plant asset for the period. The adjusting entry for depreciation affects two accounts for each type of plant asset: Depreciation Expense and Accumulated Depreciation.

▲ **Depreciation Expense**   Depreciation Expense is, of course, classified as an expense account. During a fiscal period, the account has a zero balance because the adjustment for depreciation is recorded only at the end of the fiscal period. Like other expense accounts, Depreciation Expense is reported on the income statement. It is a temporary account whose balance is transferred into Income Summary through a closing entry.

A business having many different types of plant assets needs several accounts for depreciation expense. Each depreciation expense account, therefore, is labeled with the title of the plant asset that is being depreciated. For example, the title of the depreciation expense account for delivery trucks and equipment would be Depreciation Expense—Delivery Equipment.

▲ **Accumulated Depreciation**   The Accumulated Depreciation account summarizes the total amount of depreciation that has been allocated to a plant asset since the original purchase. Examples of the titles of accumulated depreciation accounts are Accumulated Depreciation—Delivery Equipment and Accumulated Depreciation—Building.

Accumulated Depreciation is classified as a contra plant asset account. As you recall, the balance of a contra account reduces the balance of its related

Teaching Tips

■ Use T accounts to show how the balance of Accumulated Depreciation—Delivery Equipment affects the balance of the Delivery Equipment account.

ACCOUNTING *Notes*

Accumulated Depreciation is also called a valuation account. The two accounts together—asset and contra asset—provide the book value of the asset on the balance sheet.

account. In the case of an accumulated depreciation account, the related account is a plant asset account. For example, Accumulated Depreciation—Delivery Equipment is a contra account to the asset account Delivery Equipment.

Accumulated Depreciation	
Dr.	Cr.
–	+
Decrease Side	Increase Side
	Balance Side

The balance of an accumulated depreciation account represents the cost of an asset that has been allocated as depreciation expense over a period of time. As a contra asset account, the rules of debit and credit for an accumulated depreciation account are opposite those for asset accounts. An accumulated depreciation account is increased on the credit side and decreased on the debit side. It has a normal credit balance. The balance of an accumulated depreciation account is reported on the balance sheet as a decrease to its related plant asset account.

R E M E M B E R

The normal balance of an asset account, such as Delivery Equipment, is a debit. The normal balance of a contra asset account, such as Accumulated Depreciation—Delivery Equipment, is a credit.

▲ Analyzing the Adjustment for Depreciation Expense

Let's use these accounts now to analyze the adjustment needed at the end of a fiscal period for Superior's delivery truck.

Looking at the depreciation schedule in Figure 22-1 on page 489, you can see that the annual depreciation expense for the delivery truck is $3,000.00. The two accounts affected by the adjustment for depreciation of the delivery truck are Depreciation Expense—Delivery Equipment and Accumulated Depreciation—Delivery Equipment. Depreciation Expense—Delivery Equipment is debited for $3,000.00, which is the portion of the original cost of the delivery truck that is being allocated as an expense for this fiscal period. The contra asset account Accumulated Depreciation—Delivery Equipment is credited for $3,000.00 because that account is increased by the amount of the cost allocated to this fiscal year.

Depreciation Expense—Delivery Equipment		Accumulated Depreciation—Delivery Equipment	
Dr.	Cr.	Dr.	Cr.
+	–	–	+
$3,000.00			$3,000.00

Suppose this is the third year of the estimated useful life of Superior's delivery truck. At the end of the third year, the adjustment made to record the depreciation of the delivery truck is again a debit of $3,000.00 to Depreciation Expense—Delivery Equipment and a credit of $3,000.00 to Accumulated Depreciation—Delivery Equipment. This is the same adjustment that has been made each year. Look at the T accounts below. Before recording the depreciation amount, the Depreciation Expense account has a zero balance. As you recall, the balances of all expense accounts are closed at the end of each fiscal period. The Accumulated Depreciation account, however, shows the total amount of the asset's cost that has been allocated to date — that is, since the asset was purchased. As you can see, at the end of the third year, this total is $9,000.00.

Depreciation Expense—Delivery Equipment		Accumulated Depreciation—Delivery Equipment	
Dr.	Cr.	Dr.	Cr.
+	−	−	+
$3,000.00			1st Yr. $3,000.00
			2nd Yr. 3,000.00
			3rd Yr. 3,000.00
			Bal. $9,000.00

The adjustments for the depreciation of other plant assets — such as buildings, office equipment, and so on — are calculated the same way as the adjustment for the delivery equipment. Now that you know how to analyze depreciation adjustments using T accounts, let's look at how these adjustments are entered on a work sheet.

Recording Depreciation Adjustments on a Work Sheet

After the adjusting entries for depreciation are analyzed, they are entered in the Adjustments section of the work sheet. The placement of these adjustments is shown on the partial work sheet in Figure 22-3 on pages 494-495.

The balances of the Accumulated Depreciation accounts before adjustments appear on lines 9 and 11 in the Trial Balance Credit column. The depreciation expense accounts (lines 24 and 25) do not have balances in the Trial Balance section. Adjustments (e) and (f) are entered in the Adjustments section to show the depreciation expense and the increases in accumulated depreciation for this fiscal year. Note that the depreciation expense accounts are debited and the accumulated depreciation accounts are credited.

After the adjustments for depreciation are entered in the Adjustments section, each amount is extended to the other work sheet columns. The amounts for the asset accounts Delivery Equipment and Building are extended to the Adjusted Trial Balance Debit column and, eventually, to the Balance Sheet Debit column. Notice that these account balances are not affected by the adjustments for depreciation.

The balances of the accumulated depreciation accounts in the Trial Balance section are added to the amounts in the Adjustments Credit column. The total is then extended first to the Adjusted Trial Balance Credit column and then to the Balance Sheet Credit column.

The balances of the depreciation expense accounts are extended to the Adjusted Trial Balance Debit column and to the Income Statement Debit column.

Using Visuals

Point out the adjustments for depreciation in Figure 22-3. Ask students why the depreciation expense accounts had no balance prior to the adjustments. (The accounts were closed in the previous period and this period's depreciation is yet to be recorded.)

ANSWERS

1. Credit; contra asset
2. (a) $6,000; Depreciation Expense—Office Equipment; (b) $6,000; Accumulated Depreciation—Office Equipment
3. $22,000
4. $24,000

Superior
Work
For the Year Ended

ACCT. NO.	ACCOUNT NAME	TRIAL BALANCE DEBIT	TRIAL BALANCE CREDIT	ADJUSTMENTS DEBIT	ADJUSTMENTS CREDIT
8 150	Delivery Equipment	16 500 00			
9 155	Accum. Depr.–Del. Equip.		6 000 00		(e) 3 000 00
10 160	Building	50 000 00			
11 165	Accum. Depr.–Building		5 625 00		(f) 2 500 00
23 601	Advertising Expense	1 600 00			
24 605	Depr. Exp.–Del. Equip.	—		(e) 3 000 00	
25 610	Depr. Exp.–Building	—		(f) 2 500 00	

Figure 22-3 Recording the Adjustments for Accumulated Depreciation and Depreciation Expense on the Work Sheet (Left Side)

Before you read any further, do the following activity to check your understanding of the calculation of depreciation.

Check Your Learning

On January 5, the Lavalle Corporation bought office equipment for $34,000.00. The equipment has an estimated useful life of five years and a disposal value of $4,000.00. The following depreciation schedule has been set up for this equipment.

Year	Cost	Annual Depreciation	Accumulated Depreciation	Book Value
Date of purchase	$34,000.00	—	—	$34,000.00
First year		$6,000.00	$ 6,000.00	28,000.00
Second year		6,000.00	12,000.00	?
Third year		6,000.00	18,000.00	16,000.00
Fourth year		6,000.00	?	10,000.00
Fifth year		6,000.00	30,000.00	4,000.00

Using this depreciation schedule, answer the questions that follow.

1. Accumulated Depreciation has a normal __?__ balance and is classified as a __?__ account.
2. The adjusting entry made to record depreciation at the end of the first year is:
   a. a debit of $ __?__ to the __?__ account.
   b. a credit of $ __?__ to the __?__ account.
3. What is the book value at the end of the second year?
4. What is the accumulated depreciation at the end of the fourth year?

Compare your answers to those in the answers section. Re-read the preceding part of the chapter to find the correct answers to any questions you may have missed.

494

UNIT 5   Accounting for Special Procedures

Reteaching Strategies

Some students may want to credit the plant asset account for the amount of the depreciation. Explain that the only time a plant asset account is credited is when the asset is sold, traded in, or discarded. When depreciation is allocated, the amount of depreciation is recorded in the accumulated depreciation account, which is a contra asset account whose balance decreases the plant asset balance.

Appliance Center
Sheet
December 31, 19--

ADJUSTED TRIAL BALANCE		INCOME STATEMENT		BALANCE SHEET		
DEBIT	CREDIT	DEBIT	CREDIT	DEBIT	CREDIT	
1650000				1650000		8
	900000				900000	9
5000000				5000000		10
	812500				812500	11
160000		160000				23
300000		300000				24
250000		250000				25

(Right Side)

Reporting Depreciation Expense and Accumulated Depreciation on Financial Statements

The depreciation expense accounts appear on the income statement as expenses. The placement of the depreciation expense accounts is shown on the partial income statement of Superior Appliance Center shown in Figure 22-4.

Superior Appliance Center
Income Statement
For the Year Ended December 31, 19--

Operating Expenses:		
Advertising Expense	160000	
Depr. Expense-Del.Equip.	300000	
Depr. Expense-Building	250000	
Total Oper. Expenses		9435100
Operating Income		5134200

Figure 22-4   Reporting Depreciation Expense on the Income Statement

On the balance sheet, the accumulated depreciation accounts are listed immediately below their related plant asset accounts in the Assets section. Their placement is illustrated on the partial balance sheet for Superior Appliance Center shown in Figure 22-5.

Superior Appliance Center
Balance Sheet
December 31, 19--

Assets

Delivery Equipment	1650000	
Less: Accumulated Depreciation-Delivery Equip.	900000	750000
Building	5000000	
Less: Accumulated Depreciation- Building	812500	4187500

Figure 22-5   Reporting Accumulated Depreciation on the Balance Sheet

CHAPTER 22   Accounting for the Depreciation of Plant and Equipment   495

CONCEPT DEVELOPMENT
Reporting Depreciation Expense and Accumulated Depreciation on Financial Statements
Depreciation Expense represents the portion of an asset that has become an expense during a fiscal period. That expense amount is thus reported on the income statement.

The balance of an accumulated depreciation account represents a reduction in assets since the account is a contra asset account. The balance of accumulated depreciation is reported on the balance sheet to show the change in assets during the fiscal period.

Using Visuals
Point out the lines for depreciation expense in Figure 22-4. Ask students how the depreciation expense affects the net income reported on the income statement.

Call students' attention to Figure 22-5. Point out that the balance in the right column of the balance sheet represents the book value of the asset that is being depreciated.

Using Visuals

Use demonstration problem 22-4 to show students how to report depreciation expense and accumulated depreciation on the financial statements.

Making Connections

AROUND THE WORLD

One company that has benefited from the attention to global markets is Berlitz, the language-instruction company. Berlitz is the market leader in teaching foreign languages to business executives. Some U.S. executives study language to communicate with immigrants. Others want to learn to conduct business in other countries.

The most popular language for U.S. business people to learn is Spanish. Worldwide, the first choice is English.

Depreciation does not represent the physical deterioration of a plant asset or the decrease in its market value. It is simply a means of allocating the *cost* of the asset over the years in which it is used.

The balances of $7,500.00 for Delivery Equipment and $41,875.00 for Building entered in the second amount column represent the book value of those assets. As you can see, the contra account balance is subtracted from its related plant asset account to determine the book value. The book value of each plant asset reported on the balance sheet is the same as that shown on the plant asset record.

Journalizing the Adjusting Entries for Depreciation Expense

After the work sheet is completed and the financial statements are prepared, the adjustments for depreciation expense are recorded in the general journal.

The information for the journal entries is taken directly from the Adjustments section of the work sheet. The adjusting entries for depreciation shown in Figure 22-6 are made using the partial work sheet in Figure 22-3 on pages 494-495.

	GENERAL JOURNAL			PAGE 29	
DATE	DESCRIPTION	POST. REF.	DEBIT	CREDIT	
	Adjusting Entries				1
Dec. 31	Depreciation Expense–Delivery Equip.		3 0 0 0 00		10
	Accum. Depr.–Delivery Equip.			3 0 0 0 00	11
31	Depreciation Expense–Building		2 5 0 0 00		12
	Accum. Depr.–Building			2 5 0 0 00	13

Figure 22-6 Recording Adjusting Entries for Depreciation Expense

496

UNIT 5 Accounting for Special Procedures

As with all journal entries, adjusting entries for depreciation must be posted to the general ledger. A partial general ledger showing the posting of the two depreciation adjusting entries is shown in Figure 22-7.

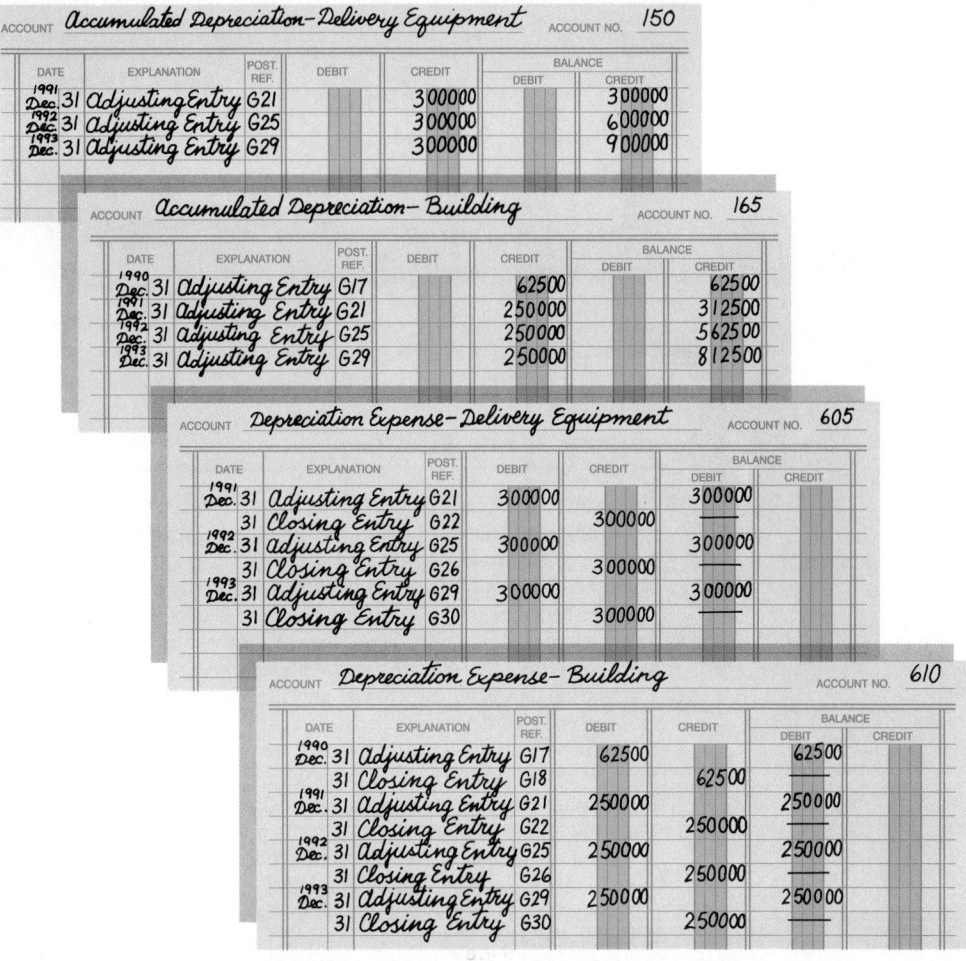

Figure 22-7 Posting Adjusting and Closing Entries for Depreciation Expense to the General Ledger

Journalizing Closing Entries for Depreciation Expense

After adjusting entries are journalized and posted, the next step in the accounting cycle is to close the ledger. In the second closing entry, you'll remember, those accounts with debit balances in the Income Statement Debit

CHAPTER 22   Accounting for the Depreciation of Plant and Equipment   **497**

Using Visuals

Have students trace the posting of the closing entry in Figure 22-8 to the ledger accounts on page 497.

Teaching Tips

■ Assign Problem 22A, page 643, to students who need extra practice calculating and recording depreciation expense.

3 CLOSE

CHAPTER SUMMARY

This summary enumerates the key information in the chapter. It is a useful tool for reinforcement and review.

---

column of the work sheet are closed into Income Summary. This closing entry includes the depreciation expense accounts. A part of that closing entry is shown in Figure 22-8.

	GENERAL JOURNAL				PAGE 30	
	DATE	DESCRIPTION	POST. REF.	DEBIT	CREDIT	
1		*Closing Entries*				1
5	*Dec. 31*	*Income Summary*		16250900		5
8		*Advertising Expense*			160000	8
9		*Depr. Expense-Delivery Equip.*			300000	9
10		*Depr. Expense-Building*			250000	10

Figure 22-8   Recording the Closing Entries

When this closing entry is posted to the general ledger, the balances of the Depreciation Expense accounts will be reduced to zero as shown in Figure 22-7 on page 497.

Summary of Key Points

1. Assets that will be used in the production or sale of other assets or services for more than one accounting period are called plant and equipment, or plant assets.
2. The useful life of a plant asset is limited because it wears out from normal use, becomes outdated, or is no longer needed by the business.
3. The original cost of a plant asset, less its disposal value, is allocated as an expense over its estimated useful life.
4. The portion of a plant asset's cost allocated as an expense during a fiscal year is called depreciation.
5. Before depreciation can be estimated, four things must be known: (a) the cost of the asset, (b) its estimated useful life in years, (c) its disposal value, and (d) the depreciation method being used.
6. The straight-line method of calculating depreciation distributes the cost of a plant asset equally over its estimated useful life. It is a widely used method for financial accounting purposes.
7. Annual depreciation is calculated by the straight-line method using the following formula:

Original Cost	−	Estimated Disposal Value	=	Estimated Amount To Be Depreciated	÷	Years of Estimated Useful Life	=	Estimated Annual Depreciation

8. A plant asset record is kept for each plant asset that is depreciated. The plant asset record usually includes a depreciation schedule that also shows the accumulated depreciation and the book value of the plant asset.
9. Accumulated depreciation is the total amount of depreciation allocated to an asset as of a certain date. Book value is the original cost of a plant asset less the accumulated depreciation.
10. An adjusting entry for depreciation is made at the end of each fiscal year.

Pop Quiz

1. Land and buildings are examples of ____ assets.
2. When a plant asset is traded in, its estimated value at the time of replacement is called ____.
3. Define straight-line depreciation.
4. The original cost of a plant asset less its accumulated depreciation is called ____.
5. What is accumulated depreciation?

ANSWERS

1. Plant.
2. Disposal value.
3. Depreciation expenses on a plant asset are equally distributed over its estimated useful life.
4. Book value.
5. It is the total amount of depreciation for a plant asset up to a specific point in time.

Review and Applications

Building Your Accounting Vocabulary

In your own words, write the definition of each of the following accounting terms. Use complete sentences for your definitions.

accumulated depreciation

book value

current asset depreciation

disposal value

plant and equipment straight-line depreciation

Reviewing Your Accounting Knowledge

1. What distinguishes a plant asset from a current asset?
2. Why is the useful life of a plant asset limited?
3. What is meant by "allocating the cost" of a plant asset?
4. Why is the cost of land not depreciated?
5. What four factors affect the estimated depreciation?
6. How is the annual depreciation expense for a plant asset calculated under the straight-line method?
7. What is the purpose of a plant asset record?
8. When is the depreciation on a plant asset recorded?
9. Which two accounts are affected by an adjusting entry for depreciation?
10. What type of account is Accumulated Depreciation?
11. Into which account are the depreciation expense accounts closed at the end of the fiscal period?

Improving Your Analysis Skills

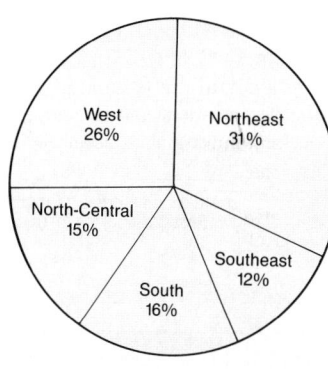

In business, graphs are often used to illustrate facts and figures in a form that is easy to "see" and understand. The three most common types of graphs are the line graph, the bar graph, and the circle graph (often called a pie chart). Being able to interpret the information presented in a graph is an important business skill.

At the left is a circle graph that illustrates the sales, by region, of the Wesley Corporation. Use the graph to answer the questions that follow.

1. Which region had the highest sales?
2. Which region had the lowest sales?
3. If total sales were $547,500, what were each region's sales?
4. How much greater than the South's sales were the sales of the Northeast region (in dollars)?

499

PRACTICE AND APPLY

- Language Development
- Comprehension and Retention
- Basic Skills

Building Your Accounting Vocabulary

See the Glossary on pages 670-679 for definitions of these terms.

Reviewing Your Accounting Knowledge

1. Plant assets are long-lived assets and are used in the production or sale of other assets or services over several accounting periods. Current assets, on the other hand, are either used up or converted to cash during one accounting period.
2. Because it will wear out from normal use or it may become outdated or no longer needed by the business.
3. A plant asset's cost is allocated over the number of years of the asset's productive life by charging the cost to depreciation expense.
4. Because land never wears out or becomes obsolete.
5. (a) Cost of the plant asset, (b) estimated useful life of the asset, (c) estimated disposal value of the asset, and (d) depreciation method used.
6. The formula for straight-line depreciation is: (Original Cost − Estimated Disposal Value) ÷ Estimated Useful Life = Estimated Annual Depreciation Expense.
7. To provide detailed information about an individual plant asset, including date of purchase, original cost, annual depreciation, accumulated depreciation, book value, estimated useful life, estimated disposal value, and depreciation method used.
8. At the end of the fiscal period through an adjusting entry.
9. Depreciation Expense and Accumulated Depreciation.
10. A contra plant asset account.
11. Income Summary.

Improving Your Analysis Skills
1. Northeast
2. Southeast
3. Northeast, $169,725; Southeast, $65,700; South, $87,600; North-Central, $82,125; West, $142,350
4. $82,125

Chapter 22

PRACTICE AND APPLY

• Concepts and Procedures

Exercise 22-1: Ch. Obj. 1

Exercise 22-2: Ch. Obj. 3
1. $370,000; $14,800
2. $150; $50
3. $350; $68
4. $4,600; $460
5. $1,500; $125

Exercise 22-3: Ch. Obj. 3, 4
1. $420; $60/year; $40
2. $5,000; $500/year; $83.33
3. $1,800; $72/year; $36
4. $30,000; $6,000/year; $1,500
5. $2,880; $144/year; $132

Exercise 22-4: Ch. Obj. 3, 5
Book Value:
1st year, $1,908
2nd year, $1,456
3rd year, $1,004
4th year, $552
5th year, $100

Applying Accounting Procedures

Exercise 22-1 Classifying Asset Accounts

Listed below are the assets of New England Sports Equipment, Inc.

Accounts Receivable	Office Equipment
Building	Office Furniture
Cash in Bank	Petty Cash Fund
Change Fund	Prepaid Insurance
Delivery Equipment	Store Equipment
Land	Supplies
Merchandise Inventory	

Instructions: Use a form similar to the one that follows. For each asset, indicate whether it is a current asset or plant and equipment by placing a check mark in the correct column.

Asset	Current Asset	Plant and Equipment
Accounts Receivable	✔	

Exercise 22-2 Calculating Estimated Annual Depreciation

Instructions: Determine the estimated amount to be depreciated and the estimated annual depreciation for each of the following plant assets. Use the straight-line method of depreciation.

Plant Asset	Original Cost	Estimated Disposal Value	Estimated Useful Life
1. Building	$385,000	$15,000	25 yrs.
2. Calculator	150	0	3 yrs.
3. Chair	360	20	5 yrs.
4. Computer	4,800	200	10 yrs.
5. Typewriter	1,600	100	12 yrs.

SPREADSHEET

PROBLEM

Exercise 22-3 Calculating Depreciation Expense for Part of a Year

Instructions: Calculate the estimated amount to be depreciated, the estimated annual depreciation, and the estimated depreciation for the first year for each of the following plant assets.

Plant Asset	Months Owned First Year	Original Cost	Estimated Disposal Value	Estimated Useful Life
1. Cash register	8	$ 450	$ 30	7 yrs.
2. Computer	2	6,500	1,500	10 yrs.
3. Conference table	6	1,900	100	25 yrs.
4. Delivery truck	3	36,400	6,400	5 yrs.
5. Desk	11	3,180	300	20 yrs.

Exercise 22-4 Preparing a Depreciation Schedule

The Quade Corporation bought a copy machine on January 7 of the current year at a cost of $2,360. The copy machine has an estimated useful life of 5 years and an estimated disposal value of $100.

500

> Refer students to the Chapter 22 review pages in the workbook, *Chapter Reviews and Working Papers*.

Additional Reinforcement

Students who need additional practice or individualized help will benefit from the *Glencoe Accounting Electronic Study Guide* or the *Glencoe Accounting* on-line multimedia program, which provide reinforcement and reteaching for vocabulary, concepts, and procedures.

Instructions: Prepare a depreciation schedule for this machine using the straight-line method of depreciation. Use a form similar to the one that follows.

Date	Cost	Annual Depreciation	Accumulated Depreciation	Book Value
January 7	$2,360	—	—	$2,360

Problem 22-1   Opening a Plant Asset Record

On July 10, Brookside Laundry purchased an Apex commercial dryer from Taunton Bros. Appliances for $1,500. Taunton Bros. charged Brookside $200 to install the dryer. The dryer has an estimated useful life of 4 years and an estimated disposal value of $260.

Instructions: Prepare a plant asset record, including the depreciation schedule, for Brookside's new dryer. Use the form provided in your working papers. Other necessary information is as follows.

> Serial number: TMC46312
> General ledger account: Laundry Equipment
> Location: Main Street store
> Depreciation method: Straight-line
> Rate of depreciation: 25%

Problem 22-2   Recording Adjusting Entries for Depreciation

The following adjustments for depreciation were entered on the work sheet for the Bushnell Company for the year ended April 30.

	Adjustments	
	Debit	Credit
Delivery Equipment		
Accumulated Depreciation—Delivery Equipment		(e) 3,800
Office Equipment		
Accumulated Depreciation—Office Equipment		(f) 1,400
Depreciation Expense—Delivery Equipment	(e) 3,800	
Depreciation Expense—Office Equipment	(f) 1,400	

Instructions: Record the adjusting entries on general journal page 11.

Problem 22-3   Reporting Depreciation Expense on the Work Sheet

The trial balance of the Cagle Company appears on the work sheet included in the working papers. All adjustments except those for depreciation have already been recorded on the work sheet.

Instructions:

(1) Record the following adjustments for depreciation expense on the work sheet.

(d) Estimated annual depreciation for office equipment is $2,500.00.
(e) Estimated annual depreciation for store equipment is $1,200.00.

(2) Complete the work sheet.

501

Problem 22-1: Ch. Obj. 1, 3, 4, 5
Book Value:
Purchase, $1,700
1st year, $1,520
2nd year, $1,160
3rd year, $800
4th year, $440
5th year, $260

Problem 22-2: Ch. Obj. 6
Adjustments:
Delivery Equipment, $3,800
Office Equipment, $1,400

Problem 22-3: Ch. Obj. 5, 6
Column totals:
Adj., $11,550
ATB, $152,900
Net income, $14,405
IS, $58,755
BS, $108,550

Teacher Notes

Chapter

Problem 22-4: Ch. Obj. 5

Gross profit on sales, $32,880
Total operating expenses, $18,475
Net income, $14,475

Ending capital, $87,320
Bal. sheet totals, $90,150

Problem 22-5: Ch. Obj. 3, 4, 5, 6

Book value:
1st yr., $403,500
2nd yr., $387,900

Depr. Expense, $6,500

Problem 22-6: Ch. Obj. 3, 4, 5, 6

COMPUTER

PROBLEM

This computer image identifies a problem that students may complete using the *Glencoe Accounting, General Ledger* software.

Adjustments:
(a) $2,700
(b) $700
(c) $5,000
(d) $1,200
(e) $3,000
(f) $6,000
(g) $250

Depr. Expense:
Laundry Equip., $1,200
Dry Cleaning, $3,000
Building, $6,000
Fed. Income Tax, $250

Work sheet totals:
Adj., $18,850
ATB, $323,000
Net income, $24,140
IS, $78,000
BS, $269,140

Problem 22-4   Reporting Depreciation on the Financial Statements

Use the work sheet you prepared in Problem 22-3 to complete this problem.

Instructions: Prepare an income statement, statement of changes in owner's equity, and balance sheet for the Cagle Company for the year ended June 30.

Problem 22-5   Calculating and Recording Depreciation Expense

The National Box Company purchased manufacturing equipment on August 1 at a total cost of $410,000. The equipment has an estimated useful life of 25 years and an estimated disposal value of $20,000. The partial depreciation schedule that follows was set up for the equipment.

Instructions:
(1) Calculate annual depreciation, accumulated depreciation, and book value for each of the first two years. The fiscal year ends December 31. Use the form provided in the workbook.
(2) Calculate the depreciation adjustment to be entered on the work sheet at the end of the first year. Use T accounts to show the accounts debited and credited.
(3) Journalize the adjustment for depreciation at the end of the first year.
(4) Post the adjusting entry to the general ledger accounts.

Date	Cost	Annual Depreciation	Accumulated Depreciation	Book Value
Purchased Aug. 1	$410,000	—	—	$410,000

COMPUTER

PROBLEM

Problem 22-6   Calculating and Recording Adjustments

The December 31 trial balance of the Olson Laundry Service is included in the working papers accompanying this textbook.

Instructions:
(1) Calculate and record the end-of-period adjustments on the work sheet.
   (a) Laundry supplies on hand total $1,200.00.
   (b) Office supplies on hand total $250.00.
   (c) The amount of the expired insurance premium is $5,000.00.
   (d) Use the following information to calculate the estimated annual depreciation expense.

Plant Asset	Cost	Estimated Disposal Value	Estimated Useful Life
Laundry Equipment	$ 13,000	$ 1,000	10 years
Dry Cleaning Equipment	32,000	2,000	10 years
Building	160,000	10,000	25 years

   (e) The total federal income tax expense for the year is $4,250.00.
(2) Complete the work sheet.
(3) Journalize and post the adjusting entries. Begin on general journal page 16.
(4) Journalize and post the closing entries.

502

CHALLENGE Problem 22-7 Examining Depreciation Adjustments

PROBLEM

The University Book Store sells both hardcover and paperback books. On May 2, the store purchased a new book-listing machine from Yong Manufacturing Co. The cost of the machine was $2,700. It has an estimated disposal value of $100 and an estimated useful life of 8 years.

On December 31, the adjustment for depreciation for the first year was entered on the work sheet. Accumulated Depreciation—Store Equipment was credited for $325 in the Adjustments section of the work sheet. Depreciation Expense—Store Equipment was debited for the same amount.

Instructions: Answer the following questions regarding this adjustment.

(1) What is wrong with the adjustment for depreciation made on December 31?
(2) What must be changed to make the entry correct?
(3) If this error is not corrected, what effect will it have on the total expenses for the period?
(4) If the error is not corrected, will the net income for the period be understated or overstated?
(5) If the error is not corrected, what effect will it have on the balances reported on the balance sheet?
(6) One year from now, another adjustment for this machine will be entered on the work sheet. Calculate the following:
   (a) Amount entered in the Adjustments section for annual depreciation.
   (b) Amount extended to the Adjusted Trial Balance section for Accumulated Depreciation—Store Equipment.
   (c) Amount extended to the Adjusted Trial Balance section for Depreciation Expense—Store Equipment.
   (d) Amount extended to the Balance Sheet section for Store Equipment.

503

Chapter 22

Problem 22-7: Ch. Obj. 3, 4, 5, 6

CHALLENGE

PROBLEM

The last problem in each chapter is a challenge problem and is identified by this "maze" symbol.

(1) Amount is overstated; adjust for 8 months, not 12.
(2) Amount should be $216.67.
(3) Expenses will be overstated by $108.33.
(4) Understated.
(5) Accum. Depr.—Store Equip. will be overstated by $108.33; assets will be understated by that amount.
(6) (a) $325.00
     (b) $541.67
     (c) $325.00
     (d) $2,700.00

---

4 ASSESS

A chapter test is available for use in assessing students' understanding of concepts in this chapter.

The testmaker software will enable you to develop tailor-made chapter, unit, semester, and final tests.

Alternative Assessment

For alternative assessment strategies, refer to *Tech Prep Strategies in Accounting.*

Use Chapter Test 22 here to assess students' understanding and retention of the concepts and procedures presented in the chapter.

Many theatrical companies, symphony orchestras, and opera companies in the United States operate near, at, or even below their break-even point. Ask students to speculate how such groups can continue to operate, even when incurring a loss.

QUESTIONS

1. How might the sale of season tickets to the theater be viewed from an accounting perspective?
2. Have students explore the various organizations for which one might work in the field of fund raising.

ANSWERS

1. Season ticket sales may be viewed in two ways: as revenue and as prepaid income, which is actually a liability until the performances for the season have been delivered.
2. Students' answers will vary but could include such companies as public relations businesses, schools and universities, charitable groups, arts foundations, and so on.

*P*laying a Supporting Role: The Theatrical Accountant

When you think of a Broadway play, who do you think of? Actors. Director. Producer. Set designer. Stage manager. After all, theater is art, and these are the artists. There's another cast of characters, however, behind the scenes who contribute to the success of any theatrical production. Producers need the specialized talents of an attorney, a manager, and a theatrical accountant—because behind all the glitter, theater is also a business.

The theatrical accountant's work begins long before opening night. Preparations for a production often take from one to five years. During this period, the accountant helps the attorney prepare the prospectus for potential financial investors. The prospectus includes budgets, profit-sharing formulas, and royalty arrangements. The accountant's expertise enables her or him to answer tax and accounting questions and to predict the backers' return on investment in the show. The accountant also helps the business manager project operating expenses and prepare a budget. The accountant works with the attorney to prepare financial reports required by the state.

Before the show is in rehearsal, the accountant is involved with the preparation of contracts and the federal and state registrations needed for payroll deductions. The accountant reviews contracts for the show's major stars that outline payment arrangements.

When rehearsals start, the accountant keeps closely detailed records and prepares weekly profit and loss statements to determine whether the production is within budget. By the time the curtain goes up, the accountant will have interacted

Theatrical accountants make sure that the business end of show business is in order so that the show can go on.

with just about all of the creative and business staff.

The next time you go to the theater, reserve some applause for the hard-working accountant. Maybe one day, that person will be *you*.

504

ACCOUNTING FOR UNCOLLECTIBLE ACCOUNTS RECEIVABLE

INTRODUCING THE CHAPTER

I n previous chapters, you learned that many businesses sell goods or services on account. These businesses have developed various procedures to choose the customers to whom they will extend credit. Credit checks help businesses determine the prospective customers' ability to make payments. They also help businesses decide the maximum amount of credit to extend to each customer.

Regardless of these procedures, some charge customers cannot or will not pay the amounts they owe. These unpaid accounts must eventually be removed from the accounting records as uncollectible. In this chapter, you will learn about two methods of accounting for charge customers who fail to pay the amounts owed.

Learning Objectives

When you have completed Chapter 23, you should be able to do the following:

1. Explain the difference between the direct write-off method and the allowance method of accounting for uncollectible accounts.
2. Journalize the entry to record the direct write-off of an uncollectible account receivable.
3. Explain how the adjustment for uncollectible accounts using the allowance method is recorded on the work sheet.
4. Journalize the adjusting entry for estimated uncollectible accounts.
5. Journalize the entry to write off an uncollectible account using the allowance method.
6. Journalize the entry to record the collection of a written-off account.
7. Describe two methods that can be used to estimate bad debts expense.
8. Define the accounting terms introduced in this chapter.

New Terms

uncollectible account
direct write-off method
allowance method
book value of accounts receivable
percentage of net sales method
aging of accounts receivable method

LOOKING BACK

In earlier chapters students learned to record transactions involving the sale of merchandise to customers on account. Businesses have determined ways to establish which potential customers are good credit risks. In spite of credit checks, however, some customers will not pay the amounts they owe. In this chapter students will learn how businesses allow for uncollectible accounts and how they adjust the accounting records to reflect unpaid customer balances.

VOCABULARY DEVELOPMENT

Discuss the definitions of the new terms in class. Ask students to give their definitions of each term, and then explain how each is used in accounting. Definitions of these terms are found in the chapter and in the glossary on pages 670-679.

505

Teaching Resources

- Lesson Plans
- TE/Chapter Reviews & Working Papers
- Demonstration Problems
- Student Study Plans
- Teaching Transparencies
- Solutions Transparencies
- Electronic Field Trips Video, Level I
- Electronic Study Guide
- Chapter 23 Test

Other Resources

- Skills Improvement Activities
- Blackline Masters
- Careers in Accounting
- Dictionary
- Math Review for Accounting
- Tech Prep Strategies in Accounting
- Video
- Test Bank with Software
- Spanish Resources/Audiotapes
- Spanish Electronic Study Guide

1 FOCUS

MAJOR CONCEPTS

- Extending Credit
- The Direct Write-Off Method
- Matching Bad Debts Expense with Revenue
- The Allowance Method
- Estimating Bad Debts Expense

BUSINESS CONNECTION

An account that is uncollectible becomes an expense to the business because it reduces owner's or stockholders' equity. The banking industry is especially susceptible to uncollectible accounts because its business is to loan people money. In 1992 Citicorp began to see increased earnings as a result of extensive changes made in their operations, but bad debts continued to erode the bank's operating margin.

2 TEACH

CONCEPT DEVELOPMENT
Extending Credit
Review the different types of credit checks a business may make before selling to a customer on credit. If time permits, use a resource person to discuss safeguards a business can take to reduce its number of uncollectible accounts. Students should understand that granting credit is risky, but most businesses believe that the increase in revenue will offset the uncollectible accounts.

Extending Credit

Selling goods and services on credit is now standard practice for businesses of all sizes and types: retailers, wholesalers, manufacturers, sole proprietorships, and corporations. Businesses sell on credit because they expect to sell more than if they accepted only cash. The additional sales result in higher profit.

Before a business extends credit, it carefully checks each prospective customer's credit rating. This credit check helps the business determine the customer's ability to pay her or his debts. Retail stores may ask potential customers to complete an application for credit. They also rely on reports from personal references, credit card companies, and local retail credit bureaus. When wholesalers and manufacturers consider extending credit to customers, they use reports from national credit-rating organizations such as Dun and Bradstreet, reports from wholesale credit bureaus, and customers' financial statements.

No matter how thorough a business's credit checks are, there will be some charge customers who cannot or will not pay the amounts they owe. Those accounts receivable accounts that cannot be collected are called **uncollectible accounts,** or bad debts. An account that is uncollectible becomes an expense to the business because it decreases owner's or stockholders' equity. It must be removed from the accounting records as an account receivable and recorded as an expense.

In this chapter, we will look at two methods of accounting for uncollectible accounts: the direct write-off method and the allowance method.

The Direct Write-Off Method

One method of accounting for uncollectible accounts is the direct write-off method. With the **direct write-off method,** the uncollectible amount is removed from the accounts receivable subsidiary ledger and the controlling account in the general ledger when the business determines that the amount owed is not going to be paid. A journal entry is made crediting Accounts Receivable and the customer's account and debiting an expense account called Bad Debts Expense. The direct write-off method is used mainly by small businesses and businesses with few charge customers. Let's look at an example of how this method is used.

Writing Off an Uncollectible Account

On June 4, Quinn's Bicycle Shop sold a bicycle on account to Mark Hamada for $250.00 plus $15.00 sales tax. When this transaction was journalized, Accounts Receivable and the Mark Hamada account were debited for $265.00, Sales was credited for $250.00, and Sales Tax Payable was credited for $15.00.

After trying for over a year to collect the amount owed, Quinn's decided that Mark Hamada was not going to pay the $265.00.

***August 25:** Wrote off Mark Hamada's account as uncollectible, $265.00, Memorandum 48.*

506

Reinforcing Study Skills

One reason that learning through listening is difficult for many students is that people speak at an average of about 200 words a minute, while they think at a rate about four times faster. Unless someone is consciously paying attention, his or her mind wanders during the extra time, daydreaming or thinking about everyday events and plans. Remind students that an important technique for active listening is to ask themselves questions during the speaker's presentation or lecture.

Provide a copy of the *Student Study Plans* to each class member to help organize study activities or to individualize practice and review activities.

In this transaction, Bad Debts Expense is debited for $265.00 because the uncollectible account has now become an expense to the business. Since the charge customer is not going to pay, the amount is no longer an account receivable. Accounts Receivable and the account Mark Hamada are, therefore, credited for $265.00.

GENERAL LEDGER

Bad Debts Expense	
Dr. +	Cr. −
$265.00	

Accounts Receivable	
Dr. +	Cr. −
	$265.00

SUBSIDIARY LEDGER

Mark Hamada	
Dr. +	Cr. −
	$265.00

Figure 23-1 shows how this transaction is recorded in the general journal and posted to the general ledger and accounts receivable subsidiary ledger accounts.

Figure 23-1 Journalizing and Posting the Direct Write-Off of an Uncollectible Account

Notice the explanation entered in Mark Hamada's account. When an account is written off as uncollectible, it is important to note this in the account. Anyone looking at the account must be able to see that it was written off, not paid off.

CONCEPT DEVELOPMENT
The Direct Write-Off Method
Give students an example of a sale of merchandise on account. After recording the transaction in general journal form, inform students that for one year or more every effort possible has been made to collect this accounts receivable account. A management decision has been made that the charge customer is not going to pay.

Analyze the write-off of the uncollectible account in T-account form. Mention that the direct write-off method is used because the expense is being charged directly for the uncollectible amount at the time it is ruled uncollectible.

Teaching Tips

■ Use T accounts to review the recording of the original sale on account to Mark Hamada.
■ Use the six-step method to analyze this transaction.

Using Visuals

Use demonstration problem 23-1 to give students practice in analyzing and journalizing uncollectible amounts.

Using Visuals

Have students look at Figure 23-1 and trace the entries in the general journal from the T-account analysis.

Making Connections

EVERYDAY LIFE
Ask students what factors they would consider before deciding whether to loan money to a friend. Relate their responses to the safeguards that businesses employ when extending credit; i.e., requiring references and financial ability to repay and completing credit checks.

REMEMBER

When using the direct write-off method, Accounts Receivable is credited because it has been determined that the charge customer is not going to pay. The amount, therefore, is no longer an account receivable. The loss of the uncollectible amount is charged to **Bad Debts Expense**, which is debited for the amount of the loss.

Collecting a Written-Off Account

Occasionally, a charge customer whose account was written off as uncollectible will later pay the amount owed. When this happens, the customer's account must first be reinstated, or returned to the accounting records. The cash receipt can then be journalized and posted.

September 5: Received $265.00 from Mark Hamada, whose account was written off as uncollectible on August 25, Memorandum 51 and Receipt 309.

This transaction requires *two* journal entries. The first journal entry, shown in Figure 23-2, reverses the August 25 entry to write off the account. The memo is the source document for this entry.

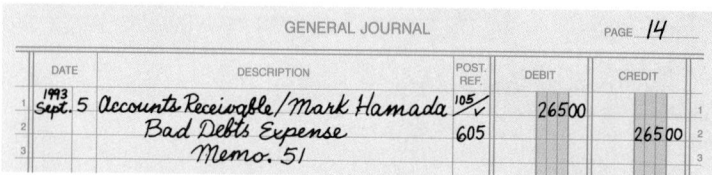

Figure 23-2 Journal Entry To Reinstate a Written-Off Account

After this transaction is posted, the cash receipt is journalized and posted. The cash receipt transaction is recorded in the cash receipts journal. Cash in Bank is debited for $265.00 and Accounts Receivable and the Mark Hamada account are credited for $265.00. The receipt is the source document for this entry.

When both of the September 5 journal entries are posted, Mark Hamada's account in the subsidiary ledger will contain all of the information about the series of transactions. Figure 23-3 shows that subsidiary ledger account.

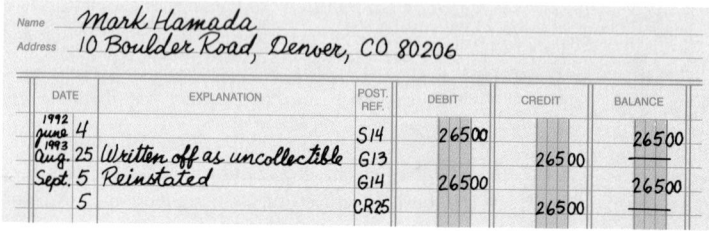

Figure 23-3 Mark Hamada Account

508

Businesses that sell on credit believe that the increase in sales revenue will offset the amount of uncollectible accounts.

The Tax Reform Act of 1986 made the direct write-off method the only method that a business can use for income tax purposes. The direct write-off method is an accepted accounting procedure for businesses that have few uncollectible accounts. A business that often sells on credit, however, should use a method of accounting for uncollectible accounts that will match revenue with the expenses incurred to earn that revenue.

Before learning about that method, complete the following activity to check your understanding of the direct write-off method.

Check Your Learning

Record the following transactions, in general journal form, on a sheet of notebook paper.

Apr. 10 *Sold merchandise on account to Sonya Dickson, $600.00 plus $30.00 sales tax, Sales Slip 928.*

Nov. 30 *Wrote off Sonya Dickson's account as uncollectible, $630.00, Memorandum 78.*

Dec. 30 *Received $630.00 from Sonya Dickson in full payment of her account, which was written off on November 30, Memorandum 89 and Receipt 277.*

Compare your answers to those in the answers section. Re-read the preceding part of the chapter to find the correct answers to any questions you may have missed.

Matching Bad Debts Expense with Revenue

When the direct write-off method of accounting for uncollectible accounts is used, an unpaid account is written off when the business determines that it will not be paid. Frequently, a year or more may pass before the business decides that an account is uncollectible. Under the direct write-off method, the bad debts expense is recorded as an expense in the period in which the account was written off, not during the period when the sale was made.

When measuring business income, one of the most fundamental principles of accounting is that *revenue must be matched with the expenses incurred in generating that revenue.* This means that expenses incurred to earn revenue should be deducted in the same fiscal period that the revenue is earned. For example, a bad debts expense is caused by selling goods on account to a customer who fails to pay. This expense, therefore, is really incurred in the year in which the sale takes place, even though the amount owed is determined to be uncollectible in some future period. That is, a 1992 credit sale that is determined to be uncollectible some time during 1993 represents an expense for 1992. In order to charge the bad debts expense against 1992 revenues, the business must estimate how much of the 1992 revenues will become uncollectible.

This advance provision for bad debts is made by an adjusting entry at the end of the fiscal period. The adjusting entry meets two objectives: (1) Accounts Receivable is reduced to the amount the business can reasonably expect to receive, and (2) the estimated potential bad debts expense is charged to the current fiscal period. Let's now look at the method of accounting for uncollectible accounts that uses this procedure.

The Allowance Method

The **allowance method** of accounting for uncollectible accounts matches potential bad debts expenses with sales made during the same fiscal period. At the end of the fiscal period, an estimate is made of the amount of uncollectible accounts that will result from the sales made during the period. The estimated uncollectible amount is then recorded as an adjustment on the work sheet. The adjusting entry shows that the estimated uncollectible amount has been entered into the accounting records of the business. The two accounts affected by this adjustment for uncollectible accounts are Bad Debts Expense and Allowance for Uncollectible Accounts.

As in the direct write-off method, the account Bad Debts Expense is used to summarize the uncollectible accounts receivable for a fiscal period. Under the allowance method, however, the amount recorded is an *estimate,* not the actual amount that proved to be uncollectible. In addition, in the allowance method, Bad Debts Expense is used only at the end of the fiscal period—when an adjustment for the estimated uncollectible amount is debited to the account.

When the adjustment is being made, it is impossible for the business to know exactly which charge customers will fail to pay the amounts they owe.

510

As a result, the estimated uncollectible amount cannot be credited to Accounts Receivable. Remember, the balance of the Accounts Receivable controlling account must always equal the total of the accounts in the accounts receivable subsidiary ledger. If a specific customer account cannot be credited, neither can Accounts Receivable. Since Accounts Receivable cannot be used to record the estimated uncollectible amount, another account must be opened. This account is Allowance for Uncollectible Accounts.

Allowance for Uncollectible Accounts	
Dr.	Cr.
–	+
Decrease Side	Increase Side
	Balance Side

Allowance for Uncollectible Accounts is used to summarize the estimated uncollectible accounts receivable of the business. It is classified as a contra asset account and appears on the balance sheet as a deduction from Accounts Receivable. By using this contra asset account, the balance of Accounts Receivable still equals the total of the customer accounts in the subsidiary ledger. The balance of Allowance for Uncollectible Accounts represents the amount the business estimates to be uncollectible. The difference between the two accounts represents the book value of accounts receivable. **Book value of accounts receivable** is the amount the business can reasonably expect to receive from all its charge customers. Let's look at the adjustment for estimated uncollectible accounts.

Adjusting for Uncollectible Accounts

Sonaguard, a company that sells burglar and fire alarm systems, uses the allowance method of accounting for uncollectible accounts. On December 31, Sonaguard estimated that its bad debts expense for the fiscal year ended December 31 was $1,350.00. (There are various methods that can be used to estimate bad debts expense. You will learn more about two frequently used methods later in the chapter.)

In this adjustment, Bad Debts Expense is being debited for $1,350.00, the estimated uncollectible amount for the year. Allowance for Uncollectible Accounts is being increased. It is credited for $1,350.00, the amount of current Accounts Receivable that Sonaguard estimates to be uncollectible.

Bad Debts Expense		Allowance for Uncollectible Accounts	
Dr.	Cr.	Dr.	Cr.
+	–	–	+
Adj. $1,350.00			Bal. $ 125.00
			Adj. 1,350.00

Figure 23-4, at the top of pages 512-513, shows how this adjustment is recorded and extended on the work sheet.

Notice that, on line 3, Allowance for Uncollectible Accounts has a $125.00 balance in the Trial Balance Credit column. This balance has been carried over from previous years. If the previous years' uncollectible accounts had exactly equaled the estimated amounts, Allowance for Uncollectible Accounts would have a zero balance. This seldom happens.

Teaching Tips
■ Allowance for Uncollectible Accounts is a valuation account. Its balance is the estimate of uncollectible accounts receivable.
■ The book value of accounts receivable represents the estimated amount of accounts receivable a business will collect from its charge customers.

Using Visuals

Use demonstration problem 23-3 to give students practice in using the allowance method of adjusting for uncollectible accounts.

Teaching Tips
■ Review the rules of debit and credit for Allowance for Uncollectible Accounts. As a contra asset account, it is increased by a credit and decreased by a debit. Its normal balance is a credit.

Critical Thinking
The normal balance side of Allowance for Uncollectible Accounts is a credit. Could the account ever have a debit balance? Explain.
(Answer: Yes. If the actual amount of accounts written off totaled more than the amount that was estimated, the account would have a debit balance instead of its normal credit balance.)

Sona-
Work-
For the Year Ended

ACCT. NO.	ACCOUNT NAME	TRIAL BALANCE DEBIT	TRIAL BALANCE CREDIT	ADJUSTMENTS DEBIT	ADJUSTMENTS CREDIT
101	Cash in Bank	1265000			
105	Accounts Receivable	4489300			
110	Allow. for Uncoll. Accts.		12500		(a) 135000
605	Advertising Expense	60000			
610	Bad Debts Expense			(a) 135000	

Figure 23-4 Recording the Adjustment for Uncollectible Accounts on the Work Sheet (Left Side)

Notice too that the new balance is determined and extended first to the Adjusted Trial Balance Credit column and then to the Balance Sheet Credit column. The new balance of the Bad Debts Expense account is extended first to the Adjusted Trial Balance Debit column and then to the Income Statement Debit column.

Reporting Estimated Uncollectible Amounts on the Financial Statements

The Bad Debts Expense account appears on Sonaguard's income statement as an expense. The placement of the Bad Debts Expense account is shown in the partial income statement in Figure 23-5.

Sonaguard
Income Statement
For the Year Ended December 31, 19— —

Operating Expenses:			
Advertising Expense		60000	
Bad Debts Expense		147500	
Total Oper. Expenses			3834500
Operating Income			2469800

Figure 23-5 Reporting Bad Debts Expense on the Income Statement

On the balance sheet, Allowance for Uncollectible Accounts is listed immediately below Accounts Receivable in the Assets section. The partial balance sheet of Sonaguard is shown in Figure 23-6.

Sonaguard
Balance Sheet
December 31, 19— —

Assets			
Cash in Bank			1265000
Accounts Receivable		4489300	
Less: Allowance for Uncollectible Accts.		147500	4341800

Figure 23-6 Reporting the Allowance for Uncollectible Accounts on the Balance Sheet

512

UNIT 5   Accounting for Special Procedures

(Right Side)

ANSWERS

1. $125.00
2. $1,350.00
3. No
4. Income statement
5. $43,418.00

ACCOUNTING ISSUES

Accountemps conducted a national survey of chief financial officers and found that 31 percent believe that credit and collections is the most important accounting function during a recession.

Notice that the balances of Accounts Receivable and Allowance for Uncollectible Accounts are entered in the first amount column. The difference between the two balances — the book value of accounts receivable — is entered in the second amount column.

R E M E M B E R

Allowance for Uncollectible Accounts is a contra asset account. It is listed on the balance sheet just below Accounts Receivable. The balance of Allowance for Uncollectible Accounts reduces the balance of Accounts Receivable.

Before continuing, complete the following activity.

Check Your Learning

Use Figures 23-4, 23-5, and 23-6 on page 512 and this page to answer these questions. Write your answers on a sheet of notebook paper.

1. What was the balance of Allowance for Uncollectible Accounts before the adjustment?
2. What is the estimated bad debts expense for this fiscal period?
3. Was the Accounts Receivable account affected by the adjustment?
4. On what financial statement is Bad Debts Expense reported?
5. What is the book value of accounts receivable on December 31?

Compare your answers to those in the answers section. Re-read the preceding part of the chapter to find the correct answers to any questions you may have missed.

Journalizing the Adjusting Entry for Uncollectible Accounts

After the work sheet is completed and the financial statements are prepared, the adjusting entries are journalized. The information for the adjusting entries, as you know, is found in the Adjustments section of the work sheet as shown in Figure 23-4.

CHAPTER 23   Accounting for Uncollectible Accounts Receivable   **513**

Reteaching Strategies

In explaining the allowance method, try to get students to think of the allowance account as a worst-case scenario. The allowance is the business's best guess as to the amount it might lose as a result of credit customers not making their payments. As the possibility of a nonpayment turns into reality, the amount of the lost revenue must be taken out of the allowance account and turned into a definite expense (Bad Debts Expense).

Figure 23-7 shows how the adjusting entry for the estimated uncollectible amount is recorded in the general journal and posted to the appropriate general ledger accounts.

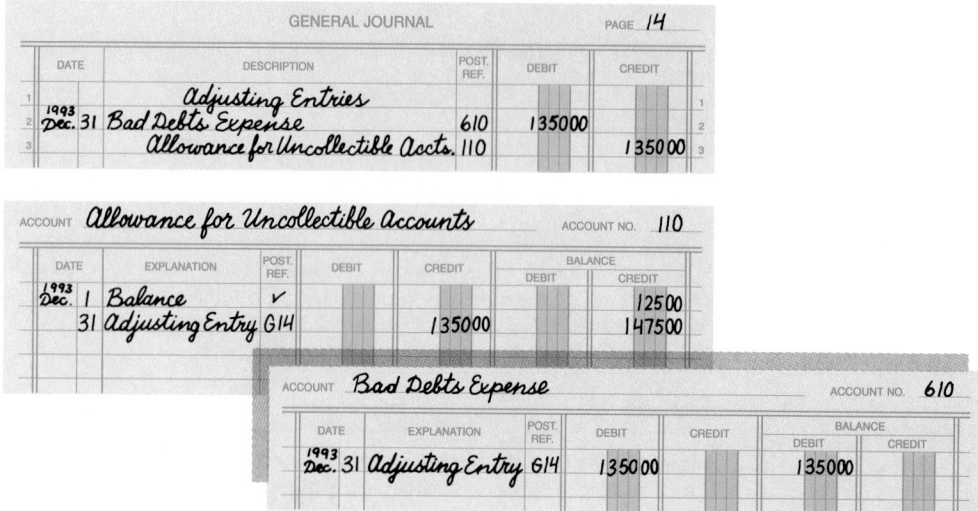

Figure 23-7 Journalizing and Posting the Adjusting Entry for Uncollectible Accounts

At the end of the fiscal period, the balance of the Bad Debts Expense account is closed, along with the balances of the other expense accounts, into Income Summary. It will have a zero balance at the beginning of the next fiscal period. The balance of Allowance for Uncollectible Accounts is not affected by the closing entries. Its balance at the beginning of the next fiscal period is $1,475.00.

R E M E M B E R

When using the allowance method of accounting for uncollectible accounts, an estimate is made at the end of the fiscal period of the amount owed by charge customers that will not be paid. The use of an estimate for bad debts expense allows a company to match expenses and revenue for a fiscal period.

Writing Off Uncollectible Accounts Receivable

When it becomes clear that a charge customer is not going to pay the amount owed, the uncollectible account must be removed from the accounting records. With the direct write-off method, Bad Debts Expense is debited and Accounts Receivable and the customer's account in the subsidiary ledger are credited.

514   UNIT 5 Accounting for Special Procedures

Most businesses require potential charge customers to complete an application for credit.

Under the allowance method, however, the expense incurred has already been provided for by the adjusting entry debiting Bad Debts Expense and crediting Allowance for Uncollectible Accounts. In the previous section, you learned that Allowance for Uncollectible Accounts is not closed at the end of the fiscal period. It acts as a reservoir: At the end of the fiscal period, it is "filled up" by the adjusting entry. The account balance is saved until it is needed some time in the future. When a charge customer's account finally proves uncollectible, the business can dip into that reservoir to write off the account. Let's look at an example.

After many attempts to collect the amount owed, Sonaguard decided to write off the account of the Sullivan Company.

April 18: *Wrote off the account of the Sullivan Company as uncollectible, $150.00, Memorandum 136.*

In this transaction, Allowance for Uncollectible Accounts is debited for $150.00. That account is decreased because the $150.00 is no longer part of an estimate; it is an actual amount. Accounts Receivable and the Sullivan Company account in the accounts receivable subsidiary ledger are credited for $150.00 since Sonaguard no longer expects to receive a payment from Sullivan.

GENERAL LEDGER

Allowance for Uncollectible Accounts		Accounts Receivable	
Dr.	Cr.	Dr.	Cr.
–	+	+	–
$150	Bal. $1,415		$150

SUBSIDIARY LEDGER

Sullivan Company	
Dr.	Cr.
+	–
Bal. $150	$150

CHAPTER 23   Accounting for Uncollectible Accounts Receivable   **515**

Using Visuals

Have students compare the journal entry in Figure 23-8 with that in Figure 23-1 (the direct write-off method) on page 507. Using the allowance method, no expense account is affected by the write-off.

Figure 23-8 shows how the journal entry to write off the account is journalized and posted. Notice that, with the allowance method, an expense account is not affected by the write-off. The expense was recorded as part of the adjusting entry in a previous year.

Figure 23-8 Journalizing and Posting the Write-Off of an Uncollectible Account under the Allowance Method

Collecting an Account Written Off by the Allowance Method

A charge customer whose account was written off as uncollectible by the allowance method may later pay the amount owed. When this happens, the customer's account must first be reinstated by an entry that is the exact opposite of the write-off entry.

> **ACCOUNTING Notes**
> A customer's account is reinstated so that the accounting records will show that the customer paid the debt.

November 19: *Received a check for $150.00 from the Sullivan Company, whose account was written off April 18, Memorandum 154 and Receipt 1243.*

The general journal entry to reinstate the account receivable and reverse the original write-off transaction is shown in Figure 23-9.

516

UNIT 5   Accounting for Special Procedures

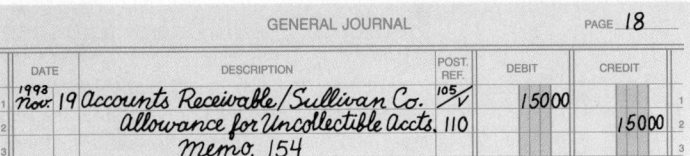

Figure 23-9 Journalizing the Entry To Reinstate a Written-Off Account Under the Allowance Method

After this transaction is posted, the cash receipt transaction can be journalized and posted. (The entry is recorded as a normal cash receipt in the cash receipts journal.) Figure 23-10 shows the Sullivan Company's account after the cash receipt transaction has been posted. Notice that the account shows that (1) the account was declared uncollectible and was written off, (2) the account was later reinstated, and (3) the amount previously written off was collected in full.

Figure 23-10 Sullivan Company Account

Before you read about how to estimate the amount of the bad debts expense, do the following activity to check your understanding of the material you have just learned.

Check Your Learning

Record the following transactions in general journal form on a sheet of notebook paper.

Dec. 31 The adjusting entry for the estimated bad debts expense for the fiscal year ended December 31 was $1,850.00.

May 4 Using the allowance method, wrote off the account of Jack Bowers as uncollectible, $1,050.00, Memorandum 241.

Nov. 18 Received $1,050.00 from Jack Bowers in full payment of his account, which was written off May 4, Memorandum 321 and Receipt 1078.

Compare your answers to those in the answers section. Re-read the preceding part of the chapter to find the correct answers to any questions you may have missed.

CHAPTER 23   Accounting for Uncollectible Accounts Receivable   **517**

CONCEPT DEVELOPMENT

Estimating Bad Debts Expense

Point out that to match revenues earned with expenses, bad debts expense must be estimated at the end of a fiscal period. Emphasize that under the allowance method, the amount of bad debts is just an estimate. Have students name some factors that could cause any estimate to be off.

Demonstrate the percentage of net sales method of estimating bad debts. After the demonstration, allow students to practice estimating bad debts. Make up several situations, giving students this information: Sales, Sales Discounts, Sales Returns and Allowances, and percentage of estimated net sales uncollectible.

Teaching Tips

■ The percentage of net sales method for estimating uncollectible accounts is used here because it is one of the easier methods. Other methods are commonly used. Each business chooses a method that is reasonable for its circumstances.

Using Visuals

 Use demonstration problem 23-6, Part A, to give students practice estimating bad debts expense.

$67,500.00
×   .02
$ 1,350.00

Estimating Bad Debts Expense

When a company uses the allowance method, it must carefully estimate the amount of uncollectible accounts. Estimates are usually based on judgment and past experience. In addition, there are various methods that can be used to estimate bad debts expense. Two common methods that are used are the percentage of net sales method and the aging of accounts receivable method.

Percentage of Net Sales Method

In the **percentage of net sales method** of estimating bad debts expense, the business assumes that a certain percentage of each year's net sales will be uncollectible. Net sales, remember, is Sales less Sales Discounts and Sales Returns and Allowances. The amount of the adjustment for bad debts is found by multiplying the amount of the current year's net sales by a certain percentage.

Sonaguard uses the percentage of net sales method to estimate its bad debts expense. Let's see how this method works. In recent years, Sonaguard's actual losses from bad debts have been approximately 2% of its net sales. On this basis, Sonaguard's accountant believes that the 2% figure should continue to be used to estimate bad debts expense. (The percentage may be changed if actual losses for several years show that it is an unreasonable figure.)

Year	Net Sales	Losses from Bad Debts
1	$ 59,000	$1,062 (1.8%)
2	65,000	1,430 (2.2%)
3	67,000	1,273 (1.9%)
Totals	$191,000	$3,765 (2.0%)

To calculate the current year's estimate of bad debts expense, Sonaguard must first determine the amount of its net sales. As shown, net sales can be found by subtracting the end-of-period balances of Sales Discounts and Sales Returns and Allowances from the end-of-period balance of Sales.

Sales		$74,500.00
Less: Sales Discounts	$3,000.00	
Sales Returns and Allowances	4,000.00	− 7,000.00
Net Sales		$67,500.00

The bad debts expense for the current year is then determined by multiplying the net sales amount ($67,500.00) by the set percentage of 2%. Sonaguard's bad debts expense for the fiscal period is, therefore, estimated to be $1,350.00.

When this method of estimating bad debts expense is used, the estimated amount is the amount recorded as the adjustment on the work sheet, regardless of any balance in Allowance for Uncollectible Accounts. The $1,350.00 amount is based on the current year's net sales. The balance in Allowance for Uncollectible Accounts represents estimates based on previous years' net sales amounts. This adjustment is shown in the T accounts on page 511.

The adjustment is first entered on the work sheet and later entered into the accounting records by journalizing the adjusting entry. At the beginning of the next fiscal period, Allowance for Uncollectible Accounts will have a credit balance of $1,475.00.

The Aging of Accounts Receivable Method

With the **aging of accounts receivable method,** each customer's account is examined and "aged," or classified according to its due date. The accounts are then separated into age groups: not yet due, 1-30 days past due, 31-60 days past due, and so on. Based on past experience, a business can estimate what percentage of each age group will be uncollectible. The total amount for each age group is multiplied by the percentage considered to be uncollectible for that group. The resulting amounts are the estimated uncollectible amounts for each age group. The total of all the estimated uncollectible amounts by age groups represents the *end-of-period balance* of Allowance for Uncollectible Accounts.

Let's look at an example. The Ink Spot, a printing business, uses the aging of accounts receivable method to estimate its bad debts expense. At the end of the fiscal period, the company examined its accounts receivable. The computer printout in Figure 23-11 is an analysis of the Ink Spot's accounts receivable accounts. As you can see, each customer's account was placed in a certain age group.

```
                        THE INK SPOT
                 Analysis of Accounts Receivable
                       December 31, 19--

                        Total                     Days Past Due
Account   Customer's    Amount   Not Yet   --------------------------------
Number      Name        Owed       Due      1-30   31-60  61-90  Over 90

  800    James Allgood  $ 300.00 $ 300.00
  805    Kathy Bell        50.00           $ 50.00
  810    J. W. Boyet      800.00                                  $800.00
  815    Eric Conner      200.00   200.00
  820    Ray DeVall       175.00                  $175.00
  825    Steve Grey     1,000.00 1,000.00
  830    Anna Jackson      40.00                          $40.00
  835    Jan Parker       225.00   225.00
  840    Lynn Stevens     306.50           306.50
  845    Betty Walsh      750.00   750.00


         TOTALS        $3,846.50 $2,475.00 $356.50 $175.00 $40.00 $800.00
```

Figure 23-11 Computer-Generated Analysis of Accounts Receivable

The computer printout in Figure 23-12 on page 520 illustrates how the estimated uncollectible amount is determined from the accounts receivable analysis in Figure 23-11. As you can see, the Ink Spot estimates that a total of $729.26 of its accounts receivable will be uncollectible.

An adjustment must now be made to bring the balance of Allowance for Uncollectible Accounts up to the estimated figure of $729.26. The balance of Allowance for Uncollectible Accounts reported in the Trial Balance Credit column is $49.80. The amount of the adjustment for bad debts expense must

ACCOUNTING PRACTICE
Students may complete Exercise 23-2 after the text relating to the percentage of net sales method.

Using Visuals

Explain each of the columns in Figure 23-11. Point out that the older an account (the longer it is past due), the less likely the business is to collect from the customer.

ACCOUNTING PRACTICE
Students may complete Exercise 23-3 after the section on aging the accounts receivable.

COMPUTERS IN ACCOUNTING

Commercial software to manage loan collections is available to banks, retailers, and finance companies. Such software can be customized to empower businesses to sort accounts according to account type, the time past due, geographical area, etc. In addition, the software program can evaluate the collection productivity of the user's employees.

Making Connections

BUSINESS ETHICS

Assume that you are an accountant for Sherwood, Inc. Data Resources, one of Sherwood's credit customers, is owned by a friend, Jan Hugo, and is having some financial problems. To save money, Hugo asks you to write off Data Resources' account, although

Data Resources could not yet be considered a bad debt. What should you do?

(Answer: Do not write off the account while there is still the possibility that it may be paid. You might suggest that Hugo talk to Sherwood's credit department about developing a more workable payment plan.)

Chapter

Using Visuals

Use Figure 23-12 to help students understand that the amount still to be collected generally decreases as the time periods of the age groups increase. The percentage of uncollectible accounts within the age groups, however, increases.

Teaching Tips

- The preparation of an aging schedule could be extremely time consuming if there were a large number of accounts receivable and if the schedule had to be prepared manually. Today computers enable even larger businesses to age their accounts receivable in a relatively short time.

Using Visuals

Use demonstration problem 23-6, Part B, to give students practice preparing an aging schedule.

3 CLOSE

CHAPTER SUMMARY

This summary enumerates the key information in the chapter. It is a useful tool for reinforcement and review.

	THE INK SPOT Aging of Accounts Receivable Estimated Uncollectible Amount December 31, 19--			
Age Group	Amount	Estimated Percentage Uncollectible	Estimated Uncollectible Amount	
Not yet due	$2,475.00	2%	$ 49.50	
1-30 days past due	356.50	4%	14.26	
31-60 days past due	175.00	10%	17.50	
61-90 days past due	40.00	20%	8.00	
Over 90 days past due	800.00	80%	640.00	
Total	$3,846.50		$729.26	

Figure 23-12 Accounts Receivable Aging Schedule

take this balance into consideration. To determine the adjustment for bad debts expense based on the aging of accounts receivable method, the balance of Allowance for Uncollectible Accounts ($49.80) is subtracted from the total estimated uncollectible amount ($729.26). The adjustment amount is, therefore, $679.46.

Bad Debts Expense			Allowance for Uncollectible Accounts	
Dr.	Cr.		Dr.	Cr.
+	–		–	+
Adj. $679.46				Bal. $ 49.80
				Adj. 679.46
				Bal. $729.26

After the adjusting entry is journalized and posted, the balance of Allowance for Uncollectible Accounts will be $729.26, the balance as determined by the aging schedule.

Summary of Key Points

1. Even though each prospective charge customer's ability to pay is carefully checked before credit is granted, some charge customers will not or cannot pay the amounts they owe. Charge customers' accounts that are declared uncollectible become an expense to the business.
2. In the direct write-off method of accounting for uncollectible accounts, Bad Debts Expense is debited and Accounts Receivable is credited when a customer's account is determined to be uncollectible.
3. The allowance method of accounting for uncollectible accounts enables the business to match bad debt expenses with sales for the same fiscal period. An adjustment is made at the end of the period debiting Bad Debts Expense and crediting Allowance for Uncollectible Accounts.
4. Allowance for Uncollectible Accounts is a contra asset account and is shown on the balance sheet as a deduction from Accounts Receivable.

520

UNIT 5   Accounting for Special Procedures

Pop Quiz

1. Define uncollectible accounts.
2. The _____ method removes the uncollectible amount from the general ledger and the controlling account.
3. The _____ method estimates the amount of uncollectible accounts resulting from sales during the period.
4. One method of estimating bad debts expense assumes that a certain percentage of each year's _____ will be uncollectible.
5. Describe the method of aging accounts receivable.

ANSWERS

1. Accounts receivable accounts that cannot be collected.
2. Direct write-off.
3. Allowance.
4. Net sales.
5. Accounts are grouped by due date.

5. The book value of accounts receivable is the difference between the balance of Accounts Receivable and the balance of Allowance for Uncollectible Accounts. It is the amount the business can reasonably expect to receive from its charge customers.

6. When it is clear that a charge customer's account is uncollectible, it must be written off. Under the allowance method, Allowance for Uncollectible Accounts is debited and Accounts Receivable is credited.

7. When a charge customer whose account has been written off pays the amount owed, the account must first be reinstated before the cash receipt can be journalized.

8. Two common methods used to estimate bad debts expense are the percentage of net sales method and the aging of accounts receivable method.

PRACTICE AND APPLY

- Language Development
- Comprehension and Retention
- Basic Skills

Building Your Accounting Vocabulary

See the Glossary on pages 670-679 for definitions of these terms.

Reviewing Your Accounting Knowledge

1. The direct write-off method and the allowance method. The allowance method is likely to be used by a large business, while the direct write-off method is likely to be used by a business that sells mainly for cash.

2. So that anyone looking at the account can see that it was written off, not paid off.

3. The first journal entry reinstates the customer's account, the second journal entry records the cash receipt.

4. The matching principle is violated because revenue is not matched with the expenses incurred to earn that revenue.

5. Bad Debts Expense is debited and Allowance for Uncollectible Accounts is credited.

6. Because it reduces the balance of Accounts Receivable.

7. The difference between the balance of the Accounts Receivable account and the balance of Allowance for Uncollectible Accounts is the book value of accounts receivable.

8. When using the direct write-off method, Accounts Receivable and the Customer's account are credited and Bad Debts Expense is debited. Under the allowance method, Accounts Receivable and the customer's account are also credited, but the account debited is Allowance for Uncollectible Accounts.

9. The percentage of net sales method and the aging of accounts receivable method.

10. The amount of the adjustment is $12,600.

11. Each accounts receivable account is analyzed when the aging of accounts receivable method is used.

Review and Applications

Building Your Accounting Vocabulary

In your own words, write the definition of each of the following accounting terms. Use complete sentences for your definitions.

aging of accounts receivable method	book value of accounts receivable	percentage of net sales method
allowance method	direct write-off method	uncollectible account

Reviewing Your Accounting Knowledge

1. Name two methods of accounting for uncollectible accounts. Which method is likely to be used by a large business with many charge customers? By a business that sells mainly on a cash basis?
2. Why should an explanation be included in the Explanation column of a charge customer's account when it is written off?
3. Why does the collection of an accounts receivable account previously written off require two journal entries?
4. Which accounting principle is violated when the direct write-off method of accounting for uncollectible accounts is used? How?
5. With the allowance method, which two general ledger accounts are affected by the adjusting entry to record the estimated uncollectible amount for the period?
6. Why is Allowance for Uncollectible Accounts classified as a contra asset account?
7. How is the book value of accounts receivable determined?
8. How does the entry to write off a charge customer's account using the direct write-off method differ from the allowance method?
9. Name two methods that can be used to estimate the bad debts expense for the fiscal period.
10. If a company had net sales of $630,000 and estimates that its bad debt losses will be 2% of net sales, what is the amount of the adjustment?
11. Which method of estimating uncollectible accounts analyzes each accounts receivable account?

Improving Your Decision-Making Skills

Andrus Jewelers, Inc., has been using the direct write-off method of accounting for uncollectible accounts. For the current fiscal year, credit sales are more than double cash sales for the first time. The Accounts Receivable account has also doubled in amount. Bad debt losses are increasing.

Should the company make a change in the way it accounts for uncollectible accounts? If so, what should it do and why? Should the credit department be notified of the increasing bad debt losses? What suggestions would you give the credit department concerning extending credit?

522

Improving Your Decision-Making Skills

Since credit sales and bad debt losses are increasing, Andrus Jewelers, Inc., should switch to the allowance method of accounting for uncollectible accounts. This action should be taken so that bad debt losses can be matched against the revenue for the period. Once this change is made, the method should be used consistently.

Yes, the credit department should be notified of the increasing bad debt losses. It should be asked to review its guidelines for extending credit. It should also be asked to make a more thorough credit check of prospective charge customers.

Applying Accounting Procedures

Exercise 23-1   Comparing the Direct Write-Off
and Allowance Methods

Listed below is a partial chart of accounts for Baker Kitchenware.

101	Cash in Bank	310	Income Summary
105	Accounts Receivable	401	Sales
107	Allowance for Uncollectible Accounts	610	Bad Debts Expense

Instructions: Use a form similar to the one shown. The first transaction has been completed as an example. For each of the following transactions,
(1) In the direct write-off method section, identify by account number the accounts that would be debited and credited. If the transaction would not be recorded, enter "NA" in the debit and credit columns.
(2) In the allowance method section, identify by account number the accounts that would be debited and credited. If the transaction would not be recorded, enter "NA" in the debit and credit columns.

Date	Direct Write-Off Method		Allowance Method	
	Debit	Credit	Debit	Credit
December 1	105	401	105	401

Transactions:

Dec. 1   Sold a shirt on account to a charge customer.
     3   Wrote off a charge customer's account as uncollectible.
     17   Reinstated a charge customer's account that had been written off in October.
     17   Collected cash from the charge customer whose account was reinstated.
     31   Recorded the adjusting entry for uncollectible accounts for the period.
     31   Recorded the closing entry for Bad Debts Expense.

SPREADSHEET   **Exercise 23-2   Estimating Bad Debts Expense**
by the Percentage of Net Sales Method

PROBLEM

Listed below are the end-of-period account balances for several companies. Each company uses the percentage of net sales method to estimate its uncollectible accounts. The percentage used by each company is also listed below.

Instructions: Calculate the amount of the adjustment for bad debts expense using the percentage of net sales method. Use the form provided in your working papers.

	Sales	Sales Discounts	Sales Returns and Allowances	Percentage of Net Sales
Andrews Co.	$142,360	$1,423	$ 936	2%
The Book Nook	209,100	3,180	1,139	1%
Cable, Inc.	173,270	1,730	1,540	$1\frac{1}{2}$%
Davis, Inc.	65,460	650	690	2%
Ever-Sharp Co.	95,085	900	1,035	$1\frac{1}{4}$%

523

PRACTICE AND APPLY

• Concepts and Procedures

Exercise 23-1: Ch. Obj. 1, 2

Exercise 23-2: Ch. Obj. 7

Adjustments:
Andrews Co., $2,800.02
Book Nook, $2,047.81
Cable, Inc., $2,550.00
Davis, Inc., $1,282.40
Ever-Sharp, $1,164.38

Additional Reinforcement

Students who need additional practice or individualized help will benefit from the *Glencoe Accounting Electronic Study Guide* or the *Glencoe Accounting* on-line multimedia program, which provide reinforcement and reteaching for vocabulary, concepts, and procedures.

Refer students to the Chapter 23 review pages in the workbook, *Chapter Reviews and Working Papers.*

Exercise 23-3: Ch. Obj. 7

Total estimated uncollectible amount:
$2,160.00

Problem 23-1: Ch. Obj. 1, 2

Ending GL account balances:
Cash in Bank, $10,938.91
Accounts Receivable, $7,325.60
Bad Debts Expense, $402.15

Problem 23-2: Ch. Obj. 3, 4

Bad Debts Expense, $8,400.00
Book value of AR, $97,600

Exercise 23-3 Completing an Aging Schedule

The Gibson Company uses the aging of accounts receivable method to estimate its uncollectible amount. The aging schedule is shown below.

Instructions: Complete the schedule, using the form in the workbook.

Age Group	Amount	Estimated Percentage Uncollectible	Estimated Uncollectible Amount
Not yet due	$14,320	2%	
1-30 days past due	3,640	5%	
31-60 days past due	3,752	10%	
61-90 days past due	2,280	20%	
91-180 days past due	1,920	25%	
Over 180 days past due	634	60%	
Totals	$26,546		

Problem 23-1 Using the Direct Write-Off Method

The Parker Supply Company uses the direct write-off method of accounting for uncollectible accounts.

Instructions:

(1) Record the following transactions in the general journal, page 14.

(2) Post the transactions to the appropriate accounts.

Transactions:

May 7 Wrote off the $288.75 account of Edward Cobb as uncollectible, Memorandum 223.

June 4 Wrote off the account of Joan Schmidt as uncollectible, $243.60, Memorandum 249.

29 Wrote off the $57.75 account of Albert Olson as uncollectible, Memorandum 255.

Sept. 12 Received $288.75 from Edward Cobb in full payment of his account, which was written off in May, Memorandum 298 and Receipt 944.

Dec. 19 Wrote off Anna Waybright's account as uncollectible, $100.80, Memorandum 329.

Problem 23-2 Calculating and Recording Estimated Bad Debts Expense

Plato Tire Company uses the allowance method of accounting for uncollectible accounts. At the end of the fiscal period, the following accounts appeared on Plato's trial balance.

Accounts Receivable	$110,000.00	
Allowance for Uncollectible Accounts		$ 4,000.00
Sales		900,000.00
Sales Discounts	10,000.00	
Sales Returns and Allowances	50,000.00	
Bad Debts Expense	0.00	

Instructions:

(1) Determine the amount of the adjustment for bad debts for the fiscal period ended December 31. Management estimates that uncollectible accounts will be 1% of net sales.

524

Teacher Notes

(2) Journalize the adjusting entry in the general journal, page 8.

(3) Post the adjusting entry to the general ledger accounts.

(4) Determine the book value of accounts receivable.

Problem 23-3 Writing Off Accounts under the Allowance Method

Taylor Furniture Company, Inc., uses the allowance method of accounting for uncollectible accounts.

Instructions:

(1) Record the following transactions in the general journal, page 9.

(2) Post the transactions to the appropriate accounts. (The opened general ledger and accounts receivable subsidiary ledger are included in the working papers.)

(3) Prepare the Assets section of the balance sheet for Taylor Furniture Company, Inc., using the partial general ledger in the working papers. The balances of other asset accounts needed are Merchandise Inventory, $33,000.00; Supplies, $2,000.00; and Prepaid Insurance, $1,200.00.

Transactions:

Apr. 2 Wrote off the $593.25 account of Tom Pernell as uncollectible, Memorandum 29.

May 17 Wrote off Roger Nagel's $262.50 account as uncollectible, Memorandum 32.

July 9 Wrote off the account of the King Company as uncollectible, $840.00, Memorandum 43.

31 Received $131.25 from the Zeron Company in full payment of its account, which had been written off on November 10, Memorandum 49 and Receipt 399.

Dec. 28 Wrote off the account of Stull, Inc., as uncollectible, $945.00, Memorandum 74.

31 Recorded the adjusting entry for estimated uncollectible accounts for the period. The bad debts expense estimate is based on 2% of the net sales of $150,000.00.

31 Recorded the closing entry for Bad Debts Expense.

Problem 23-4 Estimating Bad Debts Expense by the Aging of Accounts Receivable Method

Pilgrim Appliance Company uses the allowance method of accounting for uncollectible accounts. The company estimates the uncollectible amount by aging its accounts receivable accounts.

Instructions:

(1) Complete the analysis of accounts receivable that is included in the working papers accompanying this textbook.

(2) Calculate the estimated uncollectible amount. Use the form provided in the working papers.

(3) Journalize the December 31 adjusting entry for bad debts expense on general journal page 11. Allowance for Uncollectible Accounts has a credit balance of $142.00.

(4) Post the adjusting entry to the general ledger accounts.

(5) Calculate the book value of accounts receivable.

525

Problem 23-3: Ch. Obj. 5, 6

Adjustment for bad debts, $3,000

Ending GL account balances:
Cash in Bank, $9,437.79
Accounts Receivable, $20,461.25
Allowance for Uncollectible Accounts, $3,654.50

Total assets, $62,444.54
Book value of AR, $16,806.75

Problem 23-4: Ch. Obj. 7

Estimated uncollectible amount, $780.19
Adjustment, $638.19
Book value of AR, $6,430.81

Teacher Notes

Problem 23-5: Ch. Obj. 1, 3, 4

COMPUTER

PROBLEM

This computer image identifies a problem that students may complete using the *Glencoe Accounting, General Ledger* software.

Adjustment, $2,239.35
Net income, $36,745.85
Retained Earnings, $46,510.00
Balance sheet totals, $92,889.10

Problem 23-6: Ch. Obj. 3, 4, 5, 6

CHALLENGE

PROBLEM

The last problem in each chapter is a challenge problem and is identified by this "maze" symbol.

4 ASSESS

A chapter test is available for use in assessing students' understanding of concepts in this chapter.

The testmaker software will enable you to develop tailor-made chapter, unit, semester, and final tests.

Alternative Assessment

For alternative assessment strategies, refer to *Tech Prep Strategies in Accounting.*

COMPUTER

PROBLEM

Problem 23-5   Reporting Uncollectible Amounts on the Financial Statements

The work sheet for Anderson Paper Products, Inc., is included in the working papers accompanying this textbook. The trial balance has been completed on the work sheet, along with all adjustments except that for bad debts.

Instructions:

(1) Record the adjustment for bad debt losses in the Adjustments section of the work sheet. Bad debt losses are estimated to be 1.5% of net sales. Label the adjustment (a).

(2) Complete the work sheet.

(3) Prepare an income statement, a statement of retained earnings, and a balance sheet.

(4) Record the adjusting entries on page 18 of the general journal.

(5) Post the adjusting entries to the general ledger accounts.

(6) Record the closing entries in the general journal.

(7) Post the closing entries to the general ledger accounts.

CHALLENGE

PROBLEM

Problem 23-6   Handling Write-Offs in the Allowance Method

McCloud's Department Store uses the allowance method to account for uncollectible accounts.

Instructions: Journalize the following transactions on page 13 of the general journal. Post the transactions to Terry Mahady's account, provided in the working papers.

Transactions:

Jan. 14 Wrote off the account of Terry Mahady as uncollectible, $194.50, Memorandum 398.

June 25 Received a check for $30.00 from Terry Mahady on account, Memorandum 467 and Receipt 1298.

Dec. 10 Received notice that Terry Mahady had been declared bankrupt. Received 40% of the balance due and wrote off the remainder of his account, Receipt 1588 and Memorandum 541.

Use Chapter Test 23 here to assess students' understanding and retention of the concepts and procedures presented in the chapter.

*C*omputer Viruses:
The Enemy Within

*C*omputer viruses are small computer programs that appear harmless but, as part of their operation, "reproduce" and insert themselves into previously uninfected programs. Like a biological virus, a computer virus spreads quickly. It can cause havoc by slowing entire systems or, worse, destroying stored data. Some viruses even lie dormant, scheduled to go off months or even years in the future.

A computer virus often starts at a personal computer and winds its way through a computer network. Its victim can be anyone: governments, businesses, universities, research facilities, private citizens.

It is estimated that thousands of computers a year are attacked—from laptops to the most powerful networks. One computer virus can turn into an epidemic, affecting many computer systems. New strains surface every week.

Some viruses (called "worms") are pretty harmless, like the Cookie Monster that interrupted users with the message, "I want a cookie." Others are more destructive. In 1988 a disgruntled former employee of an insurance and brokerage company was convicted of electronically destroying over 150,000 payroll records and planting a "time bomb" virus intended to erase computer records every month.

A computer virus is often difficult to detect and usually expensive to cure. As computer viruses have increased, so too have the number of protection programs created to ward off the enemy. Disk Defender, Data Physician, and Vaccinate are just some of the many "virus busters" now on the market.

Who commits these acts of vandalism? It could be a hostile employee, but a pattern seems to be emerging. The culprits are, more often than not,

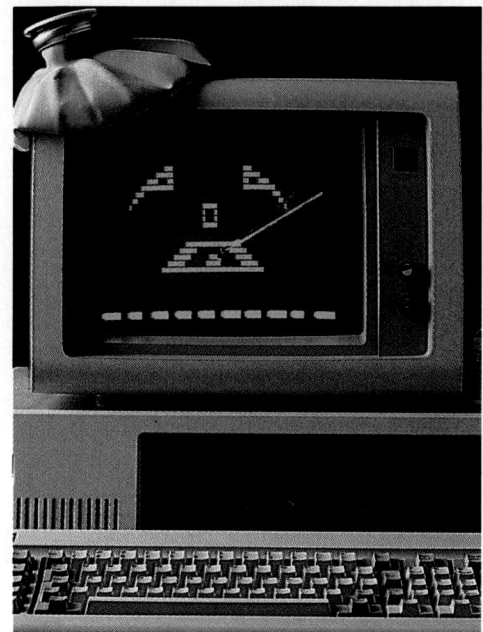

Increased security measures are needed to prevent the spread of computer viruses.

young people in their late teens or early 20s who have spent a lot of time with computers. Perhaps they're trying to prove they can beat the system. They've learned computer use, but not computer ethics.

What may have started as a prank has now mushroomed into an epidemic that is disruptive, destructive, and deeply disturbing to computer users everywhere. There's an enemy within—but where?

527

Have students read the ethics case given in the textbook and jot down ideas about what they would do in the situation described. Then review the five-step decision model (see page T44). Emphasize that there are no "right" or "wrong" answers to the questions in the decision model.

After students have discussed the first four steps, have them vote on which alternative they feel is best, or, if one alternative has clearly been chosen during the discussion, review students' reasoning for choosing that course of action.

You may want to have students compare their final decision with the one they wrote down after first reading the vignette. Did following the five-step model reinforce their "instinctual" decision or lead them to choose a different course of action? Help students realize that following a decision model when they confront an ethical dilemma can help them to organize their thinking and arrive at a satisfactory solution.

QUESTIONS

1. What are the ethical issues in this situation?
2. What are the alternatives?
3. Who are the affected parties?
4. How do the alternatives affect the parties?
5. What is the decision?

ANSWERS

1. The deliberate attempt to destroy business property—data files.
2. For the people who create computer viruses, the alternatives are to continue to test their creativity in a destructive way or to find a different way of using their computer expertise.
3. The affected parties are the virus programmers and any business or government agency whose computer files are affected by a virus.
4. The businesses that lose data files from computer viruses may have to spend a lot of money recreating those files. They could also lose business as a result.
5. Accept any answer, but require students to defend the course of action they choose.

Chapter

ACCOUNTING FOR INVENTORIES

LOOKING BACK

At the beginning of this unit, students learned to use cash funds and to describe various means of internal control for the protection of cash and other assets. One of those assets is the inventory of merchandise maintained by the business. It is equally as important to protect merchandise as it is to protect cash. In this chapter students will learn about different methods of determining the quantity of merchandise on hand and four methods for assigning a value to that merchandise.

VOCABULARY DEVELOPMENT

Have students read the list of new terms. Ask for ideas for each term's meaning. Write correct responses on the board. Review the meanings of terms that are not familiar to students. Definitions of these terms are found in the chapter and in the glossary on pages 670-679.

Electronic Field Trips

In earlier chapters, you learned how important it is for a business to maintain control over its cash. Improper control of cash can result in poor management decisions. It can also mean a lack of cash for other needs and, in some cases, business failure.

For a merchandising business, it is equally important to control merchandise. Merchandising businesses spend a great deal of time and money purchasing, storing, and selling merchandise. To exercise control over its merchandise, a merchandising business establishes a system of inventory procedures.

In this chapter, you will learn how businesses count their inventories, how they account for increases and decreases in quantities of merchandise in inventory, and how they assign a cost value to merchandise remaining in inventory.

Learning Objectives

When you have completed Chapter 24, you should be able to do the following:

1. Explain the importance of maintaining consistent inventory records.
2. Explain the difference between a periodic and a perpetual inventory system.
3. Determine the cost of a merchandise inventory using the following methods: specific identification; first in, first out; last in, first out; and weighted average cost.
4. Assign a value to merchandise inventory using the lower-of-cost-or-market rule.
5. Define the accounting terms introduced in this chapter.

New **Terms**

periodic inventory system
perpetual inventory system
online
specific identification method
first in, first out method
last in, first out method
weighted average cost method
market value
conservatism

528

Teaching Resources

- Lesson Plans
- TE/Chapter Reviews & Working Papers
- Demonstration Problems
- Student Study Plans
- Teaching Transparencies
- Solutions Transparencies
- Electronic Field Trips Video, Level I
- Electronic Study Guide
- Chapter 24 Test

Other Resources

- Skills Improvement Activities
- Blackline Masters
- Careers in Accounting
- Dictionary
- Math Review for Accounting
- Tech Prep Strategies in Accounting
- Video
- Test Bank with Software
- Spanish Resources/Audiotapes
- Spanish Electronic Study Guide

Merchandise Inventory

Earlier you learned that goods purchased by a business for resale to customers are called merchandise. The cost of all those goods still on hand at the end of a fiscal period is recorded in the Merchandise Inventory account.

Merchandise plays a very important role in any merchandising business. It is one of the business's largest asset accounts. This is because much of the business's cash is used to purchase merchandise. Like cash, merchandise must be subject to a control system that helps the business keep track of its merchandise. Businesses need to know not only how much merchandise is sold but also which items of merchandise have been sold. The business also needs to know if a certain item of merchandise is not selling. The business may stop buying that item and find some means — through sales or promotions, for example — to eliminate that item from its inventory.

In a merchandising business, the quantity and cost value of merchandise on hand are important in presenting a realistic picture of the company's financial position. Merchandise Inventory is the only account reported on both the balance sheet and the income statement. The balance of the Merchandise Inventory account at the end of the fiscal period (the ending inventory) is reported on the balance sheet because it is classified as an asset account. The beginning and ending inventory balances are reported on the income statement because they are used to determine the cost of merchandise sold.

An inventory control system requires certain information to function efficiently. That information includes the quantity of merchandise on hand at a given time and the cost of that merchandise.

ACCOUNTING Notes
A business's merchandise inventory includes all of the items on hand and available for sale, whether those items are located in the stockroom or on the sales floor.

Determining the Quantity of Inventories

The quantity of merchandise on hand must be determined before the cost of this merchandise can be calculated and reported on the financial statements. There are two systems businesses use to determine the quantity of merchandise on hand: a periodic inventory system and a perpetual inventory system.

The Periodic Inventory System

One of the most commonly used systems of determining the quantity of merchandise on hand is a periodic inventory system. A **periodic inventory system** requires a physical count of all merchandise on hand. With this system, each inventory item is counted. The total number of a particular item on hand is recorded on an inventory card or sheet. A typical inventory sheet is shown in Figure 24-1 on page 530. As you can see, the sheet lists the stock number of the item, a description of the item, the quantity on hand, the unit cost, and the total value of the inventory item on hand.

For businesses having many items in inventory, the process of identifying and counting all items of merchandise can be very time-consuming. For this reason, inventory should be counted when it is at its lowest level. Many seasonal businesses take their inventories at the end of their peak selling periods when much of their merchandise has been sold. Most businesses take a periodic inventory of their merchandise at least once a year.

Determining the Quantity of Inventories (Continued)

essential part of an inventory management system. The periodic inventory system is most familiar to students. Discuss the amount of time needed to complete this type of inventory to help students understand why most businesses cannot perform this type of inventory frequently. Businesses using a periodic inventory system need a physical count of all merchandise at least once per year.

INVENTORY SHEET

DATE _Jan. 5, 19--_   CLERK _Brian Cropp_   PAGE _1_

STOCK NO.	ITEM	UNIT	QUANTITY	UNIT COST	TOTAL VALUE
1901	Needles	Pkg.	24	1 14	27 36
2132	Thread	Spool	12	65	7 80
2136	Thread	Spool	18	55	9 90
3245	Zipper	Each	18	1 50	27 00
1917	Pins	Box	24	79	18 96
4971	Buttons	Pkg.	12	89	10 68
4993	Tape Measure	Each	15	1 49	22 35
				TOTAL FOR THIS SHEET	789 14

Figure 24-1   Inventory Sheet Used in a Periodic Inventory System

Some businesses use automated equipment to assist them in taking inventories. When automated equipment is used, the user merely enters the stock number of the item and the amount still on hand into a small hand-held computer. After the physical count of all items in stock is taken, a complete printout can be obtained from the computer. An example of a stock-on-hand printout is shown in Figure 24-2.

```
                    Abbott's Department Store
                      Physical Inventory
                        Department 34
                        June 30, 19--

   Stock                                  Unit      Total
   No.          Item          Unit  Qty   Cost      Value

   012844   Patton Desk Lamp   Each    8   32.40    259.20
   012846   Captain's Lamp     Each    4   39.95    159.80
   012852   Doon Table Lamp    Each    7   46.55    325.85
   012857   18-Inch Table Lamp Each    3   43.80    131.40
   012859   Floor Lamp         Each    9   63.60    572.40
   012862   Kline Floor Lamp   Each    3   72.69    218.07
   012864   Warnen Night Lamp  Pair    6   39.45    236.70
   012867   10-Inch Night Lamp Each    0   42.59
   012868   Patton Bulbs       Each   28    2.35     65.80
   012873   10-Inch Lamp Shade Each   12   19.50    234.00
   012875   12-Inch Lamp Shade Each   16   22.86    365.76
   012876   14-Inch Lamp Shade Each    5   27.95    139.75
   012883   Lamp Dimmer        Each    7    9.45     66.15
                                                  --------
                                                  2774.88
                                                  ========
```

Figure 24-2   Computer Printout of Inventory

UNIT 5   Accounting for Special Procedures

The Perpetual Inventory System

Computers have enabled many businesses to maintain perpetual inventory systems.

Another system that can be used to account for inventories is the perpetual inventory system. A **perpetual inventory system** requires that a constant, up-to-date record of merchandise on hand be kept. With this inventory system, a business can determine the balance of the Merchandise Inventory account at any time since all purchases and sales are recorded immediately. In addition, the cost of merchandise sold can be determined easily since the accounting records indicate merchandise purchases and balances on hand.

Businesses using a perpetual inventory system may use stock record sheets or cards. A stock card used in a perpetual inventory system is shown in Figure 24-3. Each time the level of stock is increased or decreased, the amount of the increase or decrease is recorded on the stock card. For example, when an incoming order of merchandise is received, the quantity is recorded in the In column of the stock card. Sales of the item are recorded in the Out column.

STOCK CARD

STOCK NO.	ITEM			
C 1297	Altmore Disk Player			

SUPPLIER	SUPPLIER'S CATALOGUE NO.
Star Electric	91246

UNIT	MINIMUM	MAXIMUM
Each	15	60

DATE	EXPLANATION	IN	OUT	BALANCE
7/1/--	Balance on Hand			48
7/8/--	Shipping Order 21928		6	42
7/12/-	Shipping Order 22201		10	32
7/20/-	Shipping Order 22456		8	24
7/24/-	Shipping Order 22719		12	12
7/24/-	Purchase Requisition 19426			
7/31/-	Receiving Report 21563	48		60

Figure 24-3 Stock Card Used in a Perpetual Inventory System

Manual perpetual inventory systems are generally used by businesses that sell large items. For example, a television dealer would probably find it convenient to maintain a separate stock card for every type of item in stock. Each time a new inventory item is purchased, a new card is prepared and inserted in the file. If the item is discontinued, the card is pulled from the inventory file.

Computerized Inventory Systems

With the increased use of computers, many businesses maintain computerized perpetual inventory systems. This is done through terminals or cash registers that are online to a central computer system. **Online** means that a terminal or cash register is linked directly to the computer and feeds data into the appropriate files controlled by the computer. For example, when a sale is made by a business using a computerized inventory system, the item

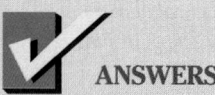
number, the quantity, and the price of the item being sold are entered into the cash register by the salesperson. The cash register is online to a computer, which updates the inventory cost records immediately. With this information stored in the computer, management may obtain inventory quantities and values at any time. An example of a computer printout for a perpetual inventory system is shown in Figure 24-4.

```
                    CENTER SPORTS SHOP
                    PERPETUAL INVENTORY
                      DEPARTMENT 28
                    SEPTEMBER 30,  19--

  STOCK                                        UNIT     TOTAL
   NO.        ITEM            UNIT    QTY      COST      VALUE

   2305   Warner Rods         Each    7       27.45     192.15
   2319   Tanner Rods         Each    9       31.48     283.32
   2320   Paterson Rods       Each   13       34.95     454.35
   2325   Junior Rods         Each   10       22.50     225.00
   2337   Weber Reel          Each   13       29.45     382.85
   2339   Art Reel            Each    8       25.85     206.80
   2345   Pro Reel # 4        Each    4       38.50     154.00
   2353   # 9 Hooks           Box    16        8.75     140.00
   2356   # 6 Hooks           Box    13        7.95     103.35
                                              -------
                                              2141.82
                                              =======
```

Figure 24-4   Computer Printout from a Perpetual Inventory System

In a perpetual inventory system, the Merchandise Inventory account always shows the balance of merchandise on hand. A physical count should be taken at least once a year, usually at the year's end, to verify the balance reported in the Merchandise Inventory account.

Before you learn how to determine the cost of inventory on hand, do the following activity to check your understanding of periodic and perpetual inventory systems.

Check Your Learning

Write the answers to these questions on notebook paper.

1. The ___?___ inventory system requires a physical count of the merchandise on hand.
2. The ___?___ inventory system provides constant inventory data.
3. Which type of inventory system might be used by a small stereo store?
4. Which type of inventory system might be used by a large supermarket?
5. Why do companies that use a perpetual inventory system still take a periodic inventory at the end of the year?

Compare your answers to those in the answers section. Re-read the preceding part of the chapter to find the correct answers to any questions you may have missed.

UNIT 5   Accounting for Special Procedures

Determining the Cost of Inventories

Once the quantity of merchandise on hand has been determined, the cost of the merchandise must be calculated. If a perpetual inventory system is used, it is easy for the business to determine the cost of the inventory because the actual cost of each item is recorded on the stock card or in the computer.

If a periodic inventory system is used, however, the cost of the inventory is more difficult to determine. Calculating the cost of each item in inventory is not always easy because businesses may buy the same item many times within a single inventory period. The cost of an item may change from one purchase to another. To simplify matters, businesses using the periodic inventory system assign costs to the items in inventory. The inventory costs may be assigned using one of four commonly accepted inventory costing methods. These four methods are specific identification; first in, first out; last in, first out; and weighted average cost.

The Specific Identification Costing Method

When the **specific identification method** is used, the exact cost of each item on the inventory sheet must be determined and assigned to that item. The actual cost of each item is usually obtained from the purchase invoice. Unfortunately, the task of looking up the actual cost of each item is very time-consuming unless you are dealing with a small number of items.

The specific identification method is most often used by businesses that have a low unit volume of merchandise with, usually, high unit prices. For example, appliance stores, automobile dealerships, and furniture stores often use this method. Specific identification is the most realistic costing method because it assigns the actual cost to each item in inventory. Let's look at an example.

The Triangle Video Store started the fiscal year with a beginning inventory of 15 video cassette recorders. The VCRs had been purchased for $250.00 each. During the period, the store purchased an additional 50 VCRs. When a periodic inventory was taken on May 31, there were 12 VCRs still on hand. The costs of the VCRs are as follows:

Beginning inventory	15 units @ $250.00 each =	$ 3,750.00
Purchased August 4	20 units @ $250.00 each =	5,000.00
Purchased December 8	10 units @ $253.00 each =	2,530.00
Purchased February 27	10 units @ $258.00 each =	2,580.00
Purchased May 1	10 units @ $260.00 each =	2,600.00
Total Available	65	$16,460.00

Using the specific identification method, Triangle must check its purchase invoices to find the actual cost of each of the 12 VCRs still on hand at the end of May. After checking its invoices, Triangle found that

4 VCRs were purchased @ $253.00 each =	$1,012.00
5 VCRs were purchased @ $258.00 each =	1,290.00
3 VCRs were purchased @ $260.00 each =	780.00
12 VCRs (ending inventory)	$3,082.00

CHAPTER 24   Accounting for Inventories   533

CONCEPT DEVELOPMENT
Determining the Cost of Inventories

Before introducing students to the methods of assigning a cost to ending inventory, discuss the problems involved in this procedure for different types of businesses. Very few businesses can assign exact costs to all items on hand, so estimated costing methods are used.

When presenting the specific identification costing method, emphasize that this is the most accurate method since exact costs are used.

Teaching Tips

- Ask students why the cost of an item could change quickly.
- Have students name different types of businesses that could use the specific identification method with success.

Using Visuals

 Use demonstration problem 24-2, Part A, to give students practice in calculating inventory cost using specific identification.

Cooperative Learning

CO-OP, CO-OP

Assign students in pairs and ask each pair to contact a local retail business to inquire about how that business maintains its inventory records. Have each pair report its findings to the class.

Refer to the "Cooperative Learning" section of *Tech Prep Strategies in Accounting* for additional cooperative learning strategies.

ACCOUNTING
PRACTICE
Students may complete
Exercise 24-1 after their study of
the specific identification
method.

Teaching Tips

■ When presenting lifo and fifo, put examples on the chalkboard and have students determine the costs under each method.
■ Mention that fifo is an acronym. Have students think of other acronyms such as CPA or FASB.

Using Visuals

Use demonstration problem 24-2, Part B, to present the fifo method.

ACCOUNTING
PRACTICE
Students may complete
Exercise 24-2 after their study of
the fifo method.

In this example, the actual cost of each VCR was determined. The total cost of the ending inventory was determined by adding the purchase costs of the 12 VCRs: $3,082.00. With this figure, the cost of merchandise sold can be calculated by subtracting the cost of the ending inventory from the cost of the merchandise available for sale. For example,

Total VCRs available for sale (65 units)	$16,460.00
Less ending inventory (12 units)	− 3,082.00
Cost of merchandise sold (53 units)	$13,378.00

The First In, First Out Costing Method

The **first in, first out method** (fifo) of assigning cost assumes that the first items purchased (first in) were the first sold (first out). When assigning costs to inventory, therefore, the fifo method assumes that the last items purchased are the ones on hand at the end of the fiscal period. For example, think about milk that is stocked by a supermarket. Since milk is perishable, the supermarket puts the milk it purchased first at the front of the shelf. As that milk is sold, later purchases of milk are added at the back of the shelves.

Let's apply the fifo costing method to our VCR example. During the period, 65 VCRs were available for sale.

Beginning inventory	15 units @ $250.00 each	=	$ 3,750.00
Purchased August 4	20 units @ $250.00 each	=	5,000.00
Purchased December 8	10 units @ $253.00 each	=	2,530.00
Purchased February 27	10 units @ $258.00 each	=	2,580.00
Purchased May 1	10 units @ $260.00 each	=	2,600.00
	65 units		$16,460.00

Under the fifo method, the first items purchased are assumed to be the first items sold. In other words, the 53 VCRs sold are assumed to be the 15 VCRs in the beginning inventory plus the 20 VCRs purchased on August 4, plus the 10 VCRs purchased on December 8, plus 8 of the 10 VCRs purchased on February 27. The items remaining in inventory are the last ones purchased: 2 VCRs purchased on February 27 and 10 VCRs purchased on May 1. The cost of the ending inventory is calculated as follows:

10 units @ $260.00 each	=	$2,600.00
2 units @ $258.00 each	=	516.00
12 units		$3,116.00

The cost of merchandise sold using the fifo method is as follows:

Total VCRs available for sale (65 units)	$16,460.00
Less ending inventory (12 units)	3,116.00
Cost of merchandise sold (53 units)	$13,344.00

The Last In, First Out Costing Method

The **last in, first out method** (lifo) of assigning inventory cost assumes that the last items purchased (last in) are the first items sold (first

534

UNIT 5 Accounting for Special Procedures

Making Connections

COMMUNICATIONS

Many new business owners depend on their accountants' advice when choosing systems and methods. Have students describe a hypothetical start-up business and explain either orally or in writing how they would recommend one of the inventory costing methods to the owner or manager.

out). When the lifo method is used, the business assumes that the first items purchased are still on hand at the end of the fiscal period. The earliest costs, therefore, are the ones used to assign a cost to the inventory.

If the Triangle Video Store uses the lifo method rather than the fifo method of assigning costs to the ending inventory, the value of the ending inventory will be different. Let's return to the VCR example.

Beginning inventory	15 units @ $250.00 each =	$ 3,750.00
Purchased August 4	20 units @ $250.00 each =	5,000.00
Purchased December 8	10 units @ $253.00 each =	2,530.00
Purchased February 27	10 units @ $258.00 each =	2,580.00
Purchased May 1	10 units @ $260.00 each =	2,600.00
	65 units	$16,460.00

Using the lifo method, the business would assume that the 12 VCRs remaining in stock are from the beginning inventory of 15 units. The cost of the ending inventory is calculated as follows:

12 units @ $250.00 each = $3,000.00

The cost of merchandise sold using the lifo method is as follows:

Total VCRs available for sale (65 units)	$16,460.00
Less ending inventory (12 units)	− 3,000.00
Cost of merchandise sold (53 units)	$13,460.00

Before you learn about the weighted average cost method of assigning costs to ending inventory, do the following activity to check your understanding of the specific identification, lifo, and fifo methods.

 Check Your Learning

The following items were purchased by Reid Leather Goods during the month of April:

April 2	36 wallets @ $7.92 each
April 8	24 wallets @ $7.84 each
April 18	18 wallets @ $7.98 each
April 26	30 wallets @ $8.06 each

1. If 46 wallets remain on hand at the end of the accounting period, find the cost of the ending inventory using the specific identification method. Of the 46 wallets in inventory, 12 were purchased on April 2; 20 were purchased on April 8; 3 were purchased on April 18; and 11 were purchased on April 26.
2. Using the ending inventory of 46 wallets, find the cost of the ending inventory using the lifo and the fifo methods.

Compare your answers to those in the answers section. Re-read the preceding part of the chapter to find the correct answers to any questions you may have missed.

 Using Visuals

Use demonstration problem 24-2, Part C, to present the lifo method.

Teaching Tips

- In periods of rising costs, the lifo method will usually yield a *lower* ending inventory amount than the fifo method.

ACCOUNTING PRACTICE
Students may complete Exercise 24-3 after their study of the lifo method.

 ANSWERS
1. $364.44
2. Lifo, $363.53; fifo, $369.48

Reteaching Strategies

Remind students that the key word to helping them remember which prices to use in the fifo and lifo methods is the *first* word. Using fifo, "F" for first tells students that the first items purchased are assumed to have been sold. Using lifo, "L" for *last* tells students that the last items purchased are assumed to have been sold.

Assign additional Problem 24A, page 643, to students who need additional practice with inventory costing methods.

Teaching Tips

■ Briefly discuss average costs. For students who need a math review, assign problems in the *Math Review for Accounting* workbook.

Using Visuals

 Use demonstration 24-2, Part D, to show students how to calculate average costs.

Teaching Tips

■ The weighted average cost method is often used by businesses dealing in such products as oil and grain.
■ The average cost method usually yields an amount between the lifo and fifo amounts.

 ACCOUNTING PRACTICE
Students may complete Exercise 24-4 at this point.

CONCEPT DEVELOPMENT
Choosing an Inventory Costing Method
Discuss the effects of the different methods on the cost of merchandise sold. Point out that there is no right or wrong method, but rather one that is best for a particular business in certain economic times. A discussion on long-term and short-term economic projections and current price trends is helpful. This section may be confusing for students, but it is important that they understand why certain decisions are made.

Teaching Tips

■ Have students discuss what would happen if businesses could change methods whenever they wanted to.

The Weighted Average Cost Method

Another method that may be used to assign costs to an inventory is the weighted average cost method. The **weighted average cost method** is a means of calculating cost by adding all the purchases of an item (units and cost) to the beginning inventory (units and cost) of that item. The total cost is then divided by the total units to obtain the average cost per unit. The average cost per unit is used to determine the cost of the ending inventory. Again, we will use the Triangle Video Store example. Purchases were as follows:

Beginning inventory	15 units @ $250.00 each	=	$ 3,750.00
Purchased August 4	20 units @ $250.00 each	=	5,000.00
Purchased December 8	10 units @ $253.00 each	=	2,530.00
Purchased February 27	10 units @ $258.00 each	=	2,580.00
Purchased May 1	10 units @ $260.00 each	=	2,600.00
	65 units		$16,460.00

To determine the cost of the ending inventory, Triangle needs to know the average cost per VCR. This cost is calculated by dividing the total cost of the VCRs available for sale ($16,460.00) by the total units available for sale (65).

$16,460.00 ÷ 65 = $253.23 (average cost per unit)

The number of items remaining in the ending inventory (12) is multiplied by the average cost per unit ($253.23). The answer is the cost of the ending merchandise inventory.

12 × $253.23 = $3,038.76

The cost of merchandise sold is again calculated as follows:

Total VCRs available for sale (65 units)	$16,460.00
Less ending inventory (12 units)	− 3,038.76
Cost of merchandise sold (53 units)	$13,421.24

This method is called the weighted average cost method because the average cost per unit is calculated on total units available for sale during the period. The more units purchased at a certain price, the more effect—or weight—that purchase price has on the average. For example, the purchase of 20 VCRs on August 4 has a greater effect than does the purchase of the 10 VCRs on May 1.

Choosing an Inventory Costing Method

A business may use any one of the four methods of assigning costs to ending inventory: specific identification, fifo, lifo, or weighted average cost. Once a company has chosen a method, however, it must use that method consistently. The consistent use of an inventory costing method helps owners and creditors compare financial reports from one period to another. The Internal Revenue Service does allow a business to change methods, but

536

Interdisciplinary Connections

MATHEMATICS
Remind students that, even when computers or calculators are being used, it is up to human beings to make sure that inventory counts and other figures are accurate. For practice, have students take an inventory of, for instance, the books on the classroom shelves. Compare their results for consistency and accuracy.

Quick access to inventory data should produce better management decisions and an advantage over competition.

the business must first get permission from the IRS. This restriction helps to ensure that the proper amount of taxes are paid to state and federal governments.

When making a decision about the inventory costing method to use, the owner or manager compares the four methods and selects the one that is likely to be the most beneficial to the company. The owner or manager should also consider both the present economic conditions and the future economic outlook. For example, the present economic condition could be a period of inflation or perhaps a recession. The outlook for the future might be higher prices for new merchandise, caused by inflation or strong demand for that particular type of merchandise. On the other hand, the outlook could be for stable prices, prices that remain the same as at the present time. Business owners and managers must consider all these factors when making decisions that will affect the profitability of the business.

To illustrate what a company may do, let's compare the four methods to see the effect that each would have on the inventory cost reported on financial statements.

Comparing the Four Methods of Determining Inventory Cost

The specific identification method requires that the actual cost be determined for each item remaining in inventory at the end of the fiscal period. This process is normally too time-consuming for all but small businesses that have few items in inventory. For this reason, few businesses use the specific identification method.

The fifo and lifo methods are based on certain assumptions about the items remaining in inventory. Fifo assumes that the items in inventory are the last ones purchased and so assigns a cost to inventory based on the last purchase price of an item. Lifo assumes that the first items purchased are the ones remaining in inventory and assigns a cost based on the first purchase price.

The weighted average cost method takes into account the costs of all the merchandise available for sale during the period. With this method, an average cost per item is determined for each type of merchandise in inventory. The average cost per item is assigned to all items remaining in inventory.

Look at the following table, which compares the gross profit calculated using the four different costing methods. For this illustration, we have assumed that the VCRs were all sold for $320.00 each for total sales of $16,960.00 (53 × $320.00).

	Specific Identification	First In, First Out	Last In, First Out	Weighted Average
Sales	$16,960.00	$16,960.00	$16,960.00	$16,960.00
Less: Cost of merchandise sold	13,378.00	13,344.00	13,460.00	13,421.24
Gross profit	$ 3,582.00	$ 3,616.00	$ 3,500.00	$ 3,538.76

The cost of the ending inventory affects the gross profit for the period, which in turn affects the operating income for the period. As you recall, operating income is calculated by subtracting operating expenses from the gross profit. Businesses pay income taxes on the operating income earned. The inventory costing method used by a business, therefore, can raise or lower its taxes. Businesses generally select the inventory costing method that will result in the lowest income taxes given current and projected future economic conditions.

Reporting Inventory Cost Using the Lower-of-Cost-or-Market Method

Once the cost of the inventory has been calculated, it is reported on the income statement and the balance sheet. When reporting the cost of the ending inventory, a business may value the inventory at the cost calculated by one of the four inventory costing methods or at market value, whichever is lower. **Market value** is the current price that is being charged for similar items of merchandise in the market. Market value is the cost at which the inventory items could be replaced at the time the inventory is taken.

Let's look at an example. Assume that Triangle Video Store determines that the current market value of the 12 VCRs it has in inventory is $248.00 each. Using the market value, the total cost of the VCRs is $2,976.00. Assume also that Triangle determines its inventory cost using the fifo method. Under this method, the cost of the ending inventory was determined as $3,116.00. Following the lower-of-cost-or-market rule, Triangle would report the value of its inventory at $2,976.00.

Cost is usually the most appropriate basis for assigning a value to the inventory, but occasionally an inventory may be valued at less than its cost. For example, some merchandise items may deteriorate or become obsolete.

Making Connections

AROUND THE WORLD

For businesses that want to compete in foreign markets, international product shows are one means of showcasing products and making contacts with prospective buyers. For example, Chrysler recently unveiled its new international car model, the Neon, at the Frankfurt International Auto Show. The Frankfurt Book Fair is another annual meeting that is attended by book publishers from around the world. Many cities host international product shows each year.

If the market value of such items is less than the cost, the difference is a loss to the business. In such a case, it is more conservative to report inventory at market value.

Conservatism is one of the fundamental guidelines of accounting. To be conservative is to take the safe route. In reporting the financial position of a business, it is best to present amounts that are least likely to result in an overstatement of income or property values. The lower-of-cost-or-market basis for inventory valuation is thought to be a conservative approach for two reasons: (1) losses, or decreases, in inventory value are recognized when they occur and increases in market value are never recorded; (2) inventory values reported on the balance sheet are never greater, but may be less, than the actual cost of the inventory.

Summary of Key Points

1. It is important for a business to keep accurate inventory records. Information about inventory is needed for inventory control and to help a business present a realistic picture of its financial position on its financial statements.
2. A periodic inventory system requires a physical count of the merchandise still on hand at the end of a fiscal period. Most businesses take a periodic inventory at least once a year.
3. A perpetual inventory system is one in which the business keeps a current record of all merchandise on hand. This system provides continuous merchandise inventory information to management.
4. The specific identification method of costing ending inventory assigns the exact cost to each item still on hand.
5. The first in, first out method (fifo) assumes that the first items purchased were the first items sold. The items still on hand at the end of the fiscal period are assumed to be the last items purchased. Inventory cost is assigned using the cost of the last items purchased.
6. The last in, first out method (lifo) assumes that the last items purchased were the first items sold. The items still on hand at the end of the period are assumed to be the first ones purchased. Inventory cost is assigned using the cost of the first items purchased.
7. The weighted average cost method uses the average cost of all items available for sale during the period to assign a cost to the ending inventory.
8. A company's gross profit on sales and net income are affected by its method of estimating inventory cost.
9. The lower-of-cost-or-market rule for reporting inventory value allows a business to follow a conservative approach in valuing its inventory.

COMPUTERS IN ACCOUNTING

About five years ago, PepsiCo invested approximately $40 million to develop hand-held computers that its 10,000 route salespeople could use to enter orders and log in data about what is on the store shelves or still in the store's inventory. The data is transmitted instantaneously via satellite network to a mainframe database at Frito-Lay headquarters. The company has gained a competitive advantage and has saved approximately $40 million each year because it reduces the amount of product that goes stale on the store shelves.

3 CLOSE

CHAPTER SUMMARY

This summary enumerates the key information in the chapter. It is a useful tool for reinforcement and review.

Pop Quiz

1. When will a business most likely complete a periodic inventory?
2. Which type of inventory system would provide a daily balance of merchandise on hand?
3. Which method of inventory costing would a grocery store likely use?
4. Calculating the average cost per unit is the _____.
5. Why would an item's market value be less than its cost?

ANSWERS

1. When inventory is at its lowest level, generally at the end of a peak selling period.
2. Perpetual.
3. First in, first out.
4. Weighted average cost method.
5. The item may have deteriorated or become obsolete.

Review and Applications

PRACTICE AND APPLY

- Language Development
- Comprehension and Retention
- Basic Skills

Building Your Accounting Vocabulary
See the Glossary on pages 670-679 for definitions of these terms.

Reviewing Your Accounting Knowledge

1. Because merchandise is the largest asset of most businesses and only by a control system can proper analysis of inventory trends be made.

2. The quantity of the inventory must be determined before the cost of that merchandise can be calculated.

3. In a periodic system, a physical count of all merchandise must be made to determine its cost. In a perpetual system, a constant, up-to-date record of merchandise is kept.

4. To provide accurate information for preparing the financial statements and to determine the accuracy of a perpetual inventory system.

5. A constant record of merchandise on hand must be kept, and for businesses selling a large volume of small items, the system would be too time consuming.

6. A business can determine at any time the balance of the Merchandise Inventory account since all purchases and sales of merchandise are recorded immediately.

7. It is the most realistic inventory costing method because it assigns the actual cost to each item remaining in inventory.

8. The fifo method assumes that the first items purchased are the first items sold. Therefore, the last items purchased are assumed to be the ones in inventory and their cost is based on the most recent costs.

9. "Weighted" means that the more units purchased at a particular price, the more effect—or weight—that purchase price has on the average unit cost.

Building Your Accounting Vocabulary

In your own words, write the definition of each of the following accounting terms. Use complete sentences for your definitions.

conservatism
first in, first out
  method
last in, first out
  method
market value

online
periodic inventory
  system
perpetual inventory
  system

specific identification
  method
weighted average
  cost method

Reviewing Your Accounting Knowledge

1. Why should a company have a control system for its merchandise inventory?
2. What must be determined before the cost of merchandise sold can be calculated?
3. What is the difference between a periodic inventory system and a perpetual inventory system?
4. Why must a periodic inventory be completed at least once a year?
5. Why is it difficult for some businesses to use a perpetual inventory system?
6. What advantage is there in using a perpetual inventory system?
7. Why is the specific identification method the most realistic method for determining inventory cost?
8. What is meant by the phrase "with the fifo method, the inventory is based on the most recent costs"?
9. What does the term "weighted" mean in relation to the weighted average cost method?
10. How does the inventory costing method affect a business's gross profit on sales and net income?
11. What is the lower-of-cost-or-market rule and why is it used?

Improving Your Human Relations Skills

Virginia Lacey and Carl White were assigned the task of taking the annual inventory. One person was to count the items, and the other would write the information on the inventory form. As they were taking the inventory, the following situations occurred. If you were Carl, what would you have done in each situation?

1. As they began work, Virginia said, "I'll do the counting since I don't like to sit and write." Carl doesn't like to sit and write either.
2. Virginia suggested that they estimate some of the inventory items.

10. The inventory method affects the cost of merchandise sold, which then changes gross profit and net income. The higher the cost of merchandise sold, the lower the gross profit and net income. The lower the cost of merchandise sold, the higher the gross profit and net income.

11. The lower-of-cost-or-market rule states that a business should value its inventory at the cost calculated by one of the four inventory costing methods or at market value, whichever is lower. This rule is used because it is a conservative approach. Losses in inventory value are recognized before the goods are sold and increases in the market value of the merchandise are never recorded.

Improving Your Human Relations Skills

1. Carl should tell Virginia that he doesn't like to sit and write either. He could then suggest to Virginia that they take turns counting and writing.

2. Carl should refuse to take shortcuts. He should reinforce the importance of obtaining an inventory count that is as accurate as possible.

Applying Accounting Procedures

Exercise 24-1   Costing Inventory by the Specific Identification Method

The Home and Garden Center made the following purchases of lawn mowers during the year.

March 24	10 mowers @ $93.00 each
April 19	12 mowers @ $94.95 each
May 16	8 mowers @ $96.00 each
June 20	15 mowers @ $97.00 each
July 18	18 mowers @ $98.50 each

Instructions: Calculate the cost of the ending inventory using the specific identification method. Of the 12 mowers on hand, 3 were purchased on April 19, 4 on May 16, 2 on June 20, and 3 on July 18. Use the form provided in the working papers.

Exercise 24-2   Costing Inventory by the Fifo Method

During the first six months of the year, the Linen Loft had the following 60″ round tablecloths available for sale.

Beginning inventory	24 tablecloths @ $7.14 each
Purchased March 1	18 tablecloths @ $7.49 each
Purchased April 10	12 tablecloths @ $7.95 each
Purchased May 12	24 tablecloths @ $8.09 each
Purchased June 6	24 tablecloths @ $8.24 each

Instructions: Calculate the cost of the ending inventory of 29 tablecloths using the fifo method. Use the form provided in the workbook.

Exercise 24-3   Costing Inventory by the Lifo Method

Noble Tire Company had the following beginning inventory and purchases of 22-inch whitewall tires during the year.

Beginning inventory	12 tires @ $19.85 each
Purchased April 18	24 tires @ $21.10 each
Purchased July 6	36 tires @ $22.00 each
Purchased September 14	18 tires @ $22.25 each
Purchased November 28	18 tires @ $24.00 each

Instructions: Calculate the cost of the ending inventory of 38 tires using the lifo method. Use the form provided in the workbook.

Exercise 24-4   Costing Inventory by the Weighted Average Cost Method

Peterson's Hardware Store began the year with 16 smoke detectors on hand, at a cost of $1.98. During the year, the business made the following purchases of smoke detectors.

January 9	48 smoke detectors @ $2.25 each
April 4	60 smoke detectors @ $2.45 each
June 30	24 smoke detectors @ $2.69 each
September 15	36 smoke detectors @ $2.62 each
December 20	72 smoke detectors @ $2.66 each

541

PRACTICE AND APPLY

• Concepts and Procedures

Exercise 24-1: Ch. Obj. 3
Cost of ending inventory,
$1,158.35

Exercise 24-2: Ch. Obj. 3
Cost of ending inventory, $238.21

Exercise 24-3: Ch. Obj. 3
Cost of ending inventory, $788.60

Exercise 24-4: Ch. Obj. 3
Cost of ending inventory, $67.23

Additional Reinforcement

Students who need additional practice or individualized help will benefit from the *Glencoe Accounting Electronic Study Guide* or the *Glencoe Accounting* on-line multimedia program, which provide reinforcement and reteaching for vocabulary, concepts, and procedures.

Refer students to the Chapter 24 review pages in the workbook, *Chapter Reviews and Working Papers.*

Problem 24-1: Ch. Obj. 3

Cost of ending inventory:
SI, $585.60
Fifo, $586.20
Lifo, $570.56
WAC, $576.96

Problem 24-2: Ch. Obj. 3, 4

SI, $2,480.15
Fifo, $2,479.55
Lifo, $2,495.19
WAC, $2,488.79

Problem 24-3: Ch. Obj. 4

Cost of ending inventory,
$2,033.46

Instructions: Calculate the cost of the ending inventory of 27 smoke detectors using the weighted average cost method. Use the form provided in the workbook.

Problem 24-1   Calculating the Cost of Ending Inventory

The Morehouse Film Shop sells inexpensive cameras. On January 2, the beginning inventory was 80 cameras. The total cost of the 80 cameras was $1,426.40. During the fiscal period, the shop bought additional cameras. The costs of the cameras available for sale during the period are as follows.

Beginning inventory	80 units @ $17.83 each	=	$1,426.40
Purchased January 3	10 units @ $17.95 each	=	179.50
Purchased March 15	25 units @ $18.15 each	=	453.75
Purchased July 27	20 units @ $18.25 each	=	365.00
Purchased September 27	15 units @ $18.30 each	=	274.50
Purchased November 29	20 units @ $18.33 each	=	366.60
	170		$3,065.75

At the end of the fiscal year, there were 32 cameras remaining in the ending inventory.

Instructions:

(1) Assign a cost to the ending inventory using the specific identification method. Of the 32 cameras on hand, 9 were purchased on July 27, 8 were purchased on September 27, and 15 were purchased on November 29.

(2) Assign a cost to the ending inventory using the fifo, lifo, and weighted average cost methods.

Problem 24-2   Calculating the Cost of Merchandise Sold

Use the inventory information of the Morehouse Film Shop in Problem 24-1 to complete this problem.

Instructions: Determine the cost of merchandise sold under each of the four costing methods. Use the form provided in the working papers accompanying this textbook.

Problem 24-3   Completing an Inventory Sheet

Tom's Bike Shop assigns a value to its inventory using the lower-of-cost-or-market rule. A partial inventory record is shown below. The first line of the inventory record has been completed as an example. The complete inventory record is included in the working papers accompanying this textbook.

		INVENTORY RECORD				
ITEM NO.	ITEM	ENDING INVENTORY	COST PER UNIT	CURRENT MARKET VALUE	PRICE TO BE USED	TOTAL COST
1	2	3	4	5	6	7
0247	Tubes 24"	24	2.67	2.83	2.67	64.08
0391	Tubes 25"	36	2.80	2.74		

542

Teacher Notes

Instructions: Complete the inventory record. To do so,

(1) Select the lower-of-cost-or-market value. Enter that amount in Column 6.
(2) Calculate the total cost of each item by multiplying the total number of each item in inventory (from Column 3) by the amount entered in Column 6.
(3) Add all the amounts in Column 7 to determine the total cost of the ending inventory.

SPREADSHEET

PROBLEM

Problem 24-4   Calculating Gross Profit on Sales

Using the four inventory costing methods, Matt Lake summarized the cost of his bookstore's ending inventory as follows.

Specific Identification	First In, First Out	Last In, First Out	Weighted Average Cost
$1,476.00	$1,581.40	$1,410.93	$1,447.36

Matt's Bookstore also reported the following amounts.

Net Sales	$2,674.92
Beginning Inventory	2,246.80
Net Purchases	374.51

Instructions: Using the above information, determine the cost of merchandise sold and the gross profit on sales using each of the four inventory costing methods.

Problem 24-5   Reporting Ending Inventory
on the Income Statement

Jen's Card Shop uses a fiscal year beginning January 1. At the beginning of the fiscal period, the shop had a beginning inventory of cards valued at $2,700.00 (6,000 cards @ 45¢ each). During the year, the business made the following purchases.

January 20	700 cards @ 47¢ each =	$ 329.00
March 5	2,500 cards @ 45¢ each =	1,125.00
April 23	2,000 cards @ 48¢ each =	960.00
August 14	1,500 cards @ 47¢ each =	705.00
October 3	1,200 cards @ 50¢ each =	600.00
November 17	3,500 cards @ 52¢ each =	1,820.00
Total Purchases 11,400		$5,539.00

During the year, the cards were sold for 95¢ each. There were 4,525 cards in inventory at the end of the period.

Instructions:

(1) Calculate the cost of the ending inventory using the fifo, lifo, and weighted average cost methods.
(2) Using the costs obtained in Step 1, determine the cost of merchandise sold for each method.
(3) Prepare a partial income statement for each method showing sales and the calculation of gross profit on sales. Assume that the sales and purchases amounts are net amounts.

543

Chapter 24

Problem 24-4: Ch. Obj. 3, 4

SPREADSHEET   Problem 24-4 can be completed using *Spreadsheet Applications,* the

PROBLEM

spreadsheet software that accompanies Glencoe Accounting.

Cost of merchandise sold:
SI, $1,145.31
Fifo, $1,039.91
Lifo, $1,210.38
WAC, $1,173.95

Gross profit:
SI, $1,529.61
Fifo, $1,635.01
Lifo, $1,464.54
WAC, $1,500.97

Problem 24-5: Ch. Obj. 4

Ending inventory:
Fifo, $2,332.50
Lifo, $2,036.25
WAC, $2,126.75

Cost of merchandise sold:
Fifo, $5,906.50
Lifo, $6,202.75
WAC, $6,112.25

Gross profit:
Fifo, $6,324.75
Lifo, $6,028.50
WAC, $6,119.00

Teacher Notes

Problem 24-6: Ch. Obj. 4

Cost of merchandise available for sale:
26", $5,415.00
24", $1,647.00
Total, $12,518.00

Ending inventory:
28", $1,516.00
26", $1,431.00
24", $816.00
Total, $3,763.00

Cost of merchandise sold:
28", $3,940.00
26", $3,984.00
24", $831.00
Total, $8,755.00

Net Sales, $17,574.00
Gross profit, $8,819.00

Problem 24-7: Ch. Obj. 3, 4

CHALLENGE

PROBLEM

The last problem in each chapter is a challenge problem and is identified by this "maze" symbol.

Problem 24-6   Reporting Ending Inventory
on the Income Statement

The Spoke and Wheel Bicycle Shop started its fiscal year on January 1 with the following inventory of bicycles.

Stock No.	Description	Units on Hand	Unit Cost	Selling Price
2-3780	28" bicycle	6	$188.00	$399.00
3-412X	26" bicycle	11	159.00	325.00
3-406Y	24" bicycle	7	136.00	299.00

During the fiscal period, the Spoke and Wheel Bicycle Shop made the following purchases.

March 9	10	28" bicycles @ $194.00 each
	5	24" bicycles @ $139.00 each
June 24	10	26" bicycles @ $165.00 each
November 6	12	28" bicycles @ $199.00 each
	12	26" bicycles @ $168.00 each

The inventory for the fiscal period ended December 31 showed the following items in stock.

8	28" bicycles
9	26" bicycles
6	24" bicycles

Instructions:

(1) Calculate the total cost of merchandise available for sale for each size of bicycle. To calculate this cost, first determine the cost of the beginning inventory for each bicycle size. Then add the cost of purchases for the period. As an example, the calculation on the cost of the 28" bicycles available for sale is shown below.

Beginning inventory	6	28" bicycles @ $188.00 each	=	$1,128.00
Purchased March 9	10	28" bicycles @ $194.00 each	=	1,940.00
Purchased November 6	12	28" bicycles @ $199.00 each	=	2,388.00
	28	28" bicycles		$5,456.00

Do the same type of calculation on the cost of merchandise available for sale for the 26" and the 24" bicycles.

(2) Using the lifo method, assign a cost to the ending inventory for each size of bicycle.

(3) Calculate the cost of merchandise sold for each bicycle size. Total the costs for the three sizes of bicycles.

(4) Prepare a partial income statement showing sales and the calculation of the gross profit on sales.

CHALLENGE

PROBLEM

**Problem 24-7   Calculating Cost of Merchandise Sold
and Gross Profit on Sales**

Lisa Moore owns and operates Encore Audio Center. The store started its fiscal period on May 1 with the following inventory of phone answering machines.

Teacher Notes

Stock No.	Brand	Units on Hand	Unit Cost
3845	Lenox	4	$57.00
4931	Lancaster	6	65.00
9265	Paterson	3	48.00
4850	McMahon	5	72.00

The transactions that follow took place during May.

The Encore Audio Center uses the fifo method to calculate the value of its merchandise inventory. The May 31 inventory indicated that the following machines were still on hand:

#3845	4 machines	#9265	7 machines
#4931	5 machines	#4850	3 machines

Although the purchase price of the answering machines varied, the selling price remained the same throughout May. The selling prices are as follows:

#3845	$89.00	#9265	$72.00
#4931	$93.00	#4850	$99.00

Instructions:

(1) Determine how many units of each of the four answering machines were sold during May.

(2) Calculate the gross profit on sales for each type of answering machine using the chart provided in the working papers.

Transactions:

May 2 Purchased 10 #4931 machines at $66.00 each.

　4 Bought 5 units of #4850 machines for $75.00 a unit.

　9 Purchased 6 machines, stock no. 3845, for $58.00 per unit plus a $12.00 transportation charge.

　14 Purchased 5 #9265 machines at a cost of $50.00 each.

　17 Purchased 8 machines at $67.00 per unit, stock no. 4931.

　19 Purchased 4 #3845 machines at $59.00 per unit plus transportation charges of $8.00.

　22 Returned 2 of the machines that had been purchased on May 17 for full credit.

　27 Bought 8 machines, stock number 9265, at a cost of $52.00 per unit.

　29 Purchased 4 #4931 machines at a cost of $68.00 each.

　30 Returned 2 of the machines purchased on May 4 for full credit.

Sales:
#3845, 10
#4931, 21
#9265, 9
#4850, 5

Gross profit:
#3845, $294.00
#4931, $568.00
#9265, $202.00
#4850, $135.00

4 ASSESS

A chapter test is available for use in assessing students' understanding of concepts in this chapter.

The testmaker software will enable you to develop tailor-made chapter, unit, semester, and final tests.

Alternative Assessment

For alternative assessment strategies, refer to *Tech Prep Strategies in Accounting.*

545

Use Chapter Test 24 here to assess students' understanding and retention of the concepts and procedures presented in the chapter.

Very few business people actually get involved in writing computer programs. Software packages make it unnecessary to do so. Ask students to investigate some of the software packages commonly used in business, especially in accounting. Have them discuss the strengths and weaknesses of the packages. (Computer magazines, which frequently make product comparisons, would be a good source of information for students.)

QUESTIONS

1. What is a computer program?
2. Have students choose one of the following topics to research and report to the class: pen-based computers, voice recognition programs, fourth-generation languages (4GLs), laptop computers (add other topics if you choose).

ANSWERS

1. A computer program is a set of instructions telling the computer what to do, how to do it, and the sequence of steps to be followed.
2. Answers will vary depending on the topic chosen.

Home Is Where the Office Is

The alarm jolts Meg out of a sound sleep at 5:30 a.m. She rolls out of bed, heads for the shower, dresses, gulps down breakfast, races for the car, makes her way to the highway, and then drives 28 miles in bumper-to-bumper traffic to the office. When she finally arrives, there are 12 phone messages stuck to her phone. The staff meeting is already underway. Back at home, Meg's husband, Jim, is already at work—and he hasn't left the house. He slept until 7:00, jogged three miles, had a hearty breakfast, skimmed The Wall Street Journal, and made five phone calls. Then he hooked up a modem to his personal computer and started work.

Jim is a "telecommuter," one of a new breed of home-based workers. Advances in computer technology have enabled workers to use home computers and modems to receive and deliver information and assignments via telephone lines. Within the last ten years, home offices have grown over 50%. The Department of Labor predicts that half of the American work force will be doing the same in the next 10 to 15 years.

The likely candidates for telecommuting are people who do not require much space or staff, such as tax and financial consultants and freelance designers, reporters, or writers. The at-home worker may also be a parent who wants to stay home to care for children.

What are the benefits? With fewer meetings and memos, telecommuters experience a lower stress level, greater productivity, and improved creativity. If they are self-employed, overhead and operating costs are usually lower. Telecommuters also have more control over their lives and greater flexibility.

There are also disadvantages. At-home workers

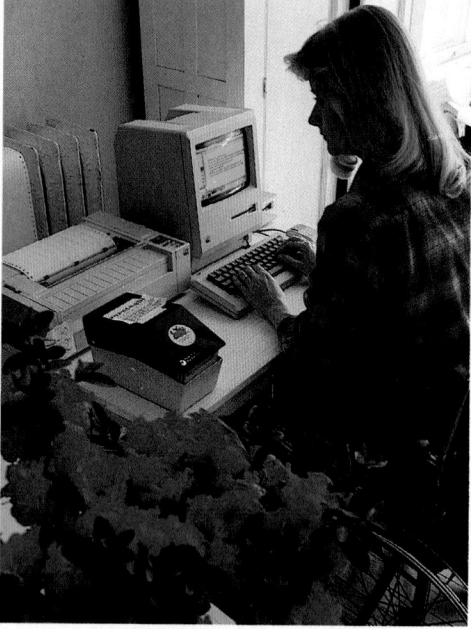

Advances in technology have enabled millions of Americans to work at home.

often need to "escape" for relaxation and lack peer interaction. If they are self-employed, their insurance costs are higher while their pay may be less.

What's best: an office in the home or outside the home? It depends on the quality of life that a worker strives for and what he or she is willing to sacrifice for it. Waiting for the bus in a Monday morning rainstorm could make working at home sound awfully sweet!

546

Chapter 25

ACCOUNTING FOR NOTES PAYABLE AND RECEIVABLE

When businesses buy on credit, current liabilities called accounts payable are created. When businesses sell on credit to charge customers, current assets called accounts receivable are created. Credit is granted on the assumption that the debt will be paid in the near future. That is, payment is expected within 30 to 60 days. These debts exist in the form of open accounts, which represent a general agreement to pay.

In this chapter, you will learn how to record formal loan agreements—both payable and receivable—in the accounting records of a business.

LOOKING BACK

Students have learned several special accounting procedures in the previous four chapters, namely, accounting for cash funds, depreciation, uncollectible accounts, and inventories. This chapter concludes the unit on accounting for special procedures and focuses on accounting for notes receivable and payable. Many businesses today use such notes both to grant long-term credit and to make use of such credit.

VOCABULARY DEVELOPMENT

Discuss the definitions of the new terms in class. Ask students to give their definitions of each term, and then explain how each is used in accounting. Definitions of these terms are found in the chapter and in the glossary on pages 670-679.

Learning Objectives

When you have completed Chapter 25, you should be able to do the following:

1. Explain how promissory notes are used by businesses.
2. Determine the due date, interest expense, and maturity value of a promissory note.
3. Explain the difference between interest-bearing and non-interest-bearing notes.
4. Record journal entries for notes payable and notes receivable.
5. Define the accounting terms introduced in this chapter.

New Terms

promissory note
issue date
term
payee
principal
face value
interest
interest rate
maturity date
maker
maturity value
note payable
interest-bearing note payable
non-interest-bearing note payable
bank discount
proceeds
other expense
note receivable
other revenue

547

Teaching Resources

- Lesson Plans
- TE/Chapter Reviews & Working Papers
- Demonstration Problems
- Student Study Plans
- Teaching Transparencies
- Solutions Transparencies
- Electronic Field Trips Video, Level I
- Electronic Study Guide
- Chapter 25 Test
- Unit 5 Objective Test for Chapters 21-25
- Unit 5 Problem Test for Chapters 21-25

Other Resources

- Skills Improvement Activities
- Blackline Masters
- Careers in Accounting
- Dictionary
- Math Review for Accounting
- Tech Prep Strategies in Accounting
- Video
- Test Bank with Software
- Spanish Resources/Audiotapes
- Spanish Electronic Study Guide

1 FOCUS

MAJOR CONCEPTS

- Promissory Notes
- Notes Payable
- Notes Receivable

USINESS CONNECTION

As Chief Executive Officer of the Chrysler Corporation, Lee Iacocca led the failing company to success. One key to Chrysler's economic survival was the U. S. Congress's agreement to help. In 1979 Chrysler received a $1.2 billion loan for 10 years from the U.S. Government. The loan was paid back in full in 1983—seven years before it was due.

2 TEACH

CONCEPT DEVELOPMENT
Promissory Notes

Invite a local banker or business person who works with notes receivable and notes payable to discuss them with the class. Prepare students for the resource person by giving them a working knowledge of notes. Be sure that students understand the purposes for either issuing or receiving a note. The resource person should give specific examples of how notes are used.

Using Visuals

Use Figure 25-1 to discuss each part of a note. Have students identify each item of information.

Teaching Tips

■ Point out that the face value plus interest is the amount that will be paid at maturity.

Promissory Notes

A **promissory note** is a written promise to pay a certain amount of money at a specific time. "Promissory note" is often shortened to simply the word "note." Promissory notes are formal documents that are evidence of credit granted or received. For example, a business may ask for a promissory note from a customer who wants more time to pay an account receivable. A business may issue a promissory note to obtain a loan from a bank.

To be upheld in a court of law, a promissory note must contain certain information. That information is shown in Figure 25-1.

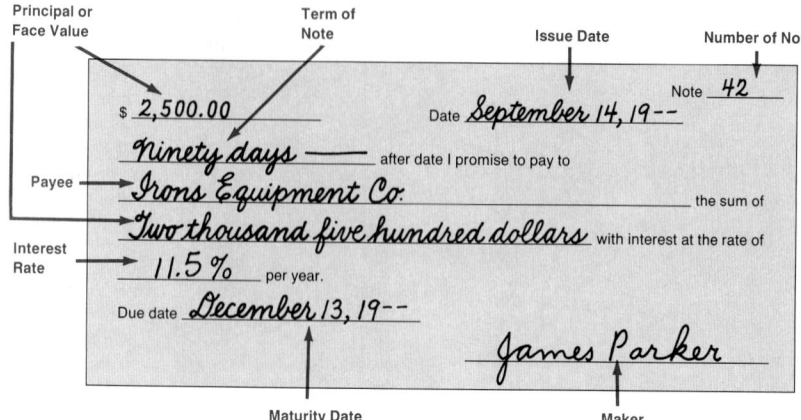

Figure 25-1
Promissory Note

The date on which a note is written is called its **issue date.** The **term** of the note is the amount of time the borrower has to repay the note, such as 90 days. The **payee** is the person or business to whom the note is payable. The **principal** of the note is the amount being borrowed. The **face value** is the amount written on the "face" of the note. The principal and the face value are usually, but not always, the same.

Interest is the fee charged for the use of money. The **interest rate** is the amount of interest to be charged stated as a percentage of the principal. The **maturity date** is the due date of the note, that is, the date on which the note must be paid. The **maker** of the note is the person or business promising to repay the principal and interest.

Determining the Maturity Date of a Note

When a note is signed, the maker agrees to repay the note within a certain period of time, usually expressed in days or months. This period of time is the term of the note. Both the term and the issue date are needed to determine the maturity date of a note.

Let's use the promissory note in Figure 25-1 as our example. In signing this note, James Parker agreed to pay Irons Equipment Co. the principal plus interest 90 days from September 14. To determine the maturity date,

1. Determine the number of days left in the month in which the note is issued. No interest is charged for the issue date, so subtract the date of the

UNIT 5   Accounting for Special Procedures

Reinforcing Study Skills

From time to time, it is useful to remind students of the steps in the reading technique SQ3R. After *surveying* the section heads and subheads, students should turn them into questions that can then guide their reading: for instance, "What is a promissory note?" or "How do you determine the maturity date of a note?"

Provide a copy of the *Student Study Plans* to each class member to help organize study activities or to individualize practice and review activities.

30	September
−14	Issue date
16	Days left in September

90	Days in term
−16	Days in September
74	

74	
−31	Days in October
43	

43	
−30	Days in November
13	

Figure 25-2
Time Calendar

note from the number of days in the month. In our example, you would subtract 14 from 30 days, leaving 16 days in September.

Remember that January, March, May, July, August, October, and December have 31 days; February has 28 days (29 days in a leap year); and April, June, September, and November have 30 days.

2. Determine the number of days the note has left after the first month. To do this, subtract the days calculated in Step 1 from the term of the note.
3. Subtract the number of days in the next month (October) from the number of days left after Step 2. In our example, the 31 days in October are subtracted from 74.
4. Subtract the number of days in the third month (November) from the days left after Step 3. The 30 days in November are subtracted from 43.
5. Since there are 13 days left after subtracting the 30 days in November, the due date will be 13 days into the next month. In other words, the due date for this particular note is December 13.

Businesses and banks use time calendars to calculate the maturity date of a note. An example of a time calendar is shown in Figure 25-2. The time calendar has two sets of days: (1) the day of the month (left and right sides), and (2) the day of the year by month.

Day of month	Jan.	Feb.	Mar.	Apr.	May	June	July	Aug.	Sept.	Oct.	Nov.	Dec.	Day of month
1	1	32	60	91	121	152	182	213	244	274	305	335	1
2	2	33	61	92	122	153	183	214	245	275	306	336	2
3	3	34	62	93	123	154	184	215	246	276	307	337	3
4	4	35	63	94	124	155	185	216	247	277	308	338	4
5	5	36	64	95	125	156	186	217	248	278	309	339	5
6	6	37	65	96	126	157	187	218	249	279	310	340	6
7	7	38	66	97	127	158	188	219	250	280	311	341	7
8	8	39	67	98	128	159	189	220	251	281	312	342	8
9	9	40	68	99	129	160	190	221	252	282	313	343	9
10	10	41	69	100	130	161	191	222	253	283	314	344	10
11	11	42	70	101	131	162	192	223	254	284	315	345	11
12	12	43	71	102	132	163	193	224	255	285	316	346	12
13	13	44	72	103	133	164	194	225	256	286	317	347	13
14	14	45	73	104	134	165	195	226	257	287	318	348	14
15	15	46	74	105	135	166	196	227	258	288	319	349	15
16	16	47	75	106	136	167	197	228	259	289	320	350	16
17	17	48	76	107	137	168	198	229	260	290	321	351	17
18	18	49	77	108	138	169	199	230	261	291	322	352	18
19	19	50	78	109	139	170	200	231	262	292	323	353	19
20	20	51	79	110	140	171	201	232	263	293	324	354	20
21	21	52	80	111	141	172	202	233	264	294	325	355	21
22	22	53	81	112	142	173	203	234	265	295	326	356	22
23	23	54	82	113	143	174	204	235	266	296	327	357	23
24	24	55	83	114	144	175	205	236	267	297	328	358	24
25	25	56	84	115	145	176	206	237	268	298	329	359	25
26	26	57	85	116	146	177	207	238	269	299	330	360	26
27	27	58	86	117	147	178	208	239	270	300	331	361	27
28	28	59	87	118	148	179	209	240	271	301	332	362	28
29	29	...	88	119	149	180	210	241	272	302	333	363	29
30	30	...	89	120	150	181	211	242	273	303	334	364	30
31	31	...	90	...	151	...	212	243	...	304	...	365	31

NOTE: For leap years, after February 28, the number of the day is one greater than that given in the table.

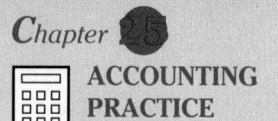

Chapter 25

ACCOUNTING
PRACTICE
**Students may complete
Exercise 25-1 at this point.**

ANSWERS

1. October 17
2. January 1
3. November 18
4. March 14
5. January 7
6. June 17

Teaching Tips

- Remind students that "term" means "time," and that "face value" is usually the same as "principal."
- The full year—365 days—is used in the examples here since banks or businesses using computers to calculate interest generally use the full year. Some businesses use 360 days as the basis for one year.
- Review with the class the arithmetic skills needed to calculate interest. Stress that interest rates are usually stated on an annual basis. Show students how to determine interest for one year. After they have mastered determining interest for one year, show how interest is determined for periods of less than one year.

Interest for One Year		Number of Days		
$287.50	×	90	=	$25,875
$25,875	÷	365	=	$70.89

To calculate a maturity date using the time calendar, follow these steps:

257
+90
347

1. Locate the issue day of the note (for example, 14) in the Day of Month column. Move across the day of the year columns until you come to the issue month (September). In our example, September 14 is the 257th day of the year.

2. Add the number of days in the term of the note (90) to the day of the year. The sum of the two numbers is 347.

3. Find the number 347 in the day of the year columns. The date for the 347th day of the year is the due date of the note, or December 13.

Before reading further, do the following activity to check your understanding of how to calculate the maturity date of a note.

Check Your Learning

Find the maturity date for each of the following notes. Use the manual method first and check your answer by the time calendar method.

	Issue Date	Term
1.	August 18	60 days
2.	October 3	90 days
3.	July 21	120 days
4.	January 14	60 days (leap year)
5.	September 9	120 days
6.	December 19	180 days

Compare your answers to those in the answers section. Re-read the preceding part of the chapter to find the correct answers to any questions you may have missed.

Calculating Interest on a Note

The interest on a promissory note is based on three factors: the principal, the interest rate, and the term of the note. The equation that is used to compute interest is

$$\text{Interest} = \text{Principal} \times \text{Interest Rate} \times \text{Time} \qquad (I = PRT)$$

Interest rates are usually stated on an annual basis; that is, they are usually based on a borrowing period of one year. To find the interest on a promissory note for one year, multiply the principal by the interest rate. For example, the interest on an 11.5%, $2,500 promissory note for one year is $287.50 ($2,500.00 × .115 = $287.50).

If the term of a promissory note is less than a year, the time used in the calculations must be expressed as a fraction of one year. The fraction may be stated in days or months. For example, on September 14, James Parker signed a note for $2,500 at 11.5% interest for 90 days. Since the term of the note is expressed in days, 365 days are used as the denominator of the time fraction. The interest is calculated as follows:

UNIT 5   Accounting for Special Procedures

Reteaching Strategies

Contrast the promissory note with an installment loan for a car. Students are probably familiar with the idea of making monthly car payments through an installment loan. A promissory note is a single-payment loan. It is repaid with one payment after a specified period of time. Such notes are generally offered for short periods of time, usually less than a year.

$$\begin{array}{ccccccc}
\text{Principal} & \times & \text{Interest Rate} & \times & \text{Time} & = & \text{Interest} \\
\$2,500.00 & \times & .115 & \times & \tfrac{90}{365} & = & \$70.89
\end{array}$$

$2,500.00 Principal
+   70.89 Interest
$2,570.89 Maturity value

The interest on the note shown in Figure 25-1 is $70.89. On the maturity date, James Parker must repay the maturity value of the note. **Maturity value** is the principal plus the interest. In our example, the maturity value is $2,570.89.

If the term of this note had been three months instead of 90 days, the denominator of the time fraction would be 12. The interest would be calculated as follows:

$$\begin{array}{ccccccc}
\text{Principal} & \times & \text{Interest Rate} & \times & \text{Time} & = & \text{Interest} \\
\$2,500.00 & \times & .115 & \times & \tfrac{3}{12} & = & \$71.88
\end{array}$$

R E M E M B E R

Interest rates are based on a borrowing period of one year. To calculate interest on a note signed for a shorter time period, express the term of the note as a fraction of one year.

Calculating Interest Using an Interest Table

To calculate interest, businesses and banks often use an interest table similar to the one shown in Figure 25-3.

To calculate interest using an interest table, first find the term of the note in the Day column. We will use James Parker's note again for this example. The term of that note is 90 days. Next, follow the row across until you reach the column for the interest rate (11.5%). As you can see, the factor where the two meet is 2.835616.

The interest table is for interest on $100.00. The amount of the principal ($2,500.00) must, therefore, be divided by $100.00. Multiply this number (25) by the factor of 2.835616 to find the total interest. The interest calculated using the interest table is also $70.89. Factors in an interest table are rounded

SIMPLE INTEREST ON $100, 365 DAY BASIS

DAY	11.50 % INTEREST	DAY	11.75 % INTEREST	DAY	12.00 % INTEREST	DAY	12.25 % INTEREST	DAY	12.50 % INTEREST	DAY	12.75 % INTEREST
30	0.945205	30	0.965753	30	0.986301	30	1.006849	30	1.027397	30	1.047945
60	1.890411	60	1.931507	60	1.972603	60	2.013699	60	2.054795	60	2.095890
90	2.835260	90	2.897260	90	2.958904	90	3.020548	90	3.082192	90	3.143836
120	3.780822	120	3.863014	120	3.945205	120	4.027397	120	4.109589	120	4.191781
150	4.726027	150	4.828767	150	4.931507	150	5.034247	150	5.136986	150	5.239726
180	5.671233	180	5.794521	180	5.917808	180	6.041096	180	6.164384	180	6.287671
210	6.616438	210	6.760274	210	6.904110	210	7.047945	210	7.191781	210	7.335616
240	7.561644	240	7.726027	240	7.890411	240	8.054795	240	8.219178	240	8.383562
270	8.506849	270	8.691781	270	8.876712	270	9.061644	270	9.246575	270	9.431507
300	9.452055	300	9.657534	300	9.863014	300	10.068493	300	10.273973	300	10.479452
330	10.397260	330	10.623288	330	10.849315	330	11.075342	330	11.301370	330	11.527397
360	11.342466	360	11.589041	360	11.835616	360	12.082192	360	12.328767	360	12.575342
365	11.500000	365	11.750000	365	12.000000	365	12.250000	365	12.500000	365	12.750000
366	11.531507	366	11.782192	366	12.032877	366	12.283562	366	12.534247	366	12.784932

Figure 25-3 Interest Table

CHAPTER 25   Accounting for Notes Payable and Receivable   **551**

Cooperative Learning

CO-OP, CO-OP

Assign students in pairs and ask them to contact a local bank or other lending institution to determine the current interest rate for car loans. Ask students to compare this rate with the current prime rate.

Refer to the "Cooperative Learning" section of *Tech Prep Strategies in Accounting* for additional cooperative learning strategies.

ANSWERS

1. $75.62; $4,075.62
2. $289.73; $10,289.73
3. $136.23; $6,636.23
4. $36.25; $936.25
5. $142.03; $2,542.03

CONCEPT DEVELOPMENT
Notes Payable

Role play borrowing $7,000 from a bank by signing an interest-bearing note. After the role play, analyze the transaction in T-account form. Then illustrate how it is recorded in the cash receipts journal. Review how interest is calculated. Use the Eastwick Office Equipment Co. note as an example. Stress that when an interest-bearing note is due, the principal *and* the interest must be paid. Illustrate how the maturity value is determined.

Businesses often issue notes when borrowing money from banks to cover short-term cash needs.

off so there may be a few cents difference from the interest calculated manually.

Using the Computer To Calculate Interest

A computer is often used to calculate the interest and maturity value of a note. With a computer program that is designed to calculate interest, a business simply enters the principal, interest rate, and term of the note. The computer calculates the interest and the maturity value. The use of a computer saves much time for businesses that issue or receive many notes.

Now that you know how to determine the maturity value of a promissory note, let's look at how businesses use such notes.

Now complete the following activity to check your understanding of how to calculate interest.

Check Your Learning

Find the interest and the maturity values for each of the following notes. First find the interest manually and then use the interest table to check your answer.

	Principal	Interest Rate	Term
1.	$ 4,000.00	11.5%	60 days
2.	10,000.00	11.75%	90 days
3.	6,500.00	12.75%	60 days
4.	900.00	12.25%	120 days
5.	2,400.00	12%	180 days

Compare your answers to those in the answers section. Re-read the preceding part of the chapter to find the correct answers to any questions you may have missed.

Notes Payable

A **note payable** is a promissory note issued to a creditor. A note payable may also be issued by a business to borrow money from a bank. A note payable is a liability of the business issuing the note. Notes issued by a business, therefore, are summarized in the Notes Payable account. Notes Payable is a liability account and has a normal credit balance.

Two types of notes that are frequently issued by businesses are interest-bearing notes payable and non-interest-bearing notes payable.

Interest-Bearing Notes Payable

A note that requires that the face value plus interest be paid on the maturity date is called an **interest-bearing note payable.** On an interest-bearing note, the face value and the principal are the same. The note we

---

used in earlier examples (issued by James Parker) is an interest-bearing note. Its maturity value is $2,570.89 ($2,500.00 face value plus interest of $70.89).

Now let's look at how an interest-bearing note payable is recorded in a business's accounting records.

▲ Recording the Issuance of an Interest-Bearing Note Payable

On April 3, the Eastwick Office Equipment Co. had the following transaction.

April 3: Borrowed $7,000.00 from the State Street Bank and issued a 90-day, 12% note payable to the bank, Note 6.

The accounts affected by this transaction are Cash in Bank and Notes Payable. In this transaction, Cash in Bank is debited for $7,000.00 because the money borrowed from the bank is increasing the business's cash. Notes Payable is credited for $7,000.00 because the transaction increases the business's liability.

Cash in Bank			Notes Payable	
Dr.	Cr.		Dr.	Cr.
+	–		–	+
$7,000.00				$7,000.00

This transaction is recorded in Eastwick's cash receipts journal as shown in Figure 25-4. The interest on the note is not recorded until it is actually paid on the maturity date.

	DATE	DOC. NO.	ACCOUNT TITLE	POST. REF.	GENERAL DEBIT	GENERAL CREDIT	SALES CREDIT	SALES TAX PAYABLE CREDIT	ACCOUNTS RECEIVABLE CREDIT	CASH IN BANK DEBIT	
1	19— Apr. 3	N6	Notes Payable			7 000 00				7 000 00	1

Figure 25-4 Recording the Issuance of an Interest-Bearing Note Payable

▲ Recording the Issuance of an Interest-Bearing Note Payable

On April 3, the Eastwick Office Equipment Co. had the following transaction:

July 2: Eastwick Office Equipment Co. issued Check 892 for $7,207.12 payable to State Street Bank in payment of the note payable issued April 3.

The check that is prepared to repay the bank loan is written for the maturity value of the note (principal plus interest). Using the interest equation, the interest on Eastwick's note is calculated as follows:

$7,000.00 Principal
+   207.12 Interest
$7,207.12 Maturity value

$$\text{Principal} \times \text{Interest Rate} \times \text{Time} = \text{Interest}$$
$$\$7,000.00 \times .12 \times \tfrac{90}{365} = \$207.12$$

CHAPTER 25   Accounting for Notes Payable and Receivable   **553**

The maturity value of the note is found by adding the interest to the principal. In this case, the maturity value is $7,207.12.

The payment of the note is recorded in the accounting records to show the decrease in the company's liability. Notes Payable is debited for $7,000.00, reducing its balance to zero. The interest charged by the bank for the use of the money is now recognized as an expense. Interest Expense is debited for $207.12. Cash in Bank is credited for $7,207.12, the total amount being paid.

Notes Payable		Interest Expense		Cash in Bank	
Dr.	Cr.	Dr.	Cr.	Dr.	Cr.
–	+	+	–	+	–
$7,000.00	Bal. $7,000.00	$207.12			$7,207.12

The entry made in the cash payments journal to record this transaction is shown in Figure 25-5.

	DATE	DOC. NO.	ACCOUNT TITLE	POST. REF.	GENERAL DEBIT	GENERAL CREDIT	ACCOUNTS PAYABLE DEBIT	PURCHASES DISCOUNTS CREDIT	CASH IN BANK CREDIT	
1	July 2	CK892	*Notes Payable*		1 000 00				7 207 12	1
2			*Interest Expense*		207 12					2

Figure 25-5 Recording the Payment of an Interest-Bearing Note Payable

Before reading further, do the following activity to check your understanding of notes payable.

Check Your Learning

Use a sheet of notebook paper to answer these questions.

1. On June 12, Frank's Lobster Pound issued a $9,000.00, 120-day, 12% note payable to the American Bank of Commerce.
   a. What is the title of the account debited? For what amount?
   b. What is the title of the account credited? For what amount?
   c. What is the classification of each account?
   d. What is the maturity value of the note?
2. On October 10, Brighton Tree Service issued Check 498 in payment of a $12,500.00, 90-day, 12.25% note payable.
   a. What is the maturity date of the note?
   b. What is the face value of the note? The maturity value?
   c. To record this transaction, which accounts are debited and credited? For what amounts?

Compare your answers to those in the answers section. Re-read the preceding section of the chapter to find the answers to any questions you may have missed.

UNIT 5   Accounting for Special Procedures

Reteaching Strategies

Before introducing how to record a note payable, have students role play borrowing $10,000 from a bank by signing a 60-day, 11 percent, interest-bearing note. After the role play, ask the students to calculate the interest, analyze the transaction, determine which ledger accounts are affected, and indicate in which journal the transaction should be recorded.

(Answers: Interest, $183.33; Cash in Bank debit, $10,000; Notes Payable credit, $10,000; cash receipts journal)

Non-Interest-Bearing Notes Payable

Sometimes a bank requires a borrower to pay the interest on a note payable in advance. The bank deducts the interest charge from the face value of the note, in effect "discounting" the amount of money received by the borrower on the issue date. A note from which the interest has been deducted in advance is called a **non-interest-bearing note payable.** The note is referred to as "non-interest-bearing" because there is no interest rate stated on the note itself. The interest deducted in advance is called the **bank discount.** The cash actually received by the borrower is called the **proceeds.** The proceeds equal the face value minus the bank discount.

Since interest on a non-interest-bearing note payable is deducted at the time the money is borrowed, the maturity value of the note is the same as the face value amount. An example of a non-interest-bearing note payable is shown in Figure 25-6.

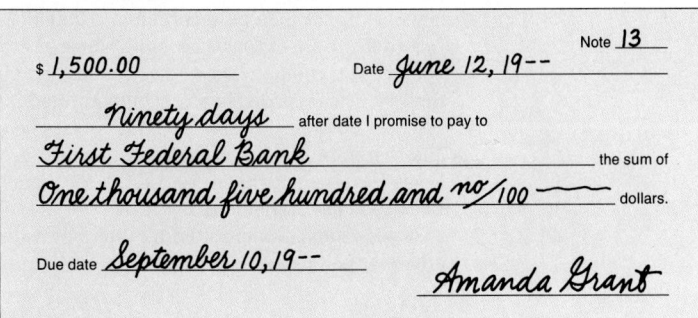

Figure 25-6   A Non-Interest-Bearing Note Payable

Let's look at how the proceeds of a non-interest-bearing note payable are calculated. The note shown in Figure 25-6 is the source document for the following transaction.

June 12: *Amanda Grant, owner of Amanda's Shoes, signed a $1,500.00, 90-day non-interest-bearing note payable that the First Federal Bank discounted at a rate of 12%, Note 13.*

The first step is to calculate the bank discount, which is the interest on the note. The bank discount is calculated the same way as the interest on an interest-bearing note. The face value of the note ($1,500.00) is multiplied by the discount rate (12%) and by the term (90 days). As you recall, the term is always expressed in years or as a fraction of a year.

		Discount Rate					
Face Value	$\times$	(Interest Rate)	$\times$	Time	=	Bank Discount
$1,500.00	$\times$	.12	$\times$	$\frac{90}{365}$	=	$44.38

$1,500.00 Face value
−   44.38 Bank discount
$1,455.62 Proceeds

The amount of the bank discount is subtracted from the face value of the note to determine the proceeds. The proceeds, the amount Amanda Grant actually receives, are $1,455.62.

Making Connections

COMMUNICATIONS

With the proliferation of "voice mail," "E mail," and other services, telephones have become more than simple machines for conversation. Discuss with students ways in which the telephone is changing how business is conducted. Ask students to predict new changes over the next ten years. Ask students to give specific examples that relate to the accounting field.

Teaching Tips

- Give students several examples of non-interest-bearing notes payable and have them analyze them using T accounts.

- Ask the class to describe how to record a non-interest-bearing note payable. Then analyze the transaction in T-account form using the six-step approach. Illustrate the recording of the transaction in the cash receipts journal.

- The Discount on Notes Payable account may be confusing for students. Point out that, although the interest is deducted in advance, the Interest Expense account is not debited until the note payable is paid.

- Discuss why the discount account is a contra account for Notes Payable.

The cost of getting a college degree seems to rise every year. The cost at public universities, though, has grown less than that at private schools. From 1968 to 1993, costs at public universities rose from $5,000 to $6,000; costs at private schools rose from $10,000 to $19,300. Many students take advantage of student loan programs to help finance their college educations.

REMEMBER

Regardless of whether a note is interest-bearing or non-interest-bearing, the interest charge is based on a percentage of the note's face value.

▲ **Recording the Issuance of a Non-Interest-Bearing Note Payable** The T accounts that follow show the three accounts affected by this transaction: Cash in Bank, Discount on Notes Payable, and Notes Payable. In this transaction, Cash in Bank is debited for $1,455.62, the proceeds of the note—or the amount of cash actually received.

The face value of a non-interest-bearing note includes two amounts: (1) the amount actually borrowed ($1,455.62) and (2) the future interest charge ($44.38). The future interest charge (the bank discount) has already been paid and is not a liability at the time the note is issued. The bank discount amount cannot then be recorded in a liability account. The $44.38 could be recorded in an expense account, since the bank discount is an interest charge. The company, however, has not yet incurred the expense. Instead, the $44.38 is recorded in an account entitled Discount on Notes Payable. The Discount on Notes Payable account is classified as a contra liability account and therefore has a normal debit balance. In this transaction, Discount on Notes Payable is debited for $44.38, the future interest charge included in the face value of the note.

Notes Payable is credited for the face value of the note, $1,500.00, increasing the business's liability.

Cash in Bank		Discount on Notes Payable		Notes Payable	
Dr.	Cr.	Dr.	Cr.	Dr.	Cr.
+	−	+	−	−	+
$1,455.62		$44.38			$1,500.00

This entry is recorded in the cash receipts journal, as shown in Figure 25-7.

	DATE	DOC. NO.	ACCOUNT TITLE	POST. REF.	GENERAL DEBIT	GENERAL CREDIT	SALES CREDIT	SALES TAX PAYABLE CREDIT	ACCOUNTS RECEIVABLE CREDIT	CASH IN BANK DEBIT	
1	19—— June 12	N13	Notes Payable			1 500 00					1
2			Discount on Notes Pay		44 38					1 455 62	2

Figure 25-7 Recording the Issuance of a Non-Interest-Bearing Note Payable

Discount on Notes Payable would be reported on the balance sheet as a deduction from Notes Payable. If a balance sheet were prepared for Amanda's Shoes on June 30, the accounts would appear as shown in Figure 25-8 at the top of page 557. The $1,455.62 amount represents the book value of notes payable.

556   UNIT 5   Accounting for Special Procedures

Interdisciplinary Connections

GOVERNMENT/SOCIAL STUDIES

The Federal Reserve System, created in 1913, influences interest rates charged by banks. The "Fed" can raise or lower the discount rate, the rate at which member banks borrow from Federal Reserve Banks. A high discount rate means banks will have less money to lend and will charge borrowers higher rates of interest.

Amanda's Shoes
Balance Sheet
June 30, 19--

Liabilities			
Notes Payable		1500 00	
Less: Discount on Notes Payable		44 38	1455 62

Figure 25-8   Reporting Non-Interest-Bearing Notes Payable on the Balance Sheet

R E M E M B E R

On interest-bearing notes, the face value is equal to the principal, or the amount borrowed. On non-interest-bearing notes, the face value equals the maturity value of the note.

▲ Recording the Payment of a Non-Interest-Bearing Note Payable

▲ Recording the Payment of a Non-Interest-Bearing Note Payable   When the non-interest-bearing note payable is due, Amanda Grant will pay First Federal Bank the face value of the note, which is also the note's maturity value.

September 10: *Amanda's Shoes issued Check 1241 for $1,500.00 to the First Federal Bank in payment of the June 12 non-interest-bearing note payable.*

ACCOUNTING **Notes**
As debts, liabilities are claims recognized by law. That is, the law gives creditors the right to force the sale of a company's assets to pay debts if the company fails to pay. Creditors have rights over owners and must be paid in full before the owners receive anything, even if payment of the debts uses up all the assets of the business.

As you can see from the T accounts, Notes Payable is debited for $1,500.00 to show the decrease in the liability. Cash in Bank is credited for $1,500.00, the amount of the check written to pay the maturity value of the note. This transaction removes the note payable from the accounting records.

Notes Payable			Cash in Bank	
Dr.	Cr.		Dr.	Cr.
–	+		+	–
$1,500.00	Bal. $1,500.00			$1,500.00

When a non-interest-bearing note payable matures, the amount of the bank discount must be recognized as an expense. It is transferred from the Discount on Notes Payable account to the Interest Expense account. As you can see from the T accounts, Interest Expense is debited for $44.38 and Discount on Notes Payable is credited for $44.38. This transaction shows that the bank discount has now become an expense.

Interest Expense			Discount on Notes Payable	
Dr.	Cr.		Dr.	Cr.
+	–		+	–
$44.38			Bal. $44.38	$44.38

Chapter

Using Visuals

Point out the entry in Figure 25-9 showing the payment of a non-interest-bearing note payable. Ask students to explain why this note has both an interest charge and a discount.

ANSWERS

1. (a) Cash in Bank is debited for $9,802.74; Discount on Notes Payable is debited for $197.26; and Notes Payable is credited for $10,000.00. (b) $197.26; $9,802.74
2. (a) Maturity value, $10,000; face value, $10,000; (b) Notes Payable is debited for $10,000.00; Interest Expense is debited for $197.26; Discount on Notes Payable is credited for $197.26, and Cash in Bank is credited for $10,000.00.

CONCEPT DEVELOPMENT
Notes Receivable

Point out the difference between a note receivable and a note payable. Review the reasons for a business to accept a note receivable. After the role playing, analyze the transaction in T account form using the six-step approach. Also show students how to record the transaction in the general journal.

Two separate journal entries could be prepared to record (1) the payment of the non-interest-bearing note payable (in the cash payments journal) and (2) the interest expense (in the general journal). It is much simpler, however, to prepare one compound entry in the cash payments journal. The entry recorded in the accounting records of Amanda's Shoes is shown in Figure 25-9.

	DATE	DOC. NO.	ACCOUNT TITLE	POST. REF.	GENERAL DEBIT	GENERAL CREDIT	ACCOUNTS PAYABLE DEBIT	PURCHASES DISCOUNTS CREDIT	CASH IN BANK CREDIT	
1	Sept. 10	C1241	Notes Payable		150000				150000	1
2			Interest Expense		4438					2
3			Discount on Notes Payable			4438				3

CASH PAYMENTS JOURNAL   PAGE 12

Figure 25-9   Recording the Payment of a Non-Interest-Bearing Note Payable

The Interest Expense account is classified as an other expense account. An **other expense** is a non-operating expense—an expense that does not result from the normal operations of the business. A separate section for other expenses appears on the income statement, as a deduction from operating income.

Before continuing, complete the following activity to check your understanding of non-interest-bearing notes.

Check Your Learning

Use a sheet of notebook paper to answer these questions.

1. On October 14, Canton Car Care Center issued a $10,000.00, 60-day, 12% non-interest-bearing note payable to the Canton National Bank.
   a. Which accounts are debited and credited? For what amounts?
   b. What is the amount of the bank discount? The proceeds?
2. On December 13, Canton Car Care Center issued Check 146 to the Canton National Bank in payment of the $10,000.00 non-interest-bearing note payable issued October 14. One entry is recorded in the business's cash payments journal.
   a. What is the maturity value of this note? The face value?
   b. Which accounts are debited and credited? For what amounts?

Compare your answers to those in the answers section. Re-read the preceding part of the chapter to find the answers to any questions you may have missed.

Notes Receivable

On occasion, a business may grant a customer additional time to pay a debt. The customer may be asked to sign a promissory note. Promissory notes that a business accepts from customers are called **notes receivable.**

558   UNIT 5   Accounting for Special Procedures

Reteaching Strategies

Have students role play borrowing $1,500 by signing a 120-day, non-interest-bearing note discounted at 11.5 percent. Ask students to note the difference between an interest-bearing and a non-interest-bearing note at the time it is signed. Have students analyze the transaction, determine which ledger accounts are affected, and indicate in which journal the transaction should be recorded.

(Answers: The interest is deducted in advance for a non-interest-bearing note. Interest, $57.50; Cash in Bank debit, $1,442.50; Discount on Notes Payable debit, $57.50; Notes Payable credit, $1,500; cash receipts journal)

Notes Receivable is an asset account and has a normal debit balance. Like a note payable, a note receivable is due on a specific future date and carries an interest charge for the term of the note.

Recording the Receipt of a Note Receivable

On March 1, Eastwick Office Equipment Co. sold $1,750.00 of merchandise on account to Peter Johnson. That transaction was recorded in Eastwick's sales journal. On April 6, Eastwick had the following transaction.

April 6: *Eastwick Office Equipment Co. received a 60-day, 12.5% note from Peter Johnson for $1,750.00 to pay the account receivable, Note 4.*

In this transaction, Eastwick agreed to accept a note receivable in payment of the amount owed by Peter Johnson. When a customer signs a promissory note as payment of an amount owed on an account receivable, the amount owed to the business becomes a note receivable. Notes Receivable is being increased, so that account is debited for $1,750.00. Accounts Receivable is credited for the same amount to decrease its balance. Peter Johnson's account in the accounts receivable subsidiary ledger is also credited for $1,750.00, decreasing the amount he owes as an account receivable.

GENERAL LEDGER

Notes Receivable	
Dr.	Cr.
+	–
$1,750.00	

SUBSIDIARY LEDGER

Accounts Receivable	
Dr.	Cr.
+	–
Bal. $1,750.00	$1,750.00

Peter Johnson	
Dr.	Cr.
+	–
Bal. $1,750.00	$1,750.00

The general journal entry for this transaction is shown in Figure 25-10.

	GENERAL JOURNAL			PAGE 10
DATE	DESCRIPTION	POST. REF.	DEBIT	CREDIT
19-- Apr. 6	Notes Receivable		1 750 00	
	Accts Receivable/Peter Johnson	✓		1 750 00
	Note 4			

Figure 25-10 Journalizing the Receipt of a Note Receivable

Recording the Receipt of Cash for a Note Receivable

On June 5, Eastwick should receive a check from Peter Johnson in payment of the note accepted on April 6. Since the note is an interest-bearing note, the check should be for the maturity value of the note (principal plus interest). The maturity value is calculated as follows:

Principal	×	Interest Rate	×	Time	=	Interest
$1,750.00	×	.125	×	$\frac{60}{365}$	=	$35.96

$1,750.00	Principal
+ 35.96	Interest
$1,785.96	Maturity value

The maturity value is, therefore, $1,785.96.

Making Connections

AROUND THE WORLD

Doing business in many different countries has created a new market for products geared to the international business traveler. One popular product is a power transformer used for U.S. computers that are not set up for the stronger foreign power sources. Other products that help international business travelers are modem and communications software and adapters that allow a modem to be connected to a foreign telephone jack.

COMPUTERS IN ACCOUNTING

Teleconferencing is becoming more popular as the available technology improves. A teleconference is essentially a long-distance meeting. At the lowest level, a teleconference is three people talking together on the telephone. A sophisticated teleconference involves a group a people (all individuals could be located in different states or countries) participating in the sharing of video, audio, written reports, and drawings. Today teleconferencing is an efficient and effective means for accounting firms to keep in touch with their clients.

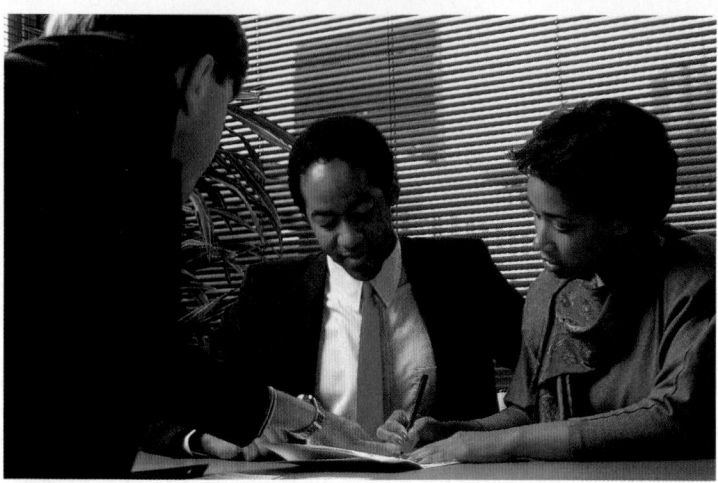

Notes offer several advantages to businesses: they are legal evidence of a debt, they earn interest, and they can be used as security for a loan.

June 5: Received a check for $1,785.96 from Peter Johnson in payment of the $1,750.00 note accepted on April 6 plus interest of $35.96, Receipt 496.

In this transaction, cash is being received so Cash in Bank is debited for $1,785.96. The collection of the note receivable reduces the balance in Notes Receivable. That account is credited for the principal, or face value, of the note, $1,750.00.

The interest received for extending the time for payment on an account receivable is revenue for the payee of the note. The amount received, $35.96, is credited to an other revenue account called Interest Income. **Other revenue** is non-operating revenue—revenue that a business receives or earns from activities outside the normal operations of the business. Like other expenses, other revenue is reported separately on the income statement.

Cash in Bank		Notes Receivable		Interest Income	
Dr.	Cr.	Dr.	Cr.	Dr.	Cr.
+	−	+	−	−	+
$1,785.96		Bal. $1,750.00	$1,750.00		$35.96

The cash receipts journal entry to record the collection of a note receivable is shown in Figure 25-11.

	DATE	DOC. NO.	ACCOUNT TITLE	POST. REF.	GENERAL DEBIT	GENERAL CREDIT	SALES CREDIT	SALES TAX PAYABLE CREDIT	ACCOUNTS RECEIVABLE CREDIT	CASH IN BANK DEBIT	
1	19-- June 5	R496	Notes Receivable			1750 00				1785 96	1
2			Interest Income			35 96					2

PAGE 21

CASH RECEIPTS JOURNAL

Figure 25-11 Journalizing the Collection of a Note Receivable

Before reading further, do the following activity to check your understanding of notes receivable.

 Check Your Learning

Use a sheet of notebook paper to answer these questions.

1. On May 30, BioTech Computers accepted a 90-day, 9%, $6,000.00 note receivable from Amy Andrus, a charge customer.
   a. Which accounts are debited and credited? For how much?
   b. Is this an interest-bearing or a non-interest-bearing note?
2. On August 28, BioTech received a check from Amy Andrus in payment of the $6,000.00 note dated May 30.
   a. What was the amount of Amy Andrus's check?
   b. Which accounts are debited and credited? For how much?

Compare your answers to those in the answers section. Re-read the preceding section of the chapter to find the answers to any questions you may have missed.

Summary of Key Points

1. A promissory note is a written promise to pay a certain amount of money at a specific future time.
2. Promissory notes issued by businesses to creditors or to banks to obtain a loan are called notes payable. Notes Payable is a liability account.
3. Interest is the fee charged to the maker of a promissory note for the use of money. Interest is calculated as a percentage of the face value of the note, based on a borrowing period of one year. Borrowing periods of less than one year are expressed as fractions of a year.
4. The equation for calculating interest on a promissory note is $I = PRT$, or Interest = Principal $\times$ Rate $\times$ Time.
5. Interest on interest-bearing notes is paid on the maturity date of the note. The maturity value of an interest-bearing note equals the face value plus the interest charge.
6. A non-interest-bearing note payable is a note from which the interest has been deducted in advance. The interest deducted from the note's face value in advance is called the bank discount. The amount of cash actually received by the maker after the interest has been deducted is called the proceeds. The maturity value of a non-interest-bearing note payable is the same as its face value.
7. When the issuance of a non-interest-bearing note payable is journalized, the amount of the bank discount is debited to the Discount on Notes Payable account. Discount on Notes Payable is a contra liability account.
8. When a non-interest-bearing note payable is paid, the interest charge is transferred from Discount on Notes Payable to Interest Expense.
9. Promissory notes accepted by businesses from charge customers are called notes receivable. Notes Receivable is an asset account.

CHAPTER 25   Accounting for Notes Payable and Receivable   **561**

3 CLOSE

CHAPTER SUMMARY

This summary enumerates the key information in the chapter. It is a useful tool for reinforcement and review.

Reteaching Strategies

Give students this example. Drew Simpkins signs a 30-day, 11.75 percent note for $3,450 to pay an account receivable. Ask students to analyze the transaction both when the note is signed and when it is paid, indicating the accounts affected and the journals used to record each transaction.

(Answer: When the note is signed, Notes Receivable is debited for $3,450 and Accounts Receivable/Drew Simpkins are credited for $3,450. The entry is recorded in the general journal. When the note is paid, Cash in Bank is debited for $3,483.70, Notes Receivable is credited for $3,450, and Interest Income is credited for $33.78. The entry is made in the cash receipts journal.)

PRACTICE AND APPLY

- Language Development
- Comprehension and Retention
- Basic Skills

Building Your Accounting Vocabulary

See the Glossary on pages 670-679 for definitions of these terms.

Reviewing Your Accounting Knowledge

1. (a) The maker is the party issuing the note. (b) The payee is the party receiving the note.
2. An example of when a business may receive a promissory note is in exchange for an account receivable when a charge customer will not be able to pay the amount owed by the due date. A business may issue a promissory note to borrow money from a bank for a short period of time.
3. Interest = Principal × Interest Rate × Time.
4. By multiplying the principal times the interest rate times the time, which is stated as a fraction of a year.
5. The principal of the note plus the interest charged equals the maturity value.
6. Interest-bearing notes and non-interest-bearing notes payable. When the interest is paid is the difference between the two. The interest on an interest-bearing note is paid at maturity. The interest on a non-interest-bearing note is paid on the day the note is issued.
7. Interest is the charge for the use of borrowed money that is paid on the maturity date of the loan. Bank discount is the charge for the use of borrowed money that is paid the day the money is borrowed.
8. First, the amount of the interest is determined (the bank discount) and is then subtracted from the principal to find the proceeds of the note.
9. It is a contra liability account and has a normal debit balance.
10. Because the revenue or expense results from activities that are outside the normal operations of the business.

Building Your Accounting Vocabulary

In your own words, write the definition of each of the following accounting terms. Use complete sentences for your definitions.

bank discount	maker	other expense
face value	maturity date	other revenue
interest	maturity value	payee
interest rate	non-interest-bearing	principal
interest-bearing note	note payable	proceeds
payable	note payable	promissory note
issue date	note receivable	term

Reviewing Your Accounting Knowledge

1. Name the two parties to a promissory note.
   a. Which party issues the note?
   b. Which party receives the note?
2. Describe a situation in which a business might (a) receive a promissory note and (b) issue a promissory note.
3. What is the basic equation for the calculation of interest?
4. How is the interest on a note calculated if the term is less than a year?
5. How is the maturity value of an interest-bearing note determined?
6. Name two types of notes a business may issue. What is the major difference between the two?
7. What is the difference between interest and a bank discount?
8. When a non-interest-bearing note payable is issued, how are the proceeds calculated?
9. How is the Discount on Notes Payable account classified? What is its normal balance?
10. Why are Interest Income and Interest Expense reported separately on the income statement?

Improving Your Math Skills

Many businesses today borrow money for capital expansion or to meet operating expenses during periods when earnings are below expectations. The interest formula can be used to calculate the cost of borrowing money. Use the formula to complete the following problems.

1. With an interest rate of 9.5%, what is the cost of borrowing $42,400 for one year?
2. What is the cost of borrowing $20,000 at 13% for one year? for six months?
3. If the amount of interest charged on a one-year, $8,400 loan is $820, what is the interest rate?

562

Improving Your Math Skills
1. $4,028   4. 9%
2. $2,600:$1,300   5. $13,809.52
3. 9.76%

4. What is the interest rate on a $22,000 loan costing $990 for six months?

5. What is the amount borrowed when interest is $725, the rate is 10.5%, and the time is six months?

Applying Accounting Procedures

Exercise 25-1   Determining the Maturity Date of Notes

Instructions: Determine the maturity date for each of the following notes.

	Issue Date	Term
1.	November 18	60 days
2.	August 3	90 days
3.	July 22	120 days
4.	February 5	3 months
5.	April 28	9 months

Exercise 25-2   Calculating Interest

Instructions: Calculate the interest charge for each of the following notes.

	Principal	Interest Rate	Term
1.	$ 600	15%	90 days
2.	3,500	12%	60 days
3.	9,600	9%	4 months
4.	2,500	10%	180 days
5.	1,500	11.5%	6 months

Exercise 25-3   Determining the Maturity Value

Instructions: Determine the interest and the maturity value of each of the following notes.

	Principal	Interest Rate	Term
1.	$ 900	9%	80 days
2.	1,200	12%	60 days
3.	3,250	10%	90 days
4.	2,430	15%	2 months
5.	210	8%	3 months

SPREADSHEET

PROBLEM

Exercise 25-4   Calculating the Bank Discount and Proceeds

Instructions: Calculate the amount of the bank discount and the proceeds for each of the following non-interest-bearing notes.

	Face Value	Term	Discount Rate
1.	$ 300	60 days	12%
2.	3,840	90 days	9%
3.	2,100	4 months	11%
4.	5,000	7 months	7%
5.	800	5 months	8%

563

Refer students to the Chapter 25 review pages in the workbook, *Chapter Reviews and Working Papers.*

Additional **Reinforcement**

Students who need additional practice or individualized help will benefit from the *Glencoe Accounting Electronic Study Guide* or the *Glencoe Accounting* on-line multimedia program, which provide reinforcement and reteaching for vocabulary, concepts, and procedures.

Chapter 25

PRACTICE AND APPLY

• Concepts and Procedures

Exercise 25-1: Ch. Obj. 2
1. January 17
2. November 1
3. November 19
4. May 5
5. January 28

Exercise 25-2: Ch. Obj. 2
1. $22.19
2. $69.04
3. $288.00
4. $123.29
5. $86.25

Exercise 25-3: Ch. Obj. 2
1. $17.75; $917.75
2. $23.67; $1,223.67
3. $80.14; $3,330.14
4. $60.75; $2,490.75
5. $4.20; $214.20

Exercise 25-4: Ch. Obj. 2, 3

SPREADSHEET

PROBLEM

Exercise 25-4 can be completed using *Spreadsheet Applications*, the spreadsheet software that accompanies *Glencoe Accounting.*

1. $5.92; $294.08
2. $85.22; $3,754.78
3. $77.00; $2,023.00
4. $204.17; $4,795.83
5. $26.67; $773.33

Chapter 25

Problem 25-1: Ch. Obj. 4
Apr. 14 interest exp., $44.38
Aug. 29 interest exp., $382.19

Problem 25-2: Ch. Obj. 4
June 10 discount, $98.63
Aug. 30 discount, $552.33

Problem 25-3: Ch. Obj. 4
Maturity value Oct. 12 note,
$1,826.63

Problem 25-1   Recording Transactions for Interest-Bearing Notes Payable

Instructions: Record the following transactions in a cash receipts journal and a cash payments journal.

Transactions:

Jan. 14   Borrowed $1,500.00 from the Beaumont Bank by issuing a 90-day, 12% interest-bearing note payable (Note 78).

Apr. 14   Issued Check 1468 for $1,544.38 to the Beaumont Bank in payment of the $1,500.00 note issued on January 14, plus interest of $44.38.

May 31   Borrowed $12,400.00 from the Merchant's Bank and Trust on a 90-day, 12.5% interest-bearing note, Note 79.

Aug. 29   Paid the Merchant's Bank and Trust the maturity value of the note issued on May 31, Check 8842 for $12,782.19.

Problem 25-2   Recording Transactions for Non-Interest-Bearing Notes Payable

Instructions: Record the following transactions in a cash receipts journal and a cash payments journal.

Transactions:

June 10   Borrowed $6,000.00 from Lincoln County National Bank by issuing a 60-day, non-interest-bearing note payable (proceeds, $5,901.37) that the bank discounted at 10% (Note 67).

Aug. 9   Issued Check 74285 for $6,000.00 in payment of the note issued June 10; recorded the interest expense.

       30   Borrowed $16,000.00 from Citizen's Bank, issuing a 120-day non-interest-bearing note payable (Note 68), less the 10.5% bank discount of $552.33.

Dec. 28   Issued Check 84298 in payment of the note issued on August 30; recorded the interest expense.

Problem 25-3   Recording Transactions for Notes Receivable

Instructions: Journalize the following transactions.

Transactions:

June 4   Received a 90-day, 8.5%, $1,450.00 note receivable from Bill Jackson for an extension on his account. The note was dated June 2 (Note 461).

Aug. 14   Accepted a 60-day, 9% note receivable for $1,800.00 from Susan Keys for an extension on her account receivable, Note 69 dated August 13.

       31   Received a $1,480.39 check from Bill Jackson in payment of the note dated June 2, Receipt 888.

Oct. 12   Received from Susan Keys a check for the maturity value of the note dated August 13, Receipt 984.

Problem 25-4   Recording Notes Payable and Notes Receivable

Instructions: Record the following transactions in a cash receipts journal (page 47), cash payments journal (page 56), and general journal (page 19).

564

Teacher Notes

Transactions:

Mar. 19 Borrowed $9,000.00 from the Hornbeck National Bank by issuing a 90-day, 12% interest-bearing note payable, Note 87.

June 4 Received a 120-day, 13% note receivable for $1,900.00 from Lee Hebert as a time extension on his account receivable, Note 6 dated June 1.

17 Paid the Hornbeck National Bank the maturity value of the note issued on March 19, Check 2784.

Sept. 29 Received a check from Lee Hebert for the maturity value of the note dated June 1, Receipt 4428.

Oct. 6 Borrowed $2,700.00 from Jonesboro Bank and Trust, signing a 60-day non-interest-bearing note payable (Note 878), discounted at 11.5%.

Dec. 5 Prepared a check for the note issued on October 6 (Check 2954) and recorded the interest expense.

COMPUTER

PROBLEM

Problem 25-5   Recording Notes Payable and Notes Receivable

The following is a partial list of accounts used by the McMahon Company.

101	Cash in Bank	205	Discount on Notes Payable
105	Notes Receivable	210	Accounts Payable
110	Accounts Receivable	710	Interest Income
201	Notes Payable	750	Interest Expense

Instructions: Record the following transactions in a cash receipts journal (page 67), cash payments journal (page 73), and general journal (page 27).

Transactions:

May 7 Borrowed $4,000.00 from the Jefferson State Bank by signing a 60-day, 9.5% non-interest-bearing note, Note 284.

15 Issued a $3,000.00, 90-day, 9% interest-bearing note (Note 283) to the Hicks Company in place of the amount owed on account.

21 Received a 120-day, 10% note for $1,200.00 from Jane Sinclair for an extension of time on her account, Note 94 dated May 20.

July 6 Issued Check 4711 in payment of the non-interest-bearing note given to the Jefferson State Bank on May 7.

Aug. 13 Issued Check 5044 for the maturity value of the note issued to the Hicks Company on May 15.

Sept. 17 Received a check from Jane Sinclair for the maturity value of the note dated May 20, Receipt 5921.

CHALLENGE

PROBLEM

Problem 25-6   Calculating Current and Future Interest

Frequently, notes that are issued or received in one fiscal period do not mature until the next fiscal period. As a result, the interest expense paid or the interest income received applies to two different fiscal periods. Listed on page 566 is the information for ten different notes.

Instructions: For each note,
(1) Determine the maturity date. Assume February has 28 days.
(2) Determine what portion of the interest applies to the current year and what portion of the interest applies to the following year. December 31 is the end of the fiscal period.

565

Problem 25-4: Ch. Obj. 4

Maturity value of note paid on June 17, $9,266.30
Maturity value of note payment received on Sept. 29, $1,981.21
Proceeds of Oct. 6 note, $2,648.96

Problem 25-5: Ch. Obj. 4

COMPUTER

PROBLEM

This computer image identifies a problem that students may complete using the *Glencoe Accounting, General Ledger* software.

Proceeds of May 7 note, $3,937.53
Maturity value of Aug. 13 note, $3,066.58
Maturity value of note payment received on Sept. 17, $1,239.45

Problem 25-6: Ch. Obj. 2, 3

CHALLENGE
PROBLEM

The last problem (or problems) in each chapter is a challenge problem and is identified by this "maze" symbol.

Maturity dates/interest:
1. Jan.9/$5.70/$2.44
2. Jan. 20/$9.21/$4.60
3. Jan. 8/$384.16/$37.48
4. Feb. 3/$42.74/$55.89
5. Mar. 10/$136.23/$184.32
6. Mar. 7/$65.59/$37.97
7. Jan. 26/$79.56/$47.02
8. Apr. 1/$19.95/$19.95
9. Mar. 1/$10.00/$20.00
10. May 1/$90.00/$72.00

Teacher Notes

Chapter 25

Problem 25-7: Ch. Obj. 2, 4

CHALLENGE

PROBLEM

The last problem (or problems) in each chapter is a challenge problem and is identified by this "maze" symbol.

Interest income for June 12 transaction, $27.96

Maturity value of Sept. 10 payment, $1,936.60

4 ASSESS

A chapter test is available for use in assessing students' understanding of concepts in this chapter.

The testmaker software will enable you to develop tailor-made chapter, unit, semester, and final tests.

Unit objective and problem tests are available to assess students' knowledge of concepts in Chapters 21-25.

Alternative Assessment

For alternative assessment strategies, refer to *Tech Prep Strategies in Accounting*.

	Amount	Issue Date	Interest Rate	Term
1.	$ 1,100	December 10	9%	30 days
2.	700	November 21	12%	60 days
3.	17,100	October 10	10%	90 days
4.	4,000	December 5	15%	60 days
5.	15,000	November 10	6.5%	120 days
6.	3,000	September 8	7%	180 days
7.	6,600	November 17	10%	70 days
8.	840	October 1	9.5%	6 months
9.	1,200	December 1	10%	3 months
10.	2,700	August 1	8%	9 months

CHALLENGE

PROBLEM

Problem 25-7   Renewing a Note Receivable

Occasionally, a note may be renewed on its maturity date instead of being paid off. When this occurs, the interest on the first note is paid, the first note is canceled, and a new note for the same principal amount is issued—usually at a higher interest rate. The Donne Company had the following transactions.

Instructions: Record the following transactions on general journal page 24.

Transactions:

Mar. 14   Sold merchandise on account to Lynn Reid for $1,800.00, plus sales tax of $90.00, terms 30 days, Sales Slip 688.

Apr. 13   Accepted a 60-day, 9% note for $1,890.00 from Lynn Reid in place of the accounts receivable amount, Note 416.

June 12   Received the interest due from Lynn Reid for the note dated April 13 and agreed to renew the note at 10% for 90 days, Receipt 2444 and Note 417.

Sept. 10   Received a check from Lynn Reid for the maturity value of the note issued June 12, Receipt 3555.

566

Use Chapter Test 25 here to assess students' understanding and retention of the concepts and procedures presented in the chapter.

Use Unit 5 Objective Test and/or Unit 5 Problem Test to assess students' retention of concepts presented in Chapters 21-25.

Computer Graphics

Without the help of models or trick photography, computers can create three-dimensional images that are shaded and can move. The most famous of these computer-generated special effects are those seen in movies such as *Star Wars* and *Terminator 3*. Moviemakers, however, aren't the only ones using computer graphics.

The business manager captures management's attention by using computer-generated charts and graphs to emphasize critical spreadsheet data. With an integrated business software program, colorful graphs and charts are created in minutes.

By manipulating stored data on the computer, the cartographer, a map maker, creates numerous configurations with awesome speed and accuracy.

Using state-of-the-art computer-aided design (CAD) software, the architect sits at the keyboard instead of the drawing board to create renderings of design concepts.

Before trying them out on an actual machine, the industrial engineer works at a computer to create simulated sequences of his company's spot-welding operations. The process is quick and reliable.

The salesperson needs to highlight a product feature for an important sales presentation the next day. With the help of her new presentation software, a microcomputer, and laser printer, she creates an impressive overhead visual in less than an hour. Her startled competition has no time to respond. She closes the sale.

You've all seen video games, which use animated computer graphics. More sophisticated graphics programs are now used to create simulations that help train pilots and astronauts, test new engineering designs, develop new drugs or chemicals to fight disease, or "see" the area around a black hole.

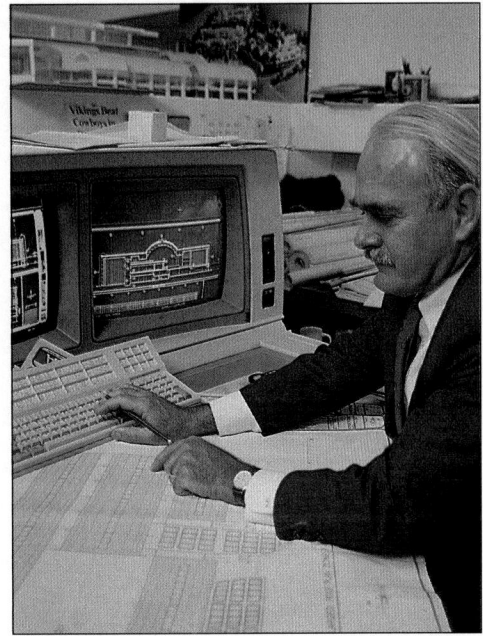

The computer gives this architect the opportunity to try out many designs before committing the ideas to costly and time-consuming models.

Thanks to the advent of computer graphics, presentations and reports are more persuasive; spreadsheets are clear and memorable; and designs are created with greater accuracy, in less time, and for less money.

Computer graphics has enabled skilled professionals to spend more time on creative tasks, less on tedious ones. Everybody wins!

Most of us have seen prototypes of products "drawn" by computer-aided design (CAD) software. Have students explain the benefits of CAD to businesses such as automakers, furniture builders, or kitchen remodelers.

QUESTIONS

1. What is multimedia computing?
2. How might a stockbroker use computer graphics in a presentation?

ANSWERS

1. Multimedia computing uses computers to combine sound and images. Multimedia technology allows business people to create product presentations or training programs that are interesting and entertaining and allow their audiences to participate through interactive activities.
2. Computer graphic capabilities allow a stockbroker, for example, to show graphic comparisons of the performance of alternative investments or the performance of stocks this year versus last year.

567

This final unit in the textbook focuses on the accounting procedures that are specific to the partnership and public corporation forms of business ownership. In Chapter 26 students learn to apportion earnings based on partnership interests. Chapter 27 covers basic accounting procedures for a publicly held corporation, including the issuance of common and preferred stock and the declaration and payment of dividends. Chapter 28 concludes the unit with a presentation of several basic analyses that are made to interpret financial information for decision making.

Chapter 26
Accounting for Partnerships
Focus on Careers

Chapter 27
Accounting for Corporations
Focus on Computers

Chapter 28
Analyzing and Interpreting
Financial Statements
Focus on Ethics

U N I T

ACCOUNTING FOR OTHER FORMS OF BUSINESS ORGANIZATION

In this last unit of the textbook, you will learn how accounting for a partnership differs from accounting for a sole proprietorship or a corporation. You will also learn about accounting for a publicly held corporation. Publicly held corporations publish their operating results in annual reports. These reports are studied and analyzed by many people, both inside and outside the corporation. People who own stock in the corporation study annual reports to analyze how well the corporation is operating. Other people may be interested in purchasing stock and want to determine whether the stock is a good investment.

568

Individualizing Instruction

To provide individualized activities within the unit, you may use any of the following:

- chapter study plans
- study guides in the student workbook
- end-of-chapter challenge problems (identified by a maze symbol)

- optional problems in the Additional Problems section at the back of the student textbook
- cases from *Tech Prep Strategies in Accounting*
- *Electronic Study Guide*

Accounting for Other Forms of Business Organization

Unit Concepts

Unit 6 expands on the concept of the private enterprise system introduced in Chapter 1. The unit explains the advantages and disadvantages of partnerships and publicly held corporations, as well as the accounting procedures that each must follow. Students are also given vital information on how business managers analyze and interpret financial statements. They learn about the important ratios that business managers use to interpret this information. Students learn why it is important to be able to compare financial statements from one accounting period to the next and how managers use these comparisons to make important decisions affecting the business.

General Unit Performance Objectives

1. Correctly use accounting terminology as it relates to the partnership and corporate forms of business organization.
2. Describe the accounting principles and practices applied to partnerships and corporations.
3. Demonstrate accounting procedures for partnerships and corporations.

PERFORMANCE OBJECTIVES

Unit Objective Test: Chapters 26-28

1. Define accounting vocabulary correctly.
2. Determine correct and incorrect accounting procedures for partnerships and corporations.
3. Analyze business transactions for partnerships and corporations.

Unit Problem Test: Chapters 26-28

1. Record transactions involving partnership equity in a general journal.
2. Record transactions involving the issuance of stock for a publicly held corporation.
3. Calculate the current ratio, quick ratio, the return on common stockholders' equity, and the return on sales using given financial data.
4. Analyze a balance sheet using vertical analysis.
5. Analyze an income statement using horizontal analysis.

Chapter	Learning Objectives
26	1. List the major characteristics, advantages, and disadvantages of the partnership form of business organization. 2. Journalize transactions involving partners' equity for a partnership. 3. Use two different methods to distribute the earnings of a partnership among the partners. 4. Prepare the financial statements for a partnership. 5. Define the accounting terms new to this chapter.
27	1. List the major characteristics, advantages, and disadvantages of the corporate form of business organization. 2. Journalize transactions involving the issuance of stock. 3. Journalize transactions involving cash dividends. 4. Prepare financial statements for a publicly held corporation. 5. Define the accounting terms new to this chapter.
28	1. List the qualitative characteristics and general accounting guidelines for accounting information. 2. Prepare a classified balance sheet and income statement. 3. Prepare horizontal and vertical analyses of financial statements. 4. Calculate commonly used liquidity and profitability ratios. 5. Use liquidity and profitability ratios to analyze a business's performance. 6. Define the accounting terms new to this chapter.

State/Local Objectives			Demonstration Problems	Check Your Learning	Basic Skills	Exercises	Problems	Challenge Problem	Additional Problems
			26-1 26-2 26-3 26-4 26-5	p. 575 p. 579	Decision Making p. 582	26-1 26-2	26-1 26-2 26-3 26-4 26-5	26-6	26A 26B p. 644
			27-1 27-2 27-3 27-4	p. 590 p. 593 p. 597	Communi-cations p. 602	27-1 27-2 27-3 27-4	27-1 27-2 27-3 27-4 27-5	27-6	27A 27B p. 645
			28-1 28-2 28-3 28-4	p. 614 p. 618 p. 621 p. 623	Decision Making p. 624	28-1 28-2 28-3 28-4	28-1 28-2 28-3 28-4	28-5 28-6	28A 28B p. 646

Chapter	Glencoe Integrated Accounting	Spreadsheet Applications	Electronic Study Guide Model Exercises/Problems	CD Rom
26	Problem 26-5	Problem 26-4	Exercise 26-2 Problem 26-3	Menu Selection 26
27	Problem 27-5	Problem 27-3	Problem 27-3	Menu Selection 27
28		Problem 28-4	Exercise 28-1 28-2 28-3 28-4	Menu Selection 28
Basic Math Review			Menu Option 29	

INTRODUCING THE CHAPTER

LOOKING BACK

In preceding chapters students have learned how to record a variety of business transactions. Recording the business transactions for a sole proprietorship, partnership, or corporation is essentially the same except for those transactions directly affecting the ownership equity accounts. Transactions differ for assets and liabilities only in the case of large businesses for which transactions become more complex as businesses become more complex. In this chapter, students will learn how to record transactions related to the capital accounts of a partnership.

VOCABULARY DEVELOPMENT

Ask students to write a sentence using each of the new terms in context. Ask for volunteers to write their sentences on the board. Discuss any differences in the use of the terms. Definitions of these terms are found in the chapter and in the glossary on pages 670-679.

Electronic Field Trips

Chapter 26
ACCOUNTING FOR PARTNERSHIPS

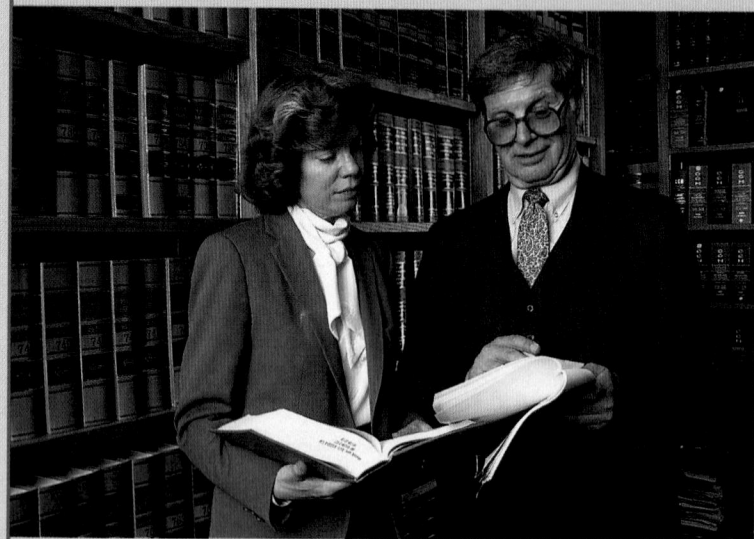

The accounting procedures that you have learned up to now have been applied to businesses organized as sole proprietorships or as closely held corporations. Most of these procedures can also be applied to businesses organized as partnerships. For example, the purchase of supplies for cash is handled in the same manner by all forms of business organizations.

You'll remember, however, that transactions involving ownership equity for a sole proprietorship and a closely held corporation were handled differently. There are also differences in accounting for the ownership equity of a partnership.

In this chapter, you will examine briefly some of the characteristics of a partnership. You will learn the procedures involved in accounting for partners' equity and in dividing the net income or loss among the partners.

Learning Objectives

When you have completed Chapter 26, you should be able to do the following:

1. List the major characteristics, advantages, and disadvantages of the partnership form of business organization.
2. Journalize transactions involving partners' equity for a partnership.
3. Use two different methods to distribute the earnings of a partnership among the partners.
4. Prepare the financial statements for a partnership.
5. Define the accounting terms introduced in this chapter.

New Terms
partnership
mutual agency
partnership agreement
statement of changes in partners' equity

570

Teaching Resources

- Lesson Plans
- TE/Chapter Reviews & Working Papers
- Demonstration Problems
- Student Study Plans
- Teaching Transparencies
- Solutions Transparencies
- Electronic Field Trips Video, Level I
- Electronic Study Guide
- Chapter 26 Test

Other Resources

- Skills Improvement Activities
- Blackline Masters
- Careers in Accounting
- Dictionary
- Math Review for Accounting
- Tech Prep Strategies in Accounting
- Video
- Test Bank with Software
- Spanish Resources/Audiotapes
- Spanish Electronic Study Guide

Accounting for a Partnership

As you learned in Chapter 1, a **partnership** is an association of two or more persons to operate, as co-owners, a business for profit. Any type of business may be organized as a partnership. Partnerships, however, are more common in the professions or in businesses that provide professional services. For example, accounting and legal firms are often organized as partnerships. Each partner can have her or his own clients, yet share with the other partners the expenses of operating an office.

Characteristics of a Partnership

The partnership form of business organization has certain unique features. Let's look at some of them.

Ease of Formation

Like a sole proprietorship, there are no special legal requirements that must be met to form a partnership. A partnership is automatically formed when two or more persons agree to operate as partners. A partnership is a voluntary arrangement. No one can be forced into a partnership or required to continue as a partner.

Unlimited Liability

Each partner is personally liable for the debts of the partnership. That means that if the partnership's creditors cannot be paid out of the assets of the partnership, a partner's personal assets may be used to pay the partnership's debts. As you recall, the owner of a sole proprietorship also has unlimited liability.

Limited Life

A partnership may be ended for a number of reasons. These reasons may include death, withdrawal, bankruptcy, or incapacity of any partner. A partnership may also be ended when the project for which the partnership was formed is completed or when the time period set by the partners has expired. For example, two architects may agree to combine their talents to design and oversee the construction of a building. When the building has been completed, the partnership is dissolved.

Mutual Agency

Each partner is an agent of the partnership. In other words, any partner can, in the name of the firm, enter into agreements that are binding on all other partners. This relationship is known as **mutual agency.**

Co-ownership of Partnership Property

When a partner invests assets in the partnership, he or she gives up all personal rights of ownership. All of the partnership assets are co-owned by the partners.

1 FOCUS

MAJOR CONCEPTS
- Accounting for a Partnership
- Characteristics of a Partnership
- The Partnership Agreement
- Accounting for Partners' Equity
- Division of Partnership Income or Loss
- Preparing Financial Statements for a Partnership
- Recording the Closing Entries for a Partnership

BUSINESS CONNECTION

Imagine a partnership that has 6,100 partners in 117 countries, all of whom think they "own" the business! That was exactly the situation at KPMG Peat Marwick, the largest of the "Big Six" accounting firms. The top-heavy organizational structure worked fine during the 1980s, but the recession of the early 1990s emphasized the need for a smaller organization. Since 1991 the firm has decreased its U.S. partners by 265, with projected savings of $52 million.

2 TEACH

CONCEPT DEVELOPMENT
Accounting for a Partnership
Of the three types of business organization discussed in this textbook, the partnership is the least common probably because it is more difficult for two or more people to agree on how a business is to be run. In addition, mutual agency often makes the partnership less acceptable to those who do not want to be bound by others' decisions.

CONCEPT DEVELOPMENT
Characteristics of a Partnership
Discuss each characteristic of a partnership and explain why each is an advantage or disadvantage to that form of business organization.

Partnerships are the least common form of business organization.

Advantages and Disadvantages of a Partnership

One of the most important advantages of a partnership is that it provides the opportunity to bring together the abilities, experiences, and resources of two or more individuals. A partnership is easy to form, the only requirement being the agreement of the partners. Members of a partnership are usually able to make decisions without having to hold a formal meeting of the partners. Although a partnership must have a legal purpose, there are few other legal restrictions. Finally, federal and state income taxes are not levied against the partnership. Each partner must pay personal income taxes on her or his share of the business's net income.

There are, of course, disadvantages to the partnership form. As discussed earlier, a partnership has a limited life, each partner is personally liable for the debts of the partnership, and all partners may be held responsible for the decision of one partner. In addition, a partner cannot transfer her or his interest in the partnership without the consent of the other partners. The ability to work together without major disagreements, however, may be the greatest test of the partnership form of organization.

The Partnership Agreement

A partnership may be formed when two or more individuals orally agree to operate a business as co-owners. However, it is advisable to have a written partnership agreement. A **partnership agreement** is a written document that sets out the terms under which the partnership will operate. There is no standard form for a partnership agreement. It should, however, include the following types of information:

1. The name and address of each partner.
2. The name, location, and nature of the partnership.
3. The date of the agreement and the length of time the partnership is to run.
4. The investment of each partner.
5. The duties, rights, and responsibilities of each partner.
6. The amount of withdrawals allowed each partner.
7. The procedures for sharing profits and losses.
8. The procedure for distributing assets when the partnership is dissolved.

Each partner should, of course, sign the agreement.

Accounting for Partners' Equity

Accounting for owners' equity for a partnership is basically the same as for a sole proprietorship. A sole proprietorship has only one capital account; a partnership has two or more capital accounts. A separate capital account is set up for each partner to record that partner's investment in the business. Each partner also has a separate withdrawals account in which to record the amount of cash or other assets the partner withdraws from the business for personal use.

In a partnership, separate capital and withdrawals accounts are set up for each partner.

Recording the Partners' Investments

When the partnership is formed, the value of cash and other assets invested by each partner is listed in the partnership agreement. Separate entries are then made to record each partner's investment in the business. Let's look at an example.

On January 1, Pat Donald and Harold Thompson agreed to form a partnership to operate an accounting firm. The name of the firm was to be Donald & Thompson, CPAs. Each partner agreed to invest the following assets in the new business (Memorandum 1):

	Donald	Thompson
Cash	$12,000	
Office supplies	1,000	
Office equipment (market value)	12,000	
Building (market value)		$30,000
Land		15,000
Total assets invested	$25,000	$45,000

The journal entries made to record the partners' initial investments are shown in Figure 26-1. Notice that the asset accounts Office Equipment and Building are debited for their current market value. Each partner's capital account is then credited for the total amount of the assets that partner invested.

GENERAL JOURNAL   PAGE 1

DATE	DESCRIPTION	POST. REF.	DEBIT	CREDIT
Jan. 1	Cash in Bank		12 000 00	
	Office Supplies		1 000 00	
	Office Equipment		12 000 00	
	Pat Donald, Capital			25 000 00
	Memo. 1			
	1 Building		30 000 00	
	Land		15 000 00	
	Harold Thompson, Capital			45 000 00
	Memo. 1			

Figure 26-1   Recording the Partners' Investments in the Business

R E M E M B E R

When a partner invests noncash assets in the business, they are recorded in the partnership records at their current market value.

Critical Thinking

Maria and Julio are eager to start a restaurant business. They have the necessary cash to get the business going but little experience in managing a restaurant. They decide to invite Shana, who has been a restaurant manager for 15 years, to join the partnership. Shana has no cash to invest, but Maria and Julio are willing to offer her an equal share in the net profits or net losses of the business.

Why would Maria and Julio offer Shana an equal share?

(Answer: Effective management will be a key factor in the success of the restaurant. With an equal share, Shana will have as much incentive as Maria and Julio to make the business successful. Also, Shana may have more responsibility in managing the business and may work more hours.)

Recording Additional Investments

Any additional investments by the partners are recorded in a similar manner. For example, in April each partner agreed to invest an additional $5,000.00 cash in the business.

April 4: *Recorded the additional investment of $5,000.00 by each partner, Memorandum 42.*

The general journal entry to record this transaction is shown in Figure 26-2.

| GENERAL JOURNAL | | | | PAGE 10 |
DATE	DESCRIPTION	POST. REF.	DEBIT	CREDIT
19-- Apr. 4	Cash in Bank		10 000 00	
	Pat Donald, Capital			5 000 00
	Harold Thompson, Capital			5 000 00
	Memo. 42			

Figure 26-2 Journalizing an Additional Investment by the Partners

Recording Withdrawals by the Partners

During the fiscal period, the partners may withdraw cash or other assets for personal use, according to the terms of the partnership agreement. Partners' withdrawals are recorded in the same way as are the withdrawals of the owner of a sole proprietorship. The amount of the withdrawal is debited to the partner's withdrawals account and credited to the appropriate asset account. The amounts withdrawn by the partners do not have to be equal.

May 12: *Pat Donald withdrew $1,200.00 cash for personal use (Check 123) and Harold Thompson withdrew $1,800.00 cash for personal use (Check 124).*

Figure 26-3 shows how these withdrawals are recorded in general-journal form.

| GENERAL JOURNAL | | | | PAGE 12 |
DATE	DESCRIPTION	POST. REF.	DEBIT	CREDIT
19-- May 12	Pat Donald, Withdrawals		1 200 00	
	Cash in Bank			1 200 00
	Check 123			
12	Harold Thompson, Withdrawals		1 800 00	
	Cash in Bank			1 800 00
	Check 124			

Figure 26-3 Journalizing Withdrawals by the Partners

Before continuing, complete the following activity to check your understanding of the material you have just studied.

UNIT 6 Accounting for Other Forms of Business Organization

Interdisciplinary Connections

HISTORY

The United States has long been a center for commerce. Some people recognized this country's potential even during the days before it became a country. The British statesman, Edmund Burke, accurately predicted this country's future as a business power when he said in 1775, "There is America—which at this day serves for little more than to amuse you with stories of savage men, and uncouth manners; yet shall, before you taste of death, show itself equal to the whole of that commerce which now attracts the envy of the world." The United States has not only equalled but has surpassed the once-mighty British empire.

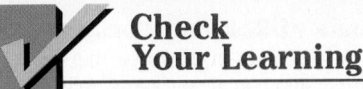

Check Your Learning

On a sheet of notebook paper, indicate whether each of the following statements is true or false.

1. A separate capital account is set up for each partner.
2. A partnership has an unlimited life.
3. A partnership pays income taxes just like a corporation.
4. The duties, rights, and responsibilities of each partner should be listed in a partnership agreement.

Compare your answers with those in the answers section. Re-read the preceding part of the chapter to find the correct answers to any questions you may have missed.

ANSWERS

1. True
2. False
3. False
4. True

Division of Partnership Income or Loss

At the end of each accounting period, the net income or net loss from partnership operations is divided among the partners. Partners may divide the net income or loss among themselves in any way they choose. The specific method should be set out in the partnership agreement. If it is not, the law provides that net income or net loss be divided equally among the partners.

There are many ways for partners to divide profits and losses. The division is generally based on the services and capital contributed by the partners to the partnership. For example, if the partners share equally in the work of the business but one partner has invested more capital, it seems only fair that the one who has invested more should stand to gain more. When the profits of the accounting period are divided, each partner's capital account is increased. If the business incurs a net loss for the accounting period, the capital account of each partner is decreased.

Let's look now at two methods that can be used to distribute partnership profits or losses. To illustrate the two methods, we'll use two examples for each method. In the first example, the partnership has a net income of $24,000. In the second example, the partnership has a net loss of $12,000.

ACCOUNTING Notes
A partnership rewards partners in the form of partnership profits. Partners, therefore, do not have take-home pay as do the employees of the partnership business. Instead, active partners commonly withdraw regular amounts of money on a weekly or monthly basis in anticipation of their share of annual profits.

R E M E M B E R

If the partnership agreement does not set out how net income or loss is to be distributed, the net income or loss is shared equally among the partners.

Dividing Profits and Losses Equally

The easiest way to divide a partnership's net income or loss is equally. This method is often used when all partners invest equal amounts of capital and share equally in the work of the business.

Teaching Tips

■ Present other net income amounts and have students calculate the division. You can also use more than two partners in these examples.
■ Remind students that closing entries are journalized as the last step in the accounting cycle.

Using Visuals

Have students look at the closing entry in Figure 26-4. Then ask for a volunteer to explain how this closing entry differs from the closing entry for a sole proprietorship? For a corporation?

Have students compare the closing entry for a net loss in Figure 26-5 with the closing entry in Figure 26-4.

Using Visuals

 Use demonstration problem 26-3 to give students practice recording the entry to divide partnership profits.

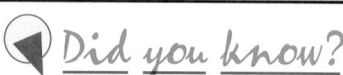

A worldwide baby boom has been taking place. By the year 2001, the world will have over 2 billion teenagers. The majority of these future teenagers live in Asia and Latin America, and, having grown up in the international economy, they will be the first "global teenagers."

▲ **Net Income of $24,000**   During the first fiscal year of operations, the Donald & Thompson, CPAs partnership earned a net income of $24,000. The partnership agreement states that the profits or losses are to be divided between the two partners equally. Each partner's share of the net income is calculated as shown here.

Donald's share:	$24,000 ÷ 2 = $12,000
Thompson's share:	$24,000 ÷ 2 = $12,000

On December 31, the closing entry for a $24,000 net income divided equally between the two partners would be journalized as shown in Figure 26-4.

	DATE	DESCRIPTION	POST. REF.	DEBIT	CREDIT	
1	19--	Closing Entries				1
15	Dec. 31	Income Summary		24 000 00		15
16		Pat Donald, Capital			12 000 00	16
17		Harold Thompson, Capital			12 000 00	17

GENERAL JOURNAL   PAGE 25

Figure 26-4   Closing Entry To Divide Net Income Equally

The effect of this division of net income on the partners' capital accounts is illustrated below.

Pat Donald, Capital		Harold Thompson, Capital	
Dr.	Cr.	Dr.	Cr.
−	+	−	+
	Bal. $30,000		Bal. $50,000
	Clos. 12,000		Clos. 12,000

▲ **Net Loss of $12,000**   If the partnership had incurred a net loss of $12,000 for the fiscal period, each partner's share would be calculated as shown here.

Donald's share:	$12,000 ÷ 2 = $6,000
Thompson's share:	$12,000 ÷ 2 = $6,000

The closing entry on December 31 to distribute the $12,000 net loss equally between the two partners would appear as in Figure 26-5.

	DATE	DESCRIPTION	POST. REF.	DEBIT	CREDIT	
1	19--	Closing Entries				1
15	Dec. 31	Pat Donald, Capital		6 000 00		15
16		Harold Thompson, Capital		6 000 00		16
17		Income Summary			12 000 00	17

GENERAL JOURNAL   PAGE 25

Figure 26-5   Closing Entry To Divide Net Loss Equally

Making Connections

AROUND THE WORLD

Over 60 joint ventures have been formed between Mexican companies and foreign partners in recent years. The majority of the businesses are in the manufacturing and processing industries, and most of the partners are U.S. businesses. Some European and Asian companies have also formed joint ventures with Mexican businesses. Their number is expected to increase in the future.

The net loss amount is debited to each partner's capital account as shown in the following T accounts.

Pat Donald, Capital				Harold Thompson, Capital			
Dr.		Cr.		Dr.		Cr.	
−		+		−		+	
Clos. $6,000		Bal. $30,000		Clos. $6,000		Bal. $50,000	

Dividing Profits and Losses on a Fractional-Share Basis

The second simplest way to divide net income or loss is to assign each partner a stated fraction of the total. The size of the fraction usually takes into consideration: (1) the amount of each partner's investment and (2) the value of each partner's services to the business.

Let's suppose that the Donald & Thompson, CPAs partnership agreement states that the profits or losses are to be divided between the two partners on this basis: Thompson, $\frac{2}{3}$, and Donald, $\frac{1}{3}$.

When partners share net income or loss on a fractional-share basis, the basis is often stated as a ratio. Thompson's $\frac{2}{3}$ and Donald's $\frac{1}{3}$ could be expressed as a 2:1 ratio (2 to 1). To turn a ratio into a fraction, add the figures and use the total as the denominator of the fraction. For example,

$$2:1 \qquad 2 + 1 = 3 \qquad \tfrac{2}{3} \text{ and } \tfrac{1}{3}$$

▲ **Net Income of $24,000** The division of the net income based on the partners' capital investments would be calculated as follows:

Donald's share:	$24,000 $\times \frac{1}{3} = $ $ 8,000
Thompson's share:	$24,000 $\times \frac{2}{3} = $ $16,000

The December 31 closing entry would appear as shown in Figure 26-6.

	GENERAL JOURNAL			PAGE 25
DATE	DESCRIPTION	POST. REF.	DEBIT	CREDIT
19--	*Closing Entries*			
Dec. 31	Income Summary		24 000 00	
	Pat Donald, Capital			8 000 00
	Harold Thompson, Capital			16 000 00

Figure 26-6   Closing Entry To Divide Net Income on a Fractional-Share Basis

The effect of this method of dividing partnership earnings on the partners' capital accounts is illustrated below.

Pat Donald, Capital				Harold Thompson, Capital			
Dr.		Cr.		Dr.		Cr.	
−		+		−		+	
		Bal. $30,000				Bal. $50,000	
		Clos. 8,000				Clos. 16,000	

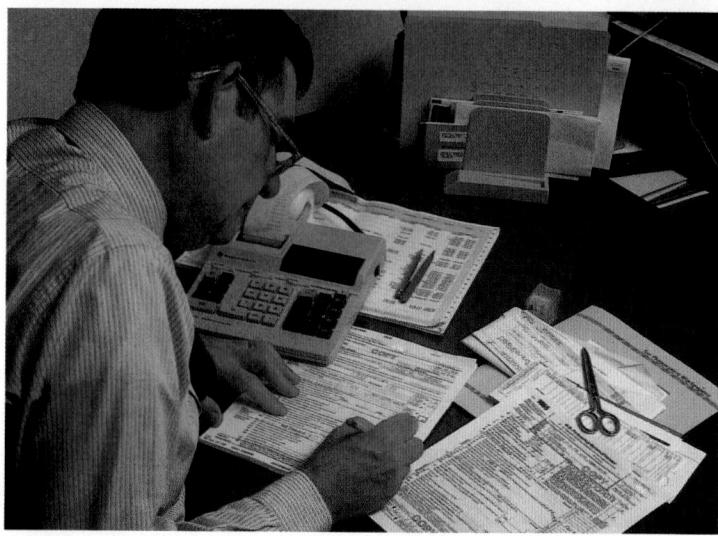

While a partnership does not pay income taxes, it is required to file an informational tax return with the IRS on Form 1065.

▲ **Net Loss of $12,000** If the partnership had incurred a net loss of $12,000 for the fiscal period, the December 31 distribution would be computed as shown here.

Donald's share: $12,000 × $\frac{1}{3}$ = $4,000
Thompson's share: $12,000 × $\frac{2}{3}$ = $8,000

On December 31, the closing entry would be prepared as shown in Figure 26-7.

	GENERAL JOURNAL			PAGE 25
DATE	DESCRIPTION	POST. REF.	DEBIT	CREDIT
19--	*Closing Entries*			
Dec 31	*Pat Donald, Capital*		4 000 00	
	Harold Thompson, Capital		8 000 00	
	Income Summary			12 000 00

Figure 26-7 Closing Entry To Divide Net Loss on a Fractional-Share Basis

The effect of this division of net loss on the partners' capital accounts is shown in the following T accounts:

Pat Donald, Capital			Harold Thompson, Capital	
Dr.	Cr.		Dr.	Cr.
–	+		–	+
Clos. $4,000	Bal. $30,000		Clos. $8,000	Bal. $50,000

578

UNIT 6   Accounting for Other Forms of Business Organization

Making Connections

BUSINESS ETHICS

Your company has a suggestion system in which employees receive a bonus for suggestions that are implemented and that result in cost savings. You submitted a suggestion for which you received a $1,000 bonus. The suggestion, however, was originally mentioned by a co-worker in a casual conversation. What should you do?

(Answer: You should share the bonus with your co-worker. How much you share may depend on how detailed the original suggestion was and the time you spent to develop the suggestion before submitting it.)

Before continuing, complete the following activity to check your understanding of how to distribute partnership earnings.

Check Your Learning

Answer these questions on a sheet of notebook paper.

Norton and Player are partners in a law firm. They share profits and losses on a fractional-share basis: Norton, $\frac{3}{8}$; Player, $\frac{5}{8}$. On December 31 (the end of the fiscal period), the partnership had a net income of $36,000.

1. What is each partner's share of the net income?
2. The ending capital balances were as follows: Norton, $32,000; Player, $40,000. What is the balance of each partner's capital account after the closing entry dividing the net income is posted?

Compare your answers to those in the answers section. Re-read the preceding part of the chapter to find the answers to any questions you missed.

Preparing Financial Statements for a Partnership

At the end of the fiscal period, a work sheet is prepared for the partnership and the financial statements are completed. The firm of Donald & Thompson, CPAs prepares an income statement, a statement of changes in partners' equity, and a balance sheet.

The Income Statement

The income statement is prepared in the same way as for any service business. Total expenses are subtracted from total revenue to determine the amount of the net income or net loss. The net income or net loss is divided among the partners and may be entered on the income statement.

The partnership agreement of Donald & Thompson, CPAs states that net income or net loss will be divided equally. At the end of the fiscal period, the firm had a net income of $24,000.00. According to the terms of the partnership agreement, each partner receives $12,000.00. If this division were included on Donald & Thompson's income statement, it would appear as shown in Figure 26-8.

Donald & Thompson, CPAs Income Statement For the Year Ended December 31, 19--		
Net Income		24 000 00
Division of Net Income:		
Pat Donald	12 000 00	
Harold Thompson	12 000 00	
Net Income		24 000 00

Figure 26-8 Reporting the Division of Net Income on the Income Statement

ANSWERS
1. Norton, $13,500; Player, $22,500
2. Norton, $45,500; Player, $62,500

CONCEPT DEVELOPMENT
Preparing Financial Statements for a Partnership
Students are familiar already with the financial statements to be prepared for a partnership. The only difference is in terminology. The capital statement for a partnership is called a statement of changes in partners' equity in contrast to a statement of changes in owner's equity for a sole proprietorship. The format is slightly different, but the results are the same.

Teaching Tips
- Review the income statement prepared for a service business with students (page 152).

Using Visuals
Walk students through the recording of each item of information in Figure 26-8. Point out that accounting rules do not make it mandatory that the income statement show a division of net income or loss between or among partners.

Reteaching Strategies

Students who are having difficulty apportioning partnership income or losses may need to review calculations involving percentages. Have such students complete appropriate activities in the *Math Review for Accounting* workbook.

For students who need extra practice calculating and recording partnership income and losses, assign items (1) and (2) of additional Problem 26B, page 644.

The Statement of Changes in Partners' Equity

The **statement of changes in partners' equity** reports the changes in each partner's capital account resulting from the business operations. It is very similar to the statement of changes in owner's equity for a sole proprietorship. The only difference between the two is that the statement of partners' equity for the partnership contains a separate column for each partner. Figure 26-9 shows the statement of changes in partners' equity for the firm of Donald & Thompson, CPAs.

Notice that the net income has been divided between the partners as set forth on the income statement.

Donald & Thompson, CPAs — Statement of Changes in Partners' Equity — For the Year Ended December 31, 19--	Donald	Thompson	Totals
Beginning Capital, January 1, 19--			
Add: Investments	30 000 00	50 000 00	80 000 00
Net Income	12 000 00	12 000 00	24 000 00
Subtotal	42 000 00	62 000 00	104 000 00
Less: Withdrawals	3 000 00	5 000 00	8 000 00
Ending Capital, December 31, 19--	39 000 00	57 000 00	96 000 00

Figure 26-9 Statement of Changes in Partners' Equity

The Balance Sheet

For a partnership, the owners' equity section of the balance sheet is referred to as the Partners' Equity section. Each partner's capital account is listed separately in the Partners' Equity section, as shown in Figure 26-10. The capital account amounts reported on the balance sheet are taken from the statement of changes in partners' equity.

Donald & Thompson, CPAs — Balance Sheet — December 31, 19--		
Partners' Equity		
Pat Donald, Capital	39 000 00	
Harold Thompson, Capital	57 000 00	
Total Partners' Equity		96 000 00
Total Liabilities and Partners' Equity		101 250 00

Figure 26-10 The Partners' Equity Section of the Balance Sheet of a Partnership

Recording the Closing Entries for a Partnership

As you remember, the four closing entries made for a sole proprietorship at the end of the period are as follows:

1. Close the revenue accounts into Income Summary.
2. Close the expense accounts into Income Summary.

UNIT 6 Accounting for Other Forms of Business Organization

---

3. Close Income Summary into the owner's capital account by the amount of the net income or net loss.
4. Close the withdrawals account into the capital account.

The first two closing entries for a partnership are the same as those listed above. In the third closing entry, Income Summary is closed into the partners' capital accounts. The amount of the net income or net loss is divided among the partners as shown on the income statement. Finally, each partner's withdrawals account is closed into that partner's capital account.

The closing entries involving the capital accounts for the partnership of Donald & Thompson, CPAs are shown in Figure 26-11. Notice that each partner's withdrawals account is closed separately.

	GENERAL JOURNAL			PAGE 25
DATE	DESCRIPTION	POST. REF.	DEBIT	CREDIT
19--	*Closing Entries*			
Dec. 31	*Income Summary*		2400000	
	Pat Donald, Capital			1200000
	Harold Thompson, Capital			1200000
31	*Pat Donald, Capital*		300000	
	Pat Donald, Withdrawals			300000
31	*Harold Thompson, Capital*		500000	
	Harold Thompson, Withdr.			500000

Figure 26-11 Partial Closing Entries for a Partnership

Summary of Key Points

1. A partnership is an association of two or more persons to carry on, as co-owners, a business for profit.
2. The actions of one partner acting on behalf of the partnership are binding on all partners. This is known as mutual agency.
3. In a partnership, a capital account and a withdrawals account are set up for each partner.
4. The net income or loss of a partnership is divided among the partners according to the terms set forth in the partnership agreement.
5. Division of partnership profits and losses is generally based on the contribution of services and capital by the partners.

Review and Applications

PRACTICE AND APPLY

- Language Development
- Comprehension and Retention
- Basic Skills

Building Your Accounting Vocabulary

See the Glossary on pages 670-679 for definitions of these terms.

Reviewing Your Accounting Knowledge

1. (a) Ease of formation, (b) unlimited liability, (c) limited life, (d) mutual agency, and (e) co-ownership of partnership property.

2. Advantages are ease of formation, few legal restrictions, and no income taxes on partnership earnings. Disadvantages are limited life, unlimited liability for partnership debts, mutual agency, no sale of equity without consent of other partners, and potential difficulty of working together.

3. Because it sets out terms under which the partnership will operate.

4. Name and address of each partner; name, location, and nature of the partnership; date of the agreement and length of time it is to run; investment of each partner; duties, rights, and responsibilities of each partner; withdrawals allowed each partner; procedures for sharing profits and losses; and procedure for distributing assets upon dissolution.

5. Partners can divide profits and losses in any manner they choose, which is often according to capital invested or the skills, services, and time provided by each partner.

6. At current market value to accurately and fairly reflect a partner's contribution.

7. Equally or on a fractional basis.

8. Income statement, statement of changes in partners' equity, and balance sheet.

9. The equity section of the balance sheet is called Partners' Equity rather than Owner's Equity and reports each partner's capital account.

Building Your Accounting Vocabulary

In your own words, write the definition of each of the following accounting terms. Use complete sentences for your definitions.

mutual agency
partnership

partnership
agreement

statement of changes
in partners' equity

Reviewing Your Accounting Knowledge

1. What are five characteristics of a partnership?
2. List three advantages and three disadvantages of the partnership form of business organization.
3. Why is a written partnership agreement important?
4. What information is usually included in a partnership agreement?
5. What do partners usually consider when deciding on how the profits and losses of the partnership will be divided?
6. When assets other than cash are invested in a partnership, at what value are these assets recorded?
7. Name two methods partners might use to divide profits and losses.
8. What three financial statements are prepared for a partnership at the end of a fiscal period?
9. How does the balance sheet for a partnership differ from that for a sole proprietorship?
10. How do the closing entries of a partnership differ from those of a sole proprietorship?

Improving Your Decision-Making Skills

Amy Palaski is the owner of a small retail business organized as a sole proprietorship. She is thinking about forming a partnership with Gene Hogan, whom she considers friendly and trustworthy. What things should Amy consider before deciding whether to form a partnership with Gene?

Applying Accounting Procedures

Exercise 26-1   Determining Partners' Fractional Shares
The ratios used by several partnerships to divide partnership earnings appear below.

Instructions: Determine the fractions that would be used to calculate each partner's share of net income or loss. Use the form provided in the working papers.

1. 3:1
2. 5:3:1
3. 3:2:1:1
4. 2:2:1
5. 3:2

10. The first two closing entries are the same. In the third closing entry, the balance of Income Summary is closed into the partners' capital accounts according to the method specified in the partnership agreement. In the fourth closing entry, each partner's withdrawals account is closed separately into that partner's capital account.

Improving Your Decision-Making Skills
Students' answers will vary but could include points listed here. Each partner brings various strengths, weaknesses, and abilities to the business. Before forming a partnership, the persons involved should agree—preferably in writing—upon key issues the business will face, including tangible assets to be contributed by each partner, the participation of each partner in the business, how disagreements will be settled, how profits or losses will be divided, and how assets will be divided if the business is dissolved. One of Amy's most important decisions is whether she can work with Gene without strife.

Exercise 26-2 Dividing Partnership Earnings

Listed below are the net income and the method of dividing net income or loss for several different partnerships.

Instructions: Use the form provided in the working papers to determine each partner's share of the net income.

Net Income	Method of Dividing Partnership Earnings
1. $45,000	Equally: 2 partners
2. $89,700	Fractional share: $\frac{2}{3}, \frac{1}{3}$
3. $22,000	Fractional share: **3:1**
4. $32,000	Fractional share: $\frac{2}{5}, \frac{2}{5}, \frac{1}{5}$
5. $92,700	Equally: 3 partners

Problem 26-1 Recording Partners' Investments

On June 1, Jennifer Thiry and Matthew Deck agreed to combine their individual sole proprietorships into a new business organized as a partnership. The partnership would take over all the assets of the two proprietorships. The assets invested by Thiry and Deck are listed below.

Instructions: Prepare the entries required to record the investment by each partner. Use page 1 of a general journal. The source document is Memorandum 1.

	Thiry	Deck
Cash	$ 2,300	$1,200
Accounts receivable	7,000	2,000
Merchandise	5,000	8,000
Equipment	12,000	5,000

Problem 26-2 Dividing Partnership Earnings Equally

On January 3, May Allrite and John Waters formed a partnership to be known as Allrite-Waters Products. The partnership agreement stated that net income or loss would be divided equally between Allrite and Waters.

Instructions:

(1) Determine each partner's share of the net income of $28,743.

(2) Record the December 31 entry, on page 4 of the general journal, to close the Income Summary account into the partners' capital accounts.

Problem 26-3 Preparing Closing Entries for a Partnership

Barbara Scott and Martin Towers are partners in the firm of Office Interiors. Their partnership agreement states that Scott and Towers respectively share net income or loss in a 3:2 ratio.

At the end of the fiscal period (December 31), the business had a net loss of $9,700. During the period, Scott had withdrawals of $6,600 and Towers had withdrawals of $5,400.

Instructions:

(1) Journalize the closing entries to divide the net loss between the partners and to close the withdrawals accounts. Use general journal page 14.

(2) Post the closing entries to the general ledger accounts.

583

PRACTICE AND APPLY

• Concepts and Procedures

Exercise 26-1: Ch. Obj. 3
1. 3/4, 1/4
2. 5/9, 3/9 (1/3), 1/9
3. 3/7, 2/7, 1/7, 1/7
4. 2/5, 2/5, 1/5
5. 3/5, 2/5

Exercise 26-2: Ch. Obj. 3
1. $22,500; $22,500
2. $59,800; $29,900
3. $16,500; $5,500
4. $12,800; $12,800; $6,400
5. $30,900; $30,900; $30,900

Problem 26-1: Ch. Obj. 2
Capital balances: Thiry, $26,300; Deck, $16,200

Problem 26-2: Ch. Obj. 3
$14,371.50 to each partner

Problem 26-3: Ch. Obj. 2
Division of net loss: Scott, ($5,820); Towers, ($3,880)
Ending capital balances: Scott, $54,892; Towers, $40,321

Problem 26-4: Ch. Obj. 4

SPREADSHEET   Problem 26-4 can be completed using *Spreadsheet Applications,* the PROBLEM   spreadsheet software that accompanies *Glencoe Accounting.*

Division of net income: $16,588 each
Ending capital balances: Hires, $59,588; Buckley, $61,088

Refer students to the Chapter 26 review pages in the workbook, *Chapter Reviews and Working Papers.*

Problem 26-5: Ch. Obj. 4

COMPUTER

PROBLEM

This computer image identifies a problem that students may complete using the *Glencoe Accounting, General Ledger* software.

Division of net income: Lions, $19,767; Castle, $6,589
Ending capital balances: Lions, $53,305; Castle, $16,027
Balance sheet totals, $77,277

Problem 26-6: Ch. Obj. 3

CHALLENGE

PROBLEM

The last problem in each chapter is a challenge problem and is identified by this "maze" symbol.

Plan 1: O'Riley, $5,833.33
      White, $5,833.33
      Garrity, $5,833.34
Plan 2: O'Riley, $7,000.00
      White, $7,000.00
      Garrity, $3,500.00
Plan 3: O'Riley, $4,149.48
      White, $5,532.65
      Garrity, $7,817.87

4 ASSESS

A chapter test is available for use in assessing students' understanding of concepts in this chapter.

The testmaker software enables you to develop tailor-made chapter, unit, semester, and final tests.

Alternative Assessment

For alternative assessment strategies, refer to *Tech Prep Strategies in Accounting*.

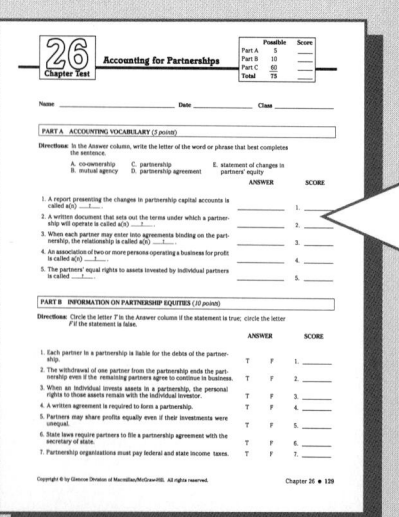

SPREADSHEET

PROBLEM

Problem 26-4   Preparing a Statement of Changes in Partners' Equity

On January 1, Jack Hires and Carol Buckley formed a partnership called Research Consultants. Each partner invested $50,000 in cash on that date. The partnership agreement stated that the net income or loss would be shared equally.

During the year, Hires invested an additional $1,500 and withdrew $8,500 for personal use. Buckley invested an additional $2,000 and withdrew a total of $7,500. Net income for the year was $33,176.

Instructions: Prepare a statement of changes in partners' equity for the year ended December 31.

COMPUTER

PROBLEM

Problem 26-5   Completing End-of-Period Activities for a Partnership

Richard Lions and Carrie Castle are partners in the firm of R & C Roofing. They have agreed to divide net income or loss on the following basis: Lions, $\frac{3}{4}$; Castle, $\frac{1}{4}$.

The completed worksheet for R & C Roofing for the year ended December 31 appears in the working papers accompanying this textbook.

Instructions:

(1) Prepare an income statement for the partnership.
(2) Prepare a statement of changes in partners' equity. During the year, the partners made the following additional investments in the business: Lions, $3,500; Castle, $200.
(3) Prepare a balance sheet.
(4) Journalize the adjusting and closing entries, beginning on page 27 of the general journal.

CHALLENGE

PROBLEM

Problem 26-6   Evaluating Methods of Dividing Partnership Earnings

Maureen O'Riley, David White, and Jo Garrity have decided to form a partnership to operate a restaurant. The partners plan to invest the following assets in the business:

	O'Riley	White	Garrity
Cash	$22,000	$40,000	
Supplies	5,000	2,000	
Equipment	7,500	4,000	
Building			$50,000
Land			15,000

They are considering the following plans for the division of net income or loss:

1. Equally.
2. O'Riley, 40%; White, 40%; Garrity, 20%.
3. In the same ratio as the beginning balances of their capital accounts.

Instructions: Assume that the business had a net income of $17,500. Calculate the division of net income under each of the three plans.

584

Use Chapter Test 26 here to assess students' understanding and retention of the concepts and procedures presented in the chapter.

*F*orensic Accountants:
Fraud Sleuths

A uditors are independent accountants who are hired to check a business's accounting records. In a corporation's annual report, the auditor's statement assures stockholders that the financial information is true, accurate, and consistent with generally accepted accounting principles.

Ideally, these audits should reveal incidents of illegal tampering. In standard audits, accountants review samples of inventory, accounts receivable, and accounts payable; check bank balances; and verify the authenticity of contracts with outside vendors. Routine audits usually end there. When fraud is suspected or when an accounting firm is sued for malpractice because it did not report accounting irregularities, it's time to call in the "fraud sleuths," officially called "forensic accountants."

Often members of small accounting firms, these specialists go beyond the routine evaluation. They delve deeply into the financial records and personnel profiles of a business in ways that an accountant performing a standard audit would not.

Like detectives, they probe relentlessly into contracts, memos, liens, property records, and banking records. They look for collusion, kickbacks, and secret bank accounts; prepare profiles of key people involved with a company, including officers, employees, and vendors; investigate computer databases to uncover suspicious or irregular activities, such as a corporate officer buying property with unaccounted income. They might use computers with special software designed to track distribution of funds and find out if checks made out to different payees eventually ended up in the same bank account.

With an increase in the incidence of fraud and malpractice suits, there's an increase in demand

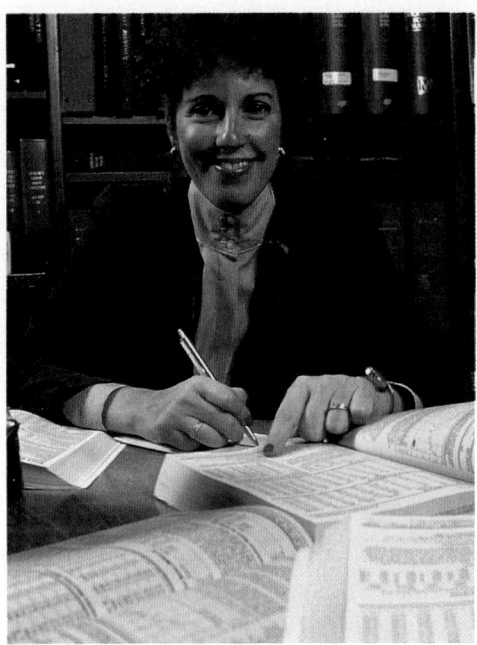

Some accountants specialize in auditing business records to uncover fraud.

for these investigative accountants. As a result, forensic accounting is a well-paying field.

If this sounds like an exciting career, get your CPA and auditing experience. You may even want to curl up with a Sherlock Holmes mystery whenever you have a chance!

Invite a forensic accountant from a local accounting firm to speak to your class. Ask the accountant to share the details of the most interesting case of fraud in which he or she has been involved.

QUESTIONS

1. What role have computers played in accounting fraud?
2. What traits or characteristics in addition to those of the typical accountant must a forensic accountant possess?

ANSWERS

1. With their speed and complexity, computers have probably made accounting fraud easier to perpetrate. Those same computers, however, make it easier to uncover and trace irregularities that lead to the embezzlers.
2. The forensic accountant must be logical, be comfortable with detail work, possess a somewhat suspicious nature, and have a clear understanding of how organizations work.

585

Chapter 27

ACCOUNTING FOR CORPORATIONS

LOOKING BACK

In Chapter 17 students learned how to prepare financial statements for a business organized as a privately held corporation. Students were introduced to the stockholders' equity accounts for capital stock and retained earnings. In this chapter students will learn about the characteristics, advantages, and disadvantages of corporations. They will also learn how corporations raise capital by issuing stock and how they distribute earnings to stockholders.

VOCABULARY DEVELOPMENT

Have students read the list of new terms. Ask for ideas for each term's meaning. Write correct responses on the board. Review the meanings of terms that are not familiar to students. Definitions of these terms are found in the chapter and in the glossary on pages 670-679.

Electronic Field Trips

Up to this point in your study of accounting, you have learned about the accounting procedures for the sole proprietorship and partnership forms of business organization. In Unit 3, you recorded the business transactions for a family-owned corporation. Most business transactions are recorded in the same manner regardless of how the business is organized. The major difference lies in accounting for ownership equity.

In this chapter, you will learn how to account for the ownership equity of the publicly held corporation. You will also learn how a corporation distributes its earnings to stockholders and how to prepare the financial statements for a publicly held corporation.

Learning Objectives

When you have completed Chapter 27, you should be able to do the following:

1. List the major characteristics, advantages, and disadvantages of the corporate form of business organization.
2. Journalize transactions involving the issuance of stock.
3. Journalize transactions involving cash dividends.
4. Prepare financial statements for a publicly held corporation.
5. Define the accounting terms introduced in this chapter.

New Terms

closely held corporation
publicly held corporation
board of directors
authorized capital stock
par value
common stock
proxy
preferred stock
paid-in capital in excess of par
dividend
statement of stockholders' equity

586

Teaching Resources

- Lesson Plans
- TE/Chapter Reviews & Working Papers
- Demonstration Problems
- Student Study Plans
- Teaching Transparencies
- Solutions Transparencies
- Electronic Field Trips Video, Level I
- Electronic Study Guide
- Chapter 27 Test

Other Resources

- Skills Improvement Activities
- Blackline Masters
- Careers in Accounting
- Dictionary
- Math Review for Accounting
- Tech Prep Strategies in Accounting
- Video
- Test Bank with Software
- Spanish Resources/Audiotapes
- Spanish Electronic Study Guide

Publicly Held Corporations

In the United States, there are more sole proprietorships and partnerships than there are corporations. Corporations, however, account for more business activity than the other two combined.

There are different types of corporations. In Unit 3, you learned how to record the business transactions for a family-owned, closely held corporation. **Closely held corporations** are corporations owned by a few persons or by a family. The stock of a closely held corporation is not sold to the general public.

In this chapter, you will learn about another type of corporation: the publicly held corporation. A **publicly held corporation** is one whose stock is widely held, has a large market, and is usually traded on a stock exchange. You're probably familiar with many corporations whose stock is traded on stock exchanges like the New York Stock Exchange or the American Stock Exchange. The stockholders of such publicly held corporations as IBM, General Motors, Polaroid, and McDonalds number in the millions.

Characteristics of a Corporation

The corporate form of business organization has several unique features. Let's look at some of them.

Legal Permission To Operate

To operate a business as a corporation, the incorporators (organizers) must file an application with state officials for permission to operate. Once the application is approved, it becomes the corporation's charter. As you learned in Chapter 1, the charter indicates the purpose of the business and spells out the rules under which the business must operate. The charter also states the type and amount of stock a corporation is authorized to issue.

Separate Legal Entity

A corporation is a separate legal entity that is created and exists only by law. A corporation may enter into contracts, borrow money, and conduct business in the same manner as a person. It may acquire, own, and sell property in its name. It can also sue and be sued in the courts.

ACCOUNTING *Notes*
How do you get to be the president of a large corporation in the United States? Probably by beginning your career as an accountant. Statistically, more accountants have risen to be presidents of large U.S. corporations than people with any other background.

Stockholders

The owners of a corporation are called stockholders. Ownership is divided into units called shares of stock. Each stockholder receives a *stock certificate* as proof of ownership. The stock certificate lists the name of the stockholder, the number of shares issued, and the date they were issued.

Professional Management

Stockholders own the corporation, but they do not manage it. The stockholders elect a **board of directors,** who govern and are responsible for the affairs of the corporation. One of the first duties of the board of directors is to hire professional managers to operate the business.

CHAPTER 27 Accounting for Corporations **587**

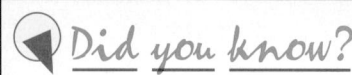

⬤ *Did you know?*

Corporate charters are issued by each of the 50 states and by the federal government. Federal charters are limited to banks, savings and loans, and quasi-corporations such as the FDIC.

Using Visuals

Read the photo caption to the class. Point out that stocks sold on a stock exchange have already been issued by a corporation; the transaction is between seller and buyer, not corporation and buyer.

Teaching Tips

▪ Organization Costs is an intangible asset account.

CONCEPT DEVELOPMENT
Advantages and Disadvantages of a Corporation

Compare the advantages and disadvantages listed here with the advantages and disadvantages of the partnership form of business organization. Point out that the advantages and disadvantages of the corporate form are the opposite of the advantages and disadvantages of the partnership form.

Using Visuals

 You may want to use the blackline master listing the characteristics of sole proprietorships, partnerships, and corporations at this point. See the blackline masters booklet accompanying Glencoe Accounting.

Altogether, about 30 million Americans (or one person out of eight) own shares in corporations.

Organization Costs

Forming a corporation is a much more costly process than forming a sole proprietorship or a partnership. To get started, corporations incur various *organization costs.* Organization costs include incorporation fees paid to the state, attorneys' fees for legal services, payments to promoters to sell stock, the cost of printing stock certificates, and other costs to bring the corporation into existence.

Advantages and Disadvantages of a Corporation

One of the most important advantages of a corporation is the *limited liability* of its owners. A corporation is a separate legal entity; it is responsible for its own actions and liabilities. The risk of an individual stockholder is limited to the amount he or she has invested. As mentioned earlier, shares of stock may be sold by one stockholder to another without disrupting the activities of the business or requiring the approval of other stockholders. Another advantage is that a corportation has a continuous existence even though the ownership may change.

There are, of course, disadvantages to the corporate form of business organization. First, corporations are more closely regulated by state and federal governments and are required to file numerous reports. Second, since stock is publicly held, corporations are required to disclose their operations more fully to the public. Third, corporate income is subject to federal and state income taxes. If the earnings of the corporation are distributed to stockholders, they too must pay taxes on that same income. This disadvantage is sometimes called *double taxation.*

588   UNIT 6   Accounting for Other Forms of Business Organization

Making Connections

EVERYDAY LIFE

Most people deal with one or more corporations every day. If you make a telephone call, you are using the services of a corporation. If you purchase gasoline for your car, you are most likely using a product of a corporation. Ask your students to think of corporations they do business with frequently.

Stockholders' Equity

Stockholders' equity, as you know, is the value of the stockholders' claims to the assets of the corporation. As you learned in Chapter 17, corporations must report stockholders' equity in two parts: (1) the equity that has been paid into the corporation by stockholders, and (2) the equity earned by the corporation and retained in the business. Let's look now at how transactions affecting stockholders' equity are handled.

Capital Stock

Capital stock refers to the shares of ownership in the corporation, the amount invested by the stockholders. When a corporation receives permission from the state to operate, it is authorized to sell a certain number of shares of stock to investors. The maximum number of shares a corporation may issue is called its **authorized capital stock.** The authorized capital stock of a corporation is usually much greater than the number of shares the corporation plans to sell right away. This allows the corporation to sell additional shares at a later time without having to ask the state to increase the authorized amount.

State laws may require that an amount or value be assigned to each share of stock before it is sold to the public. The amount assigned to each share is referred to as par value. **Par value** is simply the dollar amount printed on the stock certificates. The par value is used to determine the amount credited to the capital stock account. A corporation is free to select any par value; par values of $1, $5, and $25 are common. Most corporations set the par value low because state laws do not allow the corporation to sell the stock below its par value when it is first issued for sale to the public.

The corporate charter specifies the types of capital stock that a corporation may issue. The two main types of stock are common and preferred.

Common Stock

If the corporation issues only one class of capital stock, it is called **common stock.** The ownership of common stock usually carries certain basic rights. Common stockholders have the right to vote and elect the board of directors and, in effect, exercise control over the operations of the corporation. Each share of stock is entitled to one vote. Stockholders' meetings are usually held once a year. If a stockholder cannot attend the meeting, he or she may send in a **proxy,** which gives the stockholder's voting rights to someone else. Common stockholders have the right to share in the earnings of the corporation by receiving dividends. Common stockholders are also entitled to share in the assets of the corporation if it ceases operations.

Preferred Stock

In order to appeal to as many potential investors as possible, a corporation may issue preferred stock. **Preferred stock** has certain privileges (or

CONCEPT DEVELOPMENT
Stockholders' Equity

Remind students that stockholders' equity is made up of two parts: the capital paid into the corporation to purchase stock and prior earnings retained in the business.

CONCEPT DEVELOPMENT
Capital Stock

Remind students that all corporations—closely or publicly held—are owned in the form of capital stock. The capital stock account changes only when a corporation issues additional stock or buys its own stock from the public. Shares of stock traded on a stock exchange by members of the public do not affect the corporation's accounting records. Ask students to explain why.

Teaching Tips

■ Capital stock is also the legal capital of a corporation; that is, it cannot be paid back to the stockholders and must remain with the corporation to protect the interests of the creditors.

■ No-par stock is quite common. No-par stock requires that a "stated value" be used. Accounting for stated value and par value are the same except for the terminology.

■ Only California and Delaware allow corporations to issue stock below par.

■ Common stock carries these rights: the right to vote, to share in profits, to share in assets at liquidation, and the first option to buy additional shares issued (pre-emptive right).

Critical Thinking

Fred and Edmond co-own a plastics manufacturing business that their father started several years ago. The business currently has some large debts, but sales have grown steadily during the last five years, with revenues of more than $50 million last year. One of the brothers is contemplating leaving the business in the next few years. Recently, they have talked about incorporating the business.

What would the advantages be to incorporating the business?

(Answer: They could sell stock to raise capital for the business to help pay off the debts. If the business cannot pay its debts, there will be limited liability. Even if one of the brothers does decide to leave the business, there will be continuous existence.)

preferences) over common stock. Preferred stockholders are entitled to receive dividends before common stockholders. The preferred stock dividend is stated in specific dollars, such as $6, or as a percentage of the stock's par value, such as 6%. The stock itself is then referred to as "$6 preferred stock" or "6% preferred stock."

Preferred stockholders are also given preference to the assets of the corporation should it cease operations. In return for these special privileges, the preferred stockholder gives up the right to vote and, in turn, the right to participate in the control of the corporation.

A separate account is set up by the corporation for each class of stock.

Before continuing, complete the following activity to check your understanding of the material you have just studied.

Check Your Learning

Record your answers to these questions on notebook paper.

1. A(n) ___?___ corporation is one whose stock is traded on a stock exchange.
2. ___?___ is the amount assigned to a share of stock. It is the amount used to record entries in the capital stock account.
3. Two types of stock issued by corporations are ___?___ and ___?___ .
4. Stock with a stated dividend per share is called ___?___ .

Compare your answers to those in the answers section. Re-read the preceding part of the chapter to find the correct answers to any questions you may have missed.

Issuing Common Stock

When common stock is issued, the Common Stock account is credited for the par value of the stock. The amount of money received for the stock may not always be the par value. Let's look at some examples.

▲ **Issuing Common Stock at Par Value**   On January 1, the Sender Corporation was incorporated and authorized to sell 20,000 shares of common stock with a par value of $10. On January 3, the company had the following transaction.

January 3: *Issued 10,000 shares of $10 par common stock at $10 per share, Memorandum 3.*

$ 10,000 shares
× $10
‾‾‾‾‾‾‾‾‾
$100,000

In this transaction, the Sender Corporation received $100,000 cash in return for the 10,000 shares. Whenever shares of stock are sold at par value, the amount credited to the Common Stock account is determined by multiplying the number of shares issued by the par value. In this transaction, therefore, Cash in Bank is debited for $100,000 and Common Stock is credited for $100,000. This transaction is shown in general journal form in Figure 27-1.

Figure 27-1 Journalizing the Sale of Common Stock at Par Value

▲ **Issuing Common Stock in Excess of Par Value** Investors are often willing to pay more than par value for the stock of a corporation. When stock sells at a price above par, the excess over par is credited to a separate stockholders' equity account called **paid-in capital in excess of par.**

Paid-in Capital in Excess of Par	
Dr.	Cr.
−	+
Decrease Side	Increase Side
	Balance Side

Paid-in Capital in Excess of Par appears in the chart of accounts immediately below the Common Stock account. The amounts recorded in this account are not profits to the corporation. Rather, they represent part of the stockholders' investment in the corporation.

One year after the Sender Corporation was incorporated, it had the following transaction.

June 15: Issued 5,000 shares of $10 par common stock at $11.50 per share, Memorandum 147.

5,000 shares
×$11.50
$57,500

In this transaction, the Sender Corporation received $57,500 in exchange for 5,000 shares of its common stock. Before the transaction can be journalized, the corporation must determine how much of the $57,500 is to be credited to Common Stock and how much is to be credited to Paid-in Capital in Excess of Par. Remember, the amount credited to the Common Stock account is the par value of the shares issued.

Total cash received	$57,500
Common stock, 5,000 shares @ $10 par value	−50,000
Excess, 5,000 shares @ $1.50 per share	$ 7,500

In the transaction, Cash in Bank is debited for $57,500.00, the total amount of cash received. Common Stock is credited for $50,000.00, the total par value of the shares issued. Paid-in Capital in Excess of Par is credited for $7,500.00, the excess over par paid for the shares. The transaction is shown in general journal form in Figure 27-2 on page 592.

CHAPTER 27 Accounting for Corporations   **591**

Using Visuals

Walk students through the calculations of amounts recorded in Figure 27-2. Give students other examples and ask them to calculate the amounts to record.

Using Visuals

Review the journal entry in Figure 27-3. Ask students to describe the differences between preferred stock and common stock.

ACCOUNTING PRACTICE
Students may complete Exercise 27-1 at this point.

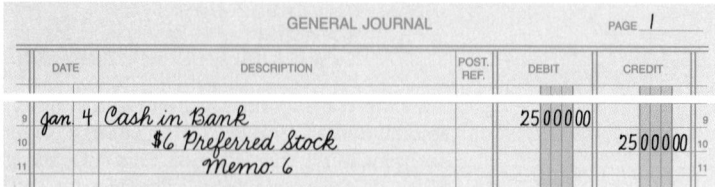

Figure 27-2   Journalizing the Sale of Common Stock at a Price in Excess of Par

ACCOUNTING *Notes*
Large issues of stock sold by a corporation to the public must have the approval of the Securities and Exchange Commission. This approval certifies that the sellers of the stock are not concealing information about the business from potential stock buyers.

R E M E M B E R

When common stock is issued by a corporation, the **Common Stock** account is credited for the par value of the stock. Any excess over par received for the sale of the stock is credited to the **Paid-in Capital in Excess of Par** account.

Issuing Preferred Stock

When preferred stock is issued, the Preferred Stock account is credited for the par value of the stock. Investors buy preferred stock to receive the stated dividend that it pays. Unlike common stock, preferred stock is almost always issued at its par value.

When the Sender Corporation was incorporated on January 2, it was also authorized to issue 1,000 shares of preferred stock with a par value of $100 and a stated dividend of $6. On January 4, the company had the following transaction.

January 4: *Issued 250 shares of $6 preferred stock, $100 par, at $100 per share, Memorandum 6.*

250 shares
× $100
$25,000

In this transaction, the Sender Corporation received $25,000 cash in return for the 250 shares of preferred stock. Whenever preferred stock is sold at par value, the amount to be credited to the $6 Preferred Stock account is determined by multiplying the number of shares issued by the par value of the stock.

In this transaction, therefore, Cash in Bank is debited for $25,000, the total amount of cash received. The $6 Preferred Stock account is credited for $25,000, the total par value of the shares issued. This transaction is shown in general journal form in Figure 27-3.

Figure 27-3   Journalizing the Sale of Preferred Stock at Par Value

592

UNIT 6   Accounting for Other Forms of Business Organization

Interdisciplinary Connections

ECONOMICS

In the twenty years from 1965 to 1985, the number of individuals who owned stock in corporations went from 20 million to 47 million—to about one person in four of the adult population. In 1985 stockholders were almost equally divided between women and men. Their median age was 44 years, down from 49 in 1965.

Before continuing, complete the following activity to check your understanding of the issuance of stock.

Check Your Learning

Write your answers to these questions on notebook paper.

1. What accounts are debited and credited when a corporation issues common stock at its par value?
2. What amount is used to determine the amount credited to the capital stock account?
3. Is Paid-in Capital in Excess of Par debited or credited when stock is sold above its par value?
4. The Gillis Corporation issued 1,500 shares of common stock, $5 par value, at $7.50. What accounts are debited and credited? For what amounts?

Compare your answers to those in the answers section. Re-read the preceding part of the chapter to find the correct answers to any questions you may have missed.

Distributing the Earnings of a Corporation

When the owner of a sole proprietorship or a partnership that has earned sufficient profits wishes to take money out of the business, a check is written on the business's checking account. The amount of the check is recorded in the owner's withdrawals account.

Owners (stockholders) of a publicly held corporation cannot withdraw cash whenever they want. Publicly held corporations distribute cash to stockholders in the form of dividends. **Dividends** are a return on the money invested by the stockholder. In other words, a corporation distributes a part of the corporation's retained earnings to its stockholders as a return on their investment. Most dividends are paid in cash and are expressed as a specific amount per share; for example, $1.25 per share. A person who owned 100 shares of stock would then receive $125.00 (100 shares × $1.25). Most publicly held corporations pay dividends on a quarterly basis.

Dividends may be declared, or authorized, only by the corporation's board of directors. Of course, before a cash dividend can be authorized, the corporation should have a sufficient amount of cash available to pay the dividend. In addition, since dividends decrease Retained Earnings, there must be an adequate balance in that account. Retained Earnings, remember, summarizes the net income earned and retained by the corporation.

Once a dividend has been declared, the board of directors must arrange to pay the dividends to stockholders on a certain date. There are three dates that are important in the dividend process.

CHAPTER 27   Accounting for Corporations   593

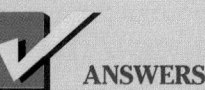
Chapter 27

ANSWERS

1. Cash in Bank is debited; Common Stock is credited.
2. Par value.
3. Credited.
4. Cash in Bank, $11,250 debit; Common Stock, $7,500 credit; Paid-in Capital in Excess of Par, $3,750 credit.

CONCEPT DEVELOPMENT
Distributing the Earnings of a Corporation

Have students look at the stock listings on the financial pages. Help them find the column indicating the dividends paid by each corporation. You may want to have students select three companies and then compare the stock price and dividends paid for each company. Ask students which stock is the best buy in terms of dividends paid. The price-earnings ratio is one that is commonly used to evaluate a corporation's financial performance.

Teaching Tips

■ Describe "return" as the income paid for using the money invested by the stockholders; it is similar to interest paid by a bank.
■ The corporation must have cash to pay any dividends declared.
■ Corporations sometimes declare property dividends or stock dividends.

Reteaching Strategies

Students sometimes confuse the buying and selling of stock on a public stock exchange with the buying and selling of stock by the corporation. The only time a corporation sells stock is when it is issued. Thereafter, any trading of the corporation's stock is handled by a stock exchange and does not affect the accounting records of the corporation. Thus, the equity of the corporation is not affected by sales of its stock on a stock exchange.

Teaching Tips

- Even in years when a profit does not exist, some corporations will pay dividends if there is adequate cash.
- Stockholders are the owners of a corporation and are entitled to a share of its profits, but dividends are not guaranteed. The size and frequency of dividends depend on the corporation's earnings, the amount of cash available, and the plans of the board of directors.
- The board of directors is under no legal obligation to declare dividends. A corporation must retain some of its assets for emergencies, for future distribution to stockholders as dividends in those years when earnings are not sufficient to pay normal dividends, and—most importantly— for use in expanding operations.

Using Visuals

 Use demonstration problem 27-2 to give students practice recording the transactions declaring and paying dividends.

1. *Date of declaration:* The date on which the board of directors declares, or votes to pay, a dividend. Once a dividend is declared, a liability is created for the amount of the total cash dividends to be paid.
2. *Date of record:* The date on which the ownership of shares is set. Persons who own stock on this date, called stockholders of record, are entitled to the dividend. The date of record is usually one or two weeks after the date of declaration.
3. *Date of payment:* The date on which the dividend is paid.

Journal entries must be recorded on the date of declaration and on the date of payment. No journal entry is required on the date of record. Let's look at the transactions involved when dividends were declared by the board of directors of the Sender Corporation during its second year of incorporation.

Preferred Stock Dividends

As mentioned earlier, preferred stockholders have certain preferences over common stockholders. The most common preference is the right to receive dividends before they are paid to common stockholders.

November 15: *The board of directors of the Sender Corporation declared an annual cash dividend on the 250 shares of $6 preferred stock issued, Memorandum 215. The dividend is payable to preferred stockholders of record as of November 29 with payment due on December 15.*

▲ **Date of Declaration**   When a dividend is declared, the total amount of the dividend is debited to an account entitled Dividends. The Dividends account is a temporary contra stockholders' equity account. It is used to summarize the dividends declared by the corporation during the fiscal period. At the end of the fiscal period, the total of the Dividends account is debited to (closed into) the Retained Earnings account. In this way, it is very similar to the sole proprietor's or partner's withdrawals account.

Dividends	
Dr.	Cr.
+	−
Increase Side	Decrease Side
Balance Side	

The amount of the dividend could be debited directly to the Retained Earnings account. Most corporations, however, prefer to use a separate account so that the dividend amounts can be easily determined.

If a corporation is authorized to issue two types of stock, a separate dividends account is set up for each type of stock. The Sender Corporation, therefore, has a Dividends—Preferred account and a Dividends—Common account.

The total amount of the preferred stock dividend declared by the Sender Corporation on November 15 is $1,500 (250 shares × $6 stated dividend). This amount is then debited to the Dividends—Preferred account. On November 15, a liability is created and the corporation has a legal obligation, or debt, to its preferred stockholders. As a result, the amount of the dividend is credited to a liability account entitled Dividends Payable— Preferred.

594

UNIT 6   Accounting for Other Forms of Business Organization

Making Connections

BUSINESS ETHICS

You are an accountant for Florence Industries. During the course of your work, you learn that the company is planning to buy a smaller company whose stock is traded on a local stock exchange. You are thinking about purchasing several thousand shares of the small-er company's stock, expecting to make a profit when the purchase goes through. Should you?

(Answer: No. Using information learned on the job to profit from buying or selling corporate securities is called insider trading and is illegal.)

The general journal entry for the November 15 transaction is shown in Figure 27-4.

		GENERAL JOURNAL		PAGE 35	
	DATE	DESCRIPTION	POST. REF.	DEBIT	CREDIT
1	19-- Nov. 15	Dividends—Preferred		1 500 00		1
2		Dividends Payable—Preferred			1 500 00	2
3		Memo. 215				3

Figure 27-4   Journalizing the Declaration of a Preferred Stock Cash Dividend

▲ **Date of Record**   On November 29, the corporation checks its records and prepares a list of preferred stockholders entitled to receive the dividend. No journal entry is required on this date.

▲ **Date of Payment**   On December 15, the Sender Corporation's accountant wrote one check for the total amount of the preferred stock dividend payable. This check was deposited in a special dividends checking account, from which separate checks made payable to each individual stockholder of record were drawn.

December 15: Issued Check 373 for $1,500.00 in payment of the preferred stock dividend declared November 15.

In this transaction, Dividends Payable—Preferred is debited for $1,500.00 since the liability is now being decreased. Cash in Bank is credited for $1,500.00, the total amount being paid out. This transaction is shown in general journal form in Figure 27-5.

		GENERAL JOURNAL		PAGE 39	
	DATE	DESCRIPTION	POST. REF.	DEBIT	CREDIT
1	19-- Dec. 15	Dividends Payable—Preferred		1 500 00		1
2		Cash in Bank			1 500 00	2
3		Check 373				3

Figure 27-5   Journalizing the Payment of a Preferred Stock Cash Dividend

The stated dividend rate for preferred stock is an *annual* rate. That is, the stated dividend indicates the dividend that will be paid to preferred stockholders per year. If the board of directors pays dividends annually, the preferred stockholders will receive the entire stated dividend at one time.

If the corporation pays dividends on a quarterly basis, for example, the stated dividend is paid to stockholders in four equal installments. For example, suppose that the Sender Corporation pays quarterly dividends on its $100 par $6 preferred stock. The quarterly dividend would be $1.50 ($6.00 ÷ 4). If the dividend were paid semiannually, the semiannual dividend would be $3.00 ($6.00 ÷ 2).

CHAPTER 27   Accounting for Corporations   595

Common Stock Dividends

Dividends are also paid to common stockholders.

November 15: *The board of directors declared a quarterly cash dividend on common stock of 50¢ per share (on 15,000 shares of common stock issued) to all stockholders of record as of December 1, payable on December 26 (Memorandum 215).*

▲ **Date of Declaration**   The total amount of the common stock dividend is $7,500.00 (15,000 shares × $0.50). This amount is debited to the Dividends—Common account. Another liability has been created by the declaration of the common stock dividend. The total amount of the dividend ($7,500.00) is credited to the liability account Dividends Payable—Common. The entry is shown in general journal form in Figure 27-6.

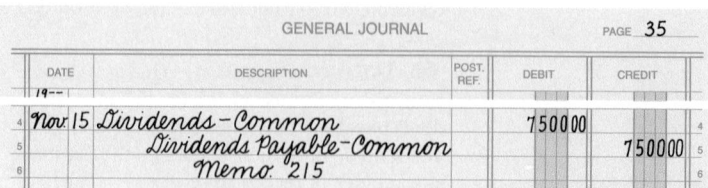

Figure 27-6   Journalizing the Declaration of a Common Stock Cash Dividend

▲ **Date of Record**   On December 1, the corporation checks its records and prepares a list of common stockholders entitled to receive the dividend. No journal entry is required on this date.

▲ **Date of Payment**   On December 26, the Sender Corporation's accountant wrote a check for the total amount of the common stock dividend payable. The check was deposited in the dividends checking account and a separate check was prepared for each common stockholder.

December 26: *Issued Check 389 for $7,500.00 in payment of the common stock dividend declared November 15.*

In this transaction, Dividends Payable—Common is debited for $7,500.00 since the liability is being decreased. Cash in Bank is credited for $7,500.00. This transaction is shown in general journal form in Figure 27-7.

	GENERAL JOURNAL			PAGE 39
DATE	DESCRIPTION	POST. REF.	DEBIT	CREDIT
19--				
17 Dec. 26	Dividends Payable—Common		7 500 00	
18	Cash in Bank			7 500 00
19	Check 389			

Figure 27-7   Journalizing the Payment of a Common Stock Cash Dividend

The total amount available for a common stock dividend may depend upon the amount paid to preferred stockholders. For example, suppose that on November 15, the board of directors of the Sender Corporation had declared a total cash dividend of $3,000. Preferred stockholders receive dividends before common stockholders, and they receive these dividends at a stated amount. The dividend for preferred stockholders, you'll remember, totaled $1,500 ($6 stated dividend × 250 shares). The amount available for dividends to common stockholders would then be only $1,500, or 10¢ per share.

Before going on, complete the following activity to check your understanding of the dividend process.

Check Your Learning

Record your answers to the following questions on notebook paper.

1. The date on which the board of directors votes to pay a dividend is called the date of ___?___ .
2. The date on which ownership of shares for dividend payment is set is called the date of ___?___ .
3. The date a dividend is paid is called the ___?___ date.
4. Journal entries for dividends are recorded on the date of ___?___ and the date of ___?___ .
5. The Engstrom Corporation has issued 2,500 shares of $5 preferred stock. If the board of directors declares an annual dividend on its preferred stock, what is the total amount of the cash dividend?

Compare your answers to those in the answers section. Re-read the preceding part of the chapter to find the answers to any questions you may have missed.

Financial Statements for the Corporation

The income statement of a publicly held corporation is similar to that prepared by a closely held corporation. As you remember, the federal income taxes paid by the corporation are reported separately on the income statement.

While publicly held corporations can prepare a statement of retained earnings, many corporations now prepare a statement of stockholders' equity. In this section, we'll examine the information reported on that statement and how it is prepared. We'll also see how stockholders' equity is reported on the corporation's balance sheet.

Statement of Stockholders' Equity

In Chapter 17, you learned how to prepare a statement of retained earnings for a closely held corporation. That statement reported the changes that had taken place in the Retained Earnings account during the period.

CHAPTER 27   Accounting for Corporations   597

ACCOUNTING PRACTICE
Students may complete Exercise 27-2 at this point.

ANSWERS
1. Declaration
2. Record
3. Payment
4. Declaration; payment
5. $12,500

CONCEPT DEVELOPMENT
Financial Statements for a Corporation
The financial statements for a publicly held corporation are similar to those students learned about in Chapter 17 for a privately held corporation. Discuss the new statement in this chapter, the statement of stockholders' equity, which reports all changes in equity accounts during the period.

Teaching Tips
■ Small corporations may be taxed on accumulated earnings if they never pay a dividend.
■ Collect several annual reports to share with students. Compare the financial statements in the reports.

Reteaching Strategies
When cash dividends are paid, the effect is a decrease in the Retained Earnings account and a decrease in the Cash in Bank account. Dividends are paid to give stockholders a return on their investments.
    For students who need additional practice recording stockholders' equity transactions, assign Problem 27A, page 645.

Today, most corporations use computers to maintain up-to-date lists of their stockholders.

The statement of retained earnings you prepared was very simple. It showed the beginning balance of Retained Earnings, the net income earned by the corporation for the period, and the ending balance of Retained Earnings.

Many corporations now prepare a statement of stockholders' equity rather than the statement of retained earnings. The **statement of stockholders' equity** reports the changes that have taken place in *all* of the stockholders' equity accounts during the fiscal period. Companies are increasingly using this statement because it reveals much more about the transactions affecting stockholders' equity during the period. The types of information reported on a statement of stockholders' equity include

1. The number of any shares of stock issued and the total amount received for those shares.
2. Net income for the period.
3. Any dividends declared during the period.

The statement of stockholders' equity prepared by the Sender Corporation at the end of its second year of incorporation appears in Figure 27-8. The information needed to prepare the statement is taken from the work sheet and from the general ledger accounts. Notice that the titles of the four stockholders' equity accounts appear at the top of the form. There is also a Total column at the far right. The first line shows the balance in the accounts at the beginning of the fiscal period. Transactions affecting the stockholders' equity accounts are then described in the wide column. The increase or decrease amounts are recorded in the individual account columns and in the total column. For example, the second line on the statement indicates that the company issued 5,000 shares of common stock during the period. The issuance of the 5,000 shares increased the balance of the Common Stock account by $50,000. Since the shares were issued at a price above par value, the Paid-in Capital in Excess of Par account was increased by $7,500.

Making Connections

AROUND THE WORLD

Investments in foreign businesses are not made just by other businesses. Individuals may also choose to invest in foreign companies. One means of investment is to purchase shares in an international stock fund. These funds are managed by large brokerage houses, which make all decisions about which stocks to purchase and sell. Several funds focus on stock shares for companies that are in "emerging markets," which are expected to be hot business areas in the future. Among the risks of investing in foreign markets are exchange rate changes that wipe out stock price increases or unstable governments that affect stock prices and earnings through economic disruption.

As you know, the net income earned by a corporation increases Retained Earnings. Any dividends declared by the corporation decrease Retained Earnings. Amounts that decrease account balances are enclosed in parentheses on the statement. Notice that the dividends declared on the preferred and common stock are listed separately. Also notice that the Retained Earnings column of the statement of stockholders' equity contains the same information that would be reported on a statement of retained earnings.

Teaching Tips

■ Remind students that when earnings are retained from profits, growth takes place through investment in assets. Without profits, there would be no growth and no technological improvements in our economy.

Sender Corporation
Statement of Stockholders' Equity
For the Year Ended December 31, 19--

	$100 Par $6 Preferred Stock	$10 Par Common Stock	Paid-in Capital in Excess of Par	Retained Earnings	Total
Balance, January 1, 19--	25 000 00	100 000 00	—	27 600 00	152 600 00
Issuance of 5,000 shares of common stock		50 000 00	7 500 00		57 500 00
Net Income				13 525 00	13 525 00
Cash Dividends:					
Preferred Stock				(1 500 00)	(1 500 00)
Common Stock				(7 500 00)	(7 500 00)
Balance, December 31, 19--	25 000 00	150 000 00	7 500 00	32 125 00	214 625 00

Figure 27-8 Statement of Stockholders' Equity

As with the statement of retained earnings, the balance calculated on the statement of stockholders' equity for Retained Earnings is used to prepare the corporation's balance sheet.

Using Visuals

Help students analyze the information in Figure 27-8. Explain why dividends decrease the Retained Earnings account.

Balance Sheet

The balance sheet of a publicly held corporation is similar to that for a closely held corporation.

The Dividends Payable accounts are reported in the liabilities section. Since the Sender Corporation paid the dividend liabilities before the end of the fiscal period, zero balances are reported for these accounts, as shown in Figure 27-9.

ACCOUNTING PRACTICE

Students may complete Exercise 27-3 after the section on the statement of stockholders' equity.

Sender Corporation
Balance Sheet
December 31, 19--

Liabilities		
Accounts Payable		14 562 10
Dividends Payable—Preferred		—
Dividends Payable—Common		—
Total Liabilities		27 016 00

Figure 27-9 Reporting the Balances of the Dividends Payable Accounts on the Balance Sheet

Using Visuals

Call students' attention to the partial balance sheet in Figure 27-9. Remind students that the asset section of the balance sheet is the same as that for a closely held corporation.

CHAPTER 27 Accounting for Corporations   599

Making Connections

COMMUNICATIONS

Corporations must often communicate financial information to their stockholders in language that non-experts can understand. The accountant should try to develop a writing style that is coherent, concise, and clear in order to prepare annual reports and other corporate communications. Ask students to prepare a brief memo summarizing the results of the statement of stockholders' equity prepared in either Problem 27-4 or Problem 27-5.

COMPUTERS IN ACCOUNTING

America Online is an online network service that features a variety of platforms including News, Stock Quotes, and Portfolio Management. Once you log on to the network, you can obtain current market information about each of the major stock exchanges as well as market indexes such as Dow-Jones averages. You can get 15-minute delayed stock quotes, and you can send and receive messages to and from your broker. You can also buy or sell stocks and even maintain a personal portfolio that will provide a record of your transactions. Other similar networks provide comparable services.

Using Visuals

Walk students through the balance sheet entries in Figure 27-10. Remind students that the stockholders' equity consists of two types: capital paid to the corporation to purchase stock and earnings retained by the corporation from revenue.

Using Visuals

Use demonstration problem 27-4 to show students how to prepare the stockholders' equity section of a balance sheet.

ACCOUNTING PRACTICE

Students may complete Exercise 27-4 at this point.

ACCOUNTING *Notes*

Even though corporations are fewer in number than sole proprietorships and partnerships, they contribute much more to the U.S. economy in monetary terms. For example, in 1986, General Motors generated more revenues than all but thirteen of the world's countries.

The stockholders' equity section of the balance sheet of a publicly held corporation is more detailed than that of a closely held corporation. As you can see in Figure 27-10, each capital stock account is listed separately under the heading "Paid-in Capital." Each listing describes the par value, the number of shares authorized, and the number of shares issued. Preferred stock is always listed before common stock. Notice also that the Dividends accounts are *not* listed in the stockholders' equity section. The Dividends accounts, remember, are closed into Retained Earnings at the end of the fiscal period. The balance of Retained Earnings shown on the balance sheet reflects the dividends declared during the period.

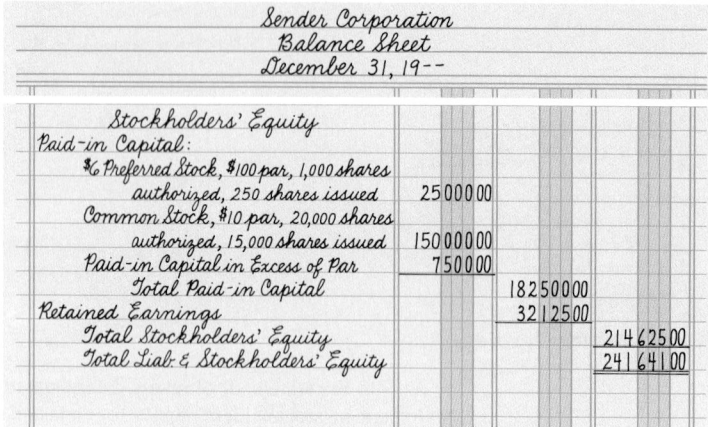

Figure 27-10 The Stockholders' Equity Section of the Balance Sheet

R E M E M B E R

The total value of all stockholders' equity is reported on the balance sheet. This total includes the total paid-in capital — the balances of $6 Preferred Stock, Common Stock, and Paid-in Capital in Excess of Par — and the balance of the Retained Earnings account.

Summary of Key Points

1. A closely held corporation is one that is owned by a few persons or by a family. A publicly held corporation is one whose stock is widely held, has a wide market, and is usually traded on a stock exchange.
2. A corporation must have permission from the state to operate, is considered to be a separate legal entity, is owned by its stockholders, and is usually run by professional managers.
3. Two types of stock a corporation may issue are common and preferred.
4. The par value of stock is the dollar amount or value assigned to each share of stock. Par value is used to determine the amount credited to the capital stock account when stock is issued.

600   UNIT 6   Accounting for Other Forms of Business Organization

---

3 CLOSE

CHAPTER SUMMARY

This summary enumerates the key information in the chapter. It is a useful tool for reinforcement and review.

Pop Quiz

1. A _____ is responsible for the affairs of the corporation.
2. If a corporation issues only one class of capital stock, it is called _____.
3. Why is the Paid-in Capital in Excess of Par account used?
4. A corporation distributes part of its earnings to its stockholders by paying _____.
5. A report that shows the changes in all of the stockholders' equity accounts during the fiscal period is a _____.

ANSWERS

1. Board of directors.
2. Common stock.
3. If stock sells above par, the account is used to record the amount over par.
4. Dividends.
5. Statement of stockholders' equity.

5. Common stockholders have the right to vote and elect the board of directors of the corporation, to share in the earnings of the corporation, and to share in the assets of the corporation should it cease operations.

6. Preferred stockholders do not have the right to vote but are entitled to receive dividends before the common stockholders.

7. If stock is issued at a price higher than its par value, the amount received over par is credited to an account called Paid-in Capital in Excess of Par.

8. Corporations distribute a part of their earnings to stockholders in the form of dividends.

9. The total amount of a cash dividend is debited to the Dividends account. Dividends is a temporary contra stockholders' equity account. At the end of the fiscal period, the balance of the Dividends account is debited to (closed into) Retained Earnings. A separate Dividends account is set up for each type of stock.

10. Corporations may prepare a statement of stockholders' equity, which reports the changes that have occurred in all of the stockholders' equity accounts during the fiscal period.

PRACTICE AND APPLY

- Language Development
- Comprehension and Retention
- Basic Skills

Building Your Accounting Vocabulary

See the Glossary on pages 670-679 for definitions of these terms.

Reviewing Your Accounting Knowledge

1. A closely held corporation does not sell stock on a public exchange and is usually owned by a small number of people. The stock of a publicly held corporation is traded on a stock exchange and is usually owned by hundreds or thousands of investors.

2. A corporation must get legal permission to operate, is considered a separate legal entity, is owned by its stockholders, is managed by professionals, and is more costly to organize.

3. Advantages: limited liability of stockholders, stock may be sold without disrupting activities of the business or requiring approval of other owners, continuous existence of the corporation. Disadvantages: closer regulation by state and federal agencies, disclosure of operations to the public, double taxation of corporate earnings.

4. The right to vote and elect the board of directors, the right to share in the earnings of the corporation, and the right to share in the assets of the corporation should it liquidate.

5. Common stock entitles its owners to attend stockholders' meetings and vote for members of the board of directors. Owners of preferred stock do not vote but have the right to receive dividends before common stockholders.

6. The total par value of shares sold.

7. Stockholders' equity account; it has a normal credit balance.

8. (a) The date of declaration, which is the date on which the hoard of directors votes to pay a dividend; (b) the date of record, which is the date on which the ownership of shares is set, and (c) the date of actual payment of the dividend.

9. A temporary contra stockholders' equity account; it has a normal debit balance.

10. Dividends account is debited and Dividends Payable is credited.

11. On the date of declaration. Once the board of directors votes to pay a dividend, it has an obligation to its stockholders to pay that dividend.

12. The issuance of stock (at par and above par), the net income, and the amount of any dividends declared.

Review and Applications

Building Your Accounting Vocabulary

In your own words, write the definition of each of the following accounting terms. Use complete sentences for your definitions.

authorized capital stock
board of directors
closely held corporation
common stock
dividend
paid-in capital in excess of par
par value
preferred stock
proxy
publicly held corporation
statement of stockholders' equity

Reviewing Your Accounting Knowledge

1. What is the difference between a closely held corporation and a publicly held corporation?
2. Name five characteristics of a corporation.
3. List three advantages and three disadvantages of the corporate form of business organization.
4. What are some of the rights of common stockholders?
5. What are the differences between common and preferred stock?
6. When stock is sold at a price above its par value, what amount is credited to the capital stock account?
7. What is the classification of the Paid-in Capital in Excess of Par account? What is its normal balance?
8. Name and explain the three dates important to the dividend process.
9. What type of account is Dividends?
10. When a dividend is declared, what accounts are debited and credited?
11. At what date does a dividend become a liability to the corporation? Explain.
12. What type of information is reported on the statement of stockholders' equity?

Improving Your Communications Skills

Using simple, concise wording will make your messages easier to read and understand. There are many wordy expressions that can be replaced with one or two simple words. For example, the wordy expression "in the event that" can be replaced with the word "if."

Change each of the following wordy expressions to make them more concise. Refer to a dictionary if necessary.

1. at the present time
2. in a satisfactory manner
3. bring to a conclusion
4. make an effort
5. due to the fact that
6. it would appear that
7. in the amount of
8. herewith enclosed please find
9. in view of the fact that

602

Improving Your Communications Skills
1. now
2. satisfactorily
3. end, conclude
4. try
5. because, since
6. it seems
7. for
8. enclosed is
9. in view of, since

Applying Accounting Procedures

Exercise 27-1 Examining Capital Stock Transactions

The Dublin Corporation was organized and authorized to issue 10,000 shares of $100 par, 8% preferred stock and 500,000 shares of $10 par common stock. The transactions illustrated in the following T accounts took place during the first month of operations.

Instructions: Describe each transaction.

Cash in Bank				8% Preferred Stock	
Dr.	**Cr.**			**Dr.**	**Cr.**
+	−			−	+
(1) $300,000					(2) $200,000
(2) 200,000					
(3) 700,000					

Common Stock				Paid-in Capital in Excess of Par	
Dr.	**Cr.**			**Dr.**	**Cr.**
--	+			−	+
	(1) $300,000				(3) $200,000
	(3) 500,000				

Exercise 27-2 Distributing Corporate Earnings

During its first year of operations, the Long-Horn Corporation issued 17,500 shares of $10 par common stock. At the end of the fiscal period, the corporation had a net income of $350,000. The board of directors declared a cash dividend of $5 per share.

Instructions: Answer the following questions.

(1) How much of the net income earned for the year was paid out to the stockholders?

(2) How much of the net income was retained by the corporation?

Exercise 27-3 Examining the Statement of Stockholders' Equity

The following transactions took place during the fiscal period of Victor Jewelry Corporation.

Instructions: Use the form provided in the working papers to indicate which of the transactions would be reported on the statement of stockholders' equity.

Transactions:

1. Paid accounts payable of $50,000.
2. Issued 2,000 shares of $10 par common stock, receiving $15 per share.
3. The board of directors declared a cash dividend of $12,000 for all common stockholders.
4. Bought equipment on account at a total cost of $125,000.
5. Paid the cash dividend declared in Transaction #3.
6. Issued 500 shares of $100 par, $7 preferred stock.
7. Paid the federal income tax installment of $5,000.
8. Earned a net income of $150,000 for the fiscal period.

603

PRACTICE AND APPLY

• Concepts and Procedures

Exercise 27-1: Ch. Obj. 2

Exercise 27-2: Ch. Obj. 3

Net income paid out:
$87,500 (25%)
Net income retained:
$262,500 (75%)

Exercise 27-3: Ch. Obj. 4

1. No
2. Yes
3. Yes
4. No
5. No
6. Yes
7. No
8. Yes

Additional Reinforcement

Students who need additional practice or individualized help will benefit from the *Glencoe Accounting Electronic Study Guide* or the *Glencoe Accounting* on-line multimedia program, which provide reinforcement and reteaching for vocabulary, concepts, and procedures.

Refer students to the Chapter 27 review pages in the workbook, *Chapter Reviews and Working Papers.*

Exercise 27-4: Ch. Obj. 2
Preferred stock, 900 shares
Common stock, 15,000 shares
Stockholders' equity, $335,000

Problem 27-1: Ch. Obj. 2

Problem 27-2: Ch. Obj. 3
Oct. 15 dividend amount, $44,800
Nov. 5 dividend amount, $43,750
Retained Earnings, $215,464

Exercise 27-4   Determining Stockholders' Equity

The balance sheet of the Speedy Transport Company, Inc., included the following amounts.

$6 Preferred Stock, $100 Par	$ 90,000
Common Stock, $10 Par	150,000
Paid-in Capital in Excess of Par	40,000
Retained Earnings	55,000

Instructions: Answer the following questions.

(1) How many shares of $6 preferred stock have been issued by Speedy Transport Company, Inc.?

(2) How many shares of common stock have been issued?

(3) What is the total stockholders' equity?

Problem 27-1   Journalizing the Issue of Stock

On June 1, the Hadley Corporation was incorporated and authorized to issue 1,000 shares of $100 par, 9% preferred stock and 10,000 shares of $25 par common stock.

Instructions: Record the following transactions on page 1 of the general journal.

Transactions:

June 1 Issued 200 shares of 9% preferred stock at $100 per share, Memorandum 3.

2 Issued 3,000 shares of common stock at $25 per share, Memorandum 7.

6 Received $31 per share for 2,000 shares of common stock issued, Memorandum 10.

7 Issued 50 shares of 9% preferred stock at par, Memorandum 11.

Problem 27-2   Journalizing Common and Preferred Stock Dividend Transactions

The Maple Corporation has issued 8,000 shares of $80 par, 7% preferred stock and 35,000 shares of $25 par common stock.

Instructions:

(1) Record the following transactions on general journal page 14.

(2) Post the transactions to the general ledger accounts provided in the working papers.

Transactions:

Oct. 15 The board of directors declared an annual cash dividend on the 7% preferred stock, payable on December 1, Memorandum 407.

Nov. 5 Declared an annual cash dividend of $1.25 on 35,000 shares of common stock, payable on December 17, Memorandum 415.

Dec. 1 Paid the preferred stock cash dividend declared on October 15, Check 1163.

17 Paid the common stock dividend declared on November 5, Check 1201.

31 Closed Income Summary into Retained Earnings for the amount of the net income of $135,000.

31 Closed the two Dividends accounts into Retained Earnings.

604

Teacher Notes

_____

_____

_____

_____

SPREADSHEET

PROBLEM

Problem 27-3   Journalizing Stockholders' Equity Transactions

The Walters Clothing Company, Inc., has issued 10,000 shares of $100 par, 9% preferred stock and 100,000 shares of $20 par common stock.

Instructions: Record the following selected transactions on general journal page 27.

Transactions:

Mar. 1 Declared the semiannual cash dividend on the preferred stock issued, payable April 15, Memorandum 1064.

1 Declared a semiannual cash dividend of $2 per share on the common stock issued, payable April 15, Memorandum 1065.

Apr. 15 Paid the preferred stock cash dividend, Check 3614.

15 Paid the common stock cash dividend, Check 3615.

May 12 Issued 1,000 shares of preferred stock at $100 per share, Memorandum 1203.

Aug. 1 Issued 25,000 shares of common stock at $22.50 per share, Memorandum 1369.

Sept. 1 Declared the semiannual cash dividend on the preferred stock issued, payable October 1, Memorandum 1568.

1 Declared a semiannual cash dividend of $1 per share on the common stock issued, payable October 15, Memorandum 1569.

Dec. 31 Closed the net income for the period of $767,400 from Income Summary into Retained Earnings.

31 Closed the two Dividends accounts into Retained Earnings.

Problem 27-4   Preparing a Statement of Stockholders' Equity

The following balances appeared in the general ledger accounts of Walters Clothing Company, Inc., on January 1, the beginning of the fiscal period.

9% Preferred Stock ($100 par)	$1,000,000
Common Stock ($20 par)	2,000,000
Paid-in Capital in Excess of Par	87,500
Retained Earnings	1,155,000
Dividends—Preferred	0
Dividends—Common	0

Instructions: Use the above information and the transactions from Problem 27-3 to prepare a statement of stockholders' equity for Walters Clothing Company, Inc.

COMPUTER

PROBLEM

Problem 27-5   Preparing Corporate Financial Statements

The Silverplate Corporation is authorized to issue 10,000 shares of $100 par, 9% preferred stock and 500,000 shares of $5 par common stock. The balances on page 606 appeared in the Balance Sheet section of the company's work sheet for the year ended December 31.

Instructions:

(1) Prepare the statement of stockholders' equity.

(a) During the period, the corporation issued 500 shares of 9% preferred stock at par and 25,000 shares of common stock at $9.

(b) The net income for the fiscal period was $425,000.

(2) Prepare the balance sheet.

605

Problem 27-3: Ch. Obj. 2, 3

SPREADSHEET

PROBLEM

Problem 27-3 can be completed using *Spreadsheet Applications,* the spreadsheet software that accompanies *Glencoe Accounting.*

Total preferred dividend Mar. 1, $45,000
Total common dividend Mar. 1, $200,000
9% Preferred Stock, $100,000
Common Stock, $500,000
Paid-in Capital in Excess of Par, $62,500
Total preferred dividend Sept. 1, $49,500
Total common dividend Sept. 1, $125,000

Problem 27-4: Ch. Obj. 4

Totals:
Preferred Stock, $1,100,000
Common Stock, $2,500,000
Paid-in Capital, $150,000
Retained Earnings, $1,502,900

Problem 27-5: Ch. Obj. 4

COMPUTER

PROBLEM

This computer image identifies a problem that students may complete using the *Glencoe Accounting, General Ledger* software.

Totals:
Preferred Stock, $500,000
Common Stock, $750,000
Paid-in Capital, $300,000
Retained Earnings, $852,500

Balance sheet totals, $2,661,912

CHALLENGE The last problem
in each chapter is
a challenge prob-
lem and is identi-
PROBLEM fied by this
"maze" symbol.

Preferred dividend Mar. 15, $6,000
Common dividend Mar. 15,
$56,250
Preferred dividend Sept. 1, $8,000
Common dividend Sept. 1,
$71,250

Total Stockholders' Equity,
$1,144,540

4 ASSESS

A chapter test is available for use in
assessing students' understanding of
concepts in this chapter.
    The testmaker software will en-
able you to develop tailor-made
chapter, unit, semester, and final
tests.

Alternative Assessment

For alternative assessment strategies,
refer to *Tech Prep Strategies in
Accounting*.

Accounts Payable	$ 62,412
Accounts Receivable (net)	150,680
Building (net)	639,298
Cash in Bank	406,010
Common Stock	750,000
Dividends — Common	262,500
Dividends — Preferred	45,000
Dividends Payable — Common	150,000
Dividends Payable — Preferred	22,500
Equipment (net)	363,009
Federal Income Tax Payable	20,000
Land	772,500
Merchandise Inventory	316,315
Paid-in Capital in Excess of Par	300,000
9% Preferred Stock	500,000
Prepaid Insurance	3,600
Retained Earnings	735,000
Sales Tax Payable	4,500
Supplies	10,500

CHALLENGE **Problem 27-6   Recording Stockholders' Equity Transactions**

Fitness for Health, Inc., is authorized to issue 100,000 shares of $5 par
common stock and 5,000 shares of $100 par, 8% preferred stock. On Janu-
ary 1, the beginning of the fiscal period, the stockholders' equity accounts
PROBLEM had the following balances:

8% Preferred Stock	$150,000
Paid-in Capital in Excess of Par — Preferred	11,250
Common Stock	225,000
Paid-in Capital in Excess of Par — Common	112,500
Retained Earnings	366,800
Dividends — Preferred	0
Dividends — Common	0

Instructions:

(1) Record the following transactions on general journal page 42.

(2) Prepare the stockholders' equity section of the balance sheet.

Transactions:

Mar. 15   The board of directors approved a semiannual cash dividend of
$62,250 for preferred and common stockholders. The dividend is
payable to stockholders of record as of April 15 with payment on
May 1, Memorandum 635.

Apr. 19   Issued 500 shares of preferred stock at $108, Memorandum 651.

May 1   Paid the dividend declared on March 15, Check 2956.

Aug. 10   Issued 12,000 shares of common stock in exchange for land valued
at $15,000 and a building valued at $55,000, Memorandum 793.

Sept. 1   The board of directors approved a semiannual cash dividend of
$79,250 for preferred and common stockholders. The dividend is
payable to stockholders of record as of October 1 with payment
on November 1, Memorandum 828.

Nov. 1   Paid the dividend declared on September 1, Check 4837.

Dec. 31   Closed Income Summary into Retained Earnings in the amount of
the net income of $296,490.

    31   Closed the Dividends accounts into Retained Earnings.

606

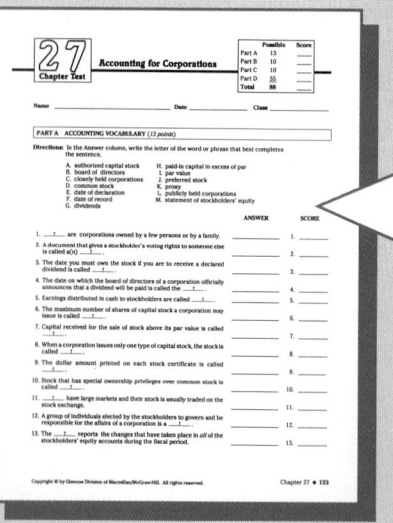

Use Chapter Test 27 here to assess students' understanding and retention of
the concepts and procedures presented
in the chapter.

*T*elecommunications

No need for you to worry about mail or messages being misplaced or delayed or sent to the wrong address. Thanks to *electronic mail systems*.

• Letters, memos, and reports can be sent in a fraction of the time mail or messenger services take.

• A salesperson can send the day's orders to the home office to be processed the next day.

• You can post or read messages on a computer bulletin board.

No need to spend hours at the card catalog and library stacks. Thanks to *information utilities*,

• A researcher can search vast databases for the specific information needed.

• An investor can get instant access to financial and stock information.

• A writer can search months of news stories for articles on a specific topic.

Forget overnight delivery. Thanks to *facsimile transmission* (FAX), exact duplicates of documents can be sent across the country as fast as you can telephone your mother.

And that's just how it's done. Using telephone lines, computers can "talk" to computers. To accomplish this marvel, all communicators need are

• Access to the telephone system.

• A computer (screen, keyboard, disk drives) to process information.

• Two modems (short for *modulator-demodulator*) to convert the computer's digital signals into audio signals that can be sent over telephone lines and then converted back into digital signals on the receiving end.

• Communications software—either written by the user or, in most cases, commercially prepared—that enables the computer, the modem, and the telephone to work together smoothly.

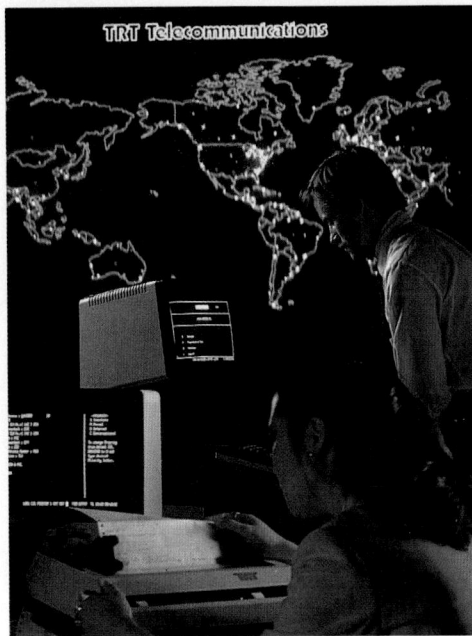

"Telecomputing" refers to sending data from one computer to another via telephone lines.

• A printer to produce "hard copy" if the receiver wishes.

Computer communications is playing an increasingly important role not only in businesses but also in schools, hospitals, libraries, and homes. More and more people are using computers to obtain information and to send it. You might say that they're "letting their fingers do the talking."

607

Students are no doubt familiar with cellular phones. Suggest that students visit a cellular phone store, talk with someone in the business, or read several media stories to determine the status of the industry. Is the market growing? What is happening to prices? Who uses cellular phones the most? Is the business profitable? Have students report their findings in class.

QUESTIONS

1. Discuss the advantages and disadvantages of electronic mail systems (E-mail).
2. What is voice processing?

ANSWERS

1. Advantages: They reduce paper usage, eliminate "telephone tag," and save time. Disadvantages: They require an ability to use computers, they are not confidential, and letters may still do a better job of communicating longer messages.
2. Voice processing permits the use of spoken language when sending or receiving information from a computer. Students may remember receiving a call (sales pitch) in which a computer was delivering the message. They may also have talked to a computer when ordering merchandise by phone.

Chapter **28**

ANALYZING AND INTERPRETING FINANCIAL STATEMENTS

LOOKING BACK

In all other chapters of the textbook, students have learned how to record and report financial information. They have also learned how to keep accounting records for different types of businesses: sole proprietorships, partnerships, and closely held and publicly held corporations. In this chapter students will learn one of the primary uses of financial information, which is the analysis of accounting data for business decision making.

VOCABULARY DEVELOPMENT

Discuss the definitions of the new terms in class. Ask students to give their definitions of each term, and then explain how each is used in accounting. Definitions of these terms are found in the chapter and in the glossary on pages 670-679.

Electronic Field Trips

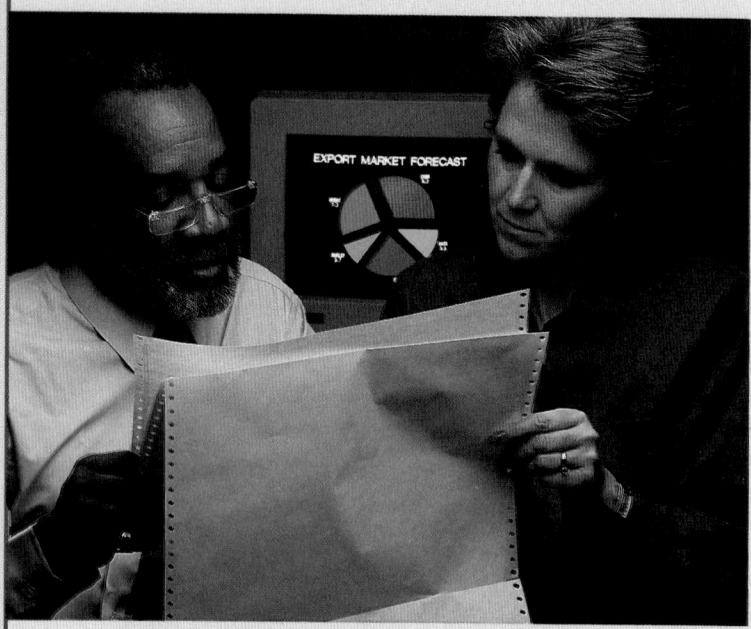

In preceding chapters, you learned about the development of an accounting system and how to prepare the system's end product: financial statements. Financial statements are issued to provide information about an organization to aid users in making decisions about that organization.

In this chapter, you will learn about the methods used to analyze and interpret financial statements. During statement analysis, relationships between dollar amounts may be discovered and used to make more fully informed decisions.

New Terms

relevance
reliability
comparability
full disclosure
materiality
investments
current liabilities
long-term liabilities
selling expenses
administrative expenses
horizontal analysis
base year
vertical analysis
working capital
ratio analysis
liquidity ratio
current ratio
quick ratio
profitability ratios

Learning Objectives

When you have completed Chapter 28, you should be able to do the following:

1. List the qualitative characteristics and general accounting guidelines for accounting information.
2. Prepare a classified balance sheet and income statement.
3. Prepare horizontal and vertical analyses of financial statements.
4. Calculate commonly used liquidity and profitability ratios.
5. Use liquidity and profitability ratios to analyze a business's performance.
6. Define the accounting terms introduced in this chapter.

608

Teaching Resources

- Lesson Plans
- TE/Chapter Reviews & Working Papers
- Demonstration Problems
- Student Study Plans
- Teaching Transparencies
- Solutions Transparencies
- Electronic Field Trips Video, Level I
- Electronic Study Guide
- Chapter 28 Test
- Unit 6 Objective Test for Chapters 26-28
- Unit 6 Problem Test for Chapters 26-28

Other Resources

- Skills Improvement Activities
- Blackline Masters
- Careers in Accounting
- Dictionary
- Math Review for Accounting
- Tech Prep Strategies in Accounting
- Video
- Test Bank with Software
- Spanish Resources/Audiotapes
- Spanish Electronic Study Guide

Evaluating Financial Statements

The financial statements issued by a business are used by many different people to evaluate the business's financial performance. The managers of a business analyze its financial statements to help them evaluate past performance and make more informed predictions and decisions that will affect the future operations of the business. Investors (owners), creditors, and unions are also interested in the financial performance of a business. Investors and creditors want to protect their equity. Unions want to obtain fair wages for the efforts of the business's employees.

If accounting information is to be useful, it must be understandable. Qualitative characteristics and other general accounting guidelines help accountants make the financial information more understandable.

Qualitative Characteristics

In accounting, *qualitative characteristics* are those characteristics that make information provided by accountants more trustworthy and useful. Three of these characteristics are relevance, reliability, and comparability.

▲ **Relevance** In accounting, **relevance** means that the information "makes a difference" to a user in reaching a decision about a business. Investors, creditors, and other users of a business's financial information need relevant information to make informed decisions. Not all information is relevant.

> *EXAMPLE: On January 30, a business reported that its sales for the preceding year were $500,000, which was an increase of 14% over sales two years ago. This information is relevant because it is useful in evaluating previous net income and in predicting future sales.*

▲ **Reliability** Users of accounting data must be able to assume that the data is reliable. **Reliability** relates to the confidence users have in the financial information. In other words, people who are making decisions based on financial data want to know that the information is free of mistakes and biased opinions of what should or should not be reported. Reliable information is based on facts, not hopes for the future.

> *EXAMPLE: A business reported a net income of $150,000 after taxes. This information is reliable because the management of the business, the accountant, and the auditor (a person who checks all of the business's accounting records) are required to agree on the amount of the company's net income before it can be publicly reported.*

▲ **Comparability** **Comparability** refers to accounting information that can be compared from one fiscal period to another or from one business to another. For example, an investor may want to compare the net income made by two similar businesses to determine which business is the better investment. Accounting reports are based on certain rules so that

CHAPTER 28 Analyzing and Interpreting Financial Statements **609**

---

1 FOCUS

MAJOR CONCEPTS
- Evaluating Financial Statements
- Classified Financial Statements
- The Analysis of Financial Statements
- Horizontal Analysis
- Vertical Analysis
- Working Capital
- Ratio Analysis

BUSINESS CONNECTION

Smart investment decisions are made with careful, intelligent analysis of a corporation's financial statements. One type of analysis is to calculate a profitability ratio to measure the return on stockholders' equity. Southwestern Bell Corporation provides telephone, cellular, cable TV, and advertising services to customers worldwide. In 1991 and 1992 Southwestern Bell Corporation's total return on stockholder's equity was 19 percent.

2 TEACH

CONCEPT DEVELOPMENT
Evaluating Financial Statements

Discuss the qualitative characteristics and guidelines accountants follow when preparing financial statements. Relate each of the qualitative characteristics to something students will understand. For example, ask students what information is relevant when reporting the outcome of a sports event.

(Continued)

Reinforcing Study Skills

Taking tests successfully is more than a question of reviewing the textbook and notes. Studying for an accounting test should be spread out, not concentrated in one night of "cramming." During a test, students should remember to pay careful attention to test instructions (both oral and written) and to pace themselves for the allotted time.

The Glencoe *Contest Review Booklet* can be used to review good test-taking techniques as well as sample test questions.

Provide a copy of the *Student Study Plans* to each class member to help organize study activities or to individualize practice and review activities.

Teaching Tips
- Reliable information is neutral, verifiable, and complete.
- When discussing comparability, ask students whether they could tell which school has the best team if game scores were reported using different rules for each school.

Evaluating Financial Statements (Continued)

Also review some of the other basic accounting concepts students have learned in previous chapters of the book: business entity, going concern, unit of measure, time period (all in Chapter 1), revenue principle, matching principle, guideline of conservatism.

Using Visuals

A teaching transparency showing the flow of data through an accounting system to the production of financial reports is available in the transparency binder accompanying Glencoe Accounting

---

Teaching Tips

■ Full disclosure requires reports to be complete enough not to mislead a reader.
■ Materiality is not just a matter of size. A decision regarding materiality requires judgment and experience.

CONCEPT DEVELOPMENT

Classified Financial Statements

Financial statements that are classified are easier to analyze than those that are not classified. You may want to bring into class examples of several annual reports to show students how published financial statements are classified.

---

users can make intelligent comparisons. In other words, users need to know that they are comparing apples to apples and not apples to potatoes.

> **EXAMPLE:** *A business reported that its after-tax net income was $300,000 in one year and $275,000 in the previous year. Since both amounts are reported on an after-tax basis, they are comparable.*

General Accounting Guidelines

Accounting is the "common language" of business. Accountants want to ensure that users understand that language by making sure financial reports are clear and consistent. To do this, accountants follow certain general guidelines. Two of these guidelines are full disclosure and materiality.

▲ **Full Disclosure**   "To disclose" means "to uncover or to make known." The guideline of **full disclosure** requires that anyone preparing a financial report include enough information so that the report is complete. Relevant information left out of a report or half truths are not acceptable. Information in the report must not lead the reader to wrong conclusions.

> **EXAMPLE:** *At the end of its report, a business included a footnote about a lawsuit it was involved in. It also stated that the case had not been settled and no financial claim had yet been made against the company. This note prepares readers for a possible financial claim the company may have to pay. The report would not meet the requirement of full disclosure if it had failed to mention the lawsuit and the possible claim.*

▲ **Materiality**   If something is "material," it carries weight. The guideline of **materiality** states that relatively important data are included in financial reports. Important data are material; unimportant data are immaterial. Accounting workers deal with many different kinds of financial transactions involving small dollar amounts. Such transactions are of little concern except to recordkeepers. When preparing financial reports—as opposed to keeping records—information is material if it is likely to influence the conclusions or decisions made by a user of the report.

> **EXAMPLE:** *In an annual report of a business reporting net income of $10 million a year, the understatement of profit by $5,000 may be immaterial. The same $5,000 understatement by a business reporting a net income of $20,000 would be material.*

Classified Financial Statements

The analysis of financial statements is made easier when the information reported is separated into related categories, or classifications.

Classifying the Balance Sheet

You have learned that there are three major categories of accounts reported on the balance sheet: assets, liabilities, and owner's equity. Information related to these accounts becomes more useful when assets and

610

Making Connections

EVERYDAY LIFE

Obtain several copies of financial reports for corporations that students know by name. Ask students to choose an annual report and to calculate a current ratio and a quick ratio using the information reported in the balance sheet.

liabilities are classified into groups. For example, assets may be classified as current assets; investments; property, plant, and equipment; and other assets. Liabilities are classified as current liabilities or long-term liabilities.

An example of a classified balance sheet is shown in Figure 28-1 on page 612. Refer to this illustration as you read the paragraphs that follow.

▲ **Current Assets**   Current assets are cash or other assets intended to be converted to cash, sold, or consumed generally within the next accounting period. Accounts such as Cash in Bank, Accounts Receivable, and Merchandise Inventory are classified as current assets. These assets are reported on the balance sheet in their order of liquidity. That is, the most liquid asset is reported first; the next most liquid asset, second; and so on.

▲ **Investments**   **Investments** are assets, generally long term in nature, that are not intended to be converted to cash or to be used in the normal operations of the business within the next accounting period. Examples of investments include land held for some future purpose of the business, stocks of other companies, and bonds of government agencies or other businesses. Companies often purchase such assets expecting to earn a return on their investment.

▲ **Property, Plant, and Equipment**   Property, plant, and equipment are the long-lived physical assets used in the normal operations of the business. These long-lived assets are used in the production and sale of goods, the performance of services, and other requirements of the business. Plant and equipment are referred to as plant assets. You were first introduced to plant assets in Chapter 22 when you learned about the depreciation of plant and equipment assets.

▲ **Other Assets**   Other assets are any assets that do not fit within any of the preceding categories. Examples of other assets are deposits for utilities and the book value of trademarks, copyrights, and patents.

▲ **Current Liabilities**   **Current liabilities** are debts of the business that must be paid within the next accounting period. Examples of current liabilities are notes payable due within the upcoming accounting period, amounts owed to creditors, and federal income taxes payable.

▲ **Long-Term Liabilities**   **Long-term liabilities** are debts that are not required to be paid within the next accounting period. Examples of long-term liabilities include mortgages and notes payable that have maturity dates longer than one year.

▲ **Stockholders' Equity**   Capital invested or contributed by stockholders of the corporation includes amounts reported in the capital stock and paid-in capital accounts. Equity earned and retained by the corporation is reported as retained earnings. These accounts are classified on the balance sheet as stockholders' equity.

CHAPTER 28   Analyzing and Interpreting Financial Statements   **611**

Teaching Tips

■ Intangible assets, such as organization costs and goodwill, are not discussed in this textbook.

■ The concept of "normal operating cycle" may be used rather than "next accounting period." A normal operating cycle for some businesses may be longer than a year.

■ "Marketable Securities" may be used for short-term investments, since excess cash is usually invested in marketable securities.

■ The test of a current liability is: If the liability is due within the next accounting period, it is classified as a current liability.

Critical Thinking

A small business that has sales of $500,000 a year purchased some office equipment for $10,000 with an estimated life of five years. Rather than recording the copier as an asset and depreciating its cost over its useful life, the business recorded the purchase as an expense. Have general accounting guidelines been violated?

(Answer: Yes, because a purchase of $10,000 is a significant amount of money for a business with revenues of $500,000, and this data is material.)

Using Visuals

Point out the classifications of assets and liabilities in Figure 28-1. You may want to give students other, unclassified balance sheets and have them classify the accounts.

ACCOUNTING ISSUES

A recent survey of U.S. corporate controllers found that drug testing is largely aimed at new hires. Half of the companies surveyed reported that they screen new job applicants for substance abuse. Only 18 percent of the companies test both applicants and current employees. The companies testing job applicants reported the following results.

Company Responses	Test Results
73%	5% positive
14%	10% positive
3%	15% positive
10%	2% positive

Fitness Forever, Inc.
Balance Sheet
December 31, 1993

Assets

Current Assets:		
Cash in Bank	$ 17,200	
Accounts Receivable	48,030	
Merchandise Inventory	53,000	
Store Supplies	4,210	
Prepaid Insurance	780	
Total Current Assets		$123,220
Investments:		
A-Z Technologies, Inc. (stock)		21,000
Property, Plant, and Equipment:		
Equipment (net)	31,000	
Building (net)	110,000	
Land	15,000	
Total Property, Plant, and Equipment		156,000
Total Assets		$300,220

Liabilities

Current Liabilities:		
Notes Payable	$ 15,000	
Accounts Payable	39,000	
Sales Tax Payable	1,765	
Total Current Liabilities		$ 55,765
Long-Term Liabilities:		
Mortgage Payable		28,000
Total Liabilities		83,765

Stockholders' Equity

Common Stock, $90 par, 4,000 shares authorized, 800 shares issued	72,000	
Retained Earnings	144,455	
Total Stockholders' Equity		216,455
Total Liabilities and Stockholders' Equity		$300,220

Figure 28-1 Classified Balance Sheet

Classifying the Income Statement

Like the balance sheet, an income statement is more useful if the information reported there is classified. The information reported on an income statement for a merchandising business is commonly divided into four categories: revenue, cost of merchandise sold, operating expenses, and other revenue and expenses. There is no cost of merchandise sold section on the income statement of a service business.

An example of a classified income statement is shown in Figure 28-2.

▲ **Revenue** As you recall, revenue is earned by providing services or selling merchandise to customers. Sales discounts and returns reduce the net sales revenue earned by a merchandising business.

Interdisciplinary Connections

LANGUAGE ARTS

Just as a corporation is regarded as a "legal person," the word itself is related to a number of other terms that refer to a physical body—in Latin, *corpus*. The term *corporation* for a business organization granted a royal charter was first used in English in 1611. Earlier it was used for town and professional organizations.

Fitness Forever, Inc.
Income Statement
For the Year Ended December 31, 1993

Revenue:			
Sales		$578,000	
Less: Sales Returns		3,000	
Net Sales			$575,000
Cost of Merchandise Sold:			
Merchandise Inventory, Jan. 1, 1993		49,000	
Net Purchases		385,000	
Merchandise Available for Sale		434,000	
Merchandise Inventory, Dec. 31, 1993		53,000	
Cost of Merchandise Sold			381,000
Gross Profit on Sales			194,000
Operating Expenses:			
Selling Expenses:			
Advertising Expense	$10,000		
Depr. Exp.—Store Equip.	4,000		
Sales Salaries Expense	50,000		
Store Supplies Expense	10,350		
Total Selling Expenses		74,350	
Administrative Expenses:			
Depr. Exp.—Office Equip.	2,800		
Insurance Expense	900		
Miscellaneous Expense	750		
Office Salaries Expense	69,000		
Total Administrative Expenses		73,450	
Total Operating Expenses			147,800
Operating Income			46,200
Other Expenses:			
Interest Expense			3,400
Net Income			$ 42,800

Figure 28-2 Classified Income Statement

▲ **Cost of Merchandise Sold** Merchandising businesses buy merchandise to resell to their customers. The cost of merchandise sold is the net amount paid by the business for merchandise sold to customers.

▲ **Operating Expenses** Operating expenses are the cash spent, assets consumed, or liabilities incurred to earn revenue for the business. To compare the separate operating expenses of a business from one period to the next, expenses are usually classified by function. Two common ways to classify operating expenses are as selling expenses and administrative expenses. **Selling expenses** are incurred to sell or market the merchandise or services sold by the business. Examples of selling expenses are the costs of advertising and the salaries of salespeople.

Administrative expenses are costs related to the management of the business. Examples of administrative expenses are office expenses and salaries of management personnel.

CHAPTER 28 Analyzing and Interpreting Financial Statements 613

Using Visuals
Call students' attention to Figure 28-2. Ask students how this income statement would differ if it were unclassified.

Cooperative Learning

CATEGORIZE

Assign students in pairs and give them a long list of account titles and balances. Ask each pair to analyze, classify, and organize the accounts, then prepare a balance sheet and an income statement.

Refer to the "Cooperative Learning" section of *Tech Prep Strategies in Accounting* for additional cooperative learning strategies.

✓ ANSWERS

1. D
2. C
3. I
4. H
5. I
6. B and C
7. F
8. A
9. B
10. J
11. G
12. E

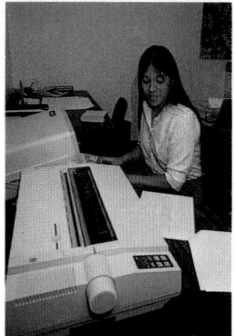

Today's computer programs can quickly and accurately produce classified financial statements from information stored in the computer's memory.

▲ **Other Revenue and Expenses**   As you learned in Chapter 25, other revenue and other expenses are non-operating revenue or expenses. That is, other revenue and expenses do not result from the normal operations of the business. Examples of other revenue or expenses are the interest paid and interest earned on notes.

R E M E M B E R

The financial statements issued by public corporations may be analyzed by many people. Classifying the accounts reported on the financial statement makes analysis easier because the accounts of the corporation are separated into related groups.

Before you read about how to analyze financial statements, complete the following activity to check your understanding of classified financial statements.

✓ Check Your Learning

Match the account in Column A with the proper classification in Column B. Write your answers on notebook paper.

Column A	Column B
1. Accounts Payable	A. Administrative Expense
2. Cash in Bank	B. Cost of Merchandise Sold
3. Equipment	C. Current Asset
4. Interest Income	D. Current Liability
5. Land	E. Investments
6. Merchandise Inventory	F. Long-Term Liability
7. Mortgage Payable	G. Selling Expense
8. Office Salaries Expense	H. Other Revenue and Expenses
9. Purchases	I. Property, Plant, and Equipment
10. Retained Earnings	J. Stockholders' Equity
11. Store Supplies Expense	
12. TBS, Inc. (stock)	

Compare your answers to those in the answers section. Re-read the preceding part of the chapter to find the correct answers to any questions you may have missed.

The Analysis of Financial Statements

As mentioned earlier, many people analyze financial statements to evaluate the financial performance of a business. The information reported on financial statements is expressed primarily in dollar amounts. Although dollar amounts are useful for many purposes, amounts by themselves generally

614   UNIT 6   Accounting for Other Forms of Business Organization

don't mean very much. The analysis of financial statements is more meaningful when the dollar relationships within the financial statements are converted to percentages. These percentages enable readers to more easily clarify and compare changes from one accounting period to another, as well as changes within one accounting period.

Three types of analyses using percentages are horizontal analysis, vertical analysis, and ratio analysis.

Horizontal Analysis

The comparison of the same items on financial statements for two or more accounting periods and the analysis of changes from one period to the next is called **horizontal analysis.** The comparison of financial statements normally begins with the comparison of the current and past year's statements. The current balance of one item is compared with the balance of the same item on the previous year's statement. Look at the comparative balance sheet shown in Figure 28-3 on page 616.

With horizontal analysis, each amount on the current statement (the first column) is compared with its corresponding amount on the previous statement (the second column). The dollar increase or decrease is calculated and reported in the third column. The percentage of the increase or decrease is also reported (fourth column). Decreases are reported by enclosing the amount and the percentage in parentheses.

Let's look at an example. On the comparative balance sheet, the ending balance of Cash in Bank for 1992 was $7,453. For the following year, 1993, the balance of Cash in Bank was $17,200. By subtracting the 1992 balance from the 1993 balance, you find that cash for the current year increased by $9,747. To calculate the percentage of the increase, divide the amount of the increase ($9,747) by the base year amount and multiply by 100. A **base year** is a year that is used for comparison, in this case, 1992.

$$\frac{\$9,747}{\$7,453} = 1.3078 \times 100 = 130.78\%$$

As you can see, both dollar amounts and percentages may be compared. Although dollar comparisons are easier to compute, percentage changes are more revealing. For example, look again at the increase in Cash in Bank of $9,747. The percentage increase more clearly shows how substantial the increase was from 1992 to 1993. The firm's cash position improved greatly. Notice also that Fitness Forever almost doubled its investment in the stock of A-Z Technologies during 1993.

R E M E M B E R

To calculate the percentage of increase or decrease, divide the dollar amount of the increase or decrease by the base year amount and multiply by 100.

CHAPTER 28   Analyzing and Interpreting Financial Statements   **615**

CONCEPT DEVELOPMENT
Horizontal Analysis
Remind students that calculating the percentages in horizontal and vertical analysis is simply an arithmetic function. You may want to review for students the calculation of a few percentages using the financial statements presented in the chapter. Refer students who need a review of percentages to the *Math Review for Accounting* workbook.

Teaching Tips
■ Point out that most businesses do not hold a lot of excess cash within the business; it is invested to earn money for the business.
■ Demonstrate that a percentage change reveals more than an actual dollar change.

ACCOUNTING PRACTICE
Students may complete Exercise 28-1 at this point.

Making Connections

COMMUNICATIONS

As students think about career goals, they need to learn how to prepare a convincing and appropriate resume of their education and experience. Have each student make up a sample resume presenting his or her real-life qualifications for a beginning job in a business or an accounting firm. This project would be an excellent collaborative effort to discuss with your English Department or with any other teacher who teaches a unit on resume writing.

CONCEPT DEVELOPMENT
Vertical Analysis

Contrast vertical analysis and horizontal analysis. Point out that vertical analysis involves amounts of the same year, while horizontal analysis involves amounts from two or more years.

Fitness Forever, Inc.
Comparative Balance Sheet
December 31, 1993 and 1992

	1993	1992	Increase (Decrease) (1993 over 1992) Dollars	Percentage
Assets				
Current Assets:				
Cash in Bank	$ 17,200	$ 7,453	$ 9,747	130.78%
Accounts Receivable	48,030	41,200	6,830	16.58%
Merchandise Inventory	53,000	49,000	4,000	8.16%
Store Supplies	4,210	4,120	90	2.18%
Prepaid Insurance	780	650	130	20.00%
Total Current Assets	123,220	102,423	20,797	20.31%
Investments:				
A-Z Technologies, Inc. (stock)	21,000	11,000	10,000	90.91%
Property, Plant, and Equipment:				
Equipment (net)	31,000	29,000	2,000	6.90%
Building (net)	110,000	115,000	(5,000)	(4.35%)
Land	15,000	15,000	0	0.00%
Total Property, Plant, and Equipment	156,000	159,000	(3,000)	(1.89%)
Total Assets	$300,220	$272,423	$27,797	10.20%
Liabilities				
Current Liabilities:				
Notes Payable	$ 15,000	$ 14,000	$ 1,000	7.14%
Accounts Payable	39,000	37,900	1,100	2.90%
Sales Tax Payable	1,765	1,345	420	31.23%
Total Current Liabilities	55,765	53,245	2,520	4.73%
Long-Term Liabilities:				
Mortgage Payable	28,000	33,000	(5,000)	(15.15%)
Total Liabilities	83,765	86,245	(2,480)	(2.88%)
Stockholders' Equity				
Common Stock, $90 par, 4,000 shares authorized, 800 shares issued	72,000	72,000	0	0.00%
Retained Earnings	144,455	114,178	30,277	26.52%
Total Stockholders' Equity	216,455	186,178	30,277	6.26%
Total Liabilities and Stockholders' Equity	$300,220	$272,423	$27,797	10.20%

Figure 28-3 Comparative Balance Sheet Showing Horizontal Analysis

Vertical Analysis

With **vertical analysis,** each dollar amount reported on a financial statement is also stated as a percentage of a base amount reported on the same statement. In other words, vertical analysis uses percentages to show the relationship of the different parts to the total on a particular financial statement. Each amount on the income statement, for example, is reported

616

UNIT 6   Accounting for Other Forms of Business Organization as a percentage of net sales. On the balance sheet, each individual asset is reported as a percentage of total assets. The individual liabilities and equities are reported as a percentage of total liabilities and stockholders' equity. Current year percentages may then be compared with percentages from past periods or with percentages from other businesses within the same industry. The percentages may also be used to construct future budgets.

Let's look at an example of vertical analysis. A comparative income statement showing vertical analysis appears in Figure 28-4. As you can see, the net sales amount for each year is assigned a percentage of 100%. Every other amount on the income statement is then compared to the net sales amount. (Amounts may not total exactly 100% because of rounding.)

Look at the amounts reported for sales. In 1992, sales were $556,000; in 1993, the amount had increased to $578,000. To calculate the percentages, each amount is divided by the net sales amount.

Fitness Forever, Inc.
Comparative Income Statement
For the Years Ended December 31, 1993 and 1992

	1993 Dollars	1993 Percentage	1992 Dollars	1992 Percentage
Revenue:				
Sales	$578,000	100.52%	$556,000	100.51%
Less: Sales Returns	3,000	0.52%	2,800	0.51%
Net Sales	575,000	100.00%	553,200	100.00%
Cost of Merchandise Sold:				
Merch. Inv., January 1	49,000	8.52%	46,000	8.32%
Net Purchases	385,000	66.96%	375,000	67.79%
Merchandise Available for Sale	434,000	75.48%	421,000	76.10%
Merch. Inv., December 31	53,000	9.22%	49,000	8.86%
Cost of Merchandise Sold	381,000	66.26%	372,000	67.25%
Gross Profit on Sales	194,000	33.74%	181,200	32.75%
Operating Expenses:				
Selling Expenses:				
Advertising Expense	10,000	1.74%	9,100	1.64%
Depr. Exp.—Store Equip.	4,000	0.70%	4,000	0.72%
Sales Salaries Expense	50,000	8.70%	47,000	8.50%
Store Supplies Expense	10,350	1.80%	9,240	1.67%
Total Selling Expenses	74,350	12.93%	69,340	12.53%
Administrative Expenses:				
Depr. Exp.—Office Equip.	2,800	0.49%	2,800	0.51%
Insurance Expense	900	0.16%	870	0.16%
Miscellaneous Expense	750	0.13%	810	0.15%
Office Salaries Expense	69,000	12.00%	66,000	11.93%
Total Administrative Exp.	73,450	12.77%	70,480	12.74%
Total Operating Expenses	147,800	25.70%	139,820	25.27%
Operating Income	46,200	8.03%	41,380	7.48%
Other Expenses:				
Interest Expense	3,400	0.59%	3,800	0.69%
Net Income	$ 42,800	7.44%	$ 37,580	6.79%

Figure 28-4 Comparative Income Statement Showing Vertical Analysis

CHAPTER 28   Analyzing and Interpreting Financial Statements   **617**

Chapter 28

ACCOUNTING PRACTICE

Students may complete Exercise 28-2 after the section on vertical analysis.

ANSWERS

1. E
2. C
3. D
4. B
5. A

	1993	1992
Sales	$578,000	$556,000
Net Sales	$575,000 = 100.52%	$553,200 = 100.51%

Look at another example. In dollar amounts, the gross profit on sales for 1992 and 1993 were different—$181,200 for 1992 and $194,000 for 1993. When converted to percentages of net sales, however, the results for the two years are almost exactly the same. In other words, gross profit on sales increased in 1993, but net sales also increased. As a result, the relationship of gross profit on sales to net sales remained the same.

R E M E M B E R

On an income statement arranged for vertical analysis, each dollar amount is expressed as a percentage of net sales. On a balance sheet arranged for vertical analysis, each asset amount is expressed as a percentage of total assets and each liability or equity amount is expressed as a percentage of total liabilities and stockholders' equity.

Vertical analysis is useful for comparing the importance of certain components in the operation of the business. It is also useful for pointing out important changes in the components from one year to the next.

The income statement and the balance sheet may also be prepared to show both horizontal and vertical analysis on the same statement.

Now do the following activity to check your understanding of horizontal and vertical analyses.

Check Your Learning

Match the items in Column A with the proper statements in Column B. Write your answers on notebook paper.

Column A	Column B
1. Comparative statement	**A.** Expresses each item on the statement as a percentage of a base item on the same statement
2. Horizontal analysis	
3. Net sales	**B.** The base used in vertical analysis of the balance sheet
4. Total assets (or Total liabilities and stockholders' equity)	**C.** Comparison of an amount on one statement with the same item on a preceding year's statement
5. Vertical analysis	**D.** The base used in vertical analysis of the income statement
	E. A statement that reports amounts for two or more fiscal periods

Compare your answers to those in the answers section. Re-read the preceding part of the chapter to find the correct answers to any questions you may have missed.

618

UNIT 6   Accounting for Other Forms of Business Organization

Reteaching Strategies

Students may need help performing the calculations for percentages in horizontal and vertical analysis. Guide students step by step through the horizontal analysis calculation on page 615 and the vertical analysis calculation on page 618, then provide several additional examples so that students can practice calculating the percentages for each.

Calculate several of the percentages in Figures 28-3 and 28-4 on the chalkboard to help students understand how to complete these analyses.

Assign Problems 28A and 28B to give students extra practice completing horizontal and vertical analyses.

Working Capital

The amount by which current assets exceed current liabilities is known as the company's **working capital.** Working capital is an important measure of a company's ability to meet its short-term liquidity needs. Because current liabilities are usually paid out of current assets, working capital represents the excess assets available to continue business operations. It represents the assets available to purchase inventory, obtain credit, and expand operations. Lack of working capital can lead to the failure of the business.

The working capital for Fitness Forever, Inc., for 1991 and 1992 is calculated as follows:

	1992	1991
Current Assets	$123,220	$102,423
− Current Liabilities	− 55,765	− 53,245
Working Capital	$ 67,455	$ 49,178

Working capital is useful when analyzing one company's financial statements. It is, however, difficult to compare one company's working capital with another company's. For example, working capital of $50,000 may be adequate for a small grocery store but totally inadequate for a large grocery store.

R E M E M B E R

Working capital is current assets less current liabilities.

Ratio Analysis

A ratio is a relationship between two numbers. **Ratio analysis** then is a comparison of two items on a financial statement, resulting in a percentage that is used to evaluate the relationship between the two items. Ratio analysis is generally used to determine a business's financial strength, activity, and the debt-paying ability. Two general measures of financial strength and debt-paying ability are liquidity ratios and profitability ratios.

All examples used in the following discussion are taken from the comparative financial statements shown in Figures 28-3 and 28-4.

Liquidity Ratios

As you recall from Chapter 5, liquidity refers to the ease with which an asset can be converted to cash. A **liquidity ratio** is a measure of a business's ability to pay its current debts as they become due and to provide for unexpected needs of cash. Two common ratios that are used to determine liquidity are the current ratio and the quick ratio.

Computer software can be used to calculate liquidity and profitability ratios, which can then be used for forecasting.

▲ **Current Ratio** The **current ratio** is the relationship between current assets and current liabilities. The current ratio is calculated by dividing the dollar amount of current assets by the dollar amount of current

CHAPTER 28 Analyzing and Interpreting Financial Statements **619**

CONCEPT DEVELOPMENT
Working Capital
Explain that working capital is really the excess net current assets of the business. The term "net working capital" is actually more accurate, but convention dictates the use of the term "working capital."

CONCEPT DEVELOPMENT
Ratio Analysis
Accountants rely upon analysis and the use of ratios to find out more about a company than would be possible simply by reading the financial data as presented. The process of comparing a set of figures and establishing their relationships enables one to gain a better understanding of a going concern. Ratios highlight unusual, unexpected, or otherwise unexplained changes in a business's performance.

Published comparative ratio information may be acquired from two basic groups or agencies. One group, which includes Dun & Bradstreet and Robert Morris Associates, compiles financial data for a number of individual industries. The other group, generally trade associations, compiles information for a particular industry or group of industries. Dun & Bradstreet, Inc., has been publishing "Key Business Ratios" annually since 1932 in *Dun's Review and Modern Industry*, a monthly magazine. Robert Morris Associates, founded in 1914, has developed ratio studies for over 225 lines of business. The most important specialized industry sources for ratio data are national trade associations. These associations publish ratio statistics covering a wide range of industries.

Using Visuals
Read the photo caption to the class. Ask students how forecasting in accounting is similar to forecasting the weather. (The business is predicting future occurrences based on current information, but sometimes the future does not happen as predicted.)

Making Connections

AROUND THE WORLD

Rock music stars have long been a part of international business. In the 1960s an English group, the Beatles, began the era of exporting rock music when they toured the United States and other countries, gaining many fans and selling hundreds of thousands of records. In even earlier generations, opera stars and other singers gave concerts in cities around the world. Music stars of today, from all countries, continue to travel and to take their music to people everywhere.

liabilities. On the comparative balance sheet in Figure 28-3 on page 616, current assets for 1993 are $123,220. Current liabilities are $55,765. The current ratio is calculated as follows:

$$\frac{\text{Current Assets}}{\text{Current Liabilities}} \quad \frac{\$123,220}{\$55,765} = 2.21 \text{ or } 2.21:1$$

Ratios are often written as $1:1$ (1 to 1) or $2:2$ (2 to 2).

The current ratio for one period may be compared to the current ratio for another period to determine whether the ratio is increasing or decreasing. For example, to find the current ratio for 1992, the current assets of $102,423 are divided by the current liabilities of $53,245.

$$\frac{\$102,423}{\$53,245} = 1.92:1$$

The current liabilities of a business must be paid within a year. These liabilities are paid from current assets. The current ratio indicates whether the business is in a good position to pay its current debts. A widely used rule-of-thumb is that the current ratio should be at least $2:1$. A current ratio of $2:1$ indicates that a business has current assets that are two times its current liabilities. In other words, the business has $2 of current assets for each $1 of current liabilities.

A ratio of $2:1$ or higher is considered favorable by creditors because it indicates that a business is able to pay its debts. A low ratio may indicate that a company could have trouble paying its current debts.

▲ **Quick Ratio**   One of the limitations of the current ratio is that it is based on total current assets. Current assets include merchandise inventory and prepaid items such as supplies and insurance. Inventory may take time to convert to cash, while prepaid items are consumed during business operations. A more rigorous measure of debt-paying ability is the quick ratio. The **quick ratio** is a measure of the relationship between short-term liquid assets and current liabilities. Short-term liquid assets—those that can be converted to cash quickly—are cash and net receivables. The quick ratio is calculated by dividing the total cash and receivables by current liabilities.

Let's look at an example. Again using the balance sheet in Figure 28-3 on page 616, cash and receivables for 1993 total $65,230. Current liabilities are $55,765. Dividing cash and receivables by current liabilities gives a ratio of 1.17:1.

$$\frac{\text{Cash and Receivables}}{\text{Current Liabilities}} \quad \frac{\$65,230}{\$55,765} = 1.17:1$$

Quick ratios may also be compared from one year to the next. For example, cash and receivables for 1992 were $48,653. Current liabilities were $53,245.

$$\frac{\$48,653}{\$53,245} = 0.91:1$$

Chapter 28

A quick ratio of 1 to 1 is considered adequate. That is, if a business has a quick ratio of 1:1 or higher, the business has $1 in liquid assets for each $1 of its current liabilities. As you can see, Fitness Forever improved its liquidity position in 1992.

Before continuing, complete the following activity to check your understanding of the material you have just studied.

Check Your Learning

Use the following accounting data to answer the questions.

Current Assets	$135,000	Cash in Bank	$ 9,500
Current Liabilities	62,000	Accounts Receivable	18,250

1. What is the working capital?
2. What is the current ratio?
3. What is the quick ratio?

Compare your answers to those in the answers section. Re-read the preceding part of the chapter to find the correct answers to any questions you may have missed.

Profitability Ratios

Profitability ratios are used to evaluate the earnings performance of the business during the accounting period. A business's earning power is an important measure of its ability to grow and to continue to earn revenue. Two commonly used profitability ratios are the return on common stockholders' equity and the return on sales.

▲ **Return on Common Stockholders' Equity** Return on common stockholders' equity shows how well a business has used the resources provided by stockholders' investments. This ratio looks at profitability from the point of view of the investor. Investors commit their dollars to a business and want to receive a fair return on their investments. Investors also want to compare the return on an investment with other possible investments.

Fitness Forever, Inc., has only one class of capital stock. As a result, the return on common stockholders' equity is calculated by dividing net income by the average common stockholders' equity. Average common stockholders' equity is found by adding the beginning stockholders' equity amount and the ending stockholders' equity amount and dividing that total by 2. (If the company also had preferred stock, the preferred stock dividends for the period would have to be subtracted from the net income amount and the balances of the preferred stock accounts subtracted from the stockholders' equity amount.)

CHAPTER 28   Analyzing and Interpreting Financial Statements   **621**

Teaching Tips

■ The quick ratio is often called the "acid test" ratio.

ACCOUNTING PRACTICE Students may complete Exercise 28-3 after the section on the quick ratio.

ANSWERS
1. $73,000
2. 2.18:1
3. 0.45:1

Teaching Tips

■ Reinforce the concept that the financial data reported by a company presents a picture of that company's financial results. For public corporations, the picture is there for anyone who wants to see or who knows how to analyze the parts of the picture.
■ Return on common stockholders' equity shows return on invested capital. This ratio measures how effectively management is using the capital to provide a return. The return on stockholders' equity is compared with the industry average, taking into account the degree of risk involved in the business.

Reteaching Strategies

Students may need help remembering how to calculate each ratio. Urge students to create a list of the ratios, including a brief description of each ratio and its formula. Students can then refer to their lists as they work the exercises and problems.

Remind students that a ratio is calculated by dividing one number by another. Ratio analysis shows the relationship between the two items. Ratios highlight unusual, unexpected, or otherwise unexplained changes in a business's performance.

Chapter 28

COMPUTERS IN ACCOUNTING

Xerox Corporation received the 1993 Industrial Design Excellence Award for the innovative technology in its new electronic blackboard that incorporates video technology. The Liveboard provides an on-line forum enabling individuals to conduct interactive meetings anywhere in the world. It utilizes a wireless pen and runs Microsoft Windows software. Liveboards can be connected through telephone lines so that accountants in one city can interact with their clients in another city.

Teaching Tips

■ Return on sales is a measure of profit margins. Again, for real analysis, this ratio should be compared with others in the industry.

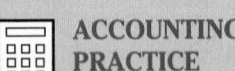

Using Visuals

Use demonstration problem 28-4 to give students practice calculating profitability ratios.

ACCOUNTING PRACTICE

Students may complete Exercise 28-4 at this point.

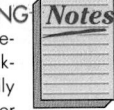

ACCOUNTING Notes
The annual report to stockholders usually includes other features besides financial statements. Among them are a message from the president and chairman of the board, descriptions and photos of products and facilities, lists of principal officers, and other items of interest.

Look again at the comparative income statement in Figure 28-4. The net income for 1993 is $42,800. On the comparative balance sheet in Figure 28-3, the beginning common stockholders' equity amount for 1993 is $186,178 and the ending stockholders' equity amount is $216,455. (The ending amount reported for 1992 is the beginning amount for 1993.) The average common stockholders' equity amount is $201,317 ($186,178 + $216,455 = $402,633 ÷ 2). The return on common stockholders' equity for 1993 then is calculated as follows:

$$\frac{\text{Net Income}}{\text{Average Common Stockholders' Equity}} \quad \frac{\$42,800}{\$201,317} = 0.2126 \text{ or } 21.26\%$$

The return on common stockholders' equity shows that the business earned more than 21 cents for each dollar invested in the business by the common stockholders.

The return on common stockholders' equity ratio can be compared to the ratios for previous periods. For example, in 1992 Fitness Forever had a net income of $37,580. The beginning stockholders' equity amount (taken from a previous statement) was $142,598 and the ending stockholders' equity amount was $186,178. The return on owners' investment for 1992 is

$$\frac{\$37,580}{\$164,388} = 0.2286 \text{ or } 22.86\%$$

As you can see, the return on common stockholders' equity decreased slightly from 1992 to 1993.

▲ **Return on Sales** The return on sales reflects the portion of each dollar of sales that represents profit. Return on sales is computed during vertical analysis of the income statement. To calculate the return on sales, divide the net income by the net sales for the period. In 1993, Fitness Forever had a net income of $42,800 and net sales of $575,000. The return on sales is calculated as follows:

$$\frac{\text{Net Income}}{\text{Net Sales}} \quad \frac{\$42,800}{\$575,000} = 0.0744 \text{ or } 7.44\%$$

This return on sales percentage indicates that each dollar of sales in 1993 produced 7.44 cents of profit. This percentage may be compared to other accounting periods to determine whether it is increasing or decreasing. For example, net income in 1992 was $37,580 and net sales were $553,200. The return on sales for 1992 is thus 6.79%.

$$\frac{\$37,580}{\$553,200} = 0.0679 \text{ or } 6.79\%$$

As you can see, profit per sales dollar increased in 1993 by 0.65 cents over 1992.

Now complete the following activity to check your understanding of profitability ratios.

622

UNIT 6   Accounting for Other Forms of Business Organization

Pop Quiz

1. Why do managers analyze financial statements?
2. Why do investors and creditors analyze financial statements?
3. Define working capital.
4. A ____ ratio is a measure of a business's ability to pay its current debts and provide for unexpected needs of cash.
5. A ratio that shows the return on common stockholders' equity looks at profitability from the ____ point of view.

ANSWERS

1. To help them evaluate past performance and make more informed decisions about future operations of the business.
2. They are interested in protecting their equity.
3. The amount by which current assets exceed current liabilities.
4. liquidity
5. investor's

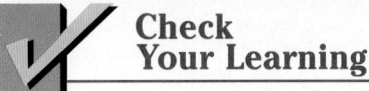

Check Your Learning

Match the descriptions in Column A with the proper items in Column B.

Column A	Column B
1. Computed during vertical analysis of the income statement	**A.** Return on common stockholders' equity
2. Measures management's success with the use of investors' capital	**B.** Return on sales
3. Allows investors to compare the return on an investment with other potential investment opportunities	
4. Represents profit per dollar of sales	

Compare your answers to those in the answers section. Re-read the preceding part of the chapter to find the correct answers to any questions you may have missed.

Summary of Key Points

1. Qualitative characteristics are those characteristics that make accounting information useful and understandable. The three qualitative characteristics are relevance, reliability, and comparability.
2. Two guidelines accountants follow when preparing financial statements are full disclosure and materiality.
3. Classified balance sheets and income statements are usually prepared by accountants to help make these financial statements more useful and easier to analyze for the user.
4. Three types of analyses made of financial statements are horizontal analysis, vertical analysis, and ratio analysis.
5. The analysis of a change between two amounts on a financial statement from one accounting period to the next is called horizontal analysis.
6. Vertical analysis requires that each amount on a financial statement be restated as a percentage of a base figure on the same statement.
7. Liquidity ratios measure the ability of a business to meet its short-term debts. Common liquidity measures are the current ratio and the quick ratio.
8. Profitability ratios analyze the earning performance of the business. Two commonly used profitability ratios are return on common stockholders' equity and return on sales.

Chapter 28

ANSWERS

1. B
2. A
3. A
4. B

3 CLOSE

CHAPTER SUMMARY

This summary enumerates the key information in the chapter. It is a useful tool for reinforcement and review.

*R*eteaching *S*trategies

Some students may need extra practice calculating ratios. Collect corporate financial statements from business simulations and have students calculate profitability ratios. Allow students to help each other by pairing students who have a good grasp of how to calculate ratios with weaker students.

Review and Applications

Building Your Accounting Vocabulary

In your own words, write the definition of each of the following accounting terms. Use complete sentences for your definitions.

administrative expenses	horizontal analysis	ratio analysis
base year	investments	relevance
comparability	liquidity ratios	reliability
current liabilities	long-term liabilities	selling expenses
current ratio	materiality	vertical analysis
full disclosure	profitability ratios	working capital
	quick ratio	

Reviewing Your Accounting Knowledge

1. Identify the people or businesses that would be interested in analyzing the financial statements of a business.
2. What are the three qualitative characteristics of accounting?
3. Name two guidelines accountants follow to make sure financial statements are clear and consistent.
4. What is the purpose of classifying financial statements?
5. What is the difference between horizontal and vertical analysis?
6. What is the purpose of computing ratios from amounts on financial statements?
7. Why might a creditor be interested in the liquidity ratios of a business?
8. How are the current ratio and the quick ratio similar? different?
9. Who might be interested in the profitability ratios of a business?
10. Which ratios will help you to answer the following questions:
    a. How effective is the firm's use of credit?
    b. Are the resources (assets) of the firm being used effectively?

Improving Your Decision-Making Skills

The following information was taken from the accounting records of the Lorain Corporation:

Current assets	$238,000
Total stockholders' equity	85,680
Current liabilities	152,320

How would you evaluate this company's debt? If you were a creditor, would you extend additional credit to the company?

Applying Accounting Procedures

Exercise 28-1   Preparing a Horizontal Analysis

The following amounts appeared on the comparative balance sheet for the Sharp Hats Co.

624

PRACTICE AND APPLY
- Language Development
- Comprehension and Retention
- Basic Skills

Building Your Accounting Vocabulary
See the Glossary on pages 670-679 for definitions of these terms.

Reviewing Your Accounting Knowledge

1. Owners, investors, creditors, labor unions, suppliers, lenders. and management would be interested in analyzing the financial statements of a business.
2. The three qualitative characteristics are relevance, reliability, and comparability.
3. Accountants follow the guidelines of full disclosure and materiality to make financial statements relevant and complete.
4. Financial statements are classified to make the analysis of financial information easier.
5. Horizontal analysis compares an amount on a financial statement with the same item on a prior statement reporting the dollar change as well as the percentage change. Vertical analysis expresses amounts on financial statements as a percentage of a base amount on the same statement.
6. Ratios take absolute amounts and convert them to relationships. Relationships can be more revealing than amounts when making comparisons.
7. A creditor might be interested in the liquidity ratios of a particular business because liquidity is a measure of a business's ability to meet current debts as they become due and to provide for unexpected needs for cash. Thus, the creditor can judge whether the business is likely to make its payments on time.
8. Both the current ratio and the quick ratio measure the relationship between current assets and current liabilities and reflect the short-term, debt-paying ability of the firm. The quick ratio includes only the most liquid current assets: cash and accounts receivable. The quick ratio is a stronger test of debt-paying ability than the current ratio.

9. Stockholders, creditors, suppliers, lenders, and management might be interested in the profitability ratios of a particular business.
10. (a) The current ratio helps one determine whether the business is in a good position to pay its current debts. A high current ratio means that current liabilities (the business's credit) are relatively low compared to current assets. (b) The return on common stockholders' equity ratio tells whether the resources of the business are being used effectively.

Improving Your Decision-Making Skills
The company's debt could be evaluated

through the use of the current ratio, which is the dollar amount of current assets divided by the dollar amount of current liabilities.

$$\frac{\$238,000}{\$152,320} = 1.56 \text{ or } 1.56:1$$

A creditor would be well advised not to extend additional credit to the Lorain Corporation. Such a low current ratio may indicate that the Lorain Corporation could have trouble paying its current debts. The creditor may also want to make additional evaluations by calculating a quick ratio or asking for a credit history report.

Instructions: Determine the amount of increase or decrease and the percentage of increase or decrease for each amount listed. Use the form in the working papers and round percentages to two decimal places.

	1992	1991
Current Assets	$540,000	$510,000
Property, Plant, and Equipment	455,000	470,000
Total Assets	$995,000	$980,000
Liabilities	$410,000	$400,000
Stockholders' Equity	585,000	580,000
Total Liabilities and Stockholders' Equity	$995,000	$980,000

Exercise 28-2   Preparing a Vertical Analysis

The following amounts appeared on the comparative income statement of the Sharp Hats Co.

Instructions: Prepare a comparative income statement using vertical analysis. Round percentages to two decimal places.

	1992	1991
Net Sales	$700,000	$625,000
Cost of Merchandise Sold	450,000	380,000
Gross Profit on Sales	250,000	245,000
Operating Expenses	175,000	175,000
Net Income	$ 75,000	$ 70,000

Exercise 28-3   Calculating Liquidity Ratios

The following account balances were taken from the financial statements of the Times-Wright Corporation.

Instructions:

(1) Determine the company's working capital.
(2) Calculate the current ratio.
(3) Calculate the quick ratio.

Cash in Bank	$ 90,000	Accounts Payable	$185,000
Accounts Receivable	185,000	Federal Inc. Tax Payable	30,000
Merchandise Inventory	165,000	Sales Tax Payable	10,000
Prepaid Expenses	11,500		

Exercise 28-4   Calculating Profitability Ratios

The following data were taken from the financial statements of the Exact Fit Company.

Instructions: For each year,

(1) Calculate the return on common stockholders' equity. The beginning common stockholders' equity amount for 1991 was $751,500.
(2) Calculate the return on sales.

	1992	1991
Net Sales	$315,000	$265,000
Net Income	25,000	23,500
Capital Stock	500,000	500,000
Retained Earnings	300,000	275,000

625

Chapter 28

PRACTICE AND APPLY

• Concepts and Procedures

Exercise 28-1: Ch. Obj. 3
Current assets, $30,000; 5.88%
PP&E, ($15,000); (3.19%)
Total assets, $15,000; 1.53%
Liabilities, $10,000; 2.50%
Stockholders' equity, $5,000; 0.86%
Total L&SE, $15,000; 1.53%

Exercise 28-2: Ch. Obj. 3
Net sales, 100.00%; 100.00%
Cost/merch. sold, 64.29%; 60.80%
Gross profit, 35.71%; 39.20%
Oper. expenses, 25.00%; 28.00%
Net income, 10.71%; 11.20%

Exercise 28-3: Ch. Obj. 4
1. $226,500
2. 2.01:1
3. 1.22:1

Exercise 28-4: Ch. Obj. 4
1992	1991
3.17%	3.08%
7.94%	8.87%

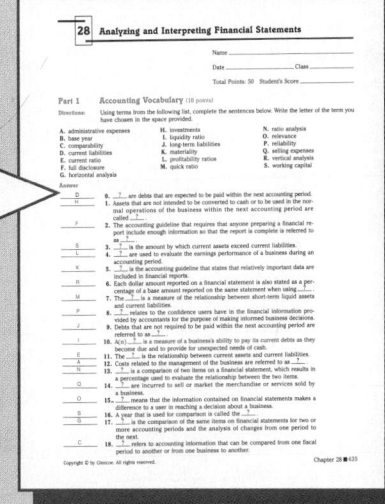

Additional Reinforcement

Students who need additional practice or individualized help will benefit from the *Glencoe Accounting Electronic Study Guide* or the *Glencoe Accounting* on-line multimedia program, which provide reinforcement and reteaching for vocabulary, concepts, and procedures.

Refer students to the Chapter 28 review pages in the workbook, *Chapter Reviews and Working Papers.*

Problem 28-1: Ch. Obj. 2

Balance sheet totals, $130,700

Problem 28-2: Ch. Obj. 3

Net income:
$8,287
47.48%

Problem 28-1 Preparing a Classified Balance Sheet

The following account balances appeared on the December 31 work sheet for the Q-Tex Company. The corporation is authorized to issue 10,000 shares of $100 par common stock.

Instructions: Prepare a classified balance sheet for the Q-Tex Company.

Accounts Payable	$10,750	Merchandise Inventory	$14,800
Accounts Receivable (net)	6,700	Mortgage Payable	25,000
Building (net)	37,500	Notes Payable	5,700
Cash in Bank	7,500	Office Equipment (net)	18,000
Common Stock	50,000	Office Supplies	1,200
Edge It Corp. (stock)	23,000	Retained Earnings	38,500
Land	22,000	Sales Tax Payable	750

Problem 28-2 Using Horizontal Analysis

The following is a partial comparative income statement for Mini-Sports Shop, Inc.

Instructions: Complete the comparative income statement using horizontal analysis. Round all percentages to two decimal places. Use the form provided in the working papers.

Mini-Sports Shop, Inc.
Comparative Income Statement
For the Years Ended August 31, 1992 and 1991

	1992	1991
Revenue:		
Sales	$232,345	$208,578
Less: Sales Returns and Allowances	4,350	3,988
Net Sales	227,995	204,590
Cost of Merchandise Sold	135,678	122,345
Gross Profit on Sales	92,317	82,245
Operating Expenses:		
Selling Expenses:		
Advertising Expense	9,500	8,700
Delivery Expense	7,678	7,456
Depr. Exp.—Store Equipment	1,000	1,000
Sales Salaries Expense	21,500	19,899
Travel Expense	4,567	4,134
Total Selling Expenses	44,245	41,189
Administrative Expenses:		
Bad Debts Expense	2,350	2,200
Depr. Exp.—Office Equipment	2,000	2,000
Insurance Expense	2,500	2,400
Miscellaneous Expense	2,367	2,200
Office Salaries Expense	12,345	11,397
Rent Expense	5,000	4,500
Total Administrative Expenses	26,562	24,697
Total Operating Expenses	70,807	65,886
Operating Income	21,510	16,359
Other Revenue	4,500	1,550
Other Expenses	270	456
Net Income	$ 25,740	$ 17,453

626

Teacher Notes

Problem 28-3   Using Vertical Analysis

The following is a partial comparative balance sheet for the Mini-Sports Shop, Inc.

Instructions: Complete the comparative balance sheet using vertical analysis. Round the percentages to two decimal places. Use the form provided in the working papers.

Problem 28-3: Ch. Obj. 3

Problem 28-4: Ch. Obj. 4

SPREADSHEET

PROBLEM

Problem 28-4 can be completed using *Spreadsheet Applications,* the spreadsheet software that accompanies *Glencoe Accounting.*

Working capital, $490,000
Current ratio, 2.88:1
Quick ratio, 1.27:1

Mini-Sports Shop, Inc.
Comparative Balance Sheet
August 31, 1993 and 1992

	1993	1992
Assets		
Current Assets:		
Cash in Bank	$ 11,900	$ 10,890
Accounts Receivable (net)	16,780	15,450
Merchandise Inventory	45,000	38,700
Prepaid Expenses	2,100	1,860
Total Current Assets	75,780	66,900
Investments:		
Runner, Inc. (stock)	10,500	8,500
Property, Plant, and Equipment:		
Equipment (net)	35,000	30,000
Building (net)	75,000	80,000
Land	15,000	15,000
Total Property, Plant, and Equip.	125,000	125,000
Total Assets	$211,280	$200,400
Liabilities		
Current Liabilities:		
Notes Payable	$ 22,500	$ 18,600
Accounts Payable	15,600	13,200
Sales Tax Payable	1,300	1,200
Total Current Liabilities	39,400	33,000
Long-Term Liabilities:		
Mortgage Payable	15,000	25,000
Total Liabilities	54,400	58,000
Stockholders' Equity		
Common Stock, $100 par, 5,000 shares authorized, 500 shares issued	50,000	50,000
Retained Earnings	106,880	92,400
Total Stockholders' Equity	156,880	142,400
Total Liabilities and Stockholders' Equity	$211,280	$200,400

SPREADSHEET

PROBLEM

Problem 28-4   Calculating Ratios

The following balances appeared on the financial statements of The Music Center, Inc.

Cash in Bank	$135,000	Notes Payable	$ 25,000
Accounts Receivable	195,000	Accounts Payable	210,000
Merchandise Inventory	387,000	Dividends Payable	0
Prepaid Insurance	20,000	Federal Inc. Tax Pay.	15,000
Supplies	13,000	Sales Tax Payable	10,000

627

Teacher Notes

Problem 28-5: Ch. Obj. 2, 3, 4, 5

Balance sheet:
Cash in Bank, $150,000
Merch. Inv., $50,000
Prop., Plant, & Equip., $300,000
Current Liabilities, $100,000
Stockholders' Equity, $175,000

Income statement:
Net Sales, $262,500
Cost of Merch. Sold, $157,500
Gross Profit on Sales, $105,000
Total Operating Exp., $94,500

Instructions:

(1) Use the account balances to compute the working capital, the current ratio, and the quick ratio.

(2) Compute the working capital, current ratio, and quick ratio after considering each of the following *independent* transactions. In other words, determine what effect each transaction would have on the three ratios.

Transactions:

1. Received cash on account, $100,000.
2. Paid accounts payable, $100,000.
3. Purchased merchandise on account, $75,000.
4. Borrowed $150,000, signing a long-term note payable.
5. Paid notes payable of $25,000.
6. Issued common stock at par, receiving $125,000.
7. Paid cash for supplies, $25,000.
8. Declared a cash dividend of $125,000.
9. Paid $50,000 on the long-term note payable.
10. Borrowed $75,000, signing a 30-day note payable.

CHALLENGE **Problem 28-5 Determining Financial Statement Amounts**

PROBLEM

The abbreviated financial statements for the Eastway Metal Company appear below. The statements have several dollar amounts missing.

Instructions: Compute the missing amounts and complete the financial statements. Assume that stockholders' equity did not change. Additional information needed is given here.

Current ratio:	2:1
Quick ratio:	1.5:1
Gross profit percentage:	40%
Return on sales:	4%
Return on common stockholders' equity:	6%

Eastway Metal Company
Balance Sheet
December 31, 19—

Cash in Bank	$?	Current Liabilities	$?
Merchandise Inventory	?	Long-Term Liabilities	225,000
Property, Plant, and Equipment	?	Stockholders' Equity	?
		Total Liabilities and	
Total Assets	**$ 500,000**	**Stockholders' Equity**	**$ 500,000**

Eastway Metal Company
Income Statement
For the Year Ended December 31, 19—

Net Sales	$?
Cost of Merchandise Sold	?
Gross Profit on Sales	?
Total Operating Expenses	?
Net Income	$ 10,500

CHALLENGE **Problem 28-6 Determining Financial Statement Amounts**

PROBLEM

An abbreviated comparative income statement for Bay State Lumber, Inc., is shown on page 629.

628

Teacher Notes

Instructions: Complete the statement by determining the missing amounts for each of the question marks. Determine percentages to the nearest tenth of a percent. Use plain paper or the form provided in the working papers.

Bay State Lumber, Inc.
Comparative Income Statement
For the Years Ended December 31, 1992 and 1991

	1992	1991	Increase (Decrease) 1992 over 1991 Dollars	Percentage
Net Sales	$690,106	?	$116,966	?
Cost of Merchandise Sold	?	$281,834	59,028	?
Gross Profit on Sales	349,244	?	?	19.9%
Total Operating Expenses	?	176,085	?	7.7%
Operating Income	159,612	115,221	?	?
Other Revenue	1,802	?	197	?
Other Expenses	?	1,403	?	(39.5%)
Net Income	?	?	?	?

Problem 28-6: Ch. Obj. 2, 3, 4, 5

CHALLENGE

PROBLEM

The last problem in each chapter is a challenge problem and is identified by this "maze" symbol.

Net Sales, $573,140; 20.4%
Cost/Merch. Sold, $340,862; 20.9%
Gross Profit, $291,306; $57,938
Total Oper. Exp., $189,632; $13,547
Operating Inc., $44,391; 38.5%
Other Revenue $1,605; 12.3%
Other Exp., $849; ($554)
Net Income, $160,565; $115,423; $45,142; 39.1%

4 ASSESS

A chapter test is available for use in assessing students' understanding of concepts in this chapter.

The testmaker software will enable you to develop tailor-made chapter, unit, semester, and final tests.

Unit objective and problem tests are available to assess students' knowledge of concepts in Chapters 26-28.

Alternative Assessment

For alternative assessment strategies, refer to *Tech Prep Strategies in Accounting.*

Use Chapter Test 28 here to assess students' understanding and retention of the concepts and procedures presented in the chapter.

Use Unit 6 Objective Test and/or Unit 6 Problem Test to assess students' retention of concepts presented in Chapters 26-28.

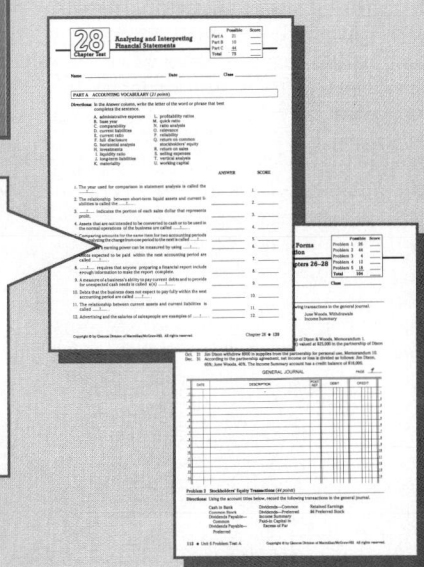

629

Have students read the ethics case given in the textbook and jot down ideas about what they would do in the situation described. Then review the five-step decision model (see page T44). Emphasize that there are no "right" or "wrong" answers to the questions in the decision model.

After students have discussed the first four steps, have them vote on which alternative they feel is best, or, if one alternative has clearly been chosen during the discussion, review students' reasoning for choosing that course of action.

You may want to have students compare their final decision with the one they wrote down after first reading the vignette. Did following the five-step model reinforce their "instinctual" decision or lead them to choose a different course of action? Help students realize that following a decision model when they confront an ethical dilemma can help them to organize their thinking and arrive at a satisfactory solution.

QUESTIONS

1. What are the ethical issues in this situation?
2. What are the alternatives?
3. Who are the affected parties?
4. How do the alternatives affect the parties?
5. What is the decision?

ANSWERS

1. Whether to put friendship above the law, above company loyalty, and above customer security.
2. Devon can report Jason to the company or protect Jason by trying to cover up his actions.
3. Devon, Jason, the company, the company's customers.
4. Answers will vary. For example, if Devon reports Jason to the company, he would probably lose Jason's friendship, might have to testify against Jason should the situation become a legal matter, and might be held responsible for not finding the problem earlier. If Devon does not report the situation, the company may continue to lose money if Jason believes that he has an ally who will not report his theft.

Does Friendship Always Come First?

Could you confront a friend who had broken company policy, or even the law, and still maintain that friendship? Would you be willing to risk a friendship if you felt that your friend's code of ethics did not match yours? Before you answer, consider the following situation.

Devon and Jason have been best friends since high school. They both went to the same college, roomed together, and majored in accounting. During their senior year, a financial firm was on campus recruiting, and both young men landed a job. Within the firm, they both did well, but diverged in their responsibilities. Jason handled most of the customer accounts while Devon pursued managerial accounting.

One day, during Devon's routine auditing of the different departments, Devon found some numbers in Jason's records that had been deliberately falsified. Devon agonized over what to do. Since Jason was the only one with access to these records, he had to have been the one who set up the phony auditing trail. Should he confront Jason personally? Should he go directly to Jason's boss? In the end, Devon decided to go directly to Jason.

Jason admitted to Devon what he had done, and said that he had been too ashamed to tell Devon about it before. The problem was that Jason was not able to immediately pay back the money he had taken. He promised Devon that he would pay back the money, but asked Devon not to tell anyone.

What is the ethical dilemma that Devon faces? If Devon reports Jason, Jason would most likely lose his job, might have criminal charges brought against him, and would probably no longer call Devon his friend. The money Jason took also might be lost for good. If Devon agrees to shield Jason,

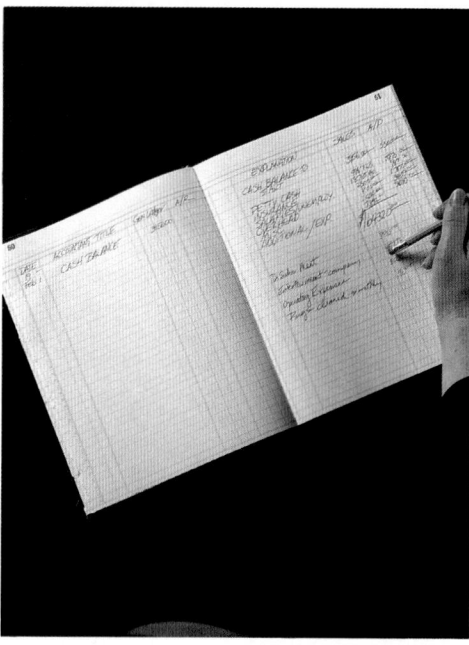

Friends often share common interests, ideas, and activities. Friendships can become very complicated, though, when a friend's code of ethics differs from yours.

the money belonging to the firm's customers might eventually be repaid, but if the theft were discovered, Devon would be implicated along with Jason. If you were in Devon's place, what would you do?

630

5. Accept any answer, but require students to defend the course of action they choose.

Additional Reinforcement Problems

Additional problems are not included for Chapter 1.

Chapter 2, Problem 2A   Determining the Effects of Business Transactions on the Accounting Equation

Ashley Moore has set up a business for herself as an accountant.

Instructions: Use a form similar to the one below. For each of the following transactions,
(1) Identify the accounts affected.
(2) Write the amount of the increase or decrease in the space provided.
(3) Determine the new balance for each account.

Trans.	ASSETS					=	LIABILITIES	+	OWNER'S EQUITY
	Cash in Bank	Accts. Rec.	Office Supp.	Comp. Equip.	Office Equip.	=	Accounts Payable	+	A. Moore, Capital
1									

Transactions:
1. Ashley Moore, the owner, opened a checking account for the business by depositing $48,000 of her personal funds.
2. Paid the monthly rent of $1,500.
3. Bought office supplies on account for $1,000.
4. Ashley Moore invested $3,000 of office equipment in the business.
5. Paid cash for a new computer for the business, $5,000.
6. Paid for an advertisement in the local newspaper, $200.
7. Completed accounting services for a client and sent a bill for $800.
8. Paid $700 on account for the office supplies bought earlier.
9. Received $500 on account from a client.
10. Ashley Moore withdrew $1,000 from the business for personal use.

Chapter 3, Problem 3A   Analyzing Transactions into Debit and Credit Parts

Paul Morales owns a cleaning service. The accounts he uses to record and report business transactions are listed on the following page.

Teacher Notes

Ending balances:
Cash in Bank, $26,875
Accounts Receivable, $50
Cleaning Supplies, $675
Cleaning Equipment, $1,900
Store Equipment, $650
Van, $19,360
Accounts Payable, $18,860
Capital, $30,650
Totals, $49,510

Problem 4A: Ch. Obj. 2, 3, 4

Ending balances:
Cash in Bank, $24,795
Accounts Receivable, $200
Equipment, $1,525
Accounts Payable, $900
Capital, $25,125
Withdrawals, $150
Landscaping Fees, $1,125
Maintenance Expense, $20
Rent Expense, $350
Utilities Expense, $110
Totals, $27,150

Cash in Bank	Store Equipment
Accounts Receivable	Van
Cleaning Supplies	Accounts Payable
Cleaning Equipment	Paul Morales, Capital

Instructions:

(1) Prepare a T account for each account listed above.

(2) Analyze and record each of the following business transactions in the appropriate T accounts. Identify each transaction by number.

(3) After recording all transactions, compute and record the account balance on the normal balance side of each T account.

(4) Add the balances of those accounts with normal debit balances.

(5) Add the balances of those accounts with normal credit balances.

(6) Compare the two totals. Are they the same?

Transactions:

1. Paul Morales invested $30,000 from his savings into the business.
2. Invested cleaning equipment, valued at $650, in the business.
3. Bought a van on account from Westside Motors for $19,360.
4. Bought cleaning supplies for $550, Check 100.
5. Bought a new rug shampooer on account from Harris Equipment for $1,250.
6. As a favor, sold some cleaning supplies on credit to a neighboring business, $50.
7. Purchased storage shelves for the business for $650, Check 101.
8. Paid $500 on account to Harris Equipment, Check 102.
9. Bought cleaning supplies for $175, Check 103.
10. Paid $1,250 on account to Westside Motors, Check 104.

Chapter 4, Problem 4A Analyzing Transactions

Jane Black owns the Arbor Landscaping Service. She plans to use the following accounts for recording and reporting business transactions.

Cash in Bank	Jane Black, Withdrawals
Accounts Receivable	Landscaping Fees
Equipment	Maintenance Expense
Accounts Payable	Rent Expense
Jane Black, Capital	Utilities Expense

Instructions:

(1) Prepare a T account for each account listed above.

(2) Analyze and record each of the following transactions, using the appropriate T accounts. Identify each transaction by number.

(3) After recording all transactions, compute a balance for each account.

(4) Test for the equality of debits and credits.

Transactions:

1. Jane Black invested $25,000 cash in the business.
2. Bought a new lawnmower on account from Mason Lawn Products, Inc., for $1,400.
3. Jane Black invested equipment valued at $125 in the business.
4. Paid the rent for the month of $350, Check 101.
5. Wrote Check 102 for $20 for minor repairs to the equipment.
6. Completed landscaping for a customer and sent a bill for $350.

632

Additional Reinforcement Problems

7. Paid the utility bill of $75, Check 103.
8. Deposited the daily receipts for landscaping services, $175.
9. Sent Check 104 for $500 to Mason Lawn Products as a payment on account.
10. Received $150 from a charge customer on account.
11. Ms. Black withdrew $150 for her personal use, Check 105.
12. Paid the telephone bill of $35, Check 106.
13. Deposited the daily receipts of $600 for landscaping services.

Problem 5A: Ch. Obj. 5

Problem 6A: Ch. Obj. 2, 3
Trial balance totals, $52,325

Chapter 5, Problem 5A   Recording Transactions in the General Journal

Six months ago, Jack Wiley opened his own engineering company. He uses the following accounts to record the business's transactions.

Cash in Bank
Accounts Receivable—
   Hempfield Township
Accounts Receivable—
   Unity Township
Engineering Supplies
Surveying Equipment
Blueprint Equipment
Motor Vehicles

Accounts Payable—Engineering Suppliers
Accounts Payable—Mohawk Van Dealers
Jack Wiley, Capital
Jack Wiley, Withdrawals
Professional Fees
Advertising Expense
Rent Expense
Utilities Expense

Instructions: Record the following transactions on page 6 of a general journal.

Transactions:

June 1   Jack Wiley invested surveying equipment valued at $800 in the business, Memorandum 202.
3   Wrote Check 150 to New Town Press for advertisements, $125.
6   Completed services for Hempfield Township and sent a bill for $750, Invoice 91.
8   Paid the $85 utility bill, Check 151.
15   Purchased $160 in engineering supplies from Engineering Suppliers on account, Invoice 1161.
18   Received a check for $375 from Hempfield Township to apply on account, Receipt 123.
20   Sent a bill for $900 to Unity Township for engineering services performed on account, Invoice 92.
22   Sent Check 152 for $160 to Engineering Suppliers on account.
25   Jack Wiley withdrew $15 in engineering supplies for personal use, Memorandum 203.
28   Received $500 from Unity Township on account, Receipt 124.
30   Purchased a $16,000 van from Mohawk Van Dealers on account, Invoice 553.

Chapter 6, Problem 6A   Posting Business Transactions

Bruno Ciani started a business to provide dental services to the community. The accounts used by the business, Bruno Ciani, D.D.S., have been opened and are included in the working papers accompanying this textbook. The general journal entries for the May business transactions are also included in the working papers.

Teacher Notes

_____

_____

_____

_____

_____

Instructions:

(1) Post each journal entry to the appropriate accounts in the ledger.

(2) Prove the ledger by preparing a trial balance.

Trial balance totals, $52,325

Problem 7A: Ch. Obj. 3
Net income, $4,053.50

Problem 8A: Ch. Obj. 2, 4, 6
Net income, $9,299
Ending Capital, $24,215
Balance sheet totals, $41,267

Chapter 7, Problem 7A Preparing a Six-Column Work Sheet

The final balances in the general ledger of the Bodyworks Fitness Center at the end of July are as follows.

No.	Account	Balance
101	Cash in Bank	$16,095.50
105	Accounts Receivable—R. D. Best	350.00
110	Supplies	612.00
115	Exercise Equipment	15,090.00
120	Office Equipment	2,600.00
125	Office Furniture	3,200.00
201	Accounts Payable—Lake Co.	688.00
205	Accounts Payable—Pro Equipment Co.	2,405.95
210	Accounts Payable—Walton Supply Co.	620.50
301	Lynn Foster, Capital	31,679.55
305	Lynn Foster, Withdrawals	1,500.00
310	Income Summary	0.00
401	Membership Fees	10,500.00
405	Class Fees	8,400.00
501	Advertising Expense	1,250.00
505	Maintenance Expense	1,619.00
510	Miscellaneous Expense	515.00
515	Rent Expense	1,900.00
520	Salaries Expense	6,100.00
525	Utilities Expense	3,462.50

Instructions: Prepare a work sheet for the month ended July 31.

Chapter 8, Problem 8A Preparing Financial Statements

The work sheet for the A-1 Driving School appears below.

A-1 Driving School
Work Sheet
For the Quarter Ended September 30, 19--

ACCT. NO.	ACCOUNT NAME	TRIAL BALANCE DEBIT	TRIAL BALANCE CREDIT	INCOME STATEMENT DEBIT	INCOME STATEMENT CREDIT	BALANCE SHEET DEBIT	BALANCE SHEET CREDIT
101	Cash in Bank	6 107 00				6 107 00	
105	Accts. Rec.-Andover Pub. Schools	450 00				450 00	
110	Accts. Rec.-Taunton Pub. Schools	1 600 00				1 600 00	
115	Office Equipment	2 510 00				2 510 00	
120	Motor Vehicles	30 600 00				30 600 00	
201	Accts. Pay.- Bay State Motors		15 423 00				15 423 00
205	Accts. Pay.- Tappley Co.		1 629 00				1 629 00
301	Mark O'Keefe, Capital		18 516 00				18 516 00
305	Mark O'Keefe, Withdrawals	3 600 00				3 600 00	
310	Income Summary	—	—	—	—		
401	Instruction Fees		15 960 00		15 960 00		
501	Advertising Expense	2 000 00		2 000 00			
505	Fuel Expense	1 656 00		1 656 00			
510	Maintenance Expense	1 800 00		1 800 00			
515	Rent Expense	900 00		900 00			
520	Utilities Expense	305 00		305 00			
		51 528 00	51 528 00	6 661 00	15 960 00	44 867 00	35 568 00
	Net Income			9 299 00			9 299 00
				15 960 00	15 960 00	44 867 00	44 867 00

634

Teacher Notes

Instructions:

(1) Prepare an income statement for the quarter ended September 30.
(2) Prepare a statement of changes in owner's equity. Mark O'Keefe made no additional investments during the period.
(3) Prepare a balance sheet in report form.

Problem 9A: Ch. Obj. 4

Problem 10A: Ch. Obj. 3, 5, 6
Reconciled balance, $13,445.46

Problem 11A: Ch. Obj. 3, 5

Chapter 9, Problem 9A   Preparing Closing Entries

The following information appeared on the work sheet of Young Air Conditioning Repair for the year ended June 30.

	Income Statement		Balance Sheet	
	Debit	Credit	Debit	Credit
Harold Young, Capital				38,000.00
Harold Young, Withdrawals			8,000.00	
Income Summary	—	—		
Repair Service Fees		37,000.00		
Advertising Expense	2,000.00			
Miscellaneous Expense	1,500.00			
Rent Expense	12,000.00			
Telephone Expense	1,200.00			
Utilities Expense	3,600.00			
	20,300.00	37,000.00	56,419.00	39,719.00
Net Income	16,700.00			16,700.00
	37,000.00	37,000.00	56,419.00	56,419.00

Instructions: Using the information above, prepare the four journal entries to close the temporary capital accounts. Use journal page 19.

Chapter 10, Problem 10A   Reconciling the Bank Statement

On April 30, the accounting clerk for Horizon Movers received the bank statement dated April 28. After comparing the company's checkbook with the bank statement, the accounting clerk found

1. The checkbook balance on April 30 was $13,462.96.
2. The ending bank statement balance was $13,883.80.
3. The bank statement showed a service charge of $17.50.
4. Deposits of $675.00 on April 28 and $925.00 on April 29 did not appear on the bank statement.
5. The following checks were outstanding:

   Check 1266 $125.00   Check 1270 $1,462.19
   Check 1268   69.42   Check 1271   381.73

Instructions:

(1) Record the bank service charge in the checkbook.
(2) Reconcile the bank statement for Horizon Movers.
(3) Record the entry for the bank service charge on general journal page 13.
(4) Post the bank service charge to the appropriate ledger accounts.

Chapter 11, Problem 11A   Recording Sales Transactions

The Home Furnishings Center is a retail furniture store. During June, it had the charge sales appearing on page 636.

Additional Reinforcement Problems

635

Teacher Notes

Column totals:
Sales Cr., $2,856.76
Sales Tax Payable Cr., $142.85
Accounts Receivable Dr., $2,999.61

Problem 12A: Ch. Obj. 1, 2, 3
Column totals:
General Cr., $25.00
Sales Cr., $4,751.31
Sales Tax Payable Cr., $190.06
Accounts Receivable Cr.,
$1,252.20
Sales Discount Dr., $12.40
Cash in Bank Dr., $6,206.17

Instructions:

(1) Record the charge sales for June on sales journal page 9.

(2) Foot, total, prove, and rule the sales journal at the end of the month.

Transactions:

June 2 Sold a chair to Elaine McGarrell for $245.00 plus sales tax of $12.25, Sales Slip 160.

4 Sold to Larry Falzarano a set of end tables, $175.00 plus $8.75 sales tax, Sales Slip 161.

10 Sold a magazine rack to Gail Buresh, $22.95 plus sales tax of $1.15, Sales Slip 162.

11 Sold to Stan Garfield a $179.00 bentwood rocker, $8.95 sales tax, Sales Slip 163.

15 Sold two earthenware lamps to Margaret Balzotti for $299.90 plus sales tax of $15.00, Sales Slip 164.

17 Sold a sofa and love seat totaling $1,495.00, sales tax $74.75, to Elaine McGarrell, Sales Slip 165.

20 Sold a telephone stand, $55.00 plus sales tax of $2.75, to Gail Buresh, Sales Slip 166.

22 Sold a coffee table to Larry Falzarano for $259.95 plus $13.00 sales tax, Sales Slip 167.

27 Sold to Elaine McGarrell for $55.00 plus a sales tax of $2.75 a set of three framed prints, Sales Slip 168.

29 Sold a $69.96 side table to Margaret Balzotti, sales tax $3.50, Sales Slip 169.

Chapter 12, Problem 12A   Journalizing and Posting Cash Receipts Transactions

Hanover House, a retail store, uses special journals and an accounts receivable subsidiary ledger to record its business transactions. The accounts receivable subsidiary ledger is included in the working papers. During the month of August, the store had the cash receipts transactions that follow.

Instructions:

(1) Record the transactions in the cash receipts journal on page 17.

(2) Post the individual amounts from the Accounts Receivable Credit column to the customers' accounts in the accounts receivable subsidiary ledger.

(3) Foot, prove, total, and rule the cash receipts journal.

Transactions:

Aug. 2 Julie Murphy sent a check for $535.50 in payment of a sales slip totaling $546.00 less a $10.50 discount, Receipt 213.

7 Received cash on account from Kathy Curley, $75.00, Receipt 214.

8 Received a check for $200.00 from Richard Stratton on account, Receipt 215.

10 Received a $96.90 check from Robert Gaudet as payment for merchandise totaling $98.80, less a $1.90 discount, Receipt 216.

12 Recorded cash sales of $1,603.15, plus $64.13 in sales taxes, Tape 96.

12 Bank card sales totaled $647.50 plus $25.90 sales taxes, Tape 96.

15 Kathy Curley sent a $75.00 check on account, Receipt 217.

18 Sold $25.00 of supplies, as a favor, to Arthur Moore, Receipt 218.

Teacher Notes

_____

_____

_____

_____

Aug. 24 Julie Murphy sent a check for $200.00 on account, Receipt 219.
    28 A $57.40 check was received on account from Robert Gaudet, Receipt 220.
    31 Recorded cash sales, $2,004.91 plus sales taxes of $80.20, Tape 97.
    31 Recorded $495.75 in bank card sales, sales tax $19.83, Tape 97.

Chapter 13, Problem 13A   Journalizing and Posting Purchases on Account

Highland Fashions uses a purchases journal to record its purchases on account. The opened general ledger accounts appear in the working papers.

Instructions:

(1) Record the following transactions on page 11 of a purchases journal.
(2) Post the amounts in the General Debit column to the general ledger.
(3) Foot, prove, total, and rule the purchases journal.
(4) Post the totals of the special amount columns to the general ledger accounts.

Transactions:

Oct. 2 Purchased merchandise on account, $1,263.59, from Liberty Sportswear, Invoice 1633.
    4 Bought supplies on account from Bowen Office Products, Invoice 4301 for $116.25.
    10 Received Invoice 7893 for merchandise purchased on account from Top Drawer Tops, $609.05.
    12 Bought $129.50 worth of merchandise on account from Liberty Sportswear, Invoice 1702.
    15 Davis, Inc., sent Invoice 4782 for merchandise purchased on account, $503.20.
    19 Purchased a new cash register (store equipment) on account from Purcell Equipment, $1,595.00, Invoice 0613.
    23 Received an invoice for merchandise bought on account from Top Drawer Tops, $352.00, Invoice 7909.
    26 Purchased $1,050.90 worth of merchandise on account from Davis, Inc., Invoice 4883.
    29 Received Invoice 4362 for $79.43 for supplies purchased on account from Bowen Office Products.

Chapter 14, Problem 14A   Recording Cash Payment Transactions

Arroyo Leather Goods uses special journals and subsidiary ledgers to record its business transactions. A portion of the company's accounts are included in the working papers.

Instructions:

(1) Record the following transactions in the cash payments journal, page 16.
(2) Post the transactions to the accounts payable subsidiary ledger daily.
(3) Foot, prove, total, and rule the cash payments journal at the end of the month.
(4) Post the total of the Accounts Payable Debit column only to the general ledger.
(5) Prepare a schedule of accounts payable.

Problem 13A: Ch. Obj. 3, 4

Column totals:
Accounts Payable Cr., $5,698.92
Purchases Dr., $3,908.24
General Dr., $1,790.68

Account balances:
Supplies, $921.18
Store Equipment, $11,011.00
Accounts Payable, $7,729.57
Purchases, $33,602.40

Problem 14A: Ch. Obj. 1, 2, 3, 4, 5

Column totals:
General Dr., $4,907.36
Accounts Payable Dr., $7,915.95
Purchases Discount Dr., $152.82
Cash in Bank Cr. $12,670.49

Schedule of Accounts Payable, $2,290.60

Teacher Notes

_____

_____

_____

_____

_____

Transactions:

Nov. 1 Wrote Check 815 to Mesa Realtors for the November rent of $1,200.00.
2 Paid Harris Luggage Co. $1,309.50 for Invoice 1642 totaling $1,350.00 less the 3% discount of $40.50, Check 816.
4 Purchased $300.00 worth of merchandise from Suede Unlimited for cash, Check 817.
8 Issued Check 818 for office supplies costing $136.95.
9 Paid the telephone bill of $214.92, Check 819.
11 Sent Check 820 to Kenwood Manufacturing, $1,225.00, for Invoice P613 for $1,250.00 less a 2% discount of $25.00.
12 Sent $500.00 to Curry Leather Co. on account, Check 821.
15 Issued Check 822 for $2,509.78 to Renaissance Leather in full payment of Invoice 4389 for $2,561.00 less a $51.22 discount.
16 Purchased a roll of stamps for $25.00 (Misc. Exp.), Check 823.
17 Paid Invoice 1427 from Bugatti Leather Works, $1,125.00 less a discount of $22.50, Check 824 for $1,102.50.
18 Paid the $305.00 electric bill by issuing Check 825.
22 Paid $1,200.00 for a one-year fire insurance policy, Check 826.
24 Purchased merchandise for $1,260.00 cash, Check 827.
25 Recorded the bank service charge of $25.00 from the November bank statement.
25 The bank card fee listed on the November bank statement was $176.60.
26 Sent Check 828 to Kenwood Manufacturing for $666.35, in payment of Invoice P668 for $679.95, less a 2% discount of $13.60.
29 Purchased office supplies for cash, Check 829 for $63.89.
30 Sent Check 830 for $450.00 to Harris Luggage Co. on account.

Chapter 15, Problem 15A Recording General Journal Transactions

Instructions: Record the following transactions of the Pottery Shoppe on page 9 of the general journal.

Transactions:

Jan. 5 Gave credit to Megan O'Hara for the return of $80.00 in merchandise sold on account, plus $4.80 sales tax, Credit Memo 36.
10 Discovered that a $320.00 payment on account from Jack Perkins had been incorrectly journalized and posted to John Parker's account, Memorandum 20.
15 Returned defective merchandise purchased on account from Phillips Corp., $270.00, Debit Memo 42.
20 Discovered that a $330.00 purchase of supplies on account from Holbrook Office Supplies had been incorrectly journalized and posted to the Purchases account, Memorandum 21.

Chapter 15, Problem 15B Analyzing Correcting Entries

The correcting entries on the following page were recorded in the general journal of the Merchandise Mart during July.

Instructions: Give a brief description of the error that was probably made when each transaction was originally recorded.

638

Teacher Notes

GENERAL JOURNAL
PAGE 7

	DATE	DESCRIPTION	POST. REF.	DEBIT	CREDIT	
1	July 5	Store Equipment		485 00		1
2		Office Equipment			485 00	2
3		Memo. 77				3
4	9	Purchases		1500 00		4
5		Merchandise Inventory			1500 00	5
6		Memo. 78				6
7	14	Steve Snider		90 00		7
8		Stan Snyder			90 00	8
9		Memo. 79				9
10	17	Sales Returns and Allowances		105 00		10
11		Sales			105 00	11
12		Memo. 80				12
13	19	Supplies		165 00		13
14		Purchases			165 00	14
15		Memo. 81				15

Chapter 16, Problem 16A Completing a Ten-Column Work Sheet

The December 31 account balances for Allston Fabrics, Inc., are listed below. Also listed is the data needed for the adjustments.

	Debit	Credit
Cash in Bank	$ 8,971.14	
Accounts Receivable	5,623.80	
Merchandise Inventory	52,339.50	
Supplies	3,250.00	
Prepaid Insurance	1,800.00	
Office Equipment	8,675.00	
Store Equipment	26,114.25	
Accounts Payable		$ 6,446.90
Federal Income Tax Payable		
Sales Tax Payable		792.97
Capital Stock		30,000.00
Retained Earnings		26,022.38
Income Summary		
Sales		177,890.25
Sales Returns and Allowances	1,316.90	
Purchases	59,296.75	
Transportation In	3,557.80	
Purchases Discounts		1,008.04
Advertising Expense	1,500.00	
Insurance Expense		
Miscellaneous Expense	3,065.40	
Rent Expense	10,800.00	
Salaries Expense	47,600.00	
Supplies Expense		
Federal Income Tax Expense	8,250.00	

Data for Adjustments

Merchandise Inventory, December 31	$ 60,062.00
Supplies on hand, December 31	1,106.50
Insurance premium expired during the period	900.00
Additional federal income taxes owed	1,930.00

Teacher Notes

_____

_____

_____

_____

_____

Instructions: Complete the ten-column work sheet for Allston Fabrics, Inc., for the year ended December 31. The account titles have already been entered on the work sheet.

Chapter 17, Problem 17A   Preparing Financial Statements

The completed work sheet for the Darnell Hobby and Crafts Center appears in the working papers.

Instructions:

(1) Prepare the income statement for the fiscal year ended June 30.
(2) Prepare a statement of retained earnings.
(3) Prepare a balance sheet.

Chapter 18, Problem 18A   Journalizing Adjusting Entries

The Bell City Fishing Supply Co. ended its fiscal period on March 31. The following appeared in the Adjustments section of the work sheet.

	Debit	Credit
Merchandise Inventory		(a) 7,000.00
Supplies		(b) 1,632.00
Prepaid Insurance		(c) 900.00
Federal Income Tax Payable		(d) 1,130.00
Income Summary	(a) 7,000.00	
Insurance Expense	(c) 900.00	
Supplies Expense	(b) 1,632.00	
Federal Income Tax Expense	(d) 1,130.00	

Instructions: Journalize the adjusting entries on general journal page 24.

Chapter 18, Problem 18B   Journalizing Closing Entries

The following account balances appeared in the Income Statement section of the work sheet for the Merryville Corporation for the year ended June 30.

	Debit	Credit
Income Summary	3,462.00	
Sales		96,412.00
Sales Discounts	867.00	
Sales Returns and Allowances	1,735.00	
Purchases	35,000.00	
Transportation In	1,700.00	
Purchases Discounts		750.00
Purchases Returns and Allowances		455.00
Advertising Expense	900.00	
Bank Card Fees Expense	647.00	
Insurance Expense	1,200.00	
Miscellaneous Expense	369.00	
Rent Expense	18,000.00	
Supplies Expense	2,612.00	
Utilities Expense	4,200.00	
Federal Income Tax Expense	5,343.00	
	76,035.00	97,617.00
Net Income	21,582.00	
	97,617.00	97,617.00

Additional Reinforcement Problems

Teacher Notes

_____

_____

_____

_____

_____

Instructions: Journalize all the closing entries on general journal page 17.

Chapter 19, Problem 19A Preparing a Payroll Register

Kelly's Supermarket has four employees. They are paid on a weekly basis with overtime paid for all hours worked over 40. The overtime rate is $1\frac{1}{2}$ times the regular rate of pay. The employee names and other information needed to prepare the payroll are as follows.

Don Bell: Married; 3 exemptions; rate per hour, $6.50; employee no. 106

Alice Kerr: Single; 1 exemption; rate per hour, $5.75; employee no. 112; union member

Eric Sullivan: Married; 2 exemptions, rate per hour, $5.25; employee no. 117; union member

Carol Vinton: Single; 0 exemptions; rate per hour, $5.90; employee no. 119; union member

During the week ended May 6, Bell worked 44 hours, Kerr and Vinton each worked 40 hours, and Sullivan worked 41 hours.

Instructions:

(1) Prepare a payroll register. The date of payment is May 6. List employees in alphabetical order by last name.
- **(a)** Compute FICA taxes at 6.2% for social security and 1.45% for medicare.
- **(b)** Use the tax charts on pages 424-425 to determine federal income taxes. There is no state income tax.
- **(c)** All four employees have deductions for hospital insurance: $3.70 for single employees and $5.10 for married employees.
- **(d)** Union members pay weekly dues of $2.50.

(2) After the payroll information is entered in the payroll register, total the columns and check the accuracy of the totals.

Chapter 20, Problem 20A Recording Payroll Transactions

The payroll register of Star Bakery for the week ended March 31 appears below.

PAYROLL REGISTER

PAY PERIOD ENDING _____ 19 ___   DATE OF PAYMENT _____

EMPLOYEE NUMBER	NAME	MAR. STATUS	EXEMP.	TOTAL HOURS	RATE	EARNINGS			DEDUCTIONS							NET PAY	CK. NO.
						REGULAR	OVERTIME	TOTAL	SOC. SEC. TAX	MEDICARE TAX	FED. INC. TAX	STATE INC. TAX	HOSP. INS.	OTHER	TOTAL		
13	Austin, Corrine	S	1	39	6.25	243 75		243 75	15 11	3 53	23 00	9 75	4 50		55 89	187 86	1
16	Fisher, Paul	M	4	40	7.00	280 00		280 00	17 36	4 06	—	11 20	5 25	UW 3 85	41 72	238 28	2
19	Lopez, Lisa	S	1	25	5.80	145 00		145 00	8 99	2 10	8 00	5 80	4 50		29 39	115 61	3
23	Rutherford, Amy	S	0	43	6.80	272 00	30 60	302 60	18 76	4 39	38 00	12 10	4 50	UW 3 00	80 75	221 85	4
26	Williams, Randy	S	2	35	6.50	227 50		227 50	14 11	3 30	13 00	9 10	4 50	5 00	49 01	178 49	5
27	Wong, Cynthia	M	3	43	5.90	236 00	26 55	262 55	16 28	3 81	2 00	10 50	5 25	UW 2 25	40 09	222 46	6
					TOTALS	1404 25	57 15	1461 40	90 61	21 19	84 00	58 95	28 50	14 10	296 85	1164 55	25

Other Deductions: Write the appropriate code letter to the left of the amount: B—U.S. Savings Bonds; C—Credit Union; UD—Union Dues; UW—United Way.

Instructions: Record the following transactions in the cash payments journal (page 21) and in the general journal (page 11).

Problem 19A: Ch. Obj. 2, 4
Regular Earnings, $936.00
Overtime, $46.88
Total, $982.88
Social Security, $60.94
Medicare, $14.26
FIT, $56.00
Hospital Insurance, $17.60
Union Dues, $7.50
Total Deductions, $156.30
Net Pay, $826.58

Problem 20A: Ch. Obj. 1, 2, 3
Payroll Tax Expense, $202.41
Social Security Tax Pay., $90.61
Medicare Tax Pay., $21.19
FUTP, $11.69
SUTP, $78.92

$687.04

Teacher Notes

Transactions:

Mar. 31 Wrote Check 603 to pay the payroll for the period ended March 31.

31 Recorded the employer's payroll taxes (FICA tax rates 6.2% for social security tax, 1.45% for medicare tax; federal unemployment tax rate, 0.8%; state unemployment tax rate, 5.4%).

31 Issued Check 604 for the amounts owed to the federal government for employees' federal income taxes ($252.00) and FICA taxes ($435.04).

31 Paid $114.00 to the Mutual Insurance Company for the employees' hospital insurance, Check 605.

Chapter 21, Problem 21A   Maintaining a Petty Cash Register

Maureen Miller owns a financial consulting business. She established a petty cash fund on July 1 by writing Check 336 for $100.00. She also records all petty cash disbursements in a petty cash register. The accounts for which petty cash disbursements are usually made include Office Supplies, Delivery Expense, Miscellaneous Expense, and Advertising Expense.

Instructions:

(1) Record the establishment of the petty cash fund on the first line of the petty cash register, page 1.

(2) Record each of the following petty cash disbursements in the petty cash register.

(3) Foot, prove, total, and rule the petty cash register at the end of the month.

(4) Reconcile the petty cash fund. An actual cash count of the fund shows a balance of $5.68.

(5) Check 362 was issued to replenish the petty cash fund. Record the replenishment information in the petty cash register.

Transactions:

July 1 Paid $1.20 for postage due on a letter, Voucher 101.

3 Purchased a $9.00 ad in the *Towne Sentinel* newspaper, Voucher 102.

5 Bought a ream of typing paper for $4.75 and issued Voucher 103.

6 Paid $6.00 for a mailgram, Voucher 104.

8 Issued Voucher 105 for $9.90 to Express Couriers in payment for the delivery of packages.

10 Paid the newscarrier $4.10 for daily newspapers and issued Voucher 106.

13 Bought pens, pencils, and memo pads for $6.60, Voucher 107.

15 Purchased a $9.50 advertisement in a local trade journal, Voucher 108.

19 Issued Voucher 109 for $8.70 for office supplies.

22 Express Couriers delivered financial data from a client, $9.90, Voucher 110.

26 Issued Voucher 111 for $2.12 for additional postage due on mail.

27 Bought an ad in the *Towne Sentinel* for $8.70 and issued Voucher 112.

29 Purchased a typewriter ribbon for $5.50, issuing Voucher 113.

30 Voided Voucher 114 due to an error.

30 Issued Voucher 115 for $4.10 to the newscarrier.

Teacher Notes

Chapter 22, Problem 22A Calculating and Recording Depreciation Expense

The American Carpet Company purchased a delivery truck on October 12, 1991, at a total cost of $78,900. The delivery truck has an estimated useful life of 3 years and an estimated disposal value of $900.

Instructions:

(1) Prepare a depreciation schedule for the delivery truck using the straight-line method. Use the form provided in the working papers.

(2) Record the following transactions on general journal page 41. Post the transactions to the ledger accounts provided.

Transactions:

1991

Oct. 12 Purchased a delivery truck for $78,900 cash, Check 1436.

Dec. 31 Recorded the adjusting entry for the depreciation expense on the delivery truck.

1992

Dec. 31 Recorded the adjusting entry for the year's depreciation expense.

Chapter 23, Problem 23A Calculating and Recording Bad Debts Expense

Quality Rugs, Inc., uses the allowance method of accounting for uncollectible accounts. At the end of the fiscal period, the following accounts appeared on Quality's trial balance.

Accounts Receivable	$18,647.25	
Allowance for Uncollectible Accounts		$ 1,060.50
Sales		452,612.00
Sales Discounts	5,431.35	
Sales Returns and Allowances	13,578.36	
Bad Debts Expense	0.00	

Instructions:

(1) Determine the amount of the adjustment for bad debts for the fiscal period ended December 31. Management estimates that uncollectible accounts will be 1.25% of net sales.

(2) Journalize the adjusting entry in the general journal, page 10.

(3) Post the adjusting entry to the general ledger accounts.

(4) Determine the book value of accounts receivable.

Chapter 24, Problem 24A Calculating the Cost of Merchandise Sold

Harvey's Camera Shop uses a one-year fiscal period beginning January 1. At the beginning of the fiscal period, the shop had a beginning inventory of film valued at $785.23 (527 rolls of film at $1.49 each). During the year, the business made the following purchases.

January 15	500 rolls of film @ $1.49 each =	$ 745.00
March 4	1,200 rolls of film @ $1.53 each =	1,836.00
April 16	1,000 rolls of film @ $1.55 each =	1,550.00
August 24	1,500 rolls of film @ $1.54 each =	2,310.00
October 15	1,750 rolls of film @ $1.59 each =	2,782.50
November 12	2,500 rolls of film @ $1.62 each =	4,050.00
Total Purchases	8,450	$13,273.50

Problem 22A: Ch. Obj. 3, 4, 5, 6

1991 adjustment, $6,500
1992 adjustment, $26,000

Problem 23A: Ch. Obj. 3, 4

Adjustment, $5,420.03
Book value of AR, $12,166.72

Problem 24A: Ch. Obj. 3, 4

Teacher Notes

Cost of ending inventory:
SI, $587.64
FIFO, $588.06
LIFO, $540.87
WAC, $669.91

Cost of merchandise sold:
SI, $13,471.06
FIFO, $13,470.67
LIFO, $13,517.86
WAC, $13,488.82

Problem 25A: Ch. Obj. 2, 4
Maturity value July 1 note,
  $7,771.23
Maturity value Sept. 10 note,
  $1,853.26
Proceeds Sept. 16, $2,429.11
Interest Expense Dec. 15, $70.89

Problem 26A: Ch. Obj. 2
Capital balances:
Adams, $602,500
Lee, $517,500

Problem 26B: Ch. Obj. 2, 3, 4

There were 363 rolls of film in inventory at the end of the period.

Instructions:

(1) Calculate the cost of the ending inventory using the specific identification, fifo, lifo, and weighted average cost methods. For the specific identification method, 350 of the rolls were purchased on November 12 and 13 rolls were purchased on October 15.

(2) Using the costs obtained in Step 1, determine the cost of merchandise sold for each method.

Chapter 25, Problem 25A   Recording Notes Payable and Notes Receivable Transactions

Instructions: Record the following transactions in a cash receipts journal (page 18), cash payments journal (page 25), and general journal (page 11).

Transactions:

Mar. 3   Borrowed $7,500.00 from the American State Bank by issuing a 120-day, 11% interest-bearing note payable, Note 7.

June 14   Received a 90-day, 12% note receivable for $1,800.00 from Marie Richards for an extension of time on her account receivable, Note 3 dated June 12.

July 1   Paid the American State Bank the maturity value of the note issued on March 3, Check 1748.

Sept. 10   Received a check from Marie Richards for the maturity value of the note receivable dated June 12, Receipt 2422.

   16   Borrowed $2,500.00 from the Peoples National Bank, signing a 90-day non-interest-bearing note payable (Note 8), discounted at 11.5%.

Dec. 15   Prepared Check 2254 for the note issued on September 16 and recorded the interest expense.

Chapter 26, Problem 26A   Recording the Partners' Investment

On June 15, Walter Adams and Janice Lee agreed to combine their individual sole proprietorships into one firm organized as a partnership. The partners were to invest all the assets of their two former businesses. Those assets are listed below.

	W. Adams	J. Lee
Cash	$247,000	$517,500
Accounts Receivable	78,000	
Merchandise Inventory	123,000	
Equipment	154,500	

Instructions: Prepare the general journal entries (page 1) required to record the partners' investments. The source document is Memorandum 1.

Chapter 26, Problem 26B   Dividing Partnership Earnings

On January 1, Susan Keith and Mike Yonan formed a partnership organized under the name Ready-to-Serve Hot Foods. Mike and Susan each invested $75,000. Because Mike was going to operate the business, he was to receive 67% of the profits and losses. Susan, who was only investing capital, was to receive 33% of the profits and losses.

Additional Reinforcement Problems

Teacher Notes

During the year, Mike Yonan invested an additional $10,000 in cash in the business and withdrew $4,800. Susan, who expected a profitable first year, withdrew $7,500. Net income for the year ended December 31 amounted to $27,500.

Instructions:

(1) Journalize the entries needed to close the Income Summary and withdrawals accounts. Use general journal page 12.

(2) Post the closing entries to the general ledger accounts.

(3) Prepare a statement of changes in partners' equity.

Chapter 27, Problem 27A Recording Stockholders' Equity Transactions

The Maxwell Corporation was organized on September 1 and authorized to issue 10,000 shares of $100 par, $8 preferred stock and 25,000 shares of $50 par common stock.

Instructions: Record the following transactions in general journal form. Use general journal page 1.

Transactions:

1991

Sept. 1 Issued 4,000 shares of $8 preferred stock at $100.00 per share, Receipt 101.

12 Issued 12,000 shares of common stock at $50.00 per share, Receipt 102.

Nov. 15 Received $52.50 per share for 2,500 shares of common stock issued, Receipt 215.

Dec. 16 Received $5,000.00 for 50 shares of $8 preferred stock issued, Receipt 298.

1992

Mar. 24 Issued 1,000 shares of common stock at $55.00 per share, Receipt 389.

Aug. 15 Declared a dividend of $32,400 on 4,050 shares of $8 preferred stock outstanding, payable on September 15 to stockholders of record on September 1, Memorandum 316.

15 Declared a cash dividend of 25¢ per share on 15,500 shares of common stock outstanding, payable on September 30 to stockholders of record on September 1, Memorandum 317.

Sept. 15 Paid the preferred stock dividend declared on August 15, Check 1763.

30 Paid the common stock dividend declared on August 15, Check 1802.

Dec. 31 Prepared the closing entries in the general journal to close Income Summary for the net income of $102,600 and to close the two Dividends accounts.

Chapter 27, Problem 27B Preparing a Statement of Stockholders' Equity

The account balances on page 646 appeared on the December 31 trial balance of Broughton Products, Inc.

Net income:
Keith, $9,075
Yonan, $18,425

Capital balances:
Keith, $76,575
Yonan, $98,625

Problem 27A: Ch. Obj. 2, 3
Total cash dividend Aug. 15, $3,875

Problem 27B: Ch. Obj. 4
Retained Earnings, $304,000

Teacher Notes

_____

_____

_____

_____

_____

$4 Preferred Stock ($50 Par)	$200,000
Common Stock ($10 Par)	400,000
Paid-in Capital in Excess of Par	200,000
Retained Earnings	275,000
Dividends—Preferred	16,000
Dividends—Common	80,000

Instructions: Prepare the statement of stockholders' equity for the year ended December 31. During the fiscal period, the corporation issued 5,000 shares of common stock at $22 per share. Net income for the period was $125,000.

Chapter 28, Problem 28A   Using Horizontal Analysis

A partial comparative income statement for Wonderland Toys, Inc., is shown below.

Instructions: Complete the comparative income statement using horizontal analysis. Round all percentages to two decimal places. Use the form provided in the working papers.

Wonderland Toys, Inc.
Comparative Income Statement
For the Years Ended August 31, 1992 and 1991

	1992	1991
Revenue:		
Sales	$243,576	$219,326
Less: Sales Returns and Allowances	3,450	4,566
Net Sales	240,126	214,760
Cost of Merchandise Sold	143,579	126,784
Gross Profit on Sales	96,547	87,976
Operating Expenses:		
Selling Expenses:		
Advertising Expense	8,700	7,600
Delivery Expense	8,674	8,796
Depr. Expense—Store Equip.	1,500	1,200
Sales Salaries Expense	23,400	20,120
Travel Expense	5,342	4,123
Total Selling Expenses	47,616	41,839
Administrative Expenses:		
Bad Debts Expense	2,250	2,320
Depr. Expense—Office Equip.	1,550	1,575
Insurance Expense	1,500	2,355
Office Salaries Expense	13,635	12,345
Rent Expense	4,000	5,000
Supplies Expense	3,245	2,100
Total Administrative Expenses	26,180	25,695
Total Operating Expenses	73,796	67,534
Operating Income	22,751	20,442
Other Income	3,000	2,550
Other Expenses	280	355
Net Income	$ 25,471	$ 22,637

Chapter 28, Problem 28B   Using Vertical Analysis

A partial comparative balance sheet for Wonderland Toys, Inc., is shown on the following page.

646

Teacher Notes

Instructions: Complete the comparative balance sheet using vertical analysis. Round the percentages to two decimal places. Use the form provided in the working papers.

Wonderland Toys, Inc.
Comparative Balance Sheet
August 31, 1993 and 1992

	1993	1992
Assets		
Current Assets:		
Cash in Bank	$ 12,790	$ 11,900
Accounts Receivable (net)	14,567	16,890
Merchandise Inventory	38,500	35,000
Prepaid Expenses	2,300	1,900
Total Current Assets	68,157	65,690
Investments:		
Runner, Inc. (stock)	12,500	10,500
Property, Plant, and Equipment:		
Equipment (net)	40,000	45,000
Building (net)	80,000	85,000
Land	15,000	15,000
Total Property, Plant, and Equipment	135,000	145,000
Total Assets	$215,657	$221,190
Liabilities		
Current Liabilities:		
Notes Payable	$ 27,600	$ 22,600
Accounts Payable	24,500	15,000
Sales Tax Payable	1,200	890
Total Current Liabilities	53,300	38,490
Long-Term Liabilities:		
Mortgage Payable	20,000	30,000
Total Liabilities	73,300	68,490
Stockholders' Equity		
Common Stock, $10 Par, 25,000 shares authorized, 5,000 shares issued	50,000	50,000
Retained Earnings	92,357	102,700
Total Stockholders' Equity	142,357	152,700
Total Liabilities and Stockholders' Equity	$215,657	$221,190

Teacher Notes

Enrichment Chapter A

Recording Transactions in the Combination Journal

In earlier chapters you learned that businesses that have a large volume of financial transactions use special journals to record those transactions. Special journals, you'll remember, are designed for recording a "special" kind of business transaction. Therefore, similar entries are recorded in one journal. Each journal has several special amount columns, which speed up the journalizing and posting process. Finally, through the use of special journals, the workload can be distributed among a number of employees.

Although special journals are ideally used in large businesses, they are not very practical for small service and retail businesses with few employees. Such businesses usually have only one accounting clerk. It is impractical for one clerk to record transactions in five different journals. At the same time, using only a general journal is very time consuming. For many small businesses, these problems are solved by using one journal—a combination journal.

The Combination Journal

As its name implies, a *combination journal* is a multicolumn journal that combines the features of the general journal and the special journals into one book of original entry. Like the special journals, the combination journal has special amount columns that are used to record transactions that occur frequently. In addition, the combination journal has General Debit and Credit columns in which to record transactions for which there are no special amount columns. Therefore, all the transactions of a business can be recorded in a single, multicolumn journal.

					COMBINATION			
DATE	ACCOUNT TITLE	DOC. NO.	POST. REF.	GENERAL		ACCOUNTS RECEIVABLE	
				DEBIT	CREDIT	DEBIT	CREDIT
1							
2							
3							
4							

Figure 1 The Combination Journal (*Left Side*)

A business designs its combination journal to fit its own special needs. The number of columns, the selection of the special columns, and the arrangement of the columns will depend upon the type of business and the transactions that take place. Most businesses, however, use combination journals with between 10 and 13 columns. Care must be taken in determining how many columns to include. Too many columns will make the journal too large and difficult to use.

R E M E M B E R

Small businesses design their combination journal to meet their own special needs.

The arrangement of the columns varies from one business to another. The columns should be arranged to make recording and posting easy and accurate. For example, look at Hi-Tech Home Entertainment Center's combination journal in Figure 1. The Date, Account Title, Document Number, and Posting Reference columns are located at the far left. These columns are followed by the General Debit and Credit columns.

The General columns are followed by the special amount columns for Accounts Receivable, Sales, Sales Tax Payable, Accounts Payable, Purchases, and Cash in Bank.

Notice too the line numbers that appear to the left and right sides of each page of the journal. These line numbers help the accounting clerk avoid writing amounts on the wrong lines.

R E M E M B E R

When recording transactions, use the line numbers as a guide to avoid writing amounts on the wrong line.

Using the Combination Journal

A properly designed combination journal can be used efficiently for recording every possible business transaction. Receipts of cash are recorded in the Cash in Bank Debit column; cash payments are entered in the Cash in Bank Credit column. The purchase of merchandise, for cash or on account,

JOURNAL						PAGE _____	
SALES CREDIT	SALES TAX PAYABLE CREDIT	ACCOUNTS PAYABLE		PURCHASES DEBIT	CASH IN BANK		
		DEBIT	CREDIT		DEBIT	CREDIT	

Recording Transactions in the Combination Journal   **649**

Using Visuals

Point out the headings in the journal in Figure 1. Have students relate these headings to the special journals they learned to use in earlier chapters of the textbook.

ACCOUNTING ISSUES

Does anyone use the combination journal anymore? Small businesses that have few transactions may still find a combination journal to be an efficient means of keeping accounting records. With the increased use of computers, though, fewer and fewer businesses are likely to use the combination journal in the future. Many accounting software programs are available for the small business. One of the most popular accounting programs is Peachtree Complete Accounting.

CONCEPT DEVELOPMENT

Using the Combination Journal

Recording entries in a combination journal is no different from recording entries in the special journals. Each business sets up column headings to meet its special needs. Business transactions are analyzed to determine the accounts affected and then recorded in the appropriate journal column.

Making Connections

AROUND THE WORLD

The governments of countries help to promote business interests by negotiating trade agreements that make it easier for companies to do business in other countries. For example, the North American Free Trade Agreement, or NAFTA, is an agreement between Canada, Mexico, and the United States to reduce trade restrictions among the three countries.

Using Visuals

Walk students through the entries in Figure 2. Remind students that the "General" columns are used for all accounts that do not fit in the "special" columns shown in the journal.

COMBINATION

DATE	ACCOUNT TITLE	DOC. NO.	POST. REF.	GENERAL DEBIT	GENERAL CREDIT	ACCOUNTS RECEIVABLE DEBIT	ACCOUNTS RECEIVABLE CREDIT
19-- June 6	Cash Sales	T61	–				
8	Sales Discounts	R62	405	8 00			
	James Angelo		✓				424 00
10	Valley Hospital	S75	✓			530 00	
13	Office Equipment	M11	135	650 00			
	Val Venturi, Capital		301		650 00		
14	Sales Returns & Allow.	CM5	410	90 00			
	Sales Tax Payable		220	5 40			
	Tracey Sands		✓				95 40
15	Clair Anderson	M12	✓			80 00	
	Carl Andersen		✓				80 00
16	Video Distributors	I003	✓				
18	Supplies	I214		100 00			
	Beste Office Supplies		✓				
21	TeleCommunications Sy.	CK350	✓				
	Purchases Discounts		505		6 00		
23	Utilities Expense	CK351	630	175 00			
24	Purchases	CK352	–				
26	Salaries Expense	CK353	625	3200 00			
	Social Security Tax Pay.		205		198 40		
	Medicare Tax Pay.		206		46 40		
	Emp. Fed. Inc. Tax Pay.		210		480 00		
	Emp. State Inc. Tax Pay.		215		70 40		
26	Payroll Tax Expense	P.Reg.	620	456 00			
	Social Security Tax Pay.		205		198 40		
	Medicare Tax Pay.		206		46 40		
	Fed. Unemploy. Tax Pay.		225		25 60		
	State Unemploy. Tax Pay.		230		185 60		
27	Val Venturi Withdrawals	CK354	310	500 00			
28	Compact Discs. Mfg.	DM10	✓				
	Purchases Returns & Allow.		510		90 00		
29	Supplies	M13	110	125 00			
	Purchases		501		125 00		
30	Totals			5309 40	2122 20	610 00	599 40
				5309 40	2122 20	610 00	599 40
				(✓)	(✓)	(103)	(103)

Figure 2 Recording Transactions in a Combination Journal (*Left Side*)

is recorded in the Purchases Debit column. Transactions affecting creditor accounts are written in the Accounts Payable Debit and Credit columns. The sale of merchandise is recorded in the Sales Credit and Sales Tax Payable Credit columns. Transactions affecting charge customer accounts are entered in the Accounts Receivable Debit and Credit columns. Finally, general ledger accounts for which there are no special columns are recorded in the General Debit and Credit columns. Adjusting and closing entries, for example, would be recorded in the General Debit and Credit columns.

R E M E M B E R

The General columns are used to record any amount for which no special columns are provided.

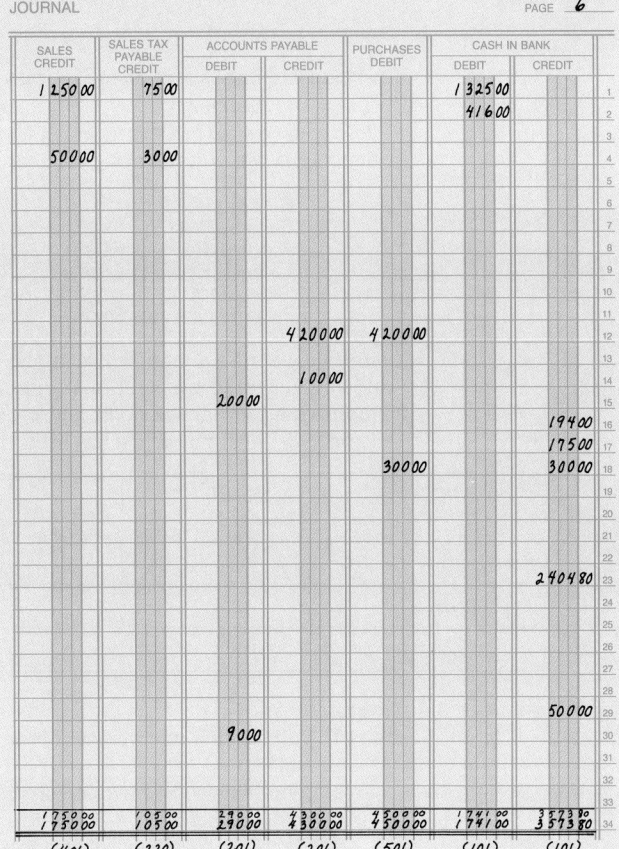

Hi-Tech Home Entertainment Center's business transactions for the month of June are recorded in the combination journal shown in Figure 2.

Proving and Posting the Journal

Like special journals, an important feature of the combination journal is that it saves time in both recording and posting transactions. The amounts entered in the General columns are posted on a daily basis to the appropriate general ledger accounts. Amounts entered in the Accounts Receivable and Accounts Payable columns are also posted on a daily basis to the appropriate charge customer or creditor accounts in the accounts receivable and accounts payable subsidiary ledgers. At the end of the month, the combination journal is footed, proved, totaled, and ruled. Totals of the special amount columns of the combination journal are then posted to the general

Recording Transactions in the Combination Journal

651

ledger accounts named in the column headings. Figure B-2 shows how the combination journal will look at the end of the month after all postings have been made.

Exercise 1   Analyzing Transactions for Combination Journal Entries

John Dunn owns The Country Store, a small retail store. He uses a combination journal with the following columns.

General Debit	Accounts Payable Debit
General Credit	Accounts Payable Credit
Accounts Receivable Debit	Purchases Debit
Accounts Receivable Credit	Cash in Bank Debit
Sales Credit	Cash in Bank Credit
Sales Tax Payable Credit	

Instructions: Use a form similar to the one that follows. For each of the following selected transactions, indicate in which column(s) of the combination journal the debit and credit parts of the entry would be recorded. The first transaction has been completed as an example.

Date	Trans.	General Dr.	General Cr.	Accounts Receivable Dr.	Accounts Receivable Cr.	Sales Cr.	Sales Tax Payable Cr.	Accounts Payable Dr.	Accounts Payable Cr.	Purchases Dr.	Cash in Bank Dr.	Cash in Bank Cr.
1	Debit	✔										
	Credit								✔			

Transactions:

Dec. 1 Purchased a microcomputer on account from King's Computer Outlet.
   2 John Dunn withdrew cash for personal use.
   5 Sold merchandise on account to Bernard Peterson, plus sales tax.
   8 Purchased merchandise on account from Cory Distributors.
   10 Issued Credit Memo 14 to Tom Tray, a charge customer, for the return of merchandise sold on account plus sales tax.
   13 Issued Debit Memo 20 to Cory Distributors for the return of merchandise purchased from them on account.
   15 Received a check from Bernard Peterson in full payment of his account.
   18 Issued a check to Cory Distributors in payment of our account less the purchases return and less a purchases discount.
   22 John Dunn invested a calculator in the business.
   25 Issued a check for the monthly payroll less deductions for FICA taxes, federal income tax, and state income tax.
   25 Recorded the employer's payroll tax liabilities for FICA taxes, federal unemployment tax, and state unemployment tax.
   30 Recorded cash sales plus sales tax.
   31 Recorded the adjusting entry for the office supplies consumed during the period.

Teacher Notes

_____

_____

_____

_____

Dec. 31 Recorded the closing entry to transfer the net income to the capital account.

Problem 1 Recording Transactions in the Combination Journal

Craig Glasser is a physician who operates a family medical practice. His practice, Glasser Family Medical Center, uses a combination journal with these amount columns.

General Debit	Accounts Payable Debit
General Credit	Accounts Payable Credit
Accounts Receivable Debit	Medical Supplies Debit
Accounts Receivable Credit	Cash in Bank Debit
Medical Fees Credit	Cash in Bank Credit
Laboratory Fees Credit	

Instructions:

(1) Record the following transactions on page 17 of the combination journal.

(2) Total, prove, and rule the combination journal.

Transactions:

Oct. 1 Received $2,100.00 in medical fees from patients, Receipt 90.

2 Issued Check 414 for the cash purchase of $120.00 of office supplies.

4 Purchased medical supplies on account from Wharton Laboratories, Invoice 1406 for $1,950.00, terms n/60.

6 Craig Glasser invested medical equipment valued at $750.00 in the medical practice, Memorandum 30.

8 Billed a patient, Daniel O'Connell, $150.00 for his annual physical, Statement 40.

9 Completed lab services for Carl Fisher and billed him $160.00, Statement 41.

11 Purchased a new examination table (medical equipment) on account from Medical Suppliers, Invoice L163 for $1,452.50, terms n/45.

13 Billed Patricia Vallano $300.00 for medical services, Statement 42.

15 Issued Check 415 for $2,004.81 for the monthly salaries expense of $2,500.00 less deductions: social security tax, $155.00, medicare tax, $36.25; employees' federal income taxes, $209.00; employees' state income taxes, $94.94.

15 Recorded the employer's payroll tax liabilities: social security tax, $155.00, medicare tax, $36.25; federal unemployment taxes, $20.00; state unemployment taxes, $145.00, payroll register.

18 Issued Debit Memo 16 to Wharton Laboratories for $200.00 for the return of medical supplies purchased on account.

20 Paid the telephone bill, Check 416 for $110.00.

22 A check for $110.00 was received from John Marshall to apply on his account, Receipt 91.

25 Craig Glasser withdrew $1,250.00 cash from the business, Check 417.

28 Received $75.00 from Daniel O'Connell to apply on his account, Receipt 92.

31 Sent Statement 43 for $95.00 to Donna Gordon for lab services completed on account.

31 Issued Check 418 for the November rent of $900.00.

Problem 1

General Dr., $7,435.25
General Cr., $1,794.44
Accounts Receivable Dr., $705.00
Accounts Receivable Cr., $185.00
Medical Fees Cr., $2,550.00
Laboratory Fees Cr., $255.00
Accounts Payable Dr., $200.00
Accounts Payable Cr., $3,402.50
Medical Supplies Dr., $1,950.00
Cash in Bank Dr., $2,285.00
Cash in Bank Cr., $4,388.81

Teacher Notes

Problem 2

General Dr., $4,077.74
General Cr., $865.81
Accounts Receivable Dr., $408.50
Accounts Receivable Cr., $506.25
Sales Cr., $3,300.00
Sales Tax Payable Cr., $148.50
Accounts Payable Dr., $660.00
Accounts Payable Cr., $900.00
Purchases Dr., $700.00
Cash in Bank Dr., $3,489.82
Cash in Bank Cr., $3,615.50

Problem 2   Recording Transactions in the Combination Journal

Jon James owns Candles 'n Things, a small merchandising business specializing in glass products, figurines, decorative candles, and other small gift items. Candles 'n Things uses a combination journal with these amount columns.

General Debit	Accounts Payable Debit
General Credit	Accounts Payable Credit
Accounts Receivable Debit	Purchases Debit
Accounts Receivable Credit	Cash in Bank Debit
Sales Credit	Cash in Bank Credit
Sales Tax Payable Credit	

Instructions:

(1) Record the following transactions on page 12 of the combination journal.

(2) Total, prove, and rule the combination journal.

Transactions:

Dec. 1 Issued Check 151 for $700.00 to Pine Valley Realty for the monthly rent.

2 Received a check for $204.82 from Wilma Hutchins in payment of her account of $209.00 less a discount of $4.18, Receipt 303.

3 Purchased $400.00 of merchandise on account from the Stained Glass Outlet, Invoice 479 dated December 2, terms 2/10, n/30.

4 Issued Check 152 for $75.00 to The Knight Crier for advertisements.

5 Issued Check 153 for $230.30 to Phoenix Glass Co. in payment of their invoice for $235.00.

6 Sent Credit Memo 35 to Stan Kopak for damaged merchandise returned, $50.00 plus $2.25 sales tax.

8 Sold merchandise on account to Mindy Silvis, $100.00 plus sales tax of $4.50, Sales Slip 205.

10 Discovered that $95.00 received on account from Mindy Silvis on November 16 had been journalized and posted to Robert Sylvan's account, Memorandum 16.

11 Recorded the monthly salaries of $2,100.00 less deductions: social security tax, $130.20; medicare tax, $30.45; employees' federal income taxes, $326.00; and employees' state income taxes, $48.09; Check 154 for $1,565.26.

11 Recorded the employer's payroll tax liabilities: social security tax, $130.20; medicare tax, $30.45; federal unemployment tax, $16.80; state unemployment tax, $121.80; payroll register.

12 Sent Check 155 for $392.00 to the Stained Glass Outlet in payment of Invoice 479 less a discount of $8.00.

15 Received $150.00 from Al Holland to apply on his account, Receipt 304.

18 Issued Debit Memo 20 to Glazing Unlimited for $25.00 for the return of merchandise purchased on account.

20 The owner, Jon James, withdrew $500.00 for personal use, Check 156.

24 Sold $200.00 in merchandise on account to Rob Vesco plus sales tax of $9.00, Sales Slip 206.

Teacher Notes

Dec. 26   Purchased $300.00 of merchandise on account from Phoenix Glass Co., Invoice 601.

     28   Purchased store equipment on account, from Abbot Enterprises, $200.00, Invoice 609.

     29   Paid a $150.00 electric bill for the month by issuing Check 157 to Dukane Power Company.

     31   Recorded cash sales of $3,000.00, plus $135.00 sales taxes, Tape 52.

Problem 3   Recording Adjusting and Closing Entries in a Combination Journal

Shown below is part of the December 31 work sheet for Balloons & Gifts Boutique.

Instructions:

(1) Record the adjusting entries in the combination journal. Then total, prove, and rule the General columns of the journal.

(2) Record the closing entries in the combination journal. Then total, prove, and rule the General columns of the journal.

ACCT. NO.	ACCOUNT NAME	ADJUSTMENTS DEBIT	ADJUSTMENTS CREDIT	INCOME STATEMENT DEBIT	INCOME STATEMENT CREDIT	BALANCE SHEET DEBIT	BALANCE SHEET CREDIT
110	Merchandise Inventory	(a) 2 000 00				26 000 00	
115	Office Supplies		(b) 270 00			95 00	
120	Store Supplies		(c) 1 840 00			327 00	
130	Prepaid Insurance		(d) 70 00			100 00	
301	Lisa Phillips, Capital						28 400 00
305	Lisa Phillips, Withdrawals					1 200 00	
310	Income Summary		(a) 2 000 00	2 000 00			
401	Sales				46 000 00		
405	Sales Returns & Allow.			405 00			
501	Purchases			18 000 00			
505	Purchases Discounts				225 00		
510	Purchases Returns & Allow.				150 00		
610	Insurance Expense	(d) 70 00		70 00			
620	Miscellaneous Expense			180 00			
630	Office Supplies Expense	(b) 270 00		270 00			
640	Rent Expense			6 000 00			
650	Store Supplies Expense	(c) 1 840 00		1 840 00			

Teacher Notes

THE ACCRUAL BASIS OF ACCOUNTING

Use of the accrual basis in accounting helps businesses attain the goal of matching revenue for a period with the expenses incurred to earn that revenue. Under the accrual basis, revenue is recognized when a sale is made regardless of whether the resulting cash has been received. Likewise, interest is matched to the fiscal period when it is earned or incurred, not when it is actually received or paid.

MAJOR CONCEPTS

- Accruals and Deferrals
- Accrued Revenue
- Accrued Expenses
- Unearned Revenue
- Prepaid Expenses

BUSINESS CONNECTION

In 1942 J. Armand Bombardier manufactured and distributed a tracked vehicle to carry passengers and cargo on snowbound roads. Today his invention is a popular recreational transportation vehicle called the Ski-Doo. Following the snowmobile boom in the 1960s, the Bombardier Corporation introduced a new product, the Sea-Doo personal watercraft. Companies like Bombardier use the accrual basis of accounting so they can recognize revenue when it is actually earned and expenses when they are actually incurred.

CONCEPT DEVELOPMENT

Accruals and Deferrals

Very few companies are able to use a cash basis of accounting because it may not allow for the matching of revenue and expenses. Review the definitions of accruals and deferrals. Accruals are items that accumulate or increase. In accounting, accruals are amounts that have accumulated

(continued)

Enrichment Chapter B

The Accrual Basis of Accounting

Some small businesses keep their financial records on a cash basis. The *cash basis* of accounting recognizes revenue and expenses only when cash is received or paid out. Often, however, cash is received from charge customers and payments are made to creditors in an accounting period other than the fiscal period in which the original transaction occurred. When this happens, financial statements may not accurately report data. To overcome this, some businesses use the *accrual basis* of accounting, which recognizes revenue when it is actually earned and expenses when they are actually incurred.

R E M E M B E R

With the accrual basis of accounting, revenue is recorded when it is earned, and expenses are recorded when they are actually incurred.

Accruals and Deferrals

The word "accrue" means to accumulate or grow in size. In accounting, an *accrual* is the recognition of revenue or an expense that has accumulated over time but has not yet been recorded. Accruals are required when

1. *There are unrecorded revenues.* An example is interest earned on a note receivable in one accounting period but not collected until the next period.
2. *There are unrecorded expenses.* An example is wages earned by employees in one fiscal period but not paid until the next fiscal period.

The word "defer" means to delay or postpone. In accounting, a *deferral* is a delay in recognizing revenue for cash already received or an expense for a bill already paid. Deferrals are required when

1. *Already recorded revenues apply to two or more accounting periods.* An example is rent received in advance when some of the rental time is in one accounting period and the rest is in the next accounting period.
2. *Already recorded expenses must be spread out over two or more accounting periods.* An example is office supplies when some of the supplies are used in one accounting period and the remainder in the next accounting period.

Adjusting entries are used to recognize unrecorded revenue and expenses and to allocate already recorded revenue and expenses to the appropriate accounting periods.

R E M E M B E R

Adjusting entries must be recorded when (1) there are unrecorded revenue and expenses at the end of the fiscal period, and (2) already recorded revenue and expenses must be allocated over two or more accounting periods.

Accruals

Accruals are revenue or expenses that are gradually earned or incurred over time. In order to report a company's financial position accurately, accruals should be recognized in the accounting period in which they occur.

Accrued Revenue

Accrued revenue is revenue that has been earned but not yet received and recorded. Examples of accrued revenue include interest earned on a note receivable and fees from advertising services earned but not yet received.

On December 5, the Circle Distributing Co. accepted a $5,000, 90-day, 9% note receivable from a charge customer, Paul Stanley. Stanley issued the note as an extension on his charge account. Circle Distributing Co. recorded the transaction as a debit of $5,000 to Notes Receivable and a credit of $5,000 to Accounts Receivable and Paul Stanley's account in the subsidiary ledger. On December 31, 26 days of interest had accrued (been earned) on the note receivable: $5,000.00 \times .09 \times \frac{26}{365} = 32.05. An adjusting entry must be made on December 31 to record the amount of interest income earned during the fiscal period.

Since the interest earned will not be received until the maturity date, the accrued interest is debited to an account called Interest Receivable. Interest Income is credited for $32.05.

December

S	M	T	W	T	F	S
1	2	3	4	5	6	7
8	9	10	11	12	13	14
15	16	17	18	19	20	21
22	23	24	25	26	27	28
29	30	31				

Interest Receivable		Interest Income	
Dr.	Cr.	Dr.	Cr.
+	–	–	+
Adj. $32.05			Adj. $32.05

The adjusting entry is shown in Figure 1.

	GENERAL JOURNAL			PAGE 18	
DATE	DESCRIPTION	POST. REF.	DEBIT	CREDIT	
	Adjusting Entries				1
19-- Dec. 31	Interest Receivable		32 05		2
	Interest Income			32 05	3

Figure 1 Recording the Adjusting Entry for Accrued Revenue

The Accrual Basis of Accounting   657

Accruals and Deferrals (Continued)

but have not yet been recorded in the accounting records.

Deferrals are items that are delayed, or "deferred." Deferrals are used in accounting when an amount applies to two or more accounting periods.

CONCEPT DEVELOPMENT
Accrued Revenue

Businesses frequently earn revenue before the actual cash is received. A primary example is interest on a note receivable. The business earns the interest each day, but that amount is not recorded until the payment of the interest is received.

Use the T accounts for Interest Receivable and Interest Income to walk students through an example of accrued revenue.

Using Visuals

Explain the rationale for the adjusting entry in Figure 1. Remind students that interest on promissory notes is paid in one payment at the maturity date; thus, no interest is paid during the term of the note.

Making Connections

AROUND THE WORLD
To help improve its operating results, Lufthansa—the German airline—has signed an agreement with the U.S. carrier, United Airlines. Under this agreement, the airlines will follow a practice called "code sharing."

Code sharing means that a single flight number is assigned to a flight even though it may require a change of planes to either a United or a Lufthansa flight. Such plans allow both airlines to increase the number of destinations they serve.

Enrichement Chapter B   657

Using Visuals

In Figure 2 walk students through the calculations for interest receivable and interest income.

CONCEPT DEVELOPMENT
Accrued Expenses
Accrued expenses are amounts the business owes that have not yet been recorded in the accounting records. Use the T accounts for Property Tax Expense and Property Tax Payable to demonstrate this idea to students.

Have students ask their parents when they pay property taxes on their homes. Many people pay property taxes through their monthly mortgage payments. The mortgage company accrues the tax money and pays it to the local government when it comes due. People who pay rent also pay property tax, but in a hidden way. Rental payments cover the building owner's costs, which include property taxes on all the rental units.

On March 5, Circle received a check from Paul Stanley for $5,110.96, the maturity value of the note ($5,000.00 principal + $110.96 interest). Of the total interest, $32.05 had been earned and reported in the previous accounting period. The remaining $78.91 should be recorded as income in the *current* fiscal period.

In the entry, Cash in Bank is debited for $5,110.96, the total amount of cash received. Notes Receivable is credited for $5,000.00. Interest Receivable is credited for $32.05 since this amount has now been received. Interest Income is credited for $78.91, the amount of the interest that applies to the current accounting period.

Cash in Bank		Notes Receivable	
Dr.	Cr.	Dr.	Cr.
+	−	+	−
$5,110.96		Bal. $5,000.00	$5,000.00

Interest Receivable		Interest Income	
Dr.	Cr.	Dr.	Cr.
+	−	−	+
Adj. $32.05	$32.05		$78.91

The entry for this transaction, shown in general journal form, appears in Figure 2.

GENERAL JOURNAL				PAGE 26
DATE	DESCRIPTION	POST. REF.	DEBIT	CREDIT
19-- Mar. 5	Cash in Bank		5 110 96	
	Notes Receivable			5 000 00
	Interest Receivable			32 05
	Interest Income			78 91
	Receipt 416			

Figure 2 Recording the Payment of a Note Receivable

Accrued Expenses

Most expenses are recorded when they are paid, or a liability is incurred. There are, however, some business expenses that build up daily but are not recorded until an adjusting entry is made at the end of the fiscal period. Some examples of these *accrued expenses* are salaries and wages earned by employees but not yet paid to them, interest incurred on unpaid notes, and property taxes owed but not yet paid.

To acquire cash with which to provide services, communities impose a tax on property. Owners usually pay the property tax twice a year, with each payment covering a six-month period and one-half of the annual tax.

Pike Department Store owns the building and land on which it operates. The value of the property is $300,000. The total annual property taxes are $7,800. Pike is located in a state where property taxes must be paid in May and November. The May payment covers the first six months of the calendar year, and the November payment covers the last six months of the calendar year.

Pike's fiscal period ends on March 31. As a result, at the end of its fiscal period, Pike owes property taxes of $1,950 ($7,800 × $\frac{3}{12}$) for the months of January, February, and March. These taxes, however, will not be paid until May. In order to show the correct amount of the property tax expense for the current fiscal period, an adjusting entry must be recorded on March 31. The adjusting entry would be recorded as shown in Figure C-3.

Property Tax Expense			Property Tax Payable	
Dr.	Cr.		Dr.	Cr.
+	−		−	+
Bal. $5,850.00				Adj. $1,950.00
Adj. $1,950.00				

GENERAL JOURNAL				PAGE 57
DATE	DESCRIPTION	POST. REF.	DEBIT	CREDIT
	Adjusting Entries			
19-- Mar. 31	Property Tax Expense		1950 00	
	Property Tax Payable			1950 00

Figure 3 Recording the Adjusting Entry for Accrued Expenses

R E M E M B E R

An adjusting entry must be made at the end of the fiscal period for expenses that have accrued but have not yet been recorded.

On May 15, Pike wrote a check for the semiannual property tax payment of $3,900. Of this amount, $1,950 is an expense charged to the prior fiscal period and $1,950 is an expense charged to the current accounting period. The entry to record this payment is shown in Figure C-4.

Property Tax Expense			Property Tax Payable	
Dr.	Cr.		Dr.	Cr.
+	−		−	+
$1,950.00			$1,950.00	Bal. $1,950.00

Cash in Bank	
Dr.	Cr.
+	−
	$3,900.00

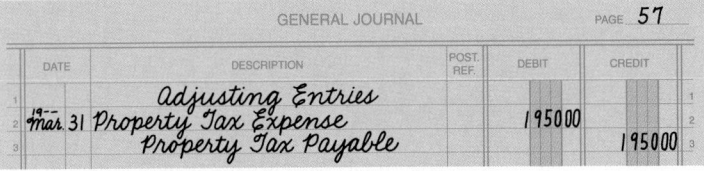

GENERAL JOURNAL				PAGE 60
DATE	DESCRIPTION	POST. REF.	DEBIT	CREDIT
19-- May 15	Property Tax Expense		1950 00	
	Property Tax Payable		1950 00	
	Cash in Bank			3900 00
	Check 401			

Figure 4 Recording the Payment of Property Taxes

Deferrals

Sometimes a business receives cash or a receivable for revenue not yet earned. Cash is also paid out for expenses before those expenses are actually incurred. So that a business can more accurately show its financial condition, unearned revenue and prepaid expenses must be deferred (postponed) to the proper fiscal period.

Unearned Revenue

Ask students whether they have ever bought tickets to a music concert or to a sporting event before the actual event. If so, their payments were unearned revenue for the companies putting on those events. Use the T accounts to demonstrate such a transaction to students.

Unearned Revenue

Unearned revenue is revenue received before it is actually earned. Examples of unearned revenue include cash received in advance for rental properties, for season tickets to various events, for insurance premiums, and for work to be done in the future. Because the business has an obligation to deliver the merchandise or perform the service for which it has already received payment, unearned revenue represents a current liability to the business.

As the business delivers the merchandise or performs the service, it earns a part of the advance payment. The earned portion must be transferred from a liability account to a revenue account through an adjusting entry made at the end of the fiscal period.

Let's look at an example. Randall Real Estate rents space in its building to a tax accountant. On November 1, the accountant paid Randall $1,200 in advance for rent for the months of November through April. The entry to record this transaction is shown in the T accounts below and in Figure 5.

Using Visuals

In Figure 5 point out the use of a different revenue account to record unearned revenue. The business uses different accounts to track all sources of revenue.

Cash in Bank		Unearned Rental Income	
Dr.	Cr.	Dr.	Cr.
+	−	−	+
$1,200.00			$1,200.00

GENERAL JOURNAL				PAGE 24	
DATE	DESCRIPTION	POST. REF.	DEBIT	CREDIT	
19-- Nov. 1	Cash in Bank		1 200 00		1
	Unearned Rental Income			1 200 00	2
	Receipt 181				3

Figure 5 Recording the Receipt of Unearned Revenue

When Randall's fiscal period ends on December 31, the company will have earned rental income of $400 for two of the six months paid in advance ($1,200 × $\frac{1}{3}$).

Unearned Rental Income		Rental Income	
Dr.	Cr.	Dr.	Cr.
−	+	−	+
Adj. $400.00	Bal. $1,200.00		Adj. $400.00

The adjusting entry to record the rental income earned through December 31 is shown in Figure 6.

GENERAL JOURNAL   PAGE 29

	DATE	DESCRIPTION	POST. REF.	DEBIT	CREDIT	
1		*Adjusting Entries*				1
2	19-- Dec. 31	*Unearned Rental Income*		400 00		2
3		*Rental Income*			400 00	3

Figure 6   Recording the Adjusting Entry for Unearned Revenue

R E M E M B E R

Revenue received in advance is recorded in a liability account. That account must be adjusted at the end of the fiscal period to recognize the revenue earned during the period.

Prepaid Expenses

A *prepaid expense* is an expense paid in advance. Examples include the purchase of office supplies, premiums paid on insurance policies, rent paid in advance of the use of the rental property, and bank discounts on non-interest-bearing notes payable.

A prepaid expense is usually recorded initially in an asset account. The portion of the asset that is used up during the accounting period is an expense for that accounting period. The portion of the asset that is *not* used up is an asset that is deferred to the next accounting period. At the end of the accounting period, an adjusting entry is made to record the amount of the expense.

The Lampley Corporation records the purchase of office supplies in the Office Supplies account. At the end of the accounting period, the Office Supplies account had a balance of $2,570. On December 31, a physical inventory showed that only $570 of office supplies were still on hand. By subtracting the ending supplies inventory from the balance of the Office Supplies account ($2,570 balance − $570 on hand = $2,000 used), the amount of office supplies used during the fiscal period is determined.

Office Supplies Expense			Office Supplies		
Dr.	Cr.		Dr.	Cr.	
+	−		+	−	
Adj. $2,000.00			Bal. $2,570.00	Adj. $2,000.00	

The adjusting entry to record the office supplies expense is shown in Figure 7.

GENERAL JOURNAL   PAGE 10

	DATE	DESCRIPTION	POST. REF.	DEBIT	CREDIT	
1		*Adjusting Entries*				1
2	19-- Dec. 31	*Office Supplies Expense*		2 000 00		2
3		*Office Supplies*			2 000 00	3

Figure 7   Recording the Adjusting Entry for a Prepaid Expense

The Accrual Basis of Accounting   **661**

PRACTICE AND APPLY
• Concepts and Procedures

Exercise 1
2. Unearned Revenue
3. Accrued Expense
4. Unearned Revenue
5. Accrued Revenue
6. Accrued Expense
7. Accrued Expense
8. Accrued Revenue
9. Prepaid Expense
10. Unearned Revenue

Problem 1
Adjustments:
(1) $7,400.00
(2) $900.00
(3) $59.18
(4) $250.00

Problem 2
Adjusting entry, $113.74
Maturity value, $9,796.71

Exercise 1 Identifying Accruals and Deferrals

Instructions: Use a form similar to the one that follows. For each item listed below, indicate whether the item is a prepaid expense, unearned revenue, an accrued expense, or accrued revenue by placing a check mark in the correct column. The first item has been completed as an example.

1. A two-year premium paid on a fire insurance policy.
2. Tuition collected in advance by a boarding school.
3. Interest on an interest-bearing note payable due in the next period.
4. Cash received for a three-year subscription to a magazine.
5. Fees due for the completed designs for three of five buildings.
6. Property taxes incurred for the last three months of the fiscal period.
7. Salaries owed but not yet paid.
8. Interest on an interest-bearing note receivable that matures in the next fiscal period.
9. Office supplies purchased.
10. Cash received for season tickets for home football games.

Item	Prepaid Expense	Unearned Revenue	Accrued Expense	Accrued Revenue
1	✔			

Problem 1 Recording Adjusting Entries

The Pinnacle Printing Company uses the accrual basis of accounting. Its fiscal period ends on June 30. The following account balances appear in the company's general ledger as of June 30.

Cash in Bank	$34,616	Office Supplies Expense	$ 0
Interest Receivable	0	Salaries Expense	76,500
Office Supplies	8,335	Rental Income	0
Salaries Payable	0	Interest Income	0
Unearned Rental Income	1,000		

Instructions: Record the adjusting entries on general journal page 14.
(1) The office supplies on hand on June 30 are valued at $935.
(2) Pinnacle's 5-day weekly payroll totals $1,500. Salaries have been earned, but not yet recorded, for June 28-30.
(3) On June 30, 30 days of interest had accrued on an $8,000, 90-day, 9% note receivable from a charge customer.
(4) Of the $1,000 recorded in the Unearned Rental Income account, $250 had been earned as of June 30.

Problem 2 Recording Transactions for Notes Payable

The Landry Corporation uses the accrual basis of accounting. Its fiscal period ends on December 31.

On November 15, the Landry Corporation borrowed $9,500 from the First Federal Savings Bank by issuing a 120-day, $9\frac{1}{2}\%$ interest-bearing note payable.

Instructions: Record the following transactions on general journal page 41.
(1) The issuance of the note payable (Note 7).
(2) The adjusting entry to record the amount of the accrued interest payable.
(3) The payment of the note on the maturity date (Check 411).

APPENDIX C   The Accrual Basis of Accounting

Teacher Notes

Answers to "Check Your Learning" Activities

Chapter 2, Page 19
1. a. $7,000; b. $1,500; c. $8,000
2. $40
3. $20
4. $14,000

Chapter 2, Page 21
1. $25,000
2. liabilities
3. $158,000

Chapter 2, Page 27
1. Cash in Bank, +$30,000; Jan Swift, Capital, +$30,000
2. Office Furniture, +$700; Jan Swift, Capital, +$700
3. Delivery Equipment, +$10,000; Cash in Bank, −$10,000
4. Office Furniture, +$5,000; Accounts Payable, +$5,000
5. Accounts Receivable, +$700; Office Furniture, −$700
6. Accounts Payable, −$2,000; Cash in Bank, −$2,000
   Ending Balances: Assets, $33,700 = Liabilities, $3,000 + Owner's Equity, $30,700

Chapter 2, Page 30
1. Jan Swift, Capital, −$50; Cash in Bank, −$50
2. Cash in Bank, +$1,000; Jan Swift, Capital, +$1,000
3. Jan Swift, Capital, −$600; Cash in Bank, −$600
4. Jan Swift, Capital, −$800; Cash in Bank, −$800
5. Cash in Bank, +$200; Accounts Receivable, −$200
   Ending Balances: Assets, $33,250 = Liabilities, $3,000 + Owner's Equity, $30,250

Chapter 3, Page 44
1. debit
2. credit
3. debit
4.

Office Equipment

Debit	Credit
+	−
$2,000	$500
1,500	
Bal. $3,000	

The balance of $3,000 is recorded on the debit side.

Chapter 3, Page 46
1. right
2. left
3. credit
4.

Accounts Payable

Debit	Credit
−	+
$600	$700
200	500
400	300
	Bal. $300

The balance of $300 is recorded on the credit side.

5.

Patrick Vance, Capital

Debit	Credit
−	+
$1,500	$ 9,000
700	3,000
	1,500
	Bal. $11,300

The balance of $11,300 is recorded on the credit side.

Chapter 4, Page 66

1. The normal balance side of any account is the side on which increases are recorded in that account.
2. A debit increases an expense account.
3. The normal balance for a revenue account is a credit balance.
4. A credit increases a revenue account.
5. A debit balance is the normal balance for an expense account.
6. A credit decreases the withdrawals account.
7. A debit balance is the normal balance for a withdrawals account.

Chapter 4, Page 75

1. Cash in Bank; Rent Expense
2. Cash in Bank is an asset account; Rent Expense is an expense account.
3. Cash in Bank is decreased; Rent Expense is increased.
4. Rent Expense is debited for $2,000.
5. Cash in Bank is credited for $2,000.
6. Rent Expense is debited for $2,000 and Cash in Bank is credited for $2,000.

Rent Expense

Debit	Credit
+	–
$2,000	

Cash in Bank

Debit	Credit
+	–
	$2,000

Chapter 5, Page 88

1. fiscal period
2. cycle; fiscal period
3. source documents
4. general journal

Chapter 5, Page 91

1. September 12
2. Office Supplies, $125
3. Cash in Bank, $125
4. Check 424

Chapter 5, Page 97

1. Advertising Expense
2. 9
3. Memorandum 2

4. October 15
5. 2
6. Global Travel completed services for Burton Company and billed them $450, Invoice 1000.

Chapter 5, Page 100

1. a. assets; b. assets; c. owner's equity; d. expenses; e. revenue; f. liabilities; g. expenses
2. a. Cash in Bank; b. Accounts Receivable — Martinez Company; c. Accounts Payable — Podaski Co.; d. B. Watson, Capital; e. Membership Fees; f. Maintenance Expense; g. Miscellaneous Expense
3. a. 1; b. 1; c. 3; d. 5; e. 4; f. 2; g. 5

Chapter 6, Page 112

1. the date: June 6, 19—
2. Accounts Payable — Monroe Products
3. $250; credit balance
4. 101

Chapter 6, Page 117

1. the letter and page number of the journal entry
2. $4,200
3. a zero balance
4. to indicate that an amount is not being posted from a journal
5. Credit Balance column

Chapter 7, Page 135

1. heading
2. Accounts appear in the same order as they appear in the chart of accounts.
3. A dash is entered in the normal balance amount column.

Chapter 7, Page 140

1. Balance Sheet
2. net income or net loss
3. capital
4. Check to see that all debit and credit balances have been extended properly. If all balances have been extended, check the addition and subtraction.

Chapter 8, Page 154

1. Who? What? When?
2. For the Quarter Ended June 30, 19—
3. individual account balances; totals
4. net income; $236

Chapter 8, Page 157
1. capital account
2. income statement
3. $23,200
4. balance sheet

Chapter 8, Page 160
1. October 31, 19—
2. heading, assets section, and liabilities and owner's equity sections
3. in the same order as they appear in the Balance Sheet section of the work sheet
4. statement of changes in owner's equity

Chapter 9, Page 173
1. a. Ticket Revenue; b. Income Summary; c. $6,000; $6,000
2. a. June 30, 19—; b. Income Summary; c. $3,100; d. Gas and Oil Expense, Miscellaneous Expense, Utilities Expense; e. $700, $600, $1,800

Chapter 9, Page 176
1. work sheet
2. 4
3. Income Summary
4. increased
5. 3

Chapter 10, Page 194
1. Global Travel Agency
2. Hilda G. Burton; Patriot Bank
3. ABA
4. account

Chapter 10, Page 199
1. $2,938.95
2. $635.00
3. $782.00
4. $2,938.95
5. Yes

Chapter 11, Page 217
1. Sales
2. sales slip
3. liability
4. credit terms
5.

Accounts Receivable	
Dr.	Cr.
+	−
$53.00	

Sales	
Dr.	Cr.
−	+
	$50.00

Sales Tax Payable	
Dr.	Cr.
−	+
	$3.00

Chapter 11, Page 223
1. sales of merchandise on account
2. that the transaction has been posted to the accounts receivable ledger
3. daily
4. an account in the general ledger that summarizes a subsidiary ledger; its balance must equal the total of all the account balances in the subsidiary ledger
5. An accounts receivable subsidiary ledger account form has lines at the top for the name and address of the customer and it has only one Balance column.

Chapter 11, Page 228
1. 3
2. to test for the equality of debits and credits before entering the totals in ink
3. by placing the Sales account number, in parentheses, below the double rule in the Sales Credit column
4. Debit
5. a check mark

Chapter 12, Page 242
1. receipt; tape; tape
2. debit side; it is a contra account to Sales, an account which has a normal credit balance
3. $105; $3,395

Chapter 12, Page 247
1. R311
2. General Credit
3. $1,790.00
4. by placing a dash in the Posting Reference column
5. $923.44

Chapter 13, Page 270
1. May 24
2. July 2

3. August 7
4. October 2
5. November 6; $70; $3,430
6. December 13; $18; $582
7. March 20; $19.04; $932.96
8. September 3; $145.10; $7,109.90

Chapter 13, Page 274
1. Purchases
2. decrease
3. debits; credits
4. Purchases; Accounts Payable
5. Store Equipment; Accounts Payable
6. all purchases other than purchases of merchandise on account

Chapter 13, Page 280
1. December 15, 19—
2. Sung International Imports
3. Accounts Payable Credit; Purchases Debit
4. accounts payable
5. check mark
6. Accounts Payable Credit; Purchases Debit; general ledger accounts
7. account number

Chapter 14, Page 293
1. the premium
2. check stub
3. credit
4. because over time such discounts can add up to a sizable reduction in costs
5. decrease

Chapter 14, Page 301
1. 7
2. 0
3. $1,135.21
4. 1
5. $1,008.36
6. no
7. general journal
8. 7

Chapter 14, Page 307
1. Purchases Discounts
2. individual accounts in the general ledger periodically
3. Accounts Payable
4. Cash in Bank
5. Accounts Payable; general
6. $5,000; yes

Chapter 15, Page 324
1. sales return
2. sales allowance
3. credit memorandum
4. Sales
5. debit

Chapter 15, Page 327
1. debit memorandum
2. A purchases return occurs when a business returns to the supplier for full credit merchandise bought on account. A purchases allowance occurs when a business keeps unsatisfactory merchandise but pays less than its original cost.
3. a contra cost of merchandise account
4. that the amount is to be posted to both the general and the subsidiary ledgers
5. cost of merchandise

Chapter 16, Page 349
1. because the balance of the account does not reflect the amount of merchandise on hand at the end of the fiscal period
2. A physical inventory can be taken at any time. It is always taken at the end of the fiscal period.
3. Merchandise Inventory (debited); Income Summary (credited)
4. Income Summary (debited); Merchandise Inventory (credited)

Chapter 16, Page 354
1. $2,503.70; Supplies Expense; Supplies
2. $290.00; Insurance Expense; Prepaid Insurance
3. greater than
4. $115.00; Federal Income Tax Expense; Federal Income Tax Payable

Chapter 16, Page 357
1. 4
2. $81,385.70; the credit adjustment of $3,535.40 was subtracted from the Trial Balance amount of $84,921.10
3. $9,895.00
4. Prepaid Insurance is an asset account; asset accounts are extended to the Balance Sheet section of the work sheet.
5. $0
6. The total of the Income Statement Debit column was subtracted from the total of the Income Statement Credit column.

Chapter 17, Page 366
1. Jane Settles, Capital
2. Capital Stock
3. stockholders' equity
4. Capital Stock and Retained Earnings

Chapter 17, Page 373
1. $78,698.40
2. $7,749.67
3. $82,889.36
4. $74,401.73
5. Net income is calculated by subtracting the federal income taxes from the operating income.

Chapter 18, Page 386
1. Income Summary; Merchandise Inventory; $2,000
2. Supplies Expense
3. Insurance Expense
4. consumed
5. $720.00

Chapter 18, Page 394
1. Income Statement
2. credit; balance
3. Retained Earnings
4. net loss
5. Each revenue and contra cost of merchandise account is debited for the amount of its balance. Income Summary is credited for $20,460.00.
6. The balance of $14,500.00 represents a net income for the period.

Chapter 18, Page 399
1. $27,625.45
2. $68,175.82
3. net income
4. 4
5. Insurance Expense, Supplies Expense, and Federal Income Tax Expense
6. balance sheet

Chapter 19, Page 420
1. a. $173.16; b. $201.24; c. $250.38
2. $441.50
3. $227.10

Chapter 19, Page 426
1. federal income tax; social security and medicare tax; city or state income tax
2. Marital status; number of exemptions
3. a. $2.00; b. $10.00

4. a. $13.89; b. $10.04

Chapter 20, Page 442
1. gross earnings
2. liabilities
3. net pay
4. cash payments

Chapter 20, Page 446
1. $56.00
2. Social Security Tax Payable; Medicare Tax Payable; Federal Unemployment Tax Payable; State Unemployment Tax Payable
3. employer
4. $2,075.07

Chapter 20, Page 448
1. 7
2. the payments were made to different government agencies and businesses
3. $571.16
4. $51.14
5. $1,323.64
6. $0

Chapter 21, Page 468
1. merchandising businesses, including such retail stores as supermarkets and drug stores
2. Change Fund is debited for $25.00; Cash in Bank is credited for $25.00.
3. short; $5
4. Cash in Bank Debit, $390.75; Cash Short and Over Debit, $3.00; Sales Credit, $375.00; Sales Tax Payable Credit, $18.75
5. Cash in Bank Debit, $647.10; Sales Credit, $620.00; Sales Tax Payable Credit, $24.80; Cash Short and Over Credit, $2.30

Chapter 21, Page 475
1. $7
2. Petty Cash Fund is debited and Cash in Bank is credited.
3. $10.35
4. Debits: Supplies, $16.00; Advertising Expense, $9.00; Delivery Expense, $15.90; and Miscellaneous Expense, $8.75. Credit: Cash in Bank, $49.65.
5. A petty cash requisition is prepared to request money to replenish the petty cash fund.

Chapter 22, Page 487

1. A current asset is an asset that is either used up or converted to cash during one accounting period. Examples include cash and accounts receivable.
2. A plant asset is a long-lived asset that is used in the production or sale of other assets or services over several accounting periods. Examples include equipment, machinery, and buildings.
3. Depreciation is the process of spreading the cost of a plant asset over the asset's useful life.
4. Businesses use depreciation to allocate the costs of their assets. The matching principle is involved. Like other expenses, the costs of assets consumed during a fiscal period must be matched with the revenue earned during the same period.
5. (a) the cost of the plant asset, (b) the estimated useful life of the asset, (c) the estimated disposal value of the asset, and (d) the depreciation method used
6. Based on estimates: b, c; based on certainty: a, d

Chapter 22, Page 489

1. $23,000 - $5,000 = $18,000
2. $18,000 ÷ 5 years = $3,600
3. $3,600 ÷ 12 months = $300
4. $3,600 × $\frac{8}{12}$ = $2,400

Chapter 22, Page 494

1. credit; contra asset
2. a. $6,000; Depreciation Expense— Office Equipment
   b. $6,000; Accumulated Depreciation— Office Equipment
3. $22,000
4. $24,000

Chapter 23, Page 509

19—			
Apr. 10	Accts. Rec./Sonya Dickson	630.00	
	Sales		600.00
	Sales Tax Payable		30.00
	Sales Slip 928		
Nov. 30	Bad Debts Expense	630.00	
	Accts. Rec./Sonya Dickson		630.00
	Memo. 78		
Dec. 30	Accts. Rec./Sonya Dickson	630.00	
	Bad Debts Expense		630.00
	Memo. 89		
30	Cash in Bank	630.00	
	Accts. Rec./Sonya Dickson		630.00
	Receipt 277		

Chapter 23, Page 513

1. $125.00
2. $1,350.00
3. no
4. income statement
5. $43,418.00

Chapter 23, Page 517

Adjusting Entry

19—			
Dec. 31	Bad Debts Expense	1,850.00	
	Allow. for Uncoll. Accts.		1,850.00
19—			
May 4	Allow. for Uncoll. Accts.	1,050.00	
	Accts. Rec./Jack Bowers		1,050.00
	Memo. 241		
Nov. 18	Accts. Rec./Jack Bowers	1,050.00	
	Allow. for Uncoll. Accts.		1,050.00
	Memo. 321		
18	Cash in Bank	1,050.00	
	Accts. Rec./Jack Bowers		1,050.00
	Receipt 1078		

Chapter 24, Page 532

1. periodic
2. perpetual
3. periodic inventory
4. computerized perpetual inventory
5. Companies that use a perpetual inventory system take a periodic inventory at the end of the period to verify the balance in Merchandise Inventory.

Chapter 24, Page 535

1. $364.44
2. lifo: $363.52; fifo: $369.48

Chapter 25, Page 550

1. October 17
2. January 1
3. November 18
4. March 14
5. January 7
6. June 17

Chapter 25, Page 552

1. $75.62; $4,075.62
2. $289.73; $10,289.73
3. $136.23; $6,636.23
4. $36.25; $936.25
5. $142.03; $2,542.03

Chapter 25, Page 554

1. a. Cash in Bank, $9,000.00
   b. Notes Payable, $9,000.00
   c. Cash in Bank, asset; Notes Payable, liability
   d. $9,355.07
2. a. January 8
   b. $12,500.00; $12,877.57
   c. Notes Payable is debited for $12,500.00; Interest Expense is debited for $377.57; and Cash in Bank is credited for $12,877.57.

Chapter 25, Page 558

1. a. Cash in Bank is debited for $9,802.74; Discount on Notes Payable is debited for $197.26; and Notes Payable is credited for $10,000.00.
   b. $197.26; $9,802.74
2. a. Maturity value, $10,000; face value, $10,000
   b. Notes Payable is debited for $10,000.00; Interest Expense is debited for $197.26; Discount on Notes Payable is credited for $197.26, and Cash in Bank is credited for $10,000.00.

Chapter 25, Page 561

1. a. Notes Receivable is debited for $6,000.00; Accounts Receivable is credited for $6,000.00; and Amy Andrus's account is credited for $6,000.00.
   b. interest-bearing
2. a. $6,133.15
   b. Cash in Bank is debited for $6,133.15; Notes Receivable is credited for $6,000.00; and Interest Income is credited for $133.15.

Chapter 26, Page 575

1. true
2. false
3. false
4. true

Chapter 26, Page 579

1. Norton, $13,500; Player, $22,500
2. Norton, $45,500; Player, $62,500

Chapter 27, Page 590

1. publicly held corporation

2. par value
3. common stock; preferred stock
4. preferred stock

Chapter 27, Page 593

1. Cash in Bank is debited; Common Stock is credited.
2. par value
3. credited
4. Cash in Bank, $11,250 debit; Common Stock, $7,500 credit; Paid-in Capital in Excess of Par, $3,750 credit

Chapter 27, Page 597

1. declaration
2. record
3. payment
4. declaration; payment
5. $12,500

Chapter 28, Page 614

1. D
2. C
3. I
4. H
5. I
6. B and C
7. F
8. A
9. B
10. J
11. G
12. E

Chapter 28, Page 618

1. E
2. C
3. D
4. B
5. A

Chapter 28, Page 621

1. $73,000
2. 2.18:1
3. 0.45:1

Chapter 28, Page 623

1. B
2. A
3. A
4. B

Glossary

a

account subdivision under the three sections of the basic accounting equation used to summarize increases and decreases in assets, liabilities, and owner's equity

accountant a person who handles a broad range of jobs related to the making of choices and decisions about the design of a business's accounting system and the preparation and explanation of financial reports

accounting clerk entry-level job that can vary with the size of the company from specialization in one part of the system to a wide range of recordkeeping tasks

accounting cycle a full range of activities that help a business keep its accounting records in an orderly fashion

accounting system a systematic process of recording and reporting the financial information resulting from business transactions

accounts payable an amount owed to a creditor for goods or services bought on credit

accounts payable subsidiary ledger a separate ledger that contains accounts for all creditors; it is summarized in the Accounts Payable account in the general ledger

accounts receivable an amount to be received from a customer for goods or services sold on credit

accounts receivable subsidiary ledger a separate ledger that contains accounts for all charge customers; it is summarized in the Accounts Receivable account in the general ledger

accumulated depreciation the total amount of depreciation for a plant asset that has been recorded up to a specific point in time

accumulated earnings an employee's year-to-date gross earnings

adjusting entries journal entries that update the general ledger accounts at the end of the fiscal period

adjustment an amount that is added to or subtracted from an account balance to bring that balance up to date

administrative expenses costs related to the management of a business (for example, office expenses)

aging of accounts receivable method a method of estimating bad debts expense in which each customer's account is examined and classified by age, the age classifications are multiplied by certain percentages, and the total estimated uncollectible amounts are added to determine the end-of-period balance of Allowance for Uncollectible Accounts

allowance method a method of accounting for uncollectible accounts in which an estimate is made of the amount of sales on account for which payment will not be received

assets property or economic resources owned by a business or individual

authorized capital stock the maximum number of shares of stock a corporation may issue

b

balance sheet a report of the final balances in all asset, liability, and owner's equity accounts at a specific time

balance side the same side of an account as the side used to increase that account

bank card a credit card issued by a bank and honored by many businesses

bank card fee a fee charged by a bank for handling a business's bank card sales; it is stated as a percentage of the total bank card sales

bank discount the interest charge deducted in advance on a non-interest-bearing note payable

bank service charge a fee charged by the bank for maintaining bank records and processing bank statement items for the depositor

bank statement an itemized record of all transactions occurring in a depositor's account over a given period, usually a month

base year a year used for comparison

basic accounting equation assets = liabilities + owner's equity; shows the relationship between assets and total equities

beginning inventory the merchandise a business has on hand at the beginning of a fiscal period

board of directors a group of people, elected by the common stockholders, who are responsible for the affairs of a corporation

book value the value of an asset at a specific point in time; for a plant asset, it equals the initial cost of the plant asset minus the accumulated depreciation

book value of accounts receivable the amount a business can realistically receive from its charge customers

business entity an organization that exists independently of its owner's personal holdings

business transaction a business event, such as the buying, selling, or exchange of goods, that causes a change in the assets, liabilities, or owner's equity of a business

c

canceled checks checks paid by the bank and deducted from the depositor's account

capital the money invested in a business by an owner; the owner's equity in a business; the owner's claim or right to a business's assets

capital stock the total amount of investment in a corporation by its stockholders

cash discount the amount a charge customer can deduct if merchandise is paid for within a specified time

cash payments journal a special journal used to record all transactions in which cash is paid out or decreased

cash receipt cash received by a business

cash receipts journal a special journal used to record all transactions in which cash is received

cash sale a transaction in which a business receives full payment for the merchandise sold at the time of the sale

certified public accountant (CPA) a public accountant who has passed the licensing exam on accounting theory, practice, auditing, and business law

change fund an amount of money, consisting of varying denominations of bills and coins, that is used for making change in cash transactions

charge customer a customer to whom a sale on account is made

chart of accounts a list of all the accounts used in journalizing a business's transactions

charter a written permission to operate as a corporation; it spells out the rules under which a business must operate

check a written order from a depositor telling the bank to pay cash to the person or business named on the check

check stub the portion remaining after a check has been detached from a checkbook; the check stub contains details of the cash payment

checking account a bank account that allows a bank customer to deposit cash and to write checks against the account balance

closely held corporation a corporation, often owned by a few people or by a family, that does not offer its stock for sale to the general public

closing entries journal entries made to close out, or reduce to zero, the balances in the temporary capital accounts and to transfer the net income or loss for the period to the capital account

Glossary

commission an amount paid to an employee based on a percentage of the employee's sales

common stock the stock issued by a corporation when it is authorized to issue only one class of stock

comparability the accounting principle that allows the financial information from one period to be compared to that of another period; also, the comparison of financial information of two or more businesses

compound entry a journal entry having two or more debits or credits

computerized accounting system a system in which financial information is recorded by entering it into a computer

conservatism accounting guideline requiring that accountants choose the "safer," or more conservative, method when there is a choice of procedures

contra account an account whose balance is a decrease to another account

controlling account an account that acts as a control on the accuracy of the accounts in a related subsidiary ledger; its balance must equal the total of all the account balances in the subsidiary ledger

corporation a business organization legally recognized to have a life of its own

correcting entry an entry made to correct an error in a journal entry discovered after posting

cost of merchandise the actual cost to the business of the merchandise to be resold to customers

cost of merchandise sold the actual cost to the business of the merchandise sold to customers

credit an agreement to pay for a purchase at a later time; an entry to the right side of a T account

credit card a card containing a customer's name and account number that is presented when buying merchandise on account

credit memorandum a form that lists the details of a sales return or sales allowance; the charge customer's account is credited for the amount of a return or allowance

credit terms terms for a sale on account that set out the time allowed for payment

creditor a person or business that has a claim to the assets of a business; a person or business to which money is owed

current assets those assets that are either used up, sold, or converted to cash during one accounting period

current liabilities debts of a business that must be paid within the next accounting period

current ratio the relationship between current assets and current liabilities; calculated by dividing the dollar amount of current assets by the dollar amount of current liabilities

d

debit an entry made to the left side of a T account

debit memorandum a form used by a business to notify a creditor of a return or allowance

deduction (payroll) an amount that is subtracted from an employee's gross earnings

deposit slip a bank form on which the currency (bills and coins) and checks to be deposited are listed

depositor a person or business that has cash on deposit in a bank

depreciation the allocation of the cost of a plant asset over its useful life

direct deposit the depositing of an employee's net pay directly into her or his personal bank account; usually made through electronic funds transfer

direct write-off method a procedure in which an uncollectible account is removed from the accounts receivable subsidiary ledger and the controlling account in the general ledger when a business determines that the amount owed is not going to be paid

discount period the period of time in which a cash discount is available

disposal value the estimated value of a plant asset at its replacement time; often called trade-in value or salvage value

dividends a return on the investments by the stockholders of a corporation;

672

charged against the corporation's retained earnings

double-entry accounting a financial recordkeeping system in which each transaction affects at least two accounts; for each debit there must be an equal credit

drawee the bank on which a check is written

drawer the person who signs a check

due date the date by which an invoice must be paid

e

electronic badge reader computerized equipment that reads a magnetic strip on an employee's time card and automatically records the employee's arrival or departure time

electronic funds transfer system a system that enables banks to transfer funds from the account of one depositor to the account of another without the immediate exchange of checks

employee's earnings record an individual payroll record prepared for each employee; includes data on earnings, deductions, net pay, and accumulated earnings

ending inventory the merchandise a business has on hand at the end of a fiscal period

endorsement an authorized signature written or stamped on the back of a check

equity the total financial claims to the assets, or property, of a business

exemption an allowance claimed by a taxpayer that reduces the amount of taxes that must be paid

expense the cost of the goods or services that are used to operate a business; expenses decrease owner's equity

external controls those controls provided outside a business (for example, controls maintained by banks to protect deposits)

f

face value the amount written on the "face" of a promissory note; usually the same as the principal

federal tax deposit coupon (Form 8109) a form sent with the payment for FICA and federal income taxes or federal unemployment taxes to indicate the total amount of taxes being paid

financial statements reports prepared to summarize the changes resulting from business transactions that have occurred during the fiscal period

first in, first out method (fifo) an inventory costing method that assumes the first items purchased (first in) were the first items sold (first out)

fiscal period the time covered by an accounting report (usually one year)

FOB destination shipping terms specifying that the supplier pays the shipping cost to the buyer's destination

FOB shipping point shipping terms specifying that the buyer pays the shipping charge from the supplier's shipping point

footing a column total written in pencil in small figures

Form 940 the employer's unemployment tax return; it includes both federal and state unemployment taxes paid during the year

Form 941 the employer's quarterly federal tax return; it reports the accumulated amounts of FICA and federal income tax withheld from employees' earnings for the quarter as well as FICA tax owed by the employer

Form W-2 a form that provides the employee with a summary of earnings and amounts withheld for federal, state, and local taxes; also called a wage and tax statement

Form W-3 a summary of the information contained on the employees' Forms W-2; also called a transmittal of income and tax statements

full disclosure accounting guideline requiring that a financial report include enough information so that it is complete

g

general bookkeeper one person who keeps all the accounting records, usually for a small- or medium-sized business

general journal an all-purpose journal in which all transactions may be recorded

general ledger the group of accounts used by a business

going concern the assumption that a business entity will continue to operate for an indefinite time

gross earnings the total amount of money earned by an employee during a pay period

gross profit the difference between the revenue earned from sales and the total cost of the merchandise sold

gross profit on sales the amount of profit made during the fiscal period before expenses are deducted; it is found by subtracting the cost of merchandise sold from net sales

h

hardware computers and related equipment, such as disk drives and printers

horizontal analysis the comparison of the same items on accounting statements for two or more accounting periods and the analysis of changes from one period to the next

i

income statement a report of the net income or net loss for a fiscal period; sometimes called a "profit and loss" statement

Income Summary account the account in the general ledger used to summarize the revenue and expenses for the fiscal period

interest the fee charged for the use of money

interest rate the fee charged for the use of the principal when a loan is made

interest-bearing note a note that requires the face value plus interest to be paid at maturity

internal controls steps a business takes to protect cash (for example, limiting the number of persons handling cash)

inventory the items of merchandise a business has in stock

investments those assets owned by a business but not used in the operation of the business

invoice a bill; a form that lists the quantity, description, unit price, and total cost of the items sold and shipped to a buyer

issue date the date on which a promissory note is written

j

journal a chronological record of a business's transactions

journalizing the process of recording business transactions in a journal

l

last in, first out method (lifo) an inventory costing method that assumes that the last items purchased are the first items sold

ledger a book or file containing a separate page for each business account; serves as a permanent record of financial transactions

ledger account form the accounting stationery used to record financial information about a specific account

liabilities amounts owed to creditors; the claims of creditors to the assets of the business

liquidity ease with which an asset can be converted to cash

liquidity ratios measures of a business's ability to meet current debts as they become due and to provide for unexpected needs for cash

long-term liabilities debts that are not required to be paid within the next accounting period

loss the result of a company's spending more than it receives in revenue

m

maker the person or business promising to repay the principal and interest when a loan is made

managerial accounting accounting within a business firm to provide financial information to management

manual accounting system a system in which accounting information is processed by hand

manufacturing business a business that transforms raw materials into finished products through the use of labor and machinery

market value the current "market" price that is being charged for a specific item; the price at which inventory items could be replaced at the time an inventory is taken

matching principle principle stating that expenses are compared to revenues for the same period

materiality an accounting guideline stating that relatively important data should be included in financial reports

maturity date the due date of a promissory note; the date on which the principal and interest must be paid

maturity value the principal plus interest on a note that must be paid on the maturity date

medicare a federal program that provides certain health insurance benefits to retired people.

merchandise goods bought for resale to customers

merchandising business a business that buys goods (for example, books or clothing) and then sells those goods for a profit

mutual agency the characteristic of partnerships under which any partner can enter into agreements for the business that are binding on all other partners

n

net income the amount left after expenses for the period have been subtracted from revenue for the same period

net loss the amount by which total expenses exceed total revenue

net pay the amount of money left after all deductions have been subtracted from gross earnings

net purchases the total cost of all merchandise purchased during a fiscal period, less any purchases discounts, returns, or allowances

net sales the amount of sales for the fiscal period, less any sales discounts, returns, or allowances

non-interest-bearing note a note from which the interest is deducted at the time the note is made; a promissory note that has no stated rate of interest on its face

normal balance the increase side of an account: assets, debit side; liabilities and capital, credit side

note payable a promissory note issued to a creditor

note receivable a promissory note that a business accepts from a customer or other person who owes the business money

not-for-profit organization an organization that does not operate for the purpose of making a profit

NSF check a check returned by the bank because there are not sufficient funds in the drawer's checking account to cover the amount of the check

o

on account buying on credit; agreeing to pay for an item later

online the direct link-up of a terminal or cash register to a centralized computer system

operating expenses the cash spent or assets consumed to earn revenue for a business; operating expenses do not include federal income tax expense

operating income the taxable income of a corporation

other expense a non-operating expense; an expense that does not result from the normal operations of the business

other revenue non-operating revenue; revenue earned for transactions outside the normal operations of the business

outstanding checks checks that have been written but not yet presented to the bank for payment

outstanding deposits deposits that have been made and recorded in the checkbook but that do not appear on the bank statement

overtime rate a rate of pay $1\frac{1}{2}$ times an employee's regular rate of pay; overtime is paid for all hours worked over 40 per week

owner's equity the owner's claims to or investment in the assets of the business

p

packing slip a form that lists the items included in a shipment

paid-in capital in excess of par the amount of cash received by a corporation over the stock's par value

par value the dollar amount assigned to each share of stock when the corporation's charter is approved; used to determine the amount credited to the capital stock account

partnership a type of business ownership in which two or more persons agree to operate the business as co-owners

partnership agreement a written document that sets out the terms under which a partnership will operate

pay period the amount of time for which an employee is paid

payee the person or business to whom a check is written; the person or business to whom a promissory note is payable

payroll a list of the employees of a business that shows the payments due to each employee for a specific pay period

payroll clerk a person whose responsibility is the preparation of the payroll

payroll register a form that summarizes information about employees' earnings for each pay period

percentage of net sales method a method of estimating bad debts expense in which a business assumes that a certain percentage of each year's net sales will be uncollectible

periodic inventory system an inventory system in which the number of items on hand is determined by a physical count

permanent accounts accounts that are continuous from one accounting period to the next; balances are carried forward to the next period (for example, assets, liabilities, and owner's capital accounts)

perpetual inventory system an inventory system in which a constant, up-to-date record of the amount of merchandise on hand is maintained

petty cash disbursement a payment made from the petty cash fund

petty cash fund cash kept on hand for making small, incidental cash payments

petty cash register a record of all disbursements made from the petty cash fund

petty cash requisition a form requesting money to replenish the petty cash fund

petty cash voucher a form that provides proof of payment from the petty cash fund

petty cashier the person responsible for maintaining the petty cash fund and for making petty cash disbursements

physical inventory an actual count of all the merchandise on hand and available for sale

piece rate the amount paid to an employee for each item, or piece, produced

plant and equipment long-lived assets that are used in the production or sale of other assets or services over several accounting periods; commonly called plant assets

post-closing trial balance the trial balance prepared after the closing entries have been journalized and posted

posting the process of transferring information in a journal entry to accounts in a ledger

preferred stock stock whose owners have certain privileges over common stockholders

premium the amount paid for insurance

principal the amount of money being borrowed on a promissory note

private enterprise economy an economy in which people are free to produce the goods and services they choose

proceeds the amount of cash actually received by a borrower on a non-interest-bearing note payable

processing stamp a stamp placed on a creditor's invoice that outlines the steps to be followed in processing the invoice for payment

profit the amount of revenue earned above the expenses incurred to operate the business

profitability ratios ratios used to evaluate the earnings performance of a business during the accounting period (for example, return on common stockholders' equity)

676

promissory note a written promise to pay a certain amount of money at a specific, future time

property items of value that are owned or controlled by a business; economic resources of a business

property rights creditors' and owners' financial claims to the assets of a business

proving cash the process of determining whether the amounts of cash recorded in a business's accounting records and in its checkbook agree

proving the ledger adding all debit balances and all credit balances of ledger accounts and then comparing the two totals to see whether they are equal

proxy a document that transfers a stockholder's voting rights to someone else

publicly held corporation a corporation whose stock is widely held, has a large market, and is usually traded on a stock exchange

purchase discount term used by the buyer to refer to a cash discount offered for early payment

purchase order a written offer to a supplier to buy certain items

purchase requisition a written request that a certain item or items be ordered

Purchases the account used to record the cost of merchandise purchased during a fiscal period

purchases allowance a price reduction given when a business keeps unsatisfactory merchandise it has bought

purchases journal a special journal used to record all transactions in which items are bought on account

purchases return the return to the supplier for full credit of merchandise bought on account

q

quick ratio a measure of the relationship between short-term liquid assets (cash and receivables) and current liabilities

r

ratio analysis a numerical comparison of two items on a financial statement that is used to evaluate the relationship of the two items

receipt a form that serves as a record of cash received

reconciling the bank statement the process of determining any differences between a bank statement balance and a checkbook balance

relevance a characteristic of accounting requiring that information "make a difference" in reaching a business decision

reliability a characteristic requiring that accounting information be reasonably free of bias and error

report form a format for preparing the balance sheet in which the classifications of accounts are one under another

restrictive endorsement a check endorsement that restricts or limits how a check may be handled (for example, "For Deposit Only")

retailer a business that sells to the final user (consumer)

retained earnings earnings held by a corporation and not paid to stockholders as a return on their investment

revenue income earned by a business from its operations; revenue increases owner's equity

revenue principle accounting principle that states that revenue is recognized and recorded on the date it is earned

ruling a single line drawn under a column of figures to signify that the entries above the rule are to be added or subtracted; a double rule under an amount signifies a total

s

salary a fixed amount of money paid to an employee for each pay period

sale on account the sale of goods that will be paid for later

sales allowance a price reduction granted by a business for damaged goods kept by the customer

sales discount a cash discount

sales journal a journal used only to record the sale of merchandise on account

sales return any merchandise returned for full credit or a cash refund

sales slip a form that lists the details of a sale

sales tax a tax levied by a city or state on the retail sale of merchandise

schedule of accounts payable a list of all creditors in the accounts payable ledger, the balance in each account, and the total amount owed to all creditors

schedule of accounts receivable a list of each charge customer, the balance in the customer's account, and the total amount due from all customers

selling expenses expenses incurred in selling or marketing the merchandise or services sold by a business

service business a business operated for profit that provides a needed service for a fee

signature card a card containing the signature(s) of the person(s) authorized to write checks on a checking account

slide accidental misplacement of a decimal point in an amount

software computer programs that direct the operation of the computer

sole proprietorship a business that has one owner

source document a paper prepared as evidence that a transaction occurred

special journals multicolumn journals with columns reserved for the recording of specific types of transactions

specific identification method an inventory costing method in which the exact cost of each item in inventory is determined and assigned; used most often by businesses that have a low unit volume of merchandise with high unit prices

statement of changes in owner's equity a financial statement prepared to summarize the effects of business transactions on the capital account

statement of changes in partners' equity a financial statement that reports the changes in each partner's capital account as a result of business operations

statement of retained earnings a statement that reports the changes that have taken place in the Retained Earnings account during the fiscal period; prepared as a supporting document for the balance sheet

statement of stockholders' equity a statement that reports the changes that have taken place in all of the stockholders' equity accounts during the period

stockholders' equity the value of the stockholders' claims to the assets of the corporation

stop payment order a demand by the depositor that a bank not honor a certain check

straight-line depreciation a method of equally distributing the cost of a plant asset over the asset's estimated useful life

subsidiary ledger a ledger that is summarized in a controlling account in the general ledger

t

T account an account shaped like a "T" that is used for analyzing transactions

temporary capital accounts accounts used to record information during the fiscal period that will be transferred to a permanent capital account at the end of the period

term the length of time the borrower has to repay a promissory note

tickler file a file that contains a folder for each day of the month; invoices are placed in the folders according to their due dates

timecard a record of the time an employee arrives at work, the time the employee leaves, and the total number of hours worked each day

transposition error the accidental reversal of two numbers

trial balance a proof of the equality of total debits and credits

u

uncollectible account an account receivable that cannot be collected

unemployment taxes taxes collected to provide funds for workers who are temporarily out of work; usually paid only by the employer

v

vertical analysis a method of analysis that requires the restating of each dollar amount reported on a financial statement as a percentage of a base amount reported on the same statement

voiding a check canceling a check by writing the word "Void" on the front of a check in ink

w

wage an amount of money paid to an employee at a specified rate per hour worked

weighted average cost method an inventory costing method in which all purchases of an item are added to the beginning inventory of that item; the total cost is then divided by the total units to obtain the average cost per unit

wholesaler a business that sells to retail businesses

withdrawal the removal of cash or another asset from the business by the owner for personal use

work sheet a working paper used to collect information from ledger accounts for use in completing end-of-fiscal-period work

working capital the amount by which current assets exceed current liabilities

Credits

Cover Photos © Marble background, Otto Rogge/The Stock Market
World Trade Center, Ben Simmons/The Stock Market

vii (t) © Roy Morsch/The Stock Market
vii (b) © Giulio Veggi/The Stock Market
iv © The Image Bank
v © C. Bowman/Picture Perfect
vi (t) © Index Stock
vi (b) © David R. Frazier/Photo Library
1 © Roy Morsch/The Stock Market
2 © Mark Harmel/FPG International
4 © Miro Vintoniv/Stock Boston
8 © Superstock
16 © Gary Gladstone/The Image Bank
17 © Comstock
18 © Peter L. Champman
29 © Charles Gupton/Stock Boston
37 © Gabe Palmer/The Stock Market
39 © Giulio Veggi/The Stock Market
41 © Comstock
47 © Paul Markow/FPG International
50 © Ron Chapple/FPG International
59 © Lowell Georgia/Photo Researchers, Inc.
60 © Four by Five
62 © Chris Noble/AllStock
71 © Richard Hutchings/Photo Researchers, Inc.
82 © David R. Frazier/Photolibrary
83 © Diane Padys/FPG International
98 © KS Studios
106 © Frank Siteman/The Picture Cube
107 © Tony Stone Images
109 © Michal Heron/Woodfin Camp & Associates
127 © Gabe Palmer/The Stock Market
128 © C.J. Pickerell/FPG International
130 © Picture Perfect
132 © Richard Hutchings/Photo Researchers, Inc.
147 © Elliott V. Smith/Int'l Stock Photo
148 © SuperStock
151 © 1987 Ed Bock/The Stock Market
167 © KS Studios
168 © Comstock
176 © Joseph Nettis/Photo Researchers, Inc.
186 © Dan McCoy From Rainbow
187 © Tom McCarthy/The Stock Market
188 © Steve Dunwell/The Image Bank
195 © Elyse Lewin/The Image Bank
206 © KS Studios
207 © Michael Krasowitz/FPG International
211 © The Image Bank
213 © Comstock
222 © G. Covian/The Image Bank
237 © Randy Duchaine/The Stock Market
238 © Janeart/The Image Bank
240 © Mark Sherman/Bruce Coleman, Inc.
246 © Susan Van Etten/The Picture Cube
264 © Jeff Smith/The Image Bank
265 © Don Smetzer/Tony Stone Images
268 © Jay Freis/The Image Bank
275 © Beth Ullmann/Taurus Photos
288 © Spencer Grant/Stock Boston
289 © Lawrence Migdale/Stock Boston
291 © Richard Hackett/Int'l Stock Photo
298 © Henley & Savage/The Stock Market

316 © Richard Hackett
317 © James Wilson/Woodfin Camp & Associates
318 © Peter L. Chapman
337 © Robert Schoen
338 © Larry Dale Gordon/The Image Bank
341 © SuperStock
346 © Comstock
363 © Camerique/E.P. Jones
364 © John Elk III/Bruce Coleman, Inc.
368 © David Hamilton/The Image Bank
375 © 1985 Chris Jones/The Stock Market
382 © KS Studios
383 © Richard Pan/The Image Bank
385 © Bill Stanton, Int'l Stock Photo
398 © KS Studios
409 © Four by Five
410 © Sheryl McNee/Tony Stone Images
415 © C. Bowman/Picture Perfect
416 © Richard Price/Westlight
418 © Jennifer Cogswell/The Picture Cube
421 © Robert Capece/Monkmeyer Press Photo Service
436 © Michael Abramson/Woodfin Camp & Associates
437 © Dick Luria/FPG International
442 © KS Studios
458 © KS Studios
459 © Tom Pantages
463 © Index Stock
464 © Allen Russell/ProFiles West
465 © Lawrence Migdale/Photo Researchers, Inc.
474 © Peter Garfield/The Stock Market
483 © Steve Strickland/Westlight
484 © Randy Wells/AllStock
486 © Alan Levenson/Tony Stone Images
496 © Janet Gill/Tony Stone Images
504 © John G. Ross/Photo Researchers, Inc.
505 © Tom McCarthy/ProFiles West
509 © Michael Salas/The Image Bank
515 © KS Studios
527 © Tim Davis/Photo Researchers, Inc.
528 © Walter Bibikow/The Image Bank
531 © Gabe Palmer/The Stock Market
537 © Joseph Nettis/Photo Researchers, Inc.
546 © Dan McCoy, From Rainbow
547 © J.R. Ferro/ProFiles West
552 © Michael K. Nichols/Magnum Photos
560 © Four by Five
567 © Spencer Grant/The Picture Cube
569 © David R. Frazier/Photolibrary
570 © Carol Lee/The Picture Cube
572 © Mark Sherman/Bruce Coleman, Inc.
578 © Dave Forbert/SuperStock
585 © Alvis Upitis/The Image Bank
586 © SuperStock
588 © Jon Feinsersh/Stock Boston
598 © Robert Schoen
607 © Gabe Palmer/The Stock Market
608 © Peter Beck/The Stock Market
614 © Lawrence Migdale/Photo Researchers, Inc.
619 © Barbara Loudis/Int'l Stock Photo
630 © K.S. Studios

680

*I*ndex

681

shipping charges and, 292, 370
credit, 19 *def.*, 42
  buying on, 19, 25, 49-50
  card, 215
  check, 506
  extending, 506
  manager, 316
  memorandum, 319
  rules of, 42-46, 63-67, 75
  terms, 216
credit card, 215
credit memorandum, 319 *def.*
credit terms, 216
creditor, 19 *def.*
current assets, 485 *def.*, 611
current liabilities, 611 *def.*
current ratio, 619 *def.*

d

dates, of posting, 111
debit, 42 *def.*
  rules of, 42-46, 63-67, 75
debit memorandum, 324 *def.*
deductions
  from gross earnings, 420-426
  section of payroll register, 427
  voluntary payroll, 423, 426
deferral, 656 *def.*, 660-661
deposit slip, 191 *def.*
depositor, 189 *def.*
deposits
  making, 191-192
  outstanding, 197
  recording, in checkbook, 192
depreciation, 485 *def.*
  accumulated, 490, 491-492
  adjusting entries for, 496-497
  adjustment for, on work sheet, 490-494
  and book value, 490
  calculating, 488
  closing entry for, 497-498
  and disposal value, 487
  estimating, 486-488
  expense, 488
  reported on financial statements, 495-496
  straight-line method of, 487
  summary form, 491
direct deposit, 428
direct write-off method, 506-509 *def.*
disclosure, full, 610
discount
  cash, 241-242, 244-245
  on notes payable, 556-558
  period, 269-270
  purchase, 269, 291-292
  sales, 242
disposal value, 487 *def.*
dividends, 593 *def.*
  account, 594

common stock, 596-597
  dates for, 594
  declaring and paying, 594-597
  journalizing, 595, 596
  payable, 595
  preferred, 594-595
dollar sign, in journal entries, 90
double-entry accounting, 42 *def.*
double taxation, of corporation, 588
drawee, 193 *def.*
drawer, 193 *def.*
due date, of invoice, 269-270, 273

e

earnings
  accumulated, 429
  employee's record of, 428-429
  gross, 417
  statement of retained, 373-374
electronic badge readers, 419 *def.*
electronic funds transfer system (EFTS), 3, 200-201, 428, 483
employee's earnings record, 429 *def.*
Employee's Withholding Allowance Certificate, 422
employer's payroll taxes, 442-448
  journalizing, 444-445
employer's quarterly federal tax return, 450, 451
ending inventory, 345 *def.*
  adjustment for, 345-348
  calculating cost of merchandise sold, 345
  determining cost of, 533-536
endorsement, 191 *def.*
  restrictive, 192
equation, accounting. *See* accounting equation
equity, 20 *def.*
  owner's, 20
  partners', 572-574
  statement of changes in owner's, 155-156
  statement of changes in partners', 580
  stockholders', 366, 597-599, 611
errors
  correcting, in journal, 96
  correcting entries for, 119-121
  finding, on trial balance, 118-119
  finding, on work sheet, 134
estimated useful life, of plant asset, 486
exemption, 422 *def.*
expense, 27 *def.*
  accrued, 658-659
  administrative, 613
  bad debts, 506
  cash payment of, 27-28, 290, 296
  deferred, 656

depreciation, 488, 491-494
  journalizing transactions, affecting, 93-95, 296
  and matching principle, 137, 510
  operating, 371, 613
  other, 558, 614
  prepaid, 661
  section of income statement, 153, 371-372
  selling, 613
expense accounts
  analyzing transactions affecting, 27-28, 68-70, 72-73
  closing, 172-173, 391-392
  rules of debit and credit for, 64-65
external controls, for cash, 188

f

face value, of note, 548
federal income tax
  adjustment for, 351-352
  payment of, 446-447
  payroll deductions for, 421-422
  reported on income statement, 371
  tables, 424-425
  withholding, 421-422
Federal Insurance Contributions Act, 423
federal tax deposit coupon, 446
federal unemployment tax, 443-444
  paying, 447-448
Federal Unemployment Tax Act, 443
FICA taxes
  employee's, 423
  employer's, 443
  payment of, 446-447
fifo (first in, first out) method of costing merchandise, 534
Financial Accounting Standards Board (FASB), 11
financial claims in accounting, 20-21
financial statements, 149 *def.*
  analyzing, 614-618
  balance sheet, 157-160, 374-375, 599-600
  classified balance sheet, 610-612
  classified income statement, 612-614
  comparative balance sheet, 615-616
  comparative income statement, 617-618
  evaluating, 609-614
  income statement, 150-154, 367-372
  for a merchandising corporation, 367-375, 597-600
  for a partnership, 579-580

prepared by computer, 160-161, 375-376
purpose of, 149, 367
for a sole proprietorship, 149-160
statement of changes in owner's equity, 155-156
statement of changes in partners' equity, 580
statement of retained earnings, 373-374
statement of stockholders' equity, 597-599
first in, first out (fifo) method of costing merchandise, 534 *def.*
fiscal period, 8 *def.*, 84
and closing entries, 169-170
on financial statements, 149
length of, 84
FOB destination, 292 *def.*
FOB shipping point, 292 *def.*
footing, 224 *def.*
Form 940, 453
Form 941, 450 *def.*, 451
Form 8109, 447, 448
Form W-2, 450 *def.*, 450-452
Form W-3, 452
Form W-4, 422
fractional share basis, of dividing partnership earnings, 577-578
full disclosure, 610

g

general bookkeeper, 9
general journal, 87 *def.*, 88 *illus.*
adjusting entries, 384-386
closing entries in, 171-175, 389-394
correcting entries, 120-121, 328-329
employer's payroll taxes in, 444
payroll transactions in, 440
posting from, 111-116, 322-323
purchases returns and allowances transactions in, 326
recording transactions in, 88-96
sales returns and allowances transactions in, 321-322
general ledger, 108 *def.*
adjusting entries posted to, 387-389
closing entries posted to, 176-178
opening accounts in, 110
posting from general journal, 111-116, 322-323, 394-398
posting from special journals, 250-251, 252-254, 277, 303, 322-323
posting special journal column

totals to, 225-227, 252-253, 278-279, 305
proving the equality of, 117-118
going concern, 7
gross earnings, 417 *def.*
calculation of, 417-420
deductions from, 420-426
gross profit, 345 *def.*
calculating, 346
on sales, 371
guidelines, general accounting, 610

h

hardware, 288, 400 *def.*
heading
on financial statements, 150, 157-158
on work sheet, 132-133
horizontal analysis, 615 *def.*
of balance sheet, 615-616
hourly wage, 418 *def.*
calculating, 418-419

i

income
division, in a partnership, 575-578
net, 137
income statement, 150 *def.*
analysis of, 617-618
classified, 612-614
comparative, 617-618
cost of merchandise sold section of, 369-371, 613
expenses section of, 153, 371, 613
gross profit reported on, 371
heading for, 150
for a merchandising corporation, 367-372
net income or loss on, 153-154, 371-372
for a partnership, 579
purpose of, 150, 367
revenue section of, 151-153, 368-369, 612
section of work sheet, 136-137
for sole proprietorship, 150-160
vertical analysis of, 617-618
Income Summary account, 170 *def.*
classification of, 170-171
closing, 173-174, 389
and closing entries, 171-173
extending, on work sheet, 354-355
need for, 170-171
income tax. *See* federal income tax
insurance, prepaid, 290, 351
interest, 548 *def.*
accrued, 657-658

calculating, 550-552
rate, 548
table, 549
interest-bearing note, 552-554
interest rate, of note, 548
internal controls for cash, 188, 290
Internal Revenue Service (IRS), 11
careers with, 409
inventory, 214 *def.*
adjustments for merchandise, 345-349
beginning, 345
card, 531
computerized system, 531-532
determining cost of, 533-536
ending, 345
lower-of-cost-or-market method of valuing, 538-539
merchandise, 214, 529-539
methods of costing, 533-536
periodic, 529-530
perpetual, 531, 532
physical, 345
sheet, 530
investments, 611 *def.*
by owner, 23-24, 47-49
by partners, 573-574
invoice, 85 *def.*, 268
due date of, 273
processing stamp on, 269
issue date, of note, 548

j

journal, 87 *def.*
cash payments, 293
cash receipts, 243
combination, 648
general, 87
purchases, 271
sales, 219
special, 219
See also specific journals
journalizing, 87 *def.*, 88-96
cash payments transactions, 294-300
cash receipts transactions, 243-247
closing entries, 171-175
correcting errors in, 96, 119-121
information required for, 87
payroll, 438-440
purchases transactions, 272-274
sales on account, 220-221

l

last in, first out (lifo) method of costing merchandise, 534-535 *def.*
ledger, 108 *def.*

accounts payable subsidiary, 275
accounts receivable subsidiary, 221
four-column form, 109-110
general, 108-110
opening accounts in, 110, 116-117
posting to, 109, 111-112, 117
proving equality of, 117-118
three-column form, 221
liabilities, 20 *def.*
  analyzing transactions affecting, 46-53
  current, 611
  long-term, 611
  payroll, 444-445, 446-448
  rules of debit and credit for, 44-45
  section of balance sheet, 158-159, 374-375
lifo (last in, first out) method of costing merchandise, 534-535
limited liability, of corporation, 588
liquidity, 98 *def.*
  ratios, *def.*, 619
long-term liabilities, 611 *def.*
loss, 3 *def.*
lower-of-cost-or-market method of valuing inventory, 538-539

m

maker, of promissory note, 548
managerial accounting, 10
manual accounting system, 87 *def.*
manufacturing business, 4
market value, 538 *def.*
matching principle, 137, 510
materiality, 610
maturity date
  determining, 548-550
  of promissory note, 548
maturity value, of promissory note, 551
memorandum, 85 *def.*
  credit, 319 *def.*
  debit, 324 *def.*
merchandise, 214 *def.*
  cash purchase of, 295
  cost of, 271
  credit purchase of, 270-271, 272-273
  sale of, 215
merchandise inventory, 214 *def.*
  adjusting, 345-348
  adjustment for, on work sheet, 348-349
  beginning, 345
  choosing a costing method, 536-538

and cost of merchandise sold, 345, 534-535
determining cost of, 533-536
determining quantities of, 529-532
ending, 345
fifo (first in, first out) method of costing, 534
lifo (last in, first out) method of costing, 534-535
lower-of-cost-or-market method of valuing, 538-539
periodic, 529-530
perpetual, 531-532
specific identification method of costing, 533-534
weighted average cost method, 536
merchandising business, 4 *def.*, 214
MICR number, on check, 190
mutual agency, 571 *def.*

n

net income, 137 *def.*
  closing entry for, 171-172, 393
  division of, for partnership, 575-578
  section of income statement, 153, 371-372
  on statement of changes in owner's equity, 155-156
  on statement of changes in partners' equity, 580
  on statement of retained earnings, 373-374
  on work sheet, 136-138, 355
net loss, 138 *def.*
  closing entry for, 393-394
  entering, on work sheet, 138-139, 355
  on income statement, 154, 371-372
net pay, 427 *def.*
net purchases, 369 *def.*
net sales, 369 *def.*
non-interest-bearing note, 555-558
normal balance. *See* balance side
not-for-profit accounting, 3, 10
note. *See* promissory note
notes payable, 552 *def.*
  book value of, 556-557
  discount on, 556-558
  interest-bearing, 552-554
  issuing, 553, 556
  journalizing, 553-554, 556-558
  non-interest-bearing, 555-558
  paying, 553-554, 557-558
  reported on balance sheet, 557
notes receivable, 558 *def.*
  accepting, 559

and accrued interest, 657-658
collection of, 559-560
journalizing, 559, 560
NSF check, 200

o

online, 531 *def.*
operating expenses, 371, 613
operating income, 372
organization, types of business, 3, 5
organization costs, of corporation, 588
other expense, 558, 614
other revenue, 558, 614
outstanding check, 197
outstanding deposit, 197
overtime rate, 420 *def.*
owner's equity, 20 *def.*
  section of balance sheet, 158-159
  statement of changes in, 155-156

p

packing slip, 268 *def.*
paid-in capital in excess of par, 591-592
par value, 589 *def.*
partners' equity, statement of changes in, 580
partnership, 5 *def.*, 571
  advantages and disadvantages of, 572
  agreement, 572
  balance sheet for, 580
  capital accounts for, 572
  characteristics of, 571
  closing entries for, 580-581
  division of income, 575-578
  financial statements for, 579-580
  income statement for, 579
  investments, by partners, 573-574
  mutual agency of, 571
  statement of changes in partners' equity, 580
  unlimited liability of, 571
partnership agreement, 572
pay period, 417 *def.*
payee
  of check, 193
  of promissory note, 548
payroll, 417 *def.*
  accounting, 416-430
  checks, preparing, 427-428
  computerized system, 419, 430
  deductions, 420-426
  employer's taxes, 442-448
  journalizing, 438-440
  liabilities, 438-439

posting transaction for, 440-441
system, 417
payroll clerk, 417
payroll register, 426 *def.*
  completing, 426-427
  deductions section of, 427
  earnings section of, 426
  net pay section of, 427
payroll taxes
  computing, 443-444
  journalizing, 444-445
  paying, 446-448
  posting, 445, 448
percentage of net sales method of
  estimating uncollectible
  accounts, 518-519
periodic inventory system, 529 *def.*
permanent accounts, 62 *def.*
perpetual inventory system, 531
  def.
petty cash disbursement, 468
petty cash fund, 468
  cash short and over in, 475-476
  envelope, 473
  establishing, 469
  increasing, 469
  making payments from, 468, 470
  reconciling, 470-471, 475-476
  recording transactions in petty
    cash register, 472-473
  replenishing, 470-472, 474
  requisition form, 471-472
  voucher for, 470
petty cash register, 472 *def.*
  recording vouchers in, 472
  totaling and proving, 472-473
petty cash requisition, 471 *def.*
petty cash voucher, 470 *def.*, 472
petty cashier, 468 *def.*
physical inventory, 345 *def.*
piece rate, 419 *def.*
plant and equipment asset, 485
  book value of, 490
  cost of, 486
  depreciation of, 487-488
  disposal value of, 487
  record, 489-490
post-closing trial balance, 169 *def.*
  for a merchandising
    corporation, 398
  preparing, 178-179
posting, 108 *def.*
  to accounts payable ledger,
    300-303
  to accounts receivable ledger,
    222-223
  adjusting entries, 387-389
  from the cash payments journal,
    300-303, 305
  from the cash receipts journal,
    247-251, 252-254
  closing entries, 175-178, 394-398

in a computerized system, 117,
  229
frequency of, 111
to general ledger accounts, 109,
  111-116, 225-227, 252-254
payroll transaction, 440-441
from purchases journal, 276-277,
  278-279
reference, 111-112
from sales journal, 222-223,
  225-227
posting reference, 111-112
preferred stock, 589-590 *def.*
  dividends, 594-595
  issuing, 592
premium, insurance, 290
prepaid expense, 661
prepaid insurance, 290, 351
principal, of promissory note, 548
private enterprise economy, 3-5
proceeds, 555 *def.*
processing stamp, on invoice, 269
profit, 3 *def.*
  gross, 345 *def.*
profitability ratios, 621 *def.*
promissory note, 548 *def.*
  bank discount, 555
  calculating interest on, 550-552
  determining maturity date of,
    548-550
  face value, 548
  interest, 548, 550-552
  interest-bearing, 552-554
  interest rate, 548
  issue date, 548
  maker, 548
  maturity date, 548-550
  maturity value, 551
  non-interest-bearing, 555-558
  payee, 548
  principal, 548
  proceeds, 555
  term, 548
  See also notes payable; notes
    receivable
property, 18 *def.*
  rights, 18, 20-21
  taxes, accrued, 658-659
property, plant, and equipment
  asset, 611
proprietorship. *See* sole
  proprietorship
proxy, 589
public accounting, 10
publicly held corporation, 587 *def.*
  See also corporation
purchase allowance, 325 *def.*
purchase discount, 269 *def.*
purchase order, 267 *def.*
purchase requisition, 266 *def.*
purchase return, 325 *def.*
purchases, 271 *def.*

on account, 49-50, 266-271,
  279-280
cash, 48, 290
in a computerized accounting
  system, 279-280
discount, 269-270, 291-292,
  296-297
journalizing, 272-274
source document for, 268
purchases journal, 271 *def.*
  posting column totals, 278-279
  posting the general column of,
    277
  posting to the accounts payable
    subsidiary ledger, 276
  recording transactions in,
    272-274
  totaling, proving, and ruling, 278
purchases returns and allowances
  account, 325
  journalizing, 326
  posting, 326-327
purchasing procedures, 266-269

q

qualitative characteristics, of
  accounting information,
  609-610
quick ratio, 620 *def.*

r

ratio
  analysis, 619-622
  current, 619-620
  liquidity, 619-621
  profitability, 621-622
  quick, 620-621
  return on common stockholders'
    equity, 621
  return on sales, 622
receipt, 85 *def.*, 239
  cash, 239
  journalizing cash, 243-247,
    294-296
  kinds of, 239-241
reconciled petty cash balance,
  470-471
reconciling
  bank statements, 196-198
  petty cash fund, 470-471
record of original entry. *See*
  journal
reinstatement, of written-off
  account receivable, 508,
  516-517
relevance, 609
reliability, 609
report form, 157 *def.*
restrictive endorsement, 191 *def.*

retailer, 214 *def.*
retained earnings, 366
  account, 366
  and closing entries, 393
  statement of, 373-374
return on common stockholders'
  equity, 621 *def.*
return on sales, 622 *def.*
revenue, 27 *def.*
  accrued, 656
  deferred, 656
  and matching principle, 137
  other, 560, 614
  section of income statement,
    151-152, 368-369, 612
  unearned, 660-661
revenue accounts
  analyzing transactions affecting,
    27-28, 70-72
  closing entries for, 171-172, 291
  rules of debit and credit for,
    63-64
rights, property, 18
ruling, 134 *def.*
  special journals, 224-225
  work sheet, 134, 138, 355

s

salary, 417 *def.*
  plus commission or bonus, 419
sale
  on account, 215-217, 220-221
  bank card, 240-241
  cash, 239, 245-246
sales, return on, 622
Sales account, 214
sales allowance, 318 *def.*
sales discount. *See* cash discount
sales journal, 219 *def.*
  completing, 224-227
  posting column totals, 225-227
  posting to accounts receivable
    ledger, 222-223
  recording transactions in,
    220-221
  totaling, proving, and ruling,
    224-225
sales on account
  analyzing, 216-217
  in a computerized system, 229
  journalizing, 220-221
sales return, 318 *def.*
sales returns and allowances
  account, 319-320
  journalizing, 321-322
  posting, 322-323
sales slip, 215 *def.*
sales tax, 216 *def.*
  calculating, 216
  recording in cash receipts
    journal, 245-246
  and sales return and allowance
    transactions, 321

schedule of accounts payable, 306
  def.
schedule of accounts receivable,
  254-255 *def.*
Securities and Exchange
  Commission, 11
selling expense, 613 *def.*
service business, 4
service charge, bank, 197
  journalizing, 199, 298-299
shipping charges, 292, 297, 298
signature card, 189 *def.*
slide error, 119
social security tax. *See* FICA taxes
software, 400 *def.*
  buying, 288
  piracy, 237
sole proprietorship, 5 *def.*
  financial statements for, 149-160
  investments by owner of, 23-24,
    27-30, 47, 49
  journalizing transactions for,
    87-90
source document, 85 *def.*
  as evidence of business
    transaction, 86
  types of, 85
special journals, 219 *def. See also*
    specific journals
specific identification method, 533
  def.
spreadsheet, computerized, 31
state income taxes, 423
  paying, 447
state unemployment taxes, 443-444
statement of account, 255
statement of changes in owner's
  equity, 155 *def.*
  preparing, 155-156
  purpose of, 155
statement of changes in partners'
  equity, 580
statement of retained earnings,
  373 *def.*
  preparing, 373-374
  showing dividends on, 599
statement of stockholders' equity,
  597-599
stock, 589 *def.*
  capital, 365, 589-592
  card, 531
  certificate, 587
  common, 589, 590-592
  preferred, 589-590, 592
stockholders' equity, 365 *def.*, 611
  reporting, 365-366, 597-599
  return on common, 621-622
  section of balance sheet, 600
  statement of, 597-599
stop payment order, 200
straight-line depreciation method,
  487 *def.*
subsidiary ledger, 221 *def.*
supplies, adjustments for, 349-351

t

T account, 42 *def.*
taxes
  accrued property, 658-659
  corporate income, 351-352
  employee's federal income,
    421-422
  employer's payroll, 442-448
  federal unemployment, 443-444
  FICA, 423, 443, 446-447
  sales, 216
  state income, 423, 447
  state unemployment, 443-444
  tables, 424-425
  tax rate, FICA, 423
temporary capital accounts, 61 *def.*
  adjustments to, 344
  closing, 170, 174-175
  rules of debit and credit for,
    62-67
term, of promissory note, 548
tickler file, 273 *def.*
time calendar, 549
time card, 418 *def.*
time period, 8. *See also* fiscal
  period
totaling
  petty cash register, 472
  special journals, 224
  work sheet, 134, 136, 355
transaction. *See* business
  transactions
transmittal of income and tax
  statements (Form W-3), 452
transportation charges, 292,
  297-298
transposition error, 119
trial balance, 76, 108 *def.*, 118
  post-closing, 169, 178-179, 398
  section of work sheet, 133-134,
    342-343

u

uncollectible accounts, 506 *def.*
  accounting for, 506-517
  aging of accounts receivable
    method, 519-520
  allowance for, 510-511
  allowance method, 510-520
  direct write off of, 506-507
  percentage of net sales method
    of estimating, 518-519
  reinstating, 508, 516-517
  writing off, 506-507, 514-516
unearned revenue, 660-661
unemployment taxes, 443 *def.*
  paying, 447-448
unit of measure, 8
unit price, 267
unlimited liability, 571
useful life, of plant assets, 486

V

value
  book, of accounts receivable,
    511
  book, of plant assets, 490
  face, 548
  market, 538
vendor number, 279
vertical analysis, 616 *def.*
  of income statement, 617-618
voiding a check, 194
voucher, petty cash, 470

W

wage, hourly, 418 *def.*
  calculating, 418-419
wage and tax statement (Form
  W-2), 450-452
weighted average cost method, 536
  def.
wholesaler, 214 *def.*

withdrawals, 29 *def.*
  analyzing transactions affecting,
    29-30, 73-74
  closing into capital account,
    174-175
  journalizing, 96
  by owner, 29-30, 73-74
  by partners, 574
  rules of debit and credit for
    owner's, 66
  on statement of changes in
    owner's equity, 155-156
withholding allowance certificate,
  422
withholding taxes, 421-422
work sheet, 131 *def.*, 139 *illus.*
  adjusted trial balance section of,
    352-354
  adjustment for bad debts
    expense, 511-512
  adjustment for depreciation on,
    490-494

  adjustments section of
    ten-column, 348
  balance sheet section of, 135,
    354
  extending amounts on, 135-136,
    354-355
  heading for, 132-133
  income statement section of,
    136, 354
  listing accounts on, 133
  for merchandising corporation,
    345-349
  net income on, 136-138, 140, 355
  net loss on, 138-139, 355
  ruling, 134, 138, 355
  six-column, 131-140
  steps in preparing, 131-139, 140
  ten-column, 342-356
  totaling, 136-139, 355
  trial balance section of, 133-134,
    342-343
working capital, 619